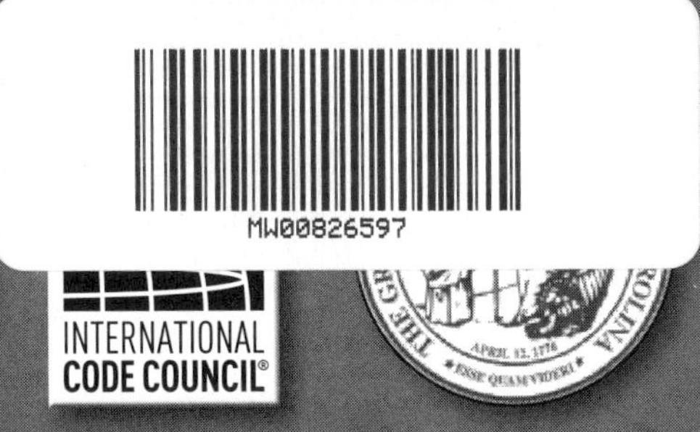

North Carolina State Building Code:

Building Code

(2009 IBC® with North Carolina Amendments)

2012

2012 North Carolina Building Code

First Printing: August 2011

ISBN-978-1-60983-116-5

PRINTED IN THE U.S.A.

NORTH CAROLINA STATE BUILDING CODE COUNCIL
JUNE 1, 2011
www.ncbuildingcodes.com

Al Bass, Jr., PE – 15
(Mechanical Engineer)
Bass, Nixon and Kennedy
6425 Chapman Court
Raleigh, NC 27612
919-782-4689

Cindy Browning, PE – 11
(State Agency)
State Construction
301 North Wilmington St.
Raleigh, NC 27601
919-807-4127

Ralph Euchner – 13
(Gas Industry)
PSNC Energy
PO Box 1398
Gastonia, NC 28053
704-810-3331

Steve Knight, PE – 15
(Structural Engineer)
Steve L. Knight, PE
1507 Mount Vernon Ave.
Statesville, NC 28677
704-878-2996

Lon McSwain – 15
(Building Inspector)
Mecklenburg County
700 North Tryon Street
Charolotte, NC 28202
704-336-4302

CHAIR

Dan Tingen – 11
(Home Builder)
Tingen Construction Co.
8411 Garvey Drive, #101
Raleigh, NC 27616
919-875-2161

Ed Moore, Sr. – 13
(Electrical Contractor)
E. Moore and Son Electric
2708 N. Graham St., Ste. D
Charlotte, NC 28206
704-358-8828

Jack Neel, PE – 10
(Municipal Representative)
City of Albemarle
1007 Colonial Drive
Albemarle, NC 28001
704-982-8434

Mack Nixon – 16
(County Representative)
Albemarle Home Builders
199 Mill Street
Elizabeth City, NC 27909
252-338-5211

Alan Perdue – 15
(Fire Services)
Guilford County
1002 Meadowood Street
Greensboro, NC 27409
336-641-7565

Kim Reitterer, PE – 13
(Electrical Engineer)
ELM Engineering
212 S. Tryon St., Ste. 1050
Charlotte, NC 28281
704-335-0396

VICE CHAIRMAN

John Hitch, AIA – 16
(Architect)
The Smith Sinnett Assoc.
4601 Lake Boone Trail
Raleigh, NC 27607
919-781-8582

Bob Ruffner, Jr. – 15
(General Contractor)
Clancy and Theys Construction
PO Box 4189
Wilmington, NC 28406
910-392-5220

David Smith – 16
(Coastal Contractor)
D. Smith Builder
905 Saltwood Lane
Wilmington, NC 28411
910-681-0394

Paula Strickland – 13
(Mechanical Contractor)
Williams PH&AC
1051 Grecade Street
Greensboro, NC 27408
336-275-1328

Hawley Truax – 11
(Public Representative)
Z. Smith Reynolds Found
147 S. Cherry St., Ste. 200
Winston-Salem, NC 27101
336-725-7541

Tom Turner, FAIA – 10
(Architect)
ADEP, PA
3225 Wickersham Road
Charlotte, NC 28211
704-770-0475

NORTH CAROLINA
DEPARTMENT OF INSURANCE

www.ncdoi.com/osfm
919-661-5880

By Statute, the Commissioner of Insurance has general supervision of the administration and enforcement of the North Carolina State Building Code, and the Engineering Division serves as the Staff for the Building Code Council. Officials of the Department of Insurance are:

WAYNE GOODWIN
Commissioner

TIM BRADLEY
Senior Deputy Commissioner

CHRIS NOLES, PE
Deputy Commissioner

BARRY GUPTON, PE
Chief Code Consultant

CARL MARTIN, RA
Building Code Consultant

COMMITTEES OF THE COUNCIL
JUNE 1, 2011

ADMINISTRATION
Dan Tingen – Chair
Al Bass, PE
John Hitch, AIA
Steve Knight, PE
Alan Perdue
Kim Reitterer, PE
Lon McSwain
David Smith
Tom Turner, FAIA

BUILDING
Lon McSwain – Chair
Cindy Browning, PE
John Hitch, AIA
Ed Moore, Sr.
Alan Perdue
Bob Ruffner, Jr.
Paula Strickland
Tom Turner, FAIA

ELECTRICAL
Kim Reitterer, PE – Chair
Al Bass, PE
Cindy Browning, PE
John Hitch, AIA
Ed Moore, Sr.
Bob Ruffner, Jr.

ENERGY
Tom Turner, FAIA – Chair
Al Bass, PE
Ralph Euchner
Mack Nixon
Kim Reitterer, PE
Bob Ruffner, Jr.
Hawley Truax

FIRE PREVENTION
Alan Perdue – Chair
Ralph Euchner
John Hitch, AIA
Jack Neel, PE
Mack Nixon
Bob Ruffner, Jr.

MECHANICAL
Al Bass, PE – Chair
Ralph Euchner
Ed Moore, Sr.
David Smith
Paula Strickland

RESIDENTIAL
David Smith – Chair
Cindy Browning, PE
Steve Knight, PE
Jack Neel, PE
Mack Nixon
Lon McSwain
Paula Strickland
Tom Turner, FAIA
Hawley Truax

STRUCTURAL
Steve Knight, PE – Chair
Al Bass, PE
John Hitch, AIA
Bob Ruffner, Jr.

PREFACE

Introduction

Internationally, code officials recognize the need for a modern, up-to-date building code addressing the design and installation of building systems through requirements emphasizing performance. The *International Building Code*®, in this 2009 edition, is designed to meet these needs through model code regulations that safeguard the public health and safety in all communities, large and small.

This comprehensive building code establishes minimum regulations for building systems using prescriptive and performance-related provisions. It is founded on broad-based principles that make possible the use of new materials and new building designs. This 2009 edition is fully compatible with all the *International Codes*® (I-Codes®) published by the International Code Council (ICC)®, including the *International Energy Conservation Code*®, *International Existing Building Code*®, *International Fire Code*®, *International Fuel Gas Code*®, *International Mechanical Code*®, ICC *Performance Code*®, *International Plumbing Code*®, *International Private Sewage Disposal Code*®, *International Property Maintenance Code*®, *International Residential Code*®, *International Wildland-Urban Interface Code*™ and *International Zoning Code*®.

The *International Building Code* provisions provide many benefits, among which is the model code development process that offers an international forum for building professionals to discuss performance and prescriptive code requirements. This forum provides an excellent arena to debate proposed revisions. This model code also encourages international consistency in the application of provisions.

Development

The first edition of the *International Building Code* (2000) was the culmination of an effort initiated in 1997 by the ICC. This included five drafting subcommittees appointed by ICC and consisting of representatives of the three statutory members of the International Code Council at that time, including: Building Officials and Code Administrators International, Inc. (BOCA), International Conference of Building Officials (ICBO) and Southern Building Code Congress International (SBCCI). The intent was to draft a comprehensive set of regulations for building systems consistent with and inclusive of the scope of the existing model codes. Technical content of the latest model codes promulgated by BOCA, ICBO and SBCCI was utilized as the basis for the development, followed by public hearings in 1997, 1998 and 1999 to consider proposed changes. This 2009 edition presents the code as originally issued, with changes reflected in the 2003 and 2006 editions and further changes approved through the ICC Code Development Process through 2008. A new edition such as this is promulgated every 3 years.

This code is founded on principles intended to establish provisions consistent with the scope of a building code that adequately protects public health, safety and welfare; provisions that do not unnecessarily increase construction costs; provisions that do not restrict the use of new materials, products or methods of construction; and provisions that do not give preferential treatment to particular types or classes of materials, products or methods of construction.

Adoption

The *International Building Code* is available for adoption and use by jurisdictions internationally. Its use within a governmental jurisdiction is intended to be accomplished through adoption by reference in accordance with proceedings establishing the jurisdiction's laws. At the time of adoption, jurisdictions should insert the appropriate information in provisions requiring specific local information, such as the name of the adopting jurisdiction. These locations are shown in bracketed words in small capital letters in the code and in the sample ordinance. The sample adoption ordinance on page xvii addresses several key elements of a code adoption ordinance, including the information required for insertion into the code text.

Maintenance

The *International Building Code* is kept up to date through the review of proposed changes submitted by code enforcing officials, industry representatives, design professionals and other interested parties. Proposed changes are carefully considered through an open code development process in which all interested and affected parties may participate.

The contents of this work are subject to change both through the Code Development Cycles and the governmental body that enacts the code into law. For more information regarding the code development process, contact the Code and Standard Development Department of the International Code Council.

While the development procedure of the *International Building Code* assures the highest degree of care, ICC, its members and those participating in the development of this code do not accept any liability resulting from compliance or noncompliance with the provisions because ICC does not have the power or authority to police or enforce compliance with the contents of this code. Only the governmental body that enacts the code into law has such authority.

Letter Designations in Front of Section Numbers

In each code development cycle, proposed changes to the code are considered at the Code Development Hearings by the applicable ICC Code Development Committee, whose action constitutes a recommendation to the voting membership for final action on the proposed change. Proposed changes to a code section that has a number beginning with a letter in brackets are considered by a different code development committee. For example, proposed changes to code sections that have [F] in front of them (e.g., [F] 903.1.1.1) are considered by the ICC Fire Code Development Committee at the code development hearings.

The content of sections in this code that begin with a letter designation are maintained by another code development committee in accordance with the following:

[E] = International Energy Conservation Code Development Committee;

[EB] = International Existing Building Code Development Committee;

[F] = International Fire Code Development Committee;

[FG] = International Fuel Gas Code Development Committee;

[M] = International Mechanical Code Development Committee; and

[P] = International Plumbing Code Development Committee.

Marginal <u>and Text</u> Markings

Solid vertical lines in the margins within the body of the code indicate a technical change from the requirements of the 2006 edition of the *International Building Code*. Deletion indicators in the form of an arrow (➡) are provided in the margin where an entire section, paragraph, exception or table has been deleted or an item in a list of items or a table has been deleted. <u>Underlining within the body of the code indicate a technical change to the 2012 *North Carolina Building Code* from the requirements of the 2009 edition of the *International Building Code*.</u>

Chapter 7 user note: Chapter 7 of the code has been reorganized from the 2006 edition as a result of an approved code change proposal. This proposal renumbered what was Section 714 in the 2006 edition to Section 704 in this edition, which in turn resulted in renumbering Sections 704 through 713 in the 2006 edition to Sections 705 through 714 in this edition. Marginal markings are included at each section number but have not been included to reflect the subsection renumbering.

Coordination between the International Building and Fire Codes

Because the coordination of technical provisions is one of the benefits of adopting the ICC family of model codes, users will find the ICC codes to be a very flexible set of model documents. To accomplish this flexibility some technical provisions are duplicated in some of the model code documents. While the International Codes are provided as a comprehensive set of model codes for the built environment, documents are occasionally adopted as a stand-alone regulation. When one of the model documents is adopted as the basis of a stand-alone code, that code should provide a complete package of requirements with enforcement assigned to the entity for which the adoption is being made.

The model codes can also be adopted as a family of complimentary codes. When adopted together there should be no conflict of any of the technical provisions. When multiple model codes are adopted in a jurisdiction it is important for the adopting authority to evaluate the provisions in each code document and determine how and by which agency(ies) they will be enforced. It is important, therefore, to understand that where technical provisions are duplicated in multiple model documents that enforcement duties must be clearly assigned by the local adopting jurisdiction. ICC remains committed to providing state-of-the-art model code documents that, when adopted locally, will reduce the cost to government of code adoption and enforcement and protect the public health, safety and welfare.

Italicized Terms

Selected terms set forth in Chapter 2, Definitions, are italicized where they appear in code text (except those in Sections 1903 through 1908 where italics indicate provisions that differ from ACI 318). Such terms are not italicized where the definition set forth in Chapter 2 does not impart the intended meaning in the use of the term. The terms selected have definitions which the user should read carefully to facilitate better understanding of the code.

Effective Use of the International Building Code

The *International Building Code*® (IBC®) is a model code that provides minimum requirements to safeguard the public health, safety and general welfare of the occupants of new and existing buildings and structures. The IBC is fully compatible with the ICC family of codes, including: *International Energy Conservation Code*® (IECC®), *International Existing Building Code*® (IEBC®), *International Fire Code*® (IFC®), *International Fuel Gas Code*® (IFGC®), *International Mechanical Code*® (IMC®), *ICC Performance Code*® (ICCPC®), *International Plumbing Code*® (IPC®), *International Private Sewage Disposal Code*® (IPSDC®), *International Property Maintenance Code*® (IPMC®), *International Residential Code*® (IRC®), *International Wildland-Urban Interface Code*™ (IWUIC®) and *International Zoning Code*® (IZC®).

The IBC addresses structural strength, means of egress, sanitation, adequate lighting and ventilation, accessibility, energy conservation and life safety in regards to new and existing buildings, facilities and systems. The codes are promulgated on a 3-year cycle to allow for new construction methods and technologies to be incorporated into the codes. Alternative materials, designs and methods not specifically addressed in the code can be approved by the code official where the proposed materials, designs or methods comply with the intent of the provisions of the code (see Section 104.11).

The IBC applies to all occupancies, including one- and two-family dwellings and townhouses that are not within the scope of the IRC. The IRC is referenced for coverage of detached one- and two-family dwellings and townhouses as defined in the Exception to Section 101.2 and the definition for "townhouse" in Chapter 2. The IBC applies to all types of buildings and structures unless exempted. Work exempted from permits is listed in Section 105.2.

Arrangement and Format of the 2009 IBC

Before applying the requirements of the IBC, it is beneficial to understand its arrangement and format. The IBC, like other codes published by ICC, is arranged and organized to follow sequential steps that generally occur during a plan review or inspection.

Chapters	Subjects
1–2	Administration and definitions
3	Use and occupancy classifications
4, 31	Special requirements for specific occupancies or elements
5–6	Height and area limitations based on type of construction
7–9	Fire resistance and protection requirements
10	Requirements for evacuation
11	Specific requirements to allow use and access to a building for persons with disabilities
12–13, 27–30	Building systems, such as lighting, HVAC, plumbing fixtures, elevators
14–26	Structural components—performance and stability
32	Encroachment outside of property lines
33	Safeguards during construction
34	Existing building allowances
35	Referenced standards
Appendices A–K	Appendices

The IBC requirements for high hazard, fire-resistance-rated construction, interior finish, fire protection systems, means of egress, emergency and standby power, and temporary structures are directly correlated with the requirements of the IFC. The following chapters/sections of the IBC are correlated to the IFC:

IBC Chapter/Section	IFC Chapter/Section	Subject
Sections 307, 414, 415	Chapters 27–44	High-hazard requirements
Chapter 7	Chapter 7	Fire-resistance-rated construction
Chapter 8	Chapter 8	Interior finish, decorative materials and furnishings
Chapter 9	Chapter 9	Fire protection systems
Chapter 10	Chapter 10	Means of egress
Chapter 27	Section 604	Standby and emergency power
Section 3103	Chapter 24	Temporary structures

The IBC requirements for smoke control systems, and smoke and fire dampers are directly correlated to the requirements of the IMC. IBC Chapter 28 is a reference to the IMC and the IFGC for chimney, fireplaces and barbeques, and all aspects of mechanical systems. The following chapters/sections of the IBC are correlated with the IMC:

IBC Chapter/Section	IMC Chapter/Section	Subject
Section 716	Section 607	Smoke and fire dampers
Section 909	Section 513	Smoke control

The IBC requirements for plumbing fixtures and toilet rooms are directly correlated to the requirements of the IPC. The following chapters/sections of the IBC are correlated with the IPC:

IBC Chapter/Section	IPC Chapter/Section	Subject
Chapter 29	Chapters 3 & 4	Plumbing fixtures and facilities

The following is a chapter-by-chapter synopsis of the scope and intent of the provisions of the *International Building Code*.

Chapter 1 Scope and Administration. Chapter 1 establishes the limits of applicability of the code and describes how the code is to be applied and enforced. Chapter 1 is in two parts, Part 1—Scope and Application (Sections 101–102) and Part 2—Administration and Enforcement (Sections 103–116). Section 101 identifies which buildings and structures come under its purview and references other ICC codes as applicable. Standards and codes are scoped to the extent referenced (see Section 102.4).

The building code is intended to be adopted as a legally enforceable document and it cannot be effective without adequate provisions for its administration and enforcement. The provisions of Chapter 1 establish the authority and duties of the code official appointed by the jurisdiction having authority and also establish the rights and privileges of the design professional, contractor and property owner.

Chapter 2 Definitions. All terms that are defined in the code are listed alphabetically in Chapter 2. Terms are defined in Chapter 2 or there is a reference to the section where the definition is located. While a defined term may be listed in one chapter or another, the meaning is applicable throughout the code.

Codes are technical documents and every word, term and punctuation mark can impact the meaning of the code text and the intended results. The code often uses terms that have a unique meaning in the code and the code meaning can differ substantially from the ordinarily understood meaning of the term as used outside of the code. Where understanding of a term's definition is especially key to or necessary for understanding a particular code provision, the term is shown in *italics* wherever it appears in the code.

This is true only for those terms that have a meaning that is unique to the code. In other words, the generally understood meaning of a term or phrase might not be sufficient or consistent with the meaning prescribed by the code; therefore, it is essential that the code-defined meaning be known.

Definitions are deemed to be of prime importance in establishing the meaning and intent of the code text that uses the terms. The user of the code should be familiar with and consult this chapter because the definitions are essential to the correct interpretation of the code and because the user may not be aware that a term is defined.

Chapter 3 Use and Occupancy Classification. Chapter 3 provides for the classification of buildings, structures and parts thereof based on the purpose or purposes for which they are used. Section 302 identifies the groups into which all buildings, structures and parts thereof must be classified. Sections 303 through 312 identify the occupancy characteristics of each group classification. In some sections, specific group classifications having requirements in common are collectively organized such that one term applies to all. For example, Groups A-1, A-2, A-3, A-4 and A-5 are individual groups for assembly-type buildings. The general term "Group A," however, includes each of these individual groups. Other groups include Business (B), Educational (E), Factory (F-1, F-2), High Hazard (H-1, H-2, H-3, H-4, H-5), Institutional (I-1, I-2, I-3, I-4), Mercantile (M), Residential (R-1, R-2, R-3, R-4), Storage (S-1, S-2) and Utility (U). In some occupancies, the smaller number means a higher hazard, but that is not always the case.

Defining the use of the buildings is very important as it sets the tone for the remaining chapters of the code. Occupancy works with the height, area and construction type requirements in Chapters 5 and 6, as well as the special provisions in Chapter 4, to determine "equivalent risk," or providing a reasonable level of protection or life safety for building occupants. The determination of equivalent risk involves three interdependent considerations: (1) the level of fire hazard associated with the specific occupancy of the facility; (2) the reduction of fire hazard by limiting the floor area(s) and the height of the building based on the fuel load (combustible contents and burnable building components) and (3) the level of overall fire resistance provided by the type of construction used for the building. The greater the potential fire hazards indicated as a function of the group, the lesser the height and area allowances for a particular construction type.

Occupancy classification also plays a key part in organizing and prescribing the appropriate protection measures. As such, threshold requirements for fire protection and means of egress systems are based on occupancy classification (see Chapters 9 and 10). Other sections of the code also contain requirements respective to the classification of building groups. For example, Section 706 deals with requirements for fire wall fire-resistance ratings that are tied to the occupancy classification of a building and Section 803.9 contains interior finish requirements that are dependent upon the occupancy classification. The use of the space, rather than the occupancy of the building is utilized for determining occupant loading (Section 1004) and live loading (Section 1607).

Chapter 4 Special Detailed Requirements Based On Use and Occupancy. Chapter 4 contains the requirements for protecting special uses and occupancies, which are supplemental to the remainder of the code. Chapter 4 contains provisions that may alter requirements found elsewhere in the code; however, the general requirements of the code still apply unless modified within the chapter. For example, the height and area limitations established in Chapter 5 apply to all special occupancies unless Chapter 4 contains height and area limitations. In this case, the limitations in Chapter 4 supersede those in other sections. An example of this is the height and area limitations for open parking garages given in Section 406.3.5, which supersede the limitations given in Section 503.

In some instances, it may not be necessary to apply the provisions of Chapter 4. For example, if a covered mall building complies with the provisions of the code for Group M, Section 402 does not apply; however, other sections that deal with a use, process or operation must be applied to that specific occupancy, such as stages and platforms, special amusement buildings and hazardous materials (Sections 410, 411 and 414).

The chapter includes requirements for buildings and conditions that apply to one or more groups, such as high-rise buildings, underground buildings or atriums. Special uses may also imply specific occupancies and operations, such as for Group H, hazardous materials, application of flammable finishes, drying rooms, organic coatings and combustible storage or hydrogen cutoff rooms, all of which are coordinated with the IFC. Unique consideration is taken for special use areas, such as covered mall buildings, motor-vehicle-related occupancies, special amusement buildings and aircraft-related occupancies. Special facilities within other occupancies are considered, such as stages and platforms, motion picture projection rooms and storm shelters. Finally, in order that the overall package of protection features can be easily understood, unique considerations for specific occupancies are addressed: Groups I-1, I-2, I-3, R-1, R-2, R-3 (by definition R-4), ambulatory care facilities and live/work units.

Chapter 5 General Building Heights and Areas. Chapter 5 contains the provisions that regulate the minimum type of construction for area limits and height limits based on the occupancy of the building. Height and area increases (including allowances for basements, mezzanines and equipment platforms) are permitted based on open frontage for fire department access, and the type of sprinkler protection provided and separation (Sections 503–506, 509). These thresholds are reduced for buildings over three stories in height in accordance with Section 506.4.1. Provisions include the protection and/or separation of incidental accessory occupancies (Table 508.2.5), accessory occupancies (Sections 508.2) and mixed uses in the same building (Sections 506.5, 508.3, 508.4 and 509). Unlimited area buildings are permitted in certain occupancies when they meet special provisions (Section 507).

Table 503 is the keystone in setting thresholds for building size based on the building's use and the materials with which it is constructed. If one then looks at Table 503, the relationship among group classification, allowable heights and areas and types of construction becomes apparent. Respective to each group classification, the greater the fire-resistance rating of structural elements, as represented by the type of construction, the greater the floor area and height allowances. The greater the potential fire hazards indicated as a function of the group, the lesser the height and area allowances for a particular construction type.

Chapter 6 Types of Construction. The interdependence of these fire safety considerations can be seen by first looking at Tables 601 and 602, which show the fire-resistance ratings of the principal structural elements comprising a building in relation to the five classifications for types of construction. Type I construction is the classification that generally requires the highest fire-resistance ratings for structural elements, whereas Type V construction, which is designated as a combustible type of construction, generally requires the least amount of fire-resistance-rated structural elements. The greater the potential fire hazards indicated as a function of the group, the lesser the height and area allowances for a particular construction type. Section 603 includes a list of combustible elements that can be part of a noncombustible building (Types I and II construction).

Chapter 7 Fire and Smoke Protection Features. The provisions of Chapter 7 present the fundamental concepts of fire performance that all buildings are expected to achieve in some form. This chapter identifies the acceptable materials, techniques and methods which proposed construction can be designed and evaluated against to determine a building's ability to limit the impact of fire. The fire-resistance-rated construction requirements within Chapter 7 provide passive resistance to the spread and effects of fire. Types of separations addressed include fire walls, fire barriers, fire partitions, horizontal assemblies, smoke barriers and smoke partitions. A fire produces heat that can weaken structural components and smoke products that cause property damage and place occupants at risk. The requirements of Chapter 7 work in unison with height and area requirements (Chapter 5), active fire detection and suppression systems (Chapter 9) and occupant egress requirements (Chapter 10) to contain a fire should it occur while helping ensure occupants are able to safely exit.

Chapter 8 Interior Finishes. This chapter contains the performance requirements for controlling fire growth within buildings by restricting interior finish and decorative materials. Past fire experience has shown that interior finish and decorative materials are key elements in the development and spread of fire. The provisions of Chapter 8 require materials used as interior finishes and decorations to meet certain flame-spread index or flame-propagation criteria based on the relative fire hazard associated with the occupancy. As smoke is also a hazard associated with fire, this chapter contains limits on the smoke development characteristics of interior finishes. The performance of the material is evaluated based on test standards.

Chapter 9 Fire Protection Systems. Chapter 9 prescribes the minimum requirements for active systems of fire protection equipment to perform the following functions: detect a fire; alert the occupants or fire department of a fire emergency; and control smoke and control or extinguish the fire. Generally, the requirements are based on the occupancy, the height and the area of the building, because these are the factors that most affect fire-fighting capabilities and the relative hazard of a specific building or portion thereof. This chapter parallels and is substantially duplicated in Chapter 9 of the *International Fire Code* (IFC); however, the IFC Chapter 9 also contains periodic testing criteria that are not contained in the IBC. In addition, the special fire protection system requirements based on use and occupancy found in IBC Chapter 4 are duplicated in IFC Chapter 9 as a user convenience.

Chapter 10 Means of Egress. The general criteria set forth in Chapter 10 regulating the design of the means of egress are established as the primary method for protection of people in buildings by allowing timely relocation or evacuation of building occupants. Both prescriptive and performance language is utilized in this chapter to provide for a basic approach in the determination of a safe exiting system for all occupancies. It addresses all portions of the egress system (i.e., exit access, exits and exit discharge) and includes design requirements as well as provisions regulating individual components. The requirements detail the size, arrangement, number and protection of means of egress components. Functional and operational characteristics also are specified for the components that will permit their safe use without special knowledge or effort. The means of egress protection requirements work in coordination with other sections of the code, such as protection of vertical openings (see Chapter 7), interior finish (see Chapter 8), fire suppression and detection systems (see Chapter 9) and numerous others, all having an impact on life safety. Chapter 10 of the IBC is duplicated in Chapter 10 of the IFC; however, the IFC contains two additional sections on the means of egress system in existing buildings.

Chapter 11 Accessibility. Chapter 11 contains provisions that set forth requirements for accessibility of buildings and their associated sites and facilities for people with physical disabilities. The fundamental philosophy of the code on the subject of accessibility is that everything is required to be accessible. This is reflected in the basic applicability requirement (see Section 1103.1). The code's scoping requirements then address the conditions under which accessibility is not required in terms of exceptions to this general mandate. While the IBC contains scoping provisions for accessibility (e.g., what, where and how many), ICC/ANSI A117.1, *Accessible and Usable Buildings and Facilities*, is the referenced standard for the technical provisions (i.e., how).

There are many accessibility issues that not only benefit people with disabilities, but also provide a tangible benefit to people without disabilities. This type of requirement can be set forth in the code as generally applicable without necessarily identifying it specifically as an accessibility-related issue. Such a requirement would then be considered as having been "mainstreamed." For example, visible alarms are located in Chapter 9 and ramp requirements are addressed in Chapter 10.

Accessibility criteria for existing buildings are addressed in Section 3411. Appendix E is supplemental information included in the code to address accessibility for items in the new Americans with Disabilities Act/Architectural Barriers Act Accessibility Guidelines (ADA/ABA) that were not typically enforceable through the standard traditional building code enforcement approach system (e.g., beds, room signage). The *International Residential Code* (IRC) references Chapter 11 for accessibility provisions; therefore, this chapter may be applicable to housing covered under the IRC.

Chapter 12 Interior Environment. Chapter 12 provides minimum standards for the interior environment of a building. The standards address the minimum sizes of spaces, minimum temperature levels, and minimum light and ventilation levels. The collection of requirements addresses limiting sound transmission through walls, ventilation of attic spaces and under floor spaces (crawl spaces). Finally, the chapter provides minimum standards for walls, partitions and floors to resist water intrusion and damage in rooms such as toilet and shower facilities, where water is frequently in use.

Chapter 13 Energy Efficiency. The purpose of Chapter 13 is to provide minimum design requirements that will promote efficient utilization of energy in buildings. The requirements are directed toward the design of building envelopes with adequate thermal resistance and low air leakage, and toward the design and selection of mechanical, water heating, electrical and illumination systems that promote effective use of depletable energy resources. For the specifics of these criteria, Chapter 13 requires design and construction in compliance with the *International Energy Conservation Code* (IECC).

Chapter 14 Exterior Walls. This chapter addresses requirements for exterior walls of buildings. Minimum standards for wall covering materials, installation of wall coverings and the ability of the wall to provide weather protection are provided. This chapter also requires exterior walls that are close to lot lines, or that are bearing walls for certain types of construction, to comply with the minimum fire-resistance ratings specified in Chapters 6 and 7. The installation of each type of wall covering, be it wood, masonry, vinyl, metal composite material or an exterior insulation and finish system, is critical to its long-term performance in protecting the interior of the building from the elements and the spread of fire. Special attention to the use of combustible materials on the exterior of the building such as balconies, eaves, decks and architectural trim is the focus of Section 1406.

Chapter 15 Roof Assemblies and Rooftop Structures. Chapter 15 provides standards for both roof assemblies as well as structures which sit on top of the roof of buildings. The criteria address roof construction and covering which includes the weather-protective barrier at the roof and, in most circumstances, a fire-resistant barrier. The chapter is prescriptive in nature and is based on decades of experience with various traditional materials. These prescriptive rules are very important for satisfying performance of one type of roof covering or another. Section 1509 addresses rooftop structures including penthouses, tanks, towers and spires. Rooftop penthouses larger than prescribed in this chapter must be treated as a story under Chapter 5.

Chapter 16 Structural Design. Chapter 16 prescribes minimum structural loading requirements for use in the design and construction of buildings and structural components. It includes minimum design loads, as well as permitted design methodologies. Standards are provided for minimum design loads (live, dead, snow, wind, rain, flood and earthquake as well as load combinations). The application of these loads and adherence to the serviceability criteria will enhance the protection of life and property. The chapter references and relies on many nationally recognized design standards. A key standard is the American Society of Civil Engineer's *Minimum Design Loads for Buildings and Other Structures* (ASCE 7). Structural design needs to address the conditions of the site and location. Therefore maps of rainfall, seismic, snow and wind criteria in different regions are provided.

Chapter 17 Structural Tests and Special Inspections. Chapter 17 provides a variety of procedures and criteria for testing materials and assemblies, for labeling materials and assemblies, and for special inspection of structural assemblies. This chapter expands on the requirements of Chapter 1 regarding the roles and responsibilities of the building official regarding approval of building components. It also provides additional duties and responsibilities for the owner, contractor, design professionals and special inspectors. Proper assembly of structural components, proper quality of materials used, and proper application of materials are essential to ensuring that a building, once constructed, complies with the structural and fire-resistance minimums of the code and the approved design. To determine this compliance often requires continuous or frequent inspection and testing. Chapter 17 establishes these special inspection and testing standards as well as reporting of the work to the building official.

Chapter 18 Soils and Foundations. Chapter 18 contains minimum requirements for design, construction and resistance to water intrusion of foundation systems for buildings and other structures. It provides criteria for the geotechnical and structural considerations in the selection and installation of adequate support for the loads transferred from the structure above. The uncertainties of foundation construction make it extremely difficult to address every potential failure within the text of the code. The chapter includes requirements for soils investigation and site preparation for receiving a foundation including the allowed load-bearing values for soils and for protecting the foundation from water intrusion. Section 1808 addresses the basic requirements for all foundation types. Later sections address foundation requirements that are specific to shallow foundations and deep foundations. Due care must be exercised in the planning and design of foundation systems based on obtaining sufficient soils information, the use of accepted engineering procedures, experience and good technical judgment.

Chapter 19 Concrete. This chapter provides minimum accepted practices to the design and construction of buildings and structural components using concrete—both plain and reinforced. Chapter 19 is formatted to parallel American Concrete Institute (ACI) 318, *Building Code Requirements for Structural Concrete*. The chapter also includes references to additional standards. Structural concrete must be designed and constructed to comply with this code and all listed standards. There are specific sections of the chapter addressing concrete slabs, anchorage to concrete, shotcrete, reinforced gypsum concrete and concrete-filled pipe columns. Because of the variable properties of material and numerous design and construction options available in the uses of concrete, due care and control throughout the construction process is necessary.

Chapter 20 Aluminum. Chapter 20 contains standards for the use of aluminum in building construction. Only the structural applications of aluminum are addressed. The chapter does not address the use of aluminum in specialty products such as storefront or window framing or architectural hardware. The use of aluminum in heating, ventilating or air-conditioning systems is addressed in the *International Mechanical Code* (IMC). The chapter references national standards from the Aluminum Association for use of aluminum in building construction, AA ASM 35, *Aluminum Sheet Metal Work in Building Construction*, and AA ADM 1, *Aluminum Design Manual*. By utilizing the standards set forth, a proper application of this material can be obtained.

Chapter 21 Masonry. This chapter provides comprehensive and practical requirements for masonry construction. The provisions of Chapter 21 require minimum accepted practices and the use of standards for the design and construction of masonry structures. The provisions address: material specifications and test methods; types of wall construction; criteria for engineered and empirical designs; required details of construction including the execution of construction. Masonry design methodologies including allowable stress design, strength design and empirical design are covered by provisions of the chapter. Also addressed are masonry fireplaces and chimneys, masonry heaters and glass unit masonry. Fire-resistant construction using masonry is also required to comply with Chapter 7. Masonry foundations are also subject to the requirements of Chapter 18.

Chapter 22 Steel. Chapter 22 provides the requirements necessary for the design and construction of structural steel (including composite construction), cold-formed steel, steel joists, steel cable structures and steel storage racks. The chapter specifies appropriate design and construction standards for these types of structures. It also provides a road map of the applicable technical requirements for steel structures. Steel is a noncombustible building material commonly associated with Types I and II construction; however, it is permitted to be used in all types of construction. The code requires that materials used in the design of structural steel members conform to designated national standards. Chapter 22 is involved with the design and use of steel materials using the specifications and standards of the American Institute for Steel Construction, the American Iron and Steel Institute, the Steel Joist Institute and the American Society of Civil Engineers.

Chapter 23 Wood. This chapter provides minimum guidance for the design of buildings and structures that use wood and wood-based products in their framing and fabrication. The chapter is organized around three design methodologies: allowable stress design (ASD), load and resistance-factor design (LRFD) and conventional light-frame construction. Included in the chapter are references to design and manufacturing standards for various wood and wood-based products; general construction requirements; design criteria for lateral-force-resisting systems and specific requirements for the application of the three design methods. In general, only Type III, IV or V buildings may be constructed of wood. Accordingly Chapter 23 is referenced when the combination of the occupancy (determined in Chapter 3) and the height and area of the building (determined in Chapter 5) indicate that construction can be Type III, IV or V.

Chapter 24 Glass and Glazing. This chapter establishes regulations for glass and glazing used in buildings and structures that, when installed, are subjected to wind, snow and dead loads. Engineering and design requirements are included in the chapter. Additional structural requirements are found in Chapter 16. A second concern of this chapter is glass and glazing used in areas where it is likely to have an impact on the occupants. Section 2406 identifies hazardous locations where glazing installed must either be safety glazing or blocked to prevent human impact. Safety glazing must meet stringent standards and be appropriately marked or identified. Additional standards for glass and glazing in guards, handrails, elevator hoistways and elevator cars, and in athletic facilities are provided.

Chapter 25 Gypsum Board and Plaster. Chapter 25 contains the provisions and referenced standards that regulate the design, construction and quality of gypsum board and plaster. These represent the most common interior and exterior finish materials in the building industry. This chapter primarily addresses quality-control-related issues with regard to material specifications and installation requirements. Most products are manufactured under the control of industry standards. The building official or inspector primarily needs to verify that the appropriate product is used and properly installed for the intended use and location. While often simply used as wall and ceiling coverings, proper design and application are necessary to provide weather resistance and required fire protection for both structural and nonstructural building components.

Chapter 26 Plastic. The use of plastics in building construction and components is addressed in Chapter 26. This chapter provides standards addressing foam plastic insulation, foam plastics used as interior finish and trim, and other plastic veneers used on the inside or outside of a building. Plastic siding is regulated by Chapter 14. Sections 2606 through 2611 address the use of light-transmitting plastics in various configurations such as walls, roof panels, skylights, signs and as glazing. Requirements for the use of fiber reinforced polymers, fiberglass reinforced polymers and reflective plastic core insulation are also contained in this chapter. Some plastics exhibit rapid flame spread and heavy smoke density characteristics when exposed to fire. Additionally, exposure to the heat generated by a fire can cause some plastics to deform, which can affect their performance. The requirements and limitations of this chapter are necessary to control the use of plastic and foam plastic products such that they do not compromise the safety of building occupants.

Chapter 27 Electrical. Since electrical systems and components are an integral part of almost all structures, it is necessary for the code to address the installation of such systems. For this purpose, Chapter 27 references the *National Electrical Code* (NEC). In addition, Section 2702 addresses emergency and standby power requirements. Such systems must comply with the *International Fire Code* (IFC) and referenced standards. This section also provides references to the various code sections requiring emergency and standby power, such as high-rise buildings and buildings containing hazardous materials.

Chapter 28 Mechanical Systems. Nearly all buildings will include mechanical systems. This chapter provides references to the *International Mechanical Code* (IMC) and the *International Fuel Gas Code* (IFGC) for the design and installation of mechanical systems. In addition, the chapter references Chapter 21 of the IBC for masonry chimneys, fireplaces and barbecues.

Chapter 29 Plumbing Systems. Chapter 29 regulates the minimum number of plumbing fixtures that must be provided for every type of building. This chapter also regulates the location of the required fixtures in various types of buildings and the construction of toilet rooms. This section requires separate facilities for males and females except for certain types of small occupancies. The regulations in this chapter come directly from Chapters 3 and 4 of the *International Plumbing Code* (IPC).

Chapter 30 Elevators and Conveying Systems. Chapter 30 provides standards for the installation of elevators into buildings. Referenced standards provide the requirements for the elevator system and mechanisms. Detailed standards are provided in the chapter for hoistway enclosures, hoistway venting and machine rooms. New provisions are added in the 2009 IBC for Fire Service Access Elevators required in high-rise buildings and for the optional choice of Occupant Evacuation Elevators (see Section 403).

Chapter 31 Special Construction. Chapter 31 contains a collection of regulations for a variety of unique structures and architectural features. Pedestrian walkways and tunnels connecting two buildings are addressed in Section 3104. Membrane and air-supported structures are addressed by Section 3102. Safeguards for swimming pool safety are found in Section 3109. Standards for temporary structures, including permit requirements are provided in Section 3103. Structures as varied as awnings, marquees, signs, telecommunication and broadcast towers and automatic vehicular gates are also addressed (see Sections 3105 through 3108 and 3110).

Chapter 32 Encroachments into the Public Right-of-way. Buildings and structures from time to time are designed to extend over a property line and into the public right-of-way. Local regulations outside of the building code usually set limits to such encroachments, and such regulations take precedence over the provisions of this chapter. Standards are provided for encroachments below grade for structural support, vaults and areaways. Encroachments above grade are divided into below 8 feet, 8 feet to 15 feet, and above 15 feet, because of headroom and vehicular height issues. This includes steps, columns, awnings, canopies, marquees, signs, windows, balconies. Similar architectural features above grade are also addressed. Pedestrian walkways must also comply with Chapter 31.

Chapter 33 Safeguards During Construction. Chapter 33 provides safety requirements during construction and demolition of buildings and structures. These requirements are intended to protect the public from injury and adjoining property from damage. In addition the chapter provides for the progressive installation and operation of exit stairways and standpipe systems during construction.

Chapter 34 Existing Structures. The provisions in Chapter 34 deal with alternative methods or reduced compliance requirements when dealing with existing building constraints. This chapter allows for a controlled departure from full compliance with the technical codes, without compromising the minimum standards for fire prevention and life safety features of the rehabilitated building. Provisions are divided by addition, alterations, repairs, change of occupancy and moved structures. There are further allowances for registered historic buildings. There are also special allowances for replacement of existing stairways, replacement of glass and accessibility requirements. The fire escape requirements in Section 3406 are consistent with the fire escape requirements in Section 1030 of the *International Fire Code* (IFC).

Section 3412, *Compliance Alternatives*, allows for existing buildings to be evaluated so as to show that alterations, while not meeting new construction requirements, will improve the current existing situation. Provisions are based on a numerical scoring system involving 18 various safety parameters and the degree of code compliance for each issue.

Chapter 34 is repeated in the *International Existing Building Code* (IEBC). Sections 3402 through 3409 are repeated as IEBC Chapter 3 and Section 3410 as Chapter 13.

Chapter 35 Referenced Standards. The code contains numerous references to standards that are used to regulate materials and methods of construction. Chapter 35 contains a comprehensive list of all standards that are referenced in the code, including the appendices. The standards are part of the code to the extent of the reference to the standard (see Section 102.4). Compliance with the referenced standard is necessary for compliance with this code. By providing specifically adopted standards, the construction and installation requirements necessary for compliance with the code can be readily determined. The basis for code compliance is, therefore, established and available on an equal basis to the building code official, contractor, designer and owner.

Chapter 35 is organized in a manner that makes it easy to locate specific standards. It lists all of the referenced standards, alphabetically, by acronym of the promulgating agency of the standard. Each agency's standards are then listed in either alphabetical or numeric order based upon the standard identification. The list also contains the title of the standard; the edition (date) of the standard referenced; any addenda included as part of the ICC adoption; and the section or sections of this code that reference the standard.

Appendices. Appendices are provided in the IBC to offer optional or supplemental criteria to the provisions in the main chapters of the code. Appendices provide additional information for administration of the Department of Building Safety as well as standards not typically administered by all building departments. Appendices have the same force and effect as the first 35 chapters of the IBC only when explicitly adopted by the jurisdiction.

Appendix A Employee Qualifications. Effective administration and enforcement of the family of *International Codes* depends on the training and expertise of the personnel employed by the jurisdiction and his or her knowledge of the codes. Section 103 of the code establishes the Department of Building Safety and calls for the appointment of a building official and deputies such as plans examiners and inspectors. Appendix A provides standards for experience, training and certification for the building official and the other staff mentioned in Chapter 1.

Appendix B Board of Appeals. Section 112 of Chapter 1 requires the establishment of a board of appeals to hear appeals regarding determinations made by the building official. Appendix B provides qualification standards for members of the board as well as operational procedures of such board.

Appendix C Group U–Agricultural Buildings. Appendix C provides a more liberal set of standards for the construction of agricultural buildings, rather than strictly following the Utility building provision, reflective of their specific usage and limited occupant load. The provisions of the appendix, when adopted, allow reasonable heights and areas commensurate with the risk of agricultural buildings.

Appendix D Fire Districts. Fire districts have been a tool used to limit conflagration hazards in areas of a city with intense and concentrated development. More frequently used under the model codes which preceded the *International Building Code* (IBC), the appendix is provided to allow jurisdictions to continue the designation and use of fire districts. Fire District standards restrict certain occupancies within the district, as well as setting higher minimum construction standards.

Appendix E Supplemental Accessibility Requirements. The Architectural and Transportation Barriers Compliance Board (U.S. Access Board) has revised and updated its accessibility guidelines for buildings and facilities covered by the Americans with Disabilities Act (ADA) and the Architectural Barriers Act (ABA). Appendix E includes scoping requirements contained in the new ADA/ABA Accessibility Guidelines that are not in Chapter 11 and not otherwise mentioned or mainstreamed throughout the code. Items in the appendix deal with subjects not typically addressed in building codes (e.g., beds, room signage, transportation facilities).

Appendix F Rodentproofing. The provisions of this appendix are minimum mechanical methods to prevent the entry of rodents into a building. These standards, when used in conjunction with cleanliness and maintenance programs, can significantly reduce the potential of rodents invading a building.

Appendix G Flood-resistant Construction. Appendix G is intended to fulfill the flood-plain management and administrative requirements of the National Flood Insurance Program (NFIP) that are not included in the code. Communities that adopt the *International Building Code* (IBC) and Appendix G will meet the minimum requirements of NFIP as set forth in Title 44 of the Code of Federal Regulations.

Appendix H Signs. Appendix H gathers in one place the various code standards that regulate the construction and protection of outdoor signs. Whenever possible, the appendix provides standards in performance language, thus allowing the widest possible application.

Appendix I Patio Covers. Appendix I provides standards applicable to the construction and use of patio covers. It is limited in application to patio covers accessory to dwelling units. Covers of patios and other outdoor areas associated with restaurants, mercantile buildings, offices, nursing homes or other nondwelling occupancies would be subject to standards in the main code and not this appendix.

Appendix J Grading. Appendix J provides standards for the grading of properties. The appendix also provides standards for administration and enforcement of a grading program including permit and inspection requirements. Appendix J was originally developed in the 1960s and used for many years in jurisdictions throughout the western states. It is intended to provide consistent and uniform code requirements anywhere grading is considered an issue.

Appendix K Administrative Provisions. Appendix K primarily provides administrative provisions for jurisdictions adopting and enforcing NFPA 70—the *National Electrical Code* (NEC). The provisions contained in this appendix are compatible with administrative and enforcement provisions contained in Chapter 1 of the IBC and the other *International Codes*. Annex H of NFPA 70 also contains administrative provisions for the NEC; however, some of its provisions are not compatible with IBC Chapter 1. Section K110 also contains technical provisions that are unique to this appendix and are in addition to technical standards of NFPA 70.

ORDINANCE

The *International Codes* are designed and promulgated to be adopted by reference by ordinance. Jurisdictions wishing to adopt the 2009 *International Building Code* as an enforceable regulation governing structures and premises should ensure that certain factual information is included in the adopting ordinance at the time adoption is being considered by the appropriate governmental body. The following sample adoption ordinance addresses several key elements of a code adoption ordinance, including the information required for insertion into the code text.

SAMPLE ORDINANCE FOR ADOPTION OF THE INTERNATIONAL BUILDING CODE ORDINANCE NO.________

An ordinance of the **[JURISDICTION]** adopting the 2009 edition of the *International Building Code*, regulating and governing the conditions and maintenance of all property, buildings and structures; by providing the standards for supplied utilities and facilities and other physical things and conditions essential to ensure that structures are safe, sanitary and fit for occupation and use; and the condemnation of buildings and structures unfit for human occupancy and use and the demolition of such structures in the **[JURISDICTION]**; providing for the issuance of permits and collection of fees therefor; repealing Ordinance No. ______ of the **[JURISDICTION]** and all other ordinances and parts of the ordinances in conflict therewith.

The **[GOVERNING BODY]** of the **[JURISDICTION]** does ordain as follows:

Section 1. That a certain document, three (3) copies of which are on file in the office of the **[TITLE OF JURISDICTION'S KEEPER OF RECORDS]** of **[NAME OF JURISDICTION]**, being marked and designated as the *International Building Code*, 2009 edition, including Appendix Chapters **[FILL IN THE APPENDIX CHAPTERS BEING ADOPTED]** (see *International Building Code* Section 101.2.1, 2009 edition), as published by the International Code Council, be and is hereby adopted as the Building Code of the **[JURISDICTION]**, in the State of **[STATE NAME]** for regulating and governing the conditions and maintenance of all property, buildings and structures; by providing the standards for supplied utilities and facilities and other physical things and conditions essential to ensure that structures are safe, sanitary and fit for occupation and use; and the condemnation of buildings and structures unfit for human occupancy and use and the demolition of such structures as herein provided; providing for the issuance of permits and collection of fees therefor; and each and all of the regulations, provisions, penalties, conditions and terms of said Building Code on file in the office of the **[JURISDICTION]** are hereby referred to, adopted, and made a part hereof, as if fully set out in this ordinance, with the additions, insertions, deletions and changes, if any, prescribed in Section 2 of this ordinance.

Section 2. The following sections are hereby revised:

Section 101.1. Insert: **[NAME OF JURISDICTION]**

Section 1612.3. Insert: **[NAME OF JURISDICTION]**

Section 1612.3. Insert: **[DATE OF ISSUANCE]**

Section 3412.2. Insert: **[DATE IN ONE LOCATION]**

Section 3. That Ordinance No. ______ of **[JURISDICTION]** entitled **[FILL IN HERE THE COMPLETE TITLE OF THE ORDINANCE OR ORDINANCES IN EFFECT AT THE PRESENT TIME SO THAT THEY WILL BE REPEALED BY DEFINITE MENTION]** and all other ordinances or parts of ordinances in conflict herewith are hereby repealed.

Section 4. That if any section, subsection, sentence, clause or phrase of this ordinance is, for any reason, held to be unconstitutional, such decision shall not affect the validity of the remaining portions of this ordinance. The **[GOVERNING BODY]** hereby declares that it would have passed this ordinance, and each section, subsection, clause or phrase thereof, irrespective of the fact that any one or more sections, subsections, sentences, clauses and phrases be declared unconstitutional.

Section 5. That nothing in this ordinance or in the Building Code hereby adopted shall be construed to affect any suit or proceeding impending in any court, or any rights acquired, or liability incurred, or any cause or causes of action acquired or existing, under any act or ordinance hereby repealed as cited in Section 3 of this ordinance; nor shall any just or legal right or remedy of any character be lost, impaired or affected by this ordinance.

Section 6. That the **[JURISDICTION'S KEEPER OF RECORDS]** is hereby ordered and directed to cause this ordinance to be published. (An additional provision may be required to direct the number of times the ordinance is to be published and to specify that it is to be in a newspaper in general circulation. Posting may also be required.)

Section 7. That this ordinance and the rules, regulations, provisions, requirements, orders and matters established and adopted hereby shall take effect and be in full force and effect **[TIME PERIOD]** from and after the date of its final passage and adoption.

TABLE OF CONTENTS

CHAPTER 1
SCOPE AND ADMINISTRATION

PART 1—SCOPE AND APPLICATION

SECTION 101 GENERAL

101.1 Title. These regulations shall be known as the *North Carolina Building Code* as adopted by the North Carolina Building Code Council on September 14, 2010 to be effective September 1, 2011. References to the *International Code* shall mean the *North Carolina Codes*. The North Carolina amendments to the *International Code* are underlined.

101.2 Scope. The provisions of this code shall apply to the construction, *alteration*, movement, enlargement, replacement, repair, equipment, use and occupancy, location, maintenance, removal and demolition of every building or structure or any appurtenances connected or attached to such buildings or structures.

Exceptions:

1. Detached one- and two-family *dwellings* and multiple single-family *dwellings* (*townhouses*) not more than three *stories* above *grade plane* in height with a separate *means of egress* and their accessory structures shall comply with the *International Residential Code*.
2. Farm *buildings* located outside of the building rules jurisdiction of any municipality.

   Exception: All *buildings* used for sleeping purposes shall conform to the provisions of the technical codes.
3. The design, construction, location, installation or operation of equipment for storing, handling and transporting liquefied petroleum gases for fuel purposes up to the outlet of the first stage pressure regulator, and anhydrous ammonia or other liquid fertilizers.
4. The design, construction, location, installation or operation of equipment or facilities of a public utility, as defined in G.S. 62-3, or an electric or telephone membership corporation, including without limitation poles, towers and other structures supporting electric or communication lines from the distribution network up to the meter location.

   Note: All *buildings* owned and operated by a public utility or an electric or telephone membership corporation shall meet the provisions of this code.
5. The Storage and Handling of Hazardous Chemicals Right to Know Act, Article 18 of Chapter 95 of the North Carolina General Statutes.

101.2.1 Appendices. Provisions in the appendices shall not apply unless specifically adopted or referenced in this code.

101.3 Intent. The purpose of this code is to establish the minimum requirements to safeguard the public health, safety and general welfare through structural strength, *means of egress* facilities, stability, sanitation, adequate light and ventilation, energy conservation, and safety to life and property from fire and other hazards attributed to the built environment and to provide safety to fire fighters and emergency responders during emergency operations.

101.4 Referenced codes. The other codes listed in Sections 101.4.1 through 101.4.6 and referenced elsewhere in this code shall be considered part of the requirements of this code to the prescribed extent of each such reference.

101.4.1 Gas. The provisions of the *International Fuel Gas Code* shall apply to the installation of gas piping from the point of delivery, gas appliances and related accessories as covered in this code. These requirements apply to gas piping systems extending from the point of delivery to the inlet connections of appliances and the installation and operation of residential and commercial gas appliances and related accessories.

101.4.2 Mechanical. The provisions of the *International Mechanical Code* shall apply to the installation, alterations, repairs and replacement of mechanical systems, including equipment, appliances, fixtures, fittings and/or appurtenances, including ventilating, heating, cooling, air-conditioning and refrigeration systems, incinerators and other energy-related systems.

101.4.3 Plumbing. The provisions of the *International Plumbing Code* shall apply to the installation, *alteration*, repair and replacement of plumbing systems, including equipment, appliances, fixtures, fittings and appurtenances, and where connected to a water or sewage system and all aspects of a medical gas system. The provisions of the *International Private Sewage Disposal Code* shall apply to private sewage disposal systems.

101.4.4 Property maintenance. Deleted.

101.4.5 Fire prevention. The provisions of the *International Fire Code* shall apply to matters affecting or relating to structures, processes and premises from the hazard of fire and explosion arising from the storage, handling or use of structures, materials or devices; from conditions hazardous to life, property or public welfare in the occupancy of structures or premises; and from the construction, extension, repair, *alteration* or removal of fire suppression and alarm systems or fire hazards in the structure or on the premises from occupancy or operation.

101.4.6 Energy. The provisions of the *International Energy Conservation Code* shall apply to all matters governing the design and construction of buildings for energy efficiency.

101.5 Requirements of other State agencies, occupational licensing boards or commissions. The North Carolina State

Building Codes do not include all additional requirements for *buildings* and structures that may be imposed by other State agencies, occupational licensing boards and commissions. It shall be the responsibility of a permit holder, registered design professional, contractor or occupational licensing holder to determine whether any additional requirements exist.

SECTION 102 APPLICABILITY

102.1 General. Where there is a conflict between a general requirement and a specific requirement, the specific requirement shall be applicable. Where, in any specific case, different sections of this code specify different materials, methods of construction or other requirements, the most restrictive shall govern.

102.2 Other laws. The provisions of this code shall not be deemed to nullify any provisions of local, state or federal law.

102.3 Application of references. References to chapter or section numbers, or to provisions not specifically identified by number, shall be construed to refer to such chapter, section or provision of this code.

102.4 Referenced codes and standards. The codes and standards referenced in this code shall be considered part of the requirements of this code to the prescribed extent of each such reference. Where differences occur between provisions of this code and referenced codes and standards, the provisions of this code shall apply.

102.5 Partial invalidity. In the event that any part or provision of this code is held to be illegal or void, this shall not have the effect of making void or illegal any of the other parts or provisions.

102.6 Existing structures. The legal occupancy of any structure existing on the date of adoption of this code shall be permitted to continue without change, except as is specifically covered in this code, the *International Property Maintenance Code* or the *International Fire Code*, or as is deemed necessary by the *building official* for the general safety and welfare of the occupants and the public.

PART 2—ADMINISTRATION AND ENFORCEMENT

SECTION 103 DEPARTMENT OF BUILDING SAFETY

Deleted. See the North Carolina Administrative Code and Policies.

SECTION 104 DUTIES AND POWERS OF BUILDING OFFICIAL

Deleted. See the North Carolina Administrative Code and Policies.

SECTION 105 PERMITS

Deleted. See the North Carolina Administrative Code and Policies.

SECTION 106 FLOOR AND ROOF DESIGN LOADS

Deleted. See the North Carolina Administrative Code and Policies.

SECTION 107 SUBMITTAL DOCUMENTS

Deleted. See the North Carolina Administrative Code and Policies.

SECTION 108 TEMPORARY STRUCTURES AND USES

Deleted. See the North Carolina Administrative Code and Policies.

SECTION 109 FEES

Deleted. See the North Carolina Administrative Code and Policies.

SECTION 110 INSPECTIONS

Deleted. See the North Carolina Administrative Code and Policies.

SECTION 111 CERTIFICATE OF OCCUPANCY

Deleted. See the North Carolina Administrative Code and Policies.

SECTION 112 SERVICE UTILITIES

Deleted. See the North Carolina Administrative Code and Policies.

SECTION 113 BOARD OF APPEALS

Deleted. See the North Carolina Administrative Code and Policies.

SECTION 114 VIOLATIONS

Deleted. See the North Carolina Administrative Code and Policies.

SECTION 115
STOP WORK ORDER

Deleted. See the North Carolina Administrative Code and Policies.

SECTION 116
UNSAFE STRUCTURES AND EQUIPMENT

Deleted. See the North Carolina Administrative Code and Policies.

CHAPTER 2
DEFINITIONS

SECTION 201
GENERAL

201.1 Scope. Unless otherwise expressly stated, the following words and terms shall, for the purposes of this code, have the meanings shown in this chapter.

201.2 Interchangeability. Words used in the present tense include the future; words stated in the masculine gender include the feminine and neuter; the singular number includes the plural and the plural, the singular.

201.3 Terms defined in other codes. Where terms are not defined in this code and are defined in the *International Fuel Gas Code, International Fire Code, International Mechanical Code* or *International Plumbing Code,* such terms shall have the meanings ascribed to them as in those codes.

201.4 Terms not defined. Where terms are not defined through the methods authorized by this section, such terms shall have ordinarily accepted meanings such as the context implies.

SECTION 202
DEFINITIONS

AAC MASONRY. See Section 2102.1.

ACCEPTED ENGINEERING PRACTICE. Design, analysis and testing methods that are used in developing design solutions for compliance with the requirements of this code. Accepted engineering practice is the level at which the average, prudent designer in a given community would practice.

ACCESSIBLE. See Section 1102.1.

ACCESSIBLE MEANS OF EGRESS. See Section 1002.1.

ACCESSIBLE ROUTE. See Section 1102.1.

ACCESSIBLE UNIT. See Section 1102.1.

ACCREDITATION BODY. See Section 2302.1.

ADDITION. An extension or increase in floor area or height of a building or structure.

ADHERED MASONRY VENEER. See Section 1402.1.

ADOBE CONSTRUCTION. See Section 2102.1.

Adobe, stabilized. See Section 2102.1.

Adobe, unstabilized. See Section 2102.1.

[F] AEROSOL. See Section 307.2.

Level 1 aerosol products. See Section 307.2.

Level 2 aerosol products. See Section 307.2.

Level 3 aerosol products. See Section 307.2.

[F] AEROSOL CONTAINER. See Section 307.2.

AGGREGATE. See Section 1502.1.

AGRICULTURAL, BUILDING. A structure designed and constructed to house farm implements, hay, grain, poultry, livestock or other horticultural products. This structure shall not be a place of human habitation or a place of employment where agricultural products are processed, treated or packaged, nor shall it be a place used by the public.

AIR-INFLATED STRUCTURE. See Section 3102.2.

AIR-SUPPORTED STRUCTURE. See Section 3102.2.

Double skin. See Section 3102.2.

Single skin. See Section 3102.2.

AISLE. See Section 1002.1.

AISLE ACCESSWAY. See Section 1002.1.

[F] ALARM NOTIFICATION APPLIANCE. See Section 902.1.

[F] ALARM SIGNAL. See Section 902.1.

[F] ALARM VERIFICATION FEATURE. See Section 902.1.

ALLOWABLE STRESS DESIGN. See Section 1602.1.

ALTERATION. Any construction or renovation to an existing structure other than repair or *addition.*

ALTERNATING TREAD DEVICE. See Section 1002.1.

AMBULATORY HEALTH CARE FACILITY. Buildings or portions thereof used to provide medical, surgical, psychiatric, nursing or similar care on a less than 24-hour basis to individuals who are rendered incapable of self-preservation.

ANCHOR. See Section 2102.1.

ANCHOR BUILDING. See Section 402.2.

ANCHORED MASONRY VENEER. See Section 1402.1.

ANNULAR SPACE. See Section 702.1.

[F] ANNUNCIATOR. See Section 902.1.

APPROVED. Acceptable to the code official or authority having jurisdiction for compliance with the provisions of the applicable code or referenced standard.

APPROVED AGENCY. See Section 1702.1.

APPROVED FABRICATOR. See Section 1702.1.

APPROVED SOURCE. An independent person, firm or corporation, *approved* by the *building official*, who is competent and experienced in the application of engineering principles to materials, methods or systems analyses.

ARCHITECTURAL TERRA COTTA. See Section 2102.1.

AREA (for masonry). See Section 2102.1.

Bedded. See Section 2102.1.

Gross cross-sectional. See Section 2102.1.

Net cross-sectional. See Section 2102.1.

AREA, BUILDING. See Section 502.1.

AREA OF REFUGE. See Section 1002.1.

AREAWAY. A subsurface space adjacent to a building open at the top or protected at the top by a grating or *guard*.

ASSISTED LIVING FACILITIES. See Section 310.2, "Residential Care/Assisted living facilities."

ATRIUM. See Section 404.1.1.

ATTIC. The space between the ceiling beams of the top *story* and the roof rafters.

[F] AUDIBLE ALARM NOTIFICATION APPLIANCE. See Section 902.1.

AUTOCLAVED AERATED CONCRETE (AAC). See Section 2102.1.

[F] AUTOMATIC. See Section 902.1.

[F] AUTOMATIC FIRE-EXTINGUISHING SYSTEM. See Section 902.1.

[F] AUTOMATIC SMOKE DETECTION SYSTEM. See Section 902.1.

[F] AUTOMATIC SPRINKLER SYSTEM. See Section 902.1.

[F] AVERAGE AMBIENT SOUND LEVEL. See Section 902.1.

AWNING. An architectural projection that provides weather protection, identity or decoration and is wholly supported by the building to which it is attached. An *awning* is comprised of a lightweight frame structure over which a covering is attached.

BACKING. See Section 1402.1.

[F] BALED COTTON. See Section 307.2.

[F] BALED COTTON, DENSELY PACKED. See Section 307.2.

BALLAST. See Section 1502.1.

[F] BARRICADE. See Section 307.2.

Artificial barricade. See Section 307.2.

Natural barricade. See Section 307.2.

BASE FLOOD. See Section 1612.2.

BASE FLOOD ELEVATION. See Section 1612.2.

BASEMENT (for other than flood loads). See Section 502.1.

BASEMENT (for flood loads). See Section 1612.2.

BEARING WALL STRUCTURE. See Section 1614.2.

BED JOINT. See Section 2102.1.

BLEACHERS. See Section 1002.1.

BOARDING HOUSE. See Section 310.2.

[F] BOILING POINT. See Section 307.2.

BOND BEAM. See Section 2102.1.

BRACED WALL LINE. See Section 2302.1.

BRACED WALL PANEL. See Section 2302.1.

BRICK. See Section 2102.1.

Calcium silicate (sand lime brick). See Section 2102.1.

Clay or shale. See Section 2102.1.

Concrete. See Section 2102.1.

BUILDING. Any structure used or intended for supporting or sheltering any use or occupancy.

BUILDING ELEMENT. See Section 702.1.

BUILDING LINE. The line established by law, beyond which a building shall not extend, except as specifically provided by law.

BUILDING OFFICIAL. The officer or other designated authority charged with the administration and enforcement of this code, or a duly authorized representative.

BUILT-UP ROOF COVERING. See Section 1502.1.

CABLE-RESTRAINED, AIR-SUPPORTED STRUCTURE. See Section 3102.2.

CANOPY. A permanent structure or architectural projection of rigid construction over which a covering is attached that provides weather protection, identity or decoration, and shall be structurally independent or supported by attachment to a building on one end and by not less than one stanchion on the outer end.

[F] CARBON DIOXIDE EXTINGUISHING SYSTEMS. See Section 902.1.

CAST STONE. See Section 2102.1.

[F] CEILING LIMIT. See Section 902.1.

CEILING RADIATION DAMPER. See Section 702.1.

CELL. See Section 408.1.1.

CELL (masonry). See Section 2102.1.

CELL TIER. See Section 408.1.1.

CEMENT PLASTER. See Section 2502.1.

CERAMIC FIBER BLANKET. See Section 721.1.1.

CERTIFICATE OF COMPLIANCE. See Section 1702.1.

CHILD CARE FACILITIES. See Section 308.3.1.

CHIMNEY. See Section 2102.1.

CHIMNEY TYPES. See Section 2102.1.

High-heat appliance type. See Section 2102.1.

Low-heat appliance type. See Section 2102.1.

Masonry type. See Section 2102.1.

Medium-heat appliance type. See Section 2102.1.

CIRCULATION PATH. See Section 1102.1.

[F] CLEAN AGENT. See Section 902.1.

CLEANOUT. See Section 2102.1.

CLINIC, OUTPATIENT. See Section 304.1.1.

[F] CLOSED SYSTEM. See Section 307.2.

COLLAR JOINT. See Section 2102.1.

COLLECTOR. See Section 2302.1.

COMBINATION FIRE/SMOKE DAMPER. See Section 702.1.

[F] COMBUSTIBLE DUST. See Section 307.2.

[F] COMBUSTIBLE FIBERS. See Section 307.2.

[F] COMBUSTIBLE LIQUID. See Section 307.2.

Class II. See Section 307.2.

Class IIIA. See Section 307.2.

Class IIIB. See Section 307.2.

COMMON USE. See Section 1102.1.

COMMON PATH OF EGRESS TRAVEL. See Section 1002.1.

[F] COMPRESSED GAS. See Section 307.2.

COMPRESSIVE STRENGTH OF MASONRY. See Section 2102.1.

CONCRETE, CARBONATE AGGREGATE. See Section 721.1.1.

CONCRETE, CELLULAR. See Section 721.1.1.

CONCRETE, LIGHTWEIGHT AGGREGATE. See Section 721.1.1.

CONCRETE, PERLITE. See Section 721.1.1.

CONCRETE, SAND-LIGHTWEIGHT. See Section 721.1.1.

CONCRETE, SILICEOUS AGGREGATE. See Section 721.1.1.

CONCRETE, VERMICULITE. See Section 721.1.1.

CONGREGATE LIVING FACILITIES. See Section 310.2.

CONNECTOR. See Section 2102.1.

[F] CONSTANTLY ATTENDED LOCATION. See Section 902.1.

CONSTRUCTION DOCUMENTS. Written, graphic and pictorial documents prepared or assembled for describing the design, location and physical characteristics of the elements of a project necessary for obtaining a building *permit*.

CONSTRUCTION TYPES. See Section 602.

Type I. See Section 602.2.

Type II. See Section 602.2.

Type III. See Section 602.3.

Type IV. See Section 602.4.

Type V. See Section 602.5.

[F] CONTINUOUS GAS DETECTION SYSTEM. See Section 415.2.

[F] CONTROL AREA. See Section 307.2.

CONTROLLED LOW-STRENGTH MATERIAL. A self-compacted, cementitious material used primarily as a backfill in place of compacted fill.

CONVENTIONAL LIGHT-FRAME CONSTRUCTION. See Section 2302.1.

COOPERATIVE INNOVATIVE HIGH SCHOOL PROGRAM. A program to supplement the required curriculum for high school students that may require attendance at a college, community college or university.

CORRIDOR. See Section 1002.1.

CORROSION RESISTANCE. The ability of a material to withstand deterioration of its surface or its properties when exposed to its environment.

[F] CORROSIVE. See Section 307.2.

COURT. An open, uncovered space, unobstructed to the sky, bounded on three or more sides by exterior building walls or other enclosing devices.

COVER. See Section 2102.1.

COVERED MALL BUILDING. See Section 402.2.

Mall. See Section 402.2.

Open mall. See Section 402.2.

Open mall building. See Section 402.2.

CRIPPLE WALL. See Section 2302.1.

[F] CRYOGENIC FLUID. See Section 307.2.

DALLE GLASS. See Section 2402.1.

DAMPER. See Section 702.1.

DANGEROUS. See Section 3402.1.

[F] DAY BOX. See Section 307.2.

DEAD LOADS. See Section 1602.1.

DECORATIVE GLASS. See Section 2402.1.

[F] DECORATIVE MATERIALS. All materials applied over the building *interior finish* for decorative, acoustical or other effect (such as curtains, draperies, fabrics, streamers and surface coverings), and all other materials utilized for decorative effect (such as batting, cloth, cotton, hay, stalks, straw, vines, leaves, trees, moss and similar items), including foam plastics and materials containing foam plastics. *Decorative materials* do not include floor coverings, ordinary window shades, *interior finish* and materials 0.025 inch (0.64 mm) or less in thickness applied directly to and adhering tightly to a substrate.

DEEP FOUNDATION. See Section 1802.1.

[F] DEFLAGRATION. See Section 307.2.

[F] DELUGE SYSTEM. See Section 902.1.

DESIGN DISPLACEMENT. See Section 1908.1.1.

DESIGN EARTHQUAKE GROUND MOTION. See Section 1613.2.

DESIGN FLOOD. See Section 1612.2.

DESIGN FLOOD ELEVATION. See Section 1612.2.

DESIGN STRENGTH. See Section 1602.1.

DESIGNATED SEISMIC SYSTEM. See Section 1702.1.

[F] DETACHED BUILDING. See Section 415.2.

DETAILED PLAIN CONCRETE STRUCTURAL WALL. See Section 1908.1.1.

DETECTABLE WARNING. See Section 1102.1.

[F] DETECTOR, HEAT. See Section 902.1.

[F] DETONATION. See Section 307.2.

DETOXIFICATION FACILITY. See Section 308.3.1.

DIAPHRAGM. See Sections 1602.1 and 2302.1.

Diaphragm, blocked. See Section 1602.1.

Diaphragm, boundary. See Section 1602.1.

Diaphragm, chord. See Section 1602.1.

Diaphragm, flexible. See Section 1602.1.

Diaphragm, rigid. See Section 1602.1.

Diaphragm, unblocked. See Section 2302.1.

DIMENSIONS. See Section 2102.1.

Actual. See Section 2102.1.

Nominal. Scc Scction 2102.1.

Specified. See Section 2102.1.

[F] DISPENSING. See Section 307.2.

DOOR, BALANCED. See Section 1002.1.

DORMITORY. See Section 310.2.

DRAFTSTOP. See Section 702.1.

DRAG STRUT. See Section 2302.1.

DRILLED SHAFT. See Section 1802.1.

Socketed drilled shaft. See Section 1802.1.

[F] DRY-CHEMICAL EXTINGUISHING AGENT. See Section 902.1.

DRY FLOODPROOFING. See Section 1612.2.

DURATION OF LOAD. See Section 1602.1.

DWELLING. A building that contains one or two *dwelling units* used, intended or designed to be used, rented, leased, let or hired out to be occupied for living purposes.

DWELLING UNIT. A single unit providing complete, independent living facilities for one or more persons, including permanent provisions for living, sleeping, eating, cooking and sanitation.

DWELLING UNIT OR SLEEPING UNIT, MULTI-STORY. See Section 1102.1.

DWELLING UNIT OR SLEEPING UNIT, TYPE A. See Section 1102.1.

DWELLING UNIT OR SLEEPING UNIT, TYPE B. See Section 1102.1.

EGRESS COURT. See Section 1002.1.

ELEVATOR GROUP. See Section 902.1.

[F] EMERGENCY ALARM SYSTEM. See Section 902.1.

[F] EMERGENCY CONTROL STATION. See Section 415.2.

EMERGENCY ESCAPE AND RESCUE OPENING. See Section 1002.1.

[F] EMERGENCY VOICE/ALARM COMMUNICATIONS. See Section 902.1.

EMPLOYEE WORK AREA. See Section 1102.1.

EQUIPMENT PLATFORM. See Section 502.1.

ESSENTIAL FACILITIES. See Section 1602.1.

[F] EXHAUSTED ENCLOSURE. See Section 415.2.

EXISTING CONSTRUCTION. See Section 1612.2.

EXISTING STRUCTURE. See Sections 1612.2 and 3402.1.

EXIT. See Section 1002.1.

EXIT ACCESS. See Section 1002.1.

EXIT ACCESS DOORWAY. See Section 1002.1.

EXIT DISCHARGE. See Section 1002.1.

EXIT DISCHARGE, LEVEL OF. See Section 1002.1.

EXIT ENCLOSURE. See Section 1002.1.

EXIT, HORIZONTAL. See Section 1002.1.

EXIT PASSAGEWAY. See Section 1002.1.

EXPANDED VINYL WALL COVERING. See Section 802.1.

[F] EXPLOSION. See Section 307.2.

[F] EXPLOSIVE. See Section 307.2.

High explosive. See Section 307.2.

Low explosive. See Section 307.2.

Mass detonating explosives. See Section 307.2.

UN/DOTn Class 1 Explosives. See Section 307.2.

Division 1.1. See Section 307.2.

Division 1.2. See Section 307.2.

Division 1.3. See Section 307.2.

Division 1.4. See Section 307.2.

Division 1.5. See Section 307.2.

Division 1.6. See Section 307.2.

EXTERIOR INSULATION AND FINISH SYSTEM (EIFS). See Section 1402.1.

EXTERIOR INSULATION AND FINISH SYSTEM (EIFS) WITH DRAINAGE. See Section 1402.1.

EXTERIOR SURFACES. See Section 2502.1.

EXTERIOR WALL. See Section 1402.1.

EXTERIOR WALL COVERING. See Section 1402.1.

EXTERIOR WALL ENVELOPE. See Section 1402.1.

F RATING. See Section 702.1.

FABRIC PARTITION. See Section 1602.1.

FABRICATED ITEM. See Section 1702.1.

[F] FABRICATION AREA. See Section 415.2.

FACILITY. See Section 1102.1.

FACTORED LOAD. See Section 1602.1.

FIBER CEMENT SIDING. See Section 1402.1.

FIBER REINFORCED POLYMER. See Section 2602.1.

Fiberglass Reinforced Polymer. See Section 2602.1.

FIBERBOARD. See Section 2302.1.

FIRE ALARM BOX, MANUAL. See Section 902.1.

[F] FIRE ALARM CONTROL UNIT. See Section 902.1.

[F] FIRE ALARM SIGNAL. See Section 902.1.

[F] FIRE ALARM SYSTEM. See Section 902.1.

FIRE AREA. See Section 902.1.

FIRE BARRIER. See Section 702.1.

[F] FIRE COMMAND CENTER. See Section 902.1.

FIRE DAMPER. See Section 702.1.

[F] FIRE DETECTOR, AUTOMATIC. See Section 902.1.

FIRE DOOR. See Section 702.1.

FIRE DOOR ASSEMBLY. See Section 702.1.

FIRE EXIT HARDWARE. See Section 1002.1.

[F] FIRE LANE. A road or other passageway developed to allow the passage of fire apparatus. A *fire lane* is not necessarily intended for vehicular traffic other than fire apparatus.

FIRE PARTITION. See Section 702.1.

FIRE PROTECTION RATING. See Section 702.1.

[F] FIRE PROTECTION SYSTEM. See Section 902.1.

FIRE RESISTANCE. See Section 702.1.

FIRE-RESISTANCE RATING. See Section 702.1.

FIRE-RESISTANT JOINT SYSTEM. See Section 702.1.

[F] FIRE SAFETY FUNCTIONS. See Section 902.1.

FIRE SEPARATION DISTANCE. See Section 702.1.

FIRE WALL. See Section 702.1.

FIRE WINDOW ASSEMBLY. See Section 702.1.

FIREBLOCKING. See Section 702.1.

FIREPLACE. See Section 2102.1.

FIREPLACE THROAT. See Section 2102.1.

[F] FIREWORKS. See Section 307.2.

Fireworks, 1.3G. See Section 307.2.

Fireworks, 1.4G. See Section 307.2.

FIXED BASE OPERATOR (FBO). See Section 412.2.

FLAME SPREAD. See Section 802.1.

FLAME SPREAD INDEX. See Section 802.1.

[F] FLAMMABLE GAS. See Section 307.2.

[F] FLAMMABLE LIQUEFIED GAS. See Section 307.2.

[F] FLAMMABLE LIQUID. See Section 307.2.

Class IA. See Section 307.2.

Class IB. See Section 307.2.

Class IC. See Section 307.2.

[F] FLAMMABLE MATERIAL. See Section 307.2.

[F] FLAMMABLE SOLID. See Section 307.2.

[F] FLAMMABLE VAPORS OR FUMES. See Section 415.2.

[F] FLASH POINT. See Section 307.2.

FLIGHT. See Section 1002.1.

FLOOD OR FLOODING. See Section 1612.2.

FLOOD DAMAGE-RESISTANT MATERIALS. See Section 1612.2.

FLOOD HAZARD AREA. See Section 1612.2.

FLOOD HAZARD AREA SUBJECT TO HIGH-VELOCITY WAVE ACTION. See Section 1612.2.

FLOOD INSURANCE RATE MAP (FIRM). See Section 1612.2.

FLOOD INSURANCE STUDY. See Section 1612.2.

FLOODWAY. See Section 1612.2.

FLOOR AREA, GROSS. See Section 1002.1.

FLOOR AREA, NET. See Section 1002.1.

FLOOR FIRE DOOR ASSEMBLY. See Section 702.1.

FLY GALLERY. See Section 410.2.

[F] FOAM-EXTINGUISHING SYSTEMS. See Section 902.1.

FOAM PLASTIC INSULATION. See Section 2602.1.

FOLDING AND TELESCOPIC SEATING. See Section 1002.1.

FOOD COURT. See Section 402.2.

FOUNDATION PIER. See Section 2102.1.

FRAME STRUCTURE. See Section 1614.2.

[F] GAS CABINET. See Section 415.2.

[F] GAS ROOM. See Section 415.2.

[F] GASEOUS HYDROGEN SYSTEM. See Section 421.2.

GLASS FIBERBOARD. See Section 721.1.1.

GLUED BUILT-UP MEMBER. See Section 2302.1.

GRADE FLOOR OPENING. A window or other opening located such that the sill height of the opening is not more than 44 inches (1118 mm) above or below the finished ground level adjacent to the opening.

GRADE (LUMBER). See Section 2302.1.

GRADE PLANE. See Section 502.1.

GRANDSTAND. See Section 1002.1.

GRIDIRON. See Section 410.2.

GROSS LEASABLE AREA. See Section 402.2.

GROUTED MASONRY. See Section 2102.1.

Grouted hollow-unit masonry. See Section 2102.1.

Grouted multiwythe masonry. See Section 2102.1.

GUARD. See Section 1002.1.

GYPSUM BOARD. See Section 2502.1.

GYPSUM PLASTER. See Section 2502.1.

GYPSUM VENEER PLASTER. See Section 2502.1.

HABITABLE SPACE. A space in a building for living, sleeping, eating or cooking. Bathrooms, toilet rooms, closets, halls, storage or utility spaces and similar areas are not considered habitable spaces.

[F] HALOGENATED EXTINGUISHING SYSTEMS. See Section 902.1.

[F] HANDLING. See Section 307.2.

HANDRAIL. See Section 1002.1.

HARDBOARD. See Section 2302.1.

[F] HAZARDOUS MATERIALS. See Section 307.2.

[F] HAZARDOUS PRODUCTION MATERIAL (HPM). See Section 415.2.

HEAD JOINT. See Section 2102.1.

[F] HEALTH HAZARD. See Section 307.2.

HEIGHT, BUILDING. See Section 502.1.

HEIGHT, WALLS. See Section 2102.1.

HELICAL PILE. See Section 1802.1.

HELIPORT. See Section 412.2.

HELISTOP. See Section 412.2.

HIGH-RISE BUILDING. A building with an occupied floor located more than 75 feet (22 860 mm) above the lowest level of fire department vehicle access.

[F] HIGHLY TOXIC. See Section 307.2.

HISTORIC BUILDINGS. Buildings that are listed in or eligible for listing in the National Register of Historic Places, or designated as historic under an appropriate state or local law (see Sections 3409 and 3411.9).

HORIZONTAL ASSEMBLY. See Section 702.1.

HOSPITALS AND MENTAL HOSPITALS. See Section 308.3.1.

HOUSING UNIT. See Section 408.1.1.

[F] HPM FLAMMABLE LIQUID. See Section 415.2.

[F] HPM ROOM. See Section 415.2.

HURRICANE-PRONE REGIONS. See Section 1609.2.

[F] HYDROGEN CUTOFF ROOM. See Section 421.2.

[F] IMMEDIATELY DANGEROUS TO LIFE AND HEALTH (IDLH). See Section 415.2.

IMPACT LOAD. See Section 1602.1.

[F] INCOMPATIBLE MATERIALS. See Section 307.2.

[F] INERT GAS. See Section 307.2.

[F] INITIATING DEVICE. See Section 902.1.

INSPECTION CERTIFICATE. See Section 1702.1.

INTENDED TO BE OCCUPIED AS A RESIDENCE. See Section 1102.1.

INTERIOR FINISH. See Section 802.1.

INTERIOR FLOOR FINISH. See Section 802.1.

[F] INTERIOR FLOOR-WALL BASE. See Section 802.1.

INTERIOR SURFACES. See Section 2502.1.

INTERIOR WALL AND CEILING FINISH. See Section 802.1.

INTERLAYMENT. See Section 1502.1.

INTUMESCENT FIRE-RESISTANT COATINGS. See Section 1702.1.

JOINT. See Section 702.1.

JURISDICTION. The governmental unit that has adopted this code under due legislative authority.

LABEL. An identification applied on a product by the manufacturer that contains the name of the manufacturer, the function and performance characteristics of the product or material, and the name and identification of an *approved agency* and that indicates that the representative sample of the product or material has been tested and evaluated by an *approved agency* (see Section 1703.5 and "Inspection certificate," "Manufacturer's designation" and "*Mark*").

LABELED. Equipment, materials or products to which has been affixed a *label*, seal, symbol or other identifying *mark* of a nationally recognized testing laboratory, inspection agency or other organization concerned with product evaluation that maintains periodic inspection of the production of the above-labeled items and whose labeling indicates either that the equipment, material or product meets identified standards or has been tested and found suitable for a specified purpose.

LIGHT-DIFFUSING SYSTEM. See Section 2602.1.

LIGHT-FRAME CONSTRUCTION. A type of construction whose vertical and horizontal structural elements are primarily formed by a system of repetitive wood or cold-formed steel framing members.

LIGHT-TRANSMITTING PLASTIC ROOF PANELS. See Section 2602.1.

LIGHT-TRANSMITTING PLASTIC WALL PANELS. See Section 2602.1.

LIMIT STATE. See Section 1602.1.

[F] LIQUID. See Section 415.2.

[F] LIQUID STORAGE ROOM. See Section 415.2.

[F] LIQUID USE, DISPENSING AND MIXING ROOM. See Section 415.2.

LISTED. Equipment, materials, products or services included in a list published by an organization acceptable to the code official and concerned with evaluation of products or services that maintains periodic inspection of production of *listed* equipment or materials or periodic evaluation of services and whose listing states either that the equipment, material, product or service meets identified standards or has been tested and found suitable for a specified purpose.

LIVE LOADS. See Section 1602.1.

LIVE LOADS (ROOF). See Section 1602.1.

LOAD AND RESISTANCE FACTOR DESIGN (LRFD). See Section 1602.1.

LOAD EFFECTS. See Section 1602.1.

LOAD FACTOR. See Section 1602.1.

LOADS. See Section 1602.1.

LOT. A portion or parcel of land considered as a unit.

LOT LINE. A line dividing one lot from another, or from a street or any public place.

[F] LOWER FLAMMABLE LIMIT (LFL). See Section 415.2.

LOWEST FLOOR. See Section 1612.2.

MAIN WINDFORCE-RESISTING SYSTEM. See Section 1702.1.

[F] MANUAL FIRE ALARM BOX. See Section 902.1.

MANUFACTURER'S DESIGNATION. An identification applied on a product by the manufacturer indicating that a product or material complies with a specified standard or set of rules (see also "Inspection certificate," "*Label*" and "*Mark*").

MARK. An identification applied on a product by the manufacturer indicating the name of the manufacturer and the function of a product or material (see also "Inspection certificate," "*Label*" and "Manufacturer's designation").

MARQUEE. A permanent roofed structure attached to and supported by the building and that projects into the public right-of-way.

MASONRY. See Section 2102.1.

Ashlar masonry. See Section 2102.1.

Coursed ashlar. See Section 2102.1.

Glass unit masonry. See Section 2102.1.

Plain masonry. See Section 2102.1.

Random ashlar. See Section 2102.1.

Reinforced masonry. See Section 2102.1.

Solid masonry. See Section 2102.1.

Unreinforced (plain) masonry. See Section 2102.1.

MASONRY UNIT. See Section 2102.1.

Clay. See Section 2102.1.

Concrete. See Section 2102.1.

Hollow. See Section 2102.1.

Solid. See Section 2102.1.

MASTIC FIRE-RESISTANT COATINGS. See Section 1702.1.

MAXIMUM CONSIDERED EARTHQUAKE GROUND MOTION. See Section 1613.2.

MEANS OF EGRESS. See Section 1002.1.

MECHANICAL-ACCESS OPEN PARKING GARAGES. See Section 406.3.2.

MECHANICAL EQUIPMENT SCREEN. See Section 1502.1.

MECHANICAL SYSTEMS. See Section 1613.2.

MEMBRANE-COVERED CABLE STRUCTURE. See Section 3102.2.

MEMBRANE-COVERED FRAME STRUCTURE. See Section 3102.2.

MEMBRANE PENETRATION. See Section 702.1.

MEMBRANE-PENETRATION FIRESTOP. See Section 702.1.

MENTAL HOSPITALS. See Section 308.3.1.

MERCHANDISE PAD. See Section 1002.1.

METAL COMPOSITE MATERIAL (MCM). See Section 1402.1.

METAL COMPOSITE MATERIAL (MCM) SYSTEM. See Section 1402.1.

METAL ROOF PANEL. See Section 1502.1.

METAL ROOF SHINGLE. See Section 1502.1.

MEZZANINE. See Section 502.1.

MICROPILE. See Section 1802.1.

MINERAL BOARD. See Section 721.1.1.

MINERAL FIBER. See Section 702.1.

MINERAL WOOL. See Section 702.1.

MODIFIED BITUMEN ROOF COVERING. See Section 1502.1.

MORTAR. See Section 2102.1.

MORTAR, SURFACE-BONDING. See Section 2102.1.

MULTILEVEL ASSEMBLY SEATING. See Section 1102.1.

[F] MULTIPLE-STATION ALARM DEVICE. See Section 902.1.

[F] MULTIPLE-STATION SMOKE ALARM. See Section 902.1.

MULTISTORY UNITS. See Section 1102.1.

NAILING, BOUNDARY. See Section 2302.1.

NAILING, EDGE. See Section 2302.1.

NAILING, FIELD. See Section 2302.1.

NATURALLY DURABLE WOOD. See Section 2302.1.

Decay resistant. See Section 2302.1.

Termite resistant. See Section 2302.1.

NIGHTCLUB. See Section 902.1.

NOMINAL LOADS. See Section 1602.1.

NOMINAL SIZE (LUMBER). See Section 2302.1.

NONCOMBUSTIBLE MEMBRANE STRUCTURE. See Section 3102.2.

[F] NORMAL TEMPERATURE AND PRESSURE (NTP). See Section 415.2.

NOSING. See Section 1002.1.

NOTIFICATION ZONE. See Section 902.1.

[F] NUISANCE ALARM. See Section 902.1.

NURSING HOMES. See Section 308.3.1.

OCCUPANCY CATEGORY. See Section 1602.1.

OCCUPANT LOAD. See Section 1002.1.

OCCUPIABLE SPACE. A room or enclosed space designed for human occupancy in which individuals congregate for amusement, educational or similar purposes or in which occupants are engaged at labor, and which is equipped with *means of egress* and light and ventilation facilities meeting the requirements of this code.

OPEN PARKING GARAGE. See Section 406.3.2.

[F] OPEN SYSTEM. See Section 307.2.

[F] OPERATING BUILDING. See Section 307.2.

ORDINARY PRECAST STRUCTURAL WALL. See Section 1908.1.1.

ORDINARY REINFORCED CONCRETE STRUCTURAL WALL. See Section 1908.1.1.

ORDINARY STRUCTURAL PLAIN CONCRETE WALL. See Section 1908.1.1.

[F] ORGANIC PEROXIDE. See Section 307.2.

Class I. See Section 307.2.

Class II. See Section 307.2.

Class III. See Section 307.2.

Class IV. See Section 307.2.

Class V. See Section 307.2.

Unclassified detonable. See Section 307.2.

ORTHOGONAL. See Section 1613.2.

OTHER STRUCTURES. See Section 1602.1.

OWNER. Any person, agent, firm or corporation having a legal or equitable interest in the property.

[F] OXIDIZER. See Section 307.2.

Class 4. See Section 307.2.

Class 3. See Section 307.2.

Class 2. See Section 307.2.

Class 1. See Section 307.2.

[F] OXIDIZING GAS. See Section 307.2.

PANEL (PART OF A STRUCTURE). See Section 1602.1.

PANIC HARDWARE. See Section 1002.1.

PARTICLEBOARD. See Section 2302.1.

PENETRATION FIRESTOP. See Section 702.1.

PENTHOUSE. See Section 1502.1.

PERMIT. An official document or certificate issued by the authority having jurisdiction which authorizes performance of a specified activity.

PERSON. An individual, heirs, executors, administrators or assigns, and also includes a firm, partnership or corporation, its or their successors or assigns, or the agent of any of the aforesaid.

PERSONAL CARE SERVICE. See Section 310.2.

PHOTOLUMINESCENT. See Section 1002.1.

[F] PHYSICAL HAZARD. See Section 307.2.

[F] PHYSIOLOGICAL WARNING THRESHOLD LEVEL. See Section 415.2.

PINRAIL. See Section 410.2.

PLASTIC, APPROVED. See Section 2602.1.

PLASTIC GLAZING. See Section 2602.1.

PLATFORM. See Section 410.2.

POSITIVE ROOF DRAINAGE. See Section 1502.1.

PREFABRICATED WOOD I-JOIST. See Section 2302.1.

PRESTRESSED MASONRY. See Section 2102.1.

PRIMARY FUNCTION. See Section 3402.1.

PRIMARY STRUCTURAL FRAME. The primary structural frame shall include all of the following structural members:

1. The columns;
2. Structural members having direct connections to the columns, including girders, beams, trusses and spandrels;
3. Members of the floor construction and roof construction having direct connections to the columns; and
4. Bracing members that are essential to the vertical stability of the primary structural frame under gravity loading shall be considered part of the primary structural frame whether or not the bracing member carries gravity loads.

PRISM. See Section 2102.1.

PROSCENIUM WALL. See Section 410.2.

PUBLIC ENTRANCE. See Section 1102.1.

PUBLIC-USE AREAS. See Section 1102.1.

PUBLIC WAY. See Section 1002.1.

[F] PYROPHORIC. See Section 307.2.

[F] PYROTECHNIC COMPOSITION. See Section 307.2.

RAMP. See Section 1002.1.

RAMP-ACCESS OPEN PARKING GARAGES. See Section 406.3.2.

[F] RECORD DRAWINGS. See Section 902.1.

REFLECTIVE PLASTIC CORE FOIL INSULATION. An insulation material packaged in rolls that is less than 0.5 inch (12.7 mm) thick, with at least one exterior low emittance surface (0.1 perm or less) and a core material containing voids or cells.

REGISTERED DESIGN PROFESSIONAL. An individual who is registered or licensed to practice their respective design profession as defined by the statutory requirements of the professional registration laws of the state or jurisdiction in which the project is to be constructed. A design by a registered design professional is not required where exempt under the registration or licensure laws.

REGISTERED DESIGN PROFESSIONAL IN RESPONSIBLE CHARGE. A *registered design professional* engaged by the owner to review and coordinate certain aspects of the project, as determined by the *building official*, for compatibility with the design of the building or structure, including submittal documents prepared by others, deferred submittal documents and phased submittal documents.

RELIGIOUS WORSHIP, PLACE OF. A building or portion thereof intended for the performance of religious services.

REPAIR. The reconstruction or renewal of any part of an existing building for the purpose of its maintenance.

REROOFING. See Section 1502.1.

RESIDENTIAL AIRCRAFT HANGAR. See Section 412.2.

RESIDENTIAL CARE/ASSISTED LIVING FACILITIES. See Section 310.2.

RESISTANCE FACTOR. See Section 1602.1.

RESTRICTED ENTRANCE. See Section 1102.1.

RETRACTABLE AWNING. See Section 3105.2.

ROOF ASSEMBLY. See Section 1502.1.

ROOF COVERING. See Section 1502.1.

ROOF COVERING SYSTEM. See Section 1502.1.

ROOF DECK. See Section 1502.1.

ROOF RECOVER. See Section 1502.1.

ROOF REPAIR. See Section 1502.1.

ROOF REPLACEMENT. See Section 1502.1.

ROOF VENTILATION. See Section 1502.1.

ROOFTOP STRUCTURE. See Section 1502.1.

RUBBLE MASONRY. See Section 2102.1.

Coursed rubble. See Section 2102.1.

Random rubble. See Section 2102.1.

Rough or ordinary rubble. See Section 2102.1.

RUNNING BOND. See Section 2102.1.

SALLYPORT. See Section 408.1.1.

SCISSOR STAIR. See Section 1002.1.

SCUPPER. See Section 1502.1.

SECONDARY MEMBERS. The following structural members shall be considered secondary members and not part of the primary structural frame:

1. Structural members not having direct connections to the columns;
2. Members of the floor construction not having direct connections to the columns; and
3. Bracing members other than those that are part of the *primary structural frame*.

SEISMIC DESIGN CATEGORY. See Section 1613.2.

SEISMIC-FORCE-RESISTING SYSTEM. See Section 1613.2.

SELF-CLOSING. See Section 702.1.

SELF-LUMINOUS. See Section 1002.1.

SELF-SERVICE STORAGE FACILITY. See Section 1102.1.

[F] SERVICE CORRIDOR. See Section 415.2.

SERVICE ENTRANCE. See Section 1102.1.

SHAFT. See Section 702.1.

SHAFT ENCLOSURE. See Section 702.1.

SHALLOW FOUNDATION. See Section 1802.1.

SHEAR WALL. See Sections 2102.1 and 2302.1.

Detailed plain masonry shear wall. See Section 2102.1.

Intermediate prestressed masonry shear wall. See Section 2102.1.

Intermediate reinforced masonry shear wall. See Section 2102.1.

Ordinary plain masonry shear wall. See Section 2102.1.

Ordinary plain prestressed masonry shear wall. See Section 2102.1.

Ordinary reinforced masonry shear wall. See Section 2102.1.

Perforated shear wall. See Section 2302.1.

Perforated shear wall segment. See Section 2302.1.

Special prestressed masonry shear wall. See Section 2102.1.

Special reinforced masonry shear wall. See Section 2102.1.

SHELL. See Section 2102.1.

SINGLE-PLY MEMBRANE. See Section 1502.1.

[F] SINGLE-STATION SMOKE ALARM. See Section 902.1.

SITE. See Section 1102.1.

SITE CLASS. See Section 1613.2.

SITE COEFFICIENTS. See Section 1613.2.

SITE-FABRICATED STRETCH SYSTEM. See Section 802.1.

SKYLIGHT, UNIT. A factory-assembled, glazed fenestration unit, containing one panel of glazing material that allows for natural lighting through an opening in the roof assembly while preserving the weather-resistant barrier of the roof.

SKYLIGHTS AND SLOPED GLAZING. Glass or other transparent or translucent glazing material installed at a slope of 15 degrees (0.26 rad) or more from vertical. Glazing material in skylights, including unit skylights, solariums, sunrooms, roofs and sloped walls, are included in this definition.

SLEEPING UNIT. A room or space in which people sleep, which can also include permanent provisions for living, eating, and either sanitation or kitchen facilities but not both. Such rooms and spaces that are also part of a *dwelling unit* are not sleeping units.

[F] SMOKE ALARM. See Section 902.1.

SMOKE BARRIER. See Section 702.1.

SMOKE COMPARTMENT. See Section 702.1.

SMOKE DAMPER. See Section 702.1.

[F] SMOKE DETECTOR. See Section 902.1.

SMOKE-DEVELOPED INDEX. See Section 802.1.

SMOKE-PROTECTED ASSEMBLY SEATING. See Section 1002.1.

SMOKEPROOF ENCLOSURE. See Section 902.1.

[F] SOLID. See Section 415.2.

SPECIAL AMUSEMENT BUILDING. See Section 411.2.

SPECIAL FLOOD HAZARD AREA. See Section 1612.2.

SPECIAL INSPECTION. See Section 1702.1.

SPECIAL INSPECTION, CONTINUOUS. See Section 1702.1.

SPECIAL INSPECTION, PERIODIC. See Section 1702.1.

SPECIAL STRUCTURAL WALL. See Section 1908.1.1.

SPECIFIED. See Section 2102.1.

SPECIFIED COMPRESSIVE STRENGTH OF MASONRY (f'_m). See Section 2102.1.

SPLICE. See Section 702.1.

SPRAYED FIRE-RESISTANT MATERIALS. See Section 1702.1.

STACK BOND. See Section 2102.1.

STAGE. See Section 410.2.

STAIR. See Section 1002.1.

STAIRWAY. See Section 1002.1.

STAIRWAY, EXTERIOR. See Section 1002.1.

STAIRWAY, INTERIOR. See Section 1002.1.

STAIRWAY, SPIRAL. See Section 1002.1.

[F] STANDPIPE SYSTEM, CLASSES OF. See Section 902.1.

Class I system. See Section 902.1.

Class II system. See Section 902.1.

Class III system. See Section 902.1.

[F] STANDPIPE, TYPES OF. See Section 902.1.

Automatic dry. See Section 902.1.

Automatic wet. See Section 902.1.

Manual dry. See Section 902.1.

Manual wet. See Section 902.1.

Semiautomatic dry. See Section 902.1.

START OF CONSTRUCTION. See Section 1612.2.

STEEL CONSTRUCTION, COLD-FORMED. See Section 2202.1.

STEEL JOIST. See Section 2202.1.

STEEL MEMBER, STRUCTURAL. See Section 2202.1.

STEEP SLOPE. A roof slope greater than two units vertical in 12 units horizontal (17-percent slope).

STONE MASONRY. See Section 2102.1.

Ashlar stone masonry. See Section 2102.1.

Rubble stone masonry. See Section 2102.1.

[F] STORAGE, HAZARDOUS MATERIALS. See Section 415.2.

STORM SHELTER. See Section 423.2.

Community storm shelter. See Section 423.2.

Residential storm shelter. See Section 423.2.

STORY. That portion of a building included between the upper surface of a floor and the upper surface of the floor or roof next above (also see "Basement," "*Mezzanine*" and Section 502.1). It is measured as the vertical distance from top to top of two successive tiers of beams or finished floor surfaces and, for the topmost *story*, from the top of the floor finish to the top of the ceiling joists or, where there is not a ceiling, to the top of the roof rafters.

STORY ABOVE GRADE PLANE. Any *story* having its finished floor surface entirely above *grade plane*, or in which the finished surface of the floor next above is:

1. More than 6 feet (1829 mm) above *grade plane*; or
2. More than 12 feet (3658 mm) above the finished ground level at any point.

STRENGTH. See Section 2102.1.

Design strength. See Section 2102.1.

Nominal strength. See Sections 1602.1 and 2102.1.

Required strength. See Sections 1602.1 and 2102.1.

STRENGTH DESIGN. See Section 1602.1.

STRUCTURAL COMPOSITE LUMBER. See Section 2302.1.

Laminated veneer lumber (LVL). See Section 2302.1.

Parallel strand lumber (PSL). See Section 2302.1.

STRUCTURAL GLUED-LAMINATED TIMBER. See Section 2302.1.

STRUCTURAL OBSERVATION. See Section 1702.1.

STRUCTURE. That which is built or constructed.

SUBDIAPHRAGM. See Section 2302.1.

SUBSTANTIAL DAMAGE. See Section 1612.2.

SUBSTANTIAL IMPROVEMENT. See Section 1612.2.

SUBSTANTIAL STRUCTURAL DAMAGE. See Section 3402.1.

SUITE. See Section 1002.1.

SUNROOM. See Section 1202.1.

[F] SUPERVISING STATION. See Section 902.1.

[F] SUPERVISORY SERVICE. See Section 902.1.

[F] SUPERVISORY SIGNAL. See Section 902.1.

[F] SUPERVISORY SIGNAL-INITIATING DEVICE. See Section 902.1.

SWIMMING POOLS. See Section 3109.2.

T RATING. See Section 702.1.

TECHNICALLY INFEASIBLE. See Section 3402.1.

TEMPORARY OVERFLOW SHELTER. A shelter that provides temporary overflow accommodations from an approved homeless shelter in accordance with Section 424.

TENT. A structure, enclosure or shelter, with or without sidewalls or drops, constructed of fabric or pliable material supported in any manner except by air or the contents it protects.

THERMAL ISOLATION. See Section 1202.1.

THERMOPLASTIC MATERIAL. See Section 2602.1.

THERMOSETTING MATERIAL. See Section 2602.1.

THIN-BED MORTAR. See Section 2102.1.

THROUGH PENETRATION. See Section 702.1.

THROUGH-PENETRATION FIRESTOP SYSTEM. See Section 702.1.

TIE-DOWN (HOLD-DOWN). See Section 2302.1.

TIE, LATERAL. See Section 2102.1.

TIE, WALL. See Section 2102.1.

TILE. See Section 2102.1.

TILE, STRUCTURAL CLAY. See Section 2102.1.

[F] TIRES, BULK STORAGE OF. See Section 902.1.

TOWNHOUSE. A single-family *dwelling unit* constructed in a group of three or more attached units in which each unit extends from the foundation to roof and with open space on at least two sides.

[F] TOXIC. See Section 307.2.

TRANSIENT. See Section 310.2.

TRANSIENT AIRCRAFT. See Section 412.2.

TREATED WOOD. See Section 2302.1.

Fire-retardant-treated wood. See Section 2302.1.

Preservative-treated wood. See Section 2302.1.

TRIM. See Section 802.1.

[F] TROUBLE SIGNAL. See Section 902.1.

TYPE A UNIT. See Section 1102.1.

TYPE B UNIT. See Section 1102.1.

UNDERLAYMENT. See Section 1502.1.

[F] UNSTABLE (REACTIVE) MATERIAL. See Section 307.2.

Class 4. See Section 307.2.

Class 3. See Section 307.2.

Class 2. See Section 307.2.

Class 1. See Section 307.2.

[F] USE (MATERIAL). See Section 415.2.

VAPOR-PERMEABLE MEMBRANE. A material or covering having a permeance rating of 5 perms (52.9×10^{-10} kg/Pa · s · m^2) or greater, when tested in accordance with the dessicant method using Procedure A of ASTM E 96. A vapor-permeable material permits the passage of moisture vapor.

VAPOR RETARDER CLASS. A measure of a material or assembly's ability to limit the amount of moisture that passes through that material or assembly. Vapor retarder class shall be defined using the desiccant method of ASTM E 96 as follows:

Class I: 0.1 perm or less.

Class II: 0.1 < perm ≤ 1.0 perm.

Class III: 1.0 < perm ≤ 10 perm.

VEHICLE BARRIER SYSTEM. See Section 1602.1.

VEHICULAR GATE. See Section 3110.2.

VENEER. See Section 1402.1.

VENTILATION. The natural or mechanical process of supplying conditioned or unconditioned air to, or removing such air from, any space.

VINYL SIDING. See Section 1402.1.

[F] VISIBLE ALARM NOTIFICATION APPLIANCE. See Section 902.1.

WALKWAY, PEDESTRIAN. A walkway used exclusively as a pedestrian trafficway.

WALL. See Section 2102.1.

Cavity wall. See Section 2102.1.

Composite wall. See Section 2102.1.

Dry-stacked, surface-bonded wall. See Section 2102.1.

Masonry-bonded hollow wall. See Section 2102.1.

Parapet wall. See Section 2102.1.

WALL, LOAD-BEARING. Any wall meeting either of the following classifications:

1. Any metal or wood stud wall that supports more than 100 pounds per linear foot (1459 N/m) of vertical load in addition to its own weight.
2. Any masonry or concrete wall that supports more than 200 pounds per linear foot (2919 N/m) of vertical load in addition to its own weight.

WALL, NONLOAD-BEARING. Any wall that is not a *load-bearing wall.*

WALL PIER. See Section 1908.1.1.

[F] WATER-REACTIVE MATERIAL. See Section 307.2.

Class 3. See Section 307.2.

Class 2. See Section 307.2.

Class 1. See Section 307.2.

WATER-RESISTIVE BARRIER. See Section 1402.1.

WEATHER-EXPOSED SURFACES. See Section 2502.1.

WEB. See Section 2102.1.

[F] WET-CHEMICAL EXTINGUISHING SYSTEM. See Section 902.1.

WHEELCHAIR SPACE. See Section 1102.1.

WIND-BORNE DEBRIS REGION. See Section 1609.2.

WINDER. See Section 1002.1.

WIRE BACKING. See Section 2502.1.

[F] WIRELESS PROTECTION SYSTEM. See Section 902.1.

WOOD SHEAR PANEL. See Section 2302.1.

WOOD STRUCTURAL PANEL. See Section 2302.1.

Composite panels. See Section 2302.1.

Oriented strand board (OSB). See Section 2302.1.

Plywood. See Section 2302.1.

[F] WORKSTATION. See Section 415.2.

WYTHE. See Section 2102.1.

YARD. An open space, other than a *court*, unobstructed from the ground to the sky, except where specifically provided by this code, on the lot on which a building is situated.

[F] ZONE. See Section 902.1.

ZONE, NOTIFICATION. See Section 902.1.

CHAPTER 3
USE AND OCCUPANCY CLASSIFICATION

SECTION 301
GENERAL

301.1 Scope. The provisions of this chapter shall control the classification of all buildings and structures as to use and occupancy.

SECTION 302
CLASSIFICATION

302.1 General. Structures or portions of structures shall be classified with respect to occupancy in one or more of the groups listed below. A room or space that is intended to be occupied at different times for different purposes shall comply with all of the requirements that are applicable to each of the purposes for which the room or space will be occupied. Structures with multiple occupancies or uses shall comply with Section 508. Where a structure is proposed for a purpose that is not specifically provided for in this code, such structure shall be classified in the group that the occupancy most nearly resembles, according to the fire safety and relative hazard involved.

1. Assembly (see Section 303): Groups A-1, A-2, A-3, A-4 and A-5
2. Business (see Section 304): Group B
3. Educational (see Section 305): Group E
4. Factory and Industrial (see Section 306): Groups F-1 and F-2
5. High Hazard (see Section 307): Groups H-1, H-2, H-3, H-4 and H-5
6. Institutional (see Section 308): Groups I-1, I-2, I-3 and I-4
7. Mercantile (see Section 309): Group M
8. Residential (see Section 310): Groups R-1, R-2, R-3 and R-4
9. Storage (see Section 311): Groups S-1 and S-2
10. Utility and Miscellaneous (see Section 312): Group U

SECTION 303
ASSEMBLY GROUP A

303.1 Assembly Group A. Assembly Group A occupancy includes, among others, the use of a building or structure, or a portion thereof, for the gathering of persons for purposes such as civic, social or religious functions; recreation, food or drink consumption or awaiting transportation.

Exceptions:

1. A building or tenant space used for assembly purposes with an *occupant load* of less than 50 persons shall be classified as a Group B occupancy.
2. A room or space used for assembly purposes with an *occupant load* of less than 50 persons and accessory to another occupancy shall be classified as a Group B occupancy or as part of that occupancy.
3. A room or space used for assembly purposes that is less than 750 square feet (70 m^2) in area and accessory to another occupancy shall be classified as a Group B occupancy or as part of that occupancy.
4. Assembly areas that are accessory to Group E occupancies are not considered separate occupancies except when applying the assembly occupancy requirements of Chapter 11.
5. Accessory religious educational rooms and religious auditoriums with occupant loads of less than 100 are not considered separate occupancies.

Assembly occupancies shall include the following:

A-1 Assembly uses, usually with fixed seating, intended for the production and viewing of the performing arts or motion pictures including, but not limited to:

Motion picture theaters
Symphony and concert halls
Television and radio studios admitting an audience
Theaters

A-2 Assembly uses intended for food and/or drink consumption including, but not limited to:

Banquet halls
Night clubs
Restaurants
Taverns and bars

A-3 Assembly uses intended for worship, recreation or amusement and other assembly uses not classified elsewhere in Group A including, but not limited to:

Amusement arcades
Art galleries
Bowling alleys
Community halls
Courtrooms
Dance halls (not including food or drink consumption)
Exhibition halls
Funeral parlors
Gymnasiums (without spectator seating)
Indoor swimming pools (without spectator seating)
Indoor tennis courts (without spectator seating)
Lecture halls
Libraries
Museums
Places of religious worship
Pool and billiard parlors
Waiting areas in transportation terminals

A-4 Assembly uses intended for viewing of indoor sporting events and activities with spectator seating including, but not limited to:

Arenas
Skating rinks
Swimming pools
Tennis courts

A-5 Assembly uses intended for participation in or viewing outdoor activities including, but not limited to:

Amusement park structures
Bleachers
Grandstands
Stadiums

SECTION 304
BUSINESS GROUP B

304.1 Business Group B. Business Group B occupancy includes, among others, the use of a building or structure, or a portion thereof, for office, professional or service-type transactions, including storage of records and accounts. Business occupancies shall include, but not be limited to, the following:

Airport traffic control towers
Ambulatory health care facilities
Animal hospitals, kennels and pounds
Banks
Barber and beauty shops
Car wash
Civic administration
Clinic—outpatient
Dry cleaning and laundries: pick-up and delivery stations and self-service
Educational occupancies for students above the 12th grade
Electronic data processing
Laboratories: testing and research
Motor vehicle showrooms
Post offices
Print shops
Professional services (architects, attorneys, dentists, physicians, engineers, etc.)
Radio and television stations
Telephone exchanges
Training and skill development not within a school or academic program
Education occupancies for high school students participating in Cooperative Innovative High School Programs taught at colleges, community colleges or universities.

304.1.1 Definitions. The following words and terms shall, for the purposes of this section and as used elsewhere in this code, have the meanings shown herein.

CLINIC, OUTPATIENT. Buildings or portions thereof used to provide medical care on less than a 24-hour basis to individuals who are not rendered incapable of self-preservation by the services provided.

SECTION 305
EDUCATIONAL GROUP E

305.1 Educational Group E. Educational Group E occupancy includes, among others, the use of a building or structure, or a portion thereof, by six or more persons at any one time for educational purposes through the 12th grade. Religious educational rooms and religious auditoriums, which are accessory to *places of religious worship* in accordance with Section 303.1 and have *occupant loads* of less than 100, shall be classified as Group A-3 occupancies. Education occupancies for high school students participating in Cooperative Innovative High School Programs taught at colleges, community colleges or universities shall be classified as Group B occupancies.

305.2 Day care. The use of a building or structure, or portion thereof, for educational, supervision or *personal care services* for more than five children older than $2^1/_2$ years of age, shall be classified as a Group E occupancy.

SECTION 306
FACTORY GROUP F

306.1 Factory Industrial Group F. Factory Industrial Group F occupancy includes, among others, the use of a building or structure, or a portion thereof, for assembling, disassembling, fabricating, finishing, manufacturing, packaging, repair or processing operations that are not classified as a Group H hazardous or Group S storage occupancy.

306.2 Factory Industrial F-1 Moderate-hazard Occupancy. Factory industrial uses which are not classified as Factory Industrial F-2 Low Hazard shall be classified as F-1 Moderate Hazard and shall include, but not be limited to, the following:

Aircraft (manufacturing, not to include repair)
Appliances
Athletic equipment
Automobiles and other motor vehicles
Bakeries
Beverages: over 16-percent alcohol content
Bicycles
Boats
Brooms or brushes
Business machines
Cameras and photo equipment
Canvas or similar fabric
Carpets and rugs (includes cleaning)
Clothing
Construction and agricultural machinery
Disinfectants
Dry cleaning and dyeing
Electric generation plants
Electronics
Engines (including rebuilding)
Food processing
Furniture
Hemp products
Jute products
Laundries
Leather products
Machinery
Metals

Millwork (sash and door)
Motion pictures and television filming (without spectators)
Musical instruments
Optical goods
Paper mills or products
Photographic film
Plastic products
Printing or publishing
Recreational vehicles
Refuse incineration
Shoes
Soaps and detergents
Textiles
Tobacco
Trailers
Upholstering
Wood; distillation
Woodworking (cabinet)

306.3 Factory Industrial F-2 Low-hazard Occupancy. Factory industrial uses that involve the fabrication or manufacturing of noncombustible materials which during finishing, packing or processing do not involve a significant fire hazard shall be classified as F-2 occupancies and shall include, but not be limited to, the following:

Beverages: up to and including 16-percent alcohol content
Brick and masonry
Ceramic products
Foundries
Glass products
Gypsum
Ice
Metal products (fabrication and assembly)

SECTION 307 HIGH-HAZARD GROUP H

[F] 307.1 High-hazard Group H. High-hazard Group H occupancy includes, among others, the use of a building or structure, or a portion thereof, that involves the manufacturing, processing, generation or storage of materials that constitute a physical or health hazard in quantities in excess of those allowed in *control areas* complying with Section 414, based on the maximum allowable quantity limits for control areas set forth in Tables 307.1(1) and 307.1(2). Hazardous occupancies are classified in Groups H-1, H-2, H-3, H-4 and H-5 and shall be in accordance with this section, the requirements of Section 415 and the *International Fire Code*. Hazardous materials stored, or used on top of roofs or canopies shall be classified as outdoor storage or use and shall comply with the *International Fire Code*.

Exceptions: The following shall not be classified as Group H, but shall be classified as the occupancy that they most nearly resemble.

1. Buildings and structures occupied for the application of flammable finishes, provided that such buildings or areas conform to the requirements of Section 416 and the *International Fire Code*.
2. Wholesale and retail sales and storage of flammable and combustible liquids in mercantile occupancies conforming to the *International Fire Code*.
3. Closed piping system containing flammable or combustible liquids or gases utilized for the operation of machinery or equipment.
4. Cleaning establishments that utilize combustible liquid solvents having a flash point of 140°F (60°C) or higher in closed systems employing equipment *listed* by an *approved* testing agency, provided that this occupancy is separated from all other areas of the building by 1-hour *fire barriers* constructed in accordance with Section 707 or 1-hour *horizontal assemblies* constructed in accordance with Section 712, or both.
5. Cleaning establishments that utilize a liquid solvent having a flash point at or above 200°F (93°C).
6. Liquor stores and distributors without bulk storage.
7. Refrigeration systems.
8. The storage or utilization of materials for agricultural purposes on the premises.
9. Stationary batteries utilized for facility emergency power, uninterrupted power supply or telecommunication facilities, provided that the batteries are provided with safety venting caps and ventilation is provided in accordance with the *International Mechanical Code*.
10. Corrosives shall not include personal or household products in their original packaging used in retail display or commonly used building materials.
11. Buildings and structures occupied for aerosol storage shall be classified as Group S-1, provided that such buildings conform to the requirements of the *International Fire Code*.
12. Display and storage of nonflammable solid and nonflammable or noncombustible liquid hazardous materials in quantities not exceeding the maximum allowable quantity per *control area* in Group M or S occupancies complying with Section 414.2.5.
13. The storage of black powder, smokeless propellant and small arms primers in Groups M and R-3 and special industrial explosive devices in Groups B, F, M and S, provided such storage conforms to the quantity limits and requirements prescribed in the *International Fire Code*.

[F] TABLE 307.1(1)
MAXIMUM ALLOWABLE QUANTITY PER CONTROL AREA OF HAZARDOUS MATERIALS POSING A PHYSICAL HAZARD[a, j, m, n, p]

MATERIAL	CLASS	GROUP WHEN THE MAXIMUM ALLOWABLE QUANTITY IS EXCEEDED	STORAGE[b]			USE-CLOSED SYSTEMS[b]			USE-OPEN SYSTEMS[b]	
			Solid pounds (cubic feet)	Liquid gallons (pounds)	Gas (cubic feet at NTP)	Solid pounds (cubic feet)	Liquid gallons (pounds)	Gas (cubic feet at NTP)	Solid pounds (cubic feet)	Liquid gallons (pounds)
Combustible liquid[c, i]	II IIIA IIIB	H-2 or H-3 H-2 or H-3 N/A	N/A	120[d, e] 330[d, e] 13,200[e, f]	N/A	N/A	120[d] 330[d] 13,200[f]	N/A	N/A	30[d] 80[d] 3,300[f]
Combustible fiber	Loose Baled[o]	H-3	(100) (1,000)	N/A	N/A	(100) (1,000)	N/A	N/A	(20) (200)	N/A
Consumer fireworks (Class C, Common)	1.4G	H-3	125[d, e, l]	N/A	N/A	N/A	N/A	N/A	N/A	N/A
Cryogenics, flammable	N/A	H-2	N/A	45[d]	N/A	N/A	45[d]	N/A	N/A	10[d]
Cryogenics, inert	N/A	N/A	N/A	N/A	NL	N/A	N/A	NL	N/A	N/A
Cryogenics, oxidizing	N/A	H-3	N/A	45[d]	N/A	N/A	45[d]	N/A	N/A	10[d]
Explosives	Division 1.1 Division 1.2 Division 1.3 Division 1.4 Division 1.4G Division 1.5 Division 1.6	H-1 H-1 H-1 or H-2 H-3 H-3 H-1 H-1	1[e, g] 1[e, g] 5[e, g] 50[e, g] 125[d, e, l] 1[e, g] 1[e, g]	(1)[e, g] (1)[e, g] (5)[e, g] (50)[e, g] N/A (1)[e, g] N/A	N/A N/A N/A N/A N/A N/A N/A	0.25[g] 0.25[g] 1[g] 50[g] N/A 0.25[g] N/A	(0.25)[g] (0.25)[g] (1)[g] (50)[g] N/A (0.25)[g] N/A	N/A N/A N/A N/A N/A N/A N/A	0.25[g] 0.25[g] 1[g] N/A N/A 0.25[g] N/A	(0.25)[g] (0.25)[g] (1)[g] N/A N/A (0.25)[g] N/A
Flammable gas	Gaseous Liquefied	H-2	N/A	N/A (150)[d, e]	1,000[d, e] N/A	N/A	N/A (150)[d, e]	1,000[d, e] N/A	N/A	N/A
Flammable liquid[c]	1A 1B and 1C	H-2 or H-3	N/A	30[d, e] 120[d, e]	N/A	N/A	30[d] 120[d]	N/A	N/A	10[d] 30[d]
Flammable liquid, combination (1A, 1B, 1C)	N/A	H-2 or H-3	N/A	120[d, e, h]	N/A	N/A	120[d, h]	N/A	N/A	30[d, h]
Flammable solid	N/A	H-3	125[d, e]	N/A	N/A	125[d]	N/A	N/A	25[d]	N/A
Inert gas	Gaseous Liquefied	N/A N/A	N/A N/A	N/A N/A	NL NL	N/A N/A	N/A N/A	NL NL	N/A N/A	N/A N/A
Organic peroxide	UD I II III IV V	H-1 H-2 H-3 H-3 N/A N/A	1[e, g] 5[d, e] 50[d, e] 125[d, e] NL NL	(1)[e, g] (5)[d, e] (50)[d, e] (125)[d, e] NL NL	N/A N/A N/A N/A N/A N/A	0.25[g] 1[d] 50[d] 125[d] NL NL	(0.25)[g] (1) (50)[d] (125)[d] NL NL	N/A N/A N/A N/A N/A N/A	0.25[g] 1[d] 10[d] 25[d] NL NL	(0.25)[g] (1)[d] (10)[d] (25)[d] NL NL
Oxidizer	4 3[k] 2 1	H-1 H-2 or H-3 H-3 N/A	1[e, g] 10[d, e] 250[d, e] 4,000[e, f]	(1)[e, g] (10)[d, e] (250)[d, e] (4,000)[e, f]	N/A N/A N/A N/A	0.25[g] 2[d] 250[d] 4,000[f]	(0.25)[g] (2)[d] (250)[d] (4,000)[f]	N/A N/A N/A N/A	0.25[g] 2[d] 50[d] 1,000[f]	(0.25)[g] (2)[d] (50)[d] (1,000)[f]

(continued)

[F] TABLE 307.1(1)—continued
MAXIMUM ALLOWABLE QUANTITY PER CONTROL AREA OF HAZARDOUS MATERIALS POSING A PHYSICAL HAZARD[a, j, m, n, p]

MATERIAL	CLASS	GROUP WHEN THE MAXIMUM ALLOWABLE QUANTITY IS EXCEEDED	STORAGE[b]			USE-CLOSED SYSTEMS[b]			USE-OPEN SYSTEMS[b]	
			Solid pounds (cubic feet)	Liquid gallons (pounds)	Gas (cubic feet at NTP)	Solid pounds (cubic feet)	Liquid gallons (pounds)	Gas (cubic feet at NTP)	Solid pounds (cubic feet)	Liquid gallons (pounds)
Oxidizing gas	Gaseous	H-3	N/A	N/A	1,500[d, e]	N/A	N/A	1,500[d, e]	N/A	N/A
	Liquefied		N/A	(150)[d, e]	N/A	N/A	(150)[d, e]	N/A	N/A	N/A
Pyrophoric material	N/A	H-2	4[e, g]	(4)[e, g]	50[e, g]	1[g]	(1)[g]	10[g]	0	0
Unstable (reactive)	4	H-1	1[e, g]	(1)[e, g]	10[g]	0.25[g]	(0.25)[g]	2[e, g]	0.25[g]	(0.25)[g]
	3	H-1 or H-2	5[d, e]	(5)[d, e]	50[d, e]	1[d]	(1)[d]	10[d, e]	1[d]	(1)[d]
	2	H-3	50[d, e]	(50)[d, e]	250[d, e]	50[d]	(50)[d]	250[d, e]	10[d]	(10)[d]
	1	N/A	NL	NL	NL	NL	NL	NL	NL	NL
Water reactive	3	H-2	5[d, e]	(5)[d, e]	N/A	5[d]	(5)[d]	N/A	1[d]	(1)[d]
	2	H-3	50[d, e]	(50)[d, e]	N/A	50[d]	(50)[d]	N/A	10[d]	(10)[d]
	1	N/A	NL	NL	N/A	NL	NL	N/A	NL	NL

For SI: 1 cubic foot = 0.028 m^3, 1 pound = 0.454 kg, 1 gallon = 3.785 L.

NL = Not Limited; N/A = Not Applicable; UD = Unclassified Detonable

a. For use of *control areas*, see Section 414.2.

b. The aggregate quantity in use and storage shall not exceed the quantity listed for storage.

c. The quantities of alcoholic beverages in retail and wholesale sales occupancies shall not be limited providing the liquids are packaged in individual containers not exceeding 1.3 gallons. In retail and wholesale sales occupancies, the quantities of medicines, foodstuffs, consumer or industrial products, and cosmetics containing not more than 50 percent by volume of water-miscible liquids with the remainder of the solutions not being flammable, shall not be limited, provided that such materials are packaged in individual containers not exceeding 1.3 gallons.

d. Maximum allowable quantities shall be increased 100 percent in buildings equipped throughout with an *automatic sprinkler system* in accordance with Section 903.3.1.1. Where Note e also applies, the increase for both notes shall be applied accumulatively.

e. Maximum allowable quantities shall be increased 100 percent when stored in *approved* storage cabinets, day boxes, gas cabinets or exhausted enclosures or in *listed* safety cans in accordance with Section 2703.9.10 of the *International Fire Code*. Where Note d also applies, the increase for both notes shall be applied accumulatively.

f. The permitted quantities shall not be limited in a building equipped throughout with an *automatic sprinkler system* in accordance with Section 903.3.1.1.

g. Permitted only in buildings equipped throughout with an *automatic sprinkler system* in accordance with Section 903.3.1.1.

h. Containing not more than the maximum allowable quantity per *control area* of Class IA, IB or IC flammable liquids.

i. The maximum allowable quantity shall not apply to fuel oil storage complying with Section 603.3.2 of the *International Fire Code*.

j. Quantities in parenthesis indicate quantity units in parenthesis at the head of each column.

k. A maximum quantity of 200 pounds of solid or 20 gallons of liquid Class 3 oxidizers is allowed when such materials are necessary for maintenance purposes, operation or sanitation of equipment. Storage containers and the manner of storage shall be approved.

l. Net weight of the pyrotechnic composition of the fireworks. Where the net weight of the pyrotechnic composition of the fireworks is not known, 25 percent of the gross weight of the fireworks, including packaging, shall be used.

m. For gallons of liquids, divide the amount in pounds by 10 in accordance with Section 2703.1.2 of the *International Fire Code*.

n. For storage and display quantities in Group M and storage quantities in Group S occupancies complying with Section 414.2.5, see Tables 414.2.5(1) and 414.2.5(2).

o. Densely packed baled cotton that complies with the packing requirements of ISO 8115 shall not be included in this material class.

p. The following shall not be included in determining the maximum allowable quantities:

1. Liquid or gaseous fuel in fuel tanks on vehicles.
2. Liquid or gaseous fuel in fuel tanks on motorized equipment operated in accordance with this code.
3. Gaseous fuels in piping systems and fixed appliances regulated by the *International Fuel Gas Code*.
4. Liquid fuels in piping systems and fixed appliances regulated by the *International Mechanical Code*.

[F] TABLE 307.1(2)
MAXIMUM ALLOWABLE QUANTITY PER CONTROL AREA OF HAZARDOUS MATERIAL POSING A HEALTH HAZARD[a, b, c, i]

MATERIAL	STORAGE[d]			USE-CLOSED SYSTEMS[d]			USE-OPEN SYSTEMS[d]	
	Solid pounds (cubic feet)	Liquid gallons (pounds)[e, f]	Gas (cubic feet at NTP)[e]	Solid pounds[e]	Liquid gallons (pounds)[e]	Gas (cubic feet at NTP)[e]	Solid pounds[e]	Liquid gallons (pounds)[e]
Corrosive	5,000	500	Gaseous 810[f] Liquefied (150)[h]	5,000	500	Gaseous 810[f] Liquefied (150)[h]	1,000	100
Highly toxic	10	(10)[h]	Gaseous 20[g] Liquefied (4)[g, h]	10	(10)[i]	Gaseous 20[g] Liquefied (4)[g, h]	3	(3)[i]
Toxic	500	(500)[h]	Gaseous 810[f] Liquefied (150)[f, h]	500	(500)[i]	Gaseous 810[f] Liquefied (150)[f, h]	125	(125)

For SI: 1 cubic foot = 0.028 m^3, 1 pound = 0.454 kg, 1 gallon = 3.785 L.

a. For use of control areas, see Section 414.2.

b. In retail and wholesale sales occupancies, the quantities of medicines, foodstuffs, consumer or industrial products, and cosmetics, containing not more than 50 percent by volume of water-miscible liquids and with the remainder of the solutions not being flammable, shall not be limited, provided that such materials are packaged in individual containers not exceeding 1.3 gallons.

c. For storage and display quantities in Group M and storage quantities in Group S occupancies complying with Section 414.2.5, see Tables 414.2.5(1) and 414.2.5(2).

d. The aggregate quantity in use and storage shall not exceed the quantity listed for storage.

e. Maximum allowable quantities shall be increased 100 percent in buildings equipped throughout with an approved automatic sprinkler system in accordance with Section 903.3.1.1. Where Note f also applies, the increase for both notes shall be applied accumulatively.

f. Maximum allowable quantities shall be increased 100 percent when stored in approved storage cabinets, gas cabinets or exhausted enclosures as specified in the *International Fire Code*. Where Note e also applies, the increase for both notes shall be applied accumulatively.

g. Allowed only when stored in approved exhausted gas cabinets or exhausted enclosures as specified in the *International Fire Code*.

h. Quantities in parenthesis indicate quantity units in parenthesis at the head of each column.

i. For gallons of liquids, divide the amount in pounds by 10 in accordance with Section 2703.1.2 of the *International Fire Code*.

307.1.1 Hazardous materials. Hazardous materials in any quantity shall conform to the requirements of this code, including Section 414, and the *International Fire Code*.

[F] 307.2 Definitions. The following words and terms shall, for the purposes of this section and as used elsewhere in this code, have the meanings shown herein.

AEROSOL. A product that is dispensed from an aerosol container by a propellant.

Aerosol products shall be classified by means of the calculation of their chemical heats of combustion and shall be designated Level 1, 2 or 3.

Level 1 aerosol products. Those with a total chemical heat of combustion that is less than or equal to 8,600 British thermal units per pound (Btu/lb) (20 kJ/g).

Level 2 aerosol products. Those with a total chemical heat of combustion that is greater than 8,600 Btu/lb (20 kJ/g), but less than or equal to 13,000 Btu/lb (30 kJ/g).

Level 3 aerosol products. Those with a total chemical heat combustion that is greater than 13,000 Btu/lb (30 kJ/g).

AEROSOL CONTAINER. A metal can or a glass or plastic bottle designed to dispense an aerosol. Metal cans shall be limited to a maximum size of 33.8 fluid ounces (1000 ml). Glass or plastic bottles shall be limited to a maximum size of 4 fluid ounces (118 ml).

BALED COTTON. A natural seed fiber wrapped in and secured with industry accepted materials, usually consisting of burlap, woven polypropylene, polyethylene or cotton or sheet polyethylene, and secured with steel, synthetic or wire bands or wire; also includes linters (lint removed from the cottonseed) and motes (residual materials from the ginning process).

BALED COTTON, DENSELY PACKED. Cotton made into banded bales with a packing density of at least 22 pounds per cubic foot (360 kg/m^3), and dimensions complying with the following: a length of 55 inches (1397 ± 20 mm), a width of 21 inches (533.4 ± 20 mm) and a height of 27.6 to 35.4 inches (701 to 899 mm).

BARRICADE. A structure that consists of a combination of walls, floor and roof, which is designed to withstand the rapid release of energy in an explosion and which is fully confined, partially vented or fully vented; or other effective method of shielding from explosive materials by a natural or artificial barrier.

Artificial barricade. An artificial mound or revetment a minimum thickness of 3 feet (914 mm).

Natural barricade. Natural features of the ground, such as hills, or timber of sufficient density that the surrounding exposures that require protection cannot be seen from the magazine or building containing explosives when the trees are bare of leaves.

BOILING POINT. The temperature at which the vapor pressure of a liquid equals the atmospheric pressure of 14.7 pounds per square inch (psi) (101 kPa) gage or 760 mm of mercury. Where an accurate boiling point is unavailable for the material in question, or for mixtures which do not have a constant boiling point, for the purposes of this classification, the 20-percent evaporated point of a distillation performed in accordance with ASTM D 86 shall be used as the boiling point of the liquid.

CLOSED SYSTEM. The use of a solid or liquid hazardous material involving a closed vessel or system that remains closed during normal operations where vapors emitted by the product are not liberated outside of the vessel or system and the product is not exposed to the atmosphere during normal operations; and all uses of compressed gases. Examples of closed systems for solids and liquids include product conveyed through a piping system into a closed vessel, system or piece of equipment.

COMBUSTIBLE DUST. Finely divided solid material that is 420 microns or less in diameter and which, when dispersed in air in the proper proportions, could be ignited by a flame, spark or other source of ignition. Combustible dust will pass through a U.S. No. 40 standard sieve.

COMBUSTIBLE FIBERS. Readily ignitable and free-burning materials in a fibrous or shredded form, such as cocoa fiber, cloth, cotton, excelsior, hay, hemp, henequen, istle, jute, kapok, oakum, rags, sisal, Spanish moss, straw, tow, wastepaper, certain synthetic fibers or other like materials. This definition does not include densely packed baled cotton.

COMBUSTIBLE LIQUID. A liquid having a closed cup flash point at or above 100°F (38°C). Combustible liquids shall be subdivided as follows:

Class II. Liquids having a closed cup flash point at or above 100°F (38°C) and below 140°F (60°C).

Class IIIA. Liquids having a closed cup flash point at or above 140°F (60°C) and below 200°F (93°C).

Class IIIB. Liquids having a closed cup flash point at or above 200°F (93°C).

The category of combustible liquids does not include compressed gases or cryogenic fluids.

COMPRESSED GAS. A material, or mixture of materials, that:

1. Is a gas at 68°F (20°C) or less at 14.7 pounds per square inch atmosphere (psia) (101 kPa) of pressure; and
2. Has a boiling point of 68°F (20°C) or less at 14.7 psia (101 kPa) which is either liquefied, nonliquefied or in solution, except those gases which have no other health- or physical-hazard properties are not considered to be compressed until the pressure in the packaging exceeds 41 psia (282 kPa) at 68°F (20°C).

The states of a compressed gas are categorized as follows:

1. Nonliquefied compressed gases are gases, other than those in solution, which are in a packaging under the charged pressure and are entirely gaseous at a temperature of 68°F (20°C).
2. Liquefied compressed gases are gases that, in a packaging under the charged pressure, are partially liquid at a temperature of 68°F (20°C).
3. Compressed gases in solution are nonliquefied gases that are dissolved in a solvent.
4. Compressed gas mixtures consist of a mixture of two or more compressed gases contained in a packaging, the hazard properties of which are represented by the properties of the mixture as a whole.

CONTROL AREA. Spaces within a building where quantities of hazardous materials not exceeding the maximum allowable quantities per *control area* are stored, dispensed, used or handled. See also the definition of "Outdoor control area" in the *International Fire Code.*

CORROSIVE. A chemical that causes visible destruction of, or irreversible alterations in, living tissue by chemical action at the point of contact. A chemical shall be considered corrosive if, when tested on the intact skin of albino rabbits by the method described in DOTn 49 CFR, Part 173.137, such a chemical destroys or changes irreversibly the structure of the tissue at the point of contact following an exposure period of 4 hours. This term does not refer to action on inanimate surfaces.

CRYOGENIC FLUID. A liquid having a boiling point lower than -130°F (-89.9°C) at 14.7 pounds per square inch atmosphere (psia) (an absolute pressure of 101 kPa).

DAY BOX. A portable magazine designed to hold explosive materials constructed in accordance with the requirements for a Type 3 magazine as defined and classified in Chapter 33 of the *International Fire Code.*

DEFLAGRATION. An exothermic reaction, such as the extremely rapid oxidation of a flammable dust or vapor in air, in which the reaction progresses through the unburned material at a rate less than the velocity of sound. A deflagration can have an explosive effect.

DETONATION. An exothermic reaction characterized by the presence of a shock wave in the material which establishes and maintains the reaction. The reaction zone progresses through the material at a rate greater than the velocity of sound. The principal heating mechanism is one of shock compression. Detonations have an explosive effect.

DISPENSING. The pouring or transferring of any material from a container, tank or similar vessel, whereby vapors, dusts, fumes, mists or gases are liberated to the atmosphere.

EXPLOSION. An effect produced by the sudden violent expansion of gases, which may be accompanied by a shock wave or disruption, or both, of enclosing materials or structures. An explosion could result from any of the following:

1. Chemical changes such as rapid oxidation, *deflagration* or *detonation*, decomposition of molecules and runaway polymerization (usually *detonation*s).
2. Physical changes such as pressure tank ruptures.
3. Atomic changes (nuclear fission or fusion).

EXPLOSIVE. A chemical compound, mixture or device, the primary or common purpose of which is to function by explosion. The term includes, but is not limited to, dynamite, black powder, pellet powder, initiating explosives, detonators, safety fuses, squibs, detonating cord, igniter cord, igniters and display fireworks, 1.3G (Class B, Special).

The term "explosive" includes any material determined to be within the scope of USC Title 18: Chapter 40 and also includes any material classified as an explosive other than consumer fireworks, 1.4G (Class C, Common) by the hazardous materials regulations of DOTn 49 CFR, Parts 100-185.

High explosive. Explosive material, such as dynamite, which can be caused to detonate by means of a No. 8 test blasting cap when unconfined.

Low explosive. Explosive material that will burn or deflagrate when ignited. It is characterized by a rate of reaction that is less than the speed of sound. Examples of low explosives include, but are not limited to, black powder; safety fuse; igniters; igniter cord; fuse lighters; fireworks, 1.3G (Class B, Special) and propellants, 1.3C.

Mass-detonating explosives. Division 1.1, 1.2 and 1.5 explosives alone or in combination, or loaded into various types of ammunition or containers, most of which can be expected to explode virtually instantaneously when a small portion is subjected to fire, severe concussion, impact, the impulse of an initiating agent or the effect of a considerable discharge of energy from without. Materials that react in this manner represent a mass explosion hazard. Such an explosive will normally cause severe structural damage to adjacent objects. Explosive propagation could occur immediately to other items of ammunition and explosives stored sufficiently close to and not adequately protected from the initially exploding pile with a time interval short enough so that two or more quantities must be considered as one for quantity-distance purposes.

UN/DOTn Class 1 explosives. The former classification system used by DOTn included the terms "high" and "low" explosives as defined herein. The following terms further define explosives under the current system applied by DOTn for all explosive materials defined as hazard Class 1 materials. Compatibility group letters are used in concert with the division to specify further limitations on each division noted (i.e., the letter G identifies the material as a pyrotechnic substance or article containing a pyrotechnic substance and similar materials).

Division 1.1. Explosives that have a mass explosion hazard. A mass explosion is one which affects almost the entire load instantaneously.

Division 1.2. Explosives that have a projection hazard but not a mass explosion hazard.

Division 1.3. Explosives that have a fire hazard and either a minor blast hazard or a minor projection hazard or both, but not a mass explosion hazard.

Division 1.4. Explosives that pose a minor explosion hazard. The explosive effects are largely confined to the package and no projection of fragments of appreciable size or range is to be expected. An external fire must not cause virtually instantaneous explosion of almost the entire contents of the package.

Division 1.5. Very insensitive explosives. This division is comprised of substances that have a mass explosion hazard, but that are so insensitive there is very little probability of initiation or of transition from burning to *detonation* under normal conditions of transport.

Division 1.6. Extremely insensitive articles which do not have a mass explosion hazard. This division is comprised of articles that contain only extremely insensitive detonating substances and which demonstrate a negligible probability of accidental initiation or propagation.

FIREWORKS. Any composition or device for the purpose of producing a visible or audible effect for entertainment purposes by combustion, deflagration or *detonation* that meets the definition of 1.4G fireworks or 1.3G fireworks as set forth herein.

Fireworks, 1.3G. (Formerly Class B, Special Fireworks.) Large fireworks devices, which are explosive materials, intended for use in fireworks displays and designed to produce audible or visible effects by combustion, deflagration or *detonation*. Such 1.3G fireworks include, but are not limited to, firecrackers containing more than 130 milligrams (2 grains) of explosive composition, aerial shells containing more than 40 grams (617 grains) of pyrotechnic composition, and other display pieces which exceed the limits for classification as 1.4G fireworks. Such 1.3G fireworks are also described as fireworks, UN0335 by the DOTn.

Fireworks, 1.4G. (Formerly Class C, Common Fireworks.) Small fireworks devices containing restricted amounts of pyrotechnic composition designed primarily to produce visible or audible effects by combustion. Such 1.4G fireworks which comply with the construction, chemical composition and labeling regulations of the DOTn for fireworks, UN0336, and the U.S. Consumer Product Safety Commission (CPSC) as set forth in CPSC 16 CFR: Parts 1500 and 1507, are not explosive materials for the purpose of this code.

FLAMMABLE GAS. A material that is a gas at 68°F (20°C) or less at 14.7 pounds per square inch atmosphere (psia) (101 kPa) of pressure [a material that has a boiling point of 68°F (20°C) or less at 14.7 psia (101 kPa)] which:

1. Is ignitable at 14.7 psia (101 kPa) when in a mixture of 13 percent or less by volume with air; or
2. Has a flammable range at 14.7 psia (101 kPa) with air of at least 12 percent, regardless of the lower limit.

The limits specified shall be determined at 14.7 psi (101 kPa) of pressure and a temperature of 68°F (20°C) in accordance with ASTM E 681.

FLAMMABLE LIQUEFIED GAS. A liquefied compressed gas which, under a charged pressure, is partially liquid at a temperature of 68°F (20°C) and which is flammable.

FLAMMABLE LIQUID. A liquid having a closed cup flash point below 100°F (38°C). Flammable liquids are further categorized into a group known as Class I liquids. The Class I category is subdivided as follows:

Class IA. Liquids having a flash point below 73°F (23°C) and a boiling point below 100°F (38°C).

Class IB. Liquids having a flash point below 73°F (23°C) and a boiling point at or above 100°F (38°C).

Class IC. Liquids having a flash point at or above 73°F (23°C) and below 100°F (38°C).

The category of flammable liquids does not include compressed gases or cryogenic fluids.

FLAMMABLE MATERIAL. A material capable of being readily ignited from common sources of heat or at a temperature of 600°F (316°C) or less.

FLAMMABLE SOLID. A solid, other than a blasting agent or explosive, that is capable of causing fire through friction, absorption or moisture, spontaneous chemical change, or retained heat from manufacturing or processing, or which has an ignition temperature below 212°F (100°C) or which burns so vigorously and persistently when ignited as to create a serious hazard. A chemical shall be considered a flammable solid as determined in accordance with the test method of CPSC 16 CFR; Part 1500.44, if it ignites and burns with a self-sustained flame at a rate greater than 0.1 inch (2.5 mm) per second along its major axis.

FLASH POINT. The minimum temperature in degrees Fahrenheit at which a liquid will give off sufficient vapors to form an ignitable mixture with air near the surface or in the container, but will not sustain combustion. The flash point of a liquid shall be determined by appropriate test procedure and apparatus as specified in ASTM D 56, ASTM D 93 or ASTM D 3278.

HANDLING. The deliberate transport by any means to a point of storage or use.

HAZARDOUS MATERIALS. Those chemicals or substances that are physical hazards or health hazards as defined and classified in this section and the *International Fire Code*, whether the materials are in usable or waste condition.

HEALTH HAZARD. A classification of a chemical for which there is statistically significant evidence that acute or chronic health effects are capable of occurring in exposed persons. The term "health hazard" includes chemicals that are *toxic* or *highly toxic*, and corrosive.

HIGHLY TOXIC. A material which produces a lethal dose or lethal concentration that falls within any of the following categories:

1. A chemical that has a median lethal dose (LD_{50}) of 50 milligrams or less per kilogram of body weight when administered orally to albino rats weighing between 200 and 300 grams each.
2. A chemical that has a median lethal dose (LD_{50}) of 200 milligrams or less per kilogram of body weight when administered by continuous contact for 24 hours (or less if death occurs within 24 hours) with the bare skin of albino rabbits weighing between 2 and 3 kilograms each.
3. A chemical that has a median lethal concentration (LC_{50}) in air of 200 parts per million by volume or less of gas or vapor, or 2 milligrams per liter or less of mist, fume or dust, when administered by continuous inhalation for 1 hour (or less if death occurs within 1 hour) to albino rats weighing between 200 and 300 grams each.

Mixtures of these materials with ordinary materials, such as water, might not warrant classification as *highly toxic*. While this system is basically simple in application, any hazard evaluation that is required for the precise categorization of this type of material shall be performed by experienced, technically competent persons.

INCOMPATIBLE MATERIALS. Materials that, when mixed, have the potential to react in a manner that generates heat, fumes, gases or byproducts which are hazardous to life or property.

INERT GAS. A gas that is capable of reacting with other materials only under abnormal conditions such as high temperatures, pressures and similar extrinsic physical forces. Within the context of the code, inert gases do not exhibit either physical or health properties as defined (other than acting as a simple asphyxiant) or hazard properties other than those of a compressed gas. Some of the more common inert gases include argon, helium, krypton, neon, nitrogen and xenon.

OPEN SYSTEM. The use of a solid or liquid hazardous material involving a vessel or system that is continuously open to the atmosphere during normal operations and where vapors are liberated, or the product is exposed to the atmosphere during normal operations. Examples of open systems for solids and liquids include dispensing from or into open beakers or containers, dip tank and plating tank operations.

OPERATING BUILDING. A building occupied in conjunction with the manufacture, transportation or use of explosive materials. Operating buildings are separated from one another with the use of intraplant or intraline distances.

ORGANIC PEROXIDE. An organic compound that contains the bivalent -O-O- structure and which may be considered to be a structural derivative of hydrogen peroxide where one or both of the hydrogen atoms have been replaced by an organic radical. Organic peroxides can pose an explosion hazard (*detonation* or deflagration) or they can be shock sensitive. They can also decompose into various unstable compounds over an extended period of time.

Class I. Those formulations that are capable of deflagration but not *detonation*.

Class II. Those formulations that burn very rapidly and that pose a moderate reactivity hazard.

Class III. Those formulations that burn rapidly and that pose a moderate reactivity hazard.

Class IV. Those formulations that burn in the same manner as ordinary combustibles and that pose a minimal reactivity hazard.

Class V. Those formulations that burn with less intensity than ordinary combustibles or do not sustain combustion and that pose no reactivity hazard.

Unclassified detonable. Organic peroxides that are capable of *detonation*. These peroxides pose an extremely high explosion hazard through rapid explosive decomposition.

OXIDIZER. A material that readily yields oxygen or other oxidizing gas, or that readily reacts to promote or initiate combustion of combustible materials and, if heated or contaminated, can result in vigorous self-sustained decomposition.

Class 4. An oxidizer that can undergo an explosive reaction due to contamination or exposure to thermal or physical shock and that causes a severe increase in the burning rate of combustible materials with which it comes into contact. Additionally, the oxidizer causes a severe increase in the burning rate and can cause spontaneous ignition of combustibles.

Class 3. An oxidizer that causes a severe increase in the burning rate of combustible materials with which it comes in contact.

Class 2. An oxidizer that will cause a moderate increase in the burning rate of combustible materials with which it comes in contact.

Class 1. An oxidizer that does not moderately increase the burning rate of combustible materials.

OXIDIZING GAS. A gas that can support and accelerate combustion of other materials.

PHYSICAL HAZARD. A chemical for which there is evidence that it is a combustible liquid, cryogenic fluid, explosive, flammable (solid, liquid or gas), organic peroxide (solid or liquid), oxidizer (solid or liquid), oxidizing gas, pyrophoric (solid, liquid or gas), unstable (reactive) material (solid, liquid or gas) or water-reactive material (solid or liquid).

PYROPHORIC. A chemical with an autoignition temperature in air, at or below a temperature of 130°F (54.4°C).

PYROTECHNIC COMPOSITION. A chemical mixture that produces visible light displays or sounds through a self-propagating, heat-releasing chemical reaction which is initiated by ignition.

TOXIC. A chemical falling within any of the following categories:

1. A chemical that has a median lethal dose (LD_{50}) of more than 50 milligrams per kilogram, but not more than 500 milligrams per kilogram of body weight when administered orally to albino rats weighing between 200 and 300 grams each.
2. A chemical that has a median lethal dose (LD_{50}) of more than 200 milligrams per kilogram, but not more than 1,000 milligrams per kilogram of body weight when administered by continuous contact for 24 hours (or less if death occurs within 24 hours) with the bare skin of albino rabbits weighing between 2 and 3 kilograms each.
3. A chemical that has a median lethal concentration (LC_{50}) in air of more than 200 parts per million, but not more than 2,000 parts per million by volume of gas or vapor, or more than 2 milligrams per liter but not more than 20 milligrams per liter of mist, fume or dust, when administered by continuous inhalation for 1 hour (or less if death occurs within 1 hour) to albino rats weighing between 200 and 300 grams each.

UNSTABLE (REACTIVE) MATERIAL. A material, other than an explosive, which in the pure state or as commercially produced, will vigorously polymerize, decompose, condense or become self-reactive and undergo other violent chemical changes, including explosion, when exposed to heat, friction or shock, or in the absence of an inhibitor, or in the presence of contaminants, or in contact with incompatible materials. Unstable (reactive) materials are subdivided as follows:

Class 4. Materials that in themselves are readily capable of *detonation* or explosive decomposition or explosive reaction at normal temperatures and pressures. This class includes materials that are sensitive to mechanical or localized thermal shock at normal temperatures and pressures.

Class 3. Materials that in themselves are capable of *detonation* or of explosive decomposition or explosive reaction but which require a strong initiating source or which must be heated under confinement before initiation. This class includes materials that are sensitive to thermal or mechanical shock at elevated temperatures and pressures.

Class 2. Materials that in themselves are normally unstable and readily undergo violent chemical change but do not detonate. This class includes materials that can undergo chemical change with rapid release of energy at normal temperatures and pressures, and that can undergo violent chemical change at elevated temperatures and pressures.

Class 1. Materials that in themselves are normally stable but which can become unstable at elevated temperatures and pressure.

WATER-REACTIVE MATERIAL. A material that explodes; violently reacts; produces flammable, *toxic* or other hazardous gases; or evolves enough heat to cause autoignition or ignition of combustibles upon exposure to water or moisture. Water-reactive materials are subdivided as follows:

Class 3. Materials that react explosively with water without requiring heat or confinement.

Class 2. Materials that react violently with water or have the ability to boil water. Materials that produce flammable, *toxic* or other hazardous gases or evolve enough heat to cause autoignition or ignition of combustibles upon exposure to water or moisture.

Class 1. Materials that react with water with some release of energy, but not violently.

[F] 307.3 High-hazard Group H-1. Buildings and structures containing materials that pose a *detonation* hazard shall be classified as Group H-1. Such materials shall include, but not be limited to, the following:

Detonable pyrophoric materials

Explosives:

Division 1.1
Division 1.2
Division 1.3

Exception: Materials that are used and maintained in a form where either confinement or configuration will not elevate the hazard from a mass fire to mass explosion hazard shall be allowed in H-2 occupancies.

Division 1.4

Exception: Articles, including articles packaged for shipment, that are not regulated as an explosive under Bureau of Alcohol, Tobacco and Firearms regulations, or unpackaged articles used in process operations that do not propagate a *detonation* or deflagration between articles shall be allowed in H-3 occupancies.

Division 1.5
Division 1.6

Organic peroxides, unclassified detonable
Oxidizers, Class 4
Unstable (reactive) materials, Class 3 detonable and Class 4

[F] 307.4 High-hazard Group H-2. Buildings and structures containing materials that pose a deflagration hazard or a hazard from accelerated burning shall be classified as Group H-2. Such materials shall include, but not be limited to, the following:

Class I, II or IIIA flammable or combustible liquids which are used or stored in normally open containers or systems, or in closed containers or systems pressurized at more than 15 psi (103.4 kPa) gage.
Combustible dusts
Cryogenic fluids, flammable
Flammable gases
Organic peroxides, Class I
Oxidizers, Class 3, that are used or stored in normally open containers or systems, or in closed containers or systems pressurized at more than 15 psi (103 kPa) gage
Pyrophoric liquids, solids and gases, nondetonable
Unstable (reactive) materials, Class 3, nondetonable
Water-reactive materials, Class 3

[F] 307.5 High-hazard Group H-3. Buildings and structures containing materials that readily support combustion or that pose a physical hazard shall be classified as Group H-3. Such materials shall include, but not be limited to, the following:

Class I, II or IIIA flammable or combustible liquids that are used or stored in normally closed containers or systems pressurized at 15 pounds per square inch gauge (103.4 kPa) or less
Combustible fibers, other than densely packed baled cotton
Consumer fireworks, 1.4G (Class C, Common)
Cryogenic fluids, oxidizing
Flammable solids
Organic peroxides, Class II and III
Oxidizers, Class 2
Oxidizers, Class 3, that are used or stored in normally closed containers or systems pressurized at 15 pounds per square inch gauge (103 kPa) or less
Oxidizing gases
Unstable (reactive) materials, Class 2
Water-reactive materials, Class 2

[F] 307.6 High-hazard Group H-4. Buildings and structures which contain materials that are health hazards shall be classified as Group H-4. Such materials shall include, but not be limited to, the following:

Corrosives
Highly toxic materials
Toxic materials

[F] 307.7 High-hazard Group H-5 structures. Semiconductor fabrication facilities and comparable research and development areas in which hazardous production materials (HPM) are used and the aggregate quantity of materials is in excess of those listed in Tables 307.1(1) and 307.1(2) shall be classified as Group H-5. Such facilities and areas shall be designed and constructed in accordance with Section 415.8.

[F] 307.8 Multiple hazards. Buildings and structures containing a material or materials representing hazards that are classified in one or more of Groups H-1, H-2, H-3 and H-4 shall conform to the code requirements for each of the occupancies so classified.

SECTION 308
INSTITUTIONAL GROUP I

308.1 Institutional Group I. Institutional Group I occupancy includes, among others, the use of a building or structure, or a portion thereof, in which people are cared for or live in a supervised environment, having physical limitations because of health or age are harbored for medical treatment or other care or treatment, or in which people are detained for penal or correctional purposes or in which the liberty of the occupants is restricted. Institutional occupancies shall be classified as Group I-1, I-2, I-3 or I-4.

308.2 Group I-1. This occupancy shall include buildings, structures or parts thereof housing more than 16 persons, on a 24-hour basis, who because of age, mental disability or other reasons, live in a supervised residential environment that provides *personal care services*. The occupants are capable of responding to an emergency situation without physical assistance from staff. This group shall include, but not be limited to, the following:

Alcohol and drug centers
Assisted living facilities
Congregate care facilities
Convalescent facilities
Group homes
Halfway houses
Residential board and care facilities
Social rehabilitation facilities

A facility such as the above with five or fewer persons shall be classified as a Group R-3 or shall comply with the *International Residential Code* in accordance with Section 101.2. A facility such as above, housing at least six and not more than 16 persons, shall be classified as Group R-4.

308.3 Group I-2. This occupancy shall include buildings and structures used for medical, surgical, psychiatric, nursing or custodial care for persons who are not capable of self-preservation. This group shall include, but not be limited to, the following:

Child care facilities
Detoxification facilities
Hospitals
Mental hospitals
Nursing homes

308.3.1 Definitions. The following words and terms shall, for the purposes of this section and as used elsewhere in this code, have the meanings shown herein.

CHILD CARE FACILITIES. Facilities that provide care on a 24-hour basis to more than five children, $2^1/_2$ years of age or less.

DETOXIFICATION FACILITIES. Facilities that serve patients who are provided treatment for substance abuse on a 24-hour basis and who are incapable of self-preservation or who are harmful to themselves or others.

HOSPITALS AND MENTAL HOSPITALS. Buildings or portions thereof used on a 24-hour basis for the medical, psychiatric, obstetrical or surgical treatment of inpatients who are incapable of self-preservation.

NURSING HOMES. Nursing homes are long-term care facilities on a 24-hour basis, including both intermediate care facilities and skilled nursing facilities, serving more than five persons and any of the persons are incapable of self-preservation.

308.4 Group I-3. This occupancy shall include buildings and structures that are inhabited by more than five persons who are under restraint or security. An I-3 facility is occupied by persons who are generally incapable of self-preservation due to security measures not under the occupants' control. This group shall include, but not be limited to, the following:

Correctional centers
Detention centers
Jails
Prerelease centers
Prisons
Reformatories

Buildings of Group I-3 shall be classified as one of the occupancy conditions indicated in Sections 308.4.1 through 308.4.5 (see Section 408.1).

308.4.1 Condition 1. This occupancy condition shall include buildings in which free movement is allowed from sleeping areas, and other spaces where access or occupancy is permitted, to the exterior via *means of egress* without restraint. A Condition 1 facility is permitted to be constructed as Group R.

308.4.2 Condition 2. This occupancy condition shall include buildings in which free movement is allowed from sleeping areas and any other occupied smoke compartment to one or more other smoke compartments. Egress to the exterior is impeded by locked *exits*.

308.4.3 Condition 3. This occupancy condition shall include buildings in which free movement is allowed within individual smoke compartments, such as within a residential unit comprised of individual *sleeping units* and group activity spaces, where egress is impeded by remote-controlled release of *means of egress* from such a smoke compartment to another smoke compartment.

308.4.4 Condition 4. This occupancy condition shall include buildings in which free movement is restricted from an occupied space. Remote-controlled release is provided to permit movement from *sleeping units*, activity spaces and other occupied areas within the smoke compartment to other smoke compartments.

308.4.5 Condition 5. This occupancy condition shall include buildings in which free movement is restricted from an occupied space. Staff-controlled manual release is provided to permit movement from *sleeping units*, activity spaces and other occupied areas within the smoke compartment to other smoke compartments.

308.5 Group I-4, day care facilities. This group shall include buildings and structures occupied by persons of any age who receive custodial care for less than 24 hours by individuals other than parents or guardians, relatives by blood, marriage or adoption, and in a place other than the home of the person cared for. A facility such as the above with five or fewer persons shall be classified as a Group R-3 or shall comply with the *International Residential Code* in accordance with Section 101.2. Places of worship during religious functions are not included.

308.5.1 Adult care facility. A facility that provides accommodations for less than 24 hours for more than five unrelated adults and provides supervision and *personal care services* shall be classified as Group I-4.

Exception: Deleted.

308.5.2 Child care facility. A facility that provides supervision and personal care on less than a 24-hour basis for more than five children $2^1/_2$ years of age or less shall be classified as Group I-4.

Exception: A child day care facility that provides care for more than five but no more than 100 children $2^1/_2$ years or less of age, where the rooms in which the children are cared for are located on a *level of exit discharge* serving such rooms and each of these child care rooms has an *exit* door directly to the exterior, shall be classified as Group E.

SECTION 309
MERCANTILE GROUP M

309.1 Mercantile Group M. Mercantile Group M occupancy includes, among others, the use of a building or structure or a portion thereof, for the display and sale of merchandise and involves stocks of goods, wares or merchandise incidental to such purposes and accessible to the public. Mercantile occupancies shall include, but not be limited to, the following:

Department stores
Drug stores
Markets
Motor fuel-dispensing facilities
Retail or wholesale stores
Sales rooms

309.2 Quantity of hazardous materials. The aggregate quantity of nonflammable solid and nonflammable or noncombustible liquid hazardous materials stored or displayed in a single *control area* of a Group M occupancy shall not exceed the quantities in Table 414.2.5(1).

SECTION 310
RESIDENTIAL GROUP R

310.1 Residential Group R. Residential Group R includes, among others, the use of a building or structure, or a portion thereof, for sleeping purposes when not classified as an Institutional Group I or when not regulated by the *International Residential Code* in accordance with Section 101.2. Residential occupancies shall include the following:

R-1 Residential occupancies containing *sleeping units* where the occupants are primarily transient in nature, including:

Boarding houses (transient)
Hotels (transient)
Motels (transient)

Congregate living facilities (transient) with 10 or fewer occupants are permitted to comply with the construction requirements for Group R-3.

R-2 Residential occupancies containing *sleeping units* or more than two *dwelling units* where the occupants are primarily permanent in nature, including:

Apartment houses
Boarding houses (nontransient)
Convents
Dormitories
Fraternities and sororities
Hotels (nontransient)
Live/work units
Monasteries
Motels (nontransient)
Vacation timeshare properties

Congregate living facilities with 16 or fewer occupants are permitted to comply with the construction requirements for Group R-3.

R-3 Residential occupancies where the occupants are primarily permanent in nature and not classified as Group R-1, R-2, R-4 or I, including:

Buildings that do not contain more than two dwelling units.
Adult care facilities that provide accommodations for five or fewer persons of any age for less than 24 hours.
Child care facilities that provide accommodations for eight or fewer persons with no more than five for a preschool for less than 24 hours.
Congregate living facilities with 16 or fewer persons.

Adult care and child care facilities that are within a single-family home are permitted to comply with the *International Residential Code.*

R-4 Residential occupancies shall include buildings arranged for occupancy as residential care/assisted living facilities, or adult and child day care facilities that provide accommodations in a residence occupied as a home by the caregiver for persons of any age for less than 24 hours, including more than five but not more than 16 occupants, excluding staff.

Group R-4 occupancies shall meet the requirements for construction as defined for Group R-3, except as otherwise provided for in this code or shall comply with the *International Residential Code* provided the building is protected by an *automatic sprinkler system* installed in accordance with Section 903.2.8.

310.2 Definitions. The following words and terms shall, for the purposes of this section and as used elsewhere in this code, have the meanings shown herein.

BOARDING HOUSE. A building arranged or used for lodging for compensation, with or without meals, and not occupied as a single-family unit.

CONGREGATE LIVING FACILITIES. A building or part thereof that contains sleeping units where residents share bathroom and/or kitchen facilities.

DORMITORY. A space in a building where group sleeping accommodations are provided in one room, or in a series of closely associated rooms, for persons not members of the same family group, under joint occupancy and single management, as in college dormitories or fraternity houses.

PERSONAL CARE SERVICE. The care of residents who do not require chronic or convalescent medical or nursing care. Personal care involves responsibility for the safety of the resident while inside the building.

RESIDENTIAL CARE/ASSISTED LIVING FACILITIES. A building or part thereof housing persons, on a 24-hour basis, who because of age, mental disability or other reasons, live in a supervised residential environment which provides *personal care services*. The occupants are capable of responding to an emergency situation without physical assistance from staff. This classification shall include, but not be limited to, the following: residential board and care facilities, assisted living facilities, halfway houses, group homes, congregate care facilities, social rehabilitation facilities, alcohol and drug abuse centers and convalescent facilities.

TRANSIENT. Occupancy of a *dwelling unit* or *sleeping unit* for not more than 30 days.

SECTION 311
STORAGE GROUP S

311.1 Storage Group S. Storage Group S occupancy includes, among others, the use of a building or structure, or a portion thereof, for storage that is not classified as a hazardous occupancy.

311.2 Moderate-hazard storage, Group S-1. Buildings occupied for storage uses that are not classified as Group S-2, including, but not limited to, storage of the following:

Aerosols, Levels 2 and 3
Aircraft hangar (storage and repair)
Bags: cloth, burlap and paper
Bamboos and rattan
Baskets
Belting: canvas and leather
Books and paper in rolls or packs
Boots and shoes
Buttons, including cloth covered, pearl or bone
Cardboard and cardboard boxes
Clothing, woolen wearing apparel
Cordage

Dry boat storage (indoor)
Furniture
Furs
Glues, mucilage, pastes and size
Grains
Horns and combs, other than celluloid
Leather
Linoleum
Lumber
Motor vehicle repair garages complying with the maximum allowable quantities of hazardous materials listed in Table 307.1(1) (see Section 406.6)
Photo engravings
Resilient flooring
Silks
Soaps
Sugar
Tires, bulk storage of
Tobacco, cigars, cigarettes and snuff
Upholstery and mattresses
Wax candles

311.3 Low-hazard storage, Group S-2. Includes, among others, buildings used for the storage of noncombustible materials such as products on wood pallets or in paper cartons with or without single thickness divisions; or in paper wrappings. Such products are permitted to have a negligible amount of plastic *trim*, such as knobs, handles or film wrapping. Group S-2 storage uses shall include, but not be limited to, storage of the following:

Asbestos
Beverages up to and including 16-percent alcohol in metal, glass or ceramic containers
Cement in bags
Chalk and crayons
Dairy products in nonwaxed coated paper containers
Dry cell batteries
Electrical coils
Electrical motors
Empty cans
Food products
Foods in noncombustible containers
Fresh fruits and vegetables in nonplastic trays or containers
Frozen foods
Glass
Glass bottles, empty or filled with noncombustible liquids
Gypsum board
Inert pigments
Ivory
Meats
Metal cabinets
Metal desks with plastic tops and *trim*
Metal parts
Metals
Mirrors
Oil-filled and other types of distribution transformers
Parking garages, open or enclosed
Porcelain and pottery
Stoves
Talc and soapstones
Washers and dryers

SECTION 312
UTILITY AND MISCELLANEOUS GROUP U

312.1 General. Buildings and structures of an accessory character and miscellaneous structures not classified in any specific occupancy shall be constructed, equipped and maintained to conform to the requirements of this code commensurate with the fire and life hazard incidental to their occupancy. Group U shall include, but not be limited to, the following:

Agricultural buildings
Aircraft hangars, accessory to a one- or two-family residence (see Section 412.5)
Barns
Carports
Fences more than 6 feet (1829 mm) high
Grain silos, accessory to a residential occupancy
Greenhouses
Livestock shelters
Private garages
Retaining walls
Sheds
Stables
Tanks
Towers

CHAPTER 4

SPECIAL DETAILED REQUIREMENTS BASED ON USE AND OCCUPANCY

SECTION 401 SCOPE

401.1 Detailed use and occupancy requirements. In addition to the occupancy and construction requirements in this code, the provisions of this chapter apply to the special uses and occupancies described herein.

SECTION 402 COVERED MALL AND OPEN MALL BUILDINGS

402.1 Scope. The provisions of this section shall apply to buildings or structures defined herein as *covered mall buildings* not exceeding three floor levels at any point nor more than three *stories above grade plane*. Except as specifically required by this section, *covered mall buildings* shall meet applicable provisions of this code.

Exceptions:

1. Foyers and lobbies of Groups B, R-1 and R-2 are not required to comply with this section.
2. Buildings need not comply with the provisions of this section when they totally comply with other applicable provisions of this code.

402.2 Definitions. The following words and terms shall, for the purposes of this chapter and as used elsewhere in this code, have the meanings shown herein.

ANCHOR BUILDING. An exterior perimeter building of a group other than H having direct access to a *covered mall building* but having required *means of egress* independent of the mall.

COVERED MALL BUILDING. A single building enclosing a number of tenants and occupants, such as retail stores, drinking and dining establishments, entertainment and amusement facilities, passenger transportation terminals, offices and other similar uses wherein two or more tenants have a main entrance into one or more malls. For the purpose of this chapter, *anchor buildings* shall not be considered as a part of the *covered mall building*. The term "*covered mall building*" shall include open mall buildings as defined below.

Mall. A roofed or covered common pedestrian area within a *covered mall building* that serves as access for two or more tenants and not to exceed three levels that are open to each other. The term "mall" shall include open malls as defined below.

Open mall. An unroofed common pedestrian way serving a number of tenants not exceeding three levels. Circulation at levels above grade shall be permitted to include open exterior balconies leading to *exits* discharging at grade.

Open mall building. Several structures housing a number of tenants, such as retail stores, drinking and dining establishments, entertainment and amusement facilities, offices, and other similar uses, wherein two or more tenants have a main entrance into one or more open malls. For the purpose of Chapter 4 of the *International Building Code*, *anchor buildings* are not considered as a part of the open mall building.

FOOD COURT. A public seating area located in the mall that serves adjacent food preparation tenant spaces.

GROSS LEASABLE AREA. The total floor area designed for tenant occupancy and exclusive use. The area of tenant occupancy is measured from the centerlines of joint partitions to the outside of the tenant walls. All tenant areas, including areas used for storage, shall be included in calculating gross leasable area.

402.3 Lease plan. Each *covered mall building* owner shall provide both the building and fire departments with a lease plan showing the location of each occupancy and its exits after the certificate of occupancy has been issued. No modifications or changes in occupancy or use shall be made from that shown on the lease plan without prior approval of the *building official*.

402.4 Means of egress. Each tenant space and the *covered mall building* shall be provided with *means of egress* as required by this section and this code. Where there is a conflict between the requirements of this code and the requirements of this section, the requirements of this section shall apply.

402.4.1 Determination of occupant load. The *occupant load* permitted in any individual tenant space in a *covered mall building* shall be determined as required by this code. *Means of egress* requirements for individual tenant spaces shall be based on the *occupant load* thus determined.

402.4.1.1 Occupant formula. In determining required *means of egress* of the mall, the number of occupants for whom *means of egress* are to be provided shall be based on gross leasable area of the *covered mall building* (excluding *anchor buildings*) and the *occupant load* factor as determined by the following equation.

$$OLF = (0.00007)(GLA) + 25 \qquad \textbf{(Equation 4-1)}$$

where:

OLF = The *occupant load* factor (square feet per person).

GLA = The gross leasable area (square feet).

Exception: Tenant spaces attached to a *covered mall building* but with a *means of egress* system that is totally independent of the *covered mall building* shall not be considered as gross leasable area for determining the required *means of egress* for the *covered mall building*.

402.4.1.2 OLF range. The *occupant load* factor (*OLF*) is not required to be less than 30 and shall not exceed 50.

402.4.1.3 Anchor buildings. The *occupant load* of *anchor buildings* opening into the mall shall not be included in computing the total number of occupants for the mall.

402.4.1.4 Food courts. The *occupant load* of a food court shall be determined in accordance with Section 1004. For the purposes of determining the *means of egress* requirements for the mall, the food court *occupant load* shall be added to the *occupant load* of the *covered mall building* as calculated above.

402.4.2 Number of means of egress. Wherever the distance of travel to the mall from any location within a tenant space used by persons other than employees exceeds 75 feet (22 860 mm) or the tenant space has an *occupant load* of 50 or more, not less than two *means of egress* shall be provided.

402.4.3 Arrangements of means of egress. Assembly occupancies with an *occupant load* of 500 or more shall be so located in the *covered mall building* that their entrance will be immediately adjacent to a principal entrance to the mall and shall have not less than one-half of their required *means of egress* opening directly to the exterior of the *covered mall building*.

402.4.3.1 Anchor building means of egress. Required *means of egress* for *anchor buildings* shall be provided independently from the mall *means of egress* system. The *occupant load* of *anchor buildings* opening into the mall shall not be included in determining *means of egress* requirements for the mall. The path of egress travel of malls shall not exit through anchor buildings. Malls terminating at an *anchor building* where no other *means of egress* has been provided shall be considered as a dead-end mall.

402.4.4 Distance to exits. Within each individual tenant space in a *covered mall building*, the maximum distance of travel from any point to an *exit* or entrance to the mall shall not exceed 200 feet (60 960 mm).

The maximum distance of travel from any point within a mall to an *exit* shall not exceed 200 feet (60 960 mm).

402.4.5 Access to exits. Where more than one *exit* is required, they shall be so arranged that it is possible to travel in either direction from any point in a mall to separate *exits*. The minimum width of an *exit passageway* or *corridor* from a mall shall be 66 inches (1676 mm).

Exception: Dead ends not exceeding a length equal to twice the width of the mall measured at the narrowest location within the dead-end portion of the mall.

402.4.5.1 Exit passageways. Where *exit passageways* provide a secondary *means of egress* from a tenant space, doorways to the exit passageway shall be protected by 1-hour *fire door assemblies* that are self- or automatic-closing by smoke detection in accordance with Section 715.4.8.3.

402.4.6 Service areas fronting on exit passageways. Mechanical rooms, electrical rooms, building service areas and service elevators are permitted to open directly into *exit passageways*, provided the exit passageway is separated from such rooms with not less than 1-hour *fire barriers* constructed in accordance with Section 707 or *horizontal assemblies* constructed in accordance with Section 712, or both. The minimum *fire protection rating* of openings in the *fire barriers* shall be 1 hour.

402.5 Mall width. For the purpose of providing required egress, malls are permitted to be considered as *corridors* but need not comply with the requirements of Section 1005.1 of this code where the width of the mall is as specified in this section.

402.5.1 Minimum width. The minimum width of the mall shall be 20 feet (6096 mm). The mall width shall be sufficient to accommodate the *occupant load* served. There shall be a minimum of 10 feet (3048 mm) clear exit width to a height of 8 feet (2438 mm) between any projection of a tenant space bordering the mall and the nearest kiosk, vending machine, bench, display opening, food court or other obstruction to *means of egress* travel.

402.5.2 Minimum width open mall. The minimum floor and roof opening width above grade shall be 20 feet (6096 mm) in open malls.

402.6 Types of construction. The area of any *covered mall building*, including *anchor buildings*, of Types I, II, III and IV construction, shall not be limited provided the *covered mall building* and attached *anchor buildings* and parking garages are surrounded on all sides by a permanent open space of not less than 60 feet (18 288 mm) and the *anchor buildings* do not exceed three *stories above grade plane*. The allowable height and area of *anchor buildings* greater than three *stories above grade plane* shall comply with Section 503, as modified by Sections 504 and 506. The construction type of *open parking garages* and enclosed parking garages shall comply with Sections 406.3 and 406.4, respectively.

402.6.1 Reduced open space. The permanent open space of 60 feet (18 288 mm) shall be permitted to be reduced to not less than 40 feet (12 192 mm), provided the following requirements are met:

1. The reduced open space shall not be allowed for more than 75 percent of the perimeter of the *covered mall building* and *anchor buildings*.
2. The *exterior wall* facing the reduced open space shall have a minimum *fire-resistance rating* of 3 hours.
3. Openings in the *exterior wall* facing the reduced open space shall have opening protectives with a minimum *fire protection rating* of 3 hours.
4. Group E, H, I or R occupancies are not within the *covered mall building* or *anchor stores*.

402.7 Fire-resistance-rated separation. Fire-resistance-rated separation is not required between tenant spaces and the mall. Fire-resistance-rated separation is not required between a food court and adjacent tenant spaces or the mall.

402.7.1 Attached garage. An attached garage for the storage of passenger vehicles having a capacity of not more than nine persons and *open parking garages* shall be considered as a separate building where it is separated from the *covered mall building* by not less than 2-hour *fire barriers* constructed in accordance with Section 707 or *horizontal assemblies* constructed in accordance with Section 712, or both.

Exception: Where an *open parking garage* or enclosed parking garage is separated from the *covered mall building* or *anchor building* a distance greater than 10 feet (3048 mm), the provisions of Table 602 shall apply. Pedestrian walkways and tunnels that attach the *open parking garage* or enclosed parking garage to the *covered mall building* or *anchor building* shall be constructed in accordance with Section 3104.

402.7.2 Tenant separations. Each tenant space shall be separated from other tenant spaces by a *fire partition* complying with Section 709. A tenant separation wall is not required between any tenant space and the mall.

402.7.3 Anchor building separation. An *anchor building* shall be separated from the *covered mall building* by *fire walls* complying with Section 706.

Exception: *Anchor buildings* of not more than three *stories above grade plane* that have an occupancy classification the same as that permitted for tenants of the *covered mall building* shall be separated by 2-hour fire-resistive *fire barriers* complying with Section 707.

402.7.3.1 Openings between anchor building and mall. Except for the separation between Group R-1 *sleeping units* and the mall, openings between *anchor buildings* of Type IA, IB, IIA and IIB construction and the mall need not be protected.

402.8 Interior finish. *Interior wall* and *ceiling finishes* within the mall and *exits* shall have a minimum *flame spread index* and smoke-developed index of Class B in accordance with Chapter 8. *Interior floor finishes* shall meet the requirements of Section 804.

[F] 402.9 Automatic sprinkler system. The *covered mall building* and buildings connected shall be equipped throughout with an *automatic sprinkler system* in accordance with Section 903.3.1.1, which shall comply with the following:

1. The *automatic sprinkler system* shall be complete and operative throughout occupied space in the *covered mall building* prior to occupancy of any of the tenant spaces. Unoccupied tenant spaces shall be similarly protected unless provided with *approved* alternative protection.
2. Sprinkler protection for the mall shall be independent from that provided for tenant spaces or anchors. Where tenant spaces are supplied by the same system, they shall be independently controlled.

Exception: An *automatic sprinkler system* shall not be required in spaces or areas of *open parking garages* constructed in accordance with Section 406.3.

[F] 402.9.1 Standpipe system. The *covered mall building* shall be equipped throughout with a standpipe system as required by Section 905.3.3.

402.10 Smoke control. Where a *covered mall building* contains an atrium, a smoke control system shall be provided in accordance with Section 404.5.

Exception: A smoke control system is not required in *covered mall buildings* where the atrium connects only two stories.

402.11 Kiosks. Kiosks and similar structures (temporary or permanent) shall meet the following requirements:

1. Combustible kiosks or other structures shall not be located within the mall unless constructed of any of the following materials:
   1.1. *Fire-retardant-treated wood* complying with Section 2303.2.
   1.2. Foam plastics having a maximum heat-release rate not greater than 100 kilowatts (105 Btu/h) when tested in accordance with the exhibit booth protocol in UL 1975.
   1.3. Aluminum composite material (ACM) meeting the requirements of Class A interior finish in accordance with Chapter 8 when tested as an assembly in the maximum thickness intended for use.
2. Kiosks or similar structures located within the mall shall be provided with *approved* fire suppression and detection devices.
3. The minimum horizontal separation between kiosks or groupings thereof and other structures within the mall shall be 20 feet (6096 mm).
4. Each kiosk or similar structure or groupings thereof shall have a maximum area of 300 square feet (28 m^2).

402.12 Children's playground structures. Structures intended as children's playgrounds that exceed 10 feet (3048 mm) in height and 150 square feet (14 m^2) in area shall comply with Sections 402.12.1 through 402.12.4.

402.12.1 Materials. Children's playground structures shall be constructed of noncombustible materials or of combustible materials that comply with the following:

1. *Fire-retardant-treated wood* complying with Section 2303.2.
2. Light-transmitting plastics complying with Section 2606.
3. Foam plastics (including the pipe foam used in soft-contained play equipment structures) having a maximum heat-release rate not greater than 100 kilowatts when tested in accordance with UL 1975.
4. Aluminum composite material (ACM) meeting the requirements of Class A *interior finish* in accordance with Chapter 8 when tested as an assembly in the maximum thickness intended for use.
5. Textiles and films complying with the flame propagation performance criteria contained in NFPA 701.
6. Plastic materials used to construct rigid components of soft-contained play equipment structures (such as tubes, windows, panels, junction boxes, pipes, slides

and decks) exhibiting a peak rate of heat release not exceeding 400 kW/m^2 when tested in accordance with ASTM E 1354 at an incident heat flux of 50 kW/m^2 in the horizontal orientation at a thickness of 6 mm.

7. Ball pool balls, used in soft-contained play equipment structures, having a maximum heat-release rate not greater than 100 kilowatts when tested in accordance with UL 1975. The minimum specimen test size shall be 36 inches by 36 inches (914 mm by 914 mm) by an average of 21 inches (533 mm) deep, and the balls shall be held in a box constructed of galvanized steel poultry netting wire mesh.
8. Foam plastics shall be covered by a fabric, coating or film meeting the flame propagation performance criteria of NFPA 701.
9. The floor covering placed under the children's playground structure shall exhibit a Class I *interior floor finish* classification, as described in Section 804, when tested in accordance with NFPA 253.

402.12.2 Fire protection. Children's playground structures located within the mall shall be provided with the same level of *approved* fire suppression and detection devices required for kiosks and similar structures.

402.12.3 Separation. Children's playground structures shall have a minimum horizontal separation from other structures within the mall of 20 feet (6090 mm).

402.12.4 Area limits. Children's playground structures shall not exceed 300 square feet (28 m^2) in area, unless a special investigation has demonstrated adequate fire safety.

402.13 Security grilles and doors. Horizontal sliding or vertical security grilles or doors that are a part of a required *means of egress* shall conform to the following:

1. They shall remain in the full open position during the period of occupancy by the general public.
2. Doors or grilles shall not be brought to the closed position when there are 10 or more persons occupying spaces served by a single exit or 50 or more persons occupying spaces served by more than one exit.
3. The doors or grilles shall be openable from within without the use of any special knowledge or effort where the space is occupied.
4. Where two or more exits are required, not more than one-half of the exits shall be permitted to include either a horizontal sliding or vertical rolling grille or door.

[F] 402.14 Standby power. *Covered mall buildings* exceeding 50,000 square feet (4645 m^2) shall be provided with standby power systems that are capable of operating the emergency voice/alarm communication system.

[F] 402.15 Emergency voice/alarm communication system. *Covered mall buildings* exceeding 50,000 square feet (4645 m^2) in total floor area shall be provided with an emergency voice/alarm communication system. Emergency voice/alarm communication systems serving a mall, required or otherwise, shall be accessible to the fire department. The system shall be provided in accordance with Section 907.5.2.2.

402.16 Plastic signs. Plastic signs affixed to the storefront of any tenant space facing the mall shall be limited as specified in Sections 402.16.1 through 402.16.5.2.

402.16.1 Area. Plastic signs shall not exceed 20 percent of the wall area facing the mall.

402.16.2 Height and width. Plastic signs shall not exceed a height of 36 inches (914 mm), except that if the sign is vertical, the height shall not exceed 96 inches (2438 mm) and the width shall not exceed 36 inches (914 mm).

402.16.3 Location. Plastic signs shall be located a minimum distance of 18 inches (457 mm) from adjacent tenants.

402.16.4 Plastics other than foam plastics. Plastics other than foam plastics used in signs shall be light-transmitting plastics complying with Section 2606.4 or shall have a self-ignition temperature of 650°F (343°C) or greater when tested in accordance with ASTM D 1929, and a *flame spread index* not greater than 75 and smoke-developed index not greater than 450 when tested in the manner intended for use in accordance with ASTM E 84 or UL 723 or meet the acceptance criteria of Section 803.1.2.1 when tested in accordance with NFPA 286.

402.16.4.1 Encasement. Edges and backs of plastic signs in the mall shall be fully encased in metal.

402.16.5 Foam plastics. Foam plastics used in signs shall have flame-retardant characteristics such that the sign has a maximum heat-release rate of 150 kilowatts when tested in accordance with UL 1975 and the foam plastics shall have the physical characteristics specified in this section. Foam plastics used in signs installed in accordance with Section 402.16 shall not be required to comply with the flame spread and smoke-developed indexes specified in Section 2603.3.

402.16.5.1 Density. The minimum density of foam plastics used in signs shall not be less than 20 pounds per cubic foot (pcf) (320 kg/m^3).

402.16.5.2 Thickness. The thickness of foam plastic signs shall not be greater than $^1/_2$ inch (12.7 mm).

[F] 402.17 Fire department access to equipment. Rooms or areas containing controls for air-conditioning systems, automatic fire-extinguishing systems or other detection, suppression or control elements shall be identified for use by the fire department.

SECTION 403 HIGH-RISE BUILDINGS

403.1 Applicability. High-rise buildings shall comply with Sections 403.2 through 403.6.

Exception: The provisions of Sections 403.2 through 403.6 shall not apply to the following buildings and structures:

1. Airport traffic control towers in accordance with Section 412.3.
2. Open parking garages in accordance with Section 406.3.

3. Buildings with a Group A-5 occupancy in accordance with Section 303.1.
4. Special industrial occupancies in accordance with Section 503.1.1.
5. Buildings with a Group H-1, H-2 or H-3 occupancy in accordance with Section 415.

403.2 Construction. The construction of high-rise buildings shall comply with the provisions of Sections 403.2.1 through 403.2.4.

403.2.1 Reduction in fire-resistance rating. The *fire-resistance-rating* reductions listed in Sections 403.2.1.1 and 403.2.1.2 shall be allowed in buildings that have sprinkler control valves equipped with supervisory initiating devices and water-flow initiating devices for each floor.

403.2.1.1 Type of construction. The following reductions in the minimum *fire-resistance rating* of the building elements in Table 601 shall be permitted as follows:

1. For buildings not greater than 420 feet (128 m) in *building height*, the *fire-resistance rating* of the building elements in Type IA construction shall be permitted to be reduced to the minimum *fire-resistance ratings* for the building elements in Type IB.

   Exception: The required *fire-resistance rating* of columns supporting floors shall not be permitted to be reduced.

2. In other than Group F-1, M and S-1 occupancies, the *fire-resistance rating* of the building elements in Type IB construction shall be permitted to be reduced to the *fire-resistance ratings* in Type IIA.
3. The *building height* and *building area* limitations of a building containing building elements with reduced *fire-resistance ratings* shall be permitted to be the same as the building without such reductions.

403.2.1.2 Shaft enclosures. For buildings not greater than 420 feet (128 m) in *building height*, the required *fire-resistance rating* of the *fire barriers* enclosing vertical shafts, other than *exit enclosures* and elevator hoistway enclosures, is permitted to be reduced to 1 hour where automatic sprinklers are installed within the shafts at the top and at alternate floor levels.

403.2.2 Seismic considerations. For seismic considerations, see Chapter 16.

403.2.3 Structural integrity of exit enclosures and elevator hoistway enclosures. For high-rise buildings of occupancy category III or IV in accordance with Section 1604.5, and for all buildings that are more than 420 feet (128 m) in *building height*, *exit enclosures* and elevator hoistway enclosures shall comply with Sections 403.2.3.1 through 403.2.3.4.

403.2.3.1 Wall assembly. The wall assemblies making up the *exit enclosures* and elevator hoistway enclosures shall meet or exceed Soft Body Impact Classification Level 2 as measured by the test method described in ASTM C 1629/C 1629M.

403.2.3.2 Wall assembly materials. The face of the wall assemblies making up the *exit enclosures* and elevator hoistway enclosures that are not exposed to the interior of the *exit enclosure* or elevator hoistway enclosure shall be constructed in accordance with one of the following methods:

1. The wall assembly shall incorporate not less than two layers of impact-resistant construction board each of which meets or exceeds Hard Body Impact Classification Level 2 as measured by the test method described in ASTM C 1629/C 1629M.
2. The wall assembly shall incorporate not less than one layer of impact-resistant construction material that meets or exceeds Hard Body Impact Classification Level 3 as measured by the test method described in ASTM C 1629/C 1629M.
3. The wall assembly incorporates multiple layers of any material, tested in tandem, that meet or exceed Hard Body Impact Classification Level 3 as measured by the test method described in ASTM C 1629/C 1629M.

403.2.3.3 Concrete and masonry walls. Concrete or masonry walls shall be deemed to satisfy the requirements of Sections 403.2.3.1 and 403.2.3.2.

403.2.3.4 Other wall assemblies. Any other wall assembly that provides impact resistance equivalent to that required by Sections 403.2.3.1 and 403.2.3.2 for Hard Body Impact Classification Level 3, as measured by the test method described in ASTM C 1629/C 1629M, shall be permitted.

403.2.4 Sprayed fire-resistant materials (SFRM). The bond strength of the SFRM installed throughout the building shall be in accordance with Table 403.2.4.

TABLE 403.2.4
MINIMUM BOND STRENGTH

HEIGHT OF BUILDING[a]	SFRM MINIMUM BOND STRENGTH
Up to 420 feet	430 psf
Greater than 420 feet	1,000 psf

For SI: 1 foot = 304.8 mm, 1 pound per square foot (psf) = 0.0479 kW/m^2.
a. Above the lowest level of fire department vehicle access.

[F] 403.3 Automatic sprinkler system. Buildings and structures shall be equipped throughout with an *automatic sprinkler system* in accordance with Section 903.3.1.1 and a secondary water supply where required by Section 903.3.5.2.

Exception: An *automatic sprinkler system* shall not be required in spaces or areas of:

1. *Open parking garages* in accordance with Section 406.3.
2. Telecommunications equipment buildings used exclusively for telecommunications equipment, associated electrical power distribution equipment, batteries and standby engines, provided that those spaces

or areas are equipped throughout with an automatic fire detection system in accordance with Section 907.2 and are separated from the remainder of the building by not less than 1-hour *fire barriers* constructed in accordance with Section 707 or not less than 2-hour *horizontal assemblies* constructed in accordance with Section 712, or both.

[F] 403.3.1 Number of sprinkler risers and system design. Each sprinkler system zone in buildings that are more than 420 feet (128 m) in *building height* shall be supplied by a minimum of two risers. Each riser shall supply sprinklers on alternate floors. If more than two risers are provided for a zone, sprinklers on adjacent floors shall not be supplied from the same riser.

[F] 403.3.1.1 Riser location. Sprinkler risers shall be placed in *exit enclosures* that are remotely located in accordance with Section 1015.2.

[F] 403.3.2 Water supply to required fire pumps. Required fire pumps shall be supplied by connections to a minimum of two water mains located in different streets. Separate supply piping shall be provided between each connection to the water main and the pumps. Each connection and the supply piping between the connection and the pumps shall be sized to supply the flow and pressure required for the pumps to operate.

Exception: Two connections to the same main shall be permitted provided the main is valved such that an interruption can be isolated so that the water supply will continue without interruption through at least one of the connections.

403.4 Emergency systems. The detection, alarm and emergency systems of high-rise buildings shall comply with Sections 403.4.1 through 403.4.8.

[F] 403.4.1 Smoke detection. Smoke detection shall be provided in accordance with Section 907.2.13.1.

[F] 403.4.2 Fire alarm system. A fire alarm system shall be provided in accordance with Section 907.2.13.

[F] 403.4.3 Emergency voice/alarm communication system. An emergency voice/alarm communication system shall be provided in accordance with Section 907.5.2.2.

[F] 403.4.4 Emergency responder radio coverage. Emergency responder radio coverage shall be provided in accordance with Section 510 of the *International Fire Code*.

[F] 403.4.5 Fire command. A fire command center complying with Section 911 shall be provided in a location *approved* by the fire department.

403.4.6 Smoke removal. To facilitate smoke removal in post-fire salvage and overhaul operations, buildings and structures shall be equipped with natural or mechanical ventilation for removal of products of combustion in accordance with one of the following:

1. Easily identifiable, manually operable windows or panels shall be distributed around the perimeter of each floor at not more than 50-foot (15 240 mm) intervals. The area of operable windows or panels shall not be less than 40 square feet (3.7 m^2) per 50 linear feet (15 240 mm) of perimeter.

   Exceptions:

   1. In Group R-1 occupancies, each *sleeping unit* or suite having an *exterior wall* shall be permitted to be provided with 2 square feet (0.19 m^2) of venting area in lieu of the area specified in Item 1.
   2. Windows shall be permitted to be fixed provided that glazing can be cleared by fire fighters.

2. Mechanical air-handling equipment providing one exhaust air change every 15 minutes for the area involved. Return and exhaust air shall be moved directly to the outside without recirculation to other portions of the building.
3. Any other *approved* design that will produce equivalent results.

[F] 403.4.7 Standby power. A standby power system complying with Chapter 27 shall be provided for standby power loads specified in Section 403.4.7.2.

[F] 403.4.7.1 Special requirements for standby power systems. If the standby system is a generator set inside a building, the system shall be located in a separate room enclosed with 2-hour *fire barriers* constructed in accordance with Section 707 or *horizontal assemblies* constructed in accordance with Section 712, or both. System supervision with manual start and transfer features shall be provided at the fire command center.

[F] 403.4.7.2 Standby power loads. The following are classified as standby power loads:

1. Power and lighting for the fire command center required by Section 403.4.5;
2. Ventilation and automatic fire detection equipment for smokeproof enclosures; and
3. Standby power shall be provided for elevators in accordance with Sections 1007.4, 3003, 3007 and 3008.

[F] 403.4.8 Emergency power systems. An emergency power system complying with Chapter 27 shall be provided for emergency power loads specified in Section 403.4.8.1.

[F] 403.4.8.1 Emergency power loads. The following are classified as emergency power loads:

1. Exit signs and *means of egress* illumination required by Chapter 10;
2. Elevator car lighting;
3. Emergency voice/alarm communications systems;
4. Automatic fire detection systems;
5. Fire alarm systems; and
6. Electrically powered fire pumps.

403.5 Means of egress and evacuation. The *means of egress* in high-rise buildings shall comply with Sections 403.5.1 through 403.5.6.

403.5.1 Remoteness of exit stairway enclosures. The required *exit stairway* enclosures shall be separated by a distance not less than 30 feet (9144 mm) or not less than one-fourth of the length of the maximum overall diagonal dimension of the building or area to be served, whichever is less. The distance shall be measured in a straight line between the nearest points of the *exit stairway* enclosures. In buildings with three or more *exit stairway* enclosures, at least two of the *exit stairway* enclosures shall comply with this section. Interlocking or *scissor stairs* shall be counted as one *exit stairway.*

403.5.2 Additional exit stairway. For buildings other than Group R-2 that are more than 420 feet (128 m) in *building height*, one additional *exit stairway* meeting the requirements of Sections 1009 and 1022 shall be provided in addition to the minimum number of *exits* required by Section 1021.1. The total width of any combination of remaining *exit stairways* with one *exit stairway* removed shall not be less than the total width required by Section 1005.1. *Scissor stairs* shall not be considered the additional *exit stairway* required by this section.

Exception: An additional *exit stairway* shall not be required to be installed in buildings having elevators used for occupant self-evacuation in accordance with Section 3008.

403.5.3 Stairway door operation. Stairway doors other than the *exit discharge* doors shall be permitted to be locked from the stairway side. Stairway doors that are locked from the stairway side shall be capable of being unlocked simultaneously without unlatching upon a signal from the fire command center.

403.5.3.1 Stairway communication system. A telephone or other two-way communications system connected to an *approved* constantly attended station shall be provided at not less than every fifth floor in each *stairway* where the doors to the *stairway* are locked.

403.5.4 Smokeproof exit enclosures. Every required *exit stairway* serving floors more than 75 feet (22 860 mm) above the lowest level of fire department vehicle access shall comply with Sections 909.20 and 1022.9.

403.5.5 Luminous egress path markings. Luminous egress path markings shall be provided in accordance with Section 1024.

403.5.6 Emergency escape and rescue. Emergency escape and rescue openings required by Section 1029 are not required.

403.6 Elevators. Elevator installation and operation in high-rise buildings shall comply with Chapter 30 and Sections 403.6.1 and 403.6.2.

403.6.1 Fire service access elevator. In buildings with an occupied floor 10 or more stories above the lowest level of fire department vehicle access, a minimum of one fire service access elevator shall be provided in accordance with Section 3007.

403.6.2 Occupant evacuation elevators. Where installed in accordance with Section 3008, passenger elevators for general public use shall be permitted to be used for occupant self-evacuation.

SECTION 404
ATRIUMS

404.1 General. In other than Group H occupancies, and where permitted by Exception 5 in Section 708.2, the provisions of this section shall apply to buildings or structures containing vertical openings defined herein as "Atriums."

404.1.1 Definition. The following word and term shall, for the purposes of this chapter and as used elsewhere in this code, have the meaning shown herein.

ATRIUM. An opening connecting two or more *stories* other than enclosed *stairways*, elevators, hoistways, escalators, plumbing, electrical, air-conditioning or other equipment, which is closed at the top and not defined as a mall. Stories, as used in this definition, do not include balconies within assembly groups or *mezzanines* that comply with Section 505.

404.2 Use. The floor of the atrium shall not be used for other than low fire hazard uses and only *approved* materials and decorations in accordance with the *International Fire Code* shall be used in the atrium space.

Exception: The atrium floor area is permitted to be used for any *approved* use where the individual space is provided with an *automatic sprinkler system* in accordance with Section 903.3.1.1.

[F] 404.3 Automatic sprinkler protection. An *approved automatic sprinkler system* shall be installed throughout the entire building.

Exceptions:

1. That area of a building adjacent to or above the atrium need not be sprinklered provided that portion of the building is separated from the atrium portion by not less than 2-hour *fire barriers* constructed in accordance with Section 707 or *horizontal assemblies* constructed in accordance with Section 712, or both.
2. Where the ceiling of the atrium is more than 55 feet (16 764 mm) above the floor, sprinkler protection at the ceiling of the atrium is not required.

[F] 404.4 Fire alarm system. A fire alarm system shall be provided in accordance with Section 907.2.14.

404.5 Smoke control. A smoke control system shall be installed in accordance with Section 909.

Exception: Smoke control is not required for atriums that connect only two *stories.*

404.6 Enclosure of atriums. Atrium spaces shall be separated from adjacent spaces by a 1-hour *fire barrier* constructed in accordance with Section 707 or a *horizontal assembly* constructed in accordance with Section 712, or both.

Exceptions:

1. A glass wall forming a smoke partition where automatic sprinklers are spaced 6 feet (1829 mm) or less along both sides of the separation wall, or on the room

side only if there is not a walkway on the atrium side, and between 4 inches and 12 inches (102 mm and 305 mm) away from the glass and designed so that the entire surface of the glass is wet upon activation of the sprinkler system without obstruction. The glass shall be installed in a gasketed frame so that the framing system deflects without breaking (loading) the glass before the sprinkler system operates.

2. A glass-block wall assembly in accordance with Section 2110 and having a $^{3}/_{4}$-hour *fire protection rating*.
3. The adjacent spaces of any three *floors* of the atrium shall not be required to be separated from the atrium where such spaces are accounted for in the design of the smoke control system.

[F] 404.7 Standby power. Equipment required to provide smoke control shall be connected to a standby power system in accordance with Section 909.11.

404.8 Interior finish. The *interior finish* of walls and ceilings of the atrium shall not be less than Class B with no reduction in class for sprinkler protection.

404.9 Travel distance. In other than the lowest level of the atrium, where the required *means of egress* is through the atrium space, the portion of exit access travel distance within the atrium space shall not exceed 200 feet (60 960 mm). The travel distance requirements for areas of buildings open to the atrium and where access to the *exits* is not through the atrium, shall comply with the requirements of Section 1016.

SECTION 405
UNDERGROUND BUILDINGS

405.1 General. The provisions of this section apply to building spaces having a floor level used for human occupancy more than 30 feet (9144 mm) below the finished floor of the lowest *level of exit discharge*.

Exceptions:

1. One- and two-family *dwellings*, sprinklered in accordance with Section 903.3.1.3.
2. Parking garages with automatic sprinkler systems in compliance with Section 405.3.
3. Fixed guideway transit systems.
4. Grandstands, *bleachers*, stadiums, arenas and similar facilities.
5. Where the lowest *story* is the only *story* that would qualify the building as an underground building and has an area not exceeding 1,500 square feet (139 m^2) and has an *occupant load* less than 10.
6. Pumping stations and other similar mechanical spaces intended only for limited periodic use by service or maintenance personnel.

405.2 Construction requirements. The underground portion of the building shall be of Type I construction.

[F] 405.3 Automatic sprinkler system. The highest level of *exit discharge* serving the underground portions of the building and all levels below shall be equipped with an *automatic sprinkler system* installed in accordance with Section 903.3.1.1. Water-flow switches and control valves shall be supervised in accordance with Section 903.4.

405.4 Compartmentation. Compartmentation shall be in accordance with Sections 405.4.1 through 405.4.3.

405.4.1 Number of compartments. A building having a floor level more than 60 feet (18 288 mm) below the finished floor of the lowest *level of exit discharge* shall be divided into a minimum of two compartments of approximately equal size. Such compartmentation shall extend through the highest *level of exit discharge* serving the underground portions of the building and all levels below.

Exception: The lowest *story* need not be compartmented where the area does not exceed 1,500 square feet (139 m^2) and has an *occupant load* of less than 10.

405.4.2 Smoke barrier penetration. The compartments shall be separated from each other by a *smoke barrier* in accordance with Section 710. Penetrations between the two compartments shall be limited to plumbing and electrical piping and conduit that are firestopped in accordance with Section 713. Doorways shall be protected by *fire door assemblies* that are automatic-closing by smoke detection in accordance with Section 715.4.8.3 and are installed in accordance with NFPA 105 and Section 715.4.3. Where provided, each compartment shall have an air supply and an exhaust system independent of the other compartments.

405.4.3 Elevators. Where elevators are provided, each compartment shall have direct access to an elevator. Where an elevator serves more than one compartment, an elevator lobby shall be provided and shall be separated from each compartment by a *smoke barrier* in accordance with Section 710. Doors shall be gasketed, have a drop sill and be automatic-closing by smoke detection in accordance with Section 715.4.8.3.

[F] 405.5 Smoke control system. A smoke control system shall be provided in accordance with Sections 405.5.1 and 405.5.2.

[F] 405.5.1 Control system. A smoke control system is required to control the migration of products of combustion in accordance with Section 909 and the provisions of this section. Smoke control shall restrict movement of smoke to the general area of fire origin and maintain *means of egress* in a usable condition.

[F] 405.5.2 Compartment smoke control system. Where compartmentation is required, each compartment shall have an independent smoke control system. The system shall be automatically activated and capable of manual operation in accordance with Sections 907.2.18 and 907.2.19.

[F] 405.6 Fire alarm systems. A fire alarm system shall be provided where required by Sections 907.2.18 and 907.2.19.

405.7 Means of egress. *Means of egress* shall be in accordance with Sections 405.7.1 and 405.7.2.

405.7.1 Number of exits. Each floor level shall be provided with a minimum of two *exits*. Where compartmentation is required by Section 405.4, each compartment shall have a minimum of one *exit* and shall also have an *exit access* doorway into the adjoining compartment.

405.7.2 Smokeproof enclosure. Every required *stairway* serving floor levels more than 30 feet (9144 mm) below the finished floor of its *level of exit discharge* shall comply with the requirements for a smokeproof enclosure as provided in Section 1022.9.

[F] 405.8 Standby power. A standby power system complying with Chapter 27 shall be provided standby power loads specified in Section 405.8.1.

[F] 405.8.1 Standby power loads. The following loads are classified as standby power loads:

1. Smoke control system.
2. Ventilation and automatic fire detection equipment for smokeproof enclosures.
3. Fire pumps.

Standby power shall be provided for elevators in accordance with Section 3003.

[F] 405.8.2 Pick-up time. The standby power system shall pick up its connected loads within 60 seconds of failure of the normal power supply.

[F] 405.9 Emergency power. An emergency power system complying with Chapter 27 shall be provided for emergency power loads specified in Section 405.9.1.

[F] 405.9.1 Emergency power loads. The following loads are classified as emergency power loads:

1. Emergency voice/alarm communications systems.
2. Fire alarm systems.
3. Automatic fire detection systems.
4. Elevator car lighting.
5. *Means of egress* and exit sign illumination as required by Chapter 10.

[F] 405.10 Standpipe system. The underground building shall be equipped throughout with a standpipe system in accordance with Section 905.

SECTION 406 MOTOR-VEHICLE-RELATED OCCUPANCIES

406.1 Private garages and carports.

406.1.1 Classification. Buildings or parts of buildings classified as Group U occupancies because of the use or character of the occupancy shall not exceed 1,000 square feet (93 m^2) in area or one *story* in height except as provided in Section 406.1.2. Any building or portion thereof that exceeds the limitations specified in this section shall be classified in the occupancy group other than Group U that it most nearly resembles.

406.1.2 Area increase. Group U occupancies used for the storage of private or pleasure-type motor vehicles where no repair work is completed or fuel is dispensed are permitted to be 3,000 square feet (279 m^2) when the following provisions are met:

1. For a mixed occupancy building, the *exterior wall* and opening protection for the Group U portion of the building shall be as required for the major occupancy of the building. For such a mixed occupancy building, the allowable floor area of the building shall be as permitted for the major occupancy contained therein.
2. For a building containing only a Group U occupancy, the *exterior wall* shall not be required to have a *fire-resistance rating* and the area of openings shall not be limited when the *fire separation distance* is 5 feet (1524 mm) or more.

More than one 3,000-square-foot (279 m^2) Group U occupancy shall be permitted to be in the same building, provided each 3,000-square-foot (279 m^2) area is separated by *fire walls* complying with Section 706.

406.1.3 Garages and carports. Carports shall be open on at least two sides. Carport floor surfaces shall be of *approved* noncombustible material. Carports not open on at least two sides shall be considered a garage and shall comply with the provisions of this section for garages.

Exception: Asphalt surfaces shall be permitted at ground level in carports.

The area of floor used for parking of automobiles or other vehicles shall be sloped to facilitate the movement of liquids to a drain or toward the main vehicle entry doorway.

406.1.4 Separation. Separations shall comply with the following:

1. The private garage shall be separated from the *dwelling unit* and its *attic* area by means of a minimum $^1/_2$-inch (12.7 mm) gypsum board applied to the garage side. Garages beneath habitable rooms shall be separated from all habitable rooms above by not less than a $^5/_8$-inch (15.9 mm) Type X gypsum board or equivalent. Door openings between a private garage and the *dwelling unit* shall be equipped with either solid wood doors or solid or honeycomb core steel doors not less than 1$^3/_8$ inches (34.9 mm) thick, or doors in compliance with Section 715.4.3. Openings from a private garage directly into a room used for sleeping purposes shall not be permitted. Doors shall be self-closing and self-latching.
2. Ducts in a private garage and ducts penetrating the walls or ceilings separating the *dwelling unit* from the garage shall be constructed of a minimum 0.019-inch (0.48 mm) sheet steel and shall have no openings into the garage.
3. A separation is not required between a Group R-3 and U carport, provided the carport is entirely open on two or more sides and there are not enclosed areas above.

406.1.5 Automatic garage door openers. Automatic garage door openers, if provided, shall be *listed* in accordance with UL 325.

406.2 Parking garages.

406.2.1 Classification. Parking garages shall be classified as either open, as defined in Section 406.3, or enclosed and shall meet the appropriate criteria in Section 406.4. Also see Section 509 for special provisions for parking garages.

406.2.2 Clear height. The clear height of each floor level in vehicle and pedestrian traffic areas shall not be less than 7 feet (2134 mm). Vehicle and pedestrian areas accommodating van-accessible parking required by Section 1106.5 shall conform to ICC A117.1.

406.2.3 Guards. *Guards* shall be provided in accordance with Section 1013. *Guards* serving as vehicle barrier systems shall comply with Sections 406.2.4 and 1013.

406.2.4 Vehicle barrier systems. Vehicle barrier systems not less than 2 feet 9 inches (835 mm) high shall be placed at the end of drive lanes, and at the end of parking spaces where the vertical distance to the ground or surface directly below is greater than 1 foot (305 mm). Vehicle barrier systems shall comply with the loading requirements of Section 1607.7.3.

Exception: Vehicle storage compartments in a mechanical access parking garage.

406.2.5 Ramps. Vehicle ramps shall not be considered as required *exits* unless pedestrian facilities are provided. Vehicle ramps that are utilized for vertical circulation as well as for parking shall not exceed a slope of 1:15 (6.67 percent).

406.2.6 Floor surface. Parking surfaces shall be of concrete or similar noncombustible and nonabsorbent materials.

The area of floor used for parking of automobiles or other vehicles shall be sloped to facilitate the movement of liquids to a drain or toward the main vehicle entry doorway.

Exceptions:

1. Asphalt parking surfaces shall be permitted at ground level.
2. Floors of Group S-2 parking garages shall not be required to have a sloped surface.

406.2.7 Mixed occupancy separation. Parking garages shall be separated from other occupancies in accordance with Section 508.1.

406.2.8 Special hazards. Connection of a parking garage with any room in which there is a fuel-fired appliance shall be by means of a vestibule providing a two-doorway separation.

Exception: A single door shall be allowed provided the sources of ignition in the appliance are at least 18 inches (457 mm) above the floor.

406.2.9 Attached to rooms. Openings from a parking garage directly into a room used for sleeping purposes shall not be permitted.

406.3 Open parking garages.

406.3.1 Scope. Except where specific provisions are made in Sections 406.3.2 through 406.3.13, other requirements of this code shall apply.

406.3.2 Definitions. The following words and terms shall, for the purposes of this chapter and as used elsewhere in this code, have the meanings shown herein.

MECHANICAL-ACCESS OPEN PARKING GARAGES. *Open parking garages* employing parking machines, lifts, elevators or other mechanical devices for vehicles moving from and to street level and in which public occupancy is prohibited above the street level.

OPEN PARKING GARAGE. A structure or portion of a structure with the openings as described in Section 406.3.3.1 on two or more sides that is used for the parking or storage of private motor vehicles as described in Section 406.3.4.

RAMP-ACCESS OPEN PARKING GARAGES. *Open parking garages* employing a series of continuously rising floors or a series of interconnecting ramps between floors permitting the movement of vehicles under their own power from and to the street level.

406.3.3 Construction. *Open parking garages* shall be of Type I, II or IV construction. *Open parking garages* shall meet the design requirements of Chapter 16. For vehicle barrier systems, see Section 406.2.4.

406.3.3.1 Openings. For natural ventilation purposes, the exterior side of the structure shall have uniformly distributed openings on two or more sides. The area of such openings in *exterior walls* on a tier must be at least 20 percent of the total perimeter wall area of each tier. The aggregate length of the openings considered to be providing natural ventilation shall constitute a minimum of 40 percent of the perimeter of the tier. Interior walls shall be at least 20 percent open with uniformly distributed openings.

Exception: Openings are not required to be distributed over 40 percent of the building perimeter where the required openings are uniformly distributed over two opposing sides of the building.

406.3.4 Uses. Mixed uses shall be allowed in the same building as an *open parking garage* subject to the provisions of Sections 402.7.1, 406.3.13, 508.1, 509.3, 509.4 and 509.7.

406.3.5 Area and height. Area and height of *open parking garages* shall be limited as set forth in Chapter 5 for Group S-2 occupancies and as further provided for in Section 508.1.

406.3.5.1 Single use. When the *open parking garage* is used exclusively for the parking or storage of private motor vehicles, with no other uses in the building, the area and height shall be permitted to comply with Table

406.3.5, along with increases allowed by Section 406.3.6.

Exception: The grade-level tier is permitted to contain an office, waiting and toilet rooms having a total combined area of not more than 1,000 square feet (93 m^2). Such area need not be separated from the *open parking garage*.

In *open parking garages* having a spiral or sloping floor, the horizontal projection of the structure at any cross section shall not exceed the allowable area per parking tier. In the case of an *open parking garage* having a continuous spiral floor, each 9 feet 6 inches (2896 mm) of height, or portion thereof, shall be considered a tier.

The clear height of a parking tier shall not be less than 7 feet (2134 mm), except that a lower clear height is permitted in mechanical-access *open parking garages* where *approved* by the *building official*.

406.3.6 Area and height increases. The allowable area and height of *open parking garages* shall be increased in accordance with the provisions of this section. Garages with sides open on three-fourths of the building's perimeter are permitted to be increased by 25 percent in area and one tier in height. Garages with sides open around the entire building's perimeter are permitted to be increased by 50 percent in area and one tier in height. For a side to be considered open under the above provisions, the total area of openings along the side shall not be less than 50 percent of the interior area of the side at each tier and such openings shall be equally distributed along the length of the tier.

Allowable tier areas in Table 406.3.5 shall be increased for *open parking garages* constructed to heights less than the table maximum. The gross tier area of the garage shall not exceed that permitted for the higher structure. At least three sides of each such larger tier shall have continuous horizontal openings not less than 30 inches (762 mm) in clear height extending for at least 80 percent of the length of the sides and no part of such larger tier shall be more than 200 feet (60 960 mm) horizontally from such an opening. In addition, each such opening shall face a street or *yard* accessible to a street with a width of at least 30 feet (9144 mm) for the full length of the opening, and standpipes shall be provided in each such tier.

Open parking garages of Type II construction, with all sides open, shall be unlimited in allowable area where the *building height* does not exceed 75 feet (22 860 mm). For a side to be considered open, the total area of openings along the side shall not be less than 50 percent of the interior area of the side at each tier and such openings shall be equally distributed along the length of the tier. All portions of tiers shall be within 200 feet (60 960 mm) horizontally from such openings or other natural ventilation openings as defined in Section 406.3.3.1. These openings shall be permitted to be provided in *courts* with a minimum dimension of 20 feet (6096 mm) for the full width of the openings.

406.3.7 Fire separation distance. *Exterior walls* and openings in *exterior walls* shall comply with Tables 601 and 602. The distance to an adjacent *lot line* shall be determined in accordance with Table 602 and Section 705.

406.3.8 Means of egress. Where persons other than parking attendants are permitted, *open parking garages* shall meet the *means of egress* requirements of Chapter 10. Where no persons other than parking attendants are permitted, there shall not be less than two 36-inch-wide (914 mm) *exit stairways*. Lifts shall be permitted to be installed for use of employees only, provided they are completely enclosed by noncombustible materials.

406.3.9 Standpipes. Standpipes shall be installed where required by the provisions of Chapter 9.

406.3.10 Sprinkler systems. Where required by other provisions of this code, *automatic sprinkler systems* and standpipes shall be installed in accordance with the provisions of Chapter 9.

406.3.11 Enclosure of vertical openings. Enclosure shall not be required for vertical openings except as specified in Section 406.3.8.

406.3.12 Ventilation. Ventilation, other than the percentage of openings specified in Section 406.3.3.1, shall not be required.

406.3.13 Prohibitions. The following uses and alterations are not permitted:

1. Vehicle repair work.
2. Parking of buses, trucks and similar vehicles.

TABLE 406.3.5
OPEN PARKING GARAGES AREA AND HEIGHT

TYPE OF CONSTRUCTION	AREA PER TIER (square feet)	HEIGHT (in tiers)		
		Ramp access	Mechanical access — Automatic sprinkler system: No	Mechanical access — Automatic sprinkler system: Yes
IA	Unlimited	Unlimited	Unlimited	Unlimited
IB	Unlimited	12 tiers	12 tiers	18 tiers
IIA	50,000	10 tiers	10 tiers	15 tiers
IIB	50,000	8 tiers	8 tiers	12 tiers
IV	50,000	4 tiers	4 tiers	4 tiers

For SI: 1 square foot = 0.0929 m^2.

3. Partial or complete closing of required openings in exterior walls by tarpaulins or any other means.
4. Dispensing of fuel.

406.4 Enclosed parking garages.

406.4.1 Heights and areas. Enclosed vehicle parking garages and portions thereof that do not meet the definition of *open parking garages* shall be limited to the allowable heights and areas specified in Table 503 as modified by Sections 504, 506 and 507. Roof parking is permitted.

406.4.2 Ventilation. A mechanical ventilation system shall be provided in accordance with the *International Mechanical Code*.

406.5 Motor fuel-dispensing facilities.

406.5.1 Construction. Motor fuel-dispensing facilities shall be constructed in accordance with the *International Fire Code* and Sections 406.5.1 through 406.5.3.

406.5.2 Vehicle fueling pad. The vehicle shall be fueled on noncoated concrete or other *approved* paving material having a resistance not exceeding 1 megohm as determined by the methodology in EN 1081.

406.5.3 Canopies. Canopies under which fuels are dispensed shall have a clear, unobstructed height of not less than 13 feet 6 inches (4115 mm) to the lowest projecting element in the vehicle drive-through area. Canopies and their supports over pumps shall be of noncombustible materials, *fire-retardant-treated wood* complying with Chapter 23, wood of Type IV sizes or of construction providing 1-hour *fire resistance*. Combustible materials used in or on a canopy shall comply with one of the following:

1. Shielded from the pumps by a noncombustible element of the canopy, or wood of Type IV sizes;
2. Plastics covered by aluminum facing having a minimum thickness of 0.010 inch (0.30 mm) or corrosion-resistant steel having a minimum base metal thickness of 0.016 inch (0.41 mm). The plastic shall have a *flame spread index* of 25 or less and a smoke-developed index of 450 or less when tested in the form intended for use in accordance with ASTM E 84 or UL 723 and a self-ignition temperature of 650°F (343°C) or greater when tested in accordance with ASTM D 1929; or
3. Panels constructed of light-transmitting plastic materials shall be permitted to be installed in canopies erected over motor vehicle fuel-dispensing station fuel dispensers, provided the panels are located at least 10 feet (3048 mm) from any building on the same lot and face yards or streets not less than 40 feet (12 192 mm) in width on the other sides. The aggregate areas of plastics shall not exceed 1,000 square feet (93 m^2). The maximum area of any individual panel shall not exceed 100 square feet (9.3 m^2).

406.5.3.1 Canopies used to support gaseous hydrogen systems. Canopies that are used to shelter dispensing operations where flammable compressed gases are located on the roof of the canopy shall be in accordance with the following:

1. The canopy shall meet or exceed Type I construction requirements.
2. Operations located under canopies shall be limited to refueling only.
3. The canopy shall be constructed in a manner that prevents the accumulation of hydrogen gas.

406.6 Repair garages.

406.6.1 General. Repair garages shall be constructed in accordance with the *International Fire Code* and Sections 406.6.1 through 406.6.6. This occupancy shall not include motor fuel-dispensing facilities, as regulated in Section 406.5.

406.6.2 Mixed uses. Mixed uses shall be allowed in the same building as a repair garage subject to the provisions of Section 508.1.

406.6.3 Ventilation. Repair garages shall be mechanically ventilated in accordance with the *International Mechanical Code*. The ventilation system shall be controlled at the entrance to the garage.

406.6.4 Floor surface. Repair garage floors shall be of concrete or similar noncombustible and nonabsorbent materials.

Exception: Slip-resistant, nonabsorbent, *interior floor finishes* having a critical radiant flux not more than 0.45 W/cm^2, as determined by NFPA 253, shall be permitted.

406.6.5 Heating equipment. Heating equipment shall be installed in accordance with the *International Mechanical Code*.

[F] 406.6.6 Gas detection system. Repair garages used for repair of vehicles fueled by nonodorized gases, such as hydrogen and nonodorized LNG, shall be provided with a flammable gas detection system.

[F] 406.6.6.1 System design. The flammable gas detection system shall be listed or approved and shall be calibrated to the types of fuels or gases used by vehicles to be repaired. Gas detectors or sensors shall be listed in accordance with UL 2075 and shall indicate the gases they are intended to detect. The gas detection system shall be designed to activate when the level of flammable gas exceeds 25 percent of the lower explosive limit. Gas detection shall also be provided in lubrication or chassis repair pits of garages used for repairing nonodorized LNG-fueled vehicles.

[F] 406.6.6.2 Operation. Activation of the gas detection system shall result in all of the following:

1. Initiation of distinct audible and visual alarm signals in the repair garage.
2. Deactivation of all heating systems located in the repair garage.
3. Activation of the mechanical ventilation system, where the system is interlocked with gas detection.

[F] 406.6.6.3 Failure of the gas detection system. Failure of the gas detection system shall result in the deactivation of the heating system, activation of the mechanical ventilation system when the system is interlocked with the gas detection system and cause a trouble signal to sound in an *approved* location.

SECTION 407
GROUP I-2

407.1 General. Occupancies in Group I-2 shall comply with the provisions of Sections 407.1 through 407.9 and other applicable provisions of this code.

407.2 Corridors. *Corridors* in occupancies in Group I-2 shall be continuous to the *exits* and separated from other areas in accordance with Section 407.3 except spaces conforming to Sections 407.2.1 through 407.2.4.

407.2.1 Waiting and similar areas. Waiting areas and similar spaces constructed as required for *corridors* shall be permitted to be open to a *corridor*, only where all of the following criteria are met:

1. The spaces are not occupied for patient *sleeping units*, treatment rooms, hazardous or incidental accessory occupancies in accordance with Section 508.2.
2. The open space is protected by an automatic fire detection system installed in accordance with Section 907.
3. The *corridors* onto which the spaces open, in the same smoke compartment, are protected by an automatic fire detection system installed in accordance with Section 907, or the smoke compartment in which the spaces are located is equipped throughout with quick-response sprinklers in accordance with Section 903.3.2.
4. The space is arranged so as not to obstruct access to the required *exits*.

407.2.2 Nurses' stations. Spaces for doctors' and nurses' charting, communications and related clerical areas shall be permitted to be open to the *corridor*, when such spaces are constructed as required for *corridors*.

407.2.3 Mental health treatment areas. Areas wherein mental health patients who are not capable of self-preservation are housed, or group meeting or multipurpose therapeutic spaces other than incidental accessory occupancies in accordance with Section 508.2.5, under continuous supervision by facility staff, shall be permitted to be open to the *corridor*, where the following criteria are met:

1. Each area does not exceed 1,500 square feet (140 m^2).
2. The area is located to permit supervision by the facility staff.
3. The area is arranged so as not to obstruct any access to the required *exits*.
4. The area is equipped with an automatic fire detection system installed in accordance with Section 907.2.
5. Not more than one such space is permitted in any one smoke compartment.
6. The walls and ceilings of the space are constructed as required for *corridors*.

407.2.4 Gift shops. Gift shops less than 500 square feet (46.5 m^2) in area shall be permitted to be open to the *corridor* provided the gift shop and storage areas are fully sprinklered and storage areas are protected in accordance with Section 508.2.5.

407.3 Corridor walls. *Corridor* walls shall be constructed as smoke partitions in accordance with Section 711.

407.3.1 Corridor doors. *Corridor* doors, other than those in a wall required to be rated by Section 508.2.5 or for the enclosure of a vertical opening or an *exit*, shall not have a required *fire protection rating* and shall not be required to be equipped with self-closing or automatic-closing devices, but shall provide an effective barrier to limit the transfer of smoke and shall be equipped with positive latching. Roller latches are not permitted. Other doors shall conform to Section 715.4.

407.3.2 Locking devices. Locking devices that restrict access to the patient room from the *corridor*, and that are operable only by staff from the *corridor* side, shall not restrict the *means of egress* from the patient room except for patient rooms in mental health facilities.

407.4 Smoke barriers. *Smoke barriers* shall be provided to subdivide every *story* used by patients for sleeping or treatment and to divide other *stories* with an *occupant load* of 50 or more persons, into at least two smoke compartments. Such *stories* shall be divided into smoke compartments with an area of not more than 22,500 square feet (2092 m^2) and the travel distance from any point in a smoke compartment to a *smoke barrier* door shall not exceed 200 feet (60 960 mm). The *smoke barrier* shall be in accordance with Section 710.

407.4.1 Refuge area. At least 30 net square feet (2.8 m^2) per patient shall be provided within the aggregate area of *corridors*, patient rooms, treatment rooms, lounge or dining areas and other low-hazard areas on each side of each *smoke barrier*. On floors not housing patients confined to a bed or litter, at least 6 net square feet (0.56 m^2) per occupant shall be provided on each side of each *smoke barrier* for the total number of occupants in adjoining smoke compartments.

407.4.2 Independent egress. A *means of egress* shall be provided from each smoke compartment created by *smoke barriers* without having to return through the smoke compartment from which *means of egress* originated.

407.4.3 Horizontal assemblies. *Horizontal assemblies* supporting *smoke barriers* required by this section shall be designed to resist the movement of smoke and shall comply with Section 712.9.

[F] 407.5 Automatic sprinkler system. Smoke compartments containing patient *sleeping units* shall be equipped throughout with an *automatic sprinkler system* in accordance with Section 903.3.1.1. The smoke compartments shall be equipped with *approved* quick-response or residential sprinklers in accordance with Section 903.3.2.

407.5.1 Dry pipe sprinkler system. When dry pipe sprinkler systems are installed, upon activation, a full flow of water shall be delivered to the most remote point of the system in no more than 60 seconds.

[F] 407.6 Fire alarm system. A fire alarm system shall be provided in accordance with Section 907.2.6.

[F] 407.7 Automatic fire detection. *Corridors* in Group I-2 nursing homes (both intermediate care and skilled nursing facilities), detoxification facilities and spaces permitted to be open to the *corridors* by Section 407.2 shall be equipped with an automatic fire detection system. Hospitals shall be equipped with smoke detection as required in Section 407.2.

Exceptions:

1. *Corridor* smoke detection is not required in smoke compartments that contain patient *sleeping units* where patient *sleeping units* are provided with smoke detectors that comply with UL 268. Such detectors shall provide a visual display on the *corridor* side of each patient *sleeping unit* and an audible and visual alarm at the nursing station attending each unit.
2. *Corridor* smoke detection is not required in smoke compartments that contain patient *sleeping units* where patient *sleeping unit* doors are equipped with automatic door-closing devices with integral smoke detectors on the unit sides installed in accordance with their listing, provided that the integral detectors perform the required alerting function.

407.8 Secured yards. Grounds are permitted to be fenced and gates therein are permitted to be equipped with locks, provided that safe dispersal areas having 30 net square feet (2.8 m^2) for bed and litter patients and 6 net square feet (0.56 m^2) for ambulatory patients and other occupants are located between the building and the fence. Such provided safe dispersal areas shall not be located less than 50 feet (15 240 mm) from the building they serve.

407.9 Hyperbaric facilities. Hyperbaric facilities in Group I-2 occupancies shall meet the requirements contained in Chapter 20 of NFPA 99.

407.10 Locks and latches. Door-locking arrangements shall be permitted in Group I-2 where the clinical or security needs of the patients require specialized locking measures for their safety or the safety of others, provided keys are carried at all times by staff that are responsible for the evacuation of the occupants within the locked building unit(s). Provisions for remote locking and unlocking of occupied rooms are required where more than 10 locks are necessary to be unlocked in order to move occupants from one smoke compartment to another smoke compartment. These locks may include mechanical locks, electromagnetic locks and other approved locking devices.

407.11 Special locking arrangements for Licensed Group I-2 and large residential care facilities as described in Section 425. Buildings protected throughout by an *automatic* fire detection system or *automatic sprinkler system* and in compliance with the following may be equipped with approved, listed locking devices:

1. Doors shall unlock upon actuation of the *automatic* fire detection system or *automatic sprinkler system.*
2. Doors shall unlock upon loss of power controlling the locking device.

   Exception: Independent standby power is acceptable as long as the automatic fire detection system, or automatic sprinkler system, when activated, has precedence over the standby power and unlocks the door. If a nonemergency situation occurs such as a power outage, the door shall be allowed to remain locked until a detection system(s) operates, provided that the power outage does not disable these detection systems. If any of the detection systems are disabled in any way, standby power controlling the locking devices will be interrupted.
3. A locking system of electromagnetic locks may be utilized when all of the following requirements are met:
   - 3.1. These types of locks may be used only in wards and wings or other portions of a facility that requires security provisions for the protection of its patients.
   - 3.2. These systems may be used, provided not more than one such system is located in any egress path.
   - 3.3. A wiring diagram and system components location map shall be provided under glass adjacent to the fire alarm panel.
   - 3.4. An on/off emergency release switch(es) must be capable of interrupting power to all electromagnetically locked doors in the facility. Release switch(es) shall be located and identified at each nurse's station serving the locked unit and any other control situation responsible for the evacuation of the occupants of the locked units that are manned 24 hours.
   - 3.5. An additional on/off emergency release switch shall be provided for each locked door and located within 3 feet (914mm) of the door and shall not depend on relays or other devices to cause the interruption of power.
   - 3.6. Any required emergency release switch shall interrupt the power to the locking device(s). If any required emergency release switch is of the locking type, all staff that are responsible for the evacuation of the occupants of the locked unit must carry emergency release switch keys. Additional convenience release devices may be provided.
4. Each locking installation shall be approved by the appropriate fire and building inspection authority prior to installation, after installation, and prior to initial use and reviewed periodically thereafter.
5. Emergency lighting shall be provided at the door.

SECTION 408
GROUP I-3

408.1 General. Occupancies in Group I-3 shall comply with the provisions of Sections 408.1 through 408.10 and other applicable provisions of this code (see Section 308.4).

408.1.1 Definitions. The following words and terms shall, for the purposes of this chapter and as used elsewhere in this code, have the meanings shown herein.

CELL. A room within a housing unit in a detention or correctional facility used to confine inmates or prisoners.

CELL TIER. Levels of cells vertically stacked above one another within a housing unit.

HOUSING UNIT. A dormitory or a group of cells with a common dayroom in Group I-3.

SALLYPORT. A security vestibule with two or more doors or gates where the intended purpose is to prevent continuous and unobstructed passage by allowing the release of only one door or gate at a time.

408.2 Other occupancies. Buildings or portions of buildings in Group I-3 occupancies where security operations necessitate the locking of required *means of egress* shall be permitted to be classified as a different occupancy. Occupancies classified as other than Group I-3 shall meet the applicable requirements of this code for that occupancy provided provisions are made for the release of occupants at all times.

Means of egress from detention and correctional occupancies that traverse other use areas shall, as a minimum, conform to requirements for detention and correctional occupancies.

Exception: It is permissible to exit through a *horizontal exit* into other contiguous occupancies that do not conform to detention and correctional occupancy egress provisions but that do comply with requirements set forth in the appropriate occupancy, as long as the occupancy is not a Group H use.

408.3 Means of egress. Except as modified or as provided for in this section, the provisions of Chapter 10 shall apply.

408.3.1 Door width. Doors to resident *sleeping units* shall have a clear width of not less than 28 inches (711 mm).

408.3.2 Sliding doors. Where doors in a *means of egress* are of the horizontal-sliding type, the force to slide the door to its fully open position shall not exceed 50 pounds (220 N) with a perpendicular force against the door of 50 pounds (220 N).

408.3.3 Guard tower doors. A hatch or trap door not less than 16 square feet (610 m^2) in area through the floor and having minimum dimensions of not less than 2 feet (610 mm) in any direction shall be permitted to be used as a portion of the *means of egress* from guard towers.

408.3.4 Spiral stairways. *Spiral stairways* that conform to the requirements of Section 1009.9 are permitted for access to and between staff locations.

408.3.5 Ship ladders. Ship ladders shall be permitted for egress from control rooms or elevated facility observation rooms in accordance with Section 1009.11.

408.3.6 Exit discharge. *Exits* are permitted to discharge into a fenced or walled courtyard. Enclosed yards or *courts* shall be of a size to accommodate all occupants, a minimum of 50 feet (15 240 mm) from the building with a net area of 15 square feet (1.4 m^2) per person.

408.3.7 Sallyports. A sallyport shall be permitted in a *means of egress* where there are provisions for continuous and unobstructed passage through the sallyport during an emergency egress condition.

408.3.8 Exit enclosures. One of the required *exit enclosures* in each building shall be permitted to have glazing installed in doors and interior walls at each landing level providing access to the enclosure, provided that the following conditions are met:

1. The *exit enclosure* shall not serve more than four floor levels.
2. Exit doors shall not be less than $^3/_4$-hour *fire door assemblies* complying with Section 715.4
3. The total area of glazing at each floor level shall not exceed 5,000 square inches (3 m^2) and individual panels of glazing shall not exceed 1,296 square inches (0.84 m^2).
4. The glazing shall be protected on both sides by an *automatic sprinkler system.* The sprinkler system shall be designed to wet completely the entire surface of any glazing affected by fire when actuated.
5. The glazing shall be in a gasketed frame and installed in such a manner that the framing system will deflect without breaking (loading) the glass before the sprinkler system operates.
6. Obstructions, such as curtain rods, drapery traverse rods, curtains, drapes or similar materials shall not be installed between the automatic sprinklers and the glazing.

408.4 Locks. Egress doors are permitted to be locked in accordance with the applicable use condition. Doors from a refuge area to the exterior are permitted to be locked with a key in lieu of locking methods described in Section 408.4.1. The keys to unlock the exterior doors shall be available at all times and the locks shall be operable from both sides of the door.

408.4.1 Remote release. Remote release of locks on doors in a *means of egress* shall be provided with reliable means of operation, remote from the resident living areas, to release locks on all required doors. In Occupancy Conditions 3 or 4, the arrangement, accessibility and security of the release mechanism(s) required for egress shall be such that with the minimum available staff at any time, the lock mechanisms are capable of being released within 2 minutes.

Exception: Provisions for remote locking and unlocking of occupied rooms in Occupancy Condition 4 are not required provided that not more than 10 locks are necessary to be unlocked in order to move occupants from one smoke compartment to a refuge area within 3 minutes. The opening of necessary locks shall be accomplished with not more than two separate keys.

408.4.2 Power-operated doors and locks. Power-operated sliding doors or power-operated locks for swinging doors shall be operable by a manual release mechanism at the door, and either emergency power or a remote mechanical operating release shall be provided.

Exception: Emergency power is not required in facilities with 10 locks or less complying with the exception to Section 408.4.1.

408.4.3 Redundant operation. Remote release, mechanically operated sliding doors or remote release, mechanically operated locks shall be provided with a mechanically operated release mechanism at each door, or shall be provided with a redundant remote release control.

408.4.4 Relock capability. Doors remotely unlocked under emergency conditions shall not automatically relock when closed unless specific action is taken at the remote location to enable doors to relock.

408.5 Protection of vertical openings. Any vertical opening shall be protected by a shaft enclosure in accordance with Section 708, or shall be in accordance with Section 408.5.1.

408.5.1 Floor openings. Openings in floors within a housing unit are permitted without a shaft enclosure, provided all of the following conditions are met:

1. The entire normally occupied areas so interconnected are open and unobstructed so as to enable observation of the areas by supervisory personnel;
2. *Means of egress* capacity is sufficient for all occupants from all interconnected cell tiers and areas;
3. The height difference between the floor levels of the highest and lowest cell tiers shall not exceed 23 feet (7010 mm); and
4. Egress from any portion of the cell tier to an *exit* or *exit access* door shall not require travel on more than one additional floor level within the housing unit.

408.5.2 Shaft openings in communicating floor levels. Where a floor opening is permitted between communicating floor levels of a housing unit in accordance with Section 408.5.1, plumbing chases serving vertically stacked individual cells contained with the housing unit shall be permitted without a shaft enclosure.

408.6 Smoke barrier. Occupancies in Group I-3 shall have *smoke barriers* complying with Sections 408.8 and 710 to divide every *story* occupied by residents for sleeping, or any other *story* having an *occupant load* of 50 or more persons, into at least two smoke compartments.

Exception: Spaces having a direct *exit* to one of the following, provided that the locking arrangement of the doors involved complies with the requirements for doors at the *smoke barrier* for the use condition involved:

1. A *public way*.
2. A building separated from the resident housing area by a 2-hour fire-resistance-rated assembly or 50 feet (15 240 mm) of open space.
3. A secured *yard* or *court* having a holding space 50 feet (15 240 mm) from the housing area that provides 6 square feet (0.56 m^2) or more of refuge area per occupant, including residents, staff and visitors.

408.6.1 Smoke compartments. The maximum number of residents in any smoke compartment shall be 200. The travel distance to a door in a *smoke barrier* from any room door required as *exit access* shall not exceed 150 feet (45 720 mm). The travel distance to a door in a *smoke barrier* from any point in a room shall not exceed 200 feet (60 960 mm).

408.6.2 Refuge area. At least 6 net square feet (0.56 m^2) per occupant shall be provided on each side of each *smoke barrier* for the total number of occupants in adjoining smoke compartments. This space shall be readily available wherever the occupants are moved across the *smoke barrier* in a fire emergency.

408.6.3 Independent egress. A *means of egress* shall be provided from each smoke compartment created by smoke barriers without having to return through the smoke compartment from which *means of egress* originates.

408.7 Security glazing. In occupancies in Group I-3, windows and doors in 1-hour fire barriers constructed in accordance with Section 707, fire partitions constructed n accordance with Section 709 and smoke barriers constructed in accordance with Section 710 shall be permitted to have security glazing installed provided that the following conditions are met.

1. Individual panels of glazing shall not exceed 1,296 square inches (0.84 m^2).
2. The glazing shall be protected on both sides by an *automatic sprinkler system*. The sprinkler system shall be designed to, when actuated, wet completely the entire surface of any glazing affected by fire.
3. The glazing shall be in a gasketed frame and installed in such a manner that the framing system will deflect without breaking (loading) the glass before the sprinkler system operates.
4. Obstructions, such as curtain rods, drapery traverse rods, curtains, drapes or similar materials shall not be installed between the automatic sprinklers and the glazing.

408.8 Subdivision of resident housing areas. Sleeping areas and any contiguous day room, group activity space or other common spaces where residents are housed shall be separated from other spaces in accordance with Sections 408.8.1 through 408.8.4.

408.8.1 Occupancy Conditions 3 and 4. Each sleeping area in Occupancy Conditions 3 and 4 shall be separated from the adjacent common spaces by a smoke-tight partition where the travel distance from the sleeping area through the common space to the *corridor* exceeds 50 feet (15 240 mm).

408.8.2 Occupancy Condition 5. Each sleeping area in Occupancy Condition 5 shall be separated from adjacent sleeping areas, *corridors* and common spaces by a smoke-tight partition. Additionally, common spaces shall be separated from the *corridor* by a smoke-tight partition.

408.8.3 Openings in room face. The aggregate area of openings in a solid sleeping room face in Occupancy Conditions 2, 3, 4 and 5 shall not exceed 120 square inches (77 419 mm^2). The aggregate area shall include all openings including door undercuts, food passes and grilles. Openings shall be not more than 36 inches (914 mm) above the floor. In

Occupancy Condition 5, the openings shall be closeable from the room side.

408.8.4 Smoke-tight doors. Doors in openings in partitions required to be smoke tight by Section 408.8 shall be substantial doors, of construction that will resist the passage of smoke. Latches and door closures are not required on cell doors.

408.9 Windowless buildings. For the purposes of this section, a windowless building or portion of a building is one with nonopenable windows, windows not readily breakable or without windows. Windowless buildings shall be provided with an engineered smoke control system to provide a tenable environment for exiting from the smoke compartment in the area of fire origin in accordance with Section 909 for each windowless smoke compartment.

[F] 408.10 Fire alarm system. A fire alarm system shall be provided in accordance with Section 907.2.6.3.

SECTION 409 MOTION PICTURE PROJECTION ROOMS

409.1 General. The provisions of Sections 409.1 through 409.5 shall apply to rooms in which ribbon-type cellulose acetate or other safety film is utilized in conjunction with electric arc, xenon or other light-source projection equipment that develops hazardous gases, dust or radiation. Where cellulose nitrate film is utilized or stored, such rooms shall comply with NFPA 40.

409.1.1 Projection room required. Every motion picture machine projecting film as mentioned within the scope of this section shall be enclosed in a projection room. Appurtenant electrical equipment, such as rheostats, transformers and generators, shall be within the projection room or in an adjacent room of equivalent construction.

409.2 Construction of projection rooms. Every projection room shall be of permanent construction consistent with the construction requirements for the type of building in which the projection room is located. Openings are not required to be protected.

The room shall have a floor area of not less than 80 square feet (7.44 m^2) for a single machine and at least 40 square feet (3.7 m^2) for each additional machine. Each motion picture projector, floodlight, spotlight or similar piece of equipment shall have a clear working space of not less than 30 inches by 30 inches (762 mm by 762 mm) on each side and at the rear thereof, but only one such space shall be required between two adjacent projectors. The projection room and the rooms appurtenant thereto shall have a ceiling height of not less than 7 feet 6 inches (2286 mm). The aggregate of openings for projection equipment shall not exceed 25 percent of the area of the wall between the projection room and the auditorium. Openings shall be provided with glass or other *approved* material, so as to close completely the opening.

409.3 Projection room and equipment ventilation. Ventilation shall be provided in accordance with the *International Mechanical Code.*

409.3.1 Supply air. Each projection room shall be provided with adequate air supply inlets so arranged as to provide well-distributed air throughout the room. Air inlet ducts shall provide an amount of air equivalent to the amount of air being exhausted by projection equipment. Air is permitted to be taken from the outside; from adjacent spaces within the building, provided the volume and infiltration rate is sufficient; or from the building air-conditioning system, provided it is so arranged as to provide sufficient air when other systems are not in operation.

409.3.2 Exhaust air. Projection rooms are permitted to be exhausted through the lamp exhaust system. The lamp exhaust system shall be positively interconnected with the lamp so that the lamp will not operate unless there is the required airflow. Exhaust air ducts shall terminate at the exterior of the building in such a location that the exhaust air cannot be readily recirculated into any air supply system. The projection room ventilation system is permitted to also serve appurtenant rooms, such as the generator and rewind rooms.

409.3.3 Projection machines. Each projection machine shall be provided with an exhaust duct that will draw air from each lamp and exhaust it directly to the outside of the building. The lamp exhaust is permitted to serve to exhaust air from the projection room to provide room air circulation. Such ducts shall be of rigid materials, except for a flexible connector *approved* for the purpose. The projection lamp or projection room exhaust system, or both, is permitted to be combined but shall not be interconnected with any other exhaust or return system, or both, within the building.

409.4 Lighting control. Provisions shall be made for control of the auditorium lighting and the *means of egress* lighting systems of theaters from inside the projection room and from at least one other convenient point in the building.

409.5 Miscellaneous equipment. Each projection room shall be provided with rewind and film storage facilities.

SECTION 410 STAGES AND PLATFORMS

410.1 Applicability. The provisions of Sections 410.1 through 410.7 shall apply to all parts of buildings and structures that contain stages or platforms and similar appurtenances as herein defined.

410.2 Definitions. The following words and terms shall, for the purposes of this section and as used elsewhere in this code, have the meanings shown herein.

FLY GALLERY. A raised floor area above a stage from which the movement of scenery and operation of other stage effects are controlled.

GRIDIRON. The structural framing over a stage supporting equipment for hanging or flying scenery and other stage effects.

PINRAIL. A rail on or above a stage through which belaying pins are inserted and to which lines are fastened.

PLATFORM. A raised area within a building used for worship, the presentation of music, plays or other entertainment; the head table for special guests; the raised area for lecturers and speakers; boxing and wrestling rings; theater-in-the-round stages; and similar purposes wherein there are no overhead hanging curtains, drops, scenery or stage effects other than lighting and sound. A temporary platform is one installed for not more than 30 days.

PROSCENIUM WALL. The wall that separates the stage from the auditorium or assembly seating area.

STAGE. A space within a building utilized for entertainment or presentations, which includes overhead hanging curtains, drops, scenery or stage effects other than lighting and sound.

410.3 Stages. Stage construction shall comply with Sections 410.3.1 through 410.3.7.

410.3.1 Stage construction. Stages shall be constructed of materials as required for floors for the type of construction of the building in which such stages are located.

Exceptions:

1. Stages of Type IIB or IV construction with a nominal 2-inch (51 mm) wood deck, provided that the stage is separated from other areas in accordance with Section 410.3.4.
2. In buildings of Types IIA, IIIA and VA construction, a fire-resistance-rated floor is not required, provided the space below the stage is equipped with an automatic fire-extinguishing system in accordance with Section 903 or 904.
3. In all types of construction, the finished floor shall be constructed of wood or *approved* noncombustible materials. Openings through stage floors shall be equipped with tight-fitting, solid wood trap doors with *approved* safety locks.

410.3.1.1 Stage height and area. Stage areas shall be measured to include the entire performance area and adjacent backstage and support areas not separated from the performance area by fire-resistance-rated construction. Stage height shall be measured from the lowest point on the stage floor to the highest point of the roof or floor deck above the stage.

410.3.2 Galleries, gridirons, catwalks and pinrails. Beams designed only for the attachment of portable or fixed theater equipment, gridirons, galleries and catwalks shall be constructed of *approved* materials consistent with the requirements for the type of construction of the building; and a *fire-resistance rating* shall not be required. These areas shall not be considered to be floors, stories, *mezzanines* or levels in applying this code.

Exception: Floors of fly galleries and catwalks shall be constructed of any *approved* material.

410.3.3 Exterior stage doors. Where protection of openings is required, exterior *exit* doors shall be protected with *fire door assemblies* that comply with Section 715. Exterior openings that are located on the stage for *means of egress* or loading and unloading purposes, and that are likely to be open during occupancy of the theater, shall be constructed with vestibules to prevent air drafts into the auditorium.

410.3.4 Proscenium wall. Where the stage height is greater than 50 feet (15 240 mm), all portions of the stage shall be completely separated from the seating area by a proscenium wall with not less than a 2-hour *fire-resistance rating* extending continuously from the foundation to the roof.

410.3.5 Proscenium curtain. Where a proscenium wall is required to have a *fire-resistance rating*, the stage opening shall be provided with a fire curtain complying with NFPA 80 or an *approved* water curtain complying with Section 903.3.1.1 or, in facilities not utilizing the provisions of smoke-protected assembly seating in accordance with Section 1028.6.2, a smoke control system complying with Section 909 or natural ventilation designed to maintain the smoke level at least 6 feet (1829 mm) above the floor of the *means of egress*.

410.3.6 Scenery. Combustible materials used in sets and scenery shall meet the fire propagation performance criteria of NFPA 701, in accordance with Section 806 and the *International Fire Code*. Foam plastics and materials containing foam plastics shall comply with Section 2603 and the *International Fire Code*.

410.3.7 Stage ventilation. Emergency ventilation shall be provided for stages larger than 1,000 square feet (93 m^2) in floor area, or with a stage height greater than 50 feet (15 240 mm). Such ventilation shall comply with Section 410.3.7.1 or 410.3.7.2.

410.3.7.1 Roof vents. Two or more vents constructed to open automatically by *approved* heat-activated devices and with an aggregate clear opening area of not less than 5 percent of the area of the stage shall be located near the center and above the highest part of the stage area. Supplemental means shall be provided for manual operation of the ventilator. Curbs shall be provided as required for skylights in Section 2610.2. Vents shall be labeled.

[F] 410.3.7.2 Smoke control. Smoke control in accordance with Section 909 shall be provided to maintain the smoke layer interface not less than 6 feet (1829 mm) above the highest level of the assembly seating or above the top of the proscenium opening where a proscenium wall is provided in compliance with Section 410.3.4.

410.4 Platform construction. Permanent platforms shall be constructed of materials as required for the type of construction of the building in which the permanent platform is located. Permanent platforms are permitted to be constructed of *fire-retardant-treated wood* for Types I, II and IV construction where the platforms are not more than 30 inches (762 mm) above the main floor, and not more than one-third of the room floor area and not more than 3,000 square feet (279 m^2) in area. Where the space beneath the permanent platform is used for storage or any purpose other than equipment, wiring or plumbing, the floor assembly shall not be less than 1-hour fire-resistance-rated construction. Where the space beneath the permanent platform is used only for equipment, wiring or plumbing, the underside of the permanent platform need not be protected.

410.4.1 Temporary platforms. Platforms installed for a period of not more than 30 days are permitted to be constructed of any materials permitted by the code. The space between the floor and the platform above shall only be used for plumbing and electrical wiring to platform equipment.

410.5 Dressing and appurtenant rooms. Dressing and appurtenant rooms shall comply with Sections 410.5.1 through 410.5.3.

410.5.1 Separation from stage. The stage shall be separated from dressing rooms, scene docks, property rooms, workshops, storerooms and compartments appurtenant to the stage and other parts of the building by *fire barriers* constructed in accordance with Section 707 or *horizontal assemblies* constructed in accordance with Section 712, or both. The minimum *fire-resistance rating* shall be 2 hours for stage heights greater than 50 feet (15 240 mm) and 1 hour for stage heights of 50 feet (15 240 mm) or less.

410.5.2 Separation from each other. Dressing rooms, scene docks, property rooms, workshops, storerooms and compartments appurtenant to the stage shall be separated from each other by not less than 1-hour *fire barriers* constructed in accordance with Section 707 or *horizontal assemblies* constructed in accordance with Section 712, or both.

410.5.3 Stage exits. At least one *approved means of egress* shall be provided from each side of the stage and from each side of the space under the stage. At least one means of escape shall be provided from each fly gallery and from the gridiron. A steel ladder, *alternating tread device* or *spiral stairway* is permitted to be provided from the gridiron to a scuttle in the stage roof.

[F] 410.6 Automatic sprinkler system. Stages shall be equipped with an automatic fire-extinguishing system in accordance with Chapter 9. Sprinklers shall be installed under the roof and gridiron and under all catwalks and galleries over the stage. Sprinklers shall be installed in dressing rooms, performer lounges, shops and storerooms accessory to such stages.

Exceptions:

1. Sprinklers are not required under stage areas less than 4 feet (1219 mm) in clear height that are utilized exclusively for storage of tables and chairs, provided the concealed space is separated from the adjacent spaces by not less than $^5/_8$-inch (15.9 mm) Type X gypsum board.
2. Sprinklers are not required for stages 1,000 square feet (93 m^2) or less in area and 50 feet (15 240 mm) or less in height where curtains, scenery or other combustible hangings are not retractable vertically. Combustible hangings shall be limited to a single main curtain, borders, legs and a single backdrop.
3. Sprinklers are not required within portable orchestra enclosures on stages.

[F] 410.7 Standpipes. Standpipe systems shall be provided in accordance with Section 905.

SECTION 411
SPECIAL AMUSEMENT BUILDINGS

411.1 General. Special *amusement buildings* having an *occupant load* of 50 or more shall comply with the requirements for the appropriate Group A occupancy and Sections 411.1 through 411.8. Amusement buildings having an *occupant load* of less than 50 shall comply with the requirements for a Group B occupancy and Sections 411.1 through 411.8.

Exception: Amusement buildings or portions thereof that are without walls or a roof and constructed to prevent the accumulation of smoke.

For flammable *decorative materials*, see the *International Fire Code.*

411.2 Definition. The following word and term shall, for the purpose of this section and as used elsewhere in this code, have the meaning shown herein.

SPECIAL AMUSEMENT BUILDING. A *special amusement building* is any temporary or permanent building or portion thereof that is occupied for amusement, entertainment or educational purposes and that contains a device or system that conveys passengers or provides a walkway along, around or over a course in any direction so arranged that the *means of egress* path is not readily apparent due to visual or audio distractions or is intentionally confounded or is not readily available because of the nature of the attraction or mode of conveyance through the building or structure.

[F] 411.3 Automatic fire detection. *Special amusement buildings* shall be equipped with an automatic fire detection system in accordance with Section 907.

[F] 411.4 Automatic sprinkler system. *Special amusement buildings* shall be equipped throughout with an *automatic sprinkler system* in accordance with Section 903.3.1.1. Where the *special amusement building* is temporary, the sprinkler water supply shall be of an *approved* temporary means.

Exception: Automatic sprinklers are not required where the total floor area of a temporary *special amusement building* is less than 1,000 square feet (93 m^2) and the travel distance from any point to an *exit* is less than 50 feet (15 240 mm).

[F] 411.5 Alarm. Actuation of a single smoke detector, the *automatic sprinkler system* or other automatic fire detection device shall immediately sound an alarm at the building at a *constantly attended location* from which emergency action can be initiated including the capability of manual initiation of requirements in Section 907.2.12.2.

[F] 411.6 Emergency voice/alarm communications system. An emergency voice/alarm communications system shall be provided in accordance with Sections 907.2.12 and 907.5.2.2, which is also permitted to serve as a public address system and shall be audible throughout the entire *special amusement building.*

411.7 Exit marking. Exit signs shall be installed at the required *exit* or *exit access* doorways of amusement buildings in accordance with this section and Section 1011. *Approved* directional exit markings shall also be provided. Where mirrors, mazes or other designs are utilized that disguise the path of egress travel such that they are not apparent, *approved* and *listed* low-level exit signs that comply with Section 1011.4, and directional path markings *listed* in accordance with UL 1994, shall be provided and located not more than 8 inches (203 mm) above the walking surface and on or near the path of egress travel. Such markings shall become visible in an emergency. The directional exit marking shall be activated by the automatic fire detection system and the *automatic sprinkler system* in accordance with Section 907.2.12.2.

411.7.1 Photo luminescent exit signs. Where photo luminescent *exit* signs are installed, activating light source and viewing distance shall be in accordance with the listing and markings of the signs.

411.8 Interior finish. The *interior finish* shall be Class A in accordance with Section 803.1.

SECTION 412
AIRCRAFT-RELATED OCCUPANCIES

412.1 General. Aircraft-related occupancies shall comply with Sections 412.1 through 412.7 and the *International Fire Code*.

412.2 Definitions. The following words and terms shall, for the purposes of this chapter and as used elsewhere in this code, have the meanings shown herein.

FIXED BASE OPERATOR (FBO). A commercial business granted the right by the airport sponsor to operate on an airport and provide aeronautical services, such as fueling, hangaring, tie-down and parking, aircraft rental, aircraft maintenance and flight instruction.

HELIPORT. An area of land or water or a structural surface that is used, or intended for the use, for the landing and taking off of helicopters, and any appurtenant areas that are used, or intended for use, for heliport buildings or other heliport facilities.

HELISTOP. The same as "heliport," except that no fueling, defueling, maintenance, repairs or storage of helicopters is permitted.

RESIDENTIAL AIRCRAFT HANGAR. An accessory building less than 2,000 square feet (186 m^2) and 20 feet (6096 mm) in *building height* constructed on a one- or two-family property where aircraft are stored. Such use will be considered as a residential accessory use incidental to the *dwelling*.

TRANSIENT AIRCRAFT. Aircraft based at another location and at the transient location for not more than 90 days.

412.3 Airport traffic control towers.

412.3.1 General. The provisions of Sections 412.3.1 through 412.3.6 shall apply to airport traffic control towers not exceeding 1,500 square feet (140 m^2) per floor occupied only for the following uses:

1. Airport traffic control cab.
2. Electrical and mechanical equipment rooms.
3. Airport terminal radar and electronics rooms.
4. Office spaces incidental to the tower operation.
5. Lounges for employees, including sanitary facilities.

412.3.2 Type of construction. Airport traffic control towers shall be constructed to comply with the height and area limitations of Table 412.3.2.

TABLE 412.3.2
HEIGHT AND AREA LIMITATIONS FOR AIRPORT TRAFFIC CONTROL TOWERS

TYPE OF CONSTRUCTION	HEIGHT[a] (feet)	MAXIMUM AREA (square feet)
IA	Unlimited	1,500
IB	240	1,500
IIA	100	1,500
IIB	85	1,500
IIIA	65	1,500

For SI: 1 foot = 304.8 mm, 1 square foot = 0.0929 m^2.
a. Height to be measured from grade plane to cab floor.

412.3.3 Egress. A minimum of one *exit stairway* shall be permitted for airport traffic control towers of any height provided that the *occupant load* per floor does not exceed 15. The *stairway* shall conform to the requirements of Section 1009. The *stairway* shall be separated from elevators by a minimum distance of one-half of the diagonal of the area served measured in a straight line. The *exit stairway* and elevator hoistway are permitted to be located in the same shaft enclosure, provided they are separated from each other by a 4-hour *fire barrier* having no openings. Such *stairway* shall be pressurized to a minimum of 0.15 inch of water column (43 Pa) and a maximum of 0.35 inch of water column (101 Pa) in the shaft relative to the building with stairway doors closed. *Stairways* need not extend to the roof as specified in Section 1009.11. The provisions of Section 403 do not apply.

Exception: Smokeproof enclosures as set forth in Section 1022.9 are not required where required *stairways* are pressurized.

[F] 412.3.4 Automatic fire detection systems. Airport traffic control towers shall be provided with an automatic fire detection system installed in accordance with Section 907.2.

[F] 412.3.5 Standby power. A standby power system that conforms to Chapter 27 shall be provided in airport traffic control towers more than 65 feet (19 812 mm) in height. Power shall be provided to the following equipment:

1. Pressurization equipment, mechanical equipment and lighting.
2. Elevator operating equipment.
3. Fire alarm and smoke detection systems.

412.3.6 Accessibility. Airport traffic control towers need not be *accessible* as specified in the provisions of Chapter 11.

412.4 Aircraft hangars. Aircraft hangars shall be in accordance with Sections 412.4.1 through 412.4.6.

412.4.1 Exterior walls. *Exterior walls* located less than 30 feet (9144 mm) from *lot lines* or a *public way* shall have a *fire-resistance rating* not less than 2 hours.

412.4.2 Basements. Where hangars have basements, floors over basements shall be of Type IA construction and shall be made tight against seepage of water, oil or vapors. There shall be no opening or communication between basements and the hangar. Access to basements shall be from outside only.

412.4.3 Floor surface. Floors shall be graded and drained to prevent water or fuel from remaining on the floor. Floor drains shall discharge through an oil separator to the sewer or to an outside vented sump.

> **Exception:** Aircraft hangars with individual lease spaces not exceeding 2,000 square feet (186 m^2) each in which servicing, repairing or washing is not conducted and fuel is not dispensed shall have floors that are graded toward the door, but shall not require a separator.

412.4.4 Heating equipment. Heating equipment shall be placed in another room separated by 2-hour *fire barriers* constructed in accordance with Section 707 or *horizontal assemblies* constructed in accordance with Section 712, or both. Entrance shall be from the outside or by means of a vestibule providing a two-doorway separation.

Exceptions:

1. Unit heaters and vented infrared radiant heating equipment suspended at least 10 feet (3048 mm) above the upper surface of wings or engine enclosures of the highest aircraft that are permitted to be housed in the hangar and at least 8 feet (2438 mm) above the floor in shops, offices and other sections of the hangar communicating with storage or service areas.
2. A single interior door shall be allowed, provided the sources of ignition in the appliances are at least 18 inches (457 mm) above the floor.

412.4.5 Finishing. The process of "doping," involving use of a volatile flammable solvent, or of painting, shall be carried on in a separate detached building equipped with automatic fire-extinguishing equipment in accordance with Section 903.

412.4.6 Fire suppression. Aircraft hangars shall be provided with a fire suppression system designed in accordance with NFPA 409, based upon the classification for the hangar given in Table 412.4.6.

> **Exception:** When a fixed base operator has separate repair facilities on site, Group II hangars operated by a fixed base operator used for storage of transient aircraft only shall have a fire suppression system, but the system is exempt from foam requirements.

412.4.6.1 Hazardous operations. Any Group III aircraft hangar according to Table 412.4.6 that contains hazardous operations including, but not limited to, the following shall be provided with a Group I or II fire suppression system in accordance with NFPA 409 as applicable:

1. Doping.
2. Hot work including, but not limited to, welding, torch cutting and torch soldering.
3. Fuel transfer.
4. Fuel tank repair or maintenance not including defueled tanks in accordance with NFPA 409, inerted tanks or tanks that have never been fueled.
5. Spray finishing operations.
6. Total fuel capacity of all aircraft within the unsprinklered single *fire area* in excess of 1,600 gallons (6057 L).
7. Total fuel capacity of all aircraft within the maximum single *fire area* in excess of 7,500 gallons (28 390 L) for a hangar with an *automatic sprinkler system* in accordance with Section 903.3.1.1.

[F] TABLE 412.4.6
HANGAR FIRE SUPPRESSION REQUIREMENTS[a, b, c]

MAXIMUM SINGLE FIRE AREA, SQ. FT.	TYPE OF CONSTRUCTION								
	IA	IB	IIA	IIB	IIIA	IIIB	IV	VA	VB
≥ 40,001	Group I	Group I	Group I	Group I	Group I	Group I	Group I	Group I	Group I
40,000	Group II	Group II	Group II	Group II	Group II	Group II	Group II	Group II	Group II
30,000	Group III	Group II	Group II	Group II	Group II	Group II	Group II	Group II	Group II
20,000	Group III	Group III	Group II	Group II	Group II	Group II	Group II	Group II	Group II
15,000	Group III	Group III	Group III	Group II	Group III	Group II	Group III	Group II	Group II
12,000	Group III	Group III	Group III	Group III	Group III	Group III	Group III	Group II	Group II
8,000	Group III	Group III	Group III	Group III	Group III	Group III	Group III	Group III	Group II
5,000	Group III	Group III	Group III	Group III	Group III	Group III	Group III	Group III	Group III

For SI: 1 foot = 304.8 mm, 1 square foot = 0.0929 m^2.

a. Aircraft hangars with a door height greater than 28 feet shall be provided with fire suppression for a Group I hangar regardless of maximum fire area.

b. Groups shall be as classified in accordance with NFPA 409.

c. Membrane structures complying with Section 3102 shall be classified as a Group IV hangar.

412.4.6.2 Separation of maximum single fire areas. Maximum single *fire areas* established in accordance with hangar classification and construction type in Table 412.4.6 shall be separated by 2-hour *fire walls* constructed in accordance with Section 706.

412.5 Residential aircraft hangars. Residential aircraft hangars as defined in Section 412.2 shall comply with Sections 412.5.1 through 412.5.5.

412.5.1 Fire separation. A hangar shall not be attached to a *dwelling* unless separated by a *fire barrier* having a *fire-resistance rating* of not less than 1 hour. Such separation shall be continuous from the foundation to the underside of the roof and unpierced except for doors leading to the *dwelling unit*. Doors into the *dwelling unit* must be equipped with self-closing devices and conform to the requirements of Section 715 with at least a 4-inch (102 mm) noncombustible raised sill. Openings from a hanger directly into a room used for sleeping purposes shall not be permitted.

412.5.2 Egress. A hangar shall provide two *means of egress*. One of the doors into the *dwelling* shall be considered as meeting only one of the two *means of egress*.

[F] 412.5.3 Smoke alarms. Smoke alarms shall be provided within the hangar in accordance with Section 907.2.21.

412.5.4 Independent systems. Electrical, mechanical and plumbing drain, waste and vent (DWV) systems installed within the hangar shall be independent of the systems installed within the *dwelling*. Building sewer lines shall be permitted to be connected outside the structures.

Exception: Smoke detector wiring and feed for electrical subpanels in the hangar.

412.5.5 Height and area limits. Residential aircraft hangars shall not exceed 2,000 square feet (186 m^2) in area and 20 feet (6096 mm) in *building height*.

[F] 412.6 Aircraft paint hangars. Aircraft painting operations where flammable liquids are used in excess of the maximum allowable quantities per *control area* listed in Table 307.1(1) shall be conducted in an aircraft paint hangar that complies with the provisions of Sections 412.6.1 through 412.6.6.

[F] 412.6.1 Occupancy group. Aircraft paint hangars shall be classified as Group H-2. Aircraft paint hangars shall comply with the applicable requirements of this code and the *International Fire Code* for such occupancy.

412.6.2 Construction. The aircraft paint hangar shall be of Type I or II construction.

[F] 412.6.3 Operations. Only those flammable liquids necessary for painting operations shall be permitted in quantities less than the maximum allowable quantities per *control area* in Table 307.1(1). Spray equipment cleaning operations shall be conducted in a liquid use, dispensing and mixing room.

[F] 412.6.4 Storage. Storage of flammable liquids shall be in a liquid storage room.

[F] 412.6.5 Fire suppression. Aircraft paint hangars shall be provided with fire suppression as required by NFPA 409.

412.6.6 Ventilation. Aircraft paint hangars shall be provided with ventilation as required in the *International Mechanical Code*.

412.7 Heliports and helistops. Heliports and helistops shall be permitted to be erected on buildings or other locations where they are constructed in accordance with Sections 412.7.1 through 412.7.4.

412.7.1 Size. The landing area for helicopters less than 3,500 pounds (1588 kg) shall be a minimum of 20 feet (6096 mm) in length and width. The landing area shall be surrounded on all sides by a clear area having a minimum average width at roof level of 15 feet (4572 mm) but with no width less than 5 feet (1524 mm).

412.7.2 Design. Helicopter landing areas and the supports thereof on the roof of a building shall be noncombustible construction. Landing areas shall be designed to confine any flammable liquid spillage to the landing area itself and provisions shall be made to drain such spillage away from any *exit* or *stairway* serving the helicopter landing area or from a structure housing such *exit* or *stairway*. For structural design requirements, see Section 1605.4.

412.7.3 Means of egress. The *means of egress* from heliports and helistops shall comply with the provisions of Chapter 10. Landing areas located on buildings or structures shall have two or more *means of egress*. For landing areas less than 60 feet (18 288 mm) in length or less than 2,000 square feet (186 m^2) in area, the second *means of egress* is permitted to be a fire escape, *alternating tread device* or ladder leading to the floor below.

412.7.4 Rooftop heliports and helistops. Rooftop heliports and helistops shall comply with NFPA 418.

SECTION 413
COMBUSTIBLE STORAGE

413.1 General. High-piled stock or rack storage in any occupancy group shall comply with the *International Fire Code*.

413.2 Attic, under-floor and concealed spaces. *Attic*, under-floor and concealed spaces used for storage of combustible materials shall be protected on the storage side as required for 1-hour fire-resistance-rated construction. Openings shall be protected by assemblies that are self-closing and are of noncombustible construction or solid wood core not less than $1^3/_4$ inch (45 mm) in thickness.

Exceptions:

1. Areas protected by *approved automatic sprinkler systems*.
2. Group R-3 and U occupancies.

SECTION 414
HAZARDOUS MATERIALS

[F] 414.1 General. The provisions of Sections 414.1 through 414.7 shall apply to buildings and structures occupied for the manufacturing, processing, dispensing, use or storage of hazardous materials.

[F] 414.1.1 Other provisions. Buildings and structures with an occupancy in Group H shall also comply with the applicable provisions of Section 415 and the *International Fire Code*.

[F] 414.1.2 Materials. The safe design of hazardous material occupancies is material dependent. Individual material requirements are also found in Sections 307 and 415, and in the *International Mechanical Code* and the *International Fire Code*.

[F] 414.1.2.1 Aerosols. Level 2 and 3 aerosol products shall be stored and displayed in accordance with the *International Fire Code*. See Section 311.2 and the *International Fire Code* for occupancy group requirements.

[F] 414.1.3 Information required. A report shall be submitted to the *building official* identifying the maximum expected quantities of hazardous materials to be stored, used in a closed system and used in an *open system*, and subdivided to separately address hazardous material classification categories based on Tables 307.1(1) and 307.1(2). The methods of protection from such hazards, including but not limited to *control areas*, fire protection systems and Group H occupancies shall be indicated in the report and on the *construction documents*. The opinion and report shall be prepared by a qualified person, firm or corporation *approved* by the *building official* and provided without charge to the enforcing agency.

For buildings and structures with an occupancy in Group H, separate floor plans shall be submitted identifying the locations of anticipated contents and processes so as to reflect the nature of each occupied portion of every building and structure.

[F] 414.2 Control areas. *Control areas* shall comply with Sections 414.2.1 through 414.2.5 and the *International Fire Code*.

414.2.1 Construction requirements. *Control areas* shall be separated from each other by *fire barriers* constructed in accordance with Section 707 or *horizontal assemblies* constructed in accordance with Section 712, or both.

[F] 414.2.2 Percentage of maximum allowable quantities. The percentage of maximum allowable quantities of hazardous materials per *control area* permitted at each floor level within a building shall be in accordance with Table 414.2.2.

[F] 414.2.3 Number. The maximum number of *control areas* within a building shall be in accordance with Table 414.2.2.

414.2.4 Fire-resistance-rating requirements. The required *fire-resistance rating* for *fire barriers* shall be in accordance with Table 414.2.2. The floor assembly of the *control area* and the construction supporting the floor of the *control area* shall have a minimum 2-hour *fire-resistance rating*.

Exception: The floor assembly of the *control area* and the construction supporting the floor of the *control area* are allowed to be 1-hour fire-resistance rated in buildings of Types IIA, IIIA and VA construction, provided that both of the following conditions exist:

1. The building is equipped throughout with an *automatic sprinkler system* in accordance with Section 903.3.1.1; and
2. The building is three *stories* or less above *grade plane*.

[F] TABLE 414.2.2
DESIGN AND NUMBER OF CONTROL AREAS

FLOOR LEVEL		PERCENTAGE OF THE MAXIMUM ALLOWABLE QUANTITY PER CONTROL AREA[a]	NUMBER OF CONTROL AREAS PER FLOOR	FIRE-RESISTANCE RATING FOR FIRE BARRIERS IN HOURS[b]
Above grade plane	Higher than 9	5	1	2
	7-9	5	2	2
	6	12.5	2	2
	5	12.5	2	2
	4	12.5	2	2
	3	50	2	1
	2	75	3	1
	1	100	4	1
Below grade plane	1	75	3	1
	2	50	2	1
	Lower than 2	Not Allowed	Not Allowed	Not Allowed

a. Percentages shall be of the maximum allowable quantity per control area shown in Tables 307.1(1) and 307.1(2), with all increases allowed in the notes to those tables.

b. Fire barriers shall include walls and floors as necessary to provide separation from other portions of the building.

[F] 414.2.5 Hazardous material in Group M display and storage areas and in Group S storage areas. The aggregate quantity of nonflammable solid and nonflammable or noncombustible liquid hazardous materials permitted within a single *control area* of a Group M display and storage area, a Group S storage area or an outdoor *control area* is permitted to exceed the maximum allowable quantities per *control area* specified in Tables 307.1(1) and 307.1(2) without classifying the building or use as a Group H occupancy, provided that the materials are displayed and stored in accordance with the *International Fire Code* and quantities do not exceed the maximum allowable specified in Table 414.2.5(1).

In Group M occupancy wholesale and retail sales uses, indoor storage of flammable and combustible liquids shall not exceed the maximum allowable quantities per *control area* as indicated in Table 414.2.5(2), provided that the materials are displayed and stored in accordance with the *International Fire Code.*

The maximum quantity of aerosol products in Group M occupancy retail display areas, storage areas adjacent to retail display areas and retail storage areas shall be in accordance with the *International Fire Code.*

[F] 414.3 Ventilation. Rooms, areas or spaces of Group H in which explosive, corrosive, combustible, flammable or *highly toxic* dusts, mists, fumes, vapors or gases are or may be emitted due to the processing, use, handling or storage of materials shall be mechanically ventilated as required by the *International Fire Code* and the *International Mechanical Code.*

Ducts conveying explosives or flammable vapors, fumes or dusts shall extend directly to the exterior of the building without entering other spaces. Exhaust ducts shall not extend into or through ducts and plenums.

Exception: Ducts conveying vapor or fumes having flammable constituents less than 25 percent of their lower flammable limit (LFL) are permitted to pass through other spaces.

Emissions generated at workstations shall be confined to the area in which they are generated as specified in the *International Fire Code* and the *International Mechanical Code.*

The location of supply and exhaust openings shall be in accordance with the *International Mechanical Code.* Exhaust air contaminated by *highly toxic* material shall be treated in accordance with the *International Fire Code.*

A manual shutoff control for ventilation equipment required by this section shall be provided outside the room adjacent to the principal access door to the room. The switch shall be of the break-glass type and shall be labeled: VENTILATION SYSTEM EMERGENCY SHUTOFF.

[F] 414.4 Hazardous material systems. Systems involving hazardous materials shall be suitable for the intended application. Controls shall be designed to prevent materials from entering or leaving process or reaction systems at other than the intended time, rate or path. Automatic controls, where provided, shall be designed to be fail safe.

[F] 414.5 Inside storage, dispensing and use. The inside storage, dispensing and use of hazardous materials in excess of the maximum allowable quantities per *control area* of Tables 307.1(1) and 307.1(2) shall be in accordance with Sections 414.5.1 through 414.5.5 of this code and the *International Fire Code.*

[F] 414.5.1 Explosion control. Explosion control shall be provided in accordance with the *International Fire Code* as required by Table 414.5.1 where quantities of hazardous materials specified in that table exceed the maximum allowable quantities in Table 307.1(1) or where a structure, room or space is occupied for purposes involving explosion hazards as required by Section 415 or the *International Fire Code.*

[F] 414.5.2 Monitor control equipment. Monitor control equipment shall be provided where required by the *International Fire Code.*

[F] 414.5.3 Automatic fire detection systems. Group H occupancies shall be provided with an automatic fire detection system in accordance with Section 907.2.

[F] 414.5.4 Standby or emergency power. Where mechanical ventilation, treatment systems, temperature control, alarm, detection or other electrically operated systems are required, such systems shall be provided with an emergency or standby power system in accordance with Chapter 27.

Exceptions:

1. Mechanical ventilation for storage of Class IB and Class IC flammable and combustible liquids in closed containers not exceeding 6.5 gallons (25 L) capacity.
2. Storage areas for Class 1 and 2 oxidizers.
3. Storage areas for Class II, III, IV and V organic peroxides.
4. Storage, use and handling areas for asphyxiant, irritant and radioactive gases.
5. For storage, use and handling areas for *highly toxic* or *toxic* materials, see Sections 3704.2.2.8 and 3704.3.4.2 of the *International Fire Code.*
6. Standby power for mechanical ventilation, treatment systems and temperature control systems shall not be required where an *approved* fail-safe engineered system is installed.

[F] 414.5.5 Spill control, drainage and containment. Rooms, buildings or areas occupied for the storage of solid and liquid hazardous materials shall be provided with a means to control spillage and to contain or drain off spillage and fire protection water discharged in the storage area where required in the *International Fire Code.* The methods of spill control shall be in accordance with the *International Fire Code.*

[F] 414.6 Outdoor storage, dispensing and use. The outdoor storage, dispensing and use of hazardous materials shall be in accordance with the *International Fire Code.*

[F] 414.6.1 Weather protection. Where weather protection is provided for sheltering outdoor hazardous material stor-

[F] TABLE 414.2.5(1)
MAXIMUM ALLOWABLE QUANTITY PER INDOOR AND OUTDOOR CONTROL AREA IN GROUP M AND S OCCUPANCIES NONFLAMMABLE SOLIDS AND NONFLAMMABLE AND NONCOMBUSTIBLE LIQUIDS [d, e, f]

CONDITION		MAXIMUM ALLOWABLE QUANTITY PER CONTROL AREA	
Material[a]	Class	Solids pounds	Liquids gallons
A. Health-hazard materials—nonflammable and noncombustible solids and liquids			
1. Corrosives[b, c]	Not Applicable	9,750	975
2. Highly toxics	Not Applicable	20[b, c]	2[b, c]
3. Toxics[b, c]	Not Applicable	1,000	100
B. Physical-hazard materials—nonflammable and noncombustible solids and liquids			
1. Oxidizers[b, c]	4	Not Allowed	Not Allowed
	3	1,150[g]	115
	2	2,250[h]	225
	1	18,000[i, j]	1,800[i, j]
2. Unstable (reactives)[b, c]	4	Not Allowed	Not Allowed
	3	550	55
	2	1,150	115
	1	Not Limited	Not Limited
3. Water (reactives)	3[b, c]	550	55
	2[b, c]	1,150	115
	1	Not Limited	Not Limited

For SI: 1 pound = 0.454 kg, 1 gallon = 3.785 L.

a. Hazard categories are as specified in the *International Fire Code*.

b. Maximum allowable quantities shall be increased 100 percent in buildings that are sprinklered in accordance with Section 903.3.1.1. When Note c also applies, the increase for both notes shall be applied accumulatively.

c. Maximum allowable quantities shall be increased 100 percent when stored in approved storage cabinets, in accordance with the *International Fire Code*. When Note b also applies, the increase for both notes shall be applied accumulatively.

d. See Table 414.2.2 for design and number of control areas.

e. Allowable quantities for other hazardous material categories shall be in accordance with Section 307.

f. Maximum quantities shall be increased 100 percent in outdoor control areas.

g. Maximum amounts are permitted to be increased to 2,250 pounds when individual packages are in the original sealed containers from the manufacturer or packager and do not exceed 10 pounds each.

h. Maximum amounts are permitted to be increased to 4,500 pounds when individual packages are in the original sealed containers from the manufacturer or packager and do not exceed 10 pounds each.

i. The permitted quantities shall not be limited in a building equipped throughout with an automatic sprinkler system in accordance with Section 903.3.1.1.

j. Quantities are unlimited in an outdoor control area.

TABLE [F] 414.2.5(2)
MAXIMUM ALLOWABLE QUANTITY OF FLAMMABLE AND COMBUSTIBLE LIQUIDS IN WHOLESALE AND RETAIL SALES OCCUPANCIES PER CONTROL AREA[a]

TYPE OF LIQUID	MAXIMUM ALLOWABLE QUANTITY PER CONTROL AREA (gallons)		
	Sprinklered in accordance with Note b densities and arrangements	Sprinklered in accordance with Tables 3404.3.6.3(4) through 3404.3.6.3(8) and Table 3404.3.7.5.1 of the *International Fire Code*	Nonsprinklered
Class IA	60	60	30
Class IB, IC, II and IIIA	7,500[c]	15,000[c]	1,600
Class IIIB	Unlimited	Unlimited	13,200

For SI: 1 foot = 304.8 mm, 1 square foot = 0.0929 m^2, 1 gallon = 3.785 L, 1 gallon per minute per square foot = 40.75 L/min/m^2.

a. Control areas shall be separated from each other by not less than a 1-hour fire barrier wall.

b. To be considered as sprinklered, a building shall be equipped throughout with an approved automatic sprinkler system with a design providing minimum densities as follows:

1. For uncartoned commodities on shelves 6 feet or less in height where the ceiling height does not exceed 18 feet, quantities are those permitted with a minimum sprinkler design density of Ordinary Hazard Group 2.
2. For cartoned, palletized or racked commodities where storage is 4 feet 6 inches or less in height and where the ceiling height does not exceed 18 feet, quantities are those permitted with a minimum sprinkler design density of 0.21 gallon per minute per square foot over the most remote 1,500-square-foot area.

c. Where wholesale and retail sales or storage areas exceed 50,000 square feet in area, the maximum allowable quantities are allowed to be increased by 2 percent for each 1,000 square feet of area in excess of 50,000 square feet, up to a maximum of 100 percent of the table amounts. A control area separation is not required. The cumulative amounts, including amounts attained by having an additional control area, shall not exceed 30,000 gallons.

[F] TABLE 414.5.1
EXPLOSION CONTROL REQUIREMENTS[a]

MATERIAL	CLASS	EXPLOSION CONTROL METHODS	
		Barricade construction	Explosion (deflagration) venting or explosion (deflagration) prevention systems[b]
HAZARD CATEGORY			
Combustible dusts[c]	—	Not Required	Required
Cryogenic flammables	—	Not Required	Required
Explosives	Division 1.1 Division 1.2 Division 1.3 Division 1.4 Division 1.5 Division 1.6	Required Required Not Required Not Required Required Required	Not Required Not Required Required Required Not Required Not Required
Flammable gas	Gaseous Liquefied	Not Required Not Required	Required Required
Flammable liquid	IA[d] IB[e]	Not Required Not Required	Required Required
Organic peroxides	U I	Required Required	Not Permitted Not Permitted
Oxidizer liquids and solids	4	Required	Not Permitted
Pyrophoric gas	—	Not Required	Required
Unstable (reactive)	4 3 Detonable 3 Nondetonable	Required Required Not Required	Not Permitted Not Permitted Required
Water-reactive liquids and solids	3 2[g]	Not Required Not Required	Required Required
SPECIAL USES			
Acetylene generator rooms	—	Not Required	Required
Grain processing	—	Not Required	Required
Liquefied petroleum gas-distribution facilities	—	Not Required	Required
Where explosion hazards exist[f]	Detonation Deflagration	Required Not Required	Not Permitted Required

a. See Section 414.1.3.
b. See the *International Fire Code.*
c. As generated during manufacturing or processing. See definition of "Combustible dust" in Chapter 3.
d. Storage or use.
e. In open use or dispensing.
f. Rooms containing dispensing and use of hazardous materials when an explosive environment can occur because of the characteristics or nature of the hazardous materials or as a result of the dispensing or use process.
g. A method of explosion control shall be provided when Class 2 water-reactive materials can form potentially explosive mixtures.

age or use areas, such areas shall be considered outdoor storage or use when the weather protection structure complies with Sections 414.6.1.1 through 414.6.1.3.

[F] 414.6.1.1 Walls. Walls shall not obstruct more than one side of the structure.

Exception: Walls shall be permitted to obstruct portions of multiple sides of the structure, provided that the obstructed area does not exceed 25 percent of the structure's perimeter.

[F] 414.6.1.2 Separation distance. The distance from the structure to buildings, *lot lines*, *public ways* or *means of egress* to a *public way* shall not be less than the distance required for an outside hazardous material storage or use area without weather protection.

[F] 414.6.1.3 Noncombustible construction. The overhead structure shall be of *approved* noncombustible construction with a maximum area of 1,500 square feet (140 m^2).

Exception: The increases permitted by Section 506 apply.

[F] 414.7 Emergency alarms. Emergency alarms for the detection and notification of an emergency condition in Group H occupancies shall be provided as set forth herein.

[F] 414.7.1 Storage. An *approved* manual emergency alarm system shall be provided in buildings, rooms or areas used for storage of hazardous materials. Emergency alarm-initiating devices shall be installed outside of each interior *exit* or *exit access* door of storage buildings, rooms or areas. Activation of an emergency alarm-initiating device shall sound a local alarm to alert occupants of an emergency situation involving hazardous materials.

[F] 414.7.2 Dispensing, use and handling. Where hazardous materials having a hazard ranking of 3 or 4 in accordance with NFPA 704 are transported through *corridors* or *exit enclosures*, there shall be an emergency telephone system, a local manual alarm station or an *approved* alarm-initiating device at not more than 150-foot (45 720 mm) intervals and at each *exit* and *exit access* doorway throughout the transport route. The signal shall be relayed to an *approved* central, proprietary or remote station service or constantly attended on-site location and shall also initiate a local audible alarm.

[F] 414.7.3 Supervision. Emergency alarm systems shall be supervised by an *approved* central, proprietary or remote station service or shall initiate an audible and visual signal at a constantly attended on-site location.

SECTION 415
GROUPS H-1, H-2, H-3, H-4 AND H-5

[F] 415.1 Scope. The provisions of Sections 415.1 through 415.8 shall apply to the storage and use of hazardous materials in excess of the maximum allowable quantities per *control area* listed in Section 307.1. Buildings and structures with an occupancy in Group H shall also comply with the applicable provisions of Section 414 and the *International Fire Code.*

[F] 415.2 Definitions. The following words and terms shall, for the purposes of this chapter and as used elsewhere in the code, have the meanings shown herein.

[F] CONTINUOUS GAS DETECTION SYSTEM. A gas detection system where the analytical instrument is maintained in continuous operation and sampling is performed without interruption. Analysis is allowed to be performed on a cyclical basis at intervals not to exceed 30 minutes.

[F] DETACHED BUILDING. A separate single-story building, without a basement or crawl space, used for the storage or use of hazardous materials and located an *approved* distance from all structures.

[F] EMERGENCY CONTROL STATION. An *approved* location on the premises where signals from emergency equipment are received and which is staffed by trained personnel.

[F] EXHAUSTED ENCLOSURE. An appliance or piece of equipment that consists of a top, a back and two sides providing a means of local exhaust for capturing gases, fumes, vapors and mists. Such enclosures include laboratory hoods, exhaust fume hoods and similar appliances and equipment used to locally retain and exhaust the gases, fumes, vapors and mists that could be released. Rooms or areas provided with general ventilation, in themselves, are not exhausted enclosures.

[F] FABRICATION AREA. An area within a semiconductor fabrication facility and related research and development areas in which there are processes using hazardous production materials. Such areas are allowed to include ancillary rooms or areas such as dressing rooms and offices that are directly related to the fabrication area processes.

[F] FLAMMABLE VAPORS OR FUMES. The concentration of flammable constituents in air that exceed 25 percent of their lower flammable limit (LFL).

[F] GAS CABINET. A fully enclosed, noncombustible enclosure used to provide an isolated environment for compressed gas cylinders in storage or use. Doors and access ports for exchanging cylinders and accessing pressure-regulating controls are allowed to be included.

[F] GAS ROOM. A separately ventilated, fully enclosed room in which only compressed gases and associated equipment and supplies are stored or used.

[F] HAZARDOUS PRODUCTION MATERIAL (HPM). A solid, liquid or gas associated with semiconductor manufacturing that has a degree-of-hazard rating in health, flammability or instability of Class 3 or 4 as ranked by NFPA 704 and which is used directly in research, laboratory or production processes which have as their end product materials that are not hazardous.

[F] HPM FLAMMABLE LIQUID. An HPM liquid that is defined as either a Class I flammable liquid or a Class II or Class IIIA combustible liquid.

[F] HPM ROOM. A room used in conjunction with or serving a Group H-5 occupancy, where HPM is stored or used and which is classified as a Group H-2, H-3 or H-4 occupancy.

[F] IMMEDIATELY DANGEROUS TO LIFE AND HEALTH (IDLH). The concentration of air-borne contaminants which poses a threat of death, immediate or delayed permanent adverse health effects, or effects that could prevent escape from such an environment. This contaminant concentration level is established by the National Institute of Occupational Safety and Health (NIOSH) based on both toxicity and flammability. It generally is expressed in parts per million by volume (ppm v/v) or milligrams per cubic meter (mg/m^3). If adequate data do not exist for precise establishment of IDLH concentrations, an independent certified industrial hygienist, industrial toxicologist, appropriate regulatory agency or other source *approved* by the *building official* shall make such determination.

[F] LIQUID. A material that has a melting point that is equal to or less than 68°F (20°C) and a boiling point that is greater than 68°F (20°C) at 14.7 pounds per square inch absolute (psia) (101 kPa). When not otherwise identified, the term "liquid" includes both flammable and combustible liquids.

[F] LIQUID STORAGE ROOM. A room classified as a Group H-3 occupancy used for the storage of flammable or combustible liquids in a closed condition.

[F] LIQUID USE, DISPENSING AND MIXING ROOM. A room in which Class I, II and IIIA flammable or combustible liquids are used, dispensed or mixed in open containers.

[F] LOWER FLAMMABLE LIMIT (LFL). The minimum concentration of vapor in air at which propagation of flame will occur in the presence of an ignition source. The LFL is sometimes referred to as "LEL" or "lower explosive limit."

[F] NORMAL TEMPERATURE AND PRESSURE (NTP). A temperature of 70°F (21°C) and a pressure of 1 atmosphere [14.7 psia (101 kPa)].

[F] PHYSIOLOGICAL WARNING THRESHOLD LEVEL. A concentration of air-borne contaminants, normally expressed in parts per million (ppm) or milligrams per cubic meter (mg/m^3), that represents the concentration at which persons can sense the presence of the contaminant due to odor, irritation or other quick-acting physiological response. When used in conjunction with the permissible exposure limit (PEL) the physiological warning threshold levels are those consistent with the classification system used to establish the PEL. See the definition of "Permissible exposure limit (PEL)" in the *International Fire Code.*

[F] SERVICE CORRIDOR. A fully enclosed passage used for transporting HPM and purposes other than required *means of egress*.

[F] SOLID. A material that has a melting point, decomposes or sublimes at a temperature greater than 68°F (20°C).

[F] STORAGE, HAZARDOUS MATERIALS.

1. The keeping, retention or leaving of hazardous materials in closed containers, tanks, cylinders or similar vessels, or
2. Vessels supplying operations through closed connections to the vessel.

[F] USE (MATERIAL). Placing a material into action, including solids, liquids and gases.

[F] WORKSTATION. A defined space or an independent principal piece of equipment using HPM within a fabrication area where a specific function, laboratory procedure or research activity occurs. *Approved* or *listed* hazardous materials storage cabinets, flammable liquid storage cabinets or gas cabinets serving a workstation are included as part of the workstation. A workstation is allowed to contain ventilation equipment, fire protection devices, detection devices, electrical devices and other processing and scientific equipment.

[F] 415.3 Fire separation distance. Group H occupancies shall be located on property in accordance with the other provisions of this chapter. In Groups H-2 and H-3, not less than 25 percent of the perimeter wall of the occupancy shall be an *exterior wall.*

Exceptions:

1. Liquid use, dispensing and mixing rooms having a floor area of not more than 500 square feet (46.5 m^2) need not be located on the outer perimeter of the building where they are in accordance with the *International Fire Code* and NFPA 30.
2. Liquid storage rooms having a floor area of not more than 1,000 square feet (93 m^2) need not be located on the outer perimeter where they are in accordance with the *International Fire Code* and NFPA 30.
3. Spray paint booths that comply with the *International Fire Code* need not be located on the outer perimeter.

[F] 415.3.1 Group H occupancy minimum fire separation distance. Regardless of any other provisions, buildings containing Group H occupancies shall be set back to the minimum *fire separation distance* as set forth in Items 1 through 4 below. Distances shall be measured from the walls enclosing the occupancy to *lot lines*, including those on a *public way*. Distances to assumed *lot lines* established for the purpose of determining *exterior wall* and opening protection are not to be used to establish the minimum *fire separation distance* for buildings on sites where explosives are manufactured or used when separation is provided in accordance with the quantity distance tables specified for explosive materials in the *International Fire Code.*

1. Group H-1. Not less than 75 feet (22 860 mm) and not less than required by the *International Fire Code*.

   Exceptions:

   1. Fireworks manufacturing buildings separated in accordance with NFPA 1124.
   2. Buildings containing the following materials when separated in accordance with Table 415.3.1:

      2.1. Organic peroxides, unclassified detonable.

      2.2. Unstable reactive materials, Class 4.

      2.3. Unstable reactive materials, Class 3 detonable.

      2.4. Detonable pyrophoric materials.

2. Group H-2. Not less than 30 feet (9144 mm) where the area of the occupancy exceeds 1,000 square feet (93 m^2) and it is not required to be located in a detached building.

3. Groups H-2 and H-3. Not less than 50 feet (15 240 mm) where a detached building is required (see Table 415.3.2).

4. Groups H-2 and H-3. Occupancies containing materials with explosive characteristics shall be separated as required by the *International Fire Code*. Where separations are not specified, the distances required shall not be less than the distances required by Table 415.3.1.

[F] 415.3.2 Detached buildings for Group H-1, H-2 or H-3 occupancy. The storage of hazardous materials in excess of those amounts listed in Table 415.3.2 shall be in accordance with the applicable provisions of Sections 415.4 and 415.5. Where a detached building is required by Table 415.3.2, there are no requirements for wall and opening protection based on *fire separation distance*.

[F] 415.4 Special provisions for Group H-1 occupancies. Group H-1 occupancies shall be in buildings used for no other purpose, shall not exceed one *story* in height and be without basements, crawl spaces or other under-floor spaces. Roofs shall be of lightweight construction with suitable thermal insulation to prevent sensitive material from reaching its decomposition temperature. Group H-1 occupancies containing materials that are in themselves both physical and health hazards in quantities exceeding the maximum allowable quantities per *control area* in Table 307.1.(2) shall comply with requirements for both Group H-1 and H-4 occupancies.

[F] 415.4.1 Floors in storage rooms. Floors in storage areas for organic peroxides, pyrophoric materials and unstable (reactive) materials shall be of liquid-tight, noncombustible construction.

[F] 415.5 Special provisions for Groups H-2 and H-3 occupancies. Groups H-2 and H-3 occupancies containing quantities of hazardous materials in excess of those set forth in Table 415.3.2 shall be in buildings used for no other purpose, shall not exceed one *story* in height and shall be without basements, crawl spaces or other under-floor spaces.

Groups H-2 and H-3 occupancies containing water-reactive materials shall be resistant to water penetration. Piping for conveying liquids shall not be over or through areas containing water reactives, unless isolated by *approved* liquid-tight construction.

Exception: Fire protection piping.

[F] 415.5.1 Floors in storage rooms. Floors in storage areas for organic peroxides, oxidizers, pyrophoric materials, unstable (reactive) materials and water-reactive solids and liquids shall be of liquid-tight, noncombustible construction.

[F] 415.5.2 Waterproof room. Rooms or areas used for the storage of water-reactive solids and liquids shall be constructed in a manner that resists the penetration of water through the use of waterproof materials. Piping carrying water for other than *approved* automatic fire sprinkler systems shall not be within such rooms or areas.

[F] 415.6 Group H-2. Occupancies in Group H-2 shall be constructed in accordance with Sections 415.6.1 through 415.6.4 and the *International Fire Code.*

[F] 415.6.1 Combustible dusts, grain processing and storage. The provisions of Sections 415.6.1.1 through 415.6.1.6 shall apply to buildings in which materials that produce combustible dusts are stored or handled. Buildings that store or handle combustible dusts shall comply with the applicable provisions of NFPA 61, NFPA 85, NFPA 120, NFPA 484, NFPA 654, NFPA 655 and NFPA 664, and the *International Fire Code.*

[F] 415.6.1.1 Type of construction and height exceptions. Buildings shall be constructed in compliance with the height and area limitations of Table 503 for Group H-2; except that where erected of Type I or II construction, the heights and areas of grain elevators and similar structures shall be unlimited, and where of Type IV construction, the maximum height shall be 65 feet (19 812 mm) and except further that, in isolated areas, the maximum height of Type IV structures shall be increased to 85 feet (25 908 mm).

[F] 415.6.1.2 Grinding rooms. Every room or space occupied for grinding or other operations that produce combustible dusts shall be enclosed with *fire barriers* constructed in accordance with Section 707 or *horizontal assemblies* constructed in accordance with Section 712, or both. The minimum *fire-resistance rating* shall be 2 hours where the area is not more than 3,000 square feet (279 m^2), and 4 hours where the area is greater than 3,000 square feet (279 m^2).

[F] 415.6.1.3 Conveyors. Conveyors, chutes, piping and similar equipment passing through the enclosures of rooms or spaces shall be constructed dirt tight and vapor tight, and be of *approved* noncombustible materials complying with Chapter 30.

[F] 415.6.1.4 Explosion control. Explosion control shall be provided as specified in the *International Fire Code*, or spaces shall be equipped with the equivalent mechanical ventilation complying with the *International Mechanical Code.*

[F] 415.6.1.5 Grain elevators. Grain elevators, malt houses and buildings for similar occupancies shall not be located within 30 feet (9144 mm) of interior *lot lines* or structures on the same lot, except where erected along a railroad right-of-way.

[F] 415.6.1.6 Coal pockets. Coal pockets located less than 30 feet (9144 mm) from interior *lot lines* or from structures on the same lot shall be constructed of not less than Type IB construction. Where more than 30 feet (9144 mm) from interior *lot lines*, or where erected along a railroad right-of-way, the minimum type of construction of such structures not more than 65 feet (19 812 mm) in *building height* shall be Type IV.

[F] TABLE 415.3.1
MINIMUM SEPARATION DISTANCES FOR BUILDINGS CONTAINING EXPLOSIVE MATERIALS

QUANTITY OF EXPLOSIVE MATERIAL[a]		MINIMUM DISTANCE (feet)		
		Lot lines[b] and inhabited buildings[c]		
Pounds over	Pounds not over	Barricaded[d]	Unbarricaded	Separation of magazines[d, e, f]
2	5	70	140	12
5	10	90	180	16
10	20	110	220	20
20	30	125	250	22
30	40	140	280	24
40	50	150	300	28
50	75	170	340	30
75	100	190	380	32
100	125	200	400	36
125	150	215	430	38
150	200	235	470	42
200	250	255	510	46
250	300	270	540	48
300	400	295	590	54
400	500	320	640	58
500	600	340	680	62
600	700	355	710	64
700	800	375	750	66
800	900	390	780	70
900	1,000	400	800	72
1,000	1,200	425	850	78
1,200	1,400	450	900	82
1,400	1,600	470	940	86
1,600	1,800	490	980	88
1,800	2,000	505	1,010	90
2,000	2,500	545	1,090	98
2,500	3,000	580	1,160	104
3,000	4,000	635	1,270	116
4,000	5,000	685	1,370	122
5,000	6,000	730	1,460	130
6,000	7,000	770	1,540	136
7,000	8,000	800	1,600	144
8,000	9,000	835	1,670	150
9,000	10,000	865	1,730	156
10,000	12,000	875	1,750	164
12,000	14,000	885	1,770	174
14,000	16,000	900	1,800	180
16,000	18,000	940	1,880	188
18,000	20,000	975	1,950	196
20,000	25,000	1,055	2,000	210
25,000	30,000	1,130	2,000	224
30,000	35,000	1,205	2,000	238
35,000	40,000	1,275	2,000	248

(continued)

TABLE 415.3.1—continued
MINIMUM SEPARATION DISTANCES FOR BUILDINGS CONTAINING EXPLOSIVE MATERIALS

QUANTITY OF EXPLOSIVE MATERIAL[a]		MINIMUM DISTANCE (feet)		
		Lot lines[b] and inhabited buildings[c]		
Pounds over	Pounds not over	Barricaded[d]	Unbarricaded	Separation of magazines[d, e, f]
40,000	45,000	1,340	2,000	258
45,000	50,000	1,400	2,000	270
50,000	55,000	1,460	2,000	280
55,000	60,000	1,515	2,000	290
60,000	65,000	1,565	2,000	300
65,000	70,000	1,610	2,000	310
70,000	75,000	1,655	2,000	320
75,000	80,000	1,695	2,000	330
80,000	85,000	1,730	2,000	340
85,000	90,000	1,760	2,000	350
90,000	95,000	1,790	2,000	360
95,000	100,000	1,815	2,000	370
100,000	110,000	1,835	2,000	390
110,000	120,000	1,855	2,000	410
120,000	130,000	1,875	2,000	430
130,000	140,000	1,890	2,000	450
140,000	150,000	1,900	2,000	470
150,000	160,000	1,935	2,000	490
160,000	170,000	1,965	2,000	510
170,000	180,000	1,990	2,000	530
180,000	190,000	2,010	2,010	550
190,000	200,000	2,030	2,030	570
200,000	210,000	2,055	2,055	590
210,000	230,000	2,100	2,100	630
230,000	250,000	2,155	2,155	670
250,000	275,000	2,215	2,215	720
275,000	300,000	2,275	2,275	770

For SI: 1 pound = 0.454 kg, 1 foot = 304.8 mm, 1 square foot = $0.0929 m^2$.

a. The number of pounds of explosives listed is the number of pounds of trinitrotoluene (TNT) or the equivalent pounds of other explosive.

b. The distance listed is the distance to lot line, including lot lines at public ways.

c. For the purpose of this table, an inhabited building is any building on the same lot that is regularly occupied by people. Where two or more buildings containing explosives or magazines are located on the same lot, each building or magazine shall comply with the minimum distances specified from inhabited buildings and, in addition, they shall be separated from each other by not less than the distance shown for "Separation of magazines," except that the quantity of explosive materials contained in detonator buildings or magazines shall govern in regard to the spacing of said detonator buildings or magazines from buildings or magazines containing other explosive materials. If any two or more buildings or magazines are separated from each other by less than the specified "Separation of Magazines" distances, then such two or more buildings or magazines, as a group, shall be considered as one building or magazine, and the total quantity of explosive materials stored in such group shall be treated as if the explosive were in a single building or magazine located on the site of any building or magazine of the group, and shall comply with the minimum distance specified from other magazines or inhabited buildings.

d. Barricades shall effectively screen the building containing explosives from other buildings, public ways or magazines. Where mounds or revetted walls of earth are used for barricades, they shall not be less than 3 feet in thickness. A straight line from the top of any side wall of the building containing explosive materials to the eave line of any other building, magazine or a point 12 feet above the centerline of a public way shall pass through the barricades.

e. Magazine is a building or structure, other than an operating building, approved for storage of explosive materials. Portable or mobile magazines not exceeding 120 square feet in area need not comply with the requirements of this code, however, all magazines shall comply with the *International Fire Code*.

f. The distance listed is permitted to be reduced by 50 percent where approved natural or artificial barriers are provided in accordance with the requirements in Note d.

[F] TABLE 415.3.2
DETACHED BUILDING REQUIRED

A DETACHED BUILDING IS REQUIRED WHEN THE QUANTITY OF MATERIAL EXCEEDS THAT LISTED HEREIN			
Material	**Class**	**Solids and Liquids (tons)[a, b]**	**Gases (cubic feet)[a, b]**
Explosives	Division 1.1 Division 1.2 Division 1.3 Division 1.4 Division 1.4[c] Division 1.5 Division 1.6	Maximum Allowable Quantity Maximum Allowable Quantity Maximum Allowable Quantity Maximum Allowable Quantity 1 Maximum Allowable Quantity Maximum Allowable Quantity	Not Applicable
Oxidizers	Class 4	Maximum Allowable Quantity	Maximum Allowable Quantity
Unstable (reactives) detonable	Class 3 or 4	Maximum Allowable Quantity	Maximum Allowable Quantity
Oxidizer, liquids and solids	Class 3 Class 2	1,200 2,000	Not Applicable Not Applicable
Organic peroxides	Detonable Class I Class II Class III	Maximum Allowable Quantity Maximum Allowable Quantity 25 50	Not Applicable Not Applicable Not Applicable Not Applicable
Unstable (reactives) nondetonable	Class 3 Class 2	1 25	2,000 10,000
Water reactives	Class 3 Class 2	1 25	Not Applicable Not Applicable
Pyrophoric gases	Not Applicable	Not Applicable	2,000

For SI: 1 ton = 906 kg, 1 cubic foot = 0.02832 m^3, 1 pound = 0.454 kg.

a. For materials that are detonable, the distance to other buildings or lot lines shall be as specified in Table 415.3.1 based on trinitrotoluene (TNT) equivalence of the material. For materials classified as explosives, see Chapter 33 the *International Fire Code*. For all other materials, the distance shall be as indicated in Section 415.3.1.

b. "Maximum Allowable Quantity" means the maximum allowable quantity per control area set forth in Table 307.1(1).

c. Limited to Division 1.4 materials and articles, including articles packaged for shipment, that are not regulated as an explosive under Bureau of Alcohol, Tobacco and Firearms (BATF) regulations or unpackaged articles used in process operations that do not propagate a detonation or deflagration between articles, providing the net explosive weight of individual articles does not exceed 1 pound.

[F] 415.6.2 Flammable and combustible liquids. The storage, handling, processing and transporting of flammable and combustible liquids in Groups H-2 and H-3 occupancies shall be in accordance with Sections 415.6.2.1 through 415.6.2.10, the *International Mechanical Code* and the *International Fire Code*.

[F] 415.6.2.1 Mixed occupancies. Where the storage tank area is located in a building of two or more occupancies and the quantity of liquid exceeds the maximum allowable quantity for one *control area*, the use shall be completely separated from adjacent occupancies in accordance with the requirements of Section 508.4.

[F] 415.6.2.1.1 Height exception. Where storage tanks are located within a building no more than one *story above grade plane*, the height limitation of Section 503 shall not apply for Group H.

[F] 415.6.2.2 Tank protection. Storage tanks shall be noncombustible and protected from physical damage. *Fire barriers* or *horizontal assemblies* or both around the storage tank(s) shall be permitted as the method of protection from physical damage.

[F] 415.6.2.3 Tanks. Storage tanks shall be *approved* tanks conforming to the requirements of the *International Fire Code*.

[F] 415.6.2.4 Suppression. Group H shall be equipped throughout with an *approved automatic sprinkler system*, installed in accordance with Section 903.

[F] 415.6.2.5 Leakage containment. A liquid-tight containment area compatible with the stored liquid shall be provided. The method of spill control, drainage control and secondary containment shall be in accordance with the *International Fire Code*.

Exception: Rooms where only double-wall storage tanks conforming to Section 415.6.2.3 are used to store Class I, II and IIIA flammable and combustible liquids shall not be required to have a leakage containment area.

[F] 415.6.2.6 Leakage alarm. An *approved* automatic alarm shall be provided to indicate a leak in a storage tank and room. The alarm shall sound an audible signal, 15 dBa above the ambient sound level, at every point of entry into the room in which the leaking storage tank is located. An *approved* sign shall be posted on every entry door to the tank storage room indicating the potential hazard of the interior room environment, or the sign shall state: WARNING, WHEN ALARM SOUNDS, THE ENVIRONMENT WITHIN THE ROOM MAY BE HAZARDOUS. The leakage alarm shall also be supervised in accordance with Chapter 9 to transmit a trouble signal.

[F] 415.6.2.7 Tank vent. Storage tank vents for Class I, II or IIIA liquids shall terminate to the outdoor air in accordance with the *International Fire Code*.

[F] 415.6.2.8 Room ventilation. Storage tank areas storing Class I, II or IIIA liquids shall be provided with mechanical ventilation. The mechanical ventilation system shall be in accordance with the *International Mechanical Code* and the *International Fire Code*.

[F] 415.6.2.9 Explosion venting. Where Class I liquids are being stored, explosion venting shall be provided in accordance with the *International Fire Code*.

[F] 415.6.2.10 Tank openings other than vents. Tank openings other than vents from tanks inside buildings shall be designed to ensure that liquids or vapor concentrations are not released inside the building.

[F] 415.6.3 Liquefied petroleum gas facilities. The construction and installation of liquefied petroleum gas facilities shall be in accordance with the requirements of this code, the *International Fire Code*, the *International Mechanical Code*, the *International Fuel Gas Code* and NFPA 58.

[F] 415.6.4 Dry cleaning plants. The construction and installation of dry cleaning plants shall be in accordance with the requirements of this code, the *International Mechanical Code*, the *International Plumbing Code* and NFPA 32. Dry cleaning solvents and systems shall be classified in accordance with the *International Fire Code*.

[F] 415.7 Groups H-3 and H-4. Groups H-3 and H-4 shall be constructed in accordance with the applicable provisions of this code and the *International Fire Code*.

[F] 415.7.1 Flammable and combustible liquids. The storage, handling, processing and transporting of flammable and combustible liquids in Group H-3 occupancies shall be in accordance with Section 415.6.2.

[F] 415.7.2 Gas rooms. When gas rooms are provided, such rooms shall be separated from other areas by not less than 1-hour *fire barriers* constructed in accordance with Section 707 or *horizontal assemblies* constructed in accordance with Section 712, or both.

[F] 415.7.3 Floors in storage rooms. Floors in storage areas for corrosive liquids and *highly toxic* or *toxic* materials shall be of liquid-tight, noncombustible construction.

[F] 415.7.4 Separation—highly toxic solids and liquids. *Highly toxic* solids and liquids not stored in *approved* hazardous materials storage cabinets shall be isolated from other hazardous materials storage by not less than 1-hour *fire barriers* constructed in accordance with Section 707 or *horizontal assemblies* constructed in accordance with Section 712, or both.

[F] 415.8 Group H-5.

[F] 415.8.1 General. In addition to the requirements set forth elsewhere in this code, Group H-5 shall comply with the provisions of Sections 415.8.1 through 415.8.11 and the *International Fire Code*.

[F] 415.8.2 Fabrication areas.

[F] 415.8.2.1 Hazardous materials in fabrication areas.

[F] 415.8.2.1.1 Aggregate quantities. The aggregate quantities of hazardous materials stored and used in a single fabrication area shall not exceed the quantities set forth in Table 415.8.2.1.1.

Exception: The quantity limitations for any hazard category in Table 415.8.2.1.1 shall not apply where the fabrication area contains quantities of hazardous materials not exceeding the maximum allowable quantities per *control area* established by Tables 307.1(1) and 307.1(2).

[F] 415.8.2.1.2 Hazardous production materials. The maximum quantities of hazardous production materials (HPM) stored in a single fabrication area shall not exceed the maximum allowable quantities per *control area* established by Tables 307.1(1) and 307.1(2).

[F] 415.8.2.2 Separation. Fabrication areas, whose sizes are limited by the quantity of hazardous materials allowed by Table 415.8.2.1.1, shall be separated from each other, from *corridors* and from other parts of the building by not less than 1-hour *fire barriers* constructed in accordance with Section 707 or *horizontal assemblies* constructed in accordance with Section 712, or both.

Exceptions:

1. Doors within such *fire barrier* walls, including doors to *corridors*, shall be only self-closing *fire door assemblies* having a *fire protection rating* of not less than $^3/_4$ hour.
2. Windows between fabrication areas and corridors are permitted to be fixed glazing *listed* and labeled for a *fire protection rating* of at least $^3/_4$ hour in accordance with Section 715.

[F] 415.8.2.3 Location of occupied levels. Occupied levels of fabrication areas shall be located at or above the first *story above grade plane*.

[F] 415.8.2.4 Floors. Except for surfacing, floors within fabrication areas shall be of noncombustible construction.

Openings through floors of fabrication areas are permitted to be unprotected where the interconnected levels are used solely for mechanical equipment directly related to such fabrication areas (see also Section 415.8.2.5).

Floors forming a part of an occupancy separation shall be liquid tight.

[F] TABLE 415.8.2.1.1
QUANTITY LIMITS FOR HAZARDOUS MATERIALS IN A SINGLE FABRICATION AREA IN GROUP H-5[a]

HAZARD CATEGORY		SOLIDS (pounds per square feet)	LIQUIDS (gallons per square feet)	GAS (feet^3 @ NTP/square feet)
PHYSICAL-HAZARD MATERIALS				
Combustible dust		Note b	Not Applicable	Not Applicable
Combustible fiber	Loose Baled	Note b Notes b, c	Not Applicable	Not Applicable
Combustible liquid Combination Class I, II and IIIA	II IIIA IIIB	Not Applicable	0.01 0.02 Not Limited 0.04	Not Applicable
Cryogenic gas	Flammable Oxidizing	Not Applicable	Not Applicable	Note d 1.25
Explosives		Note b	Note b	Note b
Flammable gas	Gaseous Liquefied	Not Applicable	Not Applicable	Note d Note d
Flammable liquid Combination Class IA, IB and IC Combination Class I, II and IIIA	IA IB IC	Not Applicable	0.0025 0.025 0.025 0.025 0.04	Not Applicable
Flammable solid		0.001	Not Applicable	Not Applicable
Organic peroxide Unclassified detonable Class I Class II Class III Class IV Class V		Note b Note b 0.025 0.1 Not Limited Not limited	Not Applicable	Not Applicable
Oxidizing gas Combination of gaseous and liquefied	Gaseous Liquefied	Not Applicable	Not Applicable	1.25 1.25 1.25
Oxidizer Combination	Class 4 Class 3 Class 2 Class 1 Class 1, 2, 3	Note b 0.003 0.003 0.003 0.003	Note b 0.03 0.03 0.03 0.03	Not Applicable
Pyrophoric material		Note b	0.00125	Notes d and e
Unstable reactive	Class 4 Class 3 Class 2 Class 1	Note b 0.025 0.1 Not Limited	Note b 0.0025 0.01 Not Limited	Note b Note b Note b Not Limited
Water reactive	Class 3 Class 2 Class 1	Note b 0.25 Not Limited	0.00125 0.025 Not Limited	Not Applicable
HEALTH-HAZARD MATERIALS				
Corrosives		Not Limited	Not Limited	Not Limited
Highly toxic		Not Limited	Not Limited	Note d
Toxics		Not Limited	Not Limited	Note d

For SI: 1 pound per square foot = 4.882 kg/m^2, 1 gallon per square foot = 40.7 L/m^2, 1 cubic foot @ NTP/square foot = 0.305 m^3 @ NTP/m^2, 1 cubic foot = 0.02832 m^3.

a. Hazardous materials within piping shall not be included in the calculated quantities.

b. Quantity of hazardous materials in a single fabrication shall not exceed the maximum allowable quantities per control area in Tables 307.1(1) and 307.1(2).

c. Densely packed baled cotton that complies with the packing requirements of ISO 8115 shall not be included in this material class.

d. The aggregate quantity of flammable, pyrophoric, toxic and highly toxic gases shall not exceed 9,000 cubic feet at NTP.

e. The aggregate quantity of pyrophoric gases in the building shall not exceed the amounts set forth in Table 415.3.2.

[F] 415.8.2.5 Shafts and openings through floors. Elevator shafts, vent shafts and other openings through floors shall be enclosed when required by Section 708. Mechanical, duct and piping penetrations within a fabrication area shall not extend through more than two floors. The *annular space* around penetrations for cables, cable trays, tubing, piping, conduit or ducts shall be sealed at the floor level to restrict the movement of air. The fabrication area, including the areas through which the ductwork and piping extend, shall be considered a single conditioned environment.

[F] 415.8.2.6 Ventilation. Mechanical exhaust ventilation at the rate of not less than 1 cubic foot per minute per square foot [0.0051 $m^3/(s \cdot m^2)$] of floor area shall be provided throughout the portions of the fabrication area where HPM are used or stored. The exhaust air duct system of one fabrication area shall not connect to another duct system outside that fabrication area within the building.

A ventilation system shall be provided to capture and exhaust gases, fumes and vapors at workstations.

Two or more operations at a workstation shall not be connected to the same exhaust system where either one or the combination of the substances removed could constitute a fire, explosion or hazardous chemical reaction within the exhaust duct system.

Exhaust ducts penetrating occupancy separations shall be contained in a shaft of equivalent fire-resistance-rated construction. Exhaust ducts shall not penetrate *fire walls*.

Fire dampers shall not be installed in exhaust ducts.

[F] 415.8.2.7 Transporting hazardous production materials to fabrication areas. HPM shall be transported to fabrication areas through enclosed piping or tubing systems that comply with Section 415.8.6.1, through service *corridors* complying with Section 415.8.4, or in *corridors* as permitted in the exception to Section 415.8.3. The handling or transporting of HPM within service *corridors* shall comply with the *International Fire Code*.

[F] 415.8.2.8 Electrical.

[F] 415.8.2.8.1 General. Electrical equipment and devices within the fabrication area shall comply with NFPA 70. The requirements for hazardous locations need not be applied where the average air change is at least four times that set forth in Section 415.8.2.6 and where the number of air changes at any location is not less than three times that required by Section 415.8.2.6. The use of recirculated air shall be permitted.

[F] 415.8.2.8.2 Workstations. Workstations shall not be energized without adequate exhaust ventilation. See Section 415.8.2.6 for workstation exhaust ventilation requirements.

[F] 415.8.3 Corridors. *Corridors* shall comply with Chapter 10 and shall be separated from fabrication areas as specified in Section 415.8.2.2. *Corridors* shall not contain HPM and shall not be used for transporting such materials, except through closed piping systems as provided in Section 415.8.6.3.

Exception: Where existing fabrication areas are altered or modified, HPM is allowed to be transported in existing *corridors,* subject to the following conditions:

1. Corridors. *Corridors* adjacent to the fabrication area where the *alteration* work is to be done shall comply with Section 1018 for a length determined as follows:
    1.1. The length of the common wall of the *corridor* and the fabrication area; and
    1.2. For the distance along the *corridor* to the point of entry of HPM into the *corridor* serving that fabrication area.
2. Emergency alarm system. There shall be an emergency telephone system, a local manual alarm station or other *approved* alarm-initiating device within *corridors* at not more than 150-foot (45 720 mm) intervals and at each *exit* and doorway. The signal shall be relayed to an *approved* central, proprietary or remote station service or the emergency control station and shall also initiate a local audible alarm.
3. Pass-throughs. Self-closing doors having a *fire protection rating* of not less than 1 hour shall separate pass-throughs from existing *corridors*. Pass-throughs shall be constructed as required for the *corridors* and protected by an *approved* automatic fire-extinguishing system.

[F] 415.8.4 Service corridors.

[F] 415.8.4.1 Occupancy. Service corridors shall be classified as Group H-5.

[F] 415.8.4.2 Use conditions. Service corridors shall be separated from *corridors* as required by Section 415.8.2.2. Service corridors shall not be used as a required *corridor*.

[F] 415.8.4.3 Mechanical ventilation. Service corridors shall be mechanically ventilated as required by Section 415.8.2.6 or at not less than six air changes per hour, whichever is greater.

[F] 415.8.4.4 Means of egress. The maximum distance of travel from any point in a service corridor to an *exit*, *exit access corridor* or door into a fabrication area shall not exceed 75 feet (22 860 mm). Dead ends shall not exceed 4 feet (1219 mm) in length. There shall be not less than two *exits*, and not more than one-half of the required *means of egress* shall require travel into a fabrication area. Doors from service corridors shall swing in the direction of egress travel and shall be self-closing.

[F] 415.8.4.5 Minimum width. The minimum clear width of a service corridor shall be 5 feet (1524 mm), or 33 inches (838 mm) wider than the widest cart or truck used in the corridor, whichever is greater.

[F] 415.8.4.6 Emergency alarm system. Emergency alarm systems shall be provided in accordance with this section and Sections 414.7.1 and 414.7.2. The maximum allowable quantity per *control area* provisions shall not apply to emergency alarm systems required for HPM.

[F] 415.8.4.6.1 Service corridors. An emergency alarm system shall be provided in service corridors, with at least one alarm device in each service corridor.

[F] 415.8.4.6.2 Exit access corridors and exit enclosures. Emergency alarms for *exit access corridors* and *exit enclosures* shall comply with Section 414.7.2.

[F] 415.8.4.6.3 Liquid storage rooms, HPM rooms and gas rooms. Emergency alarms for liquid storage rooms, HPM rooms and gas rooms shall comply with Section 414.7.1.

[F] 415.8.4.6.4 Alarm-initiating devices. An *approved* emergency telephone system, local alarm manual pull stations, or other *approved* alarm-initiating devices are allowed to be used as emergency alarm-initiating devices.

[F] 415.8.4.6.5 Alarm signals. Activation of the emergency alarm system shall sound a local alarm and transmit a signal to the emergency control station.

[F] 415.8.5 Storage of hazardous production materials.

[F] 415.8.5.1 General. Storage of HPM in fabrication areas shall be within *approved* or *listed* storage cabinets or gas cabinets or within a workstation. The storage of HPM in quantities greater than those listed in Section 1804.2 of the *International Fire Code* shall be in liquid storage rooms, HPM rooms or gas rooms as appropriate for the materials stored. The storage of other hazardous materials shall be in accordance with other applicable provisions of this code and the *International Fire Code*.

[F] 415.8.5.2 Construction.

[F] 415.8.5.2.1 HPM rooms and gas rooms. HPM rooms and gas rooms shall be separated from other areas by *fire barriers* constructed in accordance with Section 707 or *horizontal assemblies* constructed in accordance with Section 712, or both. The minimum *fire-resistance rating* shall be 2 hours where the area is 300 square feet (27.9 m^2) or more and 1 hour where the area is less than 300 square feet (27.9 m^2).

[F] 415.8.5.2.2 Liquid storage rooms. Liquid storage rooms shall be constructed in accordance with the following requirements:

1. Rooms in excess of 500 square feet (46.5 m^2) shall have at least one exterior door *approved* for fire department access.
2. Rooms shall be separated from other areas by *fire barriers* constructed in accordance with Section 707 or *horizontal assemblies* constructed in accordance with Section 712, or both. The *fire-resistance rating* shall be not less than 1 hour for rooms up to 150 square feet (13.9 m^2) in area and not less than 2 hours where the room is more than 150 square feet (13.9 m^2) in area.
3. Shelving, racks and wainscotting in such areas shall be of noncombustible construction or wood of not less than 1-inch (25 mm) nominal thickness.
4. Rooms used for the storage of Class I flammable liquids shall not be located in a basement.

[F] 415.8.5.2.3 Floors. Except for surfacing, floors of HPM rooms and liquid storage rooms shall be of noncombustible liquid-tight construction. Raised grating over floors shall be of noncombustible materials.

[F] 415.8.5.3 Location. Where HPM rooms, liquid storage rooms and gas rooms are provided, they shall have at least one *exterior wall* and such wall shall be not less than 30 feet (9144 mm) from *lot lines*, including *lot lines* adjacent to *public ways*.

[F] 415.8.5.4 Explosion control. Explosion control shall be provided where required by Section 414.5.1.

[F] 415.8.5.5 Exits. Where two exits are required from HPM rooms, liquid storage rooms and gas rooms, one shall be directly to the outside of the building.

[F] 415.8.5.6 Doors. Doors in a *fire barrier* wall, including doors to *corridors*, shall be self-closing *fire door assemblies* having a *fire-protection rating* of not less than $^3/_4$ hour.

[F] 415.8.5.7 Ventilation. Mechanical exhaust ventilation shall be provided in liquid storage rooms, HPM rooms and gas rooms at the rate of not less than 1 cubic foot per minute per square foot [0.0051 m^3/(s · m^2)] of floor area or six air changes per hour, whichever is greater, for categories of material.

Exhaust ventilation for gas rooms shall be designed to operate at a negative pressure in relation to the surrounding areas and direct the exhaust ventilation to an exhaust system.

[F] 415.8.5.8 Emergency alarm system. An *approved* emergency alarm system shall be provided for HPM rooms, liquid storage rooms and gas rooms.

Emergency alarm-initiating devices shall be installed outside of each interior exit door of such rooms.

Activation of an emergency alarm-initiating device shall sound a local alarm and transmit a signal to the emergency control station.

An *approved* emergency telephone system, local alarm manual pull stations or other *approved* alarm-initiating devices are allowed to be used as emergency alarm-initiating devices.

[F] 415.8.6 Piping and tubing.

[F] 415.8.6.1 General. Hazardous production materials piping and tubing shall comply with this section and ASME B31.3.

[F] 415.8.6.2 Supply piping and tubing.

[F] 415.8.6.2.1 HPM having a health-hazard ranking of 3 or 4. Systems supplying HPM liquids or gases having a health-hazard ranking of 3 or 4 shall be welded throughout, except for connections, to the systems that are within a ventilated enclosure if the material is a gas, or an *approved* method of drainage or containment is provided for the connections if the material is a liquid.

[F] 415.8.6.2.2 Location in service corridors. Hazardous production materials supply piping or tubing in service corridors shall be exposed to view.

[F] 415.8.6.2.3 Excess flow control. Where HPM gases or liquids are carried in pressurized piping above 15 pounds per square inch gauge (psig) (103.4 kPa), excess flow control shall be provided. Where the piping originates from within a liquid storage room, HPM room or gas room, the excess flow control shall be located within the liquid storage room, HPM room or gas room. Where the piping originates from a bulk source, the excess flow control shall be located as close to the bulk source as practical.

[F] 415.8.6.3 Installations in corridors and above other occupancies. The installation of HPM piping and tubing within the space defined by the walls of *corridors* and the floor or roof above, or in concealed spaces above other occupancies, shall be in accordance with Section 415.8.6.2 and the following conditions:

1. Automatic sprinklers shall be installed within the space unless the space is less than 6 inches (152 mm) in the least dimension.
2. Ventilation not less than six air changes per hour shall be provided. The space shall not be used to convey air from any other area.
3. Where the piping or tubing is used to transport HPM liquids, a receptor shall be installed below such piping or tubing. The receptor shall be designed to collect any discharge or leakage and drain it to an *approved* location. The 1-hour enclosure shall not be used as part of the receptor.
4. HPM supply piping and tubing and nonmetallic waste lines shall be separated from the *corridor* and from occupancies other than Group H-5 by *fire barriers* that have a *fire-resistance rating* of not less than 1 hour. Where gypsum wallboard is used, joints on the piping side of the enclosure are not required to be taped, provided the joints occur over framing members. Access openings into the enclosure shall be protected by *approved* fire protection-rated assemblies.
5. Readily accessible manual or automatic remotely activated fail-safe emergency shutoff valves shall be installed on piping and tubing other than waste lines at the following locations:
   5.1. At branch connections into the fabrication area.
   5.2. At entries into *corridors*.

Exception: Transverse crossings of the *corridors* by supply piping that is enclosed within a ferrous pipe or tube for the width of the *corridor* need not comply with Items 1 through 5.

[F] 415.8.6.4 Identification. Piping, tubing and HPM waste lines shall be identified in accordance with ANSI A13.1 to indicate the material being transported.

[F] 415.8.7 Continuous gas detection systems. A continuous gas detection system shall be provided for HPM gases when the physiological warning threshold level of the gas is at a higher level than the accepted PEL for the gas and for flammable gases in accordance with Sections 415.8.7.1 and 415.8.7.2.

[F] 415.8.7.1 Where required. A continuous gas detection system shall be provided in the areas identified in Sections 415.8.7.1.1 through 415.8.7.1.4.

[F] 415.8.7.1.1 Fabrication areas. A continuous gas detection system shall be provided in fabrication areas when gas is used in the fabrication area.

[F] 415.8.7.1.2 HPM rooms. A continuous gas detection system shall be provided in HPM rooms when gas is used in the room.

[F] 415.8.7.1.3 Gas cabinets, exhausted enclosures and gas rooms. A continuous gas detection system shall be provided in gas cabinets and exhausted enclosures. A continuous gas detection system shall be provided in gas rooms when gases are not located in gas cabinets or exhausted enclosures.

[F] 415.8.7.1.4 Corridors. When gases are transported in piping placed within the space defined by the walls of a *corridor* and the floor or roof above the *corridor*, a continuous gas detection system shall be provided where piping is located and in the *corridor*.

Exception: A continuous gas detection system is not required for occasional transverse crossings of the corridors by supply piping that is enclosed in a ferrous pipe or tube for the width of the *corridor*.

[F] 415.8.7.2 Gas detection system operation. The continuous gas detection system shall be capable of monitoring the room, area or equipment in which the gas is located at or below all the following gas concentrations:

1. Immediately dangerous to life and health (IDLH) values when the monitoring point is within an exhausted enclosure, ventilated enclosure or gas cabinet.
2. Permissible exposure limit (PEL) levels when the monitoring point is in an area outside an exhausted enclosure, ventilated enclosure or gas cabinet.

3. For flammable gases, the monitoring detection threshold level shall be vapor concentrations in excess of 25 percent of the lower flammable limit (LFL) when the monitoring is within or outside an exhausted enclosure, ventilated enclosure or gas cabinet.
4. Except as noted in this section, monitoring for *highly toxic* and *toxic* gases shall also comply with Chapter 37 of the *International Fire Code*.

[F] 415.8.7.2.1 Alarms. The gas detection system shall initiate a local alarm and transmit a signal to the emergency control station when a short-term hazard condition is detected. The alarm shall be both visual and audible and shall provide warning both inside and outside the area where the gas is detected. The audible alarm shall be distinct from all other alarms.

[F] 415.8.7.2.2 Shutoff of gas supply. The gas detection system shall automatically close the shutoff valve at the source on gas supply piping and tubing related to the system being monitored for which gas is detected when a short-term hazard condition is detected. Automatic closure of shutoff valves shall comply with the following:

1. Where the gas detection sampling point initiating the gas detection system alarm is within a gas cabinet or exhausted enclosure, the shutoff valve in the gas cabinet or exhausted enclosure for the specific gas detected shall automatically close.
2. Where the gas detection sampling point initiating the gas detection system alarm is within a room and compressed gas containers are not in gas cabinets or an exhausted enclosure, the shutoff valves on all gas lines for the specific gas detected shall automatically close.
3. Where the gas detection sampling point initiating the gas detection system alarm is within a piping distribution manifold enclosure, the shutoff valve supplying the manifold for the compressed gas container of the specific gas detected shall automatically close.

Exception: Where the gas detection sampling point initiating the gas detection system alarm is at the use location or within a gas valve enclosure of a branch line downstream of a piping distribution manifold, the shutoff valve for the branch line located in the piping distribution manifold enclosure shall automatically close.

[F] 415.8.8 Manual fire alarm system. An *approved* manual fire alarm system shall be provided throughout buildings containing Group H-5. Activation of the alarm system shall initiate a local alarm and transmit a signal to the emergency control station. The fire alarm system shall be designed and installed in accordance with Section 907.

[F] 415.8.9 Emergency control station. An emergency control station shall be provided in accordance with Sections 415.8.9.1 through 415.8.9.3.

[F] 415.8.9.1 Location. The emergency control station shall be located on the premises at an *approved* location outside the fabrication area.

[F] 415.8.9.2 Staffing. Trained personnel shall continuously staff the emergency control station.

[F] 415.8.9.3 Signals. The emergency control station shall receive signals from emergency equipment and alarm and detection systems. Such emergency equipment and alarm and detection systems shall include, but not be limited to, the following where such equipment or systems are required to be provided either in this chapter or elsewhere in this code:

1. *Automatic sprinkler system* alarm and monitoring systems.
2. Manual fire alarm systems.
3. Emergency alarm systems.
4. Continuous gas detection systems.
5. Smoke detection systems.
6. Emergency power system.
7. Automatic detection and alarm systems for pyrophoric liquids and Class 3 water-reactive liquids required in Section 1805.2.3.4 of the *International Fire Code*.
8. Exhaust ventilation flow alarm devices for pyrophoric liquids and Class 3 water-reactive liquids cabinet exhaust ventilation systems required in Section 1805.2.3.4 of the *International Fire Code*.

[F] 415.8.10 Emergency power system. An emergency power system shall be provided in Group H-5 occupancies where required in Section 415.8.10.1. The emergency power system shall be designed to supply power automatically to required electrical systems when the normal electrical supply system is interrupted.

[F] 415.8.10.1 Required electrical systems. Emergency power shall be provided for electrically operated equipment and connected control circuits for the following systems:

1. HPM exhaust ventilation systems.
2. HPM gas cabinet ventilation systems.
3. HPM exhausted enclosure ventilation systems.
4. HPM gas room ventilation systems.
5. HPM gas detection systems.
6. Emergency alarm systems.
7. Manual fire alarm systems.
8. *Automatic sprinkler system* monitoring and alarm systems.

9. Automatic alarm and detection systems for pyrophoric liquids and Class 3 water-reactive liquids required in Section 1805.2.3.4 of the *International Fire Code*.
10. Flow alarm switches for pyrophoric liquids and Class 3 water-reactive liquids cabinet exhaust ventilation systems required in Section 1805.2.3.4 of the *International Fire Code*.
11. Electrically operated systems required elsewhere in this code or in the *International Fire Code* applicable to the use, storage or handling of HPM.

[F] 415.8.10.2 Exhaust ventilation systems. Exhaust ventilation systems are allowed to be designed to operate at not less than one-half the normal fan speed on the emergency power system where it is demonstrated that the level of exhaust will maintain a safe atmosphere.

[F] 415.8.11 Automatic sprinkler system protection in exhaust ducts for HPM.

[F] 415.8.11.1 Exhaust ducts for HPM. An *approved automatic sprinkler system* shall be provided in exhaust ducts conveying gases, vapors, fumes, mists or dusts generated from HPM in accordance with this section and the *International Mechanical Code*.

[F] 415.8.11.2 Metallic and noncombustible nonmetallic exhaust ducts. An *approved automatic sprinkler system* shall be provided in metallic and noncombustible nonmetallic exhaust ducts when all of the following conditions apply:

1. Where the largest cross-sectional diameter is equal to or greater than 10 inches (254 mm).
2. The ducts are within the building.
3. The ducts are conveying flammable gases, vapors or fumes.

[F] 415.8.11.3 Combustible nonmetallic exhaust ducts. *Automatic sprinkler system* protection shall be provided in combustible nonmetallic exhaust ducts where the largest cross-sectional diameter of the duct is equal to or greater than 10 inches (254 mm).

Exceptions:

1. Ducts *listed* or *approved* for applications without automatic fire sprinkler system protection.
2. Ducts not more than 12 feet (3658 mm) in length installed below ceiling level.

[F] 415.8.11.4 Automatic sprinkler locations. Sprinkler systems shall be installed at 12-foot (3658 mm) intervals in horizontal ducts and at changes in direction. In vertical ducts, sprinklers shall be installed at the top and at alternate floor levels.

SECTION 416
APPLICATION OF FLAMMABLE FINISHES

[F] 416.1 General. The provisions of this section shall apply to the construction, installation and use of buildings and structures, or parts thereof, for the spraying of flammable paints, varnishes and lacquers or other flammable materials or mixtures or compounds used for painting, varnishing, staining or similar purposes. Such construction and equipment shall comply with the *International Fire Code*.

[F] 416.2 Spray rooms. Spray rooms shall be enclosed with not less than 1-hour *fire barriers* constructed in accordance with Section 707 or *horizontal assemblies* constructed in accordance with Section 712, or both. Floors shall be waterproofed and drained in an *approved* manner.

[F] 416.2.1 Surfaces. The interior surfaces of spray rooms shall be smooth and shall be so constructed to permit the free passage of exhaust air from all parts of the interior and to facilitate washing and cleaning, and shall be so designed to confine residues within the room. Aluminum shall not be used.

[F] 416.3 Spraying spaces. Spraying spaces shall be ventilated with an exhaust system to prevent the accumulation of flammable mist or vapors in accordance with the *International Mechanical Code*. Where such spaces are not separately enclosed, noncombustible spray curtains shall be provided to restrict the spread of flammable vapors.

[F] 416.3.1 Surfaces. The interior surfaces of spraying spaces shall be smooth and continuous without edges; shall be so constructed to permit the free passage of exhaust air from all parts of the interior and to facilitate washing and cleaning; and shall be so designed to confine residues within the spraying space. Aluminum shall not be used.

[F] 416.4 Spray booths. Spray booths shall be designed, constructed and operated in accordance with the *International Fire Code*.

[F] 416.5 Fire protection. An automatic fire-extinguishing system shall be provided in all spray, dip and immersing spaces and storage rooms and shall be installed in accordance with Chapter 9.

SECTION 417
DRYING ROOMS

[F] 417.1 General. A drying room or dry kiln installed within a building shall be constructed entirely of *approved* noncombustible materials or assemblies of such materials regulated by the *approved* rules or as required in the general and specific sections of Chapter 4 for special occupancies and where applicable to the general requirements of Chapter 28.

[F] 417.2 Piping clearance. Overhead heating pipes shall have a clearance of not less than 2 inches (51 mm) from combustible contents in the dryer.

[F] 417.3 Insulation. Where the operating temperature of the dryer is 175°F (79°C) or more, metal enclosures shall be insulated from adjacent combustible materials by not less than 12 inches (305 mm) of airspace, or the metal walls shall be lined with $^1/_4$-inch (6.35 mm) insulating mill board or other *approved* equivalent insulation.

[F] 417.4 Fire protection. Drying rooms designed for high-hazard materials and processes, including special occupancies as provided for in Chapter 4, shall be protected by an *approved* automatic fire-extinguishing system complying with the provisions of Chapter 9.

SECTION 418 ORGANIC COATINGS

[F] 418.1 Building features. Manufacturing of organic coatings shall be done only in buildings that do not have pits or basements.

[F] 418.2 Location. Organic coating manufacturing operations and operations incidental to or connected therewith shall not be located in buildings having other occupancies.

[F] 418.3 Process mills. Mills operating with close clearances and that process flammable and heat-sensitive materials, such as nitrocellulose, shall be located in a detached building or noncombustible structure.

[F] 418.4 Tank storage. Storage areas for flammable and combustible liquid tanks inside of structures shall be located at or above grade and shall be separated from the processing area by not less than 2-hour *fire barriers* constructed in accordance with Section 707 or *horizontal assemblies* constructed in accordance with Section 712, or both.

[F] 418.5 Nitrocellulose storage. Nitrocellulose storage shall be located on a detached pad or in a separate structure or a room enclosed with no less than 2-hour *fire barriers* constructed in accordance with Section 707 or *horizontal assemblies* constructed in accordance with Section 712, or both.

[F] 418.6 Finished products. Storage rooms for finished products that are flammable or combustible liquids shall be separated from the processing area by not less than 2-hour *fire barriers* constructed in accordance with Section 707 or *horizontal assemblies* constructed in accordance with Section 712, or both.

SECTION 419 LIVE/WORK UNITS

419.1 General. A live/work unit is a *dwelling unit* or *sleeping unit* in which a significant portion of the space includes a nonresidential use that is operated by the tenant and shall comply with Sections 419.1 through 419.8.

Exception: *Dwelling* or *sleeping units* that include an office that is less than 10 percent of the area of the *dwelling unit* shall not be classified as a live/work unit.

419.1.1 Limitations. The following shall apply to all live/work areas:

1. The live/work unit is permitted to be a maximum of 3,000 square feet (279 m^2);
2. The nonresidential area is permitted to be a maximum 50 percent of the area of each live/work unit;
3. The nonresidential area function shall be limited to the first or main floor only of the live/work unit; and
4. A maximum of five nonresidential workers or employees are allowed to occupy the nonresidential area at any one time.

419.2 Occupancies. Live/work units shall be classified as a Group R-2 occupancy. Separation requirements found in Sections 420 and 508 shall not apply within the live/work unit when the live/work unit is in compliance with Section 419. High-hazard and storage occupancies shall not be permitted in a live/work unit. The aggregate area of storage in the nonresidential portion of the live/work unit shall be limited to 10 percent of the space dedicated to nonresidential activities.

419.3 Means of egress. Except as modified by this section, the provisions for Group R-2 occupancies in Chapter 10 shall apply to the entire live/work unit.

419.3.1 Egress capacity. The egress capacity for each element of the live/work unit shall be based on the *occupant load* for the function served in accordance with Table 1004.1.1.

419.3.2 Sliding doors. Where doors in a *means of egress* are of the horizontal-sliding type, the force to slide the door to its fully open position shall not exceed 50 pounds (220 N) with a perpendicular force against the door of 50 pounds (220 N).

419.3.3 Spiral stairways. *Spiral stairways* that conform to the requirements of Section 1009.9 shall be permitted.

419.3.4 Locks. Egress doors shall be permitted to be locked in accordance with Item 4 of Section 1008.1.9.3.

419.4 Vertical openings. Floor openings between floor levels of a live/work unit are permitted without enclosure.

419.5 Fire protection. The live/work unit shall be provided with a monitored fire alarm system where required by Section 907.2.9 and an *automatic sprinkler system* in accordance with Section 903.2.8.

419.6 Structural. Floor loading for the areas within a live/work unit shall be designed to conform to Table 1607.1 based on the function within the space.

419.7 Accessibility. Accessibility shall be designed in accordance with Chapter 11.

419.8 Ventilation. The applicable requirements of the *International Mechanical Code* shall apply to each area within the live/work unit for the function within that space.

SECTION 420 GROUPS I-1, R-1, R-2, R-3

420.1 General. Occupancies in Groups I-1, R-1, R-2 and R-3 shall comply with the provisions of this section and other applicable provisions of this code.

420.2 Separation walls. Walls separating *dwelling units* in the same building, walls separating *sleeping units* in the same building and walls separating *dwelling* or *sleeping units* from other occupancies contiguous to them in the same building shall be constructed as *fire partitions* in accordance with Section 709.

420.3 Horizontal separation. Floor assemblies separating *dwelling units* in the same buildings, floor assemblies separating *sleeping units* in the same building and floor assemblies separating *dwelling* or *sleeping units* from other occupancies contiguous to them in the same building shall be constructed as *horizontal assemblies* in accordance with Section 712.

SECTION 421 HYDROGEN CUTOFF ROOMS

[F] 421.1 General. When required by the *International Fire Code*, hydrogen cutoff rooms shall be designed and constructed in accordance with Sections 421.1 through 421.8.

[F] 421.2 Definitions. The following words and terms shall, for the purposes of this chapter and as used elsewhere in this code, have the meanings shown herein.

[F] GASEOUS HYDROGEN SYSTEM. An assembly of piping, devices and apparatus designed to generate, store, contain, distribute or transport a nontoxic, gaseous hydrogen-containing mixture having at least 95-percent hydrogen gas by volume and not more than 1-percent oxygen by volume. Gaseous hydrogen systems consist of items such as compressed gas containers, reactors and appurtenances, including pressure regulators, pressure relief devices, manifolds, pumps, compressors and interconnecting piping and tubing and controls.

[F] HYDROGEN CUTOFF ROOM. A room or space that is intended exclusively to house a gaseous hydrogen system.

[F] 421.3 Location. Hydrogen cutoff rooms shall not be located below grade.

[F] 421.4 Design and construction. Hydrogen cutoff rooms shall be classified with respect to occupancy in accordance with Section 302.1 and separated from other areas of the building by not less than 1-hour *fire barriers* constructed in accordance with Section 707 or *horizontal assemblies* constructed in accordance with Section 712, or both; or as required by Section 508.2, 508.3 or 508.4, as applicable.

[F] 421.4.1 Opening protectives. Doors within the *fire barriers*, including doors to *corridors*, shall be self-closing in accordance with Section 715. Interior door openings shall be electronically interlocked to prevent operation of the hydrogen system when doors are opened or ajar or the room shall be provided with a mechanical exhaust ventilation system designed in accordance with Section 421.4.1.1.

[F] 421.4.1.1 Ventilation alternative. When an exhaust system is used in lieu of the interlock system required by Section 421.4.1, exhaust ventilation systems shall operate continuously and shall be designed to operate at a negative pressure in relation to the surrounding area. The average velocity of ventilation at the face of the door opening with the door in the fully open position shall not be less than 60 feet per minute (0.3048 m/s) with a minimum of 45 feet per minute (0.2287 m/s) at any point in the door opening.

[F] 421.4.2 Windows. Operable windows in interior walls shall not be permitted. Fixed windows shall be permitted when in accordance with Section 715.

[F] 421.5 Ventilation. Cutoff rooms shall be provided with mechanical ventilation in accordance with the applicable provisions for repair garages in Chapter 5 of the *International Mechanical Code*.

[F] 421.6 Gas detection system. Hydrogen cutoff rooms shall be provided with an *approved* flammable gas detection system in accordance with Sections 421.6.1 through 421.6.3.

[F] 421.6.1 System design. The flammable gas detection system shall be *listed* for use with hydrogen and any other flammable gases used in the room. The gas detection system shall be designed to activate when the level of flammable gas exceeds 25 percent of the lower flammability limit (LFL) for the gas or mixtures present at their anticipated temperature and pressure.

[F] 421.6.2 Operation. Activation of the gas detection system shall result in all of the following:

1. Initiation of distinct audible and visual alarm signals both inside and outside of the cutoff room.
2. Activation of the mechanical ventilation system.

[F] 421.6.3 Failure of the gas detection system. Failure of the gas detection system shall result in activation of the mechanical ventilation system, cessation of hydrogen generation and the sounding of a trouble signal in an *approved* location.

[F] 421.7 Explosion control. Explosion control shall be provided in accordance with Chapter 9 of the *International Fire Code*.

[F] 421.8 Standby power. Mechanical ventilation and gas detection systems shall be connected to a standby power system in accordance with Chapter 27.

SECTION 422 AMBULATORY HEALTH CARE FACILITIES

422.1 General. Occupancies classified as Group B ambulatory health care facilities shall comply with the provisions of Sections 422.1 through 422.6 and other applicable provisions of this code.

422.2 Smoke barriers. *Smoke barriers* shall be provided to subdivide every ambulatory care facility greater than 10,000 square feet (929 m^2) into a minimum of two smoke compartments per *story*. The travel distance from any point in a smoke compartment to a *smoke barrier* door shall not exceed 200 feet (60 960 mm). The *smoke barrier* shall be installed in accordance with Section 710.

422.3 Refuge area. At least 30 net square feet (2.8 m^2) per nonambulatory patient shall be provided within the aggregate area of *corridors*, patient rooms, treatment rooms, lounge or dining areas and other low-hazard areas on each side of each *smoke barrier*.

422.4 Independent egress. A *means of egress* shall be provided from each smoke compartment created by smoke barriers without having to return through the smoke compartment from which *means of egress* originated.

422.5 Automatic sprinkler systems. *Automatic sprinkler systems* shall be provided for ambulatory care facilities in accordance with Section 903.2.2.

422.6 Fire alarm systems. A fire alarm system shall be provided in accordance with Section 907.2.2.1.

SECTION 423
STORM SHELTERS

423.1 General. In addition to other applicable requirements in this code, storm shelters shall be constructed in accordance with ICC 500.

423.1.1 Scope. This section applies to the construction of storm shelters constructed as separate detached buildings or constructed as safe rooms within buildings for the purpose of providing safe refuge from storms that produce high winds, such as tornados and hurricanes. Such structures shall be designated to be hurricane shelters, tornado shelters, or combined hurricane and tornado shelters.

423.2 Definitions. The following words and terms shall, for the purposes of this chapter and as used elsewhere in this code, have the meanings shown herein.

STORM SHELTER. A building, structure or portions(s) thereof, constructed in accordance with ICC 500 and designated for use during a severe wind storm event, such as a hurricane or tornado.

Community storm shelter. A storm shelter not defined as a "Residential Storm Shelter."

Residential storm shelter. A storm shelter serving occupants of *dwelling units* and having an *occupant load* not exceeding 16 persons.

SECTION 424
TEMPORARY OVERFLOW EMERGENCY SHELTERS FOR THE HOMELESS

424.1 General. Existing A-2 and A-3 occupancies shall be permitted to provide facilities for temporary overflow emergency shelters for the homeless, provided that all of the following conditions are met and approved by the local code official and fire marshal:

424.1.1 The total number of homeless occupants is limited to 20 individuals who are ambulatory. The homeless occupants must be 18 years of age or older.

424.1.2 The building used for the temporary overflow emergency shelter must be of Type I, II, or III construction.

424.1.3 The temporary overflow emergency shelter must be staffed by a minimum of two individuals of 21 years of age or older and trained in accordance with Chapter 4 of the *North Carolina Fire Code* and at least one trained individual shall be awake to monitor the sleeping room and restrooms throughout the time the facility is occupied by the homeless.

424.1.4 Functioning smoke detection and a local fire alarm system in accordance with Section 907.2.8 shall be provided throughout the sleeping room and exit access corridors and stairs of the temporary overflow emergency shelter.

424.1.5 There shall be a minimum of two separate code compliant means of egress serving the temporary overflow emergency shelter. An evacuation route approved by the local code official and fire marshal shall be posted and be in compliance with Sections 404, 406, and 408 of the *North Carolina Fire Code.*

424.1.6 There shall be no lockable doors between sleeping rooms and required exits.

424.1.7 The temporary overflow emergency shelter sleeping room and exit access corridors and stairs shall have night lighting and emergency lighting with back-up power.

424.1.8 No fire protection sprinkler system is required in accordance with Section 903.2.8, Exception 2.

424.1.9 Heating, cooling, and ventilation must be provided by equipment installed and approved for such use. No space heaters are permitted.

424.1.10 There must be an adequate number of fire extinguishers to serve the temporary overflow emergency shelter as determined by the local fire marshal. Travel distance to an approved fire extinguisher shall not exceed 50 feet. Minimum rating of extinguishers shall be 3-A:40-BC.

424.1.11 No smoking is permitted in the temporary overflow emergency shelter.

424.1.12 The building owner must submit documentation illustrating that the fire alarm system is approved and that all emergency batteries have been tested and are operational.

424.1.13 Temporary overflow emergency shelters must be approved by the local code official for occupancy by issuance of an approved occupancy permit. Drawings of the temporary overflow emergency shelter sealed by a North Carolina licensed architect or engineer must be provided for local code official review and approval.

424.1.14 Compliance with *North Carolina Accessibility Code* for temporary overflow emergency shelters is not required, provided that the local jurisdiction has other shelter facilities that are accessible by the disabled.

424.1.15 Occupancy of a temporary overflow emergency shelter shall be for a maximum of 150 calendar days within any 365 day time span.

SECTION 425
LICENSED RESIDENTIAL CARE FACILITY

425.1 Classification. Buildings in which more than three people are harbored for medical, charitable or other care or treatment shall be classified as residential care facilities. The state agency having jurisdiction shall classify the facility as a residential care home, small residential care facility, small nonambulatory care facility or large residential care facility.

425.1.1 Fire extinguishers shall be installed in licensed residential care facilities in accordance with the *North Carolina Fire Prevention Code*.

425.1.2 Where two means of egress exits are required, the exits or exit access doors shall be so located and constructed to minimize the possibility that both may be blocked by any one fire or other emergency condition.

425.2 Residential care homes. Homes keeping no more than six adults or six unrestrained children who are able to respond and evacuate the facility without assistance, determined by the state agency having jurisdiction to be licensable, shall be classified as single-family residential (*North Carolina Residential Code*).

425.2.1 Each normally occupied story of the facility shall have two remotely located means of egress.

425.2.2 Smoke detectors shall be provided on all levels in accordance with the *North Carolina Residential Code*.

425.2.3 Interior wall and ceiling finishes shall be Class A, B or C.

425.2.4 Unvented fuel-fired heaters and portable electric heaters shall not be used.

425.3 Small residential care facilities. The following facilities when determined by the state agency having jurisdiction to be licensable, shall be classified as single-family residential.

1. Residential care facilities keeping no more than six adults or six unrestrained children with no more than three who are unable to respond and evacuate without assistance.
2. Residential care facilities keeping no more than five adults or five children who are unable to respond and evacuate without assistance, certifiable for Medicaid reimbursement; and staffed 24 hours per day with at least two staff awake at all times.
3. Residential care facilities keeping no more than nine adults or nine children who are able to respond and evacuate without assistance.

425.3.1 Either the *building* shall be of 1-hour fire-resistant construction, including all walls, partitions, floors and ceilings and bedroom doors, shall be 1.75 inches solid wood core or the building shall be sprinklered with a wet pipe system in accordance with NFPA 13D with a 30-minute water supply, including bathrooms, toilets, closets, pantries, storage and utility spaces. The sprinkler system shall be monitored in accordance with Section 903.4 (Section 903.4, Exception 1 is not applicable in this occupancy).

425.3.2 *Buildings* shall not exceed two *stories* in height or the area limitations for Group R-4. *Attics* and *basements* used as *habitable* spaces shall be counted as stories.

425.3.3 Each normally occupied story of the facility shall have two remotely located exits.

425.3.4 Facility exit stairways shall be either exterior unenclosed or interior enclosed on each level with 1-hour fire-resistant construction and a self-closing 20-minute labeled door. Other interior stairways shall be enclosed on one floor level with 1-hour fire resistant walls and self-closing 20-minute labeled door.

425.3.5 Smoke detectors shall be provided on all levels in accordance with the *North Carolina Residential Code*. Heat detectors shall be installed in all attic spaces. The *heat detectors* shall be connected to the fire alarm and detection system.

425.3.6 Any incidental use area (as defined by Table 508.2.5) shall be enclosed with 1-hour fire-resistant construction and self-closing 20-minute labeled door or provided with an *automatic sprinkler system* and smoke resistant separation from other areas.

425.3.7 A building *fire alarm system* shall be provided in accordance with NFPA 72. Provisions shall be made to activate the internal evacuation alarm at all required exits.

425.3.8 Interior wall and ceiling finish shall be gypsum wallboard, plaster or other noncombustible material.

425.3.9 Unvented fuel-fired heaters, floor furnaces, and portable electric heaters shall not be installed.

425.3.10 Occupants younger than six years of age shall sleep on the level of exit discharge with adult supervision.

425.3.11 Every facility shall formulate an evacuation plan (in cooperation with the local fire department), for the protection of all persons in the event of fire, for their evacuation to areas of refuge and from the building when necessary.

425.4 Small nonambulatory care facilities. Facilities keeping no more than six adults or six children who are unable to respond and evacuate without assistance, when determined by the state agency having jurisdiction to be licensable, shall comply with the requirements for small residential care facilities.

425.4.1 The building shall be sprinklered with a wet pipe system in accordance with NFPA 13D with a 30-minute water supply, including bathrooms, toilets, closets, pantries, storage and utility spaces. The sprinkler system shall be monitored in accordance with Section 903.4 (Section 903.4, Exception 1 is not applicable in this occupancy.)

425.5 Large residential care facilities. Facilities keeping no more than 12 residents, when determined by the state agency having jurisdiction to be licensable, shall be classified as Group R-4, residential (*North Carolina Building Code*).

425.5.1 The *building* shall be of 1-hour fire-resistant construction, sprinklered with a wet pipe system in accordance with NFPA 13R, including bathrooms, toilets, closets, pantries, storage and utility spaces, and limited to one story in height. The sprinkler system shall be monitored in accordance with Section 903.4 (Section 903.4, Exception 1 is not applicable in this occupancy.)

425.5.2 The facility shall have two remotely located exits.

425.5.3 All doorways subject to use by residents shall have an egress width of not less than 32 inches (812.8 mm) when the door is in the open position.

425.5.4 Required *corridors, ramps*, and passageways shall have a clear width of not less than 6 feet (1828 mm) when serving as part of the *means of egress* from resident areas.

425.5.5 Buildings may have spaces open to the *corridor* provided:

1. Each area does not exceed 250 square feet (23.22 m^2).
2. The spaces are not used for patient sleeping rooms, treatment rooms, or incidental use areas as defined in Table 508.2.5.
3. The area is equipped with *smoke detectors*.
4. Not more than one such area is permitted in any one *smoke compartment* when *smoke compartments* are provided.
5. The area is arranged not to obstruct access to required exits.

425.5.6 Unless required otherwise by Section 425.5.8, *corridor* partitions and doors in *corridor* partitions need not have a *fire-resistance rating* but shall be designed to resist the passage of smoke. Doors shall be equipped with approved latches that will keep the door tightly closed. All doors except those to patient sleeping rooms shall be self-closing or automatic closing by smoke detection. Interior wall and ceiling finish shall be gypsum wallboard, plaster or other noncombustible material.

425.5.7 *Corridors* shall be provided with *smoke detectors*. *Heat detectors* shall be installed in all *attic* spaces. The *heat detectors* shall be connected to the fire alarm and detection system.

425.5.8 Any incidental use area shall comply with the requirements of Table 508.2.5.

425.5.9 A building *fire alarm system* shall be provided in accordance with NFPA 72. Provisions shall be made to activate the internal evacuation alarm at all required exits.

425.5.10 Every facility shall formulate an evacuation plan (in cooperation with the local fire department and community emergency planning authority) for the protection of all persons in the event of fire, for their evacuation to areas of refuge and from the *building* when necessary.

SECTION 426
LICENSED ADULT AND CHILD DAY CARE

426.1 Exits.

426.1.1 Location. Rooms where occupants receive care in Group I-4 and R-3 adult and child day care facilities shall be on the level of *exit discharge*.

426.1.2 Number of exits. Group E and R-4 adult and child day care facilities shall have two exits.

> **Exception:** Rooms where occupants receive care are located on the level of exit discharge and each of these rooms has an exit door directly to the exterior.

426.1.3 Walls and ceilings. All walls and ceilings in rooms that are used for day care purposes and are part of the exiting path shall have surfaces of noncombustible construction (plaster or gypsum wallboard).

426.2 Ventilation. Rooms where occupants receive care in R-4 adult and child day care facilities shall comply with the *ventilation* requirements of Section 1203 of this code.

426.3 Portable fire extinguishers. In Group R-3 and R-4 adult and child day care facilities, at least one 2-A:10-BC fire extinguisher shall be provided per floor with a maximum of 40 feet (12 192 mm) travel distance to the extinguisher.

SECTION 427
PRIVATE AND PUBLIC SCHOOLS

427.1 Boiler rooms in public schools. Every fuel storage room and boiler room shall be separated by 2-hour-rated construction. Door openings shall be to the exterior and all penetrations to the interior of the building shall be protected.

427.2 Open flame heating appliances in public schools. Every comfort heating appliance installed within a building which produces an unprotected open flame shall be separated by 2-hour-rated construction. Direct vent tubular infrared heaters installed in gymnasiums at a minimum height of 20 feet (6096 mm), measured from the finished floor to the bottom of the unit, shall be permitted.

427.3 Group E in churches, private schools and public schools. Rooms used for first grade children and younger shall be located on the *level of exit discharge*. Rooms used for second grade children shall not be located more than one *story* above the *level of exit discharge*.

CHAPTER 5

GENERAL BUILDING HEIGHTS AND AREAS

SECTION 501
GENERAL

501.1 Scope. The provisions of this chapter control the height and area of structures hereafter erected and additions to existing structures.

[F] 501.2 Address identification. New and existing buildings shall be provided with *approved* address numbers or letters. Each character shall be a minimum 4 inches (102 mm) high and a minimum of 0.5 inch (12.7 mm) wide. They shall be installed on a contrasting background and be plainly visible from the street or road fronting the property. Where access is by means of a private road and the building address cannot be viewed from the *public way*, a monument, pole or other *approved* sign or means shall be used to identify the structure.

SECTION 502
DEFINITIONS

502.1 Definitions. The following words and terms shall, for the purposes of this chapter and as used elsewhere in this code, have the meanings shown herein.

AREA, BUILDING. The area included within surrounding *exterior walls* (or *exterior walls* and *fire walls*) exclusive of vent shafts and courts. Areas of the building not provided with surrounding walls shall be included in the *building area* if such areas are included within the horizontal projection of the roof or floor above.

BASEMENT. A *story* that is not a *story above grade plane* (see "*Story above grade plane*" in Section 202).

The definition of "Basement" does not apply to the provisions of Section 1612 for flood loads (see "Basement" in Section 1612.2).

EQUIPMENT PLATFORM. An unoccupied, elevated platform used exclusively for mechanical systems or industrial process equipment, including the associated elevated walkways, *stairs*, *alternating tread devices* and ladders necessary to access the platform (see Section 505.5).

GRADE PLANE. A reference plane representing the average of finished ground level adjoining the building at *exterior walls*. Where the finished ground level slopes away from the *exterior walls*, the reference plane shall be established by the lowest points within the area between the building and the *lot line* or, where the *lot line* is more than 6 feet (1829 mm) from the building, between the building and a point 6 feet (1829 mm) from the building.

HEIGHT, BUILDING. The vertical distance from *grade plane* to the average height of the highest roof surface.

MEZZANINE. An intermediate level or levels between the floor and ceiling of any *story* and in accordance with Section 505.

SECTION 503
GENERAL BUILDING HEIGHT AND AREA LIMITATIONS

503.1 General. The *building height and area* shall not exceed the limits specified in Table 503 based on the type of construction as determined by Section 602 and the occupancies as determined by Section 302 except as modified hereafter. Each portion of a building separated by one or more *fire walls* complying with Section 706 shall be considered to be a separate building.

503.1.1 Special industrial occupancies. Buildings and structures designed to house special industrial processes that require large areas and unusual *building heights* to accommodate craneways or special machinery and equipment, including, among others, rolling mills; structural metal fabrication shops and foundries; or the production and distribution of electric, gas or steam power, shall be exempt from the *building height and area* limitations of Table 503.

503.1.2 Buildings on same lot. Two or more buildings on the same lot shall be regulated as separate buildings or shall be considered as portions of one building if the *building height* of each building and the aggregate *building area* of the buildings are within the limitations of Table 503 as modified by Sections 504 and 506. The provisions of this code applicable to the aggregate building shall be applicable to each building.

503.1.3 Type I construction. Buildings of Type I construction permitted to be of unlimited tabular building heights and areas are not subject to the special requirements that allow unlimited area buildings in Section 507 or unlimited *building height* in Sections 503.1.1 and 504.3 or increased *building heights and areas* for other types of construction.

SECTION 504
BUILDING HEIGHT

504.1 General. The *building height* permitted by Table 503 shall be increased in accordance with this section.

Exception: The *building height* of one-story aircraft hangars, aircraft paint hangars and buildings used for the manufacturing of aircraft shall not be limited if the building is provided with an automatic fire-extinguishing system in accordance with Chapter 9 and is entirely surrounded by *public ways* or *yards* not less in width than one and one-half times the *building height*.

TABLE 503
ALLOWABLE BUILDING HEIGHTS AND AREAS[a]
Building height limitations shown in feet above grade plane. Story limitations shown as stories above grade plane. Building area limitations shown in square feet, as determined by the definition of "Area, building," per story

GROUP		TYPE OF CONSTRUCTION								
		TYPE I		TYPE II		TYPE III		TYPE IV	TYPE V	
		A	B	A	B	A	B	HT	A	B
	HEIGHT (feet)	UL	160	65	55	65	55	65	50	40
	STORIES (S) AREA (A)									
A-1	S	UL	5	3	2	3	2	3	2	1
	A	UL	UL	15,500	8,500	14,000	8,500	15,000	11,500	5,500
A-2	S	UL	11	3	2	3	2	3	2	1
	A	UL	UL	15,500	9,500	14,000	9,500	15,000	11,500	6,000
A-3	S	UL	11	3	2	3	2	3	2	1
	A	UL	UL	15,500	9,500	14,000	9,500	15,000	11,500	6,000
A-4	S	UL	11	3	2	3	2	3	2	1
	A	UL	UL	15,500	9,500	14,000	9,500	15,000	11,500	6,000
A-5	S	UL	UL	UL	UL	UL	UL	UL	UL	UL
	A	UL	UL	UL	UL	UL	UL	UL	UL	UL
B	S	UL	11	5	3	5	3	5	3	2
	A	UL	UL	37,500	23,000	28,500	19,000	36,000	18,000	9,000
E	S	UL	5	3	2	3	2	3	1	1
	A	UL	UL	26,500	14,500	23,500	14,500	25,500	18,500	9,500
F-1	S	UL	11	4	2	3	2	4	2	1
	A	UL	UL	25,000	15,500	19,000	12,000	33,500	14,000	8,500
F-2	S	UL	11	5	3	4	3	5	3	2
	A	UL	UL	37,500	23,000	28,500	18,000	50,500	21,000	13,000
H-1	S	1	1	1	1	1	1	1	1	NP
	A	21,000	16,500	11,000	7,000	9,500	7,000	10,500	7,500	NP
H-2[d]	S	UL	3	2	1	2	1	2	1	1
	A	21,000	16,500	11,000	7,000	9,500	7,000	10,500	7,500	3,000
H-3[d]	S	UL	6	4	2	4	2	4	2	1
	A	UL	60,000	26,500	14,000	17,500	13,000	25,500	10,000	5,000
H-4	S	UL	7	5	3	5	3	5	3	2
	A	UL	UL	37,500	17,500	28,500	17,500	36,000	18,000	6,500
H-5	S	4	4	3	3	3	3	3	3	2
	A	UL	UL	37,500	23,000	28,500	19,000	36,000	18,000	9,000
I-1	S	UL	9	4	3	4	3	4	3	2
	A	UL	55,000	19,000	10,000	16,500	10,000	18,000	10,500	4,500
I-2	S	UL	4	2	1	1	NP	1	1	NP
	A	UL	UL	15,000	11,000	12,000	NP	12,000	9,500	NP
I-3	S	UL	4	2	1	2	1	2	2	1
	A	UL	UL	15,000	10,000	10,500	7,500	12,000	7,500	5,000
I-4	S	UL	5	3	2	3	2	3	1	1
	A	UL	60,500	26,500	13,000	23,500	13,000	25,500	18,500	9,000
M	S	UL	11	4	2	4	2	4	3	1
	A	UL	UL	21,500	12,500	18,500	12,500	20,500	14,000	9,000
R-1	S	UL	11	4	4	4	4	4	3	2
	A	UL	UL	24,000	16,000	24,000	16,000	20,500	12,000	7,000
R-2	S	UL	11	4	4	4	4	4	3	2
	A	UL	UL	24,000	16,000	24,000	16,000	20,500	12,000	7,000
R-3	S	UL	11	4	4	4	4	4	3	3
	A	UL	UL	UL	UL	UL	UL	UL	UL	UL
R-4	S	UL	11	4	4	4	4	4	3	2
	A	UL	UL	24,000	16,000	24,000	16,000	20,500	12,000	7,000
S-1	S	UL	11	4	2	3	2	4	3	1
	A	UL	48,000	26,000	17,500	26,000	17,500	25,500	14,000	9,000
S-2[b, c]	S	UL	11	5	3	4	3	5	4	2
	A	UL	79,000	39,000	26,000	39,000	26,000	38,500	21,000	13,500
U[c]	S	UL	5	4	2	3	2	4	2	1
	A	UL	35,500	19,000	8,500	14,000	8,500	18,000	9,000	5,500

For SI: 1 foot = 304.8 mm, 1 square foot = 0.0929 m^2.

A = building area per story, S = stories above grade plane, UL = Unlimited, NP = Not permitted.

a. See the following sections for general exceptions to Table 503:

1. Section 504.2, Allowable building height and story increase due to automatic sprinkler system installation.
2. Section 506.2, Allowable building area increase due to street frontage.
3. Section 506.3, Allowable building area increase due to automatic sprinkler system installation.
4. Section 507, Unlimited area buildings.

b. For open parking structures, see Section 406.3.

c. For private garages, see Section 406.1.

d. See Section 415.5 for limitations.

504.2 Automatic sprinkler system increase. Where a building is equipped throughout with an *approved automatic sprinkler system* in accordance with Section 903.3.1.1, the value specified in Table 503 for maximum *building height* is increased by 20 feet (6096 mm) and the maximum number of *stories* is increased by one. These increases are permitted in addition to the *building area* increase in accordance with Sections 506.2 and 506.3. For Group R buildings equipped throughout with an *approved automatic sprinkler system* in accordance with Section 903.3.1.2, the value specified in Table 503 for maximum *building height* is increased by 20 feet (6096 mm) and the maximum number of *stories* is increased by one, but shall not exceed 60 feet (18 288 mm) or four *stories*, respectively.

Exceptions:

1. Buildings, or portions of buildings, classified as a Group I-2 occupancy of Type IIB, III, IV or V construction.
2. Buildings, or portions of buildings, classified as a Group H-1, H-2, H-3 or H-5 occupancy.
3. *Fire-resistance rating* substitution in accordance with Table 601, Note d.

504.3 Roof structures. Towers, spires, steeples and other roof structures shall be constructed of materials consistent with the required type of construction of the building except where other construction is permitted by Section 1509.2.4. Such structures shall not be used for habitation or storage. The structures shall be unlimited in height if of noncombustible materials and shall not extend more than 20 feet (6096 mm) above the allowable *building height* if of combustible materials (see Chapter 15 for additional requirements).

SECTION 505
MEZZANINES

505.1 General. A *mezzanine* or *mezzanines* in compliance with Section 505 shall be considered a portion of the *story* in which it is contained. Such *mezzanines* shall not contribute to either the *building area* or number of *stories* as regulated by Section 503.1. The area of the *mezzanine* shall be included in determining the *fire area* defined in Section 902. The clear height above and below the *mezzanine* floor construction shall not be less than 7 feet (2134 mm).

505.2 Area limitation. The aggregate area of a *mezzanine* or *mezzanines* within a room shall not exceed one-third of the floor area of that room or space in which they are located. The enclosed portion of a room shall not be included in a determination of the floor area of the room in which the *mezzanine* is located. In determining the allowable *mezzanine* area, the area of the *mezzanine* shall not be included in the floor area of the room.

Exceptions:

1. The aggregate area of *mezzanines* in buildings and structures of Type I or II construction for special industrial occupancies in accordance with Section 503.1.1 shall not exceed two-thirds of the floor area of the room.
2. The aggregate area of *mezzanines* in buildings and structures of Type I or II construction shall not exceed one-half of the floor area of the room in buildings and structures equipped throughout with an *approved automatic sprinkler system* in accordance with Section 903.3.1.1 and an *approved* emergency voice/alarm communication system in accordance with Section 907.5.2.2.

505.3 Egress. Each occupant of a *mezzanine* shall have access to at least two independent *means of egress* where the *common path of egress travel* exceeds the limitations of Section 1014.3. Where a *stairway* provides a means of *exit access* from a *mezzanine*, the maximum travel distance includes the distance traveled on the *stairway* measured in the plane of the tread nosing. *Accessible means of egress* shall be provided in accordance with Section 1007.

Exception: A single *means of egress* shall be permitted in accordance with Section 1015.1.

505.4 Openness. A *mezzanine* shall be open and unobstructed to the room in which such *mezzanine* is located except for walls not more than 42 inches (1067 mm) high, columns and posts.

Exceptions:

1. *Mezzanines* or portions thereof are not required to be open to the room in which the *mezzanines* are located, provided that the *occupant load* of the aggregate area of the enclosed space does not exceed 10.
2. A *mezzanine* having two or more *means of egress* is not required to be open to the room in which the *mezzanine* is located if at least one of the *means of egress* provides direct access to an *exit* from the *mezzanine* level.
3. *Mezzanines* or portions thereof are not required to be open to the room in which the *mezzanines* are located, provided that the aggregate floor area of the enclosed space does not exceed 10 percent of the *mezzanine* area.
4. In industrial facilities, *mezzanines* used for control equipment are permitted to be glazed on all sides.
5. In occupancies other than Groups H and I, that are no more than two *stories* above *grade plane* and equipped throughout with an *automatic sprinkler system* in accordance with Section 903.3.1.1, a *mezzanine* having two or more *means of egress* shall not be required to be open to the room in which the *mezzanine* is located.

505.5 Equipment platforms. *Equipment platforms* in buildings shall not be considered as a portion of the floor below. Such *equipment platforms* shall not contribute to either the *building area* or the number of *stories* as regulated by Section 503.1. The area of the *equipment platform* shall not be included in determining the *fire area* in accordance with Section 903. *Equipment platforms* shall not be a part of any *mezzanine* and such platforms and the walkways, *stairs*, *alternating tread devices* and ladders providing access to an *equipment platform* shall not serve as a part of the *means of egress* from the building.

505.5.1 Area limitations. The aggregate area of all *equipment platforms* within a room shall not exceed two-thirds of the area of the room in which they are located. Where an *equipment platform* is located in the same room as a *mezzanine*, the area of the *mezzanine* shall be determined by Section 505.2 and the combined aggregate area of the *equipment platforms* and *mezzanines* shall not exceed two-thirds of the room in which they are located.

[F] 505.5.2 Fire suppression. Where located in a building that is required to be protected by an *automatic sprinkler system*, *equipment platforms* shall be fully protected by sprinklers above and below the platform, where required by the standards referenced in Section 903.3.

505.5.3 Guards. *Equipment platforms* shall have *guards* where required by Section 1013.1.

SECTION 506
BUILDING AREA MODIFICATIONS

506.1 General. The *building areas* limited by Table 503 shall be permitted to be increased due to frontage (I_f) and *automatic sprinkler system* protection (I_s) in accordance with the following:

$$A_a = \{A_t + [A_t \times I_f] + [A_t \times I_s]\} \quad \textbf{(Equation 5-1)}$$

where:

A_a = Allowable *building area* per *story* (square feet).

A_t = Tabular *building area* per *story* in accordance with Table 503 (square feet).

I_f = Area increase factor due to frontage as calculated in accordance with Section 506.2.

I_s = Area increase factor due to sprinkler protection as calculated in accordance with Section 506.3.

506.2 Frontage increase. Every building shall adjoin or have access to a *public way* to receive a *building area* increase for frontage. Where a building has more than 25 percent of its perimeter on a *public way* or open space having a minimum width of 20 feet (6096 mm), the frontage increase shall be determined in accordance with the following:

$$I_f = [F / P - 0.25]W / 30 \quad \textbf{(Equation 5-2)}$$

where:

I_f = Area increase due to frontage.

F = Building perimeter that fronts on a *public way* or open space having 20 feet (6096 mm) open minimum width (feet).

P = Perimeter of entire building (feet).

W = Width of *public way* or open space (feet) in accordance with Section 506.2.1.

506.2.1 Width limits. The value of W shall be at least 20 feet (6096 mm). Where the value of W varies along the perimeter of the building, the calculation performed in accordance with Equation 5-2 shall be based on the weighted average of each portion of *exterior wall* and open space where the value of W is greater than or equal to 20 feet (6096 mm). Where the value of W exceeds 30 feet (9144 mm), a value of 30 feet (9144 mm) shall be used in calculating the weighted average, regardless of the actual width of the open space. Where two or more buildings are on the same lot, W shall be measured from the exterior face of a building to the exterior face of an opposing building, as applicable.

Exception: The value of W divided by 30 shall be permitted to be a maximum of 2 when the building meets all requirements of Section 507 except for compliance with the 60-foot (18 288 mm) *public way* or *yard* requirement, as applicable.

506.2.2 Open space limits. Such open space shall be either on the same lot or dedicated for public use and shall be accessed from a street or *approved fire lane*.

506.3 Automatic sprinkler system increase. Where a building is equipped throughout with an *approved automatic sprinkler system* in accordance with Section 903.3.1.1, the *building area* limitation in Table 503 is permitted to be increased by an additional 200 percent ($I_s = 2$) for buildings with more than one *story above grade plane* and an additional 300 percent ($I_s = 3$) for buildings with no more than one *story above grade plane*. These increases are permitted in addition to the height and *story* increases in accordance with Section 504.2.

Exception: The *building area* limitation increases shall not be permitted for the following conditions:

1. The *automatic sprinkler system* increase shall not apply to *buildings* with an occupancy in Group H-1.
2. The *automatic sprinkler system* increase shall not apply to the *building area* of an occupancy in Group H-2 or H-3. For *buildings* containing such occupancies, the allowable *building area* shall be determined in accordance with Section 508.4.2, with the sprinkler system increase applicable only to the portions of the building not classified as Group H-2 or H-3.
3. *Fire-resistance rating* substitution in accordance with Table 601, Note d.

506.4 Single occupancy buildings with more than one story. The total allowable *building area* of a single occupancy building with more than one *story above grade plane* shall be determined in accordance with this section. The actual aggregate *building area* at all *stories* in the building shall not exceed the total allowable *building area*.

Exception: A single basement need not be included in the total allowable *building area*, provided such basement does not exceed the area permitted for a building with no more than one *story above grade plane*.

506.4.1 Area determination. The total allowable *building area* of a single occupancy building with more than one *story above grade plane* shall be determined by multiplying the allowable *building area* per *story* (A_a), as determined in Section 506.1, by the number of *stories above grade plane* as listed below:

1. For buildings with two *stories above grade plane*, multiply by 2;

2. For buildings with three or more *stories above grade plane*, multiply by 3; and
3. No *story* shall exceed the allowable *building area* per *story* (A_a), as determined in Section 506.1, for the occupancies on that *story*.

Exceptions:

1. Unlimited area buildings in accordance with Section 507.
2. The maximum *building area* of a building equipped throughout with an *automatic sprinkler system* in accordance with Section 903.3.1.2 shall be determined by multiplying the allowable *building area* per *story* (A_a), as determined in Section 506.1, by the number of *stories above grade plane*.

506.5 Mixed occupancy area determination. The total allowable *building area* for buildings containing mixed occupancies shall be determined in accordance with the applicable provisions of this section. A single basement need not be included in the total allowable *building area*, provided such basement does not exceed the area permitted for a building with no more than one *story above grade plane*.

506.5.1 No more than one story above grade plane. For buildings with no more than one *story above grade plane* and containing mixed occupancies, the total *building area* shall be determined in accordance with the applicable provisions of Section 508.1.

506.5.2 More than one story above grade plane. For buildings with more than one *story above grade plane* and containing mixed occupancies, each *story* shall individually comply with the applicable requirements of Section 508.1. For buildings with more than three *stories above grade plane*, the total *building area* shall be such that the aggregate sum of the ratios of the actual area of each *story* divided by the allowable area of such *stories* based on the applicable provisions of Section 508.1 shall not exceed 3.

SECTION 507
UNLIMITED AREA BUILDINGS

507.1 General. The area of buildings of the occupancies and configurations specified herein shall not be limited.

507.2 Nonsprinklered, one story. The area of a Group F-2 or S-2 building no more than one *story* in height shall not be limited when the building is surrounded and adjoined by *public ways* or *yards* not less than 60 feet (18 288 mm) in width.

507.3 Sprinklered, one story. The area of a Group B, F, M or S building no more than one *story above grade plane*, or a Group A-4 building no more than one *story* above *grade plane* of other than Type V construction, shall not be limited when the building is provided with an *automatic sprinkler system* throughout in accordance with Section 903.3.1.1 and is surrounded and adjoined by *public ways* or *yards* not less than 60 feet (18 288 mm) in width.

Exceptions:

1. Buildings and structures of Types I and II construction for rack storage facilities that do not have access by the public shall not be limited in height, provided that such buildings conform to the requirements of Sections 507.3, 903.3.1.1 and Chapter 23 of the *International Fire Code.*
2. The *automatic sprinkler system* shall not be required in areas occupied for indoor participant sports, such as tennis, skating, swimming and equestrian activities in occupancies in Group A-4, provided that:
   2.1. *Exit* doors directly to the outside are provided for occupants of the participant sports areas; and
   2.2. The building is equipped with a fire alarm system with manual fire alarm boxes installed in accordance with Section 907.

507.3.1 Mixed occupancy buildings with Groups A-1 and A-2. Group A-1 and A-2 occupancies of other than Type V construction shall be permitted within mixed occupancy buildings of unlimited area complying with Section 507.3, provided:

1. Group A-1 and A-2 occupancies are separated from other occupancies as required for separated occupancies in Section 508.4.4 with no reduction allowed in the *fire-resistance rating* of the separation based upon the installation of an *automatic sprinkler system*;
2. Each area of the portions of the building used for Group A-1 or A-2 occupancies shall not exceed the maximum allowable area permitted for such occupancies in Section 503.1; and
3. All *exit* doors from Group A-1 and A-2 occupancies shall discharge directly to the exterior of the building.

507.4 Two story. The area of a Group B, F, M or S building no more than two *stories* above *grade plane* shall not be limited when the building is equipped throughout with an *automatic sprinkler system* in accordance with Section 903.3.1.1, and is surrounded and adjoined by *public ways* or *yards* not less than 60 feet (18 288 mm) in width.

507.5 Reduced open space. The *public ways* or *yards* of 60 feet (18 288 mm) in width required in Sections 507.2, 507.3, 507.4, 507.6 and 507.11 shall be permitted to be reduced to not less than 40 feet (12 192 mm) in width provided all of the following requirements are met:

1. The reduced width shall not be allowed for more than 75 percent of the perimeter of the building.
2. The *exterior walls* facing the reduced width shall have a minimum *fire-resistance rating* of 3 hours.
3. Openings in the *exterior walls* facing the reduced width shall have opening protectives with a minimum *fire protection rating* of 3 hours.

507.6 Group A-3 buildings of Type II construction. The area of a Group A-3 building no more than one *story* above *grade plane*, used as a *place of religious worship*, community hall, dance hall, exhibition hall, gymnasium, lecture hall, indoor swimming pool or tennis court of Type II construction, shall not be limited when all of the following criteria are met:

1. The building shall not have a stage other than a platform.

2. The building shall be equipped throughout with an *automatic sprinkler system* in accordance with Section 903.3.1.1.
3. The building shall be surrounded and adjoined by *public ways* or *yards* not less than 60 feet (18 288 mm) in width.

507.7 Group A-3 buildings of Types III and IV construction. The area of a Group A-3 building no more than one *story above grade plane*, used as a *place of religious worship*, community hall, dance hall, exhibition hall, gymnasium, lecture hall, indoor swimming pool or tennis court of Type III or IV construction, shall not be limited when all of the following criteria are met:

1. The building shall not have a stage other than a platform.
2. The building shall be equipped throughout with an *automatic sprinkler system* in accordance with Section 903.3.1.1.
3. The assembly floor shall be located at or within 21 inches (533 mm) of street or grade level and all *exits* are provided with ramps complying with Section 1010.1 to the street or grade level.
4. The building shall be surrounded and adjoined by *public ways* or *yards* not less than 60 feet (18 288 mm) in width.

507.8 Group H occupancies. Group H-2, H-3 and H-4 occupancies shall be permitted in unlimited area buildings containing Group F and S occupancies, in accordance with Sections 507.3 and 507.4 and the limitations of this section. The aggregate floor area of the Group H occupancies located at the perimeter of the unlimited area building shall not exceed 10 percent of the area of the building nor the area limitations for the Group H occupancies as specified in Table 503 as modified by Section 506.2, based upon the percentage of the perimeter of each Group H floor area that fronts on a street or other unoccupied space. The aggregate floor area of Group H occupancies not located at the perimeter of the building shall not exceed 25 percent of the area limitations for the Group H occupancies as specified in Table 503. Group H occupancies shall be separated from the rest of the unlimited area building and from each other in accordance with Table 508.4. For two-story unlimited area buildings, the Group H occupancies shall not be located more than one *story above grade plane* unless permitted by the allowable height in stories and feet as set forth in Table 503 based on the type of construction of the unlimited area building.

507.9 Aircraft paint hangar. The area of a Group H-2 aircraft paint hangar no more than one *story above grade plane* shall not be limited where such aircraft paint hangar complies with the provisions of Section 412.6 and is surrounded and adjoined by *public ways* or *yards* not less in width than one and one-half times the *building height*.

507.10 Group E buildings. The area of a Group E building no more than one *story above grade plane*, of Type II, IIIA or IV construction, shall not be limited when all of the following criteria are met:

1. Each classroom shall have not less than two *means of egress*, with one of the *means of egress* being a direct *exit* to the outside of the building complying with Section 1020.
2. The building is equipped throughout with an *automatic sprinkler system* in accordance with Section 903.3.1.1.
3. The building is surrounded and adjoined by *public ways* or *yards* not less than 60 feet (18 288 mm) in width.

507.11 Motion picture theaters. In buildings of Type II construction, the area of a motion picture theater located on the first *story above grade plane* shall not be limited when the building is provided with an *automatic sprinkler system* throughout in accordance with Section 903.3.1.1 and is surrounded and adjoined by *public ways* or *yards* not less than 60 feet (18 288 mm) in width.

507.12 Covered mall buildings and anchor stores. The area of *covered mall buildings* and *anchor stores* not exceeding three *stories* in height that comply with Section 402.6 shall not be limited.

SECTION 508 MIXED USE AND OCCUPANCY

508.1 General. Each portion of a building shall be individually classified in accordance with Section 302.1. Where a building contains more than one occupancy group, the building or portion thereof shall comply with the applicable provisions of Section 508.2, 508.3 or 508.4, or a combination of these sections.

Exceptions:

1. Occupancies separated in accordance with Section 509.
2. Where required by Table 415.3.2, areas of Group H-1, H-2 and H-3 occupancies shall be located in a separate and detached building or structure.
3. Uses within live/work units, complying with Section 419, are not considered separate occupancies.

508.2 Accessory occupancies. Accessory occupancies are those occupancies that are ancillary to the main occupancy of the building or portion thereof. Accessory occupancies shall comply with the provisions of Sections 508.2.1 through 508.2.5.3.

508.2.1 Area limitations. Aggregate accessory occupancies shall not occupy more than 10 percent of the *building area* of the *story* in which they are located and shall not exceed the tabular values in Table 503, without *building area* increases in accordance with Section 506 for such accessory occupancies.

508.2.2 Occupancy classification. Accessory occupancies shall be individually classified in accordance with Section 302.1. The requirements of this code shall apply to each portion of the building based on the occupancy classification of that space.

508.2.3 Allowable building area and height. The allowable *building area and height* of the building shall be based on the allowable *building area and height* for the main occupancy in accordance with Section 503.1. The height of each accessory occupancy shall not exceed the tabular values in

Table 503, without increases in accordance with Section 504 for such accessory occupancies. The *building area* of the accessory occupancies shall be in accordance with Section 508.2.1.

508.2.4 Separation of occupancies. No separation is required between accessory occupancies and the main occupancy.

Exceptions:

1. Group H-2, H-3, H-4 and H-5 occupancies shall be separated from all other occupancies in accordance with Section 508.4.
2. Incidental accessory occupancies required to be separated or protected by Section 508.2.5.
3. Group I-1, R-1, R-2 and R-3 *dwelling units* and *sleeping units* shall be separated from other *dwelling* or *sleeping units* and from accessory occupancies contiguous to them in accordance with the requirements of Section 420.

508.2.5 Separation of incidental accessory occupancies. The incidental accessory occupancies listed in Table 508.2.5 shall be separated from the remainder of the building or equipped with an automatic fire-extinguishing system, or both, in accordance with Table 508.2.5.

Exceptions:

1. Incidental accessory occupancies within and serving a *dwelling unit* are not required to comply with this section.
2. The 1-hour incidental accessory occupancy separation of Group I-2 waste and linen rooms and Group I-2 storage rooms over 100 square feet (9.29 m^2) shall not be reduced.

TABLE 508.2.5
INCIDENTAL ACCESSORY OCCUPANCIES

ROOM OR AREA	SEPARATION AND/OR PROTECTION
Furnace room where any piece of equipment is over 400,000 Btu per hour input	1 hour or provide automatic fire-extinguishing system
Rooms with boilers where the largest piece of equipment is over 15 psi and 10 horsepower	1 hour or provide automatic fire-extinguishing system
Refrigerant machinery room	1 hour or provide automatic sprinkler system
Hydrogen cutoff rooms, not classified as Group H	1 hour in Group B, F, M, S and U occupancies; 2 hours in Group A, E, I and R occupancies.
Incinerator rooms	2 hours and automatic sprinkler system
Paint shops, not classified as Group H, located in occupancies other than Group F	2 hours; or 1 hour and provide automatic fire-extinguishing system
Laboratories and vocational shops, not classified as Group H, located in a Group E or I-2 occupancy	1 hour or provide automatic fire-extinguishing system
Laundry rooms over 100 square feet	1 hour or provide automatic fire-extinguishing system
Group I-3 cells equipped with padded surfaces	1 hour
Group I-2 waste and linen collection rooms	1 hour
Group I-2 storage rooms over 100 square feet	1 hour
Group I-2 commercial kitchens	Smoke resistant construction and doors
Group I-2 laundries equal to or less than 100 square feet	Smoke resistant construction and doors
Group I-2 rooms or spaces that contain fuel-fired heating equipment	Smoke resistant construction and doors
Waste and linen collection rooms over 100 square feet	1 hour or provide automatic fire-extinguishing system
Stationary storage battery systems having a liquid electrolyte capacity of more than 50 gallons, or a lithium-ion capacity of 1,000 pounds used for facility standby power, emergency power or uninterrupted power supplies	1 hour in Group B, F, M, S and U occupancies; 2 hours in Group A, E, I and R occupancies.
Rooms containing fire pumps in nonhigh-rise buildings	2 hours; or 1 hour and provide automatic sprinkler system throughout the building
Rooms containing fire pumps in high-rise buildings	2 hours

For SI: 1 square foot = 0.0929 m^2, 1 pound per square inch (psi) = 6.9 kPa, 1 British thermal unit (Btu) per hour = 0.293 watts, 1 horsepower = 746 watts, 1 gallon = 3.785 L.

508.2.5.1 Fire-resistance-rated separation. Where Table 508.2.5 specifies a fire-resistance-rated separation, the incidental accessory occupancies shall be separated from the remainder of the *building* by a *fire barrier* constructed in accordance with Section 707 or a *horizontal assembly* constructed in accordance with Section 712, or both. Construction supporting 1-hour fire-resistance-rated *fire barriers* or *horizontal assemblies* used for incidental accessory occupancy separations in buildings of Type IIB, IIIB and VB construction are not required to be fire-resistance rated unless required by other sections of this code.

508.2.5.2 Nonfire-resistance-rated separation and protection. Where Table 508.2.5 permits an automatic fire-extinguishing system without a *fire barrier*, the incidental accessory occupancies shall be separated from the remainder of the building by construction capable of resisting the passage of smoke. The walls shall extend from the top of the foundation or floor assembly below to the underside of the ceiling that is a component of a fire-resistance-rated floor assembly or roof assembly above or to the underside of the floor or roof sheathing, deck or slab above. Doors shall be self- or automatic-closing upon detection of smoke in accordance with Section 715.4.8.3. Doors shall not have air transfer openings and shall not be undercut in excess of the clearance permitted in accordance with NFPA 80. Walls surrounding the incidental accessory occupancy shall not have air transfer openings unless provided with smoke dampers in accordance with Section 711.7.

508.2.5.3 Protection. Except as specified in Table 508.2.5 for certain incidental accessory occupancies, where an automatic fire-extinguishing system or an *automatic sprinkler system* is provided in accordance with Table 508.2.5, only the space occupied by the incidental accessory occupancy need be equipped with such a system.

508.3 Nonseparated occupancies. Buildings or portions of buildings that comply with the provisions of this section shall be considered as nonseparated occupancies.

508.3.1 Occupancy classification. Nonseparated occupancies shall be individually classified in accordance with Section 302.1. The requirements of this code shall apply to each portion of the building based on the occupancy classification of that space except that the most restrictive applicable provisions of Section 403 and Chapter 9 shall apply to the building or portion thereof in which the nonseparated occupancies are located.

508.3.2 Allowable building area and height. The allowable *building area and height* of the building or portion thereof shall be based on the most restrictive allowances for the occupancy groups under consideration for the type of construction of the building in accordance with Section 503.1.

508.3.3 Separation. No separation is required between nonseparated occupancies.

Exceptions:

1. Group H-2, H-3, H-4 and H-5 occupancies shall be separated from all other occupancies in accordance with Section 508.4.
2. Group I-1, R-1, R-2 and R-3 *dwelling units* and *sleeping units* shall be separated from other *dwelling* or *sleeping units* and from other occupancies contiguous to them in accordance with the requirements of Section 420.

508.4 Separated occupancies. Buildings or portions of buildings that comply with the provisions of this section shall be considered as separated occupancies.

508.4.1 Occupancy classification. Separated occupancies shall be individually classified in accordance with Section 302.1. Each separated space shall comply with this code based on the occupancy classification of that portion of the building.

508.4.2 Allowable building area. In each *story*, the *building area* shall be such that the sum of the ratios of the actual *building area* of each separated occupancy divided by the allowable *building area* of each separated occupancy shall not exceed 1.

508.4.3 Allowable height. Each separated occupancy shall comply with the *building height* limitations based on the type of construction of the building in accordance with Section 503.1.

Exception: Special provisions permitted by Section 509.

508.4.4 Separation. Individual occupancies shall be separated from adjacent occupancies in accordance with Table 508.4.

508.4.4.1 Construction. Required separations shall be fire barriers constructed in accordance with Section 707 or horizontal assemblies constructed in accordance with Section 712, or both, so as to completely separate adjacent occupancies.

TABLE 508.4
REQUIRED SEPARATION OF OCCUPANCIES (hours)

OCCUPANCY		A[d]	B	E	F-1	F-2	H-1	H-2	H-3	H-4	H-5	I-1	I-2	I-3	I-4	M	R	S-1	S-2[b]	U
A[d]	S	2[e,g]	1	1	1	N	NP	3	2	2	2	1	2	1	1	1	1	1	N	N
	NS	2[e,g]	2	2	2	1	NP	4	3	3	3[a]	2	NP	2	2	2	2	2	1	1
B	S	1	2[e]	1	2	1	NP	2	1	1	1	1	2	1	1	1	1	2	1	1
	NS	2	2[e]	2	3	2	NP	3	2	2	2[a]	2	NP	2	2	2	2	3	2	2
E	S	1	1	2[e]	1	N	NP	3	2	2	2	1	2	1	1	1	1	1	N	N
	NS	2	2	2[e]	2	1	NP	4	3	3	3[a]	2	NP	2	2	2	2	2	1	1
F-1	S	1	2	1	3[e]	1	NP	2	1	1	1	1	2	1	1	2	1	2	1	1
	NS	2	3	2	3[e]	2	NP	3	2	2	2[a]	2	NP	2	2	3	2	3	2	2
F-2	S	N	1	N	1	2[e]	NP	3	2	2	2	1	2	1	1	1	1	1	1	1
	NS	1	2	1	2	2[e]	NP	4	3	3	3[a]	2	NP	2	2	2	2	2	2	2
H-1	S	NP	NP	NP	NP	NP	4[e]	NP	NP	NP	NP	NP	NP	NP	NP	NP	NP	NP	NP	NP
	NS	NP	NP	NP	NP	NP	**NP**	NP	NP	NP	NP	NP	NP	NP	NP	NP	NP	NP	NP	NP
H-2	S	3	2	3	2	3	NP	4[e]	1	1	1	3	3	3	3	2	3	2	3	3
	NS	4	3	4	3	4	NP	**NP**	NP	NP	NP	NP	NP	NP	NP	3	NP	3	4	4
H-3	S	2	1	2	1	2	NP	1	3[e]	1	1[f]	2	2	2	2	1	2	1	2	2
	NS	3	2	3	2	3	NP	NP	**NP**	NP	NP	NP	NP	NP	NP	2	NP	2	3	3
H-4	S	2	1	2	1	2	NP	1	1	2[e]	1[f]	2	2	2	2	1	2	1	2	2
	NS	3	2	3	2	3	NP	NP	NP	**NP**	NP	NP	NP	NP	NP	2	NP	2	3	3
H-5	S	2	1	2	1	2	NP	1	1[f]	1[f]	2[e,f]	2	2	2	2	1	2	1	2	2
	NS	3[a]	2[a]	3[a]	2[a]	3[a]	NP	NP	NP	NP	**NP**	NP	NP	NP	NP	2[a]	NP	2[a]	3[a]	3[a]
I-1	S	1	1	1	1	1	NP	3	2	2	2	2[e]	2	1	1	1	1	1	1	1
	NS	2	2	2	2	2	NP	NP	NP	NP	NP	2[e]	NP	2	2	2	NP	2	2	2
I-2	S	2	2	2	2	2	NP	3	2	2	2	2	2[e]	2	2	2	2	2	2	2
	NS	NP	NP	NP	NP	NP	NP	NP	NP	NP	NP	NP	**NP**	NP	NP	NP	NP	NP	NP	NP
I-3	S	1	1	1	1	1	NP	3	2	2	2	1	2	2[e]	1	1	1	1	1	1
	NS	2	2	2	2	2	NP	NP	NP	NP	NP	2	NP	**NP**	2	2	NP	2	2	2
I-4	S	1	1	1	1	1	NP	3	2	2	2	1	2	1	2[e]	1	1	1	1	1
	NS	2	2	2	2	2	NP	NP	NP	NP	NP	2	NP	2	**NP**	2	NP	2	2	2
M	S	1	1	1	2	1	NP	2	1	1	1	1	2	1	1	2[e]	1	2	1	1
	NS	2	2	2	3	2	NP	3	2	2	2[a]	2	NP	2	2	2[e]	2	3	2	2
R	S	1	1	1	1	1	NP	3	2	2	2	1	2	1	1	1	2[e,h]	1	1[c]	1[c]
	NS	2	2	2	2	2	NP	NP	NP	NP	NP	NP	NP	NP	NP	2	2[e,h]	2	2[c]	2[c]
S-1	S	1	2	1	2	1	NP	2	1	1	1	1	2	1	1	2	1	3[e]	1	1
	NS	2	3	2	3	2	NP	3	2	2	2[a]	2	NP	2	2	3	2	3[e]	2	2
S-2[b]	S	N	1	N	1	1	NP	3	2	2	2	1	2	1	1	1	1[c]	1	2[e]	1
	NS	1	2	1	2	2	NP	4	3	3	3[a]	2	NP	2	2	2	2[c]	2	2[e]	2
U	S	N	1	N	1	1	NP	3	2	2	2	1	2	1	1	1	1[c]	1	1	1[e]
	NS	1	2	1	2	2	NP	4	3	3	3[a]	2	NP	2	2	2	2[c]	2	2	1[e]

S = Buildings equipped throughout with an automatic sprinkler system installed in accordance with Section 903.3.1.1.

NS = Buildings not equipped throughout with an automatic sprinkler system installed in accordance with Section 903.3.1.1.

N = No separation requirement.

NP = Not permitted.

a. For Group H-5 occupancies, see Section 903.2.5.2.

b. The required separation from areas used only for private or pleasure vehicles shall be reduced by 1-hour but not less than 1 hour.

c. See Section 406.1.4.

d. Commercial kitchens need not be separated from the restaurant seating areas that they serve.

e. Separation is not required between occupancies of the same classification unless separated mixed use is implemented.

f. For Group H-5 occupancies, see Section 415.8.2.2.

g. Groups A-1, A-2, A-3, A-4 and A-5 must be separated by the designated fire-resistance rating unless they are to be nonseparated mixed use.

h. Groups R-1, R-2, R-3 and R-4 must be separated by the designated fire-resistance rating unless they are to be nonseparated mixed use.

SECTION 509
SPECIAL PROVISIONS

509.1 General. The provisions in this section shall permit the use of special conditions that are exempt from, or modify, the specific requirements of this chapter regarding the allowable heights and areas of buildings based on the occupancy classification and type of construction, provided the special condition complies with the provisions specified in this section for such condition and other applicable requirements of this code. The provisions of Sections 509.2 through 509.8 are to be considered independent and separate from each other.

509.2 Horizontal building separation allowance. A building shall be considered as separate and distinct buildings for the purpose of determining area limitations, continuity of *fire walls*, limitation of number of *stories* and type of construction where all of the following conditions are met:

1. The buildings are separated with a *horizontal assembly* having a minimum 3-hour *fire-resistance rating*.
2. The building below the *horizontal assembly* is no more than one *story above grade plane*.
3. The building below the *horizontal assembly* is of Type IA construction.
4. Shaft, *stairway*, ramp and escalator enclosures through the *horizontal assembly* shall have not less than a 2-hour *fire-resistance rating* with opening protectives in accordance with Section 715.4.

   Exception: Where the enclosure walls below the *horizontal assembly* have not less than a 3-hour *fire-resistance rating* with opening protectives in accordance with Section 715.4, the enclosure walls extending above the *horizontal assembly* shall be permitted to have a 1-hour *fire-resistance rating*, provided:

   1. The building above the *horizontal assembly* is not required to be of Type I construction;
   2. The enclosure connects less than four *stories*; and
   3. The enclosure opening protectives above the *horizontal assembly* have a minimum 1-hour *fire protection rating*.
5. The building or buildings above the *horizontal assembly* shall be permitted to have multiple Group A occupancy uses, each with an *occupant load* of less than 300, or Group B, M, R or S occupancies.
6. The building below the *horizontal assembly* shall be protected throughout by an *approved automatic sprinkler system* in accordance with Section 903.3.1.1, and shall be permitted to be any of the following occupancies:

   6.1. Group S-2 parking garage used for the parking and storage of private motor vehicles;

   6.2. Multiple Group A, each with an *occupant load* of less than 300;

   6.3. Group B;

   6.4. Group M;

   6.5. Group R; and

   6.6. Uses incidental to the operation of the building (including entry lobbies, mechanical rooms, storage areas and similar uses).
7. The maximum *building height* in feet (mm) shall not exceed the limits set forth in Section 503 for the building having the smaller allowable height as measured from the *grade plane*.

509.3 Group S-2 enclosed parking garage with Group S-2 open parking garage above. A Group S-2 enclosed parking garage with no more than one *story* above *grade plane* and located below a Group S-2 *open parking garage* shall be classified as a separate and distinct building for the purpose of determining the type of construction where all of the following conditions are met:

1. The allowable area of the building shall be such that the sum of the ratios of the actual area divided by the allowable area for each separate occupancy shall not exceed 1.
2. The Group S-2 enclosed parking garage is of Type I or II construction and is at least equal to the *fire-resistance* requirements of the Group S-2 *open parking garage*.
3. The height and the number of tiers of the Group S-2 *open parking garage* shall be limited as specified in Table 406.3.5.
4. The floor assembly separating the Group S-2 enclosed parking garage and Group S-2 *open parking garage* shall be protected as required for the floor assembly of the Group S-2 enclosed parking garage. Openings between the Group S-2 enclosed parking garage and Group S-2 *open parking garage*, except *exit* openings, shall not be required to be protected.
5. The Group S-2 enclosed parking garage is used exclusively for the parking or storage of private motor vehicles, but shall be permitted to contain an office, waiting room and toilet room having a total area of not more than 1,000 square feet (93 m^2), and mechanical equipment rooms incidental to the operation of the building.

509.4 Parking beneath Group R. Where a maximum one *story above grade plane* Group S-2 parking garage, enclosed or open, or combination thereof, of Type I construction or open of Type IV construction, with grade entrance, is provided under a building of Group R, the number of stories to be used in determining the minimum type of construction shall be measured from the floor above such a parking area. The floor assembly between the parking garage and the Group R above shall comply with the type of construction required for the parking garage and shall also provide a *fire-resistance rating* not less than the mixed occupancy separation required in Section 508.4.

509.5 Group R-1 and R-2 buildings of Type IIIA construction. The height limitation for buildings of Type IIIA construction in Groups R-1 and R-2 shall be increased to six *stories* and 75 feet (22 860 mm) where the first floor assembly above the basement has a *fire-resistance rating* of not less than 3 hours and the floor area is subdivided by 2-hour fire-resistance-rated *fire walls* into areas of not more than 3,000 square feet (279 m^2).

509.6 Group R-1 and R-2 buildings of Type IIA construction. The height limitation for buildings of Type IIA construction in Groups R-1 and R-2 shall be increased to nine *stories* and 100 feet (30 480 mm) where the building is separated by not less than 50 feet (15 240 mm) from any other building on the lot and from *lot lines*, the *exits* are segregated in an area enclosed by a 2-hour fire-resistance-rated *fire wall* and the first floor assembly has a *fire-resistance rating* of not less than $1^1/_2$ hours.

509.7 Open parking garage beneath Groups A, I, B, M and R. *Open parking garages* constructed under Groups A, I, B, M and R shall not exceed the height and area limitations permitted under Section 406.3. The height and area of the portion of the building above the *open parking garage* shall not exceed the limitations in Section 503 for the upper occupancy. The height, in both feet and stories, of the portion of the building above the *open parking garage* shall be measured from *grade plane* and shall include both the *open parking garage* and the portion of the building above the parking garage.

509.7.1 Fire separation. *Fire barriers* constructed in accordance with Section 707 or *horizontal assemblies* constructed in accordance with Section 712 between the parking occupancy and the upper occupancy shall correspond to the required *fire-resistance rating* prescribed in Table 508.4 for the uses involved. The type of construction shall apply to each occupancy individually, except that structural members, including main bracing within the *open* parking structure, which is necessary to support the upper occupancy, shall be protected with the more restrictive fire-resistance-rated assemblies of the groups involved as shown in Table 601. *Means of egress* for the upper occupancy shall conform to Chapter 10 and shall be separated from the parking occupancy by *fire barriers* having at least a 2-hour *fire-resistance rating* as required by Section 706 with self-closing doors complying with Section 715 or horizontal assemblies having at least a 2-hour *fire-resistance rating* as required by Section 712, with self-closing doors complying with Section 715. *Means of egress* from the *open parking garage* shall comply with Section 406.3.

509.8 Group B or M with Group S-2 open parking garage. Group B or M occupancies located no higher than the first *story* above *grade plane* shall be considered as a separate and distinct building for the purpose of determining the type of construction where all of the following conditions are met:

1. The buildings are separated with a *horizontal assembly* having a minimum 2-hour *fire-resistance rating*.
2. The occupancies in the building below the *horizontal assembly* are limited to Groups B and M.
3. The occupancy above the *horizontal assembly* is limited to a Group S-2 *open parking garage*.
4. The building below the *horizontal assembly* is of Type I or II construction but not less than the type of construction required for the Group S-2 *open parking garage* above.
5. The height and area of the building below the *horizontal assembly* does not exceed the limits set forth in Section 503.
6. The height and area of the Group S-2 *open parking garage* does not exceed the limits set forth in Section 406.3. The height, in both feet and stories, of the Group S-2 *open parking garage* shall be measured from *grade plane* and shall include the building below the *horizontal assembly*.
7. Exits serving the Group S-2 *open parking garage* discharge directly to a street or *public way* and are separated from the building below the *horizontal assembly* by 2-hour *fire barriers* constructed in accordance with Section 707 or 2-hour *horizontal assemblies* constructed in accordance with Section 712, or both.

509.9 Multiple buildings above Group S-2 parking garages. Where two or more buildings are provided above the *horizontal assembly* separating a Group S-2 *open* or closed *parking garage* from the buildings above in accordance with the special provisions in Sections 509.2, 509.3 or 509.8, the buildings above the *horizontal assembly* shall be regarded as separate and distinct buildings from each other and shall comply with all other provisions of this code as applicable to each separate and distinct building.

CHAPTER 6

TYPES OF CONSTRUCTION

SECTION 601 GENERAL

601.1 Scope. The provisions of this chapter shall control the classification of buildings as to type of construction.

SECTION 602 CONSTRUCTION CLASSIFICATION

602.1 General. Buildings and structures erected or to be erected, altered or extended in height or area shall be classified in one of the five construction types defined in Sections 602.2 through 602.5. The building elements shall have a *fire-resistance rating* not less than that specified in Table 601 and exterior walls shall have a *fire-resistance rating* not less than that specified in Table 602. Where required to have a *fire-resistance rating* by Table 601, building elements shall comply with the applicable provisions of Section 703.2. The protection of openings, ducts and air transfer openings in building elements shall not be required unless required by other provisions of this code.

602.1.1 Minimum requirements. A building or portion thereof shall not be required to conform to the details of a type of construction higher than that type which meets the minimum requirements based on occupancy even though certain features of such a building actually conform to a higher type of construction.

602.2 Types I and II. Types I and II construction are those types of construction in which the building elements listed in Table 601 are of noncombustible materials, except as permitted in Section 603 and elsewhere in this code.

602.3 Type III. Type III construction is that type of construction in which the exterior walls are of noncombustible materials and the interior building elements are of any material permitted by this code. *Fire-retardant-treated wood* framing complying with Section 2303.2 shall be permitted within *exterior wall* assemblies of a 2-hour rating or less.

602.4 Type IV. Type IV construction (Heavy Timber, HT) is that type of construction in which the exterior walls are of noncombustible materials and the interior building elements are of solid or laminated wood without concealed spaces. The

TABLE 601
FIRE-RESISTANCE RATING REQUIREMENTS FOR BUILDING ELEMENTS (hours)

BUILDING ELEMENT	TYPE I		TYPE II		TYPE III		TYPE IV	TYPE V	
	A	B	A[d]	B	A[d]	B	HT	A[d]	B
Primary structural frame[g] (see Section 202)	3[a]	2[a]	1	0	1	0	HT	1	0
Bearing walls									
Exterior[f, g]	3	2	1	0	2	2	2	1	0
Interior	3[a]	2[a]	1	0	1	0	1/HT	1	0
Nonbearing walls and partitions Exterior	See Table 602								
Nonbearing walls and partitions Interior[e]	0	0	0	0	0	0	See Section 602.4.6	0	0
Floor construction and secondary members (see Section 202)	2	2	1	0	1	0	HT	1	0
Roof construction and secondary members (see Section 202)	$1^1/_2$[b]	1[b, c]	1[b, c]	0[c]	1[b, c]	0	HT	1[b, c]	0

For SI: 1 foot = 304.8 mm.

a. Roof supports: Fire-resistance ratings of primary structural frame and bearing walls are permitted to be reduced by 1 hour where supporting a roof only.

b. Except in Group F-1, H, M and S-1 occupancies, fire protection of structural members shall not be required, including protection of roof framing and decking where every part of the roof construction is 20 feet or more above any floor immediately below. Fire-retardant-treated wood members shall be allowed to be used for such unprotected members.

c. In all occupancies, heavy timber shall be allowed where a 1-hour or less fire-resistance rating is required.

d. An approved automatic sprinkler system in accordance with Section 903.3.1.1 shall be allowed to be substituted for 1-hour fire-resistance-rated construction, provided such system is not otherwise required by other provisions of the code or used for an allowable area increase in accordance with Section 506.3 or an allowable height increase in accordance with Section 504.2. The 1-hour substitution for the fire resistance of exterior walls shall not be permitted.

e. Not less than the fire-resistance rating required by other sections of this code.

f. Not less than the fire-resistance rating based on fire separation distance (see Table 602).

g. Not less than the fire-resistance rating as referenced in Section 704.10

details of Type IV construction shall comply with the provisions of this section. *Fire-retardant-treated wood* framing complying with Section 2303.2 shall be permitted within exterior wall assemblies with a 2-hour rating or less. Minimum solid sawn nominal dimensions are required for structures built using Type IV construction (HT). For glued-laminated members the equivalent net finished width and depths corresponding to the minimum nominal width and depths of solid sawn lumber are required as specified in Table 602.4.

602.4.1 Columns. Wood columns shall be sawn or glued laminated and shall not be less than 8 inches (203 mm), nominal, in any dimension where supporting floor loads and not less than 6 inches (152 mm) nominal in width and not less than 8 inches (203 mm) nominal in depth where supporting roof and ceiling loads only. Columns shall be continuous or superimposed and connected in an *approved* manner.

602.4.2 Floor framing. Wood beams and girders shall be of sawn or glued-laminated timber and shall be not less than 6 inches (152 mm) nominal in width and not less than 10 inches (254 mm) nominal in depth. Framed sawn or glued-laminated timber arches, which spring from the floor line and support floor loads, shall be not less than 8 inches (203 mm) nominal in any dimension. Framed timber trusses supporting floor loads shall have members of not less than 8 inches (203 mm) nominal in any dimension.

602.4.3 Roof framing. Wood-frame or glued-laminated arches for roof construction, which spring from the floor line or from grade and do not support floor loads, shall have members not less than 6 inches (152 mm) nominal in width and have not less than 8 inches (203 mm) nominal in depth for the lower half of the height and not less than 6 inches (152 mm) nominal in depth for the upper half. Framed or glued-laminated arches for roof construction that spring from the top of walls or wall abutments, framed timber trusses and other roof framing, which do not support floor loads, shall have members not less than 4 inches (102 mm) nominal in width and not less than 6 inches (152 mm) nominal in depth. Spaced members shall be permitted to be composed of two or more pieces not less than 3 inches (76 mm) nominal in thickness where blocked solidly throughout their intervening spaces or where spaces are tightly closed by a continuous wood cover plate of not less than 2 inches (51 mm) nominal in thickness secured to the underside of the members. Splice plates shall be not less than 3 inches (76 mm) nominal in thickness. Where protected by *approved* automatic sprinklers under the roof deck, framing members shall be not less than 3 inches (76 mm) nominal in width.

TABLE 602
FIRE-RESISTANCE RATING REQUIREMENTS FOR EXTERIOR WALLS BASED ON FIRE SEPARATION DISTANCE[a, e]

FIRE SEPARATION DISTANCE = X (feet)	TYPE OF CONSTRUCTION	OCCUPANCY GROUP H[f]	OCCUPANCY GROUP F-1, M, S-1[g]	OCCUPANCY GROUP A, B, E, F-2, I, R, S-2[g], U[b]
$X < 5$[c]	All	3	2	1
$5 \leq X < 10$	IA Others	3 2	2 1	1 1
$10 \leq X < 30$	IA, IB IIB, VB Others	2 1 1	1 0 1	1[d] 0 1[d]
$X \geq 30$	All	0	0	0

For SI: 1 foot = 304.8 mm.

a. Load-bearing exterior walls shall also comply with the fire-resistance rating requirements of Table 601.

b. For special requirements for Group U occupancies, see Section 406.1.2.

c. See Section 706.1.1 for party walls.

d. Open parking garages complying with Section 406 shall not be required to have a fire-resistance rating.

e. The fire-resistance rating of an exterior wall is determined based upon the fire separation distance of the exterior wall and the story in which the wall is located.

f. For special requirements for Group H occupancies, see Section 415.3.

g. For special requirements for Group S aircraft hangars, see Section 412.4.1.

TABLE 602.4
WOOD MEMBER SIZE

MINIMUM NOMINAL SOLID SAWN SIZE		MINIMUM GLUED-LAMINATED NET SIZE	
Width, inch	Depth, inch	Width, inch	Depth, inch
8	8	$6\,^3/_4$	$8^1/_4$
6	10	5	$10^1/_2$
6	8	5	$8^1/_4$
6	6	5	6
4	6	3	$6\,^7/_8$

For SI: 1 inch = 25.4 mm.

602.4.4 Floors. Floors shall be without concealed spaces. Wood floors shall be of sawn or glued-laminated planks, splined or tongue-and-groove, of not less than 3 inches (76 mm) nominal in thickness covered with 1-inch (25 mm) nominal dimension tongue-and-groove flooring, laid crosswise or diagonally, or 0.5-inch (12.7 mm) particleboard or planks not less than 4 inches (102 mm) nominal in width set on edge close together and well spiked and covered with 1-inch (25 mm) nominal dimension flooring or $^{15}/_{32}$-inch (12 mm) wood structural panel or 0.5-inch (12.7 mm) particleboard. The lumber shall be laid so that no continuous line of joints will occur except at points of support. Floors shall not extend closer than 0.5 inch (12.7 mm) to walls. Such 0.5-inch (12.7 mm) space shall be covered by a molding fastened to the wall and so arranged that it will not obstruct the swelling or shrinkage movements of the floor. Corbeling of masonry walls under the floor shall be permitted to be used in place of molding.

602.4.5 Roofs. Roofs shall be without concealed spaces and wood roof decks shall be sawn or glued laminated, splined or tongue-and-groove plank, not less than 2 inches (51 mm) nominal in thickness, $1^{1}/_{8}$-inch-thick (32 mm) wood structural panel (exterior glue), or of planks not less than 3 inches (76 mm) nominal in width, set on edge close together and laid as required for floors. Other types of decking shall be permitted to be used if providing equivalent *fire resistance* and structural properties.

602.4.6 Partitions. Partitions shall be of solid wood construction formed by not less than two layers of 1-inch (25 mm) matched boards or laminated construction 4 inches (102 mm) thick, or of 1-hour fire-resistance-rated construction.

602.4.7 Exterior structural members. Where a horizontal separation of 20 feet (6096 mm) or more is provided, wood columns and arches conforming to heavy timber sizes shall be permitted to be used externally.

602.5 Type V. Type V construction is that type of construction in which the structural elements, *exterior walls* and interior walls are of any materials permitted by this code.

SECTION 603
COMBUSTIBLE MATERIAL IN TYPE I AND II CONSTRUCTION

603.1 Allowable materials. Combustible materials shall be permitted in buildings of Type I or II construction in the following applications and in accordance with Sections 603.1.1 through 603.1.3:

1. *Fire-retardant-treated wood* shall be permitted in:
   - 1.1. Nonbearing partitions where the required *fire-resistance rating* is 2 hours or less.
   - 1.2. Nonbearing *exterior walls* where no fire rating is required.
   - 1.3. Roof construction, including girders, trusses, framing and decking.

     Exception: In buildings of Type IA construction exceeding two *stories above grade plane*, *fire-retardant-treated wood* is not permitted in roof construction when the vertical distance from the upper floor to the roof is less than 20 feet (6096 mm).
2. Thermal and acoustical insulation, other than foam plastics, having a *flame spread index* of not more than 25.

   Exceptions:

   1. Insulation placed between two layers of noncombustible materials without an intervening airspace shall be allowed to have a *flame spread index* of not more than 100.
   2. Insulation installed between a finished floor and solid decking without intervening airspace shall be allowed to have a *flame spread index* of not more than 200.
3. Foam plastics in accordance with Chapter 26.
4. Roof coverings that have an A, B or C classification.
5. *Interior floor finish* and floor covering materials installed in accordance with Section 804.
6. Millwork such as doors, door frames, window sashes and frames.
7. *Interior wall and ceiling finishes* installed in accordance with Sections 801 and 803.
8. *Trim* installed in accordance with Section 806.
9. Where not installed over 15 feet (4572 mm) above grade, show windows, nailing or furring strips and wooden bulkheads below show windows, including their frames, aprons and show cases.
10. Finish flooring installed in accordance with Section 805.
11. Partitions dividing portions of stores, offices or similar places occupied by one tenant only and that do not establish a *corridor* serving an *occupant load* of 30 or more shall be permitted to be constructed of *fire-retardant-treated wood*, 1-hour fire-resistance-rated construction or of wood panels or similar light construction up to 6 feet (1829 mm) in height.
12. Stages and platforms constructed in accordance with Sections 410.3 and 410.4, respectively.
13. Combustible *exterior wall coverings*, balconies and similar projections and bay or oriel windows in accordance with Chapter 14.
14. Blocking such as for handrails, millwork, cabinets and window and door frames.
15. Light-transmitting plastics as permitted by Chapter 26.
16. Mastics and caulking materials applied to provide flexible seals between components of *exterior wall* construction.
17. Exterior plastic veneer installed in accordance with Section 2605.2.
18. Nailing or furring strips as permitted by Section 803.4.

19. Heavy timber as permitted by Note c to Table 601 and Sections 602.4.7 and 1406.3.
20. Aggregates, component materials and admixtures as permitted by Section 703.2.2.
21. Sprayed fire-resistant materials and intumescent and mastic fire-resistant coatings, determined on the basis of *fire-resistance* tests in accordance with Section 703.2 and installed in accordance with Sections 1704.12 and 1704.13, respectively.
22. Materials used to protect penetrations in fire-resistance-rated assemblies in accordance with Section 713.
23. Materials used to protect joints in fire-resistance-rated assemblies in accordance with Section 714.
24. Materials allowed in the concealed spaces of buildings of Types I and II construction in accordance with Section 717.5.
25. Materials exposed within plenums complying with Section 602 of the *International Mechanical Code*.

603.1.1 Ducts. The use of nonmetallic ducts shall be permitted when installed in accordance with the limitations of the *International Mechanical Code*.

603.1.2 Piping. The use of combustible piping materials shall be permitted when installed in accordance with the limitations of the *International Mechanical Code* and the *International Plumbing Code*.

603.1.3 Electrical. The use of electrical wiring methods with combustible insulation, tubing, raceways and related components shall be permitted when installed in accordance with the limitations of this code.

CHAPTER 7

FIRE AND SMOKE PROTECTION FEATURES

SECTION 701 GENERAL

701.1 Scope. The provisions of this chapter shall govern the materials, systems and assemblies used for structural *fire resistance* and fire-resistance-rated construction separation of adjacent spaces to safeguard against the spread of fire and smoke within a building and the spread of fire to or from buildings.

SECTION 702 DEFINITIONS

702.1 Definitions. The following words and terms shall, for the purposes of this chapter, and as used elsewhere in this code, have the meanings shown herein.

ANNULAR SPACE. The opening around the penetrating item.

BUILDING ELEMENT. A fundamental component of building construction, listed in Table 601, which may or may not be of fire-resistance-rated construction and is constructed of materials based on the building type of construction.

CEILING RADIATION DAMPER. A *listed* device installed in a ceiling membrane of a fire-resistance-rated floor/ceiling or roof/ceiling assembly to limit automatically the radiative heat transfer through an air inlet/outlet opening.

COMBINATION FIRE/SMOKE DAMPER. A *listed* device installed in ducts and air transfer openings designed to close automatically upon the detection of heat and resist the passage of flame and smoke. The device is installed to operate automatically, controlled by a smoke detection system, and where required, is capable of being positioned from a fire command center.

DAMPER. See "*Ceiling radiation damper*," "*Combination fire/smoke damper*," "*Fire damper*" and "*Smoke damper*."

DRAFTSTOP. A material, device or construction installed to restrict the movement of air within open spaces of concealed areas of building components such as crawl spaces, floor/ceiling assemblies, roof/ceiling assemblies and *attics*.

F RATING. The time period that the *through-penetration firestop system* limits the spread of fire through the penetration when tested in accordance with ASTM E 814 or UL 1479.

FIRE BARRIER. A fire-resistance-rated wall assembly of materials designed to restrict the spread of fire in which continuity is maintained.

FIRE DAMPER. A *listed* device installed in ducts and air transfer openings designed to close automatically upon detection of heat and resist the passage of flame. *Fire dampers* are classified for use in either static systems that will automatically shut down in the event of a fire, or in dynamic systems that continue to operate during a fire. A dynamic *fire damper* is tested and rated for closure under elevated temperature airflow.

FIRE DOOR. The door component of a *fire door* assembly.

FIRE DOOR ASSEMBLY. Any combination of a *fire door*, frame, hardware and other accessories that together provide a specific degree of fire protection to the opening.

FIRE PARTITION. A vertical assembly of materials designed to restrict the spread of fire in which openings are protected.

FIRE PROTECTION RATING. The period of time that an opening protective will maintain the ability to confine a fire as determined by tests prescribed in Section 715. Ratings are stated in hours or minutes.

FIRE RESISTANCE. That property of materials or their assemblies that prevents or retards the passage of excessive heat, hot gases or flames under conditions of use.

FIRE-RESISTANCE RATING. The period of time a building element, component or assembly maintains the ability to confine a fire, continues to perform a given structural function, or both, as determined by the tests, or the methods based on tests, prescribed in Section 703.

FIRE-RESISTANT JOINT SYSTEM. An assemblage of specific materials or products that are designed, tested and fire-resistance rated in accordance with either ASTM E 1966 or UL 2079 to resist for a prescribed period of time the passage of fire through joints made in or between fire-resistance-rated assemblies.

FIRE SEPARATION DISTANCE. The distance measured from the building face to one of the following:

1. The closest interior *lot line*;
2. To the centerline of a street, an alley or public way; or
3. To an imaginary line between two buildings on the property.

The distance shall be measured at right angles from the face of the wall.

FIRE WALL. A fire-resistance-rated wall having protected openings, which restricts the spread of fire and extends continuously from the foundation to or through the roof, with sufficient structural stability under fire conditions to allow collapse of construction on either side without collapse of the wall.

FIRE WINDOW ASSEMBLY. A window constructed and glazed to give protection against the passage of fire.

FIREBLOCKING. Building materials or materials approved for use as fireblocking, installed to resist the free passage of flame to other areas of the building through concealed spaces.

FLOOR FIRE DOOR ASSEMBLY. A combination of a *fire door*, a frame, hardware and other accessories installed in a horizontal plane, which together provide a specific degree of fire protection to a through-opening in a fire-resistance-rated floor (see Section 712.8).

HORIZONTAL ASSEMBLY. A fire-resistance-rated floor or roof assembly of materials designed to restrict the spread of fire in which continuity is maintained.

JOINT. The linear opening in or between adjacent fire-resistance-rated assemblies that is designed to allow independent movement of the building in any plane caused by thermal, seismic, wind or any other loading.

MEMBRANE PENETRATION. An opening made through one side (wall, floor or ceiling membrane) of an assembly.

MEMBRANE-PENETRATION FIRESTOP. A material, device or construction installed to resist for a prescribed time period the passage of flame and heat through openings in a protective membrane in order to accommodate cables, cable trays, conduit, tubing, pipes or similar items.

MINERAL FIBER. Insulation composed principally of fibers manufactured from rock, slag or glass, with or without binders.

MINERAL WOOL. Synthetic vitreous fiber insulation made by melting predominately igneous rock or furnace slag, and other inorganic materials, and then physically forming the melt into fibers.

PENETRATION FIRESTOP. A through-penetration firestop or a *membrane-penetration firestop*.

SELF-CLOSING. As applied to a *fire door* or other opening protective, means equipped with an device that will ensure closing after having been opened.

SHAFT. An enclosed space extending through one or more *stories* of a building, connecting vertical openings in successive floors, or floors and roof.

SHAFT ENCLOSURE. The walls or construction forming the boundaries of a shaft.

SMOKE BARRIER. A continuous membrane, either vertical or horizontal, such as a wall, floor or ceiling assembly, that is designed and constructed to restrict the movement of smoke.

SMOKE COMPARTMENT. A space within a building enclosed by *smoke barriers* on all sides, including the top and bottom.

SMOKE DAMPER. A *listed* device installed in ducts and air transfer openings designed to resist the passage of smoke. The device is installed to operate automatically, controlled by a smoke detection system, and where required, is capable of being positioned from a fire command center.

SPLICE. The result of a factory and/or field method of joining or connecting two or more lengths of a *fire-resistant joint system* into a continuous entity.

T RATING. The time period that the penetration firestop system, including the penetrating item, limits the maximum temperature rise to 325°F (163°C) above its initial temperature through the penetration on the nonfire side when tested in accordance with ASTM E 814 or UL 1479.

THROUGH PENETRATION. An opening that passes through an entire assembly.

THROUGH-PENETRATION FIRESTOP SYSTEM. An assemblage of specific materials or products that are designed, tested and fire-resistance rated to resist for a prescribed period of time the spread of fire *through penetrations*. The F and T rating criteria for penetration firestop systems shall be in accordance with ASTM E 814 or UL 1479. See definitions of "F rating" and "T rating."

SECTION 703
FIRE-RESISTANCE RATINGS AND FIRE TESTS

703.1 Scope. Materials prescribed herein for *fire resistance* shall conform to the requirements of this chapter.

703.2 Fire-resistance ratings. The *fire-resistance rating* of building elements, components or assemblies shall be determined in accordance with the test procedures set forth in ASTM E 119 or UL 263 or in accordance with Section 703.3. Where materials, systems or devices that have not been tested as part of a fire-resistance-rated assembly are incorporated into the building element, component or assembly, sufficient data shall be made available to the *building official* to show that the required *fire-resistance rating* is not reduced. Materials and methods of construction used to protect joints and penetrations in fire-resistance-rated building elements, components or assemblies shall not reduce the required *fire-resistance rating*.

Exception: In determining the *fire-resistance rating* of exterior bearing walls, compliance with the ASTM E 119 or UL 263 criteria for unexposed surface temperature rise and ignition of cotton waste due to passage of flame or gases is required only for a period of time corresponding to the required *fire-resistance rating* of an exterior nonbearing wall with the same *fire separation distance*, and in a building of the same group. When the *fire-resistance rating* determined in accordance with this exception exceeds the *fire-resistance rating* determined in accordance with ASTM E 119 or UL 263, the fire exposure time period, water pressure and application duration criteria for the hose stream test of ASTM E 119 or UL 263 shall be based upon the *fire-resistance rating* determined in accordance with this exception.

703.2.1 Nonsymmetrical wall construction. Interior walls and partitions of nonsymmetrical construction shall be tested with both faces exposed to the furnace, and the assigned *fire-resistance rating* shall be the shortest duration obtained from the two tests conducted in compliance with ASTM E 119 or UL 263. When evidence is furnished to show that the wall was tested with the least fire-resistant side exposed to the furnace, subject to acceptance of the *building official*, the wall need not be subjected to tests from the opposite side (see Section 705.5 for *exterior walls*).

703.2.2 Combustible components. Combustible aggregates are permitted in gypsum and portland cement concrete mixtures for fire-resistance-rated construction. Any component material or admixture is permitted in assemblies if the resulting tested assembly meets the fire-resistance test requirements of this code.

703.2.3 Restrained classification. Fire-resistance-rated assemblies tested under ASTM E 119 or UL 263 shall not be considered to be restrained unless evidence satisfactory to the *building official* is furnished by the *registered design professional* showing that the construction qualifies for a restrained classification in accordance with ASTM E 119 or UL 263. Restrained construction shall be identified on the plans.

703.3 Alternative methods for determining fire resistance. The application of any of the alternative methods listed in this section shall be based on the fire exposure and acceptance criteria specified in ASTM E 119 or UL 263. The required *fire resistance* of a building element, component or assembly shall be permitted to be established by any of the following methods or procedures:

1. Fire-resistance designs documented in sources.
2. Prescriptive designs of fire-resistance-rated building elements, components or assemblies as prescribed in Section 720.
3. Calculations in accordance with Section 721.
4. Engineering analysis based on a comparison of building element, component or assemblies designs having *fire-resistance ratings* as determined by the test procedures set forth in ASTM E 119 or UL 263.
5. Alternative protection methods as allowed by Section 104.11.

703.4 Noncombustibility tests. The tests indicated in Sections 703.4.1 and 703.4.2 shall serve as criteria for acceptance of building materials as set forth in Sections 602.2, 602.3 and 602.4 in Type I, II, III and IV construction. The term "noncombustible" does not apply to the flame spread characteristics of *interior finish* or *trim* materials. A material shall not be classified as a noncombustible building construction material if it is subject to an increase in combustibility or flame spread beyond the limitations herein established through the effects of age, moisture or other atmospheric conditions.

703.4.1 Elementary materials. Materials required to be noncombustible shall be tested in accordance with ASTM E 136.

703.4.2 Composite materials. Materials having a structural base of noncombustible material as determined in accordance with Section 703.4.1 with a surfacing not more than 0.125 inch (3.18 mm) thick that has a *flame spread index* not greater than 50 when tested in accordance with ASTM E 84 or UL 723 shall be acceptable as noncombustible materials.

703.5 Fire-resistance-rated glazing. Fire-resistance-rated glazing, when tested in accordance with ASTM E 119 or UL 263 and complying with the requirements of Section 707, shall be permitted. Fire-resistance-rated glazing shall bear a *label* or other identification showing the name of the manufacturer, the test standard and the identifier "W-XXX," where the "XXX" is the *fire-resistance rating* in minutes. Such *label* or identification shall be issued by an agency and shall be permanently affixed to the glazing.

703.6 Marking and identification. *Fire walls*, *fire barriers*, *fire partitions*, *smoke barriers* and smoke partitions or any other wall required to have protected openings or penetrations shall be effectively and permanently identified with signs or stenciling. Such identification shall:

1. Be located in accessible concealed floor, floor-ceiling or *attic* spaces;
2. Be repeated at intervals not exceeding 30 feet (914 mm) measured horizontally along the wall or partition; and
3. Include lettering not less than 0.5 inch (12.7 mm) in height, incorporating the suggested wording: "FIRE AND/OR SMOKE BARRIER—PROTECT ALL OPENINGS," or other wording.

   Exception: Walls in Group R-2 occupancies that do not have a removable decorative ceiling allowing access to the concealed space.

SECTION 704 FIRE-RESISTANCE RATING OF STRUCTURAL MEMBERS

704.1 Requirements. The *fire-resistance ratings* of structural members and assemblies shall comply with this section and the requirements for the type of construction as specified in Table 601. The *fire-resistance ratings* shall not be less than the ratings required for the fire-resistance-rated assemblies supported by the structural members.

Exception: *Fire barriers*, *fire partitions*, *smoke barriers* and *horizontal assemblies* as provided in Sections 707.5, 709.4, 710.4 and 712.4, respectively.

704.2 Column protection. Where columns are required to be fire-resistance rated, the entire column shall be provided individual encasement protection by protecting it on all sides for the full column length, including connections to other structural members, with materials having the required *fire-resistance rating*. Where the column extends through a ceiling, the encasement protection shall be continuous from the top of the foundation or floor/ceiling assembly below through the ceiling space to the top of the column.

704.3 Protection of the primary structural frame other than columns. Members of the primary structural frame other than columns that are required to have a *fire-resistance rating* and support more than two floors or one floor and roof, or support a *load-bearing wall* or a nonload-bearing wall more than two *stories* high, shall be provided individual encasement protection by protecting them on all sides for their full length, including connections to other structural members, with materials having the required *fire-resistance* rating.

Exception: Individual encasement protection on all sides shall be permitted on all exposed sides provided the extent of protection is in accordance with the required *fire-resistance rating*, as determined in Section 703.

704.4 Protection of secondary members. Secondary members that are required to have a *fire-resistance rating* shall be protected by individual encasement protection, by the membrane or ceiling of a *horizontal assembly* in accordance with Section 712, or by a combination of both.

704.4.1 Light-frame construction. King studs and boundary elements that are integral elements in *load-bearing walls* of light-frame construction shall be permitted to have required *fire-resistance ratings* provided by the membrane protection provided for the *load-bearing wall*.

704.5 Truss protection. The required thickness and construction of fire-resistance-rated assemblies enclosing trusses shall be based on the results of full-scale tests or combinations of tests on truss components or on *approved* calculations based on such tests that satisfactorily demonstrate that the assembly has the required *fire resistance*.

704.6 Attachments to structural members. The edges of lugs, brackets, rivets and bolt heads attached to structural members shall be permitted to extend to within 1 inch (25 mm) of the surface of the fire protection.

704.7 Reinforcing. Thickness of protection for concrete or masonry reinforcement shall be measured to the outside of the reinforcement except that stirrups and spiral reinforcement ties are permitted to project not more than 0.5-inch (12.7 mm) into the protection.

704.8 Embedments and enclosures. Pipes, wires, conduits, ducts or other service facilities shall not be embedded in the required fire protective covering of a structural member that is required to be individually encased.

704.9 Impact protection. Where the fire protective covering of a structural member is subject to impact damage from moving vehicles, the handling of merchandise or other activity, the fire protective covering shall be protected by corner guards or by a substantial jacket of metal or other noncombustible material to a height adequate to provide full protection, but not less than 5 feet (1524 mm) from the finished floor.

Exception: Corner protection is not required on concrete columns in open or enclosed parking garages.

704.10 Exterior structural members. Load-bearing structural members located within the *exterior walls* or on the outside of a building or structure shall be provided with the highest *fire-resistance rating* as determined in accordance with the following:

1. As required by Table 601 for the type of building element based on the type of construction of the building;
2. As required by Table 601 for exterior bearing walls based on the type of construction; and
3. As required by Table 602 for *exterior walls* based on the *fire separation distance*.

704.11 Bottom flange protection. Fire protection is not required at the bottom flange of lintels, shelf angles and plates, spanning not more than 6 feet (1829 mm) whether part of the primary structural frame or not, and from the bottom flange of lintels, shelf angles and plates not part of the primary structural frame, regardless of span.

704.12 Seismic isolation systems. Fire-resistance ratings for the isolation system shall meet the *fire-resistance rating* required for the columns, walls or other structural elements in which the isolation system is installed in accordance with Table 601. Isolation systems required to have a *fire-resistance rating* shall be protected with *approved* materials or construction assemblies designed to provide the same degree of *fire resistance* as the structural element in which it is installed when tested in accordance with ASTM E 119 or UL 263 (see Section 703.2).

Such isolation system protection applied to isolator units shall be capable of retarding the transfer of heat to the isolator unit in such a manner that the required gravity load-carrying capacity of the isolator unit will not be impaired after exposure to the standard time-temperature curve fire test prescribed in ASTM E 119 or UL 263 for a duration not less than that required for the *fire-resistance rating* of the structure element in which it is installed.

Such isolation system protection applied to isolator units shall be suitably designed and securely installed so as not to dislodge, loosen, sustain damage or otherwise impair its ability to accommodate the seismic movements for which the isolator unit is designed and to maintain its integrity for the purpose of providing the required fire-resistance protection.

704.13 Sprayed fire-resistant materials (SFRM). Sprayed fire-resistant materials (SFRM) shall comply with Sections 704.13.1 through 704.13.5.

704.13.1 Fire-resistance rating. The application of SFRM shall be consistent with the *fire-resistance rating* and the listing, including, but not limited to, minimum thickness and dry density of the applied SFRM, method of application, substrate surface conditions and the use of bonding adhesives, sealants, reinforcing or other materials.

704.13.2 Manufacturer's installation instructions. The application of SFRM shall be in accordance with the manufacturer's installation instructions. The instructions shall include, but are not limited to, substrate temperatures and surface conditions and SFRM handling, storage, mixing, conveyance, method of application, curing and ventilation.

704.13.3 Substrate condition. The SFRM shall be applied to a substrate in compliance with Sections 704.13.3.1 through 704.13.3.2.

704.13.3.1 Surface conditions. Substrates to receive SFRM shall be free of dirt, oil, grease, release agents, loose scale and any other condition that prevents adhesion. The substrates shall also be free of primers, paints and encapsulants other than those fire tested and *listed* by a nationally recognized testing agency. Primed, painted or encapsulated steel shall be allowed, provided that testing has demonstrated that required adhesion is maintained.

704.13.3.2 Primers, paints and encapsulants. Where the SFRM is to be applied over primers, paints or encapsulants other than those specified in the listing, the material shall be field tested in accordance with ASTM E 736. Where testing of the SFRM with primers, paints or encapsulants demonstrates that required adhesion is maintained, SFRM shall be permitted to be applied to primed, painted or encapsulated wide flange steel shapes in accordance with the following conditions:

1. The beam flange width does not exceed 12 inches (305 mm); or

2. The column flange width does not exceed 16 inches (400 mm); or
3. The beam or column web depth does not exceed 16 inches (400 mm).
4. The average and minimum bond strength values shall be determined based on a minimum of five bond tests conducted in accordance with ASTM E 736. Bond tests conducted in accordance with ASTM E 736 shall indicate a minimum average bond strength of 80 percent and a minimum individual bond strength of 50 percent, when compared to the bond strength of the SFRM as applied to clean uncoated 1/8-inch-thick (3 mm) steel plate.

704.13.4 Temperature. A minimum ambient and substrate temperature of 40°F (4.44°C) shall be maintained during and for a minimum of 24 hours after the application of the SFRM, unless the manufacturer's installation instructions allow otherwise.

704.13.5 Finished condition. The finished condition of SFRM applied to structural members or assemblies shall not, upon complete drying or curing, exhibit cracks, voids, spalls, delamination or any exposure of the substrate. Surface irregularities of SFRM shall be deemed acceptable.

704.14 Soffit in Group R. In Group R *buildings* of combustible construction the soffit material shall be securely attached to framing members and shall be constructed using either noncombustible soffit material, fire-retardant-treated soffit material, vinyl soffit installed over 3/4-inch (19.05 mm) wood sheathing or 5/8-inch (15.88 mm) gypsum board, or aluminum soffit installed over 3/4-inch (19.05 mm) wood sheathing or 5/8-inch (15.88 mm) gypsum board. Venting requirements shall apply to both soffit and underlayment and shall be in accordance with Section 1203.2.

SECTION 705
EXTERIOR WALLS

705.1 General. *Exterior walls* shall comply with this section.

705.2 Projections. Cornices, eave overhangs, exterior balconies and similar projections extending beyond the *exterior wall* shall conform to the requirements of this section and Section 1406. Exterior egress balconies and *exterior exit stairways* shall also comply with Sections 1019 and 1026, respectively. Projections shall not extend beyond the distance determined by the following three methods, whichever results in the lesser projection:

1. A point one-third the distance from the exterior face of the wall to the *lot line* where protected openings or a combination of protected and unprotected openings are required in the *exterior wall.*
2. A point one-half the distance from the exterior face of the wall to the *lot line* where all openings in the *exterior wall* are permitted to be unprotected or the building is equipped throughout with an *automatic sprinkler system* installed under the provisions of Section 705.8.2.
3. More than 12 inches (305 mm) into areas where openings are prohibited.

Buildings on the same lot and considered as portions of one building in accordance with Section 705.3 are not required to comply with this section.

705.2.1 Type I and II construction. Projections from walls of Type I or II construction shall be of noncombustible materials or combustible materials as allowed by Sections 1406.3 and 1406.4.

705.2.2 Type III, IV or V construction. Projections from walls of Type III, IV or V construction shall be of any *approved* material.

705.2.3 Combustible projections. Combustible projections located where openings are not permitted or where protection of openings is required shall be of at least 1-hour fire-resistance-rated construction, Type IV construction, *fire-retardant-treated wood* or as required by Section 1406.3.

Exception: Type V construction shall be allowed for R-3 occupancies.

705.3 Buildings on the same lot. For the purposes of determining the required wall and opening protection and roof-covering requirements, buildings on the same lot shall be assumed to have an imaginary line between them.

Where a new building is to be erected on the same lot as an existing building, the location of the assumed imaginary line with relation to the existing building shall be such that the *exterior wall* and opening protection of the existing building meet the criteria as set forth in Sections 705.5 and 705.8.

Exception: Two or more buildings on the same lot shall either be regulated as separate buildings or shall be considered as portions of one building if the aggregate area of such buildings is within the limits specified in Chapter 5 for a single building. Where the buildings contain different occupancy groups or are of different types of construction, the area shall be that allowed for the most restrictive occupancy or construction.

705.4 Materials. *Exterior walls* shall be of materials permitted by the building type of construction.

705.5 Fire-resistance ratings. *Exterior walls* shall be fire-resistance rated in accordance with Tables 601 and 602 and this section. The required *fire-resistance rating* of *exterior walls* with a *fire separation distance* of greater than 10 feet (3048 mm) shall be rated for exposure to fire from the inside. The required *fire-resistance rating* of *exterior walls* with a *fire separation distance* of less than or equal to 10 feet (3048 mm) shall be rated for exposure to fire from both sides.

705.6 Structural stability. The wall shall extend to the height required by Section 705.11 and shall have sufficient structural stability such that it will remain in place for the duration of time indicated by the required *fire-resistance rating*.

705.7 Unexposed surface temperature. Where protected openings are not limited by Section 705.8, the limitation on the rise of temperature on the unexposed surface of *exterior walls* as required by ASTM E 119 or UL 263 shall not apply. Where protected openings are limited by Section 705.8, the limitation on the rise of temperature on the unexposed surface of *exterior walls* as required by ASTM E 119 or UL 263 shall not apply provided that a correction is made for radiation from the unexposed *exterior wall* surface in accordance with the following formula:

$$A_e = A + (A_f \times F_{eo}) \quad \textbf{(Equation 7-1)}$$

where:

A_e = Equivalent area of protected openings.

A = Actual area of protected openings.

A_f = Area of *exterior wall* surface in the *story* under consideration exclusive of openings, on which the temperature limitations of ASTM E 119 or UL 263 for walls are exceeded.

F_{eo} = An "equivalent opening factor" derived from Figure 705.7 based on the average temperature of the unexposed wall surface and the *fire-resistance rating* of the wall.

705.8 Openings. Openings in *exterior walls* shall comply with Sections 705.8.1 through 705.8.6.

705.8.1 Allowable area of openings. The maximum area of unprotected and protected openings permitted in an *exterior wall* in any *story* of a building shall not exceed the percentages specified in Table 705.8.

Exceptions:

1. In other than Group H occupancies, unlimited unprotected openings are permitted in the first *story* above grade either:
   1.1. Where the wall faces a street and has a *fire separation distance* of more than 15 feet (4572 mm); or
   1.2. Where the wall faces an unoccupied space. The unoccupied space shall be on the same lot or dedicated for public use, shall not be less than 30 feet (9144 mm) in width and shall have access from a street by a posted fire lane in accordance with the *International Fire Code*.
2. Buildings whose exterior bearing walls, exterior nonbearing walls and exterior primary structural frame are not required to be fire-resistance rated shall be permitted to have unlimited unprotected openings.

705.8.2 Protected openings. Where openings are required to be protected, *fire doors* and fire shutters shall comply with Section 715.4 and *fire window assemblies* shall comply with Section 715.5.

Exception: Opening protectives are not required where the building is equipped throughout with an *automatic sprinkler system* in accordance with Section 903.3.1.1 and the exterior openings are protected by a water curtain using automatic sprinklers *approved* for that use.

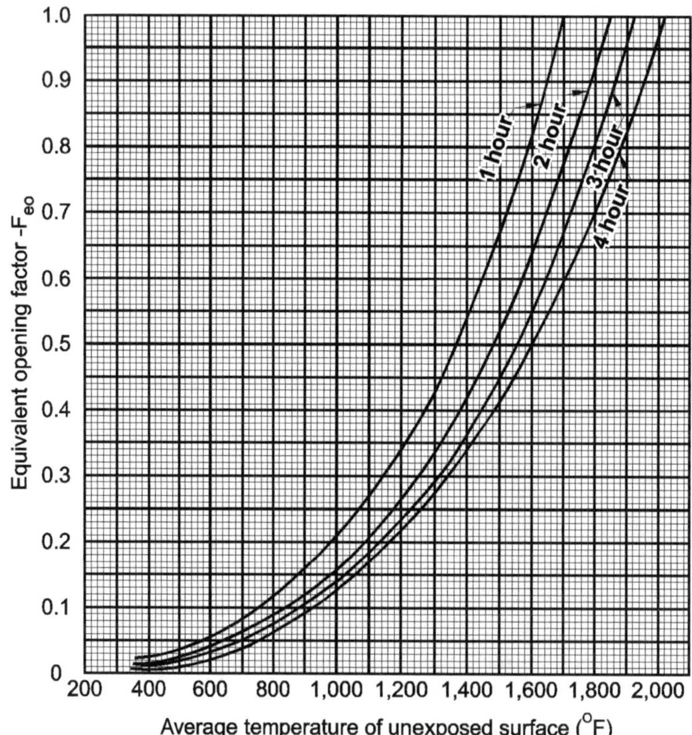

For SI: °C = [(°F) - 32] / 1.8.

FIGURE 705.7
EQUIVALENT OPENING FACTOR

TABLE 705.8
MAXIMUM AREA OF EXTERIOR WALL OPENINGS BASED ON FIRE SEPARATION DISTANCE AND DEGREE OF OPENING PROTECTION

FIRE SEPARATION DISTANCE (feet)	DEGREE OF OPENING PROTECTION	ALLOWABLE AREA[a]
0 to less than 3[b, c]	Unprotected, Nonsprinklered (UP, NS)	Not Permitted
	Unprotected, Sprinklered (UP, S)[i]	Not Permitted
	Protected (P)	Not Permitted
3 to less than 5[d, e]	Unprotected, Nonsprinklered (UP, NS)	Not Permitted
	Unprotected, Sprinklered (UP, S)[i]	15%
	Protected (P)	15%
5 to less than 10[e, f]	Unprotected, Nonsprinklered (UP, NS)	10%[h]
	Unprotected, Sprinklered (UP, S)[i]	25%
	Protected (P)	25%
10 to less than 15[e, f, g]	Unprotected, Nonsprinklered (UP, NS)	15%[h]
	Unprotected, Sprinklered (UP, S)[i]	45%
	Protected (P)	45%
15 to less than 20[f, g]	Unprotected, Nonsprinklered (UP, NS)	25%
	Unprotected, Sprinklered (UP, S)[i]	75%
	Protected (P)	75%
20 to less than 25[f, g]	Unprotected, Nonsprinklered (UP, NS)	45%
	Unprotected, Sprinklered (UP, S)[i]	No Limit
	Protected (P)	No Limit
25 to less than 30[f, g]	Unprotected, Nonsprinklered (UP, NS)	70%
	Unprotected, Sprinklered (UP, S)[i]	No Limit
	Protected (P)	No Limit
30 or greater	Unprotected, Nonsprinklered (UP, NS)	No Limit
	Unprotected, Sprinklered (UP, S)[i]	Not Required
	Protected (P)	Not Required

For SI: 1 foot = 304.8 mm.
UP, NS = Unprotected openings in buildings not equipped throughout with an automatic sprinkler system in accordance with Section 903.3.1.1.
UP, S = Unprotected openings in buildings equipped throughout with an automatic sprinkler system in accordance with Section 903.3.1.1.
P = Openings protected with an opening protective assembly in accordance with Section 705.8.2.
a. Values indicated are the percentage of the area of the exterior wall, per story.
b. For the requirements for fire walls of buildings with differing heights, see Section 706.6.1.
c. For openings in a fire wall for buildings on the same lot, see Section 706.8.
d. The maximum percentage of unprotected and protected openings shall be 25 percent for Group R-3 occupancies.
e. Unprotected openings shall not be permitted for openings with a fire separation distance of less than 15 feet for Group H-2 and H-3 occupancies.
f. The area of unprotected and protected openings shall not be limited for Group R-3 occupancies, with afire separation distance of 5 feet or greater.
g. The area of openings in an open parking structure with a fire separation distance of 10 feet or greater shall not be limited.
h. Includes buildings accessory to Group R-3.
i. Not applicable to Group H-1, H-2 and H-3 occupancies.

705.8.3 Unprotected openings. Where unprotected openings are permitted, windows and doors shall be constructed of any *approved* materials. Glazing shall conform to the requirements of Chapters 24 and 26.

705.8.4 Mixed openings. Where both unprotected and protected openings are located in the *exterior wall* in any *story* of a building, the total area of openings shall be determined in accordance with the following:

$$(A_p/a_p) + (A_u/a_u) \leq 1 \quad \textbf{(Equation 7-2)}$$

where:

A_p = Actual area of protected openings, or the equivalent area of protected openings, A_e (see Section 705.7).

a_p = Allowable area of protected openings.

A_u = Actual area of unprotected openings.

a_u = Allowable area of unprotected openings.

705.8.5 Vertical separation of openings. Openings in *exterior walls* in adjacent *stories* shall be separated vertically to protect against fire spread on the exterior of the buildings where the openings are within 5 feet (1524 mm) of each other horizontally and the opening in the lower *story* is not a protected opening with a *fire protection rating* of not less than $^3/_4$ hour. Such openings shall be separated vertically at least 3 feet (914 mm) by spandrel girders, *exterior walls* or other similar assemblies that have a *fire-resistance rating* of at least 1 hour or by flame barriers that extend horizontally at least 30 inches (762 mm) beyond the *exterior wall*. Flame barriers shall also have a *fire-resistance rating* of at least 1 hour. The unexposed surface temperature limitations specified in ASTM E 119 or UL 263 shall not apply to the flame barriers or vertical separation unless otherwise required by the provisions of this code.

Exceptions:

1. This section shall not apply to buildings that are three *stories* or less above *grade plane*.
2. This section shall not apply to buildings equipped throughout with an *automatic sprinkler system* in accordance with Section 903.3.1.1 or 903.3.1.2.
3. Open parking garages.

705.8.6 Vertical exposure. For buildings on the same lot, opening protectives having a *fire protection rating* of not less than $^3/_4$ hour shall be provided in every opening that is less than 15 feet (4572 mm) vertically above the roof of an adjacent building or structure based on assuming an imaginary line between them. The opening protectives are required where the *fire separation distance* between the imaginary line and the adjacent building or structure is less than 15 feet (4572 mm).

Exceptions:

1. Opening protectives are not required where the roof assembly of the adjacent building or structure has a *fire-resistance rating* of not less than 1 hour for a minimum distance of 10 feet (3048 mm) from the *exterior wall* facing the imaginary line and the entire length and span of the supporting elements for the fire-resistance-rated roof assembly has a *fire-resistance rating* of not less than 1 hour.
2. Buildings on the same lot and considered as portions of one building in accordance with Section 705.3 are not required to comply with Section 705.8.6.

705.9 Joints. Joints made in or between *exterior walls* required by this section to have a *fire-resistance rating* shall comply with Section 714.

Exception: Joints in *exterior walls* that are permitted to have unprotected openings.

705.9.1 Voids. The void created at the intersection of a floor/ceiling assembly and an exterior curtain wall assembly shall be protected in accordance with Section 714.4.

705.10 Ducts and air transfer openings. Penetrations by air ducts and air transfer openings in fire-resistance-rated *exterior walls* required to have protected openings shall comply with Section 716.

Exception: Foundation vents installed in accordance with this code are permitted.

705.11 Parapets. Parapets shall be provided on *exterior walls* of buildings.

Exceptions: A parapet need not be provided on an *exterior wall* where any of the following conditions exist:

1. The wall is not required to be fire-resistance rated in accordance with Table 602 because of *fire separation distance*.
2. The building has an area of not more than 1,000 square feet (93 m^2) on any floor.
3. Walls that terminate at roofs of not less than 2-hour fire-resistance-rated construction or where the roof, including the deck or slab and supporting construction, is constructed entirely of noncombustible materials.
4. One-hour fire-resistance-rated *exterior walls* that terminate at the underside of the roof sheathing, deck or slab, provided:
   - 4.1. Where the roof/ceiling framing elements are parallel to the walls, such framing and elements supporting such framing shall not be of less than 1-hour fire-resistance-rated construction for a width of 4 feet (1220 mm) for Groups R and U and 10 feet (3048 mm) for other occupancies, measured from the interior side of the wall.
   - 4.2. Where roof/ceiling framing elements are not parallel to the wall, the entire span of such framing and elements supporting such framing shall not be of less than 1-hour fire-resistance-rated construction.
   - 4.3. Openings in the roof shall not be located within 5 feet (1524 mm) of the 1-hour fire-resistance-rated *exterior wall* for Groups R and U and 10 feet (3048 mm) for other occupan-

cies, measured from the interior side of the wall.

4.4. The entire building shall be provided with not less than a Class B roof covering.

5. In Groups R-2 and R-3 where the entire building is provided with a Class C roof covering, the *exterior wall* shall be permitted to terminate at the underside of the roof sheathing or deck in Type III, IV and V construction, provided:

5.1. The roof sheathing or deck is constructed of *approved* noncombustible materials or of *fire-retardant-treated wood* for a distance of 4 feet (1220 mm); or

5.2. The roof is protected with 0.625-inch (16 mm) Type X gypsum board directly beneath the underside of the roof sheathing or deck, supported by a minimum of nominal 2-inch (51 mm) ledgers attached to the sides of the roof framing members for a minimum distance of 4 feet (1220 mm).

6. Where the wall is permitted to have at least 25 percent of the *exterior wall* areas containing unprotected openings based on *fire separation distance* as determined in accordance with Section 705.8.

705.11.1 Parapet construction. Parapets shall have the same *fire-resistance rating* as that required for the supporting wall, and on any side adjacent to a roof surface, shall have noncombustible faces for the uppermost 18 inches (457 mm), including counterflashing and coping materials. The height of the parapet shall not be less than 30 inches (762 mm) above the point where the roof surface and the wall intersect. Where the roof slopes toward a parapet at a slope greater than two units vertical in 12 units horizontal (16.7-percent slope), the parapet shall extend to the same height as any portion of the roof within a *fire separation distance* where protection of wall openings is required, but in no case shall the height be less than 30 inches (762 mm).

SECTION 706
FIRE WALLS

706.1 General. Each portion of a building separated by one or more *fire walls* that comply with the provisions of this section shall be considered a separate building. The extent and location of such *fire walls* shall provide a complete separation. Where a *fire wall* also separates occupancies that are required to be separated by a *fire barrier* wall, the most restrictive requirements of each separation shall apply.

706.1.1 Party walls. Any wall located on a *lot line* between adjacent buildings, which is used or adapted for joint service between the two buildings, shall be constructed as a *fire wall* in accordance with Section 706. Party walls shall be constructed without openings and shall create separate buildings.

Exception: Openings in a party wall separating an *anchor building* and a mall shall be in accordance with Section 402.7.3.1.

706.2 Structural stability. *Fire walls* shall have sufficient structural stability under fire conditions to allow collapse of construction on either side without collapse of the wall for the duration of time indicated by the required *fire-resistance rating*.

706.3 Materials. *Fire walls* shall be of any *approved* noncombustible materials.

Exception: Buildings of Type V construction.

706.4 Fire-resistance rating. *Fire walls* shall have a *fire-resistance rating* of not less than that required by Table 706.4.

TABLE 706.4
FIRE WALL FIRE-RESISTANCE RATINGS

GROUP	FIRE-RESISTANCE RATING (hours)
A, B, E, H-4, I, R-1, R-2, U	3[a]
F-1, H-3[b], H-5, M, S-1	3
H-1, H-2	4[b]
F-2, S-2, R-3, R-4	2

a. In Type II or V construction, walls shall be permitted to have a 2-hour fire-resistance rating.
b. For Group H-1, H-2 or H-3 buildings, also see Sections 415.4 and 415.5.

706.5 Horizontal continuity. *Fire walls* shall be continuous from *exterior wall* to *exterior wall* and shall extend at least 18 inches (457 mm) beyond the exterior surface of *exterior walls*.

Exceptions:

1. *Fire walls* shall be permitted to terminate at the interior surface of combustible exterior sheathing or siding provided the *exterior wall* has a *fire-resistance rating* of at least 1 hour for a horizontal distance of at least 4 feet (1220 mm) on both sides of the *fire wall*. Openings within such *exterior walls* shall be protected by opening protectives having a *fire protection rating* of not less than $^3/_4$ hour.
2. *Fire walls* shall be permitted to terminate at the interior surface of noncombustible exterior sheathing, exterior siding or other noncombustible exterior finishes provided the sheathing, siding, or other exterior noncombustible finish extends a horizontal distance of at least 4 feet (1220 mm) on both sides of the *fire wall*.
3. *Fire walls* shall be permitted to terminate at the interior surface of noncombustible exterior sheathing where the building on each side of the *fire wall* is protected by an *automatic sprinkler system* installed in accordance with Section 903.3.1.1 or 903.3.1.2.

706.5.1 Exterior walls. Where the *fire wall* intersects *exterior walls*, the *fire-resistance rating* and opening protection of the *exterior walls* shall comply with one of the following:

1. The *exterior walls* on both sides of the *fire wall* shall have a 1-hour *fire-resistance rating* with $^3/_4$-hour protection where opening protection is required by Section 705.8. The *fire-resistance rating* of the *exterior wall* shall extend a minimum of 4 feet (1220 mm) on

each side of the intersection of the *fire wall* to *exterior wall*. *Exterior wall* intersections at *fire walls* that form an angle equal to or greater than 180 degrees (3.14 rad) do not need *exterior wall* protection.

2. Buildings or spaces on both sides of the intersecting *fire wall* shall assume to have an imaginary *lot line* at the *fire wall* and extending beyond the exterior of the *fire wall*. The location of the assumed line in relation to the *exterior walls* and the *fire wall* shall be such that the *exterior wall* and opening protection meet the requirements set forth in Sections 705.5 and 705.8. Such protection is not required for *exterior walls* terminating at *fire walls* that form an angle equal to or greater than 180 degrees (3.14 rad).

706.5.2 Horizontal projecting elements. *Fire walls* shall extend to the outer edge of horizontal projecting elements such as balconies, roof overhangs, canopies, marquees and similar projections that are within 4 feet (1220 mm) of the *fire wall*.

Exceptions:

1. Horizontal projecting elements without concealed spaces, provided the *exterior wall* behind and below the projecting element has not less than 1-hour fire-resistance-rated construction for a distance not less than the depth of the projecting element on both sides of the *fire wall*. Openings within such *exterior walls* shall be protected by opening protectives having a *fire protection rating* of not less than $^3/_4$ hour.
2. Noncombustible horizontal projecting elements with concealed spaces, provided a minimum 1-hour fire-resistance-rated wall extends through the concealed space. The projecting element shall be separated from the building by a minimum of 1-hour fire-resistance-rated construction for a distance on each side of the *fire wall* equal to the depth of the projecting element. The wall is not required to extend under the projecting element where the building *exterior wall* is not less than 1-hour fire-resistance rated for a distance on each side of the *fire wall* equal to the depth of the projecting element. Openings within such *exterior walls* shall be protected by opening protectives having a *fire protection rating* of not less than $^3/_4$ hour.
3. For combustible horizontal projecting elements with concealed spaces, the *fire wall* need only extend through the concealed space to the outer edges of the projecting elements. The *exterior wall* behind and below the projecting element shall be of not less than 1-hour fire-resistance-rated construction for a distance not less than the depth of the projecting elements on both sides of the *fire wall*. Openings within such *exterior walls* shall be protected by opening protectives having a fire-protection rating of not less than $^3/_4$ hour.

706.6 Vertical continuity. *Fire walls* shall extend from the foundation to a termination point at least 30 inches (762 mm) above both adjacent roofs.

Exceptions:

1. Stepped buildings in accordance with Section 706.6.1.
2. Two-hour fire-resistance-rated walls shall be permitted to terminate at the underside of the roof sheathing, deck or slab, provided:
   - 2.1. The lower roof assembly within 4 feet (1220 mm) of the wall has not less than a 1-hour *fire-resistance rating* and the entire length and span of supporting elements for the rated roof assembly has a *fire-resistance rating* of not less than 1 hour.
   - 2.2. Openings in the roof shall not be located within 4 feet (1220 mm) of the *fire wall*.
   - 2.3. Each building shall be provided with not less than a Class B roof covering.
3. Walls shall be permitted to terminate at the underside of noncombustible roof sheathing, deck or slabs where both buildings are provided with not less than a Class B roof covering. Openings in the roof shall not be located within 4 feet (1220 mm) of the *fire wall*.
4. In buildings of Type III, IV and V construction, walls shall be permitted to terminate at the underside of combustible roof sheathing or decks, provided:
   - 4.1. There are no openings in the roof within 4 feet (1220 mm) of the *fire wall*,
   - 4.2. The roof is covered with a minimum Class B roof covering, and
   - 4.3. The roof sheathing or deck is constructed of *fire-retardant-treated wood* for a distance of 4 feet (1220 mm) on both sides of the wall or the roof is protected with $^5/_8$-inch (15.9 mm) Type X gypsum board directly beneath the underside of the roof sheathing or deck, supported by a minimum of 2-inch (51 mm) nominal ledgers attached to the sides of the roof framing members for a minimum distance of 4 feet (1220 mm) on both sides of the *fire wall*.
5. In buildings designed in accordance with Section 509.2, *fire walls* located above the 3-hour *horizontal assembly* required by Section 509.2, Item 1 shall be permitted to extend from the top of this *horizontal assembly*.

706.6.1 Stepped buildings. Where a *fire wall* serves as an *exterior wall* for a building and separates buildings having different roof levels, such wall shall terminate at a point not less than 30 inches (762 mm) above the lower roof level, provided the *exterior wall* for a height of 15 feet (4572 mm) above the lower roof is not less than 1-hour fire-resistance-rated construction from both sides with openings protected by fire assemblies having a *fire protection rating* of not less than $^3/_4$ hour.

Exception: Where the *fire wall* terminates at the underside of the roof sheathing, deck or slab of the lower roof, provided:

1. The lower roof assembly within 10 feet (3048 mm) of the wall has not less than a 1-hour *fire-resistance rating* and the entire length and span of supporting elements for the rated roof assembly has a fire-resistance rating of not less than 1 hour.
2. Openings in the lower roof shall not be located within 10 feet (3048 mm) of the *fire wall.*

706.7 Combustible framing in fire walls. Adjacent combustible members entering into a concrete or masonry *fire wall* from opposite sides shall not have less than a 4-inch (102 mm) distance between embedded ends. Where combustible members frame into hollow walls or walls of hollow units, hollow spaces shall be solidly filled for the full thickness of the wall and for a distance not less than 4 inches (102 mm) above, below and between the structural members, with noncombustible materials *approved* for fireblocking.

706.8 Openings. Each opening through a *fire wall* shall be protected in accordance with Section 715.4 and shall not exceed 156 square feet (15 m^2). The aggregate width of openings at any floor level shall not exceed 25 percent of the length of the wall.

Exceptions:

1. Openings are not permitted in party walls constructed in accordance with Section 706.1.1.
2. Openings shall not be limited to 156 square feet (15 m^2) where both buildings are equipped throughout with an *automatic sprinkler system* installed in accordance with Section 903.3.1.1.

706.9 Penetrations. Penetrations of *fire walls* shall comply with Section 713.

706.10 Joints. Joints made in or between *fire walls* shall comply with Section 714.

706.11 Ducts and air transfer openings. Ducts and air transfer openings shall not penetrate *fire walls.*

Exception: Penetrations by ducts and air transfer openings of *fire walls* that are not on a *lot line* shall be allowed provided the penetrations comply with Section 716. The size and aggregate width of all openings shall not exceed the limitations of Section 706.8.

SECTION 707
FIRE BARRIERS

707.1 General. *Fire barriers* installed as required elsewhere in this code or the *International Fire Code* shall comply with this section.

707.2 Materials. *Fire barriers* shall be of materials permitted by the building type of construction.

707.3 Fire-resistance rating. The *fire-resistance rating* of *fire barriers* shall comply with this section.

707.3.1 Shaft enclosures. The *fire-resistance rating* of the *fire barrier* separating building areas from a shaft shall comply with Section 708.4.

707.3.2 Exit enclosures. The *fire-resistance rating* of the *fire barrier* separating building areas from an *exit* shall comply with Section 1022.1.

707.3.3 Exit passageway. The *fire-resistance rating* of the *fire barrier* separating building areas from an *exit* passageway shall comply with Section 1023.3.

707.3.4 Horizontal exit. The *fire-resistance rating* of the separation between building areas connected by a horizontal *exit* shall comply with Section 1025.1.

707.3.5 Atriums. The *fire-resistance rating* of the *fire barrier* separating atriums shall comply with Section 404.6.

707.3.6 Incidental accessory occupancies. The *fire barrier* separating incidental accessory occupancies from other spaces in the building shall have a *fire-resistance rating* of not less than that indicated in Table 508.2.5.

707.3.7 Control areas. *Fire barriers* separating *control areas* shall have a *fire-resistance rating* of not less than that required in Section 414.2.4.

707.3.8 Separated occupancies. Where the provisions of Section 508.4 are applicable, the *fire barrier* separating mixed occupancies shall have a *fire-resistance rating* of not less than that indicated in Table 508.4 based on the occupancies being separated.

707.3.9 Fire areas. The *fire barriers* or *horizontal assemblies*, or both, separating a single occupancy or multiple occupancies into different *fire areas* shall have a *fire-resistance rating* of not less than that indicated in Table 508.4.

TABLE 707.3.9
Deleted

707.4 Exterior walls. Where *exterior walls* serve as a part of a required fire-resistance-rated shaft or *exit* enclosure, or separation, such walls shall comply with the requirements of Section 705 for *exterior walls* and the fire-resistance-rated enclosure or separation requirements shall not apply.

Exception: *Exterior walls* required to be fire-resistance rated in accordance with Section 1019 for exterior egress balconies, Section 1022.6 for *exit* enclosures and Section 1026.6 for exterior *exit* ramps and *stairways.*

707.5 Continuity. Fire barriers shall extend from the top of the foundation or floor/ceiling assembly below to the underside of the floor or roof sheathing, slab or deck above and shall be securely attached thereto. Such *fire barriers* shall be continuous through concealed spaces, such as the space above a suspended ceiling.

707.5.1 Supporting construction. The supporting construction for a *fire barrier* shall be protected to afford the required *fire-resistance rating* of the *fire barrier* supported. Hollow vertical spaces within a *fire barrier* shall be fireblocked in accordance with Section 717.2 at every floor level.

Exceptions:

1. The maximum required *fire-resistance rating* for assemblies supporting *fire barriers* separating

tank storage as provided for in Section 415.6.2.1 shall be 2 hours, but not less than required by Table 601 for the building construction type.

2. Shaft enclosures shall be permitted to terminate at a top enclosure complying with Section 708.12.

3. Supporting construction for 1-hour *fire barriers* required by Table 508.2.5 in buildings of Type IIB, IIIB and VB construction is not required to be fire-resistance rated unless required by other sections of this code.

707.6 Openings. Openings in a *fire barrier* shall be protected in accordance with Section 715. Openings shall be limited to a maximum aggregate width of 25 percent of the length of the wall, and the maximum area of any single opening shall not exceed 156 square feet (15 m^2). Openings in *exit* enclosures and *exit* passageways shall also comply with Sections 1022.3 and 1023.5, respectively.

Exceptions:

1. Openings shall not be limited to 156 square feet (15 m^2) where adjoining floor areas are equipped throughout with an *automatic sprinkler system* in accordance with Section 903.3.1.1.

2. Openings shall not be limited to 156 square feet (15 m^2) or an aggregate width of 25 percent of the length of the wall where the opening protective is a *fire door* serving an *exit* enclosure.

3. Openings shall not be limited to 156 square feet (15 m^2) or an aggregate width of 25 percent of the length of the wall where the opening protective has been tested in accordance with ASTM E 119 or UL 263 and has a minimum *fire-resistance rating* not less than the *fire-resistance rating* of the wall.

4. Fire window assemblies permitted in atrium separation walls shall not be limited to a maximum aggregate width of 25 percent of the length of the wall.

5. Openings shall not be limited to 156 square feet (15 m^2) or an aggregate width of 25 percent of the length of the wall where the opening protective is a *fire door* assembly in a *fire barrier* separating an *exit* enclosure from an *exit* passageway in accordance with Section 1022.2.1.

707.7 Penetrations. Penetrations of *fire barriers* shall comply with Section 713.

707.7.1 Prohibited penetrations. Penetrations into an *exit* enclosure or an *exit* passageway shall be allowed only when permitted by Section 1022.4 or 1023.6, respectively.

707.8 Joints. Joints made in or between *fire barriers*, and joints made at the intersection of *fire barriers* with underside of the floor or roof sheathing, slab or deck above, shall comply with Section 714.

707.9 Ducts and air transfer openings. Penetrations in a *fire barrier* by ducts and air transfer openings shall comply with Section 716.

SECTION 708
SHAFT ENCLOSURES

708.1 General. The provisions of this section shall apply to shafts required to protect openings and penetrations through floor/ceiling and roof/ceiling assemblies. Shaft enclosures shall be constructed as *fire barriers* in accordance with Section 707 or *horizontal assemblies* in accordance with Section 712, or both.

708.2 Shaft enclosure required. Openings through a floor/ceiling assembly shall be protected by a shaft enclosure complying with this section.

Exceptions:

1. A shaft enclosure is not required for openings totally within an individual residential *dwelling unit* and connecting four *stories* or less.

2. A shaft enclosure is not required in a building equipped throughout with an *automatic sprinkler system* in accordance with Section 903.3.1.1 for an escalator opening or *stairway* that is not a portion of the *means of egress* protected according to Item 2.1 or 2.2.

   2.1. Where the area of the floor opening between *stories* does not exceed twice the horizontal projected area of the escalator or *stairway* and the opening is protected by a draft curtain and closely spaced sprinklers in accordance with NFPA 13. In other than Groups B and M, this application is limited to openings that do not connect more than four *stories*.

   2.2. Where the opening is protected by *approved* power-operated automatic shutters at every penetrated floor. The shutters shall be of noncombustible construction and have a *fire-resistance rating* of not less than 1.5 hours. The shutter shall be so constructed as to close immediately upon the actuation of a smoke detector installed in accordance with Section 907.3 and shall completely shut off the well opening. Escalators shall cease operation when the shutter begins to close. The shutter shall operate at a speed of not more than 30 feet per minute (152.4 mm/s) and shall be equipped with a sensitive leading edge to arrest its progress where in contact with any obstacle, and to continue its progress on release therefrom.

3. A shaft enclosure is not required for penetrations by pipe, tube, conduit, wire, cable and vents protected in accordance with Section 713.4.

4. A shaft enclosure is not required for penetrations by ducts protected in accordance with Section 716.6. Grease ducts shall be protected in accordance with the *International Mechanical Code*.

5. In other than Group H occupancies, a shaft enclosure is not required for floor openings complying with the provisions for atriums in Section 404.

6. A shaft enclosure is not required for *approved* masonry chimneys where *annular space* is fireblocked at each floor level in accordance with Section 717.2.5.
7. In other than Groups I-2 and I-3, a shaft enclosure is not required for a floor opening or an air transfer opening that complies with the following:
   7.1. Does not connect more than two *stories*.
   7.2. Is not part of the required *means of egress* system.
   7.3. Is not concealed within the construction of a wall or a floor/ceiling assembly.
   7.4. Is not open to a *corridor* in Group I and R occupancies.
   7.5. Is not open to a *corridor* on nonsprinklered floors in any occupancy.
   7.6. Is separated from floor openings and air transfer openings serving other floors by construction conforming to required shaft enclosures.
   7.7. Is limited to the same smoke compartment.
8. A shaft enclosure is not required for automobile ramps in open and enclosed parking garages constructed in accordance with Sections 406.3 and 406.4, respectively.
9. A shaft enclosure is not required for floor openings between a *mezzanine* and the floor below.
10. A shaft enclosure is not required for joints protected by a *fire-resistant joint system* in accordance with Section 714.
11. A shaft enclosure shall not be required for floor openings created by unenclosed *stairs* or ramps in accordance with Exception 3 or 4 in Section 1016.1.
12. Floor openings protected by floor *fire doors* in accordance with Section 712.8.
13. In Group I-3 occupancies, a shaft enclosure is not required for floor openings in accordance with Section 408.5.
14. A shaft enclosure is not required for elevator hoistways in open or enclosed parking garages that serve only the parking garage.
15. In open or enclosed parking garages a shaft enclosure is not required to enclose mechanical exhaust or supply duct systems when such duct system is contained within and serves only the parking garage.
16. Where permitted by other sections of this code.

708.3 Materials. The shaft enclosure shall be of materials permitted by the building type of construction.

708.4 Fire-resistance rating. Shaft enclosures shall have a *fire-resistance rating* of not less than 2 hours where connecting four *stories* or more, and not less than 1 hour where connecting less than four *stories*. The number of *stories* connected by the shaft enclosure shall include any basements but not any *mezzanines*. Shaft enclosures shall have a *fire-resistance rating* not less than the floor assembly penetrated, but need not exceed 2 hours. Shaft enclosures shall meet the requirements of Section 703.2.1.

708.5 Continuity. Shaft enclosures shall be constructed as *fire barriers* in accordance with Section 707 or *horizontal assemblies* constructed in accordance with Section 712, or both, and shall have continuity in accordance with Section 707.5 for *fire barriers* or Section 712.4 for *horizontal assemblies* as applicable.

708.6 Exterior walls. Where *exterior walls* serve as a part of a required shaft enclosure, such walls shall comply with the requirements of Section 705 for *exterior walls* and the fire-resistance-rated enclosure requirements shall not apply.

> **Exception:** *Exterior walls* required to be fire-resistance rated in accordance with Section 1019.2 for exterior egress balconies, Section 1022.6 for *exit* enclosures and Section 1026.6 for exterior *exit* ramps and *stairways*.

708.7 Openings. Openings in a shaft enclosure shall be protected in accordance with Section 715 as required for *fire barriers*. Doors shall be self- or automatic-closing by smoke detection in accordance with Section 715.4.8.3.

708.7.1 Prohibited openings. Openings other than those necessary for the purpose of the shaft shall not be permitted in shaft enclosures.

708.8 Penetrations. Penetrations in a shaft enclosure shall be protected in accordance with Section 713 as required for *fire barriers*.

708.8.1 Prohibited penetrations. Penetrations other than those necessary for the purpose of the shaft shall not be permitted in shaft enclosures.

708.9 Joints. Joints in a shaft enclosure shall comply with Section 714.

708.10 Ducts and air transfer openings. Penetrations of a shaft enclosure by ducts and air transfer openings shall comply with Section 716.

708.11 Enclosure at the bottom. Shafts that do not extend to the bottom of the building or structure shall comply with one of the following:

1. They shall be enclosed at the lowest level with construction of the same *fire-resistance rating* as the lowest floor through which the shaft passes, but not less than the rating required for the shaft enclosure.
2. They shall terminate in a room having a use related to the purpose of the shaft. The room shall be separated from the remainder of the building by *fire barriers* constructed in accordance with Section 707 or *horizontal assemblies* constructed in accordance with Section 712, or both. The *fire-resistance rating* and opening protectives shall be at least equal to the protection required for the shaft enclosure.
3. They shall be protected by *approved fire dampers* installed in accordance with their listing at the lowest floor level within the shaft enclosure.

Exceptions:

1. The fire-resistance-rated room separation is not required, provided there are no openings in or penetrations of the shaft enclosure to the interior of the building except at the bottom. The bottom of the shaft shall be closed off around the penetrating items with materials permitted by Section 717.3.1 for draftstopping, or the room shall be provided with an *approved* automatic fire suppression system.
2. A shaft enclosure containing a refuse chute or laundry chute shall not be used for any other purpose and shall terminate in a room protected in accordance with Section 708.13.4.
3. The fire-resistance-rated room separation and the protection at the bottom of the shaft are not required provided there are no combustibles in the shaft and there are no openings or other penetrations through the shaft enclosure to the interior of the building.

708.12 Enclosure at the top. A shaft enclosure that does not extend to the underside of the roof sheathing, deck or slab of the building shall be enclosed at the top with construction of the same *fire-resistance rating* as the topmost floor penetrated by the shaft, but not less than the *fire-resistance rating* required for the shaft enclosure.

708.13 Refuse and laundry chutes. Refuse and laundry chutes, access and termination rooms and incinerator rooms shall meet the requirements of Sections 708.13.1 through 708.13.6.

Exception: Chutes serving and contained within a single *dwelling unit*.

708.13.1 Refuse and laundry chute enclosures. A shaft enclosure containing a refuse or laundry chute shall not be used for any other purpose and shall be enclosed in accordance with Section 708.4. Openings into the shaft, including those from access rooms and termination rooms, shall be protected in accordance with this section and Section 715. Openings into chutes shall not be located in *corridors*. Doors shall be self- or automatic-closing upon the actuation of a smoke detector in accordance with Section 715.4.8.3, except that heat-activated closing devices shall be permitted between the shaft and the termination room.

708.13.2 Materials. A shaft enclosure containing a refuse or laundry chute shall be constructed of materials as permitted by the building type of construction.

708.13.3 Refuse and laundry chute access rooms. Access openings for refuse and laundry chutes shall be located in rooms or compartments enclosed by not less than 1-hour *fire barriers* constructed in accordance with Section 707 or *horizontal assemblies* constructed in accordance with Section 712, or both. Openings into the access rooms shall be protected by opening protectives having a *fire protection rating* of not less than $^{3}/_{4}$ hour. Doors shall be self- or automatic-closing upon the detection of smoke in accordance with Section 715.4.8.3.

708.13.4 Termination room. Refuse and laundry chutes shall discharge into an enclosed room separated from the remainder of the building by not less than 1-hour *fire barriers* constructed in accordance with Section 707 or *horizontal assemblies* constructed in accordance with Section 712, or both. Openings into the termination room shall be protected by opening protectives having a *fire protection rating* of not less than $^{3}/_{4}$ hour. Doors shall be self- or automatic-closing upon the detection of smoke in accordance with Section 715.4.8.3. Refuse chutes shall not terminate in an incinerator room. Refuse and laundry rooms that are not provided with chutes need only comply with Table 508.2.5.

708.13.5 Incinerator room. Incinerator rooms shall comply with Table 508.2.5.

708.13.6 Automatic sprinkler system. An *approved automatic sprinkler system* shall be installed in accordance with Section 903.2.11.2.

708.14 Elevator, dumbwaiter and other hoistways. Elevator, dumbwaiter and other hoistway enclosures shall be constructed in accordance with Section 708 and Chapter 30.

708.14.1 Elevator lobby. An enclosed elevator lobby shall be provided at each floor where an elevator shaft enclosure connects more than three *stories*. The lobby enclosure shall separate the elevator shaft enclosure doors from each floor by *fire partitions*. In addition to the requirements in Section 709 for *fire partitions*, doors protecting openings in the elevator lobby enclosure walls shall also comply with Section 715.4.3 as required for *corridor* walls and penetrations of the elevator lobby enclosure by ducts and air transfer openings shall be protected as required for *corridors* in accordance with Section 716.5.4.1. Elevator lobbies shall have at least one *means of egress* complying with Chapter 10 and other provisions within this code.

Exceptions:

1. Enclosed elevator lobbies are not required at the street floor, provided the entire street floor is equipped with an *automatic sprinkler system* in accordance with Section 903.3.1.1.
2. Elevators not required to be located in a shaft in accordance with Section 708.2 are not required to have enclosed elevator lobbies.
3. Enclosed elevator lobbies are not required where additional doors are provided at the hoistway opening in accordance with Section 3002.6. Such doors shall be tested in accordance with UL 1784 without an artificial bottom seal.
4. Enclosed elevator lobbies are not required where the building is protected by an *automatic sprinkler system* installed in accordance with Section 903.3.1.1 or 903.3.1.2. This exception shall not apply to the following:
    4.1. Group I-2 occupancies;
    4.2. Group I-3 occupancies; and
    4.3. High-rise buildings.
5. Smoke partitions shall be permitted in lieu of *fire partitions* to separate the elevator lobby at each floor where the building is equipped throughout

with an *automatic sprinkler system* installed in accordance with Section 903.3.1.1 or 903.3.1.2. In addition to the requirements in Section 711 for smoke partitions, doors protecting openings in the smoke partitions shall also comply with Sections 711.5.2, 711.5.3, and 715.4.8 and duct penetrations of the smoke partitions shall be protected as required for *corridors* in accordance with Section 716.5.4.1.

6. Enclosed elevator lobbies are not required where the elevator hoistway is pressurized in accordance with Section 708.14.2.
7. Enclosed elevator lobbies are not required where the elevator serves only *open parking garages* in accordance with Section 406.3.

708.14.1.1 Areas of refuge. Areas of refuge shall be provided as required in Section 1007.

708.14.2 Enclosed elevator lobby. Where elevator hoistway pressurization is provided in lieu of required enclosed elevator lobbies, the pressurization system shall comply with this section.

708.14.2.1 Pressurization requirements. Elevator hoistways shall be pressurized to maintain a minimum positive pressure of 0.10 inch of water (25 Pa) and a maximum positive pressure of 0.25 inch of water (67 Pa) with respect to adjacent occupied space on all floors. This pressure shall be measured at the midpoint of each hoistway door, with all elevator cars at the floor of recall and all hoistway doors on the floor of recall open and all other hoistway doors closed. The opening and closing of hoistway doors at each level must be demonstrated during this test. The supply air intake shall be from an outside, uncontaminated source located a minimum distance of 20 feet (6096 mm) from any air exhaust system or outlet.

708.14.2.2 Rational analysis. A rational analysis complying with Section 909.4 shall be submitted with the *construction documents*.

708.14.2.3 Ducts for system. Any duct system that is part of the pressurization system shall be protected with the same *fire-resistance rating* as required for the elevator shaft enclosure.

708.14.2.4 Fan system. The fan system provided for the pressurization system shall be as required by this section.

708.14.2.4.1 Fire resistance. When located within the building, the fan system that provides the pressurization shall be protected with the same *fire-resistance rating* required for the elevator shaft enclosure.

708.14.2.4.2 Smoke detection. The fan system shall be equipped with a smoke detector that will automatically shut down the fan system when smoke is detected within the system.

708.14.2.4.3 Separate systems. A separate fan system shall be used for each elevator hoistway.

708.14.2.4.4 Fan capacity. The supply fan shall either be adjustable with a capacity of at least 1,000 cfm (0.4719 m^3/s) per door, or that specified by a *registered design professional* to meet the requirements of a designed pressurization system.

708.14.2.5 Standby power. The pressurization system shall be provided with standby power from the same source as other required emergency systems for the building.

708.14.2.6 Activation of pressurization system. The elevator pressurization system shall be activated upon activation of the building fire alarm system or upon activation of the elevator lobby smoke detectors. Where both a building fire alarm system and elevator lobby smoke detectors are present, each shall be independently capable of activating the pressurization system.

708.14.2.7 Special inspection. *Special inspection* for performance shall be required in accordance with Section 909.18.8. System acceptance shall be in accordance with Section 909.19.

708.14.2.8 Marking and identification. Detection and control systems shall be marked in accordance with Section 909.14.

708.14.2.9 Control diagrams. Control diagrams shall be provided in accordance with Section 909.15.

708.14.2.10 Control panel. A control panel complying with Section 909.16 shall be provided.

708.14.2.11 System response time. Hoistway pressurization systems shall comply with the requirements for smoke control system response time in Section 909.17.

SECTION 709
FIRE PARTITIONS

709.1 General. The following wall assemblies shall comply with this section.

1. Walls separating *dwelling units* in the same building as required by Section 420.2.
2. Walls separating *sleeping units* in the same building as required by Section 420.2.
3. Walls separating tenant spaces in *covered mall buildings* as required by Section 402.7.2.
4. Corridor walls as required by Section 1018.1.
5. Elevator lobby separation as required by Section 708.14.1.

709.2 Materials. The walls shall be of materials permitted by the building type of construction.

709.3 Fire-resistance rating. Fire partitions shall have a *fire-resistance rating* of not less than 1 hour.

Exceptions:

1. Corridor walls permitted to have a $^1/_2$-hour *fire-resistance rating* by Table 1018.1.

2. *Dwelling unit* and *sleeping unit* separations in buildings of Type IIB, IIIB and VB construction shall have *fire-resistance ratings* of not less than $^1/_2$-hour in buildings equipped throughout with an *automatic sprinkler system* in accordance with Section 903.3.1.1.

709.4 Continuity. Fire partitions shall extend from the top of the foundation or floor/ceiling assembly below to the underside of the floor or roof sheathing, slab or deck above or to the fire-resistance-rated floor/ceiling or roof/ceiling assembly above, and shall be securely attached thereto. If the partitions are not continuous to the sheathing, deck or slab, and where constructed of combustible construction, the space between the ceiling and the sheathing, deck or slab above shall be fireblocked or draftstopped in accordance with Sections 717.2 and 717.3 at the partition line. The supporting construction shall be protected to afford the required *fire-resistance rating* of the wall supported, except for walls separating tenant spaces in *covered mall buildings*, walls separating *dwelling units*, walls separating *sleeping units* and *corridor* walls, in buildings of Type IIB, IIIB and VB construction.

Exceptions:

1. The wall need not be extended into the crawl space below where the floor above the crawl space has a minimum 1-hour *fire-resistance rating*.
2. Where the room-side fire-resistance-rated membrane of the *corridor* is carried through to the underside of the floor or roof sheathing, deck or slab of a fire-resistance-rated floor or roof above, the ceiling of the *corridor* shall be permitted to be protected by the use of ceiling materials as required for a 1-hour fire-resistance-rated floor or roof system.
3. Where the *corridor* ceiling is constructed as required for the *corridor* walls, the walls shall be permitted to terminate at the upper membrane of such ceiling assembly.
4. The fire partitions separating tenant spaces in a *covered mall building*, complying with Section 402.7.2, are not required to extend beyond the underside of a ceiling that is not part of a fire-resistance-rated assembly. A wall is not required in *attic* or ceiling spaces above tenant separation walls.
5. Fireblocking or draftstopping is not required at the partition line in Group R-2 buildings that do not exceed four *stories above grade plane*, provided the *attic* space is subdivided by draftstopping into areas not exceeding 3,000 square feet (279 m^2) or above every two *dwelling units*, whichever is smaller.
6. Fireblocking or draftstopping is not required at the partition line in buildings equipped with an *automatic sprinkler system* installed throughout in accordance with Section 903.3.1.1 or 903.3.1.2, provided that automatic sprinklers are installed in combustible floor/ceiling and roof/ceiling spaces.

709.5 Exterior walls. Where *exterior walls* serve as a part of a required fire-resistance-rated separation, such walls shall comply with the requirements of Section 705 for *exterior walls*, and the fire-resistance-rated separation requirements shall not apply.

Exception: *Exterior walls* required to be fire-resistance rated in accordance with Section 1019.2 for exterior egress balconies, Section 1022.6 for *exit* enclosures and Section 1026.6 for exterior *exit* ramps and *stairways*.

709.6 Openings. Openings in a *fire partition* shall be protected in accordance with Section 715.

709.7 Penetrations. Penetrations of *fire partitions* shall comply with Section 713.

709.8 Joints. Joints made in or between *fire partitions* shall comply with Section 714.

709.9 Ducts and air transfer openings. Penetrations in a *fire partition* by ducts and air transfer openings shall comply with Section 716.

SECTION 710
SMOKE BARRIERS

710.1 General. *Smoke barriers* shall comply with this section.

710.2 Materials. *Smoke barriers* shall be of materials permitted by the building type of construction.

710.3 Fire-resistance rating. A 1-hour *fire-resistance rating* is required for *smoke barriers*.

Exception: *Smoke barriers* constructed of minimum 0.10-inch-thick (2.5 mm) steel in Group I-3 buildings.

710.4 Continuity. *Smoke barriers* shall form an effective membrane continuous from outside wall to outside wall and from the top of the foundation or floor/ceiling assembly below to the underside of the floor or roof sheathing, deck or slab above, including continuity through concealed spaces, such as those found above suspended ceilings, and interstitial structural and mechanical spaces. The supporting construction shall be protected to afford the required *fire-resistance rating* of the wall or floor supported in buildings of other than Type IIB, IIIB or VB construction.

Exception: Smoke-barrier walls are not required in interstitial spaces where such spaces are designed and constructed with ceilings that provide resistance to the passage of fire and smoke equivalent to that provided by the smoke-barrier walls.

710.5 Openings. Openings in a *smoke barrier* shall be protected in accordance with Section 715.

Exceptions:

1. In Group I-2, where doors are installed across *corridors*, a pair of opposite-swinging doors without a center mullion shall be installed having vision panels with fire-protection-rated glazing materials in fire-protection-rated frames, the area of which shall not exceed that tested. The doors shall be close fitting within oper-

ational tolerances, and shall not have undercuts in excess of $^3/_4$-inch, louvers or grilles. The doors shall have head and jamb stops, astragals or rabbets at meeting edges and shall be automatic-closing by smoke detection in accordance with Section 715.4.8.3. Where permitted by the door manufacturer's listing, positive-latching devices are not required.

2. In Group I-2, horizontal sliding doors installed in accordance with Section 1008.1.4.3 and protected in accordance with Section 715.

710.6 Penetrations. Penetrations of *smoke barriers* shall comply with Section 713.

710.7 Joints. Joints made in or between *smoke barriers* shall comply with Section 714.

710.8 Ducts and air transfer openings. Penetrations in a *smoke barrier* by ducts and air transfer openings shall comply with Section 716.

SECTION 711 SMOKE PARTITIONS

711.1 General. Smoke partitions installed as required elsewhere in the code shall comply with this section.

711.2 Materials. The walls shall be of materials permitted by the building type of construction.

711.3 Fire-resistance rating. Unless required elsewhere in the code, smoke partitions are not required to have a *fire-resistance rating*.

711.4 Continuity. Smoke partitions shall extend from the top of the foundation or floor below to the underside of the floor or roof sheathing, deck or slab above or to the underside of the ceiling above where the ceiling membrane is constructed to limit the transfer of smoke.

711.5 Openings. Windows shall be sealed to resist the free passage of smoke or be automatic-closing upon detection of smoke. Doors in smoke partitions shall comply with this section.

711.5.1 Louvers. Doors in smoke partitions shall not include louvers.

711.5.2 Smoke and draft control doors. Where required elsewhere in the code, doors in smoke partitions shall meet the requirements for a smoke and draft control door assembly tested in accordance with UL 1784. The air leakage rate of the door assembly shall not exceed 3.0 cubic feet per minute per square foot [0.015424 $m^3/(s \cdot m^2)$] of door opening at 0.10 inch (24.9 Pa) of water for both the ambient temperature test and the elevated temperature exposure test. Installation of smoke doors shall be in accordance with NFPA 105.

711.5.3 Self- or automatic-closing doors. Where required elsewhere in the code, doors in smoke partitions shall be self- or automatic-closing by smoke detection in accordance with Section 715.4.8.3.

711.6 Penetrations and joints. The space around penetrating items and in joints shall be filled with an *approved* material to limit the free passage of smoke.

711.7 Ducts and air transfer openings. The space around a duct penetrating a smoke partition shall be filled with an *approved* material to limit the free passage of smoke. Air transfer openings in smoke partitions shall be provided with a *smoke damper* complying with Section 716.3.2.2.

Exception: Where the installation of a *smoke damper* will interfere with the operation of a required smoke control system in accordance with Section 909, *approved* alternative protection shall be utilized.

SECTION 712 HORIZONTAL ASSEMBLIES

712.1 General. Floor and roof assemblies required to have a *fire-resistance rating* shall comply with this section. Nonfire-resistance-rated floor and roof assemblies shall comply with Section 713.4.2.

712.2 Materials. The floor and roof assemblies shall be of materials permitted by the building type of construction.

712.3 Fire-resistance rating. The *fire-resistance rating* of floor and roof assemblies shall not be less than that required by the building type of construction. Where the floor assembly separates mixed occupancies or single occupancies into different *fire areas*, the assembly shall have a *fire-resistance rating* of not less than that required by Section 508.4 based on the occupancies being separated. Horizontal assemblies separating dwelling units in the same building and horizontal assemblies separating sleeping units in the same building shall be a minimum of 1-hour fire-resistance-rated construction.

Exception: *Dwelling unit* and *sleeping unit* separations in buildings of Type IIB, IIIB and VB construction shall have *fire-resistance ratings* of not less than $^1/_2$ hour in buildings equipped throughout with an *automatic sprinkler system* in accordance with Section 903.3.1.1.

712.3.1 Ceiling panels. Where the weight of lay-in ceiling panels, used as part of fire-resistance-rated floor/ceiling or roof/ceiling assemblies, is not adequate to resist an upward force of 1 pound per square foot (48 Pa), wire or other *approved* devices shall be installed above the panels to prevent vertical displacement under such upward force.

712.3.2 Access doors. Access doors shall be permitted in ceilings of fire-resistance-rated floor/ceiling and roof/ceiling assemblies provided such doors are tested in accordance with ASTM E 119 or UL 263 as horizontal assemblies and labeled by an *approved agency* for such purpose.

712.3.3 Unusable space. In 1-hour fire-resistance-rated floor assemblies, the ceiling membrane is not required to be installed over unusable crawl spaces. In 1-hour fire-resistance-rated roof assemblies, the floor membrane is not required to be installed where unusable *attic* space occurs above.

712.4 Continuity. Assemblies shall be continuous without openings, penetrations or joints except as permitted by this section and Sections 708.2, 713.4, 714 and 1022.1. Skylights and other penetrations through a fire-resistance-rated roof deck or slab are permitted to be unprotected, provided that the structural integrity of the fire-resistance-rated roof assembly is maintained. Unprotected skylights shall not be permitted in roof assemblies required to be fire-resistance rated in accordance with Section 705.8.6. The supporting construction shall be protected to afford the required *fire-resistance rating* of the *horizontal assembly* supported.

Exception: In buildings of Type IIB, IIIB or VB construction, the construction supporting the *horizontal assembly* is not required to be fire-resistance-rated at the following:

1. Horizontal assemblies at the separations of incidental uses as specified by Table 508.2.5, provided the required *fire-resistance rating* does not exceed 1 hour.
2. Horizontal assemblies at the separations of *dwelling units* and *sleeping units* as required by Section 420.3.
3. Horizontal assemblies at *smoke barriers* constructed in accordance with Section 710.

712.5 Penetrations. Penetrations of *horizontal assemblies* shall comply with Section 713.

712.6 Joints. Joints made in or between *horizontal assemblies* shall comply with Section 714. The void created at the intersection of a floor/ceiling assembly and an exterior curtain wall assembly shall be protected in accordance with Section 714.4.

712.7 Ducts and air transfer openings. Penetrations in *horizontal assemblies* by ducts and air transfer openings shall comply with Section 716.

712.8 Floor fire door assemblies. Floor *fire door* assemblies used to protect openings in fire-resistance-rated floors shall be tested in accordance with NFPA 288, and shall achieve a *fire-resistance rating* not less than the assembly being penetrated. Floor *fire door* assemblies shall be labeled by an *approved agency*. The *label* shall be permanently affixed and shall specify the manufacturer, the test standard and the *fire-resistance rating*.

712.9 Smoke barrier. Where *horizontal assemblies* are required to resist the movement of smoke by other sections of this code in accordance with the definition of *smoke barrier*, penetrations and joints in such *horizontal assemblies* shall be protected as required for *smoke barriers* in accordance with Sections 713.5 and 714.6. Regardless of the number of *stories* connected by elevator shaft enclosures, doors located in elevator shaft enclosures that penetrate the *horizontal assembly* shall be protected by enclosed elevator lobbies complying with Section 708.14.1. Openings through *horizontal assemblies* shall be protected by shaft enclosures complying with Section 708. *Horizontal assemblies* shall not be allowed to have unprotected vertical openings.

SECTION 713
PENETRATIONS

713.1 Scope. The provisions of this section shall govern the materials and methods of construction used to protect *through penetrations* and *membrane penetrations* of *horizontal assemblies* and fire-resistance-rated wall assemblies.

713.1.1 Ducts and air transfer openings. Penetrations of fire-resistance-rated walls by ducts that are not protected with *dampers* shall comply with Sections 713.2 through 713.3.3. Penetrations of *horizontal assemblies* not protected with a shaft as permitted by Exception 4 of Section 708.2, and not required to be protected with fire *dampers* by other sections of this code, shall comply with Sections 713.4 through 713.4.2.2. Ducts and air transfer openings that are protected with *dampers* shall comply with Section 716.

713.2 Installation details. Where sleeves are used, they shall be securely fastened to the assembly penetrated. The space between the item contained in the sleeve and the sleeve itself and any space between the sleeve and the assembly penetrated shall be protected in accordance with this section. Insulation and coverings on or in the penetrating item shall not penetrate the assembly unless the specific material used has been tested as part of the assembly in accordance with this section.

713.3 Fire-resistance-rated walls. Penetrations into or through *fire walls*, *fire barriers*, *smoke barrier* walls and *fire partitions* shall comply with Sections 713.3.1 through 713.3.3. Penetrations in *smoke barrier* walls shall also comply with Section 713.5.

713.3.1 Through penetrations. Through penetrations of fire-resistance-rated walls shall comply with Section 713.3.1.1 or 713.3.1.2.

Exception: Where the penetrating items are steel, ferrous or copper pipes, tubes or conduits, the *annular space* between the penetrating item and the fire-resistance-rated wall is permitted to be protected as follows:

1. In concrete or masonry walls where the penetrating item is a maximum 6-inch (152 mm) nominal diameter and the area of the opening through the wall does not exceed 144 square inches (0.0929 m^2), concrete, grout or mortar is permitted where it is installed the full thickness of the wall or the thickness required to maintain the *fire-resistance rating*; or
2. The material used to fill the *annular space* shall prevent the passage of flame and hot gases sufficient to ignite cotton waste when subjected to ASTM E 119 or UL 263 time-temperature fire conditions under a minimum positive pressure differential of 0.01 inch (2.49 Pa) of water at the location of the penetration for the time period equivalent to the *fire-resistance rating* of the construction penetrated.

713.3.1.1 Fire-resistance-rated assemblies. Penetrations shall be installed as tested in an *approved* fire-resistance-rated assembly.

713.3.1.2 Through-penetration firestop system. *Through penetrations* shall be protected by an *approved* penetration firestop system installed as tested in accordance with ASTM E 814 or UL 1479, with a minimum positive pressure differential of 0.01 inch (2.49 Pa) of water and shall have an F rating of not less than the required *fire-resistance rating* of the wall penetrated.

713.3.2 Membrane penetrations. Membrane penetrations shall comply with Section 713.3.1. Where walls or partitions are required to have a *fire-resistance rating*, recessed fixtures shall be installed such that the required fire-resistance will not be reduced.

Exceptions:

1. Membrane penetrations of maximum 2-hour fire-resistance-rated walls and partitions by steel electrical boxes that do not exceed 16 square inches (0.0103 m^2) in area, provided the aggregate area of the openings through the membrane does not exceed 100 square inches (0.0645 m^2) in any 100 square feet (9.29 m^2) of wall area. The *annular space* between the wall membrane and the box shall not exceed $^1/_8$ inch (3.1 mm). Such boxes on opposite sides of the wall or partition shall be separated by one of the following:
   - 1.1. By a horizontal distance of not less than 24 inches (610 mm) where the wall or partition is constructed with individual noncommunicating stud cavities;
   - 1.2. By a horizontal distance of not less than the depth of the wall cavity where the wall cavity is filled with cellulose loose-fill, rockwool or slag mineral wool insulation;
   - 1.3. By solid fireblocking in accordance with Section 717.2.1;
   - 1.4. By protecting both outlet boxes with *listed* putty pads; or
   - 1.5. By other *listed* materials and methods.
2. Membrane penetrations by *listed* electrical boxes of any material, provided such boxes have been tested for use in fire-resistance-rated assemblies and are installed in accordance with the instructions included in the listing. The *annular space* between the wall membrane and the box shall not exceed $^1/_8$ inch (3.1 mm) unless *listed* otherwise. Such boxes on opposite sides of the wall or partition shall be separated by one of the following:
   - 2.1. By the horizontal distance specified in the listing of the electrical boxes;
   - 2.2. By solid fireblocking in accordance with Section 717.2.1;
   - 2.3. By protecting both boxes with *listed* putty pads; or
   - 2.4. By other *listed* materials and methods.
3. Membrane penetrations by electrical boxes of any size or type, which have been *listed* as part of a wall opening protective material system for use in fire-resistance-rated assemblies and are installed in accordance with the instructions included in the listing.
4. Membrane penetrations by boxes other than electrical boxes, provided such penetrating items and the *annular space* between the wall membrane and the box, are protected by an *approved membrane penetration* firestop system installed as tested in accordance with ASTM E 814 or UL 1479, with a minimum positive pressure differential of 0.01 inch (2.49 Pa) of water, and shall have an F and T rating of not less than the required *fire-resistance rating* of the wall penetrated and be installed in accordance with their listing.
5. The *annular space* created by the penetration of an automatic sprinkler, provided it is covered by a metal escutcheon plate.

713.3.3 Dissimilar materials. Noncombustible penetrating items shall not connect to combustible items beyond the point of firestopping unless it can be demonstrated that the fire-resistance integrity of the wall is maintained.

713.4 Horizontal assemblies. Penetrations of a floor, floor/ceiling assembly or the ceiling membrane of a roof/ceiling assembly not required to be enclosed in a shaft by Section 708.2 shall be protected in accordance with Sections 713.4.1 through 713.4.2.2.

713.4.1 Fire-resistance-rated assemblies. Penetrations of the fire-resistance-rated floor, floor/ceiling assembly or the ceiling membrane of a roof/ceiling assembly shall comply with Sections 713.4.1.1 through 713.4.1.4. Penetrations in horizontal *smoke barriers* shall also comply with 713.5.

713.4.1.1 Through penetrations. Through penetrations of fire-resistance-rated *horizontal assemblies* shall comply with Section 713.4.1.1.1 or 713.4.1.1.2.

Exceptions:

1. Penetrations by steel, ferrous or copper conduits, pipes, tubes or vents or concrete or masonry items through a single fire-resistance- rated floor assembly where the *annular space* is protected with materials that prevent the passage of flame and hot gases sufficient to ignite cotton waste when subjected to ASTM E 119 or UL 263 time-temperature fire conditions under a minimum positive pressure differential of 0.01 inch (2.49 Pa) of water at the location of the penetration for the time period equivalent to the *fire-resistance rating* of the construction penetrated. Penetrating items with a maximum 6-inch (152 mm) nominal diameter shall not be limited to the penetration of a single fire-resistance-rated floor assembly, provided the aggregate area of the openings through the assembly does not exceed 144 square inches (92 900 mm^2) in any 100 square feet (9.3 m^2) of floor area.
2. Penetrations in a single concrete floor by steel, ferrous or copper conduits, pipes, tubes or vents with a maximum 6-inch (152 mm) nominal diameter, provided the concrete, grout or mortar is installed the full thickness of the floor or the thickness required to maintain the

fire-resistance rating. The penetrating items shall not be limited to the penetration of a single concrete floor, provided the area of the opening through each floor does not exceed 144 square inches (92 900 mm^2).

3. Penetrations by *listed* electrical boxes of any material, provided such boxes have been tested for use in fire-resistance-rated assemblies and installed in accordance with the instructions included in the listing.

713.4.1.1.1 Installation. *Through penetrations* shall be installed as tested in the *approved* fire-resistance-rated assembly.

713.4.1.1.2 Through-penetration firestop system. *Through penetrations* shall be protected by an *approved through-penetration firestop system* installed and tested in accordance with ASTM E 814 or UL 1479, with a minimum positive pressure differential of 0.01 inch of water (2.49 Pa). The system shall have an F rating/T rating of not less than 1 hour but not less than the required rating of the floor penetrated.

Exception: Floor penetrations contained and located within the cavity of a wall above the floor or below the floor do not require a T rating.

713.4.1.2 Membrane penetrations. Penetrations of membranes that are part of a *horizontal assembly* shall comply with Section 713.4.1.1.1 or 713.4.1.1.2. Where floor/ceiling assemblies are required to have a *fire-resistance rating*, recessed fixtures shall be installed such that the required *fire resistance* will not be reduced.

Exceptions:

1. *Membrane penetrations* by steel, ferrous or copper conduits, pipes, tubes or vents, or concrete or masonry items where the *annular space* is protected either in accordance with Section 713.4.1.1 or to prevent the free passage of flame and the products of combustion. The aggregate area of the openings through the membrane shall not exceed 100 square inches (64 500 mm^2) in any 100 square feet (9.3 m^2) of ceiling area in assemblies tested without penetrations.
2. Ceiling membrane penetrations of maximum 2-hour *horizontal assemblies* by steel electrical boxes that do not exceed 16 square inches (10 323 mm^2) in area, provided the aggregate area of such penetrations does not exceed 100 square inches (44 500 mm^2) in any 100 square feet (9.29 m^2) of ceiling area, and the annular space between the ceiling membrane and the box does not exceed $^1/_8$ inch (3.2 mm).
3. Membrane penetrations by electrical boxes of any size or type, which have been *listed* as part of an opening protective material system for use in *horizontal assemblies* and are installed in accordance with the instructions included in the listing.
4. *Membrane penetrations* by *listed* electrical boxes of any material, provided such boxes have been tested for use in fire-resistance-rated assemblies and are installed in accordance with the instructions included in the listing. The *annular space* between the ceiling membrane and the box shall not exceed $^1/_8$ inch (3.2 mm) unless *listed* otherwise.
5. The *annular space* created by the penetration of a fire sprinkler, provided it is covered by a metal escutcheon plate.

713.4.1.3 Ducts and air transfer openings. Penetrations of *horizontal assemblies* by ducts and air transfer openings shall comply with Section 716.

713.4.1.4 Dissimilar materials. Noncombustible penetrating items shall not connect to combustible materials beyond the point of firestopping unless it can be demonstrated that the fire-resistance integrity of the *horizontal assembly* is maintained.

713.4.2 Nonfire-resistance-rated assemblies. Penetrations of nonfire-resistance-rated floor or floor/ceiling assemblies or the ceiling membrane of a nonfire-resistance-rated roof/ceiling assembly shall meet the requirements of Section 708 or shall comply with Section 713.4.2.1 or 713.4.2.2.

713.4.2.1 Noncombustible penetrating items. Noncombustible penetrating items that connect not more than three *stories* are permitted, provided that the *annular space* is filled to resist the free passage of flame and the products of combustion with an *approved* noncombustible material or with a fill, void or cavity material that is tested and classified for use in through-penetration firestop systems.

713.4.2.2 Penetrating items. Penetrating items that connect not more than two *stories* are permitted, provided that the *annular space* is filled with an *approved* material to resist the free passage of flame and the products of combustion.

713.5 Penetrations in smoke barriers. Penetrations in *smoke barriers* shall be tested in accordance with the requirements of UL 1479 for air leakage. The air leakage rate of the penetration assemblies measured at 0.30 inch (7.47 Pa) of water in both the ambient temperature and elevated temperature tests, shall not exceed:

1. 5.0 cfm per square foot ($0.025 m^3 / s \cdot m^2$) of penetration opening for each *through-penetration firestop system*; or
2. A total cumulative leakage of 50 cfm ($0.024 m^3/s$) for any 100 square feet (9.3 m^2) of wall area, or floor area.

SECTION 714
FIRE-RESISTANT JOINT SYSTEMS

714.1 General. Joints installed in or between fire-resistance-rated walls, floor or floor/ceiling assemblies and roofs or roof/ceiling assemblies shall be protected by an *approved fire-resistant joint system* designed to resist the passage of fire for a time period not less than the required *fire-resistance rating* of the wall, floor or roof in or between which it is installed. *Fire-resistant joint systems* shall be tested in accordance with Section 714.3. The void created at the intersection of a floor/ceiling assembly and an exterior curtain wall assembly shall be protected in accordance with Section 714.4.

Exception: *Fire-resistant joint systems* shall not be required for joints in all of the following locations:

1. Floors within a single *dwelling unit.*
2. Floors where the joint is protected by a shaft enclosure in accordance with Section 708.
3. Floors within atriums where the space adjacent to the atrium is included in the volume of the atrium for smoke control purposes.
4. Floors within malls.
5. Floors and ramps within open and enclosed parking garages or structures constructed in accordance with Sections 406.3 and 406.4, respectively.
6. *Mezzanine* floors.
7. Walls that are permitted to have unprotected openings.
8. Roofs where openings are permitted.
9. Control joints not exceeding a maximum width of 0.625 inch (15.9 mm) and tested in accordance with ASTM E 119 or UL 263.

714.2 Installation. *Fire-resistant joint systems* shall be securely installed in or on the joint for its entire length so as not to dislodge, loosen or otherwise impair its ability to accommodate expected building movements and to resist the passage of fire and hot gases.

714.3 Fire test criteria. *Fire-resistant joint systems* shall be tested in accordance with the requirements of either ASTM E 1966 or UL 2079. Nonsymmetrical wall joint systems shall be tested with both faces exposed to the furnace, and the assigned *fire-resistance rating* shall be the shortest duration obtained from the two tests. When evidence is furnished to show that the wall was tested with the least fire-resistant side exposed to the furnace, subject to acceptance of the *building official*, the wall need not be subjected to tests from the opposite side.

Exception: For *exterior walls* with a horizontal *fire separation distance* greater than 5 feet (1524 mm), the joint system shall be required to be tested for interior fire exposure only.

714.4 Exterior curtain wall/floor intersection. Where fire resistance-rated floor or floor/ceiling assemblies are required, voids created at the intersection of the exterior curtain wall assemblies and such floor assemblies shall be sealed with an *approved* system to prevent the interior spread of fire. Such systems shall be securely installed and tested in accordance with ASTM E 2307 to prevent the passage of flame for the time period at least equal to the *fire-resistance rating* of the floor assembly and prevent the passage of heat and hot gases sufficient to ignite cotton waste. Height and fire-resistance requirements for curtain wall spandrels shall comply with Section 705.8.5.

714.4.1 Exterior curtain wall/nonfire-resistance-rated floor assembly intersections. Voids created at the intersection of exterior curtain wall assemblies and nonfire-resistance-rated floor or floor/ceiling assemblies shall be sealed with an *approved* material or system to retard the interior spread of fire and hot gases between *stories.*

714.5 Spandrel wall. Height and fire-resistance requirements for curtain wall spandrels shall comply with Section 705.8.5. Where Section 705.8.5 does not require a fire-resistance-rated spandrel wall, the requirements of Section 714.4 shall still apply to the intersection between the spandrel wall and the floor.

714.6 Fire-resistant joint systems in smoke barriers. Fire-resistant joint systems in smoke barriers, and joints at the intersection of a horizontal *smoke barrier* and an exterior curtain wall, shall be tested in accordance with the requirements of UL 2079 for air leakage. The air leakage rate of the joint shall not exceed 5 cfm per linear foot (0.00775 $m^3/s \cdot m$) of joint at 0.30 inch (7.47 Pa) of water for both the ambient temperature and elevated temperature tests.

SECTION 715 OPENING PROTECTIVES

715.1 General. Opening protectives required by other sections of this code shall comply with the provisions of this section.

715.2 Fire-resistance-rated glazing. Fire-resistance-rated glazing tested as part of a fire-resistance-rated wall assembly in accordance with ASTM E 119 or UL 263 and labeled in accordance with Section 703.5 shall be permitted in *fire doors* and *fire window assemblies* in accordance with their listings and shall not otherwise be required to comply with this section.

715.3 Alternative methods for determining fire protection ratings. The application of any of the alternative methods *listed* in this section shall be based on the fire exposure and acceptance criteria specified in NFPA 252, NFPA 257 or UL 9. The required *fire resistance* of an opening protective shall be permitted to be established by any of the following methods or procedures:

1. Designs documented in *approved* sources.
2. Calculations performed in an *approved* manner.
3. Engineering analysis based on a comparison of opening protective designs having *fire protection ratings* as determined by the test procedures set forth in NFPA 252, NFPA 257 or UL 9.
4. Alternative protection methods as allowed by Section 104.11.

715.4 Fire door and shutter assemblies. Approved *fire door* and fire shutter assemblies shall be constructed of any material or assembly of component materials that conforms to the test requirements of Section 715.4.1, 715.4.2 or 715.4.3 and the *fire protection rating* indicated in Table 715.4. *Fire door* frames with transom lights, sidelights or both shall be permitted in accordance with Section 715.4.5. *Fire door* assemblies and shutters shall be installed in accordance with the provisions of this section and NFPA 80.

Exceptions:

1. Labeled protective assemblies that conform to the requirements of this section or UL 10A, UL 14B and UL 14C for tin-clad *fire door* assemblies.

2. Floor *fire door* assemblies in accordance with Section 712.8.

715.4.1 Side-hinged or pivoted swinging doors. *Fire door* assemblies with side-hinged and pivoted swinging doors shall be tested in accordance with NFPA 252 or UL 10C. After 5 minutes into the NFPA 252 test, the neutral pressure level in the furnace shall be established at 40 inches (1016 mm) or less above the sill.

715.4.2 Other types of assemblies. *Fire door* assemblies with other types of doors, including swinging elevator doors and fire shutter assemblies, shall be tested in accordance with NFPA 252 or UL 10B. The pressure in the furnace shall be maintained as nearly equal to the atmospheric pressure as possible. Once established, the pressure shall be maintained during the entire test period.

715.4.3 Door assemblies in corridors and smoke barriers. *Fire door* assemblies required to have a minimum *fire protection rating* of 20 minutes where located in *corridor* walls or *smoke barrier* walls having a *fire-resistance rating* in accordance with Table 715.4 shall be tested in accordance with NFPA 252 or UL 10C without the hose stream test.

Exceptions:

1. Viewports that require a hole not larger than 1 inch (25 mm) in diameter through the door, have at least a 0.25-inch-thick (6.4 mm) glass disc and the holder is of metal that will not melt out where subject to temperatures of 1,700°F (927°C).
2. *Corridor* door assemblies in occupancies of Group I-2 shall be in accordance with Section 407.3.1.
3. Unprotected openings shall be permitted for *corridors* in multitheater complexes where each motion picture auditorium has at least one-half of its required *exit* or *exit access doorways* opening directly to the exterior or into an *exit* passageway.
4. Horizontal sliding doors in *smoke barriers* that comply with Sections 408.3 and 408.8.4 in occupancies in Group I-3.

715.4.3.1 Smoke and draft control. *Fire door* assemblies shall also meet the requirements for a smoke and draft control door assembly tested in accordance with UL 1784. The air leakage rate of the door assembly shall not exceed 3.0 cubic feet per minute per square foot [0.01524 $m^3/(s \cdot m^2)$] of door opening at 0.10 inch (24.9 Pa) of water for both the ambient temperature and elevated temperature tests. Louvers shall be prohibited. Installation of smoke doors shall be in accordance with NFPA 105.

715.4.3.2 Glazing in door assemblies. In a 20-minute *fire door* assembly, the glazing material in the door itself shall have a minimum fire-protection-rated glazing of 20 minutes and shall be exempt from the hose stream test. Glazing material in any other part of the door assembly, including transom lights and sidelights, shall be tested in accordance with NFPA 257 or UL 9, including the hose stream test, in accordance with Section 715.5.

TABLE 715.4
FIRE DOOR AND FIRE SHUTTER FIRE PROTECTION RATINGS

TYPE OF ASSEMBLY	REQUIRED ASSEMBLY RATING (hours)	MINIMUM FIRE DOOR AND FIRE SHUTTER ASSEMBLY RATING (hours)
Fire walls and fire barriers having a required fire-resistance rating greater than 1 hour	4 3 2 $1^1/_2$	3 3[a] $1^1/_2$ $1^1/_2$
Fire barriers having a required fire-resistance rating of 1 hour: Shaft, exit enclosure and exit passageway walls Other fire barriers	 1 1	 1 $^3/_4$
Fire partitions: Corridor walls[c] Other fire partitions	 1 0.5 1 0.5	 $^1/_3$ [b] $^1/_3$ [b] $^3/_4$ $^1/_3$
Exterior walls	3 2 1	$1^1/_2$ $1^1/_2$ $^3/_4$
Smoke barriers	1	$^1/_3$ [b]

a. Two doors, each with a fire protection rating of $1^1/_2$ hours, installed on opposite sides of the same opening in a fire wall, shall be deemed equivalent in fire protection rating to one 3-hour fire door.

b. For testing requirements, see Section 715.4.3.

c. Fire-rated bathroom/restroom doors are not required when opening onto fire-rated halls, corridors, exit access provided:

1. No other rooms open off the bathroom/restroom;
2. No gas or electric appliances other than electric hand dryers are located in the bathroom/restroom;
3. The walls, partitions, floor and ceiling of the bathroom/restroom have a fire rating at least equal to the rating of the hall, corridor or exit access; and
4. The bathroom/restroom is not used for any other purpose than it is designed.

715.4.4 Doors in exit enclosures and exit passageways. *Fire door* assemblies in *exit* enclosures and *exit* passageways shall have a maximum transmitted temperature end point of not more than 450°F (250°C) above ambient at the end of 30 minutes of standard fire test exposure.

Exception: The maximum transmitted temperature rise is not required in buildings equipped throughout with an *automatic sprinkler system* installed in accordance with Section 903.3.1.1 or 903.3.1.2.

715.4.4.1 Glazing in doors. Fire-protection-rated glazing in excess of 100 square inches (0.065 m^2) shall be permitted in *fire door* assemblies when tested as components of the door assemblies and not as glass lights, and shall have a maximum transmitted temperature rise of 450°F (250°C) in accordance with Section 715.4.4.

Exception: The maximum transmitted temperature rise is not required in buildings equipped throughout with an *automatic sprinkler system* installed in accordance with Section 903.3.1.1 or 903.3.1.2.

715.4.5 Fire door frames with transom lights and sidelights. Door frames with transom lights, sidelights, or both, shall be permitted where a $^3/_4$-hour *fire protection rating* or less is required in accordance with Table 715.4. Where a *fire protection rating* exceeding $^3/_4$-hour is required in accordance with Table 715.4, *fire door* frames with transom lights, sidelights, or both, shall be permitted where installed with fire-resistance-rated glazing tested as an assembly in accordance with ASTM E119 or UL 263.

715.4.6 Labeled protective assemblies. *Fire door* assemblies shall be labeled by an *approved agency*. The *labels* shall comply with NFPA 80, and shall be permanently affixed to the door or frame.

715.4.6.1 Fire door labeling requirements. *Fire doors* shall be labeled showing the name of the manufacturer or other identification readily traceable back to the manufacturer, the name or trademark of the third-party inspection agency, the *fire protection rating* and, where required for *fire doors* in *exit* enclosures and *exit* passageways by Section 715.4.4, the maximum transmitted temperature end point. Smoke and draft control doors complying with UL 1784 shall be labeled as such and shall also comply with Section 715.4.6.3. Labels shall be *approved* and permanently affixed. The *label* shall be applied at the factory or location where fabrication and assembly are performed.

715.4.6.2 Oversized doors. Oversized *fire doors* shall bear an oversized *fire door label* by an *approved agency* or shall be provided with a certificate of inspection furnished by an *approved* testing agency. When a certificate of inspection is furnished by an *approved* testing agency, the certificate shall state that the door conforms to the requirements of design, materials and construction, but has not been subjected to the fire test.

715.4.6.3 Smoke and draft control door labeling requirements. Smoke and draft control doors complying with UL 1784 shall be labeled in accordance with Section 715.4.6.1 and shall show the letter "S" on the fire rating *label* of the door. This marking shall indicate that the door and frame assembly are in compliance when *listed* or labeled gasketing is also installed.

715.4.6.4 Fire door frame labeling requirements. *Fire door* frames shall be labeled showing the names of the manufacturer and the third-party inspection agency.

715.4.7 Glazing material. Fire-protection-rated glazing conforming to the opening protection requirements in Section 715.4 shall be permitted in *fire door* assemblies.

715.4.7.1 Size limitations. Fire-protection-rated glazing used in *fire doors* shall comply with the size limitations of NFPA 80.

Exceptions:

1. Fire-protection-rated glazing located in *fire walls* shall be prohibited except where serving in a *fire door* in a horizontal *exit*, a self-closing swinging door shall be permitted to have a vision panel of not more than 100 square inches (0.065 m^2) without a dimension exceeding 10 inches (254 mm).
2. Fire-protection-rated glazing shall not be installed in *fire doors* having a $1^1/_2$-hour *fire protection rating* intended for installation in *fire barriers*, unless the glazing is not more than 100 square inches (0.065 m^2) in area.

715.4.7.2 Exit and elevator protectives. *Approved* fire-protection-rated glazing used in *fire door* assemblies in elevator and *exit* enclosures shall be so located as to furnish clear vision of the passageway or approach to the elevator, ramp or *stairway*.

715.4.7.3 Labeling. Fire-protection-rated glazing shall bear a *label* or other identification showing the name of the manufacturer, the test standard and information required in Section 715.5.9.1 that shall be issued by an *approved agency* and shall be permanently affixed to the glazing.

715.4.7.3.1 Identification. For fire protection-rated glazing, the *label* shall bear the following four-part identification: "D – H or NH – T or NT – XXX." "D" indicates that the glazing shall be used in *fire door* assemblies and that the glazing meets the fire protection requirements of NFPA 252. "H" shall indicate that the glazing meets the hose stream requirements of NFPA 252. "NH" shall indicate that the glazing does not meet the hose stream requirements of the test. "T" shall indicate that the glazing meets the temperature requirements of Section 715.4.4.1. "NT" shall indicate that the glazing does not meet the temperature requirements of Section 715.4.4.1. The placeholder "XXX" shall specify the fire-protection-rating period, in minutes.

715.4.7.4 Safety glazing. Fire-protection-rated glazing installed in *fire doors* in areas subject to human impact in hazardous locations shall comply with Chapter 24.

715.4.8 Door closing. *Fire doors* shall be self- or automatic-closing in accordance with this section.

Exceptions:

1. *Fire doors* located in common walls separating *sleeping units* in Group R-1 shall be permitted without automatic- or self-closing devices.
2. The elevator car doors and the associated hoistway enclosure doors at the floor level designated for recall in accordance with Section 3003.2 shall be permitted to remain open during Phase I emergency recall operation.

715.4.8.1 Latch required. Unless otherwise specifically permitted, single *fire doors* and both leaves of pairs of side-hinged swinging *fire doors* shall be provided with an active latch bolt that will secure the door when it is closed.

715.4.8.2 Automatic-closing fire door assemblies. Automatic-closing *fire door* assemblies shall be self-closing in accordance with NFPA 80.

715.4.8.3 Smoke-activated doors. Automatic-closing doors installed in the following locations shall be automatic-closing by the actuation of smoke detectors installed in accordance with Section 907.3 or by loss of power to the smoke detector or hold-open device. Doors that are automatic-closing by smoke detection shall not have more than a 10-second delay before the door starts to close after the smoke detector is actuated:

1. Doors installed across a *corridor*.
2. Doors that protect openings in *exits* or *corridors* required to be of fire-resistance-rated construction.
3. Doors that protect openings in walls that are capable of resisting the passage of smoke in accordance with Section 508.2.5.2.
4. Doors installed in *smoke barriers* in accordance with Section 710.5.
5. Doors installed in *fire partitions* in accordance with Section 709.6.
6. Doors installed in a *fire wall* in accordance with Section 706.8.
7. Doors installed in shaft enclosures in accordance with Section 708.7.
8. Doors installed in refuse and laundry chutes and access and termination rooms in accordance with Section 708.13.
9. Doors installed in the walls for compartmentation of underground buildings in accordance with Section 405.4.2.
10. Doors installed in the elevator lobby walls of underground buildings in accordance with Section 405.4.3.
11. Doors installed in smoke partitions in accordance with Section 711.5.3.

715.4.8.4 Doors in pedestrian ways. Vertical sliding or vertical rolling steel *fire doors* in openings through which pedestrians travel shall be heat activated or activated by smoke detectors with alarm verification.

715.4.9 Swinging fire shutters. Where fire shutters of the swinging type are installed in exterior openings, not less than one row in every three vertical rows shall be arranged to be readily opened from the outside, and shall be identified by distinguishing marks or letters not less than 6 inches (152 mm) high.

715.4.10 Rolling fire shutters. Where fire shutters of the rolling type are installed, such shutters shall include *approved* automatic-closing devices.

715.5 Fire-protection-rated glazing. Glazing in *fire window assemblies* shall be fire-protection rated in accordance with this section and Table 715.5. Glazing in *fire door* assemblies shall comply with Section 715.4.7. Fire-protection-rated glazing shall be tested in accordance with and shall meet the acceptance criteria of NFPA 257 or UL 9. Fire-protection-rated glazing shall also comply with NFPA 80. Openings in nonfire-resistance-rated *exterior wall* assemblies that require protection in accordance with Section 705.3, 705.8, 705.8.5 or 705.8.6 shall have a fire-protection rating of not less than $^3/_4$ hour.

Exceptions:

1. Wired glass in accordance with Section 715.5.4.
2. Fire protection-rated glazing in 0.5-hour fire-resistance-rated partitions is permitted to have an 0.33-hour fire-protection rating.

TABLE 715.5
FIRE WINDOW ASSEMBLY FIRE PROTECTION RATINGS

TYPE OF ASSEMBLY		REQUIRED ASSEMBLY RATING (hours)	MINIMUM FIRE WINDOW ASSEMBLY RATING (hours)
Interior walls:	Fire walls	All	NP[a]
	Fire barriers	> 1 1	NP[a] $^3/_4$
	Smoke barriers	1	$^3/_4$
	Fire partitions	1 $^1/_2$	$^3/_4$ $^1/_3$
Exterior walls		> 1 1	$1^1/_2$ $^3/_4$
Party wall		All	NP

NP = Not Permitted.
a. Not permitted except as specified in Section 715.2.

715.5.1 Testing under positive pressure. NFPA 257 or UL 9 shall evaluate fire-protection-rated glazing under positive pressure. Within the first 10 minutes of a test, the pressure in the furnace shall be adjusted so at least two-thirds of the test specimen is above the neutral pressure plane, and the neutral pressure plane shall be maintained at that height for the balance of the test.

715.5.2 Nonsymmetrical glazing systems. Nonsymmetrical fire-protection-rated glazing systems in *fire partitions*, *fire barriers* or in *exterior walls* with a *fire separation distance* of 5 feet (1524 mm) or less pursuant to Section 705 shall be tested with both faces exposed to the furnace, and the assigned *fire protection rating* shall be the shortest duration obtained from the two tests conducted in compliance with NFPA 257 or UL 9.

715.5.3 Safety glazing. Fire-protection-rated glazing installed in *fire window assemblies* in areas subject to human impact in hazardous locations shall comply with Chapter 24.

715.5.4 Wired glass. Steel window frame assemblies of 0.125-inch (3.2 mm) minimum solid section or of not less than nominal 0.048-inch-thick (1.2 mm) formed sheet steel members fabricated by pressing, mitering, riveting, interlocking or welding and having provision for glazing with $^1/_4$-inch (6.4 mm) wired glass where securely installed in the building construction and glazed with $^1/_4$-inch (6.4 mm) labeled wired glass shall be deemed to meet the requirements for a $^3/_4$-hour *fire window assembly*. Wired glass panels shall conform to the size limitations set forth in Table 715.5.4.

TABLE 715.5.4
LIMITING SIZES OF WIRED GLASS PANELS

OPENING FIRE PROTECTION RATING	MAXIMUM AREA (square inches)	MAXIMUM HEIGHT (inches)	MAXIMUM WIDTH (inches)
3 hours	0	0	0
$1^1/_2$-hour doors in exterior walls	0	0	0
1 and $1^1/_2$ hours	100	33	10
$^3/_4$ hour	1,296	54	54
20 minutes	Not Limited	Not Limited	Not Limited
Fire window assemblies	1,296	54	54

For SI: 1 inch = 25.4 mm, 1 square inch = 645.2 mm^2.

715.5.5 Nonwired glass. Glazing other than wired glass in *fire window assemblies* shall be fire-protection-rated glazing installed in accordance with and complying with the size limitations set forth in NFPA 80.

715.5.6 Installation. Fire-protection-rated glazing shall be in the fixed position or be automatic-closing and shall be installed in *approved* frames.

715.5.7 Window mullions. Metal mullions that exceed a nominal height of 12 feet (3658 mm) shall be protected with materials to afford the same *fire-resistance rating* as required for the wall construction in which the protective is located.

715.5.8 Interior fire window assemblies. Fire-protection-rated glazing used in *fire window assemblies* located in *fire partitions* and *fire barriers* shall be limited to use in assemblies with a maximum *fire-resistance rating* of 1 hour in accordance with this section.

715.5.8.1 Where $^3/_4$-hour fire protection window assemblies permitted. Fire-protection-rated glazing requiring 45-minute opening protection in accordance with Table 715.5 shall be limited to *fire partitions* designed in accordance with Section 709 and *fire barriers* utilized in the applications set forth in Sections 707.3.6 and 707.3.8 where the *fire-resistance rating* does not exceed 1 hour.

715.5.8.2 Area limitations. The total area of windows shall not exceed 25 percent of the area of a common wall with any room.

715.5.9 Labeling requirements. Fire-protection-rated glazing shall bear a *label* or other identification showing the name of the manufacturer, the test standard and information required in Section 715.5.9.1 that shall be issued by an *approved agency* and shall be permanently affixed to the glazing.

715.5.9.1 Identification. For fire-protection-rated glazing, the *label* shall bear the following two-part identification: "OH – XXX." "OH" indicates that the glazing meets both the fire protection and the hose-stream requirements of NFPA 257 or UL 9 and is permitted to be used in openings. "XXX" represents the fire-protection rating period, in minutes, that was tested.

SECTION 716
DUCTS AND AIR TRANSFER OPENINGS

716.1 General. The provisions of this section shall govern the protection of duct penetrations and air transfer openings in assemblies required to be protected.

716.1.1 Ducts that penetrate fire-resistance-rated assemblies without dampers. Ducts that penetrate fire-resistance-rated assemblies and are not required by this section to have *dampers* shall comply with the requirements of Sections 713.2 through 713.3.3. Ducts that penetrate *horizontal assemblies* not required to be contained within a shaft and not required by this section to have *dampers* shall comply with the requirements of Sections 713.4 through 713.4.2.2.

716.1.1.1 Ducts that penetrate nonfire-resistance-rated assemblies. The space around a duct penetrating a nonfire-resistance-rated floor assembly shall comply with Section 716.6.3.

716.2 Installation. *Fire dampers, smoke dampers, combination fire/smoke dampers* and *ceiling radiation dampers* located within air distribution and smoke control systems shall be installed in accordance with the requirements of this section, the manufacturer's installation instructions and the *dampers'* listing.

716.2.1 Smoke control system. Where the installation of a fire *damper* will interfere with the operation of a required smoke control system in accordance with Section 909, *approved* alternative protection shall be utilized. Where mechanical systems including ducts and *dampers* utilized for normal building ventilation serve as part of the smoke control system, the expected performance of these systems in smoke control mode shall be addressed in the rational analysis required by Section 909.4.

716.2.2 Hazardous exhaust ducts. *Fire dampers* for hazardous exhaust duct systems shall comply with the *International Mechanical Code.*

716.3 Damper testing, ratings and actuation. *Damper* testing, ratings and actuation shall be in accordance with Sections 716.3.1 through 716.3.3.

716.3.1 Damper testing. *Dampers* shall be *listed* and bear the *label* of an *approved* testing agency indicating compliance with the standards in this section. *Fire dampers* shall comply with the requirements of UL 555. Only *fire dampers* labeled for use in dynamic systems shall be installed in heating, ventilation and air-conditioning systems designed to operate with fans on during a fire. *Smoke dampers* shall comply with the requirements of UL 555S. *Combination fire/smoke dampers* shall comply with the requirements of both UL 555 and UL 555S. *Ceiling radiation dampers* shall comply with the requirements of UL 555C or shall be tested as part of a fire-resistance-rated floor/ceiling or roof/ceiling assembly in accordance with ATSTM E119 or UL 263.

716.3.2 Damper rating. *Damper* ratings shall be in accordance with Sections 716.3.2.1 through 716.3.2.3.

716.3.2.1 Fire damper ratings. *Fire dampers* shall have the minimum *fire protection rating* specified in Table 716.3.2.1 for the type of penetration.

**TABLE 716.3.2.1
FIRE DAMPER RATING**

TYPE OF PENETRATION	MINIMUM DAMPER RATING (hours)
Less than 3-hour fire-resistance-rated assemblies	1.5
3-hour or greater fire-resistance-rated assemblies	3

716.3.2.2 Smoke damper ratings. *Smoke damper* leakage ratings shall not be less than Class II. Elevated temperature ratings shall not be less than 250°F (121°C).

716.3.2.3 Combination fire/smoke damper ratings. *Combination fire/smoke dampers* shall have the minimum *fire protection rating* specified for *fire dampers* in Table 716.3.2.1 for the type of penetration and shall also have a minimum Class II leakage rating and a minimum elevated temperature rating of 250°F (121°C).

716.3.3 Damper actuation. *Damper* actuation shall be in accordance with Sections 716.3.3.1 through 716.3.3.4 as applicable.

716.3.3.1 Fire damper actuation device. The *fire damper* actuation device shall meet one of the following requirements:

1. The operating temperature shall be approximately 50°F (10°C) above the normal temperature within the duct system, but not less than 160°F (71°C).
2. The operating temperature shall be not more than 350°F (177°C) where located in a smoke control system complying with Section 909.

716.3.3.2 Smoke damper actuation. The *smoke damper* shall close upon actuation of a *listed* smoke detector or detectors installed in accordance with Section 907.3 and one of the following methods, as applicable:

1. Where a *smoke damper* is installed within a duct, a smoke detector shall be installed in the duct within 5 feet (1524 mm) of the *damper* with no air outlets or inlets between the detector and the *damper*. The detector shall be *listed* for the air velocity, temperature and humidity anticipated at the point where it is installed. Other than in mechanical smoke control systems, *dampers* shall be closed upon fan shutdown where local smoke detectors require a minimum velocity to operate.
2. Where a *smoke damper* is installed above *smoke barrier* doors in a *smoke barrier*, a spot-type detector *listed* for releasing service shall be installed on either side of the *smoke barrier* door opening.
3. Where a *smoke damper* is installed within an air transfer opening in a wall, a spot-type detector *listed* for releasing service shall be installed within 5 feet (1524 mm) horizontally of the *damper*.
4. Where a *smoke damper* is installed in a *corridor* wall or ceiling, the *damper* shall be permitted to be controlled by a smoke detection system installed in the *corridor*.
5. Where a total-coverage smoke detector system is provided within areas served by a heating, ventilation and air-conditioning (HVAC) system, *smoke dampers* shall be permitted to be controlled by the smoke detection system.

716.3.3.3 Combination fire/smoke damper actuation. *Combination fire/smoke damper* actuation shall be in accordance with Sections 716.3.3.1 and 716.3.3.2. *Combination fire/smoke dampers* installed in smoke control system shaft penetrations shall not be activated by local area smoke detection unless it is secondary to the smoke management system controls.

716.3.3.4 Ceiling radiation damper actuation. The operating temperature of a *ceiling radiation damper* actuation device shall be 50°F (27.8°C) above the normal temperature within the duct system, but not less than 160°F (71°C).

716.4 Access and identification. Fire and smoke *dampers* shall be provided with an *approved* means of access, which is large enough to *permit* inspection and maintenance of the *damper* and its operating parts. The access shall not affect the integrity of fire-resistance-rated assemblies. The access openings shall not reduce the *fire-resistance rating* of the assembly. Access points shall be permanently identified on the exterior by a *label* having letters not less than $^1/_2$ inch (12.7 mm) in height reading: FIRE/SMOKE DAMPER, SMOKE DAMPER or FIRE DAMPER. Access doors in ducts shall be tight fitting and suitable for the required duct construction.

716.5 Where required. *Fire dampers, smoke dampers* and *combination fire/smoke dampers* shall be provided at the locations prescribed in Sections 716.5.1 through 716.5.7 and 716.6. Where an assembly is required to have both *fire dampers* and *smoke dampers, combination fire/smoke dampers* or a *fire damper* and a *smoke damper* shall be required.

716.5.1 Fire walls. Ducts and air transfer openings permitted in *fire walls* in accordance with Section 706.11 shall be protected with *listed fire dampers* installed in accordance with their listing.

716.5.1.1 Horizontal exits. A *listed smoke damper* designed to resist the passage of smoke shall be provided at each point a duct or air transfer opening penetrates a *fire wall* that serves as a horizontal *exit*.

716.5.2 Fire barriers. Ducts and air transfer openings of *fire barriers* shall be protected with *approved fire dampers* installed in accordance with their listing. Ducts and air transfer openings shall not penetrate *exit* enclosures and *exit* passageways except as permitted by Sections 1022.4 and 1023.6, respectively.

Exception: *Fire dampers* are not required at penetrations of *fire barriers* where any of the following apply:

1. Penetrations are tested in accordance with ASTM E 119 or UL 263 as part of the fire-resistance-rated assembly.
2. Ducts are used as part of an *approved* smoke control system in accordance with Section 909 and where the use of a *fire damper* would interfere with the operation of a smoke control system.
3. Such walls are penetrated by ducted HVAC systems, have a required *fire-resistance rating* of 1 hour or less, are in areas of other than Group H and are in buildings equipped throughout with an *automatic sprinkler system* in accordance with Section 903.3.1.1 or 903.3.1.2. For the purposes of this exception, a ducted HVAC system shall be a duct system for conveying supply, return or exhaust air as part of the structure's HVAC system. Such a duct system shall be constructed of sheet steel not less than No. 26 gage thickness and shall be continuous from the air-handling appliance or equipment to the air outlet and inlet terminals.

716.5.2.1 Horizontal exits. A *listed smoke damper* designed to resist the passage of smoke shall be provided at each point a duct or air transfer opening penetrates a *fire barrier* that serves as a horizontal *exit*.

716.5.3 Shaft enclosures. Shaft enclosures that are permitted to be penetrated by ducts and air transfer openings shall be protected with *approved* fire and smoke *dampers* installed in accordance with their listing.

Exceptions:

1. *Fire dampers* are not required at penetrations of shafts where:
   - 1.1. Steel exhaust subducts are extended at least 22 inches (559 mm) vertically in exhaust shafts, provided there is a continuous airflow upward to the outside; or
   - 1.2. Penetrations are tested in accordance with ASTM E 119 or UL 263 as part of the fire-resistance-rated assembly; or
   - 1.3. Ducts are used as part of an *approved* smoke control system designed and installed in accordance with Section 909 and where the *fire damper* will interfere with the operation of the smoke control system; or
   - 1.4. The penetrations are in parking garage exhaust or supply shafts that are separated from other building shafts by not less than 2-hour fire-resistance-rated construction.
2. In Group B and R occupancies equipped throughout with an *automatic sprinkler system* in accordance with Section 903.3.1.1, *smoke dampers* are not required at penetrations of shafts where:
   - 2.1. Kitchen, clothes dryer, bathroom and toilet room exhaust openings are installed with steel exhaust subducts, having a minimum wall thickness of 0.0187-inch (0.4712 mm) (No. 26 gage);
   - 2.2. The subducts extend at least 22 inches (559 mm) vertically; and
   - 2.3. An exhaust fan is installed at the upper terminus of the shaft that is powered continuously in accordance with the provisions of Section 909.11, so as to maintain a continuous upward airflow to the outside.
3. *Smoke dampers* are not required at penetration of exhaust or supply shafts in parking garages that are separated from other building shafts by not less than 2-hour fire-resistance-rated construction.
4. *Smoke dampers* are not required at penetrations of shafts where ducts are used as part of an *approved* mechanical smoke control system designed in accordance with Section 909 and where the *smoke damper* will interfere with the operation of the smoke control system.
5. *Fire dampers* and *combination fire/smoke dampers* are not required in kitchen and clothes dryer exhaust systems when installed in accordance with the *International Mechanical Code*.

716.5.4 Fire partitions. Ducts and air transfer openings that penetrate *fire partitions* shall be protected with *listed fire dampers* installed in accordance with their listing.

Exceptions: In occupancies other than Group H, *fire dampers* are not required where any of the following apply:

1. Corridor walls in buildings equipped throughout with an *automatic sprinkler system* in accordance with Section 903.3.1.1 or 903.3.1.2 and the duct is protected as a *through penetration* in accordance with Section 713.
2. Tenant partitions in *covered mall buildings* where the walls are not required by provisions elsewhere in the code to extend to the underside of the floor or roof sheathing, slab or deck above.
3. The duct system is constructed of *approved* materials in accordance with the *International Mechanical Code* and the duct penetrating the wall complies with all of the following requirements:
   - 3.1. The duct shall not exceed 100 square inches (0.06 m^2).
   - 3.2. The duct shall be constructed of steel a minimum of 0.0217 inch (0.55 mm) in thickness.
   - 3.3. The duct shall not have openings that communicate the *corridor* with adjacent spaces or rooms.
   - 3.4. The duct shall be installed above a ceiling.
   - 3.5. The duct shall not terminate at a wall register in the fire-resistance-rated wall.
   - 3.6. A minimum 12-inch-long (305 mm) by 0.060-inch-thick (1.52 mm) steel sleeve shall be centered in each duct opening. The sleeve shall be secured to both sides of the wall and all four sides of the sleeve with minimum $1^1/_2$-inch by $1^1/_2$-inch by 0.060-inch (38 mm by 38 mm by 1.52 mm) steel retaining angles. The retaining angles shall be secured to the sleeve and the wall with No. 10 (M5) screws. The *annular space* between the steel sleeve and the wall opening shall be filled with mineral wool batting on all sides.

716.5.4.1 Corridors. A *listed smoke damper* designed to resist the passage of smoke shall be provided at each point a duct or air transfer opening penetrates a *corridor* enclosure required to have smoke and draft control doors in accordance with Section 715.4.3.

Exceptions:

1. *Smoke dampers* are not required where the building is equipped throughout with an *approved* smoke control system in accordance with Section 909, and *smoke dampers* are not necessary for the operation and control of the system.
2. *Smoke dampers* are not required in *corridor* penetrations where the duct is constructed of steel not less than 0.019 inch (0.48 mm) in thickness and there are no openings serving the *corridor*.

716.5.5 Smoke barriers. A *listed smoke damper* designed to resist the passage of smoke shall be provided at each point a duct or air transfer opening penetrates a *smoke barrier*. *Smoke dampers* and *smoke damper* actuation methods shall comply with Section 716.3.3.2.

Exception: *Smoke dampers* are not required where the openings in ducts are limited to a single smoke compartment and the ducts are constructed of steel.

716.5.6 Exterior walls. Ducts and air transfer openings in fire-resistance-rated *exterior walls* required to have protected openings in accordance with Section 705.10 shall be protected with *listed fire dampers* installed in accordance with their listing.

716.5.7 Smoke partitions. A *listed smoke damper* designed to resist the passage of smoke shall be provided at each point that an air transfer opening penetrates a smoke partition. *Smoke dampers* and *smoke damper* actuation methods shall comply with Section 716.3.3.2.

Exception: Where the installation of a *smoke damper* will interfere with the operation of a required smoke control system in accordance with Section 909, *approved* alternative protection shall be utilized.

716.6 Horizontal assemblies. Penetrations by ducts and air transfer openings of a floor, floor/ceiling assembly or the ceiling membrane of a roof/ceiling assembly shall be protected by a shaft enclosure that complies with Section 708 or shall comply with Sections 716.6.1 through 716.6.3.

716.6.1 Through penetrations. In occupancies other than Groups I-2 and I-3, a duct constructed of *approved* materials in accordance with the *International Mechanical Code* that penetrates a fire-resistance-rated floor/ceiling assembly that connects not more than two *stories* is permitted without shaft enclosure protection, provided a *listed fire damper* is installed at the floor line or the duct is protected in accordance with Section 713.4. For air transfer openings, see Exception 7 to Section 708.2.

Exception: A duct is permitted to penetrate three floors or less without a *fire damper* at each floor, provided such duct meets all of the following requirements:

1. The duct shall be contained and located within the cavity of a wall and shall be constructed of steel having a minimum wall thickness of 0.0187 inch (0.4712 mm) (No. 26 gage).
2. The duct shall open into only one *dwelling or sleeping unit* and the duct system shall be continuous from the unit to the exterior of the building.
3. The duct shall not exceed 4-inch (102 mm) nominal diameter and the total area of such ducts shall not exceed 100 square inches (0.065 m^2) in any 100 square feet (9.3 m^2) of floor area.
4. The annular space around the duct is protected with materials that prevent the passage of flame and hot gases sufficient to ignite cotton waste where subjected to ASTM E 119 or UL 263

time-temperature conditions under a minimum positive pressure differential of 0.01 inch (2.49 Pa) of water at the location of the penetration for the time period equivalent to the *fire-resistance rating* of the construction penetrated.

5. Grille openings located in a ceiling of a fire-resistance-rated floor/ceiling or roof/ceiling assembly shall be protected with a *listed ceiling radiation damper* installed in accordance with Section 716.6.2.1.

716.6.2 Membrane penetrations. Ducts and air transfer openings constructed of *approved* materials in accordance with the *International Mechanical Code* that penetrate the ceiling membrane of a fire-resistance-rated floor/ceiling or roof/ceiling assembly shall be protected with one of the following:

1. A shaft enclosure in accordance with Section 708.
2. A *listed ceiling radiation damper* installed at the ceiling line where a duct penetrates the ceiling of a fire-resistance-rated floor/ceiling or roof/ceiling assembly.
3. A *listed ceiling radiation damper* installed at the ceiling line where a diffuser with no duct attached penetrates the ceiling of a fire-resistance-rated floor/ceiling or roof/ceiling assembly.

716.6.2.1 Ceiling radiation dampers. *Ceiling radiation dampers* shall be tested in accordance with Section 716.3.1. *Ceiling radiation dampers* shall be installed in accordance with the details *listed* in the fire-resistance-rated assembly and the manufacturer's installation instructions and the listing. *Ceiling radiation dampers* are not required where either of the following applies:

1. Tests in accordance with ASTM E 119 or UL 263 have shown that *ceiling radiation dampers* are not necessary in order to maintain the *fire-resistance rating* of the assembly.
2. Where exhaust duct penetrations are protected in accordance with Section 713.4.1.2, are located within the cavity of a wall and do not pass through another *dwelling unit* or tenant space.

716.6.3 Nonfire-resistance-rated floor assemblies. Duct systems constructed of *approved* materials in accordance with the *International Mechanical Code* that penetrate nonfire-resistance-rated floor assemblies shall be protected by any of the following methods:

1. A shaft enclosure in accordance with Section 708.
2. The duct connects not more than two *stories*, and the *annular space* around the penetrating duct is protected with an *approved* noncombustible material that resists the free passage of flame and the products of combustion.
3. The duct connects not more than three *stories*, and the *annular space* around the penetrating duct is protected with an *approved* noncombustible material that resists the free passage of flame and the products of combustion and a *fire damper* is installed at each floor line.

Exception: *Fire dampers* are not required in ducts within individual residential *dwelling units*.

716.7 Flexible ducts and air connectors. Flexible ducts and air connectors shall not pass through any fire-resistance-rated assembly. Flexible air connectors shall not pass through any wall, floor or ceiling.

SECTION 717
CONCEALED SPACES

717.1 General. Fireblocking and draftstopping shall be installed in combustible concealed locations in accordance with this section. Fireblocking shall comply with Section 717.2. Draftstopping in floor/ceiling spaces and *attic* spaces shall comply with Sections 717.3 and 717.4, respectively. The permitted use of combustible materials in concealed spaces of buildings of Type I or II construction shall be limited to the applications indicated in Section 717.5.

717.2 Fireblocking. In combustible construction, fireblocking shall be installed to cut off concealed draft openings (both vertical and horizontal) and shall form an effective barrier between floors, between a top *story* and a roof or *attic* space. Fireblocking shall be installed in the locations specified in Sections 717.2.2 through 717.2.7.

717.2.1 Fireblocking materials. Fireblocking shall consist of the following materials:

1. Two-inch (51 mm) nominal lumber.
2. Two thicknesses of 1-inch (25 mm) nominal lumber with broken lap joints.
3. One thickness of 0.719-inch (18.3 mm) wood structural panels with joints backed by 0.719-inch (18.3 mm) wood structural panels.
4. One thickness of 0.75-inch (19.1 mm) particleboard with joints backed by 0.75-inch (19 mm) particleboard.
5. One-half-inch (12.7 mm) gypsum board.
6. One-fourth-inch (6.4 mm) cement-based millboard.
7. Batts or blankets of mineral wool, mineral fiber or other *approved* materials installed in such a manner as to be securely retained in place.

717.2.1.1 Batts or blankets of mineral wool or mineral fiber. Batts or blankets of mineral wool or mineral fiber or other *approved* nonrigid materials shall be permitted for compliance with the 10-foot (3048 mm) horizontal fireblocking in walls constructed using parallel rows of studs or staggered studs.

717.2.1.2 Unfaced fiberglass. Unfaced fiberglass batt insulation used as fireblocking shall fill the entire cross section of the wall cavity to a minimum height of 16 inches (406 mm) measured vertically. When piping, conduit or similar obstructions are encountered, the insulation shall be packed tightly around the obstruction.

717.2.1.3 Loose-fill insulation material. Loose-fill insulation material, insulating foam sealants and caulk materials shall not be used as a fireblock unless specifically tested in the form and manner intended for use to demonstrate its ability to remain in place and to retard the spread of fire and hot gases.

717.2.1.4 Fireblocking integrity. The integrity of fireblocks shall be maintained.

717.2.1.5 Double stud walls. Batts or blankets of mineral or glass fiber or other *approved* nonrigid materials shall be allowed as fireblocking in walls constructed using parallel rows of studs or staggered studs.

717.2.2 Concealed wall spaces. Fireblocking shall be provided in concealed spaces of stud walls and partitions, including furred spaces, and parallel rows of studs or staggered studs, as follows:

1. Vertically at the ceiling and floor levels.
2. Horizontally at intervals not exceeding 10 feet (3048 mm).

717.2.3 Connections between horizontal and vertical spaces. Fireblocking shall be provided at interconnections between concealed vertical stud wall or partition spaces and concealed horizontal spaces created by an assembly of floor joists or trusses, and between concealed vertical and horizontal spaces such as occur at soffits, drop ceilings, cove ceilings and similar locations.

717.2.4 Stairways. Fireblocking shall be provided in concealed spaces between *stair* stringers at the top and bottom of the run. Enclosed spaces under *stairs* shall also comply with Section 1009.6.3.

717.2.5 Ceiling and floor openings. Where required by Exception 6 of Section 708.2, Exception 1 of Section 713.4.1.2 or Section 713.4.2, fireblocking of the *annular space* around vents, pipes, ducts, chimneys and fireplaces at ceilings and floor levels shall be installed with a material specifically tested in the form and manner intended for use to demonstrate its ability to remain in place and resist the free passage of flame and the products of combustion.

717.2.5.1 Factory-built chimneys and fireplaces. Factory-built chimneys and fireplaces shall be fireblocked in accordance with UL 103 and UL 127.

717.2.6 Architectural trim. Fireblocking shall be installed within concealed spaces of *exterior wall* finish and other exterior architectural elements where permitted to be of combustible construction as specified in Section 1406 or where erected with combustible frames, at maximum intervals of 20 feet (6096 mm), so that there will be no open space exceeding 100 square feet (9.3 m^3). Where wood furring strips are used, they shall be of *approved* wood of natural decay resistance or *preservative-treated wood*. If noncontinuous, such elements shall have closed ends, with at least 4 inches (102 mm) of separation between sections.

Exceptions:

1. Fireblocking of cornices is not required in single-family *dwellings*. Fireblocking of cornices of a two-family *dwelling* is required only at the line of *dwelling unit* separation.
2. Fireblocking shall not be required where installed on noncombustible framing and the face of the *exterior wall* finish exposed to the concealed space is covered by one of the following materials:
   2.1. Aluminum having a minimum thickness of 0.019 inch (0.5 mm).
   2.2. Corrosion-resistant steel having a base metal thickness not less than 0.016 inch (0.4 mm) at any point.
   2.3. Other *approved* noncombustible materials.

717.2.7 Concealed sleeper spaces. Where wood sleepers are used for laying wood flooring on masonry or concrete fire-resistance-rated floors, the space between the floor slab and the underside of the wood flooring shall be filled with an *approved* material to resist the free passage of flame and products of combustion or fireblocked in such a manner that there will be no open spaces under the flooring that will exceed 100 square feet (9.3 m^2) in area and such space shall be filled solidly under permanent partitions so that there is no communication under the flooring between adjoining rooms.

Exceptions:

1. Fireblocking is not required for slab-on-grade floors in gymnasiums.
2. Fireblocking is required only at the juncture of each alternate lane and at the ends of each lane in a bowling facility.

717.3 Draftstopping in floors. In combustible construction, draftstopping shall be installed to subdivide floor/ceiling assemblies in the locations prescribed in Sections 717.3.2 through 717.3.3.

717.3.1 Draftstopping materials. Draftstopping materials shall not be less than $^1/_2$-inch (12.7 mm) gypsum board, $^3/_8$-inch (9.5 mm) wood structural panel, $^3/_8$-inch (9.5 mm) particleboard, 1-inch (25-mm) nominal lumber, cement fiberboard, batts or blankets of mineral wool or glass fiber, or other *approved* materials adequately supported. The integrity of draftstops shall be maintained.

717.3.2 Groups R-1, R-2, R-3 and R-4. Draftstopping shall be provided in floor/ceiling spaces in Group R-1 buildings, in Group R-2 buildings with three or more *dwelling units*, in Group R-3 buildings with two *dwelling units* and in Group R-4 buildings. Draftstopping shall be located above and in line with the *dwelling unit* and *sleeping unit* separations.

Exceptions:

1. Draftstopping is not required in buildings equipped throughout with an *automatic sprinkler system* in accordance with Section 903.3.1.1.
2. Draftstopping is not required in buildings equipped throughout with an *automatic sprinkler system* in accordance with Section 903.3.1.2, pro-

vided that automatic sprinklers are also installed in the combustible concealed spaces.

717.3.3 Other groups. In other groups, draftstopping shall be installed so that horizontal floor areas do not exceed 1,000 square feet (93 m^2).

Exception: Draftstopping is not required in buildings equipped throughout with an *automatic sprinkler system* in accordance with Section 903.3.1.1.

717.4 Draftstopping in attics. In combustible construction, draftstopping shall be installed to subdivide *attic* spaces and concealed roof spaces in the locations prescribed in Sections 717.4.2 and 717.4.3. Ventilation of concealed roof spaces shall be maintained in accordance with Section 1203.2.

717.4.1 Draftstopping materials. Materials utilized for draftstopping of *attic* spaces shall comply with Section 717.3.1.

717.4.1.1 Openings. Openings in the partitions shall be protected by self-closing doors with automatic latches constructed as required for the partitions.

717.4.2 Groups R-1 and R-2. Draftstopping shall be provided in *attics*, mansards, overhangs or other concealed roof spaces of Group R-2 buildings with three or more *dwelling units* and in all Group R-1 buildings. Draftstopping shall be installed above, and in line with, *sleeping unit* and *dwelling unit* separation walls that do not extend to the underside of the roof sheathing above.

Exceptions:

1. Where *corridor* walls provide a *sleeping unit* or *dwelling unit* separation, draftstopping shall only be required above one of the *corridor* walls.
2. Draftstopping is not required in buildings equipped throughout with an *automatic sprinkler system* in accordance with Section 903.3.1.1.
3. In occupancies in Group R-2 that do not exceed four *stories above grade plane*, the *attic* space shall be subdivided by draftstops into areas not exceeding 3,000 square feet (279 m^2) or above every two *dwelling units*, whichever is smaller.
4. Draftstopping is not required in buildings equipped throughout with an *automatic sprinkler system* in accordance with Section 903.3.1.2, provided that automatic sprinklers are also installed in the combustible concealed spaces.

717.4.3 Other groups. Draftstopping shall be installed in *attics* and concealed roof spaces, such that any horizontal area does not exceed 3,000 square feet (279 m^2).

Exception: Draftstopping is not required in buildings equipped throughout with an *automatic sprinkler system* in accordance with Section 903.3.1.1.

717.5 Combustible materials in concealed spaces in Type I or II construction. Combustible materials shall not be permitted in concealed spaces of buildings of Type I or II construction.

Exceptions:

1. Combustible materials in accordance with Section 603.
2. Combustible materials exposed within plenums complying with Section 602 of the *International Mechanical Code*.
3. Class A *interior finish* materials classified in accordance with Section 803.
4. Combustible piping within partitions or shaft enclosures installed in accordance with the provisions of this code.
5. Combustible piping within concealed ceiling spaces installed in accordance with the *International Mechanical Code* and the *International Plumbing Code*.
6. Combustible insulation and covering on pipe and tubing, installed in concealed spaces other than plenums, complying with Section 719.7.

SECTION 718
FIRE-RESISTANCE REQUIREMENTS FOR PLASTER

718.1 Thickness of plaster. The minimum thickness of gypsum plaster or portland cement plaster used in a fire-resistance-rated system shall be determined by the prescribed fire tests. The plaster thickness shall be measured from the face of the lath where applied to gypsum lath or metal lath.

718.2 Plaster equivalents. For fire-resistance purposes, $^1/_2$ inch (12.7 mm) of unsanded gypsum plaster shall be deemed equivalent to $^3/_4$ inch (19.1 mm) of one-to-three gypsum sand plaster or 1 inch (25 mm) of portland cement sand plaster.

718.3 Noncombustible furring. In buildings of Type I and II construction, plaster shall be applied directly on concrete or masonry or on *approved* noncombustible plastering base and furring.

718.4 Double reinforcement. Plaster protection more than 1 inch (25 mm) in thickness shall be reinforced with an additional layer of *approved* lath embedded at least $^3/_4$ inch (19.1 mm) from the outer surface and fixed securely in place.

Exception: Solid plaster partitions or where otherwise determined by fire tests.

718.5 Plaster alternatives for concrete. In reinforced concrete construction, gypsum plaster or portland cement plaster is permitted to be substituted for $^1/_2$ inch (12.7 mm) of the required poured concrete protection, except that a minimum thickness of $^3/_8$ inch (9.5 mm) of poured concrete shall be provided in reinforced concrete floors and 1 inch (25 mm) in reinforced concrete columns in addition to the plaster finish. The concrete base shall be prepared in accordance with Section 2510.7.

SECTION 719
THERMAL- AND SOUND-INSULATING MATERIALS

719.1 General. Insulating materials, including facings such as vapor retarders and *vapor-permeable membranes*, similar coverings and all layers of single and multilayer reflective foil insulations, shall comply with the requirements of this section. Where a flame spread index or a smoke-developed index is specified in this section, such index shall be determined in accordance with ASTM E 84 or UL 723. Any material that is subject to an increase in flame spread index or smoke-developed index beyond the limits herein established through the effects of age, moisture or other atmospheric conditions shall not be permitted.

Exceptions:

1. Fiberboard insulation shall comply with Chapter 23.
2. Foam plastic insulation shall comply with Chapter 26.
3. Duct and pipe insulation and duct and pipe coverings and linings in plenums shall comply with the *International Mechanical Code*.
4. All layers of single and multilayer reflective plastic core insulation shall comply with Section 2613.

719.2 Concealed installation. Insulating materials, where concealed as installed in buildings of any type of construction, shall have a flame spread index of not more than 25 and a smoke-developed index of not more than 450.

Exception: Cellulose loose-fill insulation that is not spray applied, complying with the requirements of Section 719.6, shall only be required to meet the smoke-developed index of not more than 450.

719.2.1 Facings. Where such materials are installed in concealed spaces in buildings of Type III, IV or V construction, the flame spread and smoke-developed limitations do not apply to facings, coverings, and layers of reflective foil insulation that are installed behind and in substantial contact with the unexposed surface of the ceiling, wall or floor finish.

Exception: All layers of single and multilayer reflective plastic core insulation shall comply with Section 2613.

719.3 Exposed installation. Insulating materials, where exposed as installed in buildings of any type of construction, shall have a flame spread index of not more than 25 and a smoke-developed index of not more than 450.

Exception: Cellulose loose-fill insulation that is not spray applied complying with the requirements of Section 719.6 shall only be required to meet the smoke-developed index of not more than 450.

719.3.1 Attic floors. Exposed insulation materials installed on *attic* floors shall have a critical radiant flux of not less than 0.12 watt per square centimeter when tested in accordance with ASTM E 970.

719.4 Loose-fill insulation. Loose-fill insulation materials that cannot be mounted in the ASTM E 84 or UL 723 apparatus without a screen or artificial supports shall comply with the flame spread and smoke-developed limits of Sections 719.2 and 719.3 when tested in accordance with CAN/ULC S102.2.

Exception: Cellulose loose-fill insulation shall not be required to be tested in accordance with CAN/ULC S102.2, provided such insulation complies with the requirements of Section 719.2 or 719.3, as applicable, and Section 719.6.

719.5 Roof insulation. The use of combustible roof insulation not complying with Sections 719.2 and 719.3 shall be permitted in any type of construction provided it is covered with *approved* roof coverings directly applied thereto.

719.6 Cellulose loose-fill insulation. Cellulose loose-fill insulation shall comply with CPSC 16 CFR, Part 1209 and CPSC 16 CFR, Part 1404. Each package of such insulating material shall be clearly labeled in accordance with CPSC 16 CFR, Part 1209 and CPSC 16 CFR, Part 1404.

719.7 Insulation and covering on pipe and tubing. Insulation and covering on pipe and tubing shall have a flame spread index of not more than 25 and a smoke-developed index of not more than 450.

Exception: Insulation and covering on pipe and tubing installed in plenums shall comply with the *International Mechanical Code.*

SECTION 720
PRESCRIPTIVE FIRE RESISTANCE

720.1 General. The provisions of this section contain prescriptive details of fire-resistance-rated building elements, components or assemblies. The materials of construction listed in Tables 720.1(1), 720.1(2), and 720.1(3) shall be assumed to have the *fire-resistance ratings* prescribed therein. Where materials that change the capacity for heat dissipation are incorporated into a fire-resistance-rated assembly, fire test results or other substantiating data shall be made available to the *building official* to show that the required fire-resistance-rating time period is not reduced.

720.1.1 Thickness of protective coverings. The thickness of fire-resistant materials required for protection of structural members shall be not less than set forth in Table 720.1(1), except as modified in this section. The figures shown shall be the net thickness of the protecting materials and shall not include any hollow space in back of the protection.

720.1.2 Unit masonry protection. Where required, metal ties shall be embedded in bed joints of unit masonry for protection of steel columns. Such ties shall be as set forth in Table 720.1(1) or be equivalent thereto.

720.1.3 Reinforcement for cast-in-place concrete column protection. Cast-in-place concrete protection for steel columns shall be reinforced at the edges of such members with wire ties of not less than 0.18 inch (4.6 mm) in diameter wound spirally around the columns on a pitch of not more than 8 inches (203 mm) or by equivalent reinforcement.

720.1.4 Plaster application. The finish coat is not required for plaster protective coatings where they comply with the design mix and thickness requirements of Tables 720.1(1), 720.1(2) and 720.1(3).

720.1.5 Bonded prestressed concrete tendons. For members having a single tendon or more than one tendon installed with equal concrete cover measured from the nearest surface, the cover shall not be less than that set forth in Table 720.1(1). For members having multiple tendons installed with variable concrete cover, the average tendon cover shall not be less than that set forth in Table 720.1(1), provided:

1. The clearance from each tendon to the nearest exposed surface is used to determine the average cover.
2. In no case can the clear cover for individual tendons be less than one-half of that set forth in Table 720.1(1). A minimum cover of $^3/_4$ inch (19.1 mm) for slabs and 1 inch (25 mm) for beams is required for any aggregate concrete.
3. For the purpose of establishing a *fire-resistance rating*, tendons having a clear covering less than that set forth in Table 720.1(1) shall not contribute more than 50 percent of the required ultimate moment capacity for members less than 350 square inches (0.226 m^2) in cross-sectional area and 65 percent for larger members. For structural design purposes, however, tendons having a reduced cover are assumed to be fully effective.

SECTION 721
CALCULATED FIRE RESISTANCE

721.1 General. The provisions of this section contain procedures by which the *fire resistance* of specific materials or combinations of materials is established by calculations. These procedures apply only to the information contained in this section and shall not be otherwise used. The calculated *fire resistance* of concrete, concrete masonry and clay masonry assemblies shall be permitted in accordance with ACI 216.1/TMS 0216. The calculated *fire resistance* of steel assemblies shall be permitted in accordance with Chapter 5 of ASCE 29. The calculated *fire resistance* of exposed wood members and wood decking shall be permitted in accordance with Chapter 16 of ANSI/AF&PA *National Design Specification for Wood Construction (NDS)*.

721.1.1 Definitions. The following words and terms shall, for the purposes of this chapter and as used elsewhere in this code, have the meanings shown herein.

CERAMIC FIBER BLANKET. A mineral wool insulation material made of alumina-silica fibers and weighing 4 to 10 pounds per cubic foot (pcf) (64 to 160 kg/m^3).

CONCRETE, CARBONATE AGGREGATE. Concrete made with aggregates consisting mainly of calcium or magnesium carbonate, such as limestone or dolomite, and containing 40 percent or less quartz, chert or flint.

CONCRETE, CELLULAR. A lightweight insulating concrete made by mixing a preformed foam with portland cement slurry and having a dry unit weight of approximately 30 pcf (480 kg/m^3).

CONCRETE, LIGHTWEIGHT AGGREGATE. Concrete made with aggregates of expanded clay, shale, slag or slate or sintered fly ash or any natural lightweight aggregate meeting ASTM C 330 and possessing equivalent fire-resistance properties and weighing 85 to 115 pcf (1360 to 1840 kg/m^3).

CONCRETE, PERLITE. A lightweight insulating concrete having a dry unit weight of approximately 30 pcf (480 kg/m^3) made with perlite concrete aggregate. Perlite aggregate is produced from a volcanic rock which, when heated, expands to form a glass-like material of cellular structure.

CONCRETE, SAND-LIGHTWEIGHT. Concrete made with a combination of expanded clay, shale, slag, slate, sintered fly ash, or any natural lightweight aggregate meeting ASTM C 330 and possessing equivalent fire-resistance properties and natural sand. Its unit weight is generally between 105 and 120 pcf (1680 and 1920 kg/m^3).

CONCRETE, SILICEOUS AGGREGATE. Concrete made with normal-weight aggregates consisting mainly of silica or compounds other than calcium or magnesium carbonate, which contains more than 40-percent quartz, chert or flint.

CONCRETE, VERMICULITE. A lightweight insulating concrete made with vermiculite concrete aggregate which is laminated micaceous material produced by expanding the ore at high temperatures. When added to a portland cement slurry the resulting concrete has a dry unit weight of approximately 30 pcf (480 kg/m^3).

GLASS FIBERBOARD. Fibrous glass roof insulation consisting of inorganic glass fibers formed into rigid boards using a binder. The board has a top surface faced with asphalt and kraft reinforced with glass fiber.

MINERAL BOARD. A rigid felted thermal insulation board consisting of either felted mineral fiber or cellular beads of expanded aggregate formed into flat rectangular units.

721.2 Concrete assemblies. The provisions of this section contain procedures by which the *fire-resistance ratings* of concrete assemblies are established by calculations.

721.2.1 Concrete walls. Cast-in-place and precast concrete walls shall comply with Section 721.2.1.1. Multiwythe concrete walls shall comply with Section 721.2.1.2. Joints between precast panels shall comply with Section 721.2.1.3. Concrete walls with gypsum wallboard or plaster finish shall comply with Section 721.2.1.4.

TABLE 720.1(1)
MINIMUM PROTECTION OF STRUCTURAL PARTS BASED ON TIME PERIODS FOR VARIOUS NONCOMBUSTIBLE INSULATING MATERIALS[m]

STRUCTURAL PARTS TO BE PROTECTED	ITEM NUMBER	INSULATING MATERIAL USED	MINIMUM THICKNESS OF INSULATING MATERIAL FOR THE FOLLOWING FIRE-RESISTANCE PERIODS (inches)			
			4 hour	3 hour	2 hour	1 hour
1. Steel columns and all of primary trusses	1-1.1	Carbonate, lightweight and sand-lightweight aggregate concrete, members 6″ × 6″ or greater (not including sandstone, granite and siliceous gravel).[a]	$2^1/_2$	2	$1^1/_2$	1
	1-1.2	Carbonate, lightweight and sand-lightweight aggregate concrete, members 8″ × 8″ or greater (not including sandstone, granite and siliceous gravel).[a]	2	$1^1/_2$	1	1
	1-1.3	Carbonate, lightweight and sand-lightweight aggregate concrete, members 12″ × 12″ or greater (not including sandstone, granite and siliceous gravel).[a]	$1^1/_2$	1	1	1
	1-1.4	Siliceous aggregate concrete and concrete excluded in Item 1-1.1, members 6″ × 6″ or greater.[a]	3	2	$1^1/_2$	1
	1-1.5	Siliceous aggregate concrete and concrete excluded in Item 1-1.1, members 8″ × 8″ or greater.[a]	$2^1/_2$	2	1	1
	1-1.6	Siliceous aggregate concrete and concrete excluded in Item 1-1.1, members 12″ × 12″ or greater.[a]	2	1	1	1
	1-2.1	Clay or shale brick with brick and mortar fill.[a]	$3^3/_4$	—	—	$2^1/_4$
	1-3.1	4″ hollow clay tile in two 2″ layers; $^1/_2$″ mortar between tile and column; $^3/_8$″ metal mesh 0.046″ wire diameter in horizontal joints; tile fill.[a]	4	—	—	—
	1-3.2	2″ hollow clay tile; $^3/_4$″ mortar between tile and column; $^3/_8$″ metal mesh 0.046″ wire diameter in horizontal joints; limestone concrete fill;[a] plastered with $^3/_4$″ gypsum plaster.	3	—	—	—
	1-3.3	2″ hollow clay tile with outside wire ties 0.08″ diameter at each course of tile or $^3/_8$″ metal mesh 0.046″ diameter wire in horizontal joints; limestone or trap-rock concrete fill[a] extending 1″ outside column on all sides.	—	—	3	—
	1-3.4	2″ hollow clay tile with outside wire ties 0.08″ diameter at each course of tile with or without concrete fill; $^3/_4$″ mortar between tile and column.	—	—	—	2
	1-4.1	Cement plaster over metal lath wire tied to $^3/_4$″ cold-rolled vertical channels with 0.049″ (No. 18 B.W. gage) wire ties spaced 3″ to 6″ on center. Plaster mixed 1:2 $^1/_2$ by volume, cement to sand.	—	—	$2^1/_2$[b]	$^7/_8$
	1-5.1	Vermiculite concrete, 1:4 mix by volume over paperbacked wire fabric lath wrapped directly around column with additional 2″ × 2″ 0.065″/0.065″ (No. 16/16 B.W. gage) wire fabric placed $^3/_4$″ from outer concrete surface. Wire fabric tied with 0.049″ (No. 18 B.W. gage) wire spaced 6″ on center for inner layer and 2″ on center for outer layer.	2	—	—	—
	1-6.1	Perlite or vermiculite gypsum plaster over metal lath wrapped around column and furred $1^1/_4$″ from column flanges. Sheets lapped at ends and tied at 6″ intervals with 0.049″ (No. 18 B.W. gage) tie wire. Plaster pushed through to flanges.	$1^1/_2$	1	—	—
	1-6.2	Perlite or vermiculite gypsum plaster over self-furring metal lath wrapped directly around column, lapped 1″ and tied at 6″ intervals with 0.049″ (No. 18 B.W. gage) wire.	$1^3/_4$	$1^3/_8$	1	—
	1-6.3	Perlite or vermiculite gypsum plaster on metal lath applied to $^3/_4$″ cold-rolled channels spaced 24″ apart vertically and wrapped flatwise around column.	$1^1/_2$	—	—	—
	1-6.4	Perlite or vermiculite gypsum plaster over two layers of $^1/_2$″ plain full-length gypsum lath applied tight to column flanges. Lath wrapped with 1″ hexagonal mesh of No. 20 gage wire and tied with doubled 0.035″ diameter (No. 18 B.W. gage) wire ties spaced 23″ on center. For three-coat work, the plaster mix for the second coat shall not exceed 100 pounds of gypsum to $2^1/_2$ cubic feet of aggregate for the 3-hour system.	$2^1/_2$	2	—	—

(continued)

TABLE 720.1(1)—continued
MINIMUM PROTECTION OF STRUCTURAL PARTS BASED ON TIME PERIODS FOR VARIOUS NONCOMBUSTIBLE INSULATING MATERIALS[m]

STRUCTURAL PARTS TO BE PROTECTED	ITEM NUMBER	INSULATING MATERIAL USED	MINIMUM THICKNESS OF INSULATING MATERIAL FOR THE FOLLOWING FIRE-RESISTANCE PERIODS (inches)			
			4 hour	3 hour	2 hour	1 hour
1. Steel columns and all of primary trusses (continued)	1-6.5	Perlite or vermiculate gypsum plaster over one layer of $^1/_2''$ plain full-length gypsum lath applied tight to column flanges. Lath tied with doubled 0.049″ (No. 18 B.W. gage) wire ties spaced 23″ on center and scratch coat wrapped with 1″ hexagonal mesh 0.035″ (No. 20 B.W. gage) wire fabric. For three-coat work, the plaster mix for the second coat shall not exceed 100 pounds of gypsum to $2^1/_2$ cubic feet of aggregate.	—	2	—	—
	1-7.1	Multiple layers of $^1/_2''$ gypsum wallboard[c] adhesively[d] secured to column flanges and successive layers. Wallboard applied without horizontal joints. Corner edges of each layer staggered. Wallboard layer below outer layer secured to column with doubled 0.049″ (No. 18 B.W. gage) steel wire ties spaced 15″ on center. Exposed corners taped and treated.	—	—	2	1
	1-7.2	Three layers of $^5/_8''$ Type X gypsum wallboard.[c] First and second layer held in place by $^1/_8''$ diameter by $1^3/_8''$ long ring shank nails with $^5/_{16}''$ diameter heads spaced 24″ on center at corners. Middle layer also secured with metal straps at mid-height and 18″ from each end, and by metal corner bead at each corner held by the metal straps. Third layer attached to corner bead with 1″ long gypsum wallboard screws spaced 12″ on center.	—	—	$1^7/_8$	—
	1-7.3	Three layers of $^5/_8''$ Type X gypsum wallboard,[c] each layer screw attached to $1^5/_8''$ steel studs 0.018″ thick (No. 25 carbon sheet steel gage) at each corner of column. Middle layer also secured with 0.049″ (No. 18 B.W. gage) double-strand steel wire ties, 24″ on center. Screws are No. 6 by 1″ spaced 24″ on center for inner layer, No. 6 by $1^5/_8''$ spaced 12″ on center for middle layer and No. 8 by $2^1/_4''$ spaced 12″ on center for outer layer.	—	$1^7/_8$	—	—
	1-8.1	Wood-fibered gypsum plaster mixed 1:1 by weight gypsum-to-sand aggregate applied over metal lath. Lath lapped 1″ and tied 6″ on center at all end, edges and spacers with 0.049″ (No. 18 B.W. gage) steel tie wires. Lath applied over $^1/_2''$ spacers made of $^3/_4''$ furring channel with 2″ legs bent around each corner. Spacers located 1″ from top and bottom of member and a maximum of 40″ on center and wire tied with a single strand of 0.049″ (No. 18 B.W. gage) steel tie wires. Corner bead tied to the lath at 6″ on center along each corner to provide plaster thickness.	—	—	$1^5/_8$	—
	1-9.1	Minimum W8x35 wide flange steel column (w/d ≥ 0.75) with each web cavity filled even with the flange tip with normal weight carbonate or siliceous aggregate concrete (3,000 psi minimum compressive strength with 145 pcf ± 3 pcf unit weight). Reinforce the concrete in each web cavity with a minimum No. 4 deformed reinforcing bar installed vertically and centered in the cavity, and secured to the column web with a minimum No. 2 horizontal deformed reinforcing bar welded to the web every 18″ on center vertically. As an alternative to the No. 4 rebar, $^3/_4''$ diameter by 3″ long headed studs, spaced at 12″ on center vertically, shall be welded on each side of the web midway between the column flanges.	—	—	—	See Note n
2. Webs or flanges of steel beams and girders	2-1.1	Carbonate, lightweight and sand-lightweight aggregate concrete (not including sandstone, granite and siliceous gravel) with 3″ or finer metal mesh placed 1″ from the finished surface anchored to the top flange and providing not less than 0.025 square inch of steel area per foot in each direction.	2	$1^1/_2$	1	1
	2-1.2	Siliceous aggregate concrete and concrete excluded in Item 2-1.1 with 3″ or finer metal mesh placed 1″ from the finished surface anchored to the top flange and providing not less than 0.025 square inch of steel area per foot in each direction.	$2^1/_2$	2	$1^1/_2$	1
	2-2.1	Cement plaster on metal lath attached to $^3/_4''$ cold-rolled channels with 0.04″ (No. 18 B.W. gage) wire ties spaced 3″ to 6″ on center. Plaster mixed 1:2 $^1/_2$ by volume, cement to sand.	—	—	$2^1/_2$[b]	$^7/_8$

(continued)

TABLE 720.1(1)—continued
MINIMUM PROTECTION OF STRUCTURAL PARTS BASED ON TIME PERIODS FOR VARIOUS NONCOMBUSTIBLE INSULATING MATERIALS[m]

STRUCTURAL PARTS TO BE PROTECTED	ITEM NUMBER	INSULATING MATERIAL USED	MINIMUM THICKNESS OF INSULATING MATERIAL FOR THE FOLLOWING FIRE-RESISTANCE PERIODS (inches)			
			4 hour	3 hour	2 hour	1 hour
2. Webs or flanges of steel beams and girders (continued)	2-3.1	Vermiculite gypsum plaster on a metal lath cage, wire tied to 0.165″ diameter (No. 8 B.W. gage) steel wire hangers wrapped around beam and spaced 16″ on center. Metal lath ties spaced approximately 5″ on center at cage sides and bottom.	—	$^{7}/_{8}$	—	—
	2-4.1	Two layers of $^{5}/_{8}$″ Type X gypsum wallboard[c] are attached to U-shaped brackets spaced 24″ on center. 0.018″ thick (No. 25 carbon sheet steel gage) $1^{5}/_{8}$″ deep by 1″ galvanized steel runner channels are first installed parallel to and on each side of the top beam flange to provide a $^{1}/_{2}$″ clearance to the flange. The channel runners are attached to steel deck or concrete floor construction with approved fasteners spaced 12″ on center. U-shaped brackets are formed from members identical to the channel runners. At the bent portion of the U-shaped bracket, the flanges of the channel are cut out so that $1^{5}/_{8}$″ deep corner channels can be inserted without attachment parallel to each side of the lower flange. As an alternate, 0.021″ thick (No. 24 carbon sheet steel gage) 1″× 2″ runner and corner angles may be used in lieu of channels, and the web cutouts in the U-shaped brackets may be omitted. Each angle is attached to the bracket with $^{1}/_{2}$″-long No. 8 self-drilling screws. The vertical legs of the U-shaped bracket are attached to the runners with one $^{1}/_{2}$″ long No. 8 self-drilling screw. The completed steel framing provides a $2^{1}/_{8}$″ and $1^{1}/_{2}$″ space between the inner layer of wallboard and the sides and bottom of the steel beam, respectively. The inner layer of wallboard is attached to the top runners and bottom corner channels or corner angles with $1^{1}/_{4}$″-long No. 6 self-drilling screws spaced 16″ on center. The outer layer of wallboard is applied with $1^{3}/_{4}$″-long No. 6 self-drilling screws spaced 8″ on center. The bottom corners are reinforced with metal corner beads.	—	—	$1^{1}/_{4}$	—
	2-4.2	Three layers of $^{5}/_{8}$″ Type X gypsum wallboard[c] attached to a steel suspension system as described immediately above utilizing the 0.018″ thick (No. 25 carbon sheet steel gage) 1″ × 2″ lower corner angles. The framing is located so that a $2^{1}/_{8}$″ and 2″ space is provided between the inner layer of wallboard and the sides and bottom of the beam, respectively. The first two layers of wallboard are attached as described immediately above. A layer of 0.035″ thick (No. 20 B.W. gage) 1″ hexagonal galvanized wire mesh is applied under the soffit of the middle layer and up the sides approximately 2″. The mesh is held in position with the No. 6 $1^{5}/_{8}$″-long screws installed in the vertical leg of the bottom corner angles. The outer layer of wallboard is attached with No. 6 $2^{1}/_{4}$″-long screws spaced 8″ on center. One screw is also installed at the mid-depth of the bracket in each layer. Bottom corners are finished as described above.	—	$1^{7}/_{8}$	—	—
3. Bonded pretensioned reinforcement in prestressed concrete[e]	3-1.1	Carbonate, lightweight, sand-lightweight and siliceous[f] aggregate concrete Beams or girders Solid slabs[h]	4[g] 	3[g] 2	$2^{1}/_{2}$ $1^{1}/_{2}$	$1^{1}/_{2}$ 1
4. Bonded or unbonded post-tensioned tendons in prestressed concrete[e, i]	4-1.1	Carbonate, lightweight, sand-lightweight and siliceous[f] aggregate concrete Unrestrained members: Solid slabs[h] Beams and girders[j] 8″ wide greater than 12″ wide	— 3	2 $4^{1}/_{2}$ $2^{1}/_{2}$	$1^{1}/_{2}$ $2^{1}/_{2}$ 2	— $1^{3}/_{4}$ $1^{1}/_{2}$
	4-1.2	Carbonate, lightweight, sand-lightweight and siliceous aggregate Restrained members:[k] Solid slabs[h] Beams and girders[j] 8″ wide greater than 12″ wide	$1^{1}/_{4}$ $2^{1}/_{2}$ 2	1 2 $1^{3}/_{4}$	$^{3}/_{4}$ $1^{3}/_{4}$ $1^{1}/_{2}$	— — —

(continued)

TABLE 720.1(1)—continued
MINIMUM PROTECTION OF STRUCTURAL PARTS BASED ON TIME PERIODS FOR VARIOUS NONCOMBUSTIBLE INSULATING MATERIALS[m]

STRUCTURAL PARTS TO BE PROTECTED	ITEM NUMBER	INSULATING MATERIAL USED	MINIMUM THICKNESS OF INSULATING MATERIAL FOR THE FOLLOWING FIRE-RESISTANCE PERIODS (inches)			
			4 hour	3 hour	2 hour	1 hour
5. Reinforcing steel in reinforced concrete columns, beams girders and trusses	5-1.1	Carbonate, lightweight and sand-lightweight aggregate concrete, members 12″ or larger, square or round. (Size limit does not apply to beams and girders monolithic with floors.)	$1^1/_2$	$1^1/_2$	$1^1/_2$	$1^1/_2$
		Siliceous aggregate concrete, members 12″ or larger, square or round. (Size limit does not apply to beams and girders monolithic with floors.)	2	$1^1/_2$	$1^1/_2$	$1^1/_2$
6. Reinforcing steel in reinforced concrete joists[l]	6-1.1	Carbonate, lightweight and sand-lightweight aggregate concrete.	$1^1/_4$	$1^1/_4$	1	$^3/_4$
	6-1.2	Siliceous aggregate concrete.	$1^3/_4$	$1^1/_2$	1	$^3/_4$
7. Reinforcing and tie rods in floor and roof slabs[l]	7-1.1	Carbonate, lightweight and sand-lightweight aggregate concrete.	1	1	$^3/_4$	$^3/_4$
	7-1.2	Siliceous aggregate concrete.	$1^1/_4$	1	1	$^3/_4$

For SI: 1 inch = 25.4 mm, 1 square inch = 645.2 mm^2, 1 cubic foot = 0.0283 m^3, 1 pound per cubic foot = 16.02 kg/m^3.

a. Reentrant parts of protected members to be filled solidly.
b. Two layers of equal thickness with a $^3/_4$-inch airspace between.
c. For all of the construction with gypsum wallboard described in Table 720.1(1), gypsum base for veneer plaster of the same size, thickness and core type shall be permitted to be substituted for gypsum wallboard, provided attachment is identical to that specified for the wallboard and the joints on the face layer are reinforced, and the entire surface is covered with a minimum of $^1/_{16}$-inch gypsum veneer plaster.
d. An approved adhesive qualified under ASTM E 119 or UL 263.
e. Where lightweight or sand-lightweight concrete having an oven-dry weight of 110 pounds per cubic foot or less is used, the tabulated minimum cover shall be permitted to be reduced 25 percent, except that in no case shall the cover be less than $^3/_4$ inch in slabs or $1^1/_2$ inches in beams or girders.
f. For solid slabs of siliceous aggregate concrete, increase tendon cover 20 percent.
g. Adequate provisions against spalling shall be provided by U-shaped or hooped stirrups spaced not to exceed the depth of the member with a clear cover of 1 inch.
h. Prestressed slabs shall have a thickness not less than that required in Table 720.1(3) for the respective fire-resistance time period.
i. Fire coverage and end anchorages shall be as follows: Cover to the prestressing steel at the anchor shall be $^1/_2$ inch greater than that required away from the anchor. Minimum cover to steel-bearing plate shall be 1 inch in beams and $^3/_4$ inch in slabs.
j. For beam widths between 8 inches and 12 inches, cover thickness shall be permitted to be determined by interpolation.
k. Interior spans of continuous slabs, beams and girders shall be permitted to be considered restrained.
l. For use with concrete slabs having a comparable fire endurance where members are framed into the structure in such a manner as to provide equivalent performance to that of monolithic concrete construction.
m. Generic fire-resistance ratings (those not designated as PROPRIETARY* in the listing) in GA 600 shall be accepted as if herein listed.
n. No additional insulating material is required on the exposed outside face of the column flange to achieve a 1-hour fire-resistance rating.

TABLE 720.1(2)
RATED FIRE-RESISTANCE PERIODS FOR VARIOUS WALLS AND PARTITIONS [a, o, p]

MATERIAL	ITEM NUMBER	CONSTRUCTION	MINIMUM FINISHED THICKNESS FACE-TO-FACE[b] (inches)			
			4 hour	3 hour	2 hour	1 hour
1. Brick of clay or shale	1-1.1	Solid brick of clay or shale[c].	6	4.9	3.8	2.7
	1-1.2	Hollow brick, not filled.	5.0	4.3	3.4	2.3
	1-1.3	Hollow brick unit wall, grout or filled with perlite vermiculite or expanded shale aggregate.	6.6	5.5	4.4	3.0
	1-2.1	4″ nominal thick units at least 75 percent solid backed with a hat-shaped metal furring channel $^{3}/_{4}$″ thick formed from 0.021″ sheet metal attached to the brick wall on 24″ centers with approved fasteners, and $^{1}/_{2}$″ Type X gypsum wallboard attached to the metal furring strips with 1″-long Type S screws spaced 8″ on center.	—	—	5[d]	—
2. Combination of clay brick and load-bearing hollow clay tile	2-1.1	4″ solid brick and 4″ tile (at least 40 percent solid).	—	8	—	—
	2-1.2	4″ solid brick and 8″ tile (at least 40 percent solid).	12	—	—	—
3. Concrete masonry units	3-1.1[f, g]	Expanded slag or pumice.	4.7	4.0	3.2	2.1
	3-1.2[f, g]	Expanded clay, shale or slate.	5.1	4.4	3.6	2.6
	3-1.3[f]	Limestone, cinders or air-cooled slag.	5.9	5.0	4.0	2.7
	3-1.4[f, g]	Calcareous or siliceous gravel.	6.2	5.3	4.2	2.8
4. Solid concrete[h, i]	4-1.1	Siliceous aggregate concrete.	7.0	6.2	5.0	3.5
		Carbonate aggregate concrete.	6.6	5.7	4.6	3.2
		Sand-lightweight concrete.	5.4	4.6	3.8	2.7
		Lightweight concrete.	5.1	4.4	3.6	2.5
5. Glazed or unglazed facing tile, nonload-bearing	5-1.1	One 2″ unit cored 15 percent maximum and one 4″ unit cored 25 percent maximum with $^{3}/_{4}$″ mortar-filled collar joint. Unit positions reversed in alternate courses.	—	$6^{3}/_{8}$	—	—
	5-1.2	One 2″ unit cored 15 percent maximum and one 4″ unit cored 40 percent maximum with $^{3}/_{4}$″ mortar-filled collar joint. Unit positions side with $^{3}/_{4}$″ gypsum plaster. Two wythes tied together every fourth course with No. 22 gage corrugated metal ties.	—	$6^{3}/_{4}$	—	—
	5-1.3	One unit with three cells in wall thickness, cored 29 percent maximum.	—	—	6	—
	5-1.4	One 2″ unit cored 22 percent maximum and one 4″ unit cored 41 percent maximum with $^{1}/_{4}$″ mortar-filled collar joint. Two wythes tied together every third course with 0.030″ (No. 22 galvanized sheet steel gage) corrugated metal ties.	—	—	6	—
	5-1.5	One 4″ unit cored 25 percent maximum with $^{3}/_{4}$″ gypsum plaster on one side.	—	—	$4^{3}/_{4}$	—
	5-1.6	One 4″ unit with two cells in wall thickness, cored 22 percent maximum.	—	—	—	4
	5-1.7	One 4″ unit cored 30 percent maximum with $^{3}/_{4}$″ vermiculite gypsum plaster on one side.	—	—	$4^{1}/_{2}$	—
	5-1.8	One 4″ unit cored 39 percent maximum with $^{3}/_{4}$″ gypsum plaster on one side.	—	—	—	$4^{1}/_{2}$

(continued)

TABLE 720.1(2)—continued
RATED FIRE-RESISTANCE PERIODS FOR VARIOUS WALLS AND PARTITIONS [a, o, p]

MATERIAL	ITEM NUMBER	CONSTRUCTION	MINIMUM FINISHED THICKNESS FACE-TO-FACE[b] (inches) 4 hour	3 hour	2 hour	1 hour
6. Solid gypsum plaster	6-1.1	$^3/_4$″ by 0.055″ (No. 16 carbon sheet steel gage) vertical cold-rolled channels, 16″ on center with 2.6-pound flat metal lath applied to one face and tied with 0.049″ (No. 18 B.W. Gage) wire at 6″ spacing. Gypsum plaster each side mixed 1:2 by weight, gypsum to sand aggregate.	—	—	—	2[d]
	6-1.2	$^3/_4$″ by 0.05″ (No. 16 carbon sheet steel gage) cold-rolled channels 16″ on center with metal lath applied to one face and tied with 0.049″ (No. 18 B.W. gage) wire at 6″ spacing. Perlite or vermiculite gypsum plaster each side. For three-coat work, the plaster mix for the second coat shall not exceed 100 pounds of gypsum to $2^1/_2$ cubic feet of aggregate for the 1-hour system.	—	—	$2^1/_2$[d]	2[d]
	6-1.3	$^3/_4$″ by 0.055″ (No. 16 carbon sheet steel gage) vertical cold-rolled channels, 16″ on center with $^3/_8$″ gypsum lath applied to one face and attached with sheet metal clips. Gypsum plaster each side mixed 1:2 by weight, gypsum to sand aggregate.	—	—	—	2[d]
	6-2.1	Studless with $^1/_2$″ full-length plain gypsum lath and gypsum plaster each side. Plaster mixed 1:1 for scratch coat and 1:2 for brown coat, by weight, gypsum to sand aggregate.	—	—	—	2[d]
	6-2.2	Studless with $^1/_2$″ full-length plain gypsum lath and perlite or vermiculite gypsum plaster each side.	—	—	$2^1/_2$[d]	2[d]
	6-2.3	Studless partition with $^3/_8$″ rib metal lath installed vertically adjacent edges tied 6″ on center with No. 18 gage wire ties, gypsum plaster each side mixed 1:2 by weight, gypsum to sand aggregate.	—	—	—	2[d]
7. Solid perlite and portland cement	7-1.1	Perlite mixed in the ratio of 3 cubic feet to 100 pounds of portland cement and machine applied to stud side of $1^1/_2$″ mesh by 0.058-inch (No. 17 B.W. gage) paper-backed woven wire fabric lath wire-tied to 4″-deep steel trussed wire[j] studs 16″ on center. Wire ties of 0.049″ (No. 18 B.W. gage) galvanized steel wire 6″ on center vertically.	—	—	$3^1/_8$[d]	—
8. Solid neat wood fibered gypsum plaster	8-1.1	$^3/_4$″ by 0.055-inch (No. 16 carbon sheet steel gage) cold-rolled channels, 12″ on center with 2.5-pound flat metal lath applied to one face and tied with 0.049″ (No. 18 B.W. gage) wire at 6″ spacing. Neat gypsum plaster applied each side.	—	—	2[d]	—
9. Solid wallboard partition	9-1.1	One full-length layer $^1/_2$″ Type X gypsum wallboard[e] laminated to each side of 1″ full-length V-edge gypsum coreboard with approved laminating compound. Vertical joints of face layer and coreboard staggered at least 3″.	—	—	2[d]	—
10. Hollow (studless) gypsum wallboard partition	10-1.1	One full-length layer of $^5/_8$″ Type X gypsum wallboard[e] attached to both sides of wood or metal top and bottom runners laminated to each side of 1″ × 6″ full-length gypsum coreboard ribs spaced 2″ on center with approved laminating compound. Ribs centered at vertical joints of face plies and joints staggered 24″ in opposing faces. Ribs may be recessed 6″ from the top and bottom.	—	—	—	$2^1/_4$[d]
	10-1.2	1″ regular gypsum V-edge full-length backing board attached to both sides of wood or metal top and bottom runners with nails or $1^5/_8$″ drywall screws at 24″ on center. Minimum width of rumors $1^5/_8$″. Face layer of $^1/_2$″ regular full-length gypsum wallboard laminated to outer faces of backing board with approved laminating compound.	—	—	$4^5/_8$[d]	—

(continued)

TABLE 720.1(2)—continued
RATED FIRE-RESISTANCE PERIODS FOR VARIOUS WALLS AND PARTITIONS [a, o, p]

MATERIAL	ITEM NUMBER	CONSTRUCTION	MINIMUM FINISHED THICKNESS FACE-TO-FACE[b] (inches)			
			4 hour	3 hour	2 hour	1 hour
11. Noncombustible studs—interior partition with plaster each side	11-1.1	3 1/4″ × 0.044″ (No. 18 carbon sheet steel gage) steel studs spaced 24″ on center. 5/8″ gypsum plaster on metal lath each side mixed 1:2 by weight, gypsum to sand aggregate.	—	—	—	4 3/4[d]
	11-1.2	3 3/8″ × 0.055″ (No. 16 carbon sheet steel gage) approved nailable[k] studs spaced 24″ on center. 5/8″ neat gypsum wood-fibered plaster each side over 3/8″ rib metal lath nailed to studs with 6d common nails, 8″ on center. Nails driven 1 1/4″ and bent over.	—	—	5 5/8	—
	11-1.3	4″ × 0.044″ (No. 18 carbon sheet steel gage) channel-shaped steel studs at 16″ on center. On each side approved resilient clips pressed onto stud flange at 16″ vertical spacing, 1/4″ pencil rods snapped into or wire tied onto outer loop of clips, metal lath wire-tied to pencil rods at 6″ intervals, 1″ perlite gypsum plaster, each side.	—	7 5/8[d]	—	—
	11-1.4	2 1/2″ × 0.044″ (No. 18 carbon sheet steel gage) steel studs spaced 16″ on center. Wood fibered gypsum plaster mixed 1:1 by weight gypsum to sand aggregate applied on 3/4-pound metal lath wire tied to studs, each side. 3/4″ plaster applied over each face, including finish coat.	—	—	4 1/4[d]	—
12. Wood studs interior partition with plaster each side	12-1.1[l, m]	2″ × 4″ wood studs 16″ on center with 5/8″ gypsum plaster on metal lath. Lath attached by 4d common nails bent over or No. 14 gage by 1 1/4″ by 3/4″ crown width staples spaced 6″ on center. Plaster mixed 1:1 1/2 for scratch coat and 1:3 for brown coat, by weight, gypsum to sand aggregate.	—	—	—	5 1/8
	12-1.2[l]	2″ × 4″ wood studs 16″ on center with metal lath and 7/8″ neat wood-fibered gypsum plaster each side. Lath attached by 6d common nails, 7″ on center. Nails driven 1 1/4″ and bent over.	—	—	5 1/2[d]	—
	12-1.3[l]	2″ × 4″ wood studs 16″ on center with 3/8″ perforated or plain gypsum lath and 1/2″ gypsum plaster each side. Lath nailed with 1 1/8″ by No. 13 gage by 19/64″ head plasterboard blued nails, 4″ on center. Plaster mixed 1:2 by weight, gypsum to sand aggregate.	—	—	—	5 1/4
	12-1.4[l]	2″ × 4″ wood studs 16″ on center with 3/8″ Type X gypsum lath and 1/2″ gypsum plaster each side. Lath nailed with 1 1/8″ by No. 13 gage by 19/64″ head plasterboard blued nails, 5″ on center. Plaster mixed 1:2 by weight, gypsum to sand aggregate.	—	—	—	5 1/4
13.Noncombustible studs—interior partition with gypsum wallboard each side	13-1.1	0.018″ (No. 25 carbon sheet steel gage) channel-shaped studs 24″ on center with one full-length layer of 5/8″ Type X gypsum wallboard[e] applied vertically attached with 1″ long No. 6 drywall screws to each stud. Screws are 8″ on center around the perimeter and 12″ on center on the intermediate stud. The wallboard may be applied horizontally when attached to 3 5/8″ studs and the horizontal joints are staggered with those on the opposite side. Screws for the horizontal application shall be 8″ on center at vertical edges and 12″ on center at intermediate studs.	—	—	—	2 7/8[d]
	13-1.2	0.018″ (No. 25 carbon sheet steel gage) channel-shaped studs 25″ on center with two full-length layers of 1/2″ Type X gypsum wallboard[e] applied vertically each side. First layer attached with 1″-long, No. 6 drywall screws, 8″ on center around the perimeter and 12″ on center on the intermediate stud. Second layer applied with vertical joints offset one stud space from first layer using 1 5/8″ long, No. 6 drywall screws spaced 9″ on center along vertical joints, 12″ on center at intermediate studs and 24″ on center along top and bottom runners.	—	—	3 5/8[d]	—
	13-1.3	0.055″ (No. 16 carbon sheet steel gage) approved nailable metal studs[e] 24″ on center with full-length 5/8″ Type X gypsum wallboard[e] applied vertically and nailed 7″ on center with 6d cement-coated common nails. Approved metal fastener grips used with nails at vertical butt joints along studs.	—	—	—	4 7/8

(continued)

TABLE 720.1(2)—continued
RATED FIRE-RESISTANCE PERIODS FOR VARIOUS WALLS AND PARTITIONS [a, o, p]

MATERIAL	ITEM NUMBER	CONSTRUCTION	MINIMUM FINISHED THICKNESS FACE-TO-FACE[b] (inches)			
			4 hour	3 hour	2 hour	1 hour
14. Wood studs—interior partition with gypsum wallboard each side	14-1.1[h, m]	2″ × 4″ wood studs 16″ on center with two layers of $^3/_8$″ regular gypsum wallboard[e] each side, 4d cooler[n] or wallboard[n] nails at 8″ on center first layer, 5d cooler[n] or wallboard[n] nails at 8″ on center second layer with laminating compound between layers, joints staggered. First layer applied full length vertically, second layer applied horizontally or vertically.	—	—	—	5
	14-1.2[l, m]	2″ × 4″ wood studs 16″ on center with two layers $^1/_2$″ regular gypsum wallboard[e] applied vertically or horizontally each side[k], joints staggered. Nail base layer with 5d cooler[n] or wallboard[n] nails at 8″ on center face layer with 8d cooler[n] or wallboard[n] nails at 8″ on center.	—	—	—	5$^1/_2$
	14-1.3[l, m]	2″ × 4″ wood studs 24″ on center with $^5/_8$″ Type X gypsum wallboard[e] applied vertically or horizontally nailed with 6d cooler[n] or wallboard[n] nails at 7″ on center with end joints on nailing members. Stagger joints each side.	—	—	—	4$^3/_4$
	14-1.4[l]	2″ × 4″ fire-retardant-treated wood studs spaced 24″ on center with one layer of $^5/_8$″ Type X gypsum wallboard[e] applied with face paper grain (long dimension) parallel to studs. Wallboard attached with 6d cooler[n] or wallboard[n] nails at 7″ on center.	—	—	—	4$^3/_4$[d]
	14-1.5[l, m]	2″ × 4″ wood studs 16″ on center with two layers $^5/_8$″ Type X gypsum wallboard[e] each side. Base layers applied vertically and nailed with 6d cooler[n] or wallboard[n] nails at 9″ on center. Face layer applied vertically or horizontally and nailed with 8d cooler[n] or wallboard[n] nails at 7″ on center. For nail-adhesive application, base layers are nailed 6″ on center. Face layers applied with coating of approved wallboard adhesive and nailed 12″ on center.	—	—	6	—
	14-1.6[l]	2″ × 3″ fire-retardant-treated wood studs spaced 24″ on center with one layer of $^5/_8$″ Type X gypsum wallboard[e] applied with face paper grain (long dimension) at right angles to studs. Wallboard attached with 6d cement-coated box nails spaced 7″ on center.	—	—	—	3$^5/_8$[d]
15. Exterior or interior walls	15-1.1[l, m]	Exterior surface with $^3/_4$″ drop siding over $^1/_2$″ gypsum sheathing on 2″ × 4″ wood studs at 16″ on center, interior surface treatment as required for 1-hour-rated exterior or interior 2″ × 4″ wood stud partitions. Gypsum sheathing nailed with 1$^3/_4$″ by No. 11 gage by $^7/_{16}$″ head galvanized nails at 8″ on center. Siding nailed with 7d galvanized smooth box nails.	—	—	—	Varies
	15-1.2[l, m]	2″ × 4″ wood studs 16″ on center with metal lath and $^3/_4$″ cement plaster on each side. Lath attached with 6d common nails 7″ on center driven to 1″ minimum penetration and bent over. Plaster mix 1:4 for scratch coat and 1:5 for brown coat, by volume, cement to sand.	—	—	—	5$^3/_8$
	15-1.3[l, m]	2″ × 4″ wood studs 16″ on center with $^7/_8$″ cement plaster (measured from the face of studs) on the exterior surface with interior surface treatment as required for interior wood stud partitions in this table. Plaster mix 1:4 for scratch coat and 1:5 for brown coat, by volume, cement to sand.	—	—	—	Varies
	15-1.4	3$^5/_8$″ No. 16 gage noncombustible studs 16″ on center with $^7/_8$″ cement plaster (measured from the face of the studs) on the exterior surface with interior surface treatment as required for interior, nonbearing, noncombustible stud partitions in this table. Plaster mix 1:4 for scratch coat and 1:5 for brown coat, by volume, cement to sand.	—	—	—	Varies[d]

(continued)

TABLE 720.1(2)—continued
RATED FIRE-RESISTANCE PERIODS FOR VARIOUS WALLS AND PARTITIONS [a, o, p]

MATERIAL	ITEM NUMBER	CONSTRUCTION	MINIMUM FINISHED THICKNESS FACE-TO-FACE[b] (inches)			
			4 hour	3 hour	2 hour	1 hour
15. Exterior or interior walls (continued)	15-1.5[m]	$2^1/_4''$ × $3^3/_4''$ clay face brick with cored holes over $^1/_2''$ gypsum sheathing on exterior surface of 2″ × 4″ wood studs at 16″ on center and two layers $^5/_8''$ Type X gypsum wallboard[e] on interior surface. Sheathing placed horizontally or vertically with vertical joints over studs nailed 6″ on center with $1^3/_4''$ × No. 11 gage by $^7/_{16}''$ head galvanized nails. Inner layer of wallboard placed horizontally or vertically and nailed 8″ on center with 6d cooler[n] or wallboard[n] nails. Outer layer of wallboard placed horizontally or vertically and nailed 8″ on center with 8d cooler[n] or wallboard[n] nails. All joints staggered with vertical joints over studs. Outer layer joints taped and finished with compound. Nail heads covered with joint compound. 0.035 inch (No. 20 galvanized sheet gage) corrugated galvanized steel wall ties $^3/_4''$ by $6^5/_8''$ attached to each stud with two 8d cooler[n] or wallboard[n] nails every sixth course of bricks.	—	—	10	—
	15-1.6[l, m]	2″ × 6″ fire-retardant-treated wood studs 16″ on center. Interior face has two layers of $^5/_8''$ Type X gypsum with the base layer placed vertically and attached with 6d box nails 12″ on center. The face layer is placed horizontally and attached with 8d box nails 8″ on center at joints and 12″ on center elsewhere. The exterior face has a base layer of $^5/_8''$ Type X gypsum sheathing placed vertically with 6d box nails 8″ on center at joints and 12″ on center elsewhere. An approved building paper is next applied, followed by self-furred exterior lath attached with $2^1/_2''$, No. 12 gage galvanized roofing nails with a $^3/_8''$ diameter head and spaced 6″ on center along each stud. Cement plaster consisting of a $^1/_2''$ brown coat is then applied. The scratch coat is mixed in the proportion of 1:3 by weight, cement to sand with 10 pounds of hydrated lime and 3 pounds of approved additives or admixtures per sack of cement. The brown coat is mixed in the proportion of 1:4 by weight, cement to sand with the same amounts of hydrated lime and approved additives or admixtures used in the scratch coat.	—	—	$8^1/_4$	—
	15-1.7[l, m]	2″ × 6″ wood studs 16″ on center. The exterior face has a layer of $^5/_8''$ Type X gypsum sheathing placed vertically with 6d box nails 8″ on center at joints and 12″ on center elsewhere. An approved building paper is next applied, followed by 1″ by No. 18 gage self-furred exterior lath attached with 8d by $2^1/_2''$ long galvanized roofing nails spaced 6″ on center along each stud. Cement plaster consisting of a $^1/_2''$ scratch coat, a bonding agent and a $^1/_2''$ brown coat and a finish coat is then applied. The scratch coat is mixed in the proportion of 1:3 by weight, cement to sand with 10 pounds of hydrated lime and 3 pounds of approved additives or admixtures per sack of cement. The brown coat is mixed in the proportion of 1:4 by weight, cement to sand with the same amounts of hydrated lime and approved additives or admixtures used in the scratch coat. The interior is covered with $^3/_8''$ gypsum lath with 1″ hexagonal mesh of 0.035 inch (No. 20 B.W. gage) woven wire lath furred out $^5/_{16}''$ and 1″ perlite or vermiculite gypsum plaster. Lath nailed with $1^1/_8''$ by No. 13 gage by $^{19}/_{64}''$ head plasterboard glued nails spaced 5″ on center. Mesh attached by $1^3/_4''$ by No. 12 gage by $^3/_8''$ head nails with $^3/_8''$ furrings, spaced 8″ on center. The plaster mix shall not exceed 100 pounds of gypsum to $2^1/_2$ cubic feet of aggregate.	—	—	$8^3/_8$	—
	15-1.8[l, m]	2″ × 6″ wood studs 16″ on center. The exterior face has a layer of $^5/_8''$ Type X gypsum sheathing placed vertically with 6d box nails 8″ on center at joints and 12″ on center elsewhere. An approved building paper is next applied, followed by $1^1/_2''$ by No. 17 gage self-furred exterior lath attached with 8d by $2^1/_2''$ long galvanized roofing nails spaced 6″ on center along each stud. Cement plaster consisting of a $^1/_2''$ scratch coat, and a $^1/_2''$ brown coat is then applied. The plaster may be placed by machine. The scratch coat is mixed in the proportion of 1:4 by weight, plastic cement to sand. The brown coat is mixed in the proportion of 1:5 by weight, plastic cement to sand. The interior is covered with $^3/_8''$ gypsum lath with 1″ hexagonal mesh of No. 20 gage woven wire lath furred out $^5/_{16}''$ and 1″ perlite or vermiculite gypsum plaster. Lath nailed with $1^1/_8''$ by No. 13 gage by $^{19}/_{64}''$ head plasterboard glued nails spaced 5″ on center. Mesh attached by $1^3/_4''$ by No. 12 gage by $^3/_8''$ head nails with $^3/_8''$ furrings, spaced 8″ on center. The plaster mix shall not exceed 100 pounds of gypsum to $2^1/_2$ cubic feet of aggregate.	—	—	$8^3/_8$	—

(continued)

TABLE 720.1(2)—continued
RATED FIRE-RESISTANCE PERIODS FOR VARIOUS WALLS AND PARTITIONS [a, o, p]

MATERIAL	ITEM NUMBER	CONSTRUCTION	MINIMUM FINISHED THICKNESS FACE-TO-FACE[b] (inches)			
			4 hour	3 hour	2 hour	1 hour
15. Exterior or interior walls (continued)	15-1.9	4″ No. 18 gage, nonload-bearing metal studs, 16″ on center, with 1″ portland cement lime plaster [measured from the back side of the $^3/_4$-pound expanded metal lath] on the exterior surface. Interior surface to be covered with 1″ of gypsum plaster on $^3/_4$-pound expanded metal lath proportioned by weight—1:2 for scratch coat, 1:3 for brown, gypsum to sand. Lath on one side of the partition fastened to $^1/_4$″ diameter pencil rods supported by No. 20 gage metal clips, located 16″ on center vertically, on each stud. 3″ thick mineral fiber insulating batts friction fitted between the studs.	—	—	$6^1/_2$[d]	—
	15-1.10	Steel studs 0.060″ thick, 4″ deep or 6″ at 16″ or 24″ centers, with $^1/_2$″ Glass Fiber Reinforced Concrete (GFRC) on the exterior surface. GFRC is attached with flex anchors at 24″ on center, with 5″ leg welded to studs with two $^1/_2$″-long flare-bevel welds, and 4″ foot attached to the GFRC skin with $^5/_8$″ thick GFRC bonding pads that extend $2^1/_2$″ beyond the flex anchor foot on both sides. Interior surface to have two layers of $^1/_2$″ Type X gypsum wallboard.[e] The first layer of wallboard to be attached with 1″-long Type S buglehead screws spaced 24″ on center and the second layer is attached with $1^5/_8$″-long Type S screws spaced at 12″ on center. Cavity is to be filled with 5″ of 4 pcf (nominal) mineral fiber batts. GFRC has $1^1/_2$″ returns packed with mineral fiber and caulked on the exterior.	—	—	$6^1/_2$	—
	15-1.11	Steel studs 0.060″ thick, 4″ deep or 6″ at 16″ or 24″ centers, respectively, with $^1/_2$″ Glass Fiber Reinforced Concrete (GFRC) on the exterior surface. GFRC is attached with flex anchors at 24″ on center, with 5″ leg welded to studs with two $^1/_2$″-long flare-bevel welds, and 4″ foot attached to the GFRC skin with $^5/_8$″-thick GFRC bonding pads that extend $2^1/_2$″ beyond the flex anchor foot on both sides. Interior surface to have one layer of $^5/_8$″ Type X gypsum wallboard[e], attached with $1^1/_4$″-long Type S buglehead screws spaced 12″ on center. Cavity is to be filled with 5″ of 4 pcf (nominal) mineral fiber batts. GFRC has $1^1/_2$″ returns packed with mineral fiber and caulked on the exterior.	—	—	—	$6^1/_8$
	15-1.12[q]	2″ × 6″ wood studs at 16″ with double top plates, single bottom plate; interior and exterior sides covered with $^5/_8$″ Type X gypsum wallboard, 4′ wide, applied horizontally or vertically with vertical joints over studs, and fastened with $2^1/_4$″ Type S drywall screws, spaced 12″ on center. Cavity to be filled with $5^1/_2$″ mineral wool insulation.	—	—	—	$6^3/_4$
	15-1.13[q]	2″ × 6″ wood studs at 16″ with double top plates, single bottom plate; interior and exterior sides covered with $^5/_8$″ Type X gypsum wallboard, 4′ wide, applied vertically with all joints over framing or blocking and fastened with $2^1/_4$″ Type S drywall screws, spaced 12″ on center. R-19 mineral fiber insulation installed in stud cavity.	—	—	—	$6^3/_4$
	15-1.14[q]	2″ × 6″ wood studs at 16″ with double top plates, single bottom plate; interior and exterior sides covered with $^5/_8$″ Type X gypsum wallboard, 4′ wide, applied horizontally or vertically with vertical joints over studs, and fastened with $2^1/_4$″ Type S drywall screws, spaced 7″ on center.	—	—	—	$6^3/_4$
	15-1.15[q]	2″ × 4″ wood studs at 16″ with double top plates, single bottom plate; interior and exterior sides covered with $^5/_8$″ Type X gypsum wallboard and sheathing, respectively, 4′ wide, applied horizontally or vertically with vertical joints over studs, and fastened with $2^1/_4$″ Type S drywall screws, spaced 12″ on center. Cavity to be filled with $3^1/_2$″ mineral wool insulation.	—	—	—	$4^3/_4$
	15-1.16[q]	2″ × 6″ wood studs at 24″ centers with double top plates, single bottom plate; interior and exterior side covered with two layers of $^5/_8$″ Type X gypsum wallboard, 4′ wide, applied horizontally with vertical joints over studs. Base layer fastened with $2^1/_4$″ Type S drywall screws, spaced 24″ on center and face layer fastened with Type S drywall screws, spaced 8″ on center, wallboard joints covered with paper tape and joint compound, fastener heads covered with joint compound. Cavity to be filled with $5^1/_2$″ mineral wool insulation.	—	—	$7^3/_4$	—

(continued)

TABLE 720.1(2)—continued
RATED FIRE-RESISTANCE PERIODS FOR VARIOUS WALLS AND PARTITIONS [a, o, p]

MATERIAL	ITEM NUMBER	CONSTRUCTION	MINIMUM FINISHED THICKNESS FACE-TO-FACE[b] (inches)			
			4 hour	3 hour	2 hour	1 hour
15. Exterior or interior walls (continued)	15-2.1[d]	$3^5/_8$″ No. 16 gage steel studs at 24″ on center or 2″ × 4″ wood studs at 24″ on center. Metal lath attached to the exterior side of studs with minimum 1″ long No. 6 drywall screws at 6″ on center and covered with minimum $^3/_4$″ thick portland cement plaster. Thin veneer brick units of clay or shale complying with ASTM C 1088, Grade TBS or better, installed in running bond in accordance with Section 1405.10. Combined total thickness of the portland cement plaster, mortar and thin veneer brick units shall be not less than $1^3/_4$″. Interior side covered with one layer of $^5/_8$″ thick Type X gypsum wallboard attached to studs with 1″ long No. 6 drywall screws at 12″ on center.				6
	15-2.2[d]	$3^5/_8$″ No. 16 gage steel studs at 24″ on center or 2″ × 4″ wood studs at 24″ on center. Metal lath attached to the exterior side of studs with minimum 1″ long No. 6 drywall screws at 6″ on center and covered with minimum $^3/_4$″ thick portland cement plaster. Thin veneer brick units of clay or shale complying with ASTM C 1088, Grade TBS or better, installed in running bond in accordance with Section 1405.10. Combined total thickness of the portland cement plaster, mortar and thin veneer brick units shall be not less than 2″. Interior side covered with two layers of $^5/_8$″ thick Type X gypsum wallboard. Bottom layer attached to studs with 1″ long No. 6 drywall screws at 24″ on center. Top layer attached to studs with $1^5/_8$″ long No. 6 drywall screws at 12″ on center.			$6^7/_8$	
	15-2.3[d]	$3^5/_8$″ No. 16 gage steel studs at 16″ on center or 2″ × 4″ wood studs at 16″ on center. Where metal lath is used, attach to the exterior side of studs with minimum 1″ long No. 6 drywall screws at 6″ on center. Brick units of clay or shale not less than $2^5/_8$″ thick complying with ASTM C 216 installed in accordance with Section 1405.6 with a minimum 1″ air space. Interior side covered with one layer of $^5/_8$″ thick Type X gypsum wallboard attached to studs with 1″ long No. 6 drywall screws at 12″ on center.				$7^7/_8$
	15-2.4[d]	$3^5/_8$″ No. 16 gage steel studs at 16″ on center or 2″ × 4″ wood studs at 16″ on center. Where metal lath is used, attach to the exterior side of studs with minimum 1″ long No. 6 drywall screws at 6″ on center. Brick units of clay or shale not less than $2^5/_8$″ thick complying with ASTM C 216 installed in accordance with Section 1405.6 with a minimum 1″ air space. Interior side covered with two layers of $^5/_8$″ thick Type X gypsum wallboard. Bottom layer attached to studs with 1″ long No. 6 drywall screws at 24″ on center. Top layer attached to studs with $1^5/_8$″ long No. 6 drywall screws at 12″ on center.			$8^1/_2$	
16. Exterior walls rated for fire resistance from the inside only in accordance with Section 705.5.	16-1.1[q]	2″ × 4″ wood studs at 16″ centers with double top plates, single bottom plate; interior side covered with $^5/_8$″ Type X gypsum wallboard, 4′ wide, applied horizontally unblocked, and fastened with $2^1/_4$″ Type S drywall screws, spaced 12″ on center, wallboard joints covered with paper tape and joint compound, fastener heads covered with joint compound. Exterior covered with $^3/_8$″ wood structural panels, applied vertically, horizontal joints blocked and fastened with 6d common nails (bright) — 12″ on center in the field, and 6″ on center panel edges. Cavity to be filled with $3^1/_2$″ mineral wool insulation. Rating established for exposure from interior side only.	—	—	—	$4^1/_2$

(continued)

TABLE 720.1(2)—continued
RATED FIRE-RESISTANCE PERIODS FOR VARIOUS WALLS AND PARTITIONS [a, o, p]

MATERIAL	ITEM NUMBER	CONSTRUCTION	MINIMUM FINISHED THICKNESS FACE-TO-FACE[b] (inches)			
			4 hour	3 hour	2 hour	1 hour
16. Exterior walls rated for fire resistance from the inside only in accordance with Section 705.5. (continued)	16-1.2[q]	2″ × 6″ (51mm x 152 mm) wood studs at 16 ″ centers with double top plates, single bottom plate; interior side covered with $^5/_8$″ Type X gypsum wallboard, 4′ wide, applied horizontally or vertically with vertical joints over studs and fastened with $2^1/_4$″ Type S drywall screws, spaced 12″ on center, wallboard joints covered with paper tape and joint compound, fastener heads covered with joint compound, exterior side covered with $^7/_{16}$″ wood structural panels fastened with 6d common nails (bright) spaced 12″ on center in the field and 6″ on center along the panel edges. Cavity to be filled with $5^1/_2$″ mineral wool insulation. Rating established from the gypsum-covered side only.	—	—	—	$6^9/_{16}$
	16-1.3	2″ × 6″ wood studs at 16″ centers with double top plates, single bottom plates; interior side covered with $^5/_8$″ Type X gypsum wallboard, 4′ wide, applied vertically with all joints over framing or blocking and fastened with $2^1/_4$″ Type S drywall screws spaced 7″ on center. Joints to be covered with tape and joint compound. Exterior covered with $^3/_8$″ wood structural panels, applied vertically with edges over framing or blocking and fastened with 6d common nails (bright) at 12″ on center in the field and 6″ on center on panel edges. R-19 mineral fiber insulation installed in stud cavity. Rating established from the gypsum-covered side only.	—	—	—	$6^1/_2$

For SI: 1 inch = 25.4 mm, 1 square inch = 645.2 mm², 1 cubic foot = 0.0283 m³, 1 foot = 304.8 mm.

a. Staples with equivalent holding power and penetration shall be permitted to be used as alternate fasteners to nails for attachment to wood framing.

b. Thickness shown for brick and clay tile is nominal thicknesses unless plastered, in which case thicknesses are net. Thickness shown for concrete masonry and clay masonry is equivalent thickness defined in Section 721.3.1 for concrete masonry and Section 721.4.1.1 for clay masonry. Where all cells are solid grouted or filled with silicone-treated perlite loose-fill insulation; vermiculite loose-fill insulation; or expanded clay, shale or slate lightweight aggregate, the equivalent thickness shall be the thickness of the block or brick using specified dimensions as defined in Chapter 21. Equivalent thickness may also include the thickness of applied plaster and lath or gypsum wallboard, where specified.

c. For units in which the net cross-sectional area of cored brick in any plane parallel to the surface containing the cores is at least 75 percent of the gross cross-sectional area measured in the same plane.

d. Shall be used for nonbearing purposes only.

e. For all of the construction with gypsum wallboard described in this table, gypsum base for veneer plaster of the same size, thickness and core type shall be permitted to be substituted for gypsum wallboard, provided attachment is identical to that specified for the wallboard, and the joints on the face layer are reinforced and the entire surface is covered with a minimum of $^1/_{16}$-inch gypsum veneer plaster.

f. The fire-resistance time period for concrete masonry units meeting the equivalent thicknesses required for a 2-hour fire-resistance rating in Item 3, and having a thickness of not less than $7^5/_8$ inches is 4 hours when cores which are not grouted are filled with silicone-treated perlite loose-fill insulation; vermiculite loose-fill insulation; or expanded clay, shale or slate lightweight aggregate, sand or slag having a maximum particle size of $^3/_8$ inch.

g. The fire-resistance rating of concrete masonry units composed of a combination of aggregate types or where plaster is applied directly to the concrete masonry shall be determined in accordance with ACI 216.1/TMS 0216. Lightweight aggregates shall have a maximum combined density of 65 pounds per cubic foot.

h. See also Note b. The equivalent thickness shall be permitted to include the thickness of cement plaster or 1.5 times the thickness of gypsum plaster applied in accordance with the requirements of Chapter 25.

i. Concrete walls shall be reinforced with horizontal and vertical temperature reinforcement as required by Chapter 19.

j. Studs are welded truss wire studs with 0.18 inch (No. 7 B.W. gage) flange wire and 0.18 inch (No. 7 B.W. gage) truss wires.

k. Nailable metal studs consist of two channel studs spot welded back to back with a crimped web forming a nailing groove.

l. Wood structural panels shall be permitted to be installed between the fire protection and the wood studs on either the interior or exterior side of the wood frame assemblies in this table, provided the length of the fasteners used to attach the fire protection is increased by an amount at least equal to the thickness of the wood structural panel.

m. The design stress of studs shall be reduced to 78 percent of allowable F'_c with the maximum not greater than 78 percent of the calculated stress with studs having a slenderness ratio l_e/d of 33.

n. For properties of cooler or wallboard nails, see ASTM C 514, ASTM C 547 or ASTM F 1667.

o. Generic fire-resistance ratings (those not designated as PROPRIETARY* in the listing) in the GA 600 shall be accepted as if herein listed.

p. NCMA TEK 5-8A shall be permitted for the design of fire walls.

q. The design stress of studs shall be equal to a maximum of 100 percent of the allowable F'_c calculated in accordance with Section 2306.

TABLE 720.1(3)
MINIMUM PROTECTION FOR FLOOR AND ROOF SYSTEMS[a, q]

FLOOR OR ROOF CONSTRUCTION	ITEM NUMBER	CEILING CONSTRUCTION	THICKNESS OF FLOOR OR ROOF SLAB (inches)				MINIMUM THICKNESS OF CEILING (inches)			
			4 hour	3 hour	2 hour	1 hour	4 hour	3 hour	2 hour	1 hour
1. Siliceous aggregate concrete	1-1.1	Slab (no ceiling required). Minimum cover over nonprestressed reinforcement shall not be less than $^3/_4$″ [b].	7.0	6.2	5.0	3.5	—	—	—	—
2. Carbonate aggregate concrete	2-1.1		6.6	5.7	4.6	3.2	—	—	—	—
3. Sand-lightweight concrete	3-1.1		5.4	4.6	3.8	2.7	—	—	—	—
4. Lightweight concrete	4-1.1		5.1	4.4	3.6	2.5	—	—	—	—
5. Reinforced concrete	5-1.1	Slab with suspended ceiling of vermiculite gypsum plaster over metal lath attached to $^3/_4$″ cold-rolled channels spaced 12″ on center. Ceiling located 6″ minimum below joists.	3	2	—	—	1	$^3/_4$	—	—
	5-2.1	$^3/_8$″ Type X gypsum wallboard[c] attached to 0.018 inch (No. 25 carbon sheet steel gage) by $^7/_8$″ deep by $2^5/_8$″ hat-shaped galvanized steel channels with 1″-long No. 6 screws. The channels are spaced 24″ on center, span 35″ and are supported along their length at 35″ intervals by 0.033″ (No. 21 galvanized sheet gage) galvanized steel flat strap hangers having formed edges that engage the lips of the channel. The strap hangers are attached to the side of the concrete joists with $^5/_{32}$″ by $1^1/_4$″ long power-driven fasteners. The wallboard is installed with the long dimension perpendicular to the channels. All end joints occur on channels and supplementary channels are installed parallel to the main channels, 12″ each side, at end joint occurrences. The finished ceiling is located approximately 12″ below the soffit of the floor slab.	—	—	$2^1/_2$	—	—	—	$^5/_8$	—
6. Steel joists constructed with a poured reinforced concrete slab on metal lath forms or steel form units[d, e]	6-1.1	Gypsum plaster on metal lath attached to the bottom cord with single No. 16 gage or doubled No. 18 gage wire ties spaced 6″ on center. Plaster mixed 1:2 for scratch coat, 1:3 for brown coat, by weight, gypsum-to-sand aggregate for 2-hour system. For 3-hour system plaster is neat.	—	—	$2^1/_2$	$2^1/_4$	—	—	$^3/_4$	$^5/_8$
	6-2.1	Vermiculite gypsum plaster on metal lath attached to the bottom chord with single No.16 gage or doubled 0.049-inch (No. 18 B.W. gage) wire ties 6″ on center.	—	2	—	—	—	$^5/_8$	—	—
	6-3.1	Cement plaster over metal lath attached to the bottom chord of joists with single No. 16 gage or doubled 0.049″ (No. 18 B.W. gage) wire ties spaced 6″ on center. Plaster mixed 1:2 for scratch coat, 1:3 for brown coat for 1-hour system and 1:1 for scratch coat, 1:1 $^1/_2$ for brown coat for 2-hour system, by weight, cement to sand.	—	—	—	2	—	—	—	$^5/_8$[f]
	6-4.1	Ceiling of $^5/_8$″ Type X wallboard[c] attached to $^7/_8$″ deep by $2^5/_8$″ by 0.021 inch (No. 25 carbon sheet steel gage) hat-shaped furring channels 12″ on center with 1″ long No. 6 wallboard screws at 8″ on center. Channels wire tied to bottom chord of joists with doubled 0.049 inch (No. 18 B.W. gage) wire or suspended below joists on wire hangers.[g]	—	—	$2^1/_2$	—	—	—	$^5/_8$	—
	6-5.1	Wood-fibered gypsum plaster mixed 1:1 by weight gypsum to sand aggregate applied over metal lath. Lath tied 6″ on center to $^3/_4$″ channels spaced $13^1/_2$″ on center. Channels secured to joists at each intersection with two strands of 0.049 inch (No. 18 B.W. gage) galvanized wire.	—	—	$2^1/_2$	—	—	—	$^3/_4$	—

(continued)

TABLE 720.1(3)—continued
MINIMUM PROTECTION FOR FLOOR AND ROOF SYSTEMS[a, q]

FLOOR OR ROOF CONSTRUCTION	ITEM NUMBER	CEILING CONSTRUCTION	THICKNESS OF FLOOR OR ROOF SLAB (inches)				MINIMUM THICKNESS OF CEILING (inches)			
			4 hour	3 hour	2 hour	1 hour	4 hour	3 hour	2 hour	1 hour
7. Reinforced concrete slabs and joists with hollow clay tile fillers laid end to end in rows 2 1/2″ or more apart; reinforcement placed between rows and concrete cast around and over tile.	7-1.1	5/8″ gypsum plaster on bottom of floor or roof construction.	—	—	8[h]	—	—	—	5/8	—
	7-1.2	None	—	—	—	5 1/2[i]	—	—	—	—
8. Steel joists constructed with a reinforced concrete slab on top poured on a 1/2″ deep steel deck.[e]	8-1.1	Vermiculite gypsum plaster on metal lath attached to 3/4″ cold-rolled channels with 0.049″ (No. 18 B.W. gage) wire ties spaced 6″ on center.	2 1/2[j]	—	—	—	3/4	—	—	—
9. 3″ deep cellular steel deck with concrete slab on top. Slab thickness measured to top.	9-1.1	Suspended ceiling of vermiculite gypsum plaster base coat and vermiculite acoustical plaster on metal lath attached at 6″ intervals to 3/4″ cold-rolled channels spaced 12″ on center and secured to 1 1/2″ cold-rolled channels spaced 36″ on center with 0.065″ (No. 16 B.W. gage) wire. 1 1/2″ channels supported by No. 8 gage wire hangers at 36″ on center. Beams within envelope and with a 2 1/2″ airspace between beam soffit and lath have a 4-hour rating.	2 1/2	—	—	—	1 1/8[k]	—	—	—
10. 1 1/2″-deep steel roof deck on steel framing. Insulation board, 30 pcf density, composed of wood fibers with cement binders of thickness shown bonded to deck with unified asphalt adhesive. Covered with a Class A or B roof covering.	10-1.1	Ceiling of gypsum plaster on metal lath. Lath attached to 3/4″ furring channels with 0.049″ (No. 18 B.W. gage) wire ties spaced 6″ on center. 3/4″ channel saddle tied to 2″ channels with doubled 0.065″ (No. 16 B.W. gage) wire ties. 2″ channels spaced 36″ on center suspended 2″ below steel framing and saddle-tied with 0.165″ (No. 8 B.W. gage) wire. Plaster mixed 1:2 by weight, gypsum-to-sand aggregate.	—	—	1 7/8	1	—	—	3/4[l]	3/4[l]
11. 1 1/2″-deep steel roof deck on steel-framing wood fiber insulation board, 17.5 pcf density on top applied over a 15-lb asphalt-saturated felt. Class A or B roof covering.	11-1.1	Ceiling of gypsum plaster on metal lath. Lath attached to 3/4″ furring channels with 0.049″ (No. 18 B.W. gage) wire ties spaced 6″ on center. 3/4″ channels saddle tied to 2″ channels with doubled 0.065″ (No. 16 B.W. gage) wire ties. 2″ channels spaced 36″ on center suspended 2″ below steel framing and saddle tied with 0.165″ (No. 8 B.W. gage) wire. Plaster mixed 1:2 for scratch coat and 1:3 for brown coat, by weight, gypsum-to-sand aggregate for 1-hour system. For 2-hour system, plaster mix is 1:2 by weight, gypsum-to-sand aggregate.	—	—	1 1/2	1	—	—	7/8[g]	3/4[l]

(continued)

TABLE 720.1(3)—continued
MINIMUM PROTECTION FOR FLOOR AND ROOF SYSTEMS[a, q]

FLOOR OR ROOF CONSTRUCTION	ITEM NUMBER	CEILING CONSTRUCTION	THICKNESS OF FLOOR OR ROOF SLAB (inches)				MINIMUM THICKNESS OF CEILING (inches)			
			4 hour	3 hour	2 hour	1 hour	4 hour	3 hour	2 hour	1 hour
12. $1^1/_2''$ deep steel roof deck on steel-framing insulation of rigid board consisting of expanded perlite and fibers impregnated with integral asphalt waterproofing; density 9 to 12 pcf secured to metal roof deck by $^1/_2''$ wide ribbons of waterproof, cold-process liquid adhesive spaced 6″ apart. Steel joist or light steel construction with metal roof deck, insulation, and Class A or B built-up roof covering.[e]	12-1.1	Gypsum-vermiculite plaster on metal lath wire tied at 6″ intervals to $^3/_4''$ furring channels spaced 12″ on center and wire tied to 2″ runner channels spaced 32″ on center. Runners wire tied to bottom chord of steel joists.	—	—	1	—	—	—	$^7/_8$	—
13. Double wood floor over wood joists spaced 16″ on center.[m,n]	13-1.1	Gypsum plaster over $^3/_8''$ Type X gypsum lath. Lath initially applied with not less than four $1^1/_8''$ by No. 13 gage by $^{19}/_{64}''$ head plasterboard blued nails per bearing. Continuous stripping over lath along all joist lines. Stripping consists of 3″ wide strips of metal lath attached by $1^1/_2''$ by No. 11 gage by $^1/_2''$ head roofing nails spaced 6″ on center. Alternate stripping consists of 3″ wide 0.049″ diameter wire stripping weighing 1 pound per square yard and attached by No.16 gage by $1^1/_2''$ by $^3/_4''$ crown width staples, spaced 4″ on center. Where alternate stripping is used, the lath nailing may consist of two nails at each end and one nail at each intermediate bearing. Plaster mixed 1:2 by weight, gypsum-to-sand aggregate.	—	—	—	—	—	—	—	$^7/_8$
	13-1.2	Cement or gypsum plaster on metal lath. Lath fastened with $1^1/_2''$ by No. 11 gage by $^7/_{16}''$ head barbed shank roofing nails spaced 5″ on center. Plaster mixed 1:2 for scratch coat and 1:3 for brown coat, by weight, cement to sand aggregate.	—	—	—	—	—	—	—	$^5/_8$
	13-1.3	Perlite or vermiculite gypsum plaster on metal lath secured to joists with $1^1/_2''$ by No. 11 gage by $^7/_{16}''$ head barbed shank roofing nails spaced 5″ on center.	—	—	—	—	—	—	—	$^5/_8$
	13-1.4	$^1/_2''$ Type X gypsum wallboard[c] nailed to joists with 5d cooler[o] or wallboard[o] nails at 6″ on center. End joints of wallboard centered on joists.	—	—	—	—	—	—	—	$^1/_2$
14. Plywood stressed skin panels consisting of $^5/_8''$-thick interior C-D (exterior glue) top stressed skin on 2″ × 6″ nominal (minimum) stringers. Adjacent panel edges joined with 8d common wire nails spaced 6″ on center. Stringers spaced 12″ maximum on center.	14-1.1	$^1/_2''$-thick wood fiberboard weighing 15 to 18 pounds per cubic foot installed with long dimension parallel to stringers or $^3/_8''$ C-D (exterior glue) plywood glued and/or nailed to stringers. Nailing to be with 5d cooler[o] or wallboard[o] nails at 12″ on center. Second layer of $^1/_2''$ Type X gypsum wallboard[c] applied with long dimension perpendicular to joists and attached with 8d cooler[o] or wallboard[o] nails at 6″ on center at end joints and 8″ on center elsewhere. Wallboard joints staggered with respect to fiberboard joints.	—	—	—	—	—	—	—	1

(continued)

TABLE 720.1(3)—continued
MINIMUM PROTECTION FOR FLOOR AND ROOF SYSTEMS[a, q]

FLOOR OR ROOF CONSTRUCTION	ITEM NUMBER	CEILING CONSTRUCTION	THICKNESS OF FLOOR OR ROOF SLAB (inches)				MINIMUM THICKNESS OF CEILING (inches)			
			4 hour	3 hour	2 hour	1 hour	4 hour	3 hour	2 hour	1 hour
15. Vermiculite concrete slab proportioned 1:4 (portland cement to vermiculite aggregate) on a $1^1/_2''$-deep steel deck supported on individually protected steel framing. Maximum span of deck 6′-10″ where deck is less than 0.019 inch (No. 26 carbon steel sheet gage) or greater. Slab reinforced with 4″ × 8″ 0.109/0.083″ (No. $^{12}/_{14}$ B.W. gage) welded wire mesh.	15-1.1	None	—	—	—	3[j]	—	—	—	—
16. Perlite concrete slab proportioned 1:6 (portland cement to perlite aggregate) on a $1^1/_4''$-deep steel deck supported on individually protected steel framing. Slab reinforced with 4″ × 8″ 0.109/0.083″ (No. $^{12}/_{14}$ B.W. gage) welded wire mesh.	16-1.1	None	—	—	—	$3^1/_2$[j]	—	—	—	—
17. Perlite concrete slab proportioned 1:6 (portland cement to perlite aggregate) on a $^9/_{16}''$-deep steel deck supported by steel joists 4′ on center. Class A or B roof covering on top.	17-1.1	Perlite gypsum plaster on metal lath wire tied to $^3/_4''$ furring channels attached with 0.065″ (No. 16 B.W. gage) wire ties to lower chord of joists.	—	2[p]	2[p]	—	—	$^7/_8$	$^3/_4$	—
18. Perlite concrete slab proportioned 1:6 (portland cement to perlite aggregate) on $1^1/_4''$-deep steel deck supported on individually protected steel framing. Maximum span of deck 6′-10″ where deck is less than 0.019″ (No. 26 carbon sheet steel gage) and 8′-0″ where deck is 0.019″ (No. 26 carbon sheet steel gage) or greater. Slab reinforced with 0.042″ (No. 19 B.W. gage) hexagonal wire mesh. Class A or B roof covering on top.	18-1.1	None	—	$2^1/_4$[p]	$2^1/_4$[p]	—	—	—	—	—

(continued)

TABLE 720.1(3)—continued
MINIMUM PROTECTION FOR FLOOR AND ROOF SYSTEMS[a, q]

FLOOR OR ROOF CONSTRUCTION	ITEM NUMBER	CEILING CONSTRUCTION	THICKNESS OF FLOOR OR ROOF SLAB (inches)				MINIMUM THICKNESS OF CEILING (inches)			
			4 hour	3 hour	2 hour	1 hour	4 hour	3 hour	2 hour	1 hour
19. Floor and beam construction consisting of 3″-deep cellular steel floor unit mounted on steel members with 1:4 (proportion of portland cement to perlite aggregate) perlite-concrete floor slab on top.	19-1.1	Suspended envelope ceiling of perlite gypsum plaster on metal lath attached to $^{3}/_{4}$″ cold-rolled channels, secured to $1^{1}/_{2}$″ cold-rolled channels spaced 42″ on center supported by 0.203 inch (No. 6 B.W. gage) wire 36″ on center. Beams in envelope with 3″ minimum airspace between beam soffit and lath have a 4-hour rating.	2[p]	—	—	—	1[l]	—	—	—
20. Perlite concrete proportioned 1:6 (portland cement to perlite aggregate) poured to $^{1}/_{8}$″ thickness above top of corrugations of $1^{5}/_{16}$″-deep galvanized steel deck maximum span 8′-0″ for 0.024″ (No. 24 galvanized sheet gage) or 6′ 0″ for 0.019″ (No. 26 galvanized sheet gage) with deck supported by individually protected steel framing. Approved polystyrene foam plastic insulation board having a flame spread not exceeding 75 (1″ to 4″ thickness) with vent holes that approximate 3 percent of the board surface area placed on top of perlite slurry. A 2′ by 4′ insulation board contains six $2^{3}/_{4}$″ diameter holes. Board covered with $2^{1}/_{4}$″ minimum perlite concrete slab.	20-1.1	None	—	—	Varies	—	—	—	—	—

(continued)

TABLE 720.1(3)—continued
MINIMUM PROTECTION FOR FLOOR AND ROOF SYSTEMS[a, q]

FLOOR OR ROOF CONSTRUCTION	ITEM NUMBER	CEILING CONSTRUCTION	THICKNESS OF FLOOR OR ROOF SLAB (inches)				MINIMUM THICKNESS OF CEILING (inches)			
			4 hour	3 hour	2 hour	1 hour	4 hour	3 hour	2 hour	1 hour
(continued) 20. Slab reinforced with mesh consisting of 0.042″ (No. 19 B.W. gage) galvanized steel wire twisted together to form 2″ hexagons with straight 0.065″ (No. 16 B.W. gage) galvanized steel wire woven into mesh and spaced 3″. Alternate slab reinforcement shall be permitted to consist of 4″ × 8″, 0.109/0.238″ (No. 12/4 B.W. gage), or 2″ × 2″, 0.083/0.083″ (No. 14/14 B.W. gage) welded wire fabric. Class A or B roof covering on top.	20-1.1	None	—	—	Varies	—	—	—	—	—
21. Wood joists, wood I-joists, floor trusses and flat or pitched roof trusses spaced a maximum 24″ o.c. with $^1/_2$″ wood structural panels with exterior glue applied at right angles to top of joist or top chord of trusses with 8d nails. The wood structural panel thickness shall not be less than nominal $^1/_2$″ nor less than required by Chapter 23.	21-1.1	Base layer $^5/_8$″ Type X gypsum wallboard applied at right angles to joist or truss 24″ o.c. with $1^1/_4$″ Type S or Type W drywall screws 24″ o.c. Face layer $^5/_8$″ Type X gypsum wallboard or veneer base applied at right angles to joist or truss through base layer with $1^7/_8$″ Type S or Type W drywall screws 12″ o.c. at joints and intermediate joist or truss. Face layer Type G drywall screws placed 2″ back on either side of face layer end joints, 12″ o.c.	—	—	—	Varies	—	—	—	$1^1/_4$
22. Steel joists, floor trusses and flat or pitched roof trusses spaced a maximum 24″ o.c. with $^1/_2$″ wood structural panels with exterior glue applied at right angles to top of joist or top chord of trusses with No. 8 screws. The wood structural panel thickness shall not be less than nominal $^1/_2$″ nor less than required by Chapter 23.	22-1.1	Base layer $^5/_8$″ Type X gypsum board applied at right angles to steel framing 24″ on center with 1″ Type S drywall screws spaced 24″ on center. Face layer $^5/_8$″ Type X gypsum board applied at right angles to steel framing attached through base layer with $1^5/_8$″ Type S drywall screws 12″ on center at end joints and intermediate joints and $1^1/_2$″ Type G drywall screws 12 inches on center placed 2″ back on either side of face layer end joints. Joints of the face layer are offset 24″ from the joints of the base layer.	—	—	—	Varies	—	—	—	$1^1/_4$
23. Wood I-joist (minimum joist depth $9^1/_4$″ with a minimum flange depth of $1^5/_{16}$″ and a minimum flange cross-sectional area of 2.3 square inches) at 24″ o.c. spacing with 1 inch by 4 inch (nominal) wood furring strip spacer applied parallel to and covering the bottom of the bottom flange of each member, tacked in place. 2″ mineral wool insulation, 3.5 pcf (nominal) installed adjacent to the bottom flange of the I-joist and supported by the 1″ × 4″ furring strip spacer.	23-1.1	$^1/_2$″ deep single leg resilient channel 16″ on center (channels doubled at wallboard end joints), placed perpendicular to the furring strip and joist and attached to each joist by $1^7/_8$″ Type S drywall screws. $^5/_8$″ Type C gypsum wallboard applied perpendicular to the channel with end joints staggered at least 4′ and fastened with $1^1/_8$″ Type S drywall screws spaced 7″ on center. Wallboard joints to be taped and covered with joint compound.	—	—	—	Varies	—	—	—	$^5/_8$

(continued)

TABLE 720.1(3)—continued
MINIMUM PROTECTION FOR FLOOR AND ROOF SYSTEMS[a, q]

FLOOR OR ROOF CONSTRUCTION	ITEM NUMBER	CEILING CONSTRUCTION	THICKNESS OF FLOOR OR ROOF SLAB (inches)				MINIMUM THICKNESS OF CEILING (inches)			
			4 hour	3 hour	2 hour	1 hour	4 hour	3 hour	2 hour	1 hour
24. Wood I-joist (minimum I-joist depth $9^1/_4''$ with a minimum flange depth of $1^1/_2''$ and a minimum flange cross-sectional area of 5.25 square inches; minimum web thickness of $^3/_8''$) @ 24″ o.c., $1^1/_2''$ mineral wool insulation (2.5 pcf—nominal) resting on hat-shaped furring channels.	24-1.1	Minimum 0.026″ thick hat-shaped channel 16″ o.c. (channels doubled at wallboard end joints), placed perpendicular to the joist and attached to each joist by $1^5/_8''$ Type S drywall screws. $^5/_8''$ Type C gypsum wallboard applied perpendicular to the channel with end joints staggered and fastened with $1^1/_8''$ Type S drywall screws spaced 12″ o.c. in the field and 8″ o.c. at the wallboard ends. Wallboard joints to be taped and covered with joint compound.	—	—	—	Varies	—	—	—	$^5/_8$
25. Wood I-joist (minimum I-joist depth $9^1/_4''$ with a minimum flange depth of $1^1/_2''$ and a minimum flange cross-sectional area of 5.25 square inches; minimum web thickness of $^7/_{16}''$) @ 24″ o.c., $1^1/_2''$ mineral wool insulation (2.5 pcf—nominal) resting on resilient channels.	25-1.1	Minimum 0.019″ thick resilient channel 16″ o.c. (channels doubled at wallboard end joints), placed perpendicular to the joist and attached to each joist by $1^5/_8''$ Type S drywall screws. $^5/_8''$ Type C gypsum wallboard applied perpendicular to the channel with end joints staggered and fastened with 1″ Type S drywall screws spaced 12″ o.c. in the field and 8″ o.c. at the wallboard ends. Wallboard joints to be taped and covered with joint compound.	—	—	—	Varies	—	—	—	$^5/_8$
26. Wood I-joist (minimum I-joist depth $9^1/_4''$ with a minimum flange thickness of $1^1/_2''$ and a minimum flange cross-sectional area of 2.25 square inches; minimum web thickness of $^3/_8''$) @ 24″ o.c.	26-1.1	Two layers of $^1/_2''$ Type X gypsum wallboard applied with the long dimension perpendicular to the I-joists with end joints staggered. The base layer is fastened with $1^5/_8''$ Type S drywall screws spaced 12″ o.c. and the face layer is fastened with 2″ Type S drywall screws spaced 12″ o.c. in the field and 8″ o.c. on the edges. Face layer end joints shall not occur on the same I-joist as base layer end joints and edge joints shall be offset 24″ from base layer joints. Face layer to also be attached to base layer with $1^1/_2''$ Type G drywall screws spaced 8″ o.c. placed 6″ from face layer end joints. Face layer wallboard joints to be taped and covered with joint compound.	—	—	—	Varies	—	—	—	1
27. Wood I-joist (minimum I-joist depth $9^1/_2''$ with a minimum flange depth of $1^5/_{16}''$ and a minimum flange cross-sectional area of 1.95 square inches; minimum web thickness of $^3/_8''$) @ 24″ o.c.	27-1.1	Minimum 0.019″ thick resilient channel 16″ o.c. (channels doubled at wallboard end joints), placed perpendicular to the joist and attached to each joist by $1^5/_8''$ Type S drywall screws. Two layers of $^1/_2''$ Type X gypsum wallboard applied with the long dimension perpendicular to the I-joists with end joints staggered. The base layer is fastened with $1^1/_4''$ Type S drywall screws spaced 12″ o.c. and the face layer is fastened with $1^5/_8''$ Type S drywall screws spaced 12″ o.c. Face layer end joints shall not occur on the same I-joist as base layer end joints and edge joints shall be offset 24″ from base layer joints. Face layer to also be attached to base layer with $1^1/_2''$ Type G drywall screws spaced 8″ o.c. placed 6″ from face layer end joints. Face layer wallboard joints to be taped and covered with joint compound.	—	—	—	Varies	—	—	—	1

(continued)

TABLE 720.1(3)—continued
MINIMUM PROTECTION FOR FLOOR AND ROOF SYSTEMS[a, q]

FLOOR OR ROOF CONSTRUCTION	ITEM NUMBER	CEILING CONSTRUCTION	THICKNESS OF FLOOR OR ROOF SLAB (inches)				MINIMUM THICKNESS OF CEILING (inches)			
			4 hour	3 hour	2 hour	1 hour	4 hour	3 hour	2 hour	1 hour
28. Wood I-joist (minimum I-joist depth $9^1/_4''$ with a minimum flange depth of $1^1/_2''$ and a minimum flange cross-sectional area of 2.25 square inches; minimum web thickness of $^3/_8''$) @ 24″ o.c. Unfaced fiberglass insulation is installed between the I-joists supported on the upper surface of the flange by stay wires spaced 12″ o.c.	28-1.1	Base layer of $^5/_8''$ Type C gypsum wallboard attached directly to I-joists with $1^5/_8''$ Type S drywall screws spaced 12″ o.c. with ends staggered. Minimum 0.0179″ thick hat-shaped $^7/_8$-inch furring channel 16″ o.c. (channels doubled at wallboard end joints), placed perpendicular to the joist and attached to each joist by $1^5/_8''$ Type S drywall screws after the base layer of gypsum wallboard has been applied. The middle and face layers of $^5/_8''$ Type C gypsum wallboard applied perpendicular to the channel with end joints staggered. The middle layer is fastened with 1″ Type S drywall screws spaced 12″ o.c. The face layer is applied parallel to the middle layer but with the edge joints offset 24″ from those of the middle layer and fastened with $1^5/_8''$ Type S drywall screws 8″ o.c. The joints shall be taped and covered with joint compound.	—	—	—	Varies	—	—	$2^3/_4$	—
29. Channel-shaped 18 gage steel joists (minimum depth 8″) spaced a maximum 24″ o.c. supporting tongue-and-groove wood structural panels (nominal minimum $^3/_4''$ thick) applied perpendicular to framing members. Structural panels attached with 1-$^5/_8''$ Type S-12 screws spaced 12″ o.c.	29-1.1	Base layer $^5/_8''$ Type X gypsum board applied perpendicular to bottom of framing members with $1^1/_8''$ Type S-12 screws spaced 12″ o.c. Second layer $^5/_8''$ Type X gypsum board attached perpendicular to framing members with $1^5/_8''$ Type S-12 screws spaced 12″ o.c. Second layer joints offset 24″ from base layer. Third layer $^5/_8''$ Type X gypsum board attached perpendicular to framing members with $2^3/_8''$ Type S-12 screws spaced 12″ o.c. Third layer joints offset 12″ from second layer joints. Hat-shaped $^7/_8$-inch rigid furring channels applied at right angles to framing members over third layer with two $2^3/_8''$ Type S-12 screws at each framing member. Face layer $^5/_8''$ Type X gypsum board applied at right angles to furring channels with $1^1/_8''$ Type S screws spaced 12″ o.c.	—	—	Varies	—	—	—	$3^3/_8$	—

TABLE 720.1(3) Notes.

For SI: 1 inch = 25.4 mm, 1 foot = 304.8 mm, 1 pound = 0.454 kg, 1 cubic foot = $0.0283 m^3$,
1 pound per square inch = 6.895 kPa, 1 pound per linear foot = 1.4882 kg/m.

a. Staples with equivalent holding power and penetration shall be permitted to be used as alternate fasteners to nails for attachment to wood framing.

b. When the slab is in an unrestrained condition, minimum reinforcement cover shall not be less than $1^5/_8$ inches for 4-hour (siliceous aggregate only); $1^1/_4$ inches for 4- and 3-hour; 1 inch for 2-hour (siliceous aggregate only); and $^3/_4$ inch for all other restrained and unrestrained conditions.

c. For all of the construction with gypsum wallboard described in this table, gypsum base for veneer plaster of the same size, thickness and core type shall be permitted to be substituted for gypsum wallboard, provided attachment is identical to that specified for the wallboard, and the joints on the face layer are reinforced and the entire surface is covered with a minimum of $^1/_{16}$-inch gypsum veneer plaster.

d. Slab thickness over steel joists measured at the joists for metal lath form and at the top of the form for steel form units.

e. (a) The maximum allowable stress level for H-Series joists shall not exceed 22,000 psi.

(b) The allowable stress for K-Series joists shall not exceed 26,000 psi, the nominal depth of such joist shall not be less than 10 inches and the nominal joist weight shall not be less than 5 pounds per linear foot.

f. Cement plaster with 15 pounds of hydrated lime and 3 pounds of approved additives or admixtures per bag of cement.

g. Gypsum wallboard ceilings attached to steel framing shall be permitted to be suspended with $1^1/_2$-inch cold-formed carrying channels spaced 48 inches on center, which are suspended with No. 8 SWG galvanized wire hangers spaced 48 inches on center. Cross-furring channels are tied to the carrying channels with No. 18 SWG galvanized wire hangers spaced 48 inches on center. Cross-furring channels are tied to the carrying channels with No. 18 SWG galvanized wire (double strand) and spaced as required for direct attachment to the framing. This alternative is also applicable to those steel framing assemblies recognized under Note q.

h. Six-inch hollow clay tile with 2-inch concrete slab above.

i. Four-inch hollow clay tile with $1^1/_2$-inch concrete slab above.

j. Thickness measured to bottom of steel form units.

k. Five-eighths inch of vermiculite gypsum plaster plus $^1/_2$ inch of approved vermiculite acoustical plastic.

l. Furring channels spaced 12 inches on center.

m. Double wood floor shall be permitted to be either of the following:

(a) Subfloor of 1-inch nominal boarding, a layer of asbestos paper weighing not less than 14 pounds per 100 square feet and a layer of 1-inch nominal tongue-and-groove finished flooring; or

(b) Subfloor of 1-inch nominal tongue-and-groove boarding or $^{15}/_{32}$-inch wood structural panels with exterior glue and a layer of 1-inch nominal tongue-and-groove finished flooring or $^{19}/_{32}$-inch wood structural panel finish flooring or a layer of Type I Grade M-1 particleboard not less than $^5/_8$-inch thick.

n. The ceiling shall be permitted to be omitted over unusable space, and flooring shall be permitted to be omitted where unusable space occurs above.

o. For properties of cooler or wallboard nails, see ASTM C 514, ASTM C 547 or ASTM F 1667.

p. Thickness measured on top of steel deck unit.

q. Generic fire-resistance ratings (those not designated as PROPRIETARY* in the listing) in the GA 600 shall be accepted as if herein listed.

721.2.1.1 Cast-in-place or precast walls. The minimum equivalent thicknesses of cast-in-place or precast concrete walls for *fire-resistance ratings* of 1 hour to 4 hours are shown in Table 721.2.1.1. For solid walls with flat vertical surfaces, the equivalent thickness is the same as the actual thickness. The values in Table 721.2.1.1 apply to plain, reinforced or prestressed concrete walls.

TABLE 721.2.1.1
MINIMUM EQUIVALENT THICKNESS OF CAST-IN-PLACE OR PRECAST CONCRETE WALLS, LOAD-BEARING OR NONLOAD-BEARING

CONCRETE TYPE	MINIMUM SLAB THICKNESS (inches) FOR FIRE-RESISTANCE RATING OF				
	1-hour	$1^1/_2$-hour	2-hour	3-hour	4-hour
Siliceous	3.5	4.3	5.0	6.2	7.0
Carbonate	3.2	4.0	4.6	5.7	6.6
Sand-lightweight	2.7	3.3	3.8	4.6	5.4
Lightweight	2.5	3.1	3.6	4.4	5.1

For SI: 1 inch = 25.4 mm.

721.2.1.1.1 Hollow-core precast wall panels. For hollow-core precast concrete wall panels in which the cores are of constant cross section throughout the length, calculation of the equivalent thickness by dividing the net cross-sectional area (the gross cross section minus the area of the cores) of the panel by its width shall be permitted.

721.2.1.1.2 Core spaces filled. Where all of the core spaces of hollow-core wall panels are filled with loose-fill material, such as expanded shale, clay, or slag, or vermiculite or perlite, the *fire-resistance rating* of the wall is the same as that of a solid wall of the same concrete type and of the same overall thickness.

721.2.1.1.3 Tapered cross sections. The thickness of panels with tapered cross sections shall be that determined at a distance $2t$ or 6 inches (152 mm), whichever is less, from the point of minimum thickness, where t is the minimum thickness.

721.2.1.1.4 Ribbed or undulating surfaces. The equivalent thickness of panels with ribbed or undulating surfaces shall be determined by one of the following expressions:

For $s \geq 4t$, the thickness to be used shall be t

For $s \leq 2t$, the thickness to be used shall be t_e

For $4t > s > 2t$, the thickness to be used shall be

$$t+\left(\frac{4t}{s}-1\right)\left(t_e-t\right) \quad \textbf{(Equation 7-3)}$$

where:

s = Spacing of ribs or undulations.

t = Minimum thickness.

t_e = Equivalent thickness of the panel calculated as the net cross-sectional area of the panel divided by the width, in which the maximum thickness used in the calculation shall not exceed $2t$.

721.2.1.2 Multiwythe walls. For walls that consist of two wythes of different types of concrete, the *fire-resistance ratings* shall be permitted to be determined from Figure 721.2.1.2.

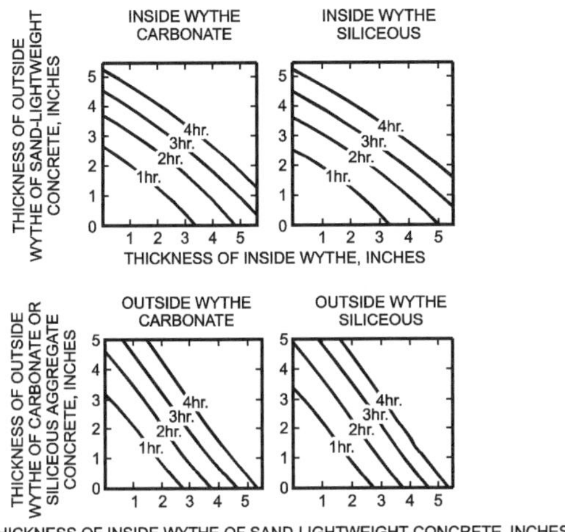

For SI: 1 inch = 25.4 mm.

FIGURE 721.2.1.2
FIRE-RESISTANCE RATINGS OF TWO-WYTHE CONCRETE WALLS

721.2.1.2.1 Two or more wythes. The *fire-resistance rating* for wall panels consisting of two or more wythes shall be permitted to be determined by the formula:

$$R = (R_1^{0.59} + R_2^{0.59} + ... + R_n^{0.59})^{1.7} \qquad \textbf{(Equation 7-4)}$$

where:

R = The fire endurance of the assembly, minutes.

R_1, R_2, and R_n = The fire endurances of the individual wythes, minutes. Values of $R_n^{0.59}$ for use in Equation 7-4 are given in Table 721.2.1.2(1). Calculated *fire-resistance ratings* are shown in Table 721.2.1.2(2).

TABLE 721.2.1.2(2)
FIRE-RESISTANCE RATINGS BASED ON $R^{0.59}$

R[a], MINUTES	$R^{0.59}$
60	11.20
120	16.85
180	21.41
240	25.37

a. Based on Equation 7-4.

721.2.1.2.2 Foam plastic insulation. The *fire-resistance ratings* of precast concrete wall panels consisting of a layer of foam plastic insulation sandwiched between two wythes of concrete shall be permitted to be determined by use of Equation 7-4. Foam plastic insulation with a total thickness of less than 1 inch (25 mm) shall be disregarded. The R_n value for thickness of foam plastic insulation of 1 inch (25 mm) or greater, for use in the calculation, is 5 minutes; therefore $R_n^{0.59} = 2.5$.

721.2.1.3 Joints between precast wall panels. Joints between precast concrete wall panels which are not insulated as required by this section shall be considered as openings in walls. Uninsulated joints shall be included in

TABLE 721.2.1.2(1)
VALUES OF $R_n^{0.59}$ FOR USE IN EQUATION 7-4

TYPE OF MATERIAL	THICKNESS OF MATERIAL (inches)											
	$1^1/_2$	2	$2^1/_2$	3	$3^1/_2$	4	$4^1/_2$	5	$5^1/_2$	6	$6^1/_2$	7
Siliceous aggregate concrete	5.3	6.5	8.1	9.5	11.3	13.0	14.9	16.9	18.8	20.7	22.8	25.1
Carbonate aggregate concrete	5.5	7.1	8.9	10.4	12.0	14.0	16.2	18.1	20.3	21.9	24.7	27.2[c]
Sand-lightweight concrete	6.5	8.2	10.5	12.8	15.5	18.1	20.7	23.3	26.0[c]	Note c	Note c	Note c
Lightweight concrete	6.6	8.8	11.2	13.7	16.5	19.1	21.9	24.7	27.8[c]	Note c	Note c	Note c
Insulating concrete[a]	9.3	13.3	16.6	18.3	23.1	26.5[c]	Note c	Note c	Note c	Note c	Note c	Note c
Airspace[b]	—	—	—	—	—	—	—	—	—	—	—	—

For SI: 1 inch = 25.4 mm, 1 pound per cubic foot = 16.02 kg/m³.

a. Dry unit weight of 35 pcf or less and consisting of cellular, perlite or vermiculite concrete.

b. The $R_n^{0.59}$ value for one $^1/_2$" to 3 $^1/_2$" airspace is 3.3. The $R_n^{0.59}$ value for two $^1/_2$" to 3 $^1/_2$" airspaces is 6.7.

c. The fire-resistance rating for this thickness exceeds 4 hours.

determining the percentage of openings permitted by Table 705.8. Where openings are not permitted or are required by this code to be protected, the provisions of this section shall be used to determine the amount of joint insulation required. Insulated joints shall not be considered openings for purposes of determining compliance with the allowable percentage of openings in Table 705.8.

721.2.1.3.1 Ceramic fiber joint protection. Figure 721.2.1.3.1 shows thicknesses of ceramic fiber blankets to be used to insulate joints between precast concrete wall panels for various panel thicknesses and for joint widths of $^3/_8$ inch (9.5 mm) and 1 inch (25 mm) for *fire-resistance ratings* of 1 hour to 4 hours. For joint widths between $^3/_8$ inch (9.5 mm) and 1 inch (25 mm), the thickness of ceramic fiber blanket is allowed to be determined by direct interpolation. Other tested and labeled materials are acceptable in place of ceramic fiber blankets.

721.2.1.4 Walls with gypsum wallboard or plaster finishes. The *fire-resistance rating* of cast-in-place or precast concrete walls with finishes of gypsum wallboard or plaster applied to one or both sides shall be permitted to be calculated in accordance with the provisions of this section.

721.2.1.4.1 Nonfire-exposed side. Where the finish of gypsum wallboard or plaster is applied to the side of the wall not exposed to fire, the contribution of the finish to the total *fire-resistance rating* shall be determined as follows: The thickness of the finish shall first be corrected by multiplying the actual thickness of the finish by the applicable factor determined from Table 721.2.1.4(1) based on the type of aggregate in the concrete. The corrected thickness of finish shall then be added to the actual or equivalent thickness of concrete and *fire-resistance rating* of the concrete and finish determined from Table 721.2.1.1, Figure 721.2.1.2 or Table 721.2.1.2(1).

721.2.1.4.2 Fire-exposed side. Where gypsum wallboard or plaster is applied to the fire-exposed side of the wall, the contribution of the finish to the total *fire-resistance rating* shall be determined as follows: The time assigned to the finish as established by Table 721.2.1.4(2) shall be added to the *fire-resistance rating* determined from Table 721.2.1.1 or Figure 721.2.1.2, or Table 721.2.1.2(1) for the concrete alone, or to the rating determined in Section 721.2.1.4.1 for the concrete and finish on the nonfire-exposed side.

721.2.1.4.3 Nonsymmetrical assemblies. For a wall having no finish on one side or different types or thicknesses of finish on each side, the calculation procedures of Sections 721.2.1.4.1 and 721.2.1.4.2 shall be performed twice, assuming either side of the wall to be the fire-exposed side. The *fire-resistance rating* of the wall shall not exceed the lower of the two values.

Exception: For an *exterior wall* with a *fire separation distance* greater than 5 feet (1524 mm) the fire shall be assumed to occur on the interior side only.

721.2.1.4.4 Minimum concrete fire-resistance rating. Where finishes applied to one or both sides of a concrete wall contribute to the *fire-resistance rating*, the concrete alone shall provide not less than one-half of the total required *fire-resistance rating*. Additionally, the contribution to the *fire resistance* of the finish on the nonfire-exposed side of a *load-bearing wall* shall not exceed one-half the contribution of the concrete alone.

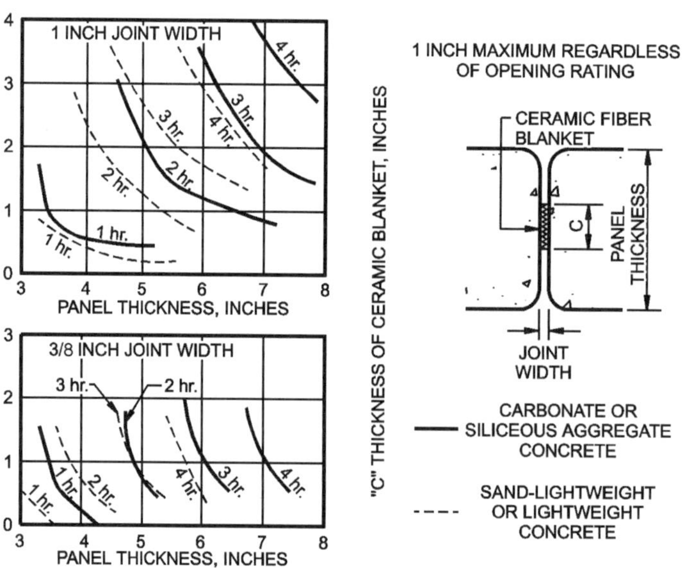

For SI: 1 inch = 25.4 mm.

FIGURE 721.2.1.3.1
CERAMIC FIBER JOINT PROTECTION

TABLE 721.2.1.4(1)
MULTIPLYING FACTOR FOR FINISHES ON NONFIRE-EXPOSED SIDE OF WALL

TYPE OF FINISH APPLIED TO CONCRETE OR CONCRETE MASONRY WALL	TYPE OF AGGREGATE USED IN CONCRETE OR CONCRETE MASONRY			
	Concrete: siliceous or carbonate Concrete Masonry: siliceous or carbonate; solid clay brick	Concrete: sand-lightweight Concrete Masonry: clay tile; hollow clay brick; concrete masonry units of expanded shale and <20% sand	Concrete: lightweight Concrete Masonry: concrete masonry units of expanded shale, expanded clay, expanded slag, or pumice < 20% sand	Concrete Masonry: concrete masonry units of expanded slag, expanded clay, or pumice
Portland cement-sand plaster	1.00	0.75[a]	0.75[a]	0.50[a]
Gypsum-sand plaster	1.25	1.00	1.00	1.00
Gypsum-vermiculite or perlite plaster	1.75	1.50	1.25	1.25
Gypsum wallboard	3.00	2.25	2.25	2.25

For SI: 1 inch = 25.4 mm.

a. For portland cement-sand plaster $^5/_8$ inch or less in thickness and applied directly to the concrete or concrete masonry on the nonfire-exposed side of the wall, the multiplying factor shall be 1.00.

TABLE 721.2.1.4(2)
TIME ASSIGNED TO FINISH MATERIALS ON FIRE-EXPOSED SIDE OF WALL

FINISH DESCRIPTION	TIME (minute)
Gypsum wallboard	
$^3/_8$ inch	10
$^1/_2$ inch	15
$^5/_8$ inch	20
2 layers of $^3/_8$ inch	25
1 layer $^3/_8$ inch, 1 layer $^1/_2$ inch	35
2 layers $^1/_2$ inch	40
Type X gypsum wallboard	
$^1/_2$ inch	25
$^5/_8$ inch	40
Portland cement-sand plaster applied directly to concrete masonry	See Note a
Portland cement-sand plaster on metal lath	
$^3/_4$ inch	20
$^7/_8$ inch	25
1 inch	30
Gypsum sand plaster on $^3/_8$-inch gypsum lath	
$^1/_2$ inch	35
$^5/_8$ inch	40
$^3/_4$ inch	50
Gypsum sand plaster on metal lath	
$^3/_4$ inch	50
$^7/_8$ inch	60
1 inch	80

For SI: 1 inch = 25.4 mm.

a. The actual thickness of portland cement-sand plaster, provided it is $^5/_8$ inch or less in thickness, shall be permitted to be included in determining the equivalent thickness of the masonry for use in Table 721.3.2.

721.2.1.4.5 Concrete finishes. Finishes on concrete walls that are assumed to contribute to the total *fire-resistance rating* of the wall shall comply with the installation requirements of Section 721.3.2.5.

721.2.2 Concrete floor and roof slabs. Reinforced and prestressed floors and roofs shall comply with Section 721.2.2.1. Multicourse floors and roofs shall comply with Sections 721.2.2.2 and 721.2.2.3, respectively.

721.2.2.1 Reinforced and prestressed floors and roofs. The minimum thicknesses of reinforced and prestressed concrete floor or roof slabs for *fire-resistance ratings* of 1 hour to 4 hours are shown in Table 721.2.2.1.

TABLE 721.2.2.1
MINIMUM SLAB THICKNESS (inches)

CONCRETE TYPE	FIRE-RESISTANCE RATING (hour)				
	1	$1^1/_2$	2	3	4
Siliceous	3.5	4.3	5.0	6.2	7.0
Carbonate	3.2	4.0	4.6	5.7	6.6
Sand-lightweight	2.7	3.3	3.8	4.6	5.4
Lightweight	2.5	3.1	3.6	4.4	5.1

For SI: 1 inch = 25.4 mm.

721.2.2.1.1 Hollow-core prestressed slabs. For hollow-core prestressed concrete slabs in which the cores are of constant cross section throughout the length, the equivalent thickness shall be permitted to be obtained by dividing the net cross-sectional area of the slab including grout in the joints, by its width.

721.2.2.1.2 Slabs with sloping soffits. The thickness of slabs with sloping soffits (see Figure 721.2.2.1.2) shall be determined at a distance $2t$ or 6 inches (152 mm), whichever is less, from the point of minimum thickness, where t is the minimum thickness.

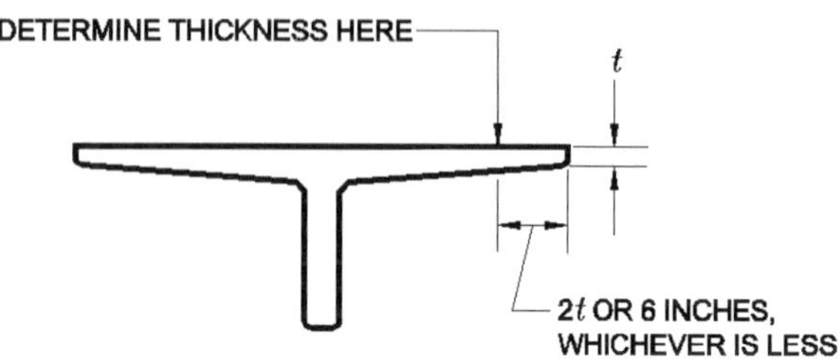

For SI: 1 inch = 25.4 mm.

FIGURE 721.2.2.1.2
DETERMINATION OF SLAB THICKNESS FOR SLOPING SOFFITS

721.2.2.1.3 Slabs with ribbed soffits. The thickness of slabs with ribbed or undulating soffits (see Figure 721.2.2.1.3) shall be determined by one of the following expressions, whichever is applicable:

For $s > 4t$, the thickness to be used shall be t

For $s \leq 2t$, the thickness to be used shall be t_e

For $4t > s > 2t$, the thickness to be used shall be

$$t + \left(\frac{4t}{s} - 1\right)\left(t_e - t\right) \qquad \textbf{(Equation 7-5)}$$

where:

s = Spacing of ribs or undulations.

t = Minimum thickness.

t_e = Equivalent thickness of the slab calculated as the net area of the slab divided by the width, in which the maximum thickness used in the calculation shall not exceed $2t$.

721.2.2.2 Multicourse floors. The *fire-resistance ratings* of floors that consist of a base slab of concrete with a topping (overlay) of a different type of concrete shall comply with Figure 721.2.2.2.

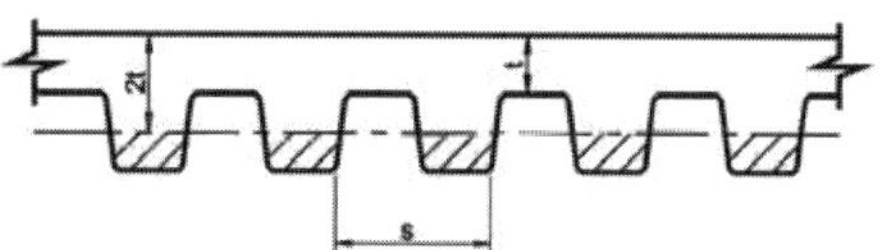

NEGLECT SHADED AREA IN CALCULATION OF EQUIVALENT THICKNESS

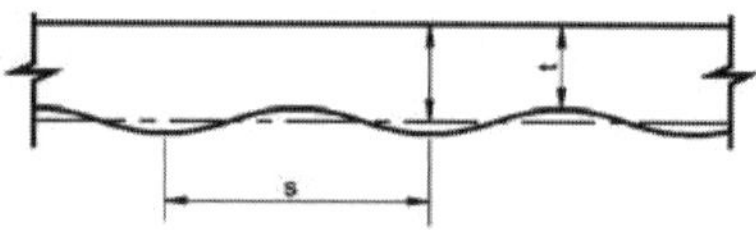

For SI: 1 inch = 25.4 mm.

FIGURE 721.2.2.1.3
SLABS WITH RIBBED OR UNDULATING SOFFITS

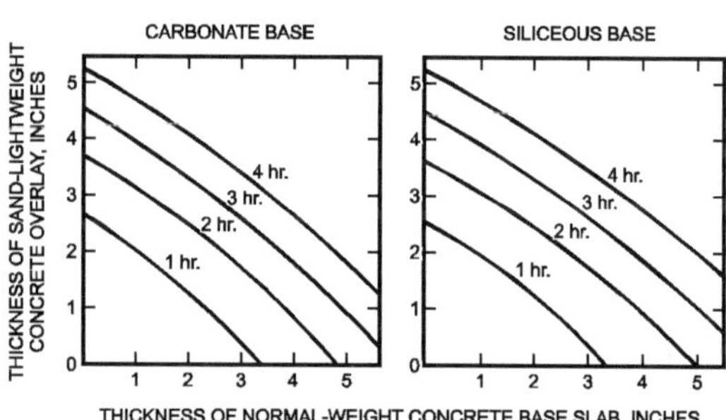

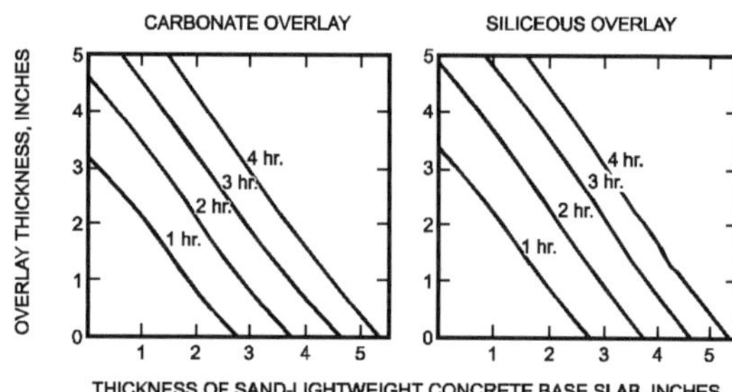

For SI: 1 inch = 25.4 mm.

FIGURE 721.2.2.2
FIRE-RESISTANCE RATINGS FOR TWO-COURSE CONCRETE FLOORS

721.2.2.3 Multicourse roofs. The *fire-resistance ratings* of roofs which consist of a base slab of concrete with a topping (overlay) of an insulating concrete or with an insulating board and built-up roofing shall comply with Figures 721.2.2.3(1) and 721.2.2.3(2).

721.2.2.3.1 Heat transfer. For the transfer of heat, three-ply built-up roofing contributes 10 minutes to the *fire-resistance rating*. The *fire-resistance rating* for concrete assemblies such as those shown in Figure 721.2.2.3(1) shall be increased by 10 minutes. This increase is not applicable to those shown in Figure 721.2.2.3(2).

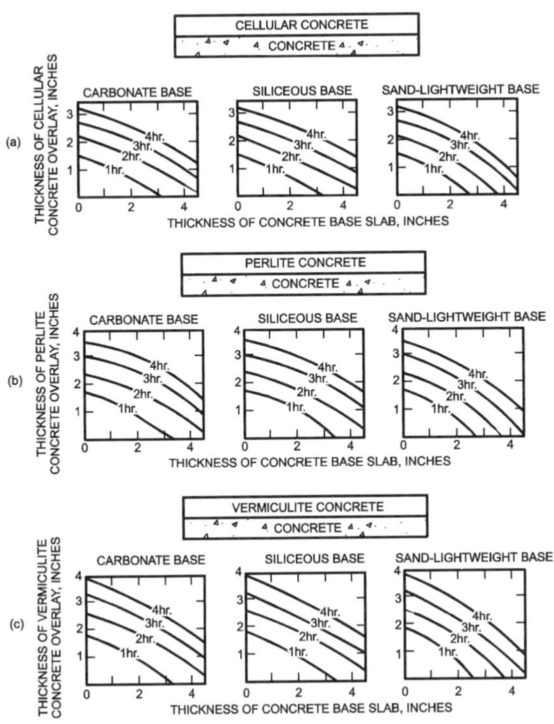

For SI: 1 inch = 25.4 mm.

FIGURE 721.2.2.3(1)
FIRE-RESISTANCE RATINGS FOR CONCRETE ROOF ASSEMBLIES

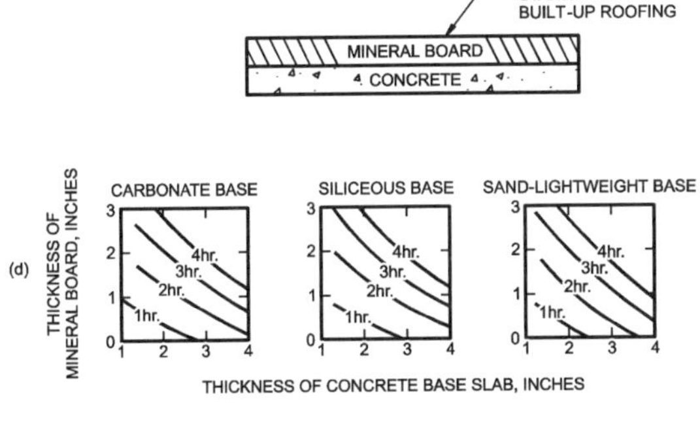

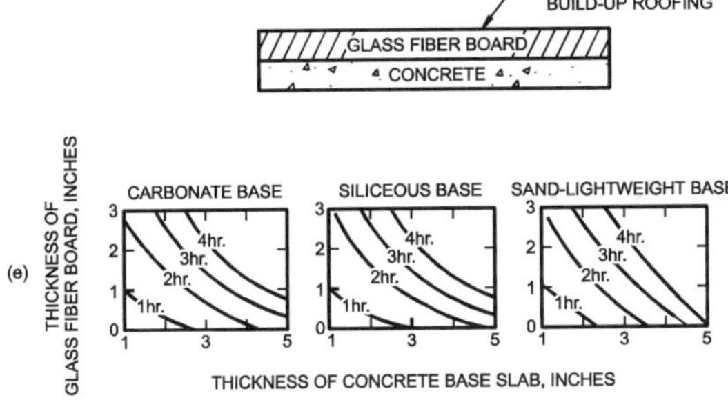

For SI: 1 inch = 25.4 mm.

FIGURE 721.2.2.3(2)
FIRE-RESISTANCE RATINGS FOR CONCRETE ROOF ASSEMBLIES

721.2.2.4 Joints in precast slabs. Joints between adjacent precast concrete slabs need not be considered in calculating the slab thickness provided that a concrete topping at least 1 inch (25 mm) thick is used. Where no concrete topping is used, joints must be grouted to a depth of at least one-third the slab thickness at the joint, but not less than 1 inch (25 mm), or the joints must be made fire resistant by other *approved* methods.

721.2.3 Concrete cover over reinforcement. The minimum thickness of concrete cover over reinforcement in concrete slabs, reinforced beams and prestressed beams shall comply with this section.

721.2.3.1 Slab cover. The minimum thickness of concrete cover to the positive moment reinforcement shall comply with Table 721.2.3(1) for reinforced concrete and Table 721.2.3(2) for prestressed concrete. These tables are applicable for solid or hollow-core one-way or two-way slabs with flat undersurfaces. These tables are applicable to slabs that are either cast in place or precast. For precast prestressed concrete not covered elsewhere, the procedures contained in PCI MNL 124 shall be acceptable.

721.2.3.2 Reinforced beam cover. The minimum thickness of concrete cover to the positive moment reinforcement (bottom steel) for reinforced concrete beams is shown in Table 721.2.3(3) for *fire-resistance ratings* of 1 hour to 4 hours.

721.2.3.3 Prestressed beam cover. The minimum thickness of concrete cover to the positive moment prestressing tendons (bottom steel) for restrained and unrestrained prestressed concrete beams and stemmed units shall comply with the values shown in Tables 721.2.3(4) and 721.2.3(5) for *fire-resistance ratings* of 1 hour to 4 hours. Values in Table 721.2.3(4) apply to beams 8 inches (203 mm) or greater in width. Values in Table 721.2.3(5) apply to beams or stems of any width, provided the cross-section area is not less than 40 square inches (25 806 mm^2). In case of differences between the values determined from Table 721.2.3(4) or 721.2.3(5), it is permitted to use the smaller value. The concrete cover shall be calculated in accordance with Section 721.2.3.3.1. The minimum concrete cover for nonprestressed reinforcement in prestressed concrete beams shall comply with Section 721.2.3.2.

721.2.3.3.1 Calculating concrete cover. The concrete cover for an individual tendon is the minimum thickness of concrete between the surface of the tendon and the fire-exposed surface of the beam, except that for ungrouted ducts, the assumed cover thickness is the minimum thickness of concrete between the surface of the duct and the fire-exposed surface of the beam. For beams in which two or more tendons are used, the cover is assumed to be the average of the minimum cover of the individual tendons. For corner tendons (tendons equal distance from the bottom and side), the minimum cover used in the calculation shall be one-half the actual value. For stemmed members with two or more prestressing tendons located along the vertical centerline of the stem, the average cover shall be the distance from the bottom of the member to the centroid of the

TABLE 721.2.3(1)
COVER THICKNESS FOR REINFORCED CONCRETE FLOOR OR ROOF SLABS (inches)

CONCRETE AGGREGATE TYPE	FIRE-RESISTANCE RATING (hours)									
	Restrained					Unrestrained				
	1	$1^1/_2$	2	3	4	1	$1^1/_2$	2	3	4
Siliceous	$^3/_4$	$^3/_4$	$^3/_4$	$^3/_4$	$^3/_4$	$^3/_4$	$^3/_4$	1	$1^1/_4$	$1^5/_8$
Carbonate	$^3/_4$	$^3/_4$	$^3/_4$	$^3/_4$	$^3/_4$	$^3/_4$	$^3/_4$	$^3/_4$	$1^1/_4$	$1^1/_4$
Sand-lightweight or lightweight	$^3/_4$	$^3/_4$	$^3/_4$	$^3/_4$	$^3/_4$	$^3/_4$	$^3/_4$	$^3/_4$	$1^1/_4$	$1^1/_4$

For SI: 1 inch = 25.4 mm.

TABLE 721.2.3(2)
COVER THICKNESS FOR PRESTRESSED CONCRETE FLOOR OR ROOF SLABS (inches)

CONCRETE AGGREGATE TYPE	FIRE-RESISTANCE RATING (hours)									
	Restrained					Unrestrained				
	1	$1^1/_2$	2	3	4	1	$1^1/_2$	2	3	4
Siliceous	$^3/_4$	$^3/_4$	$^3/_4$	$^3/_4$	$^3/_4$	$1^1/_8$	$1^1/_2$	$1^3/_4$	$2^3/_8$	$2^3/_4$
Carbonate	$^3/_4$	$^3/_4$	$^3/_4$	$^3/_4$	$^3/_4$	1	$1^3/_8$	$1^5/_8$	$2^1/_8$	$2^1/_4$
Sand-lightweight or lightweight	$^3/_4$	$^3/_4$	$^3/_4$	$^3/_4$	$^3/_4$	1	$1^3/_8$	$1^1/_2$	2	$2^1/_4$

For SI: 1 inch = 25.4 mm.

TABLE 721.2.3(3)
MINIMUM COVER FOR MAIN REINFORCING BARS OF REINFORCED CONCRETE BEAMS[c]
(APPLICABLE TO ALL TYPES OF STRUCTURAL CONCRETE)

RESTRAINED OR UNRESTRAINED[a]	BEAM WIDTH[b] (inches)	FIRE-RESISTANCE RATING (hours)				
		1	$1^1/_2$	2	3	4
Restrained	5	$^3/_4$	$^3/_4$	$^3/_4$	1[a]	$1^1/_4$[a]
	7	$^3/_4$	$^3/_4$	$^3/_4$	$^3/_4$	$^3/_4$
	≥ 10	$^3/_4$	$^3/_4$	$^3/_4$	$^3/_4$	$^3/_4$
Unrestrained	5	$^3/_4$	1	$1^1/_4$	—	—
	7	$^3/_4$	$^3/_4$	$^3/_4$	$1^3/_4$	3
	≥ 10	$^3/_4$	$^3/_4$	$^3/_4$	1	$1^3/_4$

For SI: 1 inch = 25.4 mm, 1 foot = 304.8 mm.

a. Tabulated values for restrained assemblies apply to beams spaced more than 4 feet on center. For restrained beams spaced 4 feet or less on center, minimum cover of $^3/_4$ inch is adequate for ratings of 4 hours or less.

b. For beam widths between the tabulated values, the minimum cover thickness can be determined by direct interpolation.

c. The cover for an individual reinforcing bar is the minimum thickness of concrete between the surface of the bar and the fire-exposed surface of the beam. For beams in which several bars are used, the cover for corner bars used in the calculation shall be reduced to one-half of the actual value. The cover for an individual bar must be not less than one-half of the value given in Table 721.2.3(3) nor less than $^3/_4$ inch.

TABLE 721.2.3(4)
MINIMUM COVER FOR PRESTRESSED CONCRETE BEAMS 8 INCHES OR GREATER IN WIDTH

RESTRAINED OR UNRESTRAINED[a]	CONCRETE AGGREGATE TYPE	BEAM WIDTH[b] (inches)	FIRE-RESISTANCE RATING (hours)				
			1	$1^1/_2$	2	3	4
Restrained	Carbonate or siliceous	8	$1^1/_2$	$1^1/_2$	$1^1/_2$	$1^3/_4$[a]	$2^1/_2$[a]
	Carbonate or siliceous	≥ 12	$1^1/_2$	$1^1/_2$	$1^1/_2$	$1^1/_2$	$1^7/_8$[a]
	Sand lightweight	8	$1^1/_2$	$1^1/_2$	$1^1/_2$	$1^1/_2$	2[a]
	Sand lightweight	≥ 12	$1^1/_2$	$1^1/_2$	$1^1/_2$	$1^1/_2$	$1^5/_8$[a]
Unrestrained	Carbonate or siliceous	8	$1^1/_2$	$1^3/_4$	$2^1/_2$	5[c]	—
	Carbonate or siliceous	≥ 12	$1^1/_2$	$1^1/_2$	$1^7/_8$[a]	$2^1/_2$	3
	Sand lightweight	8	$1^1/_2$	$1^1/_2$	2	$3^1/_4$	—
	Sand lightweight	≥ 12	$1^1/_2$	$1^1/_2$	$1^5/_8$	2	$2^1/_2$

For SI: 1 inch = 25.4 mm, 1 foot = 304.8 mm.

a. Tabulated values for restrained assemblies apply to beams spaced more than 4 feet on center. For restrained beams spaced 4 feet or less on center, minimum cover of $^3/_4$ inch is adequate for 4-hour ratings or less.

b. For beam widths between 8 inches and 12 inches, minimum cover thickness can be determined by direct interpolation.

c. Not practical for 8-inch-wide beam but shown for purposes of interpolation.

TABLE 721.2.3(5)
MINIMUM COVER FOR PRESTRESSED CONCRETE BEAMS OF ALL WIDTHS

RESTRAINED OR UNRESTRAINED[a]	CONCRETE AGGREGATE TYPE	BEAM AREA[b] A (square inches)	FIRE-RESISTANCE RATING (hours)				
			1	$1^1/_2$	2	3	4
Restrained	All	$40 \le A \le 150$	$1^1/_2$	$1^1/_2$	2	$2^1/_2$	—
	Carbonate or	$150 < A \le 300$	$1^1/_2$	$1^1/_2$	$1^1/_2$	$1^3/_4$	$2^1/_2$
	siliceous	$300 < A$	$1^1/_2$	$1^1/_2$	$1^1/_2$	$1^1/_2$	2
	Sand lightweight	$150 < A$	$1^1/_2$	$1^1/_2$	$1^1/_2$	$1^1/_2$	2
Unrestrained	All	$40 \le A \le 150$	2	$2^1/_2$	—	—	—
	Carbonate or	$150 < A \le 300$	$1^1/_2$	$1^3/_4$	$2^1/_2$	—	—
	siliceous	$300 < A$	$1^1/_2$	$1^1/_2$	2	3[c]	4[c]
	Sand lightweight	$150 < A$	$1^1/_2$	$1^1/_2$	2	3[c]	4[c]

For SI: 1 inch = 25.4 mm, 1 foot = 304.8 mm, 1 square inch = 645 mm².

a. Tabulated values for restrained assemblies apply to beams spaced more than 4 feet on center. For restrained beams spaced 4 feet or less on center, minimum cover of $^3/_4$ inch is adequate for 4-hour ratings or less.

b. The cross-sectional area of a stem is permitted to include a portion of the area in the flange, provided the width of the flange used in the calculation does not exceed three times the average width of the stem.

c. U-shaped or hooped stirrups spaced not to exceed the depth of the member and having a minimum cover of 1 inch shall be provided.

tendons. The actual cover for any individual tendon shall not be less than one-half the smaller value shown in Tables 721.2.3(4) and 721.2.3(5), or 1 inch (25 mm), whichever is greater.

721.2.4 Concrete columns. Concrete columns shall comply with this section.

TABLE 721.2.4
MINIMUM DIMENSION OF CONCRETE COLUMNS (inches)

TYPES OF CONCRETE	FIRE-RESISTANCE RATING (hours)				
	1	$1^1/_2$	2[a]	3[a]	4[b]
Siliceous	8	9	10	12	14
Carbonate	8	9	10	11	12
Sand-lightweight	8	$8^1/_2$	9	$10^1/_2$	12

For SI: 1 inch = 25 mm.

a. The minimum dimension is permitted to be reduced to 8 inches for rectangular columns with two parallel sides at least 36 inches in length.

b. The minimum dimension is permitted to be reduced to 10 inches for rectangular columns with two parallel sides at least 36 inches in length.

721.2.4.1 Minimum size. The minimum overall dimensions of reinforced concrete columns for *fire-resistance ratings* of 1 hour to 4 hours for exposure to fire on all sides shall comply with this section.

721.2.4.1.1 Concrete strength less than or equal to 12,000 psi. For columns made with concrete having a specified compressive strength, f'_c, of less than or equal to 12,000 psi (82.7 MPa), the minimum dimension shall comply with Table 721.2.4.

721.2.4.1.2 Concrete strength greater than 12,000 psi. For columns made with concrete having a specified compressive strength, f'_c, greater than 12,000 psi (82.7 MPa), for fire-resistance ratings of 1 hour to 4 hours the minimum dimension shall be 24 inches (610 mm).

721.2.4.2 Minimum cover for R/C columns. The minimum thickness of concrete cover to the main longitudinal reinforcement in columns, regardless of the type of aggregate used in the concrete and the specified compressive strength of concrete, f'_c, shall not be less than 1 inch (25 mm) times the number of hours of required *fire resistance* or 2 inches (51 mm), whichever is less.

721.2.4.3 Tie and spiral reinforcement. For concrete columns made with concrete having a specified compressive strength, f'_c, greater than 12,000 psi (82.7 MPa), tie and spiral reinforcement shall comply with the following:

1. The free ends of rectangular ties shall terminate with a 135-degree (2.4 rad) standard tie hook.
2. The free ends of circular ties shall terminate with a 90-degree (1.6 rad) standard tie hook.
3. The free ends of spirals, including at lap splices, shall terminate with a 90-degree (1.6 rad) standard tie hook.

The hook extension at the free end of ties and spirals shall be the larger of six bar diameters and the extension required by Section 7.1.3 of ACI 318. Hooks shall project into the core of the column.

721.2.4.4 Columns built into walls. The minimum dimensions of Table 721.2.4 do not apply to a reinforced concrete column that is built into a concrete or masonry wall provided all of the following are met:

1. The *fire-resistance rating* for the wall is equal to or greater than the required rating of the column;
2. The main longitudinal reinforcing in the column has cover not less than that required by Section 721.2.4.2; and
3. Openings in the wall are protected in accordance with Table 715.4.

Where openings in the wall are not protected as required by Section 715.4, the minimum dimension of columns required to have a *fire-resistance rating* of 3 hours or less shall be 8 inches (203 mm), and 10 inches (254 mm) for columns required to have a *fire-resistance rating* of 4 hours, regardless of the type of aggregate used in the concrete.

721.2.4.5 Precast cover units for steel columns. See Section 721.5.1.4.

721.3 Concrete masonry. The provisions of this section contain procedures by which the *fire-resistance ratings* of concrete masonry are established by calculations.

721.3.1 Equivalent thickness. The equivalent thickness of concrete masonry construction shall be determined in accordance with the provisions of this section.

721.3.1.1 Concrete masonry unit plus finishes. The equivalent thickness of concrete masonry assemblies, T_{ea}, shall be computed as the sum of the equivalent thickness of the concrete masonry unit, T_e, as determined by Section 721.3.1.2, 721.3.1.3 or 721.3.1.4, plus the equivalent thickness of finishes, T_{ef}, determined in accordance with Section 721.3.2:

$$T_{ea} = T_e + T_{ef} \quad \text{(Equation 7-6)}$$

721.3.1.2 Ungrouted or partially grouted construction. T_e shall be the value obtained for the concrete masonry unit determined in accordance with ASTM C 140.

721.3.1.3 Solid grouted construction. The equivalent thickness, T_e, of solid grouted concrete masonry units is the actual thickness of the unit.

721.3.1.4 Airspaces and cells filled with loose-fill material. The equivalent thickness of completely filled hollow concrete masonry is the actual thickness of the unit when loose-fill materials are: sand, pea gravel, crushed stone, or slag that meet ASTM C 33 requirements; pumice, scoria, expanded shale, expanded clay, expanded slate, expanded slag, expanded fly ash, or cinders that comply with ASTM C 331; or perlite or vermiculite meeting the requirements of ASTM C 549 and ASTM C 516, respectively.

721.3.2 Concrete masonry walls. The *fire-resistance rating* of walls and partitions constructed of concrete masonry units shall be determined from Table 721.3.2. The rating shall be based on the equivalent thickness of the masonry and type of aggregate used.

721.3.2.1 Finish on nonfire-exposed side. Where plaster or gypsum wallboard is applied to the side of the wall not exposed to fire, the contribution of the finish to the total *fire-resistance rating* shall be determined as follows: The thickness of gypsum wallboard or plaster shall be corrected by multiplying the actual thickness of the finish by applicable factor determined from Table 721.2.1.4(1). This corrected thickness of finish shall be added to the equivalent thickness of masonry and the *fire-resistance rating* of the masonry and finish determined from Table 721.3.2.

721.3.2.2 Finish on fire-exposed side. Where plaster or gypsum wallboard is applied to the fire-exposed side of the wall, the contribution of the finish to the total *fire-resistance rating* shall be determined as follows: The time assigned to the finish as established by Table 721.2.1.4(2) shall be added to the *fire-resistance rating* determined in Section 721.3.2 for the masonry alone, or in Section 721.3.2.1 for the masonry and finish on the nonfire-exposed side.

721.3.2.3 Nonsymmetrical assemblies. For a wall having no finish on one side or having different types or thicknesses of finish on each side, the calculation procedures of this section shall be performed twice, assuming either side of the wall to be the fire-exposed side. The *fire-resistance rating* of the wall shall not exceed the lower of the two values calculated.

> **Exception:** For *exterior walls* with a *fire separation distance* greater than 5 feet (1524 mm) the fire shall be assumed to occur on the interior side only.

TABLE 721.3.2
MINIMUM EQUIVALENT THICKNESS (inches) OF BEARING OR NONBEARING CONCRETE MASONRY WALLS[a,b,c,d]

TYPE OF AGGREGATE	FIRE-RESISTANCE RATING (hours)														
	1/2	3/4	1	1 1/4	1 1/2	1 3/4	2	2 1/4	2 1/2	2 3/4	3	3 1/4	3 1/2	3 3/4	4
Pumice or expanded slag	1.5	1.9	2.1	2.5	2.7	3.0	3.2	3.4	3.6	3.8	4.0	4.2	4.4	4.5	4.7
Expanded shale, clay or slate	1.8	2.2	2.6	2.9	3.3	3.4	3.6	3.8	4.0	4.2	4.4	4.6	4.8	4.9	5.1
Limestone, cinders or unexpanded slag	1.9	2.3	2.7	3.1	3.4	3.7	4.0	4.3	4.5	4.8	5.0	5.2	5.5	5.7	5.9
Calcareous or siliceous gravel	2.0	2.4	2.8	3.2	3.6	3.9	4.2	4.5	4.8	5.0	5.3	5.5	5.8	6.0	6.2

For SI: 1 inch = 25.4 mm.

a. Values between those shown in the table can be determined by direct interpolation.

b. Where combustible members are framed into the wall, the thickness of solid material between the end of each member and the opposite face of the wall, or between members set in from opposite sides, shall not be less than 93 percent of the thickness shown in the table.

c. Requirements of ASTM C 55, ASTM C 73, ASTM C 90 or ASTM C 744 shall apply.

d. Minimum required equivalent thickness corresponding to the hourly fire-resistance rating for units with a combination of aggregate shall be determined by linear interpolation based on the percent by volume of each aggregate used in manufacture.

721.3.2.4 Minimum concrete masonry fire-resistance rating. Where the finish applied to a concrete masonry wall contributes to its *fire-resistance rating*, the masonry alone shall provide not less than one-half the total required *fire-resistance rating*.

721.3.2.5 Attachment of finishes. Installation of finishes shall be as follows:

1. Gypsum wallboard and gypsum lath applied to concrete masonry or concrete walls shall be secured to wood or steel furring members spaced not more than 16 inches (406 mm) on center (o.c.).
2. Gypsum wallboard shall be installed with the long dimension parallel to the furring members and shall have all joints finished.
3. Other aspects of the installation of finishes shall comply with the applicable provisions of Chapters 7 and 25.

721.3.3 Multiwythe masonry walls. The *fire-resistance rating* of wall assemblies constructed of multiple wythes of masonry materials shall be permitted to be based on the *fire-resistance rating* period of each wythe and the continuous airspace between each wythe in accordance with the following formula:

$$R_A = (R_1^{0.59} + R_2^{0.59} + ... + R_n^{0.59} + A_1 + A_2 + ... + A_n)^{1.7}$$ **(Equation 7-7)**

where:

R_A = *Fire-resistance rating* of the assembly (hours).

$R_1, R_2, ..., R_n$ = *Fire-resistance rating* of wythes for 1, 2, n (hours), respectively.

$A_1, A_2, ..., A_n$ = 0.30, factor for each continuous airspace for 1, 2, ...n, respectively, having a depth of $^1/_2$ inch (12.7 mm) or more between wythes.

721.3.4 Concrete masonry lintels. *Fire-resistance ratings* for concrete masonry lintels shall be determined based upon the nominal thickness of the lintel and the minimum thickness of concrete masonry or concrete, or any combination thereof, covering the main reinforcing bars, as determined according to Table 721.3.4, or by *approved* alternate methods.

TABLE 721.3.4
MINIMUM COVER OF LONGITUDINAL REINFORCEMENT IN FIRE-RESISTANCE-RATED REINFORCED CONCRETE MASONRY LINTELS (inches)

NOMINAL WIDTH OF LINTEL (inches)	FIRE-RESISTANCE RATING (hours)			
	1	2	3	4
6	$1^1/_2$	2	—	—
8	$1^1/_2$	$1^1/_2$	$1^3/_4$	3
10 or greater	$1^1/_2$	$1^1/_2$	$1^1/_2$	$1^3/_4$

For SI: 1 inch = 25.4 mm.

721.3.5 Concrete masonry columns. The *fire-resistance rating* of concrete masonry columns shall be determined based upon the least plan dimension of the column in accordance with Table 721.3.5 or by *approved* alternate methods.

TABLE 721.3.5
MINIMUM DIMENSION OF CONCRETE MASONRY COLUMNS (inches)

FIRE-RESISTANCE RATING (hours)			
1	2	3	4
8 inches	10 inches	12 inches	14 inches

For SI: 1 inch = 25.4 mm.

721.4 Clay brick and tile masonry. The provisions of this section contain procedures by which the *fire-resistance ratings* of clay brick and tile masonry are established by calculations.

721.4.1 Masonry walls. The *fire-resistance rating* of masonry walls shall be based upon the equivalent thickness as calculated in accordance with this section. The calculation shall take into account finishes applied to the wall and airspaces between wythes in multiwythe construction.

721.4.1.1 Equivalent thickness. The *fire-resistance ratings* of walls or partitions constructed of solid or hollow clay masonry units shall be determined from Table 721.4.1(1) or 721.4.1(2). The equivalent thickness of the clay masonry unit shall be determined by Equation 7-8 when using Table 721.4.1(1). The *fire-resistance rating* determined from Table 721.4.1(1) shall be permitted to be used in the calculated *fire-resistance rating* procedure in Section 721.4.2.

$$T_e = V_n/LH$$ **(Equation 7-8)**

where:

T_e = The equivalent thickness of the clay masonry unit (inches).

V_n = The net volume of the clay masonry unit (inch^3).

L = The specified length of the clay masonry unit (inches).

H = The specified height of the clay masonry unit (inches).

721.4.1.1.1 Hollow clay units. The equivalent thickness, T_e, shall be the value obtained for hollow clay units as determined in accordance with Equation 7-8. The net volume, V_n, of the units shall be determined using the gross volume and percentage of void area determined in accordance with ASTM C 67.

721.4.1.1.2 Solid grouted clay units. The equivalent thickness of solid grouted clay masonry units shall be taken as the actual thickness of the units.

721.4.1.1.3 Units with filled cores. The equivalent thickness of the hollow clay masonry units is the actual thickness of the unit when completely filled with loose-fill materials of: sand, pea gravel, crushed stone, or slag that meet ASTM C 33 requirements; pumice, scoria, expanded shale, expanded clay, expanded slate, expanded slag, expanded fly ash, or cinders in compliance with ASTM C 331; or perlite or vermiculite meeting the requirements of ASTM C 549 and ASTM C 516, respectively.

TABLE 721.4.1(1)
FIRE-RESISTANCE PERIODS OF CLAY MASONRY WALLS

MATERIAL TYPE	MINIMUM REQUIRED EQUIVALENT THICKNESS FOR FIRE RESISTANCE[a, b, c] (inches)			
	1 hour	2 hour	3 hour	4 hour
Solid brick of clay or shale[d]	2.7	3.8	4.9	6.0
Hollow brick or tile of clay or shale, unfilled	2.3	3.4	4.3	5.0
Hollow brick or tile of clay or shale, grouted or filled with materials specified in Section 721.4.1.1.3	3.0	4.4	5.5	6.6

For SI: 1 inch = 25.4 mm.

a. Equivalent thickness as determined from Section 721.4.1.1.

b. Calculated fire resistance between the hourly increments listed shall be determined by linear interpolation.

c. Where combustible members are framed in the wall, the thickness of solid material between the end of each member and the opposite face of the wall, or between members set in from opposite sides, shall not be less than 93 percent of the thickness shown.

d. For units in which the net cross-sectional area of cored brick in any plane parallel to the surface containing the cores is at least 75 percent of the gross cross-sectional area measured in the same plane.

TABLE 721.4.1(2)
FIRE-RESISTANCE RATINGS FOR BEARING STEEL FRAME BRICK VENEER WALLS OR PARTITIONS

WALL OR PARTITION ASSEMBLY	PLASTER SIDE EXPOSED (hours)	BRICK FACED SIDE EXPOSED (hours)
Outside facing of steel studs: $^1/_2''$ wood fiberboard sheathing next to studs, $^3/_4''$ airspace formed with $^3/_4'' \times 1\,^5/_8''$ wood strips placed over the fiberboard and secured to the studs; metal or wire lath nailed to such strips, $3^3/_4''$ brick veneer held in place by filling $^3/_4''$ airspace between the brick and lath with mortar. Inside facing of studs: $^3/_4''$ unsanded gypsum plaster on metal or wire lath attached to $^5/_{16}''$ wood strips secured to edges of the studs.	1.5	4
Outside facing of steel studs: 1″ insulation board sheathing attached to studs, 1″ airspace, and $3^3/_4''$ brick veneer attached to steel frame with metal ties every 5th course. Inside facing of studs: $^7/_8''$ sanded gypsum plaster (1:2 mix) applied on metal or wire lath attached directly to the studs.	1.5	4
Same as above except use $^7/_8''$ vermiculite—gypsum plaster or 1″ sanded gypsum plaster (1:2 mix) applied to metal or wire.	2	4
Outside facing of steel studs: $^1/_2''$ gypsum sheathing board, attached to studs, and $3^3/_4''$ brick veneer attached to steel frame with metal ties every 5th course. Inside facing of studs: $^1/_2''$ sanded gypsum plaster (1:2 mix) applied to $^1/_2''$ perforated gypsum lath securely attached to studs and having strips of metal lath 3 inches wide applied to all horizontal joints of gypsum lath.	2	4

For SI: 1 inch = 25.4 mm.

721.4.1.2 Plaster finishes. Where plaster is applied to the wall, the total *fire-resistance rating* shall be determined by the formula:

$$R = (R_n^{0.59} + pl)^{1.7} \quad \textbf{(Equation 7-9)}$$

where:

R = The *fire-resistance rating* of the assembly (hours).

R_n = The *fire-resistance rating* of the individual wall (hours).

pl = Coefficient for thickness of plaster.

Values for $R_n^{0.59}$ for use in Equation 7-9 are given in Table 721.4.1(3). Coefficients for thickness of plaster shall be selected from Table 721.4.1(4) based on the actual thickness of plaster applied to the wall or partition and whether one or two sides of the wall are plastered.

721.4.1.3 Multiwythe walls with airspace. Where a continuous airspace separates multiple wythes of the wall or partition, the total *fire-resistance rating* shall be determined by the formula:

$$R = (R_1^{0.59} + R_2^{0.59} + ... + R_n^{0.59} + as)^{1.7} \quad \textbf{(Equation 7-10)}$$

where:

R = The *fire-resistance rating* of the assembly (hours).

R_1, R_2 and R_n = The *fire-resistance rating* of the individual wythes (hours).

as = Coefficient for continuous airspace.

Values for $R_n^{0.59}$ for use in Equation 7-10 are given in Table 721.4.1(3). The coefficient for each continuous airspace of $^1/_2$ inch to $3^1/_2$ inches (12.7 to 89 mm) separating two individual wythes shall be 0.3.

TABLE 721.4.1(3)
VALUES OF $R_n^{0.59}$

$R_n^{0.59}$	R (hours)
1	1.0
2	1.50
3	1.91
4	2.27

TABLE 721.4.1(4)
COEFFICIENTS FOR PLASTER, pl [a]

THICKNESS OF PLASTER (inch)	ONE SIDE	TWO SIDE
1/2	0.3	0.6
5/8	0.37	0.75
3/4	0.45	0.90

For SI: 1 inch = 25.4 mm.
a. Values listed in table are for 1:3 sanded gypsum plaster.

TABLE 721.4.1(5)
REINFORCED MASONRY LINTELS

NOMINAL LINTEL WIDTH (inches)	MINIMUM LONGITUDINAL REINFORCEMENT COVER FOR FIRE RESISTANCE (inch)			
	1 hour	2 hour	3 hour	4 hour
6	$1^1/_2$	2	NP	NP
8	$1^1/_2$	$1^1/_2$	$1^3/_4$	3
10 or more	$1^1/_2$	$1^1/_2$	$1^1/_2$	$1^3/_4$

For SI: 1 inch = 25.4 mm.
NP = Not permitted.

TABLE 721.4.1(6)
REINFORCED CLAY MASONRY COLUMNS

COLUMN SIZE	FIRE-RESISTANCE RATING (hour)			
	1	2	3	4
Minimum column dimension (inches)	8	10	12	14

For SI: 1 inch = 25.4 mm.

721.4.1.4 Nonsymmetrical assemblies. For a wall having no finish on one side or having different types or thicknesses of finish on each side, the calculation procedures of this section shall be performed twice, assuming either side to be the fire-exposed side of the wall. The *fire resistance* of the wall shall not exceed the lower of the two values determined.

Exception: For *exterior walls* with a *fire separation distance* greater than 5 feet (1524 mm), the fire shall be assumed to occur on the interior side only.

721.4.2 Multiwythe walls. The *fire-resistance rating* for walls or partitions consisting of two or more dissimilar wythes shall be permitted to be determined by the formula:

$$R = (R_1^{0.59} + R_2^{0.59} + ... + R_n^{0.59})^{1.7} \quad \textbf{(Equation 7-11)}$$

where:

R = The *fire-resistance rating* of the assembly (hours).

R_1, R_2 and R_n = The *fire-resistance rating* of the individual wythes (hours).

Values for $R_n^{0.59}$ for use in Equation 7-11 are given in Table 721.4.1(3).

721.4.2.1 Multiwythe walls of different material. For walls that consist of two or more wythes of different materials (concrete or concrete masonry units) in combination with clay masonry units, the *fire-resistance rating* of the different materials shall be permitted to be determined from Table 721.2.1.1 for concrete; Table 721.3.2 for concrete masonry units or Table 721.4.1(1) or 721.4.1(2) for clay and tile masonry units.

721.4.3 Reinforced clay masonry lintels. *Fire-resistance ratings* for clay masonry lintels shall be determined based on the nominal width of the lintel and the minimum covering for the longitudinal reinforcement in accordance with Table 721.4.1(5).

721.4.4 Reinforced clay masonry columns. The *fire-resistance ratings* shall be determined based on the last plan dimension of the column in accordance with Table 721.4.1(6). The minimum cover for longitudinal reinforcement shall be 2 inches (51 mm).

721.5 Steel assemblies. The provisions of this section contain procedures by which the *fire-resistance ratings* of steel assemblies are established by calculations.

721.5.1 Structural steel columns. The *fire-resistance ratings* of steel columns shall be based on the size of the element and the type of protection provided in accordance with this section.

721.5.1.1 General. These procedures establish a basis for determining the *fire resistance* of column assemblies as a function of the thickness of fire-resistant material and, the weight, *W*, and heated perimeter, *D*, of steel columns. As used in these sections, *W* is the average weight of a structural steel column in pounds per linear foot. The heated perimeter, *D*, is the inside perimeter of the fire-resistant material in inches as illustrated in Figure 721.5.1(1).

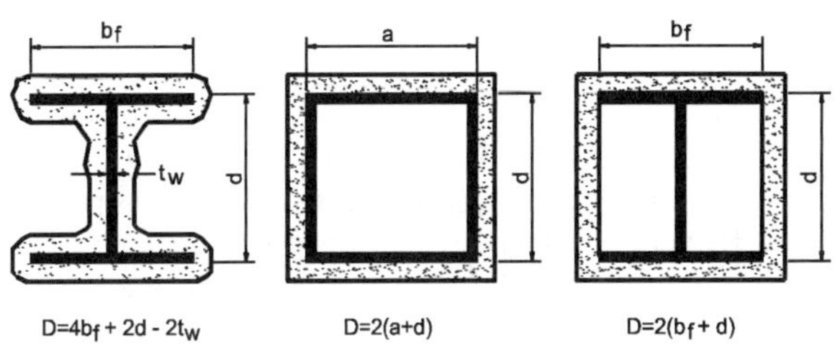

FIGURE 721.5.1(1)
DETERMINATION OF THE HEATED PERIMETER OF STRUCTURAL STEEL COLUMNS

721.5.1.1.1 Nonload-bearing protection. The application of these procedures shall be limited to column assemblies in which the fire-resistant material is not designed to carry any of the load acting on the column.

721.5.1.1.2 Embedments. In the absence of substantiating fire-endurance test results, ducts, conduit, piping, and similar mechanical, electrical, and plumbing installations shall not be embedded in any required fire-resistant materials.

721.5.1.1.3 Weight-to-perimeter ratio. Table 721.5.1(1) contains weight-to-heated-perimeter ratios (*W/D*) for both contour and box fire-resistant profiles, for the wide flange shapes most often used as columns. For different fire-resistant protection profiles or column cross sections, the weight-to-heated-perimeter ratios (*W/D*) shall be determined in accordance with the definitions given in this section.

721.5.1.2 Gypsum wallboard protection. The *fire resistance* of structural steel columns with weight-to-heated-perimeter ratios (*W/D*) less than or equal to 3.65 and which are protected with Type X gypsum wallboard shall be permitted to be determined from the following expression:

$$R = 130\left[\frac{h(W'/D)}{2}\right]^{0.75} \quad \textbf{(Equation 7-12)}$$

where:

R = *Fire resistance* (minutes).

h = Total thickness of gypsum wallboard (inches).

D = Heated perimeter of the structural steel column (inches).

W' = Total weight of the structural steel column and gypsum wallboard protection (pounds per linear foot).

$W' = W + 50hD/144$.

721.5.1.2.1 Attachment. The gypsum wallboard shall be supported as illustrated in either Figure 721.5.1(2) for *fire-resistance ratings* of 4 hours or less, or Figure 721.5.1(3) for *fire-resistance ratings* of 3 hours or less.

721.5.1.2.2 Gypsum wallboard equivalent to concrete. The determination of the *fire resistance* of structural steel columns from Figure 721.5.1(4) is permitted for various thicknesses of gypsum wallboard as a function of the weight-to-heated-perimeter ratio (*W/D*) of the column. For structural steel columns with weight-to-heated-perimeter ratios (*W/D*) greater than 3.65, the thickness of gypsum wallboard required for specified *fire-resistance ratings* shall be the same as the thickness determined for a *W*14 × 233 wide flange shape.

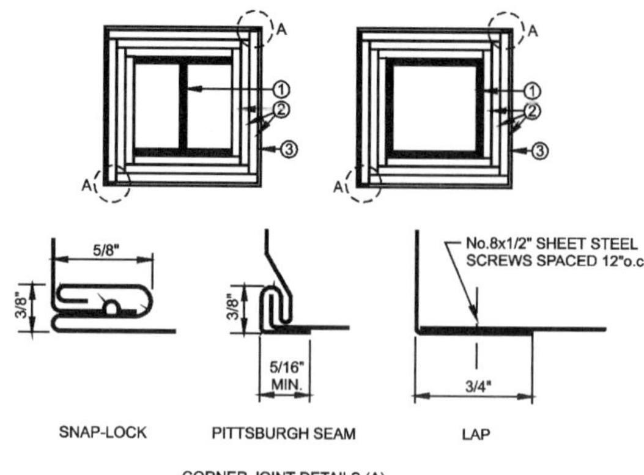

FIGURE 721.5.1(2)
GYPSUM WALLBOARD PROTECTED STRUCTURAL STEEL COLUMNS WITH SHEET STEEL COLUMN COVERS

For SI: 1 inch = 25.4 mm, 1 foot = 305 mm, 1 inch per linear foot = 83.3 mm/linear meter.

1. Structural steel column, either wide flange or tubular shapes.
2. Type X gypsum wallboard in accordance with ASTM C 36. For single-layer applications, the wallboard shall be applied vertically with no horizontal joints. For multiple-layer applications, horizontal joints are permitted at a minimum spacing of 8 feet, provided that the joints in successive layers are staggered at least 12 inches. The total required thickness of wallboard shall be determined on the basis of the specified fire-resistance rating and the weight-to-heated-perimeter ratio (*W/D*) of the column. For fire-resistance ratings of 2 hours or less, one of the required layers of gypsum wallboard may be applied to the exterior of the sheet steel column covers with 1-inch-long Type S screws spaced 1 inch from the wallboard edge and 8 inches on center. For such installations, 0.0149-inch minimum thickness galvanized steel corner beads with $1^1/_2$-inch legs shall be attached to the wallboard with Type S screws spaced 12 inches on center.
3. For fire-resistance ratings of 3 hours or less, the column covers shall be fabricated from 0.0239-inch minimum thickness galvanized or stainless steel. For 4-hour fire-resistance ratings, the column covers shall be fabricated from 0.0239-inch minimum thickness stainless steel. The column covers shall be erected with the Snap Lock or Pittsburgh joint details.

   For fire-resistance ratings of 2 hours or less, column covers fabricated from 0.0269-inch minimum thickness galvanized or stainless steel shall be permitted to be erected with lap joints. The lap joints shall be permitted to be located anywhere around the perimeter of the column cover. The lap joints shall be secured with $^1/_2$-inch-long No. 8 sheet metal screws spaced 12 inches on center.

   The column covers shall be provided with a minimum expansion clearance of $^1/_8$ inch per linear foot between the ends of the cover and any restraining construction.

721.5.1.3 Sprayed fire-resistant materials. The *fire resistance* of wide-flange structural steel columns protected with sprayed fire-resistant materials, as illustrated in Figure 721.5.1(5), shall be permitted to be determined from the following expression:

$$R = [C_1(W/D) + C_2]h \quad \textbf{(Equation 7-13)}$$

where:

R = *Fire resistance* (minutes).

h = Thickness of sprayed fire-resistant material (inches).

D = Heated perimeter of the structural steel column (inches).

C_1 and C_2 = Material-dependent constants.

W = Weight of structural steel columns (pounds per linear foot).

The *fire resistance* of structural steel columns protected with intumescent or mastic fire-resistant coatings shall be determined on the basis of fire-resistance tests in accordance with Section 703.2.

721.5.1.3.1 Material-dependent constants. The material-dependent constants, C_1 and C_2, shall be determined for specific fire-resistant materials on the basis of standard fire endurance tests in accordance with Section 703.2. Unless evidence is submitted to the *building official* substantiating a broader application, this expression shall be limited to determining the *fire resistance* of structural steel columns with weight-to-heated-perimeter ratios (W/D) between the largest and smallest columns for which standard fire-resistance test results are available.

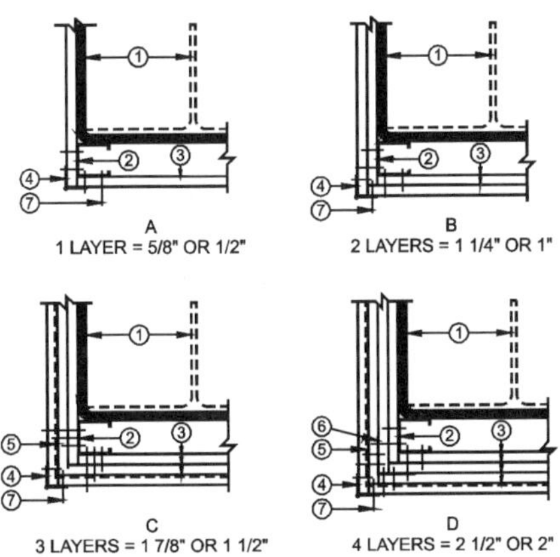

FIGURE 721.5.1(3)
GYPSUM WALLBOARD PROTECTED STRUCTURAL STEEL COLUMNS WITH STEEL STUD/SCREW ATTACHMENT SYSTEM

For SI: 1 inch = 25.4 mm, 1 foot = -305 mm.

1. Structural steel column, either wide flange or tubular shapes.
2. $1^5/_8$-inch deep studs fabricated from 0.0179-inch minimum thickness galvanized steel with $1^5/_{16}$ or $1^7/_{16}$-inch legs. The length of the steel studs shall be $^1/_2$ inch less than the height of the assembly.
3. Type X gypsum wallboard in accordance with ASTM C 36. For single-layer applications, the wallboard shall be applied vertically with no horizontal joints. For multiple-layer applications, horizontal joints are permitted at a minimum spacing of 8 feet, provided that the joints in successive layers are staggered at least 12 inches. The total required thickness of wallboard shall be determined on the basis of the specified fire-resistance rating and the weight-to-heated-perimeter ratio (W/D) of the column.
4. Galvanized 0.0149-inch minimum thickness steel corner beads with $1^1/_2$-inch legs attached to the wallboard with 1-inch-long Type S screws spaced 12 inches on center.
5. No. 18 SWG steel tie wires spaced 24 inches on center.
6. Sheet metal angles with 2-inch legs fabricated from 0.0221-inch minimum thickness galvanized steel.
7. Type S screws, 1 inch long, shall be used for attaching the first layer of wallboard to the steel studs and the third layer to the sheet metal angles at 24 inches on center. Type S screws $1^3/_4$-inch long shall be used for attaching the second layer of wallboard to the steel studs and the fourth layer to the sheet metal angles at 12 inches on center. Type S screws $2^1/_4$ inches long shall be used for attaching the third layer of wallboard to the steel studs at 12 inches on center.

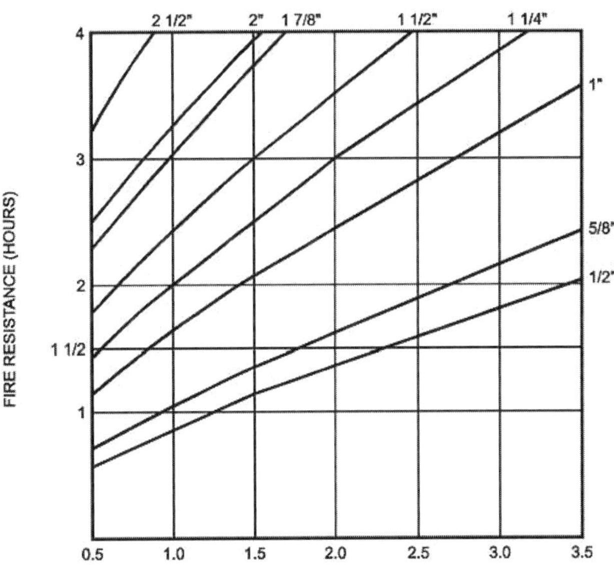

For SI: 1 inch = 25.4 mm, 1 pound per linear foot/inch = 0.059 kg/m/mm.

FIGURE 721.5.1(4)
FIRE RESISTANCE OF STRUCTURAL STEEL COLUMNS PROTECTED WITH VARIOUS THICKNESSES OF TYPE X GYPSUM WALLBOARD

a. The W/D ratios for typical wide flange columns are listed in Table 721.5.1(1). For other column shapes, the W/D ratios shall be determined in accordance with Section 720.5.1.1.

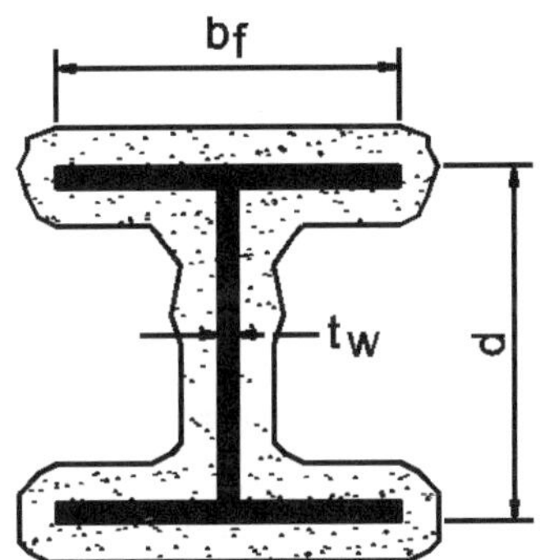

FIGURE 721.5.1(5)
WIDE FLANGE STRUCTURAL STEEL COLUMNS WITH SPRAYED FIRE-RESISTANT MATERIALS

721.5.1.3.2 Identification. Sprayed fire-resistant materials shall be identified by density and thickness required for a given *fire-resistance rating*.

721.5.1.4 Concrete-protected columns. The *fire resistance* of structural steel columns protected with concrete, as illustrated in Figure 721.5.1(6) (a) and (b), shall be permitted to be determined from the following expression:

$$R = R_o(1 + 0.03_m) \quad \textbf{(Equation 7-14)}$$

where:

$$R_o = 10(W/D)^{0.7} + 17(h^{1.6}/k_c^{0.2}) \times [1 + 26\{H/p_c c_c h(L + h)\}^{0.8}]$$

As used in these expressions:

R = Fire endurance at equilibrium moisture conditions (minutes).

R_o = Fire endurance at zero moisture content (minutes).

m = Equilibrium moisture content of the concrete by volume (percent).

W = Average weight of the steel column (pounds per linear foot).

D = Heated perimeter of the steel column (inches).

h = Thickness of the concrete cover (inches).

k_c = Ambient temperature thermal conductivity of the concrete (Btu/hr ft °F).

H = Ambient temperature thermal capacity of the steel column = 0.11W (Btu/ ft °F).

p_c = Concrete density (pounds per cubic foot).

c_c = Ambient temperature specific heat of concrete (Btu/lb °F).

L = Interior dimension of one side of a square concrete box protection (inches).

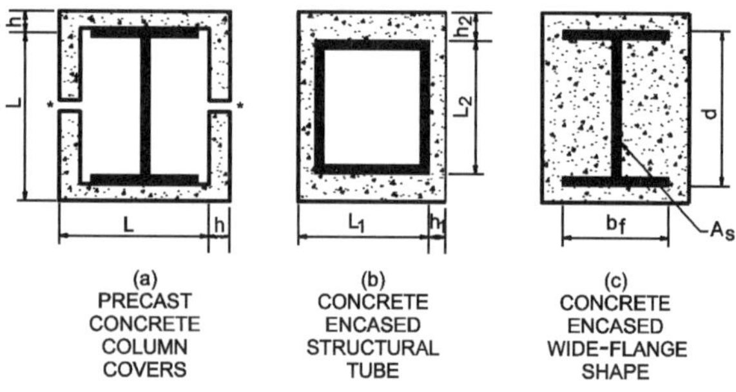

FIGURE 721.5.1(6)
CONCRETE PROTECTED STRUCTURAL STEEL COLUMNS[a,b]

a. When the inside perimeter of the concrete protection is not square, L shall be taken as the average of L_1 and L_2. When the thickness of concrete cover is not constant, h shall be taken as the average of h_1 and h_2.

b. Joints shall be protected with a minimum 1 inch thickness of ceramic fiber blanket but in no case less than one-half the thickness of the column cover (see Section 720.2.1.3).

721.5.1.4.1 Reentrant space filled. For wide-flange steel columns completely encased in concrete with all reentrant spaces filled [Figure 721.5.1(6)(c)], the thermal capacity of the concrete within the reentrant spaces shall be permitted to be added to the thermal capacity of the steel column, as follows:

$$H = 0.11W + (p_c c_c/144)(b_f d - A_s) \quad \textbf{(Equation 7-15)}$$

where:

b_f = Flange width of the steel column (inches).

d = Depth of the steel column (inches).

A_s = Cross-sectional area of the steel column (square inches).

721.5.1.4.2 Concrete properties unknown. If specific data on the properties of concrete are not available, the values given in Table 721.5.1(2) are permitted.

721.5.1.4.3 Minimum concrete cover. For structural steel column encased in concrete with all reentrant spaces filled, Figure 721.5.1(6)(c) and Tables 721.5.1(7) and 721.5.1(8) indicate the thickness of concrete cover required for various *fire-resistance ratings* for typical wide-flange sections. The thicknesses of concrete indicated in these tables also apply to structural steel columns larger than those listed.

721.5.1.4.4 Minimum precast concrete cover. For structural steel columns protected with precast concrete column covers as shown in Figure 721.5.1(6)(a), Tables 721.5.1(9) and 721.5.1(10) indicate the thickness of the column covers required for various *fire-resistance ratings* for typical wide-flange shapes. The thicknesses of concrete given in these tables also apply to structural steel columns larger than those listed.

721.5.1.4.5 Masonry protection. The *fire resistance* of structural steel columns protected with concrete masonry units or clay masonry units as illustrated in Figure 721.5.1(7), shall be permitted to be determined from the following expression:

$$R = 0.17\,(W/D)^{0.7} + [0.285\,(T_e^{1.6}/K^{0.2})]\,[1.0 + 42.7\,\{(A_s/d_m\,T_e)/(0.25p + T_e)\}^{0.8}] \quad \textbf{(Equation 7-16)}$$

where:

R = *Fire-resistance rating* of column assembly (hours).

W = Average weight of steel column (pounds per foot).

D = Heated perimeter of steel column (inches) [see Figure 721.5.1(7)].

T_e = Equivalent thickness of concrete or clay masonry unit (inches) (see Table 721.3.2 Note a or Section 721.4.1).

K = Thermal conductivity of concrete or clay masonry unit (Btu/hr · ft · °F) [see Table 721.5.1(3)].

A_s = Cross-sectional area of steel column (square inches).

d_m = Density of the concrete or clay masonry unit (pounds per cubic foot).

p = Inner perimeter of concrete or clay masonry protection (inches) [see Figure 721.5.1(7)].

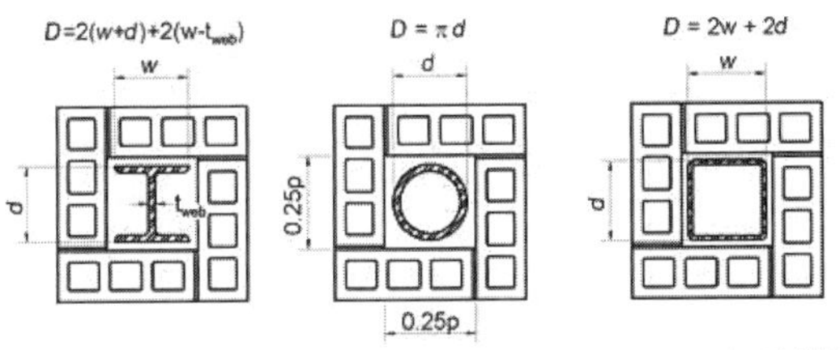

For SI: 1 inch = 25.4 mm.

FIGURE 721.5.1(7)
CONCRETE OR CLAY MASONRY PROTECTED STRUCTURAL STEEL COLUMNS

d = Depth of a wide flange column, outside diameter of pipe column, or outside dimension of structural tubing column (inches).

t_{web} = Thickness of web of wide flange column (inches).

w = Width of flange of wide flange column (inches).

721.5.1.4.6 Equivalent concrete masonry thickness. For structural steel columns protected with concrete masonry, Table 721.5.1(5) gives the equivalent thickness of concrete masonry required for various *fire-resistance ratings* for typical column shapes. For structural steel columns protected with clay masonry, Table 721.5.1(6) gives the equivalent thickness of concrete masonry required for various *fire-resistance ratings* for typical column shapes.

721.5.2 Structural steel beams and girders. The *fire-resistance ratings* of steel beams and girders shall be based upon the size of the element and the type of protection provided in accordance with this section.

721.5.2.1 Determination of *fire resistance*. These procedures establish a basis for determining resistance of structural steel beams and girders which differ in size from that specified in *approved* fire-resistance-rated assemblies as a function of the thickness of fire-resistant material and the weight (W) and heated perimeter (D) of the beam or girder. As used in these sections, W is the average weight of a structural steel member in pounds per linear foot (plf). The heated perimeter, D, is the inside perimeter of the fire-resistant material in inches as illustrated in Figure 721.5.2.

721.5.2.1.1 Weight-to-heated perimeter. The weight-to-heated-perimeter ratios (W/D), for both contour and box fire-resistant protection profiles, for the wide flange shapes most often used as beams or girders are given in Table 721.5.1(4). For different shapes, the weight-to-heated-perimeter ratios (W/D) shall be determined in accordance with the definitions given in this section.

721.5.2.1.2 Beam and girder substitutions. Except as provided for in Section 721.5.2.2, structural steel beams in *approved* fire-resistance-rated assemblies shall be considered the minimum permissible size. Other beam or girder shapes shall be permitted to be substituted provided that the weight-to-heated-perimeter ratio (W/D) of the substitute beam is equal to or greater than that of the beam specified in the *approved* assembly.

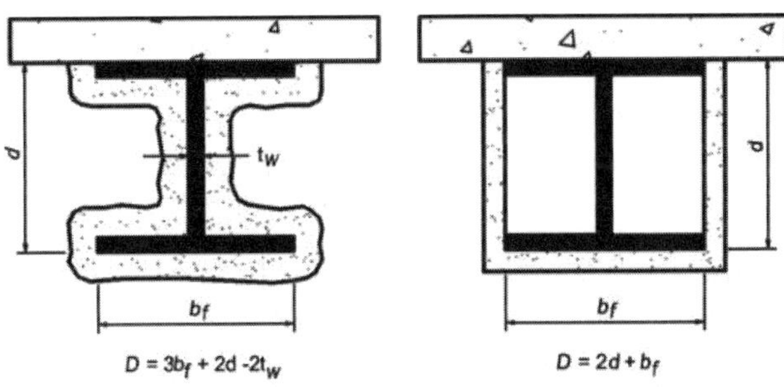

FIGURE 721.5.2
DETERMINATION OF THE HEATED PERIMETER OF STRUCTURAL STEEL BEAMS AND GIRDERS

721.5.2.2 Sprayed fire-resistant materials. The provisions in this section apply to structural steel beams and girders protected with sprayed fire-resistant materials. Larger or smaller beam and girder shapes shall be permitted to be substituted for beams specified in *approved* unrestrained or restrained fire-resistance-rated assemblies, provided that the thickness of the fire-resistant material is adjusted in accordance with the following expression:

$$h_2 = h_1\left[\left(W_1 / D_1\right) + 0.60\right] / \left[\left(W_2 / D_2\right) + 0.60\right]$$

(Equation 7-17)

where:

h = Thickness of sprayed fire-resistant material in inches.

W = Weight of the structural steel beam or girder in pounds per linear foot.

D = Heated perimeter of the structural steel beam in inches.

Subscript 1 refers to the beam and fire-resistant material thickness in the *approved* assembly.

Subscript 2 refers to the substitute beam or girder and the required thickness of fire-resistant material.

The *fire resistance* of structural steel beams and girders protected with intumescent or mastic fire-resistant coatings shall be determined on the basis of fire-resistance tests in accordance with Section 703.2.

721.5.2.2.1 Minimum thickness. The use of Equation 7-17 is subject to the following conditions:

1. The weight-to-heated-perimeter ratio for the substitute beam or girder (W_2/D_2) shall not be less than 0.37.
2. The thickness of fire protection materials calculated for the substitute beam or girder (T_1) shall not be less than $^3/_8$ inch (9.5 mm).
3. The unrestrained or restrained beam rating shall not be less than 1 hour.
4. When used to adjust the material thickness for a restrained beam, the use of this procedure is limited to steel sections classified as compact in

TABLE 721.5.1(1)
***W/D* RATIOS FOR STEEL COLUMNS**

STRUCTURAL SHAPE	CONTOUR PROFILE	BOX PROFILE	STRUCTURAL SHAPE	CONTOUR PROFILE	BOX PROFILE
W14 × 233	2.49	3.65	W10 × 112	1.78	2.57
× 211	2.28	3.35	× 100	1.61	2.33
× 193	2.10	3.09	× 88	1.43	2.08
× 176	1.93	2.85	× 77	1.26	1.85
× 159	1.75	2.60	× 68	1.13	1.66
× 145	1.61	2.39	× 60	1.00	1.48
× 132	1.52	2.25	× 54	0.91	1.34
× 120	1.39	2.06	× 49	0.83	1.23
× 109	1.27	1.88	× 45	0.87	1.24
× 99	1.16	1.72	× 39	0.76	1.09
× 90	1.06	1.58	× 33	0.65	0.93
× 82	1.20	1.68			
× 74	1.09	1.53	W8 × 67	1.34	1.94
× 68	1.01	1.41	× 58	1.18	1.71
× 61	0.91	1.28	× 48	0.99	1.44
× 53	0.89	1.21	× 40	0.83	1.23
× 48	0.81	1.10	× 35	0.73	1.08
× 43	0.73	0.99	× 31	0.65	0.97
			× 28	0.67	0.96
W12 × 190	2.46	3.51	× 24	0.58	0.83
× 170	2.22	3.20	× 21	0.57	0.77
× 152	2.01	2.90	× 18	0.49	0.67
× 136	1.82	2.63			
× 120	1.62	2.36	W6 × 25	0.69	1.00
× 106	1.44	2.11	× 20	0.56	0.82
× 96	1.32	1.93	× 16	0.57	0.78
× 87	1.20	1.76	× 15	0.42	0.63
× 79	1.10	1.61	× 12	0.43	0.60
× 72	1.00	1.48	× 9	0.33	0.46
× 65	0.91	1.35			
× 58	0.91	1.31	W5 × 19	0.64	0.93
× 53	0.84	1.20	× 16	0.54	0.80
× 50	0.89	1.23			
× 45	0.81	1.12	W4 × 13	0.54	0.79
× 40	0.72	1.00			

For SI: 1 pound per linear foot per inch = 0.059 kg/m/mm.

**TABLE 721.5.1(2)
PROPERTIES OF CONCRETE**

PROPERTY	NORMAL-WEIGHT CONCRETE	STRUCTURAL LIGHTWEIGHT CONCRETE
Thermal conductivity (k_c)	0.95 Btu/hr · ft · °F	0.35 Btu/hr · ft · °F
Specific heat (c_c)	0.20 Btu/lb °F	0.20 Btu/lb °F
Density (P_c)	145 lb/ft^3	110 lb/ft^3
Equilibrium (free) moisture content (m) by volume	4%	5%

For SI: 1 inch = 25.4 mm, 1 foot = 304.8 mm, 1 lb/ft^3 = 16.0185 kg/m^3, Btu/hr · ft · °F = 1.731 W/(m · K).

**TABLE 721.5.1(3)
THERMAL CONDUCTIVITY OF CONCRETE OR CLAY MASONRY UNITS**

DENSITY (d_m) OF UNITS (lb/ft^3)	THERMAL CONDUCTIVITY (K) OF UNITS (Btu/hr · ft · °F)
Concrete Masonry Units	
80	0.207
85	0.228
90	0.252
95	0.278
100	0.308
105	0.340
110	0.376
115	0.416
120	0.459
125	0.508
130	0.561
135	0.620
140	0.685
145	0.758
150	0.837
Clay Masonry Units	
120	1.25
130	2.25

For SI: 1 pound per cubic foot = 16.0185 kg/m^3, Btu/hr · ft · °F = 1.731 W/(m · K).

TABLE 721.5.1(4)
WEIGHT-TO-HEATED-PERIMETER RATIOS (*W/D*)
FOR TYPICAL WIDE FLANGE BEAM AND GIRDER SHAPES

STRUCTURAL SHAPE	CONTOUR PROFILE	BOX PROFILE	STRUCTURAL SHAPE	CONTOUR PROFILE	BOX PROFILE
W36 × 300	2.47	3.33	W24 × 68	0.92	1.21
× 280	2.31	3.12	× 62	0.92	1.14
× 260	2.16	2.92	× 55	0.82	1.02
× 245	2.04	2.76			
× 230	1.92	2.61	W21 × 147	1.83	2.60
× 210	1.94	2.45	× 132	1.66	2.35
× 194	1.80	2.28	× 122	1.54	2.19
× 182	1.69	2.15	× 111	1.41	2.01
× 170	1.59	2.01	× 101	1.29	1.84
× 160	1.50	1.90	× 93	1.38	1.80
× 150	1.41	1.79	× 83	1.24	1.62
× 135	1.28	1.63	× 73	1.10	1.44
			× 68	1.03	1.35
W33 × 241	2.11	2.86	× 62	0.94	1.23
× 221	1.94	2.64	× 57	0.93	1.17
× 201	1.78	2.42	× 50	0.83	1.04
× 152	1.51	1.94	× 44	0.73	0.92
× 141	1.41	1.80			
× 130	1.31	1.67	W18 × 119	1.69	2.42
× 118	1.19	1.53	× 106	1.52	2.18
			× 97	1.39	2.01
W30 × 211	2.00	2.74	× 86	1.24	1.80
× 191	1.82	2.50	× 76	1.11	1.60
× 173	1.66	2.28	× 71	1.21	1.59
× 132	1.45	1.85	× 65	1.11	1.47
× 124	1.37	1.75	× 60	1.03	1.36
× 116	1.28	1.65	× 55	0.95	1.26
× 108	1.20	1.54	× 50	0.87	1.15
× 99	1.10	1.42	× 46	0.86	1.09
			× 40	0.75	0.96
W27 × 178	1.85	2.55	× 35	0.66	0.85
× 161	1.68	2.33			
× 146	1.53	2.12	W16 × 100	1.56	2.25
× 114	1.36	1.76	× 89	1.40	2.03
× 102	1.23	1.59	× 77	1.22	1.78
× 94	1.13	1.47	× 67	1.07	1.56
× 84	1.02	1.33	× 57	1.07	1.43
			× 50	0.94	1.26
			× 45	0.85	1.15
W24 × 162	1.85	2.57	× 40	0.76	1.03
× 146	1.68	2.34	× 36	0.69	0.93
× 131	1.52	2.12	× 31	0.65	0.83
× 117	1.36	1.91	× 26	0.55	0.70
× 104	1.22	1.71			
× 94	1.26	1.63	W14 × 132	1.83	3.00
× 84	1.13	1.47	× 120	1.67	2.75
× 76	1.03	1.34	× 109	1.53	2.52

(continued)

TABLE 721.5.1(4)—continued
WEIGHT-TO-HEATED-PERIMETER RATIOS (*W/D*)
FOR TYPICAL WIDE FLANGE BEAM AND GIRDER SHAPES

STRUCTURAL SHAPE	CONTOUR PROFILE	BOX PROFILE
W14 × 99	1.39	2.31
× 90	1.27	2.11
× 82	1.41	2.12
× 74	1.28	1.93
× 68	1.19	1.78
× 61	1.07	1.61
× 53	1.03	1.48
× 48	0.94	1.35
× 43	0.85	1.22
× 38	0.79	1.09
× 34	0.71	0.98
× 30	0.63	0.87
× 26	0.61	0.79
× 22	0.52	0.68
W12 × 87	1.44	2.34
× 79	1.32	2.14
× 72	1.20	1.97
× 65	1.09	1.79
× 58	1.08	1.69
× 53	0.99	1.55
× 50	1.04	1.54
× 45	0.95	1.40
× 40	0.85	1.25
× 35	0.79	1.11
× 30	0.69	0.96
× 26	0.60	0.84
× 22	0.61	0.77
× 19	0.53	0.67
× 16	0.45	0.57
× 14	0.40	0.50
W10 × 112	2.14	3.38
× 100	1.93	3.07
× 88	1.70	2.75
× 77	1.52	2.45
× 68	1.35	2.20
× 60	1.20	1.97
× 54	1.09	1.79
× 49	0.99	1.64
× 45	1.03	1.59
× 39	0.94	1.40
× 33	0.77	1.20
W10 × 30	0.79	1.12
× 26	0.69	0.98
× 22	0.59	0.84
× 19	0.59	0.78
× 17	0.54	0.70
× 15	0.48	0.63
× 12	0.38	0.51
W8 × 67	1.61	2.55
× 58	1.41	2.26
× 48	1.18	1.91
× 40	1.00	1.63
× 35	0.88	1.44
× 31	0.79	1.29
× 28	0.80	1.24
× 24	0.69	1.07
× 21	0.66	0.96
× 18	0.57	0.84
× 15	0.54	0.74
× 13	0.47	0.65
× 10	0.37	0.51
W6 × 25	0.82	1.33
× 20	0.67	1.09
× 16	0.66	0.96
× 15	0.51	0.83
× 12	0.51	0.75
× 9	0.39	0.57
W5 × 19	0.76	1.24
× 16	0.65	1.07
W4 × 13	0.65	1.05

For SI: Pounds per linear foot per inch = 0.059 kg/m/mm.

TABLE 721.5.1(5)
FIRE RESISTANCE OF CONCRETE MASONRY PROTECTED STEEL COLUMNS

COLUMN SIZE	CONCRETE MASONRY DENSITY POUNDS PER CUBIC FOOT	MINIMUM REQUIRED EQUIVALENT THICKNESS FOR FIRE-RESISTANCE RATING OF CONCRETE MASONRY PROTECTION ASSEMBLY, T_e (inches)				COLUMN SIZE	CONCRETE MASONRY DENSITY POUNDS PER CUBIC FOOT	MINIMUM REQUIRED EQUIVALENT THICKNESS FOR FIRE-RESISTANCE RATING OF CONCRETE MASONRY PROTECTION ASSEMBLY, T_e (inches)			
		1-hour	2-hour	3-hour	4-hour			1-hour	2-hour	3-hour	4-hour
W14 × 82	80	0.74	1.61	2.36	3.04	W10 × 68	80	0.72	1.58	2.33	3.01
	100	0.89	1.85	2.67	3.40		100	0.87	1.83	2.65	3.38
	110	0.96	1.97	2.81	3.57		110	0.94	1.95	2.79	3.55
	120	1.03	2.08	2.95	3.73		120	1.01	2.06	2.94	3.72
W14 × 68	80	0.83	1.70	2.45	3.13	W10 × 54	80	0.88	1.76	2.53	3.21
	100	0.99	1.95	2.76	3.49		100	1.04	2.01	2.83	3.57
	110	1.06	2.06	2.91	3.66		110	1.11	2.12	2.98	3.73
	120	1.14	2.18	3.05	3.82		120	1.19	2.24	3.12	3.90
W14 × 53	80	0.91	1.81	2.58	3.27	W10 × 45	80	0.92	1.83	2.60	3.30
	100	1.07	2.05	2.88	3.62		100	1.08	2.07	2.90	3.64
	110	1.15	2.17	3.02	3.78		110	1.16	2.18	3.04	3.80
	120	1.22	2.28	3.16	3.94		120	1.23	2.29	3.18	3.96
W14 × 43	80	1.01	1.93	2.71	3.41	W10 × 33	80	1.06	2.00	2.79	3.49
	100	1.17	2.17	3.00	3.74		100	1.22	2.23	3.07	3.81
	110	1.25	2.28	3.14	3.90		110	1.30	2.34	3.20	3.96
	120	1.32	2.38	3.27	4.05		120	1.37	2.44	3.33	4.12
W12 × 72	80	0.81	1.66	2.41	3.09	W8 × 40	80	0.94	1.85	2.63	3.33
	100	0.91	1.88	2.70	3.43		100	1.10	2.10	2.93	3.67
	110	0.99	1.99	2.84	3.60		110	1.18	2.21	3.07	3.83
	120	1.06	2.10	2.98	3.76		120	1.25	2.32	3.20	3.99
W12 × 58	80	0.88	1.76	2.52	3.21	W8 × 31	80	1.06	2.00	2.78	3.49
	100	1.04	2.01	2.83	3.56		100	1.22	2.23	3.07	3.81
	110	1.11	2.12	2.97	3.73		110	1.29	2.33	3.20	3.97
	120	1.19	2.23	3.11	3.89		120	1.36	2.44	3.33	4.12
W12 × 50	80	0.91	1.81	2.58	3.27	W8 × 24	80	1.14	2.09	2.89	3.59
	100	1.07	2.05	2.88	3.62		100	1.29	2.31	3.16	3.90
	110	1.15	2.17	3.02	3.78		110	1.36	2.42	3.28	4.05
	120	1.22	2.28	3.16	3.94		120	1.43	2.52	3.41	4.20
W12 × 40	80	1.01	1.94	2.72	3.41	W8 × 18	80	1.22	2.20	3.01	3.72
	100	1.17	2.17	3.01	3.75		100	1.36	2.40	3.25	4.01
	110	1.25	2.28	3.14	3.90		110	1.42	2.50	3.37	4.14
	120	1.32	2.39	3.27	4.06		120	1.48	2.59	3.49	4.28

(continued)

TABLE 721.5.1(5)—continued
FIRE RESISTANCE OF CONCRETE MASONRY PROTECTED STEEL COLUMNS

NOMINAL TUBE SIZE (inches)	CONCRETE MASONRY DENSITY, POUNDS PER CUBIC FOOT	MINIMUM REQUIRED EQUIVALENT THICKNESS FOR FIRE-RESISTANCE RATING OF CONCRETE MASONRY PROTECTION ASSEMBLY, T_e (inches)				NOMINAL PIPE SIZE (inches)	CONCRETE MASONRY DENSITY, POUNDS PER CUBIC FOOT	MINIMUM REQUIRED EQUIVALENT THICKNESS FOR FIRE-RESISTANCE RATING OF CONCRETE MASONRY PROTECTION ASSEMBLY, T_e (inches)			
		1-hour	2-hour	3-hour	4-hour			1-hour	2-hour	3-hour	4-hour
4 × 4 × 1/2 wall thickness	80	0.93	1.90	2.71	3.43	4 double extra strong 0.674 wall thickness	80	0.80	1.75	2.56	3.28
	100	1.08	2.13	2.99	3.76		100	0.95	1.99	2.85	3.62
	110	1.16	2.24	3.13	3.91		110	1.02	2.10	2.99	3.78
	120	1.22	2.34	3.26	4.06		120	1.09	2.20	3.12	3.93
4 × 4 × 3/8 wall thickness	80	1.05	2.03	2.84	3.57	4 extra strong 0.337 wall thickness	80	1.12	2.11	2.93	3.65
	100	1.20	2.25	3.11	3.88		100	1.26	2.32	3.19	3.95
	110	1.27	2.35	3.24	4.02		110	1.33	2.42	3.31	4.09
	120	1.34	2.45	3.37	4.17		120	1.40	2.52	3.43	4.23
4 × 4 × 1/4 wall thickness	80	1.21	2.20	3.01	3.73	4 standard 0.237 wall thickness	80	1.26	2.25	3.07	3.79
	100	1.35	2.40	3.26	4.02		100	1.40	2.45	3.31	4.07
	110	1.41	2.50	3.38	4.16		110	1.46	2.55	3.43	4.21
	120	1.48	2.59	3.50	4.30		120	1.53	2.64	3.54	4.34
6 × 6 × 1/2 wall thickness	80	0.82	1.75	2.54	3.25	5 double extra strong 0.750 wall thickness	80	0.70	1.61	2.40	3.12
	100	0.98	1.99	2.84	3.59		100	0.85	1.86	2.71	3.47
	110	1.05	2.10	2.98	3.75		110	0.91	1.97	2.85	3.63
	120	1.12	2.21	3.11	3.91		120	0.98	2.02	2.99	3.79
6 × 6 × 3/8 wall thickness	80	0.96	1.91	2.71	3.42	5 extra strong 0.375 wall thickness	80	1.04	2.01	2.83	3.54
	100	1.12	2.14	3.00	3.75		100	1.19	2.23	3.09	3.85
	110	1.19	2.25	3.13	3.90		110	1.26	2.34	3.22	4.00
	120	1.26	2.35	3.26	4.05		120	1.32	2.44	3.34	4.14
6 × 6 × 1/4 wall thickness	80	1.14	2.11	2.92	3.63	5 standard 0.258 wall thickness	80	1.20	2.19	3.00	3.72
	100	1.29	2.32	3.18	3.93		100	1.34	2.39	3.25	4.00
	110	1.36	2.43	3.30	4.08		110	1.41	2.49	3.37	4.14
	120	1.42	2.52	3.43	4.22		120	1.47	2.58	3.49	4.28
8 × 8 × 1/2 wall thickness	80	0.77	1.66	2.44	3.13	6 double extra strong 0.864 wall thickness	80	0.59	1.46	2.23	2.92
	100	0.92	1.91	2.75	3.49		100	0.73	1.71	2.54	3.29
	110	1.00	2.02	2.89	3.66		110	0.80	1.82	2.69	3.47
	120	1.07	2.14	3.03	3.82		120	0.86	1.93	2.83	3.63
8 × 8 × 3/8 wall thickness	80	0.91	1.84	2.63	3.33	6 extra strong 0.432 wall thickness	80	0.94	1.90	2.70	3.42
	100	1.07	2.08	2.92	3.67		100	1.10	2.13	2.98	3.74
	110	1.14	2.19	3.06	3.83		110	1.17	2.23	3.11	3.89
	120	1.21	2.29	3.19	3.98		120	1.24	2.34	3.24	4.04
8 × 8 × 1/4 wall thickness	80	1.10	2.06	2.86	3.57	6 standard 0.280 wall thickness	80	1.14	2.12	2.93	3.64
	100	1.25	2.28	3.13	3.87		100	1.29	2.33	3.19	3.94
	110	1.32	2.38	3.25	4.02		110	1.36	2.43	3.31	4.08
	120	1.39	2.48	3.38	4.17		120	1.42	2.53	3.43	4.22

For SI: 1 inch = 25.4 mm, 1 pound per cubic feet = 16.02 kg/m^3.

Note: Tabulated values assume 1-inch air gap between masonry and steel section.

TABLE 721.5.1(6)
FIRE RESISTANCE OF CLAY MASONRY PROTECTED STEEL COLUMNS

COLUMN SIZE	CLAY MASONRY DENSITY, POUNDS PER CUBIC FOOT	MINIMUM REQUIRED EQUIVALENT THICKNESS FOR FIRE-RESISTANCE RATING OF CLAY MASONRY PROTECTION ASSEMBLY, T_e (inches)			
		1-hour	2-hour	3-hour	4-hour
W14 × 82	120	1.23	2.42	3.41	4.29
	130	1.40	2.70	3.78	4.74
W14 × 68	120	1.34	2.54	3.54	4.43
	130	1.51	2.82	3.91	4.87
W14 × 53	120	1.43	2.65	3.65	4.54
	130	1.61	2.93	4.02	4.98
W14 × 43	120	1.54	2.76	3.77	4.66
	130	1.72	3.04	4.13	5.09
W12 × 72	120	1.32	2.52	3.51	4.40
	130	1.50	2.80	3.88	4.84
W12 × 58	120	1.40	2.61	3.61	4.50
	130	1.57	2.89	3.98	4.94
W12 × 50	120	1.43	2.65	3.66	4.55
	130	1.61	2.93	4.02	4.99
W12 × 40	120	1.54	2.77	3.78	4.67
	130	1.72	3.05	4.14	5.10

COLUMN SIZE	CLAY MASONRY DENSITY, POUNDS PER CUBIC FOOT	MINIMUM REQUIRED EQUIVALENT THICKNESS FOR FIRE-RESISTANCE RATING OF CLAY MASONRY PROTECTION ASSEMBLY, T_e (inches)			
		1-hour	2-hour	3-hour	4-hour
W10 × 68	120	1.27	2.46	3.26	4.35
	130	1.44	2.75	3.83	4.80
W10 × 54	120	1.40	2.61	3.62	4.51
	130	1.58	2.89	3.98	4.95
W10 × 45	120	1.44	2.66	3.67	4.57
	130	1.62	2.95	4.04	5.01
W10 × 33	120	1.59	2.82	3.84	4.73
	130	1.77	3.10	4.20	5.13
W8 × 40	120	1.47	2.70	3.71	4.61
	130	1.65	2.98	4.08	5.04
W8 × 31	120	1.59	2.82	3.84	4.73
	130	1.77	3.10	4.20	5.17
W8 × 24	120	1.66	2.90	3.92	4.82
	130	1.84	3.18	4.28	5.25
W8 × 18	120	1.75	3.00	4.01	4.91
	130	1.93	3.27	4.37	5.34

STEEL TUBING

NOMINAL TUBE SIZE (inches)	CLAY MASONRY DENSITY, POUNDS PER CUBIC FOOT	MINIMUM REQUIRED EQUIVALENT THICKNESS FOR FIRE-RESISTANCE RATING OF CLAY MASONRY PROTECTION ASSEMBLY, T_e (inches)			
		1-hour	2-hour	3-hour	4-hour
4 × 4 × $^{1}/_{2}$ wall thickness	120	1.44	2.72	3.76	4.68
	130	1.62	3.00	4.12	5.11
4 × 4 × $^{3}/_{8}$ wall thickness	120	1.56	2.84	3.88	4.78
	130	1.74	3.12	4.23	5.21
4 × 4 × $^{1}/_{4}$ wall thickness	120	1.72	2.99	4.02	4.92
	130	1.89	3.26	4.37	5.34
6 × 6 × $^{1}/_{2}$ wall thickness	120	1.33	2.58	3.62	4.52
	130	1.50	2.86	3.98	4.96
6 × 6 × $^{3}/_{8}$ wall thickness	120	1.48	2.74	3.76	4.67
	130	1.65	3.01	4.13	5.10
6 × 6 × $^{1}/_{4}$ wall thickness	120	1.66	2.91	3.94	4.84
	130	1.83	3.19	4.30	5.27
8 × 8 × $^{1}/_{2}$ wall thickness	120	1.27	2.50	3.52	4.42
	130	1.44	2.78	3.89	4.86
8 × 8 × $^{3}/_{8}$ wall thickness	120	1.43	2.67	3.69	4.59
	130	1.60	2.95	4.05	5.02
8 × 8 × $^{1}/_{4}$ wall thickness	120	1.62	2.87	3.89	4.78
	130	1.79	3.14	4.24	5.21

STEEL PIPE

NOMINAL PIPE SIZE (inches)	CLAY MASONRY DENSITY, POUNDS PER CUBIC FOOT	MINIMUM REQUIRED EQUIVALENT THICKNESS FOR FIRE-RESISTANCE RATING OF CLAY MASONRY PROTECTION ASSEMBLY, T_e (inches)			
		1-hour	2-hour	3-hour	4-hour
4 double extra strong 0.674 wall thickness	120	1.26	2.55	3.60	4.52
	130	1.42	2.82	3.96	4.95
4 extra strong 0.337 wall thickness	120	1.60	2.89	3.92	4.83
	130	1.77	3.16	4.28	5.25
4 standard 0.237 wall thickness	120	1.74	3.02	4.05	4.95
	130	1.92	3.29	4.40	5.37
5 double extra strong 0.750 wall thickness	120	1.17	2.44	3.48	4.40
	130	1.33	2.72	3.84	4.83
5 extra strong 0.375 wall thickness	120	1.55	2.82	3.85	4.76
	130	1.72	3.09	4.21	5.18
5 standard 0.258 wall thickness	120	1.71	2.97	4.00	4.90
	130	1.88	3.24	4.35	5.32
6 double extra strong 0.864 wall thickness	120	1.04	2.28	3.32	4.23
	130	1.19	2.60	3.68	4.67
6 extra strong 0.432 wall thickness	120	1.45	2.71	3.75	4.65
	130	1.62	2.99	4.10	5.08
6 standard 0.280 wall thickness	120	1.65	2.91	3.94	4.84
	130	1.82	3.19	4.30	5.27

For SI: 1 inch = 25.4 mm, 1 pound per cubic feet = 16.02 kg/m^3.

**TABLE 721.5.1(7)
MINIMUM COVER (inch) FOR STEEL COLUMNS
ENCASED IN NORMAL-WEIGHT CONCRETE[a]
[FIGURE 721.5.1(6)(c)]**

<table>
<tr><th rowspan="2">STRUCTURAL SHAPE</th><th colspan="5">FIRE-RESISTANCE RATING (hours)</th></tr>
<tr><th>1</th><th>1 1/2</th><th>2</th><th>3</th><th>4</th></tr>
<tr><td>W14 × 233</td><td rowspan="7">1</td><td rowspan="5">1</td><td rowspan="3">1</td><td rowspan="2">1 1/2</td><td>2</td></tr>
<tr><td>× 176</td><td rowspan="3">2 1/2</td></tr>
<tr><td>× 132</td><td rowspan="3">2</td></tr>
<tr><td>× 90</td><td rowspan="4">1 1/2</td></tr>
<tr><td>× 61</td><td rowspan="3">3</td></tr>
<tr><td>× 48</td><td rowspan="2">1 1/2</td><td rowspan="2">2 1/2</td></tr>
<tr><td>× 43</td></tr>
<tr><td>W12 × 152</td><td rowspan="5">1</td><td rowspan="2">1</td><td rowspan="2">1</td><td rowspan="3">2</td><td rowspan="2">2 1/2</td></tr>
<tr><td>× 96</td></tr>
<tr><td>× 65</td><td rowspan="3">1 1/2</td><td rowspan="3">1 1/2</td><td rowspan="3">3</td></tr>
<tr><td>× 50</td><td rowspan="2">2 1/2</td></tr>
<tr><td>× 40</td></tr>
<tr><td>W10 × 88</td><td>1</td><td rowspan="5">1 1/2</td><td rowspan="4">1 1/2</td><td>2</td><td rowspan="3">3</td></tr>
<tr><td>× 49</td><td rowspan="4">1</td><td rowspan="4">2 1/2</td></tr>
<tr><td>× 45</td></tr>
<tr><td>× 39</td><td rowspan="2">3 1/2</td></tr>
<tr><td>× 33</td><td>2</td></tr>
<tr><td>W8 × 67</td><td rowspan="6">1</td><td rowspan="2">1</td><td rowspan="3">1 1/2</td><td rowspan="3">2 1/2</td><td rowspan="2">3</td></tr>
<tr><td>× 58</td></tr>
<tr><td>× 48</td><td rowspan="4">1 1/2</td><td rowspan="3">3 1/2</td></tr>
<tr><td>× 31</td><td rowspan="3">2</td><td rowspan="3">3</td></tr>
<tr><td>× 21</td></tr>
<tr><td>× 18</td><td>4</td></tr>
<tr><td>W6 × 25</td><td rowspan="3">1</td><td>1 1/2</td><td>2</td><td rowspan="3">3</td><td>3 1/2</td></tr>
<tr><td>× 20</td><td rowspan="4">2</td><td rowspan="4">2 1/2</td><td rowspan="4">4</td></tr>
<tr><td>× 16</td></tr>
<tr><td>× 15</td><td rowspan="2">1 1/2</td><td rowspan="2">3 1/2</td></tr>
<tr><td>× 9</td></tr>
</table>

For SI: 1 inch = 25.4 mm.

a. The tabulated thicknesses are based upon the assumed properties of normal-weight concrete given in Table 721.5.1(2).

**TABLE 721.5.1(8)
MINIMUM COVER (inch) FOR STEEL COLUMNS
ENCASED IN STRUCTURAL LIGHTWEIGHT CONCRETE[a]
[FIGURE 721.5.1(6)(c)]**

<table>
<tr><th rowspan="2">STRUCTURAL SHAPE</th><th colspan="5">FIRE-RESISTANCE RATING (HOURS)</th></tr>
<tr><th>1</th><th>1 1/2</th><th>2</th><th>3</th><th>4</th></tr>
<tr><td>W14 × 233</td><td rowspan="5">1</td><td rowspan="5">1</td><td rowspan="4">1</td><td>1</td><td rowspan="2">1 1/2</td></tr>
<tr><td>× 193</td><td rowspan="3">1 1/2</td></tr>
<tr><td>× 74</td><td>2</td></tr>
<tr><td>× 61</td><td rowspan="2">2 1/2</td></tr>
<tr><td>× 43</td><td>1 1/2</td><td>2</td></tr>
<tr><td>W12 × 65</td><td rowspan="3">1</td><td rowspan="3">1</td><td rowspan="2">1</td><td>1 1/2</td><td>2</td></tr>
<tr><td>× 53</td><td rowspan="2">2</td><td rowspan="2">2 1/2</td></tr>
<tr><td>× 40</td><td>1 1/2</td></tr>
<tr><td>W10 × 112</td><td rowspan="4">1</td><td rowspan="4">1</td><td rowspan="3">1</td><td rowspan="2">1 1/2</td><td rowspan="2">2</td></tr>
<tr><td>× 88</td></tr>
<tr><td>× 60</td><td rowspan="2">2</td><td rowspan="2">2 1/2</td></tr>
<tr><td>× 33</td><td>1 1/2</td></tr>
<tr><td>W8 × 35</td><td rowspan="4">1</td><td rowspan="3">1</td><td rowspan="4">1 1/2</td><td rowspan="2">2</td><td>2 1/2</td></tr>
<tr><td>× 28</td><td rowspan="3">3</td></tr>
<tr><td>× 24</td><td rowspan="2">2 1/2</td></tr>
<tr><td>× 18</td><td>1 1/2</td></tr>
</table>

For SI: 1 inch = 25.4 mm.

a. The tabulated thicknesses are based upon the assumed properties of structural lightweight concrete given in Table 721.5.1(2).

**TABLE 721.5.1(9)
MINIMUM COVER (inch) FOR STEEL COLUMNS
IN NORMAL-WEIGHT PRECAST COVERS[a]
[FIGURE 721.5.1(6)(a)]**

STRUCTURAL SHAPE	FIRE-RESISTANCE RATING (hours)				
	1	1 1/2	2	3	4
W14 × 233			1 1/2		3
× 211				2 1/2	
× 176					3 1/2
× 145		1 1/2	2		
× 109	1 1/2			3	
× 99					
× 61					4
× 43		2	2 1/2	3 1/2	4 1/2
W12 × 190			1 1/2	2 1/2	3 1/2
× 152					
× 120		1 1/2	2		
× 96				3	
× 87	1 1/2				4
× 58					
× 40		2	2 1/2	3 1/2	4 1/2
W10 × 112					3 1/2
× 88		1 1/2	2	3	
× 77	1 1/2				4
× 54		2	2 1/2	3 1/2	
× 33					4 1/2
W8 × 67		1 1/2	2	3	
× 58					4
× 48	1 1/2	2	2 1/2	3 1/2	
× 28					
× 21					4 1/2
× 18		2 1/2	3	4	
W6 × 25		2	2 1/2	3 1/2	
× 20	1 1/2				4 1/2
× 16			3		
× 12	2	2 1/2		4	
× 9					5

For SI: 1 inch = 25.4 mm.

a. The tabulated thicknesses are based upon the assumed properties of normal-weight concrete given in Table 721.5.1(2).

**TABLE 721.5.1(10)
MINIMUM COVER (inch) FOR STEEL COLUMNS
IN STRUCTURAL LIGHTWEIGHT PRECAST COVERS[a]
[FIGURE 721.5.1(6)(a)]**

STRUCTURAL SHAPE	FIRE-RESISTANCE RATING (hours)				
	1	1 1/2	2	3	4
W14 × 233					2 1/2
× 176				2	
× 145			1 1/2		
× 132	1 1/2	1 1/2			3
× 109					
× 99				2 1/2	
× 68			2		
× 43				3	3 1/2
W12 × 190					2 1/2
× 152				2	
× 136			1 1/2		3
× 106					
× 96	1 1/2	1 1/2		2 1/2	
× 87					
× 65			2		
× 40				3	3 1/2
W10 × 112				2	
× 100			1 1/2		3
× 88					
× 77	1 1/2	1 1/2		2 1/2	
× 60			2		
× 39				3	3 1/2
× 33		2			
W8 × 67			1 1/2	2 1/2	3
× 48		1 1/2			
× 35	1 1/2		2		3 1/2
× 28				3	
× 18		2	2 1/2		4
W6 × 25			2	3	3 1/2
× 15	1 1/2	2			4
× 9			2 1/2	3 1/2	

For SI: 1 inch = 25.4 mm.

a. The tabulated thicknesses are based upon the assumed properties of structural lightweight concrete given in Table 721.5.1(2).

accordance with the AISC *Specification for Structural Steel Buildings*, (AISC 360-05).

721.5.2.3 Structural steel trusses. The *fire resistance* of structural steel trusses protected with fire-resistant materials sprayed to each of the individual truss elements shall be permitted to be determined in accordance with this section. The thickness of the fire-resistant material shall be determined in accordance with Section 721.5.1.3. The weight-to-heated-perimeter ratio (*W/D*) of truss elements that can be simultaneously exposed to fire on all sides shall be determined on the same basis as columns, as specified in Section 721.5.1.1. The weight-to-heated-perimeter ratio (*W/D*) of truss elements that directly support floor or roof assembly shall be determined on the same basis as beams and girders, as specified in Section 721.5.2.1.

The *fire resistance* of structural steel trusses protected with intumescent or mastic fire-resistant coatings shall be determined on the basis of fire-resistance tests in accordance with Section 703.2.

721.6 Wood assemblies. The provisions of this section contain procedures by which the *fire-resistance ratings* of wood assemblies are established by calculations.

721.6.1 General. This section contains procedures for calculating the fire-resistance ratings of walls, floor/ceiling and roof/ceiling assemblies based in part on the standard method of testing referenced in Section 703.2.

721.6.1.1 Maximum fire-resistance rating. Fire resistance ratings calculated for assemblies using the methods in Section 721.6 shall be limited to a maximum of 1 hour.

721.6.1.2 Dissimilar membranes. Where dissimilar membranes are used on a wall assembly, the calculation shall be made from the least fire-resistant (weaker) side.

721.6.2 Walls, floors and roofs. These procedures apply to both load-bearing and nonload-bearing assemblies.

721.6.2.1 Fire-resistance rating of wood frame assemblies. The fire-resistance rating of a wood frame assembly is equal to the sum of the time assigned to the membrane on the fire-exposed side, the time assigned to the framing members and the time assigned for additional contribution by other protective measures such as insulation. The membrane on the unexposed side shall not be included in determining the *fire resistance* of the assembly.

721.6.2.2 Time assigned to membranes. Table 721.6.2(1) indicates the time assigned to membranes on the fire-exposed side.

721.6.2.3 Exterior walls. For an *exterior wall* with a *fire separation distance* greater than 5 feet (1524 mm), the wall is assigned a rating dependent on the interior membrane and the framing as described in Tables 721.6.2(1) and 721.6.2(2). The membrane on the outside of the nonfire-exposed side of *exterior walls* with a *fire separation distance* greater than 5 feet (1524 mm) may consist of sheathing, sheathing paper and siding as described in Table 721.6.2(3).

TABLE 721.6.2(1)
TIME ASSIGNED TO WALLBOARD MEMBRANES[a, b, c, d]

DESCRIPTION OF FINISH	TIME[e] (minutes)
$^3/_8$-inch wood structural panel bonded with exterior glue	5
$^{15}/_{32}$-inch wood structural panel bonded with exterior glue	10
$^{19}/_{32}$-inch wood structural panel bonded with exterior glue	15
$^3/_8$-inch gypsum wallboard	10
$^1/_2$-inch gypsum wallboard	15
$^5/_8$-inch gypsum wallboard	30
$^1/_2$-inch Type X gypsum wallboard	25
$^5/_8$-inch Type X gypsum wallboard	40
Double $^3/_8$-inch gypsum wallboard	25
$^1/_2$-inch + $^3/_8$-inch gypsum wallboard	35
Double $^1/_2$-inch gypsum wallboard	40

For SI: 1 inch = 25.4 mm.

a. These values apply only when membranes are installed on framing members which are spaced 16 inches o.c.

b. Gypsum wallboard installed over framing or furring shall be installed so that all edges are supported, except $^5/_8$-inch Type X gypsum wallboard shall be permitted to be installed horizontally with the horizontal joints staggered 24 inches each side and unsupported but finished.

c. On wood frame floor/ceiling or roof/ceiling assemblies, gypsum board shall be installed with the long dimension perpendicular to framing members and shall have all joints finished.

d. The membrane on the unexposed side shall not be included in determining the fire resistance of the assembly. When dissimilar membranes are used on a wall assembly, the calculation shall be made from the least fire-resistant (weaker) side.

e. The time assigned is not a finished rating.

721.6.2.4 Floors and roofs. In the case of a floor or roof, the standard test provides only for testing for fire exposure from below. Except as noted in Section 703.3, Item 5, floor or roof assemblies of wood framing shall have an upper membrane consisting of a subfloor and finished floor conforming to Table 721.6.2(4) or any other membrane that has a contribution to *fire resistance* of at least 15 minutes in Table 721.6.2(1).

721.6.2.5 Additional protection. Table 721.6.2(5) indicates the time increments to be added to the *fire resistance* where glass fiber, rockwool, slag mineral wool or cellulose insulation is incorporated in the assembly.

721.6.2.6 Fastening. Fastening of wood frame assemblies and the fastening of membranes to the wood framing members shall be done in accordance with Chapter 23.

721.6.3 Design of fire-resistant exposed wood members. The *fire-resistance rating*, in minutes, of timber beams and columns with a minimum nominal dimension of 6 inches (152 mm) is equal to:

TABLE 721.6.2(2)
TIME ASSIGNED FOR CONTRIBUTION OF WOOD FRAME [a, b, c]

DESCRIPTION	TIME ASSIGNED TO FRAME (minutes)
Wood studs 16 inches o.c.	20
Wood floor and roof joists 16 inches o.c.	10

For SI: 1 inch = 25.4 mm.
a. This table does not apply to studs or joists spaced more than 16 inches o.c.
b. All studs shall be nominal 2 × 4 and all joists shall have a nominal thickness of at least 2 inches.
c. Allowable spans for joists shall be determined in accordance with Sections 2308.8, 2308.10.2 and 2308.10.3.

TABLE 721.6.2(3)
MEMBRANE[a] ON EXTERIOR FACE OF WOOD STUD WALLS

SHEATHING	PAPER	EXTERIOR FINISH
$^{5}/_{8}$-inch T & G lumber $^{5}/_{16}$-inch exterior glue wood structural panel $^{1}/_{2}$-inch gypsum wallboard $^{5}/_{8}$-inch gypsum wallboard $^{1}/_{2}$-inch fiberboard	Sheathing paper	Lumber siding Wood shingles and shakes $^{1}/_{4}$-inch wood structural panels—exterior type $^{1}/_{4}$-inch hardboard Metal siding Stucco on metal lath Masonry veneer Vinyl siding
None	—	$^{3}/_{8}$-inch exterior-grade wood structural panels

For SI: 1 inch = 25.4 mm.
a. Any combination of sheathing, paper and exterior finish is permitted.

TABLE 721.6.2(4)
FLOORING OR ROOFING OVER WOOD FRAMING[a]

ASSEMBLY	STRUCTURAL MEMBERS	SUBFLOOR OR ROOF DECK	FINISHED FLOORING OR ROOFING
Floor	Wood	$^{15}/_{32}$-inch wood structural panels or $^{11}/_{16}$ inch T & G softwood	Hardwood or softwood flooring on building paper resilient flooring, parquet floor felted-synthetic fiber floor coverings, carpeting, or ceramic tile on $^{3}/_{8}$-inch-thick panel-type underlay Ceramic tile on $1^{1}/_{4}$-inch mortar bed
Roof	Wood	$^{15}/_{32}$-inch wood structural panels or $^{11}/_{16}$ inch T & G softwood	Finished roofing material with or without insulation

For SI: 1 inch = 25.4 mm.
a. This table applies only to wood joist construction. It is not applicable to wood truss construction.

TABLE 721.6.2(5)
TIME ASSIGNED FOR ADDITIONAL PROTECTION

DESCRIPTION OF ADDITIONAL PROTECTION	FIRE RESISTANCE (minutes)
Add to the fire-resistance rating of wood stud walls if the spaces between the studs are completely filled with glass fiber mineral wool batts weighing not less than 2 pounds per cubic foot (0.6 pound per square foot of wall surface) or rockwool or slag material wool batts weighing not less than 3.3 pounds per cubic foot (1 pound per square foot of wall surface), or cellulose insulation having a nominal density not less than 2.6 pounds per cubic foot.	15

For SI: 1 pound per cubic foot = 16.02 kg/m^3, 1 pound per square foot = 4.882 kg/m^2.

Beams: 2.54*Zb* [4 -2(*b/d*)] for beams which may be exposed to fire on four sides.

(Equation 7-18)

2.54*Zb* [4 -(*b/d*)] for beams which may be exposed to fire on three sides.

(Equation 7-19)

Columns: 2.54*Zd* [3 -(*d/b*)] for columns which may be exposed to fire on four sides

(Equation 7-20)

2.54*Zd* [3 -(*d/2b*)] for columns which may be exposed to fire on three sides.

(Equation 7-21)

where:

b = The breadth (width) of a beam or larger side of a column before exposure to fire (inches).

d = The depth of a beam or smaller side of a column before exposure to fire (inches).

Z = Load factor, based on Figure 721.6.3(1).

721.6.3.1 Equation 7-21. Equation 7-21 applies only where the unexposed face represents the smaller side of the column. If a column is recessed into a wall, its full dimension shall be used for the purpose of these calculations.

721.6.3.2 Allowable loads. Allowable loads on beams and columns are determined using design values given in AF&PA NDS.

721.6.3.3 Fastener protection. Where minimum 1-hour *fire resistance* is required, connectors and fasteners shall be protected from fire exposure by $1^1/_2$ inches (38 mm) of wood, or other *approved* covering or coating for a 1-hour rating. Typical details for commonly used fasteners and connectors are shown in AITC Technical Note 7.

721.6.3.4 Minimum size. Wood members are limited to dimensions of 6 inches (152 mm) nominal or greater. Glued-laminated timber beams utilize standard laminating combinations except that a core lamination is removed. The tension zone is moved inward and the equivalent of an extra nominal 2-inch-thick (51 mm) outer tension lamination is added.

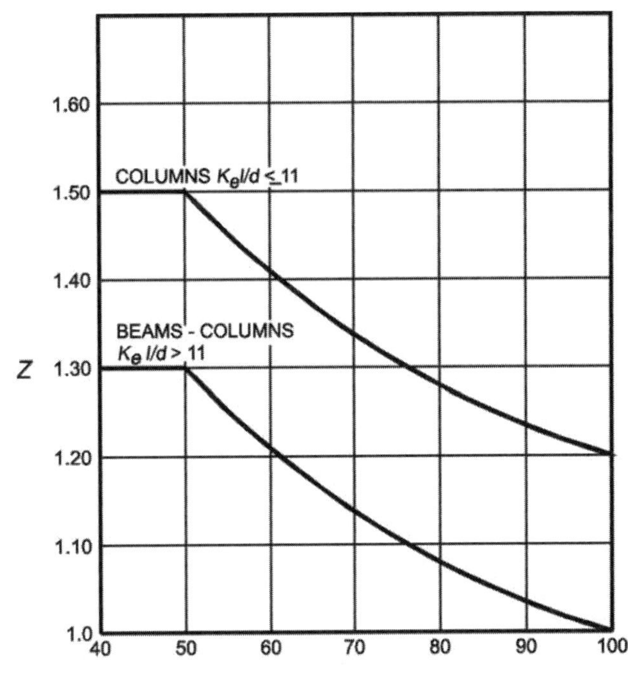

FIGURE 721.6.3(1)
LOAD FIGURE

K_e = The effective length factor as noted in Figure 721.6.3(2).
l = The unsupported length of columns (inches).

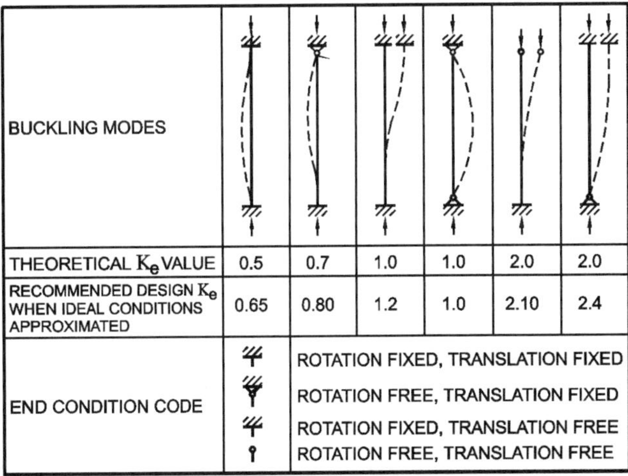

BUCKLING MODES						
THEORETICAL K_e VALUE	0.5	0.7	1.0	1.0	2.0	2.0
RECOMMENDED DESIGN K_e WHEN IDEAL CONDITIONS APPROXIMATED	0.65	0.80	1.2	1.0	2.10	2.4
END CONDITION CODE		ROTATION FIXED, TRANSLATION FIXED				
		ROTATION FREE, TRANSLATION FIXED				
		ROTATION FIXED, TRANSLATION FREE				
		ROTATION FREE, TRANSLATION FREE				

FIGURE 721.6.3(2)
EFFECTIVE LENGTH FACTORS

CHAPTER 8

INTERIOR FINISHES

SECTION 801 GENERAL

801.1 Scope. Provisions of this chapter shall govern the use of materials used as *interior finishes*, *trim* and *decorative materials*.

801.2 Interior wall and ceiling finish. The provisions of Section 803 shall limit the allowable fire performance and smoke development of *interior wall and ceiling finish* materials based on occupancy classification.

801.3 Interior floor finish. The provisions of Section 804 shall limit the allowable fire performance of *interior floor finish* materials based on occupancy classification.

[F] 801.4 Decorative materials and trim. *Decorative materials* and *trim* shall be restricted by combustibility and the flame propagation performance criteria of NFPA 701, in accordance with Section 806.

801.5 Applicability. For buildings in flood hazard areas as established in Section 1612.3, *interior finishes*, *trim* and *decorative materials* below the design flood elevation shall be flood-damage-resistant materials.

801.6 Application. Combustible materials shall be permitted to be used as finish for walls, ceilings, floors and other interior surfaces of buildings.

801.7 Windows. Show windows in the exterior walls of the first *story* above grade shall be permitted to be of wood or of unprotected metal framing.

801.8 Foam plastics. Foam plastics shall not be used as *interior finish* except as provided in Section 803.4. Foam plastics shall not be used as interior *trim* except as provided in Section 806.3 or 2604.2. This section shall apply both to exposed foam plastics and to foam plastics used in conjunction with a textile or vinyl facing or cover.

SECTION 802 DEFINITIONS

802.1 General. The following words and terms shall, for the purposes of this chapter and as used elsewhere in this code, have the meanings shown herein.

EXPANDED VINYL WALL COVERING. Wall covering consisting of a woven textile backing, an expanded vinyl base coat layer and a nonexpanded vinyl skin coat. The expanded base coat layer is a homogeneous vinyl layer that contains a blowing agent. During processing, the blowing agent decomposes, causing this layer to expand by forming closed cells. The total thickness of the wall covering is approximately 0.055 inch to 0.070 inch (1.4 mm to 1.78 mm).

FLAME SPREAD. The propagation of flame over a surface.

FLAME SPREAD INDEX. A comparative measure, expressed as a dimensionless number, derived from visual measurements of the spread of flame versus time for a material tested in accordance with ASTM E 84 or UL 723.

INTERIOR FINISH. *Interior finish* includes *interior wall and ceiling finish* and *interior floor finish*.

INTERIOR FLOOR FINISH. The exposed floor surfaces of buildings including coverings applied over a finished floor or *stair*, including risers.

[F] INTERIOR FLOOR-WALL BASE. Interior floor finish trim used to provide a functional and/or decorative border at the intersection of walls and floors.

INTERIOR WALL AND CEILING FINISH. The exposed interior surfaces of buildings, including but not limited to: fixed or movable walls and partitions; toilet room privacy partitions; columns; ceilings; and interior wainscoting, paneling or other finish applied structurally or for decoration, acoustical correction, surface insulation, structural fire resistance or similar purposes, but not including trim.

SITE-FABRICATED STRETCH SYSTEM. A system, fabricated on site and intended for acoustical, tackable or aesthetic purposes, that is comprised of three elements: (a) a frame (constructed of plastic, wood, metal or other material) used to hold fabric in place, (b) a core material (infill, with the correct properties for the application), and (c) an outside layer, comprised of a textile, fabric or vinyl, that is stretched taut and held in place by tension or mechanical fasteners via the frame.

SMOKE-DEVELOPED INDEX. A comparative measure, expressed as a dimensionless number, derived from measurements of smoke obscuration versus time for a material tested in accordance with ASTM E 84.

TRIM. Picture molds, chair rails, baseboards, handrails, door and window frames and similar decorative or protective materials used in fixed applications.

SECTION 803 WALL AND CEILING FINISHES

803.1 General. *Interior wall and ceiling finish* materials shall be classified for fire performance and smoke development in accordance with Section 803.1.1 or 803.1.2, except as shown in Sections 803.2 through 803.13. Materials tested in accordance with Section 803.1.2 shall not be required to be tested in accordance with Section 803.1.1.

803.1.1 Interior wall and ceiling finish materials. Interior wall and ceiling finish materials shall be classified in accordance with ASTM E 84 or UL 723. Such *interior finish* materials shall be grouped in the following classes in accordance with their flame spread and *smoke-developed indexes*.

Class A: Flame spread index 0-25; smoke-developed index 0-450.

Class B: Flame spread index 26-75; smoke-developed index 0-450.

Class C: Flame spread index 76-200; smoke-developed index 0-450.

Exception: Materials tested in accordance with Section 803.1.2.

803.1.2 Room corner test for interior wall or ceiling finish materials. *Interior wall or ceiling finish* materials shall be permitted to be tested in accordance with NFPA 286. Interior wall or ceiling finish materials tested in accordance with NFPA 286 shall comply with Section 803.1.2.1.

803.1.2.1 Acceptance criteria for NFPA 286. During the 40 kW exposure, the *interior finish* shall comply with Item 1. During the 160 kW exposure, the *interior finish* shall comply with Item 2. During the entire test, the *interior finish* shall comply with Items 3 and 4.

1. During the 40kW exposure, flames shall not spread to the ceiling.
2. During the 160 kW exposure, the *interior finish* shall comply with the following:
   2.1. Flame shall not spread to the outer extremity of the sample on any wall or ceiling.
   2.2. Flashover, as defined in NFPA 286, shall not occur.
3. The peak rate of heat release throughout the NFPA 286 test shall not exceed 800 kW.
4. The total smoke released throughout the NFPA 286 test shall not exceed 1,000 m^2.

803.1.3 Room corner test for textile wall coverings and expanded vinyl wall coverings. Textile wall coverings and expanded vinyl wall coverings shall meet the criteria of Section 803.1.3.1 when tested in the manner intended for use in accordance with the Method B protocol of NFPA 265 using the product-mounting system, including adhesive.

803.1.3.1 Acceptance criteria for NFPA 265. During the 40 kW exposure the *interior finish* shall comply with Item 1. During the 150 kW exposure, the *interior finish* shall comply with Item 2. During the entire test, the *interior finish* shall comply with Item 3.

1. During the 40 kW exposure, flames shall not spread to the ceiling.
2. During the 150 kW exposure, the *interior finish* shall comply with the following:
   2.1. Flame shall not spread to the outer extremities of the samples on the 8-foot by 12-foot (203 mm by 305 mm) walls.
   2.2. Flashover, as described in NFPA 265, shall not occur.
3. The total smoke released throughout the NFPA 265 test shall not exceed 1,000 m^2.

803.1.4 Acceptance criteria for textile and expanded vinyl wall or ceiling coverings tested to ASTM E 84 or UL 723. Textile wall and ceiling coverings and expanded vinyl wall and ceiling coverings shall have a Class A flame spread index in accordance with ASTM E 84 or UL 723 and be protected by an *automatic sprinkler system* installed in accordance with Section 903.3.1.1 or 903.3.1.2. Test specimen preparation and mounting shall be in accordance with ASTM E 2404.

803.2 Thickness exemption. Materials having a thickness less than 0.036 inch (0.9 mm) applied directly to the surface of walls or ceilings shall not be required to be tested.

803.3 Heavy timber exemption. Exposed portions of structural members complying with the requirements for buildings of Type IV construction in Section 602.4 shall not be subject to *interior finish* requirements.

803.4 Foam plastics. Foam plastics shall not be used as *interior finish* except as provided in Section 2603.9. This section shall apply both to exposed foam plastics and to foam plastics used in conjunction with a textile or vinyl facing or cover.

803.5 Textile wall coverings. Where used as interior wall finish materials, textile wall coverings, including materials having woven or nonwoven, napped, tufted, looped or similar surface and carpet and similar textile materials, shall be tested in the manner intended for use, using the product mounting system, including adhesive, and shall comply with the requirements of Section 803.1.2, 803.1.3 or 803.1.4.

803.6 Textile ceiling coverings. Where used as interior ceiling finish materials, textile ceiling coverings, including materials having woven or nonwoven, napped, tufted, looped or similar surface and carpet and similar textile materials, shall be tested in the manner intended for use, using the product mounting system, including adhesive, and shall comply with the requirements of Section 803.1.2 or 803.1.4.

803.7 Expanded vinyl wall coverings. Where used as interior wall finish materials, expanded vinyl wall coverings shall be tested in the manner intended for use, using the product mounting system, including adhesive, and shall comply with the requirements of Section 803.1.2, 803.1.3 or 803.1.4.

803.8 Expanded vinyl ceiling coverings. Where used as interior ceiling finish materials, expanded vinyl ceiling coverings shall be tested in the manner intended for use, using the product mounting system, including adhesive, and shall comply with the requirements of Section 803.1.2 or 803.1.4.

803.9 Interior finish requirements based on group. *Interior wall and ceiling finish* shall have a flame spread index not greater than that specified in Table 803.9 for the group and location designated. *Interior wall and ceiling finish* materials tested in accordance with NFPA 286 and meeting the acceptance criteria of Section 803.1.2.1, shall be permitted to be used where a Class A classification in accordance with ASTM E 84 or UL 723 is required.

803.10 Stability. *Interior finish* materials regulated by this chapter shall be applied or otherwise fastened in such a manner that such materials will not readily become detached where subjected to room temperatures of 200°F (93°C) for not less than 30 minutes.

TABLE 803.9
INTERIOR WALL AND CEILING FINISH REQUIREMENTS BY OCCUPANCY[k]

GROUP	SPRINKLERED[l]			NONSPRINKLERED		
	Exit enclosures and exit passageways[a, b]	Corridors	Rooms and enclosed spaces[c]	Exit enclosures and exit passageways[a, b]	Corridors	Rooms and enclosed spaces[c]
A-1 & A-2	B	B	C	A	A[d]	B[e]
A-3[f], A-4, A-5	B	B	C	A	A[d]	C
B, E, M, R-1	B	C	C	A	B	C
R-4	B	C	C	A	B	B
F	C	C	C	B	C	C
H	B	B	C[g]	A	A	B
I-1	B	C	C	A	B	B
I-2	B	B	B[h, i]	A	A	B
I-3	A	A[j]	C	A	A	B
I-4	B	B	B[h, i]	A	A	B
R-2	C	C	C	B	B	C
R-3	C	C	C	C	C	C
S	C	C	C	B	B	C
U	No restrictions			No restrictions		

For SI: 1 inch = 25.4 mm, 1 square foot = $0.0929 m^2$.

a. Class C interior finish materials shall be permitted for wainscotting or paneling of not more than 1,000 square feet of applied surface area in the grade lobby where applied directly to a noncombustible base or over furring strips applied to a noncombustible base and fireblocked as required by Section 803.11.1.

b. In exit enclosures of buildings less than three stories above grade plane of other than Group I-3, Class B interior finish for nonsprinklered buildings and Class C interior finish for sprinklered buildings shall be permitted.

c. Requirements for rooms and enclosed spaces shall be based upon spaces enclosed by partitions. Where a fire-resistance rating is required for structural elements, the enclosing partitions shall extend from the floor to the ceiling. Partitions that do not comply with this shall be considered enclosing spaces and the rooms or spaces on both sides shall be considered one. In determining the applicable requirements for rooms and enclosed spaces, the specific occupancy thereof shall be the governing factor regardless of the group classification of the building or structure.

d. Lobby areas in Group A-1, A-2 and A-3 occupancies shall not be less than Class B materials.

e. Class C interior finish materials shall be permitted in places of assembly with an occupant load of 300 persons or less.

f. For places of religious worship, wood used for ornamental purposes, trusses, paneling or chancel furnishing shall be permitted.

g. Class B material is required where the building exceeds two stories.

h. Class C interior finish materials shall be permitted in administrative spaces.

i. Class C interior finish materials shall be permitted in rooms with a capacity of four persons or less.

j. Class B materials shall be permitted as wainscotting extending not more than 48 inches above the finished floor in corridors.

k. Finish materials as provided for in other sections of this code.

l. Applies when the exit enclosures, exit passageways, corridors or rooms and enclosed spaces are protected by an automatic sprinkler system installed in accordance with Section 903.3.1.1 or 903.3.1.2.

803.11 Application of interior finish materials to fire-resistance-rated structural elements. Where *interior finish* materials are applied on walls, ceilings or structural elements required to have a *fire-resistance rating* or to be of noncombustible construction, they shall comply with the provisions of this section.

803.11.1 Direct attachment and furred construction. Where walls and ceilings are required by any provision in this code to be of fire-resistance-rated or noncombustible construction, the *interior finish* material shall be applied directly against such construction or to furring strips not exceeding $1^3/_4$ inches (44 mm) applied directly against such surfaces. The intervening spaces between such furring strips shall comply with one of the following:

1. Be filled with material that is inorganic or noncombustible;
2. Be filled with material that meets the requirements of a Class A material in accordance with Section 803.1.1 or 803.1.2; or
3. Be fireblocked at a maximum of 8 feet (2438 mm) in any direction in accordance with Section 717.

803.11.2 Set-out construction. Where walls and ceilings are required to be of fire-resistance-rated or noncombustible construction and walls are set out or ceilings are dropped distances greater than specified in Section 803.11.1, Class A finish materials, in accordance with Section 803.1.1 or 803.1.2, shall be used except where *interior finish* materials are protected on both sides by an *automatic sprinkler system* in accordance with Section 903.3.1.1 or 903.3.1.2, or attached to noncombustible backing or furring strips installed as specified in Section 803.11.1. The hangers and assembly members of such dropped ceilings that are below the main ceiling line shall be of noncombustible materials, except that in Types III and V construction, *fire-retardant-treated wood* shall be permitted. The construction of each set-out wall shall be of fire-resistance-rated construction as required elsewhere in this code.

803.11.3 Heavy timber construction. Wall and ceiling finishes of all classes as permitted in this chapter that are installed directly against the wood decking or planking of Type IV construction or to wood furring strips applied directly to the wood decking or planking shall be fireblocked as specified in Section 803.11.1.

803.11.4 Materials. An interior wall or ceiling finish that is not more than $^1/_4$ inch (6.4 mm) thick shall be applied directly against a noncombustible backing.

Exceptions:

1. Noncombustible materials.
2. Materials where the qualifying tests were made with the material suspended or furred out from the noncombustible backing.

803.12 High-density polyethylene (HDPE). Where high-density polyethylene is used as an *interior finish*, it shall comply with the requirements of Section 803.1.2.

803.13 Site-fabricated stretch systems. Where used as interior wall or interior ceiling finish materials, site-fabricated stretch systems shall be tested in the manner intended for use, and shall comply with the requirements of Section 803.1.1 or 803.1.2. If the materials are tested in accordance with ASTM E 84 or UL 723, specimen preparation and mounting shall be in accordance with ASTM E 2573.

SECTION 804 INTERIOR FLOOR FINISH

804.1 General. *Interior floor finish* and floor covering materials shall comply with Sections 804.2 through 804.4.1.

Exception: Floor finishes and coverings of a traditional type, such as wood, vinyl, linoleum or terrazzo, and resilient floor covering materials that are not comprised of fibers.

804.2 Classification. *Interior floor finish* and floor covering materials required by Section 804.4.1 to be of Class I or II materials shall be classified in accordance with NFPA 253. The classification referred to herein corresponds to the classifications determined by NFPA 253 as follows: Class I, 0.45 watts/cm^2 or greater; Class II, 0.22 watts/cm^2 or greater.

804.3 Testing and identification. *Interior floor finish* and floor covering materials shall be tested by an agency in accordance with NFPA 253 and identified by a hang tag or other suitable method so as to identify the manufacturer or supplier and style, and shall indicate the *interior floor finish* or floor covering classification according to Section 804.2. Carpet-type floor coverings shall be tested as proposed for use, including underlayment. Test reports confirming the information provided in the manufacturer's product identification shall be furnished to the building official upon request.

804.4 Interior floor finish requirements. In all occupancies, *interior floor finish* and floor covering materials in *exit* enclosures, *exit* passageways, corridors and rooms or spaces not separated from corridors by full-height partitions extending from the floor to the underside of the ceiling shall withstand a minimum critical radiant flux as specified in Section 804.4.1.

804.4.1 Minimum critical radiant flux. *Interior floor finish* and floor covering materials in exit enclosures, *exit* passageways and corridors shall not be less than Class I in Groups I-1, I-2 and I-3 and not less than Class II in Groups A, B, E, H, I-4, M, R-1, R-2 and S. In all areas, floor covering materials shall comply with the DOCFF-1 "pill test" (CPSC 16 CFR, Part 1630).

Exception: Where a building is equipped throughout with an *automatic sprinkler system* in accordance with Section 903.3.1.1 or 903.3.1.2, Class II materials are permitted in any area where Class I materials are required, and materials complying with the DOC FF-1 "pill test" (CPSC 16 CFR, Part 1630) are permitted in any area where Class II materials are required.

SECTION 805 COMBUSTIBLE MATERIALS IN TYPES I AND II CONSTRUCTION

805.1 Application. Combustible materials installed on or embedded in floors of buildings of Type I or II construction shall comply with Sections 805.1.1 through 805.1.3.

Exception: Stages and platforms constructed in accordance with Sections 410.3 and 410.4, respectively.

805.1.1 Subfloor construction. Floor sleepers, bucks and nailing blocks shall not be constructed of combustible materials, unless the space between the fire-resistance-rated floor assembly and the flooring is either solidly filled with noncombustible materials or fireblocked in accordance with Section 717, and provided that such open spaces shall not extend under or through permanent partitions or walls.

805.1.2 Wood finish flooring. Wood finish flooring is permitted to be attached directly to the embedded or fireblocked wood sleepers and shall be permitted where cemented directly to the top surface of fire-resistance-rated floor assemblies or directly to a wood subfloor attached to sleepers as provided for in Section 805.1.1.

805.1.3 Insulating boards. Combustible insulating boards not more than $^1/_2$ inch (12.7 mm) thick and covered with finish flooring are permitted where attached directly to a noncombustible floor assembly or to wood subflooring attached to sleepers as provided for in Section 805.1.1.

[F] SECTION 806 DECORATIVE MATERIALS AND TRIM

[F] 806.1 General requirements. In occupancies in Groups A, E, I and R-1 and dormitories in Group R-2, curtains, draperies, hangings and other *decorative materials* suspended from walls or ceilings shall meet the flame propagation performance criteria of NFPA 701 in accordance with Section 806.2 or be noncombustible.

Exceptions:

1. Curtains, draperies, hangings and other decorative materials suspended from walls of *sleeping units* and *dwelling units* in dormitories in Group R-2 protected by an *approved automatic sprinkler system* installed in accordance with Section 903.3.1 and such materials are limited to not more than 50 percent of the aggregate area of walls.
2. Decorative materials, including, but not limited to, photographs and paintings in dormitories in Group R-2 where such materials are of limited quantities such that a hazard of fire development or spread is not present.

In Groups I-1 and I-2, combustible *decorative materials* shall meet the flame propagation criteria of NFPA 701 unless the *decorative materials*, including, but not limited to, photographs and paintings, are of such limited quantities that a hazard of fire development or spread is not present. In Group I-3, combustible decorative materials are prohibited.

Fixed or movable walls and partitions, paneling, wall pads and crash pads applied structurally or for decoration, acoustical correction, surface insulation or other purposes shall be considered *interior finish* if they cover 10 percent or more of the wall or of the ceiling area, and shall not be considered *decorative materials* or furnishings.

In Group B and M occupancies, fabric partitions suspended from the ceiling and not supported by the floor shall meet the flame propagation performance criteria in accordance with Section 806.2 and NFPA 701 or shall be noncombustible.

[F] 806.1.1 Noncombustible materials. The permissible amount of noncombustible decorative material shall not be limited.

[F] 806.1.2 Combustible decorative materials. The permissible amount of *decorative materials* meeting the flame propagation performance criteria of NFPA 701 shall not exceed 10 percent of the specific wall or ceiling area to which it is attached.

Exceptions:

1. In auditoriums in Group A, the permissible amount of decorative material meeting the flame propagation performance criteria of NFPA 701 shall not exceed 75 percent of the aggregate wall area where the building is equipped throughout with an *automatic sprinkler system* in accordance with Section 903.3.1.1 and where the material is installed in accordance with Section 803.11.
2. The amount of fabric partitions suspended from the ceiling and not supported by the floor in Group B and M occupancies shall not be limited.

[F] 806.2 Acceptance criteria and reports. Where required by Section 806.1, *decorative materials* shall be tested by an agency and meet the flame propagation performance criteria of NFPA 701 or such materials shall be noncombustible. Reports of test results shall be prepared in accordance with NFPA 701 and furnished to the *building official* upon request.

[F] 806.3 Foam plastic. Foam plastic used as *trim* in any occupancy shall comply with Section 2604.2.

[F] 806.4 Pyroxylin plastic. Imitation leather or other material consisting of or coated with a pyroxylin or similarly hazardous base shall not be used in Group A occupancies.

[F] 806.5 Interior trim. Material, other than foam plastic used as interior *trim*, shall have a minimum Class C flame spread and smoke-developed index when tested in accordance with ASTM E 84 or UL 723, as described in Section 803.1.1. Combustible *trim*, excluding handrails and guardrails, shall not exceed 10 percent of the specific wall or ceiling area in which it is attached.

[F] 806.6 Interior floor-wall base. *Interior floor-wall base* that is 6 inches (152 mm) or less in height shall be tested in accordance with Section 804.2 and shall not be less than Class II. Where a Class I floor finish is required, the floor-wall base shall be Class I.

Exception: Interior *trim* materials that comply with Section 806.5.

SECTION 807
INSULATION

807.1 Insulation. Thermal and acoustical insulation shall comply with Section 719.

SECTION 808
ACOUSTICAL CEILING SYSTEMS

808.1 Acoustical ceiling systems. The quality, design, fabrication and erection of metal suspension systems for acoustical tile and lay-in panel ceilings in buildings or structures shall conform with generally accepted engineering practice, the provisions of this chapter and other applicable requirements of this code.

808.1.1 Materials and installation. Acoustical materials complying with the *interior finish* requirements of Section 803 shall be installed in accordance with the manufacturer's recommendations and applicable provisions for applying *interior finish.*

808.1.1.1 Suspended acoustical ceilings. Suspended acoustical ceiling systems shall be installed in accordance with the provisions of ASTM C 635 and ASTM C 636.

808.1.1.2 Fire-resistance-rated construction. Acoustical ceiling systems that are part of fire-resistance-rated construction shall be installed in the same manner used in the assembly tested and shall comply with the provisions of Chapter 7.

CHAPTER 9
FIRE PROTECTION SYSTEMS

SECTION 901
GENERAL

901.1 Scope. The provisions of this chapter shall specify where *fire protection systems* are required and shall apply to the design, installation and operation of *fire protection systems*.

901.2 Fire protection systems. *Fire protection systems* shall be installed, repaired, operated and maintained in accordance with this code and the *International Fire Code*.

Any *fire protection system* for which an exception or reduction to the provisions of this code has been granted shall be considered to be a required system.

Exception: Any *fire protection system* or portion thereof not required by this code shall be permitted to be installed for partial or complete protection provided that such system meets the requirements of this code.

901.3 Modifications. No person shall remove or modify any *fire protection system* installed or maintained under the provisions of this code or the *International Fire Code* without approval by the *building official*.

901.4 Threads. Threads provided for fire department connections to sprinkler systems, standpipes, yard hydrants or any other fire hose connection shall be compatible with the connections used by the local fire department.

901.5 Acceptance tests. *Fire protection systems* shall be tested in accordance with the requirements of this code and the *International Fire Code*. When required, the tests shall be conducted in the presence of the *building official*. Tests required by this code, the *International Fire Code* and the standards listed in this code shall be conducted at the expense of the owner or the owner's representative. It shall be unlawful to occupy portions of a structure until the required *fire protection systems* within that portion of the structure have been tested and *approved*.

901.6 Supervisory service. Where required, *fire protection systems* shall be monitored by an *approved* supervising station in accordance with NFPA 72.

901.6.1 Automatic sprinkler systems. Automatic sprinkler systems shall be monitored by an *approved* supervising station.

Exceptions:

1. A supervising station is not required for *automatic sprinkler systems* protecting one- and two-family dwellings.
2. Limited area systems serving fewer than 20 sprinklers.

901.6.2 Fire alarm systems. Fire alarm systems required by the provisions of Section 907.2 of this code and Sections 907.2 and 907.3 of the *International Fire Code* shall be monitored by an *approved* supervising station in accordance with Section 907.6.5.

Exceptions:

1. Single- and multiple-station smoke alarms required by Section 907.2.11.
2. Smoke detectors in Group I-3 occupancies.
3. Supervisory service is not required for *automatic sprinkler systems* in one- and two-family dwellings.

901.6.3 Group H. Manual fire alarm, automatic fire-extinguishing and emergency alarm systems in Group H occupancies shall be monitored by an *approved* supervising station.

Exception: When *approved* by the *building official*, on-site monitoring at a *constantly attended location* shall be permitted provided that notifications to the fire department will be equal to those provided by an *approved* supervising station.

901.7 Fire areas. Where buildings, or portions thereof, are divided into *fire areas* so as not to exceed the limits established for requiring a *fire protection system* in accordance with this chapter, such *fire areas* shall be separated by *fire barriers* constructed in accordance with Section 707 or *horizontal assemblies* constructed in accordance with Section 712, or both, having a *fire-resistance rating* of not less than that determined in accordance with Section 508.4.

SECTION 902
DEFINITIONS

902.1 Definitions. The following words and terms shall, for the purposes of this chapter, and as used elsewhere in this code, have the meanings shown herein.

[F] ALARM NOTIFICATION APPLIANCE. A fire alarm system component such as a bell, horn, speaker, light or text display that provides audible, tactile or visible outputs, or any combination thereof.

[F] ALARM SIGNAL. A signal indicating an emergency requiring immediate action, such as a signal indicative of fire.

[F] ALARM VERIFICATION FEATURE. A feature of automatic fire detection and alarm systems to reduce unwanted alarms wherein smoke detectors report alarm conditions for a minimum period of time, or confirm alarm conditions within a given time period, after being automatically reset, in order to be accepted as a valid alarm-initiation signal.

[F] ANNUNCIATOR. A unit containing one or more indicator lamps, alphanumeric displays or other equivalent means in which each indication provides status information about a circuit, condition or location.

[F] AUDIBLE ALARM NOTIFICATION APPLIANCE. A notification appliance that alerts by the sense of hearing.

[F] AUTOMATIC. As applied to fire protection devices, a device or system providing an emergency function without the necessity for human intervention and activated as a result of a predetermined temperature rise, rate of temperature rise or combustion products.

[F] AUTOMATIC FIRE-EXTINGUISHING SYSTEM. An *approved* system of devices and equipment which automatically detects a fire and discharges an *approved* fire-extinguishing agent onto or in the area of a fire.

[F] AUTOMATIC SMOKE DETECTION SYSTEM. A fire alarm system that has initiation devices that utilize smoke detectors for protection of an area such as a room or space with detectors to provide early warning of fire.

[F] AUTOMATIC SPRINKLER SYSTEM. An automatic sprinkler system, for fire protection purposes, is an integrated system of underground and overhead piping designed in accordance with fire protection engineering standards. The system includes a suitable water supply. The portion of the system above the ground is a network of specially sized or hydraulically designed piping installed in a structure or area, generally overhead, and to which automatic sprinklers are connected in a systematic pattern. The system is usually activated by heat from a fire and discharges water over the fire area.

[F] AVERAGE AMBIENT SOUND LEVEL. The root mean square, A-weighted sound pressure level measured over a 24-hour period, or the time any person is present, whichever time period is less.

[F] CARBON DIOXIDE EXTINGUISHING SYSTEMS. A system supplying carbon dioxide (CO_2) from a pressurized vessel through fixed pipes and nozzles. The system includes a manual- or automatic-actuating mechanism.

[F] CEILING LIMIT. The maximum concentration of an air-borne contaminant to which one may be exposed, as published in DOL 29 CFR Part 1910.1000.

[F] CLEAN AGENT. Electrically nonconducting, volatile or gaseous fire extinguishant that does not leave a residue upon evaporation.

[F] CONSTANTLY ATTENDED LOCATION. A designated location at a facility staffed by trained personnel on a continuous basis where alarm or supervisory signals are monitored and facilities are provided for notification of the fire department or other emergency services.

[F] DELUGE SYSTEM. A sprinkler system employing open sprinklers attached to a piping system connected to a water supply through a valve that is opened by the operation of a detection system installed in the same areas as the sprinklers. When this valve opens, water flows into the piping system and discharges from all sprinklers attached thereto.

[F] DETECTOR, HEAT. A fire detector that senses heat—either abnormally high temperature or rate of rise, or both.

[F] DRY-CHEMICAL EXTINGUISHING AGENT. A powder composed of small particles, usually of sodium bicarbonate, potassium bicarbonate, urea-potassium-based bicarbonate, potassium chloride or monoammonium phosphate, with added particulate material supplemented by special treatment to provide resistance to packing, resistance to moisture absorption (caking) and the proper flow capabilities.

[F] ELEVATOR GROUP. A grouping of elevators in a building located adjacent or directly across from one another that responds to a common hall call button(s).

[F] EMERGENCY ALARM SYSTEM. A system to provide indication and warning of emergency situations involving hazardous materials.

[F] EMERGENCY VOICE/ALARM COMMUNICATIONS. Dedicated manual or automatic facilities for originating and distributing voice instructions, as well as alert and evacuation signals pertaining to a fire emergency, to the occupants of a building.

[F] FIRE ALARM BOX, MANUAL. See "Manual fire alarm box."

[F] FIRE ALARM CONTROL UNIT. A system component that receives inputs from automatic and manual fire alarm devices and may be capable of supplying power to detection devices and transponder(s) or off-premises transmitter(s). The control unit may be capable of providing a transfer of power to the notification appliances and transfer of condition to relays or devices.

[F] FIRE ALARM SIGNAL. A signal initiated by a fire alarm-initiating device such as a manual fire alarm box, automatic fire detector, waterflow switch or other device whose activation is indicative of the presence of a fire or fire signature.

[F] FIRE ALARM SYSTEM. A system or portion of a combination system consisting of components and circuits arranged to monitor and annunciate the status of fire alarm or supervisory signal-initiating devices and to initiate the appropriate response to those signals.

[F] FIRE AREA. The aggregate floor area enclosed and bounded by fire walls, *fire barriers*, *exterior walls* or *horizontal assemblies* of a building. Areas of the building not provided with surrounding walls shall be included in the fire area if such areas are included within the horizontal projection of the roof or floor next above.

[F] FIRE COMMAND CENTER. The principal attended or unattended location where the status of detection, alarm communications and control systems is displayed, and from which the system(s) can be manually controlled.

[F] FIRE DETECTOR, AUTOMATIC. A device designed to detect the presence of a fire signature and to initiate action.

[F] FIRE PROTECTION SYSTEM. *Approved* devices, equipment and systems or combinations of systems used to detect a fire, activate an alarm, extinguish or control a fire, control or manage smoke and products of a fire or any combination thereof.

[F] FIRE SAFETY FUNCTIONS. Building and fire control functions that are intended to increase the level of life safety for occupants or to control the spread of harmful effects of fire.

[F] FOAM-EXTINGUISHING SYSTEM. A special system discharging a foam made from concentrates, either mechanically or chemically, over the area to be protected.

[F] HALOGENATED EXTINGUISHING SYSTEM. A fire-extinguishing system using one or more atoms of an element from the halogen chemical series: fluorine, chlorine, bromine and iodine.

[F] INITIATING DEVICE. A system component that originates transmission of a change-of-state condition, such as in a smoke detector, manual fire alarm box or supervisory switch.

[F] MANUAL FIRE ALARM BOX. A manually operated device used to initiate an alarm signal.

[F] MULTIPLE-STATION ALARM DEVICE. Two or more single-station alarm devices that are capable of interconnection such that actuation of one causes all integral or separate audible alarms to operate. It also can consist of one single-station alarm device having connections to other detectors or to a manual fire alarm box.

[F] MULTIPLE-STATION SMOKE ALARM. Two or more single-station alarm devices that are capable of interconnection such that actuation of one causes the appropriate alarm signal to operate in all interconnected alarms.

[F] NIGHTCLUB. An establishment meeting all of the following:

1. Has a posted capacity or occupant load that exceeds one occupant per 15 square feet (1.39 m^2) net;
2. Provides live or recorded entertainment by performing artists; and
3. Serves alcoholic beverages.

[F] NOTIFICATION ZONE. See "Zone, notification."

[F] NUISANCE ALARM. An alarm caused by mechanical failure, malfunction, improper installation or lack of proper maintenance, or an alarm activated by a cause that cannot be determined.

[F] RECORD DRAWINGS. Drawings ("as builts") that document the location of all devices, appliances, wiring sequences, wiring methods and connections of the components of a fire alarm system as installed.

[F] SINGLE-STATION SMOKE ALARM. An assembly incorporating the detector, the control equipment and the alarm-sounding device in one unit, operated from a power supply either in the unit or obtained at the point of installation.

[F] SMOKE ALARM. A single- or multiple-station alarm responsive to smoke.

[F] SMOKE DETECTOR. A *listed* device that senses visible or invisible particles of combustion.

SMOKEPROOF ENCLOSURE. An exit stairway designed and constructed so that the movement of the products of combustion produced by a fire occurring in any part of the building into the enclosure is limited.

[F] STANDPIPE SYSTEM, CLASSES OF. Standpipe classes are as follows:

Class I system. A system providing 2$^1/_2$-inch (64 mm) hose connections to supply water for use by fire departments and those trained in handling heavy fire streams.

Class II system. A system providing 1$^1/_2$-inch (38 mm) hose stations to supply water for use primarily by the building occupants or by the fire department during initial response.

Class III system. A system providing 1$^1/_2$-inch (38 mm) hose stations to supply water for use by building occupants and 2$^1/_2$-inch (64 mm) hose connections to supply a larger volume of water for use by fire departments and those trained in handling heavy fire streams.

[F] STANDPIPE, TYPES OF. Standpipe types are as follows:

Automatic dry. A dry standpipe system, normally filled with pressurized air, that is arranged through the use of a device, such as dry pipe valve, to admit water into the system piping automatically upon the opening of a hose valve. The water supply for an automatic dry standpipe system shall be capable of supplying the system demand.

Automatic wet. A wet standpipe system that has a water supply that is capable of supplying the system demand automatically.

Manual dry. A dry standpipe system that does not have a permanent water supply attached to the system. Manual dry standpipe systems require water from a fire department pumper to be pumped into the system through the fire department connection in order to meet the system demand.

Manual wet. A wet standpipe system connected to a water supply for the purpose of maintaining water within the system but does not have a water supply capable of delivering the system demand attached to the system. Manual-wet standpipe systems require water from a fire department pumper (or the like) to be pumped into the system in order to meet the system demand.

Semiautomatic dry. A dry standpipe system that is arranged through the use of a device, such as a deluge valve, to admit water into the system piping upon activation of a remote control device located at a hose connection. A remote control activation device shall be provided at each hose connection. The water supply for a semiautomatic dry standpipe system shall be capable of supplying the system demand.

[F] SUPERVISING STATION. A facility that receives signals and at which personnel are in attendance at all times to respond to these signals.

[F] SUPERVISORY SERVICE. The service required to monitor performance of guard tours and the operative condition of fixed suppression systems or other systems for the protection of life and property.

[F] SUPERVISORY SIGNAL. A signal indicating the need of action in connection with the supervision of guard tours, the fire suppression systems or equipment or the maintenance features of related systems.

[F] SUPERVISORY SIGNAL-INITIATING DEVICE. An initiation device, such as a valve supervisory switch, water-level indicator or low-air pressure switch on a dry-pipe sprinkler system, whose change of state signals an off-normal condition and its restoration to normal of a fire protection or life safety system, or a need for action in connection with guard tours, fire suppression systems or equipment or maintenance features of related systems.

[F] TIRES, BULK STORAGE OF. Storage of tires where the area available for storage exceeds 20,000 cubic feet (566 m^3).

[F] TROUBLE SIGNAL. A signal initiated by the fire alarm system or device indicative of a fault in a monitored circuit or component.

[F] VISIBLE ALARM NOTIFICATION APPLIANCE. A notification appliance that alerts by the sense of sight.

[F] WET-CHEMICAL EXTINGUISHING SYSTEM. A solution of water and potassium-carbonate-based chemical, potassium-acetate-based chemical or a combination thereof, forming an extinguishing agent.

[F] WIRELESS PROTECTION SYSTEM. A system or a part of a system that can transmit and receive signals without the aid of wire.

[F] ZONE. A defined area within the protected premises. A zone can define an area from which a signal can be received, an area to which a signal can be sent or an area in which a form of control can be executed.

[F] ZONE, NOTIFICATION. An area within a building or facility covered by notification appliances which are activated simultaneously.

SECTION 903 AUTOMATIC SPRINKLER SYSTEMS

[F] 903.1 General. *Automatic sprinkler systems* shall comply with this section.

[F] 903.1.1 Alternative protection. Alternative automatic fire-extinguishing systems complying with Section 904 shall be permitted in lieu of automatic sprinkler protection where recognized by the applicable standard and *approved* by the fire code official.

[F] 903.2 Where required. Approved *automatic sprinkler systems* in new buildings and structures shall be provided in the locations described in Sections 903.2.1 through 903.2.12.

Exception: Spaces or areas in telecommunications buildings used exclusively for telecommunications equipment, associated electrical power distribution equipment, batteries and standby engines, provided those spaces or areas are equipped throughout with an automatic smoke detection system in accordance with Section 907.2 and are separated from the remainder of the building by not less than 1-hour *fire barriers* constructed in accordance with Section 707 or not less than 2-hour *horizontal assemblies* constructed in accordance with Section 712, or both.

[F] 903.2.1 Group A. An *automatic sprinkler system* shall be provided throughout buildings and portions thereof used as Group A occupancies as provided in this section. For Group A-1, A-2, A-3 and A-4 occupancies, the *automatic sprinkler system* shall be provided throughout the floor area where the Group A-1, A-2, A-3 or A-4 occupancy is located, and in all floors from the Group A occupancy to, and including, the nearest *level of exit discharge* serving the Group A occupancy. For Group A-5 occupancies, the *automatic sprinkler system* shall be provided in the spaces indicated in Section 903.2.1.5.

[F] 903.2.1.1 Group A-1. An *automatic sprinkler system* shall be provided for Group A-1 occupancies where one of the following conditions exists:

1. The *fire area* exceeds 12,000 square feet (1115 m^2);
2. The *fire area* has an *occupant load* of 300 or more;
3. The *fire area* is located on a floor other than a *level of exit discharge* serving such occupancies; or
4. The *fire area* contains a multitheater complex.

[F] 903.2.1.2 Group A-2. An *automatic sprinkler system* shall be provided for Group A-2 occupancies where one of the following conditions exists:

1. The *fire area* exceeds 5,000 square feet (464.5 m^2);
2. The *fire area* has an *occupant load* of 300 or more, except 100 or more for *nightclubs*; or
3. The *fire area* is located on a floor other than a *level of exit discharge* serving such occupancies.

[F] 903.2.1.3 Group A-3. An *automatic sprinkler system* shall be provided for Group A-3 occupancies where one of the following conditions exists:

1. The *fire area* exceeds 12,000 square feet (1115 m^2);
2. The *fire area* has an *occupant load* of 300 or more; or
3. The *fire area* is located on a floor other than a *level of exit discharge* serving such occupancies.

Exceptions:

1. This requirement shall not apply to assembly occupancies used primarily for worship with fixed seating and part of a separted use.
2. This requirement shall not apply to assembly occupancies used primarily for worship consisting of a single multipurpose room that is not used for exhibition or display and is part of a separated use.

[F] 903.2.1.4 Group A-4. An *automatic sprinkler system* shall be provided for Group A-4 occupancies where one of the following conditions exists:

1. The *fire area* exceeds 12,000 square feet (1115 m^2);
2. The *fire area* has an *occupant load* of 300 or more; or
3. The *fire area* is located on a floor other than a *level of exit discharge* serving such occupancies.

[F] 903.2.1.5 Group A-5. An *automatic sprinkler system* shall be provided for Group A-5 occupancies in the following areas: concession stands, retail areas, press boxes and other accessory use areas in excess of 1,000 square feet (93 m^2).

[F] 903.2.2 Group B ambulatory health care facilities. An *automatic sprinkler system* shall be installed throughout all fire areas containing a Group B ambulatory health care facility occupancy when either of the following conditions exists at any time:

1. Four or more care recipients are incapable of self-preservation.
2. One or more care recipients who are incapable of self-preservation are located at other than the *level of exit discharge* serving such an occupancy.

[F] 903.2.3 Group E. An *automatic sprinkler system* shall be provided for Group E occupancies as follows:

1. Throughout all Group E *fire areas* greater than 12,000 square feet (1115 m^2) in area.
2. Throughout every portion of educational buildings below the lowest *level of exit discharge* serving that portion of the building.

   Exception: An *automatic sprinkler system* is not required in any area below the lowest *level of exit discharge* serving that area where every classroom throughout the building has at least one exterior *exit* door at ground level.

[F] 903.2.4 Group F-1. An *automatic sprinkler system* shall be provided throughout all buildings containing a Group F-1 occupancy where one of the following conditions exists:

1. A Group F-1 *fire area* exceeds 12,000 square feet (1115 m^2).
2. A Group F-1 *fire area* is located more than three stories above *grade plane*.
3. The combined area of all Group F-1 *fire areas* on all floors, including any mezzanines, exceeds 24,000 square feet (2230 m^2).

[F] 903.2.4.1 Woodworking operations. An *automatic sprinkler system* shall be provided throughout all Group F-1 occupancy *fire areas* that contain woodworking operations in excess of 2,500 square feet (232 m^2) in area which generate finely divided combustible waste or use finely divided combustible materials.

[F] 903.2.5 Group H. *Automatic sprinkler systems* shall be provided in high-hazard occupancies as required in Sections 903.2.5.1 through 903.2.5.3.

[F] 903.2.5.1 General. An *automatic sprinkler system* shall be installed in Group H occupancies.

[F] 903.2.5.2 Group H-5. An *automatic sprinkler system* shall be installed throughout buildings containing Group H-5 occupancies. The design of the sprinkler system shall not be less than that required by this code for the occupancy hazard classifications in accordance with Table 903.2.5.2. Where the design area of the sprinkler system consists of a *corridor* protected by one row of sprinklers, the maximum number of sprinklers required to be calculated is 13.

[F] TABLE 903.2.5.2
GROUP H-5 SPRINKLER DESIGN CRITERIA

LOCATION	OCCUPANCY HAZARD CLASSIFICATION
Fabrication areas	Ordinary Hazard Group 2
Service corridors	Ordinary Hazard Group 2
Storage rooms without dispensing	Ordinary Hazard Group 2
Storage rooms with dispensing	Extra Hazard Group 2
Corridors	Ordinary Hazard Group 2

[F] 903.2.5.3 Pyroxylin plastics. An *automatic sprinkler system* shall be provided in buildings, or portions thereof, where cellulose nitrate film or pyroxylin plastics are manufactured, stored or handled in quantities exceeding 100 pounds (45 kg).

[F] 903.2.6 Group I. An *automatic sprinkler system* shall be provided throughout buildings with a Group I *fire area*.

Exception: An *automatic sprinkler system* installed in accordance with Section 903.3.1.2 or 903.3.1.3 shall be allowed in Group I-1 facilities.

[F] 903.2.6.1 Dry pipe system. When dry pipe sprinkler systems are installed, upon activation, a full flow of water shall be delivered to the most remote point of the system in less than 60 seconds.

[F] 903.2.7 Group M. An *automatic sprinkler system* shall be provided throughout buildings containing a Group M occupancy where one of the following conditions exists:

1. A Group M *fire area* exceeds 12,000 square feet (1115 m^2).
2. A Group M *fire area* is located more than three stories above *grade plane*.
3. The combined area of all Group M *fire areas* on all floors, including any mezzanines, exceeds 24,000 square feet (2230 m^2).
4. Deleted.

[F] 903.2.7.1 High-piled storage. An *automatic sprinkler system* shall be provided in accordance with the *International Fire Code* in all buildings of Group M where storage of merchandise is in high-piled or rack storage arrays.

[F] 903.2.8 Group R. An *automatic sprinkler system* installed in accordance with Section 903.3 shall be provided throughout all buildings with a Group R *fire area*.

Exceptions:

1. An *automatic sprinkler system* is not required in new adult and child care facilities located in existing Group R-3 and R-4 occupancies.
2. An *automatic sprinkler system* is not required in Group R-1 *temporary overflow shelters.*

[F] 903.2.9 Group S-1. An *automatic sprinkler system* shall be provided throughout all buildings containing a Group S-1 occupancy where one of the following conditions exists:

1. A Group S-1 *fire area* exceeds 12,000 square feet (1115 m^2).
2. A Group S-1 *fire area* is located more than three stories above *grade plane*.
3. The combined area of all Group S-1 *fire areas* on all floors, including any mezzanines, exceeds 24,000 square feet (2230 m^2).
4. A Group S-1 *fire area* used for the storage of commercial trucks or buses where the *fire area* exceeds 5,000 square feet (464 m^2).

[F] 903.2.9.1 Repair garages. An *automatic sprinkler system* shall be provided throughout all buildings used as repair garages in accordance with Section 406, as shown:

1. Buildings having two or more *stories above grade plane*, including basements, with a *fire area* containing a repair garage exceeding 10,000 square feet (929 m^2).
2. Buildings no more than one *story above grade plane*, with a *fire area* containing a repair garage exceeding 12,000 square feet (1115 m^2).
3. Buildings with repair garages servicing vehicles parked in basements.
4. A Group S-1 *fire area* used for the repair of commercial trucks or buses where the *fire area* exceeds 5,000 square feet (464 m^2).

[F] 903.2.9.2 Bulk storage of tires. Buildings and structures where the area for the storage of tires exceeds 20,000 cubic feet (566 m^3) shall be equipped throughout with an *automatic sprinkler system* in accordance with Section 903.3.1.1.

[F] 903.2.10 Group S-2 enclosed parking garages. An *automatic sprinkler system* shall be provided throughout buildings classified as enclosed parking garages in accordance with Section 406.4 as follows:

1. Where the *fire area* of the enclosed parking garage exceeds 12,000 square feet (1115 m^2); or
2. Where the enclosed parking garage is located beneath other groups.

   Exception: Enclosed parking garages located beneath Group R-3 occupancies.

[F] 903.2.10.1 Commercial parking garages. An *automatic sprinkler system* shall be provided throughout buildings used for storage of commercial trucks or buses where the *fire area* exceeds 5,000 square feet (464 m^2).

[F] 903.2.11 Specific building areas and hazards. In all occupancies an *automatic sprinkler system* shall be installed for building design or hazards in the locations set forth in Sections 903.2.11.1 through 903.2.11.6.

Exception: Groups R-3 and U.

[F] 903.2.11.1 Stories without openings. An *automatic sprinkler system* shall be installed throughout all *stories*, including basements, of all buildings where the floor area exceeds 1,500 square feet (139.4 m^2) and where there is not provided at least one of the following types of *exterior wall* openings:

1. Openings below grade that lead directly to ground level by an exterior *stairway* complying with Section 1009 or an outside ramp complying with Section 1010. Openings shall be located in each 50 linear feet (15 240 mm), or fraction thereof, of *exterior wall* in the *story* on at least one side. The required openings shall be distributed such that the linear distance between adjacent openings does not exceed 50 feet (15 240 mm).
2. Openings entirely above the adjoining ground level totaling at least 20 square feet (1.86 m^2) in each 50 linear feet (15 240 mm), or fraction thereof, of *exterior wall* in the story on at least one side. The required openings shall be distributed such that the linear distance between adjacent openings does not exceed 50 feet (15 240 mm).

[F] 903.2.11.1.1 Opening dimensions and access. Openings shall have a minimum dimension of not less than 30 inches (762 mm). Such openings shall be accessible to the fire department from the exterior and shall not be obstructed in a manner that fire fighting or rescue cannot be accomplished from the exterior.

[F] 903.2.11.1.2 Openings on one side only. Where openings in a *story* are provided on only one side and the opposite wall of such *story* is more than 75 feet (22 860 mm) from such openings, the *story* shall be equipped throughout with an *approved automatic sprinkler system*, or openings as specified above shall be provided on at least two sides of the *story*.

[F] 903.2.11.1.3 Basements. Where any portion of a basement is located more than 75 feet (22 860 mm) from openings required by Section 903.2.11.1, the basement shall be equipped throughout with an *approved automatic sprinkler system*.

[F] 903.2.11.2 Rubbish and linen chutes. An *automatic sprinkler system* shall be installed at the top of rubbish and linen chutes and in their terminal rooms. Chutes extending through three or more floors shall have additional sprinkler heads installed within such chutes at alternate floors. Chute sprinklers shall be accessible for servicing.

[F] 903.2.11.3 Buildings 55 feet or more in height. An *automatic sprinkler system* shall be installed throughout buildings with a floor level having an *occupant load* of 30 or more that is located 55 feet (16 764 mm) or more above the lowest level of fire department vehicle access.

Exceptions:

1. Airport control towers.
2. Open parking structures.
3. Occupancies in Group F-2.

[F] 903.2.11.4 Ducts conveying hazardous exhausts. Where required by the *International Mechanical Code*, automatic sprinklers shall be provided in ducts conveying hazardous exhaust, or flammable or combustible materials.

Exception: Ducts in which the largest cross-sectional diameter of the duct is less than 10 inches (254 mm).

[F] 903.2.11.5 Commercial cooking operations. An *automatic sprinkler system* shall be installed in commercial kitchen exhaust hood and duct system where an *automatic sprinkler system* is used to comply with Section 904.

[F] 903.2.11.6 Other required suppression systems. In addition to the requirements of Section 903.2, the provisions indicated in Table 903.2.11.6 also require the installation of a fire suppression system for certain buildings and areas.

**[F] TABLE 903.2.11.6
ADDITIONAL REQUIRED SUPPRESSION SYSTEMS**

SECTION	SUBJECT
402.9	Covered malls
403.2, 403.3	High-rise buildings
404.3	Atriums
405.3	Underground structures
407.5	Group I-2
410.6	Stages
411.4	Special amusement buildings
412.4.6, 412.4.6.1, 412.6.5	Aircraft hangars
415.6.2.4	Group H-2
416.4	Flammable finishes
417.4	Drying rooms
507	Unlimited area buildings
508.2.5	Incidental accessory occupancies
1028.6.2.3	Smoke-protected assembly seating
IFC	Sprinkler system requirements as set forth in Section 903.2.11.6 of the *International Fire Code*

[F] 903.2.12 During construction. *Automatic sprinkler systems* required during construction, *alteration* and demolition operations shall be provided in accordance with Chapter 14 of the *International Fire Code*.

[F] 903.3 Installation requirements. *Automatic sprinkler systems* shall be designed and installed in accordance with Sections 903.3.1 through 903.3.6.

[F] 903.3.1 Standards. Sprinkler systems shall be designed and installed in accordance with Section 903.3.1.1, unless otherwise permitted by Sections 903.3.1.2 and 903.3.1.3.

[F] 903.3.1.1 NFPA 13 sprinkler systems. Where the provisions of this code require that a building or portion thereof be equipped throughout with an *automatic sprinkler system* in accordance with this section, sprinklers shall be installed throughout in accordance with NFPA 13 except as provided in Section 903.3.1.1.1.

[F] 903.3.1.1.1 Exempt locations. Automatic sprinklers shall not be required in the following rooms or areas where such rooms or areas are protected with an *approved* automatic fire detection system in accordance with Section 907.2 that will respond to visible or invisible particles of combustion. Sprinklers shall not be omitted from any room merely because it is damp, of fire-resistance-rated construction or contains electrical equipment.

1. Any room where the application of water, or flame and water, constitutes a serious life or fire hazard.
2. Any room or space where sprinklers are considered undesirable because of the nature of the contents, when *approved* by the fire code official.
3. Generator and transformer rooms separated from the remainder of the building by walls and floor/ceiling or roof/ceiling assemblies having a *fire-resistance rating* of not less than 2 hours.
4. Rooms or areas that are of noncombustible construction with wholly noncombustible contents.
5. Fire service access elevator machine rooms and machinery spaces.

[F] 903.3.1.2 NFPA 13R sprinkler systems. *Automatic sprinkler systems* in Group R occupancies up to and including four stories in height shall be permitted to be installed throughout in accordance with NFPA 13R.

[F] 903.3.1.2.1 Balconies and decks. Sprinkler protection shall be provided for exterior balconies, decks and ground floor patios of *dwelling units* where the building is of Type V construction, provided there is a roof or deck above. Sidewall sprinklers that are used to protect such areas shall be permitted to be located such that their deflectors are within 1 inch (25 mm) to 6 inches (152 mm) below the structural members and a maximum distance of 14 inches (356 mm) below the deck of the exterior balconies and decks that are constructed of open wood joist construction.

[F] 903.3.1.3 NFPA 13D sprinkler systems. Where allowed, *Automatic sprinkler systems* installed in one- and two-family *dwellings* and *townhouses* shall be permitted to be installed throughout in accordance with NFPA 13D or Appendix P2904 of the *International Residential Code*.

[F] 903.3.2 Quick-response and residential sprinklers. Where automatic sprinkler systems are required by this code, quick-response or residential automatic sprinklers shall be installed in the following areas in accordance with Section 903.3.1 and their listings:

1. Throughout all spaces within a smoke compartment containing patient sleeping units in Group I-2 in accordance with this code.
2. *Dwelling units*, and *sleeping units* in Group R and I-1 occupancies.
3. Light-hazard occupancies as defined in NFPA 13.

[F] 903.3.3 Obstructed locations. Automatic sprinklers shall be installed with due regard to obstructions that will delay activation or obstruct the water distribution pattern. Automatic sprinklers shall be installed in or under covered kiosks, displays, booths, concession stands, or equipment that exceeds 4 feet (1219 mm) in width. Not less than a 3-foot (914 mm) clearance shall be maintained between automatic sprinklers and the top of piles of combustible fibers.

Exception: Kitchen equipment under exhaust hoods protected with a fire-extinguishing system in accordance with Section 904.

[F] 903.3.4 Actuation. *Automatic sprinkler systems* shall be automatically actuated unless specifically provided for in this code.

[F] 903.3.5 Water supplies. Water supplies for *automatic sprinkler systems* shall comply with this section and the standards referenced in Section 903.3.1. The potable water supply shall be protected against backflow in accordance with the requirements of this section and the *International Plumbing Code.*

[F] 903.3.5.1 Domestic services. Where the domestic service provides the water supply for the *automatic sprinkler system*, the supply shall be in accordance with this section.

[F] 903.3.5.1.1 Limited area sprinkler systems. Limited area sprinkler systems serving fewer than 20 sprinklers on any single connection are permitted to be connected to the domestic service where a wet automatic standpipe is not available. Limited area sprinkler systems connected to domestic water supplies shall comply with each of the following requirements:

1. Valves shall not be installed between the domestic water riser control valve and the sprinklers.

   Exception: An *approved* indicating control valve supervised in the open position in accordance with Section 903.4.

2. The domestic service shall be capable of supplying the simultaneous domestic demand and the sprinkler demand required to be hydraulically calculated by NFPA 13, NFPA 13R or NFPA 13D.

[F] 903.3.5.1.2 Residential combination services. A single combination water supply shall be allowed provided that the domestic demand is added to the sprinkler demand as required by NFPA 13R.

[F] 903.3.5.2 Secondary water supply. A secondary on-site water supply equal to the hydraulically calculated sprinkler demand, including the hose stream requirement, shall be provided for high-rise buildings assigned to Seismic Design Category C, D, E or F as determined by this code. The secondary water supply shall have a duration of not less than 30 minutes as determined by the occupancy hazard classification in accordance with NFPA 13.

Exception: Existing buildings.

[F] 903.3.6 Hose threads. Fire hose threads and fittings used in connection with *automatic sprinkler systems* shall be as prescribed by the fire code official.

[F] 903.4 Sprinkler system supervision and alarms. All valves controlling the water supply for *automatic sprinkler systems*, pumps, tanks, water levels and temperatures, critical air pressures and waterflow switches on all sprinkler systems shall be electrically supervised by a *listed* fire alarm control unit.

Exceptions:

1. *Automatic sprinkler systems* protecting one- and two-family *dwellings*.
2. Limited area systems serving fewer than 20 sprinklers.
3. *Automatic sprinkler systems* installed in accordance with NFPA 13R where a common supply main is used to supply both domestic water and the *automatic sprinkler system*, and a separate shutoff valve for the *automatic sprinkler system* is not provided.
4. Jockey pump control valves that are sealed or locked in the open position.
5. Control valves to commercial kitchen hoods, paint spray booths or dip tanks that are sealed or locked in the open position.
6. Valves controlling the fuel supply to fire pump engines that are sealed or locked in the open position.
7. Trim valves to pressure switches in dry, preaction and deluge sprinkler systems that are sealed or locked in the open position.

[F] 903.4.1 Monitoring. Alarm, supervisory and trouble signals shall be distinctly different and shall be automatically transmitted to an *approved* supervising station or, when *approved* by the fire code official, shall sound an audible signal at a *constantly attended location*.

Exceptions:

1. Underground key or hub valves in roadway boxes provided by the municipality or public utility are not required to be monitored.
2. Backflow prevention device test valves located in limited area sprinkler system supply piping shall be locked in the open position. In occupancies required to be equipped with a fire alarm system, the backflow preventer valves shall be electrically supervised by a tamper switch installed in accordance with NFPA 72 and separately annunciated.

[F] 903.4.2 Alarms. *Approved* audible devices shall be connected to every *automatic sprinkler system*. Such sprinkler waterflow alarm devices shall be activated by waterflow equivalent to the flow of a single sprinkler of the smallest orifice size installed in the system. Alarm devices shall be provided on the exterior of the building in an *approved* location. Where a fire alarm system is installed, actuation of the *automatic sprinkler system* shall actuate the building fire alarm system.

[F] 903.4.3 Floor control valves. *Approved* supervised indicating control valves shall be provided at the point of connection to the riser on each floor in high-rise buildings.

[F] 903.5 Testing and maintenance. Sprinkler systems shall be tested and maintained in accordance with the *International Fire Code*.

SECTION 904 ALTERNATIVE AUTOMATIC FIRE-EXTINGUISHING SYSTEMS

[F] 904.1 General. Automatic fire-extinguishing systems, other than *automatic sprinkler systems*, shall be designed, installed, inspected, tested and maintained in accordance with the provisions of this section and the applicable referenced standards.

[F] 904.2 Where required. Automatic fire-extinguishing systems installed as an alternative to the required *automatic sprinkler systems* of Section 903 shall be *approved* by the fire code official. Automatic fire-extinguishing systems shall not be considered alternatives for the purposes of exceptions or reductions allowed by other requirements of this code.

[F] 904.2.1 Commercial hood and duct systems. Each required commercial kitchen exhaust hood and duct system required by Section 609 of the *International Fire Code* or Chapter 5 of the *International Mechanical Code* to have a Type I hood shall be protected with an approved automatic fire-extinguishing system installed in accordance with this code.

[F] 904.3 Installation. Automatic fire-extinguishing systems shall be installed in accordance with this section.

[F] 904.3.1 Electrical wiring. Electrical wiring shall be in accordance with NFPA 70.

[F] 904.3.2 Actuation. Automatic fire-extinguishing systems shall be automatically actuated and provided with a manual means of actuation in accordance with Section 904.11.1.

[F] 904.3.3 System interlocking. Automatic equipment interlocks with fuel shutoffs, ventilation controls, door closers, window shutters, conveyor openings, smoke and heat vents and other features necessary for proper operation of the fire-extinguishing system shall be provided as required by the design and installation standard utilized for the hazard.

[F] 904.3.4 Alarms and warning signs. Where alarms are required to indicate the operation of automatic fire-extinguishing systems, distinctive audible and visible alarms and warning signs shall be provided to warn of pending agent discharge. Where exposure to automatic-extinguishing agents poses a hazard to persons and a delay is required to ensure the evacuation of occupants before agent discharge, a separate warning signal shall be provided to alert occupants once agent discharge has begun. Audible signals shall be in accordance with Section 907.5.2.

[F] 904.3.5 Monitoring. Where a building fire alarm system is installed, automatic fire-extinguishing systems shall be monitored by the building fire alarm system in accordance with NFPA 72.

[F] 904.4 Inspection and testing. Automatic fire-extinguishing systems shall be inspected and tested in accordance with the provisions of this section prior to acceptance.

[F] 904.4.1 Inspection. Prior to conducting final acceptance tests, the following items shall be inspected:

1. Hazard specification for consistency with design hazard.
2. Type, location and spacing of automatic- and manual-initiating devices.
3. Size, placement and position of nozzles or discharge orifices.
4. Location and identification of audible and visible alarm devices.
5. Identification of devices with proper designations.
6. Operating instructions.

[F] 904.4.2 Alarm testing. Notification appliances, connections to fire alarm systems and connections to *approved* supervising stations shall be tested in accordance with this section and Section 907 to verify proper operation.

[F] 904.4.2.1 Audible and visible signals. The audibility and visibility of notification appliances signaling agent discharge or system operation, where required, shall be verified.

[F] 904.4.3 Monitor testing. Connections to protected premises and supervising station fire alarm systems shall be tested to verify proper identification and retransmission of alarms from automatic fire-extinguishing systems.

[F] 904.5 Wet-chemical systems. Wet-chemical extinguishing systems shall be installed, maintained, periodically inspected and tested in accordance with NFPA 17A and their listing.

[F] 904.6 Dry-chemical systems. Dry-chemical extinguishing systems shall be installed, maintained, periodically inspected and tested in accordance with NFPA 17 and their listing.

[F] 904.7 Foam systems. Foam-extinguishing systems shall be installed, maintained, periodically inspected and tested in accordance with NFPA 11 and NFPA 16 and their listing.

[F] 904.8 Carbon dioxide systems. Carbon dioxide extinguishing systems shall be installed, maintained, periodically inspected and tested in accordance with NFPA 12 and their listing.

[F] 904.9 Halon systems. Halogenated extinguishing systems shall be installed, maintained, periodically inspected and tested in accordance with NFPA 12A and their listing.

[F] 904.10 Clean-agent systems. Clean-agent fire-extinguishing systems shall be installed, maintained, periodically inspected and tested in accordance with NFPA 2001 and their listing.

[F] 904.11 Commercial cooking systems. The automatic fire-extinguishing system for commercial cooking systems shall be of a type recognized for protection of commercial cooking equipment and exhaust systems of the type and arrangement protected. Preengineered automatic dry- and wet-chemical extinguishing systems shall be tested in accordance with UL 300 and *listed* and *labeled* for the intended application. Other types of automatic fire-extinguishing systems shall be *listed* and *labeled* for specific use as protection for commercial cooking operations. The system shall be installed in accordance with this code, its listing and the manufacturer's installation instructions. Automatic fire-extinguishing systems of the following types shall be installed in accordance with the referenced standard indicated, as follows:

1. Carbon dioxide extinguishing systems, NFPA 12.
2. *Automatic sprinkler systems*, NFPA 13.
3. Foam-water sprinkler system or foam-water spray systems, NFPA 16.
4. Dry-chemical extinguishing systems, NFPA 17.
5. Wet-chemical extinguishing systems, NFPA 17A.

Exception: Factory-built commercial cooking recirculating systems that are tested in accordance with UL 710B and *listed*, *labeled* and installed in accordance with Section 304.1 of the *International Mechanical Code*.

[F] 904.11.1 Manual system operation. A manual actuation device shall be located at or near a *means of egress* from the cooking area a minimum of 10 feet (3048 mm) and a maximum of 20 feet (6096 mm) from the kitchen exhaust system. The manual actuation device shall be installed not more than 48 inches (1200 mm) or less than 42 inches (1067 mm) above the floor and shall clearly identify the hazard protected. The manual actuation shall require a maximum force of 40 pounds (178 N) and a maximum movement of 14 inches (356 mm) to actuate the fire suppression system.

Exception: *Automatic sprinkler systems* shall not be required to be equipped with manual actuation means.

[F] 904.11.2 System interconnection. The actuation of the fire suppression system shall automatically shut down the fuel or electrical power supply to the cooking equipment. The fuel and electrical supply reset shall be manual.

[F] 904.11.3 Carbon dioxide systems. When carbon dioxide systems are used, there shall be a nozzle at the top of the ventilating duct. Additional nozzles that are symmetrically arranged to give uniform distribution shall be installed within vertical ducts exceeding 20 feet (6096 mm) and horizontal ducts exceeding 50 feet (15 240 mm). *Dampers* shall be installed at either the top or the bottom of the duct and shall be arranged to operate automatically upon activation of the fire-extinguishing system. Where the *damper* is installed at the top of the duct, the top nozzle shall be immediately below the *damper.* Automatic carbon dioxide fire-extinguishing systems shall be sufficiently sized to protect against all hazards venting through a common duct simultaneously.

[F] 904.11.3.1 Ventilation system. Commercial-type cooking equipment protected by an automatic carbon dioxide-extinguishing system shall be arranged to shut off the ventilation system upon activation.

[F] 904.11.4 Special provisions for automatic sprinkler systems. *Automatic sprinkler systems* protecting commercial-type cooking equipment shall be supplied from a separate, readily accessible, indicating-type control valve that is identified.

[F] 904.11.4.1 Listed sprinklers. Sprinklers used for the protection of fryers shall be tested in accordance with UL 199E, *listed* for that application and installed in accordance with their listing.

SECTION 905
STANDPIPE SYSTEMS

[F] 905.1 General. Standpipe systems shall be provided in new buildings and structures in accordance with this section. Fire hose threads used in connection with standpipe systems shall be *approved* and shall be compatible with fire department hose threads. The location of fire department hose connections shall be *approved.* In buildings used for high-piled combustible storage, fire protection shall be in accordance with the *International Fire Code.*

[F] 905.2 Installation standard. Standpipe systems shall be installed in accordance with this section and NFPA 14.

[F] 905.3 Required installations. Standpipe systems shall be installed where required by Sections 905.3.1 through 905.3.7 and in the locations indicated in Sections 905.4, 905.5 and 905.6. Standpipe systems are allowed to be combined with *automatic sprinkler systems.*

Exception: Standpipe systems are not required in Group R-3 occupancies.

[F] 905.3.1 Height. Class III standpipe systems shall be installed throughout buildings where the floor level of the highest *story* is located more than 30 feet (9144 mm) above the lowest level of fire department vehicle access, or where the floor level of the lowest *story* is located more than 30 feet (9144 mm) below the highest level of fire department vehicle access.

Exceptions:

1. Class I standpipes are allowed in buildings equipped throughout with an *automatic sprinkler system* in accordance with Section 903.3.1.1 or 903.3.1.2.
2. Class I manual standpipes are allowed in *open parking garages* where the highest floor is located not more than 150 feet (45 720 mm) above the lowest level of fire department vehicle access.
3. Class I manual dry standpipes are allowed in *open parking garages* that are subject to freezing temperatures, provided that the hose connections are located as required for Class II standpipes in accordance with Section 905.5.
4. Class I standpipes are allowed in basements equipped throughout with an *automatic sprinkler system.*

5. In determining the lowest level of fire department vehicle access, it shall not be required to consider:

   5.1. Recessed loading docks for four vehicles or less; and

   5.2. Conditions where topography makes access from the fire department vehicle to the building impractical or impossible.

[F] 905.3.2 Group A. Class I automatic wet standpipes shall be provided in nonsprinklered Group A buildings having an *occupant load* exceeding 1,000 persons.

Exceptions:

1. Open-air-seating spaces without enclosed spaces.
2. Class I automatic dry and semiautomatic dry standpipes or manual wet standpipes are allowed in buildings where the highest floor surface used for human occupancy is 75 feet (22 860 mm) or less above the lowest level of fire department vehicle access.

[F] 905.3.3 Covered mall buildings. A *covered mall building* shall be equipped throughout with a standpipe system where required by Section 905.3.1. *Covered mall buildings* not required to be equipped with a standpipe system by Section 905.3.1 shall be equipped with Class I hose connections connected to the *automatic sprinkler system* sized to deliver water at 250 gallons per minute (946.4 L/min) at the most hydraulically remote hose connection while concurrently supplying the *automatic sprinkler system* demand. The standpipe system shall be designed not to exceed a 50 pounds per square inch (psi) (345 kPa) residual pressure loss with a flow of 250 gallons per minute (946.4 L/min) from the fire department connection to the hydraulically most remote hose connection. Hose connections shall be provided at each of the following locations:

1. Within the mall at the entrance to each *exit* passageway or *corridor*.
2. At each floor-level landing within enclosed stairways opening directly on the mall.
3. At exterior public entrances to the mall.
4. At other locations as necessary so that the distance to reach all portions of a tenant space does not exceed 200 feet (60 960 mm) from a hose connection.

[F] 905.3.4 Stages. Stages greater than 1,000 square feet in area (93 m^2) shall be equipped with a Class III wet standpipe system with $1^1/_2$-inch and $2^1/_2$-inch (38 mm and 64 mm) hose connections on each side of the stage.

Exception: Where the building or area is equipped throughout with an *automatic sprinkler system*, a $1^1/_2$-inch (38 mm) hose connection shall be installed in accordance with NFPA 13 or in accordance with NFPA 14 for Class II or III standpipes.

[F] 905.3.4.1 Hose and cabinet. The $1^1/_2$-inch (38 mm) hose connections shall be equipped with sufficient lengths of $1^1/_2$-inch (38 mm) hose to provide fire protection for the stage area. Hose connections shall be equipped with an *approved* adjustable fog nozzle and be mounted in a cabinet or on a rack.

[F] 905.3.5 Underground buildings. Underground buildings shall be equipped throughout with a Class I automatic wet or manual wet standpipe system.

[F] 905.3.6 Helistops and heliports. Buildings with a helistop or heliport that are equipped with a standpipe shall extend the standpipe to the roof level on which the helistop or heliport is located in accordance with Section 1107.5 of the *International Fire Code.*

[F] 905.3.7 Marinas and boatyards. Standpipes in marinas and boatyards shall comply with Chapter 45 of the *International Fire Code.*

[F] 905.4 Location of Class I standpipe hose connections. Class I standpipe hose connections shall be provided in all of the following locations:

1. In every required *stairway*, a hose connection shall be provided for each floor level above or below grade. Hose connections shall be located at an intermediate floor level landing between floors, unless otherwise *approved* by the fire code official.
2. On each side of the wall adjacent to the *exit* opening of a *horizontal exit.*

   Exception: Where floor areas adjacent to a *horizontal exit* are reachable from *exit stairway* hose connections by a 30-foot (9144 mm) hose stream from a nozzle attached to 100 feet (30 480 mm) of hose, a hose connection shall not be required at the *horizontal exit.*

3. In every *exit* passageway, at the entrance from the *exit* passageway to other areas of a building.

   Exception: Where floor areas adjacent to an *exit* passageway are reachable from *exit stairway* hose connections by a 30-foot (9144 mm) hose stream from a nozzle attached to 100 feet (30 480 mm) of hose, a hose connection shall not be required at the entrance from the *exit* passageway to other areas of the building.

4. In covered mall buildings, adjacent to each exterior public entrance to the mall and adjacent to each entrance from an *exit* passageway or *exit corridor* to the mall.
5. Where the roof has a slope less than four units vertical in 12 units horizontal (33.3-percent slope), each standpipe shall be provided with a hose connection located either on the roof or at the highest landing of a *stairway* with *stair* access to the roof. An additional hose connection shall be provided at the top of the most hydraulically remote standpipe for testing purposes.
6. Where the most remote portion of a nonsprinklered floor or *story* is more than 150 feet (45 720 mm) from a hose connection or the most remote portion of a sprinklered floor or *story* is more than 200 feet (60 960 mm) from a hose connection, the fire code official is authorized to require that additional hose connections be provided in *approved* locations.

[F] 905.4.1 Protection. Risers and laterals of Class I standpipe systems not located within an enclosed *stairway* or pressurized enclosure shall be protected by a degree of *fire resistance* equal to that required for vertical enclosures in the building in which they are located.

Exception: In buildings equipped throughout with an *approved automatic sprinkler system*, laterals that are not located within an enclosed *stairway* or pressurized enclosure are not required to be enclosed within fire-resistance-rated construction.

[F] 905.4.2 Interconnection. In buildings where more than one standpipe is provided, the standpipes shall be interconnected in accordance with NFPA 14.

[F] 905.5 Location of Class II standpipe hose connections. Class II standpipe hose connections shall be accessible and located so that all portions of the building are within 30 feet (9144 mm) of a nozzle attached to 100 feet (30 480 mm) of hose.

[F] 905.5.1 Groups A-1 and A-2. In Group A-1 and A-2 occupancies with *occupant loads* of more than 1,000, hose connections shall be located on each side of any stage, on each side of the rear of the auditorium, on each side of the balcony and on each tier of dressing rooms.

[F] 905.5.2 Protection. Fire-resistance-rated protection of risers and laterals of Class II standpipe systems is not required.

[F] 905.5.3 Class II system 1-inch hose. A minimum 1-inch (25 mm) hose shall be permitted to be used for hose stations in light-hazard occupancies where investigated and *listed* for this service and where *approved* by the fire code official.

[F] 905.6 Location of Class III standpipe hose connections. Class III standpipe systems shall have hose connections located as required for Class I standpipes in Section 905.4 and shall have Class II hose connections as required in Section 905.5.

[F] 905.6.1 Protection. Risers and laterals of Class III standpipe systems shall be protected as required for Class I systems in accordance with Section 905.4.1.

[F] 905.6.2 Interconnection. In buildings where more than one Class III standpipe is provided, the standpipes shall be interconnected in accordance with NFPA 14.

[F] 905.7 Cabinets. Cabinets containing fire-fighting equipment such as standpipes, fire hoses, fire extinguishers or fire department valves shall not be blocked from use or obscured from view.

[F] 905.7.1 Cabinet equipment identification. Cabinets shall be identified in an *approved* manner by a permanently attached sign with letters not less than 2 inches (51 mm) high in a color that contrasts with the background color, indicating the equipment contained therein.

Exceptions:

1. Doors not large enough to accommodate a written sign shall be marked with a permanently attached pictogram of the equipment contained therein.
2. Doors that have either an *approved* visual identification clear glass panel or a complete glass door panel are not required to be marked.

[F] 905.7.2 Locking cabinet doors. Cabinets shall be unlocked.

Exceptions:

1. Visual identification panels of glass or other *approved* transparent frangible material that is easily broken and allows access.
2. *Approved* locking arrangements.
3. Group I-3.

[F] 905.8 Dry standpipes. Dry standpipes shall not be installed.

Exception: Where subject to freezing and in accordance with NFPA 14.

[F] 905.9 Valve supervision. Valves controlling water supplies shall be supervised in the open position so that a change in the normal position of the valve will generate a supervisory signal at the supervising station required by Section 903.4. Where a fire alarm system is provided, a signal shall also be transmitted to the control unit.

Exceptions:

1. Valves to underground key or hub valves in roadway boxes provided by the municipality or public utility do not require supervision.
2. Valves locked in the normal position and inspected as provided in this code in buildings not equipped with a fire alarm system.

[F] 905.10 During construction. Standpipe systems required during construction and demolition operations shall be provided in accordance with Section 3311.

SECTION 906
PORTABLE FIRE EXTINGUISHERS

[F] 906.1 Where required. Portable fire extinguishers shall be installed in the following locations.

1. In new and existing Group A, B, E, F, H, I, M, R-1, R-2, R-4 and S occupancies.

   Exception: In new and existing Group A, B and E occupancies equipped throughout with quick response sprinklers, portable fire extinguishers shall be required only in locations specified in Items 2 through 6.

2. Within 30 feet (9144 mm) of commercial cooking equipment.
3. In areas where flammable or combustible liquids are stored, used or dispensed.
4. On each floor of structures under construction, except Group R-3 occupancies, in accordance with Section 1415.1 of the *International Fire Code*.
5. Where required by the *International Fire Code* sections indicated in Table 906.1.
6. Special-hazard areas, including but not limited to laboratories, computer rooms and generator rooms, where required by the fire code official.

[F] TABLE 906.1
ADDITIONAL REQUIRED PORTABLE FIRE EXTINGUISHERS IN THE *INTERNATIONAL FIRE CODE*

IFC SECTION	SUBJECT
303.5	Asphalt kettles
307.5	Open burning
308.1.3	Open flames—torches
309.4	Powered industrial trucks
1105.2	Aircraft towing vehicles
1105.3	Aircraft welding apparatus
1105.4	Aircraft fuel-servicing tank vehicles
1105.5	Aircraft hydrant fuel-servicing vehicles
1105.6	Aircraft fuel-dispensing stations
1107.7	Heliports and helistops
1208.4	Dry cleaning plants
1415.1	Buildings under construction or demolition
1417.3	Roofing operations
1504.4.1	Spray-finishing operations
1505.4.2	Dip-tank operations
1506.4.2	Powder-coating areas
1904.2	Lumberyards/woodworking facilities
1908.8	Recycling facilities
1909.5	Exterior lumber storage
2003.5	Organic-coating areas
2106.3	Industrial ovens
2205.5	Motor fuel-dispensing facilities
2210.6.4	Marine motor fuel-dispensing facilities
2211.6	Repair garages
2306.1	Rack storage
2404.12	Tents and membrane structures
2508.2	Tire rebuilding/storage
2604.2.6	Welding and other hot work
2903.6	Combustible fibers
3403.2.1	Flammable and combustible liquids, general
3404.3.3.1	Indoor storage of flammable and combustible liquids
3404.3.7.5.2	Liquid storage rooms for flammable and combustible liquids
3405.4.9	Solvent distillation units
3406.2.7	Farms and construction sites—flammable and combustible liquids storage
3406.4.10.1	Bulk plants and terminals for flammable and combustible liquids
3406.5.4.5	Commercial, industrial, governmental or manufacturing establishments—fuel dispensing
3406.6.4	Tank vehicles for flammable and combustible liquids
3606.5.7	Flammable solids
3808.2	LP-gas
4504.4	Marinas

[F] 906.2 General requirements. Portable fire extinguishers shall be selected, installed and maintained in accordance with this section and NFPA 10.

Exceptions:

1. The travel distance to reach an extinguisher shall not apply to the spectator seating portions of Group A-5 occupancies.
2. Thirty-day inspections shall not be required for dry-chemical or halogenated agent portable fire extinguishers that are supervised by a *listed* and *approved* electronic monitoring device, provided that all of the following conditions are met:
   2.1. Electronic monitoring shall confirm that extinguishers are properly positioned, properly charged and unobstructed.
   2.2. Loss of power or circuit continuity to the electronic monitoring device shall initiate a trouble signal.
   2.3. The extinguishers shall be installed inside of a building or cabinet in a noncorrosive environment.
   2.4. Electronic monitoring devices and supervisory circuits shall be tested every three years.
   2.5. A written log of required hydrostatic test dates for extinguishers shall be maintained by the owner to verify that hydrostatic tests are conducted at the frequency required by NFPA 10.
3. In Group I-3 occupancies, portable fire extinguishers are permitted to be located at staff locations.

[F] 906.3 Size and distribution. The size and distribution of portable fire extinguishers shall be in accordance with Sections 906.3.1 through 906.3.4.

[F] 906.3.1 Class A fire hazards. The minimum sizes and distribution of portable fire extinguishers for occupancies that involve primarily Class A fire hazards shall comply with Table 906.3(1).

[F] TABLE 906.3(1)
FIRE EXTINGUISHERS FOR CLASS A FIRE HAZARDS

	LIGHT (Low) HAZARD OCCUPANCY	ORDINARY (Moderate) HAZARD OCCUPANCY	EXTRA (High) HAZARD OCCUPANCY
Minimum Rated Single Extinguisher	2-A[c]	2-A	4-A[a]
Maximum Floor Area Per Unit of A	3,000 square feet	1,500 square feet	1,000 square feet
Maximum Floor Area for Extinguisher[b]	11,250 square feet	11,250 square feet	11,250 square feet
Maximum Travel Distance to Extinguisher	75 feet	75 feet	75 feet

For SI: 1 foot = 304.8 mm, 1 square foot = $0.0929 m^2$, 1 gallon = 3.785 L.

a. Two $2^1/_2$-gallon water-type extinguishers shall be deemed the equivalent of one 4-A rated extinguisher.

b. Annex E.3.3 of NFPA 10 provides more details concerning application of the maximum floor area criteria.

c. Two water-type extinguishers each with a 1-A rating shall be deemed the equivalent of one 2-A rated extinguisher for Light (Low) Hazard Occupancies.

[F] 906.3.2 Class B fire hazards. Portable fire extinguishers for occupancies involving flammable or combustible liquids with depths less than or equal to 0.25-inch (6.35 mm) shall be selected and placed in accordance with Table 906.3(2).

Portable fire extinguishers for occupancies involving flammable or combustible liquids with a depth of greater than 0.25-inch (6.35 mm) shall be selected and placed in accordance with NFPA 10.

[F] TABLE 906.3(2)
FLAMMABLE OR COMBUSTIBLE LIQUIDS WITH DEPTHS LESS THAN OR EQUAL TO 0.25 INCH

TYPE OF HAZARD	BASIC MINIMUM EXTINGUISHER RATING	MAXIMUM TRAVEL DISTANCE TO EXTINGUISHERS (feet)
Light (Low)	5-B 10-B	30 50
Ordinary (Moderate)	10-B 20-B	30 50
Extra (High)	40-B 80-B	30 50

For SI: 1 inch = 25.4 mm, 1 foot = 304.8 mm.

Note: For requirements on water-soluble flammable liquids and alternative sizing criteria, see Section 5.5 of NFPA 10.

[F] 906.3.3 Class C fire hazards. Portable fire extinguishers for Class C fire hazards shall be selected and placed on the basis of the anticipated Class A or B hazard.

[F] 906.3.4 Class D fire hazards. Portable fire extinguishers for occupancies involving combustible metals shall be selected and placed in accordance with NFPA 10.

[F] 906.4 Cooking grease fires. Fire extinguishers provided for the protection of cooking grease fires shall be of an *approved* type compatible with the automatic fire-extinguishing system agent and in accordance with Section 904.11.5 of the *International Fire Code.*

[F] 906.5 Conspicuous location. Portable fire extinguishers shall be located in conspicuous locations where they will be readily accessible and immediately available for use. These locations shall be along normal paths of travel, unless the fire code official determines that the hazard posed indicates the need for placement away from normal paths of travel.

[F] 906.6 Unobstructed and unobscured. Portable fire extinguishers shall not be obstructed or obscured from view. In rooms or areas in which visual obstruction cannot be completely avoided, means shall be provided to indicate the locations of extinguishers.

[F] 906.7 Hangers and brackets. Hand-held portable fire extinguishers, not housed in cabinets, shall be installed on the hangers or brackets supplied. Hangers or brackets shall be securely anchored to the mounting surface in accordance with the manufacturer's installation instructions.

[F] 906.8 Cabinets. Cabinets used to house portable fire extinguishers shall not be locked.

Exceptions:

1. Where portable fire extinguishers subject to malicious use or damage are provided with a means of ready access.
2. In Group I-3 occupancies and in mental health areas in Group I-2 occupancies, access to portable fire extinguishers shall be permitted to be locked or to be located in staff locations provided the staff has keys.

[F] 906.9 Extinguisher installation. The installation of portable fire extinguishers shall be in accordance with Sections 906.9.1 through 906.9.3.

[F] 906.9.1 Extinguishers weighing 40 pounds or less. Portable fire extinguishers having a gross weight not exceeding 40 pounds (18 kg) shall be installed so that their tops are not more than 5 feet (1524 mm) above the floor.

[F] 906.9.2 Extinguishers weighing more than 40 pounds. Hand-held portable fire extinguishers having a gross weight exceeding 40 pounds (18 kg) shall be installed so that their tops are not more than 3.5 feet (1067 mm) above the floor.

[F] 906.9.3 Floor clearance. The clearance between the floor and the bottom of installed hand-held portable fire extinguishers shall not be less than 4 inches (102 mm).

[F] 906.10 Wheeled units. Wheeled fire extinguishers shall be conspicuously located in a designated location.

SECTION 907
FIRE ALARM AND DETECTION SYSTEMS

[F] 907.1 General. This section covers the application, installation, performance and maintenance of fire alarm systems and their components.

[F] 907.1.1 Construction documents. *Construction documents* for fire alarm systems shall be of sufficient clarity to indicate the location, nature and extent of the work proposed and show in detail that it will conform to the provisions of this code, the *International Fire Code*, and relevant laws, ordinances, rules and regulations, as determined by the fire code official.

[F] 907.1.2 Fire alarm shop drawings. Shop drawings for fire alarm systems shall be submitted for review and approval prior to system installation, and shall include, but not be limited to, all of the following:

1. A floor plan that indicates the use of all rooms.
2. Locations of alarm-initiating devices.
3. Locations of alarm notification appliances, including candela ratings for visible alarm notification appliances.
4. Location of fire alarm control unit, transponders and notification power supplies.
5. Annunciators.
6. Power connection.
7. Battery calculations.
8. Conductor type and sizes.
9. Voltage drop calculations.

10. Manufacturers' data sheets indicating model numbers and listing information for equipment, devices and materials.
11. Details of ceiling height and construction.
12. The interface of fire safety control functions.
13. Classification of the supervising station.

[F] 907.1.3 Equipment. Systems and components shall be *listed* and *approved* for the purpose for which they are installed.

[F] 907.2 Where required—new buildings and structures. An *approved* fire alarm system installed in accordance with the provisions of this code and NFPA 72 shall be provided in new buildings and structures in accordance with Sections 907.2.1 through 907.2.23 and provide occupant notification in accordance with Section 907.5, unless other requirements are provided by another section of this code.

A minimum of one manual fire alarm box shall be provided in an *approved* location to initiate a fire alarm signal for fire alarm systems employing automatic fire detectors or waterflow detection devices. Where other sections of this code allow elimination of fire alarm boxes due to sprinklers, a single fire alarm box shall be installed.

Exceptions:

1. The manual fire alarm box is not required for fire alarm systems dedicated to elevator recall control and supervisory service.
2. The manual fire alarm box is not required for Group R-2 occupancies unless required by the fire code official to provide a means for fire watch personnel to initiate an alarm during a sprinkler system impairment event. Where provided, the manual fire alarm box shall not be located in an area that is accessible to the public.

[F] 907.2.1 Group A. A manual fire alarm system that activates the occupant notification system in accordance with Section 907.5 shall be installed in Group A occupancies having an *occupant load* of 300 or more. Portions of Group E occupancies occupied for assembly purposes shall be provided with a fire alarm system as required for the Group E occupancy.

Exception: Manual fire alarm boxes are not required where the building is equipped throughout with an *automatic sprinkler system* installed in accordance with Section 903.3.1.1 and the occupant notification appliances will activate throughout the notification zones upon sprinkler waterflow.

[F] 907.2.1.1 System initiation in Group A occupancies with an occupant load of 1,000 or more. Activation of the fire alarm in Group A occupancies with an *occupant load* of 1,000 or more shall initiate a signal using an emergency voice/alarm communications system in accordance with Section 907.5.2.2.

Exception: Where *approved*, the prerecorded announcement is allowed to be manually deactivated for a period of time, not to exceed 3 minutes, for the sole purpose of allowing a live voice announcement from an *approved, constantly attended location*.

[F] 907.2.2 Group B. A manual fire alarm system shall be installed in Group B occupancies where one of the following conditions exists:

1. The combined Group B *occupant load* of all floors is 500 or more.
2. The Group B *occupant load* is more than 100 persons above or below the lowest *level of exit discharge*.
3. The Group B *fire area* contains a Group B ambulatory health care facility.

Exception: Manual fire alarm boxes are not required where the building is equipped throughout with an *automatic sprinkler system* installed in accordance with Section 903.3.1.1 and the occupant notification appliances will activate throughout the notification zones upon sprinkler waterflow.

[F] 907.2.2.1 Group B ambulatory health care facilities. Fire areas containing Group B ambulatory health care facilities shall be provided with an electronically supervised automatic smoke detection system installed within the ambulatory health care facility and in public use areas outside of tenant spaces, including public *corridors* and elevator lobbies.

Exception: Buildings equipped throughout with an *automatic sprinkler system* in accordance with Section 903.3.1.1, provided the occupant notification appliances will activate throughout the notification zones upon sprinkler waterflow.

[F] 907.2.3 Group E. A manual fire alarm system that activates the occupant notification system in accordance with Section 907.5 shall be installed in Group E occupancies. When *automatic sprinkler systems* or smoke detectors are installed, such systems or detectors shall be connected to the building fire alarm system.

Exceptions:

1. In other than child day care centers, Group E occupancies with an *occupant load* of less than 50.
2. Manual fire alarm boxes are not required in Group E occupancies where all of the following apply:
   - 2.1. Interior *corridors* are protected by smoke detectors.
   - 2.2. Auditoriums, cafeterias, gymnasiums and similar areas are protected by *heat detectors* or other *approved* detection devices.
   - 2.3. Shops and laboratories involving dusts or vapors are protected by *heat detectors* or other *approved* detection devices.
   - 2.4. The capability to activate the evacuation signal from a central point is provided.
   - 2.5. In buildings where normally occupied spaces are provided with a two-way communication system between such spaces and a constantly attended receiving station

from where a general evacuation alarm can be sounded, except in locations specifically designated by the fire code official.

3. Manual fire alarm boxes shall not be required in Group E occupancies where the building is equipped throughout with an *approved automatic sprinkler system* installed in accordance with Section 903.3.1.1, the notification appliances will activate on sprinkler waterflow and manual activation is provided from a normally occupied location.

[F] 907.2.4 Group F. A manual fire alarm system that activates the occupant notification system in accordance with Section 907.5 shall be installed in Group F occupancies where both of the following conditions exist:

1. The Group F occupancy is two or more *stories* in height; and
2. The Group F occupancy has a combined *occupant load* of 500 or more above or below the lowest *level of exit discharge*.

Exception: Manual fire alarm boxes are not required where the building is equipped throughout with an *automatic sprinkler system* installed in accordance with Section 903.3.1.1 and the occupant notification appliances will activate throughout the notification zones upon sprinkler waterflow.

[F] 907.2.5 Group H. A manual fire alarm system that activates the occupant notification system shall be installed in Group H-5 occupancies and in occupancies used for the manufacture of organic coatings. An automatic smoke detection system that activates the occupant notification system shall be installed for *highly toxic* gases, organic peroxides and oxidizers in accordance with Chapters 37, 39 and 40, respectively, of the *International Fire Code.*

[F] 907.2.6 Group I. A manual fire alarm system that activates the occupant notification system shall be installed in Group I occupancies. An automatic smoke detection system that activates the occupant notification system shall be provided in accordance with Sections 907.2.6.1, 907.2.6.2 and 907.2.6.3.3.

Exceptions:

1. Manual fire alarm boxes in resident or patient sleeping areas of Group I-1 and I-2 occupancies shall not be required at *exits* if located at all nurses' control stations or other constantly attended staff locations, provided such stations are visible and continuously accessible and that travel distances required in Section 907.4.2 are not exceeded.
2. Occupant notification systems are not required to be activated where private mode signaling installed in accordance with NFPA 72 is *approved* by the fire code official.

[F] 907.2.6.1 Group I-1. An automatic smoke detection system shall be installed in *corridors*, waiting areas open to *corridors* and *habitable spaces* other than *sleeping units* and kitchens. The system shall be activated in accordance with Section 907.5.

Exceptions:

1. Smoke detection in *habitable spaces* is not required where the facility is equipped throughout with an *automatic sprinkler system* installed in accordance with Section 903.3.1.1.
2. Smoke detection is not required for exterior balconies.

[F] 907.2.6.1.1 Smoke alarms. Single- and multiple-station smoke alarms shall be installed in accordance with Section 907.2.11.

[F] 907.2.6.2 Group I-2. An automatic smoke detection system shall be installed in *corridors* in Group I-2 and spaces permitted to be open to the *corridors* by Section 407.2. The system shall be activated in accordance with Section 907.5. Hospitals shall be equipped with smoke detection as required in Section 407.

Exceptions:

1. *Corridor* smoke detection is not required in smoke compartments that contain patient sleeping units where such units are provided with smoke detectors that comply with UL 268. Such detectors shall provide a visual display on the *corridor* side of each patient *sleeping unit* and shall provide an audible and visual alarm at the nursing station attending each unit.
2. *Corridor* smoke detection is not required in smoke compartments that contain patient *sleeping units* where patient *sleeping unit* doors are equipped with automatic door-closing devices with integral smoke detectors on the unit sides installed in accordance with their listing, provided that the integral detectors perform the required alerting function.

[F] 907.2.6.3 Group I-3 occupancies. Group I-3 occupancies shall be equipped with a manual fire alarm system and automatic smoke detection system installed for alerting staff.

[F] 907.2.6.3.1 System initiation. Actuation of an automatic fire-extinguishing system, a manual fire alarm box or a fire detector shall initiate an *approved* fire alarm signal which automatically notifies staff.

[F] 907.2.6.3.2 Manual fire alarm boxes. Manual fire alarm boxes are not required to be located in accordance with Section 907.4.2 where the fire alarm boxes are provided at staff-attended locations having direct supervision over areas where manual fire alarm boxes have been omitted.

907.2.6.3.2.1 Manual fire alarm boxes in detainee areas. Manual fire alarm boxes are allowed to be locked in areas occupied by detainees, provided that staff members are present within the subject area and have keys readily available to operate the manual fire alarm boxes.

[F] 907.2.6.3.3 Automatic smoke detection system. An automatic smoke detection system shall be installed throughout resident housing areas, including *sleeping units* and contiguous day rooms, group activity spaces and other common spaces normally accessible to residents.

Exceptions:

1. Other *approved* smoke detection arrangements providing equivalent protection, including, but not limited to, placing detectors in exhaust ducts from cells or behind protective guards *listed* for the purpose, are allowed when necessary to prevent damage or tampering.
2. *Sleeping units* in Occupancy Conditions 2 and 3 as described in Section 308.
3. Smoke detectors are not required in *sleeping units* with four or fewer occupants in smoke compartments that are equipped throughout with an *automatic sprinkler system* installed in accordance with Section 903.3.1.1.

[F] 907.2.7 Group M. A manual fire alarm system that activates the occupant notification system in accordance with Section 907.5 shall be installed in Group M occupancies where one of the following conditions exists:

1. The combined Group M *occupant load* of all floors is 500 or more persons.
2. The Group M *occupant load* is more than 100 persons above or below the lowest *level of exit discharge*.

Exceptions:

1. A manual fire alarm system is not required in *covered mall buildings* complying with Section 402.
2. Manual fire alarm boxes are not required where the building is equipped throughout with an *automatic sprinkler system* installed in accordance with Section 903.3.1.1 and the occupant notification appliances will automatically activate throughout the notification zones upon sprinkler waterflow.

[F] 907.2.7.1 Occupant notification. During times that the building is occupied, the initiation of a signal from a manual fire alarm box or from a waterflow switch shall not be required to activate the alarm notification appliances when an alarm signal is activated at a *constantly attended location* from which evacuation instructions shall be initiated over an emergency voice/alarm communication system installed in accordance with Section 907.5.2.2.

[F] 907.2.8 Group R-1. Fire alarm systems and smoke alarms shall be installed in Group R-1 occupancies as required in Sections 907.2.8.1 through 907.2.8.3.

[F] 907.2.8.1 Manual fire alarm system. A manual fire alarm system that activates the occupant notification system in accordance with Section 907.5 shall be installed in Group R-1 occupancies.

Exceptions:

1. A manual fire alarm system is not required in buildings not more than two *stories* in height where all individual *sleeping units* and contiguous *attic* and crawl spaces to those units are separated from each other and public or common areas by at least 1-hour *fire partitions* and each individual *sleeping unit* has an *exit* directly to a *public way*, *egress court* or *yard*.
2. Manual fire alarm boxes are not required throughout the building when all of the following conditions are met:
   - 2.1. The building is equipped throughout with an *automatic sprinkler system* installed in accordance with Section 903.3.1.1 or 903.3.1.2;
   - 2.2. The notification appliances will activate upon sprinkler waterflow; and
   - 2.3. At least one manual fire alarm box is installed at an *approved* location.

[F] 907.2.8.2 Automatic smoke detection system. An automatic smoke detection system that activates the occupant notification system in accordance with Section 907.5 shall be installed throughout all interior *corridors* serving *sleeping units*.

Exception: An automatic smoke detection system is not required in buildings that do not have interior *corridors* serving *sleeping units* and where each *sleeping unit* has a *means of egress* door opening directly to an *exit* or to an exterior *exit access* that leads directly to an *exit*.

[F] 907.2.8.3 Smoke alarms. Single- and multiple-station smoke alarms shall be installed in accordance with Section 907.2.11.

[F] 907.2.9 Group R-2. Fire alarm systems and smoke alarms shall be installed in Group R-2 occupancies as required in Sections 907.2.9.1 and 907.2.9.2.

[F] 907.2.9.1 Manual fire alarm system. A manual fire alarm system that activates the occupant notification system in accordance with Section 907.5 shall be installed in Group R-2 occupancies where:

1. Any *dwelling unit* or *sleeping unit* is located three or more *stories* above the lowest *level of exit discharge*;
2. Any *dwelling unit* or *sleeping unit* is located more than one *story* below the highest *level of exit discharge* of *exits* serving the *dwelling unit* or *sleeping unit*; or
3. The building contains more than 16 *dwelling units* or *sleeping units*.

Exceptions:

1. A fire alarm system is not required in buildings not more than two *stories* in height where all *dwelling units* or *sleeping units* and contiguous *attic* and crawl spaces are separated from each other and public or common areas by at least

1-hour *fire partitions* and each *dwelling unit* or *sleeping unit* has an *exit* directly to a *public way, egress court* or *yard.*

2. Manual fire alarm boxes are not required where the building is equipped throughout with an *automatic sprinkler system* installed in accordance with Section 903.3.1.1 or 903.3.1.2 and the occupant notification appliances will automatically activate throughout the notification zones upon a sprinkler waterflow.
3. A fire alarm system is not required in buildings that do not have interior *corridors* serving *dwelling units* and are protected by an *approved automatic sprinkler system* installed in accordance with Section 903.3.1.1 or 903.3.1.2, provided that *dwelling units* either have a *means of egress* door opening directly to an exterior *exit access* that leads directly to the *exits* or are served by open-ended *corridors* designed in accordance with Section 1026.6, Exception 4.

[F] 907.2.9.2 Smoke alarms. Single- and multiple-station smoke alarms shall be installed in accordance with Section 907.2.11.

[F] 907.2.10 Group R-4 including adult and child day care. Fire alarm systems and smoke alarms shall be installed in Group R-4 occupancies as required in Sections 907.2.10.1 through 907.2.10.4.

[F] 907.2.10.1 Manual fire alarm system. A manual fire alarm system that activates the occupant notification system in accordance with Section 907.5 shall be installed in Group R-4 occupancies.

Exceptions:

1. A manual fire alarm system is not required in buildings not more than two *stories* in height where all individual *sleeping units* and contiguous *attic* and crawl spaces to those units are separated from each other and public or common areas by at least 1-hour *fire partitions* and each individual *sleeping unit* has an *exit* directly to a *public way, exit court* or *yard.*
2. Manual fire alarm boxes are not required throughout the building when the following conditions are met:
   - 2.1. The building is equipped throughout with an *automatic sprinkler system* installed in accordance with Section 903.3.1.1 or 903.3.1.2;
   - 2.2. The notification appliances will activate upon sprinkler waterflow; and
   - 2.3. At least one manual fire alarm box is installed at an *approved* location.
3. Manual fire alarm boxes in resident or patient sleeping areas shall not be required at *exits* where located at all nurses' control stations or other constantly attended staff locations, provided such stations are visible and continuously accessible and that travel distances required in Section 907.4.2.1 are not exceeded.

[F] 907.2.10.2 Automatic smoke detection system. An automatic smoke detection system that activates the occupant notification system in accordance with Section 907.5 shall be installed in *corridors*, waiting areas open to *corridors* and *habitable spaces* other than *sleeping units* and kitchens.

Exceptions:

1. Smoke detection in *habitable spaces* is not required where the facility is equipped throughout with an *automatic sprinkler system* installed in accordance with Section 903.3.1.1.
2. An automatic smoke detection system is not required in buildings that do not have interior *corridors* serving *sleeping units* and where each *sleeping unit* has a *means of egress* door opening directly to an *exit* or to an exterior *exit access* that leads directly to an *exit.*

[F] 907.2.10.3 Smoke alarms. Single- and multiple-station smoke alarms shall be installed in accordance with Section 907.2.11.

907.2.10.4 Adult and child day care in Group R-4. A manual fire alarm sysem listed for residential use shall be installed in new adult or child day care facilities in existing Group R-4 occupancies.

[F] 907.2.11 Single- and multiple-station smoke alarms. *Listed* single- and multiple-station smoke alarms complying with UL 217 shall be installed in accordance with Sections 907.2.11.1 through 907.2.11.4 and NFPA 72.

[F] 907.2.11.1 Group R-1. Single- or multiple-station smoke alarms shall be installed in all of the following locations in Group R-1:

1. In sleeping areas.
2. In every room in the path of the *means of egress* from the sleeping area to the door leading from the *sleeping unit.*
3. In each *story* within the *sleeping unit*, including basements. For *sleeping units* with split levels and without an intervening door between the adjacent levels, a smoke alarm installed on the upper level shall suffice for the adjacent lower level provided that the lower level is less than one full *story* below the upper level.

[F] 907.2.11.2 Groups R-2, R-3, R-4 and I-1. Single- or multiple-station smoke alarms shall be installed and maintained in Groups R-2, R-3, R-4 and I-1 regardless of *occupant load* at all of the following locations:

1. On the ceiling or wall outside of each separate sleeping area in the immediate vicinity of bedrooms.
2. In each room used for sleeping purposes.

   Exception: Single- or multiple-station smoke alarms in Group I-1 occupanices shall not be required where smoke detectors are provided in the sleeping rooms as part of an automatic smoke detection system.

3. In each *story* within a *dwelling unit*, including basements but not including crawl spaces and uninhabitable *attics*. In *dwellings* or *dwelling units* with split levels and without an intervening door between the adjacent levels, a smoke alarm installed on the upper level shall suffice for the adjacent lower level provided that the lower level is less than one full *story* below the upper level.

[F] 907.2.11.3 Interconnection. Where more than one smoke alarm is required to be installed within an individual *dwelling unit* or *sleeping unit* in Group R-1, R-2, R-3 or R-4, the smoke alarms shall be interconnected in such a manner that the activation of one alarm will activate all of the alarms in the individual unit. The alarm shall be clearly audible in all bedrooms over background noise levels with all intervening doors closed.

[F] 907.2.11.4 Power source. In new construction, required smoke alarms shall receive their primary power from the building wiring where such wiring is served from a commercial source and shall be equipped with a battery backup. Smoke alarms with integral strobes that are not equipped with battery backup shall be connected to an emergency electrical system. Smoke alarms shall emit a signal when the batteries are low. Wiring shall be permanent and without a disconnecting switch other than as required for overcurrent protection.

Exception: Smoke alarms are not required to be equipped with battery backup where they are connected to an emergency electrical system.

[F] 907.2.12 Special amusement buildings. An automatic smoke detection system shall be provided in *special amusement buildings* in accordance with Sections 907.2.12.1 through 907.2.12.3.

[F] 907.2.12.1 Alarm. Activation of any single smoke detector, the *automatic sprinkler system* or any other automatic fire detection device shall immediately sound an alarm at the building at a *constantly attended location* from which emergency action can be initiated, including the capability of manual initiation of requirements in Section 907.2.12.2.

[F] 907.2.12.2 System response. The activation of two or more smoke detectors, a single smoke detector equipped with an alarm verification feature, the *automatic sprinkler system* or other *approved* fire detection device shall automatically:

1. Cause illumination of the *means of egress* with light of not less than 1 footcandle (11 lux) at the walking surface level;
2. Stop any conflicting or confusing sounds and visual distractions;
3. Activate an *approved* directional *exit* marking that will become apparent in an emergency; and
4. Activate a prerecorded message, audible throughout the *special amusement building*, instructing patrons to proceed to the nearest *exit*. Alarm signals used in conjunction with the prerecorded message shall produce a sound which is distinctive from other sounds used during normal operation.

[F] 907.2.12.3 Emergency voice/alarm communication system. An emergency voice/alarm communication system, which is also allowed to serve as a public address system, shall be installed in accordance with Section 907.5.2.2 and be audible throughout the entire *special amusement building*.

[F] 907.2.13 High-rise buildings. High-rise buildings shall be provided with an automatic smoke detection system in accordance with Section 907.2.13.1, a fire department communication system in accordance with Section 907.2.13.2 and an emergency voice/alarm communication system in accordance with Section 907.5.2.2.

Exceptions:

1. Airport traffic control towers in accordance with Sections 907.2.22 and 412.
2. *Open parking garages* in accordance with Section 406.3.
3. Buildings with an occupancy in Group A-5 in accordance with Section 303.1.
4. Low-hazard special occupancies in accordance with Section 503.1.1.
5. Buildings with an occupancy in Group H-1, H-2 or H-3 in accordance with Section 415.
6. In Group I-1 and I-2 occupancies, the alarm shall sound at a *constantly attended location* and general occupant notification shall be broadcast by the emergency voice/alarm communication system.

[F] 907.2.13.1 Automatic smoke detection. Automatic smoke detection in high-rise buildings shall be in accordance with Sections 907.2.13.1.1 and 907.2.13.1.2.

[F] 907.2.13.1.1 Area smoke detection. Area smoke detectors shall be provided in accordance with this section. Smoke detectors shall be connected to an automatic fire alarm system. The activation of any detector required by this section shall operate the emergency voice/alarm communication system in accordance with Section 907.5.2.2. Smoke detectors shall be located as follows:

1. In each mechanical equipment, electrical, transformer, telephone equipment or similar room which is not provided with sprinkler protection.
2. In each elevator machine room and in elevator lobbies.

[F] 907.2.13.1.2 Duct smoke detection. Duct smoke detectors complying with Section 907.3.1 shall be located as follows:

1. In the main return air and exhaust air plenum of each air-conditioning system having a capacity greater than 2,000 cubic feet per minute (cfm) (0.94 m^3/s). Such detectors shall be located in a serviceable area downstream of the last duct inlet.
2. At each connection to a vertical duct or riser serving two or more stories from a return air duct or plenum of an air-conditioning system. In Group R-1 and R-2 occupancies, a smoke detector is allowed to be used in each return air riser carrying not more than 5,000 cfm (2.4 m^3/s) and serving not more than 10 air inlet openings.

[F] 907.2.13.2 Fire department communication system. Where a wired communication system is *approved* in lieu of a radio coverage system in accordance with Section 510 of the *International Fire Code*, the wired fire department communication system shall be designed and installed in accordance with NFPA 72 and shall operate between a fire command center complying with Section 911, elevators, elevator lobbies, emergency and standby power rooms, fire pump rooms, *areas of refuge* and inside enclosed *exit stairways*. The fire department communication device shall be provided at each floor level within the enclosed *exit stairway*.

[F] 907.2.14 Atriums connecting more than two stories. A fire alarm system shall be installed in occupancies with an atrium that connects more than two *stories*, with smoke detection installed throughout the atrium. The system shall be activated in accordance with Section 907.5. Such occupancies in Group A, E or M shall be provided with an emergency voice/alarm communication system complying with the requirements of Section 907.5.2.2.

[F] 907.2.15 High-piled combustible storage areas. An automatic smoke detection system shall be installed throughout high-piled combustible storage areas where required by Section 2306.5 of the *International Fire Code*.

[F] 907.2.16 Aerosol storage uses. Aerosol storage rooms and general-purpose warehouses containing aerosols shall be provided with an *approved* manual fire alarm system where required by the *International Fire Code*.

[F] 907.2.17 Lumber, wood structural panel and veneer mills. Lumber, wood structural panel and veneer mills shall be provided with a manual fire alarm system.

[F] 907.2.18 Underground buildings with smoke control systems. Where a smoke control system is installed in an underground building in accordance with this code, automatic smoke detectors shall be provided in accordance with Section 907.2.18.1.

[F] 907.2.18.1 Smoke detectors. A minimum of one smoke detector *listed* for the intended purpose shall be installed in the following areas:

1. Mechanical equipment, electrical, transformer, telephone equipment, elevator machine or similar rooms.
2. Elevator lobbies.
3. The main return and exhaust air plenum of each air-conditioning system serving more than one *story* and located in a serviceable area downstream of the last duct inlet.
4. Each connection to a vertical duct or riser serving two or more floors from return air ducts or plenums of heating, ventilating and air-conditioning systems, except that in Group R occupancies, a *listed* smoke detector is allowed to be used in each return air riser carrying not more than 5,000 cfm (2.4 m^3/s) and serving not more than 10 air inlet openings.

[F] 907.2.18.2 Alarm required. Activation of the smoke control system shall activate an audible alarm at a *constantly attended location*.

[F] 907.2.19 Deep underground buildings. Where the lowest level of a structure is more than 60 feet (18 288 mm) below the finished floor of the lowest *level of exit discharge*, the structure shall be equipped throughout with a manual fire alarm system, including an emergency voice/alarm communication system installed in accordance with Section 907.5.2.2.

[F] 907.2.20 Covered mall buildings. *Covered mall buildings* exceeding 50,000 square feet (4645 m^2) in total floor area shall be provided with an emergency voice/alarm communication system. An emergency voice/alarm communication system serving a mall, required or otherwise, shall be accessible to the fire department. The system shall be provided in accordance with Section 907.5.2.2.

[F] 907.2.21 Residential aircraft hangars. A minimum of one single-station smoke alarm shall be installed within a residential aircraft hangar as defined in Section 412.3.1 and shall be interconnected into the residential smoke alarm or other sounding device to provide an alarm which will be audible in all sleeping areas of the *dwelling*.

[F] 907.2.22 Airport traffic control towers. An automatic smoke detection system that activates the occupant notification system in accordance with Section 907.5 shall be provided in airport control towers in all occupiable and equipment spaces.

Exception: Audible appliances shall not be installed within the control tower cab.

[F] 907.2.23 Battery rooms. An automatic smoke detection system shall be installed in areas containing stationary storage battery systems with a liquid capacity of more than 50 gallons (189 L).

[F] 907.3 Fire safety functions. Automatic fire detectors utilized for the purpose of performing fire safety functions shall be connected to the building's fire alarm control unit where a fire alarm system is required by Section 907.2. Detectors shall, upon actuation, perform the intended function and activate the alarm notification appliances or activate a visible and audible supervisory signal at a *constantly attended location*. In buildings not equipped with a fire alarm system, the automatic fire detector shall be powered by normal electrical service and, upon actuation, perform the intended function. The detectors shall be located in accordance with NFPA 72.

[F] 907.3.1 Duct smoke detectors. Smoke detectors installed in ducts shall be *listed* for the air velocity, temperature and humidity present in the duct. Duct smoke detectors shall be connected to the building's fire alarm control unit when a fire alarm system is required by Section 907.2. Activation of a duct smoke detector shall initiate a visible and audible supervisory signal at a *constantly attended location* and shall perform the intended fire safety function in accordance with this code and the *International Mechanical Code*. Duct smoke detectors shall not be used as a substitute for required open area detection.

Exceptions:

1. The supervisory signal at a *constantly attended location* is not required where duct smoke detectors activate the building's alarm notification appliances.
2. In occupancies not required to be equipped with a fire alarm system, actuation of a smoke detector shall activate a visible and an audible signal in an *approved* location. Smoke detector trouble conditions shall activate a visible or audible signal in an *approved* location and shall be identified as air duct detector trouble.

[F] 907.3.2 Delayed egress locks. Where delayed egress locks are installed on *means of egress* doors in accordance with Section 1008.1.9.7, an automatic smoke or heat detection system shall be installed as required by that section.

[F] 907.3.3 Elevator emergency operation. Automatic fire detectors installed for elevator emergency operation shall be installed in accordance with the provisions of ASME A17.1 and NFPA 72.

[F] 907.3.4 Wiring. The wiring to the auxiliary devices and equipment used to accomplish the above fire safety functions shall be monitored for integrity in accordance with NFPA 72.

[F] 907.4 Initiating devices. Where manual or automatic alarm initiation is required as part of a fire alarm system, the initiating devices shall be installed in accordance with Sections 907.4.1 through 907.4.3.1.

[F] 907.4.1 Protection of fire alarm control unit. In areas that are not continuously occupied, a single smoke detector shall be provided at the location of each fire alarm control unit, notification appliance circuit power extender, and supervising station transmitting equipment.

Exceptions:

1. Where ambient conditions prohibit installation of a smoke detector, a *heat detector* shall be permitted.
2. The smoke detector shall not be required where the building is equipped throughout with an *automatic sprinkler system* in accordance with Section 903.3.1.1 or 903.3.1.2.

[F] 907.4.2 Manual fire alarm boxes. Where a manual fire alarm system is required by another section of this code, it shall be activated by fire alarm boxes installed in accordance with Sections 907.4.2.1 through 907.4.2.5.

[F] 907.4.2.1 Location. Manual fire alarm boxes shall be located not more than 5 feet (1524 mm) from the entrance to each *exit*. Additional manual fire alarm boxes shall be located so that travel distance to the nearest box does not exceed 200 feet (60 960 mm).

[F] 907.4.2.2 Height. The height of the manual fire alarm boxes shall be a minimum of 42 inches (1067 mm) and a maximum of 48 inches (1372 mm) measured vertically, from the floor level to the activating handle or lever of the box.

[F] 907.4.2.3 Color. Manual fire alarm boxes shall be red in color.

[F] 907.4.2.4 Signs. Where fire alarm systems are not monitored by a supervising station, an *approved* permanent sign shall be installed adjacent to each manual fire alarm box that reads: WHEN ALARM SOUNDS CALL FIRE DEPARTMENT.

Exception: Where the manufacturer has permanently provided this information on the manual fire alarm box.

[F] 907.4.2.5 Protective covers. The fire code official is authorized to require the installation of *listed* manual fire alarm box protective covers to prevent malicious false alarms or to provide the manual fire alarm box with protection from physical damage. The protective cover shall be transparent or red in color with a transparent face to permit visibility of the manual fire alarm box. Each cover shall include proper operating instructions. A protective cover that emits a local alarm signal shall not be installed unless *approved*. Protective covers shall not project more than that permitted by Section 1003.3.3.

[F] 907.4.3 Automatic smoke detection. Where an automatic smoke detection system is required it shall utilize smoke detectors unless ambient conditions prohibit such an installation. In spaces where smoke detectors cannot be utilized due to ambient conditions, *approved* automatic *heat detectors* shall be permitted.

907.4.3.1 Automatic sprinkler system. For conditions other than specific fire safety functions noted in Section 907.3, in areas where ambient conditions prohibit the installation of smoke detectors, an *automatic sprinkler system* installed in such areas in accordance with Section 903.3.1.1 or 903.3.1.2 and that is connected to the fire alarm system shall be *approved* as automatic heat detection.

[F] 907.5 Occupant notification systems. A fire alarm system shall annunciate at the panel and shall initiate occupant notification upon activation, in accordance with Sections 907.5.1 through 907.5.2.3.4. Where a fire alarm system is required by another section of this code, it shall be activated by:

1. Automatic fire detectors.
2. Sprinkler waterflow devices.
3. Manual fire alarm boxes.
4. Automatic fire-extinguishing systems.

Exception: Where notification systems are allowed elsewhere in Section 907 to annunciate at a *constantly attended location*.

[F] 907.5.1 Presignal feature. A presignal feature shall not be installed unless *approved* by the fire code official and the fire department. Where a presignal feature is provided, a signal shall be annunciated at a *constantly attended location approved* by the fire department, in order that occupant notification can be activated in the event of fire or other emergency.

[F] 907.5.2 Alarm notification appliances. Alarm notification appliances shall be provided and shall be *listed* for their purpose.

[F] 907.5.2.1 Audible alarms. Audible alarm notification appliances shall be provided and emit a distinctive sound that is not to be used for any purpose other than that of a fire alarm.

Exceptions:

1. Visible alarm notification appliances shall be allowed in lieu of audible alarm notification appliances in critical care areas of Group I-2 occupancies.
2. In Group I-2 occupancies, Group B ambulatory health care facilities and licensed large residential care facilities in accordance with Section 425 where occupants are incapable of evacuating themselves because of age, physical or mental disabilities, or physical restraint, audible notification appliances shall be permitted to meet the private operating mode requirements of NFPA 72 in patient care and treatment areas.

907.5.2.1.1 Average sound pressure. The audible alarm notification appliances shall provide a sound pressure level of 15 decibels (dBA) above the average ambient sound level or 5 dBA above the maximum sound level having a duration of at least 60 seconds, whichever is greater, in every *occupiable space* within the building. The minimum sound pressure levels shall be: 75 dBA in occupancies in Groups R and I-1; 90 dBA in mechanical equipment rooms and 60 dBA in other occupancies.

907.5.2.1.2 Maximum sound pressure. The maximum sound pressure level for audible alarm notification appliances shall be 110 dBA at the minimum hearing distance from the audible appliance. Where the average ambient noise is greater than 95 dBA, visible alarm notification appliances shall be provided in accordance with NFPA 72 and audible alarm notification appliances shall not be required.

907.5.2.2 Emergency voice/alarm communication systems. Emergency voice/alarm communication systems required by this code shall be designed and installed in accordance with NFPA 72. The operation of any automatic fire detector, sprinkler waterflow device or manual fire alarm box shall automatically sound an alert tone followed by voice instructions giving *approved* information and directions for a general or staged evacuation in accordance with the building's fire safety and evacuation plans required by Section 404 of the *International Fire Code*. In high-rise buildings, the system shall operate on a minimum of the alarming floor, the floor above and the floor below. Speakers shall be provided throughout the building by paging zones. At a minimum, paging zones shall be provided as follows:

1. Elevator groups.
2. *Exit stairways.*
3. Each floor.
4. *Areas of refuge* as defined in Section 1002.1.

Exception: In Group I-1 and I-2 occupancies, the alarm shall sound in a constantly attended area and a general occupant notification shall be broadcast over the overhead page.

[F] 907.5.2.2.1 Manual override. A manual override for emergency voice communication shall be provided on a selective and all-call basis for all paging zones.

[F] 907.5.2.2.2 Live voice messages. The emergency voice/alarm communication system shall also have the capability to broadcast live voice messages by paging zones on a selective and all-call basis.

[F] 907.5.2.2.3 Alternate uses. The emergency voice/alarm communication system shall be allowed to be used for other announcements, provided the manual fire alarm use takes precedence over any other use.

[F] 907.5.2.2.4 Emergency power. Emergency voice/alarm communication systems shall be provided with an *approved* emergency power source.

[F] 907.5.2.3 Visible alarms. Visible alarm notification appliances shall be provided in accordance with Sections 907.5.2.3.1 through 907.5.2.3.4.

Exceptions:

1. Visible alarm notification appliances are not required in *alterations*, except where an existing fire alarm system is upgraded or replaced, or a new fire alarm system is installed.
2. Visible alarm notification appliances shall not be required in *exits* as defined in Section 1002.1.

3. Visible alarm notification appliances shall not be required in elevator cars.

[F] 907.5.2.3.1 Public and common areas. Visible alarm notification appliances shall be provided in public areas and common areas.

[F] 907.5.2.3.2 Employee work areas. Where employee work areas have audible alarm coverage, the notification appliance circuits serving the employee work areas shall be initially designed with a minimum of 20-percent spare capacity to account for the potential of adding visible notification appliances in the future to accommodate hearing impaired employee(s).

[F] 907.5.2.3.3 Groups I-1 and R-1. Group I-1 and R-1 *dwelling units* or *sleeping units* in accordance with Table 907.5.2.3.3 shall be provided with a visible alarm notification appliance, activated by both the in-room smoke alarm and the building fire alarm system.

[F] TABLE 907.5.2.3.3
VISIBLE ALARMS

NUMBER OF SLEEP UNITS	SLEEPING ACCOMMODATIONS WITH VISIBLE ALARMS
6 to 25	2
26 to 50	4
51 to 75	7
76 to 100	9
101 to 150	12
151 to 200	14
201 to 300	17
301 to 400	20
401 to 500	22
501 to 1,000	5% of total
1,001 and over	50 plus 3 for each 100 over 1,000

[F] 907.5.2.3.4 Group R-2. In Group R-2 occupancies required by Section 907 to have a fire alarm system, all *dwelling units* and *sleeping units* shall be provided with the capability to support visible alarm notification appliances in accordance with ICC A117.1.

[F] 907.6 Installation. A fire alarm system shall be installed in accordance with this section and NFPA 72.

[F] 907.6.1 Wiring. Wiring shall comply with the requirements of NFPA 70 and NFPA 72. Wireless protection systems utilizing radio-frequency transmitting devices shall comply with the special requirements for supervision of low-power wireless systems in NFPA 72.

[F] 907.6.2 Power supply. The primary and secondary power supply for the fire alarm system shall be provided in accordance with NFPA 72.

Exception: Back-up power for single-station and multiple-station smoke alarms as required in Section 907.2.11.4.

[F] 907.6.3 Zones. Each floor shall be zoned separately and a zone shall not exceed 22,500 square feet (2090 m^2). The length of any zone shall not exceed 300 feet (91 440 mm) in any direction.

Exception: *Automatic sprinkler system* zones shall not exceed the area permitted by NFPA 13.

[F] 907.6.3.1 Zoning indicator panel. A zoning indicator panel and the associated controls shall be provided in an *approved* location. The visual zone indication shall lock in until the system is reset and shall not be canceled by the operation of an audible-alarm silencing switch.

[F] 907.6.3.2 High-rise buildings. In high-rise buildings, a separate zone by floor shall be provided for each of the following types of alarm-initiating devices where provided:

1. Smoke detectors.
2. Sprinkler waterflow devices.
3. Manual fire alarm boxes.
4. Other *approved* types of automatic fire detection devices or suppression systems.

[F] 907.6.4 Access. Access shall be provided to each fire alarm device and notification appliance for periodic inspection, maintenance and testing.

[F] 907.6.5 Monitoring. Fire alarm systems required by this chapter or by the *International Fire Code* shall be monitored by an *approved* supervising station in accordance with NFPA 72.

Exception: Monitoring by a supervising station is not required for:

1. Single- and multiple-station smoke alarms required by Section 907.2.11.
2. Smoke detectors in Group I-3 occupancies.
3. *Automatic sprinkler systems* in one- and two-family dwellings.

[F] 907.6.5.1 Automatic telephone-dialing devices. Automatic telephone-dialing devices used to transmit an emergency alarm shall not be connected to any fire department telephone number unless *approved* by the fire chief.

[F] 907.7 Acceptance tests and completion. Upon completion of the installation, the fire alarm system and all fire alarm components shall be tested in accordance with NFPA 72.

[F] 907.7.1 Single- and multiple-station alarm devices. When the installation of the alarm devices is complete, each device and interconnecting wiring for multiple-station alarm devices shall be tested in accordance with the smoke alarm provisions of NFPA 72.

[F] 907.7.2 Record of completion. A record of completion in accordance with NFPA 72 verifying that the system has been installed and tested in accordance with the *approved* plans and specifications shall be provided.

[F] 907.7.3 Instructions. Operating, testing and maintenance instructions and record drawings ("as-builts") and equipment specifications shall be provided at an *approved* location.

[F] 907.8 Inspection, testing and maintenance. The maintenance and testing schedules and procedures for fire alarm and fire detection systems shall be in accordance with Section 907.9 of the *International Fire Code*.

SECTION 908
EMERGENCY ALARM SYSTEMS

[F] 908.1 Group H occupancies. Emergency alarms for the detection and notification of an emergency condition in Group H occupancies shall be provided in accordance with Section 414.7.

[F] 908.2 Group H-5 occupancy. Emergency alarms for notification of an emergency condition in an HPM facility shall be provided as required in Section 415.8.4.6. A continuous gas-detection system shall be provided for HPM gases in accordance with Section 415.8.7.

[F] 908.3 Highly toxic and toxic materials. A gas detection system shall be provided to detect the presence of *highly toxic* or *toxic* gas at or below the permissible exposure limit (PEL) or ceiling limit of the gas for which detection is provided. The system shall be capable of monitoring the discharge from the treatment system at or below one-half the immediately dangerous to life and health (IDLH) limit.

Exception: A gas-detection system is not required for *toxic* gases when the physiological warning threshold level for the gas is at a level below the accepted PEL for the gas.

[F] 908.3.1 Alarms. The gas detection system shall initiate a local alarm and transmit a signal to a constantly attended control station when a short-term hazard condition is detected. The alarm shall be both visible and audible and shall provide warning both inside and outside the area where gas is detected. The audible alarm shall be distinct from all other alarms.

Exception: Signal transmission to a constantly attended control station is not required when not more than one cylinder of *highly toxic* or *toxic* gas is stored.

[F] 908.3.2 Shutoff of gas supply. The gas detection system shall automatically close the shutoff valve at the source on gas supply piping and tubing related to the system being monitored for whichever gas is detected.

Exception: Automatic shutdown is not required for reactors utilized for the production of *highly toxic* or *toxic* compressed gases where such reactors are:

1. Operated at pressures less than 15 pounds per square inch gauge (psig) (103.4 kPa).
2. Constantly attended.
3. Provided with readily accessible emergency shutoff valves.

[F] 908.3.3 Valve closure. The automatic closure of shutoff valves shall be in accordance with the following:

1. When the gas-detection sampling point initiating the gas detection system alarm is within a gas cabinet or exhausted enclosure, the shutoff valve in the gas cabinet or exhausted enclosure for the specific gas detected shall automatically close.
2. Where the gas-detection sampling point initiating the gas detection system alarm is within a gas room and compressed gas containers are not in gas cabinets or exhausted enclosures, the shutoff valves on all gas lines for the specific gas detected shall automatically close.
3. Where the gas-detection sampling point initiating the gas detection system alarm is within a piping distribution manifold enclosure, the shutoff valve for the compressed container of specific gas detected supplying the manifold shall automatically close.

Exception: When the gas-detection sampling point initiating the gas-detection system alarm is at a use location or within a gas valve enclosure of a branch line downstream of a piping distribution manifold, the shutoff valve in the gas valve enclosure for the branch line located in the piping distribution manifold enclosure shall automatically close.

[F] 908.4 Ozone gas-generator rooms. Ozone gas-generator rooms shall be equipped with a continuous gas-detection system that will shut off the generator and sound a local alarm when concentrations above the PEL occur.

[F] 908.5 Repair garages. A flammable-gas detection system shall be provided in repair garages for vehicles fueled by nonodorized gases in accordance with Section 406.6.6.

[F] 908.6 Refrigerant detector. Machinery rooms shall contain a refrigerant detector with an audible and visual alarm. The detector, or a sampling tube that draws air to the detector, shall be located in an area where refrigerant from a leak will concentrate. The alarm shall be actuated at a value not greater than the corresponding TLV-TWA values for the refrigerant classification indicated in the *International Mechanical Code*. Detectors and alarms shall be placed in *approved* locations.

SECTION 909
SMOKE CONTROL SYSTEMS

[F] 909.1 Scope and purpose. This section applies to mechanical or passive smoke control systems when they are required by other provisions of this code. The purpose of this section is to establish minimum requirements for the design, installation and acceptance testing of smoke control systems that are intended to provide a tenable environment for the evacuation or relocation of occupants. These provisions are not intended for the preservation of contents, the timely restoration of operations or for assistance in fire suppression or overhaul activities. Smoke control systems regulated by this section serve a different purpose than the smoke- and heat-venting provisions found in Section 910. Mechanical smoke control systems shall not be considered exhaust systems under Chapter 5 of the *International Mechanical Code*.

[F] 909.2 General design requirements. Buildings, structures or parts thereof required by this code to have a smoke control system or systems shall have such systems designed in accordance with the applicable requirements of Section 909 and the generally accepted and well-established principles of engineering relevant to the design. The *construction documents* shall include sufficient information and detail to adequately describe the elements of the design necessary for the proper implementation of the smoke control systems. These documents shall be accompanied by sufficient information and analysis to demonstrate compliance with these provisions.

[F] 909.3 Special inspection and test requirements. In addition to the ordinary inspection and test requirements which buildings, structures and parts thereof are required to undergo, smoke control systems subject to the provisions of Section 909 shall undergo *special inspections* and tests sufficient to verify the proper commissioning of the smoke control design in its final installed condition. The design submission accompanying the *construction documents* shall clearly detail procedures and methods to be used and the items subject to such inspections and tests. Such commissioning shall be in accordance with generally accepted engineering practice and, where possible, based on published standards for the particular testing involved. The special inspections and tests required by this section shall be conducted under the same terms in Section 1704.

[F] 909.4 Analysis. A rational analysis supporting the types of smoke control systems to be employed, their methods of operation, the systems supporting them and the methods of construction to be utilized shall accompany the submitted *construction documents* and shall include, but not be limited to, the items indicated in Sections 909.4.1 through 909.4.6.

[F] 909.4.1 Stack effect. The system shall be designed such that the maximum probable normal or reverse stack effect will not adversely interfere with the system's capabilities. In determining the maximum probable stack effect, altitude, elevation, weather history and interior temperatures shall be used.

[F] 909.4.2 Temperature effect of fire. Buoyancy and expansion caused by the design fire in accordance with Section 909.9 shall be analyzed. The system shall be designed such that these effects do not adversely interfere with the system's capabilities.

[F] 909.4.3 Wind effect. The design shall consider the adverse effects of wind. Such consideration shall be consistent with the wind-loading provisions of Chapter 16.

[F] 909.4.4 HVAC systems. The design shall consider the effects of the heating, ventilating and air-conditioning (HVAC) systems on both smoke and fire transport. The analysis shall include all permutations of systems status. The design shall consider the effects of the fire on the HVAC systems.

[F] 909.4.5 Climate. The design shall consider the effects of low temperatures on systems, property and occupants. Air inlets and exhausts shall be located so as to prevent snow or ice blockage.

[F] 909.4.6 Duration of operation. All portions of active or passive smoke control systems shall be capable of continued operation after detection of the fire event for a period of not less than either 20 minutes or 1.5 times the calculated egress time, whichever is less.

[F] 909.5 Smoke barrier construction. *Smoke barriers* shall comply with Section 710, and shall be constructed and sealed to limit leakage areas exclusive of protected openings. The maximum allowable leakage area shall be the aggregate area calculated using the following leakage area ratios:

1. Walls: $A/A_w = 0.00100$
2. *Exit* enclosures: $A/A_w = 0.00035$
3. All other shafts: $A/A_w = 0.00150$
4. Floors and roofs: $A/A_F = 0.00050$

where:

A = Total leakage area, square feet (m^2).

A_F = Unit floor or roof area of barrier, square feet (m^2).

A_w = Unit wall area of barrier, square feet (m^2).

The leakage area ratios shown do not include openings due to doors, operable windows or similar gaps. These shall be included in calculating the total leakage area.

[F] 909.5.1 Leakage area. The total leakage area of the barrier is the product of the *smoke barrier* gross area multiplied by the allowable leakage area ratio, plus the area of other openings such as gaps and operable windows. Compliance shall be determined by achieving the minimum air pressure difference across the barrier with the system in the smoke control mode for mechanical smoke control systems. Passive smoke control systems tested using other *approved* means such as door fan testing shall be as *approved* by the fire code official.

[F] 909.5.2 Opening protection. Openings in *smoke barriers* shall be protected by automatic-closing devices actuated by the required controls for the mechanical smoke control system. Door openings shall be protected by *fire door assemblies* complying with Section 715.4.3.

Exceptions:

1. Passive smoke control systems with automatic-closing devices actuated by spot-type smoke detectors *listed* for releasing service installed in accordance with Section 907.3.
2. Fixed openings between smoke zones that are protected utilizing the airflow method.
3. In Group I-2, where such doors are installed across corridors, a pair of opposite-swinging doors without a center mullion shall be installed having vision panels with fire protection-rated glazing materials in fire protection-rated frames, the area of which shall not exceed that tested. The doors shall be close-fitting within operational tolerances and shall not have undercuts, louvers or grilles. The doors shall have head and jamb stops, astragals or rabbets at meeting edges and shall be automatic-closing by smoke detection in accordance with Section 715.4.8.3. Positive-latching devices are not required.
4. Group I-3.

5. Openings between smoke zones with clear ceiling heights of 14 feet (4267 mm) or greater and bank-down capacity of greater than 20 minutes as determined by the design fire size.

[F] 909.5.2.1 Ducts and air transfer openings. Ducts and air transfer openings are required to be protected with a minimum Class II, 250°F (121°C) *smoke damper* complying with Section 716.

[F] 909.6 Pressurization method. The primary mechanical means of controlling smoke shall be by pressure differences across smoke barriers. Maintenance of a tenable environment is not required in the smoke control zone of fire origin.

[F] 909.6.1 Minimum pressure difference. The minimum pressure difference across a *smoke barrier* shall be 0.05-inch water gage (0.0124 kPa) in fully sprinklered buildings.

In buildings permitted to be other than fully sprinklered, the smoke control system shall be designed to achieve pressure differences at least two times the maximum calculated pressure difference produced by the design fire.

[F] 909.6.2 Maximum pressure difference. The maximum air pressure difference across a *smoke barrier* shall be determined by required door-opening or closing forces. The actual force required to open *exit* doors when the system is in the smoke control mode shall be in accordance with Section 1008.1.2. Opening and closing forces for other doors shall be determined by standard engineering methods for the resolution of forces and reactions. The calculated force to set a side-hinged, swinging door in motion shall be determined by:

$$F = F_{dc} + K(WA\Delta P)/2(W - d) \qquad \textbf{(Equation 9-1)}$$

where:

A = Door area, square feet (m^2).

d = Distance from door handle to latch edge of door, feet (m).

F = Total door opening force, pounds (N).

F_{dc} = Force required to overcome closing device, pounds (N).

K = Coefficient 5.2 (1.0).

W = Door width, feet (m).

ΔP = Design pressure difference, inches of water (Pa).

[F] 909.7 Airflow design method. When *approved* by the fire code official, smoke migration through openings fixed in a permanently open position, which are located between smoke control zones by the use of the airflow method, shall be permitted. The design airflow shall be in accordance with this section. Airflow shall be directed to limit smoke migration from the fire zone. The geometry of openings shall be considered to prevent flow reversal from turbulent effects.

[F] 909.7.1 Velocity. The minimum average velocity through a fixed opening shall not be less than:

$$v = 217.2\,[h\,(T_f - T_o)/(T_f + 460)]^{1/2} \qquad \textbf{(Equation 9-2)}$$

For SI: $v = 119.9\,[h\,(T_f - T_o)/T_f]^{1/2}$

where:

h = Height of opening, feet (m).

T_f = Temperature of smoke, °F (K).

T_o = Temperature of ambient air, °F (K).

v = Air velocity, feet per minute (m/s).

[F] 909.7.2 Prohibited conditions. This method shall not be employed where either the quantity of air or the velocity of the airflow will adversely affect other portions of the smoke control system, unduly intensify the fire, disrupt plume dynamics or interfere with exiting. In no case shall airflow toward the fire exceed 200 feet per minute (1.02 m/s). Where the formula in Section 909.7.1 requires airflow to exceed this limit, the airflow method shall not be used.

[F] 909.8 Exhaust method. When *approved* by the fire code official, mechanical smoke control for large enclosed volumes, such as in atriums or malls, shall be permitted to utilize the exhaust method. Smoke control systems using the exhaust method shall be designed in accordance with NFPA 92B.

[F] 909.8.1 Smoke layer. The height of the lowest horizontal surface of the smoke layer interface shall be maintained at least 6 feet (1829 mm) above any walking surface that forms a portion of a required egress system within the smoke zone.

[F] 909.9 Design fire. The design fire shall be based on a rational analysis performed by the *registered design professional* and *approved* by the fire code official. The design fire shall be based on the analysis in accordance with Section 909.4 and this section.

[F] 909.9.1 Factors considered. The engineering analysis shall include the characteristics of the fuel, fuel load, effects included by the fire and whether the fire is likely to be steady or unsteady.

[F] 909.9.2 Separation distance. Determination of the design fire shall include consideration of the type of fuel, fuel spacing and configuration.

[F] 909.9.3 Heat-release assumptions. The analysis shall make use of best available data from *approved* sources and shall not be based on excessively stringent limitations of combustible material.

[F] 909.9.4 Sprinkler effectiveness assumptions. A documented engineering analysis shall be provided for conditions that assume fire growth is halted at the time of sprinkler activation.

[F] 909.10 Equipment. Equipment including, but not limited to, fans, ducts, automatic *dampers* and balance *dampers*, shall be suitable for its intended use, suitable for the probable exposure temperatures that the rational analysis indicates and as *approved* by the fire code official.

[F] 909.10.1 Exhaust fans. Components of exhaust fans shall be rated and certified by the manufacturer for the probable temperature rise to which the components will be exposed. This temperature rise shall be computed by:

$$T_s = (Q_c/mc) + (T_a) \qquad \textbf{(Equation 9-3)}$$

where:

c = Specific heat of smoke at smoke layer temperature, Btu/lb · °F (kJ/kg · K).

m = Exhaust rate, pounds per second (kg/s).

Q_c = Convective heat output of fire, Btu/s (kW).

T_a = Ambient temperature, °F (K).

T_s = Smoke temperature, °F (K).

Exception: Reduced T_s as calculated based on the assurance of adequate dilution air.

[F] 909.10.2 Ducts. Duct materials and joints shall be capable of withstanding the probable temperatures and pressures to which they are exposed as determined in accordance with Section 909.10.1. Ducts shall be constructed and supported in accordance with the *International Mechanical Code.* Ducts shall be leak tested to 1.5 times the maximum design pressure in accordance with nationally accepted practices. Measured leakage shall not exceed 5 percent of design flow. Results of such testing shall be a part of the documentation procedure. Ducts shall be supported directly from fire-resistance-rated structural elements of the building by substantial, noncombustible supports.

Exception: Flexible connections (for the purpose of vibration isolation) complying with the *International Mechanical Code*, that are constructed of *approved* fire-resistance-rated materials.

[F] 909.10.3 Equipment, inlets and outlets. Equipment shall be located so as to not expose uninvolved portions of the building to an additional fire hazard. Outside air inlets shall be located so as to minimize the potential for introducing smoke or flame into the building. Exhaust outlets shall be so located as to minimize reintroduction of smoke into the building and to limit exposure of the building or adjacent buildings to an additional fire hazard.

[F] 909.10.4 Automatic dampers. Automatic *dampers*, regardless of the purpose for which they are installed within the smoke control system, shall be *listed* and conform to the requirements of *approved*, recognized standards.

[F] 909.10.5 Fans. In addition to other requirements, belt-driven fans shall have 1.5 times the number of belts required for the design duty, with the minimum number of belts being two. Fans shall be selected for stable performance based on normal temperature and, where applicable, elevated temperature. Calculations and manufacturer's fan curves shall be part of the documentation procedures. Fans shall be supported and restrained by noncombustible devices in accordance with the requirements of Chapter 16. Motors driving fans shall not be operated beyond their nameplate horsepower (kilowatts), as determined from measurement of actual current draw, and shall have a minimum service factor of 1.15.

[F] 909.11 Power systems. The smoke control system shall be supplied with two sources of power. Primary power shall be from the normal building power systems. Secondary power shall be from an *approved* standby source complying with Chapter 27 of this code. The standby power source and its transfer switches shall be in a room separate from the normal power transformers and switch gears and ventilated directly to and from the exterior. The room shall be enclosed with not less than 1-hour *fire barriers* constructed in accordance with Section 707 or horizontal assemblies constructed in accordance with Section 712, or both. The transfer to full standby power shall be automatic and within 60 seconds of failure of the primary power system.

[F] 909.11.1 Power sources and power surges. Elements of the smoke management system relying on volatile memories or the like shall be supplied with uninterruptable power sources of sufficient duration to span a 15-minute primary power interruption. Elements of the smoke management system susceptible to power surges shall be suitably protected by conditioners, suppressors or other *approved* means.

[F] 909.12 Detection and control systems. Fire detection systems providing control input or output signals to mechanical smoke control systems or elements thereof shall comply with the requirements of Section 907. Such systems shall be equipped with a control unit complying with UL 864 and *listed* as smoke control equipment.

Control systems for mechanical smoke control systems shall include provisions for verification. Verification shall include positive confirmation of actuation, testing, manual override, the presence of power downstream of all disconnects and, through a preprogrammed weekly test sequence, report abnormal conditions audibly, visually and by printed report.

[F] 909.12.1 Wiring. In addition to meeting requirements of NFPA 70, all wiring, regardless of voltage, shall be fully enclosed within continuous raceways.

[F] 909.12.2 Activation. Smoke control systems shall be activated in accordance with this section.

[F] 909.12.2.1 Pressurization, airflow or exhaust method. Mechanical smoke control systems using the pressurization, airflow or exhaust method shall have completely automatic control.

[F] 909.12.2.2 Passive method. Passive smoke control systems actuated by *approved* spot-type detectors *listed* for releasing service shall be permitted.

[F] 909.12.3 Automatic control. Where completely automatic control is required or used, the automatic-control sequences shall be initiated from an appropriately zoned *automatic sprinkler system* complying with Section 903.3.1.1, manual controls that are readily accessible to the fire department and any smoke detectors required by engineering analysis.

[F] 909.13 Control air tubing. Control air tubing shall be of sufficient size to meet the required response times. Tubing shall be flushed clean and dry prior to final connections and shall be adequately supported and protected from damage. Tubing passing through concrete or masonry shall be sleeved and protected from abrasion and electrolytic action.

[F] 909.13.1 Materials. Control-air tubing shall be hard-drawn copper, Type L, ACR in accordance with ASTM B 42, ASTM B 43, ASTM B 68, ASTM B 88, ASTM B 251 and ASTM B 280. Fittings shall be wrought copper or brass, solder type in accordance with ASME B 16.18 or ASME B16.22. Changes in direction shall be made with appropriate tool bends. Brass compression-type fittings shall be used at final connection to devices; other joints shall be brazed using a BCuP5 brazing alloy with solidus above 1,100°F (593°C) and liquids below 1,500°F (816°C). Brazing flux shall be used on copper-to-brass joints only.

Exception: Nonmetallic tubing used within control panels and at the final connection to devices provided all of the following conditions are met:

1. Tubing shall be *listed* by an *approved* agency for flame and smoke characteristics.
2. Tubing and connected devices shall be completely enclosed within a galvanized or paint-grade steel enclosure having a minimum thickness of 0.0296 inch (0.7534 mm) (No. 22 gage). Entry to the enclosure shall be by copper tubing with a protective grommet of neoprene or teflon or by suitable brass compression to male barbed adapter.
3. Tubing shall be identified by appropriately documented coding.
4. Tubing shall be neatly tied and supported within the enclosure. Tubing bridging cabinets and doors or moveable devices shall be of sufficient length to avoid tension and excessive stress. Tubing shall be protected against abrasion. Tubing serving devices on doors shall be fastened along hinges.

[F] 909.13.2 Isolation from other functions. Control tubing serving other than smoke control functions shall be isolated by automatic isolation valves or shall be an independent system.

[F] 909.13.3 Testing. Control air tubing shall be tested at three times the operating pressure for not less than 30 minutes without any noticeable loss in gauge pressure prior to final connection to devices.

[F] 909.14 Marking and identification. The detection and control systems shall be clearly marked at all junctions, accesses and terminations.

[F] 909.15 Control diagrams. Identical control diagrams showing all devices in the system and identifying their location and function shall be maintained current and kept on file with the fire code official, the fire department and in the fire command center in a format and manner *approved* by the fire chief.

[F] 909.16 Fire-fighter's smoke control panel. A fire-fighter's smoke control panel for fire department emergency response purposes only shall be provided and shall include manual control or override of automatic control for mechanical smoke control systems. The panel shall be located in a fire command center complying with Section 911 in high-rise buildings or buildings with smoke-protected assembly seating. In all other buildings, the fire-fighter's smoke control panel shall be installed in an *approved* location adjacent to the fire alarm control panel. The fire-fighter's smoke control panel shall comply with Sections 909.16.1 through 909.16.3.

[F] 909.16.1 Smoke control systems. Fans within the building shall be shown on the fire-fighter's control panel. A clear indication of the direction of airflow and the relationship of components shall be displayed. Status indicators shall be provided for all smoke control equipment, annunciated by fan and zone, and by pilot-lamp-type indicators as follows:

1. Fans, *dampers* and other operating equipment in their normal status—WHITE.
2. Fans, *dampers* and other operating equipment in their off or closed status—RED.
3. Fans, *dampers* and other operating equipment in their on or open status—GREEN.
4. Fans, *dampers* and other operating equipment in a fault status—YELLOW/AMBER.

[F] 909.16.2 Smoke control panel. The fire-fighter's control panel shall provide control capability over the complete smoke-control system equipment within the building as follows:

1. ON-AUTO-OFF control over each individual piece of operating smoke control equipment that can also be controlled from other sources within the building. This includes *stairway* pressurization fans; smoke exhaust fans; supply, return and exhaust fans; elevator shaft fans and other operating equipment used or intended for smoke control purposes.
2. OPEN-AUTO-CLOSE control over individual *dampers* relating to smoke control and that are also controlled from other sources within the building.
3. ON-OFF or OPEN-CLOSE control over smoke control and other critical equipment associated with a fire or smoke emergency and that can only be controlled from the fire-fighter's control panel.

Exceptions:

1. Complex systems, where *approved*, where the controls and indicators are combined to control and indicate all elements of a single smoke zone as a unit.
2. Complex systems, where *approved*, where the control is accomplished by computer interface using *approved*, plain English commands.

[F] 909.16.3 Control action and priorities. The fire-fighter's control panel actions shall be as follows:

1. ON-OFF and OPEN-CLOSE control actions shall have the highest priority of any control point within the building. Once issued from the fire-fighter's control panel, no automatic or manual control from any other control point within the building shall contradict the control action. Where automatic means are provided to interrupt normal, nonemergency equipment operation or produce a specific result to safeguard the building or equipment (i.e., duct freezestats, duct smoke detectors, high-temperature cutouts, tem-

perature-actuated linkage and similar devices), such means shall be capable of being overridden by the fire-fighter's control panel. The last control action as indicated by each fire-fighter's control panel switch position shall prevail. In no case shall control actions require the smoke control system to assume more than one configuration at any one time.

Exception: Power disconnects required by NFPA 70.

2. Only the AUTO position of each three-position fire-fighter's control panel switch shall allow automatic or manual control action from other control points within the building. The AUTO position shall be the NORMAL, nonemergency, building control position. Where a fire-fighter's control panel is in the AUTO position, the actual status of the device (on, off, open, closed) shall continue to be indicated by the status indicator described above. When directed by an automatic signal to assume an emergency condition, the NORMAL position shall become the emergency condition for that device or group of devices within the zone. In no case shall control actions require the smoke control system to assume more than one configuration at any one time.

[F] 909.17 System response time. Smoke-control system activation shall be initiated immediately after receipt of an appropriate automatic or manual activation command. Smoke control systems shall activate individual components (such as *dampers* and fans) in the sequence necessary to prevent physical damage to the fans, *dampers*, ducts and other equipment. For purposes of smoke control, the fire-fighter's control panel response time shall be the same for automatic or manual smoke control action initiated from any other building control point. The total response time, including that necessary for detection, shutdown of operating equipment and smoke control system startup, shall allow for full operational mode to be achieved before the conditions in the space exceed the design smoke condition. The system response time for each component and their sequential relationships shall be detailed in the required rational analysis and verification of their installed condition reported in the required final report.

[F] 909.18 Acceptance testing. Devices, equipment, components and sequences shall be individually tested. These tests, in addition to those required by other provisions of this code, shall consist of determination of function, sequence and, where applicable, capacity of their installed condition.

[F] 909.18.1 Detection devices. Smoke or fire detectors that are a part of a smoke control system shall be tested in accordance with Chapter 9 in their installed condition. When applicable, this testing shall include verification of airflow in both minimum and maximum conditions.

[F] 909.18.2 Ducts. Ducts that are part of a smoke control system shall be traversed using generally accepted practices to determine actual air quantities.

[F] 909.18.3 Dampers. *Dampers* shall be tested for function in their installed condition.

[F] 909.18.4 Inlets and outlets. Inlets and outlets shall be read using generally accepted practices to determine air quantities.

[F] 909.18.5 Fans. Fans shall be examined for correct rotation. Measurements of voltage, amperage, revolutions per minute (rpm) and belt tension shall be made.

[F] 909.18.6 Smoke barriers. Measurements using inclined manometers or other *approved* calibrated measuring devices shall be made of the pressure differences across *smoke barriers*. Such measurements shall be conducted for each possible smoke control condition.

[F] 909.18.7 Controls. Each smoke zone equipped with an automatic-initiation device shall be put into operation by the actuation of one such device. Each additional device within the zone shall be verified to cause the same sequence without requiring the operation of fan motors in order to prevent damage. Control sequences shall be verified throughout the system, including verification of override from the fire-fighter's control panel and simulation of standby power conditions.

[F] 909.18.8 Special inspections for smoke control. Smoke control systems shall be tested by a special inspector.

[F] 909.18.8.1 Scope of testing. *Special inspections* shall be conducted in accordance with the following:

1. During erection of ductwork and prior to concealment for the purposes of leakage testing and recording of device location.
2. Prior to occupancy and after sufficient completion for the purposes of pressure-difference testing, flow measurements, and detection and control verification.

[F] 909.18.8.2 Qualifications. *Special inspection* agencies for smoke control shall have expertise in fire protection engineering, mechanical engineering and certification as air balancers.

[F] 909.18.8.3 Reports. A complete report of testing shall be prepared by the special inspector or *special inspection* agency. The report shall include identification of all devices by manufacturer, nameplate data, design values, measured values and identification tag or *mark*. The report shall be reviewed by the responsible *registered design professional* and, when satisfied that the design intent has been achieved, the responsible *registered design professional* shall seal, sign and date the report.

[F] 909.18.8.3.1 Report filing. A copy of the final report shall be filed with the fire code official and an identical copy shall be maintained in an *approved* location at the building.

[F] 909.18.9 Identification and documentation. Charts, drawings and other documents identifying and locating each component of the smoke control system, and describing its proper function and maintenance requirements, shall be maintained on file at the building as an attachment to the report required by Section 909.18.8.3. Devices shall have an *approved* identifying tag or *mark* on them consistent with the other required documentation and shall be dated indicating the last time they were successfully tested and by whom.

[F] 909.19 System acceptance. Buildings, or portions thereof, required by this code to comply with this section shall not be issued a certificate of occupancy until such time that the fire code official determines that the provisions of this section have been fully complied with and that the fire department has received satisfactory instruction on the operation, both automatic and manual, of the system.

Exception: In buildings of phased construction, a temporary certificate of occupancy, as *approved* by the fire code official, shall be allowed provided that those portions of the building to be occupied meet the requirements of this section and that the remainder does not pose a significant hazard to the safety of the proposed occupants or adjacent buildings.

909.20 Smokeproof enclosures. Where required by Section 1022.9, a smokeproof enclosure shall be constructed in accordance with this section. A smokeproof enclosure shall consist of an enclosed interior *exit stairway* that conforms to Section 1022.1 and an open exterior balcony or ventilated vestibule meeting the requirements of this section. Where access to the roof is required by the *International Fire Code*, such access shall be from the smokeproof enclosure where a smokeproof enclosure is required.

909.20.1 Access. Access to the *stair* shall be by way of a vestibule or an open exterior balcony. The minimum dimension of the vestibule shall not be less than the required width of the *corridor* leading to the vestibule but shall not have a width of less than 44 inches (1118 mm) and shall not have a length of less than 72 inches (1829 mm) in the direction of egress travel.

909.20.2 Construction. The smokeproof enclosure shall be separated from the remainder of the building by not less than 2-hour *fire barriers* constructed in accordance with Section 707 or *horizontal assemblies* constructed in accordance with Section 712, or both. Openings are not permitted other than the required *means of egress* doors. The vestibule shall be separated from the *stairway* by not less than 2-hour *fire barriers* constructed in accordance with Section 707 or *horizontal assemblies* constructed in accordance with Section 712, or both. The open exterior balcony shall be constructed in accordance with the *fire-resistance rating* requirements for floor assemblies.

909.20.2.1 Door closers. Doors in a smokeproof enclosure shall be self- or automatic closing by actuation of a smoke detector in accordance with Section 715.4 and shall be installed at the floor-side entrance to the smokeproof enclosure. The actuation of the smoke detector on any door shall activate the closing devices on all doors in the smokeproof enclosure at all levels. Smoke detectors shall be installed in accordance with Section 907.3.

909.20.3 Natural ventilation alternative. The provisions of Sections 909.20.3.1 through 909.20.3.3 shall apply to ventilation of smokeproof enclosures by natural means.

909.20.3.1 Balcony doors. Where access to the *stairway* is by way of an open exterior balcony, the door assembly into the enclosure shall be a *fire door assembly* in accordance with Section 715.4.

909.20.3.2 Vestibule doors. Where access to the *stairway* is by way of a vestibule, the door assembly into the vestibule shall be a *fire door assembly* complying with Section 715.4. The door assembly from the vestibule to the *stairway* shall have not less than a 20-minute *fire protection rating* complying with Section 715.4.

909.20.3.3 Vestibule ventilation. Each vestibule shall have a minimum net area of 16 square feet (1.5 m^2) of opening in a wall facing an outer *court*, *yard* or *public way* that is at least 20 feet (6096 mm) in width.

909.20.4 Mechanical ventilation alternative. The provisions of Sections 909.20.4.1 through 909.20.4.4 shall apply to ventilation of smokeproof enclosures by mechanical means.

909.20.4.1 Vestibule doors. The door assembly from the building into the vestibule shall be a *fire door assembly* complying with Section 715.4.3. The door assembly from the vestibule to the *stairway* shall not have less than a 20-minute *fire protection rating* and meet the requirements for a smoke door assembly in accordance with Section 715.4.3. The door shall be installed in accordance with NFPA 105.

909.20.4.2 Vestibule ventilation. The vestibule shall be supplied with not less than one air change per minute and the exhaust shall not be less than 150 percent of supply. Supply air shall enter and exhaust air shall discharge from the vestibule through separate, tightly constructed ducts used only for that purpose. Supply air shall enter the vestibule within 6 inches (152 mm) of the floor level. The top of the exhaust register shall be located at the top of the smoke trap but not more than 6 inches (152 mm) down from the top of the trap, and shall be entirely within the smoke trap area. Doors in the open position shall not obstruct duct openings. Duct openings with controlling *dampers* are permitted where necessary to meet the design requirements, but *dampers* are not otherwise required.

909.20.4.2.1 Engineered ventilation system. Where a specially engineered system is used, the system shall exhaust a quantity of air equal to not less than 90 air changes per hour from any vestibule in the emergency operation mode and shall be sized to handle three vestibules simultaneously. Smoke detectors shall be located at the floor-side entrance to each vestibule and shall activate the system for the affected vestibule. Smoke detectors shall be installed in accordance with Section 907.3.

909.20.4.3 Smoke trap. The vestibule ceiling shall be at least 20 inches (508 mm) higher than the door opening into the vestibule to serve as a smoke and heat trap and to provide an upward-moving air column. The height shall not be decreased unless *approved* and justified by design and test.

909.20.4.4 Stair shaft air movement system. The *stair* shaft shall be provided with a dampered relief opening and supplied with sufficient air to maintain a minimum positive pressure of 0.10 inch of water (25 Pa) in the shaft relative to the vestibule with all doors closed.

909.20.5 Stair pressurization alternative. Where the building is equipped throughout with an *automatic sprinkler system* in accordance with Section 903.3.1.1, the vestibule is not required, provided that interior *exit stairways* are pressurized to a minimum of 0.10 inch of water (25 Pa) and a maximum of 0.35 inch of water (87 Pa) in the shaft relative to the building measured with all *stairway* doors closed under maximum anticipated conditions of stack effect and wind effect.

909.20.6 Ventilating equipment. The activation of ventilating equipment required by the alternatives in Sections 909.20.4 and 909.20.5 shall be by smoke detectors installed at each floor level at an *approved* location at the entrance to the smokeproof enclosure. When the closing device for the *stair* shaft and vestibule doors is activated by smoke detection or power failure, the mechanical equipment shall activate and operate at the required performance levels. Smoke detectors shall be installed in accordance with Section 907.3.

909.20.6.1 Ventilation systems. Smokeproof enclosure ventilation systems shall be independent of other building ventilation systems. The equipment, control wiring, power wiring and ductwork shall comply with one of the following:

1. Equipment, control wiring, power wiring and ductwork shall be located exterior to the building and directly connected to the smokeproof enclosure or connected to the smokeproof enclosure by ductwork enclosed by not less than 2-hour *fire barriers* constructed in accordance with Section 707 or *horizontal assemblies* constructed in accordance with Section 712, or both.
2. Equipment, control wiring, power wiring and ductwork shall be located within the smokeproof enclosure with intake or exhaust directly from and to the outside or through ductwork enclosed by not less than 2-hour *fire barriers* constructed in accordance with Section 707 or *horizontal assemblies* constructed in accordance with Section 712, or both.
3. Equipment, control wiring, power wiring and ductwork shall be located within the building if separated from the remainder of the building, including other mechanical equipment, by not less than 2-hour *fire barriers* constructed in accordance with Section 707 or *horizontal assemblies* constructed in accordance with Section 712, or both.

Exceptions:

1. Control wiring and power wiring utilizing a 2-hour rated cable or cable system.
2. Where encased with not less than 2 inches (51 mm) of concrete.

909.20.6.2 Standby power. Mechanical vestibule and *stair* shaft ventilation systems and automatic fire detection systems shall be powered by an *approved* standby power system conforming to Section 403.4.7 and Chapter 27.

909.20.6.3 Acceptance and testing. Before the mechanical equipment is *approved*, the system shall be tested in the presence of the *building official* to confirm that the system is operating in compliance with these requirements.

SECTION 910
SMOKE AND HEAT VENTS

[F] 910.1 General. Where required by this code or otherwise installed, smoke and heat vents, or mechanical smoke exhaust systems, and draft curtains shall conform to the requirements of this section.

Exceptions:

1. Frozen food warehouses used solely for storage of Class I and II commodities where protected by an *approved automatic sprinkler system*.
2. Where areas of buildings are equipped with early suppression fast-response (ESFR) sprinklers, automatic smoke and heat vents shall not be required within these areas.

[F] 910.2 Where required. Smoke and heat vents shall be installed in the roofs of one-story buildings or portions thereof occupied for the uses set forth in Sections 910.2.1 and 910.2.2.

[F] 910.2.1 Group F-1 or S-1. Buildings and portions thereof used as a Group F-1 or S-1 occupancy having more than 50,000 square feet (4645 m^2) in undivided area.

Exception: Group S-1 aircraft repair hangars.

[F] 910.2.2 High-piled combustible storage. Buildings and portions thereof containing high-piled combustible stock or rack storage in any occupancy group in accordance with Section 413 and the *International Fire Code*.

[F] 910.3 Design and installation. The design and installation of smoke and heat vents and draft curtains shall be as specified in Sections 910.3.1 through 910.3.5.2 and Table 910.3.

[F] 910.3.1 Design. Smoke and heat vents shall be *listed* and labeled to indicate compliance with UL 793.

[F] 910.3.2 Vent operation. Smoke and heat vents shall be capable of being operated by *approved* automatic and manual means. Automatic operation of smoke and heat vents shall conform to the provisions of Sections 910.3.2.1 through 910.3.2.3.

[F] 910.3.2.1 Gravity-operated drop-out vents. Automatic smoke and heat vents containing heat-sensitive glazing designed to shrink and drop out of the vent opening when exposed to fire shall fully open within 5 minutes after the vent cavity is exposed to a simulated fire, represented by a time-temperature gradient that reaches an air temperature of 500°F (260°C) within 5 minutes.

[F] 910.3.2.2 Sprinklered buildings. Where installed in buildings provided with an *approved automatic sprinkler system*, smoke and heat vents shall be designed to operate automatically.

[F] 910.3.2.3 Nonsprinklered buildings. Where installed in buildings not provided with an *approved automatic sprinkler system*, smoke and heat vents shall operate automatically by actuation of a heat-responsive device rated at between 100°F (38°C) and 220°F (104°C) above ambient.

Exception: Gravity-operated drop-out vents complying with Section 910.3.2.1.

[F] 910.3.3 Vent dimensions. The effective venting area shall not be less than 16 square feet (1.5 m^2) with no dimension less than 4 feet (1219 mm), excluding ribs or gutters having a total width not exceeding 6 inches (152 mm).

[F] 910.3.4 Vent locations. Smoke and heat vents shall be located 20 feet (6096 mm) or more from adjacent *lot lines* and *fire walls* and 10 feet (3048 mm) or more from *fire barriers*. Vents shall be uniformly located within the roof in the areas of the building where the vents are required to be installed by Section 910.2 with consideration given to roof pitch, draft curtain location, sprinkler location and structural members.

[F] 910.3.5 Draft curtains. Where required by Table 910.3, draft curtains shall be installed on the underside of the roof in accordance with this section.

Exception: Where areas of buildings are equipped with ESFR sprinklers, draft curtains shall not be provided within these areas. Draft curtains shall only be provided at the separation between the ESFR sprinklers and the non-ESFR sprinklers.

[F] 910.3.5.1 Construction. Draft curtains shall be constructed of sheet metal, lath and plaster, gypsum board or other *approved* materials which provide equivalent performance to resist the passage of smoke. Joints and connections shall be smoke tight.

[F] 910.3.5.2 Location and depth. The location and minimum depth of draft curtains shall be in accordance with Table 910.3.

[F] 910.4 Mechanical smoke exhaust. Where *approved* by the fire code official, engineered mechanical smoke exhaust shall be an acceptable alternate to smoke and heat vents.

[F] TABLE 910.3
REQUIREMENTS FOR DRAFT CURTAINS AND SMOKE AND HEAT VENTS[a]

OCCUPANCY GROUP AND COMMODITY CLASSIFICATION	DESIGNATED STORAGE HEIGHT (feet)	MINIMUM DRAFT CURTAIN DEPTH (feet)	MAXIMUM AREA FORMED BY DRAFT CURTAINS (square feet)	VENT-AREA-TO-FLOOR-AREA RATIO[c]	MAXIMUM SPACING OF VENT CENTERS (feet)	MAXIMUM DISTANCE FROM VENTS TO WALL OR DRAFT CURTAIN[b] (feet)
Group F-1 and S-1	—	0.2 × H[d] but ≥ 4	50,000	1:100	120	60
High-piled Storage (see Section 910.2.2) Class I-IV commodities (Option 1)	≤ 20	6	10,000	1:100	100	60
	> 20 ≤ 40	6	8,000	1:75	100	55
High-piled Storage (see Section 910.2.2) Class I-IV commodities (Option 2)	≤ 20	4	3,000	1:75	100	55
	> 20 ≤ 40	4	3,000	1:50	100	50
High-piled Storage (see Section 910.2.2) High-hazard commodities (Option 1)	≤ 20	6	6,000	1:50	100	50
	> 20 ≤ 30	6	6,000	1:40	90	45
High-piled Storage (see Section 910.2.2) High-hazard commodities (Option 2)	≤ 20	4	4,000	1:50	100	50
	> 20 ≤ 30	4	2,000	1:30	75	40

For SI: 1 foot = 304.8 mm, 1 square foot = 0.0929 m^2.

a. Additional requirements for rack storage heights in excess of those indicated shall be in accordance with Chapter 23 of the *International Fire Code*. For solid-piled storage heights in excess of those indicated, an approved engineered design shall be used.

b. Vents adjacent to walls or draft curtains shall be located within a horizontal distance not greater than the maximum distance specified in this column as measured perpendicular to the wall or draft curtain that forms the perimeter of the draft curtained area.

c. Where draft curtains are not required, the vent area to floor area ratio shall be calculated based on a minimum draft curtain depth of 6 feet (Option 1).

d. "H" is the height of the vent, in feet, above the floor.

[F] 910.4.1 Location. Exhaust fans shall be uniformly spaced within each draft-curtained area and the maximum distance between fans shall not be greater than 100 feet (30 480 mm).

[F] 910.4.2 Size. Fans shall have a maximum individual capacity of 30,000 cfm (14.2 m^3/s). The aggregate capacity of smoke exhaust fans shall be determined by the equation:

$$C = A \times 300 \qquad \textbf{(Equation 9-4)}$$

where:

C = Capacity of mechanical ventilation required, in cubic feet per minute (m^3/s).

A = Area of roof vents provided in square feet (m^2) in accordance with Table 910.3.

[F] 910.4.3 Operation. Mechanical smoke exhaust fans shall be automatically activated by the *automatic sprinkler system* or by *heat detectors* having operating characteristics equivalent to those described in Section 910.3.2. Individual manual controls of each fan unit shall also be provided.

[F] 910.4.4 Wiring and control. Wiring for operation and control of smoke exhaust fans shall be connected ahead of the main disconnect and protected against exposure to temperatures in excess of 1,000°F (538°C) for a period of not less than 15 minutes. Controls shall be located so as to be immediately accessible to the fire service from the exterior of the building and protected against interior fire exposure by not less than 1-hour *fire barriers* constructed in accordance with Section 707 or *horizontal assemblies* constructed in accordance with Section 712, or both.

[F] 910.4.5 Supply air. Supply air for exhaust fans shall be provided at or near the floor level and shall be sized to provide a minimum of 50 percent of required exhaust. Openings for supply air shall be uniformly distributed around the periphery of the area served.

[F] 910.4.6 Interlocks. In combination comfort air-handling/smoke removal systems or independent comfort air-handling systems, fans shall be controlled to shut down in accordance with the *approved* smoke control sequence.

SECTION 911 FIRE COMMAND CENTER

[F] 911.1 General. Where required by other sections of this code and in all buildings classified as high-rise buildings by this code, a fire command center for fire department operations shall be provided and shall comply with Sections 911.1.1 through 911.1.5.

[F] 911.1.1 Location and access. The location and accessibility of the fire command center shall be *approved* by the fire chief.

[F] 911.1.2 Separation. The fire command center shall be separated from the remainder of the building by not less than a 1-hour *fire barrier* constructed in accordance with Section 707 or *horizontal assembly* constructed in accordance with Section 712, or both.

[F] 911.1.3 Size. The room shall be a minimum of 200 square feet (19 m^2) with a minimum dimension of 10 feet (3048 mm).

[F] 911.1.4 Layout approval. A layout of the fire command center and all features required by Section 911.1.5 to be contained therein shall be submitted for approval prior to installation.

[F] 911.1.5 Required features. The fire command center shall comply with NFPA 72 and shall contain the following features:

1. The emergency voice/alarm communication system control unit.
2. The fire department communications system.
3. Fire detection and alarm system annunciator.
4. Annunciator unit visually indicating the location of the elevators and whether they are operational.
5. Status indicators and controls for air distribution systems.
6. The fire-fighter's control panel required by Section 909.16 for smoke control systems installed in the building.
7. Controls for unlocking *stairway* doors simultaneously.
8. Sprinkler valve and waterflow detector display panels.
9. Emergency and standby power status indicators.
10. A telephone for fire department use with controlled access to the public telephone system.
11. Fire pump status indicators.
12. Schematic building plans indicating the typical floor plan and detailing the building core, *means of egress*, fire protection systems, fire-fighting equipment and fire department access and the location of *fire walls, fire barriers, fire partitions, smoke barriers* and smoke partitions.
13. Work table.
14. Generator supervision devices, manual start and transfer features.
15. Public address system, where specifically required by other sections of this code.
16. Elevator fire recall switch in accordance with ASME A17.1.
17. Elevator emergency or standby power selector switch(es), where emergency or standby power is provided.

SECTION 912 FIRE DEPARTMENT CONNECTIONS

[F] 912.1 Installation. Fire department connections shall be installed in accordance with the NFPA standard applicable to the system design and shall comply with Sections 912.2 through 912.5.

[F] 912.2 Location. With respect to hydrants, driveways, buildings and landscaping, fire department connections shall be so located that fire apparatus and hose connected to supply the system will not obstruct access to the buildings for other fire apparatus. The location of fire department connections shall be *approved* by the fire chief.

[F] 912.2.1 Visible location. Fire department connections shall be located on the street side of buildings, fully visible and recognizable from the street or nearest point of fire department vehicle access or as otherwise *approved* by the fire chief.

[F] 912.2.2 Existing buildings. On existing buildings, wherever the fire department connection is not visible to approaching fire apparatus, the fire department connection shall be indicated by an *approved* sign mounted on the street front or on the side of the building. Such sign shall have the letters "FDC" at least 6 inches (152 mm) high and words in letters at least 2 inches (51 mm) high or an arrow to indicate the location. All such signs shall be subject to the approval of the fire code official.

[F] 912.3 Access. Immediate access to fire department connections shall be maintained at all times and without obstruction by fences, bushes, trees, walls or any other fixed or moveable object. Access to fire department connections shall be *approved* by the fire chief.

Exception: Fences, where provided with an access gate equipped with a sign complying with the legend requirements of Section 912.4 and a means of emergency operation. The gate and the means of emergency operation shall be *approved* by the fire chief and maintained operational at all times.

[F] 912.3.1 Locking fire department connection caps. The fire code official is authorized to require locking caps on fire department connections for water-based *fire protection systems* where the responding fire department carries appropriate key wrenches for removal.

[F] 912.3.2 Clear space around connections. A working space of not less than 36 inches (762 mm) in width, 36 inches (914 mm) in depth and 78 inches (1981 mm) in height shall be provided and maintained in front of and to the sides of wall-mounted fire department connections and around the circumference of free-standing fire department connections, except as otherwise required or *approved* by the fire chief.

[F] 912.3.3 Physical protection. Where fire department connections are subject to impact by a motor vehicle, vehicle impact protection shall be provided in accordance with Section 312 of the *International Fire Code.*

[F] 912.4 Signs. A metal sign with raised letters at least 1 inch (25 mm) in size shall be mounted on all fire department connections serving automatic sprinklers, standpipes or fire pump connections. Such signs shall read: AUTOMATIC SPRINKLERS or STANDPIPES or TEST CONNECTION or a combination thereof as applicable. Where the fire department connection does not serve the entire building, a sign shall be provided indicating the portions of the building served.

[P] 912.5 Backflow protection. The potable water supply to automatic sprinkler and standpipe systems shall be protected against backflow as required by the *International Plumbing Code.*

SECTION 913
FIRE PUMPS

[F] 913.1 General. Where provided, fire pumps shall be installed in accordance with this section and NFPA 20.

[F] 913.2 Protection against interruption of service. The fire pump, driver and controller shall be protected in accordance with NFPA 20 against possible interruption of service through damage caused by explosion, fire, flood, earthquake, rodents, insects, windstorm, freezing, vandalism and other adverse conditions.

913.2.1 Protection of fire pump rooms. Fire pumps shall be located in rooms that are separated from all other areas of the building by 2-hour *fire barriers* constructed in accordance with Section 707 or 2-hour *horizontal assemblies* constructed in accordance with Section 712, or both.

Exceptions:

1. In other than high-rise buildings, separation by 1-hour *fire barriers* constructed in accordance with Section 707 or 1-hour *horizontal assemblies* constructed in accordance with Section 712, or both, shall be permitted in buildings equipped throughout with an *automatic sprinkler system* in accordance with Section 903.3.1.1 or 903.3.1.2.
2. Separation is not required for fire pumps physically separated in accordance with NFPA 20.

[F] 913.3 Temperature of pump room. Suitable means shall be provided for maintaining the temperature of a pump room or pump house, where required, above 40°F (5°C).

[F] 913.3.1 Engine manufacturer's recommendation. Temperature of the pump room, pump house or area where engines are installed shall never be less than the minimum recommended by the engine manufacturer. The engine manufacturer's recommendations for oil heaters shall be followed.

[F] 913.4 Valve supervision. Where provided, the fire pump suction, discharge and bypass valves, and isolation valves on the backflow prevention device or assembly shall be supervised open by one of the following methods:

1. Central-station, proprietary or remote-station signaling service.
2. Local signaling service that will cause the sounding of an audible signal at a *constantly attended location.*
3. Locking valves open.
4. Sealing of valves and *approved* weekly recorded inspection where valves are located within fenced enclosures under the control of the owner.

[F] 913.4.1 Test outlet valve supervision. Fire pump test outlet valves shall be supervised in the closed position.

[F] 913.5 Acceptance test. Acceptance testing shall be done in accordance with the requirements of NFPA 20.

SECTION 914 EMERGENCY RESPONDER SAFETY FEATURES

[F] 914.1 Shaftway markings. Vertical shafts shall be identified as required by Sections 914.1.1 and 914.1.2.

[F] 914.1.1 Exterior access to shaftways. Outside openings accessible to the fire department and that open directly on a hoistway or shaftway communicating between two or more floors in a building shall be plainly marked with the word "SHAFTWAY" in red letters at least 6 inches (152 mm) high on a white background. Such warning signs shall be placed so as to be readily discernible from the outside of the building.

[F] 914.1.2 Interior access to shaftways. Door or window openings to a hoistway or shaftway from the interior of the building shall be plainly marked with the word "SHAFTWAY" in red letters at least 6 inches (152 mm) high on a white background. Such warning signs shall be placed so as to be readily discernible.

Exception: Markings shall not be required on shaftway openings that are readily discernible as openings onto a shaftway by the construction or arrangement.

[F] 914.2 Equipment room identification. Fire protection equipment shall be identified in an *approved* manner. Rooms containing controls for air-conditioning systems, sprinkler risers and valves or other fire detection, suppression or control elements shall be identified for the use of the fire department. *Approved* signs required to identify fire protection equipment and equipment location shall be constructed of durable materials, permanently installed and readily visible.

SECTION 915 EMERGENCY RESPONDER RADIO COVERAGE

[F] 915.1 General. Emergency responder radio coverage shall be provided in all new buildings in accordance with Section 510 of the *International Fire Code*.

CHAPTER 10

MEANS OF EGRESS

SECTION 1001 ADMINISTRATION

1001.1 General. Buildings or portions thereof shall be provided with a *means of egress* system as required by this chapter. The provisions of this chapter shall control the design, construction and arrangement of *means of egress* components required to provide an *approved means of egress* from structures and portions thereof.

1001.2 Minimum requirements. It shall be unlawful to alter a building or structure in a manner that will reduce the number of *exits* or the capacity of the *means of egress* to less than required by this code.

[F] 1001.3 Maintenance. *Means of egress* shall be maintained in accordance with the *International Fire Code*.

SECTION 1002 DEFINITIONS

1002.1 Definitions. The following words and terms shall, for the purposes of this chapter and as used elsewhere in this code, have the meanings shown herein.

ACCESSIBLE MEANS OF EGRESS. A continuous and unobstructed way of egress travel from any *accessible* point in a building or facility to a *public way*.

AISLE. An unenclosed *exit access* component that defines and provides a path of egress travel.

AISLE ACCESSWAY. That portion of an *exit access* that leads to an *aisle*.

ALTERNATING TREAD DEVICE. A device that has a series of steps between 50 and 70 degrees (0.87 and 1.22 rad) from horizontal, usually attached to a center support rail in an alternating manner so that the user does not have both feet on the same level at the same time.

AREA OF REFUGE. An area where persons unable to use *stairways* can remain temporarily to await instructions or assistance during emergency evacuation.

BLEACHERS. Tiered seating supported on a dedicated structural system and two or more rows high and is not a building element (see "*Grandstands*").

COMMON PATH OF EGRESS TRAVEL. That portion of *exit access* which the occupants are required to traverse before two separate and distinct paths of egress travel to two *exits* are available. Paths that merge are common paths of travel. Common paths of egress travel shall be included within the permitted travel distance.

CORRIDOR. An enclosed *exit access* component that defines and provides a path of egress travel to an *exit*.

DOOR, BALANCED. A door equipped with double-pivoted hardware so designed as to cause a semicounter balanced swing action when opening.

EGRESS COURT. A court or *yard* which provides access to a *public way* for one or more *exits*.

EMERGENCY ESCAPE AND RESCUE OPENING. An operable window, door or other similar device that provides for a means of escape and access for rescue in the event of an emergency.

EXIT. That portion of a *means of egress* system which is separated from other interior spaces of a building or structure by fire-resistance-rated construction and opening protectives as required to provide a protected path of egress travel between the *exit access* and the *exit discharge*. Exits include exterior exit doors at the *level of exit discharge*, vertical *exit enclosures*, *exit passageways*, *exterior exit stairways*, exterior *exit ramps* and *horizontal exits*.

EXIT ACCESS. That portion of a *means of egress* system that leads from any occupied portion of a building or structure to an *exit*.

EXIT ACCESS DOORWAY. A door or access point along the path of egress travel from an occupied room, area or space where the path of egress enters an intervening room, corridor, unenclosed *exit access stair* or unenclosed *exit access ramp*.

EXIT DISCHARGE. That portion of a *means of egress* system between the termination of an *exit* and a *public way*.

EXIT DISCHARGE, LEVEL OF. The *story* at the point at which an *exit* terminates and an *exit discharge* begins.

EXIT ENCLOSURE. An *exit* component that is separated from other interior spaces of a building or structure by fire-resistance-rated construction and opening protectives, and provides for a protected path of egress travel in a vertical or horizontal direction to the *exit discharge* or the *public way*.

EXIT, HORIZONTAL. A path of egress travel from one building to an area in another building on approximately the same level, or a path of egress travel through or around a wall or partition to an area on approximately the same level in the same building, which affords safety from fire and smoke from the area of incidence and areas communicating therewith.

EXIT PASSAGEWAY. An *exit* component that is separated from other interior spaces of a building or structure by fire-resistance-rated construction and opening protectives, and provides for a protected path of egress travel in a horizontal direction to the *exit discharge* or the *public way*.

FIRE EXIT HARDWARE. Panic hardware that is *listed* for use on *fire door assemblies*.

FLIGHT. A continuous run of rectangular treads, *winders* or combination thereof from one landing to another.

FLOOR AREA, GROSS. The floor area within the inside perimeter of the *exterior walls* of the building under consideration, exclusive of vent shafts and courts, without deduction for corridors, stairways, closets, the thickness of interior walls, columns or other features. The floor area of a building, or portion thereof, not provided with surrounding *exterior walls* shall be the usable area under the horizontal projection of the roof or floor above. The gross floor area shall not include shafts with no openings or interior courts.

FLOOR AREA, NET. The actual occupied area not including unoccupied accessory areas such as corridors, stairways, toilet rooms, mechanical rooms and closets.

FOLDING AND TELESCOPIC SEATING. Tiered seating having an overall shape and size that is capable of being reduced for purposes of moving or storing and is not a building element.

GRANDSTAND. Tiered seating supported on a dedicated structural system and two or more rows high and is not a building element (see "*Bleachers*").

GUARD. A building component or a system of building components located at or near the open sides of elevated walking surfaces that minimizes the possibility of a fall from the walking surface to a lower level.

HANDRAIL. A horizontal or sloping rail intended for grasping by the hand for guidance or support.

MEANS OF EGRESS. A continuous and unobstructed path of vertical and horizontal egress travel from any occupied portion of a building or structure to a *public way*. A means of egress consists of three separate and distinct parts: the *exit access*, the *exit* and the *exit discharge*.

MERCHANDISE PAD. A merchandise pad is an area for display of merchandise surrounded by *aisles*, permanent fixtures or walls. Merchandise pads contain elements such as nonfixed and moveable fixtures, cases, racks, counters and partitions as indicated in Section 105.2 from which customers browse or shop.

NOSING. The leading edge of treads of *stairs* and of landings at the top of *stairway flights*.

OCCUPANT LOAD. The number of persons for which the *means of egress* of a building or portion thereof is designed.

PANIC HARDWARE. A door-latching assembly incorporating a device that releases the latch upon the application of a force in the direction of egress travel.

PHOTOLUMINESCENT. Having the property of emitting light that continues for a length of time after excitation by visible or invisible light has been removed.

PUBLIC WAY. A street, alley or other parcel of land open to the outside air leading to a street, that has been deeded, dedicated or otherwise permanently appropriated to the public for public use and which has a clear width and height of not less than 10 feet (3048 mm).

RAMP. A walking surface that has a running slope steeper than one unit vertical in 20 units horizontal (5-percent slope).

SCISSOR STAIR. Two interlocking *stairways* providing two separate paths of egress located within one stairwell enclosure.

SELF-LUMINOUS. Illuminated by a self-contained power source, other than batteries, and operated independently of external power sources.

SMOKE-PROTECTED ASSEMBLY SEATING. Seating served by *means of egress* that is not subject to smoke accumulation within or under a structure.

STAIR. A change in elevation, consisting of one or more risers.

STAIRWAY. One or more *flights* of *stairs*, either exterior or interior, with the necessary landings and platforms connecting them, to form a continuous and uninterrupted passage from one level to another.

STAIRWAY, EXTERIOR. A *stairway* that is open on at least one side, except for required structural columns, beams, *handrails* and *guards*. The adjoining open areas shall be either *yards*, *courts* or *public ways*. The other sides of the exterior stairway need not be open.

STAIRWAY, INTERIOR. A *stairway* not meeting the definition of an *exterior stairway*.

STAIRWAY, SPIRAL. A *stairway* having a closed circular form in its plan view with uniform section-shaped treads attached to and radiating from a minimum-diameter supporting column.

SUITE. A group of rooms within a Group I-2 occupancy that complies with the requirements of Sections 1014.2.2 through 1014.2.7.

WINDER. A tread with nonparallel edges.

SECTION 1003
GENERAL MEANS OF EGRESS

1003.1 Applicability. The general requirements specified in Sections 1003 through 1013 shall apply to all three elements of the *means of egress* system, in addition to those specific requirements for the *exit access*, the *exit* and the *exit discharge* detailed elsewhere in this chapter.

1003.2 Ceiling height. The *means of egress* shall have a ceiling height of not less than 7 feet 6 inches (2286 mm).

Exceptions:

1. Sloped ceilings in accordance with Section 1208.2.
2. Ceilings of dwelling units and sleeping units within residential occupancies in accordance with Section 1208.2.
3. Allowable projections in accordance with Section 1003.3.
4. Stair headroom in accordance with Section 1009.2.
5. Door height in accordance with Section 1008.1.1.
6. Ramp headroom in accordance with Section 1010.5.2.

7. The clear height of floor levels in vehicular and pedestrian traffic areas in parking garages in accordance with Section 406.2.2.
8. Areas above and below *mezzanine* floors in accordance with Section 505.1.

1003.3 Protruding objects. Protruding objects shall comply with the requirements of Sections 1003.3.1 through 1003.3.4.

1003.3.1 Headroom. Protruding objects are permitted to extend below the minimum ceiling height required by Section 1003.2 provided a minimum headroom of 80 inches (2032 mm) shall be provided for any walking surface, including walks, *corridors*, *aisles* and passageways. Not more than 50 percent of the ceiling area of a *means of egress* shall be reduced in height by protruding objects.

Exception: Door closers and stops shall not reduce headroom to less than 78 inches (1981 mm).

A barrier shall be provided where the vertical clearance is less than 80 inches (2032 mm) high. The leading edge of such a barrier shall be located 27 inches (686 mm) maximum above the floor.

1003.3.2 Post-mounted objects. A free-standing object mounted on a post or pylon shall not overhang that post or pylon more than 4 inches (102 mm) where the lowest point of the leading edge is more than 27 inches (686 mm) and less than 80 inches (2032 mm) above the walking surface. Where a sign or other obstruction is mounted between posts or pylons and the clear distance between the posts or pylons is greater than 12 inches (305 mm), the lowest edge of such sign or obstruction shall be 27 inches (686 mm) maximum or 80 inches (2032 mm) minimum above the finished floor or ground.

Exception: These requirements shall not apply to sloping portions of *handrails* between the top and bottom riser of *stairs* and above the *ramp* run.

1003.3.3 Horizontal projections. Structural elements, fixtures or furnishings shall not project horizontally from either side more than 4 inches (102 mm) over any walking surface between the heights of 27 inches (686 mm) and 80 inches (2032 mm) above the walking surface.

Exception: *Handrails* are permitted to protrude $4^1/_2$ inches (114 mm) from the wall.

1003.3.4 Clear width. Protruding objects shall not reduce the minimum clear width of *accessible routes*.

1003.4 Floor surface. Walking surfaces of the *means of egress* shall have a slip-resistant surface and be securely attached.

1003.5 Elevation change. Where changes in elevation of less than 12 inches (305 mm) exist in the *means of egress*, sloped surfaces shall be used. Where the slope is greater than one unit vertical in 20 units horizontal (5-percent slope), *ramps* complying with Section 1010 shall be used. Where the difference in elevation is 6 inches (152 mm) or less, the *ramp* shall be equipped with either handrails or floor finish materials that contrast with adjacent floor finish materials.

Exceptions:

1. A single step with a maximum riser height of 7 inches (178 mm) is permitted for buildings with occupancies in Groups F, H, R-2, R-3, S and U at exterior doors not required to be *accessible* by Chapter 11.
2. A *stair* with a single riser or with two risers and a tread is permitted at locations not required to be *accessible* by Chapter 11, provided that the risers and treads comply with Section 1009.4, the minimum depth of the tread is 13 inches (330 mm) and at least one *handrail* complying with Section 1012 is provided within 30 inches (762 mm) of the centerline of the normal path of egress travel on the *stair*.
3. A step is permitted in *aisles* serving seating that has a difference in elevation less than 12 inches (305 mm) at locations not required to be *accessible* by Chapter 11, provided that the risers and treads comply with Section 1028.11 and the *aisle* is provided with a *handrail* complying with Section 1028.13.

Throughout a story in a Group I-2 occupancy, any change in elevation in portions of the *exit access* that serve nonambulatory persons shall be by means of a *ramp* or sloped walkway.

1003.6 Means of egress continuity. The path of egress travel along a *means of egress* shall not be interrupted by any building element other than a *means of egress* component as specified in this chapter. Obstructions shall not be placed in the required width of a *means of egress* except projections permitted by this chapter. The required capacity of a *means of egress* system shall not be diminished along the path of egress travel.

1003.7 Elevators, escalators and moving walks. Elevators, escalators and moving walks shall not be used as a component of a required *means of egress* from any other part of the building.

Exception: Elevators used as an *accessible means of egress* in accordance with Section 1007.4.

SECTION 1004
OCCUPANT LOAD

1004.1 Design occupant load. In determining *means of egress* requirements, the number of occupants for whom *means of egress* facilities shall be provided shall be determined in accordance with this section. Where occupants from accessory areas egress through a primary space, the calculated *occupant load* for the primary space shall include the total *occupant load* of the primary space plus the number of occupants egressing through it from the accessory area.

1004.1.1 Areas without fixed seating. The number of occupants shall be computed at the rate of one occupant per unit of area as prescribed in Table 1004.1.1. For areas without fixed seating, the *occupant load* shall not be less than that number determined by dividing the floor area under consideration by the occupant per unit of area factor assigned to the occupancy as set forth in Table 1004.1.1. Where an intended use is not listed in Table 1004.1.1, the *building official* shall establish a use based on a listed use that most nearly resembles the intended use.

Exception: Where *approved* by the *building official*, the actual number of occupants for whom each occupied space, floor or building is designed, although less than those determined by calculation, shall be permitted to be used in the determination of the design *occupant load*.

1004.2 Increased occupant load. The *occupant load* permitted in any building, or portion thereof, is permitted to be increased from that number established for the occupancies in Table 1004.1.1, provided that all other requirements of the code are also met based on such modified number and the *occupant load* does not exceed one occupant per 7 square feet (0.65 m^2) of occupiable floor space. Where required by the *building official*, an *approved aisle*, seating or fixed equipment diagram substantiating any increase in *occupant load* shall be submitted. Where required by the *building official*, such diagram shall be posted.

1004.3 Posting of occupant load. Every room or space that is an assembly occupancy shall have the *occupant load* of the room or space posted in a conspicuous place, near the main *exit* or *exit access doorway* from the room or space. Posted signs shall be of an *approved* legible permanent design and shall be maintained by the owner or authorized agent.

1004.4 Exiting from multiple levels. Where *exits* serve more than one floor, only the *occupant load* of each floor considered individually shall be used in computing the required capacity of the *exits* at that floor, provided that the *exit* capacity shall not decrease in the direction of egress travel.

1004.5 Egress convergence. Where *means of egress* from floors above and below converge at an intermediate level, the capacity of the *means of egress* from the point of convergence shall not be less than the sum of the two floors.

1004.6 Mezzanine levels. The *occupant load* of a *mezzanine* level with egress onto a room or area below shall be added to that room or area's *occupant load*, and the capacity of the exits shall be designed for the total *occupant load* thus established.

1004.7 Fixed seating. For areas having fixed seats and *aisles*, the *occupant load* shall be determined by the number of fixed seats installed therein. The *occupant load* for areas in which fixed seating is not installed, such as waiting spaces and *wheelchair spaces*, shall be determined in accordance with Section 1004.1.1 and added to the number of fixed seats.

For areas having fixed seating without dividing arms, the *occupant load* shall not be less than the number of seats based on one person for each 18 inches (457 mm) of seating length.

The *occupant load* of seating booths shall be based on one person for each 24 inches (610 mm) of booth seat length measured at the backrest of the seating booth.

1004.8 Outdoor areas. Yards, patios, courts and similar outdoor areas accessible to and usable by the building occupants shall be provided with *means of egress* as required by this chapter. The *occupant load* of such outdoor areas shall be assigned by the *building official* in accordance with the anticipated use. Where outdoor areas are to be used by persons in addition to the occupants of the building, and the path of egress travel from the outdoor areas passes through the building, *means of egress*

TABLE 1004.1.1
MAXIMUM FLOOR AREA ALLOWANCES PER OCCUPANT

FUNCTION OF SPACE	FLOOR AREA IN SQ. FT. PER OCCUPANT
Accessory storage areas, mechanical equipment room	300 gross
Agricultural building	300 gross
Aircraft hangars	500 gross
Airport terminal	
Baggage claim	20 gross
Baggage handling	300 gross
Concourse	100 gross
Waiting areas	15 gross
Assembly	
Gaming floors (keno, slots, etc.)	11 gross
Assembly with fixed seats	See Section 1004.7
Assembly without fixed seats	
Concentrated (chairs only—not fixed)	7 net
Standing space	5 net
Unconcentrated (tables and chairs)	15 net
Bowling centers, allow 5 persons for each lane including 15 feet of runway, and for additional areas	7 net
Business areas	100 gross
Courtrooms—other than fixed seating areas	40 net
Day care	35 net
Dormitories	50 gross
Educational	
Classroom area	20 net
Shops and other vocational room areas	50 net
Exercise rooms	50 gross
H-5 Fabrication and manufacturing areas	200 gross
Industrial areas	100 gross
Institutional areas	
Inpatient treatment areas	240 gross
Outpatient areas	100 gross
Sleeping areas	120 gross
Kitchens, commercial	200 gross
Library	
Reading rooms	50 net
Stack area	100 gross
Locker rooms	50 gross
Mercantile	
Areas on other floors	60 gross
Basement and grade floor areas	30 gross
Storage, stock, shipping areas	300 gross
Parking garages	200 gross
Residential	200 gross
Skating rinks, swimming pools	
Rink and pool	50 gross
Decks	15 gross
Stages and platforms	15 net
Warehouses	500 gross

For SI: 1 square foot = 0.0929 m^2.

requirements for the building shall be based on the sum of the *occupant loads* of the building plus the outdoor areas.

Exceptions:

1. Outdoor areas used exclusively for service of the building need only have one *means of egress.*
2. Both outdoor areas associated with Group R-3 and individual dwelling units of Group R-2.

1004.9 Multiple occupancies. Where a building contains two or more occupancies, the *means of egress* requirements shall apply to each portion of the building based on the occupancy of that space. Where two or more occupancies utilize portions of the same *means of egress* system, those egress components shall meet the more stringent requirements of all occupancies that are served.

SECTION 1005 EGRESS WIDTH

1005.1 Minimum required egress width. The *means of egress* width shall not be less than required by this section. The total width of *means of egress* in inches (mm) shall not be less than the total *occupant load* served by the *means of egress* multiplied by 0.3 inch (7.62 mm) per occupant for stairways and by 0.2 inch (5.08 mm) per occupant for other egress components. The width shall not be less than specified elsewhere in this code. Multiple *means of egress* shall be sized such that the loss of any one *means of egress* shall not reduce the available capacity to less than 50 percent of the required capacity. The maximum capacity required from any *story* of a building shall be maintained to the termination of the *means of egress.*

Exception: *Means of egress* complying with Section 1028.

1005.2 Door encroachment. Doors, when fully opened, and handrails shall not reduce the required *means of egress* width by more than 7 inches (178 mm). Doors in any position shall not reduce the required width by more than one-half. Other nonstructural projections such as trim and similar decorative features shall be permitted to project into the required width a maximum of $1^1/_2$ inches (38 mm) on each side.

Exception: The restrictions on a door swing shall not apply to doors within individual dwelling units and sleeping units of Group R-2 and dwelling units of Group R-3.

1005.3 Door hardware encroachment. Surface-mounted latch release hardware shall be exempt from inclusion in the 7-inch (178 mm) maximum projection requirement of Section 1005.2 when:

1. The hardware is mounted to the side of the door facing the corridor width when the door is in the open position; and
2. The hardware is mounted not less than 34 inches (865 mm) or more than 48 inches (1220 mm) above the finished floor.

SECTION 1006 MEANS OF EGRESS ILLUMINATION

1006.1 Illumination required. The *means of egress*, including the *exit discharge*, shall be illuminated at all times the building space served by the *means of egress* is occupied.

Exceptions:

1. Occupancies in Group U.
2. *Aisle accessways* in Group A.
3. Dwelling units and sleeping units in Groups R-1, R-2 and R-3.
4. Sleeping units of Group I occupancies.

1006.2 Illumination level. The *means of egress* illumination level shall not be less than 1 footcandle (11 lux) at the walking surface.

Exception: For auditoriums, theaters, concert or opera halls and similar assembly occupancies, the illumination at the walking surface is permitted to be reduced during performances to not less than 0.2 footcandle (2.15 lux), provided that the required illumination is automatically restored upon activation of a premises' fire alarm system where such system is provided.

1006.3 Illumination emergency power. The power supply for *means of egress* illumination shall normally be provided by the premises' electrical supply.

In the event of power supply failure, an emergency electrical system shall automatically illuminate all of the following areas:

1. *Aisles* and unenclosed egress *stairways* in rooms and spaces that require two or more *means of egress.*
2. *Corridors, exit enclosures* and *exit passageways* in buildings required to have two or more *exits.*
3. Exterior egress components at other than their *levels of exit discharge* until *exit discharge* is accomplished for buildings required to have two or more *exits.*
4. Interior *exit discharge* elements, as permitted in Section 1027.1, in buildings required to have two or more *exits.*
5. Exterior landings as required by Section 1008.1.6 for *exit discharge* doorways in buildings required to have two or more *exits.*

The emergency power system shall provide power for a duration of not less than 90 minutes and shall consist of storage batteries, unit equipment or an on-site generator. The installation of the emergency power system shall be in accordance with Chapter 27.

1006.4 Performance of system. Emergency lighting facilities shall be arranged to provide initial illumination that is at least an average of 1 footcandle (11 lux) and a minimum at any point of 0.1 footcandle (1 lux) measured along the path of egress at floor level. Illumination levels shall be permitted to decline to 0.6 footcandle (6 lux) average and a minimum at any point of 0.06 footcandle (0.6 lux) at the end of the emergency lighting time duration. A maximum-to-minimum illumination uniformity ratio of 40 to 1 shall not be exceeded.

SECTION 1007
ACCESSIBLE MEANS OF EGRESS

1007.1 Accessible means of egress required. *Accessible means of egress* shall comply with this section. *Accessible* spaces shall be provided with not less than one *accessible means of egress*. Where more than one *means of egress* are required by Section 1015.1 or 1021.1 from any *accessible* space, each *accessible* portion of the space shall be served by not less than two *accessible means of egress*.

Exceptions:

1. *Accessible means of egress* are not required in alterations to existing buildings.
2. One *accessible means of egress* is required from an *accessible mezzanine* level in accordance with Section 1007.3, 1007.4 or 1007.5.
3. In assembly areas with sloped or stepped *aisles*, one *accessible means of egress* is permitted where the common path of travel is *accessible* and meets the requirements in Section 1028.8.

1007.2 Continuity and components. Each required *accessible means of egress* shall be continuous to a *public way* and shall consist of one or more of the following components:

1. *Accessible routes* complying with Section 1104.
2. *Interior exit stairways* complying with Sections 1007.3 and 1022.
3. *Exterior exit stairways* complying with Sections 1007.3 and 1026.
4. Elevators complying with Section 1007.4.
5. Platform lifts complying with Section 1007.5.
6. *Horizontal exits* complying with Section 1025.
7. *Ramps* complying with Section 1010.
8. *Areas of refuge* complying with Section 1007.6.

Exceptions:

1. Where the *exit discharge* is not *accessible*, an exterior area for assisted rescue must be provided in accordance with Section 1007.7.
2. Where the *exit stairway* is open to the exterior, the *accessible means of egress* shall include either an *area of refuge* in accordance with Section 1007.6 or an exterior area for assisted rescue in accordance with Section 1007.7.

1007.2.1 Elevators required. In buildings where a required *accessible* floor is four or more stories above or below a *level of exit discharge*, at least one required *accessible means of egress* shall be an elevator complying with Section 1007.4.

Exceptions:

1. In buildings equipped throughout with an *automatic sprinkler system* installed in accordance with Section 903.3.1.1 or 903.3.1.2, the elevator shall not be required on floors provided with a *horizontal exit* and located at or above the *levels of exit discharge*.
2. In buildings equipped throughout with an *automatic sprinkler system* installed in accordance with Section 903.3.1.1 or 903.3.1.2, the elevator shall not be required on floors provided with a ramp conforming to the provisions of Section 1010.

1007.3 Stairways. In order to be considered part of an *accessible means of egress*, an *exit access stairway* as permitted by Section 1016.1 or *exit stairway* shall have a clear width of 48 inches (1219 mm) minimum between handrails and shall either incorporate an *area of refuge* within an enlarged floor-level landing or shall be accessed from either an *area of refuge* complying with Section 1007.6 or a *horizontal exit*.

Exceptions:

1. The *area of refuge* is not required at open *exit access* or *exit stairways* as permitted by Sections 1016.1 and 1022.1 in buildings that are equipped throughout with an *automatic sprinkler system* installed in accordance with Section 903.3.1.1 or 903.3.1.2.
2. The clear width of 48 inches (1219 mm) between *handrails* is not required at *exit access stairway* as permitted by Section 1016.1or *exit stairways* in buildings equipped throughout with an *automatic sprinkler system* installed in accordance with Section 903.3.1.1 or 903.3.1.2.
3. *Areas of refuge* are not required at *exit stairways* in buildings equipped throughout with an *automatic sprinkler system* installed in accordance with Section 903.3.1.1 or 903.3.1.2.
4. The clear width of 48 inches (1219 mm) between *handrails* is not required for *exit stairways* accessed from a *horizontal exit*.
5. *Areas of refuge* are not required at *exit stairways* serving *open parking garages*.
6. *Areas of refuge* are not required for smoke protected seating areas complying with Section 1028.6.2.
7. The *areas of refuge* are not required in Group R-2 occupancies.

1007.4 Elevators. In order to be considered part of an *accessible means of egress*, an elevator shall comply with the emergency operation and signaling device requirements of Section 2.27 of ASME A17.1. Standby power shall be provided in accordance with Chapter 27 and Section 3003. The elevator shall be accessed from either an *area of refuge* complying with Section 1007.6 or a *horizontal exit*.

Exceptions:

1. Elevators are not required to be accessed from an *area of refuge* or *horizontal exit* in *open parking garages*.
2. Elevators are not required to be accessed from an *area of refuge* or *horizontal exit* in buildings and facilities equipped throughout with an *automatic sprinkler system* installed in accordance with Section 903.3.1.1 or 903.3.1.2.
3. Elevators not required to be located in a shaft in accordance with Section 708.2 are not required to be accessed from an *area of refuge* or *horizontal exit*.

4. Elevators are not required to be accessed from an *area of refuge* or *horizontal exit* for smoke protected seating areas complying with Section 1028.6.2.

1007.5 Platform lifts. Platform (wheelchair) lifts shall not serve as part of an *accessible means of egress*, except where allowed as part of a required *accessible route* in Section 1109.7, Items 1 through 9. Standby power shall be provided in accordance with Chapter 27 for platform lifts permitted to serve as part of a *means of egress*.

1007.5.1 Openness. Platform lifts on an *accessible means of egress* shall not be installed in a fully enclosed hoistway.

1007.6 Areas of refuge. Every required *area of refuge* shall be *accessible* from the space it serves by an *accessible means of egress*. The maximum travel distance from any *accessible* space to an *area of refuge* shall not excee the travel distance permitted for the occupancy in accordance with Section 1016.1. Every required *area of refuge* shall have direct access to a *stairway* within an *exit enclosure* complying with Sections 1007.3 and 1022 or an elevator complying with Section 1007.4. Where an elevator lobby is used as an *area of refuge*, the shaft and lobby shall comply with Section 1022.9 for *smokeproof enclosures* except where the elevators are in an *area of refuge* formed by a *horizontal exit* or *smoke barrier*.

Exceptions:

1. A *stairway* serving an *area of refuge* is not required to be enclosed where permitted in Sections 1016.1 and 1022.1.
2. A *smokeproof enclosure* is not required for an elevator lobby used as an *area of refuge* where the elevator is not required to be enclosed.

1007.6.1 Size. Each *area of refuge* shall be sized to accommodate one *wheelchair space* of 30 inches by 48 inches (762 mm by1219 mm) for each 200 occupants or portion thereof, based on the *occupant load* of the *area of refuge* and areas served by the *area of refuge*. Such *wheelchair spaces* shall not reduce the required *means of egress* width. Access to any of the required *wheelchair spaces* in an *area of refuge* shall not be obstructed by more than one adjoining *wheelchair space*.

1007.6.2 Separation. Each *area of refuge* shall be separated from the remainder of the story by a *smoke barrier* complying with Section 710 or a *horizontal exit* complying with Section 1025. Each *area of refuge* shall be designed to minimize the intrusion of smoke.

Exception: *Areas of refuge* located within an *exit enclosure*.

1007.6.3 Two-way communication. *Areas of refuge* shall be provided with a two-way communication system complying with Sections 1007.8.1 and 1007.8.2.

1007.7 Exterior area for assisted rescue. The exterior area for assisted rescue must be open to the outside air and meet the requirements of Section 1007.6.1. Separation walls shall comply with the requirements of Section 705 for *exterior walls*. Where walls or openings are between the area for assisted rescue and the interior of the building, the building *exterior walls* within 10 feet (3048 mm) horizontally of a nonrated wall or unprotected opening shall have a *fire-resistance rating* of not less than 1 hour. Openings within such *exterior walls* shall be protected by opening protectives having a *fire protection rating* of not less than $^3/_4$ hour. This construction shall extend vertically from the ground to a point 10 feet (3048 mm) above the floor level of the area for assisted rescue or to the roof line, whichever is lower.

1007.7.1 Openness. The exterior area for assisted rescue shall be at least 50 percent open, and the open area above the guards shall be so distributed as to minimize the accumulation of smoke or toxic gases.

1007.7.2 Exterior exit stairway. *Exterior exit stairways* that are part of the *means of egress* for the exterior area for assisted rescue shall provide a clear width of 48 inches (1219 mm) between handrails.

1007.8 Two-way communication. A two-way communication system shall be provided at the elevator landing on each *accessible* floor that is one or more stories above or below the *story* of *exit discharge* complying with Sections 1007.8.1 and 1007.8.2.

Exceptions:

1. Two-way communication systems are not required at the elevator landing where the two-way communication system is provided within *areas of refuge* in accordance with Section 1007.6.3.
2. Two-way communication systems are not required on floors provided with *exit ramps* conforming to the provisions of Section 1010.

1007.8.1 System requirements. Two-way communication systems shall provide communication between each required location and the fire command center or a central control point location *approved* by the fire department. Where the central control point is not constantly attended, a two-way communication system shall have a timed automatic telephone dial-out capability to a monitoring location or 911. The two-way communication system shall include both audible and visible signals.

1007.8.2 Directions. Directions for the use of the two-way communication system, instructions for summoning assistance via the two-way communication system and written identification of the location shall be posted adjacent to the two-way communication system.

1007.9 Signage. Signage indicating special accessibility provisions shall be provided as shown:

1. Each door providing access to an *area of refuge* from an adjacent floor area shall be identified by a sign stating: AREA OF REFUGE.
2. Each door providing access to an exterior area for assisted rescue shall be identified by a sign stating: EXTERIOR AREA FOR ASSISTED RESCUE.

Signage shall comply with the ICC A117.1 requirements for visual characters and include the International Symbol of Accessibility. Where exit sign illumination is required by Section 1011.2, the signs shall be illuminated. Additionally, tactile signage complying with ICC A117.1 shall be located at each door to an *area of refuge* and exterior area for assisted rescue in accordance with Section 1011.3.

1007.10 Directional signage. Direction signage indicating the location of the other *means of egress* and which are *accessible means of egress* shall be provided at the following:

1. At *exits* serving a required *accessible* space but not providing an *approved accessible means of egress*.
2. At elevator landings.
3. Within *areas of refuge*.

1007.11 Instructions. In *areas of refuge* and exterior areas for assisted rescue, instructions on the use of the area under emergency conditions shall be posted. The instructions shall include all of the following:

1. Persons able to use the exit stairway do so as soon as possible, unless they are assisting others.
2. Information on planned availability of assistance in the use of stairs or supervised operation of elevators and how to summon such assistance.
3. Directions for use of the two-way communications system where provided.

SECTION 1008 DOORS, GATES AND TURNSTILES

1008.1 Doors. *Means of egress* doors shall meet the requirements of this section. Doors serving a *means of egress* system shall meet the requirements of this section and Section 1020.2. Doors provided for egress purposes in numbers greater than required by this code shall meet the requirements of this section.

Means of egress doors shall be readily distinguishable from the adjacent construction and finishes such that the doors are easily recognizable as doors. Mirrors or similar reflecting materials shall not be used on *means of egress* doors. *Means of egress* doors shall not be concealed by curtains, drapes, decorations or similar materials.

1008.1.1 Size of doors. The minimum width of each door opening shall be sufficient for the *occupant load* thereof and shall provide a clear width of 32 inches (813 mm). Clear openings of doorways with swinging doors shall be measured between the face of the door and the stop, with the door open 90 degrees (1.57 rad). Where this section requires a minimum clear width of 32 inches (813 mm) and a door opening includes two door leaves without a mullion, one leaf shall provide a clear opening width of 32 inches (813 mm). The maximum width of a swinging door leaf shall be 48 inches (1219 mm) nominal. *Means of egress* doors in a Group I-2 occupancy used for the movement of beds shall provide a clear width not less than $41^1/_2$ inches (1054 mm). The height of door openings shall not be less than 80 inches (2032 mm).

Exceptions:

1. The minimum and maximum width shall not apply to door openings that are not part of the required *means of egress* in Group R-2 and R-3 occupancies.
2. Door openings to resident sleeping units in Group I-3 occupancies shall have a clear width of not less than 28 inches (711 mm).
3. Door openings to storage closets less than 10 square feet (0.93 m^2) in area shall not be limited by the minimum width.
4. Width of door leaves in revolving doors that comply with Section 1008.1.4.1 shall not be limited.
5. Door openings within a dwelling unit or sleeping unit shall not be less than 78 inches (1981 mm) in height.
6. Exterior door openings in dwelling units and sleeping units, other than the required *exit* door, shall not be less than 76 inches (1930 mm) in height.
7. In other than Group R-1 occupancies, the minimum widths shall not apply to interior egress doors within a dwelling unit or sleeping unit that is not required to be an *Accessible unit*, *Type A unit* or *Type B unit*.
8. Door openings required to be accessible within Type B units shall have a minimum clear width of 31.75 inches (806 mm).

1008.1.1.1 Projections into clear width. There shall not be projections into the required clear width lower than 34 inches (864 mm) above the floor or ground. Projections into the clear opening width between 34 inches (864 mm) and 80 inches (2032 mm) above the floor or ground shall not exceed 4 inches (102 mm).

Exception: Door closers and door stops shall be permitted to be 78 inches (1980 mm) minimum above the floor.

1008.1.2 Door swing. Egress doors shall be of the pivoted or side-hinged swinging type.

Exceptions:

1. Private garages, office areas, factory and storage areas with an *occupant load* of 10 or less.
2. Group I-3 occupancies used as a place of detention.
3. Critical or intensive care patient rooms within suites of health care facilities.
4. Doors within or serving a single dwelling unit in Groups R-2 and R-3.
5. In other than Group H occupancies, revolving doors complying with Section 1008.1.4.1.
6. In other than Group H occupancies, horizontal sliding doors complying with Section 1008.1.4.3 are permitted in a *means of egress*.
7. Power-operated doors in accordance with Section 1008.1.4.2.
8. Doors serving a bathroom within an individual sleeping unit in Group R-1.

9. In other than Group H occupancies, manually operated horizontal sliding doors are permitted in a *means of egress* from spaces with an *occupant load* of 10 or less.

Doors shall swing in the direction of egress travel where serving an *occupant load* of 50 or more persons or a Group H occupancy.

1008.1.3 Door opening force. The force for pushing or pulling open interior swinging egress doors, other than *fire doors*, shall not exceed 5 pounds (22 N). For other swinging doors, as well as sliding and folding doors, the door latch shall release when subjected to a 15-pound (67 N) force. The door shall be set in motion when subjected to a 30-pound (133 N) force. The door shall swing to a full-open position when subjected to a 15-pound (67 N) force.

1008.1.3.1 Location of applied forces. Forces shall be applied to the latch side of the door.

1008.1.4 Special doors. Special doors and security grilles shall comply with the requirements of Sections 1008.1.4.1 through 1008.1.4.5.

1008.1.4.1 Revolving doors. Revolving doors shall comply with the following:

1. Each revolving door shall be capable of collapsing into a bookfold position with parallel egress paths providing an aggregate width of 36 inches (914 mm).
2. A revolving door shall not be located within 10 feet (3048 mm) of the foot of or top of *stairs* or escalators. A dispersal area shall be provided between the *stairs* or escalators and the revolving doors.
3. The revolutions per minute (rpm) for a revolving door shall not exceed those shown in Table 1008.1.4.1.
4. Each revolving door shall have a side-hinged swinging door which complies with Section 1008.1 in the same wall and within 10 feet (3048 mm) of the revolving door.
5. Revolving doors shall not be part of an *accessible route* required by Section 1007 and Chapter 11.

TABLE 1008.1.4.1
REVOLVING DOOR SPEEDS

INSIDE DIAMETER (feet-inches)	POWER-DRIVEN-TYPE SPEED CONTROL (rpm)	MANUAL-TYPE SPEED CONTROL (rpm)
6-6	11	12
7-0	10	11
7-6	9	11
8-0	9	10
8-6	8	9
9-0	8	9
9-6	7	8
10-0	7	8

For SI: 1 inch = 25.4 mm, 1 foot = 304.8 mm.

1008.1.4.1.1 Egress component. A revolving door used as a component of a *means of egress* shall comply with Section 1008.1.4.1 and the following three conditions:

1. Revolving doors shall not be given credit for more than 50 percent of the required egress capacity.
2. Each revolving door shall be credited with no more than a 50-person capacity.
3. Each revolving door shall be capable of being collapsed when a force of not more than 130 pounds (578 N) is applied within 3 inches (76 mm) of the outer edge of a wing.

1008.1.4.1.2 Other than egress component. A revolving door used as other than a component of a *means of egress* shall comply with Section 1008.1.4.1. The collapsing force of a revolving door not used as a component of a *means of egress* shall not be more than 180 pounds (801 N).

Exception: A collapsing force in excess of 180 pounds (801 N) is permitted if the collapsing force is reduced to not more than 130 pounds (578 N) when at least one of the following conditions is satisfied:

1. There is a power failure or power is removed to the device holding the door wings in position.
2. There is an actuation of the *automatic sprinkler system* where such system is provided.
3. There is an actuation of a smoke detection system which is installed in accordance with Section 907 to provide coverage in areas within the building which are within 75 feet (22 860 mm) of the revolving doors.
4. There is an actuation of a manual control switch, in an *approved* location and clearly defined, which reduces the holding force to below the 130-pound (578 N) force level.

1008.1.4.2 Power-operated doors. Where *means of egress* doors are operated by power, such as doors with a photoelectric-actuated mechanism to open the door upon the approach of a person, or doors with power-assisted manual operation, the design shall be such that in the event of power failure, the door is capable of being opened manually to permit *means of egress* travel or closed where necessary to safeguard *means of egress*. The forces required to open these doors manually shall not exceed those specified in Section 1008.1.3, except that the force to set the door in motion shall not exceed 50 pounds (220 N). The door shall be capable of swinging from any position to the full width of the opening in which such door is installed when a force is applied to the door on the side from which egress is made. Full-power-operated doors shall comply with BHMA A156.10. Power-assisted and low-energy doors shall comply with BHMA A156.19.

Exceptions:

1. Occupancies in Group I-3.
2. Horizontal sliding doors complying with Section 1008.1.4.3.
3. For a biparting door in the emergency breakout mode, a door leaf located within a multiple-leaf opening shall be exempt from the minimum 32-inch (813 mm) single-leaf requirement of Section 1008.1.1, provided a minimum 32-inch (813 mm) clear opening is provided when the two biparting leaves meeting in the center are broken out.

1008.1.4.3 Horizontal sliding doors. In other than Group H occupancies, horizontal sliding doors permitted to be a component of a *means of egress* in accordance with Exception 6 to Section 1008.1.2 shall comply with all of the following criteria:

1. The doors shall be power operated and shall be capable of being operated manually in the event of power failure.
2. The doors shall be openable by a simple method from both sides without special knowledge or effort.
3. The force required to operate the door shall not exceed 30 pounds (133 N) to set the door in motion and 15 pounds (67 N) to close the door or open it to the minimum required width.
4. The door shall be openable with a force not to exceed 15 pounds (67 N) when a force of 250 pounds (1100 N) is applied perpendicular to the door adjacent to the operating device.
5. The door assembly shall comply with the applicable *fire protection rating* and, where rated, shall be self-closing or automatic closing by smoke detection in accordance with Section 715.4.8.3, shall be installed in accordance with NFPA 80 and shall comply with Section 715.
6. The door assembly shall have an integrated standby power supply.
7. The door assembly power supply shall be electrically supervised.
8. The door shall open to the minimum required width within 10 seconds after activation of the operating device.

1008.1.4.4 Access-controlled egress doors. The entrance doors in a *means of egress* in buildings with an occupancy in Group A, B, E, I-2, M, R-1 or R-2 and entrance doors to tenant spaces in occupancies in Groups A, B, E, I-2, M, R-1 and R-2 are permitted to be equipped with an *approved* entrance and egress access control system which shall be installed in accordance with all of the following criteria:

1. A sensor shall be provided on the egress side arranged to detect an occupant approaching the doors. The doors shall be arranged to unlock by a signal from or loss of power to the sensor.
2. Loss of power to that part of the access control system which locks the doors shall automatically unlock the doors.
3. The doors shall be arranged to unlock from a manual unlocking device located 40 inches to 48 inches (1016 mm to 1219 mm) vertically above the floor and within 5 feet (1524 mm) of the secured doors. Ready access shall be provided to the manual unlocking device and the device shall be clearly identified by a sign that reads "PUSH TO EXIT." When operated, the manual unlocking device shall result in direct interruption of power to the lock—independent of the access control system electronics—and the doors shall remain unlocked for a minimum of 30 seconds.
4. Activation of the building fire alarm system, if provided, shall automatically unlock the doors, and the doors shall remain unlocked until the fire alarm system has been reset.
5. Activation of the building automatic sprinkler or fire detection system, if provided, shall automatically unlock the doors. The doors shall remain unlocked until the fire alarm system has been reset.
6. Entrance doors in buildings with an occupancy in Group A, B, E or M shall not be secured from the egress side during periods that the building is open to the general public.

1008.1.4.5 Security grilles. In Groups B, F, M and S, horizontal sliding or vertical security grilles are permitted at the main exit and shall be openable from the inside without the use of a key or special knowledge or effort during periods that the space is occupied. The grilles shall remain secured in the full-open position during the period of occupancy by the general public. Where two or more *means of egress* are required, not more than one-half of the *exits* or *exit access doorways* shall be equipped with horizontal sliding or vertical security grilles.

1008.1.5 Floor elevation. There shall be a floor or landing on each side of a door. Such floor or landing shall be at the same elevation on each side of the door. Landings shall be level except for exterior landings, which are permitted to have a slope not to exceed 0.25 unit vertical in 12 units horizontal (2-percent slope).

Exceptions:

1. Doors serving individual dwelling units in Groups R-2 and R-3 where the following apply:

1.1. A door is permitted to open at the top step of an interior *flight* of *stairs*, provided the door does not swing over the top step.

1.2. Screen doors and storm doors are permitted to swing over *stairs* or landings.

2. Exterior doors as provided for in Section 1003.5, Exception 1, and Section 1020.2, which are not on an *accessible route*.
3. In Group R-3 occupancies not required to be *Accessible units*, *Type A units* or *Type B units*, the landing at an exterior doorway shall not be more than $7^{3}/_{4}$ inches (197 mm) below the top of the threshold, provided the door, other than an exterior storm or screen door, does not swing over the landing.
4. Variations in elevation due to differences in finish materials, but not more than $^{1}/_{2}$ inch (12.7 mm).
5. Exterior decks, patios or balconies that are part of *Type B* dwelling units, have impervious surfaces and that are not more than 4 inches (102 mm) below the finished floor level of the adjacent interior space of the dwelling unit.

1008.1.6 Landings at doors. Landings shall have a width not less than the width of the *stairway* or the door, whichever is greater. Doors in the fully open position shall not reduce a required dimension by more than 7 inches (178 mm). When a landing serves an *occupant load* of 50 or more, doors in any position shall not reduce the landing to less than one-half its required width. Landings shall have a length measured in the direction of travel of not less than 44 inches (1118 mm).

Exception: Landing length in the direction of travel in Groups R-3 and U and within individual units of Group R-2 need not exceed 36 inches (914 mm).

1008.1.7 Thresholds. Thresholds at doorways shall not exceed $^{3}/_{4}$ inch (19.1 mm) in height for sliding doors serving dwelling units or $^{1}/_{2}$ inch (12.7 mm) for other doors. Raised thresholds and floor level changes greater than $^{1}/_{4}$ inch (6.4 mm) at doorways shall be beveled with a slope not greater than one unit vertical in two units horizontal (50-percent slope).

Exception: The threshold height shall be limited to $7^{3}/_{4}$ inches (197 mm) where the occupancy is Group R-2 or R-3; the door is an exterior door that is not a component of the required *means of egress*; the door, other than an exterior storm or screen door, does not swing over the landing or step; and the doorway is not on an *accessible route* as required by Chapter 11 and is not part of an *Accessible unit*, *Type A unit* or *Type B unit.*

1008.1.8 Door arrangement. Space between two doors in a series shall be 48 inches (1219 mm) minimum plus the width of a door swinging into the space. Doors in a series shall swing either in the same direction or away from the space between the doors.

Exceptions:

1. The minimum distance between horizontal sliding power-operated doors in a series shall be 48 inches (1219 mm).
2. Storm and screen doors serving individual dwelling units in Groups R-2 and R-3 need not be spaced 48 inches (1219 mm) from the other door.
3. Doors within individual dwelling units in Groups R-2 and R-3 other than within *Type A* dwelling units.

1008.1.9 Door operations. Except as specifically permitted by this section egress doors shall be readily openable from the egress side without the use of a key or special knowledge or effort.

1008.1.9.1 Hardware. Door handles, pulls, latches, locks and other operating devices on doors required to be *accessible* by Chapter 11 shall not require tight grasping, tight pinching or twisting of the wrist to operate.

1008.1.9.2 Hardware height. Door handles, pulls, latches, locks and other operating devices shall be installed 34 inches (864 mm) minimum and 48 inches (1219 mm) maximum above the finished floor. Locks used only for security purposes and not used for normal operation are permitted at any height.

Exception: Access doors or gates in barrier walls and fences protecting pools, spas and hot tubs shall be permitted to have operable parts of the release of latch on self-latching devices at 54 inches (1370 mm) maximum above the finished floor or ground, provided the self-latching devices are not also self-locking devices operated by means of a key, electronic opener or integral combination lock.

1008.1.9.3 Locks and latches. *Approved* locks and latches shall be permitted to prevent operation of doors where any of the following exists:

1. Places of detention or restraint.
2. In buildings in occupancy Group A having an *occupant load* of 100 or less and Groups B, F, M and S, the main exterior door or doors are permitted to be equipped with key-operated locking devices from the egress side provided:

   2.1. The locking device is readily distinguishable as locked and provided with a key that cannot be removed when locked from the egress side;

   2.2. A readily visible durable sign is posted on the egress side on or adjacent to the door stating: THIS DOOR TO REMAIN UNLOCKED WHEN BUILDING IS OCCUPIED. The sign shall be in letters 1 inch (25 mm) high on a contrasting background; and

   2.3. The use of the key-operated locking device is revocable by the *building official* for violations of Section 1008.1.9.3.

3. Where egress doors are used in pairs, *approved* automatic flush bolts shall be permitted to be used, provided that the door leaf having the automatic flush bolts has no doorknob or surface-mounted hardware.

4. Doors from individual dwelling or sleeping units of Group R occupancies having an *occupant load* of 10 or less are permitted to be equipped with a night latch, dead bolt or security chain, provided such devices are openable from the inside without the use of a key or tool.
5. *Fire doors* after the minimum elevated temperature has disabled the unlatching mechanism in accordance with listed fire door test procedures.

1008.1.9.4 Bolt locks. Manually operated flush bolts or surface bolts are not permitted.

Exceptions:

1. On doors not required for egress in individual dwelling units or sleeping units.
2. Where a pair of doors serves a storage or equipment room, manually operated edge- or surface-mounted bolts are permitted on the inactive leaf.
3. Where a pair of doors serves an *occupant load* of less than 50 persons in a Group B, F or S occupancy, manually operated edge- or surface-mounted bolts are permitted on the inactive leaf. The inactive leaf shall contain no doorknobs, panic bars or similar operating hardware.
4. Where a pair of doors serves a Group B, F or S occupancy, manually operated edge- or surface-mounted bolts are permitted on the inactive leaf provided such inactive leaf is not needed to meet egress width requirements and the building is equipped throughout with an *automatic sprinkler system* in accordance with Section 903.3.1.1. The inactive leaf shall contain no doorknobs, panic bars or similar operating hardware.
5. Where a pair of doors serves patient care rooms in Group I-2 occupancies, self-latching edge- or surface-mounted bolts are permitted on the inactive leaf provided that the inactive leaf is not needed to meet egress width requirements and the inactive leaf contains no doorknobs, panic bars or similar operating hardware.

1008.1.9.5 Unlatching. The unlatching of any door or leaf shall not require more than one operation.

Exceptions:

1. Places of detention or restraint.
2. Where manually operated bolt locks are permitted by Section 1008.1.9.4.
3. Doors with automatic flush bolts as permitted by Section 1008.1.9.3, Exception 3.
4. Doors from individual dwelling units and sleeping units of Group R occupancies as permitted by Section 1008.1.9.3, Exception 4.

1008.1.9.5.1 Closet and bathroom doors in Group R-4 occupancies. In Group R-4 occupancies, closet doors that latch in the closed position shall be openable from inside the closet, and bathroom doors that latch in the closed position shall be capable of being unlocked from the ingress side.

1008.1.9.6 Special locking arrangements in Group I-2. See Section 407.11.

1008.1.9.7 Delayed egress locks. *Approved, listed,* delayed egress locks shall be permitted to be installed on doors serving any occupancy except Group A, E and H occupancies in buildings that are equipped throughout with an *automatic sprinkler system* in accordance with Section 903.3.1.1 or an *approved* automatic smoke or heat detection system installed in accordance with Section 907, provided that the doors unlock in accordance with Items 1 through 6 below. A building occupant shall not be required to pass through more than one door equipped with a delayed egress lock before entering an *exit.*

1. The doors unlock upon actuation of the *automatic sprinkler system* or automatic fire detection system.
2. The doors unlock upon loss of power controlling the lock or lock mechanism.
3. The door locks shall have the capability of being unlocked by a signal from the fire command center.
4. The initiation of an irreversible process which will release the latch in not more than 15 seconds when a force of not more than 15 pounds (67 N) is applied for 1 second to the release device. Initiation of the irreversible process shall activate an audible signal in the vicinity of the door. Once the door lock has been released by the application of force to the releasing device, relocking shall be by manual means only.

   Exception: Where approved, a delay of not more than 30 seconds is permitted.
5. A sign shall be provided on the door located above and within 12 inches (305 mm) of the release device reading: PUSH UNTIL ALARM SOUNDS. DOOR CAN BE OPENED IN 15 [30] SECONDS.
6. Emergency lighting shall be provided at the door.

1008.1.9.8 Electromagnetically locked egress doors. Doors in the *means of egress* that are not otherwise required to have panic hardware in buildings with an occupancy in Group A, B, E, M, R-1 or R-2 and doors to tenant spaces in Group A, B, E, M, R-1 or R-2 shall be permitted to be electromagnetically locked if equipped with *listed* hardware that incorporates a built-in switch and meet the requirements below:

1. The *listed* hardware that is affixed to the door leaf has an obvious method of operation that is readily operated under all lighting conditions.

2. The *listed* hardware is capable of being operated with one hand.

3. Operation of the *listed* hardware releases to the electromagnetic lock and unlocks the door immediately.

4. Loss of power to the *listed* hardware automatically unlocks the door.

1008.1.9.9 Locking arrangements in correctional facilities. In occupancies in Groups A-2, A-3, A-4, B, E, F, I-2, I-3, M and S within correctional and detention facilities, doors in *means of egress* serving rooms or spaces occupied by persons whose movements are controlled for security reasons shall be permitted to be locked when equipped with egress control devices which shall unlock manually and by at least one of the following means:

1. Activation of an *automatic sprinkler system* installed in accordance with Section 903.3.1.1;
2. Activation of an *approved* manual alarm box; or
3. A signal from a *constantly attended location*.

1008.1.9.10 Stairway doors. *Interior stairway means of egress* doors shall be openable from both sides without the use of a key or special knowledge or effort.

Exceptions:

1. *Stairway* discharge doors shall be openable from the egress side and shall only be locked from the opposite side.
2. This section shall not apply to doors arranged in accordance with Section 403.5.3.
3. In *stairways* serving not more than four stories, doors are permitted to be locked from the side opposite the egress side, provided they are openable from the egress side and capable of being unlocked simultaneously without unlatching upon a signal from the fire command center, if present, or a signal by emergency personnel from a single location inside the main entrance to the building.

1008.1.10 Panic and fire exit hardware. Doors serving a Group H occupancy and doors serving rooms or spaces with an *occupant load* of 50 or more in a Group A or E occupancy shall not be provided with a latch or lock unless it is panic hardware or *fire exit hardware*.

Exception: A main *exit* of a Group A occupancy in compliance with Section 1008.1.9.3, Item 2.

Electrical rooms with equipment rated 1,200 amperes or more and over 6 feet (1829 mm) wide that contain overcurrent devices, switching devices or control devices with *exit* or *exit access* doors shall be equipped with panic hardware or *fire exit hardware*. The doors shall swing in the direction of egress travel.

1008.1.10.1 Installation. Where panic or *fire exit hardware* is installed, it shall comply with the following:

1. Panic hardware shall be *listed* in accordance with UL 305;
2. *Fire exit hardware* shall be *listed* in accordance with UL 10C and UL 305;
3. The actuating portion of the releasing device shall extend at least one-half of the door leaf width; and
4. The maximum unlatching force shall not exceed 15 pounds (67 N).

1008.1.10.2 Balanced doors. If *balanced doors* are used and panic hardware is required, the panic hardware shall be the push-pad type and the pad shall not extend more than one-half the width of the door measured from the latch side.

1008.2 Gates. Gates serving the means of egress system shall comply with the requirements of this section. Gates used as a component in a *means of egress* shall conform to the applicable requirements for doors.

Exception: Horizontal sliding or swinging gates exceeding the 4-foot (1219 mm) maximum leaf width limitation are permitted in fences and walls surrounding a stadium.

1008.2.1 Stadiums. Panic hardware is not required on gates surrounding stadiums where such gates are under constant immediate supervision while the public is present, and where safe dispersal areas based on 3 square feet (0.28 m^2) per occupant are located between the fence and enclosed space. Such required safe dispersal areas shall not be located less than 50 feet (15 240 mm) from the enclosed space. See Section 1027.6 for *means of egress* from safe dispersal areas.

1008.3 Turnstiles. Turnstiles or similar devices that restrict travel to one direction shall not be placed so as to obstruct any required *means of egress*.

Exception: Each turnstile or similar device shall be credited with no more than a 50-person capacity where all of the following provisions are met:

1. Each device shall turn free in the direction of egress travel when primary power is lost, and upon the manual release by an employee in the area.
2. Such devices are not given credit for more than 50 percent of the required egress capacity.
3. Each device is not more than 39 inches (991 mm) high.
4. Each device has at least $16^1/_2$ inches (419 mm) clear width at and below a height of 39 inches (991 mm) and at least 22 inches (559 mm) clear width at heights above 39 inches (991 mm).

Where located as part of an *accessible route*, turnstiles shall have at least 36 inches (914 mm) clear at and below a height of 34 inches (864 mm), at least 32 inches (813 mm) clear width between 34 inches (864 mm) and 80 inches (2032 mm) and shall consist of a mechanism other than a revolving device.

1008.3.1 High turnstile. Turnstiles more than 39 inches (991 mm) high shall meet the requirements for revolving doors.

1008.3.2 Additional door. Where serving an *occupant load* greater than 300, each turnstile that is not portable shall have a side-hinged swinging door which conforms to Section 1008.1 within 50 feet (15 240 mm).

SECTION 1009 STAIRWAYS

1009.1 Stairway width. The width of *stairways* shall be determined as specified in Section 1005.1, but such width shall not be less than 44 inches (1118 mm). See Section 1007.3 for *accessible means of egress stairways.*

Exceptions:

1. *Stairways* serving an *occupant load* of less than 50 shall have a width of not less than 36 inches (914 mm).
2. *Spiral stairways* as provided for in Section 1009.9.
3. *Aisle stairs* complying with Section 1028.
4. Where an incline platform lift or stairway chairlift is installed on *stairways* serving occupancies in Group R-3, or within dwelling units in occupancies in Group R-2, a clear passage width not less than 20 inches (508 mm) shall be provided. If the seat and platform can be folded when not in use, the distance shall be measured from the folded position.

1009.2 Headroom. *Stairways* shall have a minimum headroom clearance of 80 inches (2032 mm) measured vertically from a line connecting the edge of the *nosings*. Such headroom shall be continuous above the *stairway* to the point where the line intersects the landing below, one tread depth beyond the bottom riser. The minimum clearance shall be maintained the full width of the *stairway* and landing.

Exceptions:

1. *Spiral stairways* complying with Section 1009.9 are permitted a 78-inch (1981 mm) headroom clearance.
2. In Group R-3 occupancies; within dwelling units in Group R-2 occupancies; and in Group U occupancies that are accessory to a Group R-3 occupancy or accessory to individual dwelling units in Group R-2 occupancies; where the *nosings* of treads at the side of a *flight* extend under the edge of a floor opening through which the *stair* passes, the floor opening shall be allowed to project horizontally into the required headroom a maximum of $4^3/_4$ inches (121 mm).

1009.3 Walkline. The walkline across *winder* treads shall be concentric to the direction of travel through the turn and located 12 inches (305 mm) horizontally from the handrail that is adjacent to the side where the *winders* are narrower. The 12-inch (305 mm) dimension shall be measured perpendicular from the handrail surface that faces the walkline.

1009.4 Stair treads and risers. *Stair* treads and risers shall comply with Sections 1009.4.1 through 1009.4.5.

1009.4.1 Dimension reference surfaces. For the purpose of this section, all dimensions are exclusive of carpets, rugs or runners.

1009.4.2 Riser height and tread depth. *Stair* riser heights shall be 7 inches (178 mm) maximum and 4 inches (102 mm) minimum. The riser height shall be measured vertically between the leading edges of adjacent treads. Rectangular tread depths shall be 11 inches (279 mm) minimum measured horizontally between the vertical planes of the foremost projection of adjacent treads and at a right angle to the tread's leading edge. *Winder* treads shall have a minimum tread depth of 11 inches (279 mm) measured between the vertical planes of the foremost projection of adjacent treads at the intersections with the walkline and a minimum tread depth of 10 inches (254 mm) within the clear width of the *stair.*

Exceptions:

1. *Alternating tread devices* in accordance with Section 1009.10.
2. Ship ladders in accordance with Section 1009.11.
3. *Spiral stairways* in accordance with Section 1009.9.
4. *Aisle stairs* in assembly seating areas where the *stair* pitch or slope is set, for sightline reasons, by the slope of the adjacent seating area in accordance with Section 1028.11.2.
5. In Group R-3 occupancies; within dwelling units in Group R-2 occupancies; and in Group U occupancies that are accessory to a Group R-3 occupancy or accessory to individual dwelling units in Group R-2 occupancies; the maximum riser height shall be $7^3/_4$ inches (197 mm); the minimum tread depth shall be 10 inches (254 mm); the minimum *winder* tread depth at the walkline shall be 10 inches (254 mm); and the minimum *winder* tread depth shall be 6 inches (152 mm). A *nosing* not less than $^3/_4$ inch (19.1 mm) but not more than $1^1/_4$ inches (32 mm) shall be provided on *stairways* with solid risers where the tread depth is less than 11 inches (279 mm).
6. See Section 3404.1 for the replacement of existing *stairways*.
7. In Group I-3 facilities, *stairways* providing access to guard towers, observation stations and control rooms, not more than 250 square feet (23 m²) in area, shall be permitted to have a maximum riser height of 8 inches (203 mm) and a minimum tread depth of 9 inches (229 mm).

1009.4.3 Winder treads. *Winder* treads are not permitted in *means of egress stairways* except within a dwelling unit.

Exceptions:

1. Curved *stairways* in accordance with Section 1009.8.
2. *Spiral stairways* in accordance with Section 1009.9.

1009.4.4 Dimensional uniformity. *Stair* treads and risers shall be of uniform size and shape. The tolerance between the largest and smallest riser height or between the largest and smallest tread depth shall not exceed $^3/_8$ inch (9.5 mm) in any *flight* of *stairs*. The greatest *winder* tread depth at the walkline within any *flight* of *stairs* shall not exceed the smallest by more than $^3/_8$ inch (9.5 mm).

Exceptions:

1. Nonuniform riser dimensions of *aisle stairs* complying with Section 1028.11.2.
2. Consistently shaped *winders*, complying with Section 1009.4.2, differing from rectangular treads in the same *stairway flight*.

Where the bottom or top riser adjoins a sloping *public way*, walkway or driveway having an established grade and serving as a landing, the bottom or top riser is permitted to be reduced along the slope to less than 4 inches (102 mm) in height, with the variation in height of the bottom or top riser not to exceed one unit vertical in 12 units horizontal (8-percent slope) of *stairway* width. The *nosings* or leading edges of treads at such nonuniform height risers shall have a distinctive marking stripe, different from any other *nosing* marking provided on the *stair flight*. The distinctive marking stripe shall be visible in descent of the *stair* and shall have a slip-resistant surface. Marking stripes shall have a width of at least 1 inch (25 mm) but not more than 2 inches (51 mm).

1009.4.5 Profile. The radius of curvature at the leading edge of the tread shall be not greater than $^9/_{16}$ inch (14.3 mm). Beveling of *nosings* shall not exceed $^9/_{16}$ inch (14.3 mm). Risers shall be solid and vertical or sloped under the tread above from the underside of the *nosing* above at an angle not more than 30 degrees (0.52 rad) from the vertical. The leading edge (*nosings*) of treads shall project not more than $1^1/_4$ inches (32 mm) beyond the tread below and all projections of the leading edges shall be of uniform size, including the leading edge of the floor at the top of a *flight*.

Exceptions:

1. Solid risers are not required for *stairways* that are not required to comply with Section 1007.3, provided that the opening between treads does not permit the passage of a sphere with a diameter of 4 inches (102 mm).
2. Solid risers are not required for occupancies in Group I-3 or in Group F, H and S occupancies other than areas accessible to the public. There are no restrictions on the size of the opening in the riser.
3. Solid risers are not required for *spiral stairways* constructed in accordance with Section 1009.9.
4. Solid risers are not required for *alternating tread devices* constructed in accordance with Section 1009.10.

1009.5 Stairway landings. There shall be a floor or landing at the top and bottom of each *stairway*. The width of landings shall not be less than the width of *stairways* they serve. Every landing shall have a minimum dimension measured in the direction of travel equal to the width of the *stairway*. Such dimension need not exceed 48 inches (1219 mm) where the *stairway* has a straight run. Doors opening onto a landing shall not reduce the landing to less than one-half the required width. When fully open, the door shall not project more than 7 inches (178 mm) into a landing. When *wheelchair spaces* are required on the *stairway* landing in accordance with Section 1007.6.1, the *wheelchair space* shall not be located in the required width of the landing and doors shall not swing over the *wheelchair spaces*.

Exception: *Aisle stairs* complying with Section 1028.

1009.6 Stairway construction. All *stairways* shall be built of materials consistent with the types permitted for the type of construction of the building, except that wood handrails shall be permitted for all types of construction.

1009.6.1 Stairway walking surface. The walking surface of treads and landings of a *stairway* shall not be sloped steeper than one unit vertical in 48 units horizontal (2-percent slope) in any direction. *Stairway* treads and landings shall have a solid surface. Finish floor surfaces shall be securely attached.

Exceptions:

1. Openings in stair walking surfaces shall be a size that does not permit the passage of $^1/_2$-inch-diameter (12.7 mm) sphere. Elongated openings shall be placed so that the long dimension is perpendicular to the direction of travel.
2. In Group F, H and S occupancies, other than areas of parking structures accessible to the public, openings in treads and landings shall not be prohibited provided a sphere with a diameter of $1^1/_8$ inches (29 mm) cannot pass through the opening.

1009.6.2 Outdoor conditions. Outdoor *stairways* and outdoor approaches to *stairways* shall be designed so that water will not accumulate on walking surfaces.

1009.6.3 Enclosures under stairways. The walls and soffits within enclosed usable spaces under enclosed and unenclosed *stairways* shall be protected by 1-hour fire-resistance-rated construction or the *fire-resistance rating* of the stairway enclosure, whichever is greater. Access to the enclosed space shall not be directly from within the stair enclosure.

Exception: Spaces under *stairways* serving and contained within a single residential dwelling unit in Group R-2 or R-3 shall be permitted to be protected on the enclosed side with $^1/_2$-inch (12.7 mm) gypsum board.

There shall be no enclosed usable space under *exterior exit stairways* unless the space is completely enclosed in 1-hour fire-resistance-rated construction. The open space under *exterior stairways* shall not be used for any purpose.

1009.7 Vertical rise. A *flight* of *stairs* shall not have a vertical rise greater than 12 feet (3658 mm) between floor levels or landings.

Exceptions:

1. *Aisle stairs* complying with Section 1028.

2. *Alternating tread devices* used as a *means of egress* shall not have a rise greater than 20 feet (6096 mm) between floor levels or landings.

1009.8 Curved stairways. Curved *stairways* with *winder* treads shall have treads and risers in accordance with Section 1009.4 and the smallest radius shall not be less than twice the required width of the *stairway*.

Exception: The radius restriction shall not apply to curved *stairways* for occupancies in Group R-3 and within individual dwelling units in occupancies in Group R-2.

1009.9 Spiral stairways. *Spiral stairways* are permitted to be used as a component in the *means of egress* only within dwelling units or from a space not more than 250 square feet (23 m^2) in area and serving not more than five occupants, or from galleries, catwalks and *gridirons* in accordance with Section 1015.6.

A *spiral stairway* shall have a 7$^1/_2$-inch (191 mm) minimum clear tread depth at a point 12 inches (305 mm) from the narrow edge. The risers shall be sufficient to provide a headroom of 78 inches (1981 mm) minimum, but riser height shall not be more than 9$^1/_2$ inches (241 mm). The minimum *stairway* clear width at and below the *handrail* shall be 26 inches (660 mm).

1009.10 Alternating tread devices. *Alternating tread devices* are limited to an element of a *means of egress* in buildings of Groups F, H and S from a mezzanine not more than 250 square feet (23 m^2) in area and which serves not more than five occupants; in buildings of Group I-3 from a guard tower, observation station or control room not more than 250 square feet (23 m^2) in area and for access to unoccupied roofs.

1009.10.1 Handrails of alternating tread devices. *Handrails* shall be provided on both sides of *alternating tread devices* and shall comply with Section 1012.

1009.10.2 Treads of alternating tread devices. *Alternating tread devices* shall have a minimum projected tread of 5 inches (127 mm), a minimum tread depth of 8$^1/_2$ inches (216 mm), a minimum tread width of 7 inches (178 mm) and a maximum riser height of 9$^1/_2$ inches (241 mm). The projected tread depth shall be measured horizontally between the vertical planes of the foremost projections of adjacent treads. The riser height shall be measured vertically between the leading edges of adjacent treads. The combination of riser height and projected tread depth provided shall result in an alternating tread device angle that complies with Section 1002. The initial tread of the device shall begin at the same elevation as the platform, landing or floor surface.

Exception: *Alternating tread devices* used as an element of a *means of egress* in buildings from a mezzanine area not more than 250 square feet (23 m^2) in area which serves not more than five occupants shall have a minimum projected tread of 8$^1/_2$ inches (216 mm) with a minimum tread depth of 10$^1/_2$ inches (267 mm). The rise to the next alternating tread surface should not be more than 8 inches (203 mm).

1009.11 Ship ladders. Ship ladders are permitted to be used in Group I-3 as a component of a *means of egress* to and from control rooms or elevated facility observation stations not more than 250 square feet (23 m^2) with not more than three occupants and for access to unoccupied roofs.

Ship ladders shall have a pitch of 60 to 75 degrees (1.05 to 1.31 rad), maximum width of 30 inches (762 mm) to the outside of the handrails, minimum tread depth of 5 inches (127 mm), riser height of 9$^1/_2$ inches (241.3 mm) to 12 inches (304.8 mm), 1$^1/_4$-inch (31.75 mm) pipe handrail. The vertical rise between floor levels or landings shall not exceed 20 feet (6096 mm).

Handrails shall be provided on both sides of ship ladders. The minimum clear width at and below the *handrails* shall be 20 inches (508 mm).

1009.12 Handrails. *Stairways* shall have *handrails* on each side and shall comply with Section 1012. Where glass is used to provide the *handrail*, the *handrail* shall also comply with Section 2407.

Exceptions:

1. *Handrails* for *aisle stairs* are not required where permitted by Section 1028.13.
2. *Stairways* within dwelling units, *spiral stairways* and *aisle stairs* serving seating only on one side are permitted to have a *handrail* on one side only.
3. Decks, patios and walkways that have a single change in elevation where the landing depth on each side of the change of elevation is greater than what is required for a landing do not require *handrails*.
4. In Group R-3 occupancies, a change in elevation consisting of a single riser at an entrance or egress door does not require *handrails*.
5. Changes in room elevations of three or fewer risers within dwelling units and sleeping units in Group R-2 and R-3 do not require *handrails*.

1009.13 Stairway to roof. In buildings four or more stories above *grade plane*, one *stairway* shall extend to the roof surface, unless the roof has a slope steeper than four units vertical in 12 units horizontal (33-percent slope). In buildings without an occupied roof, access to the roof from the top story shall be permitted to be by an alternating tread device or a ships ladder meeting the following: a pitch of 60 to 75 degrees (1.05 to 1.31 rad) maximum, width of 30 inches (762 mm) to the outside of the handrails, minimum tread depth of 5 inches (127 mm), riser height of 9$^1/_2$ inches (241.3 mm) to 12 inches (304.8 mm), 1$^1/_4$-inch (31.75 mm) pipe handrail. The height between the top landing of the stair and the roof shall not exceed 20 feet (6096 mm).

1009.13.1 Roof access. Where a *stairway* is provided to a roof, access to the roof shall be provided through a *penthouse* complying with Section 1509.2.

Exception: In buildings without an occupied roof, access to the roof shall be permitted to be a roof hatch or trap door not less than 16 square feet (1.5 m^2) in area and having a minimum dimension of 2 feet (610 mm).

1009.13.2 Protection at roof hatch openings. Where the roof hatch opening providing the required access is located within 10 feet (3049 mm) of the roof edge, such roof access or roof edge shall be protected by *guards* installed in accordance with the provisions of Section 1013.

1009.14 Stairway to elevator equipment. Roofs and *penthouses* containing elevator equipment that must be accessed for maintenance are required to be accessed by a *stairway.*

SECTION 1010
RAMPS

1010.1 Scope. The provisions of this section shall apply to *ramps* used as a component of a *means of egress.*

Exceptions:

1. Other than *ramps* that are part of the *accessible routes* providing access in accordance with Sections 1108.2 through 1108.2.4 and 1108.2.6, ramped *aisles* within assembly rooms or spaces shall conform with the provisions in Section 1028.11.
2. Curb *ramps* shall comply with ICC A117.1.
3. Vehicle ramps in parking garages for pedestrian *exit access* shall not be required to comply with Sections 1010.3 through 1010.9 when they are not an *accessible route* serving *accessible* parking spaces, other required accessible elements or part of an *accessible means of egress.*

1010.2 Slope. *Ramps* used as part of a *means of egress* shall have a running slope not steeper than one unit vertical in 12 units horizontal (8-percent slope). The slope of other pedestrian *ramps* shall not be steeper than one unit vertical in eight units horizontal (12.5-percent slope).

Exception: *Aisle ramp* slope in occupancies of Group A or assembly occupancies accessory to Group E occupancies shall comply with Section 1028.11.

1010.3 Cross slope. The slope measured perpendicular to the direction of travel of a *ramp* shall not be steeper than one unit vertical in 48 units horizontal (2-percent slope).

1010.4 Vertical rise. The rise for any *ramp* run shall be 30 inches (762 mm) maximum.

1010.5 Minimum dimensions. The minimum dimensions of *means of egress ramps* shall comply with Sections 1010.5.1 through 1010.5.3.

1010.5.1 Width. The minimum width of a *means of egress ramp* shall not be less than that required for *corridors* by Section 1018.2. The clear width of a *ramp* between *handrails,* if provided, or other permissible projections shall be 36 inches (914 mm) minimum.

1010.5.2 Headroom. The minimum headroom in all parts of the *means of egress ramp* shall not be less than 80 inches (2032 mm).

1010.5.3 Restrictions. *Means of egress ramps* shall not reduce in width in the direction of egress travel. Projections into the required *ramp* and landing width are prohibited. Doors opening onto a landing shall not reduce the clear width to less than 42 inches (1067 mm).

1010.6 Landings. *Ramps* shall have landings at the bottom and top of each *ramp*, points of turning, entrance, exits and at doors. Landings shall comply with Sections 1010.6.1 through 1010.6.5.

1010.6.1 Slope. Landings shall have a slope not steeper than one unit vertical in 48 units horizontal (2-percent slope) in any direction. Changes in level are not permitted.

1010.6.2 Width. The landing shall be at least as wide as the widest *ramp* run adjoining the landing.

1010.6.3 Length. The landing length shall be 60 inches (1525 mm) minimum.

Exceptions:

1. In Group R-2 and R-3 individual dwelling and sleeping units that are not required to be *Accessible units, Type A units* or *Type B units* in accordance with Section 1107, landings are permitted to be 36 inches (914 mm) minimum.
2. Where the *ramp* is not a part of an *accessible route,* the length of the landing shall not be required to be more than 48 inches (1220 mm) in the direction of travel.

1010.6.4 Change in direction. Where changes in direction of travel occur at landings provided between *ramp* runs, the landing shall be 60 inches by 60 inches (1524 mm by 1524 mm) minimum.

Exception: In Group R-2 and R-3 individual dwelling or sleeping units that are not required to be *Accessible units, Type A units* or *Type B units* in accordance with Section 1107, landings are permitted to be 36 inches by 36 inches (914 mm by 914 mm) minimum.

1010.6.5 Doorways. Where doorways are located adjacent to a *ramp* landing, maneuvering clearances required by ICC A117.1 are permitted to overlap the required landing area.

1010.7 Ramp construction. All *ramps* shall be built of materials consistent with the types permitted for the type of construction of the building, except that wood *handrails* shall be permitted for all types of construction. *Ramps* used as an *exit* shall conform to the applicable requirements of Sections 1022.1 through 1022.6 for *exit enclosures.*

1010.7.1 Ramp surface. The surface of *ramps* shall be of slip-resistant materials that are securely attached.

1010.7.2 Outdoor conditions. Outdoor *ramps* and outdoor approaches to *ramps* shall be designed so that water will not accumulate on walking surfaces.

1010.8 Handrails. *Ramps* with a rise greater than 6 inches (152 mm) shall have handrails on both sides. *Handrails* shall comply with Section 1012.

Exception: *Handrails* for ramped *aisles* are not required where permitted by Section 1028.13.

1010.9 Edge protection. Edge protection complying with Section 1010.9.1 or 1010.9.2 shall be provided on each side of *ramp* runs and at each side of *ramp* landings.

Exceptions:

1. Edge protection is not required on *ramps* that are not required to have *handrails*, provided they have flared sides that comply with the ICC A117.1 curb ramp provisions.
2. Edge protection is not required on the sides of ramp landings serving an adjoining *ramp* run or *stairway*.
3. Edge protection is not required on the sides of *ramp* landings having a vertical drop off of not more than $^1/_2$ inch (12.7 mm) within 10 inches (254 mm) horizontally of the required landing area.
4. In assembly spaces with fixed seating, edge protection is not required on the sides of *ramps* where the *ramps* provide access to the adjacent seating and *aisle accessways*.

1010.9.1 Curb, rail, wall or barrier. A curb, rail, wall or barrier shall be provided to serve as edge protection. A curb shall be a minimum of 4 inches (102 mm) in height. Barriers shall be constructed so that the barrier prevents the passage of a 4-inch-diameter (102 mm) sphere, where any portion of the sphere is within 4 inches (102 mm) of the floor or ground surface.

1010.9.2 Extended floor or ground surface. The floor or ground surface of the *ramp* run or landing shall extend 12 inches (305 mm) minimum beyond the inside face of a *handrail* complying with Section 1012.

1010.10 Guards. *Guards* shall be provided where required by Section 1013 and shall be constructed in accordance with Section 1013.

SECTION 1011 EXIT SIGNS

1011.1 Where required. *Exits* and *exit access* doors shall be marked by an *approved exit* sign readily visible from any direction of egress travel. The path of egress travel to *exits* and within *exits* shall be marked by readily visible *exit* signs to clearly indicate the direction of egress travel in cases where the *exit* or the path of egress travel is not immediately visible to the occupants. Intervening *means of egress* doors within *exits* shall be marked by *exit* signs. *Exit* sign placement shall be such that no point in an *exit access corridor* or *exit passageway* is more than 100 feet (30 480 mm) or the *listed* viewing distance for the sign, whichever is less, from the nearest visible *exit* sign.

Exceptions:

1. *Exit* signs are not required in rooms or areas that require only one *exit* or *exit access*.
2. Main exterior *exit* doors or gates that are obviously and clearly identifiable as *exits* need not have *exit* signs where *approved* by the *building official*.
3. *Exit* signs are not required in occupancies in Group U and individual sleeping units or dwelling units in Group R-1, R-2 or R-3.
4. *Exit* signs are not required in dayrooms, sleeping rooms or dormitories in occupancies in Group I-3.
5. In occupancies in Groups A-4 and A-5, *exit* signs are not required on the seating side of vomitories or openings into seating areas where *exit* signs are provided in the concourse that are readily apparent from the vomitories. Egress lighting is provided to identify each vomitory or opening within the seating area in an emergency.

1011.2 Illumination. *Exit* signs shall be internally or externally illuminated.

Exception: Tactile signs required by Section 1011.3 need not be provided with illumination.

1011.3 Tactile exit signs. A tactile sign stating EXIT and complying with ICC A117.1 shall be provided adjacent to each door to an *area of refuge*, an exterior area for assisted rescue, an *exit stairway*, an *exit ramp*, an *exit passageway* and the *exit discharge*.

1011.4 Internally illuminated exit signs. Electrically powered, *self-luminous* and *photoluminescent exit* signs shall be *listed* and labeled in accordance with UL 924 and shall be installed in accordance with the manufacturer's instructions and Chapter 27. *Exit* signs shall be illuminated at all times.

1011.5 Externally illuminated exit signs. Externally illuminated *exit* signs shall comply with Sections 1011.5.1 through 1011.5.3.

1011.5.1 Graphics. Every *exit* sign and directional *exit* sign shall have plainly legible letters not less than 6 inches (152 mm) high with the principal strokes of the letters not less than $^3/_4$ inch (19.1 mm) wide. The word "EXIT" shall have letters having a width not less than 2 inches (51 mm) wide, except the letter "I," and the minimum spacing between letters shall not be less than $^3/_8$ inch (9.5 mm). Signs larger than the minimum established in this section shall have letter widths, strokes and spacing in proportion to their height.

The word "EXIT" shall be in high contrast with the background and shall be clearly discernible when the means of *exit* sign illumination is or is not energized. If a chevron directional indicator is provided as part of the *exit* sign, the construction shall be such that the direction of the chevron directional indicator cannot be readily changed.

1011.5.2 Exit sign illumination. The face of an *exit* sign illuminated from an external source shall have an intensity of not less than 5 footcandles (54 lux).

1011.5.3 Power source. *Exit* signs shall be illuminated at all times. To ensure continued illumination for a duration of not less than 90 minutes in case of primary power loss, the sign illumination means shall be connected to an emergency power system provided from storage batteries, unit equipment or an on-site generator. The installation of the emergency power system shall be in accordance with Chapter 27.

Exception: *Approved exit* sign illumination means that provide continuous illumination independent of external power sources for a duration of not less than 90 minutes, in case of primary power loss, are not required to be connected to an emergency electrical system.

SECTION 1012
HANDRAILS

1012.1 Where required. *Handrails* for *stairways* and *ramps* shall be adequate in strength and attachment in accordance with Section 1607.7. *Handrails* required for *stairways* by Section 1009.12 shall comply with Sections 1012.2 through 1012.9. *Handrails* required for *ramps* by Section 1010.8 shall comply with Sections 1012.2 through 1012.8.

1012.2 Height. *Handrail* height, measured above *stair* tread *nosings*, or finish surface of *ramp* slope, shall be uniform, not less than 34 inches (864 mm) and not more than 38 inches (965 mm). *Handrail* height of *alternating tread devices* and ship ladders, measured above tread *nosings*, shall be uniform, not less than 30 inches (762 mm) and not more than 34 inches (864 mm).

1012.3 Handrail graspability. All required *handrails* shall comply with Section 1012.3.1 or shall provide equivalent graspability.

Exception: In Group R-3 occupancies; within dwelling units in Group R-2 occupancies; and in Group U occupancies that are accessory to a Group R-3 occupancy or accessory to individual dwelling units in Group R-2 occupancies; handrails shall be Type I in accordance with Section 1012.3.1, Type II in accordance with Section 1012.3.2 or shall provide equivalent graspability.

1012.3.1 Type I. *Handrails* with a circular cross section shall have an outside diameter of at least $1^1/_4$ inches (32 mm) and not greater than 2 inches (51 mm). If the *handrail* is not circular, it shall have a perimeter dimension of at least 4 inches (102 mm) and not greater than $6^1/_4$ inches (160 mm) with a maximum cross-section dimension of $2^1/_4$ inches (57 mm). Edges shall have a minimum radius of 0.01 inch (0.25 mm).

1012.3.2 Type II. *Handrails* with a perimeter greater than $6^1/_4$ inches (160 mm) shall provide a graspable finger recess area on both sides of the profile. The finger recess shall begin within a distance of $^3/_4$ inch (19 mm) measured vertically from the tallest portion of the profile and achieve a depth of at least $^5/_{16}$ inch (8 mm) within $^7/_8$ inch (22 mm) below the widest portion of the profile. This required depth shall continue for at least $^3/_8$ inch (10 mm) to a level that is not less than $1^3/_4$ inches (45 mm) below the tallest portion of the profile. The minimum width of the *handrail* above the recess shall be $1^1/_4$ inches (32 mm) to a maximum of $2^3/_4$ inches (70 mm). Edges shall have a minimum radius of 0.01 inch (0.25 mm).

1012.4 Continuity. *Handrail* gripping surfaces shall be continuous, without interruption by newel posts or other obstructions.

Exceptions:

1. *Handrails* within dwelling units are permitted to be interrupted by a newel post at a turn or landing.
2. Within a dwelling unit, the use of a volute, turnout, starting easing or starting newel is allowed over the lowest tread.
3. *Handrail* brackets or balusters attached to the bottom surface of the *handrail* that do not project horizontally beyond the sides of the *handrail* within $1^1/_2$ inches (38 mm) of the bottom of the *handrail* shall not be considered obstructions. For each $^1/_2$ inch (12.7 mm) of additional *handrail* perimeter dimension above 4 inches (102 mm), the vertical clearance dimension of $1^1/_2$ inches (38 mm) shall be permitted to be reduced by $^1/_8$ inch (3 mm).
4. Where *handrails* are provided along walking surfaces with slopes not steeper than 1:20, the bottoms of the *handrail* gripping surfaces shall be permitted to be obstructed along their entire length where they are integral to crash rails or bumper guards.

1012.5 Fittings. *Handrails* shall not rotate within their fittings.

1012.6 Handrail extensions. *Handrails* shall return to a wall, *guard* or the walking surface or shall be continuous to the handrail of an adjacent *stair flight* or ramp run. Where *handrails* are not continuous between *flights,* the *handrails* shall extend horizontally at least 12 inches (305 mm) beyond the top riser and continue to slope for the depth of one tread beyond the bottom riser. At *ramps* where *handrails* are not continuous between runs, the *handrails* shall extend horizontally above the landing 12 inches (305 mm) minimum beyond the top and bottom of *ramp* runs. The extensions of *handrails* shall be in the same direction of the *stair flights* at *stairways* and the *ramp* runs at *ramps*.

Exceptions:

1. *Handrails* within a dwelling unit that is not required to be *accessible* need extend only from the top riser to the bottom riser.
2. *Aisle handrails* in Group A and E occupancies in accordance with Section 1028.13.
3. *Handrails* for *alternating tread devices* and ship ladders are permitted to terminate at a location vertically above the top and bottom risers. Handrails for *alternating tread devices* and ship ladders are not required to be continuous between *flights* or to extend beyond the top or bottom risers.

1012.7 Clearance. Clear space between a *handrail* and a wall or other surface shall be a minimum of $1^1/_2$ inches (38 mm). A *handrail* and a wall or other surface adjacent to the *handrail* shall be free of any sharp or abrasive elements.

1012.8 Projections. On ramps, the clear width between *handrails* shall be 36 inches (914 mm) minimum. Projections into the required width of *stairways* and *ramps* at each *handrail* shall not exceed $4^1/_2$ inches (114 mm) at or below the *handrail* height. Projections into the required width shall not be limited above the minimum headroom height required in Section 1009.2.

1012.9 Intermediate handrails. *Stairways* shall have intermediate *handrails* located in such a manner that all portions of the *stairway* width required for egress capacity are within 30 inches (762 mm) of a *handrail.* On monumental *stairs, handrails* shall be located along the most direct path of egress travel.

SECTION 1013
GUARDS

1013.1 Where required. *Guards* shall be located along open-sided walking surfaces, including *mezzanines, equipment platforms, stairs, ramps* and landings that are located more than 30 inches (762 mm) measured vertically to the floor or grade below at any point within 36 inches (914 mm) horizontally to the edge of the open side. *Guards* shall be adequate in strength and attachment in accordance with Section 1607.7.

Exception: *Guards* are not required for the following locations:

1. On the loading side of loading docks or piers.
2. On the audience side of stages and raised platforms, including steps leading up to the stage and raised platforms.
3. On raised stage and platform floor areas, such as runways, ramps and side stages used for entertainment or presentations.
4. At vertical openings in the performance area of stages and platforms.
5. At elevated walking surfaces appurtenant to stages and platforms for access to and utilization of special lighting or equipment.
6. Along vehicle service pits not accessible to the public.
7. In assembly seating where *guards* in accordance with Section 1028.14 are permitted and provided.

1013.1.1 Glazing. Where glass is used to provide a *guard* or as a portion of the *guard* system, the *guard* shall also comply with Section 2407. Where the glazing provided does not meet the strength and attachment requirements of Section 1607.7, complying *guards* shall also be located along glazed sides of open-sided walking surfaces.

1013.2 Height. Required *guards* shall be not less than 42 inches (1067 mm) high, measured vertically above the adjacent walking surfaces, adjacent fixed seating or the line connecting the leading edges of the treads.

Exceptions:

1. For occupancies in Group R-3, and within individual dwelling units in occupancies in Group R-2, *guards* on the open sides of *stairs* shall have a height not less than 34 inches (864 mm) measured vertically from a line connecting the leading edges of the treads.
2. For occupancies in Group R-3, and within individual dwelling units in occupancies in Group R-2, where the top of the *guard* also serves as a *handrail* on the open sides of *stairs*, the top of the *guard* shall not be less than 34 inches (864 mm) and not more than 38 inches (965 mm) measured vertically from a line connecting the leading edges of the treads.
3. The height in assembly seating areas shall be in accordance with Section 1028.14.
4. Along *alternating tread devices* and ship ladders, *guards* whose top rail also serves as a *handrail*, shall have height not less than 30 inches (762 mm) and not more than 34 inches (864 mm), measured vertically from the leading edge of the device tread *nosing*.

1013.3 Opening limitations. Required *guards* shall not have openings which allow passage of a sphere 4 inches (102 mm) in diameter from the walking surface to the required *guard* height. A bottom rail or curb shall be provided that will reject the passage of a 2-inch-diameter (51 mm) sphere.

Exceptions:

1. From a height of 36 inches (914 mm) to 42 inches (1067 mm), *guards* shall not have openings which allow passage of a sphere $4^3/_8$ inches (111 mm) in diameter.
2. The triangular openings at the open sides of a *stair*, formed by the riser, tread and bottom rail shall not allow passage of a sphere 6 inches (152 mm) in diameter.
3. At elevated walking surfaces for access to and use of electrical, mechanical or plumbing systems or equipment, *guards* shall not have openings which allow passage of a sphere 21 inches (533 mm) in diameter.
4. In areas that are not open to the public within occupancies in Group I-3, F, H or S, and for *alternating tread devices* and ship ladders, *guards* shall not have openings which allow passage of a sphere 21 inches (533 mm) in diameter.
5. In assembly seating areas, *guards* at the end of *aisles* where they terminate at a fascia of boxes, balconies and galleries shall not have openings which allow passage of a sphere 4 inches in diameter (102 mm) up to a height of 26 inches (660 mm). From a height of 26 inches to 42 inches (660 mm to 1067 mm) above the adjacent walking surfaces, *guards* shall not have openings which allow passage of a sphere 8 inches (203 mm) in diameter.
6. Within individual dwelling units and sleeping units in Group R-2 and R-3 occupancies, *guards* on the open sides of *stairs* shall not have openings which allow passage of a sphere $4^3/_8$ inches (111 mm) in diameter.

1013.4 Screen porches. Porches and decks which are enclosed with insect screening shall be provided with *guards* where the walking surface is located more than 30 inches (762 mm) above the floor or grade below.

1013.5 Mechanical equipment. *Guards* shall be provided where appliances, equipment, fans, roof hatch openings or other components that require service are located within 6 feet (1829 mm) of a roof edge or open side of a walking surface and such edge or open side is located more than 30 inches (762 mm) above the floor, roof or grade below. The *guard* shall be constructed so as to prevent the passage of a sphere 21 inches (533 mm) in diameter. The *guard* shall extend not less than 30 inches (762 mm) beyond each end of such appliance, equipment, fan or component.

1013.6 Roof access. *Guards* shall be provided where the roof hatch opening is located within 10 feet (3048 mm) of a roof edge or open side of a walking surface and such edge or open side is located more than 30 inches (762 mm) above the floor, roof or grade below. The *guard* shall be constructed so as to prevent the passage of a sphere 21 inches (533 mm) in diameter.

SECTION 1014 EXIT ACCESS

1014.1 General. The *exit access* shall comply with the applicable provisions of Sections 1003 through 1013. *Exit access* arrangement shall comply with Sections 1014 through 1019.

1014.2 Egress through intervening spaces. Egress through intervening spaces shall comply with this section.

1. Egress from a room or space shall not pass through adjoining or intervening rooms or areas, except where such adjoining rooms or areas and the area served are accessory to one or the other, are not a Group H occupancy and provide a discernible path of egress travel to an *exit*.

   Exception: *Means of egress* are not prohibited through adjoining or intervening rooms or spaces in a Group H, S or F occupancy when the adjoining or intervening rooms or spaces are the same or a lesser hazard occupancy group.

2. An *exit access* shall not pass through a room that can be locked to prevent egress.
3. *Means of egress* from dwelling units or sleeping areas shall not lead through other sleeping areas, toilet rooms or bathrooms.
4. Egress shall not pass through kitchens, storage rooms, closets or spaces used for similar purposes.

   Exceptions:

   1. *Means of egress* are not prohibited through a kitchen area serving adjoining rooms constituting part of the same dwelling unit or sleeping unit.
   2. *Means of egress* are not prohibited through stockrooms in Group M occupancies when all of the following are met:

      2.1. The stock is of the same hazard classification as that found in the main retail area;

      2.2. Not more than 50 percent of the *exit access* is through the stockroom;

      2.3. The stockroom is not subject to locking from the egress side; and

      2.4. There is a demarcated, minimum 44-inch-wide (1118 mm) *aisle* defined by full- or partial-height fixed walls or similar construction that will maintain the required width and lead directly from the retail area to the *exit* without obstructions.

1014.2.1 Multiple tenants. Where more than one tenant occupies any one floor of a building or structure, each tenant space, dwelling unit and sleeping unit shall be provided with access to the required *exits* without passing through adjacent tenant spaces, dwelling units and sleeping units.

Exception: The *means of egress* from a smaller tenant space shall not be prohibited from passing through a larger adjoining tenant space where such rooms or spaces of the smaller tenant occupy less than 10 percent of the area of the larger tenant space through which they pass; are the same or similar occupancy group; a discernable path of egress travel to an *exit* is provided; and the *means of egress* into the adjoining space is not subject to locking from the egress side. A required *means of egress* serving the larger tenant space shall not pass through the smaller tenant space or spaces.

1014.2.2 Group I-2. Habitable rooms or *suites* in Group I-2 occupancies shall have an *exit access* door leading directly to a *corridor.*

Exception: Rooms with *exit* doors opening directly to the outside at ground level.

1014.2.3 Suites in patient sleeping areas. Patient sleeping areas in Group I-2 occupancies shall be permitted to be divided into *suites* with one intervening room if one of the following conditions is met:

1. The intervening room within the *suite* is not used as an *exit access* for more than eight patient beds.
2. The arrangement of the *suite* allows for direct and constant visual supervision by nursing personnel.

1014.2.3.1 Area. *Suites* of sleeping rooms shall not exceed 5,000 square feet (465 m^2).

1014.2.3.2 Exit access. Any patient sleeping room, or any *suite* that includes patient sleeping rooms, of more than 1,000 square feet (93 m^2) shall have at least two *exit access* doors remotely located from each other.

1014.2.3.3 Travel distance. The travel distance between any point in a *suite* of sleeping rooms and an *exit access* door of that *suite* shall not exceed 100 feet (30 480 mm).

1014.2.4 Suites in areas other than patient sleeping areas. Areas other than patient sleeping areas in Group I-2 occupancies shall be permitted to be divided into *suites.*

1014.2.4.1 Area. *Suites* of rooms, other than patient sleeping rooms, shall not exceed 10,000 square feet (929 m^2).

1014.2.4.2 Exit access. Any room or *suite* of rooms, other than patient sleeping rooms, of more than 2,500 square feet (232 m^2) shall have at least two *exit access* doors remotely located from each other.

1014.2.4.3 One intervening room. For rooms other than patient sleeping rooms, *suites* of rooms are permitted to have one intervening room if the travel distance within the *suite* to the *exit access* door is not greater than 100 feet (30 480 mm).

1014.2.4.4 Two intervening rooms. For rooms other than patient sleeping rooms located within a *suite*, *exit access* travel from within the *suite* shall be permitted through two intervening rooms where the travel distance to the *exit access* door is not greater than 50 feet (15 240 mm).

1014.2.5 Exit access through suites. *Exit access* from all other portions of a building not classified as a *suite* in a Group I-2 occupancy shall not pass through a *suite*.

1014.2.6 Travel distance. The travel distance between any point in a Group I-2 occupancy patient sleeping room and an *exit access* door in that room shall not exceed 50 feet (15 240 mm).

1014.2.7 Separation. *Suites* in Group I-2 occupancies shall be separated from other portions of the building by a *smoke partition* complying with Section 711.

1014.3 Common path of egress travel. In occupancies other than Groups H-1, H-2 and H-3, the *common path of egress travel* shall not exceed 75 feet (22 860 mm). In Group H-1, H-2 and H-3 occupancies, the *common path of egress travel* shall not exceed 25 feet (7620 mm). For *common path of egress travel* in Group A occupancies and assembly occupancies accessory to Group E occupancies having fixed seating, see Section 1028.8.

Exceptions:

1. The length of a *common path of egress travel* in Group B, F and S occupancies shall not be more than 100 feet (30 480 mm), provided that the building is equipped throughout with an *automatic sprinkler system* installed in accordance with Section 903.3.1.1.
2. Where a tenant space in Group B, S and U occupancies has an *occupant load* of not more than 30, the length of a *common path of egress travel* shall not be more than 100 feet (30 480 mm).
3. The length of a *common path of egress travel* in a Group I-3 occupancy shall not be more than 100 feet (30 480 mm).
4. The length of a common path of egress travel in a Group R-2 occupancy shall not be more than 125 feet (38 100 mm), provided that the building is protected throughout with an *approved automatic sprinkler system* in accordance with Section 903.3.1.1 or 903.3.1.2.

SECTION 1015
EXIT AND EXIT ACCESS DOORWAYS

1015.1 Exits or exit access doorways from spaces. Two *exits* or *exit access doorways* from any space shall be provided where one of the following conditions exists:

Exception: Group I-2 occupancies shall comply with Section 1014.2.2 through 1014.2.7.

1. The *occupant load* of the space exceeds one of the values in Table 1015.1.

   Exception: In Group R-2 and R-3 occupancies, one *means of egress* is permitted within and from individual dwelling units with a maximum *occupant load* of 20 where the dwelling unit is equipped throughout with an *automatic sprinkler system* in accordance with Section 903.3.1.1 or 903.3.1.2.
2. The *common path of egress travel* exceeds one of the limitations of Section 1014.3.
3. Where required by Section 1015.3, 1015.4, 1015.5, 1015.6 or 1015.6.1.

Where a building contains mixed occupancies, each individual occupancy shall comply with the applicable requirements for that occupancy. Where applicable, cumulative *occupant loads* from adjacent occupancies shall be considered in accordance with the provisions of Section 1004.1.

TABLE 1015.1
SPACES WITH ONE EXIT OR EXIT ACCESS DOORWAY

OCCUPANCY	MAXIMUM OCCUPANT LOAD
A, B, E[a], F, M, U	49
H-1, H-2, H-3	3
H-4, H-5, I-1, I-3, I-4, R	10
S	29

a. Day care maximum occupant load is 10.

1015.1.1 Three or more exits or exit access doorways. Three *exits* or *exit access doorways* shall be provided from any space with an *occupant load* of 501 to 1,000. Four *exits* or *exit access doorways* shall be provided from any space with an *occupant load* greater than 1,000.

1015.2 Exit or exit access doorway arrangement. Required *exits* shall be located in a manner that makes their availability obvious. *Exits* shall be unobstructed at all times. *Exit* and *exit access doorways* shall be arranged in accordance with Sections 1015.2.1 and 1015.2.2.

1015.2.1 Two exits or exit access doorways. Where two *exits* or *exit access doorways* are required from any portion of the *exit access*, the *exit* doors or *exit access doorways* shall be placed a distance apart equal to not less than one-half of the length of the maximum overall diagonal dimension of the building or area to be served measured in a straight line between *exit* doors or *exit access doorways*. Interlocking or *scissor stairs* shall be counted as one *exit stairway*.

Exceptions:

1. Where *exit enclosures* are provided as a portion of the required *exit* and are interconnected by a 1-hour fire-resistance-rated *corridor* conforming to the requirements of Section 1018, the required *exit* separation shall be measured along the shortest direct line of travel within the *corridor*.
2. Where a building is equipped throughout with an *automatic sprinkler system* in accordance with Section 903.3.1.1 or 903.3.1.2, the separation distance of the *exit* doors or *exit access doorways* shall not be less than one-third of the length of the maximum overall diagonal dimension of the area served.

1015.2.2 Three or more exits or exit access doorways. Where access to three or more *exits* is required, at least two *exit* doors or *exit access doorways* shall be arranged in accordance with the provisions of Section 1015.2.1.

1015.3 Boiler, incinerator and furnace rooms. Two *exit access doorways* are required in boiler, incinerator and furnace rooms where the area is over 500 square feet (46 m^2) and any fuel-fired equipment exceeds 400,000 British thermal units (Btu) (422 000 KJ) input capacity. Where two *exit access doorways* are required, one is permitted to be a fixed ladder or an *alternating tread device. Exit access doorways* shall be separated by a horizontal distance equal to one-half the length of the maximum overall diagonal dimension of the room.

1015.4 Refrigeration machinery rooms. Machinery rooms larger than 1,000 square feet (93 m^2) shall have not less than two *exits* or *exit access* doors. Where two *exit access doorways* are required, one such doorway is permitted to be served by a fixed ladder or an *alternating tread device. Exit access doorways* shall be separated by a horizontal distance equal to one-half the maximum horizontal dimension of room.

All portions of machinery rooms shall be within 150 feet (45 720 mm) of an *exit* or *exit access doorway*. An increase in travel distance is permitted in accordance with Section 1016.1.

Doors shall swing in the direction of egress travel, regardless of the *occupant load* served. Doors shall be tight fitting and self-closing.

1015.5 Refrigerated rooms or spaces. Rooms or spaces having a floor area larger than 1,000 square feet (93 m^2), containing a refrigerant evaporator and maintained at a temperature below 68°F (20°C), shall have access to not less than two *exits* or *exit access* doors.

Travel distance shall be determined as specified in Section 1016.1, but all portions of a refrigerated room or space shall be within 150 feet (45 720 mm) of an *exit* or *exit access* door where such rooms are not protected by an *approved automatic sprinkler* system. Egress is allowed through adjoining refrigerated rooms or spaces.

Exception: Where using refrigerants in quantities limited to the amounts based on the volume set forth in the *International Mechanical Code*.

1015.6 Stage means of egress. Where two *means of egress* are required, based on the stage size or *occupant load*, one *means of egress* shall be provided on each side of the stage.

1015.6.1 Gallery, gridiron and catwalk means of egress. The *means of egress* from lighting and access catwalks, galleries and *gridirons* shall meet the requirements for occupancies in Group F-2.

Exceptions:

1. A minimum width of 22 inches (559 mm) is permitted for lighting and access catwalks.
2. *Spiral stairs* are permitted in the *means of egress*.
3. *Stairways* required by this subsection need not be enclosed.
4. *Stairways* with a minimum width of 22 inches (559 mm), ladders or *spiral stairs* are permitted in the *means of egress*.
5. A second *means of egress* is not required from these areas where a means of escape to a floor or to a roof is provided. Ladders, *alternating tread devices* or *spiral stairs* are permitted in the means of escape.
6. Ladders are permitted in the *means of egress*.

SECTION 1016
EXIT ACCESS TRAVEL DISTANCE

1016.1 Travel distance limitations. *Exits* shall be so located on each *story* such that the maximum length of *exit access* travel, measured from the most remote point within a *story* along the natural and unobstructed path of egress travel to an *exterior exit* door at the *level of exit discharge*, an entrance to a vertical *exit enclosure*, an *exit passageway*, a *horizontal exit*, an *exterior exit stairway* or an exterior *exit ramp*, shall not exceed the distances given in Table 1016.1.

Exceptions:

1. Travel distance in *open parking garages* is permitted to be measured to the closest riser of open *exit stairways*.
2. In outdoor facilities with open *exit access* components and open *exterior exit stairways* or *exit ramps*, travel distance is permitted to be measured to the closest riser of an *exit stairway* or the closest slope of the *exit ramp*.
3. In other than occupancy Groups H and I, the *exit access* travel distance to a maximum of 50 percent of the *exits* is permitted to be measured from the most remote point within a building to an *exit* using unenclosed *exit access stairways* or *ramps* when connecting a maximum of two stories. The two connected stories shall be provided with at least two *means of egress*. Such interconnected stories shall not be open to other stories.

4. In other than occupancy Groups H and I, *exit access* travel distance is permitted to be measured from the most remote point within a building to an *exit* using unenclosed *exit access stairways* or *ramps* in the first and second stories above *grade plane* in buildings equipped throughout with an *automatic sprinkler system* in accordance with Section 903.3.1.1. The first and second stories above *grade plane* shall be provided with at least two *means of egress*. Such interconnected stories shall not be open to other stories.

Where applicable, travel distance on unenclosed *exit access stairways* or *ramps* and on connecting stories shall also be included in the travel distance measurement. The measurement along *stairways* shall be made on a plane parallel and tangent to the *stair* tread *nosings* in the center of the *stairway*.

TABLE 1016.1
EXIT ACCESS TRAVEL DISTANCE[a]

OCCUPANCY	WITHOUT SPRINKLER SYSTEM (feet)	WITH SPRINKLER SYSTEM (feet)
A, E, F-1, M, R, S-1	200	250[b]
I-1	Not Permitted	250[c]
B	200	300[c]
F-2, S-2, U	300	400[c]
H-1	Not Permitted	75[c]
H-2	Not Permitted	100[c]
H-3	Not Permitted	150[c]
H-4	Not Permitted	175[c]
H-5	Not Permitted	200[c]
I-2, I-3, I-4	Not Permitted	200[c]

For SI: 1 foot = 304.8 mm.

a. See the following sections for modifications to exit access travel distance requirements:
Section 402.4: For the distance limitation in malls.
Section 404.9: For the distance limitation through an atrium space.
Section 407.4: For the distance limitation in Group I-2.
Sections 408.6.1 and 408.8.1: For the distance limitations in Group I-3.
Section 411.4: For the distance limitation in special amusement buildings.
Section 1014.2.2: For the distance limitation in Group I-2 hospital suites.
Section 1015.4: For the distance limitation in refrigeration machinery rooms.
Section 1015.5: For the distance limitation in refrigerated rooms and spaces.
Section 1021.2: For buildings with one exit.
Section 1028.7: For increased limitation in assembly seating.
Section 1028.7: For increased limitation for assembly open-air seating.
Section 3103.4: For temporary structures.
Section 3104.9: For pedestrian walkways.

b. Buildings equipped throughout with an automatic sprinkler system in accordance with Section 903.3.1.1 or 903.3.1.2. See Section 903 for occupancies where automatic sprinkler systems are permitted in accordance with Section 903.3.1.2.

c. Buildings equipped throughout with an automatic sprinkler system in accordance with Section 903.3.1.1.

1016.2 Exterior egress balcony increase. Travel distances specified in Section 1016.1 shall be increased up to an additional 100 feet (30 480 mm) provided the last portion of the *exit access* leading to the *exit* occurs on an exterior egress balcony constructed in accordance with Section 1019. The length of such balcony shall not be less than the amount of the increase taken.

SECTION 1017
AISLES

1017.1 General. *Aisles* serving as a portion of the *exit access* in the *means of egress* system shall comply with the requirements of this section. *Aisles* shall be provided from all occupied portions of the *exit access* which contain seats, tables, furnishings, displays and similar fixtures or equipment. *Aisles* serving assembly areas shall comply with Section 1028. *Aisles* serving reviewing stands, *grandstands* and *bleachers* shall also comply with Section 1028. The required width of *aisles* shall be unobstructed.

Exception: Doors complying with Section 1005.2.

1017.2 Aisles in Groups B and M. In Group B and M occupancies, the minimum clear *aisle* width shall be determined by Section 1005.1 for the *occupant load* served, but shall not be less than 36 inches (914 mm).

Exception: Nonpublic *aisles* serving less than 50 people and not required to be *accessible* by Chapter 11 need not exceed 28 inches (711 mm) in width.

1017.3 Aisle accessways in Group M. An *aisle accessway* shall be provided on at least one side of each element within the *merchandise pad*. The minimum clear width for an *aisle accessway* not required to be *accessible* shall be 30 inches (762 mm). The required clear width of the *aisle accessway* shall be measured perpendicular to the elements and merchandise within the *merchandise pad*. The 30-inch (762 mm) minimum clear width shall be maintained to provide a path to an adjacent *aisle* or *aisle accessway*. The common path of travel shall not exceed 30 feet (9144 mm) from any point in the *merchandise pad*.

Exception: For areas serving not more than 50 occupants, the common path of travel shall not exceed 75 feet (22 880 mm).

1017.4 Seating at tables. Where seating is located at a table or counter and is adjacent to an *aisle* or *aisle accessway*, the measurement of required clear width of the *aisle* or *aisle accessway* shall be made to a line 19 inches (483 mm) away from and parallel to the edge of the table or counter. The 19-inch (483 mm) distance shall be measured perpendicular to the side of the table or counter. In the case of other side boundaries for *aisle* or *aisle accessways*, the clear width shall be measured to walls, edges of seating and tread edges, except that *handrail* projections are permitted.

Exception: Where tables or counters are served by fixed seats, the width of the *aisle accessway* shall be measured from the back of the seat.

1017.4.1 Aisle accessway for tables and seating. *Aisle accessways* serving arrangements of seating at tables or counters shall have sufficient clear width to conform to the capacity requirements of Section 1005.1 but shall not have less than the appropriate minimum clear width specified in Section 1017.4.2.

1017.4.2 Table and seating accessway width. *Aisle accessways* shall provide a minimum of 12 inches (305 mm) of width plus $^1/_2$ inch (12.7 mm) of width for each additional 1 foot (305 mm), or fraction thereof, beyond 12 feet (3658 mm) of *aisle accessway* length measured from the center of the seat farthest from an *aisle*.

Exception: Portions of an *aisle accessway* having a length not exceeding 6 feet (1829 mm) and used by a total of not more than four persons.

1017.4.3 Table and seating aisle accessway length. The length of travel along the *aisle accessway* shall not exceed 30 feet (9144 mm) from any seat to the point where a person has a choice of two or more paths of egress travel to separate *exits*.

SECTION 1018 CORRIDORS

1018.1 Construction. *Corridors* shall be fire-resistance rated in accordance with Table 1018.1. The *corridor* walls required to be fire-resistance rated shall comply with Section 709 for *fire partitions*.

Exceptions:

1. A *fire-resistance rating* is not required for *corridors* in an occupancy in Group E where each room that is used for instruction has at least one door opening directly to the exterior and rooms for assembly purposes have at least one-half of the required *means of egress* doors opening directly to the exterior. Exterior doors specified in this exception are required to be at ground level.
2. A *fire-resistance rating* is not required for *corridors* contained within a dwelling or sleeping unit in an occupancy in Group R.
3. A *fire-resistance rating* is not required for *corridors* in *open parking garages*.
4. A *fire-resistance rating* is not required for *corridors* in an occupancy in Group B which is a space requiring only a single *means of egress* complying with Section 1015.1.

1018.2 Corridor width. The minimum *corridor* width shall be as determined in Section 1005.1, but not less than 44 inches (1118 mm).

Exceptions:

1. Twenty-four inches (610 mm)—For access to and utilization of electrical, mechanical or plumbing systems or equipment.
2. Thirty-six inches (914 mm)—In other than Groups I-1, I-2 and I-3 with a required occupant capacity of less than 50.
3. Thirty-six inches (914 mm)—Within a dwelling unit.
4. Seventy-two inches (1829 mm)—In Group E with a *corridor* having a required capacity of 100 or more.
5. Seventy-two inches (1829 mm)—In *corridors* and areas serving gurney traffic in occupancies where patients receive outpatient medical care, which causes the patient to be not capable of self-preservation and resident areas of Groups I-1 and I-2.
6. Ninety-six inches (2438 mm)—In Group I-2 in patient areas and in areas where required for bed movement.

1018.3 Corridor obstruction. The required width of *corridors* shall be unobstructed.

Exception: Doors complying with Section 1005.2.

1018.4 Dead ends. Where more than one *exit* or *exit access doorway* is required, the *exit access* shall be arranged such that there are no dead ends in *corridors* more than 20 feet (6096 mm) in length.

Exceptions:

1. In occupancies in Group I-3 of Occupancy Condition 2, 3 or 4 (see Section 308.4), the dead end in a *corridor* shall not exceed 50 feet (15 240 mm).
2. In occupancies in Groups B, E, F, I-1, M, R-1, R-2, R-4, S and U, where the building is equipped throughout with an *automatic sprinkler system* in accordance

TABLE 1018.1 CORRIDOR FIRE-RESISTANCE RATING[e]

OCCUPANCY	OCCUPANT LOAD SERVED BY CORRIDOR	REQUIRED FIRE-RESISTANCE RATING (hours)	
		Without sprinkler system	With sprinkler system[c]
H-1, H-2, H-3	All	Not Permitted	1
H-4, H-5	Greater than 30	Not Permitted	1
A, B[f], E[d], F, M, S, U	Greater than 30	1	0
R	Greater than 10	Not Permitted	0.5
I-2[a], I-4	All	Not Permitted	0
I-1, I-3	All	Not Permitted	1[b]

a. For requirements for occupancies in Group I-2, see Sections 407.2 and 407.3.
b. For a reduction in the fire-resistance rating for occupancies in Group I-3, see Section 408.8.
c. Buildings equipped throughout with an automatic sprinkler system in accordance with Section 903.3.1.1 or 903.3.1.2 where allowed.
d. Adult and child day care facilities without *automatic sprinkler systems* shall have 1-hour fire-resistance-rated corridors regardless of occupant load.
e. For requirements for residential care facilities, see Section 425.
f. Exit access corridors are not required to be rated on any single tenant floor or in any single tenant space, when 1-hour fire-resistance-rated tenant demising walls are provided between all tenant spaces and 1-hour fire-resistance-rated floor/ceiling assemblies are provided in multistory buildings.

with Section 903.3.1.1, the length of the dead-end *corridors* shall not exceed 50 feet (15 240 mm).

3. A dead-end *corridor* shall not be limited in length where the length of the dead-end *corridor* is less than 2.5 times the least width of the dead-end *corridor*.

1018.5 Air movement in corridors. *Corridors* shall not serve as supply, return, exhaust, relief or ventilation air ducts.

Exceptions:

1. Use of a *corridor* as a source of makeup air for exhaust systems in rooms that open directly onto such *corridors*, including toilet rooms, bathrooms, dressing rooms, smoking lounges and janitor closets, shall be permitted, provided that each such *corridor* is directly supplied with outdoor air at a rate greater than the rate of makeup air taken from the *corridor*.
2. Where located within a dwelling unit, the use of *corridors* for conveying return air shall not be prohibited.
3. Where located within tenant spaces of 1,000 square feet (93 m^2) or less in area, utilization of *corridors* for conveying return air is permitted.
4. Incidental air movement from pressurized rooms within health care facilities, provided that the *corridor* is not the primary source of supply or return to the room.

1018.5.1 Corridor ceiling. Use of the space between the *corridor* ceiling and the floor or roof structure above as a return air plenum is permitted for one or more of the following conditions:

1. The *corridor* is not required to be of fire-resistance-rated construction;
2. The *corridor* is separated from the plenum by fire-resistance-rated construction;
3. The air-handling system serving the *corridor* is shut down upon activation of the air-handling unit *smoke detectors* required by the *International Mechanical Code*;
4. The air-handling system serving the *corridor* is shut down upon detection of sprinkler waterflow where the building is equipped throughout with an *automatic sprinkler system*; or
5. The space between the *corridor* ceiling and the floor or roof structure above the *corridor* is used as a component of an *approved* engineered smoke control system.

1018.6 Corridor continuity. Fire-resistance-rated corridors shall be continuous from the point of entry to an *exit*, and shall not be interrupted by intervening rooms.

Exception: Foyers, lobbies or reception rooms constructed as required for *corridors* shall not be construed as intervening rooms.

SECTION 1019 EGRESS BALCONIES

1019.1 General. Balconies used for egress purposes shall conform to the same requirements as *corridors* for width, headroom, dead ends and projections.

1019.2 Wall separation. Exterior egress balconies shall be separated from the interior of the building by walls and opening protectives as required for *corridors*.

Exception: Separation is not required where the exterior egress balcony is served by at least two *stairs* and a dead-end travel condition does not require travel past an unprotected opening to reach a *stair*.

1019.3 Openness. The long side of an egress balcony shall be at least 50 percent open, and the open area above the guards shall be so distributed as to minimize the accumulation of smoke or toxic gases.

SECTION 1020 EXITS

1020.1 General. *Exits* shall comply with Sections 1020 through 1026 and the applicable requirements of Sections 1003 through 1013. An *exit* shall not be used for any purpose that interferes with its function as a *means of egress*. Once a given level of exit protection is achieved, such level of protection shall not be reduced until arrival at the *exit discharge*.

1020.2 Exterior exit doors. Buildings or structures used for human occupancy shall have at least one exterior door that meets the requirements of Section 1008.1.1.

1020.2.1 Detailed requirements. Exterior *exit* doors shall comply with the applicable requirements of Section 1008.1.

1020.2.2 Arrangement. Exterior *exit* doors shall lead directly to the *exit discharge* or the *public way*.

SECTION 1021 NUMBER OF EXITS AND CONTINUITY

1021.1 Exits from stories. All spaces within each *story* shall have access to the minimum number of *approved* independent *exits* as specified in Table 1021.1 based on the *occupant load* of the *story*. For the purposes of this chapter, occupied roofs shall be provided with *exits* as required for stories.

Exceptions:

1. As modified by Section 403.5.2.
2. As modified by Section 1021.2.
3. *Exit access stairways* and *ramps* that comply with Exception 3 or 4 of Section 1016.1 shall be permitted to provide the minimum number of *approved* independent *exits* required by Table 1021.1 on each *story*.
4. In Group R-2 and R-3 occupancies, one *means of egress* is permitted within and from individual dwelling units with a maximum *occupant load* of 20 where the dwelling unit is equipped throughout with an *automatic sprinkler system* in accordance with Section 903.3.1.1 or 903.3.1.2.

5. Within a *story*, rooms and spaces complying with Section 1015.1 with *exits* that discharge directly to the exterior at the *level of exit discharge*, are permitted to have one *exit*.

TABLE 1021.1
MINIMUM NUMBER OF EXITS FOR OCCUPANT LOAD

OCCUPANT LOAD (persons per story)	MINIMUM NUMBER OF EXITS (per story)
1-500	2
501-1,000	3
More than 1,000	4

1021.1.1 Exits maintained. The required number of *exits* from any *story* shall be maintained until arrival at grade or the *public way*.

1021.1.2 Parking structures. Parking structures shall not have less than two *exits* from each parking tier, except that only one *exit* is required where vehicles are mechanically parked. Vehicle ramps shall not be considered as required *exits* unless pedestrian facilities are provided.

1021.1.3 Helistops. The *means of egress* from helistops shall comply with the provisions of this chapter, provided that landing areas located on buildings or structures shall have two or more *exits*. For landing platforms or roof areas less than 60 feet (18 288 mm) long, or less than 2,000 square feet (186 m^2) in area, the second *means of egress* is permitted to be a fire escape, *alternating tread device* or ladder leading to the floor below.

1021.2 Single exits. Only one *exit* shall be required from Group R-3 occupancy buildings or from stories of other buildings as indicated in Table 1021.2. Occupancies shall be permitted to have a single *exit* in buildings otherwise required to have more than one *exit* if the areas served by the single *exit* do not exceed the limitations of Table 1021.2. Mixed occupancies shall be permitted to be served by single *exits* provided each individual occupancy complies with the applicable requirements of Table 1021.2 for that occupancy. Where applicable, cumulative *occupant loads* from adjacent occupancies shall be considered in accordance with the provisions of Section 1004.1. Basements with a single *exit* shall not be located more than one *story* below *grade plane*.

1021.3 Exit continuity. *Exits* shall be continuous from the point of entry into the *exit* to the *exit discharge*.

1021.4 Exit door arrangement. *Exit* door arrangement shall meet the requirements of Sections 1015.2 through 1015.2.2.

SECTION 1022
EXIT ENCLOSURES

1022.1 Enclosures required. *Interior exit stairways* and interior *exit ramps* shall be enclosed with *fire barriers* constructed in accordance with Section 707 or *horizontal assemblies* constructed in accordance with Section 712, or both. *Exit enclosures* shall have a *fire-resistance rating* of not less than 2 hours where connecting four stories or more and not less than 1 hour where connecting less than four stories. The number of stories connected by the *exit enclosure* shall include any basements but not any *mezzanines*. *Exit enclosures* shall have a *fire-resistance rating* not less than the floor assembly penetrated, but need not exceed 2 hours. *Exit enclosures* shall lead directly to the exterior of the building or shall be extended to the exterior of the building with an *exit passageway* conforming to the requirements of Section 1023, except as permitted in Section 1027.1. An *exit enclosure* shall not be used for any purpose other than *means of egress*.

Exceptions:

1. In all occupancies, other than Group H and I occupancies, a *stairway* is not required to be enclosed when

TABLE 1021.2
STORIES WITH ONE EXIT

STORY	OCCUPANCY	MAXIMUM OCCUPANTS (OR DWELLING UNITS) PER FLOOR AND TRAVEL DISTANCE
First story or basement	A, B[d], E[e], F[d], M, U, S[d]	49 occupants and 75 feet travel distance
	H-2, H-3	3 occupants and 25 feet travel distance
	H-4, H-5, I, R[f]	10 occupants and 75 feet travel distance
	S[a]	29 occupants and 100 feet travel distance
Second story	B[b], F, M, S[a]	29 occupants and 75 feet travel distance
	R-2	4 dwelling units and 50 feet travel distance
Third story	R-2[c]	4 dwelling units and 50 feet travel distance

For SI: 1 foot = 304.8 mm.

a. For the required number of exits for parking structures, see Section 1021.1.2.

b. For the required number of exits for air traffic control towers, see Section 412.3.

c. Buildings classified as Group R-2 equipped throughout with an automatic sprinkler system in accordance with Section 903.3.1.1 or 903.3.1.2 and provided with emergency escape and rescue openings in accordance with Section 1029.

d. Group B, F and S occupancies in buildings equipped throughout with an automatic sprinkler system in accordance with Section 903.3.1.1 shall have a maximum travel distance of 100 feet.

e. Day care occupancies shall have a maximum occupant load of 10.

f. Group R-4 adult and child day care facilities shall have two exits or the rooms where the occupants receive care shall be located on the level of exit discharge and each of these rooms shall have an exit door directly to the exterior.

the *stairway* serves an *occupant load* of less than 10 and the *stairway* complies with either Item 1.1 or 1.2. In all cases, the maximum number of connecting open stories shall not exceed two.

1.1. The *stairway* is open to not more than one *story* above its *level of exit discharge*; or

1.2. The *stairway* is open to not more than one *story* below its *level of exit discharge*.

2. *Exits* in buildings of Group A-5 where all portions of the *means of egress* are essentially open to the outside need not be enclosed.
3. *Stairways* serving and contained within a single residential dwelling unit or sleeping unit in Group R-1, R-2 or R-3 occupancies are not required to be enclosed.
4. *Stairways* in open parking structures that serve only the parking structure are not required to be enclosed.
5. *Stairways* in Group I-3 occupancies, as provided for in Section 408.3.8, are not required to be enclosed.
6. *Means of egress stairways* as required by Sections 410.5.3 and 1015.6.1 are not required to be enclosed.
7. *Means of egress stairways* from balconies, galleries or press boxes as provided for in Section 1028.5.1 are not required to be enclosed.
8. In other than Group H and I occupancies, a maximum of 50 percent of *egress stairways* serving one adjacent floor are not required to be enclosed, provided at least two *means of egress* are provided from both floors served by the unenclosed *stairways*. Any two such interconnected floors shall not open to other floors. Unenclosed *exit stairways* shall be remotely located as required in Section 1015.2.
9. In other than Group H and I occupancies, interior egress *stairways* serving only the first and second *stories* of a building equipped throughout with an *automatic sprinkler system* in accordance with Section 903.3.1.1 are not required to be enclosed, provided at least two *means of egress* are provided from both floors served by the enclosed *stairways*. Such interconnected *stories* shall not be open to other *stories*. Unenclosed *exit stairways* shall be remotely located as required in Section 1015.2.

1022.2 Termination. *Exit enclosures* shall terminate at an *exit discharge* or a *public way*.

Exception: An *exit enclosure* shall be permitted to terminate at an *exit passageway* complying with Section 1023, provided the *exit passageway* terminates at an *exit discharge* or a *public way*.

1022.2.1 Extension. Where an *exit enclosure* is extended to an *exit discharge* or a *public way* by an *exit passageway*, the *exit enclosure* shall be separated from the *exit passageway* by a *fire barrier* constructed in accordance with Section 707 or a *horizontal assembly* constructed in accordance with Section 712, or both. The *fire-resistance rating* shall be at least equal to that required for the *exit enclosure*. A *fire door assembly* complying with Section 715.4 shall be installed in the *fire barrier* to provide a *means of egress* from the *exit enclosure* to the *exit passageway*. Openings in the *fire barrier* other than the *fire door assembly* are prohibited. Penetrations of the *fire barrier* are prohibited.

Exception: Penetrations of the *fire barrier* in accordance with Section 1022.4 shall be permitted.

1022.3 Openings and penetrations. *Exit enclosure* opening protectives shall be in accordance with the requirements of Section 715.

Openings in *exit enclosures* other than unprotected exterior openings shall be limited to those necessary for *exit access* to the enclosure from normally occupied spaces and for egress from the enclosure.

Elevators shall not open into an *exit enclosure*.

1022.4 Penetrations. Penetrations into and openings through an *exit enclosure* are prohibited except for required *exit* doors, equipment and ductwork necessary for independent ventilation or pressurization, sprinkler piping, standpipes, electrical raceway for fire department communication systems and electrical raceway serving the *exit enclosure* and terminating at a steel box not exceeding 16 square inches (0.010 m^2). Such penetrations shall be protected in accordance with Section 713. There shall be no penetrations or communication openings, whether protected or not, between adjacent *exit enclosures*.

1022.5 Ventilation. Equipment and ductwork for *exit enclosure* ventilation as permitted by Section 1022.4 shall comply with one of the following items:

1. Such equipment and ductwork shall be located exterior to the building and shall be directly connected to the *exit enclosure* by ductwork enclosed in construction as required for shafts.
2. Where such equipment and ductwork is located within the *exit enclosure*, the intake air shall be taken directly from the outdoors and the exhaust air shall be discharged directly to the outdoors, or such air shall be conveyed through ducts enclosed in construction as required for shafts.
3. Where located within the building, such equipment and ductwork shall be separated from the remainder of the building, including other mechanical equipment, with construction as required for shafts.

In each case, openings into the fire-resistance-rated construction shall be limited to those needed for maintenance and operation and shall be protected by opening protectives in accordance with Section 715 for shaft enclosures.

Exit enclosure ventilation systems shall be independent of other building ventilation systems.

1022.6 Exit enclosure exterior walls. *Exterior walls* of an *exit enclosure* shall comply with the requirements of Section 705 for *exterior walls*. Where nonrated walls or unprotected openings enclose the exterior of the *stairway* and the walls or openings are exposed by other parts of the building at an angle of less than 180 degrees (3.14 rad), the building *exterior walls* within 10 feet (3048 mm) horizontally of a nonrated wall or unprotected opening shall have a *fire-resistance rating* of not less than 1 hour.

MICHAEL T WARTHON
7524 SHILLINGLAW CIR
FAYETTEVILLE NC 28314

Stu ID: 2731625
Sect ID: 102497

Fayetteville Technical Community College

Fayetteville, North Carolina

FAYETTEVILLE TECHNICAL COMMUNITY COLLEGE
ESSE QUAM VIDERI
ESTABLISHED 1961

This certifies that

MICHAEL T WARTHON

has satisfactorily completed the required hours of instruction in

GENERAL CONTRACTOR'S LICENSE PREPARATION

FOR 47.50 CONTACT HOURS
THIS COURSE CARRIES 4.75 CONTINUING EDUCATION UNITS

ASSOCIATE VICE PRESIDENT FOR CONTINUING EDUCATION

PRESIDENT

Date: 11/02/13

Division of Continuing Education

Openings within such *exterior walls* shall be protected by opening protectives having a *fire protection rating* of not less than $^3/_4$ hour. This construction shall extend vertically from the ground to a point 10 feet (3048 mm) above the topmost landing of the *stairway* or to the roof line, whichever is lower.

1022.7 Discharge identification. A *stairway* in an *exit enclosure* shall not continue below its *level of exit discharge* unless an approved barrier is provided at the *level of exit discharge* to prevent persons from unintentionally continuing into levels below. Directional *exit* signs shall be provided as specified in Section 1011.

1022.8 Floor identification signs. A sign shall be provided at each floor landing in *exit enclosures* connecting more than three stories designating the floor level, the terminus of the top and bottom of the *exit enclosure* and the identification of the *stair* or *ramp*. The signage shall also state the *story* of, and the direction to, the *exit discharge* and the availability of roof access from the enclosure for the fire department. The sign shall be located 5 feet (1524 mm) above the floor landing in a position that is readily visible when the doors are in the open and closed positions. Floor level identification signs in tactile characters complying with ICC A117.1 shall be located at each floor level landing adjacent to the door leading from the enclosure into the corridor to identify the floor level.

1022.8.1 Signage requirements. *Stairway* identification signs shall comply with all of the following requirements:

1. The signs shall be a minimum size of 18 inches by 12 inches (457 mm by 305 mm).
2. The letters designating the identification of the stair enclosure shall be a minimum of $1^1/_2$ inches (38 mm) in height.
3. The number designating the floor level shall be a minimum of 5 inches (127 mm) in height and located in the center of the sign.
4. All other lettering and numbers shall be a minimum of 1 inch (25 mm) in height.
5. Characters and their background shall have a nonglare finish. Characters shall contrast with their background, with either light characters on a dark background or dark characters on a light background.
6. When signs required by Section 1022.8 are installed in interior *exit enclosures* of buildings subject to Section 1024, the signs shall be made of the same materials as required by Section 1024.4.

1022.9 Smokeproof enclosures and pressurized stairways. In buildings required to comply with Section 403 or 405, each of the *exit enclosures* serving a *story* with a floor surface located more than 75 feet (22 860 mm) above the lowest level of fire department vehicle access or more than 30 feet (9144 mm) below the finished floor of a *level of exit discharge* serving such stories shall be a *smokeproof enclosure* or pressurized *stairway* in accordance with Section 909.20.

1022.9.1 Termination and extension. A *smokeproof enclosure* or pressurized *stairway* shall terminate at an *exit discharge* or a *public way*. The *smokeproof enclosure* or pressurized *stairway* shall be permitted to be extended by an *exit passageway* in accordance with Section 1022.2. The *exit passageway* shall be without openings other than the *fire door assembly* required by Section 1022.2 and those necessary for egress from the *exit passageway*. The *exit passageway* shall be separated from the remainder of the building by 2-hour *fire barriers* constructed in accordance with Section 707 or *horizontal assemblies* constructed in accordance with Section 712, or both.

Exceptions:

1. Openings in the *exit passageway* serving a *smokeproof enclosure* are permitted where the *exit passageway* is protected and pressurized in the same manner as the *smokeproof enclosure*, and openings are protected as required for access from other floors.
2. Openings in the *exit passageway* serving a pressurized *stairway* are permitted where the *exit passageway* is protected and pressurized in the same manner as the pressurized *stairway*.
3. The *fire barrier* separating the *smokeproof enclosure* or pressurized *stairway* from the *exit passageway* is not required, provided the *exit passageway* is protected and pressurized in the same manner as the *smokeproof enclosure* or pressurized *stairway*.
4. A *smokeproof enclosure* or pressurized *stairway* shall be permitted to egress through areas on the level of discharge or vestibules as permitted by Section 1027.

1022.9.2 Enclosure access. Access to the *stairway* within a *smokeproof enclosure* shall be by way of a vestibule or an open exterior balcony.

Exception: Access is not required by way of a vestibule or exterior balcony for *stairways* using the pressurization alternative complying with Section 909.20.5.

SECTION 1023 EXIT PASSAGEWAYS

1023.1 Exit passageway. *Exit passageways* serving as an *exit* component in a *means of egress* system shall comply with the requirements of this section. An *exit passageway* shall not be used for any purpose other than as a *means of egress*.

1023.2 Width. The width of *exit passageways* shall be determined as specified in Section 1005.1 but such width shall not be less than 44 inches (1118 mm), except that *exit passageways* serving an *occupant load* of less than 50 shall not be less than 36 inches (914 mm) in width. The required width of *exit passageways* shall be unobstructed.

Exception: Doors complying with Section 1005.2.

1023.3 Construction. *Exit passageway* enclosures shall have walls, floors and ceilings of not less than 1-hour *fire-resistance rating*, and not less than that required for any connecting *exit enclosure*. *Exit passageways* shall be constructed as *fire barriers* in accordance with Section 707 or *horizontal assemblies* constructed in accordance with Section 712, or both.

1023.4 Termination. *Exit passageways* shall terminate at an *exit discharge* or a *public way.*

1023.5 Openings and penetrations. *Exit passageway* opening protectives shall be in accordance with the requirements of Section 715.

Except as permitted in Section 402.4.6, openings in *exit passageways* other than exterior openings shall be limited to those necessary for *exit access* to the *exit passageway* from normally occupied spaces and for egress from the *exit passageway.*

Where an *exit enclosure* is extended to an *exit discharge* or a *public way* by an *exit passageway*, the *exit passageway* shall also comply with Section 1022.2.1.

Elevators shall not open into an *exit passageway.*

1023.6 Penetrations. Penetrations into and openings through an *exit passageway* are prohibited except for required *exit* doors, equipment and ductwork necessary for independent pressurization, sprinkler piping, standpipes, electrical raceway for fire department communication and electrical raceway serving the *exit passageway* and terminating at a steel box not exceeding 16 square inches (0.010 m^2). Such penetrations shall be protected in accordance with Section 713. There shall be no penetrations or communicating openings, whether protected or not, between adjacent *exit passageways*.

SECTION 1024
LUMINOUS EGRESS PATH MARKINGS

1024.1 General. *Approved* luminous egress path markings delineating the exit path shall be provided in buildings of Groups A, B, E, I, M and R-1 having occupied floors located more than 75 feet (22 860 mm) above the lowest level of fire department vehicle access in accordance with Sections 1024.1 through 1024.5.

Exceptions:

1. Luminous egress path markings shall not be required on the *level of exit discharge* in lobbies that serve as part of the exit path in accordance with Section 1027.1, Exception 1.
2. Luminous egress path markings shall not be required in areas of *open parking garages* that serve as part of the exit path in accordance with Section 1027.1, Exception 3.

1024.2 Markings within exit enclosures. Egress path markings shall be provided in *exit enclosures*, including vertical *exit enclosures* and *exit passageways*, in accordance with Sections 1024.2.1 through 1024.2.6.

1024.2.1 Steps. A solid and continuous stripe shall be applied to the horizontal leading edge of each step and shall extend for the full length of the step. Outlining stripes shall have a minimum horizontal width of 1 inch (25 mm) and a maximum width of 2 inches (51 mm). The leading edge of the stripe shall be placed at a maximum of $^1/_2$ inch (12.7 mm) from the leading edge of the step and the stripe shall overlap the leading edge of the step by not more than $^1/_2$ inch (12.7 mm) down the vertical face of the step.

Exception: The minimum width of 1 inch (25 mm) shall not apply to outlining stripes *listed* in accordance with UL 1994.

1024.2.2 Landings. The leading edge of landings shall be marked with a stripe consistent with the dimensional requirements for steps.

1024.2.3 Handrails. All *handrails* and *handrail* extensions shall be marked with a solid and continuous stripe having a minimum width of 1 inch (25 mm). The stripe shall be placed on the top surface of the *handrail* for the entire length of the *handrail*, including extensions and newel post caps. Where *handrails* or *handrail* extensions bend or turn corners, the stripe shall not have a gap of more than 4 inches (102 mm).

Exception: The minimum width of 1 inch (25 mm) shall not apply to outlining stripes *listed* in accordance with UL 1994.

1024.2.4 Perimeter demarcation lines. *Stair* landings and other floor areas within *exit enclosures*, with the exception of the sides of steps, shall be provided with solid and continuous demarcation lines on the floor or on the walls or a combination of both. The stripes shall be 1 to 2 inches (25 to 51 mm) wide with interruptions not exceeding 4 inches (102 mm).

Exception: The minimum width of 1 inch (25 mm) shall not apply to outlining stripes *listed* in accordance with UL 1994.

1024.2.4.1 Floor-mounted demarcation lines. Perimeter demarcation lines shall be placed within 4 inches (102 mm) of the wall and shall extend to within 2 inches (51 mm) of the markings on the leading edge of landings. The demarcation lines shall continue across the floor in front of all doors.

Exception: Demarcation lines shall not extend in front of *exit* doors that lead out of an *exit enclosure* and through which occupants must travel to complete the exit path.

1024.2.4.2 Wall-mounted demarcation lines. Perimeter demarcation lines shall be placed on the wall with the bottom edge of the stripe no more than 4 inches (102 mm) above the finished floor. At the top or bottom of the *stairs*, demarcation lines shall drop vertically to the floor within 2 inches (51 mm) of the step or landing edge. Demarcation lines on walls shall transition vertically to the floor and then extend across the floor where a line on the floor is the only practical method of outlining the path. Where the wall line is broken by a door, demarcation lines on walls shall continue across the face of the door or transition to the floor and extend across the floor in front of such door.

Exception: Demarcation lines shall not extend in front of *exit* doors that lead out of an *exit enclosure* and through which occupants must travel to complete the exit path.

1024.2.4.3 Transition. Where a wall-mounted demarcation line transitions to a floor-mounted demarcation line, or vice versa, the wall-mounted demarcation line shall drop vertically to the floor to meet a complementary extension of the floor-mounted demarcation line, thus forming a continuous marking.

1024.2.5 Obstacles. Obstacles at or below 6 feet 6 inches (1981 mm) in height and projecting more than 4 inches (102 mm) into the egress path shall be outlined with markings no less than 1 inch (25 mm) in width comprised of a pattern of alternating equal bands, of luminescent luminous material and black, with the alternating bands no more than 2 inches (51 mm) thick and angled at 45 degrees (0.79 rad). Obstacles shall include, but are not limited to, standpipes, hose cabinets, wall projections and restricted height areas. However, such markings shall not conceal any required information or indicators including, but not limited to, instructions to occupants for the use of standpipes.

1024.2.6 Doors from exit enclosures. Doors through which occupants within an *exit enclosure* must pass in order to complete the exit path shall be provided with markings complying with Sections 1024.2.6.1 through 1024.2.6.3.

1024.2.6.1 Emergency exit symbol. The doors shall be identified by a low-location luminous emergency exit symbol complying with NFPA 170. The exit symbol shall be a minimum of 4 inches (102 mm) in height and shall be mounted on the door, centered horizontally, with the top of the symbol no higher than 18 inches (457 mm) above the finished floor.

1024.2.6.2 Door hardware markings. Door hardware shall be marked with no less than 16 square inches (406 mm^2) of luminous material. This marking shall be located behind, immediately adjacent to or on the door handle and/or escutcheon. Where a panic bar is installed, such material shall be no less than 1 inch (25 mm) wide for the entire length of the actuating bar or touchpad.

1024.2.6.3 Door frame markings. The top and sides of the door frame shall be marked with a solid and continuous 1 inch to 2 inch (25 mm to 51 mm) wide stripe. Where the door molding does not provide sufficient flat surface on which to locate the stripe, the stripe shall be permitted to be located on the wall surrounding the frame.

1024.3 Uniformity. Placement and dimensions of markings shall be consistent and uniform throughout the same *exit enclosure*.

1024.4 Self-luminous and photoluminescent. Luminous egress path markings shall be permitted to be made of any material, including paint, provided that an electrical charge is not required to maintain the required luminance. Such materials shall include, but are not limited to, *self-luminous* materials and *photoluminescent* materials. Materials shall comply with either:

1. UL 1994; or
2. ASTM E 2072, except that the charging source shall be 1 footcandle (11 lux) of fluorescent illumination for 60 minutes, and the minimum luminance shall be 30 millicandelas per square meter at 10 minutes and 5 millicandelas per square meter after 90 minutes.

1024.5 Illumination. *Exit enclosures* where photoluminescent exit path markings are installed shall be provided with the minimum *means of egress* illumination required by Section 1006 for at least 60 minutes prior to periods when the building is occupied.

SECTION 1025
HORIZONTAL EXITS

1025.1 Horizontal exits. *Horizontal exits* serving as an *exit* in a *means of egress* system shall comply with the requirements of this section. A *horizontal exit* shall not serve as the only *exit* from a portion of a building, and where two or more *exits* are required, not more than one-half of the total number of *exits* or total *exit* width shall be *horizontal exits.*

Exceptions:

1. *Horizontal exits* are permitted to comprise two-thirds of the required *exits* from any building or floor area for occupancies in Group I-2.
2. *Horizontal exits* are permitted to comprise 100 percent of the *exits* required for occupancies in Group I-3. At least 6 square feet (0.6 m^2) of accessible space per occupant shall be provided on each side of the *horizontal exit* for the total number of people in adjoining compartments.

1025.2 Separation. The separation between buildings or refuge areas connected by a *horizontal exit* shall be provided by a *fire wall* complying with Section 706; or it shall be provided by a *fire barrier* complying with Section 707 or a *horizontal assembly* complying with Section 712, or both. The minimum *fire-resistance rating* of the separation shall be 2 hours. Opening protectives in *horizontal exits* shall also comply with Section 715. Duct and air transfer openings in a *fire wall* or *fire barrier* that serves as a *horizontal exit* shall also comply with Section 716. The *horizontal exit* separation shall extend vertically through all levels of the building unless floor assemblies have a *fire-resistance rating* of not less than 2 hours with no unprotected openings.

Exception: A *fire-resistance rating* is not required at *horizontal exits* between a building area and an above-grade *pedestrian walkway* constructed in accordance with Section 3104, provided that the distance between connected buildings is more than 20 feet (6096 mm).

Horizontal exits constructed as *fire barriers* shall be continuous from *exterior wall* to *exterior wall* so as to divide completely the floor served by the *horizontal exit.*

1025.3 Opening protectives. *Fire doors* in *horizontal exits* shall be self-closing or automatic-closing when activated by a *smoke detector* in accordance with Section 715.4.8.3. Doors, where located in a cross-corridor condition, shall be automatic-closing by activation of a *smoke detector* installed in accordance with Section 715.4.8.3.

1025.4 Capacity of refuge area. The refuge area of a *horizontal exit* shall be a space occupied by the same tenant or a public area and each such refuge area shall be adequate to accommodate the original *occupant load* of the refuge area plus the *occupant load* anticipated from the adjoining compartment. The anticipated *occupant load* from the adjoining compartment shall be based on the capacity of the *horizontal exit* doors entering the refuge area. The capacity of the refuge area shall be computed based on a net floor area allowance of 3 square feet (0.2787 m^2) for each occupant to be accommodated therein.

Exception: The net floor area allowable per occupant shall be as follows for the indicated occupancies:

1. Six square feet (0.6 m^2) per occupant for occupancies in Group I-3.
2. Fifteen square feet (1.4 m^2) per occupant for ambulatory occupancies in Group I-2.
3. Thirty square feet (2.8 m^2) per occupant for nonambulatory occupancies in Group I-2.

The refuge area into which a *horizontal exit* leads shall be provided with *exits* adequate to meet the occupant requirements of this chapter, but not including the added *occupant load* imposed by persons entering it through *horizontal exits* from other areas. At least one refuge area *exit* shall lead directly to the exterior or to an *exit enclosure*.

Exception: The adjoining compartment shall not be required to have a *stairway* or door leading directly outside, provided the refuge area into which a *horizontal exit* leads has stairways or doors leading directly outside and are so arranged that egress shall not require the occupants to return through the compartment from which egress originates.

SECTION 1026 EXTERIOR EXIT RAMPS AND STAIRWAYS

1026.1 Exterior exit ramps and stairways. *Exterior exit ramps* and *stairways* serving as an element of a required *means of egress* shall comply with this section.

Exception: *Exterior exit ramps* and *stairways* for outdoor stadiums complying with Section 1022.1, Exception 2.

1026.2 Use in a means of egress. *Exterior exit stairways* shall not be used as an element of a required *means of egress* for Group I-2 occupancies. For occupancies in other than Group I-2, *exterior exit ramps* and *stairways* shall be permitted as an element of a required *means of egress* for buildings not exceeding six stories above *grade plane* or having occupied floors more than 75 feet (22 860 mm) above the lowest level of fire department vehicle access.

1026.3 Open side. *Exterior exit ramps* and *stairways* serving as an element of a required *means of egress* shall be open on at least one side. An open side shall have a minimum of 35 square feet (3.3 m^2) of aggregate open area adjacent to each floor level and the level of each intermediate landing. The required open area shall be located not less than 42 inches (1067 mm) above the adjacent floor or landing level.

1026.4 Side yards. The open areas adjoining *exterior exit ramps* or *stairways* shall be either *yards*, *courts* or *public ways*; the remaining sides are permitted to be enclosed by the *exterior walls* of the building.

1026.5 Location. *Exterior exit ramps* and *stairways* shall be located in accordance with Section 1027.3.

1026.6 Exterior ramps and stairway protection. *Exterior exit ramps* and *stairways* shall be separated from the interior of the building as required in Section 1022.1. Openings shall be limited to those necessary for egress from normally occupied spaces.

Exceptions:

1. Separation from the interior of the building is not required for occupancies, other than those in Group R-1 or R-2, in buildings that are no more than two stories above *grade plane* where a *level of exit discharge* serving such occupancies is the first *story above grade plane*.
2. Separation from the interior of the building is not required where the *exterior ramp* or *stairway* is served by an exterior *ramp* or balcony that connects two remote *exterior stairways* or other *approved exits*, with a perimeter that is not less than 50 percent open. To be considered open, the opening shall be a minimum of 50 percent of the height of the enclosing wall, with the top of the openings no less than 7 feet (2134 mm) above the top of the balcony.
3. Separation from the interior of the building is not required for an *exterior ramp* or *stairway* located in a building or structure that is permitted to have unenclosed *interior stairways* in accordance with Section 1022.1.
4. Separation from the interior of the building is not required for *exterior ramps* or *stairways* connected to open-ended *corridors*, provided that Items 4.1 through 4.4 are met:
   - 4.1. The building, including *corridors, ramps* and *stairs*, shall be equipped throughout with an *automatic sprinkler system* in accordance with Section 903.3.1.1 or 903.3.1.2.
   - 4.2. The open-ended *corridors* comply with Section 1018.
   - 4.3. The open-ended *corridors* are connected on each end to an *exterior exit ramp* or *stairway* complying with Section 1026.
   - 4.4. At any location in an open-ended *corridor* where a change of direction exceeding 45 degrees (0.79 rad) occurs, a clear opening of not less than 35 square feet (3.3 m^2) or an *exterior ramp* or *stairway* shall be provided. Where clear openings are provided, they shall be located so as to minimize the accumulation of smoke or toxic gases.

SECTION 1027
EXIT DISCHARGE

1027.1 General. *Exits* shall discharge directly to the exterior of the building. The *exit discharge* shall be at grade or shall provide direct access to grade. The *exit discharge* shall not reenter a building. The combined use of Exceptions 1 and 2 below shall not exceed 50 percent of the number and capacity of the required *exits*.

Exceptions:

1. A maximum of 50 percent of the number and capacity of the *exit enclosures* is permitted to egress through areas on the level of discharge provided all of the following are met:
   - 1.1. Such *exit enclosures* egress to a free and unobstructed path of travel to an exterior *exit* door and such *exit* is readily visible and identifiable from the point of termination of the *exit* enclosure.
   - 1.2. The entire area of the *level of exit discharge* is separated from areas below by construction conforming to the *fire-resistance rating* for the *exit enclosure*.
   - 1.3. The egress path from the *exit enclosure* on the *level of exit discharge* is protected throughout by an *approved automatic sprinkler system*. All portions of the *level of exit discharge* with access to the egress path shall either be protected throughout with an *automatic sprinkler system* installed in accordance with Section 903.3.1.1 or 903.3.1.2, or separated from the egress path in accordance with the requirements for the enclosure of *exits*.
2. A maximum of 50 percent of the number and capacity of the *exit enclosures* is permitted to egress through a vestibule provided all of the following are met:
   - 2.1. The entire area of the vestibule is separated from areas below by construction conforming to the *fire-resistance rating* for the *exit enclosure*.
   - 2.2. The depth from the exterior of the building is not greater than 10 feet (3048 mm) and the length is not greater than 30 feet (9144 mm).
   - 2.3. The area is separated from the remainder of the *level of exit discharge* by construction providing protection at least the equivalent of *approved* wired glass in steel frames.
   - 2.4. The area is used only for *means of egress* and *exits* directly to the outside.
3. *Stairways* in *open parking garages* complying with Section 1022.1, Exception 4, are permitted to egress through the *open parking garage* at their *levels of exit discharge*.
4. *Horizontal exits* complying with Section 1025 shall not be required to discharge directly to the exterior of the building.

1027.2 Exit discharge capacity. The capacity of the *exit discharge* shall be not less than the required discharge capacity of the *exits* being served.

1027.3 Exit discharge location. Exterior balconies, *stairways* and *ramps* shall be located at least 10 feet (3048 mm) from adjacent *lot lines* and from other buildings on the same lot unless the adjacent building *exterior walls* and openings are protected in accordance with Section 705 based on *fire separation distance*.

1027.4 Exit discharge components. *Exit discharge* components shall be sufficiently open to the exterior so as to minimize the accumulation of smoke and toxic gases.

1027.5 Egress courts. *Egress courts* serving as a portion of the *exit discharge* in the *means of egress* system shall comply with the requirements of Section 1027.

1027.5.1 Width. The width of *egress courts* shall be determined as specified in Section 1005.1, but such width shall not be less than 44 inches (1118 mm), except as specified herein. *Egress courts* serving Group R-3 and U occupancies shall not be less than 36 inches (914 mm) in width. The required width of *egress courts* shall be unobstructed to a height of 7 feet (2134 mm).

Exception: Doors complying with Section 1005.2.

Where an *egress court* exceeds the minimum required width and the width of such *egress court* is then reduced along the path of *exit* travel, the reduction in width shall be gradual. The transition in width shall be affected by a guard not less than 36 inches (914 mm) in height and shall not create an angle of more than 30 degrees (0.52 rad) with respect to the axis of the *egress court* along the path of egress travel. In no case shall the width of the *egress court* be less than the required minimum.

1027.5.2 Construction and openings. Where an *egress court* serving a building or portion thereof is less than 10 feet (3048 mm) in width, the *egress court* walls shall have not less than 1-hour *fire-resistance-rated* construction for a distance of 10 feet (3048 mm) above the floor of the *court*. Openings within such walls shall be protected by opening protectives having a *fire protection rating* of not less than $^3/_4$ hour.

Exceptions:

1. *Egress courts* serving an *occupant load* of less than 10.
2. *Egress courts* serving Group R-3.

1027.6 Access to a public way. The *exit discharge* shall provide a direct and unobstructed access to a *public way*.

Exception: Where access to a *public way* cannot be provided, a safe dispersal area shall be provided where all of the following are met:

1. The area shall be of a size to accommodate at least 5 square feet (0.46 m^2) for each person.
2. The area shall be located on the same lot at least 50 feet (15 240 mm) away from the building requiring egress.

3. The area shall be permanently maintained and identified as a safe dispersal area.
4. The area shall be provided with a safe and unobstructed path of travel from the building.

SECTION 1028
ASSEMBLY

1028.1 General. Occupancies in Group A and assembly occupancies accessory to Group E which contain seats, tables, displays, equipment or other material shall comply with this section.

1028.1.1 Bleachers. *Bleachers*, *grandstands* and *folding and telescopic seating*, that are not building elements, shall comply with ICC 300.

1028.2 Assembly main exit. Group A occupancies and assembly occupancies accessory to Group E occupancies that have an *occupant load* of greater than 300 shall be provided with a main *exit*. The main *exit* shall be of sufficient width to accommodate not less than one-half of the *occupant load*, but such width shall not be less than the total required width of all *means of egress* leading to the *exit*. Where the building is classified as a Group A occupancy, the main *exit* shall front on at least one street or an unoccupied space of not less than 10 feet (3048 mm) in width that adjoins a street or *public way*.

Exception: In assembly occupancies where there is no well-defined main *exit* or where multiple main *exits* are provided, *exits* shall be permitted to be distributed around the perimeter of the building provided that the total width of egress is not less than 100 percent of the required width.

1028.3 Assembly other exits. In addition to having access to a main *exit*, each level in Group A occupancies or assembly occupancies accessory to Group E occupancies having an *occupant load* greater than 300, shall be provided with additional *means of egress* that shall provide an egress capacity for at least one-half of the total *occupant load* served by that level and comply with Section 1015.2.

Exception: In assembly occupancies where there is no well-defined main *exit* or where multiple main *exits* are provided, *exits* shall be permitted to be distributed around the perimeter of the building, provided that the total width of egress is not less than 100 percent of the required width.

1028.4 Foyers and lobbies. In Group A-1 occupancies, where persons are admitted to the building at times when seats are not available, such persons shall be allowed to wait in a lobby or similar space, provided such lobby or similar space shall not encroach upon the required clear width of the *means of egress*. Such foyer, if not directly connected to a public street by all the main entrances or *exits*, shall have a straight and unobstructed *corridor* or path of travel to every such main entrance or *exit*.

1028.5 Interior balcony and gallery means of egress. For balconies, galleries or press boxes having a seating capacity of 50 or more located in Group A occupancies, at least two *means of egress* shall be provided, with one from each side of every balcony, gallery or press box and at least one leading directly to an *exit*.

1028.5.1 Enclosure of openings. *Interior stairways* and other vertical openings shall be enclosed in an *exit enclosure* as provided in Section 1022.1, except that *stairways* are permitted to be open between the balcony, gallery or press box and the main assembly floor in occupancies such as theaters, *places of religious worship*, auditoriums and sports facilities. At least one *accessible means of egress* is required from a balcony, gallery or press box level containing accessible seating locations in accordance with Section 1007.3 or 1007.4.

1028.6 Width of means of egress for assembly. The clear width of *aisles* and other *means of egress* shall comply with Section 1028.6.1 where *smoke-protected seating* is not provided and with Section 1028.6.2 or 1028.6.3 where *smoke-protected seating* is provided. The clear width shall be measured to walls, edges of seating and tread edges except for permitted projections.

1028.6.1 Without smoke protection. The clear width of the *means of egress* shall provide sufficient capacity in accordance with all of the following, as applicable:

1. At least 0.3 inch (7.6 mm) of width for each occupant served shall be provided on *stairs* having riser heights 7 inches (178 mm) or less and tread depths 11 inches (279 mm) or greater, measured horizontally between tread *nosings*.
2. At least 0.005 inch (0.127 mm) of additional *stair* width for each occupant shall be provided for each 0.10 inch (2.5 mm) of riser height above 7 inches (178 mm).
3. Where egress requires *stair* descent, at least 0.075 inch (1.9 mm) of additional width for each occupant shall be provided on those portions of *stair* width having no *handrail* within a horizontal distance of 30 inches (762 mm).
4. Ramped *means of egress*, where slopes are steeper than one unit vertical in 12 units horizontal (8-percent slope), shall have at least 0.22 inch (5.6 mm) of clear width for each occupant served. Level or ramped *means of egress*, where slopes are not steeper than one unit vertical in 12 units horizontal (8-percent slope), shall have at least 0.20 inch (5.1 mm) of clear width for each occupant served.

1028.6.2 Smoke-protected seating. The clear width of the *means of egress* for *smoke-protected assembly seating* shall not be less than the *occupant load* served by the egress element multiplied by the appropriate factor in Table 1028.6.2. The total number of seats specified shall be those within the space exposed to the same smoke-protected environment. Interpolation is permitted between the specific values shown. A life safety evaluation, complying with NFPA 101, shall be done for a facility utilizing the reduced width requirements of Table 1028.6.2 for *smoke-protected assembly seating*.

Exception: For an outdoor smoke-protected assembly with an *occupant load* not greater than 18,000, the clear width shall be determined using the factors in Section 1028.6.3.

1028.6.2.1 Smoke control. *Means of egress* serving a *smoke-protected assembly seating* area shall be provided with a smoke control system complying with Section 909 or natural ventilation designed to maintain the smoke level at least 6 feet (1829 mm) above the floor of the *means of egress*.

1028.6.2.2 Roof height. A *smoke-protected assembly seating* area with a roof shall have the lowest portion of the roof deck not less than 15 feet (4572 mm) above the highest *aisle* or *aisle accessway*.

Exception: A roof canopy in an outdoor stadium shall be permitted to be less than 15 feet (4572 mm) above the highest *aisle* or *aisle accessway* provided that there are no objects less than 80 inches (2032 mm) above the highest *aisle* or *aisle accessway*.

1028.6.2.3 Automatic sprinklers. Enclosed areas with walls and ceilings in buildings or structures containing *smoke-protected assembly seating* shall be protected with an *approved automatic sprinkler system* in accordance with Section 903.3.1.1.

Exceptions:

1. The floor area used for contests, performances or entertainment provided the roof construction is more than 50 feet (15 240 mm) above the floor level and the use is restricted to low fire hazard uses.
2. Press boxes and storage facilities less than 1,000 square feet (93 m^2) in area.
3. Outdoor seating facilities where seating and the *means of egress* in the seating area are essentially open to the outside.

1028.6.3 Width of means of egress for outdoor smoke-protected assembly. The clear width in inches (mm) of *aisles* and other *means of egress* shall be not less than the total *occupant load* served by the egress element multiplied by 0.08 (2.0 mm) where egress is by *aisles* and *stairs* and multiplied by 0.06 (1.52 mm) where egress is by *ramps*, *corridors*, tunnels or vomitories.

Exception: The clear width in inches (mm) of *aisles* and other *means of egress* shall be permitted to comply with Section 1028.6.2 for the number of seats in the outdoor smoke-protected assembly where Section 1028.6.2 permits less width.

1028.7 Travel distance. *Exits* and *aisles* shall be so located that the travel distance to an *exit* door shall not be greater than 200 feet (60 960 mm) measured along the line of travel in nonsprinklered buildings. Travel distance shall not be more than 250 feet (76 200 mm) in sprinklered buildings. Where *aisles* are provided for seating, the distance shall be measured along the *aisles* and *aisle accessway* without travel over or on the seats.

Exceptions:

1. *Smoke-protected assembly seating*: The travel distance from each seat to the nearest entrance to a vomitory or concourse shall not exceed 200 feet (60 960 mm). The travel distance from the entrance to the vomitory or concourse to a *stair*, *ramp* or walk on the exterior of the building shall not exceed 200 feet (60 960 mm).
2. Open-air seating: The travel distance from each seat to the building exterior shall not exceed 400 feet (122 m). The travel distance shall not be limited in facilities of Type I or II construction.

1028.8 Common path of egress travel. The *common path of egress travel* shall not exceed 30 feet (9144 mm) from any seat to a point where an occupant has a choice of two paths of egress travel to two *exits*.

Exceptions:

1. For areas serving less than 50 occupants, the *common path of egress travel* shall not exceed 75 feet (22 860 mm).
2. For *smoke-protected assembly seating*, the *common path of egress travel* shall not exceed 50 feet (15 240 mm).

1028.8.1 Path through adjacent row. Where one of the two paths of travel is across the *aisle* through a row of seats to another *aisle*, there shall be not more than 24 seats between the two *aisles*, and the minimum clear width between rows for the row between the two *aisles* shall be 12

TABLE 1028.6.2
WIDTH OF AISLES FOR SMOKE-PROTECTED ASSEMBLY

TOTAL NUMBER OF SEATS IN THE SMOKE-PROTECTED ASSEMBLY OCCUPANCY	INCHES OF CLEAR WIDTH PER SEAT SERVED			
	Stairs and aisle steps with handrails within 30 inches	Stairs and aisle steps without handrails within 30 inches	Passageways, doorways and ramps not steeper than 1 in 10 in slope	Ramps steeper than 1 in 10 in slope
Equal to or less than 5,000	0.200	0.250	0.150	0.165
10,000	0.130	0.163	0.100	0.110
15,000	0.096	0.120	0.070	0.077
20,000	0.076	0.095	0.056	0.062
Equal to or greater than 25,000	0.060	0.075	0.044	0.048

For SI: 1 inch = 25.4 mm.

inches (305 mm) plus 0.6 inch (15.2 mm) for each additional seat above seven in the row between *aisles*.

Exception: For *smoke-protected assembly seating* there shall not be more than 40 seats between the two *aisles* and the minimum clear width shall be 12 inches (305 mm) plus 0.3 inch (7.6 mm) for each additional seat.

1028.9 Assembly aisles are required. Every occupied portion of any occupancy in Group A or assembly occupancies accessory to Group E that contains seats, tables, displays, similar fixtures or equipment shall be provided with *aisles* leading to *exits* or *exit access doorways* in accordance with this section. *Aisle accessways* for tables and seating shall comply with Section 1017.4.

1028.9.1 Minimum aisle width. The minimum clear width for *aisles* shall be as shown:

1. Forty-eight inches (1219 mm) for *aisle stairs* having seating on each side.

   Exception: Thirty-six inches (914 mm) where the *aisle* serves less than 50 seats.

2. Thirty-six inches (914 mm) for *aisle stairs* having seating on only one side.
3. Twenty-three inches (584 mm) between an *aisle stair handrail* or *guard* and seating where the *aisle* is subdivided by a *handrail*.
4. Forty-two inches (1067 mm) for level or ramped *aisles* having seating on both sides.

   Exceptions:

   1. Thirty-six inches (914 mm) where the *aisle* serves less that 50 seats.
   2. Thirty inches (762 mm) where the *aisle* does not serve more than 14 seats.

5. Thirty-six inches (914 mm) for level or ramped *aisles* having seating on only one side.

   Exceptions:

   1. Thirty inches (762 mm) where the aisle does not serve more than 14 seats.
   2. Twenty-three inches (584 mm) between an *aisle stair* handrail and seating where an *aisle* does not serve more than five rows on one side.

1028.9.2 Aisle width. The *aisle* width shall provide sufficient egress capacity for the number of persons accommodated by the catchment area served by the *aisle*. The catchment area served by an *aisle* is that portion of the total space that is served by that section of the *aisle*. In establishing catchment areas, the assumption shall be made that there is a balanced use of all *means of egress*, with the number of persons in proportion to egress capacity.

1028.9.3 Converging aisles. Where *aisles* converge to form a single path of egress travel, the required egress capacity of that path shall not be less than the combined required capacity of the converging *aisles*.

1028.9.4 Uniform width. Those portions of *aisles*, where egress is possible in either of two directions, shall be uniform in required width.

1028.9.5 Assembly aisle termination. Each end of an *aisle* shall terminate at cross *aisle*, foyer, doorway, vomitory or concourse having access to an *exit*.

Exceptions:

1. Dead-end *aisles* shall not be greater than 20 feet (6096 mm) in length.
2. Dead-end *aisles* longer than 20 feet (6096 mm) are permitted where seats beyond the 20-foot (6096 mm) dead-end *aisle* are no more than 24 seats from another *aisle*, measured along a row of seats having a minimum clear width of 12 inches (305 mm) plus 0.6 inch (15.2 mm) for each additional seat above seven in the row.
3. For *smoke-protected assembly seating*, the dead-end *aisle* length of vertical *aisles* shall not exceed a distance of 21 rows.
4. For *smoke-protected assembly seating*, a longer dead-end *aisle* is permitted where seats beyond the 21-row dead-end aisle are not more than 40 seats from another *aisle*, measured along a row of seats having an *aisle accessway* with a minimum clear width of 12 inches (305 mm) plus 0.3 inch (7.6 mm) for each additional seat above seven in the row.

1028.9.6 Assembly aisle obstructions. There shall be no obstructions in the required width of *aisles* except for *handrails* as provided in Section 1028.13.

1028.10 Clear width of aisle accessways serving seating. Where seating rows have 14 or fewer seats, the minimum clear *aisle accessway* width shall not be less than 12 inches (305 mm) measured as the clear horizontal distance from the back of the row ahead and the nearest projection of the row behind. Where chairs have automatic or self-rising seats, the measurement shall be made with seats in the raised position. Where any chair in the row does not have an automatic or self-rising seat, the measurements shall be made with the seat in the down position. For seats with folding tablet arms, row spacing shall be determined with the tablet arm in the used position.

Exception: For seats with folding tablet arms, row spacing is permitted to be determined with the tablet arm in the stored position where the tablet arm when raised manually to vertical position in one motion automatically returns to the stored position by force of gravity.

1028.10.1 Dual access. For rows of seating served by *aisles* or doorways at both ends, there shall not be more than 100 seats per row. The minimum clear width of 12 inches (305 mm) between rows shall be increased by 0.3 inch (7.6 mm) for every additional seat beyond 14 seats, but the minimum clear width is not required to exceed 22 inches (559 mm).

Exception: For *smoke-protected assembly seating*, the row length limits for a 12-inch-wide (305 mm) *aisle accessway*, beyond which the *aisle accessway* minimum clear width shall be increased, are in Table 1028.10.1.

TABLE 1028.10.1
SMOKE-PROTECTED
ASSEMBLY AISLE ACCESSWAYS

TOTAL NUMBER OF SEATS IN THE SMOKE-PROTECTED ASSEMBLY OCCUPANCY	MAXIMUM NUMBER OF SEATS PER ROW PERMITTED TO HAVE A MINIMUM 12-INCH CLEAR WIDTH AISLE ACCESSWAY	
	Aisle or doorway at both ends of row	Aisle or doorway at one end of row only
Less than 4,000	14	7
4,000	15	7
7,000	16	8
10,000	17	8
13,000	18	9
16,000	19	9
19,000	20	10
22,000 and greater	21	11

For SI: 1 inch = 25.4 mm.

1028.10.2 Single access. For rows of seating served by an *aisle* or doorway at only one end of the row, the minimum clear width of 12 inches (305 mm) between rows shall be increased by 0.6 inch (15.2 mm) for every additional seat beyond seven seats, but the minimum clear width is not required to exceed 22 inches (559 mm).

Exception: For *smoke-protected assembly seating*, the row length limits for a 12-inch-wide (305 mm) *aisle accessway*, beyond which the *aisle accessway* minimum clear width shall be increased, are in Table 1028.10.1.

1028.11 Assembly aisle walking surfaces. *Aisles* with a slope not exceeding one unit vertical in eight units horizontal (12.5-percent slope) shall consist of a *ramp* having a slip-resistant walking surface. *Aisles* with a slope exceeding one unit vertical in eight units horizontal (12.5-percent slope) shall consist of a series of risers and treads that extends across the full width of *aisles* and complies with Sections 1028.11.1 through 1028.11.3.

1028.11.1 Treads. Tread depths shall be a minimum of 11 inches (279 mm) and shall have dimensional uniformity.

Exception: The tolerance between adjacent treads shall not exceed $^{3}/_{16}$ inch (4.8 mm).

1028.11.2 Risers. Where the gradient of *aisle stairs* is to be the same as the gradient of adjoining seating areas, the riser height shall not be less than 4 inches (102 mm) nor more than 8 inches (203 mm) and shall be uniform within each *flight*.

Exceptions:

1. Riser height nonuniformity shall be limited to the extent necessitated by changes in the gradient of the adjoining seating area to maintain adequate sightlines. Where nonuniformities exceed 0.188 inch (4.8 mm) between adjacent risers, the exact location of such nonuniformities shall be indicated with a distinctive marking stripe on each tread at the *nosing* or leading edge adjacent to the nonuniform risers. Such stripe shall be a minimum of 1 inch (25 mm), and a maximum of 2 inches (51 mm), wide. The edge marking stripe shall be distinctively different from the contrasting marking stripe.
2. Riser heights not exceeding 9 inches (229 mm) shall be permitted where they are necessitated by the slope of the adjacent seating areas to maintain sightlines.

1028.11.3 Tread contrasting marking stripe. A contrasting marking stripe shall be provided on each tread at the *nosing* or leading edge such that the location of each tread is readily apparent when viewed in descent. Such stripe shall be a minimum of 1 inch (25 mm), and a maximum of 2 inches (51 mm), wide.

Exception: The contrasting marking stripe is permitted to be omitted where tread surfaces are such that the location of each tread is readily apparent when viewed in descent.

1028.12 Seat stability. In places of assembly, the seats shall be securely fastened to the floor.

Exceptions:

1. In places of assembly or portions thereof without ramped or tiered floors for seating and with 200 or fewer seats, the seats shall not be required to be fastened to the floor.
2. In places of assembly or portions thereof with seating at tables and without ramped or tiered floors for seating, the seats shall not be required to be fastened to the floor.
3. In places of assembly or portions thereof without ramped or tiered floors for seating and with greater than 200 seats, the seats shall be fastened together in groups of not less than three or the seats shall be securely fastened to the floor.
4. In places of assembly where flexibility of the seating arrangement is an integral part of the design and function of the space and seating is on tiered levels, a maximum of 200 seats shall not be required to be fastened to the floor. Plans showing seating, tiers and *aisles* shall be submitted for approval.
5. Groups of seats within a place of assembly separated from other seating by railings, *guards*, partial height walls or similar barriers with level floors and having no more than 14 seats per group shall not be required to be fastened to the floor.
6. Seats intended for musicians or other performers and separated by railings, *guards*, partial height walls or similar barriers shall not be required to be fastened to the floor.

1028.13 Handrails. Ramped *aisles* having a slope exceeding one unit vertical in 15 units horizontal (6.7-percent slope) and *aisle stairs* shall be provided with *handrails* located either at the side or within the *aisle* width.

Exceptions:

1. *Handrails* are not required for ramped *aisles* having a gradient no greater than one unit vertical in eight units

horizontal (12.5-percent slope) and seating on both sides.

2. *Handrails* are not required if, at the side of the *aisle*, there is a *guard* that complies with the graspability requirements of *handrails*.
3. *Handrail* extensions are not required at the top and bottom of *aisle stairs* and *aisle ramp* runs to *permit* crossovers within the *aisles*.

1028.13.1 Discontinuous handrails. Where there is seating on both sides of the *aisle*, the *handrails* shall be discontinuous with gaps or breaks at intervals not exceeding five rows to facilitate access to seating and to permit crossing from one side of the *aisle* to the other. These gaps or breaks shall have a clear width of at least 22 inches (559 mm) and not greater than 36 inches (914 mm), measured horizontally, and the *handrail* shall have rounded terminations or bends.

1028.13.2 Intermediate handrails. Where *handrails* are provided in the middle of *aisle stairs*, there shall be an additional intermediate *handrail* located approximately 12 inches (305 mm) below the main *handrail*.

1028.14 Assembly guards. Assembly *guards* shall comply with Sections 1028.14.1 through 1028.14.3.

1028.14.1 Cross aisles. Cross *aisles* located more than 30 inches (762 mm) above the floor or grade below shall have *guards* in accordance with Section 1013.

Where an elevation change of 30 inches (762 mm) or less occurs between a cross *aisle* and the adjacent floor or grade below, *guards* not less than 26 inches (660 mm) above the *aisle* floor shall be provided.

Exception: Where the backs of seats on the front of the cross *aisle* project 24 inches (610 mm) or more above the adjacent floor of the *aisle*, a *guard* need not be provided.

1028.14.2 Sightline-constrained guard heights. Unless subject to the requirements of Section 1028.14.3, a fascia or railing system in accordance with the *guard* requirements of Section 1013 and having a minimum height of 26 inches (660 mm) shall be provided where the floor or footboard elevation is more than 30 inches (762 mm) above the floor or grade below and the fascia or railing would otherwise interfere with the sightlines of immediately adjacent seating. At *bleachers*, a *guard* must be provided where required by ICC 300.

1028.14.3 Guards at the end of aisles. A fascia or railing system complying with the *guard* requirements of Section 1013 shall be provided for the full width of the *aisle* where the foot of the *aisle* is more than 30 inches (762 mm) above the floor or grade below. The fascia or railing shall be a minimum of 36 inches (914 mm) high and shall provide a minimum 42 inches (1067 mm) measured diagonally between the top of the rail and the *nosing* of the nearest tread.

1028.15 Bench seating. Where bench seating is used, the number of persons shall be based on one person for each 18 inches (457 mm) of length of the bench.

SECTION 1029
EMERGENCY ESCAPE AND RESCUE

1029.1 General. In addition to the *means of egress* required by this chapter, provisions shall be made for emergency escape and rescue in Group E classrooms, Group R and I-1 occupancies. Basements and sleeping rooms below the fourth *story above grade plane* shall have at least one exterior *emergency escape and rescue opening* in accordance with this section. Where basements contain one or more sleeping rooms, *emergency escape and rescue openings* shall be required in each sleeping room, but shall not be required in adjoining areas of the basement. Such openings shall open directly into a *public way* or to a *yard* or *court* that opens to a *public way*.

Exceptions:

1. In other than Group R-3 occupancies, buildings equipped throughout with an *approved automatic sprinkler system* in accordance with Section 903.3.1.1 or 903.3.1.2.
2. In other than Group R-3 occupancies, sleeping rooms provided with a door to a fire-resistance-rated *corridor* having access to two remote *exits* in opposite directions.
3. The *emergency escape and rescue opening* is permitted to open onto a balcony within an *atrium* in accordance with the requirements of Section 404, provided the balcony provides access to an *exit* and the dwelling unit or sleeping unit has a *means of egress* that is not open to the *atrium*.
4. Basements with a ceiling height of less than 80 inches (2032 mm) shall not be required to have emergency escape and rescue windows.
5. *High-rise buildings* in accordance with Section 403.
6. *Emergency escape and rescue openings* are not required from basements or sleeping rooms that have an *exit* door or *exit access* door that opens directly into a *public way* or to a *yard*, *court* or exterior *exit* balcony that opens to a *public way*.
7. Basements without *habitable spaces* and having no more than 200 square feet (18.6 m^2) in floor area shall not be required to have emergency escape windows.
8. In Group E where the room or space complies with the following:
   - 8.1. Doors open directly to a corridor with exit access in one direction and provide access through adjacent classrooms or directly to a separate smoke compartment with exit access in the other direction;
   - 8.2. The compartments are separated by smoke barriers having a 1-hour fire-resistance rating with self-closing or automatic closing doors;
   - 8.3. The length of travel to exits along such paths shall not exceed 150 feet (45 m);
   - 8.4. Each communicating door shall be identified; and

8.5. No locking device shall be allowed on the communicating doors.

1029.2 Minimum size. *Emergency escape and rescue openings* shall have a minimum net clear opening of 5.7 square feet (0.53 m^2).

Exception: The minimum net clear opening for *emergency escape and rescue* grade-floor *openings* shall be 5 square feet (0.46 m^2).

1029.2.1 Minimum dimensions. The minimum net clear opening height dimension shall be 24 inches (610 mm). The minimum net clear opening width dimension shall be 20 inches (508 mm). The net clear opening dimensions shall be the result of normal operation of the opening.

1029.3 Maximum height from floor. *Emergency escape and rescue openings* shall have the bottom of the clear opening not greater than 44 inches (1118 mm) measured from the floor. For classrooms serving children grade 5 and lower, the bottom of the clear opening shall be not more than 32 inches (810 mm) measured from the floor.

1029.4 Operational constraints. *Emergency escape and rescue openings* shall be operational from the inside of the room without the use of keys or tools. Bars, grilles, grates or similar devices are permitted to be placed over *emergency escape and rescue openings* provided the minimum net clear opening size complies with Section 1029.2 and such devices shall be releasable or removable from the inside without the use of a key, tool or force greater than that which is required for normal operation of the escape and rescue opening. Where such bars, grilles, grates or similar devices are installed in existing buildings, *smoke alarms* shall be installed in accordance with Section 907.2.11 regardless of the valuation of the *alteration*.

1029.5 Window wells. An *emergency escape and rescue opening* with a finished sill height below the adjacent ground level shall be provided with a window well in accordance with Sections 1029.5.1 and 1029.5.2.

1029.5.1 Minimum size. The minimum horizontal area of the window well shall be 9 square feet (0.84 m^2), with a minimum dimension of 36 inches (914 mm). The area of the window well shall allow the *emergency escape and rescue opening* to be fully opened.

1029.5.2 Ladders or steps. Window wells with a vertical depth of more than 44 inches (1118 mm) shall be equipped with an *approved* permanently affixed ladder or steps. Ladders or rungs shall have an inside width of at least 12 inches (305 mm), shall project at least 3 inches (76 mm) from the wall and shall be spaced not more than 18 inches (457 mm) on center (o.c.) vertically for the full height of the window well. The ladder or steps shall not encroach into the required dimensions of the window well by more than 6 inches (152 mm). The ladder or steps shall not be obstructed by the *emergency escape and rescue opening*. Ladders or steps required by this section are exempt from the *stairway* requirements of Section 1009.

CHAPTER 11
ACCESSIBILITY

SECTION 1101
GENERAL

1101.1 Scope. The provisions of this chapter shall control the design and construction of facilities for accessibility to physically disabled persons.

1101.2 Design. Buildings and facilities shall be designed and constructed to be *accessible* in accordance with this code and ICC A117.1.

SECTION 1102
DEFINITIONS

1102.1 Definitions. The following words and terms shall, for the purposes of this chapter and as used elsewhere in the code, have the meanings shown herein:

ACCESSIBLE. A *site*, building, *facility* or portion thereof that complies with this chapter.

ACCESSIBLE ROUTE. A continuous, unobstructed path that complies with this chapter.

ACCESSIBLE UNIT. A *dwelling unit* or *sleeping unit* that complies with this code and the provisions for *Accessible units* in ICC A117.1.

CIRCULATION PATH. An exterior or interior way of passage from one place to another for pedestrians.

COMMON USE. Interior or exterior *circulation paths*, rooms, spaces or elements that are not for public use and are made available for the shared use of two or more people.

DETECTABLE WARNING. A standardized surface feature built in or applied to walking surfaces or other elements to warn visually impaired persons of hazards on a *circulation path*.

DWELLING UNIT OR SLEEPING UNIT, MULTISTORY. See definition for "*Multistory unit*."

DWELLING UNIT OR SLEEPING UNIT, TYPE A. See definition for "*Type A unit*."

DWELLING UNIT OR SLEEPING UNIT, TYPE B. See definition for "*Type B unit*."

EMPLOYEE WORK AREA. All or any portion of a space used only by employees and only for work. *Corridors*, toilet rooms, kitchenettes and break rooms are not *employee work areas*.

FACILITY. All or any portion of buildings, structures, *site* improvements, elements and pedestrian or vehicular routes located on a site.

INTENDED TO BE OCCUPIED AS A RESIDENCE. This refers to a *dwelling unit* or *sleeping unit* that can or will be used all or part of the time as the occupant's place of abode.

MULTILEVEL ASSEMBLY SEATING. Seating that is arranged in distinct levels where each level is comprised of either multiple rows, or a single row of box seats accessed from a separate level.

MULTISTORY UNIT. A *dwelling unit* or *sleeping unit* with *habitable space* located on more than one *story*.

PUBLIC ENTRANCE. An entrance that is not a *service entrance* or a *restricted entrance*.

PUBLIC-USE AREAS. Interior or exterior rooms or spaces that are made available to the general public.

RESTRICTED ENTRANCE. An entrance that is made available for *common use* on a controlled basis, but not public use, and that is not a *service entrance*.

SELF-SERVICE STORAGE FACILITY. Real property designed and used for the purpose of renting or leasing individual storage spaces to customers for the purpose of storing and removing personal property on a self-service basis.

SERVICE ENTRANCE. An entrance intended primarily for delivery of goods or services.

SITE. A parcel of land bounded by a *lot line* or a designated portion of a public right-of-way.

TYPE A UNIT. A *dwelling unit* or *sleeping unit* designed and constructed for accessibility in accordance with this code and the provisions for *Type A units* in ICC A117.1.

TYPE B UNIT. A *dwelling unit* or *sleeping unit* designed and constructed for accessibility in accordance with this code and the provisions for *Type B units* in ICC A117.1, consistent with the design and construction requirements of the federal Fair Housing Act.

WHEELCHAIR SPACE. A space for a single wheelchair and its occupant.

SECTION 1103
SCOPING REQUIREMENTS

1103.1 Where required. *Sites*, buildings, *structures*, *facilities*, elements and spaces, temporary or permanent, shall be *accessible* to persons with physical disabilities.

1103.2 General exceptions. *Sites*, buildings, *structures*, *facilities*, elements and spaces shall be exempt from this chapter to the extent specified in this section.

1103.2.1 Specific requirements. *Accessibility* is not required in buildings and *facilities*, or portions thereof, to the extent permitted by Sections 1104 through 1110.

1103.2.2 Existing buildings. Existing buildings shall comply with Section 3411.

1103.2.3 Employee work areas. Spaces and elements within *employee work areas* shall only be required to comply with Sections 907.5.2.3.2, 1007 and 1104.3.1 and shall be designed and constructed so that individuals with disabilities can approach, enter and *exit* the work area. Work areas, or portions of work areas, other than raised courtroom stations, that are less than 300 square feet (30 m^2) in area and elevated 7 inches (178 mm) or more above the ground or finish floor where the elevation is essential to the function of the space shall be exempt from all requirements.

1103.2.4 Detached dwellings. Detached one- and two-family *dwellings* and accessory structures, and their associated *sites* and facilities, are not required to be *accessible.*

1103.2.5 Utility buildings. Occupancies in Group U are exempt from the requirements of this chapter other than the following:

1. In agricultural buildings, access is required to paved work areas and areas open to the general public.
2. Private garages or carports that contain required *accessible* parking.

1103.2.6 Construction sites. Structures, *sites* and equipment directly associated with the actual processes of construction including, but not limited to, scaffolding, bridging, materials hoists, materials storage or construction trailers are not required to be *accessible.*

1103.2.7 Raised areas. Raised areas used primarily for purposes of security, life safety or fire safety including, but not limited to, observation galleries, prison guard towers, fire towers or lifeguard stands, are not required to be *accessible* or to be served by an *accessible route.*

1103.2.8 Limited access spaces. Nonoccupiable spaces accessed only by ladders, catwalks, crawl spaces, freight elevators or very narrow passageways are not required to be *accessible.*

1103.2.9 Equipment spaces. Spaces frequented only by personnel for maintenance, repair or monitoring of equipment are not required to be *accessible.* Such spaces include, but are not limited to, elevator pits, elevator *penthouses,* mechanical, electrical or communications equipment rooms, piping or equipment catwalks, water or sewage treatment pump rooms and stations, electric substations and transformer vaults, and highway and tunnel utility facilities.

1103.2.10 Single-occupant structures. Single-occupant structures accessed only by passageways below grade or elevated above grade including, but not limited to, toll booths that are accessed only by underground tunnels, are not required to be *accessible.*

1103.2.11 Residential Group R-1. Buildings of Group R-1 containing not more than five *sleeping units* for rent or hire that are also occupied as the residence of the proprietor are not required to be *accessible.*

1103.2.12 Day care facilities. Where a day care facility (Groups A-3, E, I-4 and R-3) is part of a *dwelling unit,* only the portion of the structure utilized for the day care facility is required to be *accessible.*

1103.2.13 Live/work units. In live/work units constructed in accordance with Section 419, the portion of the unit utilized for nonresidential use is required to be *accessible.* The residential portion of the live/work unit is required to be evaluated separately in accordance with Sections 1107.6.2 and 1107.7.

1103.2.14 Detention and correctional facilities. In detention and correctional facilities, *common use* areas that are used only by inmates or detainees and security personnel, and that do not serve holding cells or housing cells required to be *accessible,* are not required to be *accessible* or to be served by an *accessible route.*

1103.2.15 Walk-in coolers and freezers. Walk-in coolers and freezers intended for employee use only are not required to be *accessible.*

SECTION 1104
ACCESSIBLE ROUTE

1104.1 Site arrival points. *Accessible routes* within the *site* shall be provided from public transportation stops; *accessible* parking; *accessible* passenger loading zones; and public streets or sidewalks to the *accessible* building entrance served. The exterior accessible path of travel shall be fixed, firm, nonslip and a minimum 48 inches (1219 mm) wide. Where handrails are provided, the measurement shall be between the handrails.

Exception: Other than in buildings or facilities containing or serving *Type B units,* an *accessible route* shall not be required between *site* arrival points and the building or facility entrance if the only means of access between them is a vehicular way not providing for pedestrian access.

1104.2 Within a site. At least one *accessible route* shall connect *accessible* buildings, *accessible* facilities, *accessible* elements and *accessible* spaces that are on the same *site.* The exterior accessible path of travel shall be fixed, firm, nonslip and a minimum 48 inches (1219 mm) wide. Where handrails are provided, the measurement shall be between the handrails.

Exception: An *accessible route* is not required between *accessible* buildings, *accessible* facilities, *accessible* elements and *accessible* spaces that have, as the only means of access between them, a vehicular way not providing for pedestrian access.

1104.3 Connected spaces. When a building or portion of a building is required to be *accessible,* an *accessible route* shall be provided to each portion of the building, to *accessible* building entrances connecting *accessible pedestrian walkways* and the public way.

Exceptions:

1. In assembly areas with fixed seating, an *accessible route* shall not be required to serve levels where *wheelchair spaces* are not provided.
2. In Group I-2 facilities, doors to *sleeping units* shall be exempted from the requirements for maneuvering clearance at the room side provided the door is a minimum of 44 inches (1118 mm) in width.

1104.3.1 Employee work areas. *Common use circulation paths* within *employee work areas* shall be *accessible routes.*

Exceptions:

1. *Common use circulation paths*, located within *employee work areas* that are less than 300 square feet (27.9 m^2) in size and defined by permanently installed partitions, counters, casework or furnishings, shall not be required to be *accessible routes.*
2. *Common use circulation paths*, located within *employee work areas*, that are an integral component of equipment, shall not be required to be *accessible routes.*
3. *Common use circulation paths*, located within exterior *employee work areas* that are fully exposed to the weather, shall not be required to be *accessible routes.*

1104.3.2 Press boxes. Press boxes in assembly areas shall be on an *accessible route.*

Exceptions:

1. An *accessible route* shall not be required to press boxes in *bleachers* that have points of entry at only one level, provided that the aggregate area of all press boxes is 500 square feet (46 m^2) maximum.
2. An *accessible route* shall not be required to free-standing press boxes that are elevated above grade 12 feet (3660 mm) minimum provided that the aggregate area of all press boxes is 500 square feet (46 m^2) maximum.

1104.4 Multilevel buildings and facilities. At least one *accessible route* shall connect each *accessible* level, including *mezzanines*, in multilevel buildings and facilities.

Exceptions:

1. An *accessible route* is not required to stories and *mezzanines* that have an aggregate area of not more than 3,000 square feet (278.7 m^2) and are located above and below *accessible* levels. This exception shall not apply to:
   1.1. Multiple tenant facilities of Group M occupancies containing five or more tenant spaces;
   1.2. Levels containing offices of health care providers (Group B or I); or
   1.3. Passenger transportation facilities and airports (Group A-3 or B).
   1.4. All buildings of state, county, or municipal government or any government agencies, including publicly owned schools, colleges, university buildings, and publicly owned dormitories, two or more stories in height.
2. Levels that do not contain *accessible* elements or other spaces as determined by Section 1107 or 1108 are not required to be served by an *accessible route* from an *accessible* level.
3. In air traffic control towers, an *accessible route* is not required to serve the cab and the floor immediately below the cab.
4. Where a two-story building or facility has one *story* with an *occupant load* of five or fewer persons that does not contain *public use* space, that *story* shall not be required to be connected by an *accessible route* to the *story* above or below.
5. Vertical access to elevated employee work stations within a courtroom is not required at the time of initial construction, provided a *ramp*, lift or elevator complying with ICC A117.1 can be installed without requiring reconfiguration or extension of the courtroom or extension of the electrical system.

1104.5 Location. *Accessible routes* shall coincide with or be located in the same area as a general *circulation path*. Where the *circulation path* is interior, the *accessible route* shall also be interior. Where only one *accessible route* is provided, the *accessible route* shall not pass through kitchens, storage rooms, restrooms, closets or similar spaces.

Exceptions:

1. *Accessible routes* from parking garages contained within and serving *Type B units* are not required to be interior.
2. A single *accessible route* is permitted to pass through a kitchen or storage room in an *Accessible unit, Type A unit* or *Type B unit.*

1104.6 Security barriers. Security barriers including, but not limited to, security bollards and security check points shall not obstruct a required *accessible route* or *accessible means of egress.*

Exception: Where security barriers incorporate elements that cannot comply with these requirements, such as certain metal detectors, fluoroscopes or other similar devices, the *accessible route* shall be permitted to be provided adjacent to security screening devices. The *accessible route* shall permit persons with disabilities passing around security barriers to maintain visual contact with their personal items to the same extent provided others passing through the security barrier.

SECTION 1105
ACCESSIBLE ENTRANCES

1105.1 Public entrances. In addition to *accessible* entrances required by Sections 1105.1.1 through 1105.1.6, at least 60 percent of all *public entrances* shall be *accessible.*

Exceptions:

1. An *accessible* entrance is not required to areas not required to be *accessible.*
2. Loading and *service entrances* that are not the only entrance to a tenant space.

1105.1.1 Parking garage entrances. Where provided, direct access for pedestrians from parking structures to buildings or facility entrances shall be *accessible*.

1105.1.2 Entrances from tunnels or elevated walkways. Where direct access is provided for pedestrians from a pedestrian tunnel or elevated walkway to a building or facility, at least one entrance to the building or facility from each tunnel or walkway shall be *accessible*.

1105.1.3 Restricted entrances. Where *restricted entrances* are provided to a building or facility, at least one *restricted entrance* to the building or facility shall be *accessible*.

1105.1.4 Entrances for inmates or detainees. Where entrances used only by inmates or detainees and security personnel are provided at judicial facilities, detention facilities or correctional facilities, at least one such entrance shall be *accessible*.

1105.1.5 Service entrances. If a *service entrance* is the only entrance to a building or a tenant space in a facility, that entrance shall be *accessible*.

1105.1.6 Tenant spaces, dwelling units and sleeping units. At least one *accessible* entrance shall be provided to each tenant, *dwelling unit* and *sleeping unit* in a facility.

Exceptions:

1. An *accessible* entrance is not required to tenants that are not required to be *accessible*.
2. An *accessible* entrance is not required to *dwelling units* and *sleeping units* that are not required to be *Accessible units*, *Type A units* or *Type B units*.

SECTION 1106
PARKING AND PASSENGER LOADING FACILITIES

1106.1 Required. Where parking is provided, *accessible* parking spaces shall be provided in compliance with Table 1106.1, except as required by Sections 1106.2 through 1106.4. Where more than one parking facility is provided on a *site*, the number of parking spaces required to be *accessible* shall be calculated separately for each parking facility.

Exception: This section does not apply to parking spaces used exclusively for buses, trucks, other delivery vehicles, law enforcement vehicles or vehicular impound and motor pools where lots accessed by the public are provided with an *accessible* passenger loading zone.

1106.2 Groups R-2 and R-3. At least 2 percent of all parking spaces, or a minimum of one space per *Type A dwelling unit*, whichever is larger, shall be provided for occupancies in Groups R-2 and Groups R-3, which are required to have *Accessible, Type A* or *Type B dwelling* or *sleeping units*, shall be *accessible*. Where parking is provided within or beneath a building, accessible parking spaces shall also be provided within or beneath the building.

TABLE 1106.1
ACCESSIBLE PARKING SPACES

TOTAL PARKING SPACES PROVIDED	REQUIRED MINIMUM NUMBER OF ACCESSIBLE SPACES
1 to 25	1
26 to 50	2
51 to 75	3
76 to 100	4
101 to 150	5
151 to 200	6
201 to 300	7
301 to 400	8
401 to 500	9
501 to 1,000	2% of total
1,001 and over	20, plus one for each 100, or fraction thereof, over 1,000

1106.3 Hospital outpatient facilities. At least 10 percent, but not less than one, of patient and visitor parking spaces provided to serve hospital outpatient facilities shall be *accessible*.

1106.4 Rehabilitation facilities and outpatient physical therapy facilities. At least 20 percent, but not less than one, of the portion of patient and visitor parking spaces serving rehabilitation facilities specializing in treating conditions that affect mobility and outpatient physical therapy facilities shall be *accessible*.

1106.5 Van spaces. For every six or fraction of six *accessible* parking spaces, at least one shall be a van-accessible parking space.

Exception: In Group R-2 and R-3 occupancies, van-accessible spaces located within private garages shall be permitted to have vehicular routes, entrances, parking spaces and access aisles with a minimum vertical clearance of 7 feet (2134 mm).

1106.6 Location. *Accessible* parking spaces shall be located on the shortest *accessible route* of travel from adjacent parking to an *accessible* building entrance. In parking facilities that do not serve a particular building, *accessible* parking spaces shall be located on the shortest route to an *accessible* pedestrian entrance to the parking facility. Where buildings have multiple *accessible* entrances with adjacent parking, *accessible* parking spaces shall be dispersed and located near the *accessible* entrances.

Exceptions:

1. In multilevel parking structures, van-accessible parking spaces are permitted on one level.
2. *Accessible* parking spaces shall be permitted to be located in different parking facilities if substantially equivalent or greater accessibility is provided in terms of distance from an *accessible* entrance or entrances, parking fee and user convenience.

1106.7 Passenger loading zones. Passenger loading zones shall be designed and constructed in accordance with ICC A117.1.

1106.7.1 Continuous loading zones. Where passenger loading zones are provided, one passenger loading zone in every continuous 100 linear feet (30.4 m) maximum of loading zone space shall be *accessible*.

1106.7.2 Medical facilities. A passenger loading zone shall be provided at an *accessible* entrance to licensed medical and long-term care facilities where people receive physical or medical treatment or care and where the period of stay exceeds 24 hours.

1106.7.3 Valet parking. A passenger loading zone shall be provided at valet parking services.

1106.7.4 Mechanical access parking garages. Mechanical access parking garages shall provide at least one passenger loading zone at vehicle drop-off and vehicle pick-up areas.

SECTION 1107
DWELLING UNITS AND SLEEPING UNITS

1107.1 General. In addition to the other requirements of this chapter, occupancies having *dwelling units* or *sleeping units* shall be provided with *accessible* features in accordance with this section.

1107.2 Design. *Dwelling units* and *sleeping units* that are required to be *Accessible units*, *Type A units* and *Type B units* shall comply with the applicable portions of Chapter 10 of ICC A117.1. Units required to be *Type A units* are permitted to be designed and constructed as *Accessible units*. Units required to be *Type B units* are permitted to be designed and constructed as *Accessible units* or as *Type A units*.

1107.3 Accessible spaces. Rooms and spaces available to the general public or available for use by residents and serving *Accessible units*, *Type A units* or *Type B units* shall be *accessible*. *Accessible* spaces shall include toilet and bathing rooms, kitchen, living and dining areas and any exterior spaces, including patios, terraces and balconies.

Exceptions:

1. Recreational facilities in accordance with Section 1109.14.
2. In Group I-2 facilities, doors to *sleeping units* shall be exempted from the requirements for maneuvering clearance at the room side provided the door is a minimum of 44 inches (1118 mm) in width.

1107.4 Accessible route. At least one *accessible route* shall connect *accessible* building or facility entrances with the primary entrance of each *Accessible unit*, *Type A unit* and *Type B unit* within the building or facility and with those exterior and interior spaces and facilities that serve the units.

Exceptions:

1. If due to circumstances outside the control of the owner, either the slope of the finished ground level between *accessible* facilities and buildings exceeds one unit vertical in 12 units horizontal (1:12), or where physical barriers or legal restrictions prevent the installation of an *accessible route*, a vehicular route with parking that complies with Section 1106 at each *public* or *common use* facility or building is permitted in place of the *accessible route*.
2. Exterior decks, patios or balconies that are part of *Type B units* and have impervious surfaces, and that are not more than 4 inches (102 mm) below the finished floor level of the adjacent interior space of the unit.

1107.5 Group I. *Accessible units* and *Type B units* shall be provided in Group I occupancies in accordance with Sections 1107.5.1 through 1107.5.5.

1107.5.1 Group I-1. *Accessible units* and *Type B units* shall be provided in Group I-1 occupancies in accordance with Sections 1107.5.1.1 and 1107.5.1.2.

1107.5.1.1 Accessible units. At least 4 percent, but not less than one, of the *dwelling units* and *sleeping units* shall be *Accessible units*.

1107.5.1.2 Type B units. In structures with four or more *dwelling units* or *sleeping units intended to be occupied as a residence*, every *dwelling unit* and *sleeping unit intended to be occupied as a residence* shall be a *Type B unit*.

Exception: The number of *Type B units* is permitted to be reduced in accordance with Section 1107.7.

1107.5.2 Group I-2 nursing homes. *Accessible units* and *Type B units* shall be provided in nursing homes of Group I-2 occupancies in accordance with Sections 1107.5.2.1 and 1107.5.2.2.

1107.5.2.1 Accessible units. At least 50 percent but not less than one of each type of the *dwelling units* and *sleeping units* shall be *Accessible units*.

1107.5.2.2 Type B units. In structures with four or more *dwelling units* or *sleeping units intended to be occupied as a residence*, every *dwelling unit* and *sleeping unit intended to be occupied as a residence* shall be a *Type B unit*.

Exception: The number of *Type B units* is permitted to be reduced in accordance with Section 1107.7.

1107.5.3 Group I-2 hospitals. *Accessible units* and *Type B units* shall be provided in general-purpose hospitals, psychiatric facilities, detoxification facilities and *residential care/assisted living facilities* of Group I-2 occupancies in accordance with Sections 1107.5.3.1 and 1107.5.3.2.

1107.5.3.1 Accessible units. At least 10 percent, but not less than one, of the *dwelling units* and *sleeping units* shall be *Accessible units*.

1107.5.3.2 Type B units. In structures with four or more *dwelling units* or *sleeping units intended to be occupied as a residence*, every *dwelling unit* and *sleeping unit intended to be occupied as a residence* shall be a *Type B unit*.

Exception: The number of *Type B units* is permitted to be reduced in accordance with Section 1107.7.

1107.5.4 Group I-2 rehabilitation facilities. In hospitals and rehabilitation facilities of Group I-2 occupancies which specialize in treating conditions that affect mobility, or units within either which specialize in treating conditions that affect mobility, 100 percent of the *dwelling units* and *sleeping units* shall be *Accessible units*.

1107.5.5 Group I-3. *Accessible units* shall be provided in Group I-3 occupancies in accordance with Sections 1107.5.5.1 through 1107.5.5.3.

1107.5.5.1 Group I-3 sleeping units. In Group I-3 occupancies, at least 2 percent, but not less than one, of the *dwelling units* and *sleeping units* shall be *Accessible units*.

1107.5.5.2 Special holding cells and special housing cells or rooms. In addition to the *Accessible units* required by Section 1107.5.5.1, where special holding cells or special housing cells or rooms are provided, at least one serving each purpose shall be an *Accessible unit*. Cells or rooms subject to this requirement include, but are not limited to, those used for purposes of orientation, protective custody, administrative or disciplinary detention or segregation, detoxification and medical isolation.

Exception: Cells or rooms specially designed without protrusions and that are used solely for purposes of suicide prevention shall not be required to include grab bars.

1107.5.5.3 Medical care facilities. Patient *sleeping units* or cells required to be *Accessible units* in medical care facilities shall be provided in addition to any medical isolation cells required to comply with Section 1107.5.5.2.

1107.6 Group R. *Accessible units*, *Type A units* and *Type B units* shall be provided in Group R occupancies in accordance with Sections 1107.6.1 through 1107.6.4.

1107.6.1 Group R-1. *Accessible units* and *Type B units* shall be provided in Group R-1 occupancies in accordance with Sections 1107.6.1.1 and 1107.6.1.2.

1107.6.1.1 Accessible units. In Group R-1 occupancies, *Accessible dwelling units* and *sleeping units* shall be provided in accordance with Table 1107.6.1.1. All R-1 units on a *site* shall be considered to determine the total number of *Accessible units*. *Accessible units* shall be dispersed among the various classes of units. Roll-in showers provided in *Accessible units* shall include a permanently mounted folding shower seat.

1107.6.1.2 Type B units. In structures with four or more *dwelling units* or *sleeping units intended to be occupied as a residence*, every *dwelling unit* and *sleeping unit intended to be occupied as a residence* shall be a *Type B unit*.

Exception: The number of *Type B units* is permitted to be reduced in accordance with Section 1107.7.

1107.6.2 Group R-2. *Accessible units*, *Type A units* and *Type B units* shall be provided in Group R-2 occupancies in accordance with Sections 1107.6.2.1 and 1107.6.2.2.

1107.6.2.1 Apartment houses, monasteries and convents. *Type A units* and *Type B units* shall be provided in apartment houses, monasteries and convents in accordance with Sections 1107.6.2.1.1 and 1107.6.2.1.2.

1107.6.2.1.1 Type A units. In Group R-2 occupancies containing 11 or more dwelling units or *sleeping units* at least 5 percent but not less than one of the units shall be a *Type A unit*. For a site with more than 100

TABLE 1107.6.1.1
ACCESSIBLE DWELLING AND SLEEPING UNITS

TOTAL NUMBER OF UNITS PROVIDED	MINIMUM REQUIRED NUMBER OF ACCESSIBLE UNITS WITHOUT ROLL-IN SHOWERS	MINIMUM REQUIRED NUMBER OF ACCESSIBLE UNITS WITH ROLL-IN SHOWERS	TOTAL NUMBER OF REQUIRED ACCESSIBLE UNITS
1 to 25	1	0	1
26 to 50	2	0	2
51 to 75	3	1	4
76 to 100	4	1	5
101 to 150	5	2	7
151 to 200	6	2	8
201 to 300	7	3	10
301 to 400	8	4	12
401 to 500	9	4	13
501 to 1,000	2% of total	1% of total	3% of total
Over 1,000	20, plus 1 for each 100, or fraction thereof, over 1,000	10 plus 1 for each 100, or fraction thereof, over 1,000	30 plus 2 for each 100, or fraction thereof, over 1,000

units, at least 2 percent of the number of units exceeding 100 shall be *Type A units.* All R-2 units on a *site* shall be considered to determine the total number of units and the required number of *Type A units*. *Type A units* shall be dispersed among the various classes of units.

Exceptions:

1. The number of *Type A units* is permitted to be reduced in accordance with Section 1107.7.
2. *Existing structures* on a *site* shall not contribute to the total number of units on a *site*.

1107.6.2.1.2 Type B units. Where there are four or more *dwelling units* or *sleeping units intended to be occupied as a residence* in a single structure, every *dwelling unit* and *sleeping unit intended to be occupied as a residence* shall be a *Type B unit*.

Exception: The number of *Type B units* is permitted to be reduced in accordance with Section 1107.7.

1107.6.2.2 Group R-2 other than apartment houses, monasteries and convents. In Group R-2 occupancies, other than apartment houses, monasteries and convents, *Accessible units* and *Type B units* shall be provided in accordance with Sections 1107.6.2.2.1 and 1107.6.2.2.2.

1107.6.2.2.1 Accessible units. *Accessible dwelling units* and *sleeping units* shall be provided in accordance with Table 1107.6.1.1.

1107.6.2.2.2 Type B units. Where there are four or more *dwelling units* or *sleeping units intended to be occupied as a residence* in a single structure, every *dwelling unit* and every *sleeping unit intended to be occupied as a residence* shall be a *Type B unit*.

Exception: The number of *Type B units* is permitted to be reduced in accordance with Section 1107.7.

1107.6.3 Group R-3. In Group R-3 occupancies where there are four or more *dwelling units* or *sleeping units intended to be occupied as a residence* in a single structure, every *dwelling unit* and *sleeping unit intended to be occupied as a residence* shall be a *Type B unit*.

Exception: The number of *Type B units* is permitted to be reduced in accordance with Section 1107.7.

1107.6.4 Group R-4. *Accessible units* and *Type B units* shall be provided in Group R-4 occupancies in accordance with Sections 1107.6.4.1 and 1107.6.4.2.

1107.6.4.1 Accessible units. At least one of the *dwelling* or *sleeping units* shall be an *Accessible unit*.

1107.6.4.2 Type B units. In structures with four or more *dwelling units* or *sleeping units intended to be occupied as a residence*, every *dwelling unit* and *sleeping unit intended to be occupied as a residence* shall be a *Type B unit*.

Exception: The number of *Type B units* is permitted to be reduced in accordance with Section 1107.7.

1107.7 General exceptions. Where specifically permitted by Section 1107.5 or 1107.6, the required number of *Type A units* and *Type B units* is permitted to be reduced in accordance with Sections 1107.7.1 through 1107.7.5.

1107.7.1 Structures without elevator service. Where no elevator service is provided in a structure, only the *dwelling units* and *sleeping units* that are located on stories indicated in Sections 1107.7.1.1 and 1107.7.1.2 are required to be *Type A units* and *Type B units*, respectively. The number of *Type A units* shall be determined in accordance with Section 1107.6.2.1.1.

1107.7.1.1 One story with Type B units required. At least one *story* containing *dwelling units* or *sleeping units intended to be occupied as a residence* shall be provided with an *accessible* entrance from the exterior of the structure and all units *intended to be occupied as a residence* on that *story* shall be *Type B units*.

1107.7.1.2 Additional stories with Type B units. On all other stories that have a building entrance in proximity to arrival points intended to serve units on that *story*, as indicated in Items 1 and 2, all *dwelling units* and *sleeping units intended to be occupied as a residence* served by that entrance on that *story* shall be *Type B units*.

1. Where the slopes of the undisturbed *site* measured between the planned entrance and all vehicular or pedestrian arrival points within 50 feet (15 240 mm) of the planned entrance are 10 percent or less, and
2. Where the slopes of the planned finished grade measured between the entrance and all vehicular or pedestrian arrival points within 50 feet (15 240 mm) of the planned entrance are 10 percent or less.

Where no such arrival points are within 50 feet (15 240 mm) of the entrance, the closest arrival point shall be used unless that arrival point serves the *story* required by Section 1107.7.1.1.

1107.7.2 Multistory units. A *multistory dwelling* or *sleeping unit* which is not provided with elevator service is not required to be a *Type B unit*. Where a *multistory unit* is provided with external elevator service to only one floor, the floor provided with elevator service shall be the primary entry to the unit, shall comply with the requirements for a *Type B unit* and a toilet facility shall be provided on that floor.

1107.7.3 Elevator service to the lowest story with units. Where elevator service in the building provides an *accessible route* only to the lowest *story* containing *dwelling* or *sleeping units intended to be occupied as a residence*, only the units on that *story* which are *intended to be occupied as a residence* are required to be *Type B units*.

1107.7.4 Site impracticality. On a *site* with multiple nonelevator buildings, the number of units required by Section 1107.7.1 to be *Type B units* is permitted to be reduced to a percentage which is equal to the percentage of the entire *site* having grades, prior to development, which are less than 10 percent, provided that all of the following conditions are met:

1. Not less than 20 percent of the units required by Section 1107.7.1 on the *site* are *Type B units*;
2. Units required by Section 1107.7.1, where the slope between the building entrance serving the units on that *story* and a pedestrian or vehicular arrival point is no greater than 8.33 percent, are *Type B units*;
3. Units required by Section 1107.7.1, where an elevated walkway is planned between a building entrance serving the units on that *story* and a pedestrian or vehicular arrival point and the slope between them is 10 percent or less are *Type B units*; and
4. Units served by an elevator in accordance with Section 1107.7.3 are *Type B units*.

1107.7.5 Design flood elevation. The required number of *Type A units* and *Type B units* shall not apply to a *site* where the required elevation of the lowest floor or the lowest horizontal structural building members of nonelevator buildings are at or above the *design flood elevation* resulting in:

1. A difference in elevation between the minimum required floor elevation at the primary entrances and vehicular and pedestrian arrival points within 50 feet (15 240 mm) exceeding 30 inches (762 mm), and
2. A slope exceeding 10 percent between the minimum required floor elevation at the primary entrances and vehicular and pedestrian arrival points within 50 feet (15.24 m).

Where no such arrival points are within 50 feet (15.24 m) of the primary entrances, the closest arrival points shall be used.

SECTION 1108 SPECIAL OCCUPANCIES

1108.1 General. In addition to the other requirements of this chapter, the requirements of Sections 1108.2 through 1108.4 shall apply to specific occupancies.

1108.2 Assembly area seating. Assembly areas with fixed seating shall comply with Sections 1108.2.1 through 1108.2.8. Dining areas shall comply with Section 1108.2.9. In addition, lawn seating shall comply with Section 1108.2.6.

1108.2.1 Services. If a service or facility is provided in an area that is not *accessible*, the same service or facility shall be provided on an *accessible* level and shall be *accessible*.

1108.2.2 Wheelchair spaces. In theaters, *bleachers*, *grandstands*, stadiums, arenas and other fixed seating assembly areas, *accessible wheelchair spaces* complying with ICC A117.1 shall be provided in accordance with Sections 1108.2.2.1 through 1108.2.2.4.

1108.2.2.1 General seating. *Wheelchair spaces* shall be provided in accordance with Table 1108.2.2.1.

1108.2.2.2 Luxury boxes, club boxes and suites. In each luxury box, club box, and suite within arenas, stadiums and *grandstands*, *wheelchair spaces* shall be provided in accordance with Table 1108.2.2.1.

1108.2.2.3 Other boxes. In boxes other than those required to comply with Section 1108.2.2.2, the total number of *wheelchair spaces* provided shall be determined in accordance with Table 1108.2.2.1. *Wheelchair spaces* shall be located in not less than 20 percent of all boxes provided.

**TABLE 1108.2.2.1
ACCESSIBLE WHEELCHAIR SPACES**

CAPACITY OF SEATING IN ASSEMBLY AREAS	MINIMUM REQUIRED NUMBER OF WHEELCHAIR SPACES
4 to 25	1
26 to 50	2
51 to 100	4
101 to 300	5
301 to 500	6
501 to 5,000	6, plus 1 for each 150, or fraction thereof, between 501 through 5,000
5,001 and over	36 plus 1 for each 200, or fraction thereof, over 5,000

1108.2.2.4 Team or player seating. At least one *wheelchair space* shall be provided in team or player seating areas serving areas of sport activity.

Exception: *Wheelchair spaces* shall not be required in team or player seating areas serving bowling lanes that are not required to be located on an *accessible route* in accordance with Section 1109.14.4.1.

1108.2.3 Companion seats. At least one companion seat complying with ICC A117.1 shall be provided for each *wheelchair space* required by Sections 1108.2.2.1 through 1108.2.2.3.

1108.2.4 Dispersion of wheelchair spaces in multilevel assembly seating areas. In *multilevel assembly seating* areas, *wheelchair spaces* shall be provided on the main floor level and on one of each two additional floor or *mezzanine* levels. *Wheelchair spaces* shall be provided in each luxury box, club box and suite within assembly facilities.

Exceptions:

1. In multilevel assembly spaces utilized for worship services where the second floor or *mezzanine* level contains 25 percent or less of the total seating capacity, *wheelchair spaces* shall be permitted to all be located on the main level.
2. In *multilevel assembly seating* where the second floor or *mezzanine* level provides 25 percent or less of the total seating capacity and 300 or fewer

seats, all *wheelchair spaces* shall be permitted to be located on the main level.

3. *Wheelchair spaces* in team or player seating serving areas of sport activity are not required to be dispersed.

1108.2.5 Designated aisle seats. At least 5 percent, but not less than one, of the total number of aisle seats provided shall be designated aisle seats and shall be the aisle seats located closest to *accessible routes*.

Exception: Designated aisle seats are not required in team or player seating serving areas of sport activity.

1108.2.6 Lawn seating. Lawn seating areas and exterior overflow seating areas, where fixed seats are not provided, shall connect to an *accessible route*.

1108.2.7 Assistive listening systems. Each assembly area where audible communications are integral to the use of the space shall have an assistive listening system.

Exception: Other than in courtrooms, an assistive listening system is not required where there is no audio amplification system.

1108.2.7.1 Receivers. Receivers shall be provided for assistive listening systems in accordance with Table 1108.2.7.1.

Exceptions:

1. Where a building contains more than one assembly area, the total number of required receivers shall be permitted to be calculated according to the total number of seats in the assembly areas in the building, provided that all receivers are usable with all systems and if assembly areas required to provide assistive listening are under one management.
2. Where all seats in an assembly area are served by an induction loop assistive listening system, the minimum number of receivers required by Table 1108.2.7.1 to be hearing-aid compatible shall not be required.

1108.2.7.2 Public address systems. Where stadiums, arenas and *grandstands* provide audible public announcements, they shall also provide equivalent text information regarding events and facilities in compliance with Sections 1108.2.7.2.1 and 1108.2.7.2.2.

1108.2.7.2.1 Prerecorded text messages. Where electronic signs are provided and have the capability to display prerecorded text messages containing information that is the same, or substantially equivalent to information that is provided audibly, signs shall display text that is equivalent to audible announcements.

Exception: Announcements that cannot be prerecorded in advance of the event shall not be required to be displayed.

1108.2.7.2.2 Real-time messages. Where electronic signs are provided and have the capability to display real-time messages containing information that is the same, or substantially equivalent, to information that is provided audibly, signs shall display text that is equivalent to audible announcements.

1108.2.8 Performance areas. An *accessible route* shall directly connect the performance area to the assembly seating area where a *circulation path* directly connects a performance area to an assembly seating area. An *accessible route* shall be provided from performance areas to ancillary areas or facilities used by performers.

1108.2.9 Dining areas. In dining areas, the total floor area allotted for seating and tables shall be *accessible*.

Exceptions:

1. In buildings or facilities not required to provide an *accessible route* between levels, an *accessible route* to a *mezzanine* seating area is not required, provided that the *mezzanine* contains less than 25 percent of the total area and the same services are provided in the *accessible* area.
2. In sports facilities, tiered dining areas providing seating required to be *accessible* shall be required to have *accessible routes* serving at least 25 percent of the dining area, provided that *accessible routes* serve *accessible* seating and where each tier is provided with the same services.

TABLE 1108.2.7.1
RECEIVERS FOR ASSISTIVE LISTENING SYSTEMS

CAPACITY OF SEATING IN ASSEMBLY AREAS	MINIMUM REQUIRED NUMBER OF RECEIVERS	MINIMUM NUMBER OF RECEIVERS TO BE HEARING-AID COMPATIBLE
50 or less	2	2
51 to 200	2, plus 1 per 25 seats over 50 seats*	2
201 to 500	2, plus 1 per 25 seats over 50 seats*	1 per 4 receivers*
501 to 1,000	20, plus 1 per 33 seats over 500 seats*	1 per 4 receivers*
1,001 to 2,000	35, plus 1 per 50 seats over 1,000 seats*	1 per 4 receivers*
Over 2,000	55, plus 1 per 100 seats over 2,000 seats*	1 per 4 receivers*

Note: * = or fraction thereof

1108.2.9.1 Dining surfaces. Where dining surfaces for the consumption of food or drink are provided, at least 5 percent, but not less than one, of the dining surfaces for the seating and standing spaces shall be *accessible* and be distributed throughout the facility and located on a level accessed by an *accessible route*.

1108.3 Self-service storage facilities. *Self-service storage facilities* shall provide *accessible* individual self-storage spaces in accordance with Table 1108.3.

TABLE 1108.3
ACCESSIBLE SELF-SERVICE STORAGE FACILITIES

TOTAL SPACES IN FACILITY	MINIMUM NUMBER OF REQUIRED ACCESSIBLE SPACES
1 to 200	5%, but not less than 1
Over 200	10, plus 2% of total number of units over 200

1108.3.1 Dispersion. *Accessible* individual self-service storage spaces shall be dispersed throughout the various classes of spaces provided. Where more classes of spaces are provided than the number of required *accessible* spaces, the number of *accessible* spaces shall not be required to exceed that required by Table 1108.3. *Accessible* spaces are permitted to be dispersed in a single building of a multibuilding facility.

1108.4 Judicial facilities. Judicial facilities shall comply with Sections 1108.4.1 through 1108.4.3.

1108.4.1 Courtrooms. Each courtroom shall be *accessible* and comply with Sections 1108.4.1.1 through 1108.4.1.5.

1108.4.1.1 Jury box. A *wheelchair space* complying with ICC A117.1 shall be provided within the jury box.

Exception: Adjacent companion seating is not required.

1108.4.1.2 Gallery seating. *Wheelchair spaces* complying with ICC A117.1 shall be provided in accordance with Table 1108.2.2.1. Designated aisle seats shall be provided in accordance with Section 1108.2.5.

1108.4.1.3 Assistive listening systems. An assistive listening system must be provided. Receivers shall be provided for the assistive listening system in accordance with Section 1108.2.7.1.

1108.4.1.4 Employee work stations. The judge's bench, clerk's station, bailiff's station, deputy clerk's station and court reporter's station shall be located on an *accessible route*. The vertical access to elevated employee work stations within a courtroom is not required at the time of initial construction, provided a *ramp*, lift or elevator complying with ICC A117.1 can be installed without requiring reconfiguration or extension of the courtroom or extension of the electrical system.

1108.4.1.5 Other work stations. The litigant's and counsel stations, including the lectern, shall be *accessible* in accordance with ICC A117.1.

1108.4.2 Holding cells. Central holding cells and court-floor holding cells shall comply with Sections 1108.4.2.1 and 1108.4.2.2.

1108.4.2.1 Central holding cells. Where separate central holding cells are provided for adult males, juvenile males, adult females or juvenile females, one of each type shall be *accessible*. Where central holding cells are provided and are not separated by age or sex, at least one *accessible* cell shall be provided.

1108.4.2.2 Court-floor holding cells. Where separate court-floor holding cells are provided for adult males, juvenile males, adult females or juvenile females, each courtroom shall be served by one *accessible* cell of each type. Where court-floor holding cells are provided and are not separated by age or sex, courtrooms shall be served by at least one *accessible* cell. *Accessible* cells shall be permitted to serve more than one courtroom.

1108.4.3 Visiting areas. Visiting areas shall comply with Sections 1108.4.3.1 and 1108.4.3.2.

1108.4.3.1 Cubicles and counters. At least 5 percent but no fewer than one of the cubicles shall be *accessible* on both the visitor and detainee sides. Where counters are provided, at least one shall be *accessible* on both the visitor and detainee sides.

Exception: This requirement shall not apply to the detainee side of cubicles or counters at noncontact visiting areas not serving *accessible* holding cells.

1108.4.3.2 Partitions. Where solid partitions or security glazing separate visitors from detainees, at least one of each type of cubicle or counter partition shall be *accessible*.

SECTION 1109
OTHER FEATURES AND FACILITIES

1109.1 General. *Accessible* building features and facilities shall be provided in accordance with Sections 1109.2 through 1109.14.

Exception: *Type A units* and *Type B units* shall comply with ICC A117.1.

1109.2 Toilet and bathing facilities. Each toilet room and bathing room shall be *accessible*. Where a floor level is not required to be connected by an *accessible route*, the only toilet rooms or bathing rooms provided within the facility shall not be located on the inaccessible floor. At least one of each type of fixture, element, control or dispenser in each *accessible* toilet room and bathing room shall be *accessible*.

Exceptions:

1. In toilet rooms or bathing rooms accessed only through a private office, not for *common* or *public use* and intended for use by a single occupant, any of the following alternatives are allowed:

   1.1. Doors are permitted to swing into the clear floor space, provided the door swing can be reversed to meet the requirements in ICC A117.1;

1.2. The height requirements for the water closet in ICC A117.1 are not applicable;

1.3. Grab bars are not required to be installed in a toilet room, provided that reinforcement has been installed in the walls and located so as to permit the installation of such grab bars; and

1.4. The requirement for height, knee and toe clearance shall not apply to a lavatory.

2. This section is not applicable to toilet and bathing rooms that serve *dwelling units* or *sleeping units* that are not required to be *accessible* by Section 1107.

3. Where multiple single-user toilet rooms or bathing rooms are clustered at a single location, at least 50 percent but not less than one room for each use at each cluster shall be *accessible.*

4. Where no more than one urinal is provided in a toilet room or bathing room, the urinal is not required to be *accessible.*

5. Toilet rooms that are part of critical care or intensive care patient sleeping rooms are not required to be *accessible.*

1109.2.1 Family or assisted-use toilet and bathing rooms. In assembly and mercantile occupancies, an *accessible* family or assisted-use toilet room shall be provided where an aggregate of six or more male and female water closets is required. In buildings of mixed occupancy, only those water closets required for the assembly or mercantile occupancy shall be used to determine the family or assisted-use toilet room requirement. In recreational facilities where separate-sex bathing rooms are provided, an *accessible* family or assisted-use bathing room shall be provided. Fixtures located within family or assisted-use toilet and bathing rooms shall be included in determining the number of fixtures provided in an occupancy.

Exception: Where each separate-sex bathing room has only one shower or bathtub fixture, a family or assisted-use bathing room is not required.

1109.2.1.1 Standard. Family or assisted-use toilet and bathing rooms shall comply with Sections 1109.2.1.2 through 1109.2.1.7 and ICC A117.1.

1109.2.1.2 Family or assisted-use toilet rooms. Family or assisted-use toilet rooms shall include only one water closet and only one lavatory. A family or assisted-use bathing room in accordance with Section 1109.2.1.3 shall be considered a family or assisted-use toilet room.

Exception: A urinal is permitted to be provided in addition to the water closet in a family or assisted-use toilet room.

1109.2.1.3 Family or assisted-use bathing rooms. Family or assisted-use bathing rooms shall include only one shower or bathtub fixture. Family or assisted-use bathing rooms shall also include one water closet and one lavatory. Where storage facilities are provided for separate-sex bathing rooms, *accessible* storage facilities shall be provided for family or assisted-use bathing rooms.

1109.2.1.4 Location. Family or assisted-use toilet and bathing rooms shall be located on an *accessible route.* Family or assisted-use toilet rooms shall be located not more than one *story* above or below separate-sex toilet rooms. The *accessible route* from any separate-sex toilet room to a family or assisted-use toilet room shall not exceed 500 feet (152 m).

1109.2.1.5 Prohibited location. In passenger transportation facilities and airports, the *accessible route* from separate-sex toilet rooms to a family or assisted-use toilet room shall not pass through security checkpoints.

1109.2.1.6 Clear floor space. Where doors swing into a family or assisted-use toilet or bathing room, a clear floor space not less than 30 inches by 48 inches (762 mm by 1219 mm) shall be provided, within the room, beyond the area of the door swing.

1109.2.1.7 Privacy. Doors to family or assisted-use toilet and bathing rooms shall be securable from within the room.

1109.2.2 Water closet compartment. Where water closet compartments are provided in a toilet room or bathing room, at least one wheelchair-*accessible* compartment shall be provided. Where the combined total water closet compartments and urinals provided in a toilet room or bathing room is six or more, at least one ambulatory-*accessible* water closet compartment shall be provided in addition to the wheelchair-*accessible* compartment. Wheelchair-*accessible* and ambulatory-*accessible* compartments shall comply with ICC A117.1.

1109.2.3 Lavatories. Where lavatories are provided, at least 5 percent, but not less than one, shall be *accessible.* Where the total lavatories provided in a toilet room or bathing facility is six or more, at least one lavatory with enhanced reach ranges in accordance with ICC A117.1, shall be provided.

1109.3 Sinks. Where sinks are provided, at least 5 percent but not less than one provided in *accessible* spaces shall comply with ICC A117.1.

Exception: Mop or service sinks are not required to be *accessible.*

1109.4 Kitchens and kitchenettes. Where kitchens and kitchenettes are provided in *accessible* spaces or rooms, they shall be *accessible* in accordance with ICC A117.1.

1. <u>A minimum 60-inch (1524 mm) clear turning space shall be provided within the kitchen of a Type A unit.</u>

2. <u>A maximum 6-inch (150 mm) deep by minimum 9-inch (230 mm) high toe space beneath a cabinet shall be permitted to provide part of the 60-inch (1524 mm) clear floor area on one side only.</u>

1109.5 Drinking fountains. Where drinking fountains are provided on an exterior site, on a floor or within a secured area, the drinking fountains shall be provided in accordance with Sections 1109.5.1 and 1109.5.2.

1109.5.1 Minimum number. No fewer than two drinking fountains shall be provided. One drinking fountain shall comply with the requirements for people who use a wheelchair and one drinking fountain shall comply with the requirements for standing persons.

Exception: A single drinking fountain that complies with the requirements for people who use a wheelchair and standing persons shall be permitted to be substituted for two separate drinking fountains.

1109.5.2 More than the minimum number. Where more than the minimum number of drinking fountains specified in Section 1109.5.1 are provided, 50 percent of the total number of drinking fountains provided shall comply with the requirements for persons who use a wheelchair and 50 percent of the total number of drinking fountains provided shall comply with the requirements for standing persons.

Exception: Where 50 percent of the drinking fountains yields a fraction, 50 percent shall be permitted to be rounded up or down, provided that the total number of drinking fountains complying with this section equals 100 percent of the drinking fountains.

1109.6 Elevators. Passenger elevators on an *accessible route* shall be *accessible* and comply with Section 3001.3.

1109.7 Lifts. Platform (wheelchair) lifts are permitted to be a part of a required *accessible route* in new construction where indicated in Items 1 through 10. Platform (wheelchair) lifts shall be installed in accordance with ASME A18.1.

1. An *accessible route* to a performing area and speaker platforms in Group A occupancies.
2. An *accessible route* to *wheelchair spaces* required to comply with the *wheelchair space* dispersion requirements of Sections 1108.2.2 through 1108.2.6.
3. An *accessible route* to spaces that are not open to the general public with an *occupant load* of not more than five.
4. An *accessible route* within a *dwelling* or *sleeping unit*.
5. An *accessible route* to wheelchair seating spaces located in outdoor dining terraces in Group A-5 occupancies where the *means of egress* from the dining terraces to a *public way* are open to the outdoors.
6. An *accessible route* to jury boxes and witness stands; raised courtroom stations including judges' benches, clerks' stations, bailiffs' stations, deputy clerks' stations and court reporters' stations; and to depressed areas such as the well of the court.
7. An *accessible route* to load and unload areas serving amusement rides.
8. An *accessible route* to play components or soft contained play structures.
9. An *accessible route* to team or player seating areas serving areas of sport activity.
10. An *accessible route* where existing exterior *site* constraints make use of a ramp or elevator infeasible.

1109.8 Storage. Where fixed or built-in storage elements such as cabinets, shelves, medicine cabinets, closets and drawers are provided in required *accessible* spaces, at least one of each type shall contain storage space complying with ICC A117.1.

1109.8.1 Lockers. Where lockers are provided in *accessible* spaces, at least five percent, but not less than one, of each type shall be *accessible*.

1109.8.2 Shelving and display units. Self-service shelves and display units shall be located on an *accessible route*. Such shelving and display units shall not be required to comply with reach-range provisions.

1109.8.3 Coat hooks and shelves. Where coat hooks and shelves are provided in toilet rooms or toilet compartments or in dressing, fitting or locker rooms, at least one of each type shall be *accessible* and shall be provided in *accessible* toilet rooms without toilet compartments, *accessible* toilet compartments and *accessible* dressing, fitting and locker rooms.

1109.9 Detectable warnings. Passenger transit platform edges bordering a drop-off and not protected by platform screens or *guards* shall have a *detectable warning*.

Exception: *Detectable warnings* are not required at bus stops.

1109.10 Seating at tables, counters and work surfaces. Where seating or standing space at fixed or built-in tables, counters or work surfaces is provided in *accessible* spaces, at least 5 percent of the seating and standing spaces, but not less than one, shall be *accessible*. In Group I-3 occupancy visiting areas at least 5 percent, but not less than one, cubicle or counter shall be *accessible* on both the visitor and detainee sides.

Exceptions:

1. Check-writing surfaces at check-out aisles not required to comply with Section 1109.11.2 are not required to be *accessible*.
2. In Group I-3 occupancies, the counter or cubicle on the detainee side is not required to be *accessible* at noncontact visiting areas or in areas not serving *accessible* holding cells or *sleeping units*.

1109.10.1 Dispersion. *Accessible* fixed or built-in seating at tables, counters or work surfaces shall be distributed throughout the space or facility containing such elements and located on a level accessed by an *accessible route*.

1109.11 Service facilities. Service facilities shall provide for *accessible* features in accordance with Sections 1109.11.1 through 1109.11.5.

1109.11.1 Dressing, fitting and locker rooms. Where dressing rooms, fitting rooms or locker rooms are provided, at least 5 percent, but not less than one, of each type of use in each cluster provided shall be *accessible*.

1109.11.2 Check-out aisles. Where check-out aisles are provided, *accessible* check-out aisles shall be provided in accordance with Table 1109.11.2. Where check-out aisles serve different functions, at least one *accessible* check-out aisle shall be provided for each function. Where check-out aisles serve different functions, *accessible* check-out aisles shall be provided in accordance with Table 1109.11.2 for each function. Where check-out aisles are dispersed throughout the building or facility, *accessible* check-out aisles shall also be dispersed. Traffic control devices, security devices and turnstiles located in *accessible* check-out aisles or lanes shall be *accessible.*

TABLE 1109.11.2
ACCESSIBLE CHECK-OUT AISLES

TOTAL CHECK-OUT AISLES OF EACH FUNCTION	MINIMUM NUMBER OF ACCESSIBLE CHECK-OUT AISLES OF EACH FUNCTION
1 to 4	1
5 to 8	2
9 to 15	3
Over 15	3, plus 20% of additional aisles

1109.11.3 Point of sale and service counters. Where counters are provided for sales or distribution of goods or services, at least one of each type provided shall be *accessible.* Where such counters are dispersed throughout the building or facility, *accessible* counters shall also be dispersed.

1109.11.4 Food service lines. Food service lines shall be *accessible.* Where self-service shelves are provided, at least 50 percent, but not less than one, of each type provided shall be *accessible.*

1109.11.5 Queue and waiting lines. Queue and waiting lines servicing *accessible* counters or check-out aisles shall be *accessible.*

1109.12 Controls, operating mechanisms and hardware. Controls, operating mechanisms and hardware intended for operation by the occupant, including switches that control lighting and ventilation and electrical convenience outlets, in *accessible* spaces, along *accessible routes* or as parts of *accessible* elements shall be *accessible.*

Exceptions:

1. Operable parts that are intended for use only by service or maintenance personnel shall not be required to be *accessible.*
2. Electrical or communication receptacles serving a dedicated use shall not be required to be *accessible.*
3. Where two or more outlets are provided in a kitchen above a length of counter top that is uninterrupted by a sink or appliance, one outlet shall not be required to be *accessible.*
4. Floor electrical receptacles shall not be required to be *accessible.*
5. HVAC diffusers shall not be required to be *accessible.*
6. Except for light switches, where redundant controls are provided for a single element, one control in each space shall not be required to be *accessible.*
7. Access doors or gates in barrier walls and fences protecting pools, spas and hot tubs shall be permitted to have operable parts of the release of latch on self-latching devices at 54 inches (1370 mm) maximum and 48 inches (1219 mm) minimum above the finished floor or ground, provided the self-latching devices are not also self-locking devices, operated by means of a key, electronic opener, or integral combination lock.

1109.12.1 Operable window. Where operable windows are provided in rooms that are required to be *accessible* in accordance with Sections 1107.5.1.1, 1107.5.2.1, 1107.5.3.1, 1107.5.4, 1107.6.1.1, 1107.6.2.1.1, 1107.6.2.2.1 and 1107.6.4.1, at least one window in each room shall be *accessible* and each required operable window shall be *accessible.*

Exception: *Accessible* windows are not required in bathrooms and kitchens.

1109.13 Fuel-dispensing systems. Fuel-dispensing systems shall comply with ICC A117.1.

1109.14 Recreational and sports facilities. Recreational and sports facilities shall be provided with *accessible* features in accordance with Sections 1109.14.1 through 1109.14.4.

1109.14.1 Facilities serving a single building. In Group R-2 and R-3 occupancies where recreational facilities are provided serving a single building containing *Type A units* or *Type B units*, 25 percent, but not less than one, of each type of recreational facility shall be *accessible.* Every recreational facility of each type on a site shall be considered to determine the total number of each type that is required to be *accessible.*

1109.14.2 Facilities serving multiple buildings. In Group R-2 and R-3 occupancies on a single *site* where multiple buildings containing *Type A units* or *Type B units* are served by recreational facilities, 25 percent, but not less than one, of each type of recreational facility serving each building shall be *accessible.* The total number of each type of recreational facility that is required to be *accessible* shall be determined by considering every recreational facility of each type serving each building on the site.

1109.14.3 Other occupancies. All recreational and sports facilities not falling within the purview of Section 1109.14.1 or 1109.14.2 shall be *accessible.*

1109.14.4 Recreational and sports facilities exceptions. Recreational and sports facilities required to be *accessible* shall be exempt from this chapter to the extent specified in this section.

1109.14.4.1 Bowling lanes. An *accessible route* shall be provided to at least 5 percent, but no less than one, of each type of bowling lane.

1109.14.4.2 Court sports. In court sports, at least one *accessible route* shall directly connect both sides of the court.

1109.14.4.3 Raised boxing or wrestling rings. Raised boxing or wrestling rings are not required to be *accessible.*

1109.14.4.4 Raised refereeing, judging and scoring areas. Raised structures used solely for refereeing, judging or scoring a sport are not required to be *accessible.*

1109.14.4.5 Raised diving boards and diving platforms. Raised diving boards and diving platforms are not required to be *accessible*.

SECTION 1110
SIGNAGE

1110.1 Signs. Required *accessible* elements shall be identified by the International Symbol of Accessibility at the following locations:

1. *Accessible* parking spaces required by Section 1106.1. Location and design of signage shall comply with the requirements of North Carolina General Statute 20-37.6 and 136-30 and the NCDOT Manual on Uniform Traffic Control Devices.
2. *Accessible* passenger loading zones.
3. *Accessible* rooms where multiple single-user toilet or bathing rooms are clustered at a single location.
4. *Accessible* entrances where not all entrances are accessible.
5. *Accessible* check-out aisles where not all aisles are accessible. The sign, where provided, shall be above the check-out aisle in the same location as the check-out aisle number or type of check-out identification.
6. Family or assisted-use toilet and bathing rooms.
7. *Accessible* dressing, fitting and locker rooms where not all such rooms are *accessible*.
8. *Accessible areas of refuge* in accordance with Section 1007.9.
9. Exterior areas for assisted rescue in accordance with Section 1007.9.

1110.2 Directional signage. Directional signage indicating the route to the nearest like *accessible* element shall be provided at the following locations. These directional signs shall include the International Symbol of Accessibility:

1. Inaccessible building entrances.
2. Inaccessible public toilets and bathing facilities.
3. Elevators not serving an *accessible route*.
4. At each separate-sex toilet and bathing room indicating the location of the nearest family or assisted-use toilet or bathing room where provided in accordance with Section 1109.2.1.
5. At *exits* and *exit stairways* serving a required *accessible* space, but not providing an *approved accessible means of egress*, signage shall be provided in accordance with Section 1007.10.

1110.3 Other signs. Signage indicating special accessibility provisions shall be provided as shown:

1. Each assembly area required to comply with Section 1108.2.7 shall provide a sign notifying patrons of the availability of assistive listening systems.

   Exception: Where ticket offices or windows are provided, signs are not required at each assembly area provided that signs are displayed at each ticket office or window informing patrons of the availability of assistive listening systems.
2. At each door to an *area of refuge*, an exterior area for assisted rescue, an egress *stairway*, *exit passageway* and *exit discharge*, signage shall be provided in accordance with Section 1011.3.
3. At *areas of refuge*, signage shall be provided in accordance with Section 1007.11.
4. At exterior areas for assisted rescue, signage shall be provided in accordance with Section 1007.11.
5. At two-way communication systems, signage shall be provided in accordance with Section 1007.8.2.
6. Within *exit enclosures*, signage shall be provided in accordance with Section 1022.8.

CHAPTER 12
INTERIOR ENVIRONMENT

SECTION 1201
GENERAL

1201.1 Scope. The provisions of this chapter shall govern ventilation, temperature control, lighting, *yards* and *courts*, sound transmission, room dimensions, surrounding materials and rodent proofing associated with the interior spaces of buildings.

SECTION 1202
DEFINITIONS

1202.1 General. The following words and terms shall, for the purposes of this chapter and as used elsewhere in this code, have the meanings shown herein.

SUNROOM. A one-story structure attached to a building with a glazing area in excess of 40 percent of the gross area of the structure's *exterior walls* and roof.

THERMAL ISOLATION. A separation of conditioned spaces, between a sunroom addition and a *dwelling unit*, consisting of existing or new wall(s), doors and/or windows.

SECTION 1203
VENTILATION

1203.1 General. Buildings shall be provided with natural ventilation in accordance with Section 1203.4, or mechanical ventilation in accordance with the *International Mechanical Code*.

1203.2 Attic spaces. Enclosed *attics* and enclosed rafter spaces formed where ceilings are applied directly to the underside of roof framing members shall have cross ventilation for each separate space by ventilating openings protected against the entrance of rain and snow. Blocking and bridging shall be arranged so as not to interfere with the movement of air. A minimum of 1 inch (25 mm) of airspace shall be provided between the insulation and the roof sheathing. The net free ventilating area shall not be less than $^1/_{300}$ of the area of the space ventilated, with 50 percent of the required ventilating area provided by ventilators located in the upper portion of the space to be ventilated at least 3 feet (914 mm) above eave or cornice vents with the balance of the required ventilation provided by eave or cornice vents.

1203.2.1 Openings into attic. Exterior openings into the *attic* space of any building intended for human occupancy shall be protected to prevent the entry of birds, squirrels, rodents, snakes and other similar creatures. Openings for ventilation having a least dimension of $^1/_{16}$ inch (1.6 mm) minimum and $^1/_4$ inch (6.4 mm) maximum shall be permitted. Openings for ventilation having a least dimension larger than $^1/_4$ inch (6.4 mm) shall be provided with corrosion-resistant wire cloth screening, hardware cloth, perforated vinyl or similar material with openings having a least dimension of $^1/_{16}$ inch (1.6 mm) minimum and $^1/_4$ inch (6.4 mm) maximum. Where combustion air is obtained from an *attic* area, it shall be in accordance with Chapter 7 of the *International Mechanical Code*.

1203.3 Under-floor ventilation. The space between the bottom of the floor joists and the earth under any building except spaces occupied by basements or cellars shall be provided with ventilation openings through foundation walls or *exterior walls*. Such openings shall be placed so as to provide cross ventilation of the under-floor space.

1203.3.1 Openings for under-floor ventilation. The minimum net area of ventilation openings shall not be less than 1 square foot for each 150 square feet (0.67 m^2 for each 100 m^2) of crawl-space area. Ventilation openings shall be covered for their height and width with any of the following materials, provided that the least dimension of the covering shall not exceed $^1/_4$ inch (6 mm):

1. Perforated sheet metal plates not less than 0.070 inch (1.8 mm) thick.
2. Expanded sheet metal plates not less than 0.047 inch (1.2 mm) thick.
3. Cast-iron grilles or gratings.
4. Extruded load-bearing vents.
5. Hardware cloth of 0.035 inch (0.89 mm) wire or heavier.
6. Corrosion-resistant wire mesh, with the least dimension not exceeding $^1/_8$ inch (3.2 mm).

1203.3.2 Exceptions. The following are exceptions to Sections 1203.3 and 1203.3.1:

1. Where warranted by climatic conditions, ventilation openings to the outdoors are not required if ventilation openings to the interior are provided.
2. The total area of ventilation openings is permitted to be reduced to $^1/_{1,500}$ of the under-floor area where the ground surface is covered with a Class I vapor retarder material and the required openings are placed so as to provide cross ventilation of the space. The installation of operable louvers shall not be prohibited.
3. Ventilation openings are not required where continuously operated mechanical ventilation is provided at a rate of 1.0 cubic foot per minute (cfm) for each 50 square feet (1.02 L/s for each 10 m^2) of crawl space floor area and the ground surface is covered with a Class I vapor retarder.
4. Ventilation openings are not required when the ground surface is covered with a Class I vapor retarder, the perimeter walls are insulated and the space is conditioned in accordance with the *International Energy Conservation Code*.

5. For buildings in flood hazard areas as established in Section 1612.3, the openings for under-floor ventilation shall be deemed as meeting the flood opening requirements of ASCE 24 provided that the ventilation openings are designed and installed in accordance with ASCE 24.

1203.4 Natural ventilation. Natural ventilation of an occupied space shall be through windows, doors, louvers or other openings to the outdoors. The operating mechanism for such openings shall be provided with ready access so that the openings are readily controllable by the building occupants.

1203.4.1 Ventilation area required. The minimum openable area to the outdoors shall be 4 percent of the floor area being ventilated.

1203.4.1.1 Adjoining spaces. Where rooms and spaces without openings to the outdoors are ventilated through an adjoining room, the opening to the adjoining room shall be unobstructed and shall have an area of not less than 8 percent of the floor area of the interior room or space, but not less than 25 square feet (2.3 m^2). The minimum openable area to the outdoors shall be based on the total floor area being ventilated.

Exception: Exterior openings required for ventilation shall be permitted to open into a *thermally isolated* sunroom addition or patio cover provided that the openable area between the sunroom addition or patio cover and the interior room shall have an area of not less than 8 percent of the floor area of the interior room or space, but not less than 20 square feet (1.86 m^2). The minimum openable area to the outdoors shall be based on the total floor area being ventilated.

1203.4.1.2 Openings below grade. Where openings below grade provide required natural ventilation, the outside horizontal clear space measured perpendicular to the opening shall be one and one-half times the depth of the opening. The depth of the opening shall be measured from the average adjoining ground level to the bottom of the opening.

1203.4.2 Contaminants exhausted. Contaminant sources in naturally ventilated spaces shall be removed in accordance with the *International Mechanical Code* and the *International Fire Code.*

1203.4.2.1 Bathrooms. Rooms containing bathtubs, showers, spas and similar bathing fixtures shall be mechanically ventilated in accordance with the *International Mechanical Code.*

1203.4.3 Openings on yards or courts. Where natural ventilation is to be provided by openings onto *yards* or *courts*, such *yards* or *courts* shall comply with Section 1206.

1203.5 Other ventilation and exhaust systems. Ventilation and exhaust systems for occupancies and operations involving flammable or combustible hazards or other contaminant sources as covered in the *International Mechanical Code* or the *International Fire Code* shall be provided as required by both codes.

SECTION 1204 TEMPERATURE CONTROL

1204.1 Equipment and systems. Interior spaces intended for human occupancy shall be provided with active or passive space-heating systems capable of maintaining a minimum indoor temperature of 68°F (20°C) at a point 3 feet (914 mm) above the floor on the design heating day.

Exception: Interior spaces where the primary purpose is not associated with human comfort.

SECTION 1205 LIGHTING

1205.1 General. Every space intended for human occupancy shall be provided with natural light by means of exterior glazed openings in accordance with Section 1205.2 or shall be provided with artificial light in accordance with Section 1205.3. Exterior glazed openings shall open directly onto a *public way* or onto a *yard* or *court* in accordance with Section 1206.

1205.2 Natural light. The minimum net glazed area shall not be less than 8 percent of the floor area of the room served.

1205.2.1 Adjoining spaces. For the purpose of natural lighting, any room is permitted to be considered as a portion of an adjoining room where one-half of the area of the common wall is open and unobstructed and provides an opening of not less than one-tenth of the floor area of the interior room or 25 square feet (2.32 m^2), whichever is greater.

Exception: Openings required for natural light shall be permitted to open into a *thermally isolated* sunroom addition or patio cover where the common wall provides a glazed area of not less than one-tenth of the floor area of the interior room or 20 square feet (1.86 m^2), whichever is greater.

1205.2.2 Exterior openings. Exterior openings required by Section 1205.2 for natural light shall open directly onto a *public way, yard* or *court*, as set forth in Section 1206.

Exceptions:

1. Required exterior openings are permitted to open into a roofed porch where the porch:
   - 1.1. Abuts a *public way, yard* or *court*;
   - 1.2. Has a ceiling height of not less than 7 feet (2134 mm); and
   - 1.3. Has a longer side at least 65 percent open and unobstructed.
2. Skylights are not required to open directly onto a *public way, yard* or *court.*

1205.3 Artificial light. Artificial light shall be provided that is adequate to provide an average illumination of 10 foot-candles (107 lux) over the area of the room at a height of 30 inches (762 mm) above the floor level.

1205.4 Stairway illumination. *Stairways* within *dwelling units* and *exterior stairways* serving a *dwelling unit* shall have an illumination level on tread runs of not less than 1 foot-candle (11 lux). *Stairs* in other occupancies shall be governed by Chapter 10.

1205.4.1 Controls. The control for activation of the required *stairway* lighting shall be in accordance with NFPA 70.

1205.5 Emergency egress lighting. The *means of egress* shall be illuminated in accordance with Section 1006.1.

SECTION 1206 YARDS OR COURTS

1206.1 General. This section shall apply to *yards* and *courts* adjacent to exterior openings that provide natural light or ventilation. Such *yards* and *courts* shall be on the same property as the building.

1206.2 Yards. *Yards* shall not be less than 3 feet (914 mm) in width for buildings two *stories* or less above *grade plane*. For buildings more than two *stories above grade plane*, the minimum width of the *yard* shall be increased at the rate of 1 foot (305 mm) for each additional *story*. For buildings exceeding 14 *stories above grade plane*, the required width of the *yard* shall be computed on the basis of 14 *stories above grade plane*.

1206.3 Courts. *Courts* shall not be less than 3 feet (914 mm) in width. *Courts* having windows opening on opposite sides shall not be less than 6 feet (1829 mm) in width. *Courts* shall not be less than 10 feet (3048 mm) in length unless bounded on one end by a *public way* or *yard*. For buildings more than two *stories above grade plane*, the *court* shall be increased 1 foot (305 mm) in width and 2 feet (610 mm) in length for each additional *story*. For buildings exceeding 14 *stories above grade plane*, the required dimensions shall be computed on the basis of 14 *stories above grade plane*.

1206.3.1 Court access. Access shall be provided to the bottom of *courts* for cleaning purposes.

1206.3.2 Air intake. *Courts* more than two *stories* in height shall be provided with a horizontal air intake at the bottom not less than 10 square feet (0.93 m^2) in area and leading to the exterior of the building unless abutting a *yard* or *public way*.

1206.3.3 Court drainage. The bottom of every *court* shall be properly graded and drained to a public sewer or other approved disposal system complying with the *International Plumbing Code*.

SECTION 1207 SOUND TRANSMISSION

1207.1 Scope. This section shall apply to common interior walls, partitions and floor/ceiling assemblies between adjacent *dwelling units* or between *dwelling units* and adjacent public areas such as halls, *corridors*, *stairs* or service areas.

1207.2 Air-borne sound. Walls, partitions and floor/ceiling assemblies separating *dwelling units* from each other or from public or service areas shall have a sound transmission class (STC) of not less than 50 (45 if field tested) for air-borne noise when tested in accordance with ASTM E 90. Penetrations or openings in construction assemblies for piping; electrical devices; recessed cabinets; bathtubs; soffits; or heating, ventilating or exhaust ducts shall be sealed, lined, insulated or otherwise treated to maintain the required ratings. This requirement shall not apply to *dwelling unit* entrance doors; however, such doors shall be tight fitting to the frame and sill.

1207.2.1 Masonry. The sound transmission class of concrete masonry and clay masonry assemblies shall be calculated in accordance with TMS 0302 or determined through testing in accordance with ASTM E 90.

1207.3 Structure-borne sound. Floor/ceiling assemblies between *dwelling units* or between a *dwelling unit* and a public or service area within the structure shall have an impact insulation class (IIC) rating of not less than 50 (45 if field tested) when tested in accordance with ASTM E 492.

SECTION 1208 INTERIOR SPACE DIMENSIONS

1208.1 Minimum room widths. *Habitable spaces*, other than a kitchen, shall not be less than 7 feet (2134 mm) in any plan dimension. Kitchens shall have a clear passageway of not less than 3 feet (914 mm) between counter fronts and appliances or counter fronts and walls.

1208.2 Minimum ceiling heights. Occupiable spaces, *habitable spaces* and *corridors* shall have a ceiling height of not less than 7 feet 6 inches (2286 mm). Bathrooms, toilet rooms, kitchens, storage rooms and laundry rooms shall be permitted to have a ceiling height of not less than 7 feet (2134 mm).

Exceptions:

1. In one- and two-family *dwellings*, beams or girders spaced not less than 4 feet (1219 mm) on center and projecting not more than 6 inches (152 mm) below the required ceiling height.
2. If any room in a building has a sloped ceiling, the prescribed ceiling height for the room is required in one-half the area thereof. Any portion of the room measuring less than 5 feet (1524 mm) from the finished floor to the ceiling shall not be included in any computation of the minimum area thereof.
3. *Mezzanines* constructed in accordance with Section 505.1.

1208.2.1 Furred ceiling. Any room with a furred ceiling shall be required to have the minimum ceiling height in two-thirds of the area thereof, but in no case shall the height of the furred ceiling be less than 7 feet (2134 mm).

1208.3 Room area. Every *dwelling unit* shall have at least one room that shall have not less than 120 square feet (13.9 m^2) of *net floor area*. Other habitable rooms shall have a *net floor area* of not less than 70 square feet (6.5 m^2).

Exception: Every kitchen in a one- and two-family *dwelling* shall have not less than 50 square feet (4.64 m^2) of *gross floor area*.

1208.4 Efficiency dwelling units. An efficiency living unit shall conform to the requirements of the code except as modified herein:

1. The unit shall have a living room of not less than 220 square feet (20.4 m^2) of floor area. An additional 100

square feet (9.3 m^2) of floor area shall be provided for each occupant of such unit in excess of two.

2. The unit shall be provided with a separate closet.
3. The unit shall be provided with a kitchen sink, cooking appliance and refrigeration facilities, each having a clear working space of not less than 30 inches (762 mm) in front. Light and ventilation conforming to this code shall be provided.
4. The unit shall be provided with a separate bathroom containing a water closet, lavatory and bathtub or shower.

SECTION 1209 ACCESS TO UNOCCUPIED SPACES

1209.1 Crawl spaces. Crawl spaces shall be provided with a minimum of one access opening not less than 18 inches by 24 inches (457 mm by 610 mm).

1209.2 Attic spaces. An opening not less than 20 inches by 30 inches (559 mm by 762 mm) shall be provided to any *attic* area having a clear height of over 30 inches (762 mm). A 30-inch (762 mm) minimum clear headroom in the *attic* space shall be provided at or above the access opening.

1209.3 Mechanical appliances. Access to mechanical appliances installed in under-floor areas, in *attic* spaces and on roofs or elevated structures shall be in accordance with the *International Mechanical Code*.

SECTION 1210 SURROUNDING MATERIALS

1210.1 Floors and wall base finish materials. In other than *dwelling units*, toilet, bathing and shower room floor finish materials shall have a smooth, hard, nonabsorbent surface. The intersections of such floors with walls shall have a smooth, hard, nonabsorbent vertical base that extends upward onto the walls at least 4 inches (102 mm).

1210.2 Walls and partitions. Walls and partitions within 2 feet (610 mm) of urinals and water closets shall have a smooth, hard, nonabsorbent surface, to a height of 4 feet (1219 mm) above the floor, and except for structural elements, the materials used in such walls shall be of a type that is not adversely affected by moisture.

Exceptions:

1. *Dwelling units* and *sleeping units*.
2. Toilet rooms that are not accessible to the public and which have not more than one water closet.

Accessories such as grab bars, towel bars, paper dispensers and soap dishes, provided on or within walls, shall be installed and sealed to protect structural elements from moisture. For walls and partitions also see Section 2903.

1210.3 Showers. Shower compartments and walls above bathtubs with installed shower heads shall be finished with a smooth, nonabsorbent surface to a height not less than 70 inches (1778 mm) above the drain inlet.

1210.4 Waterproof joints. Built-in tubs with showers shall have waterproof joints between the tub and adjacent wall.

1210.5 Toilet rooms. Toilet rooms shall not open directly into a room used for the preparation of food for service to the public.

CHAPTER 13
ENERGY EFFICIENCY

SECTION 1301
GENERAL

1301.1 Scope. This chapter governs the design and construction of buildings for energy efficiency.

1301.1.1 Criteria. Buildings shall be designed and constructed in accordance with the *International Energy Conservation Code.*

CHAPTER 14
EXTERIOR WALLS

SECTION 1401 GENERAL

1401.1 Scope. The provisions of this chapter shall establish the minimum requirements for exterior walls; *exterior wall* coverings; *exterior wall* openings; exterior windows and doors; architectural *trim*; balconies and similar projections; and bay and oriel windows.

SECTION 1402 DEFINITIONS

1402.1 General. The following words and terms shall, for the purposes of this chapter and as used elsewhere in this code, have the meanings shown herein.

ADHERED MASONRY VENEER. Veneer secured and supported through the adhesion of an *approved* bonding material applied to an *approved* backing.

ANCHORED MASONRY VENEER. Veneer secured with *approved* mechanical fasteners to an *approved* backing.

BACKING. The wall or surface to which the veneer is secured.

EXTERIOR INSULATION AND FINISH SYSTEMS (EIFS). EIFS are nonstructural, nonload-bearing, *exterior wall* cladding systems that consist of an insulation board attached either adhesively or mechanically, or both, to the substrate; an integrally reinforced base coat and a textured protective finish coat.

EXTERIOR INSULATION AND FINISH SYSTEMS (EIFS) WITH DRAINAGE. An EIFS that incorporates a means of drainage applied over a *water-resistive barrier.*

EXTERIOR WALL. A wall, bearing or nonbearing, that is used as an enclosing wall for a building, other than a *fire wall*, and that has a slope of 60 degrees (1.05 rad) or greater with the horizontal plane.

EXTERIOR WALL COVERING. A material or assembly of materials applied on the exterior side of exterior walls for the purpose of providing a weather-resisting barrier, insulation or for aesthetics, including but not limited to, veneers, siding, exterior insulation and finish systems, architectural *trim* and embellishments such as cornices, soffits, facias, gutters and leaders.

EXTERIOR WALL ENVELOPE. A system or assembly of *exterior wall* components, including *exterior wall* finish materials, that provides protection of the building structural members, including framing and sheathing materials, and conditioned interior space, from the detrimental effects of the exterior environment.

FIBER-CEMENT SIDING. A manufactured, fiber-reinforcing product made with an inorganic hydraulic or calcium silicate binder formed by chemical reaction and reinforced with discrete organic or inorganic nonasbestos fibers, or both. Additives that enhance manufacturing or product performance are permitted. Fiber-cement siding products have either smooth or textured faces and are intended for *exterior wall* and related applications.

METAL COMPOSITE MATERIAL (MCM). A factory-manufactured panel consisting of metal skins bonded to both faces of a plastic core.

METAL COMPOSITE MATERIAL (MCM) SYSTEM. An *exterior wall* covering fabricated using MCM in a specific assembly including joints, seams, attachments, substrate, framing and other details as appropriate to a particular design.

VENEER. A facing attached to a wall for the purpose of providing ornamentation, protection or insulation, but not counted as adding strength to the wall.

VINYL SIDING. A shaped material, made principally from rigid polyvinyl chloride (PVC), that is used as an *exterior wall covering.*

WATER-RESISTIVE BARRIER. A material behind an *exterior wall covering* that is intended to resist liquid water that has penetrated behind the exterior covering from further intruding into the *exterior wall* assembly.

SECTION 1403 PERFORMANCE REQUIREMENTS

1403.1 General. The provisions of this section shall apply to exterior walls, wall coverings and components thereof.

1403.2 Weather protection. Exterior walls shall provide the building with a weather-resistant *exterior wall envelope.* The *exterior wall envelope* shall include flashing, as described in Section 1405.4. The *exterior wall envelope* shall be designed and constructed in such a manner as to prevent the accumulation of water within the wall assembly by providing a *water-resistive barrier* behind the exterior veneer, as described in Section 1404.2, and a means for draining water that enters the assembly to the exterior. Protection against condensation in the *exterior wall* assembly shall be provided in accordance with Section 1405.3.

Exceptions:

1. A weather-resistant *exterior wall envelope* shall not be required over concrete or masonry walls designed in accordance with Chapters 19 and 21, respectively.
2. Compliance with the requirements for a means of drainage, and the requirements of Sections 1404.2 and 1405.4, shall not be required for an *exterior wall envelope* that has been demonstrated through testing to resist wind-driven rain, including joints, penetrations and intersections with dissimilar materials, in

accordance with ASTM E 331 under the following conditions:

2.1. *Exterior wall envelope* test assemblies shall include at least one opening, one control joint, one wall/eave interface and one wall sill. All tested openings and penetrations shall be representative of the intended end-use configuration.

2.2. *Exterior wall envelope* test assemblies shall be at least 4 feet by 8 feet (1219 mm by 2438 mm) in size.

2.3. *Exterior wall envelope* assemblies shall be tested at a minimum differential pressure of 6.24 pounds per square foot (psf) (0.297 kN/m^2).

2.4. *Exterior wall envelope* assemblies shall be subjected to a minimum test exposure duration of 2 hours.

The *exterior wall envelope* design shall be considered to resist wind-driven rain where the results of testing indicate that water did not penetrate control joints in the *exterior wall* envelope, joints at the perimeter of openings or intersections of terminations with dissimilar materials.

3. Exterior insulation and finish systems (EIFS) complying with Section 1408.4.1.

1403.3 Structural. *Exterior walls*, and the associated openings, shall be designed and constructed to resist safely the superimposed loads required by Chapter 16.

1403.4 Fire resistance. *Exterior walls* shall be fire-resistance rated as required by other sections of this code with opening protection as required by Chapter 7.

1403.5 Flood resistance. For buildings in flood hazard areas as established in Section 1612.3, *exterior walls* extending below the design flood elevation shall be resistant to water damage. Wood shall be pressure-preservative treated in accordance with AWPA U1 for the species, product and end use using a preservative *listed* in Section 4 of AWPA U1 or decay-resistant heartwood of redwood, black locust or cedar.

1403.6 Flood resistance for high-velocity wave action areas. For buildings in flood hazard areas subject to high-velocity wave action as established in Section 1612.3, electrical, mechanical and plumbing system components shall not be mounted on or penetrate through exterior walls that are designed to break away under flood loads.

SECTION 1404
MATERIALS

1404.1 General. Materials used for the construction of exterior walls shall comply with the provisions of this section. Materials not prescribed herein shall be permitted, provided that any such alternative has been *approved.*

1404.2 Water-resistive barrier. A minimum of one layer of No.15 asphalt felt, complying with ASTM D 226 for Type 1 felt or other *approved* materials, shall be attached to the studs or sheathing, with flashing as described in Section 1405.4, in such a manner as to provide a continuous *water-resistive barrier* behind the *exterior wall* veneer.

1404.3 Wood. Exterior walls of wood construction shall be designed and constructed in accordance with Chapter 23.

1404.3.1 Basic hardboard. Basic hardboard shall conform to the requirements of AHA A135.4.

1404.3.2 Hardboard siding. Hardboard siding shall conform to the requirements of AHA A135.6 and, where used structurally, shall be so identified by the *label* of an *approved* agency.

1404.4 Masonry. Exterior walls of masonry construction shall be designed and constructed in accordance with this section and Chapter 21. Masonry units, mortar and metal accessories used in anchored and adhered veneer shall meet the physical requirements of Chapter 21. The backing of anchored and adhered veneer shall be of concrete, masonry, steel framing or wood framing.

1404.5 Metal. Exterior walls of formed steel construction, structural steel or lightweight metal alloys shall be designed in accordance with Chapters 22 and 20, respectively.

1404.5.1 Aluminum siding. Aluminum siding shall conform to the requirements of AAMA 1402.

1404.5.2 Cold-rolled copper. Copper shall conform to the requirements of ASTM B 370.

1404.5.3 Lead-coated copper. Lead-coated copper shall conform to the requirements of ASTM B 101.

1404.6 Concrete. Exterior walls of concrete construction shall be designed and constructed in accordance with Chapter 19.

1404.7 Glass-unit masonry. Exterior walls of glass-unit masonry shall be designed and constructed in accordance with Chapter 21.

1404.8 Plastics. Plastic panel, apron or spandrel walls as defined in this code shall not be limited in thickness, provided that such plastics and their assemblies conform to the requirements of Chapter 26 and are constructed of *approved* weather-resistant materials of adequate strength to resist the wind loads for cladding specified in Chapter 16.

1404.9 Vinyl siding. Vinyl siding shall be certified and labeled as conforming to the requirements of ASTM D 3679 by an *approved* quality control agency.

1404.10 Fiber-cement siding. Fiber-cement siding shall conform to the requirements of ASTM C 1186, Type A, and shall be so identified on labeling listing an *approved* quality control agency.

1404.11 Exterior insulation and finish systems. Exterior insulation and finish systems (EIFS) and exterior insulation and finish systems (EIFS) with drainage shall comply with Section 1408.

TABLE 1405.2
MINIMUM THICKNESS OF WEATHER COVERINGS

COVERING TYPE	MINIMUM THICKNESS (inches)
Adhered masonry veneer	0.25
Aluminum siding	0.019
Anchored masonry veneer	2.625
Asbestos-cement boards	0.125
Asbestos shingles	0.156
Cold-rolled copper[d]	0.0216 nominal
Copper shingles[d]	0.0162 nominal
Exterior plywood (with sheathing)	0.313
Exterior plywood (without sheathing)	See Section 2304.6
Fiber-cement lap siding	0.25[c]
Fiber-cement panel siding	0.25[c]
Fiberboard siding	0.5
Glass-fiber reinforced concrete panels	0.375
Hardboard siding[c]	0.25
High-yield copper[d]	0.0162 nominal
Lead-coated copper[d]	0.0216 nominal
Lead-coated high-yield copper	0.0162 nominal
Marble slabs	1
Particleboard (with sheathing)	See Section 2304.6
Particleboard (without sheathing)	See Section 2304.6
Precast stone facing	0.625
Steel (approved corrosion resistant)	0.0149
Stone (cast artificial)	1.5
Stone (natural)	2
Structural glass	0.344
Stucco or exterior cement plaster	
Three-coat work over:	
Metal plaster base	0.875[b]
Unit masonry	0.625[b]
Cast-in-place or precast concrete	0.625[b]
Two-coat work over:	
Unit masonry	0.5[b]
Cast-in-place or precast concrete	0.375[b]
Terra cotta (anchored)	1
Terra cotta (adhered)	0.25
Vinyl siding	0.035
Wood shingles	0.375
Wood siding (without sheathing)[a]	0.5

For SI: 1 inch = 25.4 mm, 1 ounce per square foot = 0.305 kg/m².

a. Wood siding of thicknesses less than 0.5 inch shall be placed over sheathing that conforms to Section 2304.6.

b. Exclusive of texture.

c. As measured at the bottom of decorative grooves.

d. 16 ounces per square foot for cold-rolled copper and lead-coated copper, 12 ounces per square foot for copper shingles, high-yield copper and lead-coated high-yield copper.

SECTION 1405 INSTALLATION OF WALL COVERINGS

1405.1 General. *Exterior wall coverings* shall be designed and constructed in accordance with the applicable provisions of this section.

1405.2 Weather protection. *Exterior walls* shall provide weather protection for the building. The materials of the minimum nominal thickness specified in Table 1405.2 shall be acceptable as *approved* weather coverings.

1405.3 Vapor retarders. Class I or II vapor retarders shall be provided on the interior side of frame walls in Zones 5, 6, 7, 8 and Marine 4.

Exceptions:

1. Basement walls.
2. Below-grade portion of any wall.
3. Construction where moisture or its freezing will not damage the materials.

1405.3.1 Class III vapor retarders. Class III vapor retarders shall be permitted where any one of the conditions in Table 1405.3.1 is met.

TABLE 1405.3.1
CLASS III VAPOR RETARDERS

ZONE	CLASS III VAPOR RETARDERS PERMITTED FOR:[a]
Marine 4	Vented cladding over OSB Vented cladding over plywood Vented cladding over fiberboard Vented cladding over gypsum Insulated sheathing with *R*-value ≥ R2.5 over 2×4 wall Insulated sheathing with *R*-value ≥ R3.75 over 2×6 wall
5	Vented cladding over OSB Vented cladding over plywood Vented cladding over fiberboard Vented cladding over gypsum Insulated sheathing with *R*-value ≥ R5 over 2×4 wall Insulated sheathing with *R*-value ≥ R7.5 over 2×6 wall
6	Vented cladding over fiberboard Vented cladding over gypsum Insulated sheathing with *R*-value ≥ R7.5 over 2×4 wall Insulated sheathing with *R*-value ≥ R11.25 over 2×6 wall
7 and 8	Insulated sheathing with *R*-value ≥ R10 over 2×4 wall Insulated sheathing with *R*-value ≥ R15 over 2×6 wall

For SI: 1 pound per cubic foot = 16.02 kg/m³.

a. Spray foam with a minimum density of 2 pounds per cubic feet applied to the interior cavity side of OSB, plywood, fiberboard, insulating sheathing or gypsum is deemed to meet the insulating sheathing requirement where the spray foam *R*-value meets or exceeds the specified insulating sheathing *R*-value.

1405.3.2 Material vapor retarder class. The *vapor retarder class* shall be based on the manufacturer's certified testing or a tested assembly.

The following shall be deemed to meet the class specified:

Class I: Sheet polyethylene, nonperforated aluminum foil

Class II: Kraft-faced fiberglass batts or paint with a perm rating greater than 0.1 and less than or equal to 1.0

Class III: Latex or enamel paint

1405.3.3 Minimum clear airspaces and vented openings for vented cladding. For the purposes of this section, vented cladding shall include the following minimum clear airspaces.

1. Vinyl lap or horizontal aluminum siding applied over a weather-resistive barrier as specified in this chapter.
2. Brick veneer with a clear airspace as specified in this code.
3. Other *approved* vented claddings.

1405.4 Flashing. Flashing shall be installed in such a manner so as to prevent moisture from entering the wall or to redirect it to the exterior. Flashing shall be installed at the perimeters of exterior door and window assemblies, penetrations and terminations of *exterior wall* assemblies, *exterior wall* intersections with roofs, chimneys, porches, decks, balconies and similar projections and at built-in gutters and similar locations where moisture could enter the wall. Flashing with projecting flanges shall be installed on both sides and the ends of copings, under sills and continuously above projecting *trim*.

1405.4.1 Exterior wall pockets. In exterior walls of buildings or structures, wall pockets or crevices in which moisture can accumulate shall be avoided or protected with caps or drips, or other *approved* means shall be provided to prevent water damage.

1405.4.2 Masonry. Flashing and weep holes in anchored veneer shall be located in the first course of masonry above finished ground level above the foundation wall or slab, and other points of support, including structural floors, shelf angles and lintels where anchored veneers are designed in accordance with Section 1405.6.

1405.5 Wood veneers. Wood veneers on exterior walls of buildings of Type I, II, III and IV construction shall be not less than 1 inch (25 mm) nominal thickness, 0.438-inch (11.1 mm) exterior hardboard siding or 0.375-inch (9.5 mm) exterior-type wood structural panels or particleboard and shall conform to the following:

1. The veneer shall not exceed 40 feet (12 190 mm) in height above grade. Where fire-retardant-treated wood is used, the height shall not exceed 60 feet (18 290 mm) in height above grade.
2. The veneer is attached to or furred from a noncombustible backing that is fire-resistance rated as required by other provisions of this code.
3. Where open or spaced wood veneers (without concealed spaces) are used, they shall not project more than 24 inches (610 mm) from the building wall.

1405.6 Anchored masonry veneer. Anchored masonry veneer shall comply with the provisions of Sections 1405.6, 1405.7, 1405.8 and 1405.9 and Sections 6.1 and 6.2 of TMS 402/ACI 530/ASCE 5.

1405.6.1 Tolerances. Anchored masonry veneers in accordance with Chapter 14 are not required to meet the tolerances in Article 3.3 F1 of TMS 602/ACI 530.1/ASCE 6.

1405.6.2 Seismic requirements. Anchored masonry veneer located in Seismic Design Category C, D, E or F shall conform to the requirements of Section 6.2.2.10 of TMS 402/ACI 530/ASCE 5. Anchored masonry veneer located in Seismic Design Category D shall also conform to the requirements of Section 6.2.2.10.3.3 of TMS 402/ACI 530/ASCE 5.

1405.7 Stone veneer. Stone veneer units not exceeding 10 inches (254 mm) in thickness shall be anchored directly to masonry, concrete or to stud construction by one of the following methods:

1. With concrete or masonry backing, anchor ties shall be not less than 0.1055-inch (2.68 mm) corrosion-resistant wire, or *approved* equal, formed beyond the base of the backing. The legs of the loops shall be not less than 6 inches (152 mm) in length bent at right angles and laid in the mortar joint, and spaced so that the eyes or loops are 12 inches (305 mm) maximum on center (o.c.) in both directions. There shall be provided not less than a 0.1055-inch (2.68 mm) corrosion-resistant wire tie, or *approved* equal, threaded through the exposed loops for every 2 square feet (0.2 m^2) of stone veneer. This tie shall be a loop having legs not less than 15 inches (381 mm) in length bent so that it will lie in the stone veneer mortar joint. The last 2 inches (51 mm) of each wire leg shall have a right-angle bend. One-inch (25 mm) minimum thickness of cement grout shall be placed between the backing and the stone veneer.
2. With stud backing, a 2-inch by 2-inch (51 mm by 51 mm) 0.0625-inch (1.59 mm) corrosion-resistant wire mesh with two layers of *water-resistive barrier* in accordance with Section 1404.2 shall be applied directly to wood studs spaced a maximum of 16 inches (406 mm) o.c. On studs, the mesh shall be attached with 2-inch-long (51 mm) corrosion-resistant steel wire furring nails at 4 inches (102 mm) o.c. providing a minimum 1.125-inch (29 mm) penetration into each stud and with 8d common nails at 8 inches (203 mm) o.c. into top and bottom plates or with equivalent wire ties. There shall be not less than a 0.1055-inch (2.68 mm) corrosion-resistant wire, or *approved* equal, looped through the mesh for every 2 square feet (0.2 m^2) of stone veneer. This tie shall be a loop having legs not less than 15 inches (381 mm) in length, so bent that it will lie in the stone veneer mortar joint. The last 2 inches (51 mm) of each wire leg shall have a right-angle bend. One-inch (25 mm) minimum thickness of cement grout shall be placed between the backing and the stone veneer.

1405.8 Slab-type veneer. Slab-type veneer units not exceeding 2 inches (51 mm) in thickness shall be anchored directly to masonry, concrete or stud construction. For veneer units of marble, travertine, granite or other stone units of slab form ties of corrosion-resistant dowels in drilled holes shall be located in the middle third of the edge of the units, spaced a maximum of 24 inches (610 mm) apart around the periphery of each unit with not less than four ties per veneer unit. Units shall not exceed 20 square feet (1.9 m^2) in area. If the dowels are not tight fitting, the holes shall be drilled not more than 0.063 inch (1.6 mm) larger in diameter than the dowel, with the hole countersunk to a diameter and depth equal to twice the diameter of the dowel in order to provide a tight-fitting key of cement mortar at the dowel locations when the mortar in the joint has set. Veneer ties shall be corrosion-resistant metal capable of resisting, in tension or compression, a force equal to two times the weight of the attached veneer. If made of sheet metal, veneer ties shall be not smaller in area than 0.0336 by 1 inch (0.853 by 25 mm) or, if made of wire, not smaller in diameter than 0.1483-inch (3.76 mm) wire.

1405.9 Terra cotta. Anchored terra cotta or ceramic units not less than 1$^5/_8$ inches (41 mm) thick shall be anchored directly to masonry, concrete or stud construction. Tied terra cotta or ceramic veneer units shall be not less than 1$^5/_8$ inches (41 mm) thick with projecting dovetail webs on the back surface spaced approximately 8 inches (203 mm) o.c. The facing shall be tied to the backing wall with corrosion-resistant metal anchors of not less than No. 8 gage wire installed at the top of each piece in horizontal bed joints not less than 12 inches (305 mm) nor more than 18 inches (457 mm) o.c.; these anchors shall be secured to $^1/_4$-inch (6.4 mm) corrosion-resistant pencil rods that pass through the vertical aligned loop anchors in the backing wall. The veneer ties shall have sufficient strength to support the full weight of the veneer in tension. The facing shall be set with not less than a 2-inch (51 mm) space from the backing wall and the space shall be filled solidly with portland cement grout and pea gravel. Immediately prior to setting, the backing wall and the facing shall be drenched with clean water and shall be distinctly damp when the grout is poured.

1405.10 Adhered masonry veneer. Adhered masonry veneer shall comply with the applicable requirements of Section 1405.10.1 and Sections 6.1 and 6.3 of TMS 402/ACI 530/ASCE 5.

1405.10.1 Interior adhered masonry veneers. Interior adhered masonry veneers shall have a maximum weight of 20 psf (0.958 kg/m^2) and shall be installed in accordance with Section 1405.10. Where the interior adhered masonry veneer is supported by wood construction, the supporting members shall be designed to limit deflection to $^1/_{600}$ of the span of the supporting members.

1405.11 Metal veneers. Veneers of metal shall be fabricated from *approved* corrosion-resistant materials or shall be protected front and back with porcelain enamel, or otherwise be treated to render the metal resistant to corrosion. Such veneers shall not be less than 0.0149-inch (0.378 mm) nominal thickness sheet steel mounted on wood or metal furring strips or approved sheathing on the wood construction.

1405.11.1 Attachment. Exterior metal veneer shall be securely attached to the supporting masonry or framing members with corrosion-resistant fastenings, metal ties or by other *approved* devices or methods. The spacing of the fastenings or ties shall not exceed 24 inches (610 mm) either vertically or horizontally, but where units exceed 4 square feet (0.4 m^2) in area there shall be not less than four attachments per unit. The metal attachments shall have a cross-sectional area not less than provided by W 1.7 wire. Such attachments and their supports shall be capable of resisting a horizontal force in accordance with the wind loads specified in Section 1609, but in no case less than 20 psf (0.958 kg/m^2).

1405.11.2 Weather protection. Metal supports for exterior metal veneer shall be protected by painting, galvanizing or by other equivalent coating or treatment. Wood studs, furring strips or other wood supports for exterior metal veneer shall be *approved* pressure-treated wood or protected as required in Section 1403.2. Joints and edges exposed to the weather shall be caulked with *approved* durable waterproofing material or by other *approved* means to prevent penetration of moisture.

1405.11.3 Backup. Masonry backup shall not be required for metal veneer except as is necessary to meet the fire-resistance requirements of this code.

1405.11.4 Grounding. Grounding of metal veneers on buildings shall comply with the requirements of Chapter 27 of this code.

1405.12 Glass veneer. The area of a single section of thin exterior structural glass veneer shall not exceed 10 square feet (0.93 m^2) where it is not more than 15 feet (4572 mm) above the level of the sidewalk or grade level directly below, and shall not exceed 6 square feet (0.56 m^2) where it is more than 15 feet (4572 mm) above that level.

1405.12.1 Length and height. The length or height of any section of thin exterior structural glass veneer shall not exceed 48 inches (1219 mm).

1405.12.2 Thickness. The thickness of thin exterior structural glass veneer shall be not less than 0.344 inch (8.7 mm).

1405.12.3 Application. Thin exterior structural glass veneer shall be set only after backing is thoroughly dry and after application of an *approved* bond coat uniformly over the entire surface of the backing so as to effectively seal the surface. Glass shall be set in place with an *approved* mastic cement in sufficient quantity so that at least 50 percent of the area of each glass unit is directly bonded to the backing by mastic not less than $^1/_4$ inch (6.4 mm) thick and not more than $^5/_8$ inch (15.9 mm) thick. The bond coat and mastic shall be evaluated for compatibility and shall bond firmly together.

1405.12.4 Installation at sidewalk level. Where glass extends to a sidewalk surface, each section shall rest in an *approved* metal molding, and be set at least $^1/_4$ inch (6.4 mm) above the highest point of the sidewalk. The space between the molding and the sidewalk shall be thoroughly caulked and made water tight.

1405.12.4.1 Installation above sidewalk level. Where thin exterior structural glass veneer is installed above the level of the top of a bulkhead facing, or at a level more than 36 inches (914 mm) above the sidewalk level, the mastic cement binding shall be supplemented with *approved* nonferrous metal shelf angles located in the horizontal joints in every course. Such shelf angles shall be not less than 0.0478-inch (1.2 mm) thick and not less than 2 inches (51 mm) long and shall be spaced at *approved* intervals, with not less than two angles for each glass unit. Shelf angles shall be secured to the wall or backing with expansion bolts, toggle bolts or by other *approved* methods.

1405.12.5 Joints. Unless otherwise specifically *approved* by the *building official*, abutting edges of thin exterior structural glass veneer shall be ground square. Mitered joints shall not be used except where specifically *approved* for wide angles. Joints shall be uniformly buttered with an *approved* jointing compound and horizontal joints shall be held to not less than 0.063 inch (1.6 mm) by an *approved* nonrigid substance or device. Where thin exterior structural glass veneer abuts nonresilient material at sides or top, expansion joints not less than $^1/_4$ inch (6.4 mm) wide shall be provided.

1405.12.6 Mechanical fastenings. Thin exterior structural glass veneer installed above the level of the heads of show windows and veneer installed more than 12 feet (3658 mm) above sidewalk level shall, in addition to the mastic cement and shelf angles, be held in place by the use of fastenings at each vertical or horizontal edge, or at the four corners of each glass unit. Fastenings shall be secured to the wall or backing with expansion bolts, toggle bolts or by other methods. Fastenings shall be so designed as to hold the glass veneer in a vertical plane independent of the mastic cement. Shelf angles providing both support and fastenings shall be permitted.

1405.12.7 Flashing. Exposed edges of thin exterior structural glass veneer shall be flashed with overlapping corrosion-resistant metal flashing and caulked with a waterproof compound in a manner to effectively prevent the entrance of moisture between the glass veneer and the backing.

1405.13 Exterior windows and doors. Windows and doors installed in exterior walls shall conform to the testing and performance requirements of Section 1715.5.

1405.13.1 Installation. Windows and doors shall be installed in accordance with *approved* manufacturer's instructions. Fastener size and spacing shall be provided in such instructions and shall be calculated based on maximum loads and spacing used in the tests.

1405.13.2 Window sills. In Occupancy Groups R-2 and R-3, one- and two-family and multiple-family dwellings, where the opening of the sill portion of an operable window is located more than 72 inches (1829 mm) above the finished grade or other surface below, the lowest part of the clear opening of the window shall be at a height not less than 24 inches (610 mm) above the finished floor surface of the room in which the window is located. Glazing between the floor and a height of 24 inches (610 mm) shall be fixed or have openings through which a 4-inch (102 mm) diameter sphere cannot pass.

Exception: Openings that are provided with window guards that comply with ASTM F 2006 or F 2090.

1405.14 Vinyl siding. Vinyl siding conforming to the requirements of this section and complying with ASTM D 3679 shall be permitted on exterior walls of buildings located in areas where the basic wind speed specified in Chapter 16 does not exceed 100 miles per hour (45 m/s) and the *building height* is less than or equal to 40 feet (12 192 mm) in Exposure C. Where construction is located in areas where the basic wind speed exceeds 100 miles per hour (45 m/s), or building heights are in excess of 40 feet (12 192 mm), tests or calculations indicating compliance with Chapter 16 shall be submitted. Vinyl siding shall be secured to the building so as to provide weather protection for the exterior walls of the building.

1405.14.1 Application. The siding shall be applied over sheathing or materials listed in Section 2304.6. Siding shall be applied to conform with the *water-resistive barrier* requirements in Section 1403. Siding and accessories shall be installed in accordance with *approved* manufacturer's instructions. Unless otherwise specified in the *approved* manufacturer's instructions, nails used to fasten the siding and accessories shall have a minimum 0.313-inch (7.9 mm) head diameter and $^1/_8$-inch (3.18 mm) shank diameter. The nails shall be corrosion resistant and shall be long enough to penetrate the studs or nailing strip at least $^3/_4$ inch (19 mm). Where the siding is installed horizontally, the fastener spacing shall not exceed 16 inches (406 mm) horizontally and 12 inches (305 mm) vertically. Where the siding is installed vertically, the fastener spacing shall not exceed 12 inches (305 mm) horizontally and 12 inches (305 mm) vertically.

1405.14.2 Flame spread. Vinyl siding and vinyl soffit materials when used in Group R buildings shall have a flame spread index of 25 or less as tested in accordance with ASTM E 84.

1405.15 Cement plaster. Cement plaster applied to exterior walls shall conform to the requirements specified in Chapter 25.

1405.16 Fiber-cement siding. Fiber-cement siding complying with Section 1404.10 shall be permitted on exterior walls of Type I, II, III, IV and V construction for wind pressure resistance or wind speed exposures as indicated by the manufacturer's listing and *label* and *approved* installation instructions. Where specified, the siding shall be installed over sheathing or materials *listed* in Section 2304.6 and shall be installed to conform to the *water-resistive barrier* requirements in Section 1403. Siding and accessories shall be installed in accordance with *approved* manufacturer's instructions. Unless otherwise specified in the *approved* manufacturer's instructions, nails used to fasten the siding to wood studs shall be corrosion-resistant round head smooth shank and shall be long enough to penetrate the studs at least 1 inch (25 mm). For metal framing, all-weather screws shall be used and shall penetrate the metal framing at least three full threads.

1405.16.1 Panel siding. Fiber-cement panels shall comply with the requirements of ASTM C 1186, Type A, minimum Grade II. Panels shall be installed with the long dimension either parallel or perpendicular to framing. Vertical and horizontal joints shall occur over framing members and shall be sealed with caulking, covered with battens or shall be designed to comply with Section 1403.2. Panel siding shall be installed with fasteners in accordance with the *approved* manufacturer's instructions.

1405.16.2 Lap siding. Fiber-cement lap siding having a maximum width of 12 inches (305 mm) shall comply with the requirements of ASTM C 1186, Type A, minimum Grade II. Lap siding shall be lapped a minimum of $1^1/_4$ inches (32 mm) and lap siding not having tongue-and-groove end joints shall have the ends sealed with caulking, covered with an H-section joint cover, located over a strip of flashing or shall be designed to comply with Section 1403.2. Lap siding courses shall be installed with the fastener heads exposed or concealed in accordance with the *approved* manufacturer's instructions.

1405.17 Fastening. Weather boarding and wall coverings shall be securely fastened with aluminum, copper, zinc, zinc-coated or other *approved* corrosion-resistant fasteners in accordance with the nailing schedule in Table 2304.9.1 or the *approved* manufacturer's installation instructions. Shingles and other weather coverings shall be attached with appropriate standard-shingle nails to furring strips securely nailed to studs, or with *approved* mechanically bonding nails, except where sheathing is of wood not less than 1-inch (25 mm) nominal thickness or of wood structural panels as specified in Table 2308.9.3(3).

SECTION 1406
COMBUSTIBLE MATERIALS ON THE EXTERIOR SIDE OF EXTERIOR WALLS

1406.1 General. Section 1406 shall apply to *exterior wall coverings*; balconies and similar projections; and bay and oriel windows constructed of combustible materials.

1406.2 Combustible exterior wall coverings. Combustible *exterior wall coverings* shall comply with this section.

Exception: Plastics complying with Chapter 26.

1406.2.1 Ignition resistance. Combustible *exterior wall coverings* shall be tested in accordance with NFPA 268.

Exceptions:

1 Wood or wood-based products.
2. Other combustible materials covered with an exterior covering other than vinyl sidings listed in Table 1405.2.
3. Aluminum having a minimum thickness of 0.019 inch (0.48 mm).
4. *Exterior wall coverings* on *exterior walls* of Type V construction.

1406.2.1.1 Fire separation 5 feet or less. Where installed on *exterior walls* having a *fire separation distance* of 5 feet (1524 mm) or less, combustible *exterior wall coverings* shall not exhibit sustained flaming as defined in NFPA 268.

1406.2.1.2 Fire separation greater than 5 feet. For fire separation distances greater than 5 feet (1524 mm), an assembly shall be permitted that has been exposed to a reduced level of incident radiant heat flux in accordance with the NFPA 268 test method without exhibiting sustained flaming. The minimum *fire separation distance* required for the assembly shall be determined from Table 1406.2.1.2 based on the maximum tolerable level of incident radiant heat flux that does not cause sustained flaming of the assembly.

TABLE 1406.2.1.2
MINIMUM FIRE SEPARATION FOR COMBUSTIBLE VENEERS

FIRE SEPARATION DISTANCE (feet)	TOLERABLE LEVEL INCIDENT RADIANT HEAT ENERGY(kW/m^2)	FIRE SEPARATION DISTANCE (feet)	TOLERABLE LEVEL INCIDENT RADIANT HEAT ENERGY(kW/m^2)
5	12.5	16	5.9
6	11.8	17	5.5
7	11.0	18	5.2
8	10.3	19	4.9
9	9.6	20	4.6
10	8.9	21	4.4
11	8.3	22	4.1
12	7.7	23	3.9
13	7.2	24	3.7
14	6.7	25	3.5
15	6.3		

For SI: 1 foot = 304.8 mm.

1406.2.2 Type I, II, III and IV construction. On buildings of Type I, II, III and IV construction, *exterior wall coverings* shall be permitted to be constructed of wood in accordance with Section 1405.5, or other equivalent combustible material, complying with the following limitations:

1. Combustible *exterior wall coverings* shall not exceed 10 percent of an *exterior wall* surface area where the *fire separation distance* is 5 feet (1524 mm) or less.
2. Combustible architectural *trim* shall be limited to 40 feet (12 192 mm) in height above grade.
3. Combustible *exterior wall coverings* constructed of *fire-retardant-treated wood* complying with Section 2303.2 for exterior installation shall not be limited in wall surface area where the *fire separation distance* is 5 feet (1524 mm) or less and shall be permitted up to 60 feet (18 288 mm) in height above grade regardless of the *fire separation distance*.

1406.2.3 Location. Where combustible *exterior wall covering* is located along the top of *exterior walls*, such *trim* shall be completely backed up by the *exterior wall* and shall not extend over or above the top of *exterior walls*.

1406.2.4 Fireblocking. Where the combustible *exterior wall covering* is furred from the wall and forms a solid surface, the distance between the back of the covering and the wall shall not exceed $1^5/_8$ inches (41 mm). Where required by Section 717, the space thereby created shall be fireblocked.

1406.3 Balconies and similar projections. Balconies and similar projections of combustible construction other than *fire-retardant-treated wood* shall be fire-resistance rated in accordance with Table 601 for floor construction or shall be of Type IV construction in accordance with Section 602.4. The aggregate length shall not exceed 50 percent of the buildings perimeter on each floor.

Exceptions:

1. On buildings of Type I and II construction, three stories or less above *grade plane*, *fire-retardant-treated*

wood shall be permitted for balconies, porches, decks and exterior stairways not used as required exits.

2. Untreated wood is permitted for pickets and rails or similar guardrail devices that are limited to 42 inches (1067 mm) in height.
3. Balconies and similar projections on buildings of Type III, IV and V construction shall be permitted to be of Type V construction, and shall not be required to have a *fire-resistance rating* where sprinkler protection is extended to these areas.
4. Where sprinkler protection is extended to the balcony areas, the aggregate length of the balcony on each floor shall not be limited.

1406.4 Bay windows and oriel windows. Bay and oriel windows shall conform to the type of construction required for the building to which they are attached.

Exception: *Fire-retardant-treated wood* shall be permitted on buildings three stories or less of Type I, II, III and IV construction.

SECTION 1407
METAL COMPOSITE MATERIALS (MCM)

1407.1 General. The provisions of this section shall govern the materials, construction and quality of metal composite materials (MCM) for use as *exterior wall coverings* in addition to other applicable requirements of Chapters 14 and 16.

1407.1.1 Plastic core. The plastic core of the MCM shall not contain foam plastic insulation as defined in Section 2602.1.

1407.2 Exterior wall finish. MCM used as *exterior wall* finish or as elements of balconies and similar projections and bay and oriel windows to provide cladding or weather resistance shall comply with Sections 1407.4 through 1407.14.

1407.3 Architectural trim and embellishments. MCM used as architectural *trim* or embellishments shall comply with Sections 1407.7 through 1407.14.

1407.4 Structural design. MCM systems shall be designed and constructed to resist wind loads as required by Chapter 16 for components and cladding.

1407.5 Approval. Results of *approved* tests or an engineering analysis shall be submitted to the *building official* to verify compliance with the requirements of Chapter 16 for wind loads.

1407.6 Weather resistance. MCM systems shall comply with Section 1403 and shall be designed and constructed to resist wind and rain in accordance with this section and the manufacturer's installation instructions.

1407.7 Durability. MCM systems shall be constructed of *approved* materials that maintain the performance characteristics required in Section 1407 for the duration of use.

1407.8 Fire-resistance rating. Where MCM systems are used on exterior walls required to have a *fire-resistance rating* in accordance with Section 705, evidence shall be submitted to the *building official* that the required *fire-resistance rating* is maintained.

Exception: MCM systems not containing foam plastic insulation, which are installed on the outer surface of a fire-resistance-rated *exterior wall* in a manner such that the attachments do not penetrate through the entire *exterior wall* assembly, shall not be required to comply with this section.

1407.9 Surface-burning characteristics. Unless otherwise specified, MCM shall have a *flame spread index* of 75 or less and a smoke-developed index of 450 or less when tested in the maximum thickness intended for use in accordance with ASTM E 84 or UL 723.

1407.10 Type I, II, III and IV construction. Where installed on buildings of Type I, II, III and IV construction, MCM systems shall comply with Sections 1407.10.1 through 1407.10.4, or Section1407.11.

1407.10.1 Surface-burning characteristics. MCM shall have a *flame spread index* of not more than 25 and a smoke-developed index of not more than 450 when tested as an assembly in the maximum thickness intended for use in accordance with ASTM E 84 or UL 723.

1407.10.2 Thermal barriers. MCM shall be separated from the interior of a building by an *approved* thermal barrier consisting of $^1/_2$-inch (12.7 mm) gypsum wallboard or equivalent thermal barrier material that will limit the average temperature rise of the unexposed surface to not more than 250°F (121°C) after 15 minutes of fire exposure in accordance with the standard time-temperature curve of ASTM E 119 or UL 263. The thermal barrier shall be installed in such a manner that it will remain in place for not less than 15 minutes based on a test conducted in accordance with UL 1715.

1407.10.3 Thermal barrier not required. The thermal barrier specified for MCM in Section 1407.10.2 is not required where:

1. The MCM system is specifically *approved* based on tests conducted in accordance with UL 1040 or UL 1715. Such testing shall be performed with the MCM in the maximum thickness intended for use. The MCM system shall include seams, joints and other typical details used in the installation and shall be tested in the manner intended for use.
2. The MCM is used as elements of balconies and similar projections, architectural *trim* or embellishments.

1407.10.4 Full-scale tests. The MCM system shall be tested in accordance with, and comply with, the acceptance criteria of NFPA 285. Such testing shall be performed on the MCM system with the MCM in the maximum thickness intended for use.

1407.11 Alternate conditions. MCM and MCM systems shall not be required to comply with Sections 1407.10.1 through 1407.10.4 provided such systems comply with Section 1407.11.1 or 1407.11.2.

1407.11.1 Installations up to 40 feet in height. MCM shall not be installed more than 40 feet (12 190 mm) in height above grade where installed in accordance with Sections 1407.11.1.1 and 1407.11.1.2.

1407.11.1.1 Fire separation distance of 5 feet or less. Where the *fire separation distance* is 5 feet (1524 mm) or less, the area of MCM shall not exceed 10 percent of the *exterior wall* surface.

1407.11.1.2 Fire separation distance greater than 5 feet. Where the *fire separation distance* is greater than 5 feet (1524 mm), there shall be no limit on the area of *exterior wall* surface coverage using MCM.

1407.11.2 Installations up to 50 feet in height. MCM shall not be installed more than 50 feet (15 240 mm) in height above grade where installed in accordance with Sections 1407.11.2.1 and 1407.11.2.2.

1407.11.2.1 Self-ignition temperature. MCM shall have a self-ignition temperature of 650°F (343°C) or greater when tested in accordance with ASTM D 1929.

1407.11.2.2 Limitations. Sections of MCM shall not exceed 300 square feet (27.9 m^2) in area and shall be separated by a minimum of 4 feet (1219 mm) vertically.

1407.12 Type V construction. MCM shall be permitted to be installed on buildings of Type V construction.

1407.13 Foam plastic insulation. MCM systems containing foam plastic insulation shall also comply with the requirements of Section 2603.

1407.14 Labeling. MCM shall be labeled in accordance with Section 1703.5.

SECTION 1408
EXTERIOR INSULATION AND FINISH SYSTEMS (EIFS)

1408.1 General. The provisions of this section shall govern the materials, construction and quality of exterior insulation and finish systems (EIFS) for use as *exterior wall coverings* in addition to other applicable requirements of Chapters 7, 14, 16, 17 and 26.

1408.2 Performance characteristics. EIFS shall be constructed such that it meets the performance characteristics required in ASTM E 2568.

1408.3 Structural design. The underlying structural framing and substrate shall be designed and constructed to resist loads as required by Chapter 16.

1408.4 Weather resistance. EIFS shall comply with Section 1403 and shall be designed and constructed to resist wind and rain in accordance with this section and the manufacturer's application instructions.

1408.4.1 EIFS with drainage. EIFS with drainage shall have an average minimum drainage efficiency of 90 percent when tested in accordance the requirements of ASTM E 2273 and is required on framed walls of Type V construction, Group R1, R2, R3 and R4 occupancies.

1408.4.1.1 Water-resistive barrier. For EIFS with drainage, the *water-resistive barrier* shall comply with Section 1404.2 or ASTM E 2570.

1408.5 Installation. Installation of the EIFS and EIFS with drainage shall be in accordance with the EIFS manufacturer's instructions.

1408.6 Special inspections. EIFS installations shall comply with the provisions of Sections 1704.1 and 1704.14.

CHAPTER 15

ROOF ASSEMBLIES AND ROOFTOP STRUCTURES

SECTION 1501 GENERAL

1501.1 Scope. The provisions of this chapter shall govern the design, materials, construction and quality of roof assemblies, and rooftop structures.

SECTION 1502 DEFINITIONS

1502.1 General. The following words and terms shall, for the purposes of this chapter and as used elsewhere in this code, have the meanings shown herein.

AGGREGATE. In roofing, crushed stone, crushed slag or water-worn gravel used for surfacing for roof coverings.

BALLAST. In roofing, ballast comes in the form of large stones or paver systems or light-weight interlocking paver systems and is used to provide uplift resistance for roofing systems that are not adhered or mechanically attached to the roof deck.

BUILT-UP ROOF COVERING. Two or more layers of felt cemented together and surfaced with a cap sheet, mineral aggregate, smooth coating or similar surfacing material.

INTERLAYMENT. A layer of felt or nonbituminous saturated felt not less than 18 inches (457 mm) wide, shingled between each course of a wood-shake roof covering.

MECHANICAL EQUIPMENT SCREEN. A partially enclosed *rooftop structure* used to aesthetically conceal heating, ventilating and air conditioning (HVAC) electrical or mechanical equipment from view.

METAL ROOF PANEL. An interlocking metal sheet having a minimum installed weather exposure of 3 square feet (0.279 m^2) per sheet.

METAL ROOF SHINGLE. An interlocking metal sheet having an installed weather exposure less than 3 square feet (0.279 m^2) per sheet.

MODIFIED BITUMEN ROOF COVERING. One or more layers of polymer-modified asphalt sheets. The sheet materials shall be fully adhered or mechanically attached to the substrate or held in place with an *approved* ballast layer.

PENTHOUSE. An enclosed, unoccupied structure above the roof of a building, other than a tank, tower, spire, dome cupola or bulkhead.

POSITIVE ROOF DRAINAGE. The drainage condition in which consideration has been made for all loading deflections of the roof deck, and additional slope has been provided to ensure drainage of the roof within 48 hours of precipitation.

REROOFING. The process of recovering or replacing an existing roof covering. See "Roof recover" and "Roof replacement."

ROOF ASSEMBLY. A system designed to provide weather protection and resistance to design loads. The system consists of a roof covering and roof deck or a single component serving as both the roof covering and the roof deck. A roof assembly includes the roof deck, *vapor retarder*, substrate or thermal barrier, insulation, *vapor retarder* and roof covering.

The definition of "Roof assembly" is limited in application to the provisions of Chapter 15.

ROOF COVERING. The covering applied to the roof deck for weather resistance, fire classification or appearance.

ROOF COVERING SYSTEM. See "Roof assembly."

ROOF DECK. The flat or sloped surface not including its supporting members or vertical supports.

ROOF RECOVER. The process of installing an additional roof covering over a prepared existing roof covering without removing the existing roof covering.

ROOF REPAIR. Reconstruction or renewal of any part of an existing roof for the purposes of its maintenance.

ROOF REPLACEMENT. The process of removing the existing roof covering, repairing any damaged substrate and installing a new roof covering.

ROOF VENTILATION. The natural or mechanical process of supplying conditioned or unconditioned air to, or removing such air from, attics, cathedral ceilings or other enclosed spaces over which a roof assembly is installed.

ROOFTOP STRUCTURE. An enclosed structure on or above the roof of any part of a building.

SCUPPER. An opening in a wall or parapet that allows water to drain from a roof.

SINGLE-PLY MEMBRANE. A roofing membrane that is field applied using one layer of membrane material (either homogeneous or composite) rather than multiple layers.

UNDERLAYMENT. One or more layers of felt, sheathing paper, nonbituminous saturated felt or other *approved* material over which a steep-slope roof covering is applied.

SECTION 1503 WEATHER PROTECTION

1503.1 General. Roof decks shall be covered with *approved* roof coverings secured to the building or structure in accordance with the provisions of this chapter. Roof coverings shall be designed and installed in accordance with this code and the *approved* manufacturer's instructions such that the roof covering shall serve to protect the building or structure.

1503.2 Flashing. Flashing shall be installed in such a manner so as to prevent moisture entering the wall and roof through joints in copings, through moisture-permeable materials and at intersections with parapet walls and other penetrations through the roof plane.

1503.2.1 Locations. Flashing shall be installed at wall and roof intersections, at gutters, wherever there is a change in roof slope or direction and around roof openings. Where flashing is of metal, the metal shall be corrosion resistant with a thickness of not less than 0.019 inch (0.483 mm) (No. 26 galvanized sheet).

1503.3 Coping. Parapet walls shall be properly coped with noncombustible, weatherproof materials of a width no less than the thickness of the parapet wall.

[P] 1503.4 Roof drainage. Design and installation of roof drainage systems shall comply with Section 1503 and the *International Plumbing Code*.

1503.4.1 Secondary drainage required. Secondary (emergency) roof drains or scuppers shall be provided where the roof perimeter construction extends above the roof in such a manner that water will be entrapped if the primary drains allow buildup for any reason.

1503.4.2 Scuppers. When scuppers are used for secondary (emergency overflow) roof drainage, the quantity, size, location and inlet elevation of the scuppers shall be sized to prevent the depth of ponding water from exceeding that for which the roof was designed as determined by Section 1611.1. Scuppers shall not have an opening dimension of less than 4 inches (102 mm). The flow through the primary system shall not be considered when locating and sizing scuppers.

1503.4.3 Gutters. Gutters and leaders placed on the outside of buildings, other than Group R-3, private garages and buildings of Type V construction, shall be of noncombustible material or a minimum of Schedule 40 plastic pipe.

1503.5 Roof ventilation. Intake and exhaust vents shall be provided in accordance with Section 1203.2 and the manufacturer's installation instructions.

1503.6 Crickets and saddles. A cricket or saddle shall be installed on the ridge side of any chimney or penetration greater than 30 inches (762 mm) wide as measured perpendicular to the slope. Cricket or saddle coverings shall be sheet metal or of the same material as the roof covering.

SECTION 1504
PERFORMANCE REQUIREMENTS

1504.1 Wind resistance of roofs. Roof decks and roof coverings shall be designed for wind loads in accordance with Chapter 16 and Sections 1504.2, 1504.3 and 1504.4.

1504.1.1 Wind resistance of asphalt shingles. Asphalt shingles shall comply with Section 1507.2.7.

1504.2 Wind resistance of clay and concrete tile. Wind loads on clay and concrete tile roof coverings shall be in accordance with Section 1609.5.

1504.3 Wind resistance of nonballasted roofs. Roof coverings installed on roofs in accordance with Section 1507 that are mechanically attached or adhered to the roof deck shall be designed to resist the design wind load pressures for components and cladding in accordance with Section 1609.

1504.3.1 Other roof systems. Roof systems with built-up, modified bitumen, fully adhered or mechanically attached single-ply through fastened metal panel roof systems, and other types of membrane roof coverings shall also be tested in accordance with FM 4474, UL 580 or UL 1897.

1504.3.2 Metal panel roof systems. Metal panel roof systems through fastened or standing seam shall be tested in accordance with UL 580 or ASTM E 1592.

Exception: Metal roofs constructed of cold-formed steel, where the roof deck acts as the roof covering and provides both weather protection and support for structural loads, shall be permitted to be designed and tested in accordance with the applicable referenced structural design standard in Section 2209.1.

1504.4 Ballasted low-slope roof systems. Ballasted low-slope (roof slope < 2:12) single-ply roof system coverings installed in accordance with Sections 1507.12 and 1507.13 shall be designed in accordance with Section 1504.8 and ANSI/SPRI RP-4.

1504.5 Edge securement for low-slope roofs. Low-slope membrane roof system metal edge securement, except gutters, shall be designed and installed for wind loads in accordance with Chapter 16 and tested for resistance in accordance with ANSI/SPRI ES-1, except the basic wind speed shall be determined from Figure 1609.

1504.6 Physical properties. Roof coverings installed on low-slope roofs (roof slope < 2:12) in accordance with Section 1507 shall demonstrate physical integrity over the working life of the roof based upon 2,000 hours of exposure to accelerated weathering tests conducted in accordance with ASTM G 152, ASTM G 155 or ASTM G 154. Those roof coverings that are subject to cyclical flexural response due to wind loads shall not demonstrate any significant loss of tensile strength for unreinforced membranes or breaking strength for reinforced membranes when tested as herein required.

1504.7 Impact resistance. Roof coverings installed on low-slope roofs (roof slope < 2:12) in accordance with Section 1507 shall resist impact damage based on the results of tests conducted in accordance with ASTM D 3746, ASTM D 4272, CGSB 37-GP-52M or the "Resistance to Foot Traffic Test" in Section 5.5 of FM 4470.

1504.8 Aggregate. Aggregate used as surfacing for roof coverings and aggregate, gravel or stone used as ballast shall not be used on the roof of a building located in a hurricane-prone region as defined in Section 1609.2, or on any other building with a mean roof height exceeding that permitted by Table 1504.8 based on the exposure category and basic wind speed at the site.

TABLE 1504.8
MAXIMUM ALLOWABLE MEAN ROOF HEIGHT PERMITTED FOR BUILDINGS WITH AGGREGATE ON THE ROOF IN AREAS OUTSIDE A HURRICANE-PRONE REGION

BASIC WIND SPEED FROM FIGURE 1609 (mph)[b]	MAXIMUM MEAN ROOF HEIGHT (ft)[a, c]		
	Exposure category		
	B	C	D
85	170	60	30
90	110	35	15
95	75	20	NP
100	55	15	NP
105	40	NP	NP
110	30	NP	NP
115	20	NP	NP
120	15	NP	NP
Greater than 120	NP	NP	NP

For SI: 1 foot = 304.8 mm; 1 mile per hour = 0.447 m/s.

a. Mean roof height as defined in ASCE 7.

b. For intermediate values of basic wind speed, the height associated with the next higher value of wind speed shall be used, or direct interpolation is permitted.

c. NP = gravel and stone not permitted for any roof height.

SECTION 1505 FIRE CLASSIFICATION

1505.1 General. Roof assemblies shall be divided into the classes defined below. Class A, B and C roof assemblies and roof coverings required to be listed by this section shall be tested in accordance with ASTM E 108 or UL 790. In addition, *fire-retardant-treated wood* roof coverings shall be tested in accordance with ASTM D 2898. The minimum roof coverings installed on buildings shall comply with Table 1505.1 based on the type of construction of the building.

Exception: Skylights and sloped glazing that comply with Chapter 24 or Section 2610.

TABLE 1505.1[a, b]
MINIMUM ROOF COVERING CLASSIFICATION FOR TYPES OF CONSTRUCTION

IA	IB	IIA	IIB	IIIA	IIIB	IV	VA	VB
B	B	B	C[c]	B	C[c]	B	B	C[c]

For SI: 1 foot = 304.8 mm, 1 square foot = 0.0929 m^2.

a. Unless otherwise required in accordance with the *International Wildland-Urban Interface Code* or due to the location of the building within a fire district in accordance with Appendix D.

b. Nonclassified roof coverings shall be permitted on buildings of Group R-3 and Group U occupancies, where there is a minimum fire-separation distance of 6 feet measured from the leading edge of the roof.

c. Buildings that are not more than two stories above grade plane and having not more than 6,000 square feet of projected roof area and where there is a minimum 10-foot fire-separation distance from the leading edge of the roof to a lot line on all sides of the building, except for street fronts or public ways, shall be permitted to have roofs of No. 1 cedar or redwood shakes and No. 1 shingles.

1505.2 Class A roof assemblies. Class A roof assemblies are those that are effective against severe fire test exposure. Class A roof assemblies and roof coverings shall be *listed* and identified as Class A by an *approved* testing agency. Class A roof assemblies shall be permitted for use in buildings or structures of all types of construction.

Exceptions:

1. Class A roof assemblies include those with coverings of brick, masonry or an exposed concrete roof deck.
2. Class A roof assemblies also include ferrous or copper shingles or sheets, metal sheets and shingles, clay or concrete roof tile or slate installed on noncombustible decks or ferrous, copper or metal sheets installed without a roof deck on noncombustible framing.

1505.3 Class B roof assemblies. Class B roof assemblies are those that are effective against moderate fire-test exposure. Class B roof assemblies and roof coverings shall be *listed* and identified as Class B by an *approved* testing agency.

1505.4 Class C roof assemblies. Class C roof assemblies are those that are effective against light fire-test exposure. Class C roof assemblies and roof coverings shall be *listed* and identified as Class C by an *approved* testing agency.

1505.5 Nonclassified roofing. Nonclassified roofing is *approved* material that is not *listed* as a Class A, B or C roof covering.

1505.6 Fire-retardant-treated wood shingles and shakes. *Fire-retardant-treated wood* shakes and shingles shall be treated by impregnation with chemicals by the full-cell vacuum-pressure process, in accordance with AWPA C1. Each bundle shall be marked to identify the manufactured unit and the manufacturer, and shall also be labeled to identify the classification of the material in accordance with the testing required in Section 1505.1, the treating company and the quality control agency.

1505.7 Special purpose roofs. Special purpose wood shingle or wood shake roofing shall conform with the grading and application requirements of Section 1507.8 or 1507.9. In addition, an underlayment of $^5/_8$-inch (15.9 mm) Type X water-resistant gypsum backing board or gypsum sheathing shall be placed under minimum nominal $^1/_2$-inch-thick (12.7 mm) wood structural panel solid sheathing or 1-inch (25 mm) nominal spaced sheathing.

SECTION 1506 MATERIALS

1506.1 Scope. The requirements set forth in this section shall apply to the application of roof-covering materials specified herein. Roof coverings shall be applied in accordance with this chapter and the manufacturer's installation instructions. Installation of roof coverings shall comply with the applicable provisions of Section 1507.

1506.2 Compatibility of materials. Roofs and roof coverings shall be of materials that are compatible with each other and with the building or structure to which the materials are applied.

1506.3 Material specifications and physical characteristics. Roof-covering materials shall conform to the applicable standards *listed* in this chapter. In the absence of applicable standards or where materials are of questionable suitability, testing by an *approved* agency shall be required by the *building code official* to determine the character, quality and limitations of application of the materials.

1506.4 Product identification. Roof-covering materials shall be delivered in packages bearing the manufacturer's identifying marks and *approved* testing agency labels required in accordance with Section 1505. Bulk shipments of materials shall be accompanied with the same information issued in the form of a certificate or on a bill of lading by the manufacturer.

SECTION 1507 REQUIREMENTS FOR ROOF COVERINGS

1507.1 Scope. Roof coverings shall be applied in accordance with the applicable provisions of this section and the manufacturer's installation instructions.

1507.2 Asphalt shingles. The installation of asphalt shingles shall comply with the provisions of this section.

1507.2.1 Deck requirements. Asphalt shingles shall be fastened to solidly sheathed decks.

1507.2.2 Slope. Asphalt shingles shall only be used on roof slopes of two units vertical in 12 units horizontal (17-percent slope) or greater. For roof slopes from two units vertical in 12 units horizontal (17-percent slope) up to four units vertical in 12 units horizontal (33-percent slope), double underlayment application is required in accordance with Section 1507.2.8.

1507.2.3 Underlayment. Unless otherwise noted, required underlayment shall conform to ASTM D 226, Type I, ASTM D 4869, Type I, or ASTM D 6757.

1507.2.4 Self-adhering polymer modified bitumen sheet. Self-adhering polymer modified bitumen sheet shall comply with ASTM D 1970.

1507.2.5 Asphalt shingles. Asphalt shingles shall comply with ASTM D 225 or ASTM D 3462.

1507.2.6 Fasteners. Fasteners for asphalt shingles shall be galvanized, stainless steel, aluminum or copper roofing nails, minimum 12 gage [0.105 inch (2.67 mm)] shank with a minimum $^3/_8$ inch-diameter (9.5 mm) head, of a length to penetrate through the roofing materials and a minimum of $^3/_4$ inch (19.1 mm) into the roof sheathing. Where the roof sheathing is less than $^3/_4$ inch (19.1 mm) thick, the nails shall penetrate through the sheathing. Fasteners shall comply with ASTM F 1667.

1507.2.7 Attachment. Asphalt shingles shall have the minimum number of fasteners required by the manufacturer, but not less than four fasteners per strip shingle or two fasteners per individual shingle. Where the roof slope exceeds 21 units vertical in 12 units horizontal (21:12), shingles shall be installed as required by the manufacturer.

1507.2.7.1 Wind resistance. Asphalt shingles shall be tested in accordance with ASTM D 7158. Asphalt shingles shall meet the classification requirements of Table 1507.2.7.1(1) for the appropriate maximum basic wind speed. Asphalt shingle packaging shall bear a label to indicate compliance with ASTM D 7158 and the required classification in Table 1507.2.7.1(1).

Exception: Asphalt shingles not included in the scope of ASTM D 7158 shall be tested and labeled to indicate compliance with ASTM D 3161 and the required classification in Table 1507.2.7.1(2).

TABLE 1507.2.7.1(1) CLASSIFICATION OF ASPHALT ROOF SHINGLES PER ASTM D 7158[a]

MAXIMUM BASIC WIND SPEED (mph) FROM FIGURE 1609	CLASSIFICATION REQUIREMENT
85	D, G or H
90	D, G or H
100	G or H
110	G or H
120	G or H
130	H
140	H
150	H

For SI: 1 foot = 304.8 mm, 1 mile per hour = 0.447 m/s.

a. The standard calculations contained in ASTM D 7158 assume exposure category B or C and building height of 60 feet (18 288 mm) or less. Additional calculations are required for conditions outside of these assumptions.

TABLE 1507.2.7.1(2) CLASSIFICATION OF ASPHALT SHINGLES PER ASTM D 3161

MAXIMUM BASIC WIND SPEED (mph) FROM FIGURE 1609	CLASSIFICATION REQUIREMENT
85	A, D or F
90	A, D or F
100	A, D or F
110	F
120	F
130	F
140	F
150	F

For SI: 1 mile per hour = 0.447 m/s.

1507.2.8 Underlayment application. For roof slopes from two units vertical in 12 units horizontal (17-percent slope) and up to four units vertical in 12 units horizontal (33-percent slope), underlayment shall be two layers applied in the following manner. Apply a minimum 19-inch-wide (483 mm) strip of underlayment felt parallel with and starting at the eaves, fastened sufficiently to hold in place. Starting at the eave, apply 36-inch-wide (914 mm) sheets of underlayment overlapping successive sheets 19 inches (483 mm), by fastened sufficiently to hold in place. Distortions in the underlayment shall not interfere with the ability of the shingles to seal. For roof slopes of four units vertical in 12 units horizontal (33-percent slope) or greater, underlayment shall be one layer applied in the following manner. Underlayment shall be applied shingle fashion, parallel to and starting from the eave and lapped 2 inches (51 mm), fastened sufficiently to hold in place. Distortions in the underlayment shall not interfere with the ability of the shingles to seal.

1507.2.8.1 High wind attachment. Underlayment applied in areas subject to high winds [greater than 110 mph (49.2 m/s) in accordance with Figure 1609] shall be applied with corrosion-resistant fasteners in accordance with the manufacturer's instructions. Fasteners are to be applied along the overlap at a maximum spacing of 36 inches (914 mm) on center.

1507.2.8.2 Ice barrier. In areas where there has been a history of ice forming along the eaves causing a backup of water, an ice barrier that consists of at least two layers of underlayment cemented together or of a self-adhering polymer modified bitumen sheet shall be used in lieu of normal underlayment and extend from the lowest edges of all roof surfaces to a point at least 24 inches (610 mm) inside the *exterior wall* line of the building.

Exception: Detached accessory structures that contain no conditioned floor area.

1507.2.9 Flashings. Flashing for asphalt shingles shall comply with this section. Flashing shall be applied in accordance with this section and the asphalt shingle manufacturer's printed instructions.

1507.2.9.1 Base and cap flashing. Base and cap flashing shall be installed in accordance with the manufacturer's instructions. Base flashing shall be of either corrosion-resistant metal of minimum nominal 0.019-inch (0.483 mm) thickness or mineral-surfaced roll roofing weighing a minimum of 77 pounds per 100 square feet (3.76 kg/m^2). Cap flashing shall be corrosion-resistant metal of minimum nominal 0.019-inch (0.483 mm) thickness.

1507.2.9.2 Valleys. Valley linings shall be installed in accordance with the manufacturer's instructions before applying shingles. Valley linings of the following types shall be permitted:

1. For open valleys (valley lining exposed) lined with metal, the valley lining shall be at least 24 inches (610 mm) wide and of any of the corrosion-resistant metals in Table 1507.2.9.2.
2. For open valleys, valley lining of two plies of mineral-surfaced roll roofing complying with ASTM D 3909 or ASTM D 6380 shall be permitted. The bottom layer shall be 18 inches (457 mm) and the top layer a minimum of 36 inches (914 mm) wide.
3. For closed valleys (valleys covered with shingles), valley lining of one ply of smooth roll roofing complying with ASTM D 6380, and at least 36 inches (914 mm) wide or types as described in Item 1 or 2 above shall be permitted. Self-adhering polymer modified bitumen underlayment complying with ASTM D 1970 shall be permitted in lieu of the lining material.

1507.2.9.3 Drip edge. Provide drip edge at eaves and gables of shingle roofs. Overlap to be a minimum of 2 inches (51 mm). Eave drip edges shall extend $^1/_4$ inch (6.4 mm) below sheathing and extend back on the roof a minimum of 2 inches (51 mm). Drip edge shall be mechanically fastened a maximum of 12 inches (305 mm) o.c.

1507.3 Clay and concrete tile. The installation of clay and concrete tile shall comply with the provisions of this section.

1507.3.1 Deck requirements. Concrete and clay tile shall be installed only over solid sheathing or spaced structural sheathing boards.

1507.3.2 Deck slope. Clay and concrete roof tile shall be installed on roof slopes of 2$^1/_2$ units vertical in 12 units horizontal (21-percent slope) or greater. For roof slopes from

**TABLE 1507.2.9.2
VALLEY LINING MATERIAL**

MATERIAL	MINIMUM THICKNESS	GAGE	WEIGHT
Aluminum	0.024 in.	—	—
Cold-rolled copper	0.0216 in.	—	ASTM B 370, 16 oz. per square ft.
Copper	—	—	16 oz
Galvanized steel	0.0179 in.	26 (zinc-coated G90)	—
High-yield copper	0.0162 in.	—	ASTM B 370, 12 oz. per square ft.
Lead	—	—	2.5 pounds
Lead-coated copper	0.0216 in.	—	ASTM B 101, 16 oz. per square ft.
Lead-coated high-yield copper	0.0162 in.	—	ASTM B 101, 12 oz. per square ft.
Painted terne	—	—	20 pounds
Stainless steel	—	28	—
Zinc alloy	0.027 in.	—	—

For SI: 1 inch = 25.4 mm, 1 pound = 0.454 kg, 1 ounce = 28.35 g, 1 ounce per square foot = 305.15 g/m^2.

$2^1/_2$ units vertical in 12 units horizontal (21-percent slope) to four units vertical in 12 units horizontal (33-percent slope), double underlayment application is required in accordance with Section 1507.3.3.

1507.3.3 Underlayment. Unless otherwise noted, required underlayment shall conform to: ASTM D 226, Type II; ASTM D 2626 or ASTM D 6380, Class M mineral-surfaced roll roofing.

1507.3.3.1 Low-slope roofs. For roof slopes from $2^1/_2$ units vertical in 12 units horizontal (21-percent slope), up to four units vertical in 12 units horizontal (33-percent slope), underlayment shall be a minimum of two layers applied as follows:

1. Starting at the eave, a 19-inch (483 mm) strip of underlayment shall be applied parallel with the eave and fastened sufficiently in place.
2. Starting at the eave, 36-inch-wide (914 mm) strips of underlayment felt shall be applied overlapping successive sheets 19 inches (483 mm) and fastened sufficiently in place.

1507.3.3.2 High-slope roofs. For roof slopes of four units vertical in 12 units horizontal (33-percent slope) or greater, underlayment shall be a minimum of one layer of underlayment felt applied shingle fashion, parallel to, and starting from the eaves and lapped 2 inches (51 mm), fastened only as necessary to hold in place.

1507.3.4 Clay tile. Clay roof tile shall comply with ASTM C 1167.

1507.3.5 Concrete tile. Concrete roof tile shall comply with ASTM C 1492.

1507.3.6 Fasteners. Tile fasteners shall be corrosion resistant and not less than 11 gage, $^5/_{16}$-inch (8.0 mm) head, and of sufficient length to penetrate the deck a minimum of $^3/_4$ inch (19.1 mm) or through the thickness of the deck, whichever is less. Attaching wire for clay or concrete tile shall not be smaller than 0.083 inch (2.1 mm). Perimeter fastening areas include three tile courses but not less than 36 inches (914 mm) from either side of hips or ridges and edges of eaves and gable rakes.

1507.3.7 Attachment. Clay and concrete roof tiles shall be fastened in accordance with Table 1507.3.7.

1507.3.8 Application. Tile shall be applied according to the manufacturer's installation instructions, based on the following:

1. Climatic conditions.
2. Roof slope.
3. Underlayment system.
4. Type of tile being installed.

1507.3.9 Flashing. At the juncture of the roof vertical surfaces, flashing and counterflashing shall be provided in accordance with the manufacturer's installation instructions, and where of metal, shall not be less than 0.019-inch (0.48 mm) (No. 26 galvanized sheet gage) corrosion-resistant metal. The valley flashing shall extend at least 11 inches (279 mm) from the centerline each way and have a splash diverter rib not less than 1 inch (25 mm) high at the flow line formed as part of the flashing. Sections of flashing shall have an end lap of not less than 4 inches (102 mm). For roof slopes of three units vertical in 12 units horizontal (25-percent slope) and over, the valley flashing shall have a 36-inch-wide (914 mm) underlayment of either one layer of Type I underlayment running the full length of the valley, or a self-adhering polymer-modified bitumen sheet complying with ASTM D 1970, in addition to other required underlayment. In areas where the average daily temperature in January is 25°F (-4°C) or less or where there is a possibility of ice forming along the eaves causing a backup of water, the metal valley flashing underlayment shall be solid cemented to the roofing underlayment for slopes under seven units vertical in 12 units horizontal (58-percent slope) or self-adhering polymer-modified bitumen sheet shall be installed.

1507.4 Metal roof panels. The installation of metal roof panels shall comply with the provisions of this section.

1507.4.1 Deck requirements. Metal roof panel roof coverings shall be applied to a solid or closely fitted deck, except where the roof covering is specifically designed to be applied to spaced supports.

1507.4.2 Deck slope. Minimum slopes for metal roof panels shall comply with the following:

1. The minimum slope for lapped, nonsoldered seam metal roofs without applied lap sealant shall be three units vertical in 12 units horizontal (25-percent slope).
2. The minimum slope for lapped, nonsoldered seam metal roofs with applied lap sealant shall be one-half unit vertical in 12 units horizontal (4-percent slope). Lap sealants shall be applied in accordance with the *approved* manufacturer's installation instructions.
3. The minimum slope for standing seam of roof systems shall be one-quarter unit vertical in 12 units horizontal (2-percent slope).

1507.4.3 Material standards. Metal-sheet roof covering systems that incorporate supporting structural members shall be designed in accordance with Chapter 22. Metal-sheet roof coverings installed over structural decking shall comply with Table 1507.4.3(1). The materials used for metal-sheet roof coverings shall be naturally corrosion resistant or provided with corrosion resistance in accordance with the standards and minimum thicknesses shown in Table 1507.4.3(2).

TABLE 1507.3.7
CLAY AND CONCRETE TILE ATTACHMENT[a,b,c]

<table>
<tr><th colspan="5">GENERAL—CLAY OR CONCRETE ROOF TILE</th></tr>
<tr><th>Maximum basic wind speed (mph)</th><th>Mean roof height (feet)</th><th>Roof slope up to < 3:12</th><th colspan="2">Roof slope 3:12 and over</th></tr>
<tr><td>85</td><td>0-60</td><td rowspan="2">One fastener per tile. Flat tile without vertical laps, two fasteners per tile.</td><td colspan="2" rowspan="2">Two fasteners per tile. Only one fastener on slopes of 7:12 and less for tiles with installed weight exceeding 7.5 lbs./sq. ft. having a width no greater than 16 inches.</td></tr>
<tr><td>100</td><td>0-40</td></tr>
<tr><td>100</td><td>> 40-60</td><td colspan="3">The head of all tiles shall be nailed. The nose of all eave tiles shall be fastened with approved clips. All rake tiles shall be nailed with two nails. The nose of all ridge, hip and rake tiles shall be set in a bead of roofer's mastic.</td></tr>
<tr><td>110</td><td>0-60</td><td colspan="3">The fastening system shall resist the wind forces in Section 1609.5.3.</td></tr>
<tr><td>120</td><td>0-60</td><td colspan="3">The fastening system shall resist the wind forces in Section 1609.5.3.</td></tr>
<tr><td>130</td><td>0-60</td><td colspan="3">The fastening system shall resist the wind forces in Section 1609.5.3.</td></tr>
<tr><td>All</td><td>> 60</td><td colspan="3">The fastening system shall resist the wind forces in Section 1609.5.3.</td></tr>
<tr><th colspan="5">INTERLOCKING CLAY OR CONCRETE ROOF TILE WITH PROJECTING ANCHOR LUGS[d,e]
(Installations on spaced/solid sheathing with battens or spaced sheathing)</th></tr>
<tr><th>Maximum basic wind speed (mph)</th><th>Mean roof height (feet)</th><th>Roof slope up to < 5:12</th><th>Roof slope 5:12 < 12:12</th><th>Roof slope 12:12 and over</th></tr>
<tr><td>85</td><td>0-60</td><td rowspan="2">Fasteners are not required. Tiles with installed weight less than 9 lbs./sq. ft. require a minimum of one fastener per tile.</td><td rowspan="2">One fastener per tile every other row. All perimeter tiles require one fastener. Tiles with installed weight less than 9 lbs./sq. ft. require a minimum of one fastener per tile.</td><td rowspan="2">One fastener required for every tile. Tiles with installed weight less than 9 lbs./sq. ft. require a minimum of one fastener per tile.</td></tr>
<tr><td>100</td><td>0-40</td></tr>
<tr><td>100</td><td>> 40-60</td><td colspan="3">The head of all tiles shall be nailed. The nose of all eave tiles shall be fastened with approved clips. All rake tiles shall be nailed with two nails The nose of all ridge, hip and rake tiles shall be set in a bead of roofers's mastic.</td></tr>
<tr><td>110</td><td>0-60</td><td colspan="3">The fastening system shall resist the wind forces in Section 1609.5.3.</td></tr>
<tr><td>120</td><td>0-60</td><td colspan="3">The fastening system shall resist the wind forces in Section 1609.5.3.</td></tr>
<tr><td>130</td><td>0-60</td><td colspan="3">The fastening system shall resist the wind forces in Section 1609.5.3.</td></tr>
<tr><td>All</td><td>> 60</td><td colspan="3">The fastening system shall resist the wind forces in Section 1609.5.3.</td></tr>
<tr><th colspan="5">INTERLOCKING CLAY OR CONCRETE ROOF TILE WITH PROJECTING ANCHOR LUGS
(Installations on solid sheathing without battens)</th></tr>
<tr><th>Maximum basic wind speed (mph)</th><th>Mean roof height (feet)</th><th colspan="3">All roof slopes</th></tr>
<tr><td>85</td><td>0-60</td><td colspan="3">One fastener per tile.</td></tr>
<tr><td>100</td><td>0-40</td><td colspan="3">One fastener per tile.</td></tr>
<tr><td>100</td><td>> 40-60</td><td colspan="3">The head of all tiles shall be nailed. The nose of all eave tiles shall be fastened with approved clips. All rake tiles shall be nailed with two nails The nose of all ridge, hip and rake tiles shall be set in a bead of roofer's mastic.</td></tr>
<tr><td>110</td><td>0-60</td><td colspan="3">The fastening system shall resist the wind forces in Section 1609.5.3.</td></tr>
<tr><td>120</td><td>0-60</td><td colspan="3">The fastening system shall resist the wind forces in Section 1609.5.3.</td></tr>
<tr><td>130</td><td>0-60</td><td colspan="3">The fastening system shall resist the wind forces in Section 1609.5.3.</td></tr>
<tr><td>All</td><td>> 60</td><td colspan="3">The fastening system shall resist the wind forces in Section 1609.5.3.</td></tr>
</table>

For SI: 1 inch = 25.4 mm, 1 foot = 304.8 mm, 1 mile per hour = 0.447 m/s, 1 pound per square foot = 4.882 kg/m².

a. Minimum fastener size. Corrosion-resistant nails not less than No. 11 gage with $^5/_{16}$-inch head. Fasteners shall be long enough to penetrate into the sheathing $^3/_4$ inch or through the thickness of the sheathing, whichever is less. Attaching wire for clay and concrete tile shall not be smaller than 0.083 inch.

b. Snow areas. A minimum of two fasteners per tile are required or battens and one fastener.

c. Roof slopes greater than 24:12. The nose of all tiles shall be securely fastened.

d. Horizontal battens. Battens shall be not less than 1 inch by 2 inch nominal. Provisions shall be made for drainage by a minimum of $^1/_8$-inch riser at each nail or by 4-foot-long battens with at least a $^1/_2$-inch separation between battens. Horizontal battens are required for slopes over 7:12.

e. Perimeter fastening areas include three tile courses but not less than 36 inches from either side of hips or ridges and edges of eaves and gable rakes.

TABLE 1507.4.3(1)
METAL ROOF COVERINGS

ROOF COVERING TYPE	STANDARD APPLICATION RATE/THICKNESS
Aluminum	ASTM B 209, 0.024 inch minimum thickness for roll-formed panels and 0.019 inch minimum thickness for press-formed shingles.
Aluminum-zinc alloy coated steel	ASTM A 792 AZ 50
Cold-rolled copper	ASTM B 370 minimum 16 oz./sq. ft. and 12 oz./sq. ft. high yield copper for metal-sheet roof covering systems: 12 oz/sq. ft. for preformed metal shingle systems.
Copper	16 oz./sq. ft. for metal-sheet roof-covering systems; 12 oz./sq. ft. for preformed metal shingle systems.
Galvanized steel	ASTM A 653 G-90 zinc-coated[a].
Hard lead	2 lbs./sq. ft.
Lead-coated copper	ASTM B 101
Prepainted steel	ASTM A 755
Soft lead	3 lbs./sq. ft.
Stainless steel	ASTM A 240, 300 Series Alloys
Steel	ASTM A 924
Terne and terne-coated stainless	Terne coating of 40 lbs. per double base box, field painted where applicable in accordance with manufacturer's installation instructions.
Zinc	0.027 inch minimum thickness; 99.995% electrolytic high grade zinc with alloy additives of copper (0.08% - 0.20%), titanium (0.07% - 0.12%) and aluminum (0.015%).

For SI: 1 ounce per square foot = 0.305 kg/m^2,
1 pound per square foot = 4.882 kg/m^2,
1 inch = 25.4 mm, 1 pound = 0.454 kg.

a. For Group U buildings, the minimum coating thickness for ASTM A 653 galvanized steel roofing shall be G-60.

TABLE 1507.4.3(2)
MINIMUM CORROSION RESISTANCE

55% Aluminum-zinc alloy coated steel	ASTM A 792 AZ 50
5% Aluminum alloy-coated steel	ASTM A 875 GF60
Aluminum-coated steel	ASTM A 463 T2 65
Galvanized steel	ASTM A 653 G-90
Prepainted steel	ASTM A 755[a]

a. Paint systems in accordance with ASTM A 755 shall be applied over steel products with corrosion resistant coatings complying with ASTM A 463, ASTM A 653, ASTM A 792 or ASTM A 875.

1507.4.4 Attachment. Metal roof panels shall be secured to the supports in accordance with the *approved* manufacturer's fasteners. In the absence of manufacturer recommendations, the following fasteners shall be used:

1. Galvanized fasteners shall be used for steel roofs.
2. Copper, brass, bronze, copper alloy or 300 series stainless-steel fasteners shall be used for copper roofs.
3. Stainless-steel fasteners are acceptable for all types of metal roofs.

1507.5 Metal roof shingles. The installation of metal roof shingles shall comply with the provisions of this section.

1507.5.1 Deck requirements. Metal roof shingles shall be applied to a solid or closely fitted deck, except where the roof covering is specifically designed to be applied to spaced sheathing.

1507.5.2 Deck slope. Metal roof shingles shall not be installed on roof slopes below three units vertical in 12 units horizontal (25-percent slope).

1507.5.3 Underlayment. Underlayment shall comply with ASTM D 226, Type I or ASTM D 4869.

1507.5.4 Ice barrier. In areas where there has been a history of ice forming along the eaves causing a backup of water, an ice barrier that consists of at least two layers of underlayment cemented together or of a self-adhering polymer-modified bitumen sheet shall be used in lieu of normal underlayment and extend from the lowest edges of all roof surfaces to a point at least 24 inches (610 mm) inside the exterior wall line of the building.

Exception: Detached accessory structures that contain no conditioned floor area.

1507.5.5 Material standards. Metal roof shingle roof coverings shall comply with Table 1507.4.3(1). The materials used for metal-roof shingle roof coverings shall be naturally corrosion resistant or provided with corrosion resistance in accordance with the standards and minimum thicknesses specified in the standards listed in Table 1507.4.3(2).

1507.5.6 Attachment. Metal roof shingles shall be secured to the roof in accordance with the *approved* manufacturer's installation instructions.

1507.5.7 Flashing. Roof valley flashing shall be of corrosion-resistant metal of the same material as the roof covering or shall comply with the standards in Table 1507.4.3(1). The valley flashing shall extend at least 8 inches (203 mm) from the centerline each way and shall have a splash diverter rib not less than $^3/_4$ inch (19.1 mm) high at the flow line formed as part of the flashing. Sections of flashing shall have an end lap of not less than 4 inches (102 mm). In areas where the average daily temperature in January is 25°F (-4°C) or less or where there is a possibility of ice forming along the eaves causing a backup of water, the metal valley flashing shall have a 36-inch-wide (914 mm) underlayment directly under it consisting of either one layer of underlayment running the full length of the valley or a self-adhering polymer-modified bitumen sheet complying with ASTM D 1970, in addition to underlayment required for metal roof shingles. The metal valley flashing underlayment shall be solidly cemented to the roofing underlayment for roof slopes under seven units vertical in 12 units horizontal (58-percent slope) or self-adhering polymer-modified bitumen sheet shall be installed.

1507.6 Mineral-surfaced roll roofing. The installation of mineral-surfaced roll roofing shall comply with this section.

1507.6.1 Deck requirements. Mineral-surfaced roll roofing shall be fastened to solidly sheathed roofs.

1507.6.2 Deck slope. Mineral-surfaced roll roofing shall not be applied on roof slopes below one unit vertical in 12 units horizontal (8-percent slope).

1507.6.3 Underlayment. Underlayment shall comply with ASTM D 226, Type I or ASTM D 4869.

1507.6.4 Ice barrier. In areas where there has been a history of ice forming along the eaves causing a backup of water, an ice barrier that consists of at least two layers of underlayment cemented together or of a self-adhering polymer-modified bitumen sheet shall be used in lieu of normal underlayment and extend from the lowest edges of all roof surfaces to a point at least 24 inches (610 mm) inside the exterior wall line of the building.

Exception: Detached accessory structures that contain no conditioned floor area.

1507.6.5 Material standards. Mineral-surfaced roll roofing shall conform to ASTM D 3909 or ASTM D 6380.

1507.7 Slate shingles. The installation of slate shingles shall comply with the provisions of this section.

1507.7.1 Deck requirements. Slate shingles shall be fastened to solidly sheathed roofs.

1507.7.2 Deck slope. Slate shingles shall only be used on slopes of four units vertical in 12 units horizontal (4:12) or greater.

1507.7.3 Underlayment. Underlayment shall comply with ASTM D 226, Type I or ASTM D 4869.

1507.7.4 Ice barrier. In areas where the average daily temperature in January is 25°F (-4°C) or less or where there is a possibility of ice forming along the eaves causing a backup of water, an ice barrier that consists of at least two layers of underlayment cemented together or of a self-adhering polymer-modified bitumen sheet shall extend from the lowest edges of all roof surfaces to a point at least 24 inches (610 mm) inside the exterior wall line of the building.

Exception: Detached accessory structures that contain no conditioned floor area.

1507.7.5 Material standards. Slate shingles shall comply with ASTM C 406.

1507.7.6 Application. Minimum headlap for slate shingles shall be in accordance with Table 1507.7.6. Slate shingles shall be secured to the roof with two fasteners per slate.

TABLE 1507.7.6
SLATE SHINGLE HEADLAP

SLOPE	HEADLAP (inches)
4:12 < slope < 8:12	4
8:12 < slope < 20:12	3
slope ≥ 20:12	2

For SI: 1 inch = 25.4 mm.

1507.7.7 Flashing. Flashing and counterflashing shall be made with sheet metal. Valley flashing shall be a minimum of 15 inches (381 mm) wide. Valley and flashing metal shall be a minimum uncoated thickness of 0.0179-inch (0.455 mm) zinc-coated G90. Chimneys, stucco or brick walls shall have a minimum of two plies of felt for a cap flashing consisting of a 4-inch-wide (102 mm) strip of felt set in plastic cement and extending 1 inch (25 mm) above the first felt and a top coating of plastic cement. The felt shall extend over the base flashing 2 inches (51 mm).

1507.8 Wood shingles. The installation of wood shingles shall comply with the provisions of this section and Table 1507.8.

1507.8.1 Deck requirements. Wood shingles shall be installed on solid or spaced sheathing. Where spaced sheathing is used, sheathing boards shall not be less than 1-inch by 4-inch (25 mm by 102 mm) nominal dimensions and shall be spaced on centers equal to the weather exposure to coincide with the placement of fasteners.

1507.8.1.1 Solid sheathing required. Solid sheathing is required in areas where the average daily temperature in January is 25°F (-4°C) or less or where there is a possibility of ice forming along the eaves causing a backup of water.

1507.8.2 Deck slope. Wood shingles shall be installed on slopes of three units vertical in 12 units horizontal (25-percent slope) or greater.

1507.8.3 Underlayment. Underlayment shall comply with ASTM D 226, Type I or ASTM D 4869.

1507.8.4 Ice barrier. In areas where there has been a history of ice forming along the eaves causing a backup of water, an ice barrier that consists of at least two layers of underlayment cemented together or of a self-adhering polymer-modified bitumen sheet shall be used in lieu of normal underlayment and extend from the lowest edges of all roof surfaces to a point at least 24 inches (610 mm) inside the exterior wall line of the building.

Exception: Detached accessory structures that contain no conditioned floor area.

TABLE 1507.8
WOOD SHINGLE AND SHAKE INSTALLATION

ROOF ITEM	WOOD SHINGLES	WOOD SHAKES
1. Roof slope	Wood shingles shall be installed on slopes of three units vertical in 12 units horizontal (3:12) or greater.	Wood shakes shall be installed on slopes of four units vertical in 12 units horizontal (4:12) or greater.
2. Deck requirement		
Temperate climate	Shingles shall be applied to roofs with solid or spaced sheathing. Where spaced sheathing is used, sheathing boards shall not be less than 1″ × 4″ nominal dimensions and shall be spaced on center equal to the weather exposure to coincide with the placement of fasteners.	Shakes shall be applied to roofs with solid or spaced sheathing.Where spaced sheathing is used, sheathing boards shall not be less than 1″ × 4″ nominal dimensions and shall be spaced on center equal to the weather exposure to coincide with the placement of fasteners. When 1″ × 4″ spaced sheathing is installed at 10 inches, boards must be installed between the sheathing boards.
In areas where the average daily temperature in January is 25°F or less or where there is a possibility of ice forming along the eaves causing a backup of water.	Solid sheathing required.	Solid sheathing is required.
3. Interlayment	No requirements.	Interlayment shall comply with ASTM D 226, Type 1.
4. Underlayment		
Temperate climate	Underlayment shall comply with ASTM D 226, Type 1.	Underlayment shall comply with ASTM D 226, Type 1.
In areas where there is a possibility of ice forming along the eaves causing a backup of water.	An ice barrier that consists of at least two layers of underlayment cemented together or of a self-adhering polymer-modified bitumen sheet shall extend from the eave's edge to a point at least 24 inches inside the exterior wall line of the building.	An ice barrier that consists of at least two layers of underlayment cemented together or of a self-adhering polymer-modified bitumen sheet shall extend from the lowest edges of all roof surfaces to a point at least 24 inches inside the exterior wall line of the building.
5. Application		
Attachment	Fasteners for wood shingles shall be hot-dipped galvanized or Type 304 (Type 316 for coastal areas) stainless steel with a minimum penetration of 0.75 inch into the sheathing. For sheathing less than 0.5 inch thick, the fasteners shall extend through the sheathing.	Fasteners for wood shakes shall be hot-dipped galvanized or Type 304 (Type 316 for coastal areas) with a minimum penetration of 0.75 inch into the sheathing. For sheathing less than 0.5 inch thick, the fasteners shall extend through the sheathing.
No. of fasteners	Two per shingle.	Two per shake.
Exposure	Weather exposures shall not exceed those set forth in Table 1507.8.7.	Weather exposures shall not exceed those set forth in Table 1507.9.8.
Method	Shingles shall be laid with a side lap of not less than 1.5 inches between joints in courses, and no two joints in any three adjacent courses shall be in direct alignment. Spacing between shingles shall be 0.25 to 0.375 inch.	Shakes shall be laid with a side lap of not less than 1.5 inches between joints in adjacent courses. Spacing between shakes shall not be less than 0.375 inch or more than 0.625 inch for shakes and taper sawn shakes of naturally durable wood and shall be 0.25 to 0.375 inch for preservative-treated taper sawn shakes.
Flashing	In accordance with Section 1507.8.8.	In accordance with Section 1507.9.9.

For SI: 1 inch = 25.4 mm, °C = [(°F) - 32]/1.8.

1507.8.5 Material standards. Wood shingles shall be of naturally durable wood and comply with the requirements of Table 1507.8.5.

TABLE 1507.8.5
WOOD SHINGLE MATERIAL REQUIREMENTS

MATERIAL	APPLICABLE MINIMUM GRADES	GRADING RULES
Wood shingles of naturally durable wood	1, 2 or 3	CSSB

CSSB = Cedar Shake and Shingle Bureau

1507.8.6 Attachment. Fasteners for wood shingles shall be corrosion resistant with a minimum penetration of $^3/_4$ inch (19.1 mm) into the sheathing. For sheathing less than $^1/_2$ inch (12.7 mm) in thickness, the fasteners shall extend through the sheathing. Each shingle shall be attached with a minimum of two fasteners.

1507.8.7 Application. Wood shingles shall be laid with a side lap not less than $1^1/_2$ inches (38 mm) between joints in adjacent courses, and not be in direct alignment in alternate courses. Spacing between shingles shall be $^1/_4$ to $^3/_8$ inches (6.4 to 9.5 mm). Weather exposure for wood shingles shall not exceed that set in Table 1507.8.7.

TABLE 1507.8.7
WOOD SHINGLE WEATHER EXPOSURE AND ROOF SLOPE

ROOFING MATERIAL	LENGTH (inches)	GRADE	EXPOSURE (inches) 3:12 pitch to < 4:12	EXPOSURE (inches) 4:12 pitch or steeper
Shingles of naturally durable wood	16	No. 1	3.75	5
		No. 2	3.5	4
		No. 3	3	3.5
	18	No. 1	4.25	5.5
		No. 2	4	4.5
		No. 3	3.5	4
	24	No. 1	5.75	7.5
		No. 2	5.5	6.5
		No. 3	5	5.5

For SI: 1 inch = 25.4 mm.

1507.8.8 Flashing. At the juncture of the roof and vertical surfaces, flashing and counterflashing shall be provided in accordance with the manufacturer's installation instructions, and where of metal, shall not be less than 0.019-inch (0.48 mm) (No. 26 galvanized sheet gage) corrosion-resistant metal. The valley flashing shall extend at least 11 inches (279 mm) from the centerline each way and have a splash diverter rib not less than 1 inch (25 mm) high at the flow line formed as part of the flashing. Sections of flashing shall have an end lap of not less than 4 inches (102 mm). For roof slopes of three units vertical in 12 units horizontal (25-percent slope) and over, the valley flashing shall have a 36-inch-wide (914 mm) underlayment of either one layer of Type I underlayment running the full length of the valley or a self-adhering polymer-modified bitumen sheet complying with ASTM D 1970, in addition to other required underlayment. In areas where the average daily temperature in January is 25°F (-4°C) or less or where there is a possibility of ice forming along the eaves causing a backup of water, the metal valley flashing underlayment shall be solidly cemented to the roofing underlayment for slopes under seven units vertical in 12 units horizontal (58-percent slope) or self-adhering polymer-modified bitumen sheet shall be installed.

1507.9 Wood shakes. The installation of wood shakes shall comply with the provisions of this section and Table 1507.8.

1507.9.1 Deck requirements. Wood shakes shall only be used on solid or spaced sheathing. Where spaced sheathing is used, sheathing boards shall not be less than 1-inch by 4-inch (25 mm by 102 mm) nominal dimensions and shall be spaced on centers equal to the weather exposure to coincide with the placement of fasteners. Where 1-inch by 4-inch (25 mm by 102 mm) spaced sheathing is installed at 10 inches (254 mm) o.c., additional 1-inch by 4-inch (25 mm by 102 mm) boards shall be installed between the sheathing boards.

1507.9.1.1 Solid sheathing required. Solid sheathing is required in areas where the average daily temperature in January is 25°F (-4°C) or less or where there is a possibility of ice forming along the eaves causing a backup of water.

1507.9.2 Deck slope. Wood shakes shall only be used on slopes of four units vertical in 12 units horizontal (33-percent slope) or greater.

1507.9.3 Underlayment. Underlayment shall comply with ASTM D 226, Type I or ASTM D 4869.

1507.9.4 Ice barrier. In areas where there has been a history of ice forming along the eaves causing a backup of water, an ice barrier that consists of at least two layers of underlayment cemented together or of a self-adhering polymer-modified bitumen sheet shall be used in lieu of normal underlayment and extend from the lowest edges of all roof surfaces to a point at least 24 inches (610 mm) inside the exterior wall line of the building.

Exception: Detached accessory structures that contain no conditioned floor area.

1507.9.5 Interlayment. Interlayment shall comply with ASTM D 226, Type I.

1507.9.6 Material standards. Wood shakes shall comply with the requirements of Table 1507.9.6.

TABLE 1507.9.6
WOOD SHAKE MATERIAL REQUIREMENTS

MATERIAL	MINIMUM GRADES	APPLICABLE GRADING RULES
Wood shakes of naturally durable wood	1	CSSB
Taper sawn shakes of naturally durable wood	1 or 2	CSSB
Preservative-treated shakes and shingles of naturally durable wood	1	CSSB
Fire-retardant-treated shakes and shingles of naturally durable wood	1	CSSB
Preservative-treated taper sawn shakes of Southern pine treated in accordance with AWPA U1 (Commodity Specification A, Use Category 3B and Section 5.6)	1 or 2	TFS

CSSB = Cedar Shake and Shingle Bureau.
TFS = Forest Products Laboratory of the Texas Forest Services.

1507.9.7 Attachment. Fasteners for wood shakes shall be corrosion resistant with a minimum penetration of $^3/_4$ inch (19.1 mm) into the sheathing. For sheathing less than $^1/_2$ inch (12.7 mm) in thickness, the fasteners shall extend through the sheathing. Each shake shall be attached with a minimum of two fasteners.

1507.9.8 Application. Wood shakes shall be laid with a side lap not less than $1^1/_2$ inches (38 mm) between joints in adjacent courses. Spacing between shakes in the same course shall be $^3/_8$ to $^5/_8$ inches (9.5 to 15.9 mm) for shakes and taper sawn shakes of naturally durable wood and shall be $^1/_4$ to $^3/_8$ inch (6.4 to 9.5 mm) for preservative taper sawn shakes. Weather exposure for wood shakes shall not exceed those set in Table 1507.9.8.

TABLE 1507.9.8
WOOD SHAKE WEATHER EXPOSURE AND ROOF SLOPE

ROOFING MATERIAL	LENGTH (inches)	GRADE	EXPOSURE (inches) 4:12 PITCH OR STEEPER
Shakes of naturally durable wood	18 24	No. 1 No. 1	7.5 10[a]
Preservative-treated taper sawn shakes of Southern yellow pine	18 24	No. 1 No. 1	7.5 10
	18 24	No. 2 No. 2	5.5 7.5
Taper sawn shakes of naturally durable wood	18 24	No. 1 No. 1	7.5 10
	18 24	No. 2 No. 2	5.5 7.5

For SI: 1 inch = 25.4 mm.
a. For 24-inch by 0.375-inch handsplit shakes, the maximum exposure is 7.5 inches.

1507.9.9 Flashing. At the juncture of the roof and vertical surfaces, flashing and counterflashing shall be provided in accordance with the manufacturer's installation instructions, and where of metal, shall not be less than 0.019-inch (0.48 mm) (No. 26 galvanized sheet gage) corrosion-resistant metal. The valley flashing shall extend at least 11 inches (279 mm) from the centerline each way and have a splash diverter rib not less than 1 inch (25 mm) high at the flow line formed as part of the flashing. Sections of flashing shall have an end lap of not less than 4 inches (102 mm). For roof slopes of three units vertical in 12 units horizontal (25-percent slope) and over, the valley flashing shall have a 36-inch-wide (914 mm) underlayment of either one layer of Type I underlayment running the full length of the valley or a self-adhering polymer-modified bitumen sheet complying with ASTM D 1970, in addition to other required underlayment. In areas where the average daily temperature in January is 25°F (-4°C) or less or where there is a possibility of ice forming along the eaves causing a backup of water, the metal valley flashing underlayment shall be solidly cemented to the roofing underlayment for slopes under seven units vertical in 12 units horizontal (58-percent slope) or self-adhering polymer-modified bitumen sheet shall be installed.

1507.10 Built-up roofs. The installation of built-up roofs shall comply with the provisions of this section.

1507.10.1 Slope. Built-up roofs shall have a design slope of a minimum of one-fourth unit vertical in 12 units horizontal (2-percent slope) for drainage, except for coal-tar built-up roofs that shall have a design slope of a minimum one-eighth unit vertical in 12 units horizontal (1-percent slope).

1507.10.2 Material standards. Built-up roof covering materials shall comply with the standards in Table 1507.10.2.

1507.11 Modified bitumen roofing. The installation of modified bitumen roofing shall comply with the provisions of this section.

1507.11.1 Slope. Modified bitumen membrane roofs shall have a design slope of a minimum of one-fourth unit vertical in 12 units horizontal (2-percent slope) for drainage.

1507.11.2 Material standards. Modified bitumen roof coverings shall comply with CGSB 37-GP-56M, ASTM D 6162, ASTM D 6163, ASTM D 6164, ASTM D 6222, ASTM D 6223, ASTM D 6298 or ASTM D 6509.

1507.12 Thermoset single-ply roofing. The installation of thermoset single-ply roofing shall comply with the provisions of this section.

1507.12.1 Slope. Thermoset single-ply membrane roofs shall have a design slope of a minimum of one-fourth unit vertical in 12 units horizontal (2-percent slope) for drainage.

1507.12.2 Material standards. Thermoset single-ply roof coverings shall comply with ASTM D 4637, ASTM D 5019 or CGSB 37-GP-52M.

1507.12.3 Ballasted thermoset low-slope roofs. Ballasted thermoset low-slope roofs (roof slope < 2:12) shall be installed in accordance with this section and Section 1504.4. Stone used as ballast shall comply with ASTM D 448.

**TABLE 1507.10.2
BUILT-UP ROOFING MATERIAL STANDARDS**

MATERIAL STANDARD	STANDARD
Acrylic coatings used in roofing	ASTM D 6083
Aggregate surfacing	ASTM D 1863
Asphalt adhesive used in roofing	ASTM D 3747
Asphalt cements used in roofing	ASTM D 3019; D 2822; D 4586
Asphalt-coated glass fiber base sheet	ASTM D 4601
Asphalt coatings used in roofing	ASTM D1227; D 2823; D 4479
Asphalt glass felt	ASTM D 2178
Asphalt primer used in roofing	ASTM D 41
Asphalt-saturated and asphalt-coated organic felt base sheet	ASTM D 2626
Asphalt-saturated organic felt (perforated)	ASTM D 226
Asphalt used in roofing	ASTM D 312
Coal-tar cements used in roofing	ASTM D 4022; D 5643
Coal-tar saturated organic felt	ASTM D 227
Coal-tar pitch used in roofing	ASTM D 450; Type I or II
Coal-tar primer used in roofing, dampproofing and waterproofing	ASTM D 43
Glass mat, coal tar	ASTM D 4990
Glass mat, venting type	ASTM D 4897
Mineral-surfaced inorganic cap sheet	ASTM D 3909
Thermoplastic fabrics used in roofing	ASTM D 5665, D 5726

1507.13 Thermoplastic single-ply roofing. The installation of thermoplastic single-ply roofing shall comply with the provisions of this section.

1507.13.1 Slope. Thermoplastic single-ply membrane roofs shall have a design slope of a minimum of one-fourth unit vertical in 12 units horizontal (2-percent slope).

1507.13.2 Material standards. Thermoplastic single-ply roof coverings shall comply with ASTM D 4434, ASTM D 6754, ASTM D 6878 or CGSB CAN/CGSB 37-54.

1507.13.3 Ballasted thermoplastic low-slope roofs. Ballasted thermoplastic low-slope roofs (roof slope < 2:12) shall be installed in accordance with this section and Section 1504.4. Stone used as ballast shall comply with ASTM D448.

1507.14 Sprayed polyurethane foam roofing. The installation of sprayed polyurethane foam roofing shall comply with the provisions of this section.

1507.14.1 Slope. Sprayed polyurethane foam roofs shall have a design slope of a minimum of one-fourth unit vertical in 12 units horizontal (2-percent slope) for drainage.

1507.14.2 Material standards. Spray-applied polyurethane foam insulation shall comply with Type III or IV as defined in ASTM C 1029.

1507.14.3 Application. Foamed-in-place roof insulation shall be installed in accordance with the manufacturer's instructions. A liquid-applied protective coating that complies with Section 1507.15 shall be applied no less than 2 hours nor more than 72 hours following the application of the foam.

1507.14.4 Foam plastics. Foam plastic materials and installation shall comply with Chapter 26.

1507.15 Liquid-applied coatings. The installation of liquid-applied coatings shall comply with the provisions of this section.

1507.15.1 Slope. Liquid-applied roofs shall have a design slope of a minimum of one-fourth unit vertical in 12 units horizontal (2-percent slope).

1507.15.2 Material standards. Liquid-applied roof coatings shall comply with ASTM C 836, ASTM C 957, ASTM D 1227 or ASTM D 3468, ASTM D 6083, ASTM D 6694 or ASTM D 6947.

1507.16 Roof gardens and landscaped roofs. Roof gardens and landscaped roofs shall comply with the requirements of this chapter and Sections 1607.11.2.2 and 1607.11.3.

SECTION 1508
ROOF INSULATION

1508.1 General. The use of above-deck thermal insulation shall be permitted provided such insulation is covered with an *approved* roof covering and passes the tests of FM 4450 or UL 1256 when tested as an assembly.

Exceptions:

1. Foam plastic roof insulation shall conform to the material and installation requirements of Chapter 26.
2. Where a concrete roof deck is used and the above-deck thermal insulation is covered with an *approved* roof covering.

1508.1.1 Cellulosic fiberboard. Cellulosic fiberboard roof insulation shall conform to the material and installation requirements of Chapter 23.

1508.2 Material standards. Above-deck thermal insulation board shall comply with the standards in Table 1508.2.

**TABLE 1508.2
MATERIAL STANDARDS FOR ROOF INSULATION**

Cellular glass board	ASTM C 552
Composite boards	ASTM C 1289, Type III, IV, V or VI
Expanded polystyrene	ASTM C 578
Extruded polystyrene board	ASTM C 578
Perlite board	ASTM C 728
Polyisocyanurate board	ASTM C 1289, Type I or Type II
Wood fiberboard	ASTM C 208

SECTION 1509 ROOFTOP STRUCTURES

1509.1 General. The provisions of this section shall govern the construction of rooftop structures.

1509.2 Penthouses. A *penthouse* or *penthouses* in compliance with Sections 1509.2.1 through 1509.2.4 shall be considered as a portion of the *story* below.

1509.2.1 Height above roof. A *penthouse* or other projection above the roof in structures of other than Type I construction shall not exceed 28 feet (8534 mm) above the roof where used as an enclosure for tanks or for elevators that run to the roof and in all other cases shall not extend more than 18 feet (5486 mm) above the roof.

1509.2.2 Area limitation. The aggregate area of penthouses and other rooftop structures shall not exceed one-third the area of the supporting roof. Such penthouses shall not contribute to either the *building area* or number of stories as regulated by Section 503.1. The area of the penthouse shall not be included in determining the *fire area* defined in Section 902.

1509.2.3 Use limitations. A *penthouse*, bulkhead or any other similar projection above the roof shall not be used for purposes other than shelter of mechanical equipment or shelter of vertical shaft openings in the roof. Provisions such as louvers, louver blades or flashing shall be made to protect the mechanical equipment and the building interior from the elements. Penthouses or bulkheads used for purposes other than permitted by this section shall conform to the requirements of this code for an additional *story*. The restrictions of this section shall not prohibit the placing of wood flagpoles or similar structures on the roof of any building.

1509.2.4 Type of construction. Penthouses shall be constructed with walls, floors and roof as required for the building.

Exceptions:

1. On buildings of Type I construction, the exterior walls and roofs of penthouses with a *fire separation distance* of more than 5 feet (1524 mm) and less than 20 feet (6096 mm) shall be of at least 1-hour fire resistance-rated noncombustible construction. Walls and roofs with a *fire separation distance* of 20 feet (6096 mm) or greater shall be of noncombustible construction. Interior framing and walls shall be of noncombustible construction.
2. On buildings of Type I construction two stories above *grade plane* or less and Type II construction, the exterior walls and roofs of penthouses with a *fire separation distance* of more than 5 feet (1524 mm) and less than 20 feet (6096 mm) shall be of at least 1-hour fire-resistance-rated noncombustible or *fire-retardant-treated wood* construction. Walls and roofs with a *fire separation distance* of 20 feet (6096 mm) or greater shall be of noncombustible or *fire-retardant-treated wood* construction. Interior framing and walls shall be of noncombustible or *fire-retardant-treated wood* construction.
3. On buildings of Type III, IV and V construction, the exterior walls of penthouses with a *fire separation distance* of more than 5 feet (1524 mm) and less than 20 feet (6096 mm) shall be at least 1-hour fire-resistance-rated construction. Walls with a *fire separation distance* of 20 feet (6096 mm) or greater from a common property line shall be of Type IV construction or noncombustible, or *fire-retardant-treated wood* construction. Roofs shall be constructed of materials and fire-resistance rated as required in Table 601 and Section 603, Item 25.3. Interior framing and walls shall be Type IV construction or noncombustible or *fire-retardant-treated wood* construction.
4. On buildings of Type I construction, unprotected noncombustible enclosures housing only mechanical equipment and located with a minimum *fire separation distance* of 20 feet (6096 mm) shall be permitted.
5. On buildings of Type I construction two stories or less above *grade plane* or Type II, III, IV and V construction, unprotected noncombustible or *fire-retardant-treated wood* enclosures housing only mechanical equipment and located with a minimum *fire separation distance* of 20 feet (6096 mm) shall be permitted.
6. On one-story buildings, combustible unroofed mechanical equipment screens, fences or similar enclosures are permitted where located with a *fire separation distance* of at least 20 feet (6096 mm) from adjacent property lines and where not exceeding 4 feet (1219 mm) in height above the roof surface.
7. Dormers shall be of the same type of construction as the roof on which they are placed, or of the exterior walls of the building.

1509.3 Tanks. Tanks having a capacity of more than 500 gallons (2 m^3) placed in or on a building shall be supported on masonry, reinforced concrete, steel or Type IV construction provided that, where such supports are located in the building above the lowest *story*, the support shall be fire-resistance rated as required for Type IA construction.

1509.3.1 Valve. Such tanks shall have in the bottom or on the side near the bottom, a pipe or outlet, fitted with a suitable quick opening valve for discharging the contents in an emergency through an adequate drain.

1509.3.2 Location. Such tanks shall not be placed over or near a line of stairs or an elevator shaft, unless there is a solid roof or floor underneath the tank.

1509.3.3 Tank cover. Unenclosed roof tanks shall have covers sloping toward the outer edges.

1509.4 Cooling towers. Cooling towers in excess of 250 square feet (23.2 m^2) in base area or in excess of 15 feet (4572 mm) high where located on building roofs more than 50 feet (15 240 mm) high shall be of noncombustible construction. Cooling towers shall not exceed one-third of the supporting roof area.

Exception: Drip boards and the enclosing construction of wood not less than 1 inch (25 mm) nominal thickness, provided the wood is covered on the exterior of the tower with noncombustible material.

1509.5 Towers, spires, domes and cupolas. Any tower, spire, dome or cupola shall be of a type of construction not less in *fire-resistance rating* than required for the building to which it is attached, except that any such tower, spire, dome or cupola that exceeds 85 feet (25 908 mm) in height above *grade plane*, exceeds 200 square feet (18.6 m^2) in horizontal area or is used for any purpose other than a belfry or an architectural embellishment shall be constructed of and supported on Type I or II construction.

1509.5.1 Noncombustible construction required. Any tower, spire, dome or cupola that exceeds 60 feet (18 288 mm) in height above the highest point at which it comes in contact with the roof, or that exceeds 200 square feet (18.6 m^2) in area at any horizontal section, or which is intended to be used for any purpose other than a belfry or architectural embellishment, shall be entirely constructed of and supported by noncombustible materials. Such structures shall be separated from the building below by construction having a fire-resistance rating of not less than 1.5 hours with openings protected with a minimum 1.5-hour fire protection rating. Structures, except aerial supports 12 feet (3658 mm) high or less, flagpoles, water tanks and cooling towers, placed above the roof of any building more than 50 feet (15 240 mm) in building height, shall be of noncombustible material and shall be supported by construction of noncombustible material.

1509.5.2 Towers and spires. Towers and spires where enclosed shall have exterior walls as required for the building to which they are attached. The roof covering of spires shall be of a class of roof covering as required for the main roof of the rest of the structure.

SECTION 1510
REROOFING

1510.1 General. Materials and methods of application used for recovering or replacing an existing roof covering shall comply with the requirements of Chapter 15.

Exception: Reroofing shall not be required to meet the minimum design slope requirement of one-quarter unit vertical in 12 units horizontal (2-percent slope) in Section 1507 for roofs that provide positive roof drainage.

1510.2 Structural and construction loads. Structural roof components shall be capable of supporting the roof-covering system and the material and equipment loads that will be encountered during installation of the system.

1510.3 Recovering versus replacement. New roof coverings shall not be installed without first removing all existing layers of roof coverings down to the roof deck where any of the following conditions occur:

1. Where the existing roof or roof covering is water soaked or has deteriorated to the point that the existing roof or roof covering is not adequate as a base for additional roofing.
2. Where the existing roof covering is wood shake, slate, clay, cement or asbestos-cement tile.
3. Where the existing roof has two or more applications of any type of roof covering.

Exceptions:

1. Complete and separate roofing systems, such as standing-seam metal roof systems, that are designed to transmit the roof loads directly to the building's structural system and that do not rely on existing roofs and roof coverings for support, shall not require the removal of existing roof coverings.
2. Metal panel, metal shingle and concrete and clay tile roof coverings shall be permitted to be installed over existing wood shake roofs when applied in accordance with Section 1510.4.
3. The application of a new protective coating over an existing spray polyurethane foam roofing system shall be permitted without tear-off of existing roof coverings.

1510.4 Roof recovering. Where the application of a new roof covering over wood shingle or shake roofs creates a combustible concealed space, the entire existing surface shall be covered with gypsum board, mineral fiber, glass fiber or other *approved* materials securely fastened in place.

1510.5 Reinstallation of materials. Existing slate, clay or cement tile shall be permitted for reinstallation, except that damaged, cracked or broken slate or tile shall not be reinstalled. Existing vent flashing, metal edgings, drain outlets, collars and metal counterflashings shall not be reinstalled where rusted, damaged or deteriorated. Aggregate surfacing materials shall not be reinstalled.

1510.6 Flashings. Flashings shall be reconstructed in accordance with *approved* manufacturer's installation instructions. Metal flashing to which bituminous materials are to be adhered shall be primed prior to installation.

CHAPTER 16
STRUCTURAL DESIGN

SECTION 1601 GENERAL

1601.1 Scope. The provisions of this chapter shall govern the structural design of buildings, structures and portions thereof regulated by this code.

SECTION 1602 DEFINITIONS AND NOTATIONS

1602.1 Definitions. The following words and terms shall, for the purposes of this chapter, have the meanings shown herein.

ALLOWABLE STRESS DESIGN. A method of proportioning structural members, such that elastically computed stresses produced in the members by *nominal loads* do not exceed specified allowable stresses (also called "working stress design").

➡ **DEAD LOADS.** The weight of materials of construction incorporated into the building, including but not limited to walls, floors, roofs, ceilings, stairways, built-in partitions, finishes, cladding and other similarly incorporated architectural and structural items, and the weight of fixed service equipment, such as cranes, plumbing stacks and risers, electrical feeders, heating, ventilating and air-conditioning systems and automatic sprinkler systems.

➡ **DESIGN STRENGTH.** The product of the nominal strength and a resistance factor (or strength reduction factor).

DIAPHRAGM. A horizontal or sloped system acting to transmit lateral forces to the vertical-resisting elements. When the term "diaphragm" is used, it shall include horizontal bracing systems.

Diaphragm, blocked. In light-frame construction, a diaphragm in which all sheathing edges not occurring on a framing member are supported on and fastened to blocking.

Diaphragm boundary. In light-frame construction, a location where shear is transferred into or out of the diaphragm sheathing. Transfer is either to a boundary element or to another force-resisting element.

Diaphragm chord. A diaphragm boundary element perpendicular to the applied load that is assumed to take axial stresses due to the diaphragm moment.

Diaphragm flexible. A diaphragm is flexible for the purpose of distribution of story shear and torsional moment where so indicated in Section 12.3.1 of ASCE 7, as modified in Section 1613.6.1.

Diaphragm, rigid. A diaphragm is rigid for the purpose of distribution of story shear and torsional moment when the lateral deformation of the diaphragm is less than or equal to two times the average story drift.

DURATION OF LOAD. The period of continuous application of a given load, or the aggregate of periods of intermittent applications of the same load.

ESSENTIAL FACILITIES. Buildings and other structures that are intended to remain operational in the event of extreme environmental loading from flood, wind, snow or earthquakes.

FABRIC PARTITION. A partition consisting of a finished surface made of fabric, without a continuous rigid backing, that is directly attached to a framing system in which the vertical framing members are spaced greater than 4 feet (1219 mm) on center.

FACTORED LOAD. The product of a nominal load and a load factor.

GUARD. See Section 1002.1.

IMPACT LOAD. The load resulting from moving machinery, elevators, craneways, vehicles and other similar forces and kinetic loads, pressure and possible surcharge from fixed or moving loads.

LIMIT STATE. A condition beyond which a structure or member becomes unfit for service and is judged to be no longer useful for its intended function (serviceability limit state) or to be unsafe (strength limit state).

LIVE LOADS. Those loads produced by the use and occupancy of the building or other structure and do not include construction or environmental loads such as wind load, snow load, rain load, earthquake load, flood load or dead load.

LIVE LOADS (ROOF). Those loads produced (1) during maintenance by workers, equipment and materials; and (2) during the life of the structure by movable objects such as planters and by people.

LOAD AND RESISTANCE FACTOR DESIGN (LRFD). A method of proportioning structural members and their connections using load and resistance factors such that no applicable limit state is reached when the structure is subjected to appropriate load combinations. The term "LRFD" is used in the design of steel and wood structures.

LOAD EFFECTS. Forces and deformations produced in structural members by the applied loads.

LOAD FACTOR. A factor that accounts for deviations of the actual load from the *nominal load*, for uncertainties in the analysis that transforms the load into a load effect, and for the probability that more than one extreme load will occur simultaneously.

LOADS. Forces or other actions that result from the weight of building materials, occupants and their possessions, environmental effects, differential movement and restrained dimensional changes. Permanent loads are those loads in which variations over time are rare or of small magnitude, such as dead loads. All other loads are variable loads (see also "*Nominal loads*").

NOMINAL LOADS. The magnitudes of the loads specified in this chapter (dead, live, soil, wind, snow, rain, flood and earthquake).

OCCUPANCY CATEGORY. A category used to determine structural requirements based on occupancy.

OTHER STRUCTURES. Structures, other than buildings, for which loads are specified in this chapter.

PANEL (PART OF A STRUCTURE). The section of a floor, wall or roof comprised between the supporting frame of two adjacent rows of columns and girders or column bands of floor or roof construction.

RESISTANCE FACTOR. A factor that accounts for deviations of the actual strength from the nominal strength and the manner and consequences of failure (also called "strength reduction factor").

STRENGTH, NOMINAL. The capacity of a structure or member to resist the effects of loads, as determined by computations using specified material strengths and dimensions and equations derived from accepted principles of structural mechanics or by field tests or laboratory tests of scaled models, allowing for modeling effects and differences between laboratory and field conditions.

STRENGTH, REQUIRED. Strength of a member, cross section or connection required to resist factored loads or related internal moments and forces in such combinations as stipulated by these provisions.

STRENGTH DESIGN. A method of proportioning structural members such that the computed forces produced in the members by factored loads do not exceed the member design strength [also called "*load and resistance factor design*" (LRFD)]. The term "strength design" is used in the design of concrete and masonry structural elements.

VEHICLE BARRIER SYSTEM. A system of building components near open sides of a garage floor or ramp or building walls that act as restraints for vehicles.

NOTATIONS.

D = Dead load.

E = Combined effect of horizontal and vertical earthquake induced forces as defined in Section 12.4.2 of ASCE 7.

F = Load due to fluids with well-defined pressures and maximum heights.

F_a = Flood load in accordance with Chapter 5 of ASCE 7.

H = Load due to lateral earth pressures, ground water pressure or pressure of bulk materials.

L = Live load, except roof live load, including any permitted live load reduction.

L_r = Roof live load including any permitted live load reduction.

R = Rain load.

S = Snow load.

T = Self-straining force arising from contraction or expansion resulting from temperature change, shrinkage, moisture change, creep in component materials, movement due to differential settlement or combinations thereof.

W = Load due to wind pressure.

SECTION 1603 CONSTRUCTION DOCUMENTS

1603.1 General. *Construction documents* shall show the size, section and relative locations of structural members with floor levels, column centers and offsets dimensioned. The design loads and other information pertinent to the structural design required by Sections 1603.1.1 through 1603.1.9 shall be indicated on the *construction documents*.

Exception: *Construction documents* for buildings constructed in accordance with the *conventional light-frame construction* provisions of Section 2308 shall indicate the following structural design information:

1. Floor and roof live loads.
2. Ground snow load, P_g.
3. Basic wind speed (3-second gust), miles per hour (mph) (m/s) and wind exposure.
4. *Seismic design category* and *site class*.
5. Flood design data, if located in *flood hazard areas* established in Section 1612.3.
6. Design load-bearing values of soils.

1603.1.1 Floor live load. The uniformly distributed, concentrated and impact floor live load used in the design shall be indicated for floor areas. Use of live load reduction in accordance with Section 1607.9 shall be indicated for each type of live load used in the design.

1603.1.2 Roof live load. The roof live load used in the design shall be indicated for roof areas (Section 1607.11).

1603.1.3 Roof snow load. The ground snow load, P_g, shall be indicated. In areas where the ground snow load, P_g, exceeds 10 pounds per square foot (psf) (0.479 kN/m^2), the following additional information shall also be provided, regardless of whether snow loads govern the design of the roof:

1. Flat-roof snow load, P_f.
2. Snow exposure factor, C_e.
3. Snow load importance factor, I.
4. Thermal factor, C_t.

1603.1.4 Wind design data. The following information related to wind loads shall be shown, regardless of whether wind loads govern the design of the lateral-force-resisting system of the building:

1. Basic wind speed (3-second gust), miles per hour (m/s).
2. Wind importance factor, I, and *occupancy category*.
3. Wind exposure. Where more than one wind exposure is utilized, the wind exposure and applicable wind direction shall be indicated.

4. The applicable internal pressure coefficient.
5. Components and cladding. The design wind pressures in terms of psf (kN/m^2) to be used for the design of exterior component and cladding materials not specifically designed by the *registered design professional*.

1603.1.5 Earthquake design data. The following information related to seismic loads shall be shown, regardless of whether seismic loads govern the design of the lateral-force-resisting system of the building:

1. Seismic importance factor, I, and *occupancy category*.
2. Mapped spectral response accelerations, S_S and S_1.
3. *Site class*.
4. Spectral response coefficients, S_{DS} and S_{D1}.
5. *Seismic design category*.
6. Basic seismic-force-resisting system(s).
7. Design base shear.
8. Seismic response coefficient(s), C_S.
9. Response modification factor(s), R.
10. Analysis procedure used.

1603.1.6 Geotechnical information. The design load-bearing values of soils shall be shown on the *construction documents*.

1603.1.7 Flood design data. For buildings located in whole or in part in *flood hazard areas* as established in Section 1612.3, the documentation pertaining to design, if required in Section 1612.5, shall be included and the following information, referenced to the datum on the community's Flood Insurance Rate Map (FIRM), shall be shown, regardless of whether flood loads govern the design of the building:

1. In *flood hazard areas* not subject to high-velocity wave action, the elevation of the proposed lowest floor, including the basement.
2. In *flood hazard areas* not subject to high-velocity wave action, the elevation to which any nonresidential building will be dry floodproofed.
3. In *flood hazard areas* subject to high-velocity wave action, the proposed elevation of the bottom of the lowest horizontal structural member of the lowest floor, including the basement.

1603.1.8 Special loads. Special loads that are applicable to the design of the building, structure or portions thereof shall be indicated along with the specified section of this code that addresses the special loading condition.

1603.1.9 Systems and components requiring special inspections for seismic resistance. *Construction documents* or specifications shall be prepared for those systems and components requiring *special inspection* for seismic resistance as specified in Section 1707.1 by the *registered design professional* responsible for their design and shall be submitted for approval in accordance with Section 107.1. Reference to seismic standards in lieu of detailed drawings is acceptable.

SECTION 1604
GENERAL DESIGN REQUIREMENTS

1604.1 General. Building, structures and parts thereof shall be designed and constructed in accordance with strength design, *load and resistance factor design*, *allowable stress design*, empirical design or conventional construction methods, as permitted by the applicable material chapters.

1604.2 Strength. Buildings and other structures, and parts thereof, shall be designed and constructed to support safely the factored loads in load combinations defined in this code without exceeding the appropriate strength limit states for the materials of construction. Alternatively, buildings and other structures, and parts thereof, shall be designed and constructed to support safely the *nominal loads* in load combinations defined in this code without exceeding the appropriate specified allowable stresses for the materials of construction.

Loads and forces for occupancies or uses not covered in this chapter shall be subject to the approval of the *building official*.

1604.3 Serviceability. Structural systems and members thereof shall be designed to have adequate stiffness to limit deflections and lateral drift. See Section 12.12.1 of ASCE 7 for drift limits applicable to earthquake loading.

1604.3.1 Deflections. The deflections of structural members shall not exceed the more restrictive of the limitations of Sections 1604.3.2 through 1604.3.5 or that permitted by Table 1604.3.

TABLE 1604.3
DEFLECTION LIMITS[a, b, c, h, i]

CONSTRUCTION	L	S or W[f]	$D + L$[d, g]
Roof members:[e]			
Supporting plaster ceiling	l/360	l/360	l/240
Supporting nonplaster ceiling	l/240	l/240	l/180
Not supporting ceiling	l/180	l/180	l/120
Floor members	l/360	—	l/240
Exterior walls and interior partitions:			
With brittle finishes	—	l/240	—
With flexible finishes	—	l/120	—
Farm buildings	—	—	l/180
Greenhouses	—	—	l/120

For SI: 1 foot = 304.8 mm.

a. For structural roofing and siding made of formed metal sheets, the total load deflection shall not exceed l/60. For secondary roof structural members supporting formed metal roofing, the live load deflection shall not exceed l/150. For secondary wall members supporting formed metal siding, the design wind load deflection shall not exceed l/90. For roofs, this exception only applies when the metal sheets have no roof covering.

b. Interior partitions not exceeding 6 feet in height and flexible, folding and portable partitions are not governed by the provisions of this section. The deflection criterion for interior partitions is based on the horizontal load defined in Section 1607.13.

c. See Section 2403 for glass supports.

(Table notes continued)

d. For wood structural members having a moisture content of less than 16 percent at time of installation and used under dry conditions, the deflection resulting from $L + 0.5D$ is permitted to be substituted for the deflection resulting from $L + D$.

e. The above deflections do not ensure against ponding. Roofs that do not have sufficient slope or camber to assure adequate drainage shall be investigated for ponding. See Section 1611 for rain and ponding requirements and Section 1503.4 for roof drainage requirements.

f. The wind load is permitted to be taken as 0.7 times the "component and cladding" loads for the purpose of determining deflection limits herein.

g. For steel structural members, the dead load shall be taken as zero.

h. For aluminum structural members or aluminum panels used in skylights and sloped glazing framing, roofs or walls of sunroom additions or patio covers, not supporting edge of glass or aluminum sandwich panels, the total load deflection shall not exceed $l/60$. For continuous aluminum structural members supporting edge of glass, the total load deflection shall not exceed $l/175$ for each glass lite or $l/60$ for the entire length of the member, whichever is more stringent. For aluminum sandwich panels used in roofs or walls of sunroom additions or patio covers, the total load deflection shall not exceed $l/120$.

i. For cantilever members, l shall be taken as twice the length of the cantilever.

1604.3.2 Reinforced concrete. The deflection of reinforced concrete structural members shall not exceed that permitted by ACI 318.

1604.3.3 Steel. The deflection of steel structural members shall not exceed that permitted by AISC 360, AISI S100, ASCE 3, ASCE 8, SJI CJ-1.0, SJI JG-1.1, SJI K-1.1 or SJI LH/DLH-1.1, as applicable.

1604.3.4 Masonry. The deflection of masonry structural members shall not exceed that permitted by TMS 402/ACI 530/ASCE 5.

1604.3.5 Aluminum. The deflection of aluminum structural members shall not exceed that permitted by AA ADM1.

1604.3.6 Limits. Deflection of structural members over span, l, shall not exceed that permitted by Table 1604.3.

1604.4 Analysis. *Load effects* on structural members and their connections shall be determined by methods of structural analysis that take into account equilibrium, general stability, geometric compatibility and both short- and long-term material properties.

Members that tend to accumulate residual deformations under repeated service loads shall have included in their analysis the added eccentricities expected to occur during their service life.

Any system or method of construction to be used shall be based on a rational analysis in accordance with well-established principles of mechanics. Such analysis shall result in a system that provides a complete load path capable of transferring loads from their point of origin to the load-resisting elements.

The total lateral force shall be distributed to the various vertical elements of the lateral-force-resisting system in proportion to their rigidities, considering the rigidity of the horizontal bracing system or diaphragm. Rigid elements assumed not to be a part of the lateral-force-resisting system are permitted to be incorporated into buildings provided their effect on the action of the system is considered and provided for in the design. Except where diaphragms are flexible, or are permitted to be analyzed as flexible, provisions shall be made for the increased forces induced on resisting elements of the structural system resulting from torsion due to eccentricity between the center of application of the lateral forces and the center of rigidity of the lateral-force-resisting system.

Every structure shall be designed to resist the overturning effects caused by the lateral forces specified in this chapter. See Section 1609 for wind loads, Section 1610 for lateral soil loads and Section 1613 for earthquake loads.

1604.5 Occupancy category. Each building and structure shall be assigned an *occupancy category* in accordance with Table 1604.5.

1604.5.1 Multiple occupancies. Where a building or structure is occupied by two or more occupancies not included in the same *occupancy category*, it shall be assigned the classification of the highest *occupancy category* corresponding to the various occupancies. Where buildings or structures have two or more portions that are structurally separated, each portion shall be separately classified. Where a separated portion of a building or structure provides required access to, required egress from or shares life safety components with another portion having a higher *occupancy category*, both portions shall be assigned to the higher *occupancy category*.

1604.6 In-situ load tests. The *building official* is authorized to require an engineering analysis or a load test, or both, of any construction whenever there is reason to question the safety of the construction for the intended occupancy. Engineering analysis and load tests shall be conducted in accordance with Section 1714.

1604.7 Preconstruction load tests. Materials and methods of construction that are not capable of being designed by *approved* engineering analysis or that do not comply with the applicable material design standards listed in Chapter 35, or alternative test procedures in accordance with Section 1712, shall be load tested in accordance with Section 1715.

1604.8 Anchorage.

1604.8.1 General. Anchorage of the roof to walls and columns, and of walls and columns to foundations, shall be provided to resist the uplift and sliding forces that result from the application of the prescribed loads.

1604.8.2 Walls. Walls shall be anchored to floors, roofs and other structural elements that provide lateral support for the wall. Such anchorage shall provide a positive direct connection capable of resisting the horizontal forces specified in this chapter but not less than the minimum strength design horizontal force specified in Section 11.7.3 of ASCE 7, substituted for "E" in the load combinations of Section 1605.2 or 1605.3. Concrete and masonry walls shall be designed to resist bending between anchors where the anchor spacing exceeds 4 feet (1219 mm). Required anchors in masonry walls of hollow units or cavity walls shall be embedded in a reinforced grouted structural element of the wall. See Sections 1609 for wind design requirements and 1613 for earthquake design requirements.

1604.8.3 Decks. Where supported by attachment to an *exterior wall*, decks shall be positively anchored to the primary structure and designed for both vertical and lateral loads as applicable. Such attachment shall not be accomplished by the use of toenails or nails subject to withdrawal. Where positive connection to the primary building structure cannot be verified during inspection, decks shall be self-supporting. Connections of decks with cantilevered framing members to exterior walls or other framing members shall be designed for both of the following:

1. The reactions resulting from the dead load and live load specified in Table 1607.1, or the snow load specified in Section 1608, in accordance with Section 1605, acting on all portions of the deck.
2. The reactions resulting from the dead load and live load specified in Table 1607.1, or the snow load specified in Section 1608, in accordance with Section 1605, acting on the cantilevered portion of the deck, and no live load or snow load on the remaining portion of the deck.

1604.9 Counteracting structural actions. Structural members, systems, components and cladding shall be designed to resist forces due to earthquake and wind, with consideration of overturning, sliding and uplift. Continuous load paths shall be provided for transmitting these forces to the foundation. Where sliding is used to isolate the elements, the effects of friction between sliding elements shall be included as a force.

1604.10 Wind and seismic detailing. Lateral-force-resisting systems shall meet seismic detailing requirements and limitations prescribed in this code and ASCE 7, excluding Chapter 14 and Appendix 11A, even when wind *load effects* are greater than seismic *load effects*.

TABLE 1604.5
OCCUPANCY CATEGORY OF BUILDINGS AND OTHER STRUCTURES

OCCUPANCY CATEGORY	NATURE OF OCCUPANCY
I	Buildings and other structures that represent a low hazard to human life in the event of failure, including but not limited to: • Agricultural facilities. • Certain temporary facilities. • Minor storage facilities.
II	Buildings and other structures except those listed in Occupancy Categories I, III and IV
III	Buildings and other structures that represent a substantial hazard to human life in the event of failure, including but not limited to: • Buildings and other structures whose primary occupancy is public assembly with an occupant load greater than 300. • Buildings and other structures containing elementary school, secondary school or day care facilities with an occupant load greater than 250. • Buildings and other structures containing adult education facilities, such as colleges and universities, with an occupant load greater than 500. • Group I-2 occupancies with an occupant load of 50 or more resident patients but not having surgery or emergency treatment facilities. • Group I-3 occupancies. • Any other occupancy with an occupant load greater than 5,000[a]. • Power-generating stations, water treatment facilities for potable water, waste water treatment facilities and other public utility facilities not included in Occupancy Category IV. • Buildings and other structures not included in Occupancy Category IV containing sufficient quantities of toxic or explosive substances to be dangerous to the public if released.
IV	Buildings and other structures designated as essential facilities, including but not limited to: • Group I-2 occupancies having surgery or emergency treatment facilities. • Fire, rescue, ambulance and police stations and emergency vehicle garages. • Designated earthquake, hurricane or other emergency shelters. • Designated emergency preparedness, communications and operations centers and other facilities required for emergency response. • Power-generating stations and other public utility facilities required as emergency backup facilities for Occupancy Category IV structures. • Structures containing highly toxic materials as defined by Section 307 where the quantity of the material exceeds the maximum allowable quantities of Table 307.1(2). • Aviation control towers, air traffic control centers and emergency aircraft hangars. • Buildings and other structures having critical national defense functions. • Water storage facilities and pump structures required to maintain water pressure for fire suppression[b].

a. For purposes of occupant load calculation, occupancies required by Table 1004.1.1 to use gross floor area calculations shall be permitted to use net floor areas to determine the total occupant load.
b. Not intended for such uses in Categories I, II and III.

SECTION 1605
LOAD COMBINATIONS

1605.1 General. Buildings and other structures and portions thereof shall be designed to resist:

1. The load combinations specified in Section 1605.2, 1605.3.1 or 1605.3.2,
2. The load combinations specified in Chapters 18 through 23, and
3. The load combinations with overstrength factor specified in Section 12.4.3.2 of ASCE 7 where required by Section 12.2.5.2, 12.3.3.3 or 12.10.2.1 of ASCE 7. With the simplified procedure of ASCE 7 Section 12.14, the load combinations with overstrength factor of Section 12.14.3.2 of ASCE 7 shall be used.

Applicable loads shall be considered, including both earthquake and wind, in accordance with the specified load combinations. Each load combination shall also be investigated with one or more of the variable loads set to zero.

Where the load combinations with overstrength factor in Section 12.4.3.2 of ASCE 7 apply, they shall be used as follows:

1. The basic combinations for strength design with overstrength factor in lieu of Equations 16-5 and 16-7 in Section 1605.2.1.
2. The basic combinations for *allowable stress design* with overstrength factor in lieu of Equations 16-12, 16-13 and 16-15 in Section 1605.3.1.
3. The basic combinations for *allowable stress design* with overstrength factor in lieu of Equations 16-20 and 16-21 in Section 1605.3.2.

1605.1.1 Stability. Regardless of which load combinations are used to design for strength, where overall structure stability (such as stability against overturning, sliding, or buoyancy) is being verified, use of the load combinations specified in Section 1605.2 or 1605.3 shall be permitted. Where the load combinations specified in Section 1605.2 are used, strength reduction factors applicable to soil resistance shall be provided by a *registered design professional*. The stability of retaining walls shall be verified in accordance with Section 1807.2.3.

1605.2 Load combinations using strength design or load and resistance factor design.

1605.2.1 Basic load combinations. Where strength design or *load and resistance factor design* is used, structures and portions thereof shall resist the most critical effects from the following combinations of factored loads:

$1.4(D+F)$ **(Equation 16-1)**

$1.2(D+F+T)+1.6(L+H)+0.5(L_r \text{ or } S \text{ or } R)$ **(Equation 16-2)**

$1.2D+1.6(L_r \text{ or } S \text{ or } R)+(f_1 L \text{ or } 0.8W)$ **(Equation 16-3)**

$1.2D+1.6W+f_1 L+0.5(L_r \text{ or } S \text{ or } R)$ **(Equation 16-4)**

$1.2D+1.0E+f_1 L+f_2 S$ **(Equation 16-5)**

$0.9D+1.6W+1.6H$ **(Equation 16-6)**

$0.9D+1.0E+1.6H$ **(Equation 16-7)**

where:

f_1 = 1 for floors in places of public assembly, for live loads in excess of 100 pounds per square foot (4.79 kN/m^2), and for parking garage live load, and

= 0.5 for other live loads.

f_2 = 0.7 for roof configurations (such as saw tooth) that do not shed snow off the structure, and

= 0.2 for other roof configurations.

Exception: Where other factored load combinations are specifically required by the provisions of this code, such combinations shall take precedence.

1605.2.2 Flood loads. Where flood loads, F_a, are to be considered in the design, the load combinations of Section 2.3.3 of ASCE 7 shall be used.

1605.3 Load combinations using allowable stress design.

1605.3.1 Basic load combinations. Where *allowable stress design* (working stress design), as permitted by this code, is used, structures and portions thereof shall resist the most critical effects resulting from the following combinations of loads:

$D+F$ **(Equation 16-8)**

$D+H+F+L+T$ **(Equation 16-9)**

$D+H+F+(L_r \text{ or } S \text{ or } R)$ **(Equation 16-10)**

$D+H+F+0.75(L+T)+0.75(L_r \text{ or } S \text{ or } R)$ **(Equation 16-11)**

$D+H+F+(W \text{ or } 0.7E)$ **(Equation 16-12)**

$D+H+F+0.75(W \text{ or } 0.7E)+0.75L+0.75(L_r \text{ or } S \text{ or } R)$ **(Equation 16-13)**

$0.6D+W+H$ **(Equation 16-14)**

$0.6D+0.7E+H$ **(Equation 16-15)**

Exceptions:

1. Crane hook loads need not be combined with roof live load or with more than three-fourths of the snow load or one-half of the wind load.
2. Flat roof snow loads of 30 psf (1.44 kN/m^2) or less and roof live loads of 30 psf (1.44 kN/m^2) or less need not be combined with seismic loads. Where flat roof snow loads exceed 30 psf (1.44 kN/m^2), 20 percent shall be combined with seismic loads.

1605.3.1.1 Stress increases. Increases in allowable stresses specified in the appropriate material chapter or the referenced standards shall not be used with the load combinations of Section 1605.3.1, except that increases shall be permitted in accordance with Chapter 23.

1605.3.1.2 Flood loads. Where flood loads, F_a, are to be considered in design, the load combinations of Section 2.4.2 of ASCE 7 shall be used.

1605.3.2 Alternative basic load combinations. In lieu of the basic load combinations specified in Section 1605.3.1, structures and portions thereof shall be permitted to be designed for the most critical effects resulting from the following combinations. When using these alternative basic load combinations that include wind or seismic loads, allowable stresses are permitted to be increased or load combinations reduced where permitted by the material chapter of this code or the referenced standards. For load combinations that include the counteracting effects of dead and wind loads, only two-thirds of the minimum dead load likely to be in place during a design wind event shall be used. Where wind loads are calculated in accordance with Chapter 6 of ASCE 7, the coefficient ω in the following equations shall be taken as 1.3. For other wind loads, ω shall be taken as 1. When using these alternative load combinations to evaluate sliding, overturning and soil bearing at the soil-structure interface, the reduction of foundation overturning from Section 12.13.4 in ASCE 7 shall not be used. When using these alternative basic load combinations for proportioning foundations for loadings, which include seismic loads, the vertical seismic *load effect*, E_v, in Equation 12.4-4 of ASCE 7 is permitted to be taken equal to zero.

$$D + L + (L_r \text{ or } S \text{ or } R) \quad \textbf{(Equation 16-16)}$$

$$D + L + (\omega W) \quad \textbf{(Equation 16-17)}$$

$$D + L + \omega W + S/2 \quad \textbf{(Equation 16-18)}$$

$$D + L + S + \omega W/2 \quad \textbf{(Equation 16-19)}$$

$$D + L + S + E/1.4 \quad \textbf{(Equation 16-20)}$$

$$0.9D + E/1.4 \quad \textbf{(Equation 16-21)}$$

Exceptions:

1. Crane hook loads need not be combined with roof live loads or with more than three-fourths of the snow load or one-half of the wind load.
2. Flat roof snow loads of 30 psf (1.44 kN/m^2) or less and roof live loads of 30 psf (1.44 kN/m^2) or less need not be combined with seismic loads. Where flat roof snow loads exceed 30 psf (1.44 kN/m^2), 20 percent shall be combined with seismic loads.

1605.3.2.1 Other loads. Where *F, H* or *T* are to be considered in the design, each applicable load shall be added to the combinations specified in Section 1605.3.2.

1605.4 Heliports and helistops. Heliport and helistop landing areas shall be designed for the following loads, combined in accordance with Section 1605:

1. Dead load, *D*, plus the gross weight of the helicopter, D_h, plus snow load, *S*.
2. Dead load, *D*, plus two single concentrated impact loads, *L*, approximately 8 feet (2438 mm) apart applied anywhere on the touchdown pad (representing each of the helicopter's two main landing gear, whether skid type or wheeled type), having a magnitude of 0.75 times the gross weight of the helicopter. Both loads acting together total 1.5 times the gross weight of the helicopter.
3. Dead load, *D*, plus a uniform live load, *L*, of 100 psf (4.79 kN/m^2).

Exception: Landing areas designed for helicopters with gross weights not exceeding 3,000 pounds (13.34 kN) in accordance with Items 1 and 2 shall be permitted to be designed using a 40 psf (1.92 kN/m^2) uniform live load in Item 3, provided the landing area is identified with a 3,000-pound (13.34 kN) weight limitation. This 40-psf (1.92 kN/m^2) uniform live load shall not be reduced. The landing area weight limitation shall be indicated by the numeral "3" (kips) located in the bottom right corner of the landing area as viewed from the primary approach path. The indication for the landing area weight limitation shall be a minimum 5 feet (1524 mm) in height.

SECTION 1606 DEAD LOADS

1606.1 General. Dead loads are those loads defined in Section 1602.1. Dead loads shall be considered permanent loads.

1606.2 Design dead load. For purposes of design, the actual weights of materials of construction and fixed service equipment shall be used. In the absence of definite information, values used shall be subject to the approval of the *building official*.

SECTION 1607 LIVE LOADS

1607.1 General. Live loads are those loads defined in Section 1602.1.

1607.2 Loads not specified. For occupancies or uses not designated in Table 1607.1, the live load shall be determined in accordance with a method *approved* by the *building official*.

1607.3 Uniform live loads. The live loads used in the design of buildings and other structures shall be the maximum loads expected by the intended use or occupancy but shall in no case be less than the minimum uniformly distributed unit loads required by Table 1607.1.

1607.4 Concentrated loads. Floors and other similar surfaces shall be designed to support the uniformly distributed live loads prescribed in Section 1607.3 or the concentrated load, in pounds (kilonewtons), given in Table 1607.1, whichever produces the greater *load effects*. Unless otherwise specified, the indicated concentration shall be assumed to be uniformly distributed over an area $2^1/_2$ feet by $2^1/_2$ feet (0.76 m by 0.76 m) [$6^1/_4$ square feet (0.58 m^2)] and shall be located so as to produce the maximum *load effects* in the structural members.

1607.5 Partition loads. In office buildings and in other buildings where partition locations are subject to change, provisions for partition weight shall be made, whether or not partitions are shown on the *construction documents*, unless the specified live load exceeds 80 psf (3.83 kN/m^2). The partition load shall not be less than a uniformly distributed live load of 15 psf (0.72 kN/m^2).

TABLE 1607.1
MINIMUM UNIFORMLY DISTRIBUTED LIVE LOADS, L_o, AND MINIMUM CONCENTRATED LIVE LOADS[g]

OCCUPANCY OR USE	UNIFORM (psf)	CONCENTRATED (lbs.)
1. Apartments (see residential)	—	—
2. Access floor systems Office use Computer use	 50 100	 2,000 2,000
3. Armories and drill rooms	150	—
4. Assembly areas and theaters Fixed seats (fastened to floor) Follow spot, projections and control rooms Lobbies Movable seats Stages and platforms Other assembly areas	 60 50 100 100 125 100	—
5. Balconies (exterior) and decks[h]	Same as occupancy served	—
6. Bowling alleys	75	—
7. Catwalks	40	300
8. Cornices	60	—
9. Corridors, except as otherwise indicated	100	—
10. Dance halls and ballrooms	100	—
11. Dining rooms and restaurants	100	—
12. Dwellings (see residential)	—	—
13. Elevator machine room grating (on area of 4 in²)	—	300
14. Finish light floor plate construction (on area of 1 in²)	—	200
15. Fire escapes On single-family dwellings only	100 40	—
16. Garages (passenger vehicles only) Trucks and buses	40 See Section 1607.6	Note a
17. Grandstands (see stadium and arena bleachers)	—	—
18. Gymnasiums, main floors and balconies	100	—
19. Handrails, guards and grab bars	See Section 1607.7	
20. Hospitals Corridors above first floor Operating rooms, laboratories Patient rooms	 80 60 40	 1,000 1,000 1,000
21. Hotels (see residential)	—	—
22. Libraries Corridors above first floor Reading rooms Stack rooms	 80 60 150[b]	 1,000 1,000 1,000
23. Manufacturing Heavy Light	 250 125	 3,000 2,000
24. Marquees	75	—
25. Office buildings Corridors above first floor File and computer rooms shall be designed for heavier loads based on anticipated occupancy Lobbies and first-floor corridors Offices	 80 — 100 50	 2,000 — 2,000 2,000
26. Penal institutions Cell blocks Corridors	 40 100	—
27. Residential One- and two-family dwellings Uninhabitable attics without storage[i] Uninhabitable attics with limited storage[i, j, k] Habitable attics and sleeping areas All other areas Hotels and multifamily dwellings Private rooms and corridors serving them Public rooms and corridors serving them	 10 20 30 40 40 100	—
28. Reviewing stands, grandstands and bleachers	Note c	
29. Roofs All roof surfaces subject to maintenance workers Awnings and canopies Fabric construction supported by a lightweight rigid skeleton structure All other construction Ordinary flat, pitched, and curved roofs Primary roof members, exposed to a work floor Single panel point of lower chord of roof trusses or any point along primary structural members supporting roofs: Over manufacturing, storage warehouses, and repair garages All other occupancies Roofs used for other special purposes Roofs used for promenade purposes Roofs used for roof gardens or assembly purposes	 5 nonreducible 20 20 Note 1 60 100	 300 2,000 300 Note 1
30. Schools Classrooms Corridors above first floor First-floor corridors	 40 80 100	 1,000 1,000 1,000
31. Scuttles, skylight ribs and accessible ceilings	—	200
32. Sidewalks, vehicular driveways and yards, subject to trucking	250[d]	8,000[e]
33. Skating rinks	100	—

continued

TABLE 1607.1—continued
MINIMUM UNIFORMLY DISTRIBUTED LIVE LOADS, L_o, AND MINIMUM CONCENTRATED LIVE LOADS[g]

OCCUPANCY OR USE	UNIFORM (psf)	CONCENTRATED (lbs.)
34. Stadiums and arenas Bleachers Fixed seats (fastened to floor)	 100[c] 60[c]	 —
35. Stairs and exits One- and two-family dwellings All other	 40 100	Note f
36. Storage warehouses (shall be designed for heavier loads if required for anticipated storage) Heavy Light	 250 125	
37. Stores Retail First floor Upper floors Wholesale, all floors	 100 75 125	 1,000 1,000 1,000
38. Vehicle barrier systems	See Section 1607.7.3	
39. Walkways and elevated platforms (other than exitways)	60	—
40. Yards and terraces, pedestrians	100	—

For SI: 1 inch = 25.4 mm, 1 foot = 304.8 mm, 1 square inch = 645.16 mm^2,
1 square foot = 0.0929 m^2,
1 pound per square foot = 0.0479 kN/m^2, 1 pound = 0.004448 kN,

a. Floors in garages or portions of buildings used for the storage of motor vehicles shall be designed for the uniformly distributed live loads of Table 1607.1 or the following concentrated loads: (1) for garages restricted to passenger vehicles accommodating not more than nine passengers, 3,000 pounds acting on an area of 4.5 inches by 4.5 inches; (2) for mechanical parking structures without slab or deck which are used for storing passenger vehicles only, 2,250 pounds per wheel.

b. The loading applies to stack room floors that support nonmobile, double-faced library bookstacks, subject to the following limitations:
   1. The nominal bookstack unit height shall not exceed 90 inches;
   2. The nominal shelf depth shall not exceed 12 inches for each face; and
   3. Parallel rows of double-faced bookstacks shall be separated by aisles not less than 36 inches wide.

c. Design in accordance with ICC 300.

d. Other uniform loads in accordance with an approved method which contains provisions for truck loadings shall also be considered where appropriate.

e. The concentrated wheel load shall be applied on an area of 4.5 inches by 4.5 inches.

f. Minimum concentrated load on stair treads (on area of 4 square inches) is 300 pounds.

g. Where snow loads occur that are in excess of the design conditions, the structure shall be designed to support the loads due to the increased loads caused by drift buildup or a greater snow design determined by the building official (see Section 1608). For special-purpose roofs, see Section 1607.11.2.2.

h. See Section 1604.8.3 for decks attached to exterior walls.

i. Attics without storage are those where the maximum clear height between the joist and rafter is less than 42 inches, or where there are not two or more adjacent trusses with the same web configuration capable of containing a rectangle 42 inches high by 2 feet wide, or greater, located within the plane of the truss. For attics without storage, this live load need not be assumed to act concurrently with any other live load requirements.

j. For attics with limited storage and constructed with trusses, this live load need only be applied to those portions of the bottom chord where there are two or more adjacent trusses with the same web configuration capable of containing a rectangle 42 inches high by 2 feet wide or greater, located within the plane of the truss. The rectangle shall fit between the top of the bottom chord and the bottom of any other truss member, provided that each of the following criteria is met:
   i. The attic area is accessible by a pull-down stairway or framed opening in accordance with Section 1209.2, and
   ii. The truss shall have a bottom chord pitch less than 2:12.
   iii. Bottom chords of trusses shall be designed for the greater of actual imposed dead load or 10 psf, uniformly distributed over the entire span.

k. Attic spaces served by a fixed stair shall be designed to support the minimum live load specified for habitable attics and sleeping rooms.

l. Roofs used for other special purposes shall be designed for appropriate loads as approved by the building official.

1607.6 Truck and bus garages. Minimum live loads for garages having trucks or buses shall be as specified in Table 1607.6, but shall not be less than 50 psf (2.40 kN/m^2), unless other loads are specifically justified and *approved* by the *building official*. Actual loads shall be used where they are greater than the loads specified in the table.

1607.6.1 Truck and bus garage live load application. The concentrated load and uniform load shall be uniformly distributed over a 10-foot (3048 mm) width on a line normal to the centerline of the lane placed within a 12-foot-wide (3658 mm) lane. The loads shall be placed within their individual lanes so as to produce the maximum stress in each structural member. Single spans shall be designed for the uniform load in Table 1607.6 and one simultaneous concentrated load positioned to produce the maximum effect. Multiple spans shall be designed for the uniform load in Table 1607.6 on the spans and two simultaneous concentrated loads in two spans positioned to produce the maximum negative moment effect. Multiple span design loads, for other effects, shall be the same as for single spans.

TABLE 1607.6
UNIFORM AND CONCENTRATED LOADS

LOADING CLASS[a]	UNIFORM LOAD (pounds/linear foot of lane)	CONCENTRATED LOAD (pounds)[b]	
		For moment design	For shear design
H20-44 and HS20-44	640	18,000	26,000
H15-44 and HS15-44	480	13,500	19,500

For SI: 1 pound per linear foot = 0.01459 kN/m, 1 pound = 0.004448 kN,
1 ton = 8.90 kN.

a. An H loading class designates a two-axle truck with a semitrailer. An HS loading class designates a tractor truck with a semitrailer. The numbers following the letter classification indicate the gross weight in tons of the standard truck and the year the loadings were instituted.

b. See Section 1607.6.1 for the loading of multiple spans.

1607.7 Loads on handrails, guards, grab bars, seats and vehicle barrier systems. Handrails, *guards*, grab bars, accessible seats, accessible benches and vehicle barrier systems shall be designed and constructed to the structural loading conditions set forth in this section.

1607.7.1 Handrails and guards. Handrails and *guards* shall be designed to resist a load of 50 pounds per linear foot (plf) (0.73 kN/m) applied in any direction at the top and to transfer this load through the supports to the structure. Glass handrail assemblies and *guards* shall also comply with Section 2407.

Exceptions:

1. For one- and two-family dwellings, only the single concentrated load required by Section 1607.7.1.1 shall be applied.
2. In Group I-3, F, H and S occupancies, for areas that are not accessible to the general public and that have an *occupant load* less than 50, the minimum load shall be 20 pounds per foot (0.29 kN/m).

1607.7.1.1 Concentrated load. Handrails and *guards* shall be able to resist a single concentrated load of 200 pounds (0.89 kN), applied in any direction at any point along the top, and to transfer this load through the supports to the structure. This load need not be assumed to act concurrently with the loads specified in Section 1607.7.1.

1607.7.1.2 Components. Intermediate rails (all those except the handrail), balusters and panel fillers shall be designed to withstand a horizontally applied normal load of 50 pounds (0.22 kN) on an area equal to 1 square foot (0.0929 m^2), including openings and space between rails. Reactions due to this loading are not required to be superimposed with those of Section 1607.7.1 or 1607.7.1.1.

1607.7.2 Grab bars, shower seats and dressing room bench seats. Grab bars, shower seats and dressing room bench seat systems shall be designed to resist a single concentrated load of 250 pounds (1.11 kN) applied in any direction at any point.

1607.7.3 Vehicle barrier systems. Vehicle barrier systems for passenger vehicles shall be designed to resist a single load of 6,000 pounds (26.70 kN) applied horizontally in any direction to the barrier system and shall have anchorage or attachment capable of transmitting this load to the structure. For design of the system, two loading conditions shall be analyzed. The first condition shall apply the load at a height of 1 foot, 6 inches (457 mm) above the floor or ramp surface. The second loading condition shall apply the load at 2 feet, 3 inches (686 mm) above the floor or ramp surface. The more severe load condition shall govern the design of the barrier restraint system. The load shall be assumed to act on an area not to exceed 1 square foot (0.0929 m^2), and is not required to be assumed to act concurrently with any handrail or *guard* loadings specified in Section 1607.7.1. Garages accommodating trucks and buses shall be designed in accordance with an *approved* method that contains provisions for traffic railings.

1607.8 Impact loads. The live loads specified in Section 1607.3 include allowance for impact conditions. Provisions shall be made in the structural design for uses and loads that involve unusual vibration and impact forces.

1607.8.1 Elevators. Elevator loads shall be increased by 100 percent for impact and the structural supports shall be designed within the limits of deflection prescribed by ASME A17.1.

1607.8.2 Machinery. For the purpose of design, the weight of machinery and moving loads shall be increased as follows to allow for impact: (1) elevator machinery, 100 percent; (2) light machinery, shaft- or motor-driven, 20 percent; (3) reciprocating machinery or power-driven units, 50 percent; (4) hangers for floors or balconies, 33 percent. Percentages shall be increased where specified by the manufacturer.

1607.9 Reduction in live loads. Except for uniform live loads at roofs, all other minimum uniformly distributed live loads, L_o, in Table 1607.1 are permitted to be reduced in accordance with Section 1607.9.1 or 1607.9.2. Roof uniform live loads, other than special purpose roofs of Section 1607.11.2.2, are permitted to be reduced in accordance with Section 1607.11.2. Roof uniform live loads of special purpose roofs are permitted to be reduced in accordance with Section 1607.9.1 or 1607.9.2.

1607.9.1 General. Subject to the limitations of Sections 1607.9.1.1 through 1607.9.1.4, members for which a value of $K_{LL}A_T$ is 400 square feet (37.16 m^2) or more are permitted to be designed for a reduced live load in accordance with the following equation:

$$L = L_o\left(0.25+\frac{15}{\sqrt{K_{LL}A_T}}\right) \quad \textbf{(Equation 16-22)}$$

For SI: $L = L_o\left(0.25+\frac{4.57}{\sqrt{K_{LL}A_T}}\right)$

where:

L = Reduced design live load per square foot (square meter) of area supported by the member.

L_o = Unreduced design live load per square foot (square meter) of area supported by the member (see Table 1607.1).

K_{LL} = Live load element factor (see Table 1607.9.1).

A_T = Tributary area, in square feet (square meters).

L shall not be less than $0.50L_o$ for members supporting one floor and L shall not be less than $0.40L_o$ for members supporting two or more floors.

TABLE 1607.9.1
LIVE LOAD ELEMENT FACTOR, K_{LL}

ELEMENT	K_{LL}
Interior columns Exterior columns without cantilever slabs	4 4
Edge columns with cantilever slabs	3
Corner columns with cantilever slabs Edge beams without cantilever slabs Interior beams	2 2 2
All other members not identified above including: Edge beams with cantilever slabs Cantilever beams One-way slabs Two-way slabs Members without provisions for continuous shear transfer normal to their span	1

1607.9.1.1 One-way slabs. The tributary area, A_T, for use in Equation 16-22 for one-way slabs shall not exceed an area defined by the slab span times a width normal to the span of 1.5 times the slab span.

1607.9.1.2 Heavy live loads. Live loads that exceed 100 psf (4.79 kN/m^2) shall not be reduced.

Exceptions:

1. The live loads for members supporting two or more floors are permitted to be reduced by a maximum of 20 percent, but the live load shall

not be less than L as calculated in Section 1607.9.1.

2. For uses other than storage, where *approved*, additional live load reductions shall be permitted where shown by the *registered design professional* that a rational approach has been used and that such reductions are warranted.

1607.9.1.3 Passenger vehicle garages. The live loads shall not be reduced in passenger vehicle garages.

Exception: The live loads for members supporting two or more floors are permitted to be reduced by a maximum of 20 percent, but the live load shall not be less than L as calculated in Section 1607.9.1.

1607.9.1.4 Group A occupancies. Live loads of 100 psf (4.79 kN/m^2) and at areas where fixed seats are located shall not be reduced in Group A occupancies.

1607.9.1.5 Roof members. Live loads of 100 psf (4.79 kN/m^2) or less shall not be reduced for roof members except as specified in Section 1607.11.2.

1607.9.2 Alternate floor live load reduction. As an alternative to Section 1607.9.1, floor live loads are permitted to be reduced in accordance with the following provisions. Such reductions shall apply to slab systems, beams, girders, columns, piers, walls and foundations.

1. A reduction shall not be permitted in Group A occupancies.
2. A reduction shall not be permitted where the live load exceeds 100 psf (4.79 kN/m^2) except that the design live load for members supporting two or more floors is permitted to be reduced by 20 percent.

   Exception: For uses other than storage, where *approved*, additional live load reductions shall be permitted where shown by the *registered design professional* that a rational approach has been used and that such reductions are warranted.

3. A reduction shall not be permitted in passenger vehicle parking garages except that the live loads for members supporting two or more floors are permitted to be reduced by a maximum of 20 percent.
4. For live loads not exceeding 100 psf (4.79 kN/m^2), the design live load for any structural member supporting 150 square feet (13.94 m^2) or more is permitted to be reduced in accordance with Equation 16-23.
5. For one-way slabs, the area, A, for use in Equation 16-23 shall not exceed the product of the slab span and a width normal to the span of 0.5 times the slab span.

$$R = 0.08(A - 150) \qquad \textbf{(Equation 16-23)}$$

For SI: $R = 0.861(A - 13.94)$

Such reduction shall not exceed the smallest of:

1. 40 percent for horizontal members;
2. 60 percent for vertical members; or
3. R as determined by the following equation.

$$R = 23.1(1 + D/L_o) \qquad \textbf{(Equation 16-24)}$$

where:

A = Area of floor supported by the member, square feet (m^2).

D = Dead load per square foot (m^2) of area supported.

L_o = Unreduced live load per square foot (m^2) of area supported.

R = Reduction in percent.

1607.10 Distribution of floor loads. Where uniform floor live loads are involved in the design of structural members arranged so as to create continuity, the minimum applied loads shall be the full dead loads on all spans in combination with the floor live loads on spans selected to produce the greatest effect at each location under consideration. It shall be permitted to reduce floor live loads in accordance with Section 1607.9.

1607.11 Roof loads. The structural supports of roofs and marquees shall be designed to resist wind and, where applicable, snow and earthquake loads, in addition to the dead load of construction and the appropriate live loads as prescribed in this section, or as set forth in Table 1607.1. The live loads acting on a sloping surface shall be assumed to act vertically on the horizontal projection of that surface.

1607.11.1 Distribution of roof loads. Where uniform roof live loads are reduced to less than 20 psf (0.96 kN/m^2) in accordance with Section 1607.11.2.1 and are applied to the design of structural members arranged so as to create continuity, the reduced roof live load shall be applied to adjacent spans or to alternate spans, whichever produces the most unfavorable *load effect*. See Section 1607.11.2 for reductions in minimum roof live loads and Section 7.5 of ASCE 7 for partial snow loading.

1607.11.2 Reduction in roof live loads. The minimum uniformly distributed live loads of roofs and marquees, L_o, in Table 1607.1 are permitted to be reduced in accordance with Section 1607.11.2.1 or 1607.11.2.2.

1607.11.2.1 Flat, pitched and curved roofs. Ordinary flat, pitched and curved roofs, and awnings and canopies other than of fabric construction supported by lightweight rigid skeleton structures, are permitted to be designed for a reduced roof live load as specified in the following equations or other controlling combinations of loads in Section 1605, whichever produces the greater load.

In structures such as greenhouses, where special scaffolding is used as a work surface for workers and materials during maintenance and repair operations, a lower roof load than specified in the following equations shall not be used unless *approved* by the *building official*. Such structures shall be designed for a minimum roof live load of 12 psf (0.58 kN/m^2).

$$L_r = L_o R_1 R_2 \qquad \textbf{(Equation 16-25)}$$

where: $12 \le L_r \le 20$

For SI: $L_r = L_o R_1 R_2$

where: $0.58 \leq L_r \leq 0.96$

L_r = Reduced live load per square foot (m^2) of horizontal projection in pounds per square foot (kN/m^2).

The reduction factors R_1 and R_2 shall be determined as follows:

$R_1 = 1$ for $A_t \leq 200$ square feet (18.58 m^2) **(Equation 16-26)**

$R_1 = 1.2 - 0.001A_t$ for 200 square feet $< A_t <$ 600 square feet **(Equation 16-27)**

For SI: $1.2 - 0.011A_t$ for 18.58 square meters $< A_t <$ 55.74 square meters

$R_1 = 0.6$ for $A_t \geq 600$ square feet (55.74 m^2) **(Equation 16-28)**

where:

A_t = Tributary area (span length multiplied by effective width) in square feet (m^2) supported by any structural member, and

$R_2 = 1$ for $F \leq 4$ **(Equation 16-29)**

$R_2 = 1.2 - 0.05\,F$ for $4 < F < 12$ **(Equation 16-30)**

$R_2 = 0.6$ for $F \geq 12$ **(Equation 16-31)**

where:

F = For a sloped roof, the number of inches of rise per foot (for SI: $F = 0.12 \times$ slope, with slope expressed as a percentage), or for an arch or dome, the rise-to-span ratio multiplied by 32.

1607.11.2.2 Special-purpose roofs. Roofs used for promenade purposes, roof gardens, assembly purposes or other special purposes, and marquees, shall be designed for a minimum live load, L_o, as specified in Table 1607.1. Such live loads are permitted to be reduced in accordance with Section 1607.9. Live loads of 100 psf (4.79 kN/m^2) or more at areas of roofs classified as Group A occupancies shall not be reduced.

1607.11.3 Landscaped roofs. Where roofs are to be landscaped, the uniform design live load in the landscaped area shall be 20 psf (0.958 kN/m^2). The weight of the landscaping materials shall be considered as dead load and shall be computed on the basis of saturation of the soil.

1607.11.4 Awnings and canopies. Awnings and canopies shall be designed for uniform live loads as required in Table 1607.1 as well as for snow loads and wind loads as specified in Sections 1608 and 1609.

1607.12 Crane loads. The crane live load shall be the rated capacity of the crane. Design loads for the runway beams, including connections and support brackets, of moving bridge cranes and monorail cranes shall include the maximum wheel loads of the crane and the vertical impact, lateral and longitudinal forces induced by the moving crane.

1607.12.1 Maximum wheel load. The maximum wheel loads shall be the wheel loads produced by the weight of the bridge, as applicable, plus the sum of the rated capacity and the weight of the trolley with the trolley positioned on its runway at the location where the resulting load effect is maximum.

1607.12.2 Vertical impact force. The maximum wheel loads of the crane shall be increased by the percentages shown below to determine the induced vertical impact or vibration force:

Monorail cranes (powered) . . . . 25 percent

Cab-operated or remotely operated bridge cranes (powered) . . . . 25 percent

Pendant-operated bridge cranes (powered) . . . . 10 percent

Bridge cranes or monorail cranes with hand-geared bridge, trolley and hoist . . . . . 0 percent

1607.12.3 Lateral force. The lateral force on crane runway beams with electrically powered trolleys shall be calculated as 20 percent of the sum of the rated capacity of the crane and the weight of the hoist and trolley. The lateral force shall be assumed to act horizontally at the traction surface of a runway beam, in either direction perpendicular to the beam, and shall be distributed according to the lateral stiffness of the runway beam and supporting structure.

1607.12.4 Longitudinal force. The longitudinal force on crane runway beams, except for bridge cranes with hand-geared bridges, shall be calculated as 10 percent of the maximum wheel loads of the crane. The longitudinal force shall be assumed to act horizontally at the traction surface of a runway beam, in either direction parallel to the beam.

1607.13 Interior walls and partitions. Interior walls and partitions that exceed 6 feet (1829 mm) in height, including their finish materials, shall have adequate strength to resist the loads to which they are subjected but not less than a horizontal load of 5 psf (0.240 kN/m^2).

Exception: Fabric partitions complying with Section 1607.13.1 shall not be required to resist the minimum horizontal load of 5 psf (0.24 kN/m^2).

1607.13.1 Fabric partitions. Fabric partitions that exceed 6 feet (1829 mm) in height, including their finish materials, shall have adequate strength to resist the following load conditions:

1. A horizontal distributed load of 5 psf (0.24 kN/m^2) applied to the partition framing. The total area used to determine the distributed load shall be the area of the fabric face between the framing members to which the fabric is attached. The total distributed load shall be uniformly applied to such framing members in proportion to the length of each member.

2. A concentrated load of 40 pounds (0.176 kN) applied to an 8-inch diameter (203 mm) area [50.3 square inches (32 452 mm^2)] of the fabric face at a height of 54 inches (1372 mm) above the floor.

SECTION 1608
SNOW LOADS

1608.1 General. Design snow loads shall be determined in accordance with Chapter 7 of ASCE 7, but the design roof load shall not be less than that determined by Section 1607.

1608.2 Ground snow loads. The ground snow loads to be used in determining the design snow loads for roofs shall be determined in accordance with ASCE 7 or Figure 1608.2 for North Carolina. Site-specific case studies shall be made in areas designated "CS" in Figure 1608.2. Ground snow loads for sites at elevations above the limits indicated in Figure 1608.2 and for all sites within the CS areas shall be *approved*. Ground snow load determination for such sites shall be based on an extreme value statistical analysis of data available in the vicinity of the site using a value with a 2-percent annual probability of being exceeded (50-year mean recurrence interval).

SECTION 1609
WIND LOADS

1609.1 Applications. Buildings, structures and parts thereof shall be designed to withstand the minimum wind loads prescribed herein. Decreases in wind loads shall not be made for the effect of shielding by other structures.

1609.1.1 Determination of wind loads. Wind loads on every building or structure shall be determined in accordance with Chapter 6 of ASCE 7 or provisions of the alternate all-heights method in Section 1609.6. The type of opening protection required, the basic wind speed and the exposure category for a site is permitted to be determined in accordance with Section 1609 or ASCE 7. Wind shall be assumed to come from any horizontal direction and wind pressures shall be assumed to act normal to the surface considered.

Exceptions:

1. Subject to the limitations of Section 1609.1.1.1, the provisions of ICC 600 shall be permitted for applicable Group R-2 and R-3 buildings.
2. Subject to the limitations of Section 1609.1.1.1, residential structures using the provisions of the AF&PA WFCM.
3. Subject to the limitations of Section 1609.1.1.1, residential structures using the provisions of AISI S230.
4. Designs using NAAMM FP 1001.
5. Designs using TIA-222 for antenna-supporting structures and antennas.
6. Wind tunnel tests in accordance with Section 6.6 of ASCE 7, subject to the limitations in Section 1609.1.1.2.

1609.1.1.1 Applicability. The provisions of ICC 600 are applicable only to buildings located within Exposure B or C as defined in Section 1609.4. The provisions of ICC 600, AF&PA WFCM and AISI S230 shall not apply to buildings sited on the upper half of an isolated hill, ridge or escarpment meeting the following conditions:

1. The hill, ridge or escarpment is 60 feet (18 288 mm) or higher if located in Exposure B or 30 feet (9144 mm) or higher if located in Exposure C;
2. The maximum average slope of the hill exceeds 10 percent; and
3. The hill, ridge or escarpment is unobstructed upwind by other such topographic features for a distance from the high point of 50 times the height of the hill or 1 mile (1.61 km), whichever is greater.

1609.1.1.2 Wind tunnel test limitations. The lower limit on pressures for main wind-force-resisting systems and components and cladding shall be in accordance with Sections 1609.1.1.2.1 and 1609.1.1.2.2.

1609.1.1.2.1 Lower limits on main wind-force-resisting system. Base overturning moments determined from wind tunnel testing shall be limited to not less than 80 percent of the design base overturning moments determined in accordance with Section 6.5 of ASCE 7, unless specific testing is performed that demonstrates it is the aerodynamic coefficient of the building, rather than shielding from other structures, that is responsible for the lower values. The 80-percent limit shall be permitted to be adjusted by the ratio of the frame load at critical wind directions as determined from wind tunnel testing without specific adjacent buildings, but including appropriate upwind roughness, to that determined in Section 6.5 of ASCE 7.

1609.1.1.2.2 Lower limits on components and cladding. The design pressures for components and cladding on walls or roofs shall be selected as the greater of the wind tunnel test results or 80 percent of the pressure obtained for Zone 4 for walls and Zone 1 for roofs as determined in Section 6.5 of ASCE 7, unless specific testing is performed that demonstrates it is the aerodynamic coefficient of the building, rather than shielding from nearby structures, that is responsible for the lower values. Alternatively, limited tests at a few wind directions without specific adjacent buildings, but in the presence of an appropriate upwind roughness, shall be permitted to be used to demonstrate that the lower pressures are due to the shape of the building and not to shielding.

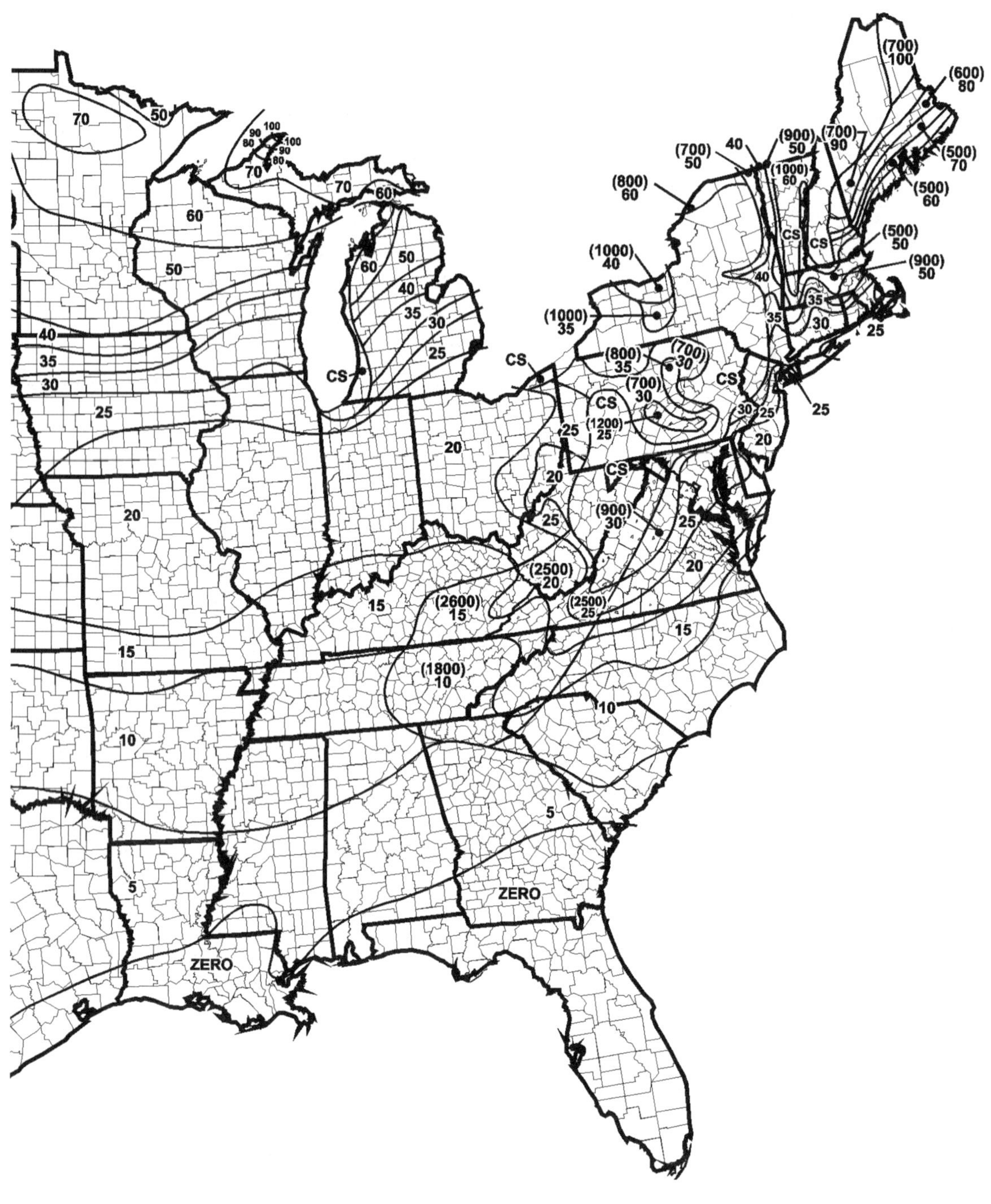

FIGURE 1608.2–continued
GROUND SNOW LOADS, p_g, FOR THE UNITED STATES (psf)

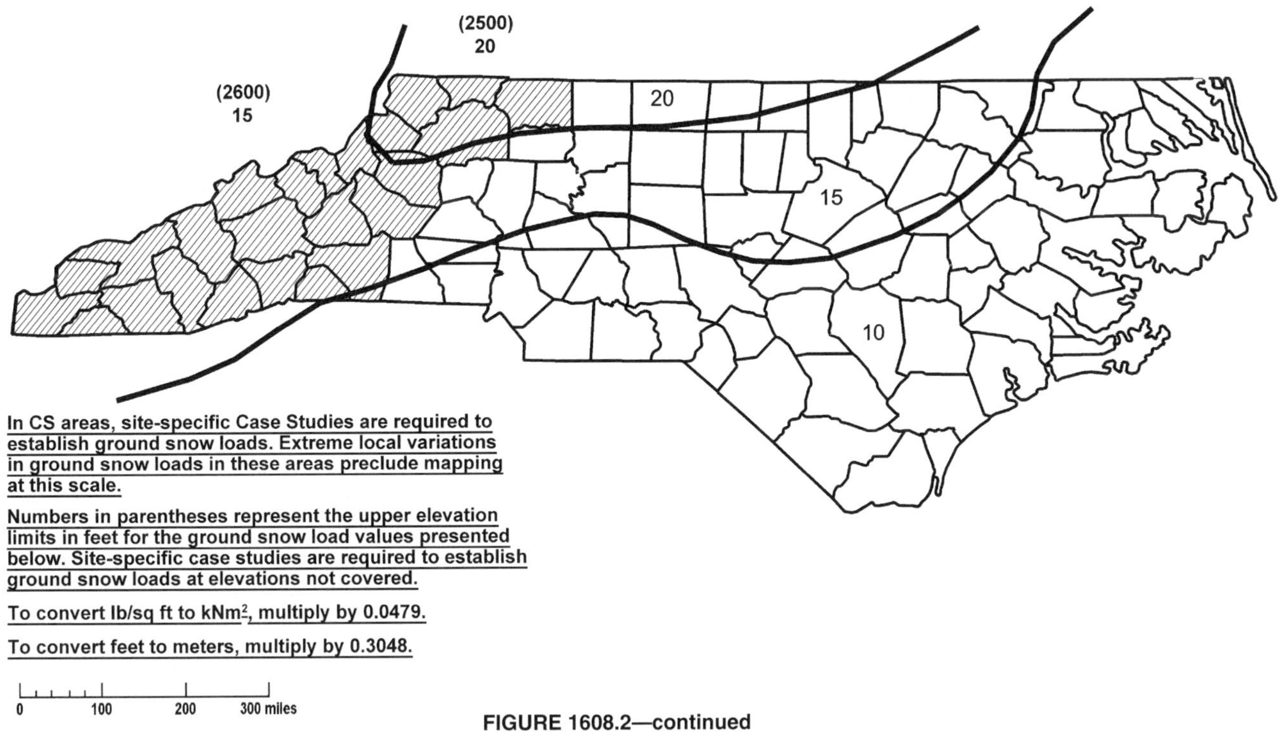

(2500)
20
(2600)
15
20
15
10
In CS areas, site-specific Case Studies are required to establish ground snow loads. Extreme local variations in ground snow loads in these areas preclude mapping at this scale.
Numbers in parentheses represent the upper elevation limits in feet for the ground snow load values presented below. Site-specific case studies are required to establish ground snow loads at elevations not covered.
To convert lb/sq ft to kNm², multiply by 0.0479.
To convert feet to meters, multiply by 0.3048.
0
100
200
300 miles

FIGURE 1608.2—continued
GROUND SNOW LOADS, *Pg*, FOR THE STATE OF NORTH CAROLINA (psf)

1609.1.2 Protection of openings. In *wind-borne debris regions*, glazing in buildings shall be impact resistant or protected with an impact-resistant covering meeting the requirements of an *approved* impact-resistant standard or ASTM E 1996 and ASTM E 1886 referenced herein as follows:

1. Glazed openings located within 30 feet (9144 mm) of grade shall meet the requirements of the large missile test of ASTM E 1996.
2. Glazed openings located more than 30 feet (9144 mm) above grade shall meet the provisions of the small missile test of ASTM E 1996.

Exceptions:

1. Wood structural panels with a minimum thickness of $^{7}/_{16}$ inch (11.1mm) and maximum panel span of 8 feet (2438 mm) shall be permitted for opening protection in buildings with a mean roof height of 45 feet (13 716 mm) or less. Panels shall be precut so that they shall be attached to the framing surrounding the opening containing the product with the glazed opening. Panels shall be secured with the attachment hardware provided. Attachments shall be designed to resist the components and cladding loads determined in accordance with the provisions of ASCE 7. Attachment in accordance with Table 1609.1.2 is permitted for buildings with a mean roof height of 45 feet (13 716 mm) or less where wind speeds do not exceed 140 mph (63 m/s).
2. Glazing in *Occupancy Category* I buildings as defined in Section 1604.5, including greenhouses that are occupied for growing plants on a production or research basis, without public access shall be permitted to be unprotected.
3. Glazing in *Occupancy Category* II, III or IV buildings located over 60 feet (18 288 mm) above the ground and over 30 feet (9144 mm) above aggregate surfaced (stone ballast or gravel) roofs located within 1,500 feet (458 m) of the building shall be permitted to be unprotected.

1609.1.2.1 Louvers. Operable louvers protecting intake and exhaust ventilation ducts not assumed to be open that are located within 30 feet (9144 mm) of grade shall meet requirements of an *approved* impact-resisting standard or the large missile test of ASTM E 1996.

1609.1.2.2 Garage doors. Garage door glazed opening protection for wind-borne debris shall meet the requirements of an *approved* impact-resisting standard or ANSI/DASMA 115.

1609.2 Definitions. The following words and terms shall, for the purposes of Section 1609, have the meanings shown herein.

TABLE 1609.1.2
WIND-BORNE DEBRIS PROTECTION FASTENING SCHEDULE FOR WOOD STRUCTURAL PANELS[a, b, c, d]

FASTENER TYPE	FASTENER SPACING (inches)		
	Panel Span ≤ 4 feet	4 feet < Panel Span ≤ 6 feet	6 feet < Panel Span ≤ 8 feet
No. 8 wood-screw-based anchor with 2-inch embedment length	16	10	8
No. 10 wood-screw-based anchor with 2-inch embedment length	16	12	9
$^{1}/_{4}$-inch diameter lag-screw-based anchor with 2-inch embedment length	16	16	16

For SI: 1 inch = 25.4 mm, 1 foot = 304.8 mm, 1 pound = 4.448 N, 1 mile per hour = 0.447 m/s.

a. This table is based on 140 mph wind speeds and a 45-foot mean roof height.

b. Fasteners shall be installed at opposing ends of the wood structural panel. Fasteners shall be located a minimum of 1 inch from the edge of the panel.

c. Anchors shall penetrate through the exterior wall covering with an embedment length of 2 inches minimum into the building frame. Fasteners shall be located a minimum of $2^{1}/_{2}$ inches from the edge of concrete block or concrete.

d. Where panels are attached to masonry or masonry/stucco, they shall be attached using vibration-resistant anchors having a minimum ultimate withdrawal capacity of 1,500 pounds.

HURRICANE-PRONE REGIONS. Areas vulnerable to hurricanes defined as:

1. The U. S. Atlantic Ocean and Gulf of Mexico coasts where the basic wind speed is greater than 90 mph (40 m/s) and
2. Hawaii, Puerto Rico, Guam, Virgin Islands and American Samoa.

WIND-BORNE DEBRIS REGION. Areas within hurricane-prone regions defined as that area east of the inland waterway from the North Carolina/South Carolina state line north to Beaufort Inlet and from that point to include the barrier islands to the North Carolina/Virginia state line.

1609.3 Basic wind speed. The basic wind speed, in mph, for the determination of the wind loads shall be determined by Figure 1609. Basic wind speed for the special wind regions indicated, near mountainous terrain and near gorges shall be in accordance with local jurisdiction requirements. Basic wind speeds determined by the local jurisdiction shall be in accordance with Section 6.5.4 of ASCE 7.

In nonhurricane-prone regions, when the basic wind speed is estimated from regional climatic data, the basic wind speed shall be not less than the wind speed associated with an annual probability of 0.02 (50-year mean recurrence interval), and the estimate shall be adjusted for equivalence to a 3-second gust wind speed at 33 feet (10 m) above ground in Exposure Category C. The data analysis shall be performed in accordance with Section 6.5.4.2 of ASCE 7.

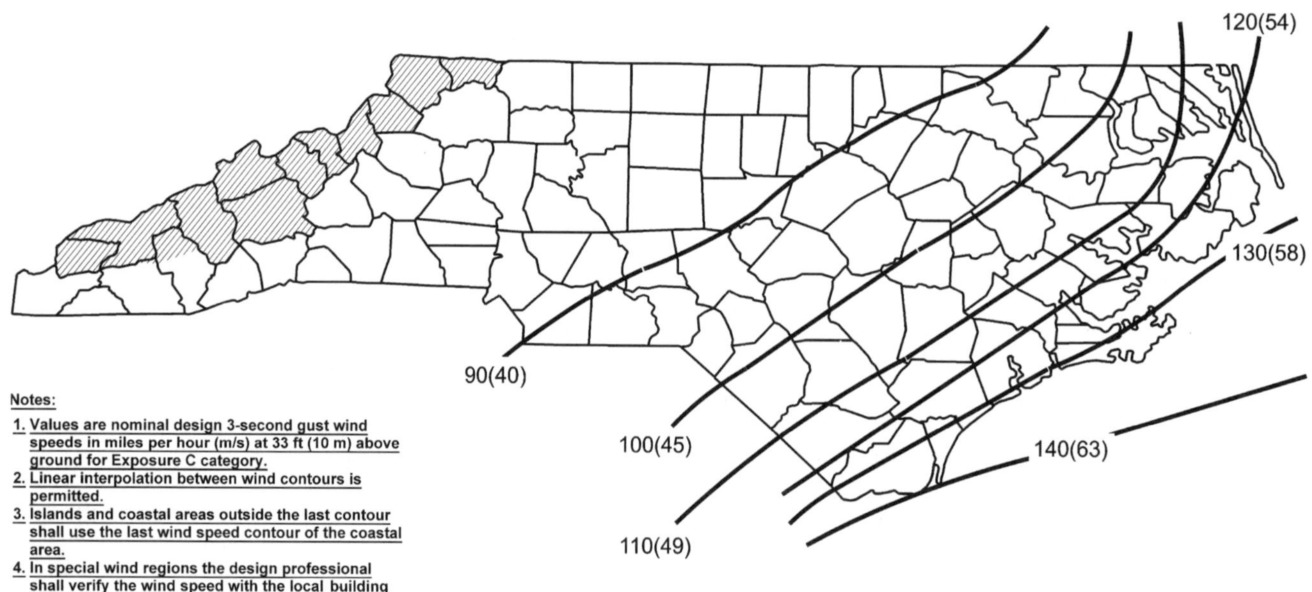
120(54)
130(58)
90(40)
100(45)
140(63)
110(49)
Notes:
1. Values are nominal design 3-second gust wind speeds in miles per hour (m/s) at 33 ft (10 m) above ground for Exposure C category.
2. Linear interpolation between wind contours is permitted.
3. Islands and coastal areas outside the last contour shall use the last wind speed contour of the coastal area.
4. In special wind regions the design professional shall verify the wind speed with the local building official.

FIGURE 1609
NORTH CAROLINA BASIC WIND SPEED

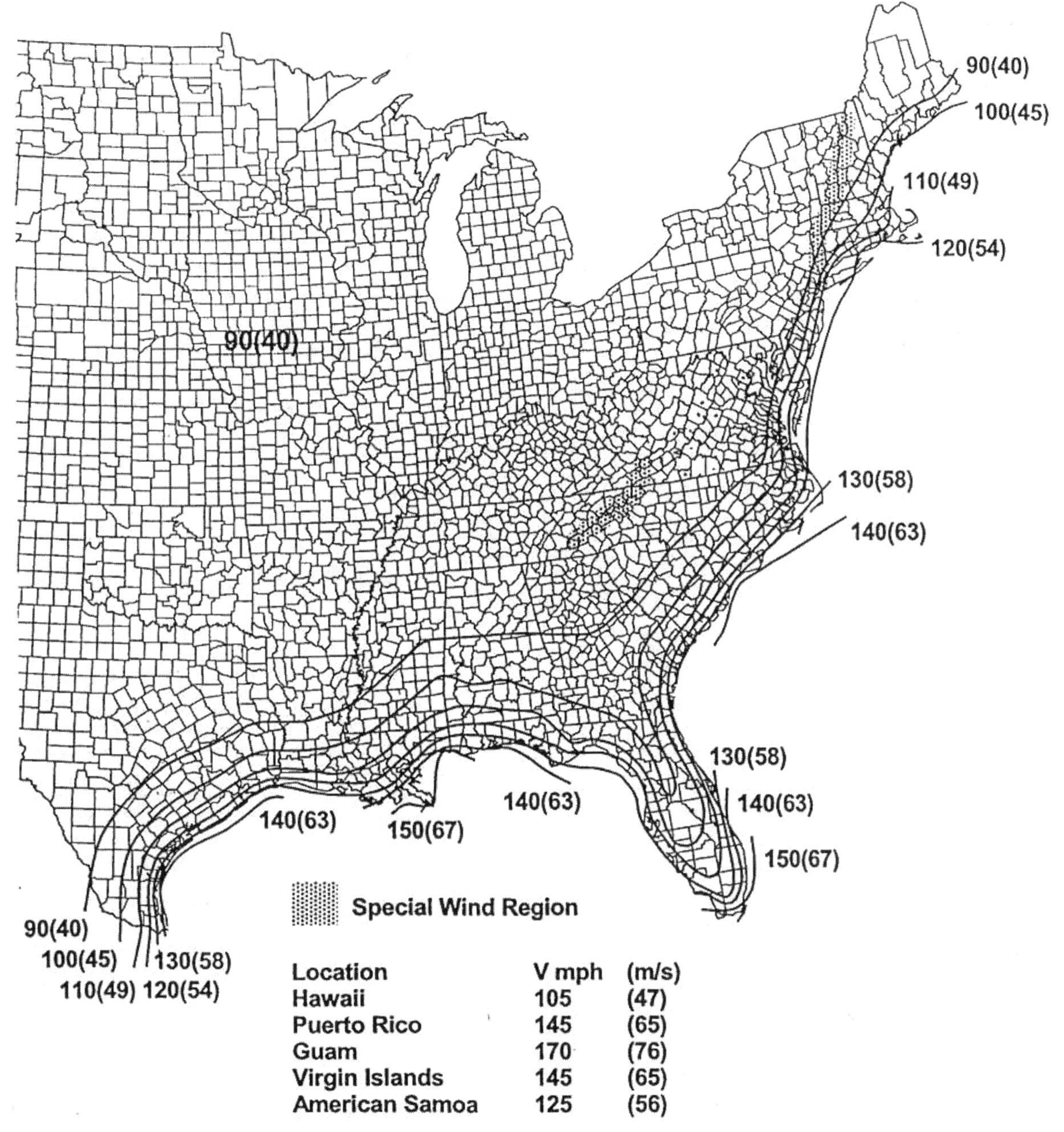

Location	V mph	(m/s)
Hawaii	105	(47)
Puerto Rico	145	(65)
Guam	170	(76)
Virgin Islands	145	(65)
American Samoa	125	(56)

Notes:

1. Values are nominal design 3-second gust wind speeds in miles per hour (m/s) at 33 ft (10 m) above ground for Exposure C category.
2. Linear Interpolation between wind contours is permitted.
3. Islands and coastal areas outside the last contour shall use the last wind speed contour of the coastal area.
4. Mountainous terrain, gorges, ocean promontories, and special wind regions shall be examined for unusual wind conditions.

FIGURE 1609—continued
BASIC WIND SPEED (3-SECOND GUST)

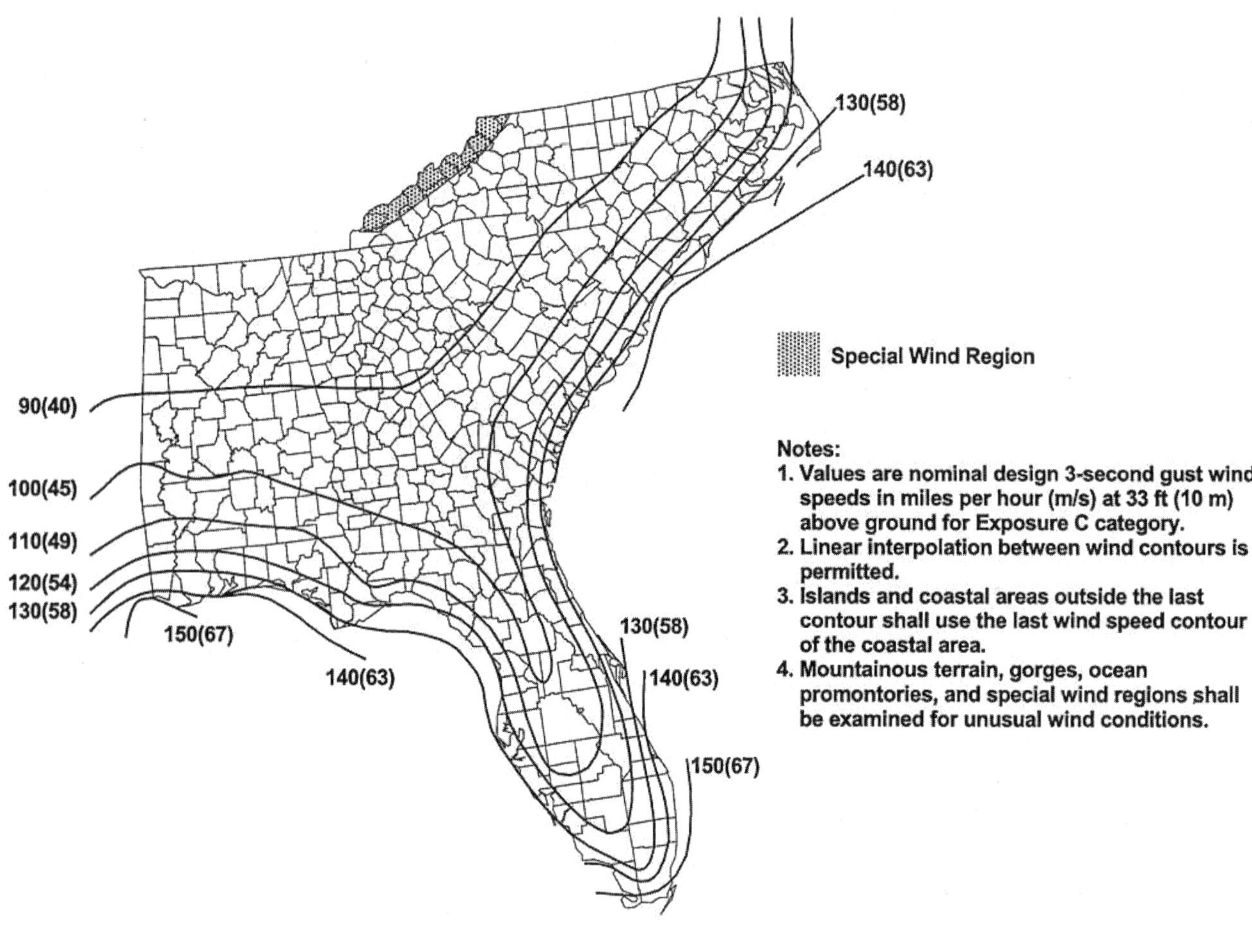
130(58)
140(63)
Special Wind Region
90(40)
100(45)
110(49)
120(54)
130(58)
150(67)
140(63)
130(58)
140(63)
150(67)
Notes:
1. Values are nominal design 3-second gust wind speeds in miles per hour (m/s) at 33 ft (10 m) above ground for Exposure C category.
2. Linear interpolation between wind contours is permitted.
3. Islands and coastal areas outside the last contour shall use the last wind speed contour of the coastal area.
4. Mountainous terrain, gorges, ocean promontories, and special wind regions shall be examined for unusual wind conditions.

FIGURE 1609—continued
BASIC WIND SPEED (3-SECOND GUST)
EASTERN GULF OF MEXICO AND SOUTHEASTERN U.S. HURRICANE COASTLINE

1609.3.1 Wind speed conversion. When required, the 3-second gust basic wind speeds of Figure 1609 shall be converted to fastest-mile wind speeds, V_{fm}, using Table 1609.3.1 or Equation 16-32.

$$V_{fm} = \frac{(V_{3S} - 10.5)}{1.05} \quad \textbf{(Equation 16-32)}$$

where:

V_{3S} = 3-second gust basic wind speed from Figure 1609.

1609.4 Exposure category. For each wind direction considered, an exposure category that adequately reflects the characteristics of ground surface irregularities shall be determined for the site at which the building or structure is to be constructed. Account shall be taken of variations in ground surface roughness that arise from natural topography and vegetation as well as from constructed features.

1609.4.1 Wind directions and sectors. For each selected wind direction at which the wind loads are to be evaluated, the exposure of the building or structure shall be determined for the two upwind sectors extending 45 degrees (0.79 rad) either side of the selected wind direction. The exposures in these two sectors shall be determined in accordance with Sections 1609.4.2 and 1609.4.3 and the exposure resulting in the highest wind loads shall be used to represent winds from that direction.

1609.4.2 Surface roughness categories. A ground surface roughness within each 45-degree (0.79 rad) sector shall be determined for a distance upwind of the site as defined in Section 1609.4.3 from the categories defined below, for the purpose of assigning an exposure category as defined in Section 1609.4.3.

Surface Roughness B. Urban and suburban areas, wooded areas or other terrain with numerous closely spaced obstructions having the size of single-family dwellings or larger.

Surface Roughness C. Open terrain with scattered obstructions having heights generally less than 30 feet (9144 mm). This category includes flat open country, grasslands, and all water surfaces in *hurricane-prone regions*.

Surface Roughness D. Flat, unobstructed areas and water surfaces outside *hurricane-prone regions*. This category includes smooth mud flats, salt flats and unbroken ice.

1609.4.3 Exposure categories. An exposure category shall be determined in accordance with the following:

Exposure B. Exposure B shall apply where the ground surface roughness condition, as defined by Surface Roughness B, prevails in the upwind direction for a distance of at least 2,600 feet (792 m) or 20 times the height of the building, whichever is greater.

Exception: For buildings whose mean roof height is less than or equal to 30 feet (9144 mm), the upwind distance is permitted to be reduced to 1,500 feet (457 m).

Exposure C. Exposure C shall apply for all cases where Exposures B or D do not apply.

Exposure D. Exposure D shall apply where the ground surface roughness, as defined by Surface Roughness D, prevails in the upwind direction for a distance of at least 5,000 feet (1524 m) or 20 times the height of the building, whichever is greater. Exposure D shall extend inland from the shoreline for a distance of 600 feet (183 m) or 20 times the height of the building, whichever is greater.

1609.5 Roof systems.

1609.5.1 Roof deck. The roof deck shall be designed to withstand the wind pressures determined in accordance with ASCE 7.

1609.5.2 Roof coverings. Roof coverings shall comply with Section 1609.5.1.

Exception: Rigid tile roof coverings that are air permeable and installed over a roof deck complying with Section 1609.5.1 are permitted to be designed in accordance with Section 1609.5.3.

Asphalt shingles installed over a roof deck complying with Section 1609.5.1 shall comply with the wind-resistance requirements of Section 1507.2.7.1.

1609.5.3 Rigid tile. Wind loads on rigid tile roof coverings shall be determined in accordance with the following equation:

$$M_a = q_h C_L b L L_a [1.0 - GC_p] \quad \textbf{(Equation 16-33)}$$

For SI: $M_a = \frac{q_h C_L b L L_a [1.0 - GC_p]}{1,000}$

where:

b = Exposed width, feet (mm) of the roof tile.

TABLE 1609.3.1
EQUIVALENT BASIC WIND SPEEDS[a, b, c]

V_{3S}	85	90	100	105	110	120	125	130	140	145	150	160	170
V_{fm}	71	76	85	90	95	104	109	114	123	128	133	142	152

For SI: 1 mile per hour = 0.447 m/s.

a. Linear interpolation is permitted.

b. V_{3S} is the 3-second gust wind speed (mph).

c. V_{fm} is the fastest mile wind speed (mph).

C_L = Lift coefficient. The lift coefficient for concrete and clay tile shall be 0.2 or shall be determined by test in accordance with Section 1716.2.

GC_p = Roof pressure coefficient for each applicable roof zone determined from Chapter 6 of ASCE 7. Roof coefficients shall not be adjusted for internal pressure.

L = Length, feet (mm) of the roof tile.

L_a = Moment arm, feet (mm) from the axis of rotation to the point of uplift on the roof tile. The point of uplift shall be taken at $0.76L$ from the head of the tile and the middle of the exposed width. For roof tiles with nails or screws (with or without a tail clip), the axis of rotation shall be taken as the head of the tile for direct deck application or as the top edge of the batten for battened applications. For roof tiles fastened only by a nail or screw along the side of the tile, the axis of rotation shall be determined by testing. For roof tiles installed with battens and fastened only by a clip near the tail of the tile, the moment arm shall be determined about the top edge of the batten with consideration given for the point of rotation of the tiles based on straight bond or broken bond and the tile profile.

M_a = Aerodynamic uplift moment, feet-pounds (N-mm) acting to raise the tail of the tile.

q_h = Wind velocity pressure, psf (kN/m^2) determined from Section 6.5.10 of ASCE 7.

Concrete and clay roof tiles complying with the following limitations shall be designed to withstand the aerodynamic uplift moment as determined by this section.

1. The roof tiles shall be either loose laid on battens, mechanically fastened, mortar set or adhesive set.
2. The roof tiles shall be installed on solid sheathing which has been designed as components and cladding.
3. An underlayment shall be installed in accordance with Chapter 15.
4. The tile shall be single lapped interlocking with a minimum head lap of not less than 2 inches (51 mm).
5. The length of the tile shall be between 1.0 and 1.75 feet (305 mm and 533 mm).
6. The exposed width of the tile shall be between 0.67 and 1.25 feet (204 mm and 381 mm).
7. The maximum thickness of the tail of the tile shall not exceed 1.3 inches (33 mm).
8. Roof tiles using mortar set or adhesive set systems shall have at least two-thirds of the tile's area free of mortar or adhesive contact.

1609.6 Alternate all-heights method. The alternate wind design provisions in this section are simplifications of the ASCE 7 Method 2—Analytical Procedure.

1609.6.1 Scope. As an alternative to ASCE 7 Section 6.5, the following provisions are permitted to be used to determine the wind effects on regularly shaped buildings, or other structures that are regularly shaped, which meet all of the following conditions:

1. The building or other structure is less than or equal to 75 feet (22 860 mm) in height with a height-to-least-width ratio of 4 or less, or the building or other structure has a fundamental frequency greater than or equal to 1 hertz.
2. The building or other structure is not sensitive to dynamic effects.
3. The building or other structure is not located on a site for which channeling effects or buffeting in the wake of upwind obstructions warrant special consideration.
4. The building shall meet the requirements of a simple diaphragm building as defined in ASCE 7 Section 6.2, where wind loads are only transmitted to the main wind-force-resisting system (MWFRS) at the diaphragms.
5. For open buildings, multispan gable roofs, stepped roofs, sawtooth roofs, domed roofs, roofs with slopes greater than 45 degrees (0.79 rad), solid free-standing walls and solid signs, and rooftop equipment, apply ASCE 7 provisions.

1609.6.1.1 Modifications. The following modifications shall be made to certain subsections in ASCE 7: in Section 1609.6.2, symbols and notations that are specific to this section are used in conjunction with the symbols and notations in ASCE 7 Section 6.3.

1609.6.2 Symbols and notations. Coefficients and variables used in the alternative all-heights method equations are as follows:

C_{net} = Net-pressure coefficient based on K_d [(G) (C_p) – (GC_{pi})], in accordance with Table 1609.6.2(2).

G = Gust effect factor for rigid structures in accordance with ASCE 7 Section 6.5.8.1.

K_d = Wind directionality factor in accordance with ASCE 7 Table 6-4.

P_{net} = Design wind pressure to be used in determination of wind loads on buildings or other structures or their components and cladding, in psf (kN/m^2).

q_s = Wind stagnation pressure in psf (kN/m^2) in accordance with Table 1609.6.2(1).

TABLE 1609.6.2(1)
WIND STAGNATION PRESSURE (q_s) AT STANDARD HEIGHT OF 33 FEET[a]

BASIC WIND SPEED (mph)	85	90	100	105	110	120	125	130	140	150	160	170
PRESSURE, q_s (psf)	18.5	20.7	25.6	28.2	31.0	36.9	40.0	43.3	50.2	57.6	65.5	74.0

For SI: 1 foot = 304.8 mm, 1 mile per hour = 0.447 m/s, 1 pound per square foot = 47.88 Pa.
a. For basic wind speeds not shown, use $q_s = 0.00256\ V^2$.

TABLE 1609.6.2(2)
NET PRESSURE COEFFICIENTS, C_{net}[a, b]

STRUCTURE OR PART THEREOF	DESCRIPTION		C_{net} FACTOR			
1. Main wind-force-resisting frames and systems			Enclosed		Partially enclosed	
	Walls:		+ Internal pressure	- Internal pressure	+ Internal pressure	- Internal pressure
	Windward wall		0.43	0.73	0.11	1.05
	Leeward wall		-0.51	-0.21	-0.83	0.11
	Sidewall		-0.66	-0.35	-0.97	-0.04
	Parapet wall	Windward	1.28		1.28	
		Leeward	-0.85		-0.85	
	Roofs:		Enclosed		Partially enclosed	
	Wind perpendicular to ridge		+ Internal pressure	- Internal pressure	+ Internal pressure	- Internal pressure
	Leeward roof or flat roof		-0.66	-0.35	-0.97	-0.04
	Windward roof slopes					
	Slope = 2:12 (10°)	Condition 1	-1.09	-0.79	-1.41	-0.47
		Condition 2	-0.28	0.02	-0.60	0.34
	Slope = 4:12 (18°)	Condition 1	-0.73	-0.42	-1.04	-0.11
		Condition 2	-0.05	0.25	-0.37	0.57
	Slope = 5:12 (23°)	Condition 1	-0.58	-0.28	-0.90	0.04
		Condition 2	0.03	0.34	-0.29	0.65
	Slope = 6:12 (27°)	Condition 1	-0.47	-0.16	-0.78	0.15
		Condition 2	0.06	0.37	-0.25	0.68
	Slope = 7:12 (30°)	Condition 1	-0.37	-0.06	-0.68	0.25
		Condition 2	0.07	0.37	-0.25	0.69
	Slope = 9:12 (37°)	Condition 1	-0.27	0.04	-0.58	0.35
		Condition 2	0.14	0.44	-0.18	0.76
	Slope = 12:12 (45°)		0.14	0.44	-0.18	0.76
	Wind parallel to ridge and flat roofs		-1.09	-0.79	-1.41	-0.47
	Nonbuilding Structures: Chimneys, Tanks and Similar Structures:					
				h/D		
				1	7	25
	Square (Wind normal to face)			0.99	1.07	1.53
	Square (Wind on diagonal)			0.77	0.84	1.15
	Hexagonal or Octagonal			0.81	0.97	1.13
	Round			0.65	0.81	0.97
	Open signs and lattice frameworks			Ratio of solid to gross area		
				< 0.1	0.1 to 0.29	0.3 to 0.7
	Flat			1.45	1.30	1.16
	Round			0.87	0.94	1.08

(continued)

TABLE 1609.6.2(2)—continued
NET PRESSURE COEFFICIENTS, C_{net}[a, b]

STRUCTURE OR PART THEREOF	DESCRIPTION		C_{net} FACTOR	
2. Components and cladding not in areas of disconti-nuity—roofs and overhangs	**Roof elements and slopes**		**Enclosed**	**Partially enclosed**
	Gable of hipped configurations (Zone 1)			
	Flat < Slope < 6:12 (27°) See ASCE 7 Figure 6-11C Zone 1			
	Positive	10 square feet or less	0.58	0.89
		100 square feet or more	0.41	0.72
	Negative	10 square feet or less	-1.00	-1.32
		100 square feet or more	-0.92	-1.23
	Overhang: Flat < Slope < 6:12 (27°) See ASCE 7 Figure 6-11B Zone 1			
	Negative	10 square feet or less	-1.45	
		100 square feet or more	-1.36	
		500 square feet or more	-0.94	
	6:12 (27°) < Slope < 12:12 (45°) See ASCE 7 Figure 6-11D Zone 1			
	Positive	10 square feet or less	0.92	1.23
		100 square feet or more	0.83	1.15
	Negative	10 square feet or less	-1.00	-1.32
		100 square feet or more	-0.83	-1.15
	Monosloped configurations (Zone 1)		**Enclosed**	**Partially enclosed**
	Flat < Slope < 7:12 (30°) See ASCE 7 Figure 6-14B Zone 1			
	Positive	10 square feet or less	0.49	0.81
		100 square feet or more	0.41	0.72
	Negative	10 square feet or less	-1.26	-1.57
		100 square feet or more	-1.09	-1.40
	Tall flat-topped roofs $h > 60'$		**Enclosed**	**Partially enclosed**
	Flat < Slope < 2:12 (10°) (Zone 1) See ASCE 7 Figure 6-17 Zone 1			
	Negative	10 square feet or less	-1.34	-1.66
		500 square feet or more	-0.92	-1.23

(continued)

TABLE 1609.6.2(2)—continued
NET PRESSURE COEFFICIENTS, C_{net}[a, b]

STRUCTURE OR PART THEREOF	DESCRIPTION		C_{net} FACTOR	
	Roof elements and slopes		**Enclosed**	**Partially enclosed**
3. Components and cladding in areas of discontinuities—roofs and overhangs	Gable or hipped configurations at ridges, eaves and rakes (Zone 2)			
	Flat < Slope < 6:12 (27°) See ASCE 7 Figure 6-11C Zone 2			
	Positive	10 square feet or less	0.58	0.89
		100 square feet or more	0.41	10.72
	Negative	10 square feet or less	-1.68	-2.00
		100 square feet or more	-1.17	-1.49
	Overhang for Slope Flat < Slope < 6:12 (27°) See ASCE 7 Figure 6-11C Zone 2			
	Negative	10 square feet or less	-1.87	
		100 square feet or more	-1.87	
	6:12 (27°) < Slope < 12:12 (45°) Figure 6-11D		**Enclosed**	**Partially enclosed**
	Positive	10 square feet or less	0.92	1.23
		100 square feet or more	0.83	1.15
	Negative	10 square feet or less	-1.17	-1.49
		100 square feet or more	-1.00	-1.32
	Overhang for 6:12 (27°) < Slope < 12:12 (45°) See ASCE 7 Figure 6-11D Zone 2			
	Negative	10 square feet or less	-1.70	
		500 square feet or more	-1.53	
	Monosloped configurations at ridges, eaves and rakes (Zone 2)			
	Flat < Slope < 7:12 (30°) See ASCE 7 Figure 6-14B Zone 2			
	Positive	10 square feet or less	0.49	0.81
		100 square feet or more	0.41	0.72
	Negative	10 square feet or less	-1.51	-1.83
		100 square feet or more	-1.43	-1.74
	Tall flat topped roofs $h > 60'$		**Enclosed**	**Partially enclosed**
	Flat < Slope < 2:12 (10°) (Zone 2) See ASCE 7 Figure 6-17 Zone 2			
	Negative	10 square feet or less	-2.11	-2.42
		500 square feet or more	-1.51	-1.83
	Gable or hipped configurations at corners (Zone 3) See ASCE 7 Figure 6-11C Zone 3			
	Flat < Slope < 6:12 (27°)		**Enclosed**	**Partially enclosed**
	Positive	10 square feet or less	0.58	0.89
		100 square feet or more	0.41	0.72
	Negative	10 square feet or less	-2.53	-2.85
		100 square feet or more	-1.85	-2.17

(continued)

TABLE 1609.6.2(2)—continued
NET PRESSURE COEFFICIENTS, C_{net}[a, b]

STRUCTURE OR PART THEREOF	DESCRIPTION		C_{net} FACTOR	
3. Components and cladding in areas of discontinuity—roofs and overhangs (continued)	Overhang for Slope Flat < Slope < 6:12 (27°) See ASCE 7 Figure 6-11C Zone 3			
	Negative	10 square feet or less	-3.15	
		100 square feet or more	-2.13	
	6:12 (27°) < 12:12 (45°) See ASCE 7 Figure 6-11D Zone 3			
	Positive	10 square feet or less	0.92	1.23
		100 square feet or more	0.83	1.15
	Negative	10 square feet or less	-1.17	-1.49
		100 square feet or more	-1.00	-1.32
	Overhang for 6:12 (27°) < Slope < 12:12 (45°)		**Enclosed**	**Partially enclosed**
	Negative	10 square feet or less	-1.70	
		100 square feet or more	-1.53	
	Monosloped Configurations at corners (Zone 3) See ASCE 7 Figure 6-14B Zone 3			
	Flat < Slope < 7:12 (30°)			
	Positive	10 square feet or less	0.49	0.81
		100 square feet or more	0.41	0.72
	Negative	10 square feet or less	-2.62	-2.93
		100 square feet or more	-1.85	-2.17
	Tall flat topped roofs $h > 60'$		**Enclosed**	**Partially enclosed**
	Flat < Slope < 2:12 (10°) (Zone 3) See ASCE 7 Figure 6-17 Zone 3			
	Negative	10 square feet or less	-2.87	-3.19
		500 square feet or more	-2.11	-2.42
4. Components and cladding not in areas of discontinuity—walls and parapets	Wall Elements: $h = 60'$ (Zone 4) Figure 6-11A		**Enclosed**	**Partially enclosed**
	Positive	10 square feetor less	1.00	1.32
		500 square feet or more	0.75	1.06
	Negative	10 square feet or less	-1.09	-1.40
		500 square feet or more	-0.83	-1.15
	Wall Elements: $h > 60'$ (Zone 4) See ASCE 7 Figure 6-17 Zone 4			
	Positive	20 square feet or less	0.92	1.23
		500 square feet or more	0.66	0.98
	Negative	20 square feet or less	-0.92	-1.23
		500 square feet or more	-0.75	-1.06
	Parapet Walls			
	Positive		2.87	3.19
	Negative		-1.68	-2.00

TABLE 1609.6.2(2)—continued
NET PRESSURE COEFFICIENTS, C_{net}[a, b]

STRUCTURE OR PART THEREOF	DESCRIPTION		C_{net} FACTOR	
5. Components and cladding in areas of discontinuity—walls and parapets	Wall elements: $h \leq 60'$ (Zone 5) Figure 6-11A		Enclosed	Partially enclosed
	Positive	10 square feet or less	1.00	1.32
		500 square feet or more	0.75	1.06
	Negative	10 square feet or less	-1.34	-1.66
		500 square feet or more	-0.83	-1.15
	Wall elements: $h > 60'$ (Zone 5) See ASCE 7 Figure 6-17 Zone 4			
	Positive	20 square feet or less	0.92	1.23
		500 square feet or more	0.66	0.98
	Negative	20 square feet or less	-1.68	-2.00
		500 square feet or more	-1.00	-1.32
	Parapet walls			
	Positive		3.64	3.95
	Negative		-2.45	-2.76

For SI: 1 foot = 304.8 mm, 1 square foot = 0.0929 m^2, 1 degree = 0.0175 rad.

a. Linear interpolation between values in the table is permitted.

b. Some C_{net} values have been grouped together. Less conservative results may be obtained by applying ASCE 7 provisions.

1609.6.3 Design equations. When using the alternative all-heights method, the MWFRS, and components and cladding of every structure shall be designed to resist the effects of wind pressures on the building envelope in accordance with Equation 16-34.

$$P_{net} = q_s K_z C_{net} [IK_{zt}] \quad \textbf{(Equation 16-34)}$$

Design wind forces for the MWFRS shall not be less than 10 psf (0.48 kN/m^2) multiplied by the area of the structure projected on a plane normal to the assumed wind direction (see ASCE 7 Section 6.1.4 for criteria). Design net wind pressure for components and cladding shall not be less than 10 psf (0.48 kN/m^2) acting in either direction normal to the surface.

1609.6.4 Design procedure. The MWFRS and the components and cladding of every building or other structure shall be designed for the pressures calculated using Equation 16-34.

1609.6.4.1 Main wind-force-resisting systems. The MWFRS shall be investigated for the torsional effects identified in ASCE 7 Figure 6-9.

1609.6.4.2 Determination of K_z and K_{zt}. Velocity pressure exposure coefficient, K_z, shall be determined in accordance with ASCE 7 Section 6.5.6.6 and the topographic factor, K_{zt}, shall be determined in accordance with ASCE 7 Section 6.5.7.

1. For the windward side of a structure, K_{zt} and K_z shall be based on height z.
2. For leeward and sidewalls, and for windward and leeward roofs, K_{zt} and K_z shall be based on mean roof height h.

1609.6.4.3 Determination of net pressure coefficients, C_{net}. For the design of the MWFRS and for components and cladding, the sum of the internal and external net pressure shall be based on the net pressure coefficient, C_{net}.

1. The pressure coefficient, C_{net}, for walls and roofs shall be determined from Table 1609.6.2(2).
2. Where C_{net} has more than one value, the more severe wind load condition shall be used for design.

1609.6.4.4 Application of wind pressures. When using the alternative all-heights method, wind pressures shall be applied simultaneously on, and in a direction normal to, all building envelope wall and roof surfaces.

1609.6.4.4.1 Components and cladding. Wind pressure for each component or cladding element is applied as follows using C_{net} values based on the effective wind area, A, contained within the zones in areas of discontinuity of width and/or length "a," "2a" or "4a" at: corners of roofs and walls; edge strips for ridges, rakes and eaves; or field areas on walls or roofs as indicated in figures in tables in ASCE 7 as referenced in Table 1609.6.2(2) in accordance with the following:

1. Calculated pressures at local discontinuities acting over specific edge strips or corner boundary areas.
2. Include "field" (Zone 1, 2 or 4, as applicable) pressures applied to areas beyond the boundaries of the areas of discontinuity.
3. Where applicable, the calculated pressures at discontinuities (Zones 2 or 3) shall be combined with design pressures that apply specifically on rakes or eave overhangs.

SECTION 1610
SOIL LATERAL LOADS

1610.1 General. Foundation walls and retaining walls shall be designed to resist lateral soil loads. Soil loads specified in Table 1610.1 shall be used as the minimum design lateral soil loads unless determined otherwise by a geotechnical investigation in accordance with Section 1803. Foundation walls and other walls in which horizontal movement is restricted at the top shall be designed for at-rest pressure. Retaining walls free to move and rotate at the top shall be permitted to be designed for active pressure. Design lateral pressure from surcharge loads shall be added to the lateral earth pressure load. Design lateral pressure shall be increased if soils at the site are expansive. Foundation walls shall be designed to support the weight of the full hydrostatic pressure of undrained backfill unless a drainage system is installed in accordance with Sections 1805.4.2 and 1805.4.3.

Exception: Foundation walls extending not more than 8 feet (2438 mm) below grade and laterally supported at the top by flexible diaphragms shall be permitted to be designed for active pressure.

TABLE 1610.1
LATERAL SOIL LOAD

DESCRIPTION OF BACKFILL MATERIAL[c]	UNIFIED SOIL CLASSIFICATION	DESIGN LATERAL SOIL LOAD[a] (pound per square foot per foot of depth)	
		Active pressure	At-rest pressure
Well-graded, clean gravels; gravel-sand mixes	GW	30	60
Poorly graded clean gravels; gravel-sand mixes	GP	30	60
Silty gravels, poorly graded gravel-sand mixes	GM	40	60
Clayey gravels, poorly graded gravel-and-clay mixes	GC	45	60
Well-graded, clean sands; gravelly sand mixes	SW	30	60
Poorly graded clean sands; sand-gravel mixes	SP	30	60
Silty sands, poorly graded sand-silt mixes	SM	45	60
Sand-silt clay mix with plastic fines	SM-SC	45	100
Clayey sands, poorly graded sand-clay mixes	SC	60	100
Inorganic silts and clayey silts	ML	45	100
Mixture of inorganic silt and clay	ML-CL	60	100
Inorganic clays of low to medium plasticity	CL	60	100
Organic silts and silt clays, low plasticity	OL	Note b	Note b
Inorganic clayey silts, elastic silts	MH	Note b	Note b
Inorganic clays of high plasticity	CH	Note b	Note b
Organic clays and silty clays	OH	Note b	Note b

For SI: 1 pound per square foot per foot of depth = 0.157 kPa/m, 1 foot = 304.8 mm.

a. Design lateral soil loads are given for moist conditions for the specified soils at their optimum densities. Actual field conditions shall govern. Submerged or saturated soil pressures shall include the weight of the buoyant soil plus the hydrostatic loads.

b. Unsuitable as backfill material.

c. The definition and classification of soil materials shall be in accordance with ASTM D 2487.

SECTION 1611
RAIN LOADS

1611.1 Design rain loads. Each portion of a roof shall be designed to sustain the load of rainwater that will accumulate on it if the primary drainage system for that portion is blocked plus the uniform load caused by water that rises above the inlet of the secondary drainage system at its design flow. The design rainfall shall be based on the 100-year hourly rainfall rate indicated in Figure 1611.1 or on other rainfall rates determined from *approved* local weather data.

$R = 5.2(d_s + d_h)$ **(Equation 16-35)**

For SI: $R = 0.0098(d_s + d_h)$

where:

d_h = Additional depth of water on the undeflected roof above the inlet of secondary drainage system at its design flow (i.e., the hydraulic head), in inches (mm).

d_s = Depth of water on the undeflected roof up to the inlet of secondary drainage system when the primary drainage system is blocked (i.e., the static head), in inches (mm).

R = Rain load on the undeflected roof, in psf (kN/m_2). When the phrase "undeflected roof" is used, deflections from loads (including dead loads) shall not be considered when determining the amount of rain on the roof.

1611.2 Ponding instability. For roofs with a slope less than $^1/_4$ inch per foot [1.19 degrees (0.0208 rad)], the design calculations shall include verification of adequate stiffness to preclude progressive deflection in accordance with Section 8.4 of ASCE 7.

1611.3 Controlled drainage. Roofs equipped with hardware to control the rate of drainage shall be equipped with a secondary drainage system at a higher elevation that limits accumulation of water on the roof above that elevation. Such roofs shall be designed to sustain the load of rainwater that will accumulate on them to the elevation of the secondary drainage system plus the uniform load caused by water that rises above the inlet of the secondary drainage system at its design flow determined from Section 1611.1. Such roofs shall also be checked for ponding instability in accordance with Section 1611.2.

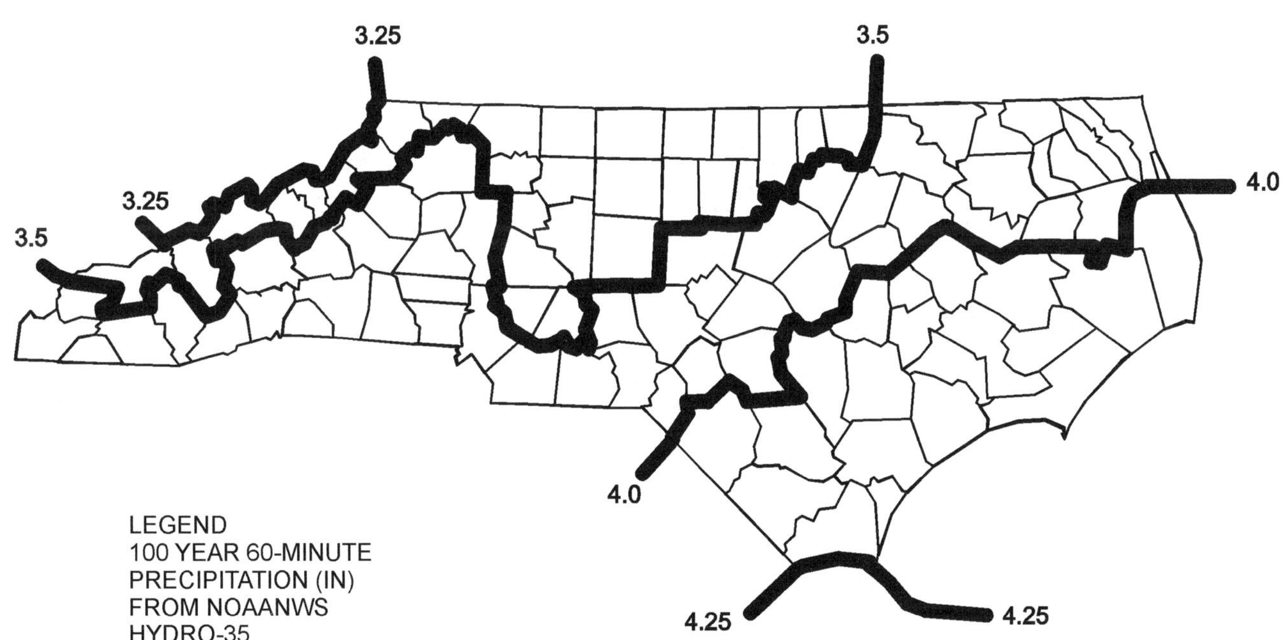

FIGURE 1611.1
100-YEAR, 1-HOUR RAINFALL (INCHES/HOUR) NORTH CAROLINA FOR PRIMARY ROOF DRAINS

For SI: 1 inch = 25.4 mm.
Source: National Weather Service, National Oceanic and Atmospheric Administration, Washington D.C.

[P] FIGURE 1611.1—continued
100-YEAR, 1-HOUR RAINFALL (INCHES) EASTERN UNITED STATES

For SI: 1 inch = 25.4 mm.

Source: National Weather Service, National Oceanic and Atmospheric Administration, Washington, DC.

SECTION 1612
FLOOD LOADS

1612.1 General. Within *flood hazard areas* as established in Section 1612.3, all new construction of buildings, structures and portions of buildings and structures, including substantial improvement and restoration of substantial damage to buildings and structures, shall be designed and constructed to resist the effects of flood hazards and flood loads. For buildings that are located in more than one *flood hazard area*, the provisions associated with the most restrictive *flood hazard area* shall apply.

1612.2 Definitions. The following words and terms shall, for the purposes of this section, have the meanings shown herein.

BASE FLOOD. The flood having a 1-percent chance of being equaled or exceeded in any given year.

BASE FLOOD ELEVATION. The elevation of the *base flood*, including wave height, relative to the National Geodetic Vertical Datum (NGVD), North American Vertical Datum (NAVD) or other datum specified on the Flood Insurance Rate Map (FIRM).

BASEMENT. The portion of a building having its floor subgrade (below ground level) on all sides.

This definition of "Basement" is limited in application to the provisions of Section 1612 (see "Basement" in Section 502.1).

DESIGN FLOOD. The flood associated with the greater of the following two areas:

1. Area with a flood plain subject to a 1-percent or greater chance of flooding in any year; or
2. Area designated as a *flood hazard area* on a community's flood hazard map, or otherwise legally designated.

DESIGN FLOOD ELEVATION. The elevation of the "*design flood*," including wave height, relative to the datum specified on the community's legally designated flood hazard map. In areas designated as Zone AO, the design flood elevation shall be the elevation of the highest existing grade of the building's perimeter plus the depth number (in feet) specified on the flood hazard map. In areas designated as Zone AO where a depth number is not specified on the map, the depth number shall be taken as being equal to 2 feet (610 mm).

DRY FLOODPROOFING. A combination of design modifications that results in a building or structure, including the attendant utility and sanitary facilities, being water tight with walls substantially impermeable to the passage of water and with structural components having the capacity to resist loads as identified in ASCE 7.

EXISTING CONSTRUCTION. Any buildings and structures for which the "start of construction" commenced before the effective date of the community's first flood plain management code, ordinance or standard. "Existing construction" is also referred to as "existing structures."

EXISTING STRUCTURE. See "Existing construction."

FLOOD or FLOODING. A general and temporary condition of partial or complete inundation of normally dry land from:

1. The overflow of inland or tidal waters.
2. The unusual and rapid accumulation or runoff of surface waters from any source.

FLOOD DAMAGE-RESISTANT MATERIALS. Any construction material capable of withstanding direct and prolonged contact with floodwaters without sustaining any damage that requires more than cosmetic repair.

FLOOD HAZARD AREA. The greater of the following two areas:

1. The area within a flood plain subject to a 1-percent or greater chance of flooding in any year.
2. The area designated as a *flood hazard area* on a community's flood hazard map, or otherwise legally designated.

FLOOD HAZARD AREA SUBJECT TO HIGH-VELOCITY WAVE ACTION. Area within the *flood hazard area* that is subject to high-velocity wave action, and shown on a Flood Insurance Rate Map (FIRM) or other flood hazard map as Zone V, VO, VE or V1-30.

FLOOD INSURANCE RATE MAP (FIRM). An official map of a community on which the Federal Emergency Management Agency (FEMA) has delineated both the special flood hazard areas and the risk premium zones applicable to the community.

FLOOD INSURANCE STUDY. The official report provided by the Federal Emergency Management Agency containing the Flood Insurance Rate Map (FIRM), the Flood Boundary and Floodway Map (FBFM), the water surface elevation of the *base flood* and supporting technical data.

FLOODWAY. The channel of the river, creek or other watercourse and the adjacent land areas that must be reserved in order to discharge the *base flood* without cumulatively increasing the water surface elevation more than a designated height.

LOWEST FLOOR. The floor of the lowest enclosed area, including basement, but excluding any unfinished or flood-resistant enclosure, usable solely for vehicle parking, building access or limited storage provided that such enclosure is not built so as to render the structure in violation of this section.

SPECIAL FLOOD HAZARD AREA. The land area subject to flood hazards and shown on a Flood Insurance Rate Map or other flood hazard map as Zone A, AE, A1-30, A99, AR, AO, AH, V, VO, VE or V1-30.

START OF CONSTRUCTION. The date of issuance for new construction and substantial improvements to existing structures, provided the actual start of construction, repair, reconstruction, rehabilitation, *addition*, placement or other improvement is within 180 days after the date of issuance. The actual start of construction means the first placement of permanent construction of a building (including a manufactured home) on a site, such as the pouring of a slab or footings, installation of pilings or construction of columns.

Permanent construction does not include land preparation (such as clearing, excavation, grading or filling), the installation of streets or walkways, excavation for a basement, footings, piers or foundations, the erection of temporary forms or the installation of accessory buildings such as garages or sheds not occupied as *dwelling units* or not part of the main building. For a substantial improvement, the actual "start of construction" means the first *alteration* of any wall, ceiling, floor or other structural part of a building, whether or not that *alteration* affects the external dimensions of the building.

SUBSTANTIAL DAMAGE. Damage of any origin sustained by a structure whereby the cost of restoring the structure to its before-damaged condition would equal or exceed 50 percent of the market value of the structure before the damage occurred.

SUBSTANTIAL IMPROVEMENT. Any repair, reconstruction, rehabilitation, *addition* or improvement of a building or structure, the cost of which equals or exceeds 50 percent of the market value of the structure before the improvement or repair is started. If the structure has sustained substantial damage, any repairs are considered substantial improvement regardless of the actual repair work performed. The term does not, however, include either:

1. Any project for improvement of a building required to correct existing health, sanitary or safety code violations identified by the *building official* and that are the minimum necessary to assure safe living conditions.
2. Any *alteration* of a historic structure provided that the *alteration* will not preclude the structure's continued designation as a historic structure.

1612.3 Establishment of flood hazard areas. To establish *flood hazard areas*, the applicable governing authority shall adopt a flood hazard map and supporting data. The flood hazard map shall include, at a minimum, areas of special flood hazard as identified by the Federal Emergency Management Agency in an engineering report entitled "The Flood Insurance Study for [INSERT NAME OF JURISDICTION]," dated [INSERT DATE OF ISSUANCE], as amended or revised with the accompanying Flood Insurance Rate Map (FIRM) and Flood Boundary and Floodway Map (FBFM) and related supporting data along with any revisions thereto. The adopted flood hazard map and supporting data are hereby adopted by reference and declared to be part of this section.

1612.3.1 Design flood elevations. Where design flood elevations are not included in the *flood hazard areas* established in Section 1612.3, or where floodways are not designated, the *building official* is authorized to require the applicant to:

1. Obtain and reasonably utilize any design flood elevation and floodway data available from a federal, state or other source; or
2. Determine the design flood elevation and/or floodway in accordance with accepted hydrologic and hydraulic engineering practices used to define special flood hazard areas. Determinations shall be undertaken by a *registered design professional* who shall document that the technical methods used reflect currently accepted engineering practice.

1612.3.2 Determination of impacts. In riverine *flood hazard areas* where design flood elevations are specified but floodways have not been designated, the applicant shall provide a floodway analysis that demonstrates that the proposed work will not increase the design flood elevation more than 1 foot (305 mm) at any point within the jurisdiction of the applicable governing authority.

1612.4 Design and construction. The design and construction of buildings and structures located in *flood hazard areas*, including flood hazard areas subject to high-velocity wave action, shall be in accordance with Chapter 5 of ASCE 7 and with ASCE 24.

1612.5 Flood hazard documentation. The following documentation shall be prepared and sealed by a *registered design professional* and submitted to the *building official*:

1. For construction in *flood hazard areas* not subject to high-velocity wave action:
   1.1. The elevation of the lowest floor, including the basement, as required by the lowest floor elevation inspection in Section 110.3.3.
   1.2. For fully enclosed areas below the design flood elevation where provisions to allow for the automatic entry and exit of floodwaters do not meet the minimum requirements in Section 2.6.2.1 of ASCE 24, *construction documents* shall include a statement that the design will provide for equalization of hydrostatic flood forces in accordance with Section 2.6.2.2 of ASCE 24.
   1.3. For dry floodproofed nonresidential buildings, *construction documents* shall include a statement that the dry floodproofing is designed in accordance with ASCE 24.
2. For construction in flood hazard areas subject to high-velocity wave action:
   2.1. The elevation of the bottom of the lowest horizontal structural member as required by the lowest floor elevation inspection in Section 110.3.3.
   2.2. *Construction documents* shall include a statement that the building is designed in accordance with ASCE 24, including that the pile or column foundation and building or structure to be attached thereto is designed to be anchored to resist flotation, collapse and lateral movement due to the effects of wind and flood loads acting simultaneously on all building components, and other load requirements of Chapter 16.
   2.3. For breakaway walls designed to resist a nominal load of less than 10 psf (0.48 kN/m^2) or more than 20 psf (0.96 kN/m^2), *construction documents* shall include a statement that the breakaway wall is designed in accordance with ASCE 24.

SECTION 1613 EARTHQUAKE LOADS

1613.1 Scope. Every structure, and portion thereof, including nonstructural components that are permanently attached to structures and their supports and attachments, shall be designed and constructed to resist the effects of earthquake motions in accordance with ASCE 7, excluding Chapter 14 and

Appendix 11A. The *seismic design category* for a structure is permitted to be determined in accordance with Section 1613 or ASCE 7.

Exceptions:

1. Detached one- and two-family dwellings, assigned to *Seismic Design Category* A, B or C, or located where the mapped short-period spectral response acceleration, S_S, is less than 0.4 g.
2. The seismic-force-resisting system of wood-frame buildings that conform to the provisions of Section 2308 are not required to be analyzed as specified in this section.
3. Agricultural storage structures intended only for incidental human occupancy.
4. Structures that require special consideration of their response characteristics and environment that are not addressed by this code or ASCE 7 and for which other regulations provide seismic criteria, such as vehicular bridges, electrical transmission towers, hydraulic structures, buried utility lines and their appurtenances and nuclear reactors.

1613.2 Definitions. The following words and terms shall, for the purposes of this section, have the meanings shown herein.

DESIGN EARTHQUAKE GROUND MOTION. The earthquake ground motion that buildings and structures are specifically proportioned to resist in Section 1613.

MAXIMUM CONSIDERED EARTHQUAKE GROUND MOTION. The most severe earthquake effects considered by this code.

MECHANICAL SYSTEMS. For the purposes of determining seismic loads in ASCE 7, mechanical systems shall include plumbing systems as specified therein.

ORTHOGONAL. To be in two horizontal directions, at 90 degrees (1.57 rad) to each other.

SEISMIC DESIGN CATEGORY. A classification assigned to a structure based on its *occupancy category* and the severity of the design earthquake ground motion at the site.

SEISMIC-FORCE-RESISTING SYSTEM. That part of the structural system that has been considered in the design to provide the required resistance to the prescribed seismic forces.

SITE CLASS. A classification assigned to a site based on the types of soils present and their engineering properties as defined in Section 1613.5.2.

SITE COEFFICIENTS. The values of F_a and F_v indicated in Tables 1613.5.3(1) and 1613.5.3(2), respectively.

1613.3 Existing buildings. *Additions*, *alterations*, repairs or change of occupancy of existing buildings shall be in accordance with Chapter 34.

1613.4 Special inspections. Where required by Sections 1705.3 through 1705.3.5, the statement of special inspections shall include the *special inspections* required by Section 1705.3.6.

1613.5 Seismic ground motion values. Seismic ground motion values shall be determined in accordance with this section.

1613.5.1 Mapped acceleration parameters. The parameters S_s and S_1 shall be determined from the 0.2 and 1-second spectral response accelerations shown on Figures 1613.5(1) through 1613.5(14). Where S_1 is less than or equal to 0.04 and S_s is less than or equal to 0.15, the structure is permitted to be assigned to *Seismic Design Category* A.

1613.5.2 Site class definitions. Based on the site soil properties, the site shall be classified as either *Site Class* A, B, C, D, E or F in accordance with Table 1613.5.2. When the soil properties are not known in sufficient detail to determine the *site class*, *Site Class* D shall be used unless the *building official* or geotechnical data determines that *Site Class* E or F soil is likely to be present at the site.

1613.5.3 Site coefficients and adjusted maximum considered earthquake spectral response acceleration parameters. The maximum considered earthquake spectral response acceleration for short periods, S_{MS}, and at 1-second period, S_{M1}, adjusted for *site class* effects shall be determined by Equations 16-36 and 16-37, respectively:

$$S_{MS} = F_a S_s \quad \textbf{(Equation 16-36)}$$

$$S_{M1} = F_v S_1 \quad \textbf{(Equation 16-37)}$$

where:

F_a = Site coefficient defined in Table 1613.5.3(1).

F_v = Site coefficient defined in Table 1613.5.3(2).

S_S = The mapped spectral accelerations for short periods as determined in Section 1613.5.1.

S_1 = The mapped spectral accelerations for a 1-second period as determined in Section 1613.5.1.

1613.5.4 Design spectral response acceleration parameters. Five-percent damped design spectral response acceleration at short periods, S_{DS}, and at 1-second period, S_{D1}, shall be determined from Equations 16-38 and 16-39, respectively:

$$S_{DS} = \frac{2}{3} S_{MS} \quad \textbf{(Equation 16-38)}$$

$$S_{D1} = \frac{2}{3} S_{M1} \quad \textbf{(Equation 16-39)}$$

where:

S_{MS} = The maximum considered earthquake spectral response accelerations for short period as determined in Section 1613.5.3.

S_{M1} = The maximum considered earthquake spectral response accelerations for 1-second period as determined in Section 1613.5.3.

TABLE 1613.5.2
SITE CLASS DEFINITIONS

SITE CLASS	SOIL PROFILE NAME	AVERAGE PROPERTIES IN TOP 100 feet, SEE SECTION 1613.5.5		
		Soil shear wave velocity, $\bar{v}_s$, (ft/s)	Standard penetration resistance, $\bar{N}$	Soil undrained shear strength, $\bar{s}_u$, (psf)
A	Hard rock	$\bar{v}_s > 5,000$	N/A	N/A
B	Rock	$2,500 < \bar{v}_s \leq 5,000$	N/A	N/A
C	Very dense soil and soft rock	$1,200 < \bar{v}_s \leq 2,500$	$\bar{N} > 50$	$\bar{s}_u \geq 2,000$
D	Stiff soil profile	$600 \leq \bar{v}_s \leq 1,200$	$15 \leq \bar{N} \leq 50$	$1,000 \leq \bar{s}_u \leq 2,000$
E	Soft soil profile	$\bar{v}_s < 600$	$\bar{N} < 15$	$\bar{s}_u < 1,000$
E	—	Any profile with more than 10 feet of soil having the following characteristics: 1. Plasticity index $PI > 20$, 2. Moisture content $w \geq 40\%$, and 3. Undrained shear strength $\bar{s}_u < 500$ psf		
F	—	Any profile containing soils having one or more of the following characteristics: 1. Soils vulnerable to potential failure or collapse under seismic loading such as liquefiable soils, quick and highly sensitive clays, collapsible weakly cemented soils. 2. Peats and/or highly organic clays ($H > 10$ feet of peat and/or highly organic clay where H = thickness of soil) 3. Very high plasticity clays ($H > 25$ feet with plasticity index $PI > 75$) 4. Very thick soft/medium stiff clays ($H > 120$ feet)		

TABLE 1613.5.3(1)
VALUES OF SITE COEFFICIENT F_a [a]

SITE CLASS	MAPPED SPECTRAL RESPONSE ACCELERATION AT SHORT PERIOD				
	$S_s \leq 0.25$	$S_s = 0.50$	$S_s = 0.75$	$S_s = 1.00$	$S_s \geq 1.25$
A	0.8	0.8	0.8	0.8	0.8
B	1.0	1.0	1.0	1.0	1.0
C	1.2	1.2	1.1	1.0	1.0
D	1.6	1.4	1.2	1.1	1.0
E	2.5	1.7	1.2	0.9	0.9
F	Note b	Note b	Note b	Note b	Note b

a. Use straight-line interpolation for intermediate values of mapped spectral response acceleration at short period, S_s.
b. Values shall be determined in accordance with Section 11.4.7 of ASCE 7.

TABLE 1613.5.3(2)
VALUES OF SITE COEFFICIENT F_V [a]

SITE CLASS	MAPPED SPECTRAL RESPONSE ACCELERATION AT 1-SECOND PERIOD				
	$S_1 \leq 0.1$	$S_1 = 0.2$	$S_1 = 0.3$	$S_1 = 0.4$	$S_1 \geq 0.5$
A	0.8	0.8	0.8	0.8	0.8
B	1.0	1.0	1.0	1.0	1.0
C	1.7	1.6	1.5	1.4	1.3
D	2.4	2.0	1.8	1.6	1.5
E	3.5	3.2	2.8	2.4	2.4
F	Note b	Note b	Note b	Note b	Note b

a. Use straight-line interpolation for intermediate values of mapped spectral response acceleration at 1-second period, S_1.
b. Values shall be determined in accordance with Section 11.4.7 of ASCE 7.

1613.5.5 Site classification for seismic design. Site classification for *Site Class* C, D or E shall be determined from Table 1613.5.5.

The notations presented below apply to the upper 100 feet (30 480 mm) of the site profile. Profiles containing distinctly different soil and/or rock layers shall be subdivided into those layers designated by a number that ranges from 1 to *n* at the bottom where there is a total of *n* distinct layers in the upper 100 feet (30 480 mm). The symbol *i* then refers to any one of the layers between 1 and *n*.

where:

v_{si} = The shear wave velocity in feet per second (m/s).

d_i = The thickness of any layer between 0 and 100 feet (30 480 mm).

where:

$$\bar{v}_s = \frac{\sum_{i=1}^{n} d_i}{\sum_{i=1}^{n} \frac{d_i}{v_{si}}} \quad \textbf{(Equation 16-40)}$$

$$\sum_{i=1}^{n} d_i = 100 \text{ feet } (30\,480 \text{ mm})$$

N_i is the Standard Penetration Resistance (ASTM D 1586) not to exceed 100 blows/foot (328 blows/m) as directly measured in the field without corrections. When refusal is met for a rock layer, N_i shall be taken as 100 blows/foot (328 blows/m).

$$\bar{N} = \frac{\sum_{i=1}^{n} d_i}{\sum_{i=1}^{n} \frac{d_i}{N_i}} \quad \textbf{(Equation 16-41)}$$

where N_i and d_i in Equation 16-41 are for cohesionless soil, cohesive soil and rock layers.

$$\bar{N}_{ch} = \frac{d_s}{\sum_{i=1}^{m} \frac{d_i}{N_i}} \quad \textbf{(Equation 16-42)}$$

where:

$$\sum_{i=1}^{m} d_i = d_s$$

Use d_i and N_i for cohesionless soil layers only in Equation 16-42.

d_s = The total thickness of cohesionless soil layers in the top 100 feet (30 480 mm).

m = The number of cohesionless soil layers in the top 100 feet (30 480 mm).

s_{ui} = The undrained shear strength in psf (kPa), not to exceed 5,000 psf (240 kPa), ASTM D 2166 or D 2850.

$$\bar{s}_u = \frac{d_c}{\sum_{i=1}^{k} \frac{d_i}{s_{ui}}} \quad \textbf{(Equation 16-43)}$$

where:

$$\sum_{i=1}^{k} d_i = d_c$$

d_c = The total thickness of cohesive soil layers in the top 100 feet (30 480 mm).

k = The number of cohesive soil layers in the top 100 feet (30 480 mm).

PI = The plasticity index, ASTM D 4318.

w = The moisture content in percent, ASTM D 2216.

Where a site does not qualify under the criteria for *Site Class* F and there is a total thickness of soft clay greater than 10 feet (3048 mm) where a soft clay layer is defined by: $\bar{s}_u < 500$ psf (24 kPa), $w \geq 40$ percent, and PI > 20, it shall be classified as *Site Class* E.

The shear wave velocity for rock, *Site Class* B, shall be either measured on site or estimated by a geotechnical engineer or engineering geologist/seismologist for competent rock with moderate fracturing and weathering. Softer and more highly fractured and weathered rock shall either be measured on site for shear wave velocity or classified as *Site Class* C.

The hard rock category, *Site Class* A, shall be supported by shear wave velocity measurements either on site or on profiles of the same rock type in the same formation with an equal or greater degree of weathering and fracturing. Where hard rock conditions are known to be continuous to a depth of 100 feet (30 480 mm), surficial shear wave velocity measurements are permitted to be extrapolated to assess $\bar{v}_s$.

TABLE 1613.5.5
SITE CLASSIFICATION[a]

SITE CLASS	$\bar{v}_s$	$\bar{N}$ or $\bar{N}_{ch}$	$\bar{s}_u$
E	< 600 ft/s	< 15	< 1,000 psf
D	600 to 1,200 ft/s	15 to 50	1,000 to 2,000 psf
C	1,200 to 2,500 ft/s	> 50	> 2,000

For SI: 1 foot per second = 304.8 mm per second, 1 pound per square foot = 0.0479kN/m^2.

a. If the $\bar{s}_u$ method is used and the $\bar{N}_{ch}$ and $\bar{s}_u$ criteria differ, select the category with the softer soils (for example, use Site Class E instead of D).

The rock categories, *Site Classes* A and B, shall not be used if there is more than 10 feet (3048 mm) of soil between the rock surface and the bottom of the spread footing or mat foundation.

1613.5.5.1 Steps for classifying a site.

1. Check for the four categories of *Site Class* F requiring site-specific evaluation. If the site corresponds to any of these categories, classify the site as *Site Class* F and conduct a site-specific evaluation.
2. Check for the existence of a total thickness of soft clay > 10 feet (3048 mm) where a soft clay layer is defined by: $\bar{s}_u$ < 500 psf (24 kPa), $w \geq 40$ percent and $PI > 20$. If these criteria are satisfied, classify the site as *Site Class* E.
3. Categorize the site using one of the following three methods with $\bar{v}_s$, $\bar{N}$, and $\bar{s}_u$ and computed in all cases as specified.

   3.1. $\bar{v}_s$ for the top 100 feet (30 480 mm) ($\bar{v}_s$ method).

   3.2. $\bar{N}$ for the top 100 feet (30 480 mm) ($\bar{N}$ method).

   3.3. $\bar{N}_{ch}$ for cohesionless soil layers ($PI < 20$) in the top 100 feet (30 480 mm) and average, $\bar{s}_u$ for cohesive soil layers ($PI > 20$) in the top 100 feet (30 480 mm) ($\bar{s}_u$ method).

1613.5.6 Determination of seismic design category. Structures classified as *Occupancy Category* I, II or III that are located where the mapped spectral response acceleration parameter at 1-second period, S_1, is greater than or equal to 0.75 shall be assigned to *Seismic Design Category* E. Structures classified as *Occupancy Category* IV that are located where the mapped spectral response acceleration parameter at 1-second period, S_1, is greater than or equal to 0.75 shall be assigned to *Seismic Design Category* F. All other structures shall be assigned to a *seismic design category* based on their *occupancy category* and the design spectral response acceleration coefficients, S_{DS} and S_{D1}, determined in accordance with Section 1613.5.4 or the site-specific procedures of ASCE 7. Each building and structure shall be assigned to the more severe *seismic design category* in accordance with Table 1613.5.6(1) or 1613.5.6(2), irrespective of the fundamental period of vibration of the structure, *T*.

**TABLE 1613.5.6(1)
SEISMIC DESIGN CATEGORY BASED ON
SHORT-PERIOD RESPONSE ACCELERATIONS**

VALUE OF S_{DS}	OCCUPANCY CATEGORY		
	I or II	III	IV
$S_{DS} < 0.167g$	A	A	A
$0.167g \leq S_{DS} < 0.33g$	B	B	C
$0.33g \leq S_{DS} < 0.50g$	C	C	D
$0.50g \leq S_{DS}$	D	D	D

**TABLE 1613.5.6(2)
SEISMIC DESIGN CATEGORY BASED ON
1-SECOND PERIOD RESPONSE ACCELERATION**

VALUE OF S_{D1}	OCCUPANCY CATEGORY		
	I or II	III	IV
$S_{D1} < 0.067g$	A	A	A
$0.067g \leq S_{D1} < 0.133g$	B	B	C
$0.133g \leq S_{D1} < 0.20g$	C	C	D
$0.20g \leq S_{D1}$	D	D	D

1613.5.6.1 Alternative seismic design category determination. Where S_1 is less than 0.75, the *seismic design category* is permitted to be determined from Table 1613.5.6(1) alone when all of the following apply:

1. In each of the two orthogonal directions, the approximate fundamental period of the structure, Ta, in each of the two orthogonal directions determined in accordance with Section 12.8.2.1 of ASCE 7, is less than 0.8 T_s determined in accordance with Section 11.4.5 of ASCE 7.
2. In each of the two orthogonal directions, the fundamental period of the structure used to calculate the story drift is less than T_s.
3. Equation 12.8-2 of ASCE 7 is used to determine the seismic response coefficient, C_s.
4. The diaphragms are rigid as defined in Section 12.3.1 of ASCE 7 or, for diaphragms that are flexible, the distances between vertical elements of the seismic-force-resisting system do not exceed 40 feet (12 192 mm).

1613.5.6.2 Simplified design procedure. Where the alternate simplified design procedure of ASCE 7 is used, the *seismic design category* shall be determined in accordance with ASCE 7.

1613.6 Alternatives to ASCE 7. The provisions of Section 1613.6 shall be permitted as alternatives to the relevant provisions of ASCE 7.

1613.6.1 Assumption of flexible diaphragm. Add the following text at the end of Section 12.3.1.1 of ASCE 7.

Diaphragms constructed of wood structural panels or untopped steel decking shall also be permitted to be idealized as flexible, provided all of the following conditions are met:

1. Toppings of concrete or similar materials are not placed over wood structural panel diaphragms except for nonstructural toppings no greater than $1^1/_2$ inches (38 mm) thick.
2. Each line of vertical elements of the seismic-force-resisting system complies with the allowable story drift of Table 12.12-1.
3. Vertical elements of the seismic-force-resisting system are light-frame walls sheathed with wood structural panels rated for shear resistance or steel sheets.

4. Portions of wood structural panel diaphragms that cantilever beyond the vertical elements of the lateral-force-resisting system are designed in accordance with Section 4.2.5.2 of AF&PA SDPWS.

1613.6.2 Additional seismic-force-resisting systems for seismically isolated structures. Add the following exception to the end of Section 17.5.4.2 of ASCE 7:

Exception: For isolated structures designed in accordance with this standard, the Structural System Limitations and the Building Height Limitations in Table 12.2-1 for ordinary steel concentrically braced frames (OCBFs) as defined in Chapter 11 and ordinary moment frames (OMFs) as defined in Chapter 11 are permitted to be taken as 160 feet (48 768 mm) for structures assigned to *Seismic Design Category* D, E or F, provided that the following conditions are satisfied:

1. The value of R_I as defined in Chapter 17 is taken as 1.
2. For OMFs and OCBFs, design is in accordance with AISC 341.

1613.6.3 Automatic sprinkler systems. *Automatic sprinkler systems* designed and installed in accordance with NFPA 13 shall be deemed to meet the requirements of Section 13.6.8 of ASCE 7.

1613.6.4 Autoclaved aerated concrete (AAC) masonry shear wall design coefficients and system limitations. Add the following text at the end of Section 12.2.1 of ASCE 7:

For ordinary reinforced AAC masonry shear walls used in the seismic-force-resisting system of structures, the response modification factor, R, shall be permitted to be taken as 2, the deflection amplification factor, C_d, shall be permitted to be taken as 2 and the system overstrength factor, Ω_o, shall be permitted to be taken as $2^1/_2$. Ordinary reinforced AAC masonry shear walls shall not be limited in height for buildings assigned to *Seismic Design Category* B, shall be limited in height to 35 feet (10 668 mm) for buildings assigned to *Seismic Design Category* C and are not permitted for buildings assigned to *Seismic Design Categories* D, E and F.

For ordinary plain (unreinforced) AAC masonry shear walls used in the seismic-force-resisting system of structures, the response modification factor, R, shall be permitted to be taken as $1^1/_2$, the deflection amplification factor, C_d, shall be permitted to be taken as $1^1/_2$ and the system overstrength factor, Ω_o, shall be permitted to be taken as $2^1/_2$. Ordinary plain (unreinforced) AAC masonry shear walls shall not be limited in height for buildings assigned to *Seismic Design Category* B and are not permitted for buildings assigned to *Seismic Design Categories* C, D, E and F.

1613.6.5 Seismic controls for elevators. Seismic switches in accordance with Section 8.4.10 of ASME A17.1 shall be deemed to comply with Section 13.6.10.3 of ASCE 7.

1613.6.6 Steel plate shear wall height limits. Modify Section 12.2.5.4 of ASCE 7 to read as follows:

12.2.5.4 Increased building height limit for steel-braced frames, special steel plate shear walls and special reinforced concrete shear walls. The height limits in Table 12.2-1 are permitted to be increased from 160 feet (48 768 mm) to 240 feet (75 152 mm) for structures assigned to *Seismic Design Category* D or E and from 100 feet (30 480 mm) to 160 feet (48 768 mm) for structures assigned to *Seismic Design Category* F that have steel-braced frames, special steel plate shear walls or special reinforced concrete cast-in-place shear walls and that meet both of the following requirements:

1. The structure shall not have an extreme torsional irregularity as defined in Table 12.2-1 (horizontal structural irregularity Type 1b).
2. The braced frames or shear walls in any one plane shall resist no more than 60 percent of the total seismic forces in each direction, neglecting accidental torsional effects.

1613.6.7 Minimum distance for building separation. All buildings and structures shall be separated from adjoining structures. Separations shall allow for the maximum inelastic response displacement (δ_M). δ_M shall be determined at critical locations with consideration for both translational and torsional displacements of the structure using Equation 16-44.

$$\delta_M = \frac{C_d \delta_{max}}{I}$$ **(Equation 16-44)**

where:

C_d = Deflection amplification factor in Table 12.2-1 of ASCE 7.

δ_{max} = Maximum displacement defined in Section 12.8.4.3 of ASCE 7.

I = Importance factor in accordance with Section 11.5.1 of ASCE 7.

Adjacent buildings on the same property shall be separated by a distance not less than δ_{MT}, determined by Equation 16-45.

$$\delta_{MT} = \sqrt{(\delta_{M1})^2 + (\delta_{M2})^2}$$ **(Equation 16-45)**

where:

δ_{M1}, δ_{M2} = The maximum inelastic response displacements of the adjacent buildings in accordance with Equation 16-44.

Where a structure adjoins a property line not common to a public way, the structure shall also be set back from the property line by not less than the maximum inelastic response displacement, δ_M, of that structure.

Exceptions:

1. Smaller separations or property line setbacks shall be permitted when justified by rational analyses.
2. Buildings and structures assigned to *Seismic Design Category* A, B or C.

1613.6.8 HVAC ductwork with I_p = 1.5. Seismic supports are not required for HVAC ductwork with I_p = 1.5 if either of the following conditions is met for the full length of each duct run:

1. HVAC ducts are suspended from hangers 12 inches (305 mm) or less in length with hangers detailed to avoid significant bending of the hangers and their attachments, or
2. HVAC ducts have a cross-sectional area of less than 6 square feet (0.557 m^2)..

1613.7 ASCE 7, Section 11.7.5. Modify ASCE 7, Section 11.7.5 to read as follows:

11.7.5 Anchorage of walls. Walls shall be anchored to the roof and all floors and members that provide lateral support for the wall or that are supported by the wall. The anchorage shall provide a direct connection between the walls and the roof or floor construction. The connections shall be capable of resisting the forces specified in Section 11.7.3 applied horizontally, substituted for *E* in load combinations of Section 2.3 or 2.4.

SECTION 1614 STRUCTURAL INTEGRITY

1614.1 General. Buildings classified as high-rise buildings in accordance with Section 403 and assigned to *Occupancy Category* III or IV shall comply with the requirements of this section. Frame structures shall comply with the requirements of Section 1614.3. Bearing wall structures shall comply with the requirements of Section 1614.4.

1614.2 Definitions. The following words and terms shall, for the purposes of Section 1614, have the meanings shown herein.

BEARING WALL STRUCTURE. A building or other structure in which vertical loads from floors and roofs are primarily supported by walls.

FRAME STRUCTURE. A building or other structure in which vertical loads from floors and roofs are primarily supported by columns.

1614.3 Frame structures. Frame structures shall comply with the requirements of this section.

1614.3.1 Concrete frame structures. Frame structures constructed primarily of reinforced or prestressed concrete, either cast-in-place or precast, or a combination of these, shall conform to the requirements of ACI 318 Sections 7.13, 13.3.8.5, 13.3.8.6, 16.5, 18.12.6, 18.12.7 and 18.12.8 as applicable. Where ACI 318 requires that nonprestressed reinforcing or prestressing steel pass through the region bounded by the longitudinal column reinforcement, that reinforcing or prestressing steel shall have a minimum nominal tensile strength equal to two-thirds of the required one-way vertical strength of the connection of the floor or roof system to the column in each direction of beam or slab reinforcement passing through the column.

Exception: Where concrete slabs with continuous reinforcing having an area not less than 0.0015 times the concrete area in each of two orthogonal directions are present and are either monolithic with or equivalently bonded to beams, girders or columns, the longitudinal reinforcing or prestressing steel passing through the column reinforcement shall have a nominal tensile strength of one-third of the required one-way vertical strength of the connection of the floor or roof system to the column in each direction of beam or slab reinforcement passing through the column.

1614.3.2 Structural steel, open web steel joist or joist girder, or composite steel and concrete frame structures. Frame structures constructed with a structural steel frame or a frame composed of open web steel joists, joist girders with or without other structural steel elements or a frame composed of composite steel or composite steel joists and reinforced concrete elements shall conform to the requirements of this section.

1614.3.2.1 Columns. Each column splice shall have the minimum design strength in tension to transfer the design dead and live load tributary to the column between the splice and the splice or base immediately below.

1614.3.2.2 Beams. End connections of all beams and girders shall have a minimum nominal axial tensile strength equal to the required vertical shear strength for *allowable stress design* (ASD) or two-thirds of the required shear strength for *load and resistance factor design* (LRFD) but not less than 10 kips (45 kN). For the purpose of this section, the shear force and the axial tensile force need not be considered to act simultaneously.

Exception: Where beams, girders, open web joist and joist girders support a concrete slab or concrete slab on metal deck that is attached to the beam or girder with not less than $^3/_8$-inch-diameter (9.5 mm) headed shear studs, at a spacing of not more than 12 inches (305 mm) on center, averaged over the length of the member, or other attachment having equivalent shear strength, and the slab contains continuous distributed reinforcement in each of two orthogonal directions with an area not less than 0.0015 times the concrete area, the nominal axial tension strength of the end connection shall be permitted to be taken as half the required vertical shear strength for ASD or one-third of the required shear strength for LRFD, but not less than 10 kips (45 kN).

1614.4 Bearing wall structures. Bearing wall structures shall have vertical ties in all load-bearing walls and longitudinal ties, transverse ties and perimeter ties at each floor level in accordance with this section and as shown in Figure 1614.4.

1614.4.1 Concrete wall structures. Precast bearing wall structures constructed solely of reinforced or prestressed concrete, or combinations of these shall conform to the requirements of Sections 7.13, 13.3.8.5 and 16.5 of ACI 318.

1614.4.2 Other bearing wall structures. Ties in bearing wall structures other than those covered in Section 1614.4.1 shall conform to this section.

1614.4.2.1 Longitudinal ties. Longitudinal ties shall consist of continuous reinforcement in slabs; continuous or spliced decks or sheathing; continuous or spliced members framing to, within or across walls; or connections of continuous framing members to walls. Longitudinal ties shall extend across interior load-bearing walls and shall connect to exterior load-bearing walls and shall be spaced at not greater than 10 feet (3038 mm) on center. Ties shall have a minimum nominal tensile strength, T_T, given by Equation 16-46. For ASD the minimum nominal tensile strength shall be permitted to be taken as 1.5 times the allowable tensile stress times the area of the tie.

$$T_T = wLS \leq \alpha_T S \quad \textbf{(Equation 16-46)}$$

where:

L = The span of the horizontal element in the direction of the tie, between bearing walls, feet (m).

w = The weight per unit area of the floor or roof in the span being tied to or across the wall, psf (N/m^2).

S = The spacing between ties, feet (m).

α_T = A coefficient with a value of 1,500 pounds per foot (2.25 kN/m) for masonry bearing wall structures and a value of 375 pounds per foot (0.6 kN/m) for structures with bearing walls of cold-formed steel light-frame construction.

1614.4.2.2 Transverse ties. Transverse ties shall consist of continuous reinforcement in slabs; continuous or spliced decks or sheathing; continuous or spliced members framing to, within or across walls; or connections of continuous framing members to walls. Transverse ties shall be placed no farther apart than the spacing of load-bearing walls. Transverse ties shall have minimum nominal tensile strength T_T, given by Equation 16-46. For ASD the minimum nominal tensile strength shall be permitted to be taken as 1.5 times the allowable tensile stress times the area of the tie.

1614.4.2.3 Perimeter ties. Perimeter ties shall consist of continuous reinforcement in slabs; continuous or spliced decks or sheathing; continuous or spliced members framing to, within or across walls; or connections of continuous framing members to walls. Ties around the perimeter of each floor and roof shall be located within 4 feet (1219 mm) of the edge and shall provide a nominal strength in tension not less than T_p, given by Equation 16-47. For ASD the minimum nominal tensile strength shall be permitted to be taken as 1.5 times the allowable tensile stress times the area of the tie.

$$T_p = 200w \leq \beta_T \quad \textbf{(Equation 16-47)}$$

For SI:

$$T_p = 90.7w \leq \beta_T$$

where:

w = As defined in Section 1614.4.2.1.

β_T = A coefficient with a value of 16,000 pounds (7200 kN) for structures with masonry bearing walls and a value of 4,000 pounds (1300 kN) for structures with bearing walls of cold-formed steel light-frame construction.

1614.4.2.4 Vertical ties. Vertical ties shall consist of continuous or spliced reinforcing, continuous or spliced members, wall sheathing or other engineered systems. Vertical tension ties shall be provided in bearing walls and shall be continuous over the height of the building. The minimum nominal tensile strength for vertical ties within a bearing wall shall be equal to the weight of the wall within that *story* plus the weight of the diaphragm tributary to the wall in the *story* below. No fewer than two ties shall be provided for each wall. The strength of each tie need not exceed 3,000 pounds per foot (450 kN/m) of wall tributary to the tie for walls of masonry construction or 750 pounds per foot (140 kN/m) of wall tributary to the tie for walls of cold-formed steel light-frame construction.

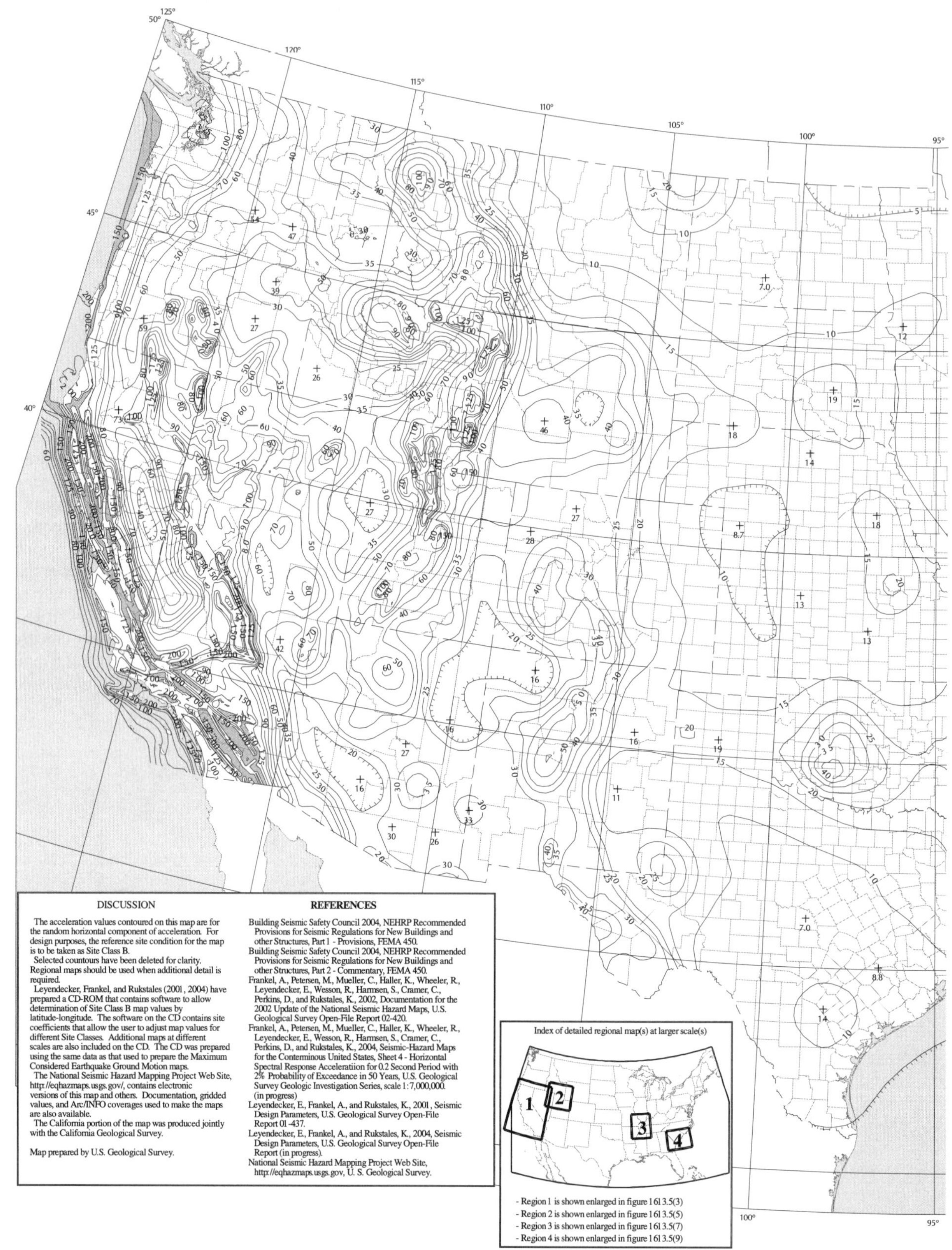

125°
50°
120°
115°
110°
105°
100°
95°
45°
40°
DISCUSSION
The acceleration values contoured on this map are for the random horizontal component of acceleration. For design purposes, the reference site condition for the map is to be taken as Site Class B.
Selected countours have been deleted for clarity. Regional maps should be used when additional detail is required.
Leyendecker, Frankel, and Rukstales (2001, 2004) have prepared a CD-ROM that contains software to allow determination of Site Class B map values by latitude-longitude. The software on the CD contains site coefficients that allow the user to adjust map values for different Site Classes. Additional maps at different scales are also included on the CD. The CD was prepared using the same data as that used to prepare the Maximum Considered Earthquake Ground Motion maps.
The National Seismic Hazard Mapping Project Web Site, http://eqhazmaps.usgs.gov/, contains electronic versions of this map and others. Documentation, gridded values, and Arc/INFO coverages used to make the maps are also available.
The California portion of the map was produced jointly with the California Geological Survey.
Map prepared by U.S. Geological Survey.
REFERENCES
Building Seismic Safety Council 2004, NEHRP Recommended Provisions for Seismic Regulations for New Buildings and other Structures, Part 1 - Provisions, FEMA 450.
Building Seismic Safety Council 2004, NEHRP Recommended Provisions for Seismic Regulations for New Buildings and other Structures, Part 2 - Commentary, FEMA 450.
Frankel, A., Petersen, M., Mueller, C., Haller, K., Wheeler, R., Leyendecker, E., Wesson, R., Harmsen, S., Cramer, C., Perkins, D., and Rukstales, K., 2002, Documentation for the 2002 Update of the National Seismic Hazard Maps, U.S. Geological Survey Open-File Report 02-420.
Frankel, A., Petersen, M., Mueller, C., Haller, K., Wheeler, R., Leyendecker, E., Wesson, R., Harmsen, S., Cramer, C., Perkins, D., and Rukstales, K., 2004, Seismic-Hazard Maps for the Conterminous United States, Sheet 4 - Horizontal Spectral Response Acceleratiion for 0.2 Second Period with 2% Probability of Exceedance in 50 Years, U.S. Geological Survey Geologic Investigation Series, scale 1:7,000,000. (in progress)
Leyendecker, E., Frankel, A., and Rukstales, K., 2001, Seismic Design Parameters, U.S. Geological Survey Open-File Report 01-437.
Leyendecker, E., Frankel, A., and Rukstales, K., 2004, Seismic Design Parameters, U.S. Geological Survey Open-File Report (in progress).
National Seismic Hazard Mapping Project Web Site, http://eqhazmaps.usgs.gov, U. S. Geological Survey.
Index of detailed regional map(s) at larger scale(s)
1
2
3
4
- Region 1 is shown enlarged in figure 1613.5(3)
- Region 2 is shown enlarged in figure 1613.5(5)
- Region 3 is shown enlarged in figure 1613.5(7)
- Region 4 is shown enlarged in figure 1613.5(9)

FIGURE 1613.5(1)
MAXIMUM CONSIDERED EARTHQUAKE GROUND MOTION FOR THE CONTERMINOUS UNITED STATES OF 0.2 SEC SPECTRAL RESPONSE ACCELERATION (5% OF CRITICAL DAMPING), SITE CLASS B

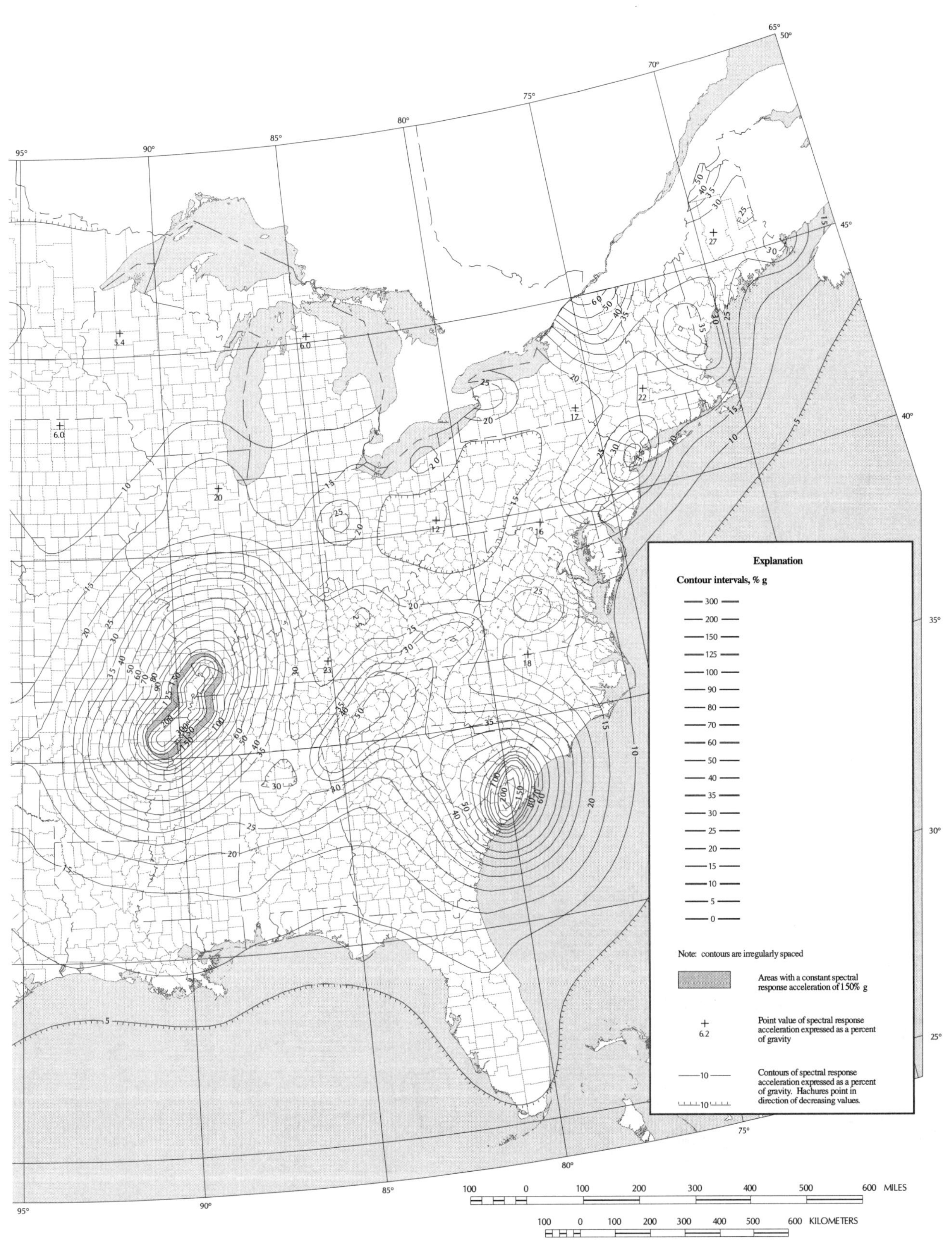

FIGURE 1613.5(1)—continued
MAXIMUM CONSIDERED EARTHQUAKE GROUND MOTION FOR THE CONTERMINOUS UNITED STATES OF 0.2 SEC SPECTRAL RESPONSE ACCELERATION (5% OF CRITICAL DAMPING), SITE CLASS B

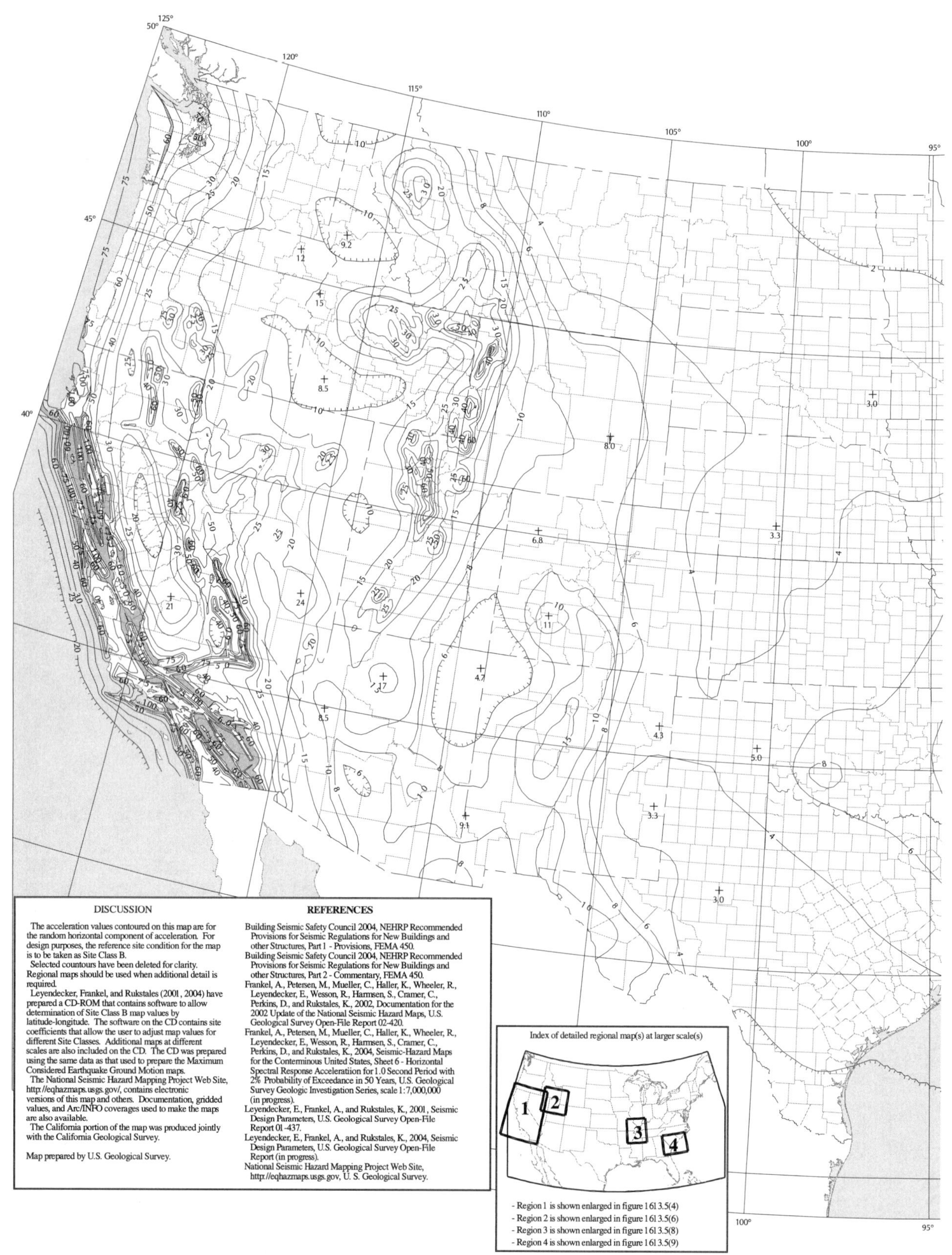

FIGURE 1613.5(2)
MAXIMUM CONSIDERED EARTHQUAKE GROUND MOTION FOR THE CONTERMINOUS UNITED STATES OF 1.0 SEC SPECTRAL RESPONSE ACCELERATION (5% OF CRITICAL DAMPING), SITE CLASS B

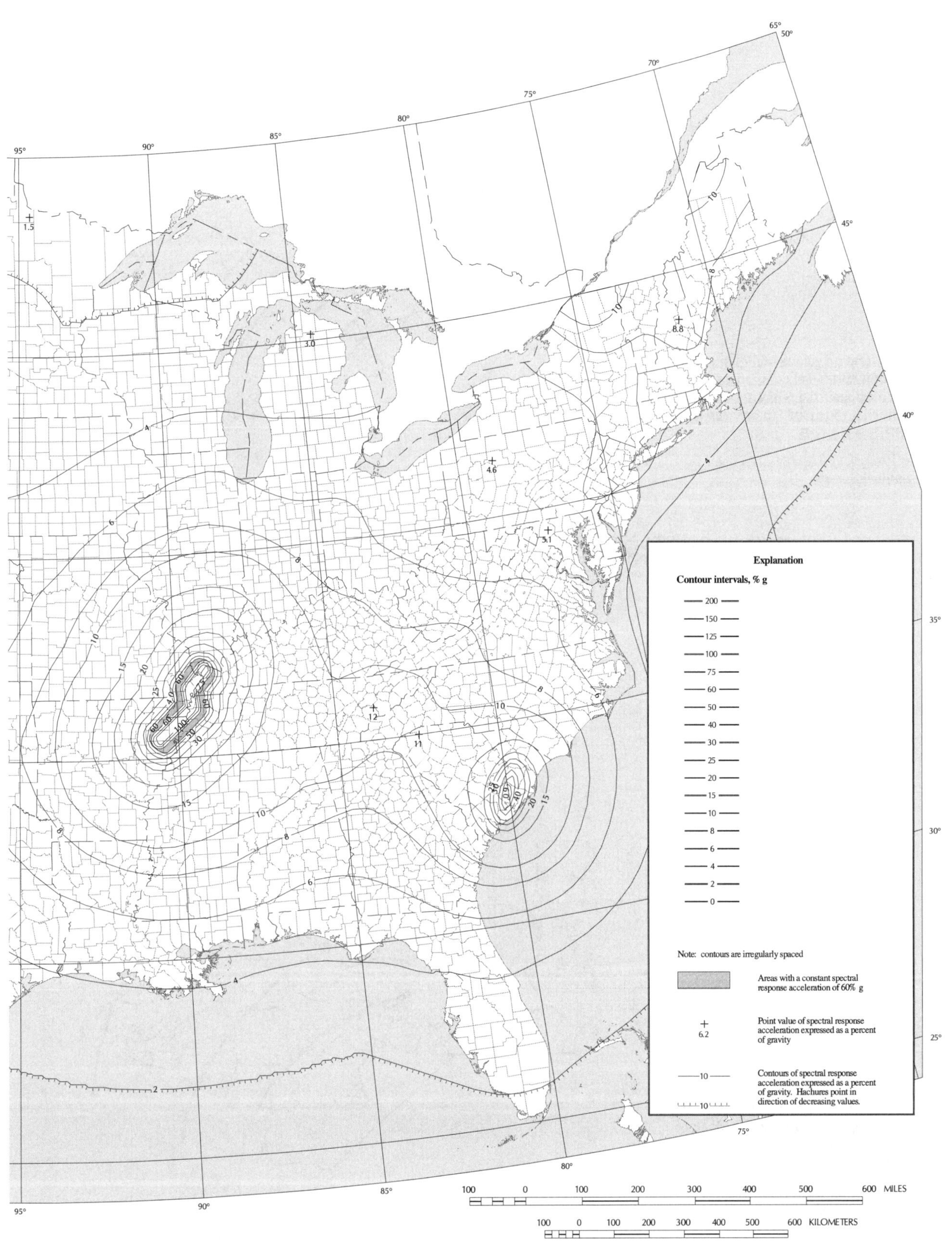

FIGURE 1613.5(2)—continued
MAXIMUM CONSIDERED EARTHQUAKE GROUND MOTION FOR THE CONTERMINOUS UNITED STATES OF 1.0 SEC SPECTRAL RESPONSE ACCELERATION (5% OF CRITICAL DAMPING), SITE CLASS B

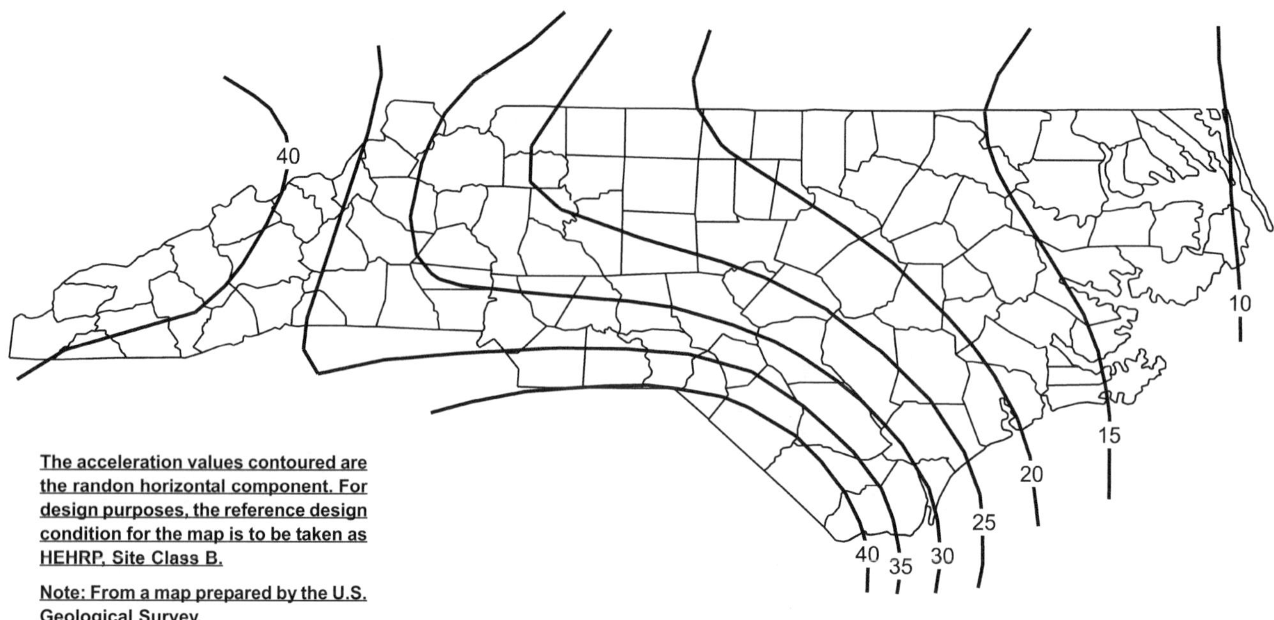

FIGURE 1613.5(3)
MAXIMUM CONSIDERED EARTHQUAKE GROUND MOTION FOR NORTH CAROLINA OF 0.2 SECOND SPECTRAL RESPONSE ACCELERATION (5 PERCENT OF CRITICAL DAMPING), SITE CLASS B

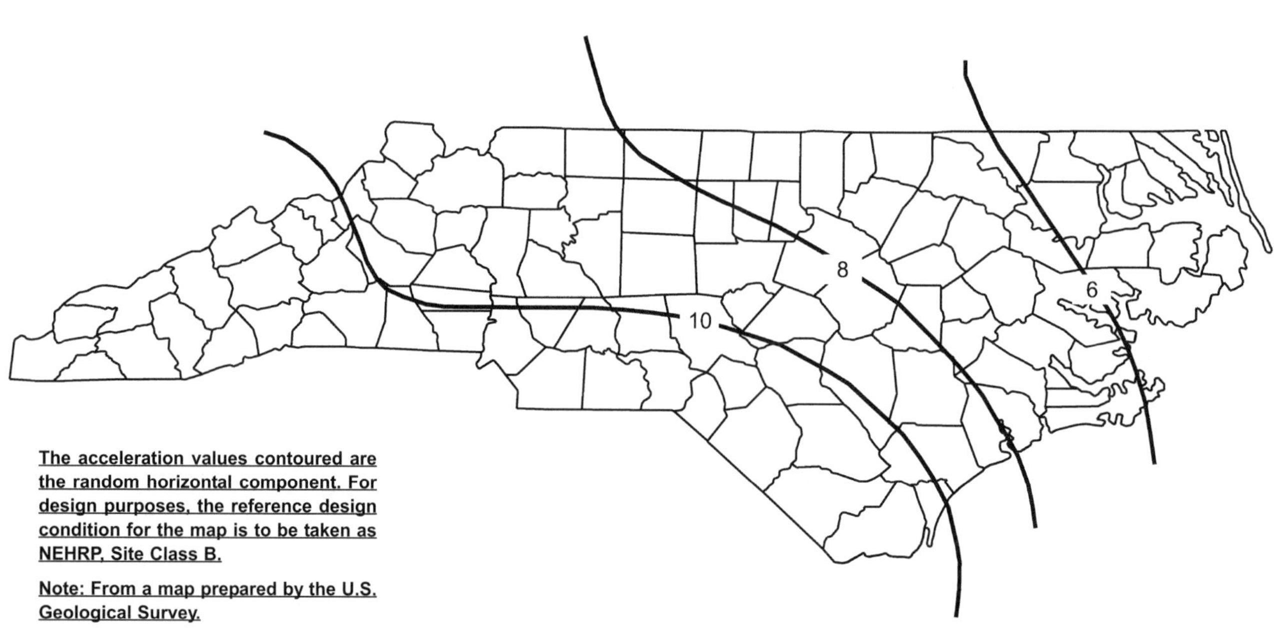

8
6
10
The acceleration values contoured are the random horizontal component. For design purposes, the reference design condition for the map is to be taken as NEHRP, Site Class B.
Note: From a map prepared by the U.S. Geological Survey.

FIGURE 1613.5(4)
MAXIMUM CONSIDERED EARTHQUAKE GROUND MOTION FOR NORTH CAROLINA OF 1.0 SECOND SPECTRAL RESPONSE ACCELERATION (5 PERCENT OF CRITICAL DAMPING), SITE CLASS B

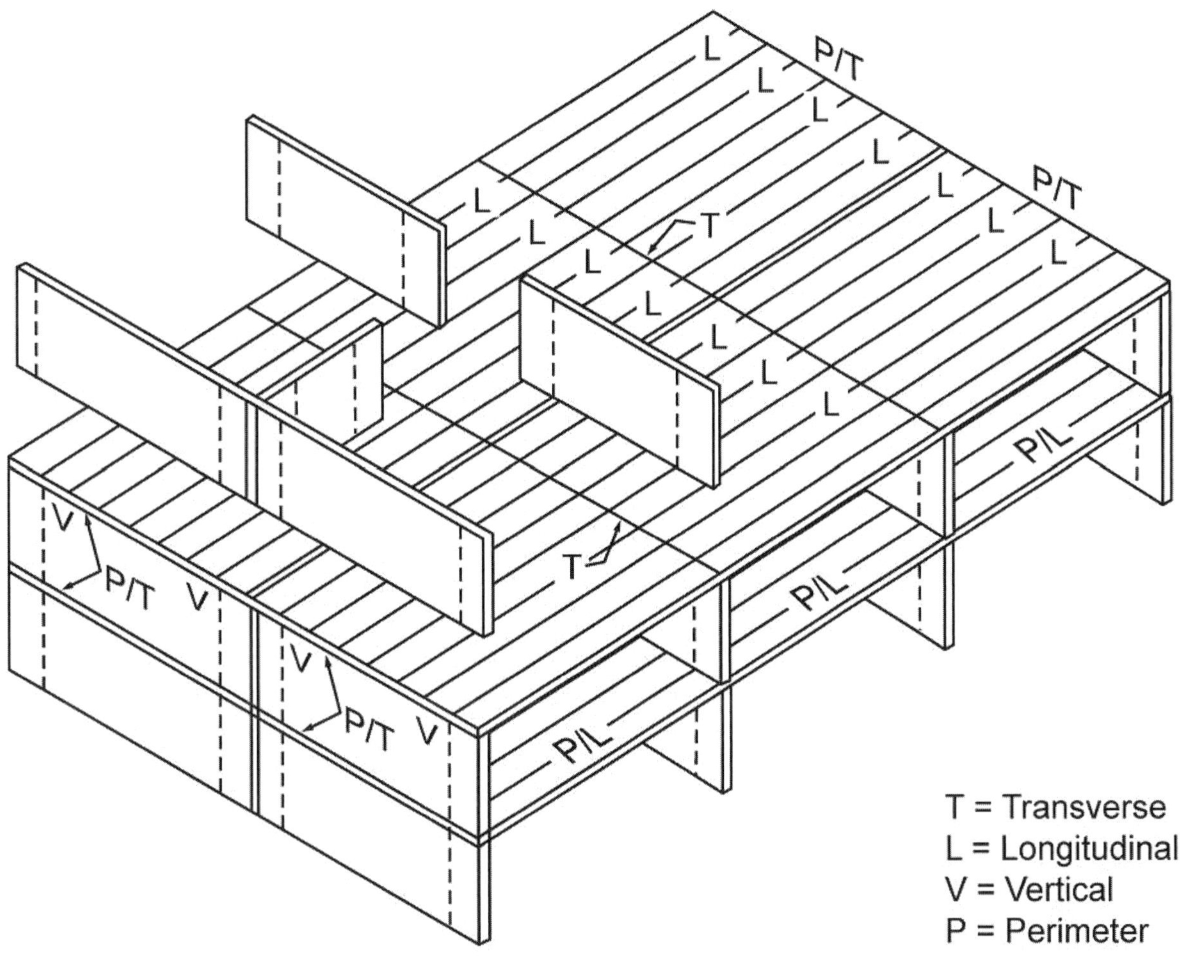

FIGURE 1614.4
LONGITUDINAL, PERIMETER, TRANSVERSE AND VERTICAL TIES

CHAPTER 17

STRUCTURAL TESTS AND SPECIAL INSPECTIONS

SECTION 1701 GENERAL

1701.1 Scope. The provisions of this chapter shall govern the quality, workmanship and requirements for materials covered. Materials of construction and tests shall conform to the applicable standards listed in this code.

1701.2 New materials. New building materials, equipment, appliances, systems or methods of construction not provided for in this code, and any material of questioned suitability proposed for use in the construction of a building or structure, shall be subjected to the tests prescribed in this chapter and in the *approved* rules to determine character, quality and limitations of use.

1701.3 Used materials. The use of second-hand materials that meet the minimum requirements of this code for new materials shall be permitted.

SECTION 1702 DEFINITIONS

1702.1 General. The following words and terms shall, for the purposes of this chapter and as used elsewhere in this code, have the meanings shown herein.

APPROVED AGENCY. An established and recognized agency regularly engaged in conducting tests or furnishing inspection services, when such agency has been *approved*.

APPROVED FABRICATOR. An established and qualified person, firm or corporation *approved* by the *building official* pursuant to Chapter 17 of this code.

CERTIFICATE OF COMPLIANCE. A certificate stating that materials and products meet specified standards or that work was done in compliance with *approved construction documents*.

DESIGNATED SEISMIC SYSTEM. Those architectural, electrical and mechanical systems and their components that require design in accordance with Chapter 13 of ASCE 7 and for which the component importance factor, I_p, is greater than 1 in accordance with Section 13.1.3 of ASCE 7.

FABRICATED ITEM. Structural, load-bearing or lateral load-resisting assemblies consisting of materials assembled prior to installation in a building or structure, or subjected to operations such as heat treatment, thermal cutting, cold working or reforming after manufacture and prior to installation in a building or structure. Materials produced in accordance with standard specifications referenced by this code, such as rolled structural steel shapes, steel-reinforcing bars, masonry units, and wood structural panels or in accordance with a standard, listed in Chapter 35, which provides requirements for quality control done under the supervision of a third-party quality control agency shall not be considered "fabricated items."

INSPECTION CERTIFICATE. An identification applied on a product by an *approved agency* containing the name of the manufacturer, the function and performance characteristics, and the name and identification of an *approved agency* that indicates that the product or material has been inspected and evaluated by an *approved agency* (see Section 1703.5 and "*Label*," "Manufacturer's designation" and "*Mark*").

INTUMESCENT FIRE-RESISTANT COATINGS. Thin film liquid mixture applied to substrates by brush, roller, spray or trowel which expands into a protective foamed layer to provide fire-resistant protection of the substrates when exposed to flame or intense heat.

MAIN WINDFORCE-RESISTING SYSTEM. An assemblage of structural elements assigned to provide support and stability for the overall structure. The system generally receives wind loading from more than one surface.

MASTIC FIRE-RESISTANT COATINGS. Liquid mixture applied to a substrate by brush, roller, spray or trowel that provides fire-resistant protection of a substrate when exposed to flame or intense heat.

SPECIAL INSPECTION. Inspection as herein required of the materials, installation, fabrication, erection or placement of components and connections requiring special expertise to ensure compliance with *approved construction documents* and referenced standards (see Section 1704).

SPECIAL INSPECTION, CONTINUOUS. The full-time observation of work requiring *special inspection* by an *approved* special inspector who is present in the area where the work is being performed.

SPECIAL INSPECTION, PERIODIC. The part-time or intermittent observation of work requiring *special inspection* by an *approved* special inspector who is present in the area where the work has been or is being performed and at the completion of the work.

SPRAYED FIRE-RESISTANT MATERIALS. Cementitious or fibrous materials that are sprayed to provide fire-resistant protection of the substrates.

STRUCTURAL OBSERVATION. The visual observation of the structural system by a *registered design professional* for general conformance to the *approved construction documents*. Structural observation does not include or waive the responsibility for the inspection required by Section 110, 1704 or other sections of this code.

SECTION 1703 APPROVALS

1703.1 Approved agency. An *approved agency* shall provide all information as necessary for the *building official* to determine that the agency meets the applicable requirements.

1703.1.1 Independence. An *approved agency* shall be objective, competent and independent from the contractor responsible for the work being inspected. The agency shall also disclose possible conflicts of interest so that objectivity can be confirmed.

1703.1.2 Equipment. An *approved agency* shall have adequate equipment to perform required tests. The equipment shall be periodically calibrated.

1703.1.3 Personnel. An *approved agency* shall employ experienced personnel educated in conducting, supervising and evaluating tests and/or inspections.

1703.2 Written approval. Any material, appliance, equipment, system or method of construction meeting the requirements of this code shall be *approved* in writing after satisfactory completion of the required tests and submission of required test reports.

1703.3 Approved record. For any material, appliance, equipment, system or method of construction that has been *approved*, a record of such approval, including the conditions and limitations of the approval, shall be kept on file in the *building official's* office and shall be open to public inspection at appropriate times.

1703.4 Performance. Specific information consisting of test reports conducted by an *approved* testing agency in accordance with standards referenced in Chapter 35, or other such information as necessary, shall be provided for the *building official* to determine that the material meets the applicable code requirements.

1703.4.1 Research and investigation. Sufficient technical data shall be submitted to the *building official* to substantiate the proposed use of any material or assembly. If it is determined that the evidence submitted is satisfactory proof of performance for the use intended, the *building official* shall approve the use of the material or assembly subject to the requirements of this code. The costs, reports and investigations required under these provisions shall be paid by the applicant.

1703.4.2 Research reports. Supporting data, where necessary to assist in the approval of materials or assemblies not specifically provided for in this code, shall consist of valid research reports from *approved* sources.

1703.5 Labeling. Where materials or assemblies are required by this code to be *labeled*, such materials and assemblies shall be *labeled* by an *approved agency* in accordance with Section 1703. Products and materials required to be labeled shall be labeled in accordance with the procedures set forth in Sections 1703.5.1 through 1703.5.3.

1703.5.1 Testing. An *approved agency* shall test a representative sample of the product or material being *labeled* to the relevant standard or standards. The *approved agency* shall maintain a record of the tests performed. The record shall provide sufficient detail to verify compliance with the test standard.

1703.5.2 Inspection and identification. The *approved agency* shall periodically perform an inspection, which shall be in-plant if necessary, of the product or material that is to be *labeled*. The inspection shall verify that the labeled product or material is representative of the product or material tested.

1703.5.3 Label information. The *label* shall contain the manufacturer's or distributor's identification, model number, serial number or definitive information describing the product or material's performance characteristics and *approved agency's* identification.

1703.6 Evaluation and follow-up inspection services. Where structural components or other items regulated by this code are not visible for inspection after completion of a prefabricated assembly, the applicant shall submit a report of each prefabricated assembly. The report shall indicate the complete details of the assembly, including a description of the assembly and its components, the basis upon which the assembly is being evaluated, test results and similar information and other data as necessary for the *building official* to determine conformance to this code. Such a report shall be *approved* by the *building official.*

1703.6.1 Follow-up inspection. The applicant shall provide for *special inspections* of fabricated items in accordance with Section 1704.2.

1703.6.2 Test and inspection records. Copies of necessary test and inspection records shall be filed with the *building official.*

SECTION 1704
SPECIAL INSPECTIONS

1704.1 General. Where application is made for construction as described in this section, the owner shall employ one or more special inspectors to provide inspections during construction on the types of work listed in accordance with Section 1704.1.2. These inspections are in addition to the inspections specified in the *North Carolina Administrative Code and Policies.*

The special inspector shall be a person who shall demonstrate competence, to the satisfaction of the *building official*, for the inspection of the particular type of construction or operation requiring *special inspection*. The *registered design professional in responsible charge* and engineers of record involved in the design of the project are permitted to act as the *approved agency* and their personnel are permitted to act as the special inspector for the work designed by them, provided those personnel meet the qualification requirements of this section to the satisfaction of the *building official*. The special inspector shall provide written documentation to the *building official* demonstrating his or her competence and relevant experience or training. Experience or training shall be considered relevant when the documented experience or training is related in complexity to the same type of *special inspection* activities for projects of similar complexity and material qualities. These qualifications are in addition to qualifications specified in other sections of this code.

Exceptions: Deleted.

1704.1.1 Building permit requirement. The permit applicant shall submit a statement of special inspections prepared by the registered design professional in responsible charge in accordance with the *North Carolina Administrative Code and Policies* as a condition for permit issuance. This statement shall include a list of materials and work requiring special inspections by Section 1704.1.1, the inspections to be performed and a list of the individuals, approved agencies or firms intended to be retained for conducting such inspections.

Exceptions: Deleted.

1704.1.2 Special inspections requirement. Special inspections in accordance with Section 1704 are required for building, building components or other structures according to the following:

1. Buildings or other structures listed in Table 1604.5 in Occupancy Category II if:
   - 1.1. Building height exceeds 45 feet (13.7 m) or three stories, or
   - 1.2. The building is an underground building in accordance with Section 405.1.
2. Buildings or other structures listed in Table 1604.5 in Occupancy Categories III or IV;
3. Piles, piers and special foundations in accoardance with Sections 1704.8 through 1704.11, 1810.3.5.2.4 and 1810.3.5.2.5;
4. Retaining walls exceeding 5 feet (1524 mm) height in accordance with Section 1807.2;
5. Smoke control and smoke exhaust systems;
6. Sprayed fire-resistant materials; or
7. Special case described in Section 1704.15.

1704.1.3 Report requirement. Special inspectors shall keep records of inspections. The special inspector shall furnish inspection reports to the *building official*, and to the *registered design professional in responsible charge*. Reports shall indicate that work inspected was or was not completed in conformance to *approved construction documents*. Discrepancies shall be brought to the immediate attention of the contractor for correction. If they are not corrected, the discrepancies shall be brought to the attention of the *building official* and to the *registered design professional in responsible charge* prior to the completion of that phase of the work. A final report documenting required *special inspections* and correction of any discrepancies noted in the inspections shall be submitted at a point in time agreed upon prior to the start of work by the applicant and the *building official*.

1704.2 Inspection of fabricators. Where fabrication of structural load-bearing members and assemblies is being performed on the premises of a fabricator's shop, *special inspection* of the fabricated items shall be required by this section and as required elsewhere in this code.

1704.2.1 Fabrication and implementation procedures. The special inspector shall verify that the fabricator maintains detailed fabrication and quality control procedures that provide a basis for inspection control of the workmanship and the fabricator's ability to conform to *approved construction documents* and referenced standards. The special inspector shall review the procedures for completeness and adequacy relative to the code requirements for the fabricator's scope of work.

Exception: *Special inspections* as required by Section 1704.2 shall not be required where the fabricator is *approved* in accordance with Section 1704.2.2.

1704.2.2 Fabricator approval. *Special inspections* required by Section 1704 are not required where the work is done on the premises of a fabricator registered and *approved* to perform such work without *special inspection*. Approval shall be based upon review of the fabricator's written procedural and quality control manuals and periodic auditing of fabrication practices by an *approved special inspection* agency. At completion of fabrication, the *approved* fabricator shall submit a *certificate of compliance* to the *building official* stating that the work was performed in accordance with the *approved construction documents*.

1704.3 Steel construction. The *special inspections* for steel elements of buildings and structures shall be as required by Section 1704.3 and Table 1704.3.

Exceptions:

1. *Special inspection* of the steel fabrication process shall not be required where the fabricator does not perform any welding, thermal cutting or heating operation of any kind as part of the fabrication process. In such cases, the fabricator shall be required to submit a detailed procedure for material control that demonstrates the fabricator's ability to maintain suitable records and procedures such that, at any time during the fabrication process, the material specification, grade and mill test reports for the main stress-carrying elements are capable of being determined.
2. The special inspector need not be continuously present during welding of the following items, provided the materials, welding procedures and qualifications of welders are verified prior to the start of the work; periodic inspections are made of the work in progress and a visual inspection of all welds is made prior to completion or prior to shipment of shop welding.
   - 2.1. Single-pass fillet welds not exceeding $^5/_{16}$ inch (7.9 mm) in size.
   - 2.2. Floor and roof deck welding.
   - 2.3. Welded studs when used for structural diaphragm.
   - 2.4. Welded sheet steel for cold-formed steel members.
   - 2.5. Welding of stairs and railing systems.

1704.3.1 Welding. Welding inspection and welding inspector qualification shall be in accordance with this section.

TABLE 1704.3
REQUIRED VERIFICATION AND INSPECTION OF STEEL CONSTRUCTION

VERIFICATION AND INSPECTION	CONTINUOUS	PERIODIC	REFERENCED STANDARD[a]	IBC REFERENCE
1. Material verification of high-strength bolts, nuts and washers:				
a. Identification markings to conform to ASTM standards specified in the approved construction documents.	—	X	AISC 360, Section A3.3 and applicable ASTM material standards	
b. Manufacturer's certificate of compliance required.	—	X	—	—
2. Inspection of high-strength bolting:				
a. Snug-tight joints.	—	X	AISC 360, Section M2.5	1704.3.3
b. Pretensioned and slip-critical joints using turn-of-nut with matchmarking, twist-off bolt or direct tension indicator methods of installation.	—	X		
c. Pretensioned and slip-critical joints using turn-of-nut without matchmarking or calibrated wrench methods of installation.	X	—		
3. Material verification of structural steel and cold-formed steel deck:				
a. For structural steel, identification markings to conform to AISC 360.	—	X	AISC 360, Section M5.5	
b. For other steel, identification markings to conform to ASTM standards specified in the approved construction documents.	—	X	Applicable ASTM material standards	
c. Manufacturer's certified test reports.	—	X		
4. Material verification of weld filler materials:				
a. Identification markings to conform to AWS specification in the approved construction documents.	—	X	AISC 360, Section A3.5 and applicable AWS A5 documents	—
b. Manufacturer's certificate of compliance required.	—	X	—	—
5. Inspection of welding:				
a. Structural steel and cold-formed steel deck:				
1) Complete and partial joint penetration groove welds.	X	—	AWS D1.1	1704.3.1
2) Multipass fillet welds.	X	—		
3) Single-pass fillet welds > $^{5}/_{16}''$	X	—		
4) Plug and slot welds.	X	—		
5) Single-pass fillet welds ≤ $^{5}/_{16}''$	—	X		
6) Floor and roof deck welds.	—	X	AWS D1.3	

(continued)

TABLE 1704.3—continued
REQUIRED VERIFICATION AND INSPECTION OF STEEL CONSTRUCTION

VERIFICATION AND INSPECTION	CONTINUOUS	PERIODIC	REFERENCED STANDARD[a]	IBC REFERENCE
b.Reinforcing steel:				—
1) Verification of weldability of reinforcing steel other than ASTM A 706.	—	X	AWS D1.4 ACI 318: Section 3.5.2	
2) Reinforcing steel resisting flexural and axial forces in intermediate and special moment frames, and boundary elements of special structural walls of concrete and shear reinforcement.	X	—		
3) Shear reinforcement.	X	—		
4) Other reinforcing steel.	—	X		
6. Inspection of steel frame joint details for compliance:				
a. Details such as bracing and stiffening.	—	X	—	1704.3.2
b. Member locations.	—	X		
c. Application of joint details at each connection.	—	X		

For SI: 1 inch = 25.4 mm.

a. Where applicable, see also Section 1707.1, Special inspection for seismic resistance.

1704.3.1.1 Structural steel. Welding inspection and welding inspector qualification for structural steel shall be in accordance with AWS D1.1.

1704.3.1.2 Cold-formed steel. Welding inspection and welding inspector qualification for cold-formed steel floor and roof decks shall be in accordance with AWS D1.3.

1704.3.1.3 Reinforcing steel. Welding inspection and welding inspector qualification for reinforcing steel shall be in accordance with AWS D1.4 and ACI 318.

1704.3.2 Details. The special inspector shall perform an inspection of the steel frame to verify compliance with the details shown on the *approved construction documents*, such as bracing, stiffening, member locations and proper application of joint details at each connection.

1704.3.3 High-strength bolts. Installation of high-strength bolts shall be inspected in accordance with AISC 360.

1704.3.3.1 General. While the work is in progress, the special inspector shall determine that the requirements for bolts, nuts, washers and paint; bolted parts and installation and tightening in such standards are met. For bolts requiring pretensioning, the special inspector shall observe the preinstallation testing and calibration procedures when such procedures are required by the installation method or by project plans or specifications; determine that all plies of connected materials have been drawn together and properly snugged and monitor the installation of bolts to verify that the selected procedure for installation is properly used to tighten bolts. For joints required to be tightened only to the snug-tight condition, the special inspector need only verify that the connected materials have been drawn together and properly snugged.

1704.3.3.2 Periodic monitoring. Monitoring of bolt installation for pretensioning is permitted to be performed on a periodic basis when using the turn-of-nut method with matchmarking techniques, the direct tension indicator method or the alternate design fastener (twist-off bolt) method. Joints designated as snug tight need be inspected only on a periodic basis.

1704.3.3.3 Continuous monitoring. Monitoring of bolt installation for pretensioning using the calibrated wrench method or the turn-of-nut method without matchmarking shall be performed on a continuous basis.

1704.3.4 Cold-formed steel trusses spanning 60 feet or greater. Where a cold-formed steel truss clear span is 60 feet (18 288 mm) or greater, the special inspector shall verify that the temporary installation restraint/bracing and the permanent individual truss member restraint/bracing are installed in accordance with the *approved* truss submittal package.

1704.4 Concrete construction. The *special inspections* and verifications for concrete construction shall be as required by this section and Table 1704.4.

Exception: *Special inspections* shall not be required for:

1. Isolated spread concrete footings of buildings three stories or less above *grade plane* that are fully supported on earth or rock.

2. Continuous concrete footings supporting walls of buildings three stories or less above *grade plane* that are fully supported on earth or rock where:
   2.1. The footings support walls of light-frame construction;
   2.2. The footings are designed in accordance with Table 1809.7; or
   2.3. The structural design of the footing is based on a specified compressive strength, f'_c, no greater than 2,500 pounds per square inch (psi) (17.2 MPa), regardless of the compressive strength specified in the *construction documents* or used in the footing construction.
3. Nonstructural concrete slabs supported directly on the ground, including prestressed slabs on grade, where the effective prestress in the concrete is less than 150 psi (1.03 MPa).
4. Concrete foundation walls constructed in accordance with Table 1807.1.6.2.
5. Concrete patios, driveways and sidewalks, on grade.

TABLE 1704.4
REQUIRED VERIFICATION AND INSPECTION OF CONCRETE CONSTRUCTION

VERIFICATION AND INSPECTION	CONTINUOUS	PERIODIC	REFERENCED STANDARD[a]	IBC REFERENCE
1. Inspection of reinforcing steel, including prestressing tendons, and placement.	—	X	ACI 318: 3.5, 7.1-7.7	1913.4
2. Inspection of reinforcing steel welding in accordance with Table 1704.3, Item 5b.	—	—	AWS D1.4 ACI 318: 3.5.2	—
3. Inspection of bolts to be installed in concrete prior to and during placement of concrete where allowable loads have been increased or where strength design is used.	X	—	ACI 318: 8.1.3, 21.2.8	1911.5, 1912.1
4. Inspection of anchors installed in hardened concrete.	—	X	ACI 318: 3.8.6, 8.1.3, 21.2.8	1912.1
5. Verifying use of required design mix.	—	X	ACI 318: Ch. 4, 5.2-5.4	1904.3, 1913.2, 1913.3
6. At the time fresh concrete is sampled to fabricate specimens for strength tests, perform slump and air content tests, and determine the temperature of the concrete.	X	—	ASTM C 172 ASTM C 31 ACI 318: 5.6, 5.8	1913.10
7. Inspection of concrete and shotcrete placement for proper application techniques.	X	—	ACI 318: 5.9, 5.10	1913.6, 1913.7, 1913.8
8. Inspection for maintenance of specified curing temperature and techniques.	—	X	ACI 318: 5.11-5.13	1913.9
9. Inspection of prestressed concrete: a. Application of prestressing forces. b. Grouting of bonded prestressing tendons in the seismic-force-resisting system.	X X	—	ACI 318: 18.20 ACI 318: 18.18.4	—
10. Erection of precast concrete members.	—	X	ACI 318: Ch. 16	—
11. Verification of in-situ concrete strength, prior to stressing of tendons in posttensioned concrete and prior to removal of shores and forms from beams and structural slabs.	—	X	ACI 318: 6.2	—
12. Inspect formwork for shape, location and dimensions of the concrete member being formed.	—	X	ACI 318: 6.1.1	—

For SI: 1 inch = 25.4 mm.

a. Where applicable, see also Section 1707.1, Special inspection for seismic resistance.

1704.4.1 Materials. In the absence of sufficient data or documentation providing evidence of conformance to quality standards for materials in Chapter 3 of ACI 318, the building official shall require testing of materials in accordance with the appropriate standards and criteria for the material in Chapter 3 of ACI 318. Weldability of reinforcement, except that which conforms to ASTM A 706, shall be determined in accordance with the requirements of Section 3.5.2 of ACI 318.

1704.5 Masonry construction. Masonry construction shall be inspected and verified in accordance with the requirements of Sections 1704.5.1 through 1704.5.3, depending on the *occupancy category* of the building or structure.

Exception: *Special inspections* shall not be required for:

1. Empirically designed masonry, glass unit masonry or masonry veneer designed by Section 2109, 2110 or Chapter 14, respectively, or by Chapter 5, 6 or 7 of TMS 402/ACI 530/ASCE 5, respectively, when they are part of structures classified as *Occupancy Category* I, II or III in accordance with Section 1604.5.
2. Masonry foundation walls constructed in accordance with Table 1807.1.6.3(1), 1807.1.6.3(2), 1807.1.6.3(3) or 1807.1.6.3(4).
3. Masonry fireplaces, masonry heaters or masonry chimneys installed or constructed in accordance with Section 2111, 2112 or 2113, respectively.

1704.5.1 Empirically designed masonry, glass unit masonry and masonry veneer in Occupancy Category IV. The minimum *special inspection* program for empirically designed masonry, glass unit masonry or masonry veneer designed by Section 2109, 2110 or Chapter 14, respectively, or by Chapter 5, 6 or 7 of TMS 402/ACI 530/ASCE 5, respectively, in structures classified as *Occupancy Category* IV, in accordance with Section 1604.5, shall comply with Table 1704.5.1.

1704.5.2 Engineered masonry in Occupancy Category I, II or III. The minimum *special inspection* program for masonry designed by Section 2107 or 2108 or by chapters other than Chapter 5, 6 or 7 of TMS 402/ACI 530/ASCE 5 in structures classified as *Occupancy Category* I, II or III, in accordance with Section 1604.5, shall comply with Table 1704.5.1.

1704.5.3 Engineered masonry in Occupancy Category IV. The minimum *special inspection* program for masonry designed by Section 2107 or 2108 or by chapters other than Chapter 5, 6 or 7 of TMS 402/ACI 530/ASCE 5 in structures classified as *Occupancy Category* IV, in accordance with Section 1604.5, shall comply with Table 1704.5.3.

1704.6 Wood construction. *Special inspections* of the fabrication process of prefabricated wood structural elements and assemblies shall be in accordance with Section 1704.2. *Special inspections* of site-built assemblies shall be in accordance with this section.

1704.6.1 High-load diaphragms. High-load diaphragms designed in accordance with Table 2306.2.1(2) shall be installed with *special inspections* as indicated in Section 1704.1. The special inspector shall inspect the wood structural panel sheathing to ascertain whether it is of the grade and thickness shown on the *approved* building plans. Additionally, the special inspector must verify the nominal size of framing members at adjoining panel edges, the nail or staple diameter and length, the number of fastener lines and that the spacing between fasteners in each line and at edge margins agrees with the *approved* building plans.

1704.6.2 Metal-plate-connected wood trusses spanning 60 feet or greater. Where a truss clear span is 60 feet (18 288 mm) or greater, the special inspector shall verify that the temporary installation restraint/bracing and the permanent individual truss member restraint/bracing are installed in accordance with the *approved* truss submittal package.

1704.7 Soils. *Special inspections* for existing site soil conditions, fill placement and load-bearing requirements shall be as required by this section and Table 1704.7. The *approved* geotechnical report, and the *construction documents* prepared by the *registered design professionals* shall be used to determine compliance. During fill placement, the special inspector shall determine that proper materials and procedures are used in accordance with the provisions of the *approved* geotechnical report.

Exception: Where Section 1803 does not require reporting of materials and procedures for fill placement, the special inspector shall verify that the in-place dry density of the compacted fill is not less than 90 percent of the maximum dry density at optimum moisture content determined in accordance with ASTM D 1557.

1704.8 Driven deep foundations. *Special inspections* shall be performed during installation and testing of driven deep foundation elements as required by Table 1704.8. The *approved* geotechnical report, and the *construction documents* prepared by the *registered design professionals*, shall be used to determine compliance.

1704.9 Cast-in-place deep foundations. *Special inspections* shall be performed during installation and testing of cast-in-place deep foundation elements as required by Table 1704.9. The *approved* geotechnical report, and the *construction documents* prepared by the *registered design professionals*, shall be used to determine compliance.

1704.10 Helical pile foundations. *Special inspections* shall be performed continuously during installation of helical pile foundations. The information recorded shall include installation equipment used, pile dimensions, tip elevations, final depth, final installation torque and other pertinent installation data as required by the *registered design professional in responsible charge*. The *approved* geotechnical report and the *construction documents* prepared by the *registered design professional* shall be used to determine compliance.

1704.11 Vertical masonry foundation elements. *Special inspection* shall be performed in accordance with Section 1704.5 for vertical masonry foundation elements.

TABLE 1704.5.1
LEVEL 1 REQUIRED VERIFICATION AND INSPECTION OF MASONRY CONSTRUCTION

VERIFICATION AND INSPECTION	FREQUENCY OF INSPECTION		REFERENCE FOR CRITERIA		
	CONTINUOUS	PERIODIC	IBC SECTION	TMS 402/ACI 530/ASCE 5[a]	TMS 602/ACI 530.1/ASCE 6[a]
1. Compliance with required inspection provisions of the construction documents and the approved submittals shall be verified.	—	X	—	—	Art. 1.5
2. Verification of f'_m and f'_{AAC} prior to construction except where specifically exempted by this code.	—	X	—	—	Art. 1.4B
3. Verification of slump flow and VSI as delivered to the site for self-consolidating grout.	X	—	—	—	Art. 1.5B.1.b.3
4. As masonry construction begins, the following shall be verified to ensure compliance:					
a. Proportions of site-prepared mortar.	—	X	—	—	Art. 2.6A
b. Construction of mortar joints.	—	X	—	—	Art. 3.3B
c. Location of reinforcement, connectors, prestressing tendons and anchorages.	—	X	—	—	Art. 3.4, 3.6A
d. Prestressing technique.	—	X	—	—	Art. 3.6B
e. Grade and size of prestressing tendons and anchorages.	—	X	—	—	Art. 2.4B, 2.4H
5. During construction the inspection program shall verify:					
a. Size and location of structural elements.	—	X	—	—	Art. 3.3F
b. Type, size and location of anchors, including other details of anchorage of masonry to structural members, frames or other construction.	—	X	—	Sec. 1.2.2(e), 1.16.1	—
c. Specified size, grade and type of reinforcement, anchor bolts, prestressing tendons and anchorages.	—	X	—	Sec. 1.15	Art. 2.4, 3.4
d. Welding of reinforcing bars.	X	—	—	Sec. 2.1.9.7.2, 3.3.3.4(b)	—
e. Preparation, construction and protection of masonry during cold weather (temperature below 40°F) or hot weather (temperature above 90°F).	—	X	Sec. 2104.3, 2104.4	—	Art. 1.8C, 1.8D
f. Application and measurement of prestressing force.	X	—	—	—	Art. 3.6B

(continued)

TABLE 1704.5.1—continued
LEVEL 1 REQUIRED VERIFICATION AND INSPECTION OF MASONRY CONSTRUCTION

VERIFICATION AND INSPECTION	FREQUENCY OF INSPECTION		REFERENCE FOR CRITERIA		
	CONTINUOUS	PERIODIC	IBC SECTION	TMS 402/ACI 530/ASCE 5[a]	TMS 602/ACI 530.1/ASCE 6[a]
6. Prior to grouting, the following shall be verified to ensure compliance:					
a. Grout space is clean.	—	X	—	—	Art. 3.2D
b. Placement of reinforcement and connectors, and prestressing tendons and anchorages.	—	X	—	Sec. 1.13	Art. 3.4
c. Proportions of site-prepared grout and prestressing grout for bonded tendons.	—	X	—	—	Art. 2.6B
d. Construction of mortar joints.	—	X	—	—	Art. 3.3B
7. Grout placement shall be verified to ensure compliance:	X	—	—	—	Art. 3.5
a. Grouting of prestressing bonded tendons.	X	—	—	—	Art. 3.6C
8. Preparation of any required grout specimens, mortar specimens and/or prisms shall be observed.	—	X	Sec. 2105.2.2, 2105.3	—	Art. 1.4

For SI: °C = [(°F) - 32]/1.8.

a. The specific standards referenced are those listed in Chapter 35.

TABLE 1704.5.3
LEVEL 2 REQUIRED VERIFICATION AND INSPECTION OF MASONRY CONSTRUCTION

VERIFICATION AND INSPECTION	CONTINUOUS	PERIODIC	REFERENCE FOR CRITERIA		
			IBC SECTION	TMS 402/ACI 530/ASCE 5[a]	TMS 602/ACI 530.1/ASCE 6[a]
1. Compliance with required inspection provisions of the construction documents and the approved submittals.	—	X	—	—	Art. 1.5
2. Verification of f'_m and f'_{AAC} prior to construction and for every 5,000 square feet during construction.	—	X	—	—	Art. 1.4B
3. Verification of proportions of materials in premixed or preblended mortar and grout as delivered to the site.	—	X	—	—	Art. 1.5B
4. Verification of slump flow and VSI as delivered to the site for self-consolidating grout.	X	—	—	—	Art. 1.5B.1.b.3
5. The following shall be verified to ensure compliance:					
a. Proportions of site-prepared mortar, grout and prestressing grout for bonded tendons.	—	X	—	—	Art. 2.6A
b. Placement of masonry units and construction of mortar joints.	—	X	—	—	Art. 3.3B
c. Placement of reinforcement, connectors and prestressing tendons and anchorages.	—	X	—	Sec. 1.15	Art. 3.4, 3.6A
d. Grout space prior to grout.	X	—	—	—	Art. 3.2D
e. Placement of grout.	X	—	—	—	Art. 3.5
f. Placement of prestressing grout.	X	—	—	—	Art. 3.6C
g. Size and location of structural elements.	—	X	—	—	Art. 3.3F
h. Type, size and location of anchors, including other details of anchorage of masonry to structural members, frames or other construction.	X	—	—	Sec.1.2.2(e), 1.16.1	—
i. Specified size, grade and type of reinforcement, anchor bolts, prestressing tendons and anchorages.	—	X	—	Sec. 1.15	Art. 2.4, 3.4
j. Welding of reinforcing bars.	X	—	—	Sec. 2.1.9.7.2, 3.3.3.4 (b)	—
k. Preparation, construction and protection of masonry during cold weather (temperature below 40°F) or hot weather (temperature above 90°F).	—	X	Sec. 2104.3, 2104.4	—	Art. 1.8C, 1.8D
l. Application and measurement of prestressing force.	X	—	—	—	Art. 3.6B
6. Preparation of any required grout specimens and/or prisms shall be observed.	X	—	Sec. 2105.2.2, 2105.3	—	Art. 1.4

For SI: °C = [(°F) - 32]/1.8, 1 square foot = 0.0929 m^2.

a. The specific standards referenced are those listed in Chapter 35.

TABLE 1704.7
REQUIRED VERIFICATION AND INSPECTION OF SOILS

VERIFICATION AND INSPECTION TASK	CONTINUOUS DURING TASK LISTED	PERIODICALLY DURING TASK LISTED
1. Verify materials below shallow foundations are adequate to achieve the design bearing capacity.	—	X
2. Verify excavations are extended to proper depth and have reached proper material.	—	X
3. Perform classification and testing of compacted fill materials.	—	X
4. Verify use of proper materials, densities and lift thicknesses during placement and compaction of compacted fill.	X	—
5. Prior to placement of compacted fill, observe subgrade and verify that site has been prepared properly.	—	X

TABLE 1704.8
REQUIRED VERIFICATION AND INSPECTION OF DRIVEN DEEP FOUNDATION ELEMENTS

VERIFICATION AND INSPECTION TASK	CONTINUOUS DURING TASK LISTED	PERIODICALLY DURING TASK LISTED
1. Verify element materials, sizes and lengths comply with the requirements.	X	—
2. Determine capacities of test elements and conduct additional load tests, as required.	X	—
3. Observe driving operations and maintain complete and accurate records for each element.	X	—
4. Verify placement locations and plumbness, confirm type and size of hammer, record number of blows per foot of penetration, determine required penetrations to achieve design capacity, record tip and butt elevations and document any damage to foundation element.	X	—
5. For steel elements, perform additional inspections in accordance with Section 1704.3.	—	—
6. For concrete elements and concrete-filled elements, perform additional inspections in accordance with Section 1704.4.	—	—
7. For specialty elements, perform additional inspections as determined by the registered design professional in responsible charge.	—	—

TABLE 1704.9
REQUIRED VERIFICATION AND INSPECTION OF CAST-IN-PLACE DEEP FOUNDATION ELEMENTS

VERIFICATION AND INSPECTION TASK	CONTINUOUS DURING TASK LISTED	PERIODICALLY DURING TASK LISTED
1. Observe drilling operations and maintain complete and accurate records for each element.	X	—
2. Verify placement locations and plumbness, confirm element diameters, bell diameters (if applicable), lengths, embedment into bedrock (if applicable) and adequate end-bearing strata capacity. Record concrete or grout volumes.	X	—
3. For concrete elements, perform additional inspections in accordance with Section 1704.4.	—	—

1704.12 Sprayed fire-resistant materials. *Special inspections* for sprayed fire-resistant materials applied to floor, roof and wall assemblies and structural members shall be in accordance with Sections 1704.12.1 through 1704.12.6. *Special inspections* shall be based on the fire-resistance design as designated in the *approved construction documents*. The tests set forth in this section shall be based on samplings from specific floor, roof and wall assemblies and structural members. *Special inspections* shall be performed after the rough installation of electrical, automatic sprinkler, mechanical and plumbing systems and suspension systems for ceilings, where applicable.

1704.12.1 Physical and visual tests. The *special inspections* shall include the following tests and observations to demonstrate compliance with the listing and the fire-resistance rating:

1. Condition of substrates.
2. Thickness of application.
3. Density in pounds per cubic foot (kg/m^3).
4. Bond strength adhesion/cohesion.
5. Condition of finished application.

1704.12.2 Structural member surface conditions. The surfaces shall be prepared in accordance with the *approved* fire-resistance design and the written instructions of *approved* manufacturers. The prepared surface of structural members to be sprayed shall be inspected before the application of the sprayed fire-resistant material.

1704.12.3 Application. The substrate shall have a minimum ambient temperature before and after application as specified in the written instructions of *approved* manufacturers. The area for application shall be ventilated during and after application as required by the written instructions of *approved* manufacturers.

1704.12.4 Thickness. No more than 10 percent of the thickness measurements of the sprayed fire-resistant materials applied to floor, roof and wall assemblies and structural members shall be less than the thickness required by the *approved* fire-resistance design, but in no case less than the minimum allowable thickness required by Section 1704.12.4.1.

1704.12.4.1 Minimum allowable thickness. For design thicknesses 1 inch (25 mm) or greater, the minimum allowable individual thickness shall be the design thickness minus $^1/_4$ inch (6.4 mm). For design thicknesses less than 1 inch (25 mm), the minimum allowable individual thickness shall be the design thickness minus 25 percent. Thickness shall be determined in accordance with ASTM E 605. Samples of the sprayed fire-resistant materials shall be selected in accordance with Sections 1704.12.4.2 and 1704.12.4.3.

1704.12.4.2 Floor, roof and wall assemblies. The thickness of the sprayed fire-resistant material applied to floor, roof and wall assemblies shall be determined in accordance with ASTM E 605, making not less than four measurements for each 1,000 square feet (93 m^2) of the sprayed area in each *story* or portion thereof.

1704.12.4.2.1 Cellular decks. Thickness measurements shall be selected from a square area, 12 inches by 12 inches (305 mm by 305 mm) in size. A minimum of four measurements shall be made, located symmetrically within the square area.

1704.12.4.2.2 Fluted decks. Thickness measurements shall be selected from a square area, 12 inches by 12 inches (305 mm by 305 mm) in size. A minimum of four measurements shall be made, located symmetrically within the square area, including one each of the following: valley, crest and sides. The average of the measurements shall be reported.

1704.12.4.3 Structural members. The thickness of the sprayed fire-resistant material applied to structural members shall be determined in accordance with ASTM E 605. Thickness testing shall be performed on not less than 25 percent of the structural members on each floor.

1704.12.4.3.1 Beams and girders. At beams and girders thickness measurements shall be made at nine locations around the beam or girder at each end of a 12-inch (305 mm) length.

1704.12.4.3.2 Joists and trusses. At joists and trusses, thickness measurements shall be made at seven locations around the joist or truss at each end of a 12-inch (305 mm) length.

1704.12.4.3.3 Wide-flanged columns. At wide-flanged columns, thickness measurements shall be made at 12 locations around the column at each end of a 12-inch (305 mm) length.

1704.12.4.3.4 Hollow structural section and pipe columns. At hollow structural section and pipe columns, thickness measurements shall be made at a minimum of four locations around the column at each end of a 12-inch (305 mm) length.

1704.12.5 Density. The density of the sprayed fire-resistant material shall not be less than the density specified in the *approved* fire-resistance design. Density of the sprayed fire-resistant material shall be determined in accordance with ASTM E 605. The test samples for determining the density of the sprayed fire-resistant materials shall be selected as follows:

1. From each floor, roof and wall assembly at the rate of not less than one sample for every 2,500 square feet (232 m^2) or portion thereof of the sprayed area in each *story*.
2. From beams, girders, trusses and columns at the rate of not less than one sample for each type of structural member for each 2,500 square feet (232 m^2) of floor area or portion thereof in each *story*.

1704.12.6 Bond strength. The cohesive/adhesive bond strength of the cured sprayed fire-resistant material applied to floor, roof and wall assemblies and structural members shall not be less than 150 pounds per square foot (psf) (7.18 kN/m^2). The cohesive/adhesive bond strength shall be determined in accordance with the field test specified in ASTM E 736 by testing in-place samples of the sprayed fire-resistant material selected in accordance with Sections 1704.12.6.1 through 1704.12.6.3.

1704.12.6.1 Floor, roof and wall assemblies. The test samples for determining the cohesive/adhesive bond strength of the sprayed fire-resistant materials shall be selected from each floor, roof and wall assembly at the rate of not less than one sample for every 2,500 square feet (232 m^2) of the sprayed area in each *story* or portion thereof.

1704.12.6.2 Structural members. The test samples for determining the cohesive/adhesive bond strength of the sprayed fire-resistant materials shall be selected from beams, girders, trusses, columns and other structural members at the rate of not less than one sample for each type of structural member for each 2,500 square feet (232 m^2) of floor area or portion thereof in each *story*.

1704.12.6.3 Primer, paint and encapsulant bond tests. Bond tests to qualify a primer, paint or encapsulant shall be conducted when the sprayed fire-resistant material is applied to a primed, painted or encapsulated surface for which acceptable bond-strength performance between these coatings and the fire-resistant material has not been determined. A bonding agent *approved* by the SFRM manufacturer shall be applied to a primed, painted or encapsulated surface where the bond strengths are found to be less than required values.

1704.13 Mastic and intumescent fire-resistant coatings. *Special inspections* for mastic and intumescent fire-resistant coatings applied to structural elements and decks shall be in accordance with AWCI 12-B. *Special inspections* shall be based on the fire-resistance design as designated in the *approved construction documents*.

1704.14 Exterior insulation and finish systems (EIFS). *Special inspections* shall be required for all EIFS applications.

Exceptions:

1. *Special inspections* shall not be required for EIFS applications installed over a *water-resistive barrier* with a means of draining moisture to the exterior.
2. *Special inspections* shall not be required for EIFS applications installed over masonry or concrete walls.

1704.14.1 Water-resistive barrier coating. A *water-resistive barrier* coating complying with ASTM E 2570 requires *special inspection* of the *water-resistive barrier* coating when installed over a sheathing substrate.

1704.15 Special cases. *Special inspections* shall be required for proposed work that is, in the opinion of the *building official*, unusual in its nature, such as, but not limited to, the following examples:

1. Construction materials and systems that are alternatives to materials and systems prescribed by this code.
2. Unusual design applications of materials described in this code.
3. Materials and systems required to be installed in accordance with additional manufacturer's instructions that prescribe requirements not contained in this code or in standards referenced by this code.

[F] 1704.16 Special inspection for smoke control. Smoke control systems shall be tested by a special inspector.

[F] 1704.16.1 Testing scope. The test scope shall be as follows:

1. During erection of ductwork and prior to concealment for the purposes of leakage testing and recording of device location.
2. Prior to occupancy and after sufficient completion for the purposes of pressure difference testing, flow measurements and detection and control verification.

[F] 1704.16.2 Qualifications. *Special inspection* agencies for smoke control shall have expertise in fire protection engineering, mechanical engineering and certification as air balancers.

SECTION 1705
STATEMENT OF SPECIAL INSPECTIONS

1705.1 General. Where *special inspection* or testing is required by Section 1704, 1707 or 1708, the *registered design professional in responsible charge* shall prepare a statement of special inspections in accordance with Section 1705 for submittal by the applicant (see Section 1704.1.1).

1705.2 Content of statement of special inspections. The statement of special inspections shall identify the following:

1. The materials, systems, components and work required to have *special inspection* or testing by the *building official* or by the *registered design professional* responsible for each portion of the work.
2. The type and extent of each *special inspection*.
3. The type and extent of each test.
4. Additional requirements for *special inspection* or testing for seismic or wind resistance as specified in Section 1705.3, 1705.4, 1707 or 1708.
5. For each type of *special inspection*, identification as to whether it will be continuous *special inspection* or periodic *special inspection*.

1705.3 Seismic resistance. The statement of special inspections shall include seismic requirements for cases covered in Sections 1705.3.1 through 1705.3.5.

Exception: Seismic requirements are permitted to be excluded from the statement of special inspections for structures designed and constructed in accordance with the following:

1. The structure consists of light-frame construction; the design spectral response acceleration at short periods, S_{DS}, as determined in Section 1613.5.4, does not

exceed 0.5g; and the height of the structure does not exceed 35 feet (10 668 mm) above *grade plane*; or

2. The structure is constructed using a reinforced masonry structural system or reinforced concrete structural system; the design spectral response acceleration at short periods, S_{DS}, as determined in Section 1613.5.4, does not exceed 0.5g, and the height of the structure does not exceed 25 feet (7620 mm) above *grade plane*; or
3. Detached one- or two-family dwellings not exceeding two *stories above grade plane*, provided the structure does not have any of the following plan or vertical irregularities in accordance with Section 12.3.2 of ASCE 7:
   - 3.1. Torsional irregularity.
   - 3.2. Nonparallel systems.
   - 3.3. Stiffness irregularity—extreme soft story and soft story.
   - 3.4. Discontinuity in capacity—weak story.

1705.3.1 Seismic-force-resisting systems. The seismic-force-resisting systems in structures assigned to *Seismic Design Category* C, D, E or F, in accordance with Section 1613.

Exception: Requirements for the seismic-force-resisting system are permitted to be excluded from the statement of special inspections for steel systems in structures assigned to *Seismic Design Category* C that are not specifically detailed for seismic resistance, with a response modification coefficient, *R*, of 3 or less, excluding cantilever column systems.

1705.3.2 Designated seismic systems. Designated seismic systems in structures assigned to *Seismic Design Category* D, E or F.

1705.3.3 Seismic Design Category C. The following additional systems and components in structures assigned to *Seismic Design Category* C:

1. Heating, ventilating and air-conditioning (HVAC) ductwork containing hazardous materials and anchorage of such ductwork.
2. Piping systems and mechanical units containing flammable, combustible or highly *toxic* materials.
3. Anchorage of electrical equipment used for emergency or standby power systems.

1705.3.4 Seismic Design Category D. The following additional systems and components in structures assigned to *Seismic Design Category* D:

1. Systems required for *Seismic Design Category* C.
2. Exterior wall panels and their anchorage.
3. Suspended ceiling systems and their anchorage.
4. Access floors and their anchorage.
5. Steel storage racks and their anchorage, where the importance factor is equal to 1.5 in accordance with Section 15.5.3 of ASCE 7.

1705.3.5 Seismic Design Category E or F. The following additional systems and components in structures assigned to *Seismic Design Category* E or F:

1. Systems required for *Seismic Design Categories* C and D.
2. Electrical equipment.

1705.3.6 Seismic requirements in the statement of special inspections. When Sections 1705.3 through 1705.3.5 specify that seismic requirements be included, the statement of special inspections shall identify the following:

1. The designated seismic systems and seismic-force-resisting systems that are subject to *special inspections* in accordance with Sections 1705.3 through 1705.3.5.
2. The additional *special inspections* and testing to be provided as required by Sections 1707 and 1708 and other applicable sections of this code, including the applicable standards referenced by this code.

1705.4 Wind resistance. The statement of special inspections shall include wind requirements for structures constructed in the following areas:

1. In wind Exposure Category B, where the 3-second-gust basic wind speed is 120 miles per hour (mph) (52.8 m/s) or greater.
2. In wind Exposure Category C or D, where the 3-second-gust basic wind speed is 110 mph (49 m/s) or greater.

1705.4.1 Wind requirements in the statement of special inspections. When Section 1705.4 specifies that wind requirements be included, the statement of special inspections shall identify the main wind-force-resisting systems and wind-resisting components subject to *special inspections* as specified in Section 1705.4.2.

1705.4.2 Detailed requirements. The statement of special inspections shall include at least the following systems and components:

1. Roof cladding and roof framing connections.
2. Wall connections to roof and floor diaphragms and framing.
3. Roof and floor diaphragm systems, including collectors, drag struts and boundary elements.
4. Vertical wind-force-resisting systems, including braced frames, moment frames and shear walls.
5. Wind-force-resisting system connections to the foundation.

6. Fabrication and installation of systems or components required to meet the impact-resistance requirements of Section 1609.1.2.

Exception: Fabrication of manufactured systems or components that have a *label* indicating compliance with the wind-load and impact-resistance requirements of this code.

SECTION 1706
SPECIAL INSPECTIONS FOR WIND REQUIREMENTS

1706.1 Special inspections for wind requirements. *Special inspections* itemized in Section 1704.1.2 and Sections 1706.2 through 1706.4 are required for buildings and structures constructed in the following areas:

1. In wind Exposure Category B, where the 3-second-gust basic wind speed is 120 miles per hour (52.8 m/sec) or greater.
2. In wind Exposure Categories C or D, where the 3-second-gust basic wind speed is 110 mph (49 m/sec) or greater.

1706.2 Structural wood. Continuous special inspection is required during field gluing operations of elements of the main windforce-resisting system. Periodic special inspection is required for nailing, bolting, anchoring and other fastening of components within the main windforce-resisting system, including wood shear walls, wood diaphragms, drag struts, braces and hold-downs.

Exception: *Special inspection* is not required for wood shear walls, shear panels and diaphragms, including nailing, bolting, anchoring and other fastening to other components of the main windforce-resisting system, where the fastener spacing of the sheathing is more than 4 inches (102 mm) on center.

1706.3 Cold-formed steel light-frame construction. Periodic special inspection is required during welding operations of elements of the main windforce-resisting system. Periodic special inspection is required for screw attachment, bolting, anchoring and other fastening of components within the main windforce-resisting system, including shear walls, braces, diaphragms, collectors (drag struts) and hold-downs.

Exception: *Special inspection* is not required for cold-formed steel light-frame shear walls, braces, diaphragms, collectors (drag struts) and hold-downs where either of the following apply:

1. The sheathing is gypsum board or fiberboard.
2. The sheathing is wood structural panel or steel sheets on only one side of the shear wall, shear panel or diaphragm assembly and the fastener spacing of the sheathing is more than 4 inches (102 mm) on center (o.c.).

1706.4 Wind-resisting components. Periodic special inspection is required for the following systems and components:

1. Roof cladding.
2. Wall cladding.

SECTION 1707
SPECIAL INSPECTIONS FOR SEISMIC RESISTANCE

1707.1 Special inspections for seismic resistance. *Special inspections* itemized in Sections 1707.2 through 1707.9, and where required by Section 1704.1.2 unless exempted by the exceptions of Section 1705.3 or 1705.3.1, are required for the following:

1. The seismic-force-resisting systems in structures assigned to *Seismic Design Category* C, D, E or F, as determined in Section 1613.
2. Designated seismic systems in structures assigned to *Seismic Design Category* D, E or F.
3. Architectural, mechanical and electrical components in structures assigned to *Seismic Design Category* C, D, E or F that are required in Sections 1707.6 and 1707.7.

1707.2 Structural steel. *Special inspection* for structural steel shall be in accordance with the quality assurance plan requirements of AISC 341.

Exceptions:

1. *Special inspections* of structural steel in structures assigned to *Seismic Design Category* C that are not specifically detailed for seismic resistance, with a response modification coefficient, *R*, of 3 or less, excluding cantilever column systems.
2. For ordinary moment frames, ultrasonic and magnetic particle testing of complete joint penetration groove welds are only required for demand critical welds.

1707.3 Structural wood. Continuous special inspection is required during field gluing operations of elements of the seismic-force-resisting system. Periodic special inspection is required for nailing, bolting, anchoring and other fastening of components within the seismic-force-resisting system, including wood shear walls, wood diaphragms, drag struts, braces, shear panels and hold-downs.

Exception: *Special inspection* is not required for wood shear walls, shear panels and diaphragms, including nailing, bolting, anchoring and other fastening to other components of the seismic-force-resisting system, where the fastener spacing of the sheathing is more than 4 inches (102 mm) on center (o.c.).

1707.4 Cold-formed steel light-frame construction. Periodic special inspection is required during welding operations of elements of the seismic-force-resisting system. Periodic special inspection is required for screw attachment, bolting, anchoring and other fastening of components within the seismic-force-resisting system, including shear walls, braces, diaphragms, collectors (drag struts) and hold-downs.

Exception: *Special inspection* is not required for cold-formed steel light-frame shear walls, braces, diaphragms, collectors (drag struts) and hold-downs where either of the following apply:

1. The sheathing is gypsum board or fiberboard.
2. The sheathing is wood structural panel or steel sheets on only one side of the shear wall, shear panel or diaphragm assembly and the fastener spacing of the sheathing is more than 4 inches (102 mm) o.c.

1707.5 Storage racks and access floors. Periodic *special inspection* is required during the anchorage of access floors and storage racks 8 feet (2438 mm) or greater in height in structures assigned to *Seismic Design Category* D, E or F.

1707.6 Architectural components. Periodic *special inspection* during the erection and fastening of exterior cladding, interior and exterior nonbearing walls and interior and exterior veneer in structures assigned to *Seismic Design Category* D, E or F.

Exceptions:

1. *Special inspection* is not required for exterior cladding, interior and exterior nonbearing walls and interior and exterior veneer 30 feet (9144 mm) or less in height above grade or walking surface.
2. *Special inspection* is not required for exterior cladding and interior and exterior veneer weighing 5 psf (24.5 N/m^2) or less.
3. *Special inspection* is not required for interior nonbearing walls weighing 15 psf (73.5 N/m^2) or less.

1707.7 Mechanical and electrical components. *Special inspection* for mechanical and electrical equipment shall be as follows:

1. Periodic special inspection is required during the anchorage of electrical equipment for emergency or standby power systems in structures assigned to *Seismic Design Category* C, D, E or F;
2. Periodic special inspection is required during the installation of anchorage of other electrical equipment in structures assigned to *Seismic Design Category* E or F;
3. Periodic special inspection is required during installation of piping systems intended to carry flammable, combustible or *highly toxic* contents and their associated mechanical units in structures assigned to *Seismic Design Category* C, D, E or F;
4. Periodic special inspection is required during the installation of HVAC ductwork that will contain hazardous materials in structures assigned to *Seismic Design Category* C, D, E or F; and
5. Periodic special inspection is required during the installation of vibration isolation systems in structures assigned to *Seismic Design Category* C, D, E or F where the *construction documents* require a nominal clearance of $^1/_4$ inch (6.4 mm) or less between the equipment support frame and restraint.

1707.8 Designated seismic system verifications. The special inspector shall examine designated seismic systems requiring seismic qualification in accordance with Section 1708.4 and verify that the *label*, anchorage or mounting conforms to the *certificate of compliance.*

1707.9 Seismic isolation system. Periodic special inspection is required during the fabrication and installation of isolator units and energy dissipation devices that are part of the seismic isolation system.

SECTION 1708
STRUCTURAL TESTING FOR SEISMIC RESISTANCE

1708.1 Testing and qualification for seismic resistance. The testing and qualification specified in Sections 1708.2 through 1708.5, and where required by Section 1704.1.2 unless exempted from *special inspections* by the exceptions of Section 1705.3 or 1705.3.1 are required as follows:

1. The seismic-force-resisting systems in structures assigned to *Seismic Design Category* C, D, E or F, as determined in Section 1613 shall meet the requirements of Sections 1708.2 and 1708.3, as applicable.
2. Designated seismic systems in structures assigned to *Seismic Design Category* C, D, E or F subject to the special certification requirements of ASCE 7 Section 13.2.2 are required to be tested in accordance with Section 1708.4.
3. Architectural, mechanical and electrical components in structures assigned to *Seismic Design Category* C, D, E or F with an I_p = 1.0 are required to be tested in accordance with Section 1708.4 where the general design requirements of ASCE 7 Section 13.2.1, Item 2 for manufacturer's certification are satisfied by testing.
4. The seismic isolation system in seismically isolated structures shall meet the testing requirements of Section 1708.5.

1708.2 Concrete reinforcement. Where reinforcement complying with ASTM A 615 is used to resist earthquake-induced flexural and axial forces in special moment frames, special structural walls and coupling beams connecting special structural walls, in structures assigned to *Seismic Design Category* B, C, D, E or F as determined in Section 1613, the reinforcement shall comply with Section 21.1.5.2 of ACI 318. Certified mill test reports shall be provided for each shipment of such reinforcement. Where reinforcement complying with ASTM A 615 is to be welded, chemical tests shall be performed to determine weldability in accordance with Section 3.5.2 of ACI 318.

1708.3 Structural steel. Testing for structural steel shall be in accordance with the quality assurance plan requirements of AISC 341.

Exceptions:

1. Testing for structural steel in structures assigned to *Seismic Design Category* C that are not specifically

detailed for seismic resistance, with a response modification coefficient, *R*, of 3 or less, excluding cantilever column systems.

2. For ordinary moment frames, ultrasonic and magnetic particle testing of complete joint penetration groove welds are only required for demand critical welds.

1708.4 Seismic certification of nonstructural components. The *registered design professional* shall state the applicable seismic certification requirements for nonstructural components and designated seismic systems on the *construction documents*.

1. The manufacturer of each designated seismic system component subject to the provisions of ASCE 7 Section 13.2.2 shall test or analyze the component and its mounting system or anchorage and submit a *certificate of compliance* for review and acceptance by the *registered design professional* responsible for the design of the designated seismic system and for approval by the *building official*. Certification shall be based on an actual test on a shake table, by three-dimensional shock tests, by an analytical method using dynamic characteristics and forces, by the use of experience data (i.e., historical data demonstrating acceptable seismic performance) or by more rigorous analysis providing for equivalent safety.
2. Manufacturer's certification of compliance for the general design requirements of ASCE 7 Section 13.2.1 shall be based on analysis, testing or experience data.

1708.5 Seismically isolated structures. For required system tests, see Section 17.8 of ASCE 7.

SECTION 1709 CONTRACTOR RESPONSIBILITY

1709.1 Contractor responsibility. Each contractor responsible for the construction of a main wind- or seismic-force-resisting system, designated seismic system or a wind- or seismic-resisting component listed in the statement of special inspections shall submit a written statement of responsibility to the *building official* and the owner prior to the commencement of work on the system or component. The contractor's statement of responsibility shall contain acknowledgement of awareness of the special requirements contained in the statement of *special inspection*.

SECTION 1710 STRUCTURAL OBSERVATIONS

1710.1 General. Where required by the provisions of Section 1710.2 or 1710.3, the owner shall employ a *registered design professional* to perform structural observations as defined in Section 1702.

Prior to the commencement of observations, the structural observer shall submit to the *building official* a written statement identifying the frequency and extent of structural observations.

At the conclusion of the work included in the permit, the structural observer shall submit to the *building official* a written statement that the site visits have been made and identify any reported deficiencies which, to the best of the structural observer's knowledge, have not been resolved.

1710.2 Structural observations for seismic resistance. Structural observations shall be provided for those structures assigned to *Seismic Design Category* D, E or F, as determined in Section 1613, where one or more of the following conditions exist:

1. The structure is classified as *Occupancy Category* III or IV in accordance with Table 1604.5.
2. The height of the structure is greater than 75 feet (22 860 mm) above the base.
3. The structure is assigned to *Seismic Design Category* E, is classified as *Occupancy Category* I or II in accordance with Table 1604.5, and is greater than two *stories above grade plane*.
4. When so designated by the *registered design professional* responsible for the structural design.
5. When such observation is specifically required by the *building official*.

1710.3 Structural observations for wind requirements. Structural observations shall be provided for those structures sited where the basic wind speed exceeds 110 mph (49 m/sec) determined from Figure 1609, where one or more of the following conditions exist:

1. The structure is classified as *Occupancy Category* III or IV in accordance with Table 1604.5.
2. The *building height* of the structure is greater than 75 feet (22 860 mm).
3. When so designated by the *registered design professional* responsible for the structural design.
4. When such observation is specifically required by the *building official*.

SECTION 1711 DESIGN STRENGTHS OF MATERIALS

1711.1 Conformance to standards. The design strengths and permissible stresses of any structural material that are identified by a manufacturer's designation as to manufacture and grade by mill tests, or the strength and stress grade is otherwise confirmed to the satisfaction of the *building official*, shall conform to the specifications and methods of design of accepted engineering practice or the *approved* rules in the absence of applicable standards.

1711.2 New materials. For materials that are not specifically provided for in this code, the design strengths and permissible stresses shall be established by tests as provided for in Section 1712.

SECTION 1712
ALTERNATIVE TEST PROCEDURE

1712.1 General. In the absence of *approved* rules or other *approved* standards, the *building official* shall make, or cause to be made, the necessary tests and investigations; or the *building official* shall accept duly authenticated reports from *approved agencies* in respect to the quality and manner of use of new materials or assemblies as provided for in Section 104.11. The cost of all tests and other investigations required under the provisions of this code shall be borne by the applicant.

SECTION 1713
TEST SAFE LOAD

1713.1 Where required. Where proposed construction is not capable of being designed by *approved* engineering analysis, or where proposed construction design method does not comply with the applicable material design standard, the system of construction or the structural unit and the connections shall be subjected to the tests prescribed in Section 1715. The *building official* shall accept certified reports of such tests conducted by an *approved* testing agency, provided that such tests meet the requirements of this code and *approved* procedures.

SECTION 1714
IN-SITU LOAD TESTS

1714.1 General. Whenever there is a reasonable doubt as to the stability or load-bearing capacity of a completed building, structure or portion thereof for the expected loads, an engineering assessment shall be required. The engineering assessment shall involve either a structural analysis or an in-situ load test, or both. The structural analysis shall be based on actual material properties and other as-built conditions that affect stability or load-bearing capacity, and shall be conducted in accordance with the applicable design standard. If the structural assessment determines that the load-bearing capacity is less than that required by the code, load tests shall be conducted in accordance with Section 1714.2. If the building, structure or portion thereof is found to have inadequate stability or load-bearing capacity for the expected loads, modifications to ensure structural adequacy or the removal of the inadequate construction shall be required.

1714.2 Test standards. Structural components and assemblies shall be tested in accordance with the appropriate material standards listed in Chapter 35. In the absence of a standard that contains an applicable load test procedure, the test procedure shall be developed by a *registered design professional* and *approved*. The test procedure shall simulate loads and conditions of application that the completed structure or portion thereof will be subjected to in normal use.

1714.3 In-situ load tests. In-situ load tests shall be conducted in accordance with Section 1714.3.1 or 1714.3.2 and shall be supervised by a *registered design professional*. The test shall simulate the applicable loading conditions specified in Chapter 16 as necessary to address the concerns regarding structural stability of the building, structure or portion thereof.

1714.3.1 Load test procedure specified. Where a standard listed in Chapter 35 contains an applicable load test procedure and acceptance criteria, the test procedure and acceptance criteria in the standard shall apply. In the absence of specific load factors or acceptance criteria, the load factors and acceptance criteria in Section 1714.3.2 shall apply.

1714.3.2 Load test procedure not specified. In the absence of applicable load test procedures contained within a standard referenced by this code or acceptance criteria for a specific material or method of construction, such *existing structure* shall be subjected to a test procedure developed by a *registered design professional* that simulates applicable loading and deformation conditions. For components that are not a part of the seismic-load-resisting system, the test load shall be equal to two times the unfactored design loads. The test load shall be left in place for a period of 24 hours. The structure shall be considered to have successfully met the test requirements where the following criteria are satisfied:

1. Under the design load, the deflection shall not exceed the limitations specified in Section 1604.3.
2. Within 24 hours after removal of the test load, the structure shall have recovered not less than 75 percent of the maximum deflection.
3. During and immediately after the test, the structure shall not show evidence of failure.

SECTION 1715
PRECONSTRUCTION LOAD TESTS

1715.1 General. In evaluating the physical properties of materials and methods of construction that are not capable of being designed by *approved* engineering analysis or do not comply with applicable material design standards listed in Chapter 35, the structural adequacy shall be predetermined based on the load test criteria established in this section.

1715.2 Load test procedures specified. Where specific load test procedures, load factors and acceptance criteria are included in the applicable design standards listed in Chapter 35, such test procedures, load factors and acceptance criteria shall apply. In the absence of specific test procedures, load factors or acceptance criteria, the corresponding provisions in Section 1715.3 shall apply.

1715.3 Load test procedures not specified. Where load test procedures are not specified in the applicable design standards listed in Chapter 35, the load-bearing and deformation capacity of structural components and assemblies shall be determined on the basis of a test procedure developed by a *registered design professional* that simulates applicable loading and deformation conditions. For components and assemblies that are not a part of the seismic-force-resisting system, the test shall be as specified in Section 1715.3.1. Load tests shall simulate the applicable loading conditions specified in Chapter 16.

1715.3.1 Test procedure. The test assembly shall be subjected to an increasing superimposed load equal to not less than two times the superimposed design load. The test load shall be left in place for a period of 24 hours. The tested assembly shall be considered to have successfully met the test requirements if the assembly recovers not less than 75 percent of the maximum deflection within 24 hours after the removal of the test load. The test assembly shall then be reloaded and subjected to an increasing superimposed load until either structural failure occurs or the superimposed load is equal to two and one-half times the load at which the deflection limitations specified in Section 1715.3.2 were reached, or the load is equal to two and one-half times the superimposed design load. In the case of structural components and assemblies for which deflection limitations are not specified in Section 1715.3.2, the test specimen shall be subjected to an increasing superimposed load until structural failure occurs or the load is equal to two and one-half times the desired superimposed design load. The allowable superimposed design load shall be taken as the lesser of:

1. The load at the deflection limitation given in Section 1715.3.2.
2. The failure load divided by 2.5.
3. The maximum load applied divided by 2.5.

1715.3.2 Deflection. The deflection of structural members under the design load shall not exceed the limitations in Section 1604.3.

1715.4 Wall and partition assemblies. *Load-bearing wall* and partition assemblies shall sustain the test load both with and without window framing. The test load shall include all design load components. Wall and partition assemblies shall be tested both with and without door and window framing.

1715.5 Exterior window and door assemblies. The design pressure rating of exterior windows and doors in buildings shall be determined in accordance with Section 1715.5.1 or 1715.5.2.

Exception: Structural wind load design pressures for window units smaller than the size tested in accordance with Section 1715.5.1 or 1715.5.2 shall be permitted to be higher than the design value of the tested unit provided such higher pressures are determined by accepted engineering analysis. All components of the small unit shall be the same as the tested unit. Where such calculated design pressures are used, they shall be validated by an additional test of the window unit having the highest allowable design pressure.

1715.5.1 Exterior windows and doors. Exterior windows and sliding doors shall be tested and labeled as conforming to AAMA/WDMA/CSA101/I.S.2/A440. The *label* shall state the name of the manufacturer, the *approved* labeling agency and the product designation as specified in AAMA/WDMA/CSA101/I.S.2/A440. Exterior side-hinged doors shall be tested and *labeled* as conforming to AAMA/WDMA/CSA101/I.S.2/A440 or comply with Section 1715.5.2. Products tested and labeled as conforming to AAMA/WDMA/CSA 101/I.S.2/A440 shall not be subject to the requirements of Sections 2403.2 and 2403.3.

1715.5.2 Exterior windows and door assemblies not provided for in Section 1715.5.1. Exterior window and door assemblies shall be tested in accordance with ASTM E 330. Structural performance of garage doors shall be determined in accordance with either ASTM E 330 or ANSI/DASMA 108, and shall meet the acceptance criteria of ANSI/DASMA 108. Exterior window and door assemblies containing glass shall comply with Section 2403. The design pressure for testing shall be calculated in accordance with Chapter 16. Each assembly shall be tested for 10 seconds at a load equal to 1.5 times the design pressure.

1715.6 Test specimens. Test specimens and construction shall be representative of the materials, workmanship and details normally used in practice. The properties of the materials used to construct the test assembly shall be determined on the basis of tests on samples taken from the load assembly or on representative samples of the materials used to construct the load test assembly. Required tests shall be conducted or witnessed by an *approved agency.*

SECTION 1716
MATERIAL AND TEST STANDARDS

1716.1 Test standards for joist hangers and connectors.

1716.1.1 Test standards for joist hangers. The vertical load-bearing capacity, torsional moment capacity and deflection characteristics of joist hangers shall be determined in accordance with ASTM D 1761 using lumber having a specific gravity of 0.49 or greater, but not greater than 0.55, as determined in accordance with AF&PA NDS for the joist and headers.

Exception: The joist length shall not be required to exceed 24 inches (610 mm).

1716.1.2 Vertical load capacity for joist hangers. The vertical load capacity for the joist hanger shall be determined by testing a minimum of three joist hanger assemblies as specified in ASTM D 1761. If the ultimate vertical load for any one of the tests varies more than 20 percent from the average ultimate vertical load, at least three additional tests shall be conducted. The allowable vertical load of the joist hanger shall be the lowest value determined from the following:

1. The lowest ultimate vertical load for a single hanger from any test divided by three (where three tests are conducted and each ultimate vertical load does not vary more than 20 percent from the average ultimate vertical load).
2. The average ultimate vertical load for a single hanger from all tests divided by three (where six or more tests are conducted).
3. The average from all tests of the vertical loads that produce a vertical movement of the joist with respect to the header of $^1/_8$ inch (3.2 mm).
4. The sum of the allowable design loads for nails or other fasteners utilized to secure the joist hanger to the wood members and allowable bearing loads that contribute to the capacity of the hanger.
5. The allowable design load for the wood members forming the connection.

1716.1.3 Torsional moment capacity for joist hangers. The torsional moment capacity for the joist hanger shall be determined by testing at least three joist hanger assemblies as specified in ASTM D 1761. The allowable torsional moment of the joist hanger shall be the average torsional moment at which the lateral movement of the top or bottom of the joist with respect to the original position of the joist is $^1/_8$ inch (3.2 mm).

1716.1.4 Design value modifications for joist hangers. Allowable design values for joist hangers that are determined by Item 4 or 5 in Section 1716.1.2 shall be permitted to be modified by the appropriate duration of loading factors as specified in AF&PA NDS but shall not exceed the direct loads as determined by Item 1, 2 or 3 in Section 1716.1.2. Allowable design values determined by Item 1, 2 or 3 in Section 1716.1.2 shall not be modified by duration of loading factors.

1716.2 Concrete and clay roof tiles.

1716.2.1 Overturning resistance. Concrete and clay roof tiles shall be tested to determine their resistance to overturning due to wind in accordance with SBCCI SSTD 11 and Chapter 15.

1716.2.2 Wind tunnel testing. When roof tiles do not satisfy the limitations in Chapter 16 for rigid tile, a wind tunnel test shall be used to determine the wind characteristics of the concrete or clay tile roof covering in accordance with SBCCI SSTD 11 and Chapter 15.

CHAPTER 18
SOILS AND FOUNDATIONS

This chapter has been revised in its entirety; there will be no marginal markings.

SECTION 1801
GENERAL

1801.1 Scope. The provisions of this chapter shall apply to building and foundation systems.

1801.2 Design basis. Allowable bearing pressures, allowable stresses and design formulas provided in this chapter shall be used with the *allowable stress design* load combinations specified in Section 1605.3. The quality and design of materials used structurally in excavations and foundations shall comply with the requirements specified in Chapters 16, 19, 21, 22 and 23 of this code. Excavations and fills shall also comply with Chapter 33.

SECTION 1802
DEFINITIONS

1802.1 Definitions. The following words and terms shall, for the purposes of this chapter, have the meanings shown herein.

DEEP FOUNDATION. A deep foundation is a foundation element that does not satisfy the definition of a shallow foundation.

DRILLED SHAFT. A drilled shaft is a cast-in-place deep foundation element constructed by drilling a hole (with or without permanent casing) into soil or rock and filling it with fluid concrete.

> **Socketed drilled shaft.** A socketed drilled shaft is a drilled shaft with a permanent pipe or tube casing that extends down to bedrock and an uncased socket drilled into the bedrock.

HELICAL PILE. Manufactured steel deep foundation element consisting of a central shaft and one or more helical bearing plates. A helical pile is installed by rotating it into the ground. Each helical bearing plate is formed into a screw thread with a uniform defined pitch.

MICROPILE. A micropile is a bored, grouted-in-place deep foundation element that develops its load-carrying capacity by means of a bond zone in soil, bedrock or a combination of soil and bedrock.

SHALLOW FOUNDATION. A shallow foundation is an individual or strip footing, a mat foundation, a slab-on-grade foundation or a similar foundation element.

SECTION 1803
GEOTECHNICAL INVESTIGATIONS

1803.1 General. Geotechnical investigations shall be conducted in accordance with Section 1803.2 and reported in accordance with Section 1803.6. Where required by the *building official* or where geotechnical investigations involve in-situ testing, laboratory testing or engineering calculations, such investigations shall be conducted by a *registered design professional*.

1803.2 Investigations required. Geotechnical investigations shall be conducted in accordance with Sections 1803.3 through 1803.5.

> **Exception:** The *building official* shall be permitted to waive the requirement for a geotechnical investigation where satisfactory data from adjacent areas is available that demonstrates an investigation is not necessary for any of the conditions in Sections 1803.5.1 through 1803.5.6 and Sections 1803.5.10 and 1803.5.11.

1803.3 Basis of investigation. Soil classification shall be based on observation and any necessary tests of the materials disclosed by borings, test pits or other subsurface exploration made in appropriate locations. Additional studies shall be made as necessary to evaluate slope stability, soil strength, position and adequacy of load-bearing soils, the effect of moisture variation on soil-bearing capacity, compressibility, liquefaction and expansiveness.

1803.3.1 Scope of investigation. The scope of the geotechnical investigation including the number and types of borings or soundings, the equipment used to drill or sample, the in-situ testing equipment and the laboratory testing program shall be determined by a *registered design professional*.

1803.4 Qualified representative. The investigation procedure and apparatus shall be in accordance with generally accepted engineering practice. The *registered design professional* shall have a fully qualified representative on site during all boring or sampling operations.

1803.5 Investigated conditions. Geotechnical investigations shall be conducted as indicated in Sections 1803.5.1 through 1803.5.12.

1803.5.1 Classification. Soil materials shall be classified in accordance with ASTM D 2487.

1803.5.2 Questionable soil. Where the classification, strength or compressibility of the soil is in doubt or where a load-bearing value superior to that specified in this code is claimed, the *building official* shall be permitted to require that a geotechnical investigation be conducted.

1803.5.3 Expansive soil. In areas likely to have expansive soil, the *building official* shall require soil tests to determine where such soils do exist.

Soils meeting all four of the following provisions shall be considered expansive, except that tests to show compliance with Items 1, 2 and 3 shall not be required if the test prescribed in Item 4 is conducted:

1. Plasticity index (PI) of 15 or greater, determined in accordance with ASTM D 4318.
2. More than 10 percent of the soil particles pass a No. 200 sieve (75 μm), determined in accordance with ASTM D 422.
3. More than 10 percent of the soil particles are less than 5 micrometers in size, determined in accordance with ASTM D 422.
4. Expansion index greater than 20, determined in accordance with ASTM D 4829.

1803.5.4 Ground-water table. A subsurface soil investigation shall be performed to determine whether the existing ground-water table is above or within 5 feet (1524 mm) below the elevation of the lowest floor level where such floor is located below the finished ground level adjacent to the foundation.

Exception: A subsurface soil investigation to determine the location of the ground-water table shall not be required where waterproofing is provided in accordance with Section 1805.

1803.5.5 Deep foundations. Where deep foundations will be used, a geotechnical investigation shall be conducted and shall include all of the following, unless sufficient data upon which to base the design and installation is otherwise available:

1. Recommended deep foundation types and installed capacities.
2. Recommended center-to-center spacing of deep foundation elements.
3. Driving criteria.
4. Installation procedures.
5. Field inspection and reporting procedures (to include procedures for verification of the installed bearing capacity where required).
6. Load test requirements.
7. Suitability of deep foundation materials for the intended environment.
8. Designation of bearing stratum or strata.
9. Reductions for group action, where necessary.

1803.5.6 Rock strata. Where subsurface explorations at the project site indicate variations or doubtful characteristics in the structure of the rock upon which foundations are to be constructed, a sufficient number of borings shall be made to a depth of not less than 10 feet (3048 mm) below the level of the foundations to provide assurance of the soundness of the foundation bed and its load-bearing capacity.

1803.5.7 Excavation near foundations. Where excavation will remove lateral support from any foundation, an investigation shall be conducted to assess the potential consequences and address mitigation measures.

1803.5.8 Compacted fill material. Where shallow foundations will bear on compacted fill material more than 12 inches (305 mm) in depth, a geotechnical investigation shall be conducted and shall include all of the following:

1. Specifications for the preparation of the site prior to placement of compacted fill material.
2. Specifications for material to be used as compacted fill.
3. Test methods to be used to determine the maximum dry density and optimum moisture content of the material to be used as compacted fill.
4. Maximum allowable thickness of each lift of compacted fill material.
5. Field test method for determining the in-place dry density of the compacted fill.
6. Minimum acceptable in-place dry density expressed as a percentage of the maximum dry density determined in accordance with Item 3.
7. Number and frequency of field tests required to determine compliance with Item 6.

1803.5.9 Controlled low-strength material (CLSM). Where shallow foundations will bear on controlled low-strength material (CLSM), a geotechnical investigation shall be conducted and shall include all of the following:

1. Specifications for the preparation of the site prior to placement of the CLSM.
2. Specifications for the CLSM.
3. Laboratory or field test method(s) to be used to determine the compressive strength or bearing capacity of the CLSM.
4. Test methods for determining the acceptance of the CLSM in the field.
5. Number and frequency of field tests required to determine compliance with Item 4.

1803.5.10 Alternate setback and clearance. Where setbacks or clearances other than those required in Section 1808.7 are desired, the *building official* shall be permitted to require a geotechnical investigation by a *registered design professional* to demonstrate that the intent of Section 1808.7 would be satisfied. Such an investigation shall include consideration of material, height of slope, slope gradient, load intensity and erosion characteristics of slope material.

1803.5.11 Seismic Design Categories C through F. For structures assigned to *Seismic Design Category* C, D, E or F in accordance with Section 1613, a geotechnical investigation shall be conducted, and shall include an evaluation of all of the following potential geologic and seismic hazards:

1. Slope instability.
2. Liquefaction.
3. Differential settlement.
4. Surface displacement due to faulting or lateral spreading.

1803.5.12 Seismic Design Categories D through F. For structures assigned to *Seismic Design Category* D, E or F in accordance with Section 1613, the geotechnical investigation required by Section 1803.5.11, shall also include:

1. The determination of lateral pressures on foundation walls and retaining walls due to earthquake motions.
2. The potential for liquefaction and soil strength loss evaluated for site peak ground accelerations, magnitudes and source characteristics consistent with the design earthquake ground motions. Peak ground acceleration shall be permitted to be determined based on a site-specific study taking into account soil amplification effects, as specified in Chapter 21 of ASCE 7, or, in the absence of such a study, peak ground accelerations shall be assumed equal to $S_{DS}/2.5$, where S_{DS} is determined in accordance with Section 1613.5.4.
3. An assessment of potential consequences of liquefaction and soil strength loss, including estimation of differential settlement, lateral movement, lateral loads on foundations, reduction in foundation soil-bearing capacity, increases in lateral pressures on retaining walls and flotation of buried structures.
4. Discussion of mitigation measures such as, but not limited to, ground stabilization, selection of appropriate foundation type and depths, selection of appropriate structural systems to accommodate anticipated displacements and forces, or any combination of these measures and how they shall be considered in the design of the structure.

1803.6 Reporting. Where geotechnical investigations are required, a written report of the investigations shall be submitted to the *building official* by the owner or authorized agent at the time of *permit* application. This geotechnical report shall include, but need not be limited to, the following information:

1. A plot showing the location of the soil investigations.
2. A complete record of the soil boring and penetration test logs and soil samples.
3. A record of the soil profile.
4. Elevation of the water table, if encountered.
5. Recommendations for foundation type and design criteria, including but not limited to: bearing capacity of natural or compacted soil; provisions to mitigate the effects of expansive soils; mitigation of the effects of liquefaction, differential settlement and varying soil strength; and the effects of adjacent loads.
6. Expected total and differential settlement.
7. Deep foundation information in accordance with Section 1803.5.5.
8. Special design and construction provisions for foundations of structures founded on expansive soils, as necessary.
9. Compacted fill material properties and testing in accordance with Section 1803.5.8.
10. Controlled low-strength material properties and testing in accordance with Section 1803.5.9.

SECTION 1804 EXCAVATION, GRADING AND FILL

1804.1 Excavation near foundations. Excavation for any purpose shall not remove lateral support from any foundation without first underpinning or protecting the foundation against settlement or lateral translation.

1804.2 Placement of backfill. The excavation outside the foundation shall be backfilled with soil that is free of organic material, construction debris, cobbles and boulders or with a controlled low-strength material (CLSM). The backfill shall be placed in lifts and compacted in a manner that does not damage the foundation or the waterproofing or dampproofing material.

Exception: CLSM need not be compacted.

1804.3 Site grading. The ground immediately adjacent to the foundation shall be sloped away from the building at a slope of not less than one unit vertical in 20 units horizontal (5-percent slope) for a minimum distance of 10 feet (3048 mm) measured perpendicular to the face of the wall. If physical obstructions or lot lines prohibit 10 feet (3048 mm) of horizontal distance, a 5-percent slope shall be provided to an *approved* alternative method of diverting water away from the foundation. Swales used for this purpose shall be sloped a minimum of 2 percent where located within 10 feet (3048 mm) of the building foundation. Impervious surfaces within 10 feet (3048 mm) of the building foundation shall be sloped a minimum of 2 percent away from the building.

Exception: Where climatic or soil conditions warrant, the slope of the ground away from the building foundation shall be permitted to be reduced to not less than one unit vertical in 48 units horizontal (2-percent slope).

The procedure used to establish the final ground level adjacent to the foundation shall account for additional settlement of the backfill.

1804.4 Grading and fill in flood hazard areas. In *flood hazard areas* established in Section 1612.3, grading and/or fill shall not be *approved*:

1. Unless such fill is placed, compacted and sloped to minimize shifting, slumping and erosion during the rise and fall of flood water and, as applicable, wave action.
2. In floodways, unless it has been demonstrated through hydrologic and hydraulic analyses performed by a *registered design professional* in accordance with standard engineering practice that the proposed grading or fill, or both, will not result in any increase in flood levels during the occurrence of the *design flood*.
3. In flood hazard areas subject to high-velocity wave action, unless such fill is conducted and/or placed to avoid diversion of water and waves toward any building or structure.
4. Where design flood elevations are specified but floodways have not been designated, unless it has been demonstrated that the cumulative effect of the proposed

flood hazard area encroachment, when combined with all other existing and anticipated *flood hazard area* encroachment, will not increase the design flood elevation more than 1 foot (305 mm) at any point.

1804.5 Compacted fill material. Where shallow foundations will bear on compacted fill material, the compacted fill shall comply with the provisions of an *approved* geotechnical report, as set forth in Section 1803.

Exception: Compacted fill material 12 inches (305 mm) in depth or less need not comply with an *approved* report, provided the in-place dry density is not less than 90 percent of the maximum dry density at optimum moisture content determined in accordance with ASTM D 1557. The compaction shall be verified by *special inspection* in accordance with Section 1704.7.

1804.6 Controlled low-strength material (CLSM). Where shallow foundations will bear on controlled low-strength material (CLSM), the CLSM shall comply with the provisions of an *approved* geotechnical report, as set forth in Section 1803.

SECTION 1805
DAMPPROOFING AND WATERPROOFING

1805.1 General. Walls or portions thereof that retain earth and enclose interior spaces and floors below grade shall be waterproofed and dampproofed in accordance with this section.

Ventilation for crawl spaces shall comply with Section 1203.4.

1805.1.1 Story above grade plane. Where a basement is considered a *story above grade plane* and the finished ground level adjacent to the basement wall is below the basement floor elevation for 25 percent or more of the perimeter, the floor and walls shall be dampproofed in accordance with Section 1805.2 and a foundation drain shall be installed in accordance with Section 1805.4.2. The foundation drain shall be installed around the portion of the perimeter where the basement floor is below ground level. The provisions of Sections 1803.5.4, 1805.3 and 1805.4.1 shall not apply in this case.

1805.1.2 Under-floor space. The finished ground level of an under-floor space such as a crawl space shall not be located below the bottom of the footings. Where there is evidence that the ground-water table rises to within 6 inches (152 mm) of the ground level at the outside building perimeter, or that the surface water does not readily drain from the building site, the ground level of the under-floor space shall be as high as the outside finished ground level, unless an *approved* drainage system is provided. The provisions of Sections 1803.5.4, 1805.2, 1805.3 and 1805.4 shall not apply in this case.

1805.1.2.1 Flood hazard areas. For buildings and structures in flood hazard areas as established in Section 1612.3, the finished ground level of an under-floor space such as a crawl space shall be equal to or higher than the outside finished ground level on at least one side.

Exception: Under-floor spaces of Group R-3 buildings that meet the requirements of FEMA/FIA-TB-11.

1805.1.3 Ground-water control. Where the ground-water table is lowered and maintained at an elevation not less than 6 inches (152 mm) below the bottom of the lowest floor, the floor and walls shall be dampproofed in accordance with Section 1805.2. The design of the system to lower the ground-water table shall be based on accepted principles of engineering that shall consider, but not necessarily be limited to, permeability of the soil, rate at which water enters the drainage system, rated capacity of pumps, head against which pumps are to operate and the rated capacity of the disposal area of the system.

1805.2 Dampproofing. Where hydrostatic pressure will not occur as determined by Section 1803.5.4, floors and walls for other than wood foundation systems shall be dampproofed in accordance with this section. Wood foundation systems shall be constructed in accordance with AF&PA PWF.

1805.2.1 Floors. Dampproofing materials for floors shall be installed between the floor and the base course required by Section 1805.4.1, except where a separate floor is provided above a concrete slab.

Where installed beneath the slab, dampproofing shall consist of not less than 6-mil (0.006 inch; 0.152 mm) polyethylene with joints lapped not less than 6 inches (152 mm), or other *approved* methods or materials. Where permitted to be installed on top of the slab, dampproofing shall consist of mopped-on bitumen, not less than 4-mil (0.004 inch; 0.102 mm) polyethylene, or other *approved* methods or materials. Joints in the membrane shall be lapped and sealed in accordance with the manufacturer's installation instructions.

1805.2.2 Walls. Dampproofing materials for walls shall be installed on the exterior surface of the wall, and shall extend from the top of the footing to above ground level.

Dampproofing shall consist of a bituminous material, 3 pounds per square *yard* (16 N/m^2) of acrylic modified cement, $^1/_8$ inch (3.2 mm) coat of surface-bonding mortar complying with ASTM C 887, any of the materials permitted for waterproofing by Section 1805.3.2 or other *approved* methods or materials.

1805.2.2.1 Surface preparation of walls. Prior to application of dampproofing materials on concrete walls, holes and recesses resulting from the removal of form ties shall be sealed with a bituminous material or other *approved* methods or materials. Unit masonry walls shall be parged on the exterior surface below ground level with not less than $^3/_8$ inch (9.5 mm) of portland cement mortar. The parging shall be coved at the footing.

Exception: Parging of unit masonry walls is not required where a material is *approved* for direct application to the masonry.

1805.3 Waterproofing. Where the ground-water investigation required by Section 1803.5.4 indicates that a hydrostatic pressure condition exists, and the design does not include a ground-water control system as described in Section 1805.1.3, walls and floors shall be waterproofed in accordance with this section.

1805.3.1 Floors. Floors required to be waterproofed shall be of concrete and designed and constructed to withstand the hydrostatic pressures to which the floors will be subjected.

Waterproofing shall be accomplished by placing a membrane of rubberized asphalt, butyl rubber, fully adhered/fully bonded HDPE or polyolefin composite membrane or not less than 6-mil [0.006 inch (0.152 mm)] polyvinyl chloride with joints lapped not less than 6 inches (152 mm) or other *approved* materials under the slab. Joints in the membrane shall be lapped and sealed in accordance with the manufacturer's installation instructions.

1805.3.2 Walls. Walls required to be waterproofed shall be of concrete or masonry and shall be designed and constructed to withstand the hydrostatic pressures and other lateral loads to which the walls will be subjected.

Waterproofing shall be applied from the bottom of the wall to not less than 12 inches (305 mm) above the maximum elevation of the ground-water table. The remainder of the wall shall be dampproofed in accordance with Section 1805.2.2. Waterproofing shall consist of two-ply hot-mopped felts, not less than 6-mil (0.006 inch; 0.152 mm) polyvinyl chloride, 40-mil (0.040 inch; 1.02 mm) polymer-modified asphalt, 6-mil (0.006 inch; 0.152 mm) polyethylene or other *approved* methods or materials capable of bridging nonstructural cracks. Joints in the membrane shall be lapped and sealed in accordance with the manufacturer's installation instructions.

1805.3.2.1 Surface preparation of walls. Prior to the application of waterproofing materials on concrete or masonry walls, the walls shall be prepared in accordance with Section 1805.2.2.1.

1805.3.3 Joints and penetrations. Joints in walls and floors, joints between the wall and floor and penetrations of the wall and floor shall be made water-tight utilizing *approved* methods and materials.

1805.4 Subsoil drainage system. Where a hydrostatic pressure condition does not exist, dampproofing shall be provided and a base shall be installed under the floor and a drain installed around the foundation perimeter. A subsoil drainage system designed and constructed in accordance with Section 1805.1.3 shall be deemed adequate for lowering the ground-water table.

1805.4.1 Floor base course. Floors of basements, except as provided for in Section 1805.1.1, shall be placed over a floor base course not less than 4 inches (102 mm) in thickness that consists of gravel or crushed stone containing not more than 10 percent of material that passes through a No. 4 (4.75 mm) sieve.

Exception: Where a site is located in well-drained gravel or sand/gravel mixture soils, a floor base course is not required.

1805.4.2 Foundation drain. A drain shall be placed around the perimeter of a foundation that consists of gravel or crushed stone containing not more than 10-percent material that passes through a No. 4 (4.75 mm) sieve. The drain shall extend a minimum of 12 inches (305 mm) beyond the outside edge of the footing. The thickness shall be such that the bottom of the drain is not higher than the bottom of the base under the floor, and that the top of the drain is not less than 6 inches (152 mm) above the top of the footing. Where a drain tile or perforated pipe is used, the invert of the pipe or tile shall not be higher than the floor elevation. The top of joints or the top of perforations shall be protected with an *approved* filter membrane material. The pipe or tile shall be placed on not less than 2 inches (51 mm) of gravel or crushed stone complying with Section 1805.4.1, and shall be covered with not less than 6 inches (152 mm) of the same material. The gravel or crushed stone shall be wrapped with an approved *geotextile* fabric.

1805.4.3 Drainage discharge. The floor base and foundation perimeter drain shall discharge by gravity or mechanical means into an *approved* drainage system that complies with the *International Plumbing Code*.

Exception: Where a site is located in well-drained gravel or sand/gravel mixture soils, a dedicated drainage system is not required.

SECTION 1806
PRESUMPTIVE LOAD-BEARING VALUES OF SOILS

1806.1 Load combinations. The presumptive load-bearing values provided in Table 1806.2 shall be used with the *allowable stress design* load combinations specified in Section 1605.3. The values of vertical foundation pressure and lateral bearing pressure given in Table 1806.2 shall be permitted to be increased by one-third where used with the alternative basic load combinations of Section 1605.3.2 that include wind or earthquake loads.

1806.2 Presumptive load-bearing values. The load-bearing values used in design for supporting soils near the surface shall not exceed the values specified in Table 1806.2 provided that all of the following criteria are satisfied.

1. Presumptive bearing pressures are acceptable only for structures where column loads are less than 50 kips per column and wall loads do not exceed 3.0 kips per linear foot.
2. Finished grades, including cut or fill operations, do not differ from the natural grades by more than 5 feet (1524 mm).
3. Histories of favorable foundation performance are available from adjoining sites for similar loading conditions.

Where the building official has reason to doubt the classification, strength or compressibility of the soil, the requirements of Section 1803.5.2 shall be satisfied.

Presumptive load-bearing values shall apply to materials with similar physical characteristics and dispositions.

Mud, organic silt, organic clays, peat or unprepared fill shall not be assumed to have a presumptive load-bearing capacity unless data to substantiate the use of such a value are submitted.

Exception: A presumptive load-bearing capacity shall be permitted to be used where the *building official* deems the load-bearing capacity of mud, organic silt or unprepared fill is adequate for the support of lightweight or temporary structures.

1806.3 Lateral load resistance. Where the presumptive values of Table 1806.2 are used to determine resistance to lateral loads, the calculations shall be in accordance with Sections 1806.3.1 through 1806.3.4.

1806.3.1 Combined resistance. The total resistance to lateral loads shall be permitted to be determined by combining the values derived from the lateral bearing pressure and the lateral sliding resistance specified in Table 1806.2.

1806.3.2 Lateral sliding resistance limit. For clay, sandy clay, silty clay, clayey silt, silt and sandy silt, in no case shall the lateral sliding resistance exceed one-half the dead load.

1806.3.3 Increase for depth. The lateral bearing pressures specified in Table 1806.2 shall be permitted to be increased by the tabular value for each additional foot (305 mm) of depth to a maximum of 15 times the tabular value.

1806.3.4 Increase for poles. Isolated poles for uses such as flagpoles or signs and poles used to support buildings that are not adversely affected by a $^1/_2$ inch (12.7 mm) motion at the ground surface due to short-term lateral loads shall be permitted to be designed using lateral bearing pressures equal to two times the tabular values.

SECTION 1807 FOUNDATION WALLS, RETAINING WALLS AND EMBEDDED POSTS AND POLES

1807.1 Foundation walls. Foundation walls shall be designed and constructed in accordance with Sections 1807.1.1 through 1807.1.6. Foundation walls shall be supported by foundations designed in accordance with Section 1808.

1807.1.1 Design lateral soil loads. Foundation walls shall be designed for the lateral soil loads set forth in Section 1610.

1807.1.2 Unbalanced backfill height. Unbalanced backfill height is the difference in height between the exterior finish ground level and the lower of the top of the concrete footing that supports the foundation wall or the interior finish ground level. Where an interior concrete slab on grade is provided and is in contact with the interior surface of the foundation wall, the unbalanced backfill height shall be permitted to be measured from the exterior finish ground level to the top of the interior concrete slab.

1807.1.3 Rubble stone foundation walls. Foundation walls of rough or random rubble stone shall not be less than 16 inches (406 mm) thick. Rubble stone shall not be used for foundation walls of structures assigned to *Seismic Design Category* C, D, E or F.

1807.1.4 Permanent wood foundation systems. Permanent wood foundation systems shall be designed and installed in accordance with AF&PA PWF. Lumber and plywood shall be treated in accordance with AWPA U1 (Commodity Specification A, Use Category 4B and Section 5.2) and shall be identified in accordance with Section 2303.1.8.1.

1807.1.5 Concrete and masonry foundation walls. Concrete and masonry foundation walls shall be designed in accordance with Chapter 19 or 21, as applicable.

Exception: Concrete and masonry foundation walls shall be permitted to be designed and constructed in accordance with Section 1807.1.6.

TABLE 1806.2
PRESUMPTIVE LOAD-BEARING VALUES

CLASS OF MATERIALS	VERTICAL FOUNDATION PRESSURE (psf)	LATERAL BEARING PRESSURE (psf/ft below natural grade)	LATERAL SLIDING RESISTANCE	
			Coefficient of friction[a]	Cohesion (psf)[b]
1. Crystalline bedrock	12,000	1,200	0.70	—
2. Sedimentary and foliated rock	4,000	400	0.35	—
3. Sandy gravel and/or gravel (GW and GP)	3,000	200	0.35	—
4. Sand, silty sand, clayey sand, silty gravel and clayey gravel (SW, SP, SM, SC, GM and GC)	2,000	150	0.25	—
5. Clay, sandy clay, silty clay, clayey silt, silt and sandy silt (CL, ML, MH and CH)	1,500	100	—	130

For SI: 1 pound per square foot = 0.0479 kPa, 1 pound per square foot per foot = 0.157 kPa/m.

a. Coefficient to be multiplied by the dead load.

b. Cohesion value to be multiplied by the contact area, as limited by Section 1806.3.2.

1807.1.6 Prescriptive design of concrete and masonry foundation walls. Concrete and masonry foundation walls that are laterally supported at the top and bottom shall be permitted to be designed and constructed in accordance with this section.

1807.1.6.1 Foundation wall thickness. The thickness of prescriptively designed foundation walls shall not be less than the thickness of the wall supported, except that foundation walls of at least 8-inch (203 mm) nominal width shall be permitted to support brick-veneered frame walls and 10-inch-wide (254 mm) cavity walls provided the requirements of Section 1807.1.6.2 or 1807.1.6.3 are met.

1807.1.6.2 Concrete foundation walls. Concrete foundation walls shall comply with the following:

1. The thickness shall comply with the requirements of Table 1807.1.6.2.
2. The size and spacing of vertical reinforcement shown in Table 1807.1.6.2 is based on the use of reinforcement with a minimum yield strength of 60,000 pounds per square inch (psi) (414 MPa). Vertical reinforcement with a minimum yield strength of 40,000 psi (276 MPa) or 50,000 psi (345 MPa) shall be permitted, provided the same size bar is used and the spacing shown in the table is reduced by multiplying the spacing by 0.67 or 0.83, respectively.

TABLE 1807.1.6.2
CONCRETE FOUNDATION WALLS[b, c]

MAXIMUM WALL HEIGHT (feet)	MAXIMUM UNBALANCED BACKFILL HEIGHT[e] (feet)	MINIMUM VERTICAL REINFORCEMENT-BAR SIZE AND SPACING (inches)								
		Design lateral soil load[a] (psf per foot of depth)								
		30[d]			45[d]			60		
		Minimum wall thickness (inches)								
		7.5	9.5	11.5	7.5	9.5	11.5	7.5	9.5	11.5
5	4	PC	PC	PC	PC	PC	PC	PC	PC	PC
	5	PC	PC	PC	PC	PC	PC	PC	PC	PC
6	4	PC	PC	PC	PC	PC	PC	PC	PC	PC
	5	PC	PC	PC	PC	PC	PC	PC	PC	PC
	6	PC	PC	PC	PC	PC	PC	PC	PC	PC
7	4	PC	PC	PC	PC	PC	PC	PC	PC	PC
	5	PC	PC	PC	PC	PC	PC	PC	PC	PC
	6	PC	PC	PC	PC	PC	PC	#5 at 48	PC	PC
	7	PC	PC	PC	#5 at 46	PC	PC	#6 at 48	PC	PC
8	4	PC	PC	PC	PC	PC	PC	PC	PC	PC
	5	PC	PC	PC	PC	PC	PC	PC	PC	PC
	6	PC	PC	PC	PC	PC	PC	#5 at 43	PC	PC
	7	PC	PC	PC	#5 at 41	PC	PC	#6 at 43	PC	PC
	8	#5 at 47	PC	PC	#6 at 43	PC	PC	#6 at 32	#6 at 44	PC
9	4	PC	PC	PC	PC	PC	PC	PC	PC	PC
	5	PC	PC	PC	PC	PC	PC	PC	PC	PC
	6	PC	PC	PC	PC	PC	PC	#5 at 39	PC	PC
	7	PC	PC	PC	#5 at 37	PC	PC	#6 at 38	#5 at 37	PC
	8	#5 at 41	PC	PC	#6 at 38	#5 at 37	PC	#7 at 39	#6 at 39	#4 at 48
	9[d]	#6 at 46	PC	PC	#7 at 41	#6 at 41	PC	#7 at 31	#7 at 41	#6 at 39
10	4	PC	PC	PC	PC	PC	PC	PC	PC	PC
	5	PC	PC	PC	PC	PC	PC	PC	PC	PC
	6	PC	PC	PC	PC	PC	PC	#5 at 37	PC	PC
	7	PC	PC	PC	#6 at 48	PC	PC	#6 at 35	#6 at 48	PC
	8	#5 at 38	PC	PC	#7 at 47	#6 at 47	PC	#7 at 35	#7 at 47	#6 at 45
	9[d]	#6 at 41	#4 at 48	PC	#7 at 37	#7 at 48	#4 at 48	#6 at 22	#7 at 37	#7 at 47
	10[d]	#7 at 45	#6 at 45	PC	#7 at 31	#7 at 40	#6 at 38	#6 at 22	#7 at 30	#7 at 38

For SI: 1 inch = 25.4 mm, 1 foot = 304.8 mm, 1 pound per square foot per foot = 0.157 kPa/m.

a. For design lateral soil loads, see Section 1610.

b. Provisions for this table are based on design and construction requirements specified in Section 1807.1.6.2.

c. "PC" means plain concrete.

d. Where unbalanced backfill height exceeds 8 feet and design lateral soil loads from Table 1610.1 are used, the requirements for 30 and 45 psf per foot of depth are not applicable (see Section 1610).

e. For height of unbalanced backfill, see Section 1807.1.2.

3. Vertical reinforcement, when required, shall be placed nearest the inside face of the wall a distance, *d*, from the outside face (soil face) of the wall. The distance, *d*, is equal to the wall thickness, *t*, minus 1.25 inches (32 mm) plus one-half the bar diameter, d_b, [$d = t - (1.25 + d_b/2)$]. The reinforcement shall be placed within a tolerance of ± $^3/_8$ inch (9.5 mm) where *d* is less than or equal to 8 inches (203 mm) or ± $^1/_2$ inch (12.7 mm) where *d* is greater than 8 inches (203 mm).
4. In lieu of the reinforcement shown in Table 1807.1.6.2, smaller reinforcing bar sizes with closer spacings that provide an equivalent cross-sectional area of reinforcement per unit length shall be permitted.
5. Concrete cover for reinforcement measured from the inside face of the wall shall not be less than $^3/_4$ inch (19.1 mm). Concrete cover for reinforcement measured from the outside face of the wall shall not be less than 1$^1/_2$ inches (38 mm) for No. 5 bars and smaller, and not less than 2 inches (51 mm) for larger bars.
6. Concrete shall have a specified compressive strength, f'_c, of not less than 2,500 psi (17.2 MPa).
7. The unfactored axial load per linear foot of wall shall not exceed 1.2 $t f'_c$ where *t* is the specified wall thickness in inches.

1807.1.6.2.1 Seismic requirements. Based on the *seismic design category* assigned to the structure in accordance with Section 1613, concrete foundation walls designed using Table 1807.1.6.2 shall be subject to the following limitations:

1. *Seismic Design Categories* A and B. No additional seismic requirements, except provide reinforcement around openings in accordance with Section 1909.6.3.
2. *Seismic Design Categories* C, D, E and F. Tables shall not be used except as allowed for plain concrete members in Section 1908.1.8.

1807.1.6.3 Masonry foundation walls. Masonry foundation walls shall comply with the following:

1. The thickness shall comply with the requirements of Table 1807.1.6.3(1) for plain masonry walls or Table 1807.1.6.3(2), 1807.1.6.3(3) or 1807.1.6.3(4) for masonry walls with reinforcement.
2. Vertical reinforcement shall have a minimum yield strength of 60,000 psi (414 MPa).
3. The specified location of the reinforcement shall equal or exceed the effective depth distance, *d*, noted in Tables 1807.1.6.3(2), 1807.1.6.3(3) and 1807.1.6.3(4) and shall be measured from the face of the exterior (soil) side of the wall to the

TABLE 1807.1.6.3(1)
PLAIN MASONRY FOUNDATION WALLS[a, b, c]

MAXIMUM WALL HEIGHT (feet)	MAXIMUM UNBALANCED BACKFILL HEIGHT[e] (feet)	MINIMUM NOMINAL WALL THICKNESS (inches) Design lateral soil load[a] (psf per foot of depth) 30[f]	45[f]	60
7	4 (or less)	8	8	8
	5	8	10	10
	6	10	12	10 (solid[c])
	7	12	10 (solid[c])	10 (solid[c])
8	4 (or less)	8	8	8
	5	8	10	12
	6	10	12	12 (solid[c])
	7	12	12 (solid[c])	Note d
	8	10 (solid[c])	12 (solid[c])	Note d
9	4 (or less)	8	8	8
	5	8	10	12
	6	12	12	12 (solid[c])
	7	12 (solid[c])	12 (solid[c])	Note d
	8	12 (solid[c])	Note d	Note d
	9[f]	Note d	Note d	Note d

For SI: 1 inch = 25.4 mm, 1 foot = 304.8 mm, 1 pound per square foot per foot = 0.157 kPa/m.

a. For design lateral soil loads, see Section 1610.
b. Provisions for this table are based on design and construction requirements specified in Section 1807.1.6.3.
c. Solid grouted hollow units or solid masonry units.
d. A design in compliance with Chapter 21 or reinforcement in accordance with Table 1807.1.6.3(2) is required.
e. For height of unbalanced backfill, see Section 1807.1.2.
f. Where unbalanced backfill height exceeds 8 feet and design lateral soil loads from Table 1610.1 are used, the requirements for 30 and 45 psf per foot of depth are not applicable (see Section 1610).

center of the vertical reinforcement. The reinforcement shall be placed within the tolerances specified in TMS 602/ACI 530.1/ASCE 6, Article 3.4.B.8 of the specified location.

4. Grout shall comply with Section 2103.12.
5. Concrete masonry units shall comply with ASTM C 90.
6. Clay masonry units shall comply with ASTM C 652 for hollow brick, except compliance with ASTM C 62 or ASTM C 216 shall be permitted where solid masonry units are installed in accordance with Table 1807.1.6.3(1) for plain masonry.
7. Masonry units shall be laid in running bond and installed with Type M or S mortar in accordance with Section 2103.8.
8. The unfactored axial load per linear foot of wall shall not exceed 1.2 $t f'_m$ where t is the specified wall thickness in inches and f'_m is the specified compressive strength of masonry in pounds per square inch.
9. At least 4 inches (102 mm) of solid masonry shall be provided at girder supports at the top of hollow masonry unit foundation walls.
10. Corbeling of masonry shall be in accordance with Section 2104.2. Where an 8-inch (203 mm) wall is corbeled, the top corbel shall not extend

TABLE 1807.1.6.3(2)
8-INCH MASONRY FOUNDATION WALLS WITH REINFORCEMENT WHERE $d \geq 5$ INCHES[a, b, c]

MAXIMUM WALL HEIGHT (feet-inches)	MAXIMUM UNBALANCED BACKFILL HEIGHT[d] (feet-inches)	MINIMUM VERTICAL REINFORCEMENT-BAR SIZE AND SPACING (inches)		
		Design lateral soil load[a] (psf per foot of depth)		
		30[e]	45[e]	60
7-4	4-0 (or less)	#4 at 48	#4 at 48	#4 at 48
	5-0	#4 at 48	#4 at 48	#4 at 48
	6-0	#4 at 48	#5 at 48	#5 at 48
	7-4	#5 at 48	#6 at 48	#7 at 48
8-0	4-0 (or less)	#4 at 48	#4 at 48	#4 at 48
	5-0	#4 at 48	#4 at 48	#4 at 48
	6-0	#4 at 48	#5 at 48	#5 at 48
	7-0	#5 at 48	#6 at 48	#7 at 48
	8-0	#5 at 48	#6 at 48	#7 at 48
8-8	4-0 (or less)	#4 at 48	#4 at 48	#4 at 48
	5-0	#4 at 48	#4 at 48	#5 at 48
	6-0	#4 at 48	#5 at 48	#6 at 48
	7-0	#5 at 48	#6 at 48	#7 at 48
	8-8[e]	#6 at 48	#7 at 48	#8 at 48
9-4	4-0 (or less)	#4 at 48	#4 at 48	#4 at 48
	5-0	#4 at 48	#4 at 48	#5 at 48
	6-0	#4 at 48	#5 at 48	#6 at 48
	7-0	#5 at 48	#6 at 48	#7 at 48
	8-0	#6 at 48	#7 at 48	#8 at 48
	9-4[e]	#7 at 48	#8 at 48	#9 at 48
10-0	4-0 (or less)	#4 at 48	#4 at 48	#4 at 48
	5-0	#4 at 48	#4 at 48	#5 at 48
	6-0	#4 at 48	#5 at 48	#6 at 48
	7-0	#5 at 48	#6 at 48	#7 at 48
	8-0	#6 at 48	#7 at 48	#8 at 48
	9-0[e]	#7 at 48	#8 at 48	#9 at 48
	10-0[e]	#7 at 48	#9 at 48	#9 at 48

For SI: 1 inch = 25.4 mm, 1 foot = 304.8 mm, 1 pound per square foot per foot = 0.157 kPa/m.
a. For design lateral soil loads, see Section 1610.
b. Provisions for this table are based on design and construction requirements specified in Section 1807.1.6.3.
c. For alternative reinforcement, see Section 1807.1.6.3.1.
d. For height of unbalanced backfill, see Section 1807.1.2.
e. Where unbalanced backfill height exceeds 8 feet and design lateral soil loads from Table 1610.1 are used, the requirements for 30 and 45 psf per foot of depth are not applicable. See Section 1610.

higher than the bottom of the floor framing and shall be a full course of headers at least 6 inches (152 mm) in length or the top course bed joint shall be tied to the vertical wall projection. The tie shall be W2.8 (4.8 mm) and spaced at a maximum horizontal distance of 36 inches (914 mm). The hollow space behind the corbelled masonry shall be filled with mortar or grout.

1807.1.6.3.1 Alternative foundation wall reinforcement. In lieu of the reinforcement provisions for masonry foundation walls in Table 1807.1.6.3(2), 1807.1.6.3(3) or 1807.1.6.3(4), alternative reinforcing bar sizes and spacings having an equivalent cross-sectional area of reinforcement per linear foot (mm) of wall shall be permitted to be used, provided the spacing of reinforcement does not exceed 72 inches (1829 mm) and reinforcing bar sizes do not exceed No. 11.

1807.1.6.3.2 Seismic requirements. Based on the *seismic design category* assigned to the structure in accordance with Section 1613, masonry foundation walls designed using Tables 1807.1.6.3(1) through 1807.1.6.3(4) shall be subject to the following limitations:

1. *Seismic Design Categories* A and B. No additional seismic requirements.
2. *Seismic Design Category* C. A design using Tables 1807.1.6.3(1) through 1807.1.6.3(4) is

TABLE 1807.1.6.3(3)
10-INCH MASONRY FOUNDATION WALLS WITH REINFORCEMENT WHERE d ≥ 6.75 INCHES [a, b, c]

MAXIMUM WALL HEIGHT (feet-inches)	MAXIMUM UNBALANCED BACKFILL HEIGHT[d] (feet-inches)	MINIMUM VERTICAL REINFORCEMENT-BAR SIZE AND SPACING (inches)		
		Design lateral soil load[a] (psf per foot of depth)		
		30[e]	45[e]	60
7-4	4-0 (or less)	#4 at 56	#4 at 56	#4 at 56
	5-0	#4 at 56	#4 at 56	#4 at 56
	6-0	#4 at 56	#4 at 56	#5 at 56
	7-4	#4 at 56	#5 at 56	#6 at 56
8-0	4-0 (or less)	#4 at 56	#4 at 56	#4 at 56
	5-0	#4 at 56	#4 at 56	#4 at 56
	6-0	#4 at 56	#4 at 56	#5 at 56
	7-0	#4 at 56	#5 at 56	#6 at 56
	8-0	#5 at 56	#6 at 56	#7 at 56
8-8	4-0 (or less)	#4 at 56	#4 at 56	#4 at 56
	5-0	#4 at 56	#4 at 56	#4 at 56
	6-0	#4 at 56	#4 at 56	#5 at 56
	7-0	#4 at 56	#5 at 56	#6 at 56
	8-8[e]	#5 at 56	#7 at 56	#8 at 56
9-4	4-0 (or less)	#4 at 56	#4 at 56	#4 at 56
	5-0	#4 at 56	#4 at 56	#4 at 56
	6-0	#4 at 56	#5 at 56	#5 at 56
	7-0	#4 at 56	#5 at 56	#6 at 56
	8-0	#5 at 56	#6 at 56	#7 at 56
	9-4[e]	#6 at 56	#7 at 56	#7 at 56
10-0	4-0 (or less)	#4 at 56	#4 at 56	#4 at 56
	5-0	#4 at 56	#4 at 56	#4 at 56
	6-0	#4 at 56	#5 at 56	#5 at 56
	7-0	#5 at 56	#6 at 56	#7 at 56
	8-0	#5 at 56	#7 at 56	#8 at 56
	9-0[e]	#6 at 56	#7 at 56	#9 at 56
	10-0[e]	#7 at 56	#8 at 56	#9 at 56

For SI: 1 inch = 25.4 mm, 1 foot = 304.8, 1 pound per square foot per foot = 0.157 kPa/m.

a. For design lateral soil loads, see Section 1610.

b. Provisions for this table are based on design and construction requirements specified in Section 1807.1.6.3.

c. For alternative reinforcement, see Section 1807.1.6.3.1.

d. For height of unbalanced backfill, See Section 1807.1.2.

e. Where unbalanced backfill height exceeds 8 feet and design lateral soil loads from Table 1610.1 are used, the requirements for 30 and 45 psf per foot of depth are not applicable. See Section 1610.

subject to the seismic requirements of Section 1.17.4.3 of TMS 402/ACI 530/ASCE 5.

3. *Seismic Design Category* D. A design using Tables 1807.1.6.3(2) through 1807.1.6.3(4) is subject to the seismic requirements of Section 1.17.4.4 of TMS 402/ACI 530/ASCE 5.

4. *Seismic Design Categories* E and F. A design using Tables 1807.1.6.3(2) through 1807.1.6.3(4) is subject to the seismic requirements of Section 1.17.4.5 of TMS 402/ACI 530/ASCE 5.

1807.2 Retaining walls. Retaining walls shall be designed in accordance with Sections 1807.2.1 through 1807.2.3.

1807.2.1 General. Retaining walls shall be designed to ensure stability against overturning, sliding, excessive foundation pressure and water uplift. Where a keyway is extended below the wall base with the intent to engage passive pressure and enhance sliding stability, lateral soil pressures on both sides of the keyway shall be considered in the sliding analysis.

1807.2.2 Design lateral soil loads. Retaining walls shall be designed for the lateral soil loads set forth in Section 1610.

1807.2.3 Safety factor. Retaining walls shall be designed to resist the lateral action of soil to produce sliding and overturning with a minimum safety factor of 1.5 in each case. The load combinations of Section 1605 shall not apply to this requirement. Instead, design shall be based on 0.7 times nominal earthquake loads, 1.0 times other *nominal loads*, and investigation with one or more of the variable loads set to zero. The safety factor against lateral sliding shall be taken as the available soil resistance at the base of the retain-

TABLE 1807.1.6.3(4)
12-INCH MASONRY FOUNDATION WALLS WITH REINFORCEMENT WHERE d ≥ 8.75 INCHES[a, b, c]

MAXIMUM WALL HEIGHT (feet-inches)	MAXIMUM UNBALANCED BACKFILL HEIGHT[d] (feet-inches)	MINIMUM VERTICAL REINFORCEMENT-BAR SIZE AND SPACING (inches)		
		Design lateral soil load[a] (psf per foot of depth)		
		30[e]	45[e]	60
7-4	4 (or less)	#4 at 72	#4 at 72	#4 at 72
	5-0	#4 at 72	#4 at 72	#4 at 72
	6-0	#4 at 72	#4 at 72	#5 at 72
	7-4	#4 at 72	#5 at 72	#6 at 72
8-0	4 (or less)	#4 at 72	#4 at 72	#4 at 72
	5-0	#4 at 72	#4 at 72	#4 at 72
	6-0	#4 at 72	#4 at 72	#5 at 72
	7-0	#4 at 72	#5 at 72	#6 at 72
	8-0	#5 at 72	#6 at 72	#8 at 72
8-8	4 (or less)	#4 at 72	#4 at 72	#4 at 72
	5-0	#4 at 72	#4 at 72	#4 at 72
	6-0	#4 at 72	#4 at 72	#5 at 72
	7-0	#4 at 72	#5 at 72	#6 at 72
	8-8[e]	#5 at 72	#7 at 72	#8 at 72
9-4	4 (or less)	#4 at 72	#4 at 72	#4 at 72
	5-0	#4 at 72	#4 at 72	#4 at 72
	6-0	#4 at 72	#5 at 72	#5 at 72
	7-0	#4 at 72	#5 at 72	#6 at 72
	8-0	#5 at 72	#6 at 72	#7 at 72
	9-4[e]	#6 at 72	#7 at 72	#8 at 72
10-0	4 (or less)	#4 at 72	#4 at 72	#4 at 72
	5-0	#4 at 72	#4 at 72	#4 at 72
	6-0	#4 at 72	#5 at 72	#5 at 72
	7-0	#4 at 72	#6 at 72	#6 at 72
	8-0	#5 at 72	#6 at 72	#7 at 72
	9-0[e]	#6 at 72	#7 at 72	#8 at 72
	10-0[e]	#7 at 72	#8 at 72	#9 at 72

For SI: 1 inch = 25.4 mm, 1 foot = 304.8 mm, 1 pound per square foot per foot = 0.157 kPa/m.

a. For design lateral soil loads, see Section 1610.

b. Provisions for this table are based on design and construction requirements specified in Section 1807.1.6.3.

c. For alternative reinforcement, see Section 1807.1.6.3.1.

d. For height of unbalanced backfill, see Section 1807.1.2.

e. Where unbalanced backfill height exceeds 8 feet and design lateral soil loads from Table 1610.1 are used, the requirements for 30 and 45 psf per foot of depth are not applicable. See Section 1610.

ing wall foundation divided by the net lateral force applied to the retaining wall.

Exception: Where earthquake loads are included, the minimum safety factor for retaining wall sliding and overturning shall be 1.1.

1807.2.4 Retaining systems adjacent to structures. Retaining systems less than 5 feet (1524 mm) in cumulative vertical relief and adjacent to a structure located closer than the vertical relief shall be designed under the responsible charge of a registered design professional.

1807.2.5 Retaining systems. Retaining systems providing a cumulative vertical relief greater than 5 feet (1524 mm) in height within a horizontal separation distance of 50 feet (15 m) or less, including retaining walls or mechanically stabilized earth walls, shall be designed under the responsible charge of a registered design professional. Retaining systems shall meet the requirements of Section 1610. Testing and inspection reports shall comply with Section 1704.1.2 and shall verify:

1. Foundation support system is adequate for the intended site conditions;
2. Measurement of the quality of construction materials for conformance with specifications;
3. Determination of similarity of actual soil conditions to those anticipated in design; and
4. Examination of backfill materials and any drainage systems for compliance with plans and specifications.

1807.3 Embedded posts and poles. Designs to resist both axial and lateral loads employing posts or poles as columns embedded in earth or in concrete footings in earth shall be in accordance with Sections 1807.3.1 through 1807.3.3.

1807.3.1 Limitations. The design procedures outlined in this section are subject to the following limitations:

1. The frictional resistance for structural walls and slabs on silts and clays shall be limited to one-half of the normal force imposed on the soil by the weight of the footing or slab.
2. Posts embedded in earth shall not be used to provide lateral support for structural or nonstructural materials such as plaster, masonry or concrete unless bracing is provided that develops the limited deflection required.

Wood poles shall be treated in accordance with AWPA U1 for sawn timber posts (Commodity Specification A, Use Category 4B) and for round timber posts (Commodity Specification B, Use Category 4B).

1807.3.2 Design criteria. The depth to resist lateral loads shall be determined using the design criteria established in Sections 1807.3.2.1 through 1807.3.2.3, or by other methods *approved* by the *building official*.

1807.3.2.1 Nonconstrained. The following formula shall be used in determining the depth of embedment required to resist lateral loads where no lateral constraint is provided at the ground surface, such as by a rigid floor or rigid ground surface pavement, and where no lateral constraint is provided above the ground surface, such as by a structural diaphragm.

$$d = 0.5A\{1 + [1 + (4.36h/A)]^{1/2}\} \qquad \textbf{(Equation 18-1)}$$

where:

A = $2.34P/S_1\, b$.

b = Diameter of round post or footing or diagonal dimension of square post or footing, feet (m).

d = Depth of embedment in earth in feet (m) but not over 12 feet (3658 mm) for purpose of computing lateral pressure.

h = Distance in feet (m) from ground surface to point of application of "P."

P = Applied lateral force in pounds (kN).

S_1 = Allowable lateral soil-bearing pressure as set forth in Section 1806.2 based on a depth of one-third the depth of embedment in pounds per square foot (psf) (kPa).

1807.3.2.2 Constrained. The following formula shall be used to determine the depth of embedment required to resist lateral loads where lateral constraint is provided at the ground surface, such as by a rigid floor or pavement.

$$d = \sqrt{\frac{4.25Ph}{S_3 b}} \qquad \textbf{(Equation 18-2)}$$

or alternatively

$$d = \sqrt{\frac{4.25M_g}{S_3 b}} \qquad \textbf{(Equation 18-3)}$$

where:

M_g = Moment in the post at grade, in foot-pounds (kN-m).

S_3 = Allowable lateral soil-bearing pressure as set forth in Section 1806.2 based on a depth equal to the depth of embedment in pounds per square foot (kPa).

1807.3.2.3 Vertical load. The resistance to vertical loads shall be determined using the vertical foundation pressure set forth in Table 1806.2.

1807.3.3 Backfill. The backfill in the annular space around columns not embedded in poured footings shall be by one of the following methods:

1. Backfill shall be of concrete with a specified compressive strength of not less than 2,000 psi (13.8 MPa). The hole shall not be less than 4 inches (102 mm) larger than the diameter of the column at its bottom or 4 inches (102 mm) larger than the diagonal dimension of a square or rectangular column.
2. Backfill shall be of clean sand. The sand shall be thoroughly compacted by tamping in layers not more than 8 inches (203 mm) in depth.
3. Backfill shall be of controlled low-strength material (CLSM).

SECTION 1808
FOUNDATIONS

1808.1 General. Foundations shall be designed and constructed in accordance with Sections 1808.2 through 1808.9. Shallow foundations shall also satisfy the requirements of Section 1809. Deep foundations shall also satisfy the requirements of Section 1810.

1808.2 Design for capacity and settlement. Foundations shall be so designed that the allowable bearing capacity of the soil is not exceeded, and that differential settlement is minimized. Foundations in areas with expansive soils shall be designed in accordance with the provisions of Section 1808.6.

1808.3 Design loads. Foundations shall be designed for the most unfavorable effects due to the combinations of loads specified in Section 1605.2 or 1605.3. The dead load is permitted to include the weight of foundations and overlying fill. Reduced live loads, as specified in Sections 1607.9 and 1607.11, shall be permitted to be used in the design of foundations.

1808.3.1 Seismic overturning. Where foundations are proportioned using the load combinations of Section 1605.2 or 1605.3.1, and the computation of seismic overturning effects is by equivalent lateral force analysis or modal analysis, the proportioning shall be in accordance with Section 12.13.4 of ASCE 7.

1808.4 Vibratory loads. Where machinery operations or other vibrations are transmitted through the foundation, consideration shall be given in the foundation design to prevent detrimental disturbances of the soil.

1808.5 Shifting or moving soils. Where it is known that the shallow subsoils are of a shifting or moving character, foundations shall be carried to a sufficient depth to ensure stability.

1808.6 Design for expansive soils. Foundations for buildings and structures founded on expansive soils shall be designed in accordance with Section 1808.6.1 or 1808.6.2.

Exception: Foundation design need not comply with Section 1808.6.1 or 1808.6.2 where one of the following conditions is satisfied:

1. The soil is removed in accordance with Section 1808.6.3; or
2. The *building official* approves stabilization of the soil in accordance with Section 1808.6.4.

1808.6.1 Foundations. Foundations placed on or within the active zone of expansive soils shall be designed to resist differential volume changes and to prevent structural damage to the supported structure. Deflection and racking of the supported structure shall be limited to that which will not interfere with the usability and serviceability of the structure.

Foundations placed below where volume change occurs or below expansive soil shall comply with the following provisions:

1. Foundations extending into or penetrating expansive soils shall be designed to prevent uplift of the supported structure.
2. Foundations penetrating expansive soils shall be designed to resist forces exerted on the foundation due to soil volume changes or shall be isolated from the expansive soil.

1808.6.2 Slab-on-ground foundations. Moments, shears and deflections for use in designing slab-on-ground, mat or raft foundations on expansive soils shall be determined in accordance with *WRI/CRSI Design of Slab-on-Ground Foundations* or *PTI Standard Requirements for Analysis of Shallow Concrete Foundations on Expansive Soils.* Using the moments, shears and deflections determined above, nonprestressed slabs-on-ground, mat or raft foundations on expansive soils shall be designed in accordance with *WRI/CRSI Design of Slab-on-Ground Foundations* and post-tensioned slab-on-ground, mat or raft foundations on expansive soils shall be designed in accordance with *PTI Standard Requirements for Design of Shallow Post-Tensioned Concrete Foundations on Expansive Soils.* It shall be permitted to analyze and design such slabs by other methods that account for soil-structure interaction, the deformed shape of the soil support, the plate or stiffened plate action of the slab as well as both center lift and edge lift conditions. Such alternative methods shall be rational and the basis for all aspects and parameters of the method shall be available for peer review.

1808.6.3 Removal of expansive soil. Where expansive soil is removed in lieu of designing foundations in accordance with Section 1808.6.1 or 1808.6.2, the soil shall be removed to a depth sufficient to ensure a constant moisture content in the remaining soil. Fill material shall not contain expansive soils and shall comply with Section 1804.5 or 1804.6.

Exception: Expansive soil need not be removed to the depth of constant moisture, provided the confining pressure in the expansive soil created by the fill and supported structure exceeds the swell pressure.

1808.6.4 Stabilization. Where the active zone of expansive soils is stabilized in lieu of designing foundations in accordance with Section 1808.6.1 or 1808.6.2, the soil shall be stabilized by chemical, dewatering, presaturation or equivalent techniques.

1808.7 Foundations on or adjacent to slopes. The placement of buildings and structures on or adjacent to slopes steeper than one unit vertical in three units horizontal (33.3-percent slope) shall comply with Sections 1808.7.1 through 1808.7.5.

1808.7.1 Building clearance from ascending slopes. In general, buildings below slopes shall be set a sufficient distance from the slope to provide protection from slope drainage, erosion and shallow failures. Except as provided in Section 1808.7.5 and Figure 1808.7.1, the following criteria will be assumed to provide this protection. Where the existing slope is steeper than one unit vertical in one unit horizontal (100-percent slope), the toe of the slope shall be assumed to be at the intersection of a horizontal plane drawn from the top of the foundation and a plane drawn tangent to the slope at an angle of 45 degrees (0.79 rad) to the horizontal. Where a retaining wall is constructed at the toe of the slope, the height of the slope shall be measured from the top of the wall to the top of the slope.

1808.7.2 Foundation setback from descending slope surface. Foundations on or adjacent to slope surfaces shall be founded in firm material with an embedment and set back from the slope surface sufficient to provide vertical and lateral support for the foundation without detrimental settlement. Except as provided for in Section 1808.7.5 and Figure 1808.7.1, the following setback is deemed adequate to meet the criteria. Where the slope is steeper than 1 unit vertical in 1 unit horizontal (100-percent slope), the required setback shall be measured from an imaginary plane 45 degrees (0.79 rad) to the horizontal, projected upward from the toe of the slope.

1808.7.3 Pools. The setback between pools regulated by this code and slopes shall be equal to one-half the building footing setback distance required by this section. That portion of the pool wall within a horizontal distance of 7 feet (2134 mm) from the top of the slope shall be capable of supporting the water in the pool without soil support.

1808.7.4 Foundation elevation. On graded sites, the top of any exterior foundation shall extend above the elevation of the street gutter at point of discharge or the inlet of an *approved* drainage device a minimum of 12 inches (305 mm) plus 2 percent. Alternate elevations are permitted subject to the approval of the *building official*, provided it can be demonstrated that required drainage to the point of discharge and away from the structure is provided at all locations on the site.

1808.7.5 Alternate setback and clearance. Alternate setbacks and clearances are permitted, subject to the approval of the *building official*. The *building official* shall be permitted to require a geotechnical investigation as set forth in Section 1803.5.10.

1808.8 Concrete foundations. The design, materials and construction of concrete foundations shall comply with Sections 1808.8.1 through 1808.8.6 and the provisions of Chapter 19.

Exception: Where concrete footings supporting walls of light-frame construction are designed in accordance with Table 1809.7, a specific design in accordance with Chapter 19 is not required.

1808.8.1 Concrete or grout strength and mix proportioning. Concrete or grout in foundations shall have a specified compressive strength (f'_c) not less than the largest applicable value indicated in Table 1808.8.1.

Where concrete is placed through a funnel hopper at the top of a deep foundation element, the concrete mix shall be designed and proportioned so as to produce a cohesive workable mix having a slump of not less than 4 inches (102 mm) and not more than 8 inches (204 mm). Where concrete or grout is to be pumped, the mix design including slump shall be adjusted to produce a pumpable mixture.

1808.8.2 Concrete cover. The concrete cover provided for prestressed and nonprestressed reinforcement in foundations shall be no less than the largest applicable value specified in Table 1808.8.2. Longitudinal bars spaced less than $1^1/_2$ inches (38 mm) clear distance apart shall be considered bundled bars for which the concrete cover provided shall also be no less than that required by Section 7.7.4 of ACI 318. Concrete cover shall be measured from the concrete surface to the outermost surface of the steel to which the cover requirement applies. Where concrete is placed in a temporary or permanent casing or a mandrel, the inside face of the casing or mandrel shall be considered the concrete surface.

1808.8.3 Placement of concrete. Concrete shall be placed in such a manner as to ensure the exclusion of any foreign matter and to secure a full-size foundation. Concrete shall not be placed through water unless a tremie or other method *approved* by the *building official* is used. Where placed under or in the presence of water, the concrete shall be deposited by *approved* means to ensure minimum segregation of the mix and negligible turbulence of the water. Where depositing concrete from the top of a deep foundation element, the concrete shall be chuted directly into smooth-sided pipes or tubes or placed in a rapid and continuous operation through a funnel hopper centered at the top of the element.

1808.8.4 Protection of concrete. Concrete foundations shall be protected from freezing during depositing and for a period of not less than five days thereafter. Water shall not be allowed to flow through the deposited concrete.

1808.8.5 Forming of concrete. Concrete foundations are permitted to be cast against the earth where, in the opinion of the *building official*, soil conditions do not require formwork. Where formwork is required, it shall be in accordance with Chapter 6 of ACI 318.

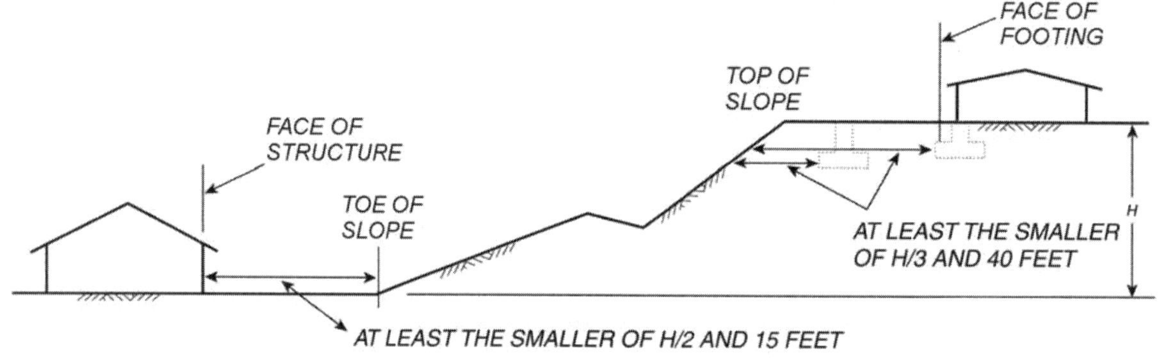

For SI: 1 foot = 304.8 mm.

FIGURE 1808.7.1
FOUNDATION CLEARANCES FROM SLOPES

TABLE 1808.8.1
MINIMUM SPECIFIED COMPRESSIVE STRENGTH f'_c OF CONCRETE OR GROUT

FOUNDATION ELEMENT OR CONDITION	SPECIFIED COMPRESSIVE STRENGTH, f'_c
1. Foundations for structures assigned to Seismic Design Category A, B or C	2,500 psi
2a. Foundations for Group R or U occupancies of light-frame construction, two stories or less in height, assigned to Seismic Design Category D, E or F	2,500 psi
2b. Foundations for other structures assigned to Seismic Design Category D, E or F	3,000 psi
3. Precast nonprestressed driven piles	4,000 psi
4. Socketed drilled shafts	4,000 psi
5. Micropiles	4,000 psi
6. Precast prestressed driven piles	5,000 psi

For SI: 1 pound per square inch = 0.00689 MPa.

TABLE 1808.8.2
MINIMUM CONCRETE COVER

FOUNDATION ELEMENT OR CONDITION	MINIMUM COVER
1. Shallow foundations	In accordance with Section 7.7 of ACI 318
2. Precast nonprestressed deep foundation elements Exposed to seawater Not manufactured under plant conditions Manufactured under plant control conditions	 3 inches 2 inches In accordance with Section 7.7.3 of ACI 318
3. Precast prestressed deep foundation elements Exposed to seawater Other	 2.5 inches In accordance with Section 7.7.3 of ACI 318
4. Cast-in-place deep foundation elements not enclosed by a steel pipe, tube or permanent casing	2.5 inches
5. Cast-in-place deep foundation elements enclosed by a steel pipe, tube or permanent casing	1 inch
6. Structural steel core within a steel pipe, tube or permanent casing	2 inches
7. Cast-in-place drilled shafts enclosed by a stable rock socket	1.5 inches

For SI: 1 inch = 25.4 mm.

1808.8.6 Seismic requirements. See Section 1908 for additional requirements for foundations of structures assigned to *Seismic Design Category* C, D, E or F.

For structures assigned to *Seismic Design Category* D, E or F, provisions of ACI 318, Sections 21.12.1 through 21.12.4, shall apply where not in conflict with the provisions of Sections 1808 through 1810.

Exceptions:

1. Detached one- and two-family dwellings of light-frame construction and two stories or less above *grade plane* are not required to comply with the provisions of ACI 318, Sections 21.12.1 through 21.12.4.
2. Section 21.12.4.4(a) of ACI 318 shall not apply.

1808.9 Vertical masonry foundation elements. Vertical masonry foundation elements that are not foundation piers as defined in Section 2102.1 shall be designed as piers, walls or columns, as applicable, in accordance with TMS 402/ACI 530/ASCE 5.

SECTION 1809
SHALLOW FOUNDATIONS

1809.1 General. Shallow foundations shall be designed and constructed in accordance with Sections 1809.2 through 1809.13.

1809.2 Supporting soils. Shallow foundations shall be built on undisturbed soil, compacted fill material or controlled low-strength material (CLSM). Compacted fill material shall be placed in accordance with Section 1804.5. CLSM shall be placed in accordance with Section 1804.6.

1809.3 Stepped footings. The top surface of footings shall be level. The bottom surface of footings shall be permitted to have a slope not exceeding one unit vertical in 10 units horizontal (10-percent slope). Footings shall be stepped where it is necessary to change the elevation of the top surface of the footing or where the surface of the ground slopes more than one unit vertical in 10 units horizontal (10-percent slope).

1809.4 Depth and width of footings. The minimum depth of footings below the undisturbed ground surface shall be 12 inches (305 mm). Where applicable, the requirements of Section 1809.5 shall also be satisfied. The minimum width of footings shall be 16 inches (406 mm). Minimum width of turned down slabs shall be 12 inches (305 mm) unless engineering analysis is provided.

1809.5 Frost protection. Except where otherwise protected from frost, foundations and other permanent supports of buildings and structures shall be protected from frost by one or more of the following methods:

1. Extending below the frost line of the locality;
2. Constructing in accordance with ASCE 32; or
3. Erecting on solid rock.

Exception: Free-standing buildings meeting all of the following conditions shall not be required to be protected:

1. Assigned to *Occupancy Category* I, in accordance with Section 1604.5;
2. Area of 600 square feet (56 m^2) or less for light-frame construction or 400 square feet (37 m^2) or less for other than light-frame construction; and
3. Eave height of 10 feet (3048 mm) or less.

Shallow foundations shall not bear on frozen soil unless such frozen condition is of a permanent character.

1809.6 Location of footings. Footings on granular soil shall be so located that the line drawn between the lower edges of adjoining footings shall not have a slope steeper than 30 degrees (0.52 rad) with the horizontal, unless the material supporting the higher footing is braced or retained or otherwise laterally supported in an *approved* manner or a greater slope has been properly established by engineering analysis.

1809.7 Prescriptive footings for light-frame construction. Where a specific design is not provided, concrete or masonry-unit footings supporting walls of light-frame construction shall be permitted to be designed in accordance with Table 1809.7.

TABLE 1809.7
PRESCRIPTIVE FOOTINGS SUPPORTING WALLS OF LIGHT-FRAME CONSTRUCTION[a, b, c, d, e]

NUMBER OF FLOORS SUPPORTED BY THE FOOTING[f]	WIDTH OF FOOTING (inches)	THICKNESS OF FOOTING (inches)
1	16	6
2	16	6
3	18	8[g]

For SI: 1 inch = 25.4 mm, 1 foot = 304.8 mm.

a. Depth of footings shall be in accordance with Section 1809.4.
b. The ground under the floor shall be permitted to be excavated to the elevation of the top of the footing.
c. Interior stud-bearing walls shall be permitted to be supported by isolated footings. The footing width and length shall be twice the width shown in this table, and footings shall be spaced not more than 6 feet on center.
d. See Section 1908 for additional requirements for concrete footings of structures assigned to Seismic Design Category C, D, E or F.
e. For thickness of foundation walls, see Section 1807.1.6.
f. Footings shall be permitted to support a roof in addition to the stipulated number of floors. Footings supporting roof only shall be as required for supporting one floor.
g. Plain concrete footings for Group R-3 occupancies shall be permitted to be 6 inches thick.

1809.8 Plain concrete footings. The edge thickness of plain concrete footings supporting walls of other than light-frame construction shall not be less than 8 inches (203 mm) where placed on soil or rock.

Exception: For plain concrete footings supporting Group R-3 occupancies, the edge thickness is permitted to be 6 inches (152 mm), provided that the footing does not extend beyond a distance greater than the thickness of the footing on either side of the supported wall.

1809.9 Masonry-unit footings. The design, materials and construction of masonry-unit footings shall comply with Sections 1809.9.1 and 1809.9.2, and the provisions of Chapter 21.

Exception: Where a specific design is not provided, masonry-unit footings supporting walls of light-frame construction shall be permitted to be designed in accordance with Table 1809.7.

1809.9.1 Dimensions. Masonry-unit footings shall be laid in Type M or S mortar complying with Section 2103.8 and the depth shall not be less than twice the projection beyond the wall, pier or column. The width shall not be less than 8 inches (203 mm) wider than the wall supported thereon.

1809.9.2 Offsets. The maximum offset of each course in brick foundation walls stepped up from the footings shall be $1^1/_2$ inches (38 mm) where laid in single courses, and 3 inches (76 mm) where laid in double courses.

1809.10 Pier and curtain wall foundations. Except in *Seismic Design Categories* D, E and F, pier and curtain wall foundations shall be permitted to be used to support light-frame construction not more than two *stories above grade plane*, provided the following requirements are met:

1. All load-bearing walls shall be placed on continuous concrete footings bonded integrally with the *exterior wall* footings.
2. The minimum actual thickness of a load-bearing masonry wall shall not be less than 4 inches (102 mm) nominal or $3^5/_8$ inches (92 mm) actual thickness, and shall be bonded integrally with piers spaced 6 feet (1829 mm) on center (o.c.).
3. Piers shall be constructed in accordance with Chapter 21 and the following:
    - 3.1. The unsupported height of the masonry piers shall not exceed 10 times their least dimension.
    - 3.2. Where structural clay tile or hollow concrete masonry units are used for piers supporting beams and girders, the cellular spaces shall be filled solidly with concrete or Type M or S mortar.

    Exception: Unfilled hollow piers shall be permitted where the unsupported height of the pier is not more than four times its least dimension.

    - 3.3. Hollow piers shall be capped with 4 inches (102 mm) of solid masonry or concrete or the cavities of the top course shall be filled with concrete or grout.
4. The maximum height of a 4-inch (102 mm) load-bearing masonry foundation wall supporting wood frame walls and floors shall not be more than 4 feet (1219 mm) in height.
5. The unbalanced fill for 4-inch (102 mm) foundation walls shall not exceed 24 inches (610 mm) for solid masonry, nor 12 inches (305 mm) for hollow masonry.

1809.11 Steel grillage footings. Grillage footings of structural steel shapes shall be separated with *approved* steel spacers and be entirely encased in concrete with at least 6 inches (152 mm) on the bottom and at least 4 inches (102 mm) at all other points. The spaces between the shapes shall be completely filled with concrete or cement grout.

1809.12 Timber footings. Timber footings shall be permitted for buildings of Type V construction and as otherwise *approved* by the *building official*. Such footings shall be treated in accordance with AWPA U1 (Commodity Specification A, Use Category 4B). Treated timbers are not required where placed entirely below permanent water level, or where used as capping for wood piles that project above the water level over submerged or marsh lands. The compressive stresses perpendicular to grain in untreated timber footings supported upon treated piles shall not exceed 70 percent of the allowable stresses for the species and grade of timber as specified in the AF&PA NDS.

1809.13 Footing seismic ties. Where a structure is assigned to *Seismic Design Category* D, E or F in accordance with Section 1613, individual spread footings founded on soil defined in Section 1613.5.2 as *Site Class* E or F shall be interconnected by ties. Unless it is demonstrated that equivalent restraint is provided by reinforced concrete beams within slabs on grade or reinforced concrete slabs on grade, ties shall be capable of carrying, in tension or compression, a force equal to the lesser of the product of the larger footing design gravity load times the seismic coefficient, S_{DS}, divided by 10 and 25 percent of the smaller footing design gravity load.

SECTION 1810
DEEP FOUNDATIONS

1810.1 General. Deep foundations shall be analyzed, designed, detailed and installed in accordance with Sections 1810.1 through 1810.4.

1810.1.1 Geotechnical investigation. Deep foundations shall be designed and installed on the basis of a geotechnical investigation as set forth in Section 1803.

1810.1.2 Use of existing deep foundation elements. Deep foundation elements left in place where a structure has been demolished shall not be used for the support of new construction unless satisfactory evidence is submitted to the *building official*, which indicates that the elements are sound and meet the requirements of this code. Such elements shall be load tested or redriven to verify their capacities. The design load applied to such elements shall be the lowest allowable load as determined by tests or redriving data.

1810.1.3 Deep foundation elements classified as columns. Deep foundation elements standing unbraced in air, water or fluid soils shall be classified as columns and designed as such in accordance with the provisions of this code from their top down to the point where adequate lateral support is provided in accordance with Section 1810.2.1.

Exception: Where the unsupported height to least horizontal dimension of a cast-in-place deep foundation element does not exceed three, it shall be permitted to design and construct such an element as a pedestal in accordance with ACI 318.

1810.1.4 Special types of deep foundations. The use of types of deep foundation elements not specifically mentioned herein is permitted, subject to the approval of the *building official*, upon the submission of acceptable test data, calculations and other information relating to the structural properties and load capacity of such elements.

The allowable stresses for materials shall not in any case exceed the limitations specified herein.

1810.2 Analysis. The analysis of deep foundations for design shall be in accordance with Sections 1810.2.1 through 1810.2.5.

1810.2.1 Lateral support. Any soil other than fluid soil shall be deemed to afford sufficient lateral support to prevent buckling of deep foundation elements and to permit the design of the elements in accordance with accepted engineering practice and the applicable provisions of this code.

Where deep foundation elements stand unbraced in air, water or fluid soils, it shall be permitted to consider them laterally supported at a point 5 feet (1524 mm) into stiff soil or 10 feet (3048 mm) into soft soil unless otherwise *approved* by the *building official* on the basis of a geotechnical investigation by a *registered design professional*.

1810.2.2 Stability. Deep foundation elements shall be braced to provide lateral stability in all directions. Three or more elements connected by a rigid cap shall be considered braced, provided that the elements are located in radial directions from the centroid of the group not less than 60 degrees (1 rad) apart. A two-element group in a rigid cap shall be considered to be braced along the axis connecting the two elements. Methods used to brace deep foundation elements shall be subject to the approval of the *building official*.

Deep foundation elements supporting walls shall be placed alternately in lines spaced at least 1 foot (305 mm) apart and located symmetrically under the center of gravity of the wall load carried, unless effective measures are taken to provide for eccentricity and lateral forces, or the foundation elements are adequately braced to provide for lateral stability.

Exceptions:

1. Isolated cast-in-place deep foundation elements without lateral bracing shall be permitted where the least horizontal dimension is no less than 2 feet (610 mm), adequate lateral support in accordance with Section 1810.2.1 is provided for the entire height and the height does not exceed 12 times the least horizontal dimension.
2. Deleted.

1810.2.3 Settlement. The settlement of a single deep foundation element or group thereof shall be estimated based on *approved* methods of analysis. The predicted settlement shall cause neither harmful distortion of, nor instability in, the structure, nor cause any element to be loaded beyond its capacity.

1810.2.4 Lateral loads. The moments, shears and lateral deflections used for design of deep foundation elements shall be established considering the nonlinear interaction of the shaft and soil, as determined by a *registered design professional*. Where the ratio of the depth of embedment of the element to its least horizontal dimension is less than or equal to six, it shall be permitted to assume the element is rigid.

1810.2.4.1 Seismic Design Categories D through F. For structures assigned to *Seismic Design Category* D, E or F, deep foundation elements on *Site Class* E or F sites, as determined in Section 1613.5.2, shall be designed and constructed to withstand maximum imposed curvatures from earthquake ground motions and structure response. Curvatures shall include free-field soil strains modified for soil-foundation-structure interaction coupled with foundation element deformations associated with earthquake loads imparted to the foundation by the structure.

Exception: Deep foundation elements that satisfy the following additional detailing requirements shall be deemed to comply with the curvature capacity requirements of this section.

1. Precast prestressed concrete piles detailed in accordance with Section 1810.3.8.3.3.
2. Cast-in-place deep foundation elements with a minimum longitudinal reinforcement ratio of 0.005 extending the full length of the element and detailed in accordance with Sections 21.6.4.2, 21.6.4.3 and 21.6.4.4 of ACI 318 as required by Section 1810.3.9.4.2.2.

1810.2.5 Group effects. The analysis shall include group effects on lateral behavior where the center-to-center spacing of deep foundation elements in the direction of lateral force is less than eight times the least horizontal dimension of an element. The analysis shall include group effects on axial behavior where the center-to-center spacing of deep foundation elements is less than three times the least horizontal dimension of an element.

1810.3 Design and detailing. Deep foundations shall be designed and detailed in accordance with Sections 1810.3.1 through 1810.3.12.

1810.3.1 Design conditions. Design of deep foundations shall include the design conditions specified in Sections 1810.3.1.1 through 1810.3.1.6, as applicable.

1810.3.1.1 Design methods for concrete elements. Where concrete deep foundations are laterally supported in accordance with Section 1810.2.1 for the entire height and applied forces cause bending moments no greater than those resulting from accidental eccentricities, structural design of the element using the load combinations of Section 1605.3 and the allowable stresses specified in this chapter shall be permitted. Otherwise, the structural design of concrete deep foundation elements shall use the load combinations of Section 1605.2 and *approved* strength design methods.

1810.3.1.2 Composite elements. Where a single deep foundation element comprises two or more sections of different materials or different types spliced together, each section of the composite assembly shall satisfy the applicable requirements of this code, and the maximum allowable load in each section shall be limited by the structural capacity of that section.

1810.3.1.3 Mislocation. The foundation or superstructure shall be designed to resist the effects of the mislocation of any deep foundation element by no less than 3 inches (76 mm). To resist the effects of mislocation, compressive overload of deep foundation elements to 110 percent of the allowable design load shall be permitted.

1810.3.1.4 Driven piles. Driven piles shall be designed and manufactured in accordance with accepted engineering practice to resist all stresses induced by handling, driving and service loads.

1810.3.1.5 Helical piles. Helical piles shall be designed and manufactured in accordance with accepted engineering practice to resist all stresses induced by installation into the ground and service loads.

1810.3.1.6 Casings. Temporary and permanent casings shall be of steel and shall be sufficiently strong to resist collapse and sufficiently water tight to exclude any foreign materials during the placing of concrete. Where a permanent casing is considered reinforcing steel, the steel shall be protected under the conditions specified in Section 1810.3.2.5. Horizontal joints in the casing shall be spliced in accordance with Section 1810.3.6.

1810.3.2 Materials. The materials used in deep foundation elements shall satisfy the requirements of Sections 1810.3.2.1 through 1810.3.2.8, as applicable.

1810.3.2.1 Concrete. Where concrete is cast in a steel pipe or where an enlarged base is formed by compacting concrete, the maximum size for coarse aggregate shall be $^3/_4$ inch (19.1 mm). Concrete to be compacted shall have a zero slump.

1810.3.2.1.1 Seismic hooks. For structures assigned to *Seismic Design Category* C, D, E or F in accordance with Section 1613, the ends of hoops, spirals and ties used in concrete deep foundation elements shall be terminated with seismic hooks, as defined in ACI 318, and shall be turned into the confined concrete core.

1810.3.2.1.2 ACI 318 Equation (10-5). Where this chapter requires detailing of concrete deep foundation elements in accordance with Section 21.6.4.4 of ACI 318, compliance with Equation (10-5) of ACI 318 shall not be required.

1810.3.2.2 Prestressing steel. Prestressing steel shall conform to ASTM A 416.

1810.3.2.3 Structural steel. Structural steel piles, steel pipe and fully welded steel piles fabricated from plates shall conform to ASTM A 36, ASTM A 252, ASTM A 283, ASTM A 572, ASTM A 588, ASTM A 690, ASTM A 913 or ASTM A 992.

1810.3.2.4 Timber. Timber deep foundation elements shall be designed as piles or poles in accordance with AF&PA NDS. Round timber elements shall conform to ASTM D 25. Sawn timber elements shall conform to DOC PS-20.

1810.3.2.4.1 Preservative treatment. Timber deep foundation elements used to support permanent structures shall be treated in accordance with this section unless it is established that the tops of the untreated timber elements will be below the lowest ground-water level assumed to exist during the life of the structure. Preservative and minimum final retention shall be in accordance with AWPA U1 (Commodity Specification E, Use Category 4C) for round timber elements and AWPA U1 (Commodity Specification A, Use Category 4B) for sawn timber elements. Preservative-treated timber elements shall be subject to a quality control program administered by an *approved agency*. Element cutoffs shall be treated in accordance with AWPA M4.

1810.3.2.5 Protection of materials. Where boring records or site conditions indicate possible deleterious action on the materials used in deep foundation elements because of soil constituents, changing water levels or other factors, the elements shall be adequately protected by materials, methods or processes *approved* by the *building official*. Protective materials shall be applied to the elements so as not to be rendered ineffective by installation. The effectiveness of such protective measures for the particular purpose shall have been thoroughly established by satisfactory service records or other evidence.

1810.3.2.6 Allowable stresses. The allowable stresses for materials used in deep foundation elements shall not exceed those specified in Table 1810.3.2.6.

1810.3.2.7 Increased allowable compressive stress for cased cast-in-place elements. The allowable compressive stress in the concrete shall be permitted to be increased as specified in Table 1810.3.2.6 for those portions of permanently cased cast-in-place elements that satisfy all of the following conditions:

1. The design shall not use the casing to resist any portion of the axial load imposed.
2. The casing shall have a sealed tip and be mandrel driven.
3. The thickness of the casing shall not be less than manufacturer's standard gage No. 14 (0.068 inch) (1.75 mm).
4. The casing shall be seamless or provided with seams of strength equal to the basic material and be of a configuration that will provide confinement to the cast-in-place concrete.
5. The ratio of steel yield strength (F_y) to specified compressive strength (f'_c) shall not be less than six.
6. The nominal diameter of the element shall not be greater than 16 inches (406 mm).

1810.3.2.8 Justification of higher allowable stresses. Use of allowable stresses greater than those specified in Section 1810.3.2.6 shall be permitted where supporting data justifying such higher stresses is filed with the *building official*. Such substantiating data shall include:

1. A geotechnical investigation in accordance with Section 1803; and
2. Load tests in accordance with Section 1810.3.3.1.2, regardless of the load supported by the element.

TABLE 1810.3.2.6
ALLOWABLE STRESSES FOR MATERIALS USED IN DEEP FOUNDATION ELEMENTS

MATERIAL TYPE AND CONDITION	MAXIMUM ALLOWABLE STRESS[a]
1. Concrete or grout in compression[b]	
Cast-in-place with a permanent casing in accordance with Section 1810.3.2.7	$0.4 f'_c$
Cast-in-place in a pipe, tube, other permanent casing or rock	$0.33 f'_c$
Cast-in-place without a permanent casing	$0.3 f'_c$
Precast nonprestressed	$0.33 f'_c$
Precast prestressed	$0.33 f'_c - 0.27 f_{pc}$
2. Nonprestressed reinforcement in compression	$0.4 f_y \leq 30{,}000$ psi
3. Structural steel in compression	
Cores within concrete-filled pipes or tubes	$0.5\ F_y \leq 32{,}000$ psi
Pipes, tubes or H-piles, where justified in accordance with Section 1810.3.2.8	$0.5\ F_y \leq 32{,}000$ psi
Pipes or tubes for micropiles	$0.4\ F_y \leq 32{,}000$ psi
Other pipes, tubes or H-piles	$0.35\ F_y \leq 16{,}000$ psi
Helical piles	$0.6\ F_y \leq 0.5\ F_u$
4. Nonprestressed reinforcement in tension	
Within micropiles	$0.6 f_y$
Other conditions	$0.5 f_y \leq 24{,}000$ psi
5. Structural steel in tension	
Pipes, tubes or H-piles, where justified in accordance with Section 1810.3.2.8	$0.5\ F_y \leq 32{,}000$ psi
Other pipes, tubes or H-piles	$0.35\ F_y \leq 16{,}000$ psi
Helical piles	$0.6\ F_y \leq 0.5\ F_u$
6. Timber	In accordance with the AF&PA NDS

For SI: 1 pound per square inch = 6.895 kPa.

a. f'_c is the specified compressive strength of the concrete or grout; f_{pc} is the compressive stress on the gross concrete section due to effective prestress forces only; f_y is the specified yield strength of reinforcement; F_y is the specified minimum yield stress of structural steel; F_u is the specified minimum tensile stress of structural steel.

b. The stresses specified apply to the gross cross-sectional area within the concrete surface. Where a temporary or permanent casing is used, the inside face of the casing shall be considered the concrete surface.

The design and installation of the deep foundation elements shall be under the direct supervision of a *registered design professional* knowledgeable in the field of soil mechanics and deep foundations who shall submit a report to the *building official* stating that the elements as installed satisfy the design criteria.

1810.3.3 Determination of allowable loads. The allowable axial and lateral loads on deep foundation elements shall be determined by an *approved* formula, load tests or method of analysis.

1810.3.3.1 Allowable axial load. The allowable axial load on a deep foundation element shall be determined in accordance with Sections 1810.3.3.1.1 through 1810.3.3.1.9.

1810.3.3.1.1 Driving criteria. The allowable compressive load on any driven deep foundation element where determined by the application of an *approved* driving formula shall not exceed 40 tons (356 kN). For allowable loads above 40 tons (356 kN), the wave equation method of analysis shall be used to estimate driveability for both driving stresses and net displacement per blow at the ultimate load. Allowable loads shall be verified by load tests in accordance with Section 1810.3.3.1.2. The formula or wave equation load shall be determined for gravity-drop or power-actuated hammers and the hammer energy used shall be the maximum consistent with the size, strength and weight of the driven elements. The use of a follower is permitted only with the approval of the *building official*. The introduction of fresh hammer cushion or pile cushion material just prior to final penetration is not permitted.

1810.3.3.1.2 Load tests. Where design compressive loads are greater than those determined using the allowable stresses specified in Section 1810.3.2.6, where the design load for any deep foundation element is in doubt, or where cast-in-place deep foundation elements have an enlarged base formed either by compacting concrete or by driving a precast base, control test elements shall be tested in accordance with ASTM D 1143 or ASTM D 4945. At least one element shall be load tested in each area of uniform subsoil conditions. Where required by the *building official*, additional elements shall be load tested where necessary to establish the safe design capacity. The resulting allowable loads shall not be more than one-half of the ultimate axial load capacity of the test element as assessed by one of the published methods listed in Section 1810.3.3.1.3 with consideration for the test type, duration and subsoil. The ultimate axial load capacity shall be determined by a *registered design professional* with consideration given to tolerable total and differential settlements at design load in accordance with Section 1810.2.3. In subsequent installation of the balance of deep foundation elements, all elements shall be deemed to have a supporting capacity equal to that of the control element where such elements are of the same type, size and relative length as the test element; are installed using the same or comparable methods and equipment as the test element; are installed in similar subsoil conditions as the test element; and, for driven elements, where the rate of penetration (e.g., net displacement per blow) of such elements is equal to or less than that of the test element driven with the same hammer through a comparable driving distance.

1810.3.3.1.3 Load test evaluation methods. It shall be permitted to evaluate load tests of deep foundation elements using any of the following methods:

1. Davisson Offset Limit.
2. Brinch-Hansen 90% Criterion.
3. Butler-Hoy Criterion.
4. Other methods *approved* by the *building official*.

1810.3.3.1.4 Allowable frictional resistance. The assumed frictional resistance developed by any uncased cast-in-place deep foundation element shall not exceed one-sixth of the bearing value of the soil material at minimum depth as set forth in Table 1806.2, up to a maximum of 500 psf (24 kPa), unless a greater value is allowed by the *building official* on the basis of a geotechnical investigation as specified in Section 1803 or a greater value is substantiated by a load test in accordance with Section 1810.3.3.1.2. Frictional resistance and bearing resistance shall not be assumed to act simultaneously unless determined by a geotechnical investigation in accordance with Section 1803.

1810.3.3.1.5 Uplift capacity of a single deep foundation element. Where required by the design, the uplift capacity of a single deep foundation element shall be determined by an *approved* method of analysis based on a minimum factor of safety of three or by load tests conducted in accordance with ASTM D 3689. The maximum allowable uplift load shall not exceed the ultimate load capacity as determined in Section 1810.3.3.1.2, using the results of load tests conducted in accordance with ASTM D 3689, divided by a factor of safety of two.

> **Exception:** Where uplift is due to wind or seismic loading, the minimum factor of safety shall be two where capacity is determined by an analysis and one and one-half where capacity is determined by load tests.

1810.3.3.1.6 Uplift capacity of grouped deep foundation elements. For grouped deep foundation elements subjected to uplift, the allowable working uplift load for the group shall be calculated by an *approved* method of analysis. Where the deep foundation elements in the group are placed at a center-to-center spacing of at least 2.5 times the least horizontal dimension of the largest single element, the allowable working uplift load for the group is permitted to be calculated as the lesser of:

1. The proposed individual uplift working load times the number of elements in the group.
2. Two-thirds of the effective weight of the group and the soil contained within a block defined by the perimeter of the group and the length of the element.

1810.3.3.1.7 Load-bearing capacity. Deep foundation elements shall develop ultimate load capacities of at least twice the design working loads in the designated load-bearing layers. Analysis shall show that no soil layer underlying the designated load-bearing layers causes the load-bearing capacity safety factor to be less than two.

1810.3.3.1.8 Bent deep foundation elements. The load-bearing capacity of deep foundation elements discovered to have a sharp or sweeping bend shall be determined by an *approved* method of analysis or by load testing a representative element.

1810.3.3.1.9 Helical piles. The allowable axial design load, P_a, of helical piles shall be determined as follows:

$$P_a = 0.5\,P_u \qquad \textbf{(Equation 18-4)}$$

where P_u is the least value of:

1. Sum of the areas of the helical bearing plates times the ultimate bearing capacity of the soil or rock comprising the bearing stratum.
2. Ultimate capacity determined from well-documented correlations with installation torque.
3. Ultimate capacity determined from load tests.
4. Ultimate axial capacity of pile shaft.
5. Ultimate axial capacity of pile shaft couplings.
6. Sum of the ultimate axial capacity of helical bearing plates affixed to pile.

1810.3.3.2 Allowable lateral load. Where required by the design, the lateral load capacity of a single deep foundation element or a group thereof shall be determined by an *approved* method of analysis or by lateral load tests to at least twice the proposed design working load. The resulting allowable load shall not be more than one-half of the load that produces a gross lateral movement of 1 inch (25 mm) at the lower of the top of foundation element and the ground surface, unless it can be shown that the predicted lateral movement shall cause neither harmful distortion of, nor instability in, the structure, nor cause any element to be loaded beyond its capacity.

1810.3.4 Subsiding soils. Where deep foundation elements are installed through subsiding fills or other subsiding strata and derive support from underlying firmer materials, consideration shall be given to the downward frictional forces that may be imposed on the elements by the subsiding upper strata.

Where the influence of subsiding fills is considered as imposing loads on the element, the allowable stresses specified in this chapter shall be permitted to be increased where satisfactory substantiating data are submitted.

1810.3.5 Dimensions of deep foundation elements. The dimensions of deep foundation elements shall be in accordance with Sections 1810.3.5.1 through 1810.3.5.3, as applicable.

1810.3.5.1 Precast. The minimum lateral dimension of precast concrete deep foundation elements shall be 8 inches (203 mm). Corners of square elements shall be chamfered.

1810.3.5.2 Cast-in-place or grouted-in-place. Cast-in-place and grouted-in-place deep foundation elements shall satisfy the requirements of this section.

1810.3.5.2.1 Cased. Cast-in-place deep foundation elements with a permanent casing shall have a nominal outside diameter of not less than 8 inches (203 mm).

1810.3.5.2.2 Uncased. Cast-in-place deep foundation elements without a permanent casing shall have a diameter of not less than 12 inches (305 mm). The element length shall not exceed 30 times the average diameter.

Exception: The length of the element is permitted to exceed 30 times the diameter, provided the design and installation of the deep foundations are under the direct supervision of a *registered design professional* knowledgeable in the field of soil mechanics and deep foundations. The *registered design professional* shall submit a report to the *building official* stating that the elements were installed in compliance with the *approved construction documents*.

1810.3.5.2.3 Micropiles. Micropiles shall have an outside diameter of 12 inches (305 mm) or less. The minimum diameter set forth elsewhere in Section 1810.3.5 shall not apply to micropiles.

1810.3.5.2.4 Pile test. A pile load test shall be performed if 400 psi (2758 kPa) shaft stress is exceeded. The pile load test shall be in accordance with Section 1810.3.3.1.2.

1810.3.5.2.5 Quality control. For piles having a shaft stress exceeding 400 psi (2758 kPa), the following quality control procedures shall be met:

1. Calibrate pile installation equipment to accurately measure grout volumes and pressure prior to test pile installation. This calibration shall be expressed in cubic feet per pump stroke.
2. Document the amount of grout injected into the test pile by recording the number of pump strokes per linear foot or number of pump strokes per 5 linear foot (1524 mm) section.
3. Subject the installation procedures to a static load test in accordance with ASTM D 1143.
4. If the load test is successful, ensure that each production pile is installed using the same procedure that installed the successful test pile.
5. A *registered design professional* shall certify to the code enforcement official that all pilings were installed in accordance with the *approved* design and tested installation procedure. The *registered design professional* shall be prepared to submit upon request a report showing the following information:
   - 5.1. Pile identification;
   - 5.2. Pile length;
   - 5.3. Date;
   - 5.4. Rate of auger withdrawal (grouting time); and
   - 5.5. Grout volume in cubic feet per linear foot or cubic feet per 5 foot (1524 mm) section.

1810.3.5.3 Steel. Steel deep foundation elements shall satisfy the requirements of this section.

1810.3.5.3.1 H-piles. Sections of H-piles shall comply with the following:

1. The flange projections shall not exceed 14 times the minimum thickness of metal in either the flange or the web and the flange widths shall not be less than 80 percent of the depth of the section.
2. The nominal depth in the direction of the web shall not be less than 8 inches (203 mm).
3. Flanges and web shall have a minimum nominal thickness of $^3/_8$ inch (9.5 mm).

1810.3.5.3.2 Steel pipes and tubes. Steel pipes and tubes used as deep foundation elements shall have a nominal outside diameter of not less than 8 inches (203 mm). Where steel pipes or tubes are driven open ended, they shall have a minimum of 0.34 square inch (219 mm^2) of steel in cross section to resist each 1,000 foot-pounds (1356 Nm) of pile hammer energy, or shall have the equivalent strength for steels having a yield strength greater than 35,000 psi (241 MPa) or the wave equation analysis shall be permitted to be used to assess compression stresses induced by driving to evaluate if the pile section is appropriate for the selected hammer. Where a pipe or tube with wall thickness less than 0.179 inch (4.6 mm) is driven open ended, a suitable cutting shoe shall be provided. Concrete-filled steel pipes or tubes in structures assigned to *Seismic Design Category* C, D, E or F shall have a wall thickness of not less than $^3/_{16}$ inch (5 mm). The pipe or tube casing for socketed drilled shafts shall have a nominal outside diameter of not less than 18 inches (457 mm), a wall thickness of not less than $^3/_8$ inch (9.5 mm) and a suitable steel driving shoe welded to the bottom; the diameter of the rock socket shall be approximately equal to the inside diameter of the casing.

Exceptions:

1. There is no minimum diameter for steel pipes or tubes used in micropiles.
2. For mandrel-driven pipes or tubes, the minimum wall thickness shall be $^1/_{10}$ inch (2.5 mm).

1810.3.5.3.3 Helical piles. Dimensions of the central shaft and the number, size and thickness of helical bearing plates shall be sufficient to support the design loads.

1810.3.6 Splices. Splices shall be constructed so as to provide and maintain true alignment and position of the component parts of the deep foundation element during installation and subsequent thereto and shall be designed to resist the axial and shear forces and moments occurring at the location of the splice during driving and for design load combinations. Where deep foundation elements of the same type are being spliced, splices shall develop not less than 50 percent of the bending strength of the weaker section. Where deep foundation elements of different materials or different types are being spliced, splices shall develop the full compressive strength and not less than 50 percent of the tension and bending strength of the weaker section. Where structural steel cores are to be spliced, the ends shall be milled or ground to provide full contact and shall be full-depth welded.

Splices occurring in the upper 10 feet (3048 mm) of the embedded portion of an element shall be designed to resist at allowable stresses the moment and shear that would result from an assumed eccentricity of the axial load of 3 inches (76 mm), or the element shall be braced in accordance with Section 1810.2.2 to other deep foundation elements that do not have splices in the upper 10 feet (3048 mm) of embedment.

1810.3.6.1 Seismic Design Categories C through F. For structures assigned to *Seismic Design Category* C, D, E or F splices of deep foundation elements shall develop the lesser of the following:

1. The full strength of the deep foundation element; and
2. The axial and shear forces and moments from the load combinations with overstrength factor in Section 12.4.3.2 of ASCE 7.

1810.3.7 Top of element detailing at cutoffs. Where a minimum length for reinforcement or the extent of closely spaced confinement reinforcement is specified at the top of a deep foundation element, provisions shall be made so that those specified lengths or extents are maintained after cutoff.

1810.3.8 Precast concrete piles. Precast concrete piles shall be designed and detailed in accordance with Sections 1810.3.8.1 through 1810.3.8.3.

1810.3.8.1 Reinforcement. Longitudinal steel shall be arranged in a symmetrical pattern and be laterally tied with steel ties or wire spiral spaced center to center as follows:

1. At not more than 1 inch (25 mm) for the first five ties or spirals at each end; then
2. At not more than 4 inches (102 mm), for the remainder of the first 2 feet (610 mm) from each end; and then
3. At not more than 6 inches (152 mm) elsewhere.

The size of ties and spirals shall be as follows:

1. For piles having a least horizontal dimension of 16 inches (406 mm) or less, wire shall not be smaller than 0.22 inch (5.6 mm) (No. 5 gage).
2. For piles having a least horizontal dimension of more than 16 inches (406 mm) and less than 20 inches (508 mm), wire shall not be smaller than 0.238 inch (6 mm) (No. 4 gage).
3. For piles having a least horizontal dimension of 20 inches (508 mm) and larger, wire shall not be smaller than $^1/_4$ inch (6.4 mm) round or 0.259 inch (6.6 mm) (No. 3 gage).

1810.3.8.2 Precast nonprestressed piles. Precast nonprestressed concrete piles shall comply with the requirements of Sections 1810.3.8.2.1 through 1810.3.8.2.3.

1810.3.8.2.1 Minimum reinforcement. Longitudinal reinforcement shall consist of at least four bars with a minimum longitudinal reinforcement ratio of 0.008.

1810.3.8.2.2 Seismic reinforcement in Seismic Design Categories C through F. For structures assigned to *Seismic Design Category* C, D, E or F in accordance with Section 1613, precast nonprestressed piles shall be reinforced as specified in this section. The minimum longitudinal reinforcement ratio shall be 0.01 throughout the length. Transverse reinforcement shall consist of closed ties or spirals with a minimum $^3/_8$ inch (9.5 mm) diameter. Spacing of transverse reinforcement shall not exceed the smaller of eight times the diameter of the smallest longitudinal bar or 6 inches (152 mm) within a distance of three times the least pile dimension from the bottom of the pile cap. Spacing of transverse reinforcement shall not exceed 6 inches (152 mm) throughout the remainder of the pile.

1810.3.8.2.3 Additional seismic reinforcement in Seismic Design Categories D through F. For structures assigned to *Seismic Design Category* D, E or F in accordance with Section 1613, transverse reinforcement shall be in accordance with Section 1810.3.9.4.2.

1810.3.8.3 Precast prestressed piles. Precast prestressed concrete piles shall comply with the requirements of Sections 1810.3.8.3.1 through 1810.3.8.3.3.

1810.3.8.3.1 Effective prestress. The effective prestress in the pile shall not be less than 400 psi (2.76 MPa) for piles up to 30 feet (9144 mm) in length, 550 psi (3.79 MPa) for piles up to 50 feet (15 240 mm) in length and 700 psi (4.83 MPa) for piles greater than 50 feet (15 240 mm) in length.

Effective prestress shall be based on an assumed loss of 30,000 psi (207 MPa) in the prestressing steel. The tensile stress in the prestressing steel shall not exceed the values specified in ACI 318.

1810.3.8.3.2 Seismic reinforcement in Seismic Design Category C. For structures assigned to *Seismic Design Category* C in accordance with Section 1613, precast prestressed piles shall have transverse reinforcement in accordance with this section. The volumetric ratio of spiral reinforcement shall not be less than the amount required by the following formula for the upper 20 feet (6096 mm) of the pile.

$$\rho_s = 0.12 f'_c / f_{yh}$$ **(Equation 18-5)**

where:

f'_c = Specified compressive strength of concrete, psi (MPa).

f_{yh} = Yield strength of spiral reinforcement $\leq$ 85,000 psi (586 MPa).

ρ_s = Spiral reinforcement index (vol. spiral/vol. core).

At least one-half the volumetric ratio required by Equation 18-5 shall be provided below the upper 20 feet (6096 mm) of the pile.

1810.3.8.3.3 Seismic reinforcement in Seismic Design Categories D through F. For structures assigned to *Seismic Design Category* D, E or F in accordance with Section 1613, precast prestressed piles shall have transverse reinforcement in accordance with the following:

1. Requirements in ACI 318, Chapter 21, need not apply, unless specifically referenced.
2. Where the total pile length in the soil is 35 feet (10 668 mm) or less, the lateral transverse reinforcement in the ductile region shall occur through the length of the pile. Where the pile length exceeds 35 feet (10 668 mm), the ductile pile region shall be taken as the greater of 35 feet (10 668 mm) or the distance from the underside of the pile cap to the point of zero curvature plus three times the least pile dimension.
3. In the ductile region, the center-to-center spacing of the spirals or hoop reinforcement shall not exceed one-fifth of the least pile dimension, six times the diameter of the longitudinal strand or 8 inches (203 mm), whichever is smallest.
4. Circular spiral reinforcement shall be spliced by lapping one full turn and bending the end of each spiral to a 90-degree hook or by use of a mechanical or welded splice complying with Section 12.14.3 of ACI 318.
5. Where the transverse reinforcement consists of circular spirals, the volumetric ratio of spiral transverse reinforcement in the ductile region shall comply with the following:

$$\rho_s = 0.25(f'_c / f_{yh})(A_g / A_{ch} - 1.0)\,[0.5 + 1.4P/(f'_c A_g)]$$

(Equation 18-6)

but not less than:

$$\rho_s = 0.12(f'_c / f_{yh})\,[0.5 + 1.4P/(f'_c A_g)] \geq 0.12 f'_c / f_{yh}$$

(Equation 18-7)

and need not exceed:

$$\rho_s = 0.021$$ **(Equation 18-8)**

where:

A_g = Pile cross-sectional area, square inches (mm^2).

A_{ch} = Core area defined by spiral outside diameter, square inches (mm^2).

f'_c = Specified compressive strength of concrete, psi (MPa).

f_{yh} = Yield strength of spiral reinforcement $\leq$ 85,000 psi (586 MPa).

P = Axial load on pile, pounds (kN), as determined from Equations 16-5 and 16-7.

ρ_s = Volumetric ratio (vol. spiral/ vol. core).

This required amount of spiral reinforcement is permitted to be obtained by providing an inner and outer spiral.

6. Where transverse reinforcement consists of rectangular hoops and cross ties, the total cross-sectional area of lateral transverse reinforcement in the ductile region with spacing, s, and perpendicular dimension, h_c, shall conform to:

$$A_{sh} = 0.3 s\, h_c\,(f'_c / f_{yh})(A_g / A_{ch} - 1.0)\,[0.5 + 1.4P/(f'_c A_g)]$$

(Equation 18-9)

but not less than:

$$A_{sh} = 0.12 s\, h_c\,(f'_c / f_{yh})\,[0.5 + 1.4P/(f'_c A_g)]$$

(Equation 18-10)

where:

f_{yh} = ≤ 70,000 psi (483 MPa).

h_c = Cross-sectional dimension of pile core measured center to center of hoop reinforcement, inch (mm).

s = Spacing of transverse reinforcement measured along length of pile, inch (mm).

A_{sh} = Cross-sectional area of tranverse reinforcement, square inches (mm²).

f'_c = Specified compressive strength of concrete, psi (MPa).

The hoops and cross ties shall be equivalent to deformed bars not less than No. 3 in size. Rectangular hoop ends shall terminate at a corner with seismic hooks.

Outside of the length of the pile requiring transverse confinement reinforcing, the spiral or hoop reinforcing with a volumetric ratio not less than one-half of that required for transverse confinement reinforcing shall be provided.

1810.3.9 Cast-in-place deep foundations. Cast-in-place deep foundation elements shall be designed and detailed in accordance with Sections 1810.3.9.1 through 1810.3.9.6.

1810.3.9.1 Design cracking moment. The design cracking moment (ϕM_n) for a cast-in-place deep foundation element not enclosed by a structural steel pipe or tube shall be determined using the following equation:

$$\phi M_n = 3\sqrt{f'_c} \times S_m \qquad \textbf{(Equation 18-11)}$$

For SI: $\phi M_n = 0.25\sqrt{f'_c} \times S_m$

where:

f'_c = Specified compressive strength of concrete or grout, psi (MPa).

S_m = Elastic section modulus, neglecting reinforcement and casing, cubic inches (mm³).

1810.3.9.2 Required reinforcement. Where subject to uplift or where the required moment strength determined using the load combinations of Section 1605.2 exceeds the design cracking moment determined in accordance with Section 1810.3.9.1, cast-in-place deep foundations not enclosed by a structural steel pipe or tube shall be reinforced.

1810.3.9.3 Placement of reinforcement. Reinforcement where required shall be assembled and tied together and shall be placed in the deep foundation element as a unit before the reinforced portion of the element is filled with concrete.

Exceptions:

1. Steel dowels embedded 5 feet (1524 mm) or less shall be permitted to be placed after concreting, while the concrete is still in a semifluid state.
2. For deep foundation elements installed with a hollow-stem auger, tied reinforcement shall be placed after elements are concreted, while the concrete is still in a semifluid state. Longitudinal reinforcement without lateral ties shall be placed either through the hollow stem of the auger prior to concreting or after concreting, while the concrete is still in a semifluid state.
3. For Group R-3 and U occupancies not exceeding two stories of light-frame construction, reinforcement is permitted to be placed after concreting, while the concrete is still in a semifluid state, and the concrete cover requirement is permitted to be reduced to 2 inches (51 mm), provided the construction method can be demonstrated to the satisfaction of the *building official*.

1810.3.9.4 Seismic reinforcement. Where a structure is assigned to *Seismic Design Category* C, reinforcement shall be provided in accordance with Section 1810.3.9.4.1. Where a structure is assigned to *Seismic Design Category* D, E or F, reinforcement shall be provided in accordance with Section 1810.3.9.4.2.

Exceptions:

1. Isolated deep foundation elements supporting posts of Group R-3 and U occupancies not exceeding two stories of light-frame construction shall be permitted to be reinforced as required by rational analysis but with not less than one No. 4 bar, without ties or spirals, where detailed so the element is not subject to lateral loads and the soil provides adequate lateral support in accordance with Section 1810.2.1.
2. Isolated deep foundation elements supporting posts and bracing from decks and patios appurtenant to Group R-3 and U occupancies not exceeding two stories of light-frame construction shall be permitted to be reinforced as required by rational analysis but with not less than one No. 4 bar, without ties or spirals, where the lateral load, E, to the top of the element does not exceed 200 pounds (890 N) and the soil provides adequate lateral support in accordance with Section 1810.2.1.
3. Deep foundation elements supporting the concrete foundation wall of Group R-3 and U occupancies not exceeding two stories of light-frame construction shall be permitted to be reinforced as required by rational analysis but with not less than two No. 4 bars, without ties or spirals, where the design cracking moment determined in accordance with Section 1810.3.9.1 exceeds the required moment strength determined using the load combinations with overstrength factor in Section 12.4.3.2 of ASCE 7 and the soil provides ade-

quate lateral support in accordance with Section 1810.2.1.

4. Closed ties or spirals where required by Section 1810.3.9.4.2 shall be permitted to be limited to the top 3 feet (914 mm) of deep foundation elements 10 feet (3048 mm) or less in depth supporting Group R-3 and U occupancies of *Seismic Design Category* D, not exceeding two stories of light-frame construction.

1810.3.9.4.1 Seismic reinforcement in Seismic Design Category C. For structures assigned to *Seismic Design Category* C in accordance with Section 1613, cast-in-place deep foundation elements shall be reinforced as specified in this section. Reinforcement shall be provided where required by analysis.

A minimum of four longitudinal bars, with a minimum longitudinal reinforcement ratio of 0.0025, shall be provided throughout the minimum reinforced length of the element as defined below starting at the top of the element. The minimum reinforced length of the element shall be taken as the greatest of the following:

1. One-third of the element length;
2. A distance of 10 feet (3048 mm);
3. Three times the least element dimension; and
4. The distance from the top of the element to the point where the design cracking moment determined in accordance with Section 1810.3.9.1 exceeds the required moment strength determined using the load combinations of Section 1605.2.

Transverse reinforcement shall consist of closed ties or spirals with a minimum $^{3}/_{8}$ inch (9.5 mm) diameter. Spacing of transverse reinforcement shall not exceed the smaller of 6 inches (152 mm) or 8-longitudinal-bar diameters, within a distance of three times the least element dimension from the bottom of the pile cap. Spacing of transverse reinforcement shall not exceed 16 longitudinal bar diameters throughout the remainder of the reinforced length.

Exceptions:

1. The requirements of this section shall not apply to concrete cast in structural steel pipes or tubes.
2. A spiral-welded metal casing of a thickness not less than manufacturer's standard gage No. 14 gage (0.068 inch) is permitted to provide concrete confinement in lieu of the closed ties or spirals. Where used as such, the metal casing shall be protected against possible deleterious action due to soil constituents, changing water levels or other factors indicated by boring records of site conditions.

1810.3.9.4.2 Seismic reinforcement in Seismic Design Categories D through F. For structures assigned to *Seismic Design Category* D, E or F in accordance with Section 1613, cast-in-place deep foundation elements shall be reinforced as specified in this section. Reinforcement shall be provided where required by analysis.

A minimum of four longitudinal bars, with a minimum longitudinal reinforcement ratio of 0.005, shall be provided throughout the minimum reinforced length of the element as defined below starting at the top of the element. The minimum reinforced length of the element shall be taken as the greatest of the following:

1. One-half of the element length;
2. A distance of 10 feet (3048 mm);
3. Three times the least element dimension; and
4. The distance from the top of the element to the point where the design cracking moment determined in accordance with Section 1810.3.9.1 exceeds the required moment strength determined using the load combinations of Section 1605.2.

Transverse reinforcement shall consist of closed ties or spirals no smaller than No. 3 bars for elements with a least dimension up to 20 inches (508 mm), and No. 4 bars for larger elements. Throughout the remainder of the reinforced length outside the regions with transverse confinement reinforcement, as specified in Section 1810.3.9.4.2.1 or 1810.3.9.4.2.2, the spacing of transverse reinforcement shall not exceed the least of the following:

1. 12 longitudinal bar diameters;
2. One-half the least dimension of the element; and
3. 12 inches (305 mm).

Exceptions:

1. The requirements of this section shall not apply to concrete cast in structural steel pipes or tubes.
2. A spiral-welded metal casing of a thickness not less than manufacturer's standard gage No. 14 gage (0.068 inch) is permitted to provide concrete confinement in lieu of the closed ties or spirals. Where used as such, the metal casing shall be protected against possible deleterious action due to soil constituents, changing water levels or other factors indicated by boring records of site conditions.

1810.3.9.4.2.1 Site Classes A through D. For *Site Class* A, B, C or D sites, transverse confinement reinforcement shall be provided in the element in accordance with Sections 21.6.4.2, 21.6.4.3 and 21.6.4.4 of ACI 318 within three times the least element dimension of the bottom of the pile cap. A transverse spiral reinforcement ratio of not less than one-half of that required in Section 21.6.4.4(a) of ACI 318 shall be permitted.

1810.3.9.4.2.2 Site Classes E and F. For *Site Class* E or F sites, transverse confinement reinforcement shall be provided in the element in accordance with Sections 21.6.4.2, 21.6.4.3 and 21.6.4.4 of ACI 318 within seven times the least element dimension of the pile cap and within seven times the least element dimension of the interfaces of strata that are hard or stiff and strata that are liquefiable or are composed of soft- to medium-stiff clay.

1810.3.9.5 Belled drilled shafts. Where drilled shafts are belled at the bottom, the edge thickness of the bell shall not be less than that required for the edge of footings. Where the sides of the bell slope at an angle less than 60 degrees (1 rad) from the horizontal, the effects of vertical shear shall be considered.

1810.3.9.6 Socketed drilled shafts. Socketed drilled shafts shall have a permanent pipe or tube casing that extends down to bedrock and an uncased socket drilled into the bedrock, both filled with concrete. Socketed drilled shafts shall have reinforcement or a structural steel core for the length as indicated by an *approved* method of analysis.

The depth of the rock socket shall be sufficient to develop the full load-bearing capacity of the element with a minimum safety factor of two, but the depth shall not be less than the outside diameter of the pipe or tube casing. The design of the rock socket is permitted to be predicated on the sum of the allowable load-bearing pressure on the bottom of the socket plus bond along the sides of the socket.

Where a structural steel core is used, the gross cross-sectional area of the core shall not exceed 25 percent of the gross area of the drilled shaft.

1810.3.10 Micropiles. Micropiles shall be designed and detailed in accordance with Sections 1810.3.10.1 through 1810.3.10.4.

1810.3.10.1 Construction. Micropiles shall develop their load-carrying capacity by means of a bond zone in soil, bedrock or a combination of soil and bedrock. Micropiles shall be grouted and have either a steel pipe or tube or steel reinforcement at every section along the length. It shall be permitted to transition from deformed reinforcing bars to steel pipe or tube reinforcement by extending the bars into the pipe or tube section by at least their development length in tension in accordance with ACI 318.

1810.3.10.2 Materials. Reinforcement shall consist of deformed reinforcing bars in accordance with ASTM A 615 Grade 60 or 75 or ASTM A 722 Grade 150.

The steel pipe or tube shall have a minimum wall thickness of $^3/_{16}$ inch (4.8 mm). Splices shall comply with Section 1810.3.6. The steel pipe or tube shall have a minimum yield strength of 45,000 psi (310 MPa) and a minimum elongation of 15 percent as shown by mill certifications or two coupon test samples per 40,000 pounds (18 160 kg) of pipe or tube.

1810.3.10.3 Reinforcement. For micropiles or portions thereof grouted inside a temporary or permanent casing or inside a hole drilled into bedrock or a hole drilled with grout, the steel pipe or tube or steel reinforcement shall be designed to carry at least 40 percent of the design compression load. Micropiles or portions thereof grouted in an open hole in soil without temporary or permanent casing and without suitable means of verifying the hole diameter during grouting shall be designed to carry the entire compression load in the reinforcing steel. Where a steel pipe or tube is used for reinforcement, the portion of the grout enclosed within the pipe is permitted to be included in the determination of the allowable stress in the grout.

1810.3.10.4 Seismic reinforcement. For structures assigned to *Seismic Design Category* C, a permanent steel casing shall be provided from the top of the micropile down to the point of zero curvature. For structures assigned to *Seismic Design Category* D, E or F, the micropile shall be considered as an alternative system in accordance with Section 104.11. The alternative system design, supporting documentation and test data shall be submitted to the *building official* for review and approval.

1810.3.11 Pile caps. Pile caps shall be of reinforced concrete, and shall include all elements to which vertical deep foundation elements are connected, including grade beams and mats. The soil immediately below the pile cap shall not be considered as carrying any vertical load. The tops of vertical deep foundation elements shall be embedded not less than 3 inches (76 mm) into pile caps and the caps shall extend at least 4 inches (102 mm) beyond the edges of the elements. The tops of elements shall be cut or chipped back to sound material before capping.

1810.3.11.1 Seismic Design Categories C through F. For structures assigned to *Seismic Design Category* C, D, E or F in accordance with Section 1613, concrete deep foundation elements shall be connected to the pile cap by embedding the element reinforcement or field-placed dowels anchored in the element into the pile cap for a distance equal to their development length in accordance with ACI 318. It shall be permitted to connect precast prestressed piles to the pile cap by developing the element prestressing strands into the pile cap provided the connection is ductile. For deformed bars, the development length is the full development length for compression, or tension in the case of uplift, without reduction for excess reinforcement in accordance with Section 12.2.5 of ACI 318. Alternative measures for laterally confining concrete and maintaining toughness and ductile-like behavior at the top of the element shall be permitted provided the design is such that any hinging occurs in the confined region.

The minimum transverse steel ratio for confinement shall not be less than one-half of that required for columns.

For resistance to uplift forces, anchorage of steel pipes, tubes or H-piles to the pile cap shall be made by means other than concrete bond to the bare steel section. Concrete-filled steel pipes or tubes shall have reinforcement of not less than 0.01 times the cross-sectional area of the concrete fill developed into the cap and extending into the fill a length equal to two times the required cap embedment, but not less than the development length in tension of the reinforcement.

1810.3.11.2 Seismic Design Categories D through F. For structures assigned to *Seismic Design Category* D, E or F in accordance with Section 1613, deep foundation element resistance to uplift forces or rotational restraint shall be provided by anchorage into the pile cap, designed considering the combined effect of axial forces due to uplift and bending moments due to fixity to the pile cap. Anchorage shall develop a minimum of 25 percent of the strength of the element in tension. Anchorage into the pile cap shall be capable of developing the following:

1. In the case of uplift, the least of the following: nominal tensile strength of the longitudinal reinforcement in a concrete element; the nominal tensile strength of a steel element; the frictional force developed between the element and the soil multiplied by 1.3; and the axial tension force resulting from the load combinations with overstrength factor in Section 12.4.3.2 of ASCE 7.
2. In the case of rotational restraint, the lesser of the following: the axial force, shear forces and bending moments resulting from the load combinations with overstrength factor in Section 12.4.3.2 of ASCE 7 or development of the full axial, bending and shear nominal strength of the element.

Where the vertical lateral-force-resisting elements are columns, the pile cap flexural strengths shall exceed the column flexural strength. The connection between batter piles and pile caps shall be designed to resist the nominal strength of the pile acting as a short column. Batter piles and their connection shall be capable of resisting forces and moments from the load combinations with overstrength factor in Section 12.4.3.2 of ASCE 7.

1810.3.12 Grade beams. For structures assigned to *Seismic Design Category* D, E or F in accordance with Section 1613, grade beams shall comply with the provisions in Section 21.12.3 of ACI 318 for grade beams, except where they have the capacity to resist the forces from the load combinations with overstrength factor in Section 12.4.3.2 of ASCE 7.

1810.3.13 Seismic ties. For structures assigned to *Seismic Design Category* C, D, E or F in accordance with Section 1613, individual deep foundations shall be interconnected by ties. Unless it can be demonstrated that equivalent restraint is provided by reinforced concrete beams within slabs on grade or reinforced concrete slabs on grade or confinement by competent rock, hard cohesive soils or very dense granular soils, ties shall be capable of carrying, in tension or compression, a force equal to the lesser of the product of the larger pile cap or column design gravity load times the seismic coefficient, S_{DS}, divided by 10, and 25 percent of the smaller pile or column design gravity load.

Exception: In Group R-3 and U occupancies of light-frame construction, deep foundation elements supporting foundation walls, isolated interior posts detailed so the element is not subject to lateral loads or exterior decks and patios are not subject to interconnection where the soils are of adequate stiffness, subject to the approval of the *building official*.

1810.4 Installation. Deep foundations shall be installed in accordance with Section 1810.4. Where a single deep foundation element comprises two or more sections of different materials or different types spliced together, each section shall satisfy the applicable conditions of installation.

1810.4.1 Structural integrity. Deep foundation elements shall be installed in such a manner and sequence as to prevent distortion or damage that may adversely affect the structural integrity of adjacent structures or of foundation elements being installed or already in place and as to avoid compacting the surrounding soil to the extent that other foundation elements cannot be installed properly.

1810.4.1.1 Compressive strength of precast concrete piles. A precast concrete pile shall not be driven before the concrete has attained a compressive strength of at least 75 percent of the specified compressive strength (f'_c), but not less than the strength sufficient to withstand handling and driving forces.

1810.4.1.2 Casing. Where cast-in-place deep foundation elements are formed through unstable soils and concrete is placed in an open-drilled hole, a casing shall be inserted in the hole prior to placing the concrete. Where the casing is withdrawn during concreting, the level of concrete shall be maintained above the bottom of the casing at a sufficient height to offset any hydrostatic or lateral soil pressure. Driven casings shall be mandrel driven their full length in contact with the surrounding soil.

1810.4.1.3 Driving near uncased concrete. Deep foundation elements shall not be driven within six element diameters center to center in granular soils or within one-half the element length in cohesive soils of an uncased element filled with concrete less than 48 hours old unless *approved* by the *building official*. If the concrete surface in any completed element rises or drops, the element shall be replaced. Driven uncased deep foundation elements shall not be installed in soils that could cause heave.

1810.4.1.4 Driving near cased concrete. Deep foundation elements shall not be driven within four and one-half average diameters of a cased element filled with concrete less than 24 hours old unless *approved* by the *building official*. Concrete shall not be placed in casings within heave range of driving.

1810.4.1.5 Defective timber piles. Any substantial sudden increase in rate of penetration of a timber pile shall be investigated for possible damage. If the sudden increase in rate of penetration cannot be correlated to soil strata, the pile shall be removed for inspection or rejected.

1810.4.2 Identification. Deep foundation materials shall be identified for conformity to the specified grade with this identity maintained continuously from the point of manufacture to the point of installation or shall be tested by an *approved agency* to determine conformity to the specified grade. The *approved agency* shall furnish an affidavit of compliance to the *building official*.

1810.4.3 Location plan. A plan showing the location and designation of deep foundation elements by an identification system shall be filed with the *building official* prior to installation of such elements. Detailed records for elements shall bear an identification corresponding to that shown on the plan.

1810.4.4 Preexcavation. The use of jetting, augering or other methods of preexcavation shall be subject to the approval of the *building official*. Where permitted, preexcavation shall be carried out in the same manner as used for deep foundation elements subject to load tests and in such a manner that will not impair the carrying capacity of the elements already in place or damage adjacent structures. Element tips shall be driven below the preexcavated depth until the required resistance or penetration is obtained.

1810.4.5 Vibratory driving. Vibratory drivers shall only be used to install deep foundation elements where the element load capacity is verified by load tests in accordance with Section 1810.3.3.1.2. The installation of production elements shall be controlled according to power consumption, rate of penetration or other *approved* means that ensure element capacities equal or exceed those of the test elements.

1810.4.6 Heaved elements. Deep foundation elements that have heaved during the driving of adjacent elements shall be redriven as necessary to develop the required capacity and penetration, or the capacity of the element shall be verified by load tests in accordance with Section 1810.3.3.1.2.

1810.4.7 Enlarged base cast-in-place elements. Enlarged bases for cast-in-place deep foundation elements formed by compacting concrete or by driving a precast base shall be formed in or driven into granular soils. Such elements shall be constructed in the same manner as successful prototype test elements driven for the project. Shafts extending through peat or other organic soil shall be encased in a permanent steel casing. Where a cased shaft is used, the shaft shall be adequately reinforced to resist column action or the annular space around the shaft shall be filled sufficiently to reestablish lateral support by the soil. Where heave occurs, the element shall be replaced unless it is demonstrated that the element is undamaged and capable of carrying twice its design load.

1810.4.8 Hollow-stem augered, cast-in-place elements. Where concrete or grout is placed by pumping through a hollow-stem auger, the auger shall be permitted to rotate in a clockwise direction during withdrawal. As the auger is withdrawn at a steady rate or in increments not to exceed 1 foot (305 mm), concreting or grouting pumping pressures shall be measured and maintained high enough at all times to offset hydrostatic and lateral earth pressures. Concrete or grout volumes shall be measured to ensure that the volume of concrete or grout placed in each element is equal to or greater than the theoretical volume of the hole created by the auger. Where the installation process of any element is interrupted or a loss of concreting or grouting pressure occurs, the element shall be redrilled to 5 feet (1524 mm) below the elevation of the tip of the auger when the installation was interrupted or concrete or grout pressure was lost and reformed. Augered cast-in-place elements shall not be installed within six diameters center to center of an element filled with concrete or grout less than 12 hours old, unless *approved* by the *building official*. If the concrete or grout level in any completed element drops due to installation of an adjacent element, the element shall be replaced.

1810.4.9 Socketed drilled shafts. The rock socket and pipe or tube casing of socketed drilled shafts shall be thoroughly cleaned of foreign materials before filling with concrete. Steel cores shall be bedded in cement grout at the base of the rock socket.

1810.4.10 Micropiles. Micropile deep foundation elements shall be permitted to be formed in holes advanced by rotary or percussive drilling methods, with or without casing. The elements shall be grouted with a fluid cement grout. The grout shall be pumped through a tremie pipe extending to the bottom of the element until grout of suitable quality returns at the top of the element. The following requirements apply to specific installation methods:

1. For micropiles grouted inside a temporary casing, the reinforcing bars shall be inserted prior to withdrawal of the casing. The casing shall be withdrawn in a controlled manner with the grout level maintained at the top of the element to ensure that the grout completely fills the drill hole. During withdrawal of the casing, the grout level inside the casing shall be monitored to verify that the flow of grout inside the casing is not obstructed.
2. For a micropile or portion thereof grouted in an open drill hole in soil without temporary casing, the minimum design diameter of the drill hole shall be verified by a suitable device during grouting.
3. For micropiles designed for end bearing, a suitable means shall be employed to verify that the bearing surface is properly cleaned prior to grouting.
4. Subsequent micropiles shall not be drilled near elements that have been grouted until the grout has had sufficient time to harden.
5. Micropiles shall be grouted as soon as possible after drilling is completed.
6. For micropiles designed with a full-length casing, the casing shall be pulled back to the top of the bond zone and reinserted or some other suitable means employed to assure grout coverage outside the casing.

1810.4.11 Helical piles. Helical piles shall be installed to specified embedment depth and torsional resistance criteria as determined by a *registered design professional*. The torque applied during installation shall not exceed the maximum allowable installation torque of the helical pile.

1810.4.12 Special inspection. *Special inspections* in accordance with Sections 1704.8 and 1704.9 shall be provided for driven and cast-in-place deep foundation elements, respectively. *Special inspections* in accordance with Section 1704.10 shall be provided for helical piles.

CHAPTER 19
CONCRETE

Italics are used for text within Sections 1903 through 1908 of this code to indicate provisions that differ from ACI 318.

SECTION 1901 GENERAL

1901.1 Scope. The provisions of this chapter shall govern the materials, quality control, design and construction of concrete used in structures.

1901.2 Plain and reinforced concrete. Structural concrete shall be designed and constructed in accordance with the requirements of this chapter and ACI 318 as amended in Section 1908 of this code. Except for the provisions of Sections 1904 and 1910, the design and construction of slabs on grade shall not be governed by this chapter unless they transmit vertical loads or lateral forces from other parts of the structure to the soil.

1901.3 Source and applicability. The format and subject matter of Sections 1902 through 1907 of this chapter are patterned after, and in general conformity with, the provisions for structural concrete in ACI 318.

1901.4 Construction documents. The *construction documents* for structural concrete construction shall include:

1. The specified compressive strength of concrete at the stated ages or stages of construction for which each concrete element is designed.
2. The specified strength or grade of reinforcement.
3. The size and location of structural elements, reinforcement and anchors.
4. Provision for dimensional changes resulting from creep, shrinkage and temperature.
5. The magnitude and location of prestressing forces.
6. Anchorage length of reinforcement and location and length of lap splices.
7. Type and location of mechanical and welded splices of reinforcement.
8. Details and location of contraction or isolation joints specified for plain concrete.
9. Minimum concrete compressive strength at time of posttensioning.
10. Stressing sequence for posttensioning tendons.
11. For structures assigned to *Seismic Design Category* D, E or F, a statement if slab on grade is designed as a structural diaphragm (see Section 21.12.3.4 of ACI 318).

1901.5 Special inspection. The *special inspection* of concrete elements of buildings and structures and concreting operations shall be as required by Chapter 17.

SECTION 1902 DEFINITIONS

1902.1 General. The words and terms defined in ACI 318 shall, for the purposes of this chapter and as used elsewhere in this code for concrete construction, have the meanings shown in ACI 318 as modified by Section 1908.1.1.

SECTION 1903 SPECIFICATIONS FOR TESTS AND MATERIALS

1903.1 General. Materials used to produce concrete, concrete itself and testing thereof shall comply with the applicable standards listed in ACI 318. *Where required, special inspections and tests shall be in accordance with Chapter 17.*

1903.2 Glass fiber reinforced concrete. *Glass fiber reinforced concrete (GFRC) and the materials used in such concrete shall be in accordance with the PCI MNL 128 standard.*

SECTION 1904 DURABILITY REQUIREMENTS

1904.1 Water-cementitious materials ratio. Where maximum water-cementitious materials ratios are specified in ACI 318, they shall be calculated in accordance with ACI 318, Section 4.1.

1904.2 Exposure categories and classes. Concrete shall be assigned to exposure classes in accordance with ACI 318, Section 4.2, based on:

1. Exposure to freezing and thawing in a moist condition or deicer chemicals;
2. Exposure to sulfates in water or soil;
3. Exposure to water where the concrete is intended to have low permeability; and
4. Exposure to chlorides from deicing chemicals, salt, saltwater, brackish water, seawater or spray from these sources, where the concrete has steel reinforcement.

1904.3 Concrete properties. Concrete mixtures shall conform to the most restrictive maximum water-cementitious materials ratios and minimum specified concrete compressive strength requirements of ACI 318, Section 4.3, based on the exposure classes assigned in Section 1904.2.

> ***Exception:*** *For occupancies and appurtenances thereto in Group R occupancies that are in buildings less than four stories above grade plane, normal-weight aggregate concrete is permitted to comply with the requirements of Table 1904.3 based on the weathering classification (freezing and thawing) determined from Figure 1904.3 in lieu of the requirements of ACI 318, Table 4.3.1.*

TABLE 1904.3
MINIMUM SPECIFIED COMPRESSIVE STRENGTH (f'_c)

TYPE OR LOCATION OF CONCRETE CONSTRUCTION	MINIMUM SPECIFIED COMPRESSIVE STRENGTH (f'_c at 28 days, psi)		
	Negligible exposure	Moderate exposure	Severe exposure
Basement walls[c] and foundations not exposed to the weather	2,500	2,500	2,500[a]
Basement slabs and interior slabs on grade, except garage floor slabs	2,500	2,500	2,500[a]
Basement walls[c], foundation walls, exterior walls and other vertical concrete surfaces exposed to the weather	2,500	3,000[b]	3,000[b]
Driveways, curbs, walks, patios, porches, carport slabs, steps and other flatwork exposed to the weather, and garage floor slabs	2,500	3,000[b, d]	3,500[b, d]

For SI: 1 pound per square inch = 0.00689 MPa.

a. Concrete in these locations that can be subjected to freezing and thawing during construction shall be of air-entrained concrete in accordance with Section 1904.2.1.

b. Concrete shall be air entrained in accordance with Section 1904.4.1.

c. Structural plain concrete basement walls are exempt from the requirements for exposure conditions of Section 1904.3 (see Section 1909.6.1).

d. For garage floor slabs where a steel trowel finish is used, the total air content required by Section 1904.4.1 is permitted to be reduced to not less than 3 percent, provided the minimum specified compressive strength of the concrete is increased to 4,000 psi.

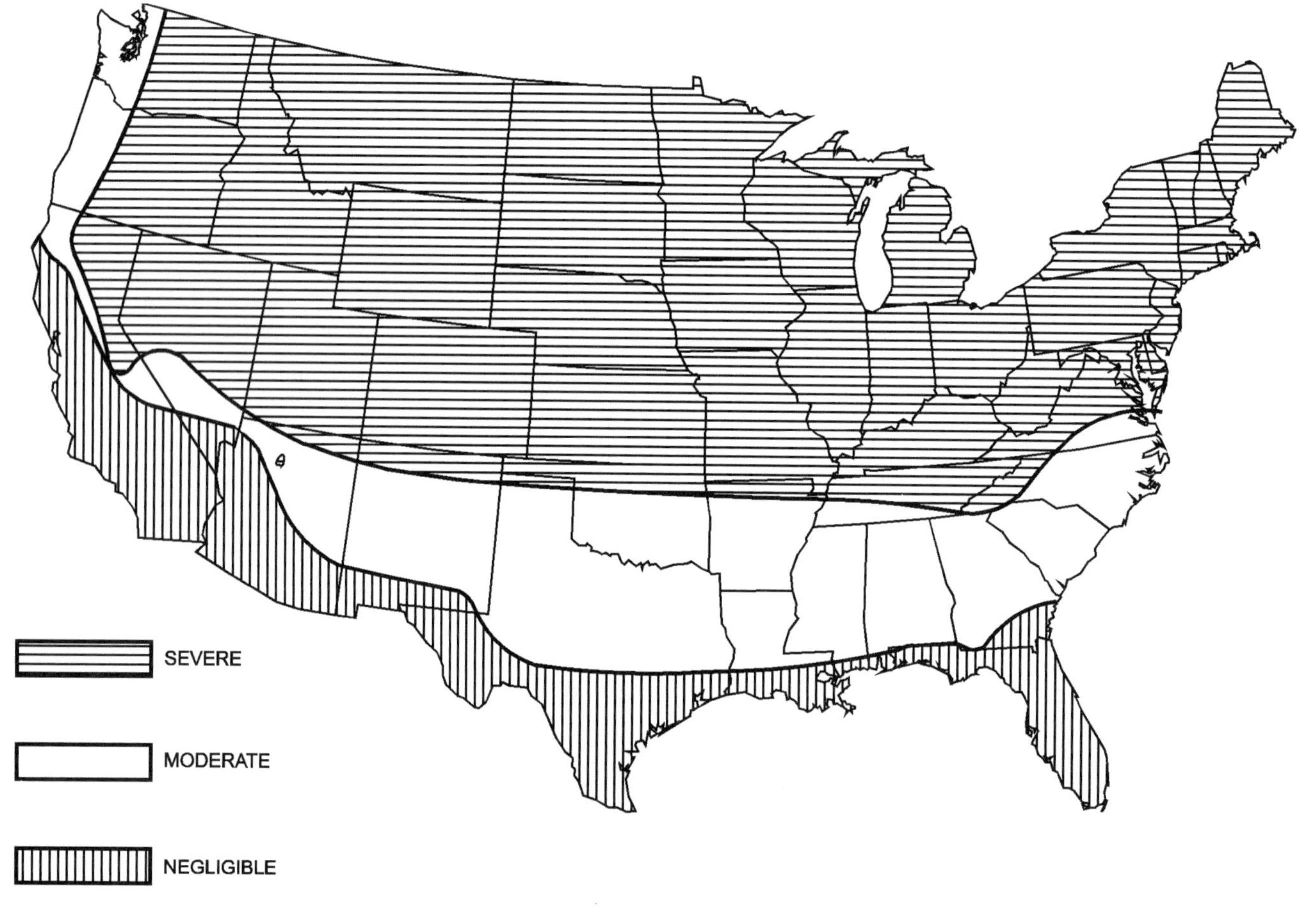

FIGURE 1904.3
WEATHERING PROBABILITY MAP FOR CONCRETE[a, b, c]

a. Lines defining areas are approximate only. Local areas can be more or less severe than indicated by the region classification.

b. A "severe" classification is where weather conditions encourage or require the use of deicing chemicals or where there is potential for a continuous presence of moisture during frequent cycles of freezing and thawing. A "moderate" classification is where weather conditions occasionally expose concrete in the presence of moisture to freezing and thawing, but where deicing chemicals are not generally used. A "negligible" classification is where weather conditions rarely expose concrete in the presence of moisture to freezing and thawing.

c. Alaska and Hawaii are classified as severe and negligible, respectively.

1904.4 Freezing and thawing exposures. Concrete that will be exposed to freezing and thawing, in the presence of moisture, with or without deicing chemicals being present, shall comply with Sections 1904.4.1 and 1904.4.2.

1904.4.1 Air entrainment. Concrete exposed to freezing and thawing while moist shall be air entrained in accordance with ACI 318, Section 4.4.1.

1904.4.2 Deicing chemicals. For concrete exposed to freezing and thawing in the presence of moisture and deicing chemicals, the maximum weight of fly ash, other pozzolans, silica fume or slag that is included in the concrete shall not exceed the percentages of the total weight of cementitious materials permitted by ACI 318, Section 4.4.2.

1904.5 Alternative cementitious materials for sulfate exposure. Alternative combinations of cementitious materials for use in sulfate-resistant concrete to those listed in ACI 318, Table 4.3.1 shall be permitted in accordance with ACI 318, Section 4.5.1.

SECTION 1905
CONCRETE QUALITY, MIXING AND PLACING

1905.1 General. The required strength and durability of concrete shall be determined by compliance with the proportioning, testing, mixing and placing provisions of Sections 1905.1.1 through 1905.13.

1905.1.1 Strength. Concrete shall be proportioned to provide an average compressive strength as prescribed in Section 1905.3 and shall satisfy the durability criteria of Section 1904. Concrete shall be produced to minimize the frequency of strengths below f'_c as prescribed in Section 1905.6.3. *For concrete designed and constructed in accordance with this chapter, f'_c shall not be less than 2,500 psi (17.22 MPa).* No maximum specified compressive strength shall apply unless restricted by a specific provision of this code or ACI 318.

1905.2 Selection of concrete proportions. Concrete proportions shall be determined in accordance with the provisions of ACI 318, Section 5.2.

1905.3 Proportioning on the basis of field experience and/or trial mixtures. Concrete proportioning determined on the basis of field experience and/or trial mixtures shall be done in accordance with ACI 318, Section 5.3.

1905.4 Proportioning without field experience or trial mixtures. Concrete proportioning determined without field experience or trial mixtures shall be done in accordance with ACI 318, Section 5.4.

1905.5 Average strength reduction. As data become available during construction, it is permissible to reduce the amount by which the average compressive strength (f'_c) is required to exceed the specified value of f'_c in accordance with ACI 318, Section 5.5.

1905.6 Evaluation and acceptance of concrete. The criteria for evaluation and acceptance of concrete shall be as specified in Sections 1905.6.2 through 1905.6.5.

1905.6.1 Qualified technicians. Concrete shall be tested in accordance with the requirements in Sections 1905.6.2 through 1905.6.5. Qualified field testing technicians shall perform tests on fresh concrete at the job site, prepare specimens required for curing under field conditions, prepare specimens required for testing in the laboratory and record the temperature of the fresh concrete when preparing specimens for strength tests. Qualified laboratory technicians shall perform all required laboratory tests.

1905.6.2 Frequency of testing. The frequency of conducting strength tests of concrete and the minimum number of tests shall be as specified in ACI 318, Section 5.6.2.

Exception: When the total volume of a given class of concrete is less than 50 cubic yards (38 m^3), strength tests are not required when evidence of satisfactory strength is submitted to and approved by the building official.

1905.6.3 Strength test specimens. Specimens prepared for acceptance testing of concrete in accordance with Section 1905.6.2 and strength test acceptance criteria shall comply with the provisions of ACI 318, Section 5.6.3.

1905.6.4 Field-cured specimens. Where required by the building official to determine adequacy of curing and protection of concrete in the structure, specimens shall be prepared, cured, tested and test results evaluated for acceptance in accordance with ACI 318, Section 5.6.4.

1905.6.5 Low-strength test results. Where any strength test (see ACI 318, Section 5.6.2.4) falls below the specified value of f'_c, the provisions of ACI 318, Section 5.6.5, shall apply.

1905.7 Preparation of equipment and place of deposit. Prior to concrete being placed, the space to receive the concrete and the equipment used to deposit it shall comply with ACI 318, Section 5.7.

1905.8 Mixing. Mixing of concrete shall be performed in accordance with ACI 318, Section 5.8.

1905.9 Conveying. The method and equipment for conveying concrete to the place of deposit shall comply with ACI 318, Section 5.9.

1905.10 Depositing. The depositing of concrete shall comply with the provisions of ACI 318, Section 5.10.

1905.11 Curing. The length of time, temperature and moisture conditions for curing of concrete shall be in accordance with ACI 318, Section 5.11.

1905.12 Cold weather requirements. Concrete to be placed during freezing or near-freezing weather shall comply with the requirements of ACI 318, Section 5.12.

1905.13 Hot weather requirements. Concrete to be placed during hot weather shall comply with the requirements of ACI 318, Section 5.13.

SECTION 1906 FORMWORK, EMBEDDED PIPES AND CONSTRUCTION JOINTS

1906.1 Formwork. The design, fabrication and erection of forms shall comply with ACI 318, Section 6.1.

1906.2 Removal of forms, shores and reshores. The removal of forms and shores, including from slabs and beams (except where cast on the ground), and the installation of reshores shall comply with ACI 318, Section 6.2.

1906.3 Conduits and pipes embedded in concrete. Conduits, pipes and sleeves of any material not harmful to concrete and within the limitations of ACI 318, Section 6.3, are permitted to be embedded in concrete with approval of the registered design professional.

1906.4 Construction joints. Construction joints, including their location, shall comply with the provisions of ACI 318, Section 6.4.

SECTION 1907 DETAILS OF REINFORCEMENT

1907.1 Hooks. Standard hooks on reinforcing bars used in concrete construction shall comply with ACI 318, Section 7.1.

1907.2 Minimum bend diameters. Minimum reinforcement bend diameters utilized in concrete construction shall comply with ACI 318, Section 7.2.

1907.3 Bending. The bending of reinforcement shall comply with ACI 318, Section 7.3.

1907.4 Surface conditions of reinforcement. The surface conditions of reinforcement shall comply with the provisions of ACI 318, Section 7.4.

1907.5 Placing reinforcement. The placement of reinforcement, including tolerances on depth and cover, shall comply with the provisions of ACI 318, Section 7.5. Reinforcement shall be accurately placed and adequately supported before concrete is placed.

1907.6 Spacing limits for reinforcement. The clear distance between reinforcing bars, bundled bars, tendons and ducts shall comply with ACI 318, Section 7.6.

1907.7 Concrete protection for reinforcement. The minimum specified concrete cover for reinforcement shall comply with Sections 1907.7.1 through 1907.7.8.

1907.7.1 Cast-in-place concrete (nonprestressed). Minimum specified concrete cover shall be provided for reinforcement in nonprestressed, cast-in-place concrete construction in accordance with ACI 318, Section 7.7.1.

1907.7.2 Cast-in-place concrete (prestressed). The minimum specified concrete cover for prestressed and nonprestressed reinforcement, ducts and end fittings in cast-in-place prestressed concrete shall comply with ACI 318, Section 7.7.2.

1907.7.3 Precast concrete (manufactured under plant control conditions). The minimum specified concrete cover for prestressed and nonprestressed reinforcement, ducts and end fittings in precast concrete manufactured under plant control conditions shall comply with ACI 318, Section 7.7.3.

1907.7.4 Bundled bars. The minimum specified concrete cover for bundled bars shall comply with ACI 318, Section 7.7.4.

1907.7.5 Headed shear stud reinforcement. For headed shear stud reinforcement, the minimum specified concrete cover shall comply with ACI 318, Section 7.7.5.

1907.7.6 Corrosive environments. In corrosive environments or other severe exposure conditions, prestressed and nonprestressed reinforcement shall be provided with additional protection in accordance with ACI 318, Section 7.7.6.

1907.7.7 Future extensions. Exposed reinforcement, inserts and plates intended for bonding with future extensions shall be protected from corrosion.

1907.7.8 Fire protection. When this code requires a thickness of cover for fire protection greater than the minimum concrete cover in Section 1907.7, such greater thickness shall be specified.

1907.8 Special reinforcement details for columns. Offset bent longitudinal bars in columns and load transfer in structural steel cores of composite compression members shall comply with the provisions of ACI 318, Section 7.8.

1907.9 Connections. Connections between concrete framing members shall comply with the provisions of ACI 318, Section 7.9.

1907.10 Lateral reinforcement for compression members. Lateral reinforcement for concrete compression members shall comply with the provisions of ACI 318, Section 7.10.

1907.11 Lateral reinforcement for flexural members. Lateral reinforcement for compression reinforcement in concrete flexural members shall comply with the provisions of ACI 318, Section 7.11.

1907.12 Shrinkage and temperature reinforcement. Reinforcement for shrinkage and temperature stresses in concrete members shall comply with the provisions of ACI 318, Section 7.12.

1907.13 Requirements for structural integrity. The detailing of reinforcement and connections between concrete members shall comply with the provisions of ACI 318, Section 7.13, to improve structural integrity.

SECTION 1908 MODIFICATIONS TO ACI 318

1908.1 General. The text of ACI 318 shall be modified as indicated in Sections 1908.1.1 through 1908.1.10.

1908.1.1 ACI 318, Section 2.2. Modify existing definitions and add the following definitions to ACI 318, Section 2.2.

DESIGN DISPLACEMENT. Total lateral displacement expected for the design-basis earthquake, *as specified by Section 12.8.6 of ASCE 7.*

DETAILED PLAIN CONCRETE STRUCTURAL WALL. *A wall complying with the requirements of Chapter 22, including 22.6.7.*

ORDINARY PRECAST STRUCTURAL WALL. *A precast wall complying with the requirements of Chapters 1 through 18.*

ORDINARY REINFORCED CONCRETE STRUCTURAL WALL. A *cast-in-place* wall complying with the requirements of Chapters 1 through 18.

ORDINARY STRUCTURAL PLAIN CONCRETE WALL. A wall complying with the requirements of Chapter 22, *excluding 22.6.7.*

SPECIAL STRUCTURAL WALL. A cast-in-place or precast wall complying with the requirements of 21.1.3 through 21.1.7, 21.9 and 21.10, as applicable, in addition to the requirements for ordinary reinforced concrete structural walls *or ordinary precast structural walls, as applicable. Where ASCE 7 refers to a "special reinforced concrete structural wall," it shall be deemed to mean a "special structural wall."*

WALL PIER. *A wall segment with a horizontal length-to-thickness ratio of at least 2.5, but not exceeding 6, whose clear height is at least two times its horizontal length.*

1908.1.2 ACI 318, Section 21.1.1. Modify ACI 318 Sections 21.1.1.3 and 21.1.1.7 to read as follows:

21.1.1.3 – Structures assigned to Seismic Design Category A shall satisfy requirements of Chapters 1 to 19 and 22; *Chapter 21 does not apply.* Structures assigned to *Seismic Design Category* B, C, D, E or F also shall satisfy 21.1.1.4 through 21.1.1.8, as applicable. *Except for structural elements of plain concrete complying with Section 1908.1.8 of the International Building Code, structural elements of plain concrete are prohibited in structures assigned to Seismic Design Category C, D, E or F.*

21.1.1.7 – Structural systems designated as part of the seismic-force-resisting system shall be restricted to those *permitted by ASCE 7.* Except for *Seismic Design Category* A, for which Chapter 21 does not apply, the following provisions shall be satisfied for each structural system designated as part of the seismic-force-resisting system, regardless of the *Seismic Design Category*:

(a) Ordinary moment frames shall satisfy 21.2.

(b) Ordinary reinforced concrete structural walls *and ordinary precast structural walls* need not satisfy any provisions in Chapter 21.

(c) Intermediate moment frames shall satisfy 21.3.

(d) Intermediate precast *structural* walls shall satisfy 21.4.

(e) Special moment frames shall satisfy 21.5 through 21.8.

(f) Special structural walls shall satisfy 21.9.

(g) Special structural walls constructed using precast concrete shall satisfy 21.10.

All special moment frames and special structural walls shall also satisfy 21.1.3 through 21.1.7.

1908.1.3 ACI 318, Section 21.4. Modify ACI 318, Section 21.4, by renumbering Section 21.4.3 to become 21.4.4 and adding new Sections 21.4.3, 21.4.5 and 21.4.6 to read as follows:

21.4.3 – Connections that are designed to yield shall be capable of maintaining 80 percent of their design strength at the deformation induced by the design displacement or shall use Type 2 mechanical splices.

21.4.4 – Elements of the connection that are not designed to yield shall develop at least 1.5 *Sy*.

21.4.5 – Wall piers not designed as part of a moment frame shall have transverse reinforcement designed to resist the shear forces determined from 21.3.3. Spacing of transverse reinforcement shall not exceed 8 inches (203 mm). Transverse reinforcement shall be extended beyond the pier clear height for at least 12 inches (305 mm).

Exceptions:

1. *Wall piers that satisfy 21.13.*
2. *Wall piers along a wall line within a story where other shear wall segments provide lateral support to the wall piers and such segments have a total stiffness of at least six times the sum of the stiffnesses of all the wall piers.*

21.4.6 – Wall segments with a horizontal length-to-thickness ratio less than 2.5 shall be designed as columns.

1908.1.4 ACI 318, Section 21.9. Modify ACI 318, Section 21.9, by adding new Section 21.9.10 to read as follows:

21.9.10 – Wall piers and wall segments.

21.9.10.1 – Wall piers not designed as a part of a special moment frame shall have transverse reinforcement designed to satisfy the requirements in 21.9.10.2.

Exceptions:

1. *Wall piers that satisfy 21.13.*
2. *Wall piers along a wall line within a story where other shear wall segments provide lateral support to the wall piers and such segments have a total stiffness of at least six times the sum of the stiffnesses of all the wall piers.*

21.9.10.2 – Transverse reinforcement with seismic hooks at both ends shall be designed to resist the shear forces determined from 21.6.5.1. Spacing of transverse reinforcement shall not exceed 6 inches (152 mm). Transverse reinforcement shall be extended beyond the pier clear height for at least 12 inches (305 mm).

21.9.10.3 – Wall segments with a horizontal length-to-thickness ratio less than 2.5 shall be designed as columns.

1908.1.5 ACI 318, Section 21.10. Modify ACI 318, Section 21.10.2, to read as follows:

21.10.2 – Special structural walls constructed using precast concrete shall satisfy all the requirements of 21.9 for cast-in-place special structural walls in addition to Sections 21.4.2 *through* 21.4.4.

1908.1.6 ACI 318, Section 21.12.1.1. Modify ACI 318, Section 21.12.1.1, to read as follows:

21.12.1.1 – Foundations resisting earthquake-induced forces or transferring earthquake-induced forces between a structure and ground shall comply with the requirements of Section 21.12 and other applicable provisions of ACI 318 *unless modified by Chapter 18 of the International Building Code.*

1908.1.7 ACI 318, Section 22.6. Modify ACI 318, Section 22.6, by adding new Section 22.6.7 to read as follows:

22.6.7 – Detailed plain concrete structural walls.

22.6.7.1 – Detailed plain concrete structural walls are walls conforming to the requirements of ordinary structural plain concrete walls and 22.6.7.2.

22.6.7.2 – Reinforcement shall be provided as follows:

(a) Vertical reinforcement of at least 0.20 square inch (129 mm²) in cross-sectional area shall be provided continuously from support to support at each corner, at each side of each opening and at the ends of walls. The continuous vertical bar required beside an opening is permitted to substitute for one of the two No. 5 bars required by 22.6.6.5.

(b) Horizontal reinforcement at least 0.20 square inch (129 mm²) in cross-sectional area shall be provided:

1. Continuously at structurally connected roof and floor levels and at the top of walls;

2. At the bottom of load-bearing walls or in the top of foundations where doweled to the wall; and

3. At a maximum spacing of 120 inches (3048 mm).

Reinforcement at the top and bottom of openings, where used in determining the maximum spacing specified in Item 3 above, shall be continuous in the wall.

1908.1.8 ACI 318, Section 22.10. Delete ACI 318, Section 22.10, and replace with the following:

22.10 – Plain concrete in structures assigned to Seismic Design Category C, D, E or F.

22.10.1 – Structures assigned to Seismic Design Category C, D, E or F shall not have elements of structural plain concrete, except as follows:

(a) Structural plain concrete basement, foundation or other walls below the base are permitted in detached one- and two-family dwellings three stories or less in height constructed with stud-bearing walls. In dwellings assigned to Seismic Design Category D or E, the height of the wall shall not exceed 8 feet (2438 mm), the thickness shall not be less than $7^1/_2$ inches (190 mm), and the wall shall retain no more than 4 feet (1219 mm) of unbalanced fill. Walls shall have reinforcement in accordance with 22.6.6.5.

(b) Isolated footings of plain concrete supporting pedestals or columns are permitted, provided the projection of the footing beyond the face of the supported member does not exceed the footing thickness.

***Exception:** In detached one- and two-family dwellings three stories or less in height, the projection of the footing beyond the face of the supported member is permitted to exceed the footing thickness.*

(c) Plain concrete footings supporting walls are permitted, provided the footings have at least two continuous longitudinal reinforcing bars. Bars shall not be smaller than No. 4 and shall have a total area of not less than 0.002 times the gross cross-sectional area of the footing. For footings that exceed 8 inches (203 mm) in thickness, a minimum of one bar shall be provided at the top and bottom of the footing. Continuity of reinforcement shall be provided at corners and intersections.

Exceptions:

1. In detached one- and two-family dwellings three stories or less in height and constructed with stud-bearing walls, plain concrete footings without longitudinal reinforcement supporting walls are permitted.

2. For foundation systems consisting of a plain concrete footing and a plain concrete stemwall, a minimum of one bar shall be provided at the top of the stemwall and at the bottom of the footing.

3. Where a slab on ground is cast monolithically with the footing, one No. 5 bar is permitted to be located at either the top of the slab or bottom of the footing.

1908.1.9 ACI 318, Section D.3.3. Modify ACI 318, Sections D.3.3.4 and D.3.3.5 to read as follows:

D.3.3.4 – Anchors shall be designed to be governed by the steel strength of a ductile steel element as determined in accordance with D.5.1 and D.6.1, unless either D.3.3.5 or D.3.3.6 is satisfied.

Exceptions:

1. Anchors in concrete designed to support nonstructural components in accordance with ASCE 7 Section 13.4.2 need not satisfy Section D.3.3.4.

2. Anchors designed to resist wall out-of-plane forces with design strengths equal to or greater than the force determined in accordance with ASCE 7 Equation 12.11-1 or 12.14-10 need not satisfy Section D.3.3.4.

D.3.3.5 – Instead of D.3.3.4, the attachment that the anchor is connecting to the structure shall be designed so that the attachment will undergo ductile yielding at a force level corresponding to anchor forces no greater than the design strength of anchors specified in D.3.3.3.

Exceptions:

1. *Anchors in concrete designed to support nonstructural components in accordance with ASCE 7 Section 13.4.2 need not satisfy Section D.3.3.5.*
2. *Anchors designed to resist wall out-of-plane forces with design strengths equal to or greater than the force determined in accordance with ASCE 7 Equation 12.11-1 or 12.14-10 need not satisfy Section D.3.3.5.*

1908.1.10 ACI 318, Section D.4.2.2. Delete ACI 318, Section D.4.2.2, and replace with the following:

D.4.2.2 – The concrete breakout strength requirements for anchors in tension shall be considered satisfied by the design procedure of D.5.2 provided Equation D-8 is not used for anchor embedments exceeding 25 inches (635 mm). The concrete breakout strength requirements for anchors in shear with diameters not exceeding 2 inches (51 mm) shall be considered satisfied by the design procedure of D.6.2. For anchors in shear with diameters exceeding 2 inches (51 mm), shear anchor reinforcement shall be provided in accordance with the procedures of D.6.2.9.

SECTION 1909
STRUCTURAL PLAIN CONCRETE

1909.1 Scope. The design and construction of structural plain concrete, both cast-in-place and precast, shall comply with the minimum requirements of Section 1909 and ACI 318, Chapter 22, as modified in Section 1908.

1909.1.1 Special structures. For special structures, such as arches, underground utility structures, gravity walls and shielding walls, the provisions of this section shall govern where applicable.

1909.2 Limitations. The use of structural plain concrete shall be limited to:

1. Members that are continuously supported by soil, such as walls and footings, or by other structural members capable of providing continuous vertical support.
2. Members for which arch action provides compression under all conditions of loading.
3. Walls and pedestals.

The use of structural plain concrete columns and structural plain concrete footings on piles is not permitted. See Section 1908.1.8 for additional limitations on the use of structural plain concrete.

1909.3 Joints. Contraction or isolation joints shall be provided to divide structural plain concrete members into flexurally discontinuous elements in accordance with ACI 318, Section 22.3.

1909.4 Design. Structural plain concrete walls, footings and pedestals shall be designed for adequate strength in accordance with ACI 318, Sections 22.4 through 22.8.

Exception: For Group R-3 occupancies and buildings of other occupancies less than two *stories above grade plane* of light-frame construction, the required edge thickness of ACI 318 is permitted to be reduced to 6 inches (152 mm), provided that the footing does not extend more than 4 inches (102 mm) on either side of the supported wall.

1909.5 Precast members. The design, fabrication, transportation and erection of precast, structural plain concrete elements shall be in accordance with ACI 318, Section 22.9.

1909.6 Walls. In addition to the requirements of this section, structural plain concrete walls shall comply with the applicable requirements of ACI 318, Chapter 22.

1909.6.1 Basement walls. The thickness of exterior basement walls and foundation walls shall be not less than $7^1/_2$ inches (191 mm).

1909.6.2 Other walls. Except as provided for in Section 1909.6.1, the thickness of bearing walls shall be not less than $^1/_{24}$ the unsupported height or length, whichever is shorter, but not less than $5^1/_2$ inches (140 mm).

1909.6.3 Openings in walls. Not less than one No. 5 bar shall be provided around window, door and similar sized openings. The bar shall be anchored to develop f_y in tension at the corners of openings.

SECTION 1910
MINIMUM SLAB PROVISIONS

1910.1 General. The thickness of concrete floor slabs supported directly on the ground shall not be less than $3^1/_2$ inches (89 mm). A 6-mil (0.006 inch; 0.15 mm) polyethylene vapor retarder with joints lapped not less than 6 inches (152 mm) shall be placed between the base course or subgrade and the concrete floor slab, or other *approved* equivalent methods or materials shall be used to retard vapor transmission through the floor slab.

Exception: A vapor retarder is not required:

1. For detached structures accessory to occupancies in Group R-3, such as garages, utility buildings or other unheated facilities.
2. For unheated storage rooms having an area of less than 70 square feet (6.5 m^2) and carports attached to occupancies in Group R-3.
3. For buildings of other occupancies where migration of moisture through the slab from below will not be detrimental to the intended occupancy of the building.

4. For driveways, walks, patios and other flatwork which will not be enclosed at a later date.
5. Where *approved* based on local site conditions.

SECTION 1911 ANCHORAGE TO CONCRETE— ALLOWABLE STRESS DESIGN

1911.1 Scope. The provisions of this section shall govern the *allowable stress design* of headed bolts and headed stud anchors cast in normal-weight concrete for purposes of transmitting structural loads from one connected element to the other. These provisions do not apply to anchors installed in hardened concrete or where load combinations include earthquake loads or effects. The bearing area of headed anchors shall be not less than one and one-half times the shank area. Where strength design is used, or where load combinations include earthquake loads or effects, the design strength of anchors shall be determined in accordance with Scction 1912. Bolts shall conform to ASTM A 307 or an *approved* equivalent.

1911.2 Allowable service load. The allowable service load for headed anchors in shear or tension shall be as indicated in Table 1911.2. Where anchors are subject to combined shear and tension, the following relationship shall be satisfied:

$$(P_s / P_t)^{5/3} + (V_s / V_t)^{5/3} \leq 1 \qquad \textbf{(Equation 19-1)}$$

where:

P_s = Applied tension service load, pounds (N).

P_t = Allowable tension service load from Table 1911.2, pounds (N).

V_s = Applied shear service load, pounds (N).

V_t = Allowable shear service load from Table 1911.2, pounds (N).

1911.3 Required edge distance and spacing. The allowable service loads in tension and shear specified in Table 1911.2 are for the edge distance and spacing specified. The edge distance and spacing are permitted to be reduced to 50 percent of the values specified with an equal reduction in allowable service load. Where edge distance and spacing are reduced less than 50 percent, the allowable service load shall be determined by linear interpolation.

1911.4 Increase in allowable load. Increase of the values in Table 1911.2 by one-third is permitted where the provisions of Section 1605.3.2 permit an increase in allowable stress for wind loading.

1911.5 Increase for special inspection. Where *special inspection* is provided for the installation of anchors, a 100-percent increase in the allowable tension values of Table 1911.2 is permitted. No increase in shear value is permitted.

SECTION 1912 ANCHORAGE TO CONCRETE— STRENGTH DESIGN

1912.1 Scope. The provisions of this section shall govern the strength design of anchors installed in concrete for purposes of transmitting structural loads from one connected element to the other. Headed bolts, headed studs and hooked (J- or L-) bolts cast in concrete and expansion anchors and undercut anchors installed in hardened concrete shall be designed in accordance with Appendix D of ACI 318 as modified by Sections 1908.1.9 and 1908.1.10, provided they are within the scope of Appendix D.

The strength design of anchors that are not within the scope of Appendix D of ACI 318, and as amended in Sections 1908.1.9 and 1908.1.10, shall be in accordance with an *approved* procedure.

TABLE 1911.2
ALLOWABLE SERVICE LOAD ON EMBEDDED BOLTS (pounds)

BOLT DIAMETER (inches)	MINIMUM EMBEDMENT (inches)	EDGE DISTANCE (inches)	SPACING (inches)	MINIMUM CONCRETE STRENGTH (psi)					
				f'_c = 2,500		f'_c = 3,000		f'_c = 4,000	
				Tension	Shear	Tension	Shear	Tension	Shear
1/4	2 1/2	1 1/2	3	200	500	200	500	200	500
3/8	3	2 1/4	4 1/2	500	1,100	500	1,100	500	1,100
1/2	4 4	3 5	6 6	950 1,450	1,250 1,600	950 1,500	1,250 1,650	950 1,550	1,250 1,750
5/8	4 1/2 4 1/2	3 3/4 6 1/4	7 1/2 7 1/2	1,500 2,125	2,750 2,950	1,500 2,200	2,750 3,000	1,500 2,400	2,750 3,050
3/4	5 5	4 1/2 7 1/2	9 9	2,250 2,825	3,250 4,275	2,250 2,950	3,560 4,300	2,250 3,200	3,560 4,400
7/8	6	5 1/4	10 1/2	2,550	3,700	2,550	4,050	2,550	4,050
1	7	6	12	3,050	4,125	3,250	4,500	3,650	5,300
1 1/8	8	6 3/4	13 1/2	3,400	4,750	3,400	4,750	3,400	4,750
1 1/4	9	7 1/2	15	4,000	5,800	4,000	5,800	4,000	5,800

For SI: 1 inch = 25.4 mm, 1 pound per square inch = 0.00689 MPa, 1 pound = 4.45 N.

SECTION 1913 SHOTCRETE

1913.1 General. Shotcrete is mortar or concrete that is pneumatically projected at high velocity onto a surface. Except as specified in this section, shotcrete shall conform to the requirements of this chapter for plain or reinforced concrete.

1913.2 Proportions and materials. Shotcrete proportions shall be selected that allow suitable placement procedures using the delivery equipment selected and shall result in finished in-place hardened shotcrete meeting the strength requirements of this code.

1913.3 Aggregate. Coarse aggregate, if used, shall not exceed $^3/_4$ inch (19.1 mm).

1913.4 Reinforcement. Reinforcement used in shotcrete construction shall comply with the provisions of Sections 1913.4.1 through 1913.4.4.

1913.4.1 Size. The maximum size of reinforcement shall be No. 5 bars unless it is demonstrated by preconstruction tests that adequate encasement of larger bars will be achieved.

1913.4.2 Clearance. When No. 5 or smaller bars are used, there shall be a minimum clearance between parallel reinforcement bars of $2^1/_2$ inches (64 mm). When bars larger than No. 5 are permitted, there shall be a minimum clearance between parallel bars equal to six diameters of the bars used. When two curtains of steel are provided, the curtain nearer the nozzle shall have a minimum spacing equal to 12 bar diameters and the remaining curtain shall have a minimum spacing of six bar diameters.

Exception: Subject to the approval of the *building official*, required clearances shall be reduced where it is demonstrated by preconstruction tests that adequate encasement of the bars used in the design will be achieved.

1913.4.3 Splices. Lap splices of reinforcing bars shall utilize the noncontact lap splice method with a minimum clearance of 2 inches (51 mm) between bars. The use of contact lap splices necessary for support of the reinforcing is permitted when *approved* by the *building official*, based on satisfactory preconstruction tests that show that adequate encasement of the bars will be achieved, and provided that the splice is oriented so that a plane through the center of the spliced bars is perpendicular to the surface of the shotcrete.

1913.4.4 Spirally tied columns. Shotcrete shall not be applied to spirally tied columns.

1913.5 Preconstruction tests. When required by the *building official*, a test panel shall be shot, cured, cored or sawn, examined and tested prior to commencement of the project. The sample panel shall be representative of the project and simulate job conditions as closely as possible. The panel thickness and reinforcing shall reproduce the thickest and most congested area specified in the structural design. It shall be shot at the same angle, using the same nozzleman and with the same concrete mix design that will be used on the project. The equipment used in preconstruction testing shall be the same equipment used in the work requiring such testing, unless substitute equipment is *approved* by the *building official*.

1913.6 Rebound. Any rebound or accumulated loose aggregate shall be removed from the surfaces to be covered prior to placing the initial or any succeeding layers of shotcrete. Rebound shall not be used as aggregate.

1913.7 Joints. Except where permitted herein, unfinished work shall not be allowed to stand for more than 30 minutes unless edges are sloped to a thin edge. For structural elements that will be under compression and for construction joints shown on the *approved construction documents*, square joints are permitted. Before placing additional material adjacent to previously applied work, sloping and square edges shall be cleaned and wetted.

1913.8 Damage. In-place shotcrete that exhibits sags, sloughs, segregation, honeycombing, sand pockets or other obvious defects shall be removed and replaced. Shotcrete above sags and sloughs shall be removed and replaced while still plastic.

1913.9 Curing. During the curing periods specified herein, shotcrete shall be maintained above 40°F (4°C) and in moist condition.

1913.9.1 Initial curing. Shotcrete shall be kept continuously moist for 24 hours after shotcreting is complete or shall be sealed with an *approved* curing compound.

1913.9.2 Final curing. Final curing shall continue for seven days after shotcreting, or for three days if high-early-strength cement is used, or until the specified strength is obtained. Final curing shall consist of the initial curing process or the shotcrete shall be covered with an *approved* moisture-retaining cover.

1913.9.3 Natural curing. Natural curing shall not be used in lieu of that specified in this section unless the relative humidity remains at or above 85 percent, and is authorized by the *registered design professional* and *approved* by the *building official*.

1913.10 Strength tests. Strength tests for shotcrete shall be made by an *approved agency* on specimens that are representative of the work and which have been water soaked for at least 24 hours prior to testing. When the maximum-size aggregate is larger than $^3/_8$ inch (9.5 mm), specimens shall consist of not less than three 3-inch-diameter (76 mm) cores or 3-inch (76 mm) cubes. When the maximum-size aggregate is $^3/_8$ inch (9.5 mm) or smaller, specimens shall consist of not less than 2-inch-diameter (51 mm) cores or 2-inch (51 mm) cubes.

1913.10.1 Sampling. Specimens shall be taken from the in-place work or from test panels, and shall be taken at least once each shift, but not less than one for each 50 cubic yards (38.2 m^3) of shotcrete.

1913.10.2 Panel criteria. When the maximum-size aggregate is larger than $^3/_8$ inch (9.5 mm), the test panels shall have minimum dimensions of 18 inches by 18 inches (457 mm by 457 mm). When the maximum size aggregate is $^3/_8$ inch (9.5 mm) or smaller, the test panels shall have minimum dimensions of 12 inches by 12 inches (305 mm by 305 mm). Panels shall be shot in the same position as the work, during the course of the work and by the nozzlemen doing the work. The conditions under which the panels are cured shall be the same as the work.

1913.10.3 Acceptance criteria. The average compressive strength of three cores from the in-place work or a single test panel shall equal or exceed $0.85 f'_c$ with no single core less than $0.75 f'_c$. The average compressive strength of three cubes taken from the in-place work or a single test panel shall equal or exceed f'_c with no individual cube less than $0.88 f'_c$. To check accuracy, locations represented by erratic core or cube strengths shall be retested.

SECTION 1914 REINFORCED GYPSUM CONCRETE

1914.1 General. Reinforced gypsum concrete shall comply with the requirements of ASTM C 317 and ASTM C 956.

1914.2 Minimum thickness. The minimum thickness of reinforced gypsum concrete shall be 2 inches (51 mm) except the minimum required thickness shall be reduced to $1^1/_2$ inches (38 mm), provided the following conditions are satisfied:

1. The overall thickness, including the formboard, is not less than 2 inches (51 mm).
2. The clear span of the gypsum concrete between supports does not exceed 33 inches (838 mm).
3. Diaphragm action is not required.
4. The design live load does not exceed 40 pounds per square foot (psf) (1915 Pa).

SECTION 1915 CONCRETE-FILLED PIPE COLUMNS

1915.1 General. Concrete-filled pipe columns shall be manufactured from standard, extra-strong or double-extra-strong steel pipe or tubing that is filled with concrete so placed and manipulated as to secure maximum density and to ensure complete filling of the pipe without voids.

1915.2 Design. The safe supporting capacity of concrete-filled pipe columns shall be computed in accordance with the *approved* rules or as determined by a test.

1915.3 Connections. Caps, base plates and connections shall be of *approved* types and shall be positively attached to the shell and anchored to the concrete core. Welding of brackets without mechanical anchorage shall be prohibited. Where the pipe is slotted to accommodate webs of brackets or other connections, the integrity of the shell shall be restored by welding to ensure hooping action of the composite section.

1915.4 Reinforcement. To increase the safe load-supporting capacity of concrete-filled pipe columns, the steel reinforcement shall be in the form of rods, structural shapes or pipe embedded in the concrete core with sufficient clearance to ensure the composite action of the section, but not nearer than 1 inch (25 mm) to the exterior steel shell. Structural shapes used as reinforcement shall be milled to ensure bearing on cap and base plates.

1915.5 Fire-resistance-rating protection. Pipe columns shall be of such size or so protected as to develop the required fire-resistance ratings specified in Table 601. Where an outer steel shell is used to enclose the fire protective covering, the shell shall not be included in the calculations for strength of the column section. The minimum diameter of pipe columns shall be 4 inches (102 mm) except that in structures of Type V construction not exceeding three *stories above grade plane* or 40 feet (12 192 mm) in *building height*, pipe columns used in basements and as secondary steel members shall have a minimum diameter of 3 inches (76 mm).

1915.6 Approvals. Details of column connections and splices shall be shop fabricated by *approved* methods and shall be *approved* only after tests in accordance with the *approved* rules. Shop-fabricated concrete-filled pipe columns shall be inspected by the *building official* or by an *approved* representative of the manufacturer at the plant.

CHAPTER 20
ALUMINUM

SECTION 2001
GENERAL

2001.1 Scope. This chapter shall govern the quality, design, fabrication and erection of aluminum.

SECTION 2002
MATERIALS

2002.1 General. Aluminum used for structural purposes in buildings and structures shall comply with AA ASM 35 and AA ADM 1. The *nominal loads* shall be the minimum design loads required by Chapter 16.

CHAPTER 21
MASONRY

SECTION 2101
GENERAL

2101.1 Scope. This chapter shall govern the materials, design, construction and quality of masonry.

2101.2 Design methods. Masonry shall comply with the provisions of one of the following design methods in this chapter as well as the requirements of Sections 2101 through 2104. Masonry designed by the *allowable stress design* provisions of Section 2101.2.1, the strength design provisions of Section 2101.2.2 or the prestressed masonry provisions of Section 2101.2.3 shall comply with Section 2105.

2101.2.1 Allowable stress design. Masonry designed by the *allowable stress design* method shall comply with the provisions of Sections 2106 and 2107.

2101.2.2 Strength design. Masonry designed by the strength design method shall comply with the provisions of Sections 2106 and 2108, except that autoclaved aerated concrete (AAC) masonry shall comply with the provisions of Section 2106, Section 1613.6.4 and Chapter 1 and Appendix A of TMS 402/ACI 530/ASCE 5.

2101.2.3 Prestressed masonry. Prestressed masonry shall be designed in accordance with Chapters 1 and 4 of TMS 402/ACI 530/ASCE 5 and Section 2106. *Special inspection* during construction shall be provided as set forth in Section 1704.5.

2101.2.4 Empirical design. Masonry designed by the empirical design method shall comply with the provisions of Sections 2106 and 2109 or Chapter 5 of TMS 402/ACI 530/ASCE 5.

2101.2.5 Glass unit masonry. Glass unit masonry shall comply with the provisions of Section 2110 or Chapter 7 of TMS 402/ACI 530/ASCE 5.

2101.2.6 Masonry veneer. Masonry veneer shall comply with the provisions of Chapter 14 or Chapter 6 of TMS 402/ACI 530/ASCE 5.

2101.3 Construction documents. The *construction documents* shall show all of the items required by this code including the following:

1. Specified size, grade, type and location of reinforcement, anchors and wall ties.
2. Reinforcing bars to be welded and welding procedure.
3. Size and location of structural elements.
4. Provisions for dimensional changes resulting from elastic deformation, creep, shrinkage, temperature and moisture.
5. Deleted.
6. Specified compressive strength of masonry at stated ages or stages of construction for which masonry is designed, except where specifically exempted by this code.
7. Details of anchorage of masonry to structural members, frames and other construction, including the type, size and location of connectors.
8. Deleted.
9. Deleted.

2101.3.1 Fireplace drawings. The *construction documents* shall describe in sufficient detail the location, size and construction of masonry fireplaces. The thickness and characteristics of materials and the clearances from walls, partitions and ceilings shall be indicated.

SECTION 2102
DEFINITIONS AND NOTATIONS

2102.1 General. The following words and terms shall, for the purposes of this chapter and as used elsewhere in this code, have the meanings shown herein.

AAC MASONRY. Masonry made of autoclaved aerated concrete (AAC) units, manufactured without internal reinforcement and bonded together using thin- or thick-bed mortar.

ADOBE CONSTRUCTION. Construction in which the exterior *load-bearing* and nonload-bearing walls and partitions are of unfired clay masonry units, and floors, roofs and interior framing are wholly or partly of wood or other *approved* materials.

Adobe, stabilized. Unfired clay masonry units to which admixtures, such as emulsified asphalt, are added during the manufacturing process to limit the units' water absorption so as to increase their durability.

Adobe, unstabilized. Unfired clay masonry units that do not meet the definition of "Adobe, stabilized."

ANCHOR. Metal rod, wire or strap that secures masonry to its structural support.

ARCHITECTURAL TERRA COTTA. Plain or ornamental hard-burned modified clay units, larger in size than brick, with glazed or unglazed ceramic finish.

AREA.

Bedded. The area of the surface of a masonry unit that is in contact with mortar in the plane of the joint.

Gross cross-sectional. The area delineated by the out-to-out specified dimensions of masonry in the plane under consideration.

Net cross-sectional. The area of masonry units, grout and mortar crossed by the plane under consideration based on out-to-out specified dimensions.

AUTOCLAVED AERATED CONCRETE (AAC). Low-density cementitious product of calcium silicate hydrates, whose material specifications are defined in ASTM C 1386.

BED JOINT. The horizontal layer of mortar on which a masonry unit is laid.

BOND BEAM. A horizontal grouted element within masonry in which reinforcement is embedded.

BRICK.

Calcium silicate (sand lime brick). A masonry unit made of sand and lime.

Clay or shale. A masonry unit made of clay or shale, usually formed into a rectangular prism while in the plastic state and burned or fired in a kiln.

Concrete. A masonry unit having the approximate shape of a rectangular prism and composed of inert aggregate particles embedded in a hardened cementitious matrix.

CAST STONE. A building stone manufactured from portland cement concrete precast and used as a *trim*, veneer or facing on or in buildings or structures.

CELL. A void space having a gross cross-sectional area greater than $1^1/_2$ square inches (967 mm^2).

CHIMNEY. A primarily vertical enclosure containing one or more passageways for conveying flue gases to the outside atmosphere.

CHIMNEY TYPES.

High-heat appliance type. An *approved* chimney for removing the products of combustion from fuel-burning, high-heat appliances producing combustion gases in excess of 2,000°F (1093°C) measured at the appliance flue outlet (see Section 2113.11.3).

Low-heat appliance type. An *approved* chimney for removing the products of combustion from fuel-burning, low-heat appliances producing combustion gases not in excess of 1,000°F (538°C) under normal operating conditions, but capable of producing combustion gases of 1,400°F (760°C) during intermittent forces firing for periods up to 1 hour. Temperatures shall be measured at the appliance flue outlet.

Masonry type. A field-constructed chimney of solid masonry units or stones.

Medium-heat appliance type. An *approved* chimney for removing the products of combustion from fuel-burning, medium-heat appliances producing combustion gases not exceeding 2,000°F (1093°C) measured at the appliance flue outlet (see Section 2113.11.2).

CLEANOUT. An opening to the bottom of a grout space of sufficient size and spacing to allow the removal of debris.

COLLAR JOINT. Vertical longitudinal joint between wythes of masonry or between masonry and backup construction that is permitted to be filled with mortar or grout.

COMPRESSIVE STRENGTH OF MASONRY. Maximum compressive force resisted per unit of net cross-sectional area of masonry, determined by the testing of masonry prisms or a function of individual masonry units, mortar and grout.

CONNECTOR. A mechanical device for securing two or more pieces, parts or members together, including anchors, wall ties and fasteners.

COVER. Distance between surface of reinforcing bar and edge of member.

DIMENSIONS.

Actual. The measured dimension of a masonry unit or element.

Nominal. The specified dimension plus an allowance for the joints with which the units are to be laid. Thickness is given first, followed by height and then length.

Specified. The dimensions specified for the manufacture or construction of masonry, masonry units, joints or any other component of a structure.

FIREPLACE. A hearth and fire chamber or similar prepared place in which a fire may be made and which is built in conjunction with a chimney.

FIREPLACE THROAT. The opening between the top of the firebox and the smoke chamber.

FOUNDATION PIER. An isolated vertical foundation member whose horizontal dimension measured at right angles to its thickness does not exceed three times its thickness and whose height is equal to or less than four times its thickness.

GROUTED MASONRY.

Grouted hollow-unit masonry. That form of grouted masonry construction in which certain designated cells of hollow units are continuously filled with grout.

Grouted multiwythe masonry. That form of grouted masonry construction in which the space between the wythes is solidly or periodically filled with grout.

HEAD JOINT. Vertical mortar joint placed between masonry units within the wythe at the time the masonry units are laid.

HEIGHT, WALLS. The vertical distance from the foundation wall or other immediate support of such wall to the top of the wall.

MASONRY. A built-up construction or combination of building units or materials of clay, shale, concrete, glass, gypsum, stone or other *approved* units bonded together with or without mortar or grout or other accepted methods of joining.

Ashlar masonry. Masonry composed of various-sized rectangular units having sawed, dressed or squared bed surfaces, properly bonded and laid in mortar.

Coursed ashlar. Ashlar masonry laid in courses of stone of equal height for each course, although different courses shall be permitted to be of varying height.

Glass unit masonry. Masonry composed of glass units bonded by mortar.

Plain masonry. Masonry in which the tensile resistance of the masonry is taken into consideration and the effects of stresses in reinforcement are neglected.

Random ashlar. Ashlar masonry laid in courses of stone set without continuous joints and laid up without drawn patterns. When composed of material cut into modular heights, discontinuous but aligned horizontal joints are discernible.

Reinforced masonry. Masonry construction in which reinforcement acting in conjunction with the masonry is used to resist forces.

Solid masonry. Masonry consisting of solid masonry units laid contiguously with the joints between the units filled with mortar.

Unreinforced (plain) masonry. Masonry in which the tensile resistance of masonry is taken into consideration and the resistance of the reinforcing steel, if present, is neglected.

MASONRY UNIT. Brick, tile, stone, glass block or concrete block conforming to the requirements specified in Section 2103.

Clay. A building unit larger in size than a brick, composed of burned clay, shale, fired clay or mixtures thereof.

Concrete. A building unit or block larger in size than 12 inches by 4 inches by 4 inches (305 mm by 102 mm by 102 mm) made of cement and suitable aggregates.

Hollow. A masonry unit whose net cross-sectional area in any plane parallel to the load-bearing surface is less than 75 percent of its gross cross-sectional area measured in the same plane.

Solid. A masonry unit whose net cross-sectional area in every plane parallel to the load-bearing surface is 75 percent or more of its gross cross-sectional area measured in the same plane.

MORTAR. A plastic mixture of *approved* cementitious materials, fine aggregates and water used to bond masonry or other structural units.

MORTAR, SURFACE-BONDING. A mixture to bond concrete masonry units that contains hydraulic cement, glass fiber reinforcement with or without inorganic fillers or organic modifiers and water.

PRESTRESSED MASONRY. Masonry in which internal stresses have been introduced to counteract potential tensile stresses in masonry resulting from applied loads.

PRISM. An assemblage of masonry units and mortar with or without grout used as a test specimen for determining properties of the masonry.

RUBBLE MASONRY. Masonry composed of roughly shaped stones.

Coursed rubble. Masonry composed of roughly shaped stones fitting approximately on level beds and well bonded.

Random rubble. Masonry composed of roughly shaped stones laid without regularity of coursing but well bonded and fitted together to form well-divided joints.

Rough or ordinary rubble. Masonry composed of unsquared field stones laid without regularity of coursing but well bonded.

RUNNING BOND. The placement of masonry units such that head joints in successive courses are horizontally offset at least one-quarter the unit length.

SHEAR WALL.

Detailed plain masonry shear wall. A masonry shear wall designed to resist lateral forces neglecting stresses in reinforcement, and designed in accordance with Section 2106.1.

Intermediate prestressed masonry shear wall. A prestressed masonry shear wall designed to resist lateral forces considering stresses in reinforcement, and designed in accordance with Section 2106.1.

Intermediate reinforced masonry shear wall. A masonry shear wall designed to resist lateral forces considering stresses in reinforcement, and designed in accordance with Section 2106.1.

Ordinary plain masonry shear wall. A masonry shear wall designed to resist lateral forces neglecting stresses in reinforcement, and designed in accordance with Section 2106.1.

Ordinary plain prestressed masonry shear wall. A prestressed masonry shear wall designed to resist lateral forces considering stresses in reinforcement, and designed in accordance with Section 2106.1.

Ordinary reinforced masonry shear wall. A masonry shear wall designed to resist lateral forces considering stresses in reinforcement, and designed in accordance with Section 2106.1.

Special prestressed masonry shear wall. A prestressed masonry shear wall designed to resist lateral forces considering stresses in reinforcement and designed in accordance with Section 2106.1 except that only grouted, laterally restrained tendons are used.

Special reinforced masonry shear wall. A masonry shear wall designed to resist lateral forces considering stresses in reinforcement, and designed in accordance with Section 2106.1.

SHELL. The outer portion of a hollow masonry unit as placed in masonry.

SPECIFIED. Required by *construction documents*.

SPECIFIED COMPRESSIVE STRENGTH OF MASONRY, f'_m. Minimum compressive strength, expressed as force per unit of net cross-sectional area, required of the masonry used in construction by the *construction documents*, and upon which the project design is based. Whenever the quantity f'_m is under the radical sign, the square root of numerical value only is intended and the result has units of pounds per square inch (psi) (MPa).

STACK BOND. The placement of masonry units in a bond pattern is such that head joints in successive courses are vertically aligned. For the purpose of this code, requirements for stack bond shall apply to masonry laid in other than running bond.

STONE MASONRY. Masonry composed of field, quarried or cast stone units bonded by mortar.

Ashlar stone masonry. Stone masonry composed of rectangular units having sawed, dressed or squared bed surfaces and bonded by mortar.

Rubble stone masonry. Stone masonry composed of irregular-shaped units bonded by mortar.

STRENGTH.

Design strength. Nominal strength multiplied by a strength reduction factor.

Nominal strength. Strength of a member or cross section calculated in accordance with these provisions before application of any strength-reduction factors.

Required strength. Strength of a member or cross section required to resist factored loads.

THIN-BED MORTAR. Mortar for use in construction of AAC unit masonry with joints 0.06 inch (1.5 mm) or less.

TIE, LATERAL. Loop of reinforcing bar or wire enclosing longitudinal reinforcement.

TIE, WALL. A connector that connects wythes of masonry walls together.

TILE. A ceramic surface unit, usually relatively thin in relation to facial area, made from clay or a mixture of clay or other ceramic materials, called the body of the tile, having either a "glazed" or "unglazed" face and fired above red heat in the course of manufacture to a temperature sufficiently high enough to produce specific physical properties and characteristics.

TILE, STRUCTURAL CLAY. A hollow masonry unit composed of burned clay, shale, fire clay or mixture thereof, and having parallel cells.

WALL. A vertical element with a horizontal length-to-thickness ratio greater than three, used to enclose space.

Cavity wall. A wall built of masonry units or of concrete, or a combination of these materials, arranged to provide an airspace within the wall, and in which the inner and outer parts of the wall are tied together with metal ties.

Composite wall. A wall built of a combination of two or more masonry units bonded together, one forming the backup and the other forming the facing elements.

Dry-stacked, surface-bonded wall. A wall built of concrete masonry units where the units are stacked dry, without mortar on the bed or head joints, and where both sides of the wall are coated with a surface-bonding mortar.

Masonry-bonded hollow wall. A wall built of masonry units so arranged as to provide an airspace within the wall, and in which the facing and backing of the wall are bonded together with masonry units.

Parapet wall. The part of any wall entirely above the roof line.

WEB. An interior solid portion of a hollow masonry unit as placed in masonry.

WYTHE. Each continuous, vertical section of a wall, one masonry unit in thickness.

NOTATIONS.

d_b = Diameter of reinforcement, inches (mm).

F_s = Allowable tensile or compressive stress in reinforcement, psi (MPa).

f_r = Modulus of rupture, psi (MPa).

f'_{AAC} = Specified compressive strength of AAC masonry, the minimum compressive strength for a class of AAC masonry as specified in ASTM C 1386, psi (MPa).

f'_m = Specified compressive strength of masonry at age of 28 days, psi (MPa).

f'_{mi} = Specified compressive strength of masonry at the time of prestress transfer, psi (MPa).

K = The lesser of the masonry cover, clear spacing between adjacent reinforcement, or five times d_b, inches (mm).

L_s = Distance between supports, inches (mm).

l_d = Required development length or lap length of reinforcement, inches (mm).

P = The applied load at failure, pounds (N).

S_t = Thickness of the test specimen measured parallel to the direction of load, inches (mm).

S_w = Width of the test specimen measured parallel to the loading cylinder, inches (mm).

SECTION 2103 MASONRY CONSTRUCTION MATERIALS

2103.1 Concrete masonry units. Concrete masonry units shall conform to the following standards: ASTM C 55 for concrete brick; ASTM C 73 for calcium silicate face brick; ASTM C 90 for load-bearing concrete masonry units or ASTM C 744 for prefaced concrete and calcium silicate masonry units.

2103.2 Clay or shale masonry units. Clay or shale masonry units shall conform to the following standards: ASTM C 34 for structural clay *load-bearing wall* tile; ASTM C 56 for structural clay nonload-bearing wall tile; ASTM C 62 for building brick (solid masonry units made from clay or shale); ASTM C 1088 for solid units of thin veneer brick; ASTM C 126 for ceramic-glazed structural clay facing tile, facing brick and solid masonry units; ASTM C 212 for structural clay facing tile; ASTM C 216 for facing brick (solid masonry units made from clay or shale); ASTM C 652 for hollow brick (hollow masonry units made from clay or shale) or ASTM C 1405 for glazed brick (single-fired solid brick units).

Exception: Structural clay tile for nonstructural use in fireproofing of structural members and in wall furring shall not be required to meet the compressive strength specifications. The fire-resistance rating shall be determined in accordance with ASTM E 119 or UL 263 and shall comply with the requirements of Table 602.

2103.3 AAC masonry. AAC masonry units shall conform to ASTM C 1386 for the strength class specified.

2103.4 Stone masonry units. Stone masonry units shall conform to the following standards: ASTM C 503 for marble building stone (exterior); ASTM C 568 for limestone building stone; ASTM C 615 for granite building stone; ASTM C 616 for sandstone building stone; or ASTM C 629 for slate building stone.

2103.5 Ceramic tile. Ceramic tile shall be as defined in, and shall conform to the requirements of, ANSI A137.1.

2103.6 Glass unit masonry. Hollow glass units shall be partially evacuated and have a minimum average glass face thickness of $^{3}/_{16}$ inch (4.8 mm). Solid glass-block units shall be provided when required. The surfaces of units intended to be in contact with mortar shall be treated with a polyvinyl butyral coating or latex-based paint. Reclaimed units shall not be used.

2103.7 Second-hand units. Second-hand masonry units shall not be reused unless they conform to the requirements of new units. The units shall be of whole, sound materials and free from cracks and other defects that will interfere with proper laying or use. Old mortar shall be cleaned from the unit before reuse.

2103.8 Mortar. Mortar for use in masonry construction shall conform to ASTM C 270 and Articles 2.1 and 2.6 A of TMS 602/ACI 530.1/ASCE 6, except for mortars listed in Sections 2103.9, 2103.10 and 2103.11. Type S or N mortar conforming to ASTM C 270 shall be used for glass unit masonry.

2103.9 Surface-bonding mortar. Surface-bonding mortar shall comply with ASTM C 887. Surface bonding of concrete masonry units shall comply with ASTM C 946.

2103.10 Mortars for ceramic wall and floor tile. Portland cement mortars for installing ceramic wall and floor tile shall comply with ANSI A108.1A and ANSI A108.1B and be of the compositions indicated in Table 2103.10.

TABLE 2103.10
CERAMIC TILE MORTAR COMPOSITIONS

LOCATION	MORTAR	COMPOSITION
Walls	Scratchcoat	1 cement; $^{1}/_{5}$ hydrated lime; 4 dry or 5 damp sand
	Setting bed and leveling coat	1 cement; $^{1}/_{2}$ hydrated lime; 5 damp sand to 1 cement 1 hydrated lime, 7 damp sand
Floors	Setting bed	1 cement; $^{1}/_{10}$ hydrated lime; 5 dry or 6 damp sand; or 1 cement; 5 dry or 6 damp sand
Ceilings	Scratchcoat and sand bed	1 cement; $^{1}/_{2}$ hydrated lime; $2^{1}/_{2}$ dry sand or 3 damp sand

2103.10.1 Dry-set portland cement mortars. Premixed prepared portland cement mortars, which require only the addition of water and are used in the installation of ceramic tile, shall comply with ANSI A118.1. The shear bond strength for tile set in such mortar shall be as required in accordance with ANSI A118.1. Tile set in dry-set portland cement mortar shall be installed in accordance with ANSI A108.5.

2103.10.2 Latex-modified portland cement mortar. Latex-modified portland cement thin-set mortars in which latex is added to dry-set mortar as a replacement for all or part of the gauging water that are used for the installation of ceramic tile shall comply with ANSI A118.4. Tile set in latex-modified portland cement shall be installed in accordance with ANSI A108.5.

2103.10.3 Epoxy mortar. Ceramic tile set and grouted with chemical-resistant epoxy shall comply with ANSI A118.3. Tile set and grouted with epoxy shall be installed in accordance with ANSI A108.6.

2103.10.4 Furan mortar and grout. Chemical-resistant furan mortar and grout that are used to install ceramic tile shall comply with ANSI A118.5. Tile set and grouted with furan shall be installed in accordance with ANSI A108.8.

2103.10.5 Modified epoxy-emulsion mortar and grout. Modified epoxy-emulsion mortar and grout that are used to install ceramic tile shall comply with ANSI A118.8. Tile set and grouted with modified epoxy-emulsion mortar and grout shall be installed in accordance with ANSI A108.9.

2103.10.6 Organic adhesives. Water-resistant organic adhesives used for the installation of ceramic tile shall comply with ANSI A136.1. The shear bond strength after water immersion shall not be less than 40 psi (275 kPa) for Type I adhesive and not less than 20 psi (138 kPa) for Type II adhesive when tested in accordance with ANSI A136.1. Tile set in organic adhesives shall be installed in accordance with ANSI A108.4.

2103.10.7 Portland cement grouts. Portland cement grouts used for the installation of ceramic tile shall comply with ANSI A118.6. Portland cement grouts for tile work shall be installed in accordance with ANSI A108.10.

2103.11 Mortar for AAC masonry. Thin-bed mortar for AAC masonry shall comply with Article 2.1 C.1 of TMS 602/ACI 530.1/ASCE 6. Mortar used for the leveling courses of AAC masonry shall comply with Article 2.1 C.2 of TMS 602/ACI 530.1/ASCE 6.

2103.12 Grout. Grout shall comply with Article 2.2 of TMS 602/ACI 530.1/ASCE 6.

2103.13 Metal reinforcement and accessories. Metal reinforcement and accessories shall conform to Article 2.4 of TMS 602/ACI 530.1/ASCE 6. Where unidentified reinforcement is *approved* for use, not less than three tension and three bending tests shall be made on representative specimens of the reinforcement from each shipment and grade of reinforcing steel proposed for use in the work.

SECTION 2104
CONSTRUCTION

2104.1 Masonry construction. Masonry construction shall comply with the requirements of Sections 2104.1.1 through 2104.4 and with TMS 602/ACI 530.1/ASCE 6.

2104.1.1 Tolerances. Masonry, except masonry veneer, shall be constructed within the tolerances specified in TMS 602/ACI 530.1/ASCE 6.

2104.1.2 Placing mortar and units. Placement of mortar, grout, and clay, concrete, glass, and AAC masonry units shall comply with TMS 602/ACI 530.1/ASCE 6.

2104.1.3 Installation of wall ties. Wall ties shall be installed in accordance with TMS 602/ACI 530.1/ASCE 6.

2104.1.4 Chases and recesses. Chases and recesses shall be constructed as masonry units are laid. Masonry directly above chases or recesses wider than 12 inches (305 mm) shall be supported on lintels.

2104.1.5 Lintels. The design for lintels shall be in accordance with the masonry design provisions of either Section 2107 or 2108.

2104.1.6 Support on wood. Masonry shall not be supported on wood girders or other forms of wood construction except as permitted in Section 2304.12.

2104.2 Corbeled masonry. Corbeled masonry shall comply with the requirements of Section 1.12 of TMS 402/ACI 530/ASCE 5.

2104.2.1 Molded cornices. Unless structural support and anchorage are provided to resist the overturning moment, the center of gravity of projecting masonry or molded cornices shall lie within the middle one-third of the supporting wall. Terra cotta and metal cornices shall be provided with a structural frame of *approved* noncombustible material anchored in an *approved* manner.

2104.3 Cold weather construction. The cold weather construction provisions of TMS 602/ACI 530.1/ASCE 6, Article 1.8 C, shall be implemented when the ambient temperature falls below 40°F (4°C).

2104.4 Hot weather construction. The hot weather construction provisions of TMS 602/ACI 530.1/ASCE 6, Article 1.8 D, shall be implemented when the ambient air temperature exceeds 100°F (37.8°C), or 90°F (32.2°C) with a wind velocity greater than 8 mph (3.58 m/s).

SECTION 2105 QUALITY ASSURANCE

2105.1 General. A quality assurance program shall be used to ensure that the constructed masonry is in compliance with the *construction documents*.

The quality assurance program shall comply with the inspection and testing requirements of Chapter 17.

2105.2 Acceptance relative to strength requirements.

2105.2.1 Compliance with f'_m and f'_{AAC}. Compressive strength of masonry shall be considered satisfactory if the compressive strength of each masonry wythe and grouted collar joint equals or exceeds the value of f'_m for clay and concrete masonry and f'_{AAC} for AAC masonry. For partially grouted clay and concrete masonry, the compressive strength of both the grouted and ungrouted masonry shall equal or exceed the applicable f'_m. At the time of prestress, the compressive strength of the masonry shall equal or exceed f'_{mi}, which shall be less than or equal to f'_m.

2105.2.2 Determination of compressive strength. The compressive strength for each wythe shall be determined by the unit strength method or by the prism test method as specified herein.

2105.2.2.1 Unit strength method.

2105.2.2.1.1 Clay masonry. The compressive strength of masonry shall be determined based on the strength of the units and the type of mortar specified using Table 2105.2.2.1.1, provided:

1. Units are sampled and tested to verify compliance with ASTM C 62, ASTM C 216 or ASTM C 652.
2. Thickness of bed joints does not exceed $^5/_8$ inch (15.9 mm).
3. For grouted masonry, the grout meets one of the following requirements:
   3.1. Grout conforms to Article 2.2 of TMS 602/ACI 530.1/ASCE 6.
   3.2. Minimum grout compressive strength equals or exceeds f'_m but not less than 2,000 psi (13.79 MPa). The compressive strength of grout shall be determined in accordance with ASTM C 1019.

TABLE 2105.2.2.1.1
COMPRESSIVE STRENGTH OF CLAY MASONRY

NET AREA COMPRESSIVE STRENGTH OF CLAY MASONRY UNITS (psi)		NET AREA COMPRESSIVE STRENGTH OF MASONRY (psi)
Type M or S mortar	Type N mortar	
1,700	2,100	1,000
3,350	4,150	1,500
4,950	6,200	2,000
6,600	8,250	2,500
8,250	10,300	3,000
9,900	—	3,500
11,500	—	4,000

For SI: 1 pound per square inch = 0.00689 MPa.

2105.2.2.1.2 Concrete masonry. The compressive strength of masonry shall be determined based on the strength of the unit and type of mortar specified using Table 2105.2.2.1.2, provided:

1. Units are sampled and tested to verify compliance with ASTM C 55 or ASTM C 90.
2. Thickness of bed joints does not exceed $^5/_8$ inch (15.9 mm).
3. For grouted masonry, the grout meets one of the following requirements:
   3.1. Grout conforms to Article 2.2 of TMS 602/ACI 530.1/ASCE 6.
   3.2. Minimum grout compressive strength equals or exceeds f'_m but not less than

2,000 psi (13.79 MPa). The compressive strength of grout shall be determined in accordance with ASTM C 1019.

TABLE 2105.2.2.1.2
COMPRESSIVE STRENGTH OF CONCRETE MASONRY

NET AREA COMPRESSIVE STRENGTH OF CONCRETE MASONRY UNITS (psi)		NET AREA COMPRESSIVE STRENGTH OF MASONRY (psi)[a]
Type M or S mortar	Type N mortar	
1,250	1,300	1,000
1,900	2,150	1,500
2,800	3,050	2,000
3,750	4,050	2,500
4,800	5,250	3,000

For SI: 1 inch = 25.4 mm, 1 pound per square inch = 0.00689 MPa.
a. For units less than 4 inches in height, 85 percent of the values listed.

2105.2.2.1.3 AAC masonry. The compressive strength of AAC masonry shall be based on the strength of the AAC masonry unit only and the following shall be met:

1. Units conform to ASTM C 1386.
2. Thickness of bed joints does not exceed $^1/_8$ inch (3.2 mm).
3. For grouted masonry, the grout meets one of the following requirements:
   - 3.1. Grout conforms to Article 2.2 of TMS 602/ACI 530.1/ASCE 6.
   - 3.2. Minimum grout compressive strength equals or exceeds f'_{AAC} but not less than 2,000 psi (13.79 MPa). The compressive strength of grout shall be determined in accordance with ASTM C 1019.

2105.2.2.2 Prism test method.

2105.2.2.2.1 General. The compressive strength of clay and concrete masonry shall be determined by the prism test method:

1. Where specified in the *construction documents*.
2. Where masonry does not meet the requirements for application of the unit strength method in Section 2105.2.2.1.

2105.2.2.2.2 Number of prisms per test. A prism test shall consist of three prisms constructed and tested in accordance with ASTM C 1314.

2105.3 Testing prisms from constructed masonry. When *approved* by the *building official*, acceptance of masonry that does not meet the requirements of Section 2105.2.2.1 or 2105.2.2.2 shall be permitted to be based on tests of prisms cut from the masonry construction in accordance with Sections 2105.3.1, 2105.3.2 and 2105.3.3.

2105.3.1 Prism sampling and removal. A set of three masonry prisms that are at least 28 days old shall be saw cut from the masonry for each 5,000 square feet (465 m^2) of the wall area that is in question but not less than one set of three masonry prisms for the project. The length, width and height dimensions of the prisms shall comply with the requirements of ASTM C 1314. Transporting, preparation and testing of prisms shall be in accordance with ASTM C 1314.

2105.3.2 Compressive strength calculations. The compressive strength of prisms shall be the value calculated in accordance ASTM C 1314, except that the net cross-sectional area of the prism shall be based on the net mortar bedded area.

2105.3.3 Compliance. Compliance with the requirement for the specified compressive strength of masonry, f'_m, shall be considered satisfied provided the modified compressive strength equals or exceeds the specified f'_m. Additional testing of specimens cut from locations in question shall be permitted.

SECTION 2106
SEISMIC DESIGN

2106.1 Seismic design requirements for masonry. Masonry structures and components shall comply with the requirements in Section 1.17 of TMS 402/ACI 530/ASCE 5 depending on the structure's *seismic design category* as determined in Section 1613.

SECTION 2107
ALLOWABLE STRESS DESIGN

2107.1 General. The design of masonry structures using *allowable stress design* shall comply with Section 2106 and the requirements of Chapters 1 and 2 of TMS 402/ACI 530/ASCE 5 except as modified by Sections 2107.2 through 2107.5.

2107.2 TMS 402/ACI 530/ASCE 5, Section 2.1.2, load combinations. Delete Section 2.1.2.1.

2107.3 TMS 402/ACI 530/ASCE 5, Section 2.1.9.7.1.1, lap splices. Modify Section 2.1.9.7.1.1 as follows:

2.1.9.7.1.1 The minimum length of lap splices for reinforcing bars in tension or compression, l_d, shall be

$$l_d = 0.002 d_b f_s \quad \textbf{(Equation 21-1)}$$

For SI: $l_d = 0.29 d_b f_s$

but not less than 12 inches (305 mm). In no case shall the length of the lapped splice be less than 40 bar diameters.

where:

d_b = Diameter of reinforcement, inches (mm).

f_s = Computed stress in reinforcement due to design loads, psi (MPa).

In regions of moment where the design tensile stresses in the reinforcement are greater than 80 percent of the allowable steel tension stress, F_s, the lap length of splices shall be increased not less than 50 percent of the minimum required length. Other equivalent means of stress transfer to accomplish the same 50 percent increase shall be permitted. Where epoxy coated bars are used, lap length shall be increased by 50 percent.

2107.4 TMS 402/ACI 530/ASCE 5, Section 2.1.9.7, splices of reinforcement. Modify Section 2.1.9.7 as follows:

2.1.9.7 Splices of reinforcement. Lap splices, welded splices or mechanical splices are permitted in accordance with the provisions of this section. All welding shall conform to AWS D1.4. Welded splices shall be of ASTM A706 steel reinforcement. Reinforcement larger than No. 9 (M #29) shall be spliced using mechanical connections in accordance with Section 2.1.9.7.3.

2107.5 TMS 402/ACI 530/ASCE 5, Section 2.3.6, maximum bar size. Add the following to Chapter 2:

2.3.6 Maximum bar size. The bar diameter shall not exceed one-eighth of the nominal wall thickness and shall not exceed one-quarter of the least dimension of the cell, course or collar joint in which it is placed.

SECTION 2108 STRENGTH DESIGN OF MASONRY

2108.1 General. The design of masonry structures using strength design shall comply with Section 2106 and the requirements of Chapters 1 and 3 of TMS 402/ACI 530/ASCE 5, except as modified by Sections 2108.2 through 2108.3.

Exception: AAC masonry shall comply with the requirements of Chapter 1 and Appendix A of TMS 402/ACI 530/ASCE 5.

2108.2 TMS 402/ACI 530/ASCE 5, Section 3.3.3.3 development. Modify the second paragraph of Section 3.3.3.3 as follows:

The required development length of reinforcement shall be determined by Equation (3-16), but shall not be less than 12 inches (305 mm) and need not be greater than 72 d_b.

2108.3 TMS 402/ACI 530/ASCE 5, Section 3.3.3.4, splices. Modify items (b) and (c) of Section 3.3.3.4 as follows:

3.3.3.4 (b). A welded splice shall have the bars butted and welded to develop at least 125 percent of the yield strength, f_y, of the bar in tension or compression, as required. Welded splices shall be of ASTM A 706 steel reinforcement. Welded splices shall not be permitted in plastic hinge zones of intermediate or special reinforced walls or special moment frames of masonry.

3.3.3.4 (c). Mechanical splices shall be classified as Type 1 or 2 according to Section 21.2.6.1 of ACI 318. Type 1 mechanical splices shall not be used within a plastic hinge zone or within a beam-column joint of intermediate or special reinforced masonry shear walls or special moment frames. Type 2 mechanical splices are permitted in any location within a member.

SECTION 2109 EMPIRICAL DESIGN OF MASONRY

2109.1 General. Empirically designed masonry shall conform to this chapter.

2109.1.1 Limitations. The use of empirical design of masonry shall be limited as follows (see Table 2109.1.1 for clarification):

1. Empirical design shall not be used for buildings assigned to Seismic Design Category D, E or F as specified in Section 1613, nor for the design of the seismic-force-resisting system for buildings assigned to Seismic Design Category B or C.
2. Empirical design shall not be used for masonry elements where the basic wind speed exceeds 130 mph (58 m/s).
3. Empirical design shall be permitted to be used for interior masonry elements that are not part of the lateral-force-resisting system in buildings other than enclosed buildings as defined in Chapter 6 of ASCE 7 and the buildings meet the following conditions:
   - 3.1. Buildings 60 feet (18 400 mm) or more but equal to or less than 180 feet (55 100 mm) in height where the basic wind speed is 90 mph (40 m/s) or less.
   - 3.2. Buildings 35 feet (10 700 mm) or more but less than 60 feet (18 400 mm) in height where the basic wind speed is 100 mph (45 m/s) or less.
   - 3.3. Deleted.
   - 3.4. Deleted.
4. Empirical design shall be permitted to be used for exterior masonry elements that are not part of the lateral-force-resisting system in buildings and the buildings meet the following conditions:
   - 4.1. Buildings 60 feet (18 400 mm) or more but equal to or less than 180 feet (55 100 mm) in height where the basic wind speed is 90 mph (40 m/s) or less.
   - 4.2. Buildings 35 feet (10 700 mm) or more but less than 60 feet (18 400 mm) in height where the basic wind speed is 100 mph (45 m/s) or less.
   - 4.3. Deleted.
5. Deleted.
6. Empirical design shall only be used when the resultant of gravity loads is within the center third of the wall thickness and within the central area bounded by lines at one-third of each cross-sectional dimension of foundation piers.
7. Empirical design shall not be used for AAC masonry. In buildings that exceed one or more of the above limitations, masonry shall be designed in accordance with the engineered design provisions of Section 2107 or 2108 or the foundation wall provisions of Section 1807.1.5.

TABLE 2109.1a
H/t LATERAL SUPPORT RATIOS FOR UNREINFORCED EXTERIOR MASONRY WALLS[a, b, c, d]

	OTHER THAN ENCLOSED BUILDINGS DESIGN WIND SPEED, mph				
Wall construction	90	100	110	120	130
Solid masonry units	19	17	14	13	11
Hollow concrete mas. units or masonry bonded hollow walls	14	12	10	9	8
Cavity walls identical wythes	The *H/t* ratio shall be 0.70 of the *H/t* ratio for single wyth walls. The *t* value shall be the sum of the nominal thickness of the individual wythes.				
Cavity walls with wythes of different types or size masonry	The wall shall be designed based on ACI-530 or the *H/t* ratio may be 0.70 of the *H/t* ratio of a single wyth hollow wall. The *t* value shall be the sum of the nominal thickness of the individual wyths.				

For SI: 1 mile per hour = 0.44 m/s.

a. *H* = clear height or length between lateral supports.
t = nominal wall thickness.

b. All masonry units shall be laid in Type M, S or N mortar. Where Type N mortar is used and the wall spans in the vertical direction, the ratios shall be reduced by 10 percent.

c. These values are based on using masonry cement mortar. If nonair-entrained portland cement/lime mortar is used, the values in the table may be increased by 1.15.

d. Larger *H/t* ratios may be used if the design is done in accordance with engineered design based on TMS 402/ACI 530/ASCE 5.

TABLE 2109.1b
H/t LATERAL SUPPORT RATIOS FOR UNREINFORCED EXTERIOR MASONRY WALLS[a, b, c, d]

	ENCLOSED BUILDING DESIGN WIND SPEED, mph				
Wall construction	90	100	110	120	130
Solid masonry units	23	20	16	15	13
Hollow concrete mas. units or masonry bonded hollow walls	16	14	11	10	9
Cavity walls identical wythes	The *H/t* ratio shall be 0.70 of the *H/t* ratio for single wythe walls. The *t* value shall be the sum of the nominal thickness of the individual wythes.				
Cavity walls with wythes of different types or size masonry	The wall shall be designed based on ACI-530 or the *H/t* ratio may be 0.70 of the *H/t* ratio of a single wythe hollow wall. The *t* value shall be the sum of the nominal thickness of the individual wythes.				

For SI: 1 mile per hour = 0.44 m/s.

a. *H* = clear height or length between lateral supports.
t = nominal wall thickness.

b. All masonry units shall be laid in Type M, S or N mortar. Where Type N mortar is used and the wall spans in the vertical direction, the ratios shall be reduced by 10 percent.

c. These values are based on using masonry cement mortar. If nonair-entrained portland cement/lime mortar is used, the values in the table may be increased by 1.15.

d. Larger *H/t* ratios may be used if the design is done in accordance with engineered design based on TMS 402/ACI 530/ASCE 5.

2109.2 Lateral stability.

2109.2.1 Shear walls. Where the structure depends upon masonry walls for lateral stability, shear walls shall be provided parallel to the direction of the lateral forces resisted.

2109.2.1.1 Cumulative length of shear walls. In each direction in which shearwalls are required for lateral stability, shear walls shall be positioned in two separate planes. The minimum cumulative length of shear walls provided shall be 0.4 times the long dimension of the building. Cumulative length of shear walls shall not include openings or any element with a length that is less than one-half its height.

2109.2.1.2 Maximum diaphragm ratio. Masonry shear walls shall be spaced so that the length-to-width ratio of each diaphragm transferring lateral forces to the shear walls does not exceed the values given in Table 2109.2.1.2.

TABLE 2109.2.1.2
DIAPHRAGM LENGTH-TO-WIDTH RATIOS

FLOOR OR ROOF DIAPHRAGM CONSTRUCTION	MAXIMUM LENGTH-TO-WIDTH RATIO OF DIAPHRAGM PANEL
Cast-in-place concrete	5:1
Precast concrete	4:1
Metal deck with concrete fill	3:1
Metal deck with no fill	2:1
Wood	2:1

TABLE 2109.1.1
EMPIRICAL WIND LIMITATIONS TABLE

	BUILDING HEIGHT, ft (m)	BASIC WIND SPEED, MPH (m/s) (kph)				
		V_{3S} = < 90 (40)	90 < V_{3S} = < 100 (45)	100 (45) < V_{3S} = < 110 (49)	110 (49) < V_{3S} = < 130 (58)	130 (58) < V_{3S}
All masonry elements that are part of the lateral force-resisting[a]	H = < 35 (H = < 11)	Permitted			Not Permitted	
Interior masonry elements that are **not** part of the lateral force-resisting system in buildings other than enclosed as defined by ASCE 7	H > 180 (H > 55)	Not Permitted				
	60 < H = < 180 (18 < H = 55)	Permitted	Not Permitted			
	35 < H = < 60 (11 < H = < 18)	Permitted		Not Permitted		
	H = < 35 (H = < 11)	Permitted				Not Permitted
Exterior masonry elements that are **not** part of the lateral force-resisting system that are more than 35 ft (11 m) above ground	H > 180 (H > 55)	Not Permitted				
	60 < H = < 180 (18 < H = < 55)	Permitted	Not Permitted			
	35 < H = < 60 (11 < H < 18)	Permitted		Not Permitted		
All masonry elements that are **not** part of the lateral force-resisting system[a]	H = < 35 (H = < 11)	Permitted				Not Permitted

For SI: 1 mile per hour = 0.44 m/s.
a. Includes interior and exterior walls for enclosed, partially enclosed, and open buildings as defined by ASCE 7.

2109.2.2 Roofs. The roof construction shall be designed so as not to impart out-of-plane lateral thrust to the walls under roof gravity load.

2109.2.3 Surface-bonded walls. Dry-stacked, surface-bonded concrete masonry walls shall comply with the requirements of this code for masonry wall construction, except where otherwise noted in this section.

2109.2.3.1 Strength. Dry-stacked, surface-bonded concrete masonry walls shall be of adequate strength and proportions to support all superimposed loads without exceeding the allowable stresses listed in Table 2109.2.3.1. Allowable stresses not specified in Table 2109.2.3.1 shall comply with the requirements of ACI 530/ASCE 5/TMS 402.

TABLE 2109.2.3.1
ALLOWABLE STRESS GROSS CROSS-SECTIONAL AREA FOR DRY-STACKED, SURFACE-BONDED CONCRETE MASONRY WALLS

DESCRIPTION	MAXIMUM ALLOWABLE STRESS (psi)
Compression standard block	45
Flexural tension	
Horizontal span	30
Vertical span	18
Shear	10

For SI: 1 pound per square inch = 0.006895 MPa.

2109.2.3.2 Construction. Construction of dry-stacked, surface-bonded masonry walls, including stacking and leveling of units, mixing and application of mortar and curing and protection shall comply with ASTM C 946.

2109.3 Compressive stress requirements.

2109.3.1 Calculations. Compressive stresses in masonry because of vertical dead plus live loads, excluding wind or seismic loads, shall be determined in accordance with Section 2109.3.2.1. Dead and live loads shall be in accordance with Chapter 16, with live load reductions as permitted in Section 1607.9.

2109.3.2 Allowable compressive stresses. The compressive stresses in masonry shall not exceed the values given in Table 2109.3.2. Stress shall be calculated based on specified rather than nominal dimensions.

2109.3.2.1 Calculated compressive stresses. Calculated compressive stresses for single wythe walls and for multiwythe composite masonrywalls shall be determined by dividing the design load by the gross cross-sectional area of the member. The area of openings, chases or recesses in walls shall not be included in the gross cross-sectional area of the wall.

2109.3.2.2 Multiwythe walls. The allowable stress shall be as given in Table 2109.3.2 for the weakest combination of the units used in each wythe.

TABLE 2109.3.2
ALLOWABLE COMPRESSIVE STRESSES FOR EMPIRICAL DESIGN OF MASONRY

CONSTRUCTION COMPRESSIVE STRENGTH OF UNIT GROSS AREA (psi)	ALLOWABLE COMPRESSIVE STRESSES[a] GROSS CROSS-SECTIONAL AREA (psi)	
	Type M or S mortar	Type N mortar
Solid masonry of brick and other solid units of clay or shale; sand-lime or concrete brick:		
8,000 or greater	350	300
4,500	225	200
2,500	160	140
1,500	115	100
Grouted masonry, of clay or shale; sand-lime or concrete:		
4,500 or greater	225	200
2,500	160	140
1,500	115	100
Solid masonry of solid concrete masonry units:		
3,000 or greater	225	200
2,000	160	140
1,200	115	100
Masonry of hollow load-bearing units:		
2,000 or greater	140	120
1,500	115	100
1,000	75	70
700	60	55
Hollow walls (noncomposite masonry bonded)[b]		
Solid units:		
2,500 or greater	160	140
1,500	115	100
Hollow units	75	70
Stone ashlar masonry:		
Granite	720	640
Limestone or marble	450	400
Sandstone or cast stone	360	320
Rubble stone masonry		
Coursed, rough or random	120	100

For SI: 1 pound per square inch = 0.006895 MPa.

a. Linear interpolation for determining allowable stresses for masonry units having compressive strengths which are intermediate between those given in the table is permitted.

b. Where floor and roof loads are carried upon one wythe, the gross cross-sectional area is that of the wythe under load; if both wythes are loaded, the gross cross-sectional area is that of the wall minus the area of the cavity between the wythes. Walls bonded with metal ties shall be considered as noncomposite walls unless collar joints are filled with mortar or grout.

2109.4 Lateral support.

2109.4.1 Intervals. Masonry walls shall be laterally supported in either the horizontal or vertical direction at intervals not exceeding those given in Table 2109.4.1.

2109.4.2 Thickness. Except for cavity walls and cantilever walls, the thickness of a wall shall be its nominal thickness measured perpendicular to the face of the wall. For cavity walls, the thickness shall be determined as the sum of the nominal thicknesses of the individual wythes. For cantilever walls, except for parapets, the ratio of height-to-nominal thickness shall not exceed six for solid masonry or four for hollow masonry. For parapets, see Section 2109.5.4.

TABLE 2109.4.1
INTERIOR WALLS LATERAL SUPPORT REQUIREMENTS IN WIND SPEEDS 110 MPH OR LESS

CONSTRUCTION	MAXIMUM WALL LENGTH TO THICKNESS OR WALL HEIGHT TO THICKNESS
Bearing walls	
Solid units or fully grouted	20
All others	18
Nonbearing walls	
Interior	36

For SI: 1 mile per hour = 0.44 m/s.

Note: Interior walls in windspeeds greater than 110 mph may be designed as exterior walls using Table 2109.1a or Table 2109.1b.

2109.4.3 Support elements. Lateral support shall be provided by crosswalls, pilasters, buttresses or structural frame members when the limiting distance is taken horizontally, or by floors, roofs acting as diaphragms or structural frame members when the limiting distance is taken vertically.

2109.5 Thickness of masonry. Minimum thickness requirements shall be based on nominal dimensions of masonry.

2109.5.1 Thickness of walls. The thickness of masonry walls shall conform to the requirements of Section 2109.5.

2109.5.2 Minimum thickness.

2109.5.2.1 Bearing walls. The minimum thickness of masonry bearing walls more than one story high shall be 8 inches (203 mm). Bearing walls of one-story buildings shall not be less than 6 inches (152 mm) thick.

2109.5.2.2 Rubble stone walls. The minimum thickness of rough, random or coursed rubble stone walls shall be 16 inches (406 mm).

2109.5.2.3 Shear walls. The minimum thickness of masonry shear walls shall be 8 inches (203 mm).

2109.5.2.4 Foundation walls. The minimum thickness of foundation walls shall be 8 inches (203 mm) and as required by Section 2109.5.3.1.

2109.5.2.5 Foundation piers. The minimum thickness of foundation piers shall be 8 inches (203 mm).

2109.5.2.6 Parapet walls. The minimum thickness of parapet walls shall be 8 inches (203 mm) and as required by Section 2109.5.4.1.

2109.5.2.7 Change in thickness. Where walls of masonry of hollow units or masonry bonded hollow walls are decreased in thickness, a course or courses of solid masonry shall be interposed between the wall below and the thinner wall above, or special units or construction shall be used to transmit the loads from face shells or wythes above to those below.

2109.5.3 Foundation walls. Foundation walls shall comply with the requirements of Section 2109.5.3.1 or 2109.5.3.2.

2109.5.3.1 Minimum thickness. Minimum thickness for foundation walls shall comply with the requirements of Table 2109.5.3.1. The provisions of Table 2109.5.3.1 are only applicable where the following conditions are met:

1. The foundation wall does not exceed 8 feet (2438 mm) in height between lateral supports;
2. The terrain surrounding foundation walls is graded to drain surface water away from foundation walls;
3. Backfill is drained to remove ground water away from foundation walls;
4. Lateral support is provided at the top of foundation walls prior to backfilling;
5. The length of foundation walls between perpendicular masonry walls or pilasters is a maximum of three times the basement wall height;
6. The backfill is granular and soil conditions in the area are nonexpansive; and
7. Masonry is laid in running bond using Type M or S mortar.

2109.5.3.2 Design requirements. Where the requirements of Section 2109.5.3.1 are not met, foundation walls shall be designed in accordance with Section 1807.1.5.

2109.5.4 Parapet walls.

2109.5.4.1 Minimum thickness. The minimum thickness of unreinforced masonry parapets shall meet Section 2109.5.2.6 and their height shall not exceed three times their thickness.

2109.5.4.2 Additional provisions. Additional provisions for parapet walls are contained in Sections 1503.2 and 1503.3.

2109.6 Bond.

2109.6.1 General. The facing and backing of multiwythe masonry walls shall be bonded in accordance with Section 2109.6.2, 2109.6.3 or 2109.6.4.

2109.6.2 Bonding with masonry headers.

2109.6.2.1 Solid units. Where the facing and backing (adjacent wythes) of solid masonry construction are bonded by means of masonry headers, no less than 4 percent of thewall surface of each face shall be composed of headers extending not less than 3 inches (76 mm) into the backing. The distance between adjacent full-length headers shall not exceed 24 inches (610 mm) either vertically or horizontally. In walls in which a single header does not extend through thewall, headers from the opposite sides shall overlap at least 3 inches (76 mm), or headers from opposite sides shall be covered with another header course overlapping the header below at least 3 inches (76 mm).

2109.6.2.2 Hollow units. Where two or more hollow units are used to make up the thickness of a wall, the stretcher courses shall be bonded at vertical intervals not exceeding 34 inches (864 mm) by lapping at least 3 inches (76 mm) over the unit below, or by lapping at vertical intervals not exceeding 17 inches (432 mm) with units that are at least 50 percent greater in thickness than the units below.

2109.6.2.3 Masonry bonded hollow walls. In masonry bonded hollow walls, the facing and backing shall be bonded so that not less than 4 percent of the wall surface of each face is composed of masonry bonded units extending not less than 3 inches (76 mm) into the backing. The distance between adjacent bonders shall not exceed 24 inches (610 mm) either vertically or horizontally.

2109.6.3 Bonding with wall ties or joint reinforcement.

2109.6.3.1 Bonding with wall ties. Except as required by Section 2109.6.3.1.1, where the facing and backing (adjacent wythes) of masonrywalls are bonded with wire size W2.8 (MW18) wall ties or metal wire of equivalent stiffness embedded in the horizontal mortar joints, there shall be at least one metal tie for each $4^1/_2$ square feet (0.42 m^2) of wall area. The maximum vertical distance between ties shall not exceed 24 inches (610 mm), and the maximum horizontal distance shall not exceed 36 inches (914 mm). Rods or ties bent to rectangular shape shall be used with hollow masonry units laid with the cells vertical. In other walls, the ends of ties shall be bent to 90-degree (1.57 rad) angles to provide hooks no less than 2 inches (51 mm) long. Wall ties shall be without drips. Additional bonding ties shall be provided at all openings, spaced not more than 36 inches (914 mm) apart around the perimeter and within 12 inches (305 mm) of the opening.

2109.6.3.1.1 Bonding with adjustable wall ties. Where the facing and backing (adjacent wythes) of masonry are bonded with adjustable wall ties, there shall be at least one tie for each 1.77 square feet (0.164m^2) of wall area. Neither the vertical nor horizontal spacing of the adjustable wall ties shall exceed 16 inches (406 mm). The maximum vertical offset of bed joints from one wythe to the other shall be $1^1/_4$ inches (32 mm). The maximum clearance between connecting parts of the ties shall be $^1/_{16}$ inch (1.6 mm). When pintle legs are used, ties shall have at least two wire size W2.8 (MW18) legs.

2109.6.3.2 Bonding with prefabricated joint reinforcement. Where the facing and backing (adjacent wythes) ofmasonry are bonded with prefabricated joint reinforcement, there shall be at least one cross wire serving as a tie for each $2^2/_3$ square feet (0.25m^2) ofwall area. The vertical spacing of the joint reinforcing shall not exceed 24 inches (610 mm). Cross wires on prefabricated joint reinforcement shall not be less than W1.7 (MW11) and shall be without drips. The longitudinal wires shall be embedded in the mortar.

2109.6.4 Bonding with natural or cast stone.

2109.6.4.1 Ashlar masonry. In ashlar masonry, bonder units, uniformly distributed, shall be provided to the extent of not less than 10 percent of the wall area. Such bonder units shall extend not less than 4 inches (102 mm) into the backing wall.

2109.6.4.2 Rubble stone masonry. Rubble stone masonry 24 inches (610 mm) or less in thickness shall have bonder units with a maximum spacing of 36 inches (914 mm) vertically and 36 inches (914 mm) horizontally, and if the masonry is of greater thickness than 24 inches (610 mm), shall have one bonder unit for each 6 square feet (0.56 m^2) of wall surface on both sides.

2109.6.5 Masonry bonding pattern.

2109.6.5.1 Masonry laid in running bond. Each wythe of masonry shall be laid in running bond, head joints in successive courses shall be offset by not less than one-fourth the unit length or the masonry walls shall be reinforced longitudinally as required in Section 2109.6.5.2.

2109.6.5.2 Masonry laid in stack bond. Where unit masonry is laid with less head joint offset than in Section 2109.6.5.1, the minimum area of horizontal reinforcement placed in mortar bed joints or in bond beams spaced not more than 48 inches (1219 mm) apart, shall be 0.0003 times the vertical cross-sectional area of the wall.

2109.7 Anchorage.

2109.7.1 General. Masonry elements shall be anchored in accordance with Sections 2109.7.2 through 2109.7.4.

2109.7.2 Intersecting walls. Masonry walls depending upon one another for lateral support shall be anchored or bonded at locations where they meet or intersect by one of the methods indicated in Sections 2109.7.2.1 through 2109.7.2.5.

2109.7.2.1 Bonding pattern. Fifty percent of the units at the intersection shall be laid in an overlapping masonry bonding pattern, with alternative units having a bearing of not less than 3 inches (76 mm) on the unit below.

2109.7.2.2 Steel connectors. Walls shall be anchored by steel connectors having a minimum section of $^1/_4$ inch (6.4 mm) by $1^1/_2$ inches (38 mm), with ends bent up at least 2 inches (51 mm) or with cross pins to form anchorage. Such anchors shall be at least 24 inches (610 mm) long and the maximum spacing shall be 48 inches (1219 mm).

2109.7.2.3 Joint reinforcement. Walls shall be anchored by joint reinforcement spaced at a maximum distance of 8 inches (203 mm). Longitudinal wires of such reinforcement shall be at least wire size W1.7 (MW 11) and shall extend at least 30 inches (762 mm) in each direction at the intersection.

2109.7.2.4 Interior nonload-bearing walls. Interior nonload-bearing walls shall be anchored at their intersection, at vertical intervals of not more than 16 inches (406 mm) with joint reinforcement or $^1/_4$-inch (6.4 mm) mesh galvanized hardware cloth.

2109.7.2.5 Ties, joint reinforcement or anchors. Other metal ties, joint reinforcement or anchors, if used, shall be spaced to provide equivalent area of anchorage to that required by this section.

2109.7.3 Floor and roof anchorage. Floor and roof diaphragms providing lateral support to masonry shall comply with the live loads in Section 1607.3 and shall be connected to the masonry in accordance with Sections 2109.7.3.1 through 2109.7.3.3. Roof loading shall be determined in accordance with Chapter 16 and, when net uplift occurs, uplift shall be resisted entirely by an anchorage system designed in accordance with the provisions of Sections 2.1 and 2.3, Sections 3.1 and 3.3 or Chapter 4 of ACI 530/ASCE 5/TMS 402.

2109.7.3.1Wood floor joists. Wood floor joists bearing on masonry walls shall be anchored to the wall at intervals not to exceed 72 inches (1829 mm) by metal strap anchors. Joists parallel to the wall shall be anchored with metal straps spaced not more than 72 inches (1829 mm) o.c. extending over or under and secured to at least three joists. Blocking shall be provided between joists at each strap anchor.

2109.7.3.2 Steel floor joists. Steel joists that are supported by masonry walls shall bear on and be connected to steel bearing plates. Maximum joist spacing shall be 6 feet (1.83 m) on center. Each bearing plate shall be anchored to the wall with a minimum of two $^1/_2$ inch (12.7 mm) diameter bolts, or their equivalent. Where steel joists are parallel to the wall, anchors shall be located where joist bridging terminates at the wall and additional anchorage shall be provided to comply with Section 2109.7.3.3.

2109.7.3.3 Roof diaphragms. Roof diaphragms shall be anchored to masonry walls with $^1/_2$-inch-diameter (12.7 mm) bolts, 72 inches (1829 mm) on center or their equivalent. Bolts shall extend and be embedded at least 15 inches (381 mm) into the masonry, or be hooked or welded to not less than 0.20 square inch (129 mm^2) of bond beam reinforcement placed not less than 6 inches (152 mm) from the top of the wall.

2109.7.4 Walls adjoining structural framing. Where walls are dependent upon the structural frame for lateral support, they shall be anchored to the structural members with metal anchors or otherwise keyed to the structural members. Metal anchors shall consist of $^1/_2$-inch (12.7 mm) bolts spaced at 48 inches (1219 mm) on center embedded 4 inches (102 mm) into the masonry, or their equivalent area.

2109.8 Adobe construction. Adobe construction shall comply with this section and shall be subject to the requirements of this code for Type V construction, Chapter 5 of TMS 402/ACI 530/ASCE 5, and this section.

2109.8.1 Unstabilized adobe.

2109.8.1.1 Compressive strength. Adobe units shall have an average compressive strength of 300 psi (2068 kPa) when tested in accordance with ASTM C 67. Five samples shall be tested and no individual unit is permitted to have a compressive strength of less than 250 psi (1724 kPa).

2109.8.1.2 Modulus of rupture. Adobe units shall have an average modulus of rupture of 50 psi (345 kPa) when tested in accordance with the following procedure. Five samples shall be tested and no individual unit shall have a modulus of rupture of less than 35 psi (241 kPa).

2109.8.1.2.1 Support conditions. A cured unit shall be simply supported by 2-inch-diameter (51 mm) cylindrical supports located 2 inches (51 mm) in from each end and extending the full width of the unit.

2109.8.1.2.2 Loading conditions. A 2-inch-diameter (51 mm) cylinder shall be placed at midspan parallel to the supports.

2109.8.1.2.3 Testing procedure. A vertical load shall be applied to the cylinder at the rate of 500 pounds per minute (37 N/s) until failure occurs.

2109.8.1.2.4 Modulus of rupture determination. The modulus of rupture shall be determined by the equation:

$$f_r = 3\,PL_s / 2\,S_w (S_t^2) \quad \textbf{(Equation 21-2)}$$

where, for the purposes of this section only:

S_w = Width of the test specimen measured parallel to the loading cylinder, inches (mm).

f_r = Modulus of rupture, psi (MPa).

L_s = Distance between supports, inches (mm).

S_t = Thickness of the test specimen measured parallel to the direction of load, inches (mm).

P = The applied load at failure, pounds (N).

2109.8.1.3 Moisture content requirements. Adobe units shall have a moisture content not exceeding 4 percent by weight.

2109.8.1.4 Shrinkage cracks. Adobe units shall not contain more than three shrinkage cracks and any single shrinkage crack shall not exceed 3 inches (76 mm) in length or $^1/_8$ inch (3.2 mm) in width.

2109.8.2 Stabilized adobe.

2109.8.2.1 Material requirements. Stabilized adobe shall comply with the material requirements of unstabilized adobe in addition to Sections 2108.3.2.1.1 and 2108.3.2.1.2.

2109.8.2.1.1 Soil requirements. Soil used for stabilized adobe units shall be chemically compatible with the stabilizing material.

2109.8.2.1.2 Absorption requirements. A 4-inch (102 mm) cube, cut from a stabilized adobe unit dried to a constant weight in a ventilated oven at 212°F to 239°F (100°C to 115°C), shall not absorb more than $2^1/_2$ percent moisture by weight when placed upon a constantly water-saturated, porous surface for seven days. A minimum of five specimens shall be tested and each specimen shall be cut from a separate unit.

2109.8.3 Allowable stress. The allowable compressive stress based on gross cross-sectional area of adobe shall not exceed 30 psi (207 kPa).

2109.8.3.1 Bolts. Bolt values shall not exceed those set forth in Table 2109.8.3.1.

TABLE 2109.8.3.1
ALLOWABLE SHEAR ON BOLTS IN ADOBE MASONRY

DIAMETER OF BOLTS (inches)	MINIMUM EMBEDMENT (inches)	SHEAR (pounds)
$^1/_2$	—	—
$^5/_8$	12	200
$^3/_4$	15	300
$^7/_8$	18	400
1	21	500
$1^1/_8$	24	600

For SI: 1 inch = 25.4 mm, 1 pound = 4.448 N.

2109.8.4 Construction.

2109.8.4.1 General. Adobe construction shall be limited as stated in Sections 2109.3.4.1.1 through 2109.3.4.1.4.

2109.8.4.1.1 Height restrictions. Adobe construction shall be limited to buildings not exceeding one *story*, except that two-*story* construction is allowed when designed by a *registered design professional*.

2109.8.4.1.2 Mortar restrictions. Mortar for stabilized adobe units shall comply with Chapter 21 or adobe soil. Adobe soil used as mortar shall comply with material requirements for stabilized adobe. Mortar for unstabilized adobe shall be portland cement mortar.

2109.8.4.1.3 Mortar joints. Adobe units shall be laid with full head and bed joints and in full running bond.

2109.8.4.1.4 Parapet walls. Parapet walls constructed of adobe units shall be waterproofed.

2109.8.4.2 Wall thickness. The minimum thickness of *exterior walls* in one-story buildings shall be 10 inches (254 mm). The walls shall be laterally supported at intervals not exceeding 24 feet (7315 mm). The minimum thickness of interior *load-bearing walls* shall be 8 inches (203 mm). In no case shall the unsupported height of any wall constructed of adobe units exceed 10 times the thickness of such wall.

2109.8.4.3 Foundations. Foundations for adobe construction shall be in accordance with Sections 2109.8.4.3.1 and 2109.8.4.3.2.

2109.8.4.3.1 Foundation support. Walls and partitions constructed of adobe units shall be supported by foundations or footings that extend not less than 6 inches (152 mm) above adjacent ground surfaces and are constructed of solid masonry (excluding adobe) or concrete. Footings and foundations shall comply with Chapter 18.

2109.8.4.3.2 Lower course requirements. Stabilized adobe units shall be used in adobe walls for the first 4 inches (102 mm) above the finished first-floor elevation.

2109.8.4.4 Isolated piers or columns. Adobe units shall not be used for isolated piers or columns in a load-bearing capacity. Walls less than 24 inches (610 mm) in length shall be considered isolated piers or columns.

2109.8.4.5 Tie beams. *Exterior walls* and interior *load-bearing walls* constructed of adobe units shall have a continuous tie beam at the level of the floor or roof bearing and meeting the following requirements.

2109.8.4.5.1 Concrete tie beams. Concrete tie beams shall be a minimum depth of 6 inches (152 mm) and a minimum width of 10 inches (254 mm). Concrete tie beams shall be continuously reinforced with a minimum of two No. 4 reinforcing bars. The specified compressive strength of concrete shall be at least 2,500 psi (17.2 MPa).

2109.8.4.5.2 Wood tie beams. Wood tie beams shall be solid or built up of lumber having a minimum nominal thickness of 1 inch (25 mm), and shall have a minimum depth of 6 inches (152 mm) and a minimum width of 10 inches (254 mm). Joints in wood tie beams shall be spliced a minimum of 6 inches (152 mm). No splices shall be allowed within 12 inches (305 mm) of an opening. Wood used in tie beams shall be *approved* naturally decay-resistant or preservative-treated wood.

2109.8.4.6 Exterior finish. *Exterior walls* constructed of unstabilized adobe units shall have their exterior surface covered with a minimum of two coats of portland cement plaster having a minimum thickness of $^3/_4$ inch (19.1 mm) and conforming to ASTM C 926. Lathing shall comply with ASTM C 1063. Fasteners shall be spaced at 16 inches (406 mm) o.c. maximum. Exposed wood surfaces shall be treated with an *approved* wood preservative or other protective coating prior to lath application.

2109.8.4.7 Lintels. Lintels shall be considered structural members and shall be designed in accordance with the applicable provisions of Chapter 16.

SECTION 2110 GLASS UNIT MASONRY

2110.1 General. Glass unit masonry construction shall comply with Chapter 7 of TMS 402/ACI 530/ASCE 5 and this section.

2110.1.1 Limitations. Solid or hollow *approved* glass block shall not be used in fire walls, party walls, fire barriers, fire partitions or smoke barriers, or for load-bearing construction. Such blocks shall be erected with mortar and reinforcement in metal channel-type frames, structural frames, masonry or concrete recesses, embedded panel anchors as provided for both exterior and interior walls or other *approved* joint materials. Wood strip framing shall not be used in walls required to have a fire-resistance rating by other provisions of this code.

Exceptions:

1. Glass-block assemblies having a fire protection rating of not less than $^3/_4$ hour shall be permitted as opening protectives in accordance with Section 715 in fire barriers, fire partitions and smoke barriers that have a required fire-resistance rating of 1 hour or less and do not enclose exit stairways, exit ramps or exit passageways.
2. Glass-block assemblies as permitted in Section 404.6, Exception 2.

SECTION 2111 MASONRY FIREPLACES

2111.1 Definition. A masonry fireplace is a fireplace constructed of concrete or masonry. Masonry fireplaces shall be constructed in accordance with this section, Table 2111.1 and Figure 2111.1.

2111.2 Footings and foundations. Footings for masonry fireplaces and their chimneys shall be constructed of concrete or solid masonry at least 12 inches (305 mm) thick and shall extend at least 12 inches (305 mm) beyond the face of the fireplace or foundation wall on all sides. Footings shall be founded on natural undisturbed earth or engineered fill below frost depth. In areas not subjected to freezing, footings shall be at least 12 inches (305 mm) below finished grade.

TABLE 2111.1
SUMMARY OF REQUIREMENTS FOR MASONRY FIREPLACES AND CHIMNEYS[a]

ITEM	LETTER	REQUIREMENTS	SECTION
Hearth and hearth extension thickness	A	4-inch minimum thickness for hearth, 2-inch minimum thickness for hearth extension.	2111.9
Hearth extension (each side of opening)	B	8 inches for fireplace opening less than 6 square feet. 12 inches for fireplace opening greater than or equal to 6 square feet.	2111.10
Hearth extension (front of opening)	C	16 inches for fireplace opening less than 6 square feet. 20 inches for fireplace opening greater than or equal to 6 square feet.	2111.10
Firebox dimensions	—	20-inch minimum firebox depth. 12-inch minimum firebox depth for Rumford fireplaces.	2111.6
Hearth and hearth extension reinforcing	D	Reinforced to carry its own weight and all imposed loads.	2111.9
Thickness of wall of firebox	E	10 inches solid masonry or 8 inches where firebrick lining is used.	2111.5
Distance from top of opening to throat	F	8 inches minimum.	2111.7 2111.7.1
Smoke chamber wall thickness dimensions	G	6 inches lined; 8 inches unlined. Not taller than opening width; walls not inclined more than 45 degrees from vertical for prefabricated smoke chamber linings or 30 degrees from vertical for corbeled masonry.	2111.8
Chimney vertical reinforcing	H	Four No. 4 full-length bars for chimney up to 40 inches wide. Add two No. 4 bars for each additional 40 inches or fraction of width, or for each additional flue.	2111.3.1, 2113.3.1
Chimney horizontal reinforcing	J	$^{1}/_{4}$-inch ties at each 18 inches, and two ties at each bend in vertical steel.	2111.3.2, 2113.3.2
Fireplace lintel	L	Noncombustible material with 4-inch bearing length of each side of opening.	2111.7
Chimney walls with flue lining	M	4-inch-thick solid masonry with $^{5}/_{8}$-inch fireclay liner or equivalent. $^{1}/_{2}$-inch grout or airspace between fireclay liner and wall.	2113.11.1
Effective flue area (based on area of fireplace opening and chimney)	P	See Section 2113.16.	2113.16
Clearances From chimney From fireplace From combustible trim or materials Above roof	R	 2 inches interior, 1 inch exterior or 12 inches from lining. 2 inches back or sides or 12 inches from lining. 6 inches from opening 3 feet above roof penetration, 2 feet above part of structure within 10 feet.	 2113.19 2111.11 2111.12 2113.9
Anchorage strap Number required Embedment into chimney Fasten to Number of bolts	S	$^{3}/_{16}$ inch by 1 inch Two 12 inches hooked around outer bar with 6-inch extension. 4 joists Two $^{1}/_{2}$-inch diameter.	2111.4 2113.4.1
Footing Thickness Width	T	 12-inch minimum. 12 inches each side of fireplace wall.	2111.2

For SI: 1 inch = 25.4 mm, 1 foot = 304.8 mm, 1 square foot = 0.0929 m², 1 degree = 0.017 rad.

a. This table provides a summary of major requirements for the construction of masonry chimneys and fireplaces. Letter references are to Figure 2111.1, which shows examples of typical construction. This table does not cover all requirements, nor does it cover all aspects of the indicated requirements. For the actual mandatory requirements of the code, see the indicated section of text.

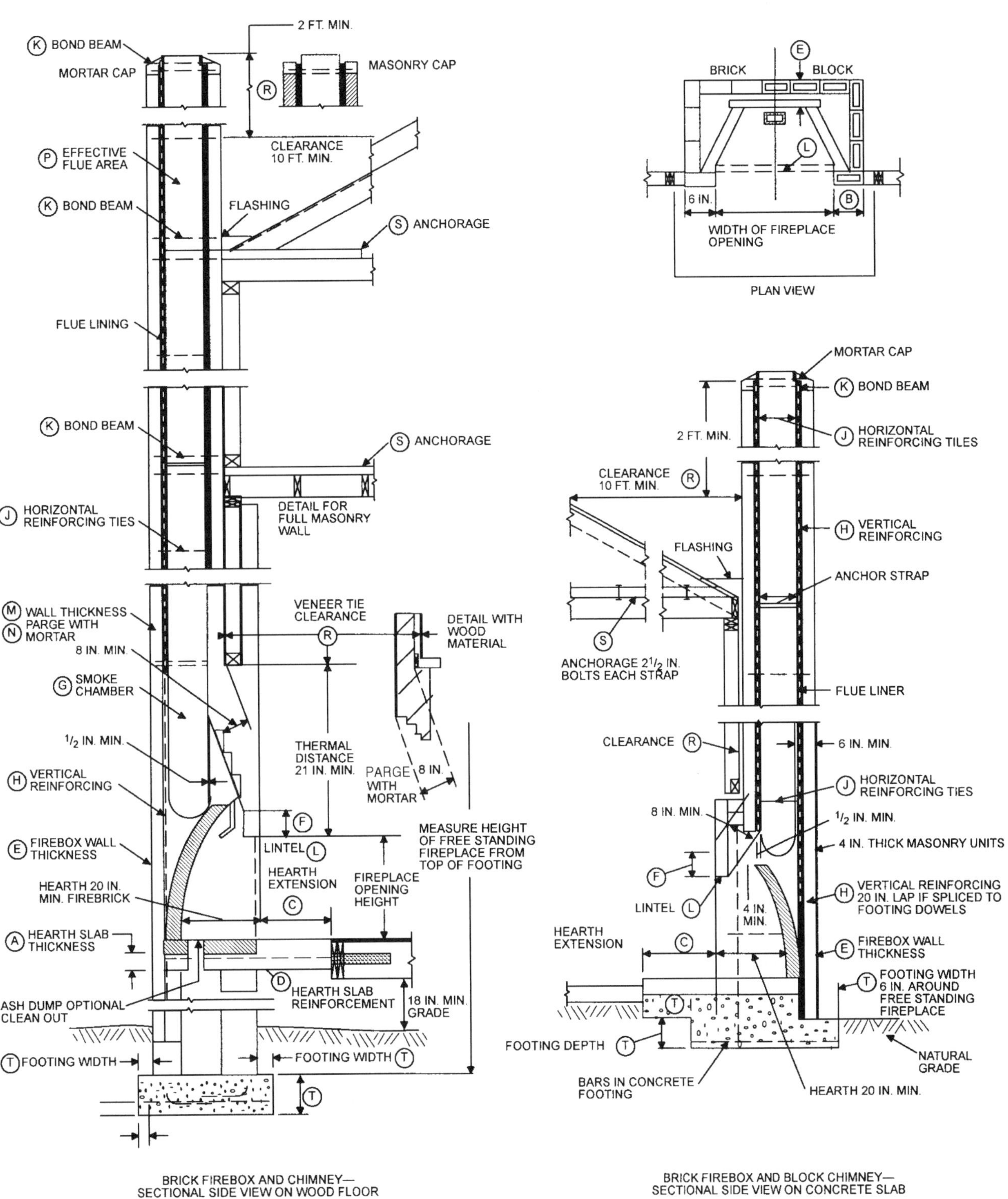

For SI: 1 inch = 25.4 mm, 1 foot = 304.8 mm.

FIGURE 2111.1
FIREPLACE AND CHIMNEY DETAILS

2111.2.1 Ash dump cleanout. Cleanout openings, located within foundation walls below fireboxes, when provided, shall be equipped with ferrous metal or masonry doors and frames constructed to remain tightly closed, except when in use. Cleanouts shall be accessible and located so that ash removal will not create a hazard to combustible materials.

2111.3 Seismic reinforcing. Masonry or concrete fireplaces shall be constructed, anchored, supported and reinforced as required in this chapter. In *Seismic Design Category* C or D, masonry and concrete fireplaces shall be reinforced and anchored as detailed in Sections 2111.3.1, 2111.3.2, 2111.4 and 2111.4.1 for chimneys serving fireplaces. In *Seismic Design Category* A or B, reinforcement and seismic anchorage is not required. In *Seismic Design Category* E or F, masonry and concrete chimneys shall be reinforced in accordance with the requirements of Sections 2101 through 2108.

2111.3.1 Vertical reinforcing. For fireplaces with chimneys up to 40 inches (1016 mm) wide, four No. 4 continuous vertical bars, anchored in the foundation, shall be placed in the concrete between wythes of solid masonry or within the cells of hollow unit masonry and grouted in accordance with Section 2103.12. For fireplaces with chimneys greater than 40 inches (1016 mm) wide, two additional No. 4 vertical bars shall be provided for each additional 40 inches (1016 mm) in width or fraction thereof.

2111.3.2 Horizontal reinforcing. Vertical reinforcement shall be placed enclosed within $^1/_4$-inch (6.4 mm) ties or other reinforcing of equivalent net cross-sectional area, spaced not to exceed 18 inches (457 mm) on center in concrete; or placed in the bed joints of unit masonry at a minimum of every 18 inches (457 mm) of vertical height. Two such ties shall be provided at each bend in the vertical bars.

2111.4 Seismic anchorage. Masonry and concrete chimneys in *Seismic Design Category* C or D shall be anchored at each floor, ceiling or roof line more than 6 feet (1829 mm) above grade, except where constructed completely within the *exterior walls*. Anchorage shall conform to the following requirements.

2111.4.1 Anchorage. Two $^3/_{16}$-inch by 1-inch (4.8 mm by 25.4 mm) straps shall be embedded a minimum of 12 inches (305 mm) into the chimney. Straps shall be hooked around the outer bars and extend 6 inches (152 mm) beyond the bend. Each strap shall be fastened to a minimum of four floor joists with two $^1/_2$-inch (12.7 mm) bolts.

2111.5 Firebox walls. Masonry fireboxes shall be constructed of solid masonry units, hollow masonry units grouted solid, stone or concrete. When a lining of firebrick at least 2 inches (51 mm) in thickness or other *approved* lining is provided, the minimum thickness of back and sidewalls shall each be 8 inches (203 mm) of solid masonry, including the lining. The width of joints between firebricks shall not be greater than $^1/_4$ inch (6.4 mm). When no lining is provided, the total minimum thickness of back and sidewalls shall be 10 inches (254 mm) of solid masonry. Firebrick shall conform to ASTM C 27 or ASTM C 1261 and shall be laid with medium-duty refractory mortar conforming to ASTM C 199.

2111.5.1 Steel fireplace units. Steel fireplace units are permitted to be installed with solid masonry to form a masonry fireplace provided they are installed according to either the requirements of their listing or the requirements of this section. Steel fireplace units incorporating a steel firebox lining shall be constructed with steel not less than $^1/_4$ inch (6.4 mm) in thickness, and an air-circulating chamber which is ducted to the interior of the building. The firebox lining shall be encased with solid masonry to provide a total thickness at the back and sides of not less than 8 inches (203 mm), of which not less than 4 inches (102 mm) shall be of solid masonry or concrete. Circulating air ducts employed with steel fireplace units shall be constructed of metal or masonry.

2111.6 Firebox dimensions. The firebox of a concrete or masonry fireplace shall have a minimum depth of 20 inches (508 mm). The throat shall not be less than 8 inches (203 mm) above the fireplace opening. The throat opening shall not be less than 4 inches (102 mm) in depth. The cross-sectional area of the passageway above the firebox, including the throat, damper and smoke chamber, shall not be less than the cross-sectional area of the flue.

Exception: Rumford fireplaces shall be permitted provided that the depth of the fireplace is at least 12 inches (305 mm) and at least one-third of the width of the fireplace opening, and the throat is at least 12 inches (305 mm) above the lintel, and at least $^1/_{20}$ the cross-sectional area of the fireplace opening.

2111.7 Lintel and throat. Masonry over a fireplace opening shall be supported by a lintel of noncombustible material. The minimum required bearing length on each end of the fireplace opening shall be 4 inches (102 mm). The fireplace throat or damper shall be located a minimum of 8 inches (203 mm) above the top of the fireplace opening.

2111.7.1 Damper. Masonry fireplaces shall be equipped with a ferrous metal damper located at least 8 inches (203 mm) above the top of the fireplace opening. Dampers shall be installed in the fireplace or at the top of the flue venting the fireplace, and shall be operable from the room containing the fireplace. Damper controls shall be permitted to be located in the fireplace.

2111.8 Smoke chamber walls. Smoke chamber walls shall be constructed of solid masonry units, hollow masonry units grouted solid, stone or concrete. The total minimum thickness of front, back and sidewalls shall be 8 inches (203 mm) of solid masonry. The inside surface shall be parged smooth with refractory mortar conforming to ASTM C 199. When a lining of firebrick at least 2 inches (51 mm) thick, or a lining of vitrified clay at least $^5/_8$ inch (15.9 mm) thick, is provided, the total minimum thickness of front, back and sidewalls shall be 6 inches (152 mm) of solid masonry, including the lining. Firebrick shall conform to ASTM C 1261 and shall be laid with refractory mortar conforming to ASTM C 199. Vitrified clay linings shall conform to ASTM C 315.

2111.8.1 Smoke chamber dimensions. The inside height of the smoke chamber from the fireplace throat to the beginning of the flue shall not be greater than the inside width of the fireplace opening. The inside surface of the smoke chamber shall not be inclined more than 45 degrees (0.76 rad) from vertical when prefabricated smoke chamber linings are used or when the smoke chamber walls are rolled or sloped rather than corbeled. When the inside surface of the smoke chamber is formed by corbeled masonry, the walls shall not be corbeled more than 30 degrees (0.52 rad) from vertical.

2111.9 Hearth and hearth extension. Masonry fireplace hearths and hearth extensions shall be constructed of concrete or masonry, supported by noncombustible materials, and reinforced to carry their own weight and all imposed loads. No combustible material shall remain against the underside of hearths or hearth extensions after construction.

2111.9.1 Hearth thickness. The minimum thickness of fireplace hearths shall be 4 inches (102 mm).

2111.9.2 Hearth extension thickness. The minimum thickness of hearth extensions shall be 2 inches (51 mm).

Exception: When the bottom of the firebox opening is raised at least 8 inches (203 mm) above the top of the hearth extension, a hearth extension of not less than $^3/_8$-inch-thick (9.5 mm) brick, concrete, stone, tile or other *approved* noncombustible material is permitted.

2111.10 Hearth extension dimensions. Hearth extensions shall extend at least 16 inches (406 mm) in front of, and at least 8 inches (203 mm) beyond, each side of the fireplace opening. Where the fireplace opening is 6 square feet (0.557 m^2) or larger, the hearth extension shall extend at least 20 inches (508 mm) in front of, and at least 12 inches (305 mm) beyond, each side of the fireplace opening.

2111.11 Fireplace clearance. Any portion of a masonry fireplace located in the interior of a building or within the *exterior wall* of a building shall have a clearance to combustibles of not less than 2 inches (51 mm) from the front faces and sides of masonry fireplaces and not less than 4 inches (102 mm) from the back faces of masonry fireplaces. The airspace shall not be filled, except to provide fireblocking in accordance with Section 2111.12.

Exceptions:

1. Masonry fireplaces *listed* and labeled for use in contact with combustibles in accordance with UL 127 and installed in accordance with the manufacturer's installation instructions are permitted to have combustible material in contact with their exterior surfaces.
2. When masonry fireplaces are constructed as part of masonry or concrete walls, combustible materials shall not be in contact with the masonry or concrete walls less than 12 inches (306 mm) from the inside surface of the nearest firebox lining.
3. Exposed combustible *trim* and the edges of sheathing materials, such as wood siding, flooring and drywall, are permitted to abut the masonry fireplace sidewalls and hearth extension, in accordance with Figure 2111.11, provided such combustible *trim* or sheathing is a minimum of 12 inches (306 mm) from the inside surface of the nearest firebox lining.
4. Exposed combustible mantels or *trim* is permitted to be placed directly on the masonry fireplace front surrounding the fireplace opening, provided such combustible materials shall not be placed within 6 inches (153 mm) of a fireplace opening. Combustible material directly above and within 12 inches (305 mm) of the fireplace opening shall not project more than $^1/_8$ inch (3.2 mm) for each 1-inch (25 mm) distance from such opening. Combustible materials located along the sides of the fireplace opening that project more than $1^1/_2$ inches (38 mm) from the face of the fireplace shall have an additional clearance equal to the projection.

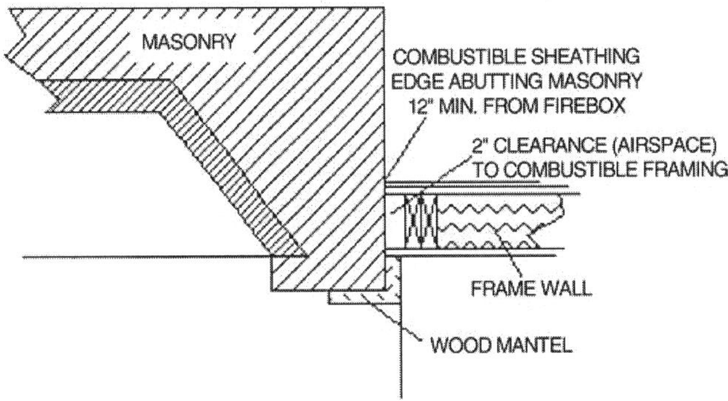

For SI: 1 inch = 25.4 mm.

FIGURE 2111.11
ILLUSTRATION OF EXCEPTION TO FIREPLACE CLEARANCE PROVISION

2111.12 Fireplace fireblocking. All spaces between fireplaces and floors and ceilings through which fireplaces pass shall be fireblocked with noncombustible material securely fastened in place. The fireblocking of spaces between wood joists, beams or headers shall be to a depth of 1 inch (25 mm) and shall only be placed on strips of metal or metal lath laid across the spaces between combustible material and the chimney.

2111.13 Exterior air. Factory-built or masonry fireplaces covered in this section shall be equipped with an exterior air supply to ensure proper fuel combustion unless the room is mechanically ventilated and controlled so that the indoor pressure is neutral or positive.

2111.13.1 Factory-built fireplaces. Exterior combustion air ducts for factory-built fireplaces shall be *listed* components of the fireplace, and installed according to the fireplace manufacturer's instructions.

2111.13.2 Masonry fireplaces. *Listed* combustion air ducts for masonry fireplaces shall be installed according to the terms of their listing and manufacturer's instructions.

2111.13.3 Exterior air intake. The exterior air intake shall be capable of providing all combustion air from the exterior of the *dwelling*. The exterior air intake shall not be located within a garage, *attic*, basement or crawl space of the *dwelling* nor shall the air intake be located at an elevation higher than the firebox. The exterior air intake shall be covered with a corrosion-resistant screen of $^1/_4$-inch (6.4 mm) mesh.

2111.13.4 Clearance. Unlisted combustion air ducts shall be installed with a minimum 1-inch (25 mm) clearance to combustibles for all parts of the duct within 5 feet (1524 mm) of the duct outlet.

2111.13.5 Passageway. The combustion air passageway shall be a minimum of 6 square inches (3870 mm^2) and not more than 55 square inches (0.035 m^2), except that combustion air systems for *listed* fireplaces or for fireplaces tested for emissions shall be constructed according to the fireplace manufacturer's instructions.

2111.13.6 Outlet. The exterior air outlet is permitted to be located in the back or sides of the firebox chamber or within 24 inches (610 mm) of the firebox opening on or near the floor. The outlet shall be closable and designed to prevent burning material from dropping into concealed combustible spaces.

SECTION 2112 MASONRY HEATERS

2112.1 Definition. A masonry heater is a heating appliance constructed of concrete or solid masonry, hereinafter referred to as "masonry," which is designed to absorb and store heat from a solid fuel fire built in the firebox by routing the exhaust gases through internal heat exchange channels in which the flow path downstream of the firebox may include flow in a horizontal or downward direction before entering the chimney and which delivers heat by radiation from the masonry surface of the heater.

2112.2 Installation. Masonry heaters shall be installed in accordance with this section and comply with one of the following:

1. Masonry heaters shall comply with the requirements of ASTM E 1602; or
2. Masonry heaters shall be *listed* and labeled in accordance with UL 1482 and installed in accordance with the manufacturer's installation instructions.

2112.3 Footings and foundation. The firebox floor of a masonry heater shall be a minimum thickness of 4 inches (102 mm) of noncombustible material and be supported on a noncombustible footing and foundation in accordance with Section 2113.2.

2112.4 Seismic reinforcing. In *Seismic Design Category* D, E and F, masonry heaters shall be anchored to the masonry foundation in accordance with Section 2113.3. Seismic reinforcing shall not be required within the body of a masonry heater with a height that is equal to or less than 3.5 times its body width and where the masonry chimney serving the heater is not supported by the body of the heater. Where the masonry chimney shares a common wall with the facing of the masonry heater, the chimney portion of the structure shall be reinforced in accordance with Section 2113.

2112.5 Masonry heater clearance. Combustible materials shall not be placed within 36 inches (765 mm) of the outside surface of a masonry heater in accordance with NFPA 211, Section 8-7 (clearances for solid fuel-burning appliances), and the required space between the heater and combustible material shall be fully vented to permit the free flow of air around all heater surfaces.

Exceptions:

1. When the masonry heater wall thickness is at least 8 inches (203 mm) thick of solid masonry and the wall thickness of the heat exchange channels is at least 5 inches (127 mm) thick of solid masonry, combustible materials shall not be placed within 4 inches (102 mm) of the outside surface of a masonry heater. A clearance of at least 8 inches (203 mm) shall be provided between the gas-tight capping slab of the heater and a combustible ceiling.
2. Masonry heaters *listed* and labeled in accordance with UL 1482 and installed in accordance with the manufacturer's instructions.

SECTION 2113 MASONRY CHIMNEYS

2113.1 Definition. A masonry chimney is a chimney constructed of concrete or masonry, hereinafter referred to as "masonry." Masonry chimneys shall be constructed, anchored, supported and reinforced as required in this chapter.

2113.2 Footings and foundations. Footings for masonry chimneys shall be constructed of concrete or solid masonry at least 12 inches (305 mm) thick and shall extend at least 6 inches (152 mm) beyond the face of the foundation or support wall on all sides. Footings shall be founded on natural undisturbed earth or engineered fill below frost depth. In areas not subjected to freezing, footings shall be at least 12 inches (305 mm) below finished grade.

2113.3 Seismic reinforcing. Masonry or concrete chimneys shall be constructed, anchored, supported and reinforced as required in this chapter. In *Seismic Design Category* C or D, masonry and concrete chimneys shall be reinforced and anchored as detailed in Sections 2113.3.1, 2113.3.2 and 2113.4. In *Seismic Design Category* A or B, reinforcement and seismic anchorage is not required. In *Seismic Design Category* E or F, masonry and concrete chimneys shall be reinforced in accordance with the requirements of Sections 2101 through 2108.

2113.3.1 Vertical reinforcing. For chimneys up to 40 inches (1016 mm) wide, four No. 4 continuous vertical bars anchored in the foundation shall be placed in the concrete between wythes of solid masonry or within the cells of hollow unit masonry and grouted in accordance with Section 2103.12. Grout shall be prevented from bonding with the flue liner so that the flue liner is free to move with thermal expansion. For chimneys greater than 40 inches (1016 mm) wide, two additional No. 4 vertical bars shall be provided for each additional 40 inches (1016 mm) in width or fraction thereof.

2113.3.2 Horizontal reinforcing. Vertical reinforcement shall be placed enclosed within $^1/_4$-inch (6.4 mm) ties, or other reinforcing of equivalent net cross-sectional area, spaced not to exceed 18 inches (457 mm) o.c. in concrete, or placed in the bed joints of unit masonry, at a minimum of every 18 inches (457 mm) of vertical height. Two such ties shall be provided at each bend in the vertical bars.

2113.4 Seismic anchorage. Masonry and concrete chimneys and foundations in *Seismic Design Category* C or D shall be anchored at each floor, ceiling or roof line more than 6 feet (1829 mm) above grade, except where constructed completely within the *exterior walls*. Anchorage shall conform to the following requirements.

2113.4.1 Anchorage. Two $^3/_{16}$-inch by 1-inch (4.8 mm by 25 mm) straps shall be embedded a minimum of 12 inches (305 mm) into the chimney. Straps shall be hooked around the outer bars and extend 6 inches (152 mm) beyond the bend. Each strap shall be fastened to a minimum of four floor joists with two $^1/_2$-inch (12.7 mm) bolts.

2113.5 Corbeling. Masonry chimneys shall not be corbeled more than half of the chimney's wall thickness from a wall or foundation, nor shall a chimney be corbeled from a wall or foundation that is less than 12 inches (305 mm) in thickness unless it projects equally on each side of the wall, except that on the second *story* of a two-story *dwelling*, corbeling of chimneys on the exterior of the enclosing walls is permitted to equal the wall thickness. The projection of a single course shall not exceed one-half the unit height or one-third of the unit bed depth, whichever is less.

2113.6 Changes in dimension. The chimney wall or chimney flue lining shall not change in size or shape within 6 inches (152 mm) above or below where the chimney passes through floor components, ceiling components or roof components.

2113.7 Offsets. Where a masonry chimney is constructed with a fireclay flue liner surrounded by one wythe of masonry, the maximum offset shall be such that the centerline of the flue above the offset does not extend beyond the center of the chimney wall below the offset. Where the chimney offset is supported by masonry below the offset in an *approved* manner, the maximum offset limitations shall not apply. Each individual corbeled masonry course of the offset shall not exceed the projection limitations specified in Section 2113.5.

2113.8 Additional load. Chimneys shall not support loads other than their own weight unless they are designed and constructed to support the additional load. Masonry chimneys are permitted to be constructed as part of the masonry walls or concrete walls of the building.

2113.9 Termination. Chimneys shall extend at least 2 feet (610 mm) higher than any portion of the building within 10 feet (3048 mm), but shall not be less than 3 feet (914 mm) above the highest point where the chimney passes through the roof.

2113.9.1 Spark arrestors. Where a spark arrestor is installed on a masonry chimney, the spark arrestor shall meet all of the following requirements:

1. The net free area of the arrestor shall not be less than four times the net free area of the outlet of the chimney flue it serves.
2. The arrestor screen shall have heat and corrosion resistance equivalent to 19-gage galvanized steel or 24-gage stainless steel.
3. Openings shall not permit the passage of spheres having a diameter greater than $^1/_2$ inch (12.7 mm) nor block the passage of spheres having a diameter less than $^3/_8$ inch (11 mm).
4. The spark arrestor shall be accessible for cleaning and the screen or chimney cap shall be removable to allow for cleaning of the chimney flue.

2113.10 Wall thickness. Masonry chimney walls shall be constructed of concrete, solid masonry units or hollow masonry units grouted solid with not less than 4 inches (102 mm) nominal thickness.

2113.10.1 Masonry veneer chimneys. Where masonry is used as veneer for a framed chimney, through flashing and weep holes shall be provided as required by Chapter 14.

2113.11 Flue lining (material). Masonry chimneys shall be lined. The lining material shall be appropriate for the type of appliance connected, according to the terms of the appliance listing and the manufacturer's instructions.

2113.11.1 Residential-type appliances (general). Flue lining systems shall comply with one of the following:

1. Clay flue lining complying with the requirements of ASTM C 315.
2. *Listed* chimney lining systems complying with UL 1777.
3. Factory-built chimneys or chimney units *listed* for installation within masonry chimneys.
4. Other *approved* materials that will resist corrosion, erosion, softening or cracking from flue gases and condensate at temperatures up to 1,800°F (982°C).

2113.11.1.1 Flue linings for specific appliances. Flue linings other than those covered in Section 2113.11.1 intended for use with specific appliances shall comply with Sections 2113.11.1.2 through 2113.11.1.4 and Sections 2113.11.2 and 2113.11.3.

2113.11.1.2 Gas appliances. Flue lining systems for gas appliances shall be in accordance with the *International Fuel Gas Code*.

2113.11.1.3 Pellet fuel-burning appliances. Flue lining and vent systems for use in masonry chimneys with pellet fuel-burning appliances shall be limited to flue lining systems complying with Section 2113.11.1 and pellet vents *listed* for installation within masonry chimneys (see Section 2113.11.1.5 for marking).

2113.11.1.4 Oil-fired appliances approved for use with L-vent. Flue lining and vent systems for use in masonry chimneys with oil-fired appliances *approved* for use with Type L vent shall be limited to flue lining systems complying with Section 2113.11.1 and *listed* chimney liners complying with UL 641 (see Section 2113.11.1.5 for marking).

2113.11.1.5 Notice of usage. When a flue is relined with a material not complying with Section 2113.11.1, the chimney shall be plainly and permanently identified by a *label* attached to a wall, ceiling or other conspicuous location adjacent to where the connector enters the chimney. The *label* shall include the following message or equivalent language: "This chimney is for use only with (type or category of appliance) that burns (type of fuel). Do not connect other types of appliances."

2113.11.2 Concrete and masonry chimneys for medium-heat appliances.

2113.11.2.1 General. Concrete and masonry chimneys for medium-heat appliances shall comply with Sections 2113.1 through 2113.5.

2113.11.2.2 Construction. Chimneys for medium-heat appliances shall be constructed of solid masonry units or of concrete with walls a minimum of 8 inches (203 mm) thick, or with stone masonry a minimum of 12 inches (305 mm) thick.

2113.11.2.3 Lining. Concrete and masonry chimneys shall be lined with an *approved* medium-duty refractory brick a minimum of $4^1/_2$ inches (114 mm) thick laid on the $4^1/_2$-inch bed (114 mm) in an *approved* medium-duty refractory mortar. The lining shall start 2 feet (610 mm) or more below the lowest chimney connector entrance. Chimneys terminating 25 feet (7620 mm) or less above a chimney connector entrance shall be lined to the top.

2113.11.2.4 Multiple passageway. Concrete and masonry chimneys containing more than one passageway shall have the liners separated by a minimum 4-inch-thick (102 mm) concrete or solid masonry wall.

2113.11.2.5 Termination height. Concrete and masonry chimneys for medium-heat appliances shall extend a minimum of 10 feet (3048 mm) higher than any portion of any building within 25 feet (7620 mm).

2113.11.2.6 Clearance. A minimum clearance of 4 inches (102 mm) shall be provided between the exterior surfaces of a concrete or masonry chimney for medium-heat appliances and combustible material.

2113.11.3 Concrete and masonry chimneys for high-heat appliances.

2113.11.3.1 General. Concrete and masonry chimneys for high-heat appliances shall comply with Sections 2113.1 through 2113.5.

2113.11.3.2 Construction. Chimneys for high-heat appliances shall be constructed with double walls of solid masonry units or of concrete, each wall to be a minimum of 8 inches (203 mm) thick with a minimum airspace of 2 inches (51 mm) between the walls.

2113.11.3.3 Lining. The inside of the interior wall shall be lined with an *approved* high-duty refractory brick, a minimum of $4^1/_2$ inches (114 mm) thick laid on the $4^1/_2$-inch bed (114 mm) in an *approved* high-duty refractory mortar. The lining shall start at the base of the chimney and extend continuously to the top.

2113.11.3.4 Termination height. Concrete and masonry chimneys for high-heat appliances shall extend a minimum of 20 feet (6096 mm) higher than any portion of any building within 50 feet (15 240 mm).

2113.11.3.5 Clearance. Concrete and masonry chimneys for high-heat appliances shall have *approved* clearance from buildings and structures to prevent overheating combustible materials, permit inspection and maintenance operations on the chimney and prevent danger of burns to persons.

2113.12 Clay flue lining (installation). Clay flue liners shall be installed in accordance with ASTM C 1283 and extend from a point not less than 8 inches (203 mm) below the lowest inlet or, in the case of fireplaces, from the top of the smoke chamber to a point above the enclosing walls. The lining shall be carried up vertically, with a maximum slope no greater than 30 degrees (0.52 rad) from the vertical.

Clay flue liners shall be laid in medium-duty refractory mortar conforming to ASTM C 199 with tight mortar joints left smooth on the inside and installed to maintain an air space or insulation not to exceed the thickness of the flue liner separating the flue liners from the interior face of the chimney masonry walls. Flue lining shall be supported on all sides. Only enough mortar shall be placed to make the joint and hold the liners in position.

2113.13 Additional requirements.

2113.13.1 Listed materials. *Listed* materials used as flue linings shall be installed in accordance with the terms of their listings and the manufacturer's instructions.

2113.13.2 Space around lining. The space surrounding a chimney lining system or vent installed within a masonry chimney shall not be used to vent any other appliance.

Exception: This shall not prevent the installation of a separate flue lining in accordance with the manufacturer's instructions.

2113.14 Multiple flues. When two or more flues are located in the same chimney, masonry wythes shall be built between adjacent flue linings. The masonry wythes shall be at least 4 inches (102 mm) thick and bonded into the walls of the chimney.

Exception: When venting only one appliance, two flues are permitted to adjoin each other in the same chimney with only the flue lining separation between them. The joints of the adjacent flue linings shall be staggered at least 4 inches (102 mm).

2113.15 Flue area (appliance). Chimney flues shall not be smaller in area than the area of the connector from the appliance. Chimney flues connected to more than one appliance shall not be less than the area of the largest connector plus 50 percent of the areas of additional chimney connectors.

Exceptions:

1. Chimney flues serving oil-fired appliances sized in accordance with NFPA 31.
2. Chimney flues serving gas-fired appliances sized in accordance with the *International Fuel Gas Code*.

2113.16 Flue area (masonry fireplace). Flue sizing for chimneys serving fireplaces shall be in accordance with Section 2113.16.1 or 2113.16.2.

2113.16.1 Minimum area. Round chimney flues shall have a minimum net cross-sectional area of at least $^1/_{12}$ of the fireplace opening. Square chimney flues shall have a minimum net cross-sectional area of at least $^1/_{10}$ of the fireplace opening. Rectangular chimney flues with an aspect ratio less than 2 to 1 shall have a minimum net cross-sectional area of at least $^1/_{10}$ of the fireplace opening. Rectangular chimney flues with an aspect ratio of 2 to 1 or more shall have a minimum net cross-sectional area of at least $^1/_8$ of the fireplace opening.

2113.16.2 Determination of minimum area. The minimum net cross-sectional area of the flue shall be determined in accordance with Figure 2113.16. A flue size providing at least the equivalent net cross-sectional area shall be used. Cross-sectional areas of clay flue linings are as provided in Tables 2113.16(1) and 2113.16(2) or as provided by the manufacturer or as measured in the field. The height of the chimney shall be measured from the firebox floor to the top of the chimney flue.

TABLE 2113.16(1)
NET CROSS-SECTIONAL AREA OF ROUND FLUE SIZES[a]

FLUE SIZE, INSIDE DIAMETER (inches)	CROSS-SECTIONAL AREA (square inches)
6	28
7	38
8	50
10	78
$10^3/_4$	90
12	113
15	176
18	254

For SI: 1 inch = 25.4 mm, 1 square inch = 645 mm².
a. Flue sizes are based on ASTM C 315.

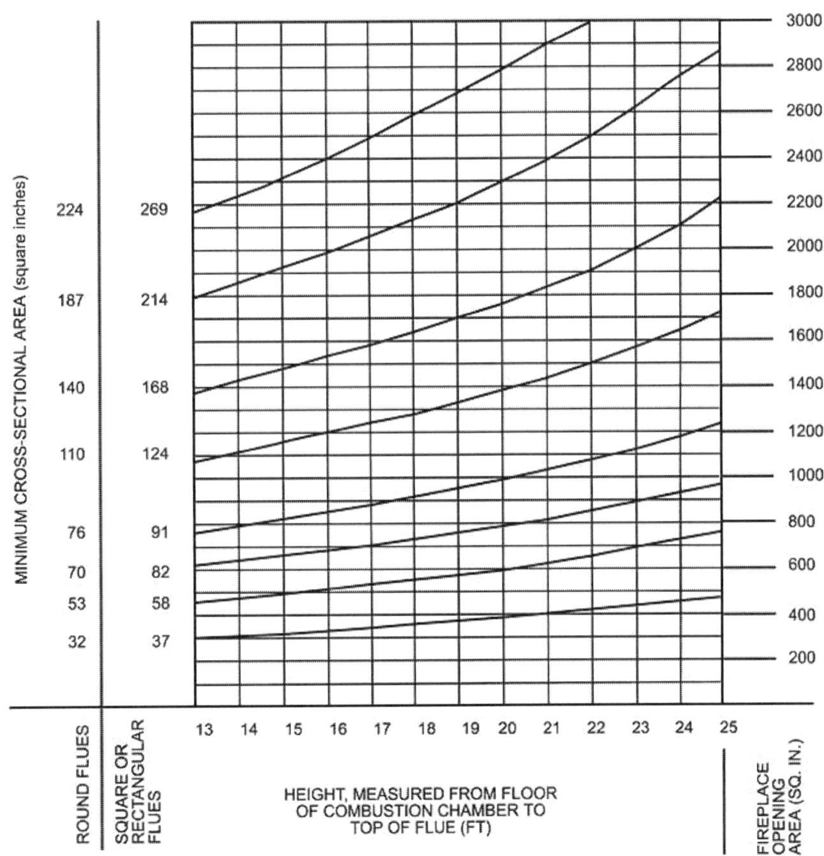

For SI: 1 foot = 304.8 mm, 1 square inch = 645 mm².

FIGURE 2113.16
FLUE SIZES FOR MASONRY CHIMNEYS

TABLE 2113.16(2)
NET CROSS-SECTIONAL AREA OF SQUARE AND RECTANGULAR FLUE SIZES

FLUE SIZE, OUTSIDE NOMINAL DIMENSIONS (inches)	CROSS-SECTIONAL AREA (square inches)
4.5 × 8.5	23
4.5 × 13	34
8 × 8	42
8.5 × 8.5	49
8 × 12	67
8.5 × 13	76
12 × 12	102
8.5 × 18	101
13 × 13	127
12 × 16	131
13 × 18	173
16 × 16	181
16 × 20	222
18 × 18	233
20 × 20	298
20 × 24	335
24 × 24	431

For SI: 1 inch = 25.4 mm, 1 square inch = 645 mm^2.

2113.17 Inlet. Inlets to masonry chimneys shall enter from the side. Inlets shall have a thimble of fireclay, rigid refractory material or metal that will prevent the connector from pulling out of the inlet or from extending beyond the wall of the liner.

2113.18 Masonry chimney cleanout openings. Cleanout openings shall be provided within 6 inches (152 mm) of the base of each flue within every masonry chimney. The upper edge of the cleanout shall be located at least 6 inches (152 mm) below the lowest chimney inlet opening. The height of the opening shall be at least 6 inches (152 mm). The cleanout shall be provided with a noncombustible cover.

Exception: Chimney flues serving masonry fireplaces, where cleaning is possible through the fireplace opening.

2113.19 Chimney clearances. Any portion of a masonry chimney located in the interior of the building or within the *exterior wall* of the building shall have a minimum airspace clearance to combustibles of 2 inches (51 mm). Chimneys located entirely outside the *exterior walls* of the building, including chimneys that pass through the soffit or cornice, shall have a minimum airspace clearance of 1 inch (25 mm). The airspace shall not be filled, except to provide fireblocking in accordance with Section 2113.20.

Exceptions:

1. Masonry chimneys equipped with a chimney lining system *listed* and labeled for use in chimneys in contact with combustibles in accordance with UL 1777, and installed in accordance with the manufacturer's instructions, are permitted to have combustible material in contact with their exterior surfaces.
2. Where masonry chimneys are constructed as part of masonry or concrete walls, combustible materials shall not be in contact with the masonry or concrete wall less than 12 inches (305 mm) from the inside surface of the nearest flue lining.
3. Exposed combustible *trim* and the edges of sheathing materials, such as wood siding, are permitted to abut the masonry chimney sidewalls, in accordance with Figure 2113.19, provided such combustible *trim* or sheathing is a minimum of 12 inches (305 mm) from the inside surface of the nearest flue lining. Combustible material and *trim* shall not overlap the corners of the chimney by more than 1 inch (25 mm).

2113.20 Chimney fireblocking. All spaces between chimneys and floors and ceilings through which chimneys pass shall be fireblocked with noncombustible material securely fastened in place. The fireblocking of spaces between wood joists, beams or headers shall be to a depth of 1 inch (25 mm) and shall only be placed on strips of metal or metal lath laid across the spaces between combustible material and the chimney.

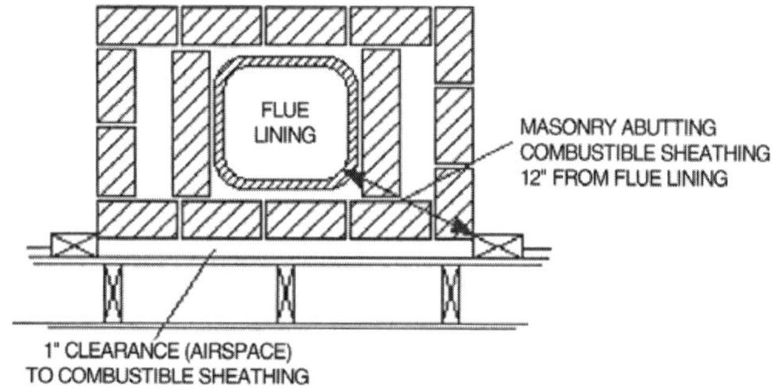

For SI: 1 inch = 25.4 mm.

FIGURE 2113.19
ILLUSTRATION OF EXCEPTION THREE

CHAPTER 22

STEEL

SECTION 2201 GENERAL

2201.1 Scope. The provisions of this chapter govern the quality, design, fabrication and erection of steel used structurally in buildings or structures.

SECTION 2202 DEFINITIONS

2202.1 Definitions. The following words and terms shall, for the purposes of this chapter and as used elsewhere in this code, have the meaning shown herein.

STEEL CONSTRUCTION, COLD-FORMED. That type of construction made up entirely or in part of steel structural members cold formed to shape from sheet or strip steel such as roof deck, floor and wall panels, studs, floor joists, roof joists and other structural elements.

STEEL JOIST. Any steel structural member of a building or structure made of hot-rolled or cold-formed solid or open-web sections, or riveted or welded bars, strip or sheet steel members, or slotted and expanded, or otherwise deformed rolled sections.

STEEL MEMBER, STRUCTURAL. Any steel structural member of a building or structure consisting of a rolled steel structural shape other than cold-formed steel, or steel joist members.

SECTION 2203 IDENTIFICATION AND PROTECTION OF STEEL FOR STRUCTURAL PURPOSES

2203.1 Identification. Identification of structural steel members shall comply with the requirements contained in AISC 360. Identification of cold-formed steel members shall comply with the requirements contained in AISI S100. Identification of cold-formed steel light-frame construction shall also comply with the requirements contained in AISI S200. Other steel furnished for structural load-carrying purposes shall be properly identified for conformity to the ordered grade in accordance with the specified ASTM standard or other specification and the provisions of this chapter. Steel that is not readily identifiable as to grade from marking and test records shall be tested to determine conformity to such standards.

2203.2 Protection. Painting of structural steel members shall comply with the requirements contained in AISC 360. Painting of open-web steel joists and joist girders shall comply with the requirements of SJI CJ-1.0, SJI JG-1.1, SJI K-1.1 and SJI LH/DLH-1.1. Individual structural members and assembled panels of cold-formed steel construction shall be protected against corrosion in accordance with the requirements contained in AISI S100. Protection of cold-formed steel light-frame construction shall also comply with the requirements contained in AISI S200.

SECTION 2204 CONNECTIONS

2204.1 Welding. The details of design, workmanship and technique for welding, inspection of welding and qualification of welding operators shall conform to the requirements of the specifications listed in Sections 2205, 2206, 2207, 2209 and 2210. *Special inspection* of welding shall be provided where required by Section 1704.

2204.2 Bolting. The design, installation and inspection of bolts shall be in accordance with the requirements of the specifications listed in Sections 2205, 2206, 2209 and 2210. *Special inspection* of the installation of high-strength bolts shall be provided where required by Section 1704.

2204.2.1 Anchor rods. Anchor rods shall be set accurately to the pattern and dimensions called for on the plans. The protrusion of the threaded ends through the connected material shall be sufficient to fully engage the threads of the nuts, but shall not be greater than the length of the threads on the bolts.

SECTION 2205 STRUCTURAL STEEL

2205.1 General. The design, fabrication and erection of structural steel for buildings and structures shall be in accordance with AISC 360. Where required, the seismic design of steel structures shall be in accordance with the additional provisions of Section 2205.2.

2205.2 Seismic requirements for steel structures. The design of structural steel structures to resist seismic forces shall be in accordance with the provisions of Section 2205.2.1 or 2205.2.2 for the appropriate *seismic design category*.

2205.2.1 Seismic Design Category A, B or C. Structural steel structures assigned to *Seismic Design Category* A, B or C shall be of any construction permitted in Section 2205. An R factor as set forth in Section 12.2.1 of ASCE 7 for the appropriate steel system is permitted where the structure is designed and detailed in accordance with the provisions of AISC 341, Part I. Systems not detailed in accordance with the above shall use the R factor in Section 12.2.1 of ASCE 7 designated for "structural steel systems not specifically detailed for seismic resistance."

2205.2.2 Seismic Design Category D, E or F. Structural steel structures assigned to *Seismic Design Category* D, E or F shall be designed and detailed in accordance with AISC 341, Part I.

2205.3 Seismic requirements for composite construction. The design, construction and quality of composite steel and concrete components that resist seismic forces shall conform to the requirements of the AISC 360 and ACI 318. An R factor as set forth in Section 12.2.1 of ASCE 7 for the appropriate composite steel and concrete system is permitted where the structure is designed and detailed in accordance with the provisions of AISC 341, Part II. In *Seismic Design Category* B or above, the design of such systems shall conform to the requirements of AISC 341, Part II.

2205.3.1 Seismic Design Categories D, E and F. Composite structures are permitted in *Seismic Design Categories* D , E and F, subject to the limitations in Section 12.2.1 of ASCE 7, where substantiating evidence is provided to demonstrate that the proposed system will perform as intended by AISC 341, Part II. The substantiating evidence shall be subject to *building official* approval. Where composite elements or connections are required to sustain inelastic deformations, the substantiating evidence shall be based on cyclic testing.

SECTION 2206
STEEL JOISTS

2206.1 General. The design, manufacture and use of open web steel joists and joist girders shall be in accordance with one of the following Steel Joist Institute (SJI) specifications:

1. SJI CJ-1.0
2. SJI K-1.1
3. SJI LH/DLH-1.1
4. SJI JG-1.1

Where required, the seismic design of buildings shall be in accordance with the additional provisions of Section 2205.2 or 2210.5.

2206.2 Design. The *registered design professional* shall indicate on the *construction documents* the steel joist and/or steel joist girder designations from the specifications *listed* in Section 2206.1 and shall indicate the requirements for joist and joist girder design, layout, end supports, anchorage, non-SJI standard bridging, bridging termination connections and bearing connection design to resist uplift and lateral loads. These documents shall indicate special requirements as follows:

1. Special loads including:
   - 1.1. Concentrated loads;
   - 1.2. Nonuniform loads;
   - 1.3. Net uplift loads;
   - 1.4. Axial loads;
   - 1.5. End moments; and
   - 1.6. Connection forces.
2. Special considerations including:
   - 2.1. Profiles for nonstandard joist and joist girder configurations (standard joist and joist girder configurations are as indicated in the SJI catalog);
   - 2.2. Oversized or other nonstandard web openings; and
   - 2.3. Extended ends.
3. Deflection criteria for live and total loads for non-SJI standard joists.

2206.3 Calculations. The steel joist and joist girder manufacturer shall design the steel joists and/or steel joist girders in accordance with the current SJI specifications and load tables to support the load requirements of Section 2206.2. The *registered design professional* may require submission of the steel joist and joist girder calculations as prepared by a *registered design professional* responsible for the product design. If requested by the *registered design professional*, the steel joist manufacturer shall submit design calculations with a cover letter bearing the seal and signature of the joist manufacturer's *registered design professional*. In addition to standard calculations under this seal and signature, submittal of the following shall be included:

1. Non-SJI standard bridging details (e.g., for cantilevered conditions, net uplift, etc.).
2. Connection details for:
   - 2.1. Non-SJI standard connections (e.g., flush-framed or framed connections);
   - 2.2. Field splices; and
   - 2.3. Joist headers.

2206.4 Steel joist drawings. Steel joist placement plans shall be provided to show the steel joist products as specified on the *construction documents* and are to be utilized for field installation in accordance with specific project requirements as stated in Section 2206.2. Steel placement plans shall include, at a minimum, the following:

1. Listing of all applicable loads as stated in Section 2206.2 and used in the design of the steel joists and joist girders as specified in the *construction documents*.
2. Profiles for nonstandard joist and joist girder configurations (standard joist and joist girder configurations are as indicated in the SJI catalog).
3. Connection requirements for:
   - 3.1. Joist supports;
   - 3.2. Joist girder supports;
   - 3.3. Field splices; and
   - 3.4. Bridging attachments.
4. Deflection criteria for live and total loads for non-SJI standard joists.
5. Size, location and connections for all bridging.
6. Joist headers.

Steel joist placement plans do not require the seal and signature of the joist manufacturer's *registered design professional*.

2206.5 Certification. At completion of manufacture, the steel joist manufacturer shall submit a *certificate of compliance* in accordance with Section 1704.2.2 stating that work was performed in accordance with *approved construction documents* and with SJI standard specifications.

SECTION 2207
STEEL CABLE STRUCTURES

2207.1 General. The design, fabrication and erection including related connections, and protective coatings of steel cables for buildings shall be in accordance with ASCE 19.

2207.2 Seismic requirements for steel cable. The design strength of steel cables shall be determined by the provisions of ASCE 19 except as modified by these provisions.

1. A load factor of 1.1 shall be applied to the prestress force included in T_3 and T_4 as defined in Section 3.12.
2. In Section 3.2.1, Item (c) shall be replaced with "1.5 T_3" and Item (d) shall be replaced with "1.5 T_4."

SECTION 2208
STEEL STORAGE RACKS

2208.1 Storage racks. The design, testing and utilization of industrial steel storage racks made of cold-formed or hot-rolled steel structural members, shall be in accordance with the RMI/ANSI MH 16.1. Where required by ASCE 7, the seismic design of storage racks shall be in accordance with the provisions of Section 15.5.3 of ASCE 7, except that Items (1), (2) and (3) of Section 15.5.3 of ASCE 7 do not apply when the rack design satisfies RMI/ANSI MH 16.1.

SECTION 2209
COLD-FORMED STEEL

2209.1 General. The design of cold-formed carbon and low-alloy steel structural members shall be in accordance with AISI S100. The design of cold-formed stainless-steel structural members shall be in accordance with ASCE 8. Cold-formed steel light-frame construction shall also comply with Section 2210.

2209.2 Steel decks. The design and construction of cold-formed steel decks shall be in accordance with this section.

2209.2.1 Composite slabs on steel decks. Composite slabs of concrete and steel deck shall be designed and constructed in accordance with ASCE 3.

2209.2.2 Noncomposite steel floor decks. Noncomposite steel floor decks shall be permitted to be designed and constructed in accordance with ANSI/SDI-NC1.0, as modified in Section 2209.2.2.1.

2209.9.2.2.1 ANSI/SDI-NC1.0 Section 2.4B1. Replace Section 2.4B1 of ANSI/SDI-NC1.0 with the following:

1. General: The design of the concrete slabs shall be done in accordance with the ACI *Building Code Requirements for Reinforced Concrete*. The minimum concrete thickness above the top of the deck shall be $1^1/_2$ inches (38 mm).

2209.2.3 Steel roof deck. Steel roof decks shall be permitted to be designed and constructed in accordance with ANSI/SDI-RD1.0.

SECTION 2210
COLD-FORMED STEEL
LIGHT-FRAME CONSTRUCTION

2210.1 General. The design and installation of structural members and nonstructural members utilized in cold-formed steel light-frame construction where the specified minimum base steel thickness is between 0.0179 inches (0.455 mm) and 0.1180 inches (2.997 mm) shall be in accordance with AISI S200 and Sections 2210.2 through 2210.7, as applicable.

2210.2 Header design. Headers, including box and back-to-back headers, and double and single L-headers shall be designed in accordance with AISI S212 or AISI S100.

2210.3 Trusses.

2210.3.1 Design. Cold-formed steel trusses and the placement diagram shall be designed and detailed by a *registered design professional* and in accordance with AISI S214, Sections 2210.3.1 through 2210.3.5 and accepted engineering practice.

2210.3.2 Truss design drawings. The truss design drawings shall conform to the requirements of Section B2.3 of AISI S214 and shall be provided with the shipment of trusses delivered to the job site. The truss design drawings shall include the details of permanent individual truss member restraint/bracing in accordance with Section B6(a) or B6(c) of AISI S214 where these methods are utilized to provide restraint/bracing. Each individual truss design drawing shall bear the seal and signature of the truss designer.

2210.3.3 Truss design drawings. AISI S214 Section B4.2 shall be deleted. The truss submittal package shall consist of each individual truss design drawing, the truss placement diagram for the project, the truss member permanent bracing specification and, as applicable, the cover sheet/truss index sheet. The submittal package shall be submitted to the project *registered design professional* for final approval prior to fabrication of trusses.

2210.3.4 Trussses spanning 60 feet or greater. The owner shall contract with a *registered design professional* for the design of the temporary installation restraint/bracing and the permanent individual truss member restraint/bracing for trusses with clear spans 60 feet (18 288 mm) or greater. *Special inspection* of trusses over 60 feet (18 288 mm) in length shall conform to Section 1704.

2210.3.5 Truss quality assurance. Trusses not part of a manufacturing process that provides requirements for quality control done under the supervision of a third-party quality control agency, shall be manufactured in compliance with Sections 1704.2 and 1704.3, as applicable.

2210.4 Wall stud design. Wall studs shall be designed in accordance with either AISI S211 or AISI S100.

2210.5 Floor and roof system design. Framing for floor and roof systems in buildings shall be designed in accordance with either AISI S210 or AISI S100.

2210.6 Lateral design. Light-frame shear walls, diagonal strap bracing that is part of a structural wall and diaphragms used to resist wind, seismic and other in-plane lateral loads shall be designed in accordance with AISI S213.

2210.7 Prescriptive framing. Detached one- and two-family *dwellings* and *townhouses*, less than or equal to three *stories above grade plane*, shall be permitted to be constructed in accordance with AISI S230 subject to the limitations therein.

CHAPTER 23
WOOD

SECTION 2301
GENERAL

2301.1 Scope. The provisions of this chapter shall govern the materials, design, construction and quality of wood members and their fasteners. Refer to Chapter 7 for fireblocking, draftstopping and fire-resistance requirements.

2301.1.1 Minimum lumber grades. The minimum grade of lumber used for light-frame construction shall be:

1. For joists and rafters, those obtained in AF&PA Design Values for Joists and Rafters.
2. For load-bearing studs, No. 3 grade, standard grade or stud grade, utility grade may be used to support roof and ceiling loads only.
3. For nonload-bearing studs, utility grade.
4. For wall top plates, utility grade.

2301.1.2 Moisture content. All lumber shall have a maximum moisture content of 19 percent at time of grading.

2301.2 General design requirements. The design of structural elements or systems, constructed partially or wholly of wood or wood-based products, shall be in accordance with one of the following methods:

1. *Allowable stress design* in accordance with Sections 2304, 2305 and 2306.
2. *Load and resistance factor design* in accordance with Sections 2304, 2305 and 2307.
3. *Conventional light-frame construction* in accordance with Sections 2304 and 2308.

   Exception: Buildings designed in accordance with the provisions of the AF&PA WFCM shall be deemed to meet the requirements of the provisions of Section 2308.

4. The design and construction of log structures shall be in accordance with the provisions of ICC 400.

2301.3 Nominal sizes. For the purposes of this chapter, where dimensions of lumber are specified, they shall be deemed to be nominal dimensions unless specifically designated as actual dimensions (see Section 2304.2).

SECTION 2302
DEFINITIONS

2302.1 Definitions. The following words and terms shall, for the purposes of this chapter, have the meanings shown herein.

ACCREDITATION BODY. An *approved*, third-party organization that is independent of the grading and inspection agencies, and the lumber mills, and that initially accredits and subsequently monitors, on a continuing basis, the competency and performance of a grading or inspection agency related to carrying out specific tasks.

BRACED WALL LINE. A series of braced wall panels in a single *story* that meets the requirements of Section 2308.3 or 2308.12.4.

BRACED WALL PANEL. A section of wall braced in accordance with Section 2308.9.3 or 2308.12.4.

COLLECTOR. A horizontal diaphragm element parallel and in line with the applied force that collects and transfers diaphragm shear forces to the vertical elements of the lateral-force-resisting system and/or distributes forces within the diaphragm.

CONVENTIONAL LIGHT-FRAME CONSTRUCTION. A type of construction whose primary structural elements are formed by a system of repetitive wood-framing members. See Section 2308 for *conventional light-frame construction* provisions.

CRIPPLE WALL. A framed stud wall extending from the top of the foundation to the underside of floor framing for the lowest occupied floor level.

DIAPHRAGM, UNBLOCKED. A diaphragm that has edge nailing at supporting members only. Blocking between supporting structural members at panel edges is not included. Diaphragm panels are field nailed to supporting members.

DRAG STRUT. See "Collector."

FIBERBOARD. A fibrous, homogeneous panel made from lignocellulosic fibers (usually wood or cane) and having a density of less than 31 pounds per cubic foot (pcf) (497 kg/m^3) but more than 10 pcf (160 kg/m^3).

GLUED BUILT-UP MEMBER. A structural element, the section of which is composed of built-up lumber, wood structural panels or wood structural panels in combination with lumber, all parts bonded together with structural adhesives.

GRADE (LUMBER). The classification of lumber in regard to strength and utility in accordance with American Softwood Lumber Standard DOC PS 20 and the grading rules of an *approved* lumber rules-writing agency.

HARDBOARD. A fibrous-felted, homogeneous panel made from lignocellulosic fibers consolidated under heat and pressure in a hot press to a density not less than 31 pcf (497 kg/m^3).

NAILING, BOUNDARY. A special nailing pattern required by design at the boundaries of diaphragms.

NAILING, EDGE. A special nailing pattern required by design at the edges of each panel within the assembly of a diaphragm or shear wall.

NAILING, FIELD. Nailing required between the sheathing panels and framing members at locations other than boundary nailing and edge nailing.

NATURALLY DURABLE WOOD. The heartwood of the following species with the exception that an occasional piece with corner sapwood is permitted if 90 percent or more of the width of each side on which it occurs is heartwood.

Decay resistant. Redwood, cedar, black locust and black walnut.

Termite resistant. Redwood, Alaska yellow-cedar, Eastern red cedar and both heartwood and all sapwood of Western red cedar.

NOMINAL SIZE (LUMBER). The commercial size designation of width and depth, in standard sawn lumber and glued-laminated lumber grades; somewhat larger than the standard net size of dressed lumber, in accordance with DOC PS 20 for sawn lumber and with the AF&PA NDS for glued-laminated lumber.

PARTICLEBOARD. A generic term for a panel primarily composed of cellulosic materials (usually wood), generally in the form of discrete pieces or particles, as distinguished from fibers. The cellulosic material is combined with synthetic resin or other suitable bonding system by a process in which the interparticle bond is created by the bonding system under heat and pressure.

PREFABRICATED WOOD I-JOIST. Structural member manufactured using sawn or structural composite lumber flanges and wood structural panel webs bonded together with exterior exposure adhesives, which forms an "I" cross-sectional shape.

SHEAR WALL. A wall designed to resist lateral forces parallel to the plane of a wall.

Shear wall, perforated. A wood structural panel sheathed wall with openings, that has not been specifically designed and detailed for force transfer around openings.

Shear wall segment, perforated. A section of shear wall with full-height sheathing that meets the height-to-width ratio limits of Section 4.3.4 of AF&PA SDPWS.

STRUCTURAL COMPOSITE LUMBER. Structural member manufactured using wood elements bonded together with exterior adhesives. Examples of structural composite lumber are:

Laminated veneer lumber (LVL). A composite of wood veneer sheet elements with wood fibers primarily oriented along the length of the member.

Parallel strand lumber (PSL). A composite of wood strand elements with wood fibers primarily oriented along the length of the member.

STRUCTURAL GLUED-LAMINATED TIMBER. An engineered, stress-rated product of a timber laminating plant, comprised of assemblies of specially selected and prepared wood laminations in which the grain of all laminations is approximately parallel longitudinally and the laminations are bonded with adhesives.

SUBDIAPHRAGM. A portion of a larger wood diaphragm designed to anchor and transfer local forces to primary diaphragm struts and the main diaphragm.

TIE-DOWN (HOLD-DOWN). A device used to resist uplift of the chords of shear walls.

TREATED WOOD. Wood and wood-based materials that use vacuum-pressure impregnation processes to enhance fire retardant or preservative properties.

Fire-retardant-treated wood. Pressure-treated lumber and plywood that exhibit reduced surface-burning characteristics and resist propagation of fire.

Preservative-treated wood. Pressure-treated wood products that exhibit reduced susceptibility to damage by fungi, insects or marine borers.

WOOD SHEAR PANEL. A wood floor, roof or wall component sheathed to act as a shear wall or diaphragm.

WOOD STRUCTURAL PANEL. A panel manufactured from veneers, wood strands or wafers or a combination of veneer and wood strands or wafers bonded together with waterproof synthetic resins or other suitable bonding systems. Examples of wood structural panels are:

Composite panels. A wood structural panel that is comprised of wood veneer and reconstituted wood-based material and bonded together with waterproof adhesive;

Oriented strand board (OSB). A mat-formed wood structural panel comprised of thin rectangular wood strands arranged in cross-aligned layers with surface layers normally arranged in the long panel direction and bonded with waterproof adhesive; or

Plywood. A wood structural panel comprised of plies of wood veneer arranged in cross-aligned layers. The plies are bonded with waterproof adhesive that cures on application of heat and pressure.

SECTION 2303
MINIMUM STANDARDS AND QUALITY

2303.1 General. Structural sawn lumber; end-jointed lumber; prefabricated wood I-joists; structural glued-laminated timber; wood structural panels, fiberboard sheathing (when used structurally); hardboard siding (when used structurally); particleboard; *preservative-treated wood*; structural log members; structural composite lumber; round timber poles and piles; *fire-retardant-treated wood*; hardwood plywood; wood trusses; joist hangers; nails; and staples shall conform to the applicable provisions of this section.

2303.1.1 Sawn lumber. Sawn lumber used for load-supporting purposes, including end-jointed or edge-glued lumber, machine stress-rated or machine-evaluated lumber, shall be identified by the grade *mark* of a lumber grading or inspection agency that has been approved by an accreditation body that complies with DOC PS 20 or equivalent. Grading practices and identification shall comply with rules published by an agency approved in accordance with the procedures of DOC PS 20 or equivalent procedures. In lieu of a grade *mark* on the material, a certificate of inspection as to species and grade issued by a lumber grading or inspection agency meeting the requirements of this section is permitted to be accepted for precut, remanufactured or rough-sawn lumber and for sizes larger than 3 inches (76 mm) nominal thickness.

Approved end-jointed lumber is permitted to be used interchangeably with solid-sawn members of the same species and grade.

2303.1.2 Prefabricated wood I-joists. Structural capacities and design provisions for prefabricated wood I-joists shall be established and monitored in accordance with ASTM D 5055.

2303.1.3 Structural glued-laminated timber. Glued-laminated timbers shall be manufactured and identified as required in ANSI/AITC A 190.1 and ASTM D 3737.

2303.1.4 Wood structural panels. Wood structural panels, when used structurally (including those used for siding, roof and wall sheathing, subflooring, diaphragms and built-up members), shall conform to the requirements for their type in DOC PS 1 or PS 2. Each panel or member shall be identified for grade and glue type by the trademarks of an *approved* testing and grading agency. Wood structural panel components shall be designed and fabricated in accordance with the applicable standards listed in Section 2306.1 and identified by the trademarks of an *approved* testing and inspection agency indicating conformance with the applicable standard. In addition, wood structural panels when permanently exposed in outdoor applications shall be of exterior type, except that wood structural panel roof sheathing exposed to the outdoors on the underside is permitted to be interior type bonded with exterior glue, Exposure 1.

2303.1.5 Fiberboard. Fiberboard for its various uses shall conform to ASTM C 208. Fiberboard sheathing, when used structurally, shall be identified by an *approved* agency as conforming to ASTM C 208.

2303.1.5.1 Jointing. To ensure tight-fitting assemblies, edges shall be manufactured with square, shiplapped, beveled, tongue-and-groove or U-shaped joints.

2303.1.5.2 Roof insulation. Where used as roof insulation in all types of construction, fiberboard shall be protected with an *approved* roof covering.

2303.1.5.3 Wall insulation. Where installed and fireblocked to comply with Chapter 7, fiberboards are permitted as wall insulation in all types of construction. In fire walls and fire barriers, unless treated to comply with Section 803.1 for Class A materials, the boards shall be cemented directly to the concrete, masonry or other noncombustible base and shall be protected with an *approved* noncombustible veneer anchored to the base without intervening airspaces.

2303.1.5.3.1 Protection. Fiberboard wall insulation applied on the exterior of foundation walls shall be protected below ground level with a bituminous coating.

2303.1.6 Hardboard. Hardboard siding used structurally shall be identified by an *approved agency* conforming to CPA/ANSI A135.6. Hardboard underlayment shall meet the strength requirements of $^{7}/_{32}$-inch (5.6 mm) or $^{1}/_{4}$-inch (6.4 mm) service class hardboard planed or sanded on one side to a uniform thickness of not less than 0.200 inch (5.1 mm). Prefinished hardboard paneling shall meet the requirements of CPA/ANSI A135.5. Other basic hardboard products shall meet the requirements of CPA/ANSI A135.4. Hardboard products shall be installed in accordance with manufacturer's recommendations.

2303.1.7 Particleboard. Particleboard shall conform to ANSI A208.1. Particleboard shall be identified by the grade *mark* or certificate of inspection issued by an *approved agency*. Particleboard shall not be utilized for applications other than indicated in this section unless the particleboard complies with the provisions of Section 2306.5.

2303.1.7.1 Floor underlayment. Particleboard floor underlayment shall conform to Type PBU of ANSI A208.1. Type PBU underlayment shall not be less than $^{1}/_{4}$-inch (6.4 mm) thick and shall be installed in accordance with the instructions of the Composite Panel Association.

2303.1.8 Preservative-treated wood. Lumber, timber, plywood, piles and poles supporting permanent structures required by Section 2304.11 to be preservative treated shall conform to the requirements of the applicable AWPA Standard U1 and M4 for the species, product, preservative and end use. Preservatives shall be listed in Section 4 of AWPA U1. Lumber and plywood used in wood foundation systems shall conform to Chapter 18.

2303.1.8.1 Identification. Wood required by Section 2304.11 to be preservative treated shall bear the quality *mark* of an inspection agency that maintains continuing supervision, testing and inspection over the quality of the *preservative-treated wood*. Inspection agencies for *preservative-treated wood* shall be *listed* by an accreditation body that complies with the requirements of the American Lumber Standards Treated Wood Program, or equivalent. The quality *mark* shall be on a stamp or *label* affixed to the *preservative-treated wood*, and shall include the following information:

1. Identification of treating manufacturer.
2. Type of preservative used.
3. Minimum preservative retention (pcf).
4. End use for which the product is treated.
5. AWPA standard to which the product was treated.
6. Identity of the accredited inspection agency.

2303.1.8.2 Moisture content. Where *preservative-treated wood* is used in enclosed locations where drying in service cannot readily occur, such wood shall be at a moisture content of 19 percent or less before being covered with insulation, interior wall finish, floor covering or other materials.

2303.1.9 Structural composite lumber. Structural capacities for structural composite lumber shall be established and monitored in accordance with ASTM D 5456.

2303.1.10 Structural log members. Stress grading of structural log members of nonrectangular shape, as typically used in log buildings, shall be in accordance with ASTM D 3957. Such structural log members shall be identified by the grade *mark* of an *approved* lumber grading or inspection agency. In lieu of a grade *mark* on the material, a certificate of inspection as to species and grade issued by a lumber grading or inspection agency meeting the requirements of this section shall be permitted.

2303.1.11 Round timber poles and piles. Round timber poles and piles shall comply with ASTM D 3200 and ASTM D 25, respectively.

2303.2 Fire-retardant-treated wood. *Fire-retardant-treated wood* is any wood product which, when impregnated with chemicals by a pressure process or other means during manufacture, shall have, when tested in accordance with ASTM E 84 or UL 723, a *listed* flame spread index of 25 or less and show no evidence of significant progressive combustion when the test is continued for an additional 20-minute period. Additionally, the flame front shall not progress more than $10^1/_2$ feet (3200 mm) beyond the centerline of the burners at any time during the test.

2303.2.1 Pressure process. For wood products impregnated with chemicals by a pressure process, the process shall be performed in closed vessels under pressures not less than 50 pounds per square inch gauge (psig) (345 kPa).

2303.2.2 Other means during manufacture. For wood products produced by other means during manufacture, the treatment shall be an integral part of the manufacturing process of the wood product. The treatment shall provide permanent protection to all surfaces of the wood product.

2303.2.3 Testing. For wood products produced by other means during manufacture, other than a pressure process, all sides of the wood product shall be tested in accordance with and produce the results required in Section 2303.2. Wood structural panels shall be permitted to test only the front and back faces.

2303.2.4 Labeling. Fire-retardant-treated lumber and wood structural panels shall be labeled. The *label* shall contain the following items:

1. The identification *mark* of an *approved agency* in accordance with Section 1703.5.
2. Identification of the treating manufacturer.
3. The name of the fire-retardant treatment.
4. The species of wood treated.
5. Flame spread and smoke-developed index.
6. Method of drying after treatment.
7. Conformance to appropriate standards in accordance with Sections 2303.2.5 through 2303.2.8.
8. For *fire-retardant-treated wood* exposed to weather, damp or wet locations, include the words "No increase in the *listed* classification when subjected to the Standard Rain Test" (ASTM D 2898).

2303.2.5 Strength adjustments. Design values for untreated lumber and wood structural panels, as specified in Section 2303.1, shall be adjusted for *fire-retardant-treated wood*. Adjustments to design values shall be based on an *approved* method of investigation that takes into consideration the effects of the anticipated temperature and humidity to which the *fire-retardant-treated wood* will be subjected, the type of treatment and redrying procedures.

2303.2.5.1 Wood structural panels. The effect of treatment and the method of redrying after treatment, and exposure to high temperatures and high humidities on the flexure properties of fire-retardant-treated softwood plywood shall be determined in accordance with ASTM D 5516. The test data developed by ASTM D 5516 shall be used to develop adjustment factors, maximum loads and spans, or both, for untreated plywood design values in accordance with ASTM D 6305. Each manufacturer shall publish the allowable maximum loads and spans for service as floor and roof sheathing for its treatment.

2303.2.5.2 Lumber. For each species of wood that is treated, the effects of the treatment, the method of redrying after treatment and exposure to high temperatures and high humidities on the allowable design properties of fire-retardant-treated lumber shall be determined in accordance with ASTM D 5664. The test data developed by ASTM D 5664 shall be used to develop modification factors for use at or near room temperature and at elevated temperatures and humidity in accordance with ASTM D 6841. Each manufacturer shall publish the modification factors for service at temperatures of not less than 80°F (27°C) and for roof framing. The roof framing modification factors shall take into consideration the climatological location.

2303.2.6 Exposure to weather, damp or wet locations. Where *fire-retardant-treated wood* is exposed to weather, or damp or wet locations, it shall be identified as "Exterior" to indicate there is no increase in the *listed* flame spread index as defined in Section 2303.2 when subjected to ASTM D 2898.

2303.2.7 Interior applications. Interior *fire-retardant-treated wood* shall have moisture content of not over 28 percent when tested in accordance with ASTM D 3201 procedures at 92-percent relative humidity. Interior *fire-retardant-treated wood* shall be tested in accordance with Section 2303.2.5.1 or 2303.2.5.2. Interior *fire-retardant-treated wood* designated as Type A shall be tested in accordance with the provisions of this section.

2303.2.8 Moisture content. *Fire-retardant-treated wood* shall be dried to a moisture content of 19 percent or less for lumber and 15 percent or less for wood structural panels before use. For wood kiln dried after treatment (KDAT), the kiln temperatures shall not exceed those used in kiln drying the lumber and plywood submitted for the tests described in Section 2303.2.5.1 for plywood and 2303.2.5.2 for lumber.

2303.2.9 Type I and II construction applications. See Section 603.1 for limitations on the use of *fire-retardant-treated wood* in buildings of Type I or II construction.

2303.3 Hardwood and plywood. Hardwood and decorative plywood shall be manufactured and identified as required in HPVA HP-1.

2303.4 Trusses.

2303.4.1 Design. Wood trusses shall be designed in accordance with the provisions of this code and accepted engineering practice. Members are permitted to be joined by nails, glue, bolts, timber connectors, metal connector plates or other *approved* framing devices.

2303.4.1.1 Truss design drawings. The written, graphic and pictorial depiction of each individual truss shall be provided to the *building official* for approval prior to installation. Truss design drawings shall also be provided with the shipment of trusses delivered to the job site. Truss design drawings shall include, at a minimum, the information specified below:

1. Slope or depth, span and spacing;
2. Location of all joints and support locations;
3. Number of plies if greater than one;
4. Required bearing widths;
5. Design loads as applicable, including:
   5.1. Top chord live load;
   5.2. Top chord dead load;
   5.3. Bottom chord live load;
   5.4. Bottom chord dead load;
   5.5. Additional loads and locations; and
   5.6. Environmental design criteria and loads (wind, rain, snow, seismic, etc.);
6. Other lateral loads, including drag strut loads;
7. Adjustments to wood member and metal connector plate design value for conditions of use;
8. Maximum reaction force and direction, including maximum uplift reaction forces where applicable;
9. Metal-connector-plate type, size and thickness or gage, and the dimensioned location of each metal connector plate except where symmetrically located relative to the joint interface;
10. Size, species and grade for each wood member;
11. Truss-to-truss connections and truss field assembly requirements;
12. Calculated span-to-deflection ratio and maximum vertical and horizontal deflection for live and total load as applicable;
13. Maximum axial tension and compression forces in the truss members; and
14. Required permanent individual truss member restraint location and the method and details of restraint/bracing to be used in accordance with Section 2303.4.1.2.

2303.4.1.2 Permanent individual truss member restraint. Where permanent restraint of truss members is required on the truss design drawings, it shall be accomplished by one of the following methods:

1. Permanent individual truss member restraint/bracing shall be installed using standard industry lateral restraint/bracing details in accordance with generally accepted engineering practice. Locations for lateral restraint shall be identified on the truss design drawing.
2. The trusses shall be designed so that the buckling of any individual truss member is resisted internally by the individual truss through suitable means (i.e., buckling reinforcement by T-reinforcement or L-reinforcement, proprietary reinforcement, etc.). The buckling reinforcement of individual members of the trusses shall be installed as shown on the truss design drawing or on supplemental truss member buckling reinforcement details provided by the truss designer.
3. A project-specific permanent individual truss member restraint/bracing design shall be permitted to be specified by any *registered design professional*.

2303.4.1.3 Trusses spanning 60 feet or greater. The owner shall contract with any qualified *registered design professional* for the design of the temporary installation restraint/bracing and the permanent individual truss member restraint/bracing for all trusses with clear spans 60 feet (18 288 mm) or greater.

2303.4.1.4 Truss designer. The truss designer is the individual or organization responsible for the design of trusses who is a *registered design professional*.

2303.4.1.4.1 Truss design drawings. Each individual truss design drawing shall bear the seal and signature of the truss designer.

Exceptions: Deleted.

2303.4.2 Truss placement diagram. The truss manufacturer shall provide a truss placement diagram that identifies the proposed location for each individually designated truss and references the corresponding truss design drawing. The truss placement diagram shall be provided as part of the truss submittal package, and with the shipment of trusses delivered to the job site. Truss placement diagrams that serve only as a guide for installation and do not deviate from the *permit* submittal drawings shall not be required to bear the seal or signature of the truss designer.

2303.4.3 Truss submittal package. The truss submittal package provided by the truss manufacturer shall consist of each individual truss design drawing, the truss placement diagram, the permanent individual truss member restraint/bracing method and details and any other structural details germane to the trusses; and, as applicable, the cover/truss index sheet. The submittal package shall be submitted to the *registered design professional in responsible charge* for final approval prior to fabrication of trusses.

2303.4.4 Anchorage. The design for the transfer of loads and anchorage of each truss to the supporting structure is the responsibility of the *registered design professional*.

2303.4.5 Alterations to trusses. Truss members and components shall not be cut, notched, drilled, spliced or otherwise altered in any way without written concurrence and approval of a *registered design professional*. Alterations resulting in the addition of loads to any member (e.g., HVAC equipment, piping, additional roofing or insulation, etc.) shall not be permitted without verification that the truss is capable of supporting such additional loading.

2303.4.6 TPI 1 specifications. In addition to Sections 2303.4.1 through 2303.4.5, the design, manufacture and quality assurance of metal-plate-connected wood trusses shall be in accordance with TPI 1. Job-site inspections shall be in compliance with Section 110.4, as applicable.

2303.4.7 Truss quality assurance. Trusses not part of a manufacturing process in accordance with either Section 2303.4.6 or a standard listed in Chapter 35, which provides requirements for quality control done under the supervision of a third-party quality control agency, shall be manufactured in compliance with Sections 1704.2 and 1704.6, as applicable.

2303.5 Test standard for joist hangers and connectors. For the required test standards for joist hangers and connectors, see Section 1716.1.

2303.6 Nails and staples. Nails and staples shall conform to requirements of ASTM F 1667. Nails used for framing and sheathing connections shall have minimum average bending yield strengths as follows: 80 kips per square inch (ksi) (551 MPa) for shank diameters larger than 0.177 inch (4.50 mm) but not larger than 0.254 inch (6.45 mm), 90 ksi (620 MPa) for shank diameters larger than 0.142 inch (3.61 mm) but not larger than 0.177 inch (4.50 mm) and 100 ksi (689 MPa) for shank diameters of at least 0.099 inch (2.51 mm) but not larger than 0.142 inch (3.61 mm).

2303.7 Shrinkage. Deleted.

SECTION 2304 GENERAL CONSTRUCTION REQUIREMENTS

2304.1 General. The provisions of this section apply to design methods specified in Section 2301.2.

2304.2 Size of structural members. Computations to determine the required sizes of members shall be based on the net dimensions (actual sizes) and not nominal sizes.

2304.3 Wall framing. The framing of exterior and interior walls shall be in accordance with the provisions specified in Section 2308 unless a specific design is furnished.

2304.3.1 Bottom plates. Studs shall have full bearing on a 2-inch-thick (actual $1^1/_2$-inch, 38 mm) or larger plate or sill having a width at least equal to the width of the studs.

2304.3.2 Framing over openings. Headers, double joists, trusses or other *approved* assemblies that are of adequate size to transfer loads to the vertical members shall be provided over window and door openings in load-bearing walls and partitions.

2304.3.3 Shrinkage. Wood walls and bearing partitions shall not support more than two floors and a roof unless an analysis satisfactory to the *building official* shows that shrinkage of the wood framing will not have adverse effects on the structure or any plumbing, electrical or mechanical systems, or other equipment installed therein due to excessive shrinkage or differential movements caused by shrinkage. The analysis shall also show that the roof drainage system and the foregoing systems or equipment will not be adversely affected or, as an alternate, such systems shall be designed to accommodate the differential shrinkage or movements.

2304.4 Floor and roof framing. The framing of wood-joisted floors and wood framed roofs shall be in accordance with the provisions specified in Section 2308 unless a specific design is furnished.

2304.5 Framing around flues and chimneys. Combustible framing shall be a minimum of 2 inches (51 mm), but shall not be less than the distance specified in Sections 2111 and 2113 and the *International Mechanical Code*, from flues, chimneys and fireplaces, and 6 inches (152 mm) away from flue openings.

2304.6 Wall sheathing. Except as provided for in Section 1405 for weatherboarding or where stucco construction that complies with Section 2510 is installed, enclosed buildings shall be sheathed with one of the materials of the nominal thickness specified in Table 2304.6 or any other *approved* material of equivalent strength or durability.

TABLE 2304.6 MINIMUM THICKNESS OF WALL SHEATHING

SHEATHING TYPE	MINIMUM THICKNESS	MAXIMUM WALL STUD SPACING
Wood boards	$^5/_8$ inch	24 inches on center
Fiberboard	$^1/_2$ inch	16 inches on center
Wood structural panel	In accordance with Tables 2308.9.3(2) and 2308.9.3(3)	—
M-S "Exterior Glue" and M-2 "Exterior Glue" Particleboard	In accordance with Tables 2306.5 and 2308.9.3(4)	—
Gypsum sheathing	$^1/_2$ inch	16 inches on center
Gypsum wallboard	$^1/_2$ inch	24 inches on center
Reinforced cement mortar	1 inch	24 inches on center

For SI: 1 inch = 25.4 mm.

2304.6.1 Wood structural panel sheathing. Where wood structural panel sheathing is used as the exposed finish on the exterior of outside walls, it shall have an exterior exposure durability classification. Where wood structural panel sheathing is used elsewhere, but not as the exposed finish, it shall be of a type manufactured with exterior glue (Exposure 1 or Exterior). Wood structural panel wall sheathing or siding used as structural sheathing shall be capable of resisting wind pressures in accordance with Section 1609. Maximum wind speeds for wood structural panel sheathing used to resist wind pressures shall be in accordance with Table 2304.6.1 for enclosed buildings with a mean roof height not greater than 30 feet (9144 mm), an importance factor (I) of 1.0 and a topographic factor (K_{zt}) of 1.0.

2304.6.2 Interior paneling. Softwood wood structural panels used for interior paneling shall conform to the provisions of Chapter 8 and shall be installed in accordance with Table 2304.9.1. Panels shall comply with DOC PS 1 or PS 2. Prefinished hardboard paneling shall meet the requirements of CPA/ANSI A135.5. Hardwood plywood shall conform to HPVA HP-1.

2304.7 Floor and roof sheathing.

2304.7.1 Structural floor sheathing. Structural floor sheathing shall be designed in accordance with the general provisions of this code and the special provisions in this section.

Floor sheathing conforming to the provisions of Table 2304.7(1), 2304.7(2), 2304.7(3) or 2304.7(4) shall be deemed to meet the requirements of this section.

2304.7.2 Structural roof sheathing. Structural roof sheathing shall be designed in accordance with the general provisions of this code and the special provisions in this section.

Roof sheathing conforming to the provisions of Table 2304.7(1), 2304.7(2), 2304.7(3) or 2304.7(5) shall be deemed to meet the requirements of this section. Wood structural panel roof sheathing shall be bonded by exterior glue.

TABLE 2304.6.1
MAXIMUM BASIC WIND SPEED (mph) (3-SECOND GUST) PERMITTED FOR WOOD STRUCTURAL PANEL WALL SHEATHING USED TO RESIST WIND PRESSURES[a, b, c]

MINIMUM NAIL		MINIMUM WOOD STRUCTURAL PANEL SPAN RATING	MINIMUM NOMINAL PANEL THICKNESS (inches)	MAXIMUM WALL STUD SPACING (inches)	PANEL NAIL SPACING		MAXIMUM WIND SPEED (mph)		
Size	Penetration (inches)				Edges (inches o.c.)	Field (inches o.c.)	Wind exposure category B	C	D
6d common (2.0″ × 0.113″)	1.5	24/0	3/8	16	6	12	110	90	85
		24/16	7/16	16	6	12	110	100	90
						6	150	125	110
8d common (2.5″ × 0.131″)	1.75	24/16	7/16	16	6	12	130	110	105
						6	150	125	110
				24	6	12	110	90	85
						6	110	90	85

For SI: 1 inch = 25.4 mm, 1 mile per hour = 0.447 m/s.

a. Panel strength axis shall be parallel or perpendicular to supports. Three-ply plywood sheathing with studs spaced more than 16 inches on center shall be applied with panel strength axis perpendicular to supports.

b. The table is based on wind pressures acting toward and away from building surfaces in accordance with Section 6.4.2.2 of ASCE 7. Lateral requirements shall be in accordance with Section 2305 or 2308.

c. Wood structural panels with span ratings of wall-16 or wall-24 shall be permitted as an alternative to panels with a 24/0 span rating. Plywood siding rated 16 o.c. or 24 o.c. shall be permitted as an alternative to panels with a 24/16 span rating. Wall-16 and plywood siding 16 o.c. shall be used with studs spaced a maximum of 16 inches o.c.

TABLE 2304.7(1)
ALLOWABLE SPANS FOR LUMBER FLOOR AND ROOF SHEATHING[a, b]

SPAN (inches)	MINIMUM NET THICKNESS (inches) OF LUMBER PLACED			
	Perpendicular to supports		Diagonally to supports	
	Surfaced dry[c]	Surfaced unseasoned	Surfaced dry[c]	Surfaced unseasoned
Floors				
24	3/4	25/32	3/4	25/32
16	5/8	11/16	5/8	11/16
Roofs				
24	5/8	11/16	3/4	25/32

For SI: 1 inch = 25.4 mm.

a. Installation details shall conform to Sections 2304.7.1 and 2304.7.2 for floor and roof sheathing, respectively.

b. Floor or roof sheathing conforming with this table shall be deemed to meet the design criteria of Section 2304.7.

c. Maximum 19-percent moisture content.

TABLE 2304.7(2)
SHEATHING LUMBER, MINIMUM GRADE REQUIREMENTS: BOARD GRADE

SOLID FLOOR OR ROOF SHEATHING	SPACED ROOF SHEATHING	GRADING RULES
Utility	Standard	NLGA, WCLIB, WWPA
4 common or utility	3 common or standard	NLGA, WCLIB, WWPA, NSLB or NELMA
No. 3	No. 2	SPIB
Merchantable	Construction common	RIS

TABLE 2304.7(3)
ALLOWABLE SPANS AND LOADS FOR WOOD STRUCTURAL PANEL SHEATHING AND SINGLE-FLOOR GRADES CONTINUOUS OVER TWO OR MORE SPANS WITH STRENGTH AXIS PERPENDICULAR TO SUPPORTS[a, b]

SHEATHING GRADES		ROOF[c]				FLOOR[d]
Panel span rating roof/floor span	Panel thickness (inches)	Maximum span (inches)		Load[e] (psf)		Maximum span (inches)
		With edge support[f]	Without edge support	Total load	Live load	
16/0	$^3/_8$	16	16	40	30	0
20/0	$^3/_8$	20	20	40	30	0
24/0	$^3/_8$, $^7/_{16}$, $^1/_2$	24	20[g]	40	30	0
24/16	$^7/_{16}$, $^1/_2$	24	24	50	40	16
32/16	$^{15}/_{32}$, $^1/_2$, $^5/_8$	32	28	40	30	16[h]
40/20	$^{19}/_{32}$, $^5/_8$, $^3/_4$, $^7/_8$	40	32	40	30	20[h,i]
48/24	$^{23}/_{32}$, $^3/_4$, $^7/_8$	48	36	45	35	24
54/32	$^7/_8$, 1	54	40	45	35	32
60/32	$^7/_8$, $1^1/_8$	60	48	45	35	32
SINGLE FLOOR GRADES		ROOF[c]				FLOOR[d]
Panel span rating	Panel thickness (inches)	Maximum span (inches)		Load[e] (psf)		Maximum span (inches)
		With edge support[f]	Without edge support	Total load	Live load	
16 o.c.	$^1/_2$, $^{19}/_{32}$, $^5/_8$	24	24	50	40	16[h]
20 o.c.	$^{19}/_{32}$, $^5/_8$, $^3/_4$	32	32	40	30	20[h,i]
24 o.c.	$^{23}/_{32}$, $^3/_4$	48	36	35	25	24
32 o.c.	$^7/_8$, 1	48	40	50	40	32
48 o.c.	$1^3/_{32}$, $1^1/_8$	60	48	50	40	48

For SI: 1 inch = 25.4 mm, 1 pound per square foot = 0.0479 kN/m^2.

a. Applies to panels 24 inches or wider.

b. Floor and roof sheathing conforming with this table shall be deemed to meet the design criteria of Section 2304.7.

c. Uniform load deflection limitations $^1/_{180}$ of span under live load plus dead load, $^1/_{240}$ under live load only.

d. Panel edges shall have approved tongue-and-groove joints or shall be supported with blocking unless $^1/_4$-inch minimum thickness underlayment or $1^1/_2$ inches of approved cellular or lightweight concrete is placed over the subfloor, or finish floor is $^3/_4$-inch wood strip. Allowable uniform load based on deflection of $^1/_{360}$ of span is 100 pounds per square foot except the span rating of 48 inches on center is based on a total load of 65 pounds per square foot.

e. Allowable load at maximum span.

f. Tongue-and-groove edges, panel edge clips (one midway between each support, except two equally spaced between supports 48 inches on center), lumber blocking or other. Only lumber blocking shall satisfy blocked diaphragm requirements.

g. For $^1/_2$-inch panel, maximum span shall be 24 inches.

h. Span is permitted to be 24 inches on center where $^3/_4$-inch wood strip flooring is installed at right angles to joist.

i. Span is permitted to be 24 inches on center for floors where $1^1/_2$ inches of cellular or lightweight concrete is applied over the panels.

TABLE 2304.7(4)
ALLOWABLE SPAN FOR WOOD STRUCTURAL PANEL COMBINATION SUBFLOOR-UNDERLAYMENT (SINGLE FLOOR)[a, b]
(Panels Continuous Over Two or More Spans and Strength Axis Perpendicular to Supports)

IDENTIFICATION	MAXIMUM SPACING OF JOISTS (inches)				
	16	20	24	32	48
Species group[c]	Thickness (inches)				
1	$^{1}/_{2}$	$^{5}/_{8}$	$^{3}/_{4}$	—	—
2, 3	$^{5}/_{8}$	$^{3}/_{4}$	$^{7}/_{8}$	—	—
4	$^{3}/_{4}$	$^{7}/_{8}$	1	—	—
Single floor span rating[d]	16 o.c.	20 o.c.	24 o.c.	32 o.c.	48 o.c.

For SI: 1 inch = 25.4 mm, 1 pound per square foot = 0.0479 kN/m^2.

a. Spans limited to value shown because of possible effects of concentrated loads. Allowable uniform loads based on deflection of $^{1}/_{360}$ of span is 100 pounds per square foot except allowable total uniform load for 1 $^{1}/_{8}$-inch wood structural panels over joists spaced 48 inches on center is 65 pounds per square foot. Panel edges shall have approved tongue-and-groove joints or shall be supported with blocking, unless $^{1}/_{4}$-inch minimum thickness underlayment or 1 $^{1}/_{2}$ inches of approved cellular or lightweight concrete is placed over the subfloor, or finish floor is $^{3}/_{4}$-inch wood strip.

b. Floor panels conforming with this table shall be deemed to meet the design criteria of Section 2304.7.

c. Applicable to all grades of sanded exterior-type plywood. See DOC PS 1 for plywood species groups.

d. Applicable to Underlayment grade, C-C (Plugged) plywood, and Single Floor grade wood structural panels.

TABLE 2304.7(5)
ALLOWABLE LOAD (PSF) FOR WOOD STRUCTURAL PANEL ROOF SHEATHING CONTINUOUS OVER TWO OR MORE SPANS AND STRENGTH AXIS PARALLEL TO SUPPORTS
(Plywood Structural Panels Are Five-Ply, Five-Layer Unless Otherwise Noted)[a, b]

PANEL GRADE	THICKNESS (inch)	MAXIMUM SPAN (inches)	LOAD AT MAXIMUM SPAN (psf)	
			Live	Total
Structural I sheathing	$^{7}/_{16}$	24	20	30
	$^{15}/_{32}$	24	35[c]	45[c]
	$^{1}/_{2}$	24	40[c]	50[c]
	$^{19}/_{32}$, $^{5}/_{8}$	24	70	80
	$^{23}/_{32}$, $^{3}/_{4}$	24	90	100
Sheathing, other grades covered in DOC PS 1 or DOC PS 2	$^{7}/_{16}$	16	40	50
	$^{15}/_{32}$	24	20	25
	$^{1}/_{2}$	24	25	30
	$^{19}/_{32}$	24	40[c]	50[c]
	$^{5}/_{8}$	24	45[c]	55[c]
	$^{23}/_{32}$, $^{3}/_{4}$	24	60[c]	65[c]

For SI: 1 inch = 25.4 mm, 1 pound per square foot = 0.0479 kN/m^2.

a. Roof sheathing conforming with this table shall be deemed to meet the design criteria of Section 2304.7.

b. Uniform load deflection limitations $^{1}/_{180}$ of span under live load plus dead load, $^{1}/_{240}$ under live load only. Edges shall be blocked with lumber or other approved type of edge supports.

c. For composite and four-ply plywood structural panel, load shall be reduced by 15 pounds per square foot.

2304.8 Lumber decking.

2304.8.1 General. Lumber decking shall be designed and installed in accordance with the general provisions of this code and Section 2304.8. Each piece shall be square end trimmed. When random lengths are furnished, each piece shall be square end trimmed across the face so that at least 90 percent of the pieces are within 0.5 degrees (0.00873 rad) of square. The ends of the pieces shall be permitted to be beveled up to 2 degrees (0.0349 rad) from the vertical with the exposed face of the piece slightly longer than the opposite face of the piece. Tongue-and-groove decking shall be installed with the tongues up on sloped or pitched roofs with pattern faces down.

2304.8.2 Layup patterns. Lumber decking is permitted to be laid up following one of five standard patterns as defined in Sections 2304.8.2.1 through 2304.8.2.5. Other patterns are permitted to be used provided they are substantiated through engineering analysis.

2304.8.2.1 Simple span pattern. All pieces shall be supported on their ends (i.e., by two supports).

2304.8.2.2 Two-span continuous pattern. All pieces shall be supported by three supports, and all end joints shall occur in line on alternating supports. Supporting members shall be designed to accommodate the load redistribution caused by this pattern.

2304.8.2.3 Combination simple and two-span continuous pattern. Courses in end spans shall be alternating simple-span pattern and two-span continuous pattern. End joints shall be staggered in adjacent courses and shall bear on supports.

2304.8.2.4 Cantilevered pieces intermixed pattern. The decking shall extend across a minimum of three spans. Pieces in each starter course and every third course shall be simple span pattern. Pieces in other courses shall be cantilevered over the supports with end joints at alternating quarter or third points of the spans. Each piece shall bear on at least one support.

2304.8.2.5 Controlled random pattern. The decking shall extend across a minimum of three spans. End joints of pieces within 6 inches (152 mm) of the end joints of the adjacent pieces in either direction shall be separated by at least two intervening courses. In the end bays, each piece shall bear on at least one support. Where an end joint occurs in an end bay, the next piece in the same course shall continue over the first inner support for at least 24 inches (610 mm). The details of the controlled random pattern shall be as specified for each decking material in Section 2304.8.3.3, 2304.8.4.3 or 2304.8.5.3.

Decking that cantilevers beyond a support for a horizontal distance greater than 18 inches (457 mm), 24 inches (610 mm) or 36 inches (914 mm) for 2-inch (51 mm), 3-inch (76 mm) and 4-inch (102 mm) nominal thickness decking, respectively, shall comply with the following:

1. The maximum cantilevered length shall be 30 percent of the length of the first adjacent interior span.
2. A structural fascia shall be fastened to each decking piece to maintain a continuous, straight line.
3. There shall be no end joints in the decking between the cantilevered end of the decking and the centerline of the first adjacent interior span.

2304.8.3 Mechanically laminated decking.

2304.8.3.1 General. Mechanically laminated decking consists of square-edged dimension lumber laminations set on edge and nailed to the adjacent pieces and to the supports.

2304.8.3.2 Nailing. The length of nails connecting laminations shall not be less than two and one-half times the net thickness of each lamination. Where decking supports are 48 inches (1219 mm) on center (o.c.) or less, side nails shall be installed not more than 30 inches (762 mm) o.c. alternating between top and bottom edges, and staggered one-third of the spacing in adjacent laminations. Where supports are spaced more than 48 inches (1219 mm) o.c., side nails shall be installed not more than 18 inches (457 mm) o.c. alternating between top and bottom edges and staggered one-third of the spacing in adjacent laminations. Two side nails shall be installed at each end of butt-jointed pieces.

Laminations shall be toenailed to supports with 20d or larger common nails. Where the supports are 48 inches (1219 mm) o.c. or less, alternate laminations shall be toenailed to alternate supports; where supports are spaced more than 48 inches (1219 mm) o.c., alternate laminations shall be toenailed to every support.

2304.8.3.3 Controlled random pattern. There shall be a minimum distance of 24 inches (610 mm) between end joints in adjacent courses. The pieces in the first and second courses shall bear on at least two supports with end joints in these two courses occurring on alternate supports. A maximum of seven intervening courses shall be permitted before this pattern is repeated.

2304.8.4 Two-inch sawn tongue-and-groove decking.

2304.8.4.1 General. Two-inch (51 mm) decking shall have a maximum moisture content of 15 percent. Decking shall be machined with a single tongue-and-groove pattern. Each decking piece shall be nailed to each support.

2304.8.4.2 Nailing. Each piece of decking shall be toenailed at each support with one 16d common nail through the tongue and face-nailed with one 16d common nail.

2304.8.4.3 Controlled random pattern. There shall be a minimum distance of 24 inches (610 mm) between end joints in adjacent courses. The pieces in the first and second courses shall bear on at least two supports with end joints in these two courses occurring on alternate supports. A maximum of seven intervening courses shall be permitted before this pattern is repeated.

2304.8.5 Three- and 4-inch sawn tongue-and-groove decking.

2304.8.5.1 General. Three-inch (76 mm) and 4-inch (102 mm) decking shall have a maximum moisture content of 19 percent. Decking shall be machined with a double tongue-and-groove pattern. Decking pieces shall be interconnected and nailed to the supports.

2304.8.5.2 Nailing. Each piece shall be toenailed at each support with one 40d common nail and face-nailed with one 60d common nail. Courses shall be spiked to each other with 8-inch (203 mm) spikes at maximum intervals of 30 inches (762 mm) through predrilled edge holes penetrating to a depth of approximately 4 inches (102 mm). One spike shall be installed at a distance not exceeding 10 inches (254 mm) from the end of each piece.

2304.8.5.3 Controlled random pattern. There shall be a minimum distance of 48 inches (1219 mm) between end joints in adjacent courses. Pieces not bearing on a support are permitted to be located in interior bays provided the adjacent pieces in the same course continue over the support for at least 24 inches (610 mm). This condition shall not occur more than once in every six courses in each interior bay.

2304.9 Connections and fasteners.

2304.9.1 Fastener requirements. Connections for wood members shall be designed in accordance with the appropriate methodology in Section 2301.2. The number and size of fasteners connecting wood members shall not be less than that set forth in Tables 2304.9.1.1, 2304.9.1.2, 2304.9.1.3, 2304.9.1.4, 2304.9.1.5 and 2304.9.1.6.

2304.9.2 Sheathing fasteners. Sheathing nails or other *approved* sheathing connectors shall be driven so that their head or crown is flush with the surface of the sheathing.

2304.9.3 Joist hangers and framing anchors. Connections depending on joist hangers or framing anchors, ties and other mechanical fastenings not otherwise covered are permitted where *approved*. The vertical load-bearing capacity, torsional moment capacity and deflection characteristics of joist hangers shall be determined in accordance with Section 1716.1.

2304.9.4 Other fasteners. Clips, staples, glues and other *approved* methods of fastening are permitted where *approved*.

2304.9.5 Fasteners and connectors in contact with preservative-treated and fire-retardant-treated wood. Fasteners and connectors in contact with *preservative-treated* and *fire-retardant-treated wood* shall be in accordance with Sections 2304.9.5.1 through 2304.9.5.4. The coating weights for zinc-coated fasteners shall be in accordance with ASTM A 153.

2304.9.5.1 Fasteners and connectors for preservative-treated wood. Fasteners in contact with *preservative-treated wood* shall be of hot-dipped zinc-coated galvanized steel, stainless steel, silicon bronze or copper. Fasteners other than nails, timber rivets, wood screws and lag screws shall be permitted to be of mechanically deposited zinc-coated steel with coating weights in accordance with ASTM B 695, Class 55 minimum. Connectors that are used in exterior applications and in contact with *preservative-treated wood* shall have coating types and weights in accordance with the treated wood or connector manufacturer's recommendations. In the absence of manufacturer's recommendations, a minimum of ASTM A 653, type G185 zinc-coated galvanized steel, or equivalent, shall be used.

Exception: Plain carbon steel fasteners in SBX/DOT and zinc borate *preservative-treated wood* in an interior, dry environment shall be permitted.

2304.9.5.2 Fastenings for wood foundations. Fastenings for wood foundations shall be as required in AF&PA PWF.

2304.9.5.3 Fasteners for fire-retardant-treated wood used in exterior applications or wet or damp locations. Fasteners for *fire-retardant-treated wood* used in exterior applications or wet or damp locations shall be of hot-dipped zinc-coated galvanized steel, stainless steel, silicon bronze or copper. Fasteners other than nails, timber rivets, wood screws and lag screws shall be permitted to be of mechanically deposited zinc-coated steel with coating weights in accordance with ASTM B 695, Class 55 minimum.

2304.9.5.4 Fasteners for fire-retardant-treated wood used in interior applications. Fasteners for *fire-retardant-treated wood* used in interior locations shall be in accordance with the manufacturer's recommendations. In the absence of manufacturer's recommendations, Section 2304.9.5.3 shall apply.

2304.9.6 Load path. Where wall framing members are not continuous from foundation sill to roof, the members shall be secured to ensure a continuous load path. Where required, sheet metal clamps, ties or clips shall be formed of galvanized steel or other *approved* corrosion-resistant material not less than 0.040 inch (1.01 mm) nominal thickness.

2304.9.7 Framing requirements. Wood columns and posts shall be framed to provide full end bearing. Alternatively, column-and-post end connections shall be designed to resist the full compressive loads, neglecting end-bearing capacity. Column-and-post end connections shall be fastened to resist lateral and net induced uplift forces.

2304.10 Heavy timber construction.

2304.10.1 Columns. Columns shall be continuous or superimposed throughout all stories by means of reinforced concrete or metal caps with brackets, or shall be connected by properly designed steel or iron caps, with pintles and base plates, or by timber splice plates affixed to the columns by metal connectors housed within the contact faces, or by other *approved* methods.

2304.10.1.1 Column connections. Girders and beams shall be closely fitted around columns and adjoining ends shall be cross tied to each other, or intertied by caps or ties, to transfer horizontal loads across joints. Wood bolsters shall not be placed on tops of columns unless the columns support roof loads only.

TABLE 2304.9.1.1
NOMINAL DIMENSIONS OF NAILS FREQUENTLY LISTED IN MODEL BUILDING CODES AND THIS REPORT[b]

NAILS DESCRIBED BY PENNYWEIGHT SYSTEM		
Pennyweight	**Length (inches)**	**Shank diameter (inches)**
Box		
6d	2	0.099
8d	$2\frac{1}{2}$	0.113
10d	3	0.128
Casing		
6d	$2\frac{1}{4}$	0.099
8d	$2\frac{1}{2}$	0.113
10d	3	0.128
Common		
6d	2	0.113
8d	$2\frac{1}{2}$	0.131
10d	3	0.148
16d	$3\frac{1}{2}$	0.162
20d	4	0.192
Cooler		
5d	$1\frac{5}{8}$	0.086
6d	$1\frac{7}{8}$	0.092
8d	$2\frac{3}{8}$	0.113
Deformed[a]		
3d	$1\frac{1}{4}$	0.099
4d	$1\frac{1}{2}$	0.099
6d	2	0.120
8d	$2\frac{1}{2}$	0.120
Finish		
8d	$2\frac{1}{2}$	0.099
10d	3	0.113
Siding		
6d	$1\frac{7}{8}$	0.106
8d	$2\frac{3}{8}$	0.128
Additional Recognized Nails		
Smooth shank nails	$2\frac{1}{4}$	0.092
	$2\frac{1}{4}$	0.105
	3	0.120
	$3\frac{1}{4}$	
	$1\frac{1}{2}$	0.131
	3	
	$3\frac{1}{4}$	
	$1\frac{1}{2}$	0.148
	$2\frac{1}{2}$	0.162
Deformed shank nails[a]	$2\frac{1}{4}$	0.099
	2	0.113
	$2\frac{3}{8}$	
	$2\frac{1}{2}$	0.131

For SI: 1 inch = 25.4 mm.

a. A deformed shank nail must have either a helical (screw) shank or an annular (ring) shank.

b. Reprinted by permission of the ICC Evaluation Service, LLC from Evaluation Report ESR-1539.

TABLE 2304.9.1.2
WALL FRAMING[a, e]

CONNECTION[b] (NAIL SIZE AND POSITION EXAGGERATED FOR ILLUSTRATIVE PURPOSES)	FASTENER MINIMUM NOMINAL LENGTH IN INCHES X MINIMUM NOMINAL NAIL DIAMETER IN INCHES	QUANTITY PER CONNECTION, OR SPACING BETWEEN FASTENERS (INCHES ON CENTER)[d]
Top or sole plate to stud (face nail)	3-1/2" × 0.162" (16d common)[c]	2
	3" × 0.148" nail (10d common)	3
	3-1/4" × 0.131" nail	
	3" × 0.131" nail	
	3-1/4" × 0.120" nail	4
	3" × 0.120" nail	
Stud to top or sole plate (toe nail)	2-1/2" × 0.131" nail (16d common)[c]	4
	3-1/2" × 0.162" nail (16d common)	3
	3" × 0.148" nail (10d common)	4
	3-1/4" × 0.131" nail	
	3" × 0.131" nail	
	3-1/4" × 0.120" nail	
	3" × 0.120" nail	
	2-3/8" × 0.113" nail	5
	2" × 0.113" nail	
	2-1/4" × 0.105" nail	
	2-1/4" × 0.099" nail	
Cap/top plate laps and intersections	3-1/2" × 0.162" nail (16 common)[c]	2 each side of lap
	3" × 0.148" nail	3 each side of lap
	3-1/4" × 0.131" nail	
	3" × 0.131" nail	
	3-1/4" × 0.120" nail	
	3" × 0.120" nail	
Diagonal bracing	3-1/2" × 0.162" nail (16d common)	2
	2-1/2" × 0.131" nail (8d common)[c]	
	3" × 0.148" nail (10d common)	
	3-1/4" × 0.131" nail	
	3" × 0.131" nail	
	3-1/4" × 0.120" nail	3
	3" × 0.120" nail	
	2-3/8" × 0.113" nail	
	2" × 0.113" nail	4
	2-1/4" × 0.105" nail	
	2-1/4" × 0.099" nail	
Sole plate to joist or blocking at braced panels	3-1/2" × 0.135" nail (16d box)[c]	3 per 16" space
	3-1/2" × 0.162" nail (16d common)	2 per 16" space
	3" × 0.148 nail (10d common)	3 per 16" space
	3-1/4" × 0.131" nail	
	3" × 0.131" nail	4 per 16" space
	3-1/4" × 0.120" nail	
	3" × 0.120" nail	
Sole plate to joist or blocking	3-1/2" × 0.162" nail (16d common)[c]	16" o.c.
	3" × 0.148" nail (10d common)	8" o.c.
	3-1/4" × 0.131" nail	
	3" × 0.131" nail	
	3-1/4" × 0.120" nail	
	3" × 0.120" nail	

(continued)

TABLE 2304.9.1.2—continued
WALL FRAMING[a, e]

CONNECTION[b] (NAIL SIZE AND POSITION EXAGGERATED FOR ILLUSTRATIVE PURPOSES)	FASTENER MINIMUM NOMINAL LENGTH IN INCHES X MINIMUM NOMINAL NAIL DIAMETER IN INCHES	QUANTITY PER CONNECTION, OR SPACING BETWEEN FASTENERS (INCHES ON CENTER)[d]
Double top plate	3" × 0.148" nail (10d common)[c]	16" o.c.
	$3^1/_2$" × 0.162" nail (16d common)	
	$3^1/_4$" × 0.131" nail	12" o.c.
	3" × 0.131"	
	$3^1/_4$" × 0.120" nail	
	3" × 0.120" nail	
Double Studs	3" × 0.148" nail (10d common)[c]	12" o.c.
	$3^1/_2$" × 0.162" nail (16d common)	
	$3^1/_4$" × 0.131" nail	8" o.c.
	3" × 0.131" nail	
	$3^1/_4$" × 0.120" nail	
	3" × 0.120" nail	
Corner Studs	$3^1/_2$" × 0.162" nail (16d common)[c]	24" o.c.
	3" × 0.148" nail (10d common)	16" o.c.
	$3^1/_4$" × 0.131" nail	
	3" × 0.131" nail	
	$3^1/_4$" × 0.120" nail	12" o.c.
	3" × 0.120" nail	

For SI: 1 inch = 25.4 mm, 1 foot = 304.8 mm, 1 mile per hour = 0.44 m/s..

a. This fastening schedule applies to framing members having an actual thickness of $1^1/_2$" (nominal "2-by" lumber).

b. Fastenings listed above may also be used for other connections that are not listed but that have the same configuration and the same code requirement for fastener quantity/spacing and fastener size (pennyweight and style, e.g., 8d common, "8-penny common nail").

c. This fastener, in the quantity or spacing shown in the rightmost column, comprises the most stringent fastening of the connection listed in the International, National, *International One- and Two-family Dwelling*, International Residential, Standard or Uniform Building Codes.

d. Fastening schedule only applies to buildings of conventional wood frame construction where wind or seismic analysis is not required by the applicable code. In areas where wind or seismic analysis is required, required fastening must be determined by structural analysis. Following are conditions for which codes require structural analysis:

i. *International Building Code*—buildings located in areas where design wind speeds exceed 100 mph (3-second gust) or 110 mph (3-second gust) in Exposure Categories A or B. Structural analysis is also required on buildings assigned to Seismic Design Categories B, C, D or E, with exception of detached Group R-3 dwellings assigned to Seismic Design Category B and some detached Group R-3 dwellings assigned to Seismic Design Category C.

ii. *International Residential Code*—buildings located in areas where the design wind speed equals or exceeds 110 mph (177.1 km/h) (3-second gust) or assigned to Seismic Design Categories C, D_1 and D_2 (with detached one- and two-family dwellings in Category C being exempt).

iii. BOCA *National Building Code*—buildings in any location.

iv. *Standard Building Code*—buildings located in areas where design wind speeds prescribed exceed 80 mph or which do not qualify for one of the exceptions outlined in Section 1607.1 of the code.

v. SBCCI *Standard SSTD 10*—this fastening schedule is equivalent to that contained in Appendix E of the standard. However, note that specific provisions in the standard may supersede or supplement this schedule.

vi. *Uniform Building Code*—buildings located in areas where the design wind speeds prescribed are 80 mph or higher. See Sections 2320.4 and 2320.5 of the code for additional requirements in various seismic zones.

vii. *International One- and Two-family Dwelling Code*—buildings other than one story buildings in height in exposure classification A/B unless over 50 feet in height, or with unusual construction or geometric shapes, with overhanging eave projections greater than 24 inches, or located in special wind regions or localities.

e. Reprinted by permission of the ICC Evaluation Service, LLC from Evaluation Report ESR-1539.

FIGURE 2304.9.1.3 CEILING AND ROOF FRAMING[a, e]

CONNECTION[b] (NAIL SIZE AND POSITION EXAGGERATED FOR ILLUSTRATIVE PURPOSES)	FASTENER MINIMUM NOMINAL LENGTH IN INCHES X MINIMUM NOMINAL NAIL DIAMETER IN INCHES	QUANTITY PER CONNECTION, OR SPACING BETWEEN FASTENERS (INCHES ON CENTER)[d]
Ceiling joist to plate 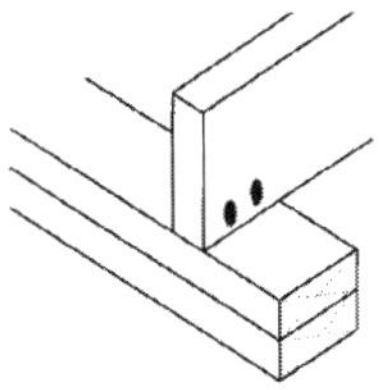	$3^{1}/_{2}$" × 0.162" nail (16d common)[c]	3
	3" × 0.148" nail (10d common)	4
	$3^{1}/_{4}$" × 0.131" nail	5
	3" × 0.131" nail	
	$3^{1}/_{4}$" × 0.120" nail	
	3" × 0.120" nail	
	$2^{3}/_{8}$" × 0.113" nail	6
Ceiling joists, laps over partitions; 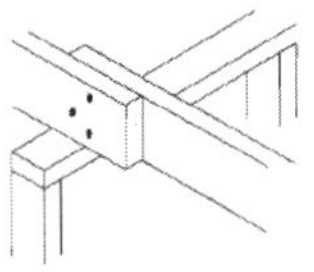 Ceiling joist to parallel rafter 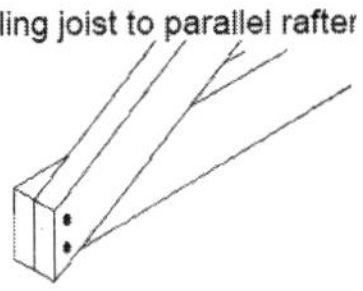	$3^{1}/_{2}$" × 0.162" nail (16d common)[c]	3
	3" × 0.148" nail (10d common)	4
	$3^{1}/_{4}$" × 0.131" nail	
	3" × 0.131" nail	
	$3^{1}/_{4}$" × 0.120" nail	
	3" × 0.120" nail	
Collar tie to rafter 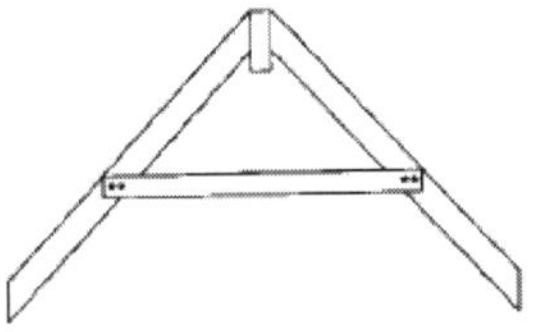	3" × 0.148" nail (10d common)[c]	3
	$3^{1}/_{2}$" × 0.162" nail (16d common)	
	$3^{1}/_{4}$" × 0.131" nail	4
	3" × 0.131" nail	
	$3^{1}/_{4}$" × 0.120" nail	
	3" × 0.120" nail	
Jack rafter to hip, toe-nailed 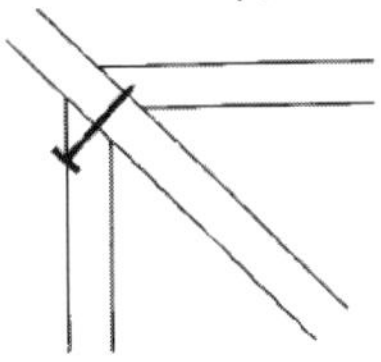	3" × 0.148" nail (10d common)[c]	3
	$3^{1}/_{2}$" × 0.162" nail (16d common)	
	$3^{1}/_{4}$" × 0.131" nail	4
	3" × 0.131" nail	
	$3^{1}/_{4}$" × 0.120" nail	
	3" × 0.120" nail	
Jack rafter to hip, face nailed 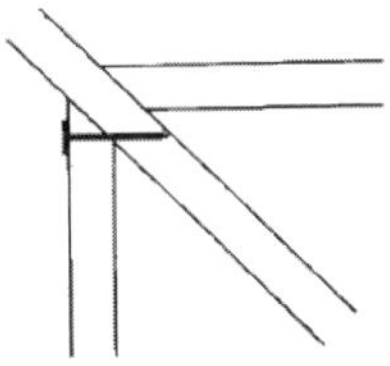	$3^{1}/_{2}$" × 0.162" nail (16d common)[c]	2
	3" × 0.148" nail (10d common)	3
	$3^{1}/_{4}$" × 0.131" nail	
	3" × 0.131" nail	
	$3^{1}/_{4}$" × 0.120" nail	4
	3" x 0.120" nail	
Roof rafter to plate (toe-nailed) 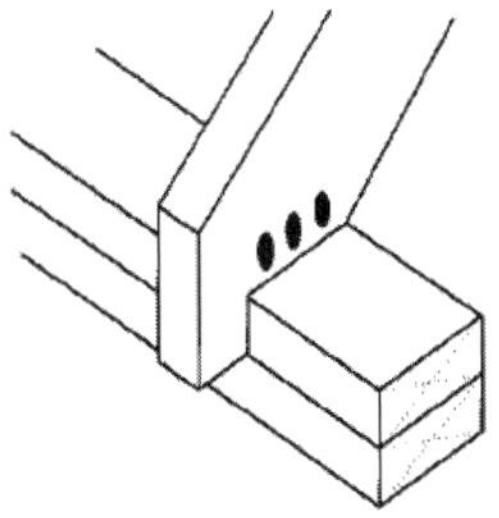	$2^{1}/_{2}$" × 0.131" nail (8d common)[c]	3
	$3^{1}/_{2}$" × 0.162" nail (16d common)	
	3" × 0.148" nail (10d common)	
	$3^{1}/_{4}$" × 0.131" nail	
	3" × 0.131" nail	
	$3^{1}/_{4}$" × 0.120" nail	4
	3" × 0.120" nail	
	$2^{3}/_{8}$" × 0.113" nail	5
	2" × 0.113" nail	
	$2^{1}/_{4}$" × 0.105" nail	
	$2^{1}/_{4}$" × 0.099" nail	6

(continued)

FIGURE 2304.9.1.3—continued
CEILING AND ROOF FRAMING[a, e]

CONNECTION[b] (NAIL SIZE AND POSITION EXAGGERATED FOR ILLUSTRATIVE PURPOSES)	FASTENER MINIMUM NOMINAL LENGTH IN INCHES X MINIMUM NOMINAL NAIL DIAMETER IN INCHES	QUANTITY PER CONNECTION, OR SPACING BETWEEN FASTENERS (INCHES ON CENTER)[d]
Roof rafter to 2-by ridge beam, face nailed (only the attachment of the top rafter is illustrated	$3^1/_2$" × 0.162" nail (16d common)[c]	2
	3" × 0.148 nail (10d common)	3
	$3^1/_4$" × 0.131" nail	
	3" × 0.131" nail	
	$3^1/_4$" × 0.120" nail	4
	3" × 0.120" nail	
Roof rafter to 2-by ridge beam, toe-nailed	$3^1/_2$" × 0.162" nail (16d common)[c]	2
	3" × 0.148" nail (10d common)	3
	$3^1/_4$" × 0.131" nail	
	3" × 0.131" nail	
	$3^1/_4$" × 0.120" nail	4
	3" x 0.120" nail	

For SI: 1 inch = 25.4 mm.

a. This fastening schedule applies to framing members having an actual thickness of $1^1/_2$" (nominal "2-by" lumber).

b. Fastenings listed above may also be used for other connections that are not listed but that have the same configuration and the same code requirement for fastener quantity/spacing and fastener size (pennyweight and style, e.g., 8d common, "8-penny common nail").

c. This fastener, in the quantity or spacing shown in the rightmost column, comprises the most stringent fastening of the connection listed in the International, National, *International One- and Two-family Dwelling*, International Residential, Standard or Uniform Building Codes.

d. Fastening schedule only applies to buildings of conventional wood frame construction where wind or seismic analysis is not required by the applicable code. In areas where wind or seismic analysis is required, required fastening must be determined by structural analysis. Following are conditions for which codes require structural analysis:

i. *International Building Code*—buildings located in areas where design wind speeds exceed 100 mph (3-second gust) or 110 mph (3-second gust) in Exposure Categories A or B. Structural analysis is also required on buildings assigned to Seismic Design Categories B, C, D or E, with exception of detached Group R-3 dwellings assigned to Seismic Design Category B and some detached Group R-3 dwellings assigned to Seismic Design Category C.

ii. *International Residential Code*—buildings located in areas where the design wind speed equals or exceeds 110 mph (3-second gust) or assigned to Seismic Design Categories C, D_1 and D_2 (with detached one- and two-family dwellings in Category C being exempt).

iii. BOCA *National Building Code*—buildings in any location.

iv. *Standard Building Code*—buildings located in areas where design wind speeds prescribed exceed 80 mph or which do not qualify for one of the exceptions outlined in Section 1607.1 of the code.

v. SBCCI *Standard SSTD 10*—this fastening schedule is equivalent to that contained in Appendix E of the standard. However, note that specific provisions in the standard may supersede or supplement this schedule.

vi. *Uniform Building Code*—buildings located in areas where the design wind speeds prescribed are 80 mph or higher. See Sections 2320.4 and 2320.5 of the code for additional requirements in various seismic zones.

vii. *International One- and Two-family Dwelling Code*—buildings other than one story buildings in height in exposure classification A/B unless over 50 feet in height, or with unusual construction or geometric shapes, with overhanging eave projections greater than 24 inches, or located in special wind regions or localities.

e. Reprinted by permission of the ICC Evaluation Service, LLC from Evaluation Report ESR-1539.

TABLE 2304.9.1.4 FLOOR FRAMING[a, e]

CONNECTION[b] (NAIL SIZE AND POSITION EXAGGERATED FOR ILLUSTRATIVE PURPOSES)	FASTENER MINIMUM NOMINAL LENGTH IN INCHES X MINIMUM NOMINAL NAIL DIAMETER IN INCHES	QUANTITY PER CONNECTION, OR SPACING BETWEEN FASTENERS[d]
joist to band joist	3 1/2" × 0.162" nail (16d common)[c]	3
	3" × 0.148" nail (10d common)	5
	3 1/4" × 0.131" nail	
	3" × 0.131" nail	
	3 1/4" × 0.120" nail	6
	3" × 0.120" nail	
Ledger strip	3 1/2" × 0.162" nail (16d common)[c]	3
	3" × 0.148" nail (10d common)	4
	3 1/4" × 0.131" nail	
	3" × 0.131" nail	
	3 1/4" × 0.120" nail	
	3" × 0.120" nail	
Joist to sill or girder toe-nailed; Blocking between joist or rafter to top plate (toe-nailed)	2 1/2" × 0.131" nail (8d common)[c]	3
	3" × 0.148" nail (10d common)	
	3 1/4" × 0.131" nail	
	3" × 0.131" nail	4
	3 1/4" × 0.120" nail	
	3" × 0.120" nail	
Bridging to joist (listed number of fasteners at each end	2 1/2" × 0.131" nail (8d common)[c]	2
	3 1/4" × 0.120" nail	3
	3" × 0.120" nail	
	2 3/8" × 0.113" nail	
	2" × 0.113" nail (6d common)	4
	2 1/4" × 0.105" nail	3
	2 1/4" × 0.099" nail	4
Rim joist to top plate (toe-nailed)	2 1/2" × 0.113" (3d box)[c]	6" o.c.
	3 1/2" × 0162" nail (16d common)	8" o.c.
	3" × 0.148" nail (10d common)	6" o.c.
	3 1/4" × 0.131" nail	
	3" × 0.131" nail	
	3 1/4" × 0.120" nail	
	3" × 0.120" nail	4" o.c.
	2 3/8" × 0.113" nail	6" o.c.
	2" × 0.113" nail (6d common)	3" o.c.
	2 1/4" × 0.105" nail	
	2 1/4" x 0.099" nail	

Connection[b] (Nail size and position Exaggerated for Illustrative purposes)	Fastner minimum nominal length in inches × minimum nominal nail diameter in inches	Spacing of fasteners along the top and bottom of beam, staggered on each side of each layer	Number of fasteners at each end and splice for each layer
Built-up girders and beams	4" × 0.192" nail (20d common)[c]	32" o.c.	2
	3 1/2" × 0.162" nail (16d common)	24" o.c.	3
	3" × 0.148" nail (10d common)		
	3 1/4" × 0.131" nail		
	3" × 0.131" nail		
	3 1/4" × 0.120" nail	16" o.c.	3
	3" × 0.120" nail		
	2 1/2" × 0.131" nail (8d common)	16" o.c.	4

For SI: 1 inch = 25.4 mm, 1 mile per hour = 0.44 m/s, 1 foot = 304.8 mm.

(continued)

FIGURE 2304.9.1.4—continued
FLOOR FRAMING[a, e]

a. This fastening schedule applies to framing members having an actual thickness of $1^1/_2$" (nominal "2-by" lumber).

b. Fastenings listed above may also be used for other connections that are not listed but that have the same configuration and the same code requirement for fastener quantity/spacing and fastener size (pennyweight and style, e.g., 8d common, "8-penny common nail").

c. This fastener, in the quantity or spacing shown in the rightmost column, comprises the most stringent fastening of the connection listed in the International, National, *International One- and Two-family Dwelling*, International Residential, Standard or Uniform Building Codes.

d. Fastening schedule only applies to buildings of conventional wood frame construction where wind or seismic analysis is not required by the applicable code. In areas where wind or seismic analysis is required, required fastening must be determined by structural analysis. Following are conditions for which codes require structural analysis:

   i. *International Building Code*—buildings located in areas where design wind speeds exceed 100 mph (3-second gust) or 110 mph (3-second gust) in Exposure Categories A or B. Structural analysis is also required on buildings assigned to Seismic Design Categories B, C, D or E, with exception of detached Group R-3 dwellings assigned to Seismic Design Category B and some detached Group R-3 dwellings assigned to Seismic Design Category C

   ii. *International Residential Code*—buildings located in areas where the design wind speed equals or exceeds 110 mph (177.1 km/h) (3 second gust) or assigned to seismic design categories C, D_1 and D_2 (with detached one- and two-family dwellings in Category C being exempt).

   iii. BOCA *National Building Code*—buildings in any location.

   iv. *Standard Building Code*—buildings located in areas where design wind speeds prescribed exceed 80 mph or which do not qualify for one of the exceptions outlined in Section 1607.1 of the code.

   v. SBCCI *Standard SSTD 10*—this fastening schedule is equivalent to that contained in Appendix E of the standard. However, note that specific provisions in the standard may supersede or supplement this schedule.

   vi. *Uniform Building Code*—buildings located in areas where the design wind speeds prescribed are 80 mph or higher. See Sections 2320.4 and 2320.5 of the code for additional requirements in various seismic zones.

   vii. *International One- and Two-family Dwelling Code*—buildings other than one story buildings in height in exposure classification A/B unless over 50 feet in height, or with unusual construction or geometric shapes, with overhanging eave projections greater than 24 inches, or located in special wind regions or localities.

e. Reprinted by permission of the ICC Evaluation Service, LLC from Evaluation Report ESR-1539.

TABLE 2304.9.1.5
SUMMARY OF USE OF FASTENERS FOR FRAMING[a, d]

CONNECTION[b, c]	NUMBER, OR SPACING, OF FASTENERS REQUIRED PER CONNECTION Nail lengths are minimum, nominal lengths, in inches. Nail shank diameters are minimum, nominal diameters, in inches.										
	$3^1/_2$ × 0.162	3 × 0.148	$3^1/_4$ × 0.131	3 × 0.131	$2^1/_2$ × 0.131	$3^1/_4$ × 0.120	3 × 0.120	$2^3/_8$ × 0.113	2 × 0.113	$2^1/_4$ × 0.105	$2^1/_4$ × 0.099
	Floor Framing										
Joist to band joist	3	5	5	5	N/A	6	6	N/A	N/A	N/A	N/A
Ledger strip	3	4	4	4	6	4	4	N/A	N/A	N/A	N/A
Joist to sill or girder	3	3	3	3	3	4	4	N/A	N/A	N/A	N/A
Blocking between joist or rafter to top plate	3	3	3	4	3	4	4	N/A	N/A	N/A	N/A
Bridging to joist	N/A	N/A	N/A	N/A	2	3	3	3	4	3	4
Rim joist to top plate	8" o.c.	6" o.c.	6" o.c.	6" o.c.	6" o.c.	6" o.c.	4" o.c.	6" o.c.	3" o.c.	3" o.c.	3" o.c.
Built-up Girders and Beams — Spacing along edges,	24" o.c.	24" o.c.	24" o.c.	24" o.c.	16" o.c.	16" o.c.	16" o.c.	N/A	N/A	N/A	N/A
— # at ends and splices	3	3	3	3	4	3	3				
	Ceiling and Roof Framing										
Ceiling joist to plate	3	4	5	5	5	5	5	6	N/A	N/A	N/A
Ceiling joists, laps over partitions	3	4	4	4	6	4	4	N/A	N/A	N/A	N/A
Ceiling joist to parallel rafter	3	4	4	4	6	4	4	N/A	N/A	N/A	N/A
Collar tie to rafter	3	3	4	4	5	4	4	N/A	N/A	N/A	N/A
Jack rafter to hip, to-nailed	3	3	4	4	5	4	4	N/A	N/A	N/A	N/A
Jack rafter to hip, face nailed	2	3	3	3	3	4	4	N/A	N/A	N/A	N/A
Roof rafter to plate	3	3	3	3	3	4	4	5	5	5	6
Roof rafter to 2-by ridge beam (driven through beam into end of ridge)	2	3	3	3	N/A	4	4	N/A	N/A	N/A	N/A
Roof rafter to 2-by ridge beam (toe-nail rafter to beam)	2	3	3	3	3	4	4	N/A	N/A	N/A	N/A
	Wall Framing										
Top or sole plate to stud (end nailed)	2	3	3	3	5	4	4	N/A	N/A	N/A	N/A
Stud to top or sole plate (toe-nailed)	3	4	4	4	4	4	4	5	5	5	5
Cap/top plate laps and intersections (each side of lap)	2	3	3	3	4	3	3	N/A	N/A	N/A	N/A
Diagonal bracing	2	2	2	2	2	3	3	3	4	4	4
Sole plate to joist or blocking at braced panels (number per 16" joist space)	2	3	3	4	N/A	4	4	N/A	N/A	N/A	N/A
Sole plate to joist or blocking	16" o.c.	8" o.c.	8" o.c.	8" o.c.	6" o.c.	8" o.c.	8" o.c.	N/A	N/A	N/A	N/A
Double top plate	16" o.c.	16" o.c.	12" o.c.	12" o.c.	8" o.c.	12" o.c.	12" o.c.	N/A	N/A	N/A	N/A
Double studs	12" o.c.	12" o.c.	8" o.c.	8" o.c.	6" o.c.	8" o.c.	8" o.c.	N/A	N/A	N/A	N/A
Corner studs	24" o.c.	16" o.c.	16" o.c.	16" o.c.	8" o.c.	12" o.c.	12" o.c.	N/A	N/A	N/A	N/A

For SI: 1 inch = 25.4 mm, 1 foot = 304.8 mm, 1 mile per hour = 0.44 m/s.

N/A = Fastener not applicable to connection.

a. This fastening schedule applies to framing members having an actual thickness of $1^1/_2$ inches (nominal "2-by" lumber).

b. Fastenings listed above may also be used for other connections that are not listed but that have the same configuration and the same code requirement for fastener quantity/spacing and fastener size (pennyweight and style, e.g., 8d common, "8-penny common nail").

c. Fastening schedule only applies to buildings of conventional wood frame construction where wind or seismic analysis is not required by the applicable code. In areas where wind or seismic analysis is required, required fastening must be determined by structural analysis. Following are conditions for which codes require structural analysis:

   i. *International Building Code*—buildings located in areas where design wind speeds exceed 100 mph (3-second gust) or 110 mph (3-second gust) in Exposure Categories A or B. Structural analysis is also required on buildings assigned to Seismic Design Categories B, C, D or E, with exception of detached Group R-3 dwellings assigned to Seismic Design Category B and some detached Group R-3 dwellings assigned to Seismic Design Category C.

   ii. *International Residential Code*—buildings located in areas where the design wind speed equals or exceeds 110 mph (3-second gust) or assigned to Seismic Design Categories C, D_1 and D_2 (with detached one- and two-family dwellings in Category C being exempt).

   iii. BOCA *National Building Code*—buildings in any location.

   iv. *Standard Building Code*—buildings located in areas where design wind speeds prescribed exceed 80 mph or which do not qualify for one of the exceptions outlined in Section 1607.1 of the code.

   v. SBCCI *Standard SSTD 10*—this fastening schedule is equivalent to that contained in Appendix E of the standard. However, note that specific provisions in the standard may supersede or supplement this schedule.

   vi. *International One- and Two-family Dwelling Code*—buildings other than one story buildings in height in exposure classification A/B unless over 50 feet in height, or with unusual construction or geometric shapes, with overhanging eave projections greater than 24 inches, or located in special wind regions or localities.

   vii. *Uniform Building Code*—buildings located in areas where the design wind speeds prescribed are 80 mph or higher. See Sections 2320.4 and 2320.5 of the code for additional requirements in various seismic zones.

d. Reprinted by permission of the ICC Evaluation Service, LLC from Evaluation Report ESR-1539.

TABLE 2304.9.1.6
ALLOWABLE SPACING OF ALTERNATE FASTENERS[a] FOR THE ATTACHMENT OF 19/32-, 5/8-, 23/32-, AND 3/4[e]-INCH WOOD STRUCTURAL PANEL AND PARTICLEBOARD COMBINATION SUBFLOOR/UNDERLAYMENT TO WOOD FRAMING MEMBERS[f]

FASTENER TYPE (MINIMUM NOMINAL NAIL[b] SHANK DIAMETER, IN INCHES, OR STAPLE[c] GAGE)	MINIMUM NOMINAL LENGTH (inches)	SPACING OF FASTENERS	
		At edges (and at intermediate supports where spans are 48" or more)	At intermediate supports
0.131" nail (8d common nail)	2 1/2	6	12
0.120" deformed shank nail	2		
0.092" nail	2 1/4	3	6
0.099" nail	2 1/4	4	8
0.099" deformed shank nail	2 1/4		
0.113" nail	2	3	6
0.113" deformed shank nail	2	4	8
0.113" nail (8d cooler)	2 3/8		
0.113" deformed shank nail	2 3/8		
0.120" nail	3		
0.131" deformed shank nail	2 1/2	6	12
16-gage staple	1 3/4	3	6
	2	4	8
15-gage staple	1 3/4	3	6
	2	4	8
	2 1/4		
	2 1/2		
14-gage staple	2	4	8
	2 1/4		
	2 1/2		
	3		

For SI: 1 inch = 25.4 mm.

a. For fastening of wood structural panel horizontal diaphragms and shear walls refer to design tables (Table 4 through 20) for sufficient lateral strength.
b. A deformed shank nail shall have either a helical (screw) shank or an annular (ring) shank.
c. Staples shall have minimum 7/16-inch crown widths.
d. In areas using the *Standard Building Code*, only deformed shank nails are permitted to fasten combination subfloor/underlayment.
e. Thicker panels may be applied but fastener length must be increased by change in panel thickness so that fastener penetration into framing members does not decrease.
f. Reprinted by permission of the ICC Evaluation Service, LLC from Evaluation Report ESR-1539.

2304.10.2 Floor framing. *Approved* wall plate boxes or hangers shall be provided where wood beams, girders or trusses rest on masonry or concrete walls. Where intermediate beams are used to support a floor, they shall rest on top of girders, or shall be supported by ledgers or blocks securely fastened to the sides of the girders, or they shall be supported by an *approved* metal hanger into which the ends of the beams shall be closely fitted.

2304.10.3 Roof framing. Every roof girder and at least every alternate roof beam shall be anchored to its supporting member; and every monitor and every sawtooth construction shall be anchored to the main roof construction. Such anchors shall be of sufficient strength to resist vertical uplift of the roof.

2304.10.4 Floor decks. Floor decks and covering shall not extend closer than $^1/_2$ inch (12.7 mm) to walls. Such $^1/_2$-inch (12.7 mm) spaces shall be covered by a molding fastened to the wall either above or below the floor and arranged such that the molding will not obstruct the expansion or contraction movements of the floor. Corbeling of masonry walls under floors is permitted in place of such molding.

2304.10.5 Roof decks. Where supported by a wall, roof decks shall be anchored to walls to resist uplift forces determined in accordance with Chapter 16. Such anchors shall be of sufficient strength to resist vertical uplift of the roof.

2304.11 Protection against decay and termites.

2304.11.1 General. Where required by this section, protection from decay and termites shall be provided by the use of naturally durable or *preservative-treated wood*.

2304.11.2 Wood used above ground. Wood used above ground in the locations specified in Sections 2304.11.2.1 through 2304.11.2.7, 2304.11.3 and 2304.11.5 shall be naturally durable wood or *preservative-treated wood* using water-borne preservatives, in accordance with AWPA U1 (Commodity Specifications A or F) for above-ground use.

2304.11.2.1 Joists, girders and subfloor. Where wood joists or the bottom of a wood structural floor without joists are closer than 18 inches (457 mm), or wood girders are closer than 12 inches (305 mm) to the exposed ground in crawl spaces or unexcavated areas located within the perimeter of the building foundation, the floor construction (including posts, girders, joists and subfloor) shall be of naturally durable or *preservative-treated wood*.

2304.11.2.2 Wood supported by exterior foundation walls. Wood framing members, including wood sheathing, that rest on exterior foundation walls and are less than 8 inches (203 mm) from exposed earth shall be of naturally durable or *preservative-treated wood*.

2304.11.2.3 Exterior walls below grade. Wood framing members and furring strips attached directly to the interior of exterior masonry or concrete walls below grade shall be of *approved* naturally durable or *preservative-treated wood*.

2304.11.2.4 Sleepers and sills. Sleepers and sills on a concrete or masonry slab that is in direct contact with earth shall be of naturally durable or *preservative-treated wood*.

2304.11.2.5 Girder ends. The ends of wood girders entering exterior masonry or concrete walls shall be provided with a $^1/_2$-inch (12.7 mm) air space on top, sides and end, unless naturally durable or *preservative-treated wood* is used.

2304.11.2.6 Wood siding. Clearance between wood siding and earth on the exterior of a building shall not be less than 6 inches (152 mm) or less than 2 inches (51 mm) vertical from concrete steps, porch slabs, patio slabs and similar horizontal surfaces exposed to the weather except where siding, sheathing and wall framing are of naturally durable or *preservative-treated wood*.

2304.11.2.7 Posts or columns. Posts or columns supporting permanent structures and supported by a concrete or masonry slab or footing that is in direct contact with the earth shall be of naturally durable or *preservative-treated wood*.

Exceptions:

1. Posts or columns that are either exposed to the weather or located in basements or cellars, supported by concrete piers or metal pedestals projected at least 1 inch (25 mm) above the slab or deck and 6 inches (152 mm) above exposed earth, and are separated therefrom by an impervious moisture barrier.
2. Posts or columns in enclosed crawl spaces or unexcavated areas located within the periphery of the building, supported by a concrete pier or metal pedestal at a height greater than 8 inches (203 mm) from exposed ground, and are separated therefrom by an impervious moisture barrier.

2304.11.3 Laminated timbers. The portions of glued-laminated timbers that form the structural supports of a building or other structure and are exposed to weather and not fully protected from moisture by a roof, eave or similar covering shall be pressure treated with preservative or be manufactured from naturally durable or *preservative-treated wood*.

2304.11.4 Wood in contact with the ground or fresh water. Wood used in contact with the ground (exposed earth) in the locations specified in Sections 2304.11.4.1 and 2304.11.4.2 shall be naturally durable (species for both decay and termite resistance) or preservative treated using water-borne preservatives in accordance with AWPA U1 (Commodity Specifications A or F) for soil or fresh water use.

Exception: Untreated wood is permitted where such wood is continuously and entirely below the groundwater level or submerged in fresh water.

2304.11.4.1 Posts or columns. Posts and columns supporting permanent structures that are embedded in concrete that is in direct contact with the earth, embedded in concrete that is exposed to the weather or in direct contact with the earth shall be of *preservative-treated wood*.

2304.11.4.2 Wood structural members. Wood structural members that support moisture-permeable floors or roofs that are exposed to the weather, such as concrete or masonry slabs, shall be of naturally durable or *preserva-*

tive-treated wood unless separated from such floors or roofs by an impervious moisture barrier.

2304.11.5 Supporting member for permanent appurtenances. Naturally durable or *preservative-treated wood* shall be utilized for those portions of wood members that form the structural supports of buildings, balconies, porches or similar permanent building appurtenances where such members are exposed to the weather without adequate protection from a roof, eave, overhang or other covering to prevent moisture or water accumulation on the surface or at joints between members.

Exception: When a building is located in a geographical region where experience has demonstrated that climatic conditions preclude the need to use durable materials where the structure is exposed to the weather.

2304.11.6 Termite control methods. Protection shall be one of the following methods or a combination of these methods:

1. Chemical termiticide treatment, as provided in Section 2304.11.6.2.
2. Termite baiting system installed and maintained according to the label.
3. Pressure-preservative-treated wood in accordance with the AWPA standards listed in Section 2303.
4. Naturally termite-resistant wood as provided in Section 2304.11.6.3.
5. Physical barriers as provided in Section 2304.11.6.4.

2304.11.6.1 Field treatment. Field-cut ends, notches and drilled holes of pressure-preservative-treated wood shall be retreated in the field in accordance with AWPA M4.

2304.11.6.2 Chemical termiticide treatment. Chemical termiticide treatment shall include soil treatment and field-applied-wood treatment. The concentration, rate of application and method of treatment of the chemical termiticide shall be in accordance with the termiticide label and applied according to the rules adopted by the North Carolina Structural Pest Control Committee.

2304.11.6.3 Naturally resistant wood. Heartwood of redwood and eastern red cedar shall be considered termite resistant.

2304.11.6.4 Barriers. *Approved* physical barriers, such as metal or plastic sheeting or collars specifically designed for termite prevention, shall be installed in a manner to prevent termites from entering the structure. Shields placed on top of an exterior foundation wall are permitted to be used only if in combination with another method of protection.

2304.11.7 Wood used in retaining walls and cribs. Wood installed in retaining or crib walls shall be preservative treated in accordance with AWPA U1 (Commodity Specifications A or F) for soil and fresh water use.

2304.11.8 Attic ventilation. For *attic* ventilation, see Section 1203.2.

2304.11.9 Under-floor ventilation (crawl space). For under-floor ventilation (crawl space), see Section 1203.3.

2304.12 Long-term loading. Wood members supporting concrete, masonry or similar materials shall be checked for the effects of long-term loading using the provisions of the AF&PA NDS. The total deflection, including the effects of long-term loading, shall be limited in accordance with Section 1604.3.1 for these supported materials.

Exception: Horizontal wood members supporting masonry or concrete nonstructural floor or roof surfacing not more than 4 inches (102 mm) thick need not be checked for long-term loading.

SECTION 2305
GENERAL DESIGN REQUIREMENTS FOR LATERAL-FORCE-RESISTING SYSTEMS

2305.1 General. Structures using wood shear walls and diaphragms to resist wind, seismic and other lateral loads shall be designed and constructed in accordance with AF&PA SDPWS and the provisions of Sections 2305, 2306 and 2307.

2305.1.1 Openings in shear panels. Openings in shear panels that materially affect their strength shall be detailed on the plans, and shall have their edges adequately reinforced to transfer all shearing stresses.

2305.2 Diaphragm deflection. The deflection (Δ) of a blocked wood structural panel diaphragm uniformly fastened throughout with staples is permitted to be calculated by using the following equation. If not uniformly fastened, the constant 0.188 (For SI: 1/1627) in the third term shall be modified accordingly.

$$\Delta = \frac{5vL^3}{8EAb} + \frac{vL}{4Gt} + 0.188Le_n + \frac{\Sigma(\Delta_c X)}{2b} \qquad \textbf{(Equation 23-1)}$$

For SI: $$\Delta = \frac{0.052vL^3}{EAb} + \frac{vL}{4Gt} + \frac{Le_n}{1627} + \frac{\Sigma(\Delta_c X)}{2b}$$

where:

A	=	Area of chord cross section, in square inches (mm²).
B	=	Diaphragm width, in feet (mm).
E	=	Elastic modulus of chords, in pounds per square inch (N/mm²).
e_n	=	Staple deformation, in inches (mm) [see Table 2305.2(1)].
Gt	=	Panel rigidity through the thickness, in pounds per inch (N/mm) of panel width or depth [see Table 2305.2(2)].
L	=	Diaphragm length, in feet (mm).
v	=	Maximum shear due to design loads in the direction under consideration, in pounds per linear foot (plf) (N/mm).
Δ	=	The calculated deflection, in inches (mm).

$\Sigma (\Delta_c X)$ = Sum of individual chord-splice slip values on both sides of the diaphragm, each multiplied by its distance to the nearest support.

TABLE 2305.2(1)
e_n VALUES (inches) FOR USE IN CALCULATING DIAPHRAGM AND SHEAR WALL DEFLECTION DUE TO FASTENER SLIP (Structural I)[a, c]

LOAD PER FASTENER[b] (pounds)	FASTENER DESIGNATIONS
	14-Ga staple x 2 inches long
60	0.011
80	0.018
100	0.028
120	0.04
140	0.053
160	0.068

For SI: 1 inch = 25.4 mm, 1 foot = 304.8 mm, 1 pound = 4.448 N.

a. Increase e_n values 20 percent for plywood grades other than Structural I.

b. Load per fastener = maximum shear per foot divided by the number of fasteners per foot at interior panel edges.

c. Decrease e_n values 50 percent for seasoned lumber (moisture content < 19 percent).

2305.3 Shear wall deflection. The deflection (Δ) of a blocked wood structural panel shear wall uniformly fastened throughout with staples is permitted to be calculated by the use of the following equation:

$$\Delta = \frac{8vh^3}{EAb} + \frac{vh}{Gt} + 0.75he_n + d_a\frac{h}{b} \qquad \textbf{(Equation 23-2)}$$

For SI: $$\Delta = \frac{vh^3}{3EAb} + \frac{vh}{Gt} + \frac{he_n}{407.6} + d_a\frac{h}{b}$$

where:

A = Area of boundary element cross section in square inches (mm²) (vertical member at shear wall boundary).

b = Wall width, in feet (mm).

d_a = Vertical elongation of overturning anchorage (including fastener slip, device elongation, anchor rod elongation, etc.) at the design shear load (v).

E = Elastic modulus of boundary element (vertical member at shear wall boundary), in pounds per square inch (N/mm²).

e_n = Staple deformation, in inches (mm) [see Table 2305.2(1)].

Gt = Panel rigidity through the thickness, in pounds per inch (N/mm) of panel width or depth [see Table 2305.2(2)].

h = Wall height, in feet (mm).

v = Maximum shear due to design loads at the top of the wall, in pounds per linear foot (N/mm).

Δ = The calculated deflection, in inches (mm).

SECTION 2306
ALLOWABLE STRESS DESIGN

2306.1 Allowable stress design. The structural analysis and construction of wood elements in structures using *allowable stress design* shall be in accordance with the following applicable standards:

American Forest & Paper Association.

NDS — National Design Specification for Wood Construction

SDPWS — Special Design Provisions for Wind and Seismic

American Institute of Timber Construction.

AITC 104 — Typical Construction Details

AITC 110 — Standard Appearance Grades for Structural Glued Laminated Timber

AITC 113 — Standard for Dimensions of Structural Glued Laminated Timber

AITC 117 — Standard Specifications for Structural Glued Laminated Timber of Softwood Species

AITC 119 — Standard Specifications for Structural Glued Laminated Timber of Hardwood Species

ANSI/ AITC A190.1 — Structural Glued Laminated Timber

AITC 200 — Inspection Manual

American Society of Agricultural and Biological Engineers.

ASABE EP 484.2 — Diaphragm Design of Metal-clad, Post-Frame Rectangular Buildings

ASABE EP 486.1 — Shallow Post Foundation Design

ASABE 559 — Design Requirements and Bending Properties for Mechanically Laminated Columns

APA—The Engineered Wood Association.

Panel Design Specification

Plywood Design Specification Supplement 1 - Design & Fabrication of Plywood Curved Panel

Plywood Design Specification Supplement 2 - Design & Fabrication of Glued Plywood-lumber Beams

Plywood Design Specification Supplement 3 - Design & Fabrication of Plywood Stressed-skin Panels

Plywood Design Specification Supplement 4 - Design & Fabrication of Plywood Sandwich Panels

Plywood Design Specification Supplement 5 - Design & Fabrication of All-plywood Beams

EWS T300 — Glulam Connection Details

EWS S560 — Field Notching and Drilling of Glued Laminated Timber Beams

EWS S475 — Glued Laminated Beam Design Tables

EWS X450 — Glulam in Residential Construction

TABLE 2305.2(2)
VALUES OF *Gt* FOR USE IN CALCULATING DEFLECTION OF WOOD STRUCTURAL PANEL SHEAR WALLS AND DIAPHRAGMS

PANEL TYPE	SPAN RATING	VALUES OF *Gt* (lb/in. panel depth or width)							
		OTHER				STRUCTURAL I			
		3-ply Plywood	4-ply Plywood	5-ply Plywood[a]	OSB	3-ply Plywood	4-ply Plywood	5-ply Plywood[a]	OSB
Sheathing	24/0	25,000	32,500	37,500	77,500	32,500	42,500	41,500	77,500
	24/16	27,000	35,000	40,500	83,500	35,000	45,500	44,500	83,500
	32/16	27,000	35,000	40,500	83,500	35,000	45,500	44,500	83,500
	40/20	28,500	37,000	43,000	88,500	37,000	48,000	47,500	88,500
	48/24	31,000	40,500	46,500	96,000	40,500	52,500	51,000	96,000
Single Floor	16 o.c.	27,000	35,000	40,500	83,500	35,000	45,500	44,500	83,500
	20 o.c.	28,000	36,500	42,000	87,000	36,500	47,500	46,000	87,000
	24 o.c.	30,000	39,000	45,000	93,000	39,000	50,500	49,500	93,000
	32 o.c.	36,000	47,000	54,000	110,000	47,000	61,000	59,500	110,000
	48 o.c.	50,500	65,500	76,000	155,000	65,500	85,000	83,500	155,000

		OTHER			STRUCTURAL I		
	Thickness (inches)	A-A, A-C	Marine	All Other Grades	A-A, A-C	Marine	All Other Grades
Sanded Plywood	$^1/_4$	24,000	31,000	24,000	31,000	31,000	31,000
	$^{11}/_{32}$	25,500	33,000	25,500	33,000	33,000	33,000
	$^3/_8$	26,000	34,000	26,000	34,000	34,000	34,000
	$^{15}/_{32}$	38,000	49,500	38,000	49,500	49,500	49,500
	$^1/_2$	38,500	50,000	38,500	50,000	50,000	50,000
	$^{19}/_{32}$	49,000	63,500	49,000	63,500	63,500	63,500
	$^5/_8$	49,500	64,500	49,500	64,500	64,500	64,500
	$^{23}/_{32}$	50,500	65,500	50,500	65,500	65,500	65,500
	$^3/_4$	51,000	66,500	51,000	66,500	66,500	66,500
	$^7/_8$	52,500	68,500	52,500	68,500	68,500	68,500
	1	73,500	95,500	73,500	95,500	95,500	95,500
	$1^1/_8$	75,000	97,500	75,000	97,500	97,500	97,500

For SI: 1 inch = 25.4 mm, 1 pound per inch = 0.1751 N/mm.
a. Applies to plywood with five or more layers; for five-ply/three-layer plywood, use values for four ply.

EWS X440	Product and Application Guide: Glulam
EWS R540	Builders Tips: Proper Storage and Handling of Glulam Beams

Truss Plate Institute, Inc.

TPI 1	National Design Standard for Metal Plate Connected Wood Truss Construction

2306.1.1 Joists and rafters. The design of rafter spans is permitted to be in accordance with the *AF&PA Span Tables for Joists and Rafters*.

2306.1.2 Plank and beam flooring. The design of plank and beam flooring is permitted to be in accordance with the *AF&PA Wood Construction Data No. 4*.

2306.1.3 Treated wood stress adjustments. The allowable unit stresses for *preservative-treated wood* need no adjustment for treatment, but are subject to other adjustments.

The allowable unit stresses for *fire-retardant-treated wood*, including fastener values, shall be developed from an *approved* method of investigation that considers the effects of anticipated temperature and humidity to which the *fire-retardant-treated wood* will be subjected, the type of treatment and the redrying process. Other adjustments are applicable except that the impact load duration shall not apply.

2306.1.4 Lumber decking. The capacity of lumber decking arranged according to the patterns described in Section 2304.8.2 shall be the lesser of the capacities determined for flexure and deflection according to the formulas in Table 2306.1.4.

TABLE 2306.1.4
ALLOWABLE LOADS FOR LUMBER DECKING

PATTERN	ALLOWABLE AREA LOAD[a, b] Flexure	Deflection
Simple span	$\sigma_b = \frac{8F_b'}{l^2}\frac{d^2}{6}$	$\sigma_\Delta = \frac{384\Delta E'}{5l^4}\frac{d^3}{12}$
Two-span continuous	$\sigma_b = \frac{8F_b'}{l^2}\frac{d^2}{6}$	$\sigma_\Delta = \frac{185\Delta E'}{l^4}\frac{d^3}{12}$
Combination simple- and two-span continuous	$\sigma_b = \frac{8F_b'}{l^2}\frac{d^2}{6}$	$\sigma_\Delta = \frac{131\Delta E'}{l^4}\frac{d^3}{12}$
Cantilevered pieces intermixed	$\sigma_b = \frac{20F_b'}{3l^2}\frac{d^2}{6}$	$\sigma_\Delta = \frac{105\Delta E'}{l^4}\frac{d^3}{12}$
Controlled random layup		
Mechanically laminated decking	$\sigma_b = \frac{20F_b'}{3l^2}\frac{d^2}{6}$	$\sigma_\Delta = \frac{100\Delta E'}{l^4}\frac{d^3}{12}$
2-inch decking	$\sigma_b = \frac{20F_b'}{3l^2}\frac{d^2}{6}$	$\sigma_\Delta = \frac{100\Delta E'}{l^4}\frac{d^3}{12}$
3-inch and 4-inch decking	$\sigma_b = \frac{20F_b'}{3l^2}\frac{d^2}{6}$	$\sigma_\Delta = \frac{116\Delta E'}{l^4}\frac{d^3}{12}$

For SI: 1 inch = 25.4 mm.

a. σ_b = Allowable total uniform load limited by bending.
σ_Δ = Allowable total uniform load limited by deflection.

b. d = Actual decking thickness.
l = Span of decking.
F_b' = Allowable bending stress adjusted by applicable factors.
E' = Modulus of elasticity adjusted by applicable factors.

2306.2 Wood diaphragms.

2306.2.1 Wood structural panel diaphragms. Wood structural panel diaphragms shall be designed and constructed in accordance with AF&PA SDPWS. Wood structural panel diaphragms are permitted to resist horizontal forces using the allowable shear capacities set forth in Table 2306.2.1(1) or 2306.2.1(2). The allowable shear capacities in Tables 2306.2.1(1) and 2306.2.1(2) are permitted to be increased 40 percent for wind design.

2306.2.2 Single diagonally sheathed lumber diaphragms. Single diagonally sheathed lumber diaphragms shall be designed and constructed in accordance with AF&PA SDPWS.

2306.2.3 Double diagonally sheathed lumber diaphragms. Double diagonally sheathed lumber diaphragms shall be designed and constructed in accordance with AF&PA SDPWS.

2306.2.4 Gypsum board diaphragm ceilings. Gypsum board diaphragm ceilings shall be in accordance with Section 2508.5.

2306.3 Wood structural panel shear walls. Wood structural panel shear walls shall be designed and constructed in accordance with AF&PA SDPWS. Wood structural panel shear walls are permitted to resist horizontal forces using the allowable capacities set forth in Table 2306.3. Allowable capacities in Table 2306.3 are permitted to be increased 40 percent for wind design.

2306.4 Lumber sheathed shear walls. Single and double diagonally sheathed lumber shear walls shall be designed and constructed in accordance with AF&PA SDPWS. Single and double diagonally sheathed lumber walls shall not be used to resist seismic forces in structures assigned to *Seismic Design Category* E or F.

2306.5 Particleboard shear walls. Particleboard shear walls shall be designed and constructed in accordance with AF&PA SDPWS. Particleboard shear walls shall be permitted to resist horizontal forces using the allowable shear capacities set forth in Table 2306.5. Allowable capacities in Table 2306.5 are permitted to be increased 40 percent for wind design. Particleboard shall not be used to resist seismic forces in structures assigned to *Seismic Design Category* D, E or F.

2306.6 Fiberboard shear walls. Fiberboard shear walls shall be designed and constructed in accordance with AF&PA SDPWS. Fiberboard shear walls are permitted to resist horizontal forces using the allowable shear capacities set forth in Table 2306.6. Allowable capacities in Table 2306.6 are permitted to be increased 40 percent for wind design. Fiberboard shall not be used to resist seismic forces in structures assigned to *Seismic Design Category* D, E or F.

2306.7 Shear walls sheathed with other materials. Shear walls sheathed with portland cement plaster, gypsum lath, gypsum sheathing or gypsum board shall be designed and constructed in accordance with AF&PA SDPWS. Shear walls sheathed with these materials are permitted to resist horizontal forces using the allowable shear capacities set forth in Table 2306.7. Shear walls sheathed with portland cement plaster, gypsum lath, gypsum sheathing or gypsum board shall not be used to resist seismic forces in structures assigned to *Seismic Design Category* E or F.

SECTION 2307
LOAD AND RESISTANCE FACTOR DESIGN

2307.1 Load and resistance factor design. The structural analysis and construction of wood elements and structures using *load and resistance factor design* shall be in accordance with AF&PA NDS and AF&PA SDPWS.

2307.1.1 Wood structural panel shear walls. In *Seismic Design Category* D, E or F, where shear design values exceed 490 pounds per foot (7154 N/m), all framing members receiving edge nailing from abutting panels shall not be less than a single 3-inch (76 mm) nominal member or two 2-inch (51 mm) nominal members fastened together in accordance with AF&PA NDS to transfer the design shear value between framing members. Wood structural panel joint and sill plate nailing shall be staggered at all panel edges. See Sections 4.3.6.1 and 4.3.6.4.3 of AF&PA SDPWS for sill plate size and anchorage requirements.

TABLE 2306.2.1(1)
ALLOWABLE SHEAR (POUNDS PER FOOT) FOR WOOD STRUCTURAL PANEL DIAPHRAGMS WITH FRAMING OF DOUGLAS FIR-LARCH, OR SOUTHERN PINE[a] FOR WIND OR SEISMIC LOADING[h]

PANEL GRADE	COMMON NAIL SIZE OR STAPLE[f] LENGTH AND GAGE	MINIMUM FASTENER PENETRATION IN FRAMING (inches)	MINIMUM NOMINAL PANEL THICKNESS (inch)	MINIMUM NOMINAL WIDTH OF FRAMING MEMBERS AT ADJOINING PANEL EDGES AND BOUNDARIES[g] (inches)	BLOCKED DIAPHRAGMS: Fastener spacing (inches) at diaphragm boundaries (all cases) at continuous panel edges parallel to load (Cases 3, 4), and at all panel edges (Cases 5, 6)[b]				UNBLOCKED DIAPHRAGMS: Fasteners spaced 6″ max. at supported edges[b]	
					6	4	$2^1/_2$[c]	2[c]		
					Fastener spacing (inches) at other panel edges (Cases 1, 2, 3 and 4)[b]					
					6	6	4	3	Case 1 (No unblocked edges or continuous joints parallel to load)	All other configurations (Cases 2, 3, 4, 5 and 6)
Structural I grades	8d ($2^1/_2$″ × 0.131″)	$1^3/_8$	$^3/_8$	2	270	360	530	600	240	180
				3	300	400	600	675	265	200
	$1^1/_2$ 16 Gage	1		2	175	235	350	400	155	115
				3	200	265	395	450	175	130
	10d[d] (3″ × 0.148″)	$1^1/_2$	$^{15}/_{32}$	2	320	425	640	730	285	215
				3	360	480	720	820	320	240
	$1^1/_2$ 16 Gage	1		2	175	235	350	400	155	120
				3	200	265	395	450	175	130
Sheathing, single floor and other grades covered in DOC PS 1 and PS 2	6d[e] (2″ × 0.113″)	$1^1/_4$	$^3/_8$	2	185	250	375	420	165	125
	8d ($2^1/_2$″ × 0.131″)	$1^3/_8$		3	210	280	420	475	185	140
				2	240	320	480	545	215	160
				3	270	360	540	610	240	180
	$1^1/_2$ 16 Gage	1		2	160	210	315	360	140	105
				3	180	235	355	400	160	120
	8d ($2^1/_2$″ × 0.131″)	$1^3/_8$	$^7/_{16}$	2	255	340	505	575	230	170
				3	285	380	570	645	255	190
	$1^1/_2$ 16 Gage	1		2	165	225	335	380	150	110
				3	190	250	375	425	165	125
	8d ($2^1/_2$″ × 0.131″)	$1^3/_8$	$^{15}/_{32}$	2	270	360	530	600	240	180
				3	300	400	600	675	265	200
	10d[d] (3″ × 0.148″)	$1^1/_2$		2	290	385	575	655	255	190
				3	325	430	650	735	290	215
	$1^1/_2$ 16 Gage	1		2	160	210	315	360	140	105
				3	180	235	355	405	160	120
	10d[d] (3″ × 0.148″)	$1^1/_2$	$^{19}/_{32}$	2	320	425	640	730	285	215
				3	360	480	720	820	320	240
	$1^3/_4$ 16 Gage	1		2	175	235	350	400	155	115
				3	200	265	395	450	175	130

continued

TABLE 2306.2.1(1)—continued
ALLOWABLE SHEAR (POUNDS PER FOOT) FOR WOOD STRUCTURAL PANEL DIAPHRAGMS WITH FRAMING OF DOUGLAS FIR-LARCH, OR SOUTHERN PINE[a] FOR WIND OR SEISMIC LOADING[h]

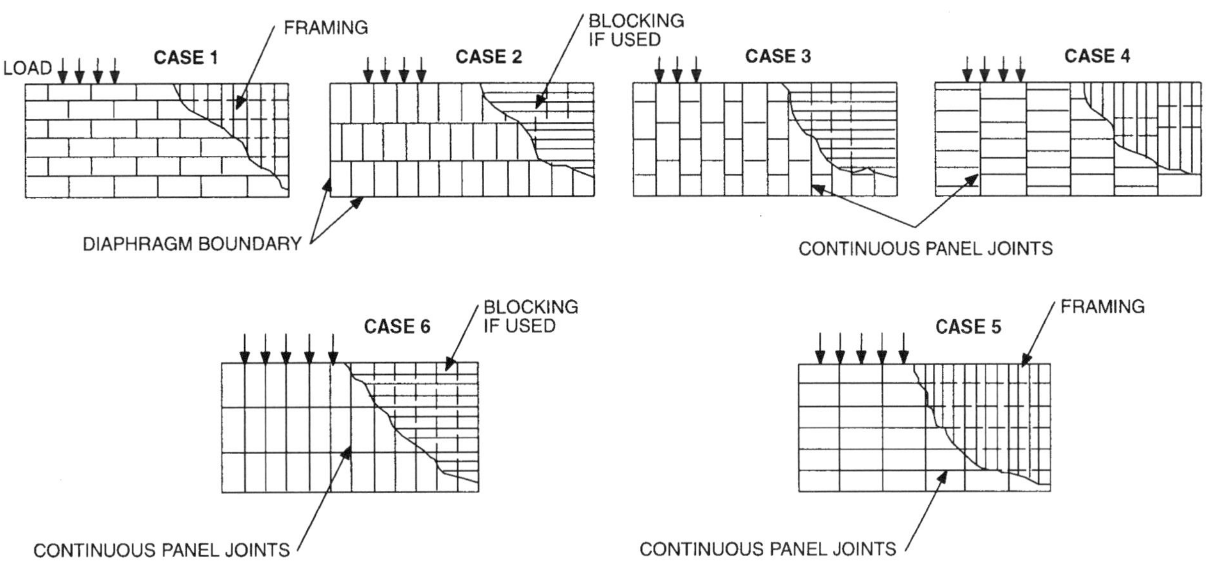

For SI: 1 inch = 25.4 mm, 1 pound per foot = 14.5939 N/m.

a. For framing of other species: (1) Find specific gravity for species of lumber in AF&PA NDS. (2) For staples find shear value from table above for Structural I panels (regardless of actual grade) and multiply value by 0.82 for species with specific gravity of 0.42 or greater, or 0.65 for all other species. (3) For nails find shear value from table above for nail size for actual grade and multiply value by the following adjustment factor: Specific Gravity Adjustment Factor = [1-(0.5 - SG)], where SG = Specific Gravity of the framing lumber. This adjustment factor shall not be greater than 1.

b. Space fasteners maximum 12 inches o.c. along intermediate framing members (6 inches o.c. where supports are spaced 48 inches o.c.).

c. Framing at adjoining panel edges shall be 3 inches nominal or wider, and nails at all panel edges shall be staggered where panel edge nailing is specified at $2^1/_2$ inches o.c. or less.

d. Framing at adjoining panel edges shall be 3 inches nominal or wider, and nails at all panel edges shall be staggered where both of the following conditions are met: (1) 10d nails having penetration into framing of more than $1^1/_2$ inches and (2) panel edge nailing is specified at 3 inches o.c. or less.

e. 8d is recommended minimum for roofs due to negative pressures of high winds.

f. Staples shall have a minimum crown width of $^7/_{16}$ inch and shall be installed with their crowns parallel to the long dimension of the framing members.

g. The minimum nominal width of framing members not located at boundaries or adjoining panel edges shall be 2 inches.

h. For shear loads of normal or permanent load duration as defined by the AF&PA NDS, the values in the table above shall be multiplied by 0.63 or 0.56, respectively.

TABLE 2306.2.1(2)
ALLOWABLE SHEAR (POUNDS PER FOOT) FOR WOOD STRUCTURAL PANEL BLOCKED DIAPHRAGMS UTILIZING MULTIPLE ROWS OF FASTENERS (HIGH LOAD DIAPHRAGMS) WITH FRAMING OF DOUGLAS FIR-LARCH OR SOUTHERN PINE[a] FOR WIND OR SEISMIC LOADING[b, g, h]

PANEL GRADE[c]	COMMON NAIL SIZE OR STAPLE[f] GAGE	MINIMUM FASTENER PENETRATION IN FRAMING (inches)	MINIMUM NOMINAL PANEL THICKNESS (inch)	MINIMUM NOMINAL WIDTH OF FRAMING MEMBER AT ADJOINING PANEL EDGES AND BOUNDARIES[e]	LINES OF FASTENERS	BLOCKED DIAPHRAGMS Cases 1 and 2[d] Fastener Spacing Per Line at Boundaries (inches): 4		2$^1/_2$		2	
						Fastener Spacing Per Line at Other Panel Edges (inches): 6	4	4	3	3	2
Structural I grades	10d common nails	1$^1/_2$	$^{15}/_{32}$	3	2	605	815	875	1,150	—	—
				4	2	700	915	1,005	1,290	—	—
				4	3	875	1,220	1,285	1,395	—	—
			$^{19}/_{32}$	3	2	670	880	965	1,255	—	—
				4	2	780	990	1,110	1,440	—	—
				4	3	965	1,320	1,405	1,790	—	—
			$^{23}/_{32}$	3	2	730	955	1,050	1,365	—	—
				4	2	855	1,070	1,210	1,565	—	—
				4	3	1,050	1,430	1,525	1,800	—	—
	14 gage staples	2	$^{15}/_{32}$	3	2	600	600	860	960	1,060	1,200
				4	3	860	900	1,160	1,295	1,295	1,400
			$^{19}/_{32}$	3	2	600	600	875	960	1,075	1,200
				4	3	875	900	1,175	1,440	1,475	1,795
Sheathing single floor and other grades covered in DOC PS 1 and PS 2	10d common nails	1$^1/_2$	$^{15}/_{32}$	3	2	525	725	765	1,010	—	—
				4	2	605	815	875	1,105	—	—
				4	3	765	1,085	1,130	1,195	—	—
			$^{19}/_{32}$	3	2	650	860	935	1,225	—	—
				4	2	755	965	1,080	1,370	—	—
				4	3	935	1,290	1,365	1,485	—	—
			$^{23}/_{32}$	3	2	710	935	1,020	1,335	—	—
				4	2	825	1,050	1,175	1,445	—	—
				4	3	1,020	1,400	1,480	1,565	—	—
	14 gage staples	2	$^{15}/_{32}$	3	2	540	540	735	865	915	1,080
				4	3	735	810	1,005	1,105	1,105	1,195
			$^{19}/_{32}$	3	2	600	600	865	960	1,065	1,200
				4	3	865	900	1,130	1,430	1,370	1,485
			$^{23}/_{32}$	4	3	865	900	1,130	1,490	1,430	1,545

For SI: 1 inch = 25.4 mm, 1 pound per foot = 14.5939 N/m.

a. For framing of other species: (1) Find specific gravity for species of framing lumber in AF&PA NDS. (2) For staples, find shear value from table above for Structural I panels (regardless of actual grade) and multiply value by 0.82 for species with specific gravity of 0.42 or greater, or 0.65 for all other species. (3) For nails, find shear value from table above for nail size of actual grade and multiply value by the following adjustment factor: Specific Gravity Adjustment Factor = [1 - (0.5 - SG)], where SG = Specific gravity of the framing lumber. This adjustment factor shall not be greater than 1.

b. Fastening along intermediate framing members: Space fasteners a maximum of 12 inches on center, except 6 inches on center for spans greater than 32 inches.

c. Panels conforming to PS 1 or PS 2.

d. This table gives shear values for Cases 1 and 2 as shown in Table 2306.2.1(1). The values shown are applicable to Cases 3, 4, 5 and 6 as shown in Table 2306.2.1(1), providing fasteners at all continuous panel edges are spaced in accordance with the boundary fastener spacing.

e. The minimum nominal depth of framing members shall be 3 inches nominal. The minimum nominal width of framing members not located at boundaries or adjoining panel edges shall be 2 inches.

f. Staples shall have a minimum crown width of $^7/_{16}$ inch, and shall be installed with their crowns parallel to the long dimension of the framing members.

g. High load diaphragms shall be subject to special inspection in accordance with Section 1704.6.1.

h. For shear loads of normal or permanent load duration as defined by the AF&PA NDS, the values in the table above shall be multiplied by 0.63 or 0.56, respectively.

TABLE 2306.2.1(2)—continued
ALLOWABLE SHEAR (POUNDS PER FOOT) FOR WOOD STRUCTURAL PANEL BLOCKED DIAPHRAGMS UTILIZING MULTIPLE ROWS OF FASTENERS (HIGH LOAD DIAPHRAGMS) WITH FRAMING OF DOUGLAS FIR-LARCH OR SOUTHERN PINE FOR WIND OR SEISMIC LOADING

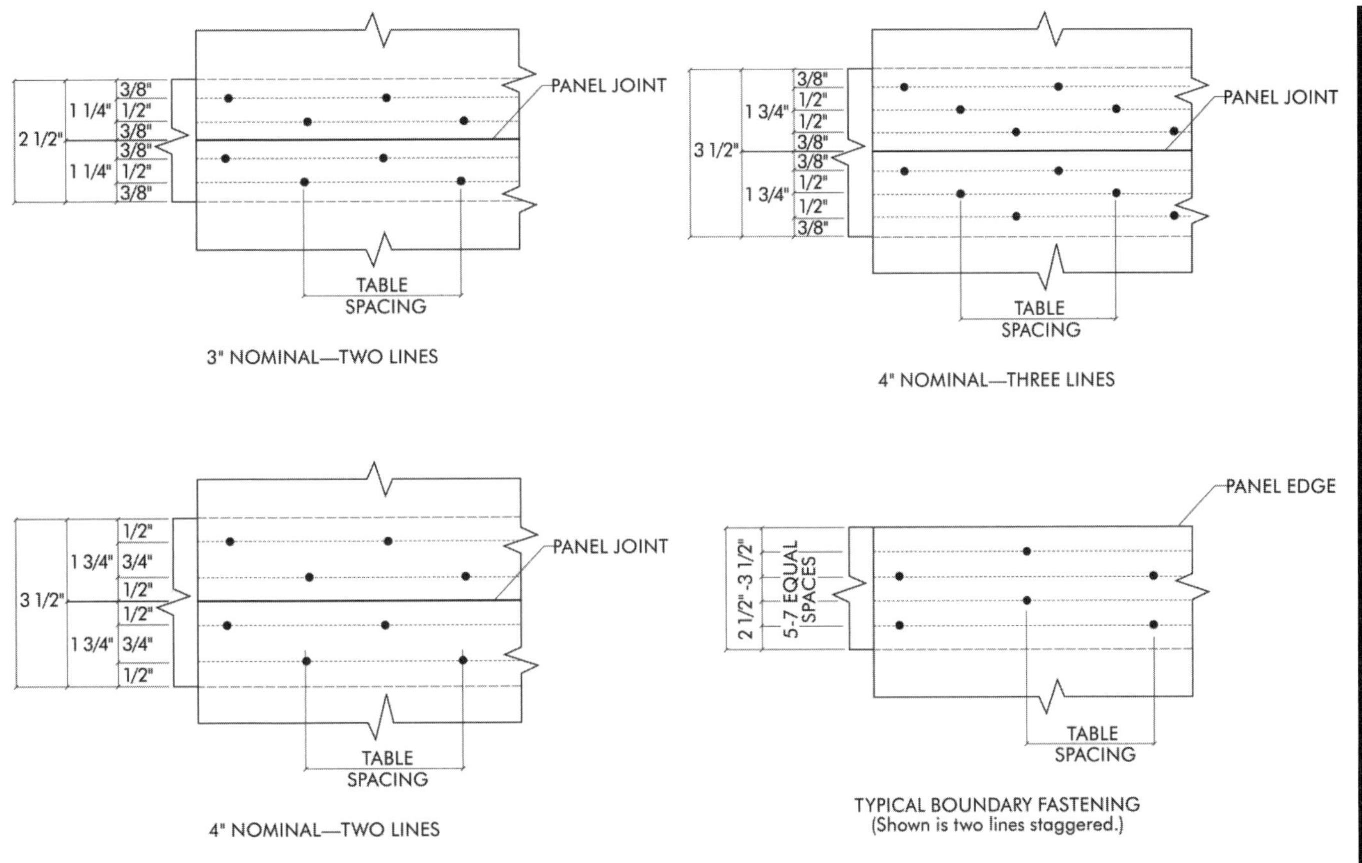

NOTE: SPACE PANEL END AND EDGE JOINT 1/8-INCH. REDUCE SPACING BETWEEN LINES OF NAILS AS NECESSARY TO MAINTAIN MINIMUM 3/8-INCH FASTENER EDGE MARGINS, MINIMUM SPACING BETWEEN LINES IS 3/8-INCH

TABLE 2306.3
ALLOWABLE SHEAR (POUNDS PER FOOT) FOR WOOD STRUCTURAL PANEL SHEAR WALLS WITH FRAMING OF DOUGLAS FIR-LARCH OR SOUTHERN PINE[a] FOR WIND OR SEISMIC LOADING[b, h, i, j, l]

PANEL GRADE	MINIMUM NOMINAL PANEL THICKNESS (inch)	MINIMUM FASTENER PENETRATION IN FRAMING (inches)	PANELS APPLIED DIRECT TO FRAMING: NAIL (common or galvanized box) or staple size[k]	Fastener spacing at panel edges (inches): 6	4	3	2[e]	PANELS APPLIED OVER 1/2″ OR 5/8″ GYPSUM SHEATHING: NAIL (common or galvanized box) or staple size[k]	Fastener spacing at panel edges (inches): 6	4	3	2[e]
Structural I sheathing	3/8	1 3/8	8d (2 1/2″ × 0.131″ common, 2 1/2″ × 0.113″ galvanized box)	230[d]	360[d]	460[d]	610[d]	10d (3″ × 0.148″ common, 3″ × 0.128″ galvanized box)	280	430	550[f]	730
		1	1 1/2 16 Gage	155	235	315	400	2 16 Gage	155	235	310	400
	7/16	1 3/8	8d (2 1/2″ × 0.131″ common, 2 1/2″ × 0.113″ galvanized box)	255[d]	395[d]	505[d]	670[d]	10d (3″ × 0.148″ common, 3″ × 0.128″ galvanized box)	280	430	550[f]	730
		1	1 1/2 16 Gage	170	260	345	440	2 16 Gage	155	235	310	400
	15/32	1 3/8	8d (2 1/2″ × 0.131″ common, 2 1/2″ × 0.113″ galvanized box)	280	430	550	730	10d (3″ × 0.148″ common, 3″ × 0.128″ galvanized box)	280	430	550[f]	730
		1	1 1/2 16 Gage	185	280	375	475	2 16 Gage	155	235	300	400
		1 1/2	10d (3″ × 0.148″ common, 3″ × 0.128″ galvanized box)	340	510	665[f]	870	—	—	—	—	—
Sheathing, plywood siding[e, g] except Group 5 Species	5/16[c] or 1/4[c]	1 1/4	6d (2″ × 0.113″ common, 2″ × 0.099″ galvanized box)	180	270	350	450	8d (2 1/2″ × 0.131″ common, 2 1/2″ × 0.113″ galvanized box)	180	270	350	450
		1	1 1/2 16 Gage	145	220	295	375	2 16 Gage	110	165	220	285
	3/8	1 1/4	6d (2″ × 0.113″ common, 2″ × 0.099″ galvanized box)	200	300	390	510	8d (2 1/2″ × 0.131″ common, 2 1/2″ × 0.113″ galvanized box)	200	300	390	510
		1 3/8	8d (2 1/2″ × 0.131″ common, 2 1/2″ × 0.113″ galvanized box)	220[d]	320[d]	410[d]	530[d]	10d (3″ × 0.148″ common, 3″ × 0.128″ galvanized box)	260	380	490[f]	640
		1	1 1/2 16 Gage	140	210	280	360	2 16 Gage	140	210	280	360
	7/16	1 3/8	8d (2 1/2″ × 0.131″ common, 2 1/2″ × 0.113″ galvanized box)	240[d]	350[d]	450[d]	585[d]	10d (3″ × 0.148″ common, 3″ × 0.128″ galvanized box)	260	380	490[f]	640
		1	1 1/2 16 Gage	155	230	310	395	2 16 Gage	140	210	280	360
	15/32	1 3/8	8d (2 1/2″ × 0.131″ common, 2 1/2″ × 0.113″ galvanized box)	260	380	490	640	10d (3″ × 0.148″ common, 3″ × 0.128″ galvanized box)	260	380	490[f]	640
		1 1/2	10d (3″ × 0.148″ common, 3″ × 0.128″ galvanized box)	310	460	600[f]	770	—	—	—	—	—
		1	1 1/2 16 Gage	170	255	335	430	2 16 Gage	140	210	280	360
	19/32	1 1/2	10d (3″ × 0.148″ common, 3″ × 0.128″ galvanized box)	340	510	665[f]	870	—	—	—	—	—
		1	1 3/4 16 Gage	185	280	375	475	—	—	—	—	—
			Nail Size (galvanized casing)					Nail Size (galvanized casing)				
	5/16[c]	1 1/4	6d (2″ × 0.099″)	140	210	275	360	8d (2 1/2″ × 0.113″)	140	210	275	360
	3/8[c]	1 3/8	8d (2 1/2″ × 0.113″)	160	240	310	410	10d (3″ × 0.128″)	160	240	310[f]	410

For SI: 1 inch = 25.4 mm, 1 pound per foot = 14.5939 N/m.

a. For framing of other species: (1) Find specific gravity for species of lumber in AF&PA NDS. (2) For staples find shear value from table above for Structural I panels (regardless of actual grade) and multiply value by 0.82 for species with specific gravity of 0.42 or greater, or 0.65 for all other species. (3) For nails find shear value from table above for nail size for actual grade and multiply value by the following adjustment factor: Specific Gravity Adjustment Factor = [1-(0.5 - SG)], where SG = Specific Gravity of the framing lumber. This adjustment factor shall not be greater than 1.

b. Panel edges backed with 2-inch nominal or wider framing. Install panels either horizontally or vertically. Space fasteners maximum 6 inches on center along intermediate framing members for 3/8-inch and 7/16-inch panels installed on studs spaced 24 inches on center. For other conditions and panel thickness, space fasteners maximum 12 inches on center on intermediate supports.

c. 3/8-inch panel thickness or siding with a span rating of 16 inches on center is the minimum recommended where applied directly to framing as exterior siding. For grooved panel siding, the nominal panel thickness is the thickness of the panel measured at the point of nailing.

(continued)

TABLE 2306.3—continued
ALLOWABLE SHEAR (POUNDS PER FOOT) FOR WOOD STRUCTURAL PANEL SHEAR WALLS WITH FRAMING OF DOUGLAS FIR-LARCH OR SOUTHERN PINE[a] FOR WIND OR SEISMIC LOADING[b, h, i, j, l]

d. Allowable shear values are permitted to be increased to values shown for $^{15}/_{32}$-inch sheathing with same nailing provided (a) studs are spaced a maximum of 16 inches on center, or (b) panels are applied with long dimension across studs.

e. Framing at adjoining panel edges shall be 3 inches nominal or wider, and nails at all panel edges shall be staggered where panel edge nailing is specified at 2 inches on center or less.

f. Framing at adjoining panel edges shall be 3 inches nominal or wider, and nails at all panel edges shall be staggered where both of the following conditions are met: (1) 10d (3″ × 0.148″) nails having penetration into framing of more than $1^1/_2$ inches and (2) panel edge nailing is specified at 3 inches on center or less.

g. Values apply to all-veneer plywood. Thickness at point of fastening on panel edges governs shear values.

h. Where panels are applied on both faces of a wall and nail spacing is less than 6 inches o.c. on either side, panel joints shall be offset to fall on different framing members. Or framing shall be 3-inch nominal or thicker at adjoining panel edges and nails at all panel edges shall be staggered.

i. In Seismic Design Category D, E or F, where shear design values exceed 350 pounds per linear foot, all framing members receiving edge nailing from abutting panels shall not be less than a single 3-inch nominal member, or two 2-inch nominal members fastened together in accordance with Section 2306.1 to transfer the design shear value between framing members. Wood structural panel joint and sill plate nailing shall be staggered at all panel edges. See Sections 4.3.6.1 and 4.3.6.4.3 of AF&PA SDPWS for sill plate size and anchorage requirements.

j. Galvanized nails shall be hot dipped or tumbled.

k. Staples shall have a minimum crown width of $^7/_{16}$ inch and shall be installed with their crowns parallel to the long dimension of the framing members.

l. For shear loads of normal or permanent load duration as defined by the AF&PA NDS, the values in the table above shall be multiplied by 0.63 or 0.56, respectively.

TABLE 2306.5
ALLOWABLE SHEAR FOR PARTICLEBOARD SHEAR WALL SHEATHING[b]

PANEL GRADE	MINIMUM NOMINAL PANEL THICKNESS (inch)	MINIMUM NAIL PENETRATION IN FRAMING (inches)	PANELS APPLIED DIRECT TO FRAMING				
			Nail size (common or galvanized box)	Allowable shear (pounds per foot) nail spacing at panel edges (inches)[a]			
				6	4	3	2
M-S "Exterior Glue" and M-2 "Exterior Glue"	$^3/_8$	$1^1/_2$	6d	120	180	230	300
	$^3/_8$	$1^1/_2$	8d	130	190	240	315
	$^1/_2$			140	210	270	350
	$^1/_2$	$1^5/_8$	10d	185	275	360	460
	$^5/_8$			200	305	395	520

For SI: 1 inch = 25.4 mm, 1 pound per foot = 14.5939 N/m.

a. Values are not permitted in Seismic Design Category D, E or F.

b. Galvanized nails shall be hot-dipped or tumbled.

TABLE 2306.6
ALLOWABLE SHEAR VALUES (plf) FOR WIND OR SEISMIC LOADING ON SHEAR WALLS OF FIBERBOARD SHEATHING BOARD CONSTRUCTION FOR TYPE V CONSTRUCTION ONLY[a, b, c, d, e]

THICKNESS AND GRADE	FASTENER SIZE	ALLOWABLE SHEAR VALUE (pounds per linear foot) NAIL SPACING AT PANEL EDGES (inches)[a]		
		4	3	2
$^1/_2$″ or $^{25}/_{32}$″ Structural	No. 11 gage galvanized roofing nail $1^1/_2$″ long for $^1/_2$″, $1^3/_4$″ long for $^{25}/_{32}$″ with $^3/_8$″ head	170	230	260
	No. 11 gage galvanized staple, $^7/_{16}$″ crown[f]	150	200	225
	No. 11 gage galvanized staple, 1″ crown[f]	220	290	325

For SI: 1 inch = 25.4 mm, 1 pound per linear foot = 14.5939 N/m.

a. Fiberboard sheathing shall not be used to brace concrete or masonry walls.

b. Panel edges shall be backed with 2-inch or wider framing of Douglas fir-larch or Southern pine. For framing of other species: (1) Find specific gravity for species of framing lumber in AF&PA NDS. (2) For staples, multiply the shear value from the table above by 0.82 for species with specific gravity of 0.42 or greater, or 0.65 for all other species. (3) For nails, multiply the shear value from the table above by the following adjustment factor: specific gravity adjustment factor = [1-(0.5-SG)], where SG = Specific gravity of the framing lumber.

c. Values shown are for fiberboard sheathing on one side only with long panel dimension either parallel or perpendicular to studs.

d. Fastener shall be spaced 6 inches on center along intermediate framing members.

e. Values are not permitted in Seismic Design Category D, E or F.

f. Staple length shall not be less than $1^1/_2$ inches for $^{25}/_{32}$-inch sheathing or $1^1/_4$ inches for $^1/_2$-inch sheathing.

TABLE 2306.7
ALLOWABLE SHEAR FOR WIND OR SEISMIC FORCES FOR SHEAR WALLS OF LATH AND PLASTER OR GYPSUM BOARD WOOD FRAMED WALL ASSEMBLIES

TYPE OF MATERIAL	THICKNESS OF MATERIAL	WALL CONSTRUCTION	FASTENER SPACING[b] MAXIMUM (inches)	SHEAR VALUE[a, e] (plf)	MINIMUM FASTENER SIZE[c, d, j, k]
1. Expanded metal or woven wire lath and portland cement plaster	7/8″	Unblocked	6	180	No. 11 gage 1 1/2″ long, 7/16″ head No. 16 gage galv. staple, 7/8″ legs
2. Gypsum lath, plain or perforated with vertical joints staggered	3/8″ lath and 1/2″ plaster	Unblocked	5	180	No. 13 gage galv. 1 1/8″ long, 19/64″ head, plasterboard nail
3. Gypsum lath, plain or perforated	3/8″ lath and 1/2″ plaster	Unblocked	5	100	No. 16 gage galv. staple 1 1/8″ long, 0.120″ nail min. 3/8″ head, 1 1/4 long
4. Gypsum sheathing	1/2″ × 2′ × 8′	Unblocked	4	75	No. 11 gage, 1 3/4″ long, 7/16″ head, diamond-point, galvanized 16 Ga. Galv. Stable, 1 3/4″ long
	1/2″ × 4′	Blocked[d]	4	175	
		Unblocked	7	100	
	5/8″ × 4′	Blocked	4″ edge/7″ field	200	6d galvanized 0.120″ Nail, min. 3/8″ head, 1 3/4″ long
5. Gypsum board, gypsum veneer base or water-resistant gypsum backing board	1/2″	Unblocked[f]	7	75	5d cooler (1 5/8″ × 0.086″) or wallboard 0.120″ nail, min. 3/8″ head, 1 1/2″ long No. 16 gage galv. staple, 1 1/2″ long
		Unblocked[f]	4	110	
		Unblocked	7	100	
		Unblocked	4	125	
		Blocked[g]	7	125	
		Blocked[g]	4	150	
		Unblocked	8/12[h]	60	No. 6—1 1/4″ screws[i]
		Blocked[g]	4/16[h]	160	
		Blocked[f, g]	4/12[h]	155	
		Blocked[g]	8/12[h]	70	
		Blocked[g]	6/12[h]	90	
	5/8″	Unblocked[f]	7	115	6d cooler (1 7/8″ × 0.092″) or wallboard 0.120″ nail, min. 3/8″ head, 1 3/4″ long No. 16 gage galv. staple, 1 1/2″ legs, 1 5/8″ long
			4	145	
		Blocked[g]	7	145	
			4	175	
		Blocked[g] Two-ply	Base ply: 9 Face ply: 7	250	Base ply-6d cooler (1 7/8″ × 0.092″) or wallboard 1 3/4″ × 0.120″ nail, min. 3/8″ head 1 5/8″ 16 gage galv. staple Face ply-8d cooler (2 3/8″ × 0.113″) or wallboard 0.120″ nail, min. 3/8″ head, 2 3/8″ long No. 15 gage galv. staple, 2 1/4″ long
		Unblocked	8/12[h]	70	No. 6—1 1/4″ screws[i]
		Blocked[g]	8/12[h]	90	
5. Gypsum sheathing	1/2″ × 2′ × 8′	Unblocked	4	75	No. 11 gage, 1 3/4″ long, 7/16″ head, diamond point, galvanized
	1/2″ × 4′	Blocked	4[f]	175	16 gage galvanized staple, 1 3/4″ long
		Unblocked	7	100	
	5/8″ × 4′	Blocked	4″ edge/ 7″ field	200	6d galvanized 0.120″ nail, minimum 3/8″ head, 1 3/4″ long

For SI: 1 inch = 25.4 mm, 1 foot = 304.8 mm, 1 pound per linear foot = 14.5939 N/m.

a. These shear walls shall not be used to resist loads imposed by masonry or concrete walls (see Section 4.1.5 of AF & PA SDPWS). Values shown are for short-term loading due to wind or seismic loading. Walls resisting seismic loads shall be subject to the limitations in Section 12.2.1 of ASCE 7. Values shown shall be reduced 25 percent for normal loading.

b. Applies to fastening at studs, top and bottom plates and blocking.

c. Alternate fasteners are permitted to be used if their dimensions are not less than the specified dimensions. Drywall screws are permitted to substitute for the 5d (1 5/8″ × 0.086″), and 6d (1 7/8″ × 0.092″)(cooler) nails listed above, and No. 6 1 1/4 inch Type S or W screws for 6d (1 7/8″ × 0.092) (cooler) nails.

d. For properties of cooler nails, see ASTM C 514.

e. Except as noted, shear values are based on a maximum framing spacing of 16 inches on center.

f. Maximum framing spacing of 24 inches on center.

g. All edges are blocked, and edge fastening is provided at all supports and all panel edges.

h. First number denotes fastener spacing at the edges; second number denotes fastener spacing at intermediate framing members.

i. Screws are Type W or S.

j. Staples shall have a minimum crown width of 7/16 inch, measured outside the legs, and shall be installed with their crowns parallel to the long dimension of the framing members.

k. Staples for the attachment of gypsum lath and woven-wire lath shall have a minimum crown width of 3/4 inch, measured outside the legs.

SECTION 2308
CONVENTIONAL LIGHT-FRAME CONSTRUCTION

2308.1 General. The requirements of this section are intended for *conventional light-frame construction*. Other methods are permitted to be used, provided a satisfactory design is submitted showing compliance with other provisions of this code. Interior nonload-bearing partitions, ceilings and curtain walls of *conventional light-frame construction* are not subject to the limitations of this section. Alternatively, compliance with AF&PA WFCM shall be permitted subject to the limitations therein and the limitations of this code. Detached one- and two-family dwellings and multiple single-family dwellings (townhouses) not more than three *stories above grade plane* in height with a separate *means of egress* and their accessory structures shall comply with the *International Residential Code*.

2308.1.1 Portions exceeding limitations of conventional construction. When portions of a building of otherwise conventional construction exceed the limits of Section 2308.2, these portions and the supporting load path shall be designed in accordance with accepted engineering practice and the provisions of this code. For the purposes of this section, the term "portions" shall mean parts of buildings containing volume and area such as a room or a series of rooms.

2308.2 Limitations. Buildings are permitted to be constructed in accordance with the provisions of *conventional light-frame construction*, subject to the following limitations, and to further limitations of Sections 2308.11 and 2308.12.

1. Buildings shall be limited to a maximum of three *stories above grade plane*. For the purposes of this section, for buildings in *Seismic Design Category* D or E as determined in Section 1613, cripple stud walls shall be considered to be a *story*.

   Exception: Solid blocked cripple walls not exceeding 14 inches (356 mm) in height need not be considered a *story*.

2. Maximum floor-to-floor height shall not exceed 11 feet, 7 inches (3531 mm). Bearing wall height shall not exceed a stud height of 10 feet (3048 mm).

3. Loads as determined in Chapter 16 shall not exceed the following:

   3.1. Average dead loads shall not exceed 15 psf (718 N/m^2) for combined roof and ceiling, exterior walls, floors and partitions.

   Exceptions:

   1. Subject to the limitations of Sections 2308.11.2 and 2308.12.2, stone or masonry veneer up to the lesser of 5 inches (127 mm) thick or 50 psf (2395 N/m^2) and installed in accordance with Chapter 14 is permitted to a height of 30 feet (9144 mm) above a noncombustible foundation, with an additional 8 feet (2438 mm) permitted for gable ends.
   2. Concrete or masonry fireplaces, heaters and chimneys shall be permitted in accordance with the provisions of this code.

   3.2. Live loads shall not exceed 40 psf (1916 N/m^2) for floors.

   3.3. Ground snow loads shall not exceed 50 psf (2395 N/m^2).

4. Wind speeds shall not exceed 100 miles per hour (mph) (44 m/s) (3-second gust).

   Exception: Wind speeds shall not exceed 110 mph (48.4 m/s) (3-second gust) for buildings in Exposure Category B that are not located in a *hurricane-prone region*.

5. Roof trusses and rafters shall not span more than 40 feet (12 192 mm) between points of vertical support.

6. The use of the provisions for *conventional light-frame construction* in this section shall not be permitted for *Occupancy Category* IV buildings assigned to *Seismic Design Category* B, C, D, E or F, as determined in Section 1613.

7. *Conventional light-frame construction* is limited in irregular structures in *Seismic Design Category* D or E, as specified in Section 2308.12.6.

2308.2.1 Basic wind speed greater than 100 mph (3-second gust). Where the basic wind speed exceeds 100 mph (3-second gust), the provisions of either AF&PA WFCM or ICC 600 are permitted to be used.

2308.2.2 Buildings in Seismic Design Category B, C, D or E. Buildings of *conventional light-frame construction* in *Seismic Design Category* B or C, as determined in Section 1613, shall comply with the additional requirements in Section 2308.11.

Buildings of *conventional light-frame construction* in *Seismic Design Category* D or E, as determined in Section 1613, shall comply with the additional requirements in Section 2308.12.

2308.3 Braced wall lines. Buildings shall be provided with exterior and interior braced wall lines as described in Section 2308.9.3 and installed in accordance with Sections 2308.3.1 through 2308.3.4.

2308.3.1 Spacing. Spacing of braced wall lines shall not exceed 35 feet (10 668 mm) o.c. in both the longitudinal and transverse directions in each *story*.

2308.3.2 Braced wall line connections. Wind and seismic lateral forces shall be transferred from the roofs and floors to braced wall lines and from the braced wall lines in upper stories to the braced wall lines in the *story* below in accordance with this section.

Braced wall line top plates shall be fastened to joists, rafters or full-depth blocking above in accordance with Table 2304.9.1 as applicable based on the orientation of the joists or rafters to the braced wall line. Braced wall line bottom plates shall be connected to joists or blocking below in accordance with Table 2304.9.1 or to foundations in accordance with Section 2308.3.3. At exterior gable end walls, braced wall panel sheathing in the top *story* shall be extended and fastened to roof framing where the spacing between parallel exterior braced wall lines is greater than 50 feet (15 240 mm).

Exception: Where roof trusses are used and are installed perpendicular to an exterior braced wall line, lateral forces shall be transferred from the roof diaphragm to the braced wall by blocking of the ends of the trusses or by other *approved* methods providing equivalent lateral force transfer. Blocking shall be a minimum of 2 inches (51 mm) nominal in thickness and equal to the depth of the truss at the wall line and shall be fastened to the braced wall line top plate as specified in Table 2304.9.1.

2308.3.3 Sill anchorage. Where foundations are required by Section 2308.3.4, braced wall line sills shall be anchored to concrete or masonry foundations. Such anchorage shall conform to the requirements of Section 2308.6 except that such anchors shall be spaced at not more than 4 feet (1219 mm) o.c. for structures over two *stories above grade plane*. The anchors shall be distributed along the length of the braced wall line. Other anchorage devices having equivalent capacity are permitted.

2308.3.3.1 Anchorage to all-wood foundations. Where all-wood foundations are used, the force transfer from the braced wall lines shall be determined based on calculation and shall have a capacity greater than or equal to the connections required by Section 2308.3.3.

2308.3.4 Braced wall line support. Braced wall lines shall be supported by continuous foundations.

Exception: For structures with a maximum plan dimension not over 50 feet (15 240 mm), continuous foundations are required at exterior walls only.

2308.4 Design of elements. Combining of engineered elements or systems and conventionally specified elements or systems is permitted subject to the following limits:

2308.4.1 Elements exceeding limitations of conventional construction. When a building of otherwise conventional construction contains structural elements exceeding the limits of Section 2308.2, these elements and the supporting load path shall be designed in accordance with accepted engineering practice and the provisions of this code.

2308.4.2 Structural elements or systems not described herein. When a building of otherwise conventional construction contains structural elements or systems not described in Section 2308, these elements or systems shall be designed in accordance with accepted engineering practice and the provisions of this code. The extent of such design need only demonstrate compliance of the nonconventional elements with other applicable provisions of this code and shall be compatible with the performance of the conventionally framed system.

2308.5 Connections and fasteners. Connections and fasteners used in conventional construction shall comply with the requirements of Section 2304.9.

2308.6 Foundation plates or sills. Foundations and footings shall be as specified in Chapter 18. Foundation plates or sills resting on concrete or masonry foundations shall comply with Section 2304.3.1. Foundation plates or sills shall be bolted or anchored to the foundation with not less than $^1/_2$-inch-diameter (12.7 mm) steel bolts or *approved* anchors spaced to provide equivalent anchorage as the steel bolts. Bolts shall be embedded at least 7 inches (178 mm) into concrete or masonry, and spaced not more than 6 feet (1829 mm) apart. There shall be a minimum of two bolts or anchor straps per piece with one bolt or anchor strap located not more than 12 inches (305 mm) or less than 4 inches (102 mm) from each end of each piece. A properly sized nut and washer shall be tightened on each bolt to the plate.

2308.7 Girders. Girders for single-story construction or girders supporting loads from a single floor shall not be less than 4 inches by 6 inches (102 mm by 152 mm) for spans 6 feet (1829 mm) or less, provided that girders are spaced not more than 8 feet (2438 mm) o.c. Spans for built-up 2-inch (51 mm) girders shall be in accordance with Table 2308.9.5 or 2308.9.6. Other girders shall be designed to support the loads specified in this code. Girder end joints shall occur over supports.

Where a girder is spliced over a support, an adequate tie shall be provided. The ends of beams or girders supported on masonry or concrete shall not have less than 3 inches (76 mm) of bearing.

2308.8 Floor joists. Spans for floor joists shall be in accordance with Table 2308.8(1) or 2308.8(2). For other grades and or species, refer to the *AF&PA Span Tables for Joists and Rafters*.

2308.8.1 Bearing. Except where supported on a 1-inch by 4-inch (25.4 mm by 102 mm) ribbon strip and nailed to the adjoining stud, the ends of each joist shall not have less than $1^1/_2$ inches (38 mm) of bearing on wood or metal, or less than 3 inches (76 mm) on masonry.

2308.8.2 Framing details. Joists shall be supported laterally at the ends and at each support by solid blocking except where the ends of the joists are nailed to a header, band or rim joist or to an adjoining stud or by other means. Solid blocking shall not be less than 2 inches (51mm) in thickness and the full depth of the joist. Notches on the ends of joists shall not exceed one-fourth the joist depth. Holes bored in joists shall not be within 2 inches (51 mm) of the top or bottom of the joist, and the diameter of any such hole shall not exceed one-third the depth of the joist. Notches in the top or bottom of joists shall not exceed one-sixth the depth and shall not be located in the middle third of the span.

Joist framing from opposite sides of a beam, girder or partition shall be lapped at least 3 inches (76 mm) or the opposing joists shall be tied together in an approved manner.

Joists framing into the side of a wood girder shall be supported by framing anchors or on ledger strips not less than 2 inches by 2 inches (51 mm by 51 mm).

2308.8.2.1 Engineered wood products. Cuts, notches and holes bored in trusses, structural composite lumber, structural glue-laminated members or I-joists are not permitted except where permitted by the manufacturer's recommendations or where the effects of such alterations are specifically considered in the design of the member by a *registered design professional.*

TABLE 2308.8(1)
FLOOR JOIST SPANS FOR COMMON LUMBER SPECIES
(Residential Sleeping Areas, Live Load = 30 pounds per square foot, $L/\Delta = 360$)

JOIST SPACING (inches)	SPECIES AND GRADE		DEAD LOAD = 10 psf				DEAD LOAD = 20 psf			
			2 x 6	2 x 8	2 x 10	2 x 12	2 x 6	2 x 8	2 x 10	2 x 12
			Maximum floor joist spans							
			(ft. - in.)	(ft. - in.)	(ft. - in.)	(ft. - in.)	(ft. - in.)	(ft. - in.)	(ft. - in.)	(ft. - in.)
12	Douglas Fir-Larch	SS	12-6	16-6	21-0	25-7	12-6	16-6	21-0	25-7
	Douglas Fir-Larch	#1	12-0	15-10	20-3	24-8	12-0	15-7	19-0	22-0
	Douglas Fir-Larch	#2	11-10	15-7	19-10	23-0	11-6	14-7	17-9	20-7
	Douglas Fir-Larch	#3	9-8	12-4	15-0	17-5	8-8	11-0	13-5	15-7
	Hem-Fir	SS	11-10	15-7	19-10	24-2	11-10	15-7	19-10	24-2
	Hem-Fir	#1	11-7	15-3	19-5	23-7	11-7	15-2	18-6	21-6
	Hem-Fir	#2	11-0	14-6	18-6	22-6	11-0	14-4	17-6	20-4
	Hem-Fir	#3	9-8	12-4	15-0	17-5	8-8	11-0	13-5	15-7
	Southern Pine	SS	12-3	16-2	20-8	25-1	12-3	16-2	20-8	25-1
	Southern Pine	#1	12-0	15-10	20-3	24-8	12-0	15-10	20-3	24-8
	Southern Pine	#2	11-10	15-7	19-10	24-2	11-10	15-7	18-7	21-9
	Southern Pine	#3	10-5	13-3	15-8	18-8	9-4	11-11	14-0	16-8
	Spruce-Pine-Fir	SS	11-7	15-3	19-5	23-7	11-7	15-3	19-5	23-7
	Spruce-Pine-Fir	#1	11-3	14-11	19-0	23-0	11-3	14-7	17-9	20-7
	Spruce-Pine-Fir	#2	11-3	14-11	19-0	23-0	11-3	14-7	17-9	20-7
	Spruce-Pine-Fir	#3	9-8	12-4	15-0	17-5	8-8	11-0	13-5	15-7
16	Douglas Fir-Larch	SS	11-4	15-0	19-1	23-3	11-4	15-0	19-1	23-0
	Douglas Fir-Larch	#1	10-11	14-5	18-5	21-4	10-8	13-6	16-5	19-1
	Douglas Fir-Larch	#2	10-9	14-1	17-2	19-11	9-11	12-7	15-5	17-10
	Douglas Fir-Larch	#3	8-5	10-8	13-0	15-1	7-6	9-6	11-8	13-6
	Hem-Fir	SS	10-9	14-2	18-0	21-11	10-9	14-2	18-0	21-11
	Hem-Fir	#1	10-6	13-10	17-8	20-9	10-4	13-1	16-0	18-7
	Hem-Fir	#2	10-0	13-2	16-10	19-8	9-10	12-5	15-2	17-7
	Hem-Fir	#3	8-5	10-8	13-0	15-1	7-6	9-6	11-8	13-6
	Southern Pine	SS	11-2	14-8	18-9	22-10	11-2	14-8	18-9	22-10
	Southern Pine	#1	10-11	14-5	18-5	22-5	10-11	14-5	17-11	21-4
	Southern Pine	#2	10-9	14-2	18-0	21-1	10-5	13-6	16-1	18-10
	Southern Pine	#3	9-0	11-6	13-7	16-2	8-1	10-3	12-2	14-6
	Spruce-Pine-Fir	SS	10-6	13-10	17-8	21-6	10-6	13-10	17-8	21-4
	Spruce-Pine-Fir	#1	10-3	13-6	17-2	19-11	9-11	12-7	15-5	17-10
	Spruce-Pine-Fir	#2	10-3	13-6	17-2	19-11	9-11	12-7	15-5	17-10
	Spruce-Pine-Fir	#3	8-5	10-8	13-0	15-1	7-6	9-6	11-8	13-6

(continued)

TABLE 2308.8(1)—continued
FLOOR JOIST SPANS FOR COMMON LUMBER SPECIES
(Residential Sleeping Areas, Live Load = 30 pounds per square foot, L/Δ = 360)

JOIST SPACING (inches)	SPECIES AND GRADE		DEAD LOAD = 10 psf				DEAD LOAD = 20 psf			
			2 x 6	2 x 8	2 x 10	2 x 12	2 x 6	2 x 8	2 x 10	2 x 12
			Maximum floor joist spans							
			(ft. - in.)	(ft. - in.)	(ft. - in.)	(ft. - in.)	(ft. - in.)	(ft. - in.)	(ft. - in.)	(ft. - in.)
19.2	Douglas Fir-Larch	SS	10-8	14-1	18-0	21-10	10-8	14-1	18-0	21-0
	Douglas Fir-Larch	#1	10-4	13-7	16-9	19-6	9-8	12-4	15-0	17-5
	Douglas Fir-Larch	#2	10-1	12-10	15-8	18-3	9-1	11-6	14-1	16-3
	Douglas Fir-Larch	#3	7-8	9-9	11-10	13-9	6-10	8-8	10-7	12-4
	Hem-Fir	SS	10-1	13-4	17-0	20-8	10-1	13-4	17-0	20-7
	Hem-Fir	#1	9-10	13-0	16-4	19-0	9-6	12-0	14-8	17-0
	Hem-Fir	#2	9-5	12-5	15-6	17-1	8-11	11-4	13-10	16-1
	Hem-Fir	#3	7-8	9-9	11-10	13-9	6-10	8-8	10-7	12-4
	Southern Pine	SS	10-6	13-10	17-8	21-6	10-6	13-10	17-8	21-6
	Southern Pine	#1	10-4	13-7	17-4	21-1	10-4	13-7	16-4	19-6
	Southern Pine	#2	10-1	13-4	16-5	19-3	9-6	12-4	14-8	17-2
	Southern Pine	#3	8-3	10-6	12-5	14-9	7-4	9-5	11-1	13-2
	Spruce-Pine-Fir	SS	9-10	13-0	16-7	20-2	9-10	13-0	16-7	19-6
	Spruce-Pine-Fir	#1	9-8	12-9	15-8	18-3	9-1	11-6	14-1	16-3
	Spruce-Pine-Fir	#2	9-8	12-9	15-8	18-3	9-1	11-6	14-1	16-3
	Spruce-Pine-Fir	#3	7-8	9-9	11-10	13-9	6-10	8-8	10-7	12-4
24	Douglas Fir-Larch	SS	9-11	13-1	16-8	20-3	9-11	13-1	16-2	18-9
	Douglas Fir-Larch	#1	9-7	12-4	15-0	17-5	8-8	11-0	13-5	15-7
	Douglas Fir-Larch	#2	9-1	11-6	14-1	16-3	8-1	10-3	12-7	14-7
	Douglas Fir-Larch	#3	6-10	8-8	10-7	12-4	6-2	7-9	9-6	11-0
	Hem-Fir	SS	9-4	12-4	15-9	19-2	9-4	12-4	15-9	18-5
	Hem-Fir	#1	9-2	12-0	14-8	17-0	8-6	10-9	13-1	15-2
	Hem-Fir	#2	8-9	11-4	13-10	16-1	8-0	10-2	12-5	14-4
	Hem-Fir	#3	6-10	8-8	10-7	12-4	6-2	7-9	9-6	11-0
	Southern Pine	SS	9-9	12-10	16-5	19-11	9-9	12-10	16-5	19-11
	Southern Pine	#1	9-7	12-7	16-1	19-6	9-7	12-4	14-7	17-5
	Southern Pine	#2	9-4	12-4	14-8	17-2	8-6	11-0	13-1	15-5
	Southern Pine	#3	7-4	9-5	11-1	13-2	6-7	8-5	9-11	11-10
	Spruce-Pine-Fir	SS	9-2	12-1	15-5	18-9	9-2	12-1	15-0	17-5
	Spruce-Pine-Fir	#1	8-11	11-6	14-1	16-3	8-1	10-3	12-7	14-7
	Spruce-Pine-Fir	#2	8-11	11-6	14-1	16-3	8-1	10-3	12-7	14-7
	Spruce-Pine-Fir	#3	6-10	8-8	10-7	12-4	6-2	7-9	9-6	11-0

Check sources for availability of lumber in lengths greater than 20 feet.

For SI: 1 inch = 25.4 mm, 1 foot = 304.8 mm, 1 pound per square foot = 47.8 N/m^2.

TABLE 2308.8(2)
FLOOR JOIST SPANS FOR COMMON LUMBER SPECIES
(Residential Living Areas, Live Load = 40 pounds per square foot, $L/\Delta = 360$)

JOIST SPACING (inches)	SPECIES AND GRADE		DEAD LOAD = 10 psf				DEAD LOAD = 20 psf			
			2 x 6	2 x 8	2 x 10	2 x 12	2 x 6	2 x 8	2 x 10	2 x 12
			Maximum floor joist spans							
			(ft. - in.)	(ft. - in.)	(ft. - in.)	(ft. - in.)	(ft. - in.)	(ft. - in.)	(ft. - in.)	(ft. - in.)
12	Douglas Fir-Larch	SS	11-4	15-0	19-1	23-3	11-4	15-0	19-1	23-3
	Douglas Fir-Larch	#1	10-11	14-5	18-5	22-0	10-11	14-2	17-4	20-1
	Douglas Fir-Larch	#2	10-9	14-2	17-9	20-7	10-6	13-3	16-3	18-10
	Douglas Fir-Larch	#3	8-8	11-0	13-5	15-7	7-11	10-0	12-3	14-3
	Hem-Fir	SS	10-9	14-2	18-0	21-11	10-9	14-2	18-0	21-11
	Hem-Fir	#1	10-6	13-10	17-8	21-6	10-6	13-10	16-11	19-7
	Hem-Fir	#2	10-0	13-2	16-10	20-4	10-0	13-1	16-0	18-6
	Hem-Fir	#3	8-8	11-0	13-5	15-7	7-11	10-0	12-3	14-3
	Southern Pine	SS	11-2	14-8	18-9	22-10	11-2	14-8	18-9	22-10
	Southern Pine	#1	10-11	14-5	18-5	22-5	10-11	14-5	18-5	22-5
	Southern Pine	#2	10-9	14-2	18-0	21-9	10-9	14-2	16-11	19-10
	Southern Pine	#3	9-4	11-11	14-0	16-8	8-6	10-10	12-10	15-3
	Spruce-Pine-Fir	SS	10-6	13-10	17-8	21-6	10-6	13-10	17-8	21-6
	Spruce-Pine-Fir	#1	10-3	13-6	17-3	20-7	10-3	13-3	16-3	18-10
	Spruce-Pine-Fir	#2	10-3	13-6	17-3	20-7	10-3	13-3	16-3	18-10
	Spruce-Pine-Fir	#3	8-8	11-0	13-5	15-7	7-11	10-0	12-3	14-3
16	Douglas Fir-Larch	SS	10-4	13-7	17-4	21-1	10-4	13-7	17-4	21-0
	Douglas Fir-Larch	#1	9-11	13-1	16-5	19-1	9-8	12-4	15-0	17-5
	Douglas Fir-Larch	#2	9-9	12-7	15-5	17-10	9-1	11-6	14-1	16-3
	Douglas Fir-Larch	#3	7-6	9-6	11-8	13-6	6-10	8-8	10-7	12-4
	Hem-Fir	SS	9-9	12-10	16-5	19-11	9-9	12-10	16-5	19-11
	Hem-Fir	#1	9-6	12-7	16-0	18-7	9-6	12-0	14-8	17-0
	Hem-Fir	#2	9-1	12-0	15-2	17-7	8-11	11-4	13-10	16-1
	Hem-Fir	#3	7-6	9-6	11-8	13-6	6-10	8-8	10-7	12-4
	Southern Pine	SS	10-2	13-4	17-0	20-9	10-2	13-4	17-0	20-9
	Southern Pine	#1	9-11	13-1	16-9	20-4	9-11	13-1	16-4	19-6
	Southern Pine	#2	9-9	12-10	16-1	18-10	9-6	12-4	14-8	17-2
	Southern Pine	#3	8-1	10-3	12-2	14-6	7-4	9-5	11-1	13-2
	Spruce-Pine-Fir	SS	9-6	12-7	16-0	19-6	9-6	12-7	16-0	19-6
	Spruce-Pine-Fir	#1	9-4	12-3	15-5	17-10	9-1	11-6	14-1	16-3
	Spruce-Pine-Fir	#2	9-4	12-3	15-5	17-10	9-1	11-6	14-1	16-3
	Spruce-Pine-Fir	#3	7-6	9-6	11-8	13-6	6-10	8-8	10-7	12-4

(continued)

TABLE 2308.8(2)—continued
FLOOR JOIST SPANS FOR COMMON LUMBER SPECIES
(Residential Living Areas, Live Load = 40 pounds per square foot, L/Δ = 360)

JOIST SPACING (inches)	SPECIES AND GRADE		DEAD LOAD = 10 psf				DEAD LOAD = 20 psf			
			2 x 6	2 x 8	2 x 10	2 x 12	2 x 6	2 x 8	2 x 10	2 x 12
			Maximum floor joist spans							
			(ft. - in.)	(ft. - in.)	(ft. - in.)	(ft. - in.)	(ft. - in.)	(ft. - in.)	(ft. - in.)	(ft. - in.)
19.2	Douglas Fir-Larch	SS	9-8	12-10	16-4	19-10	9-8	12-10	16-4	19-2
	Douglas Fir-Larch	#1	9-4	12-4	15-0	17-5	8-10	11-3	13-8	15-11
	Douglas Fir-Larch	#2	9-1	11-6	14-1	16-3	8-3	10-6	12-10	14-10
	Douglas Fir-Larch	#3	6-10	8-8	10-7	12-4	6-3	7-11	9-8	11-3
	Hem-Fir	SS	9-2	12-1	15-5	18-9	9-2	12-1	15-5	18-9
	Hem-Fir	#1	9-0	11-10	14-8	17-0	8-8	10-11	13-4	15-6
	Hem-Fir	#2	8-7	11-3	13-10	16-1	8-2	10-4	12-8	14-8
	Hem-Fir	#3	6-10	8-8	10-7	12-4	6-3	7-11	9-8	11-3
	Southern Pine	SS	9-6	12-7	16-0	19-6	9-6	12-7	16-0	19-6
	Southern Pine	#1	9-4	12-4	15-9	19-2	9-4	12-4	14-11	17-9
	Southern Pine	#2	9-2	12 -1	14-8	17-2	8-8	11-3	13-5	15-8
	Southern Pine	#3	7-4	9-5	11-1	13-2	6-9	8-7	10-1	12-1
	Spruce-Pine-Fir	SS	9-0	11-10	15-1	18-4	9-0	11-10	15-1	17-9
	Spruce-Pine-Fir	#1	8-9	11-6	14-1	16-3	8-3	10-6	12-10	14-10
	Spruce-Pine-Fir	#2	8-9	11-6	14-1	16-3	8-3	10-6	12-10	14-10
	Spruce-Pine-Fir	#3	6-10	8-8	10-7	12-4	6-3	7-11	9-8	11-3
24	Douglas Fir-Larch	SS	9-0	11-11	15-2	18-5	9-0	11-11	14-9	17-1
	Douglas Fir-Larch	#1	8-8	11-0	13-5	15-7	7-11	10-0	12-3	14-3
	Douglas Fir-Larch	#2	8-1	10-3	12-7	14-7	7-5	9-5	11-6	13-4
	Douglas Fir-Larch	#3	6-2	7-9	9-6	11-0	5-7	7-1	8-8	10-1
	Hem-Fir	SS	8-6	11-3	14-4	17-5	8-6	11-3	14-4	16-10[a]
	Hem-Fir	#1	8-4	10-9	13-1	15-2	7-9	9-9	11-11	13-10
	Hem-Fir	#2	7-11	10-2	12-5	14-4	7-4	9-3	11-4	13-1
	Hem-Fir	#3	6-2	7-9	9-6	11-0	5-7	7-1	8-8	10-1
	Southern Pine	SS	8-10	11-8	14-11	18-1	8-10	11-8	14-11	18-1
	Southern Pine	#1	8-8	11-5	14-7	17-5	8-8	11-3	13-4	15-11
	Southern Pine	#2	8-6	11-0	13-1	15-5	7-9	10-0	12-0	14-0
	Southern Pine	#3	6-7	8-5	9-11	11-10	6-0	7-8	9-1	10-9
	Spruce-Pine-Fir	SS	8-4	11-0	14-0	17-0	8-4	11-0	13-8	15-11
	Spruce-Pine-Fir	#1	8-1	10-3	12-7	14-7	7-5	9-5	11-6	13-4
	Spruce-Pine-Fir	#2	8-1	10-3	12-7	14-7	7-5	9-5	11-6	13-4
	Spruce-Pine-Fir	#3	6-2	7-9	9-6	11-0	5-7	7-1	8-8	10-1

Check sources for availability of lumber in lengths greater than 20 feet.

For SI: 1 inch = 25.4 mm, 1 foot = 304.8 mm, 1 pound per square foot = 47.8 N/m^2.

a. End bearing length shall be increased to 2 inches.

2308.8.3 Framing around openings. Trimmer and header joists shall be doubled, or of lumber of equivalent cross section, where the span of the header exceeds 4 feet (1219 mm). The ends of header joists more than 6 feet (1829 mm) long shall be supported by framing anchors or joist hangers unless bearing on a beam, partition or wall. Tail joists over 12 feet (3658 mm) long shall be supported at the header by framing anchors or on ledger strips not less than 2 inches by 2 inches (51 mm by 51 mm).

2308.8.4 Supporting bearing partitions. Bearing partitions parallel to joists shall be supported on beams, girders, doubled joists, walls or other bearing partitions. Bearing partitions perpendicular to joists shall not be offset from supporting girders, walls or partitions more than the joist depth unless such joists are of sufficient size to carry the additional load.

2308.8.5 Lateral support. Floor, *attic* and roof framing with a nominal depth-to-thickness ratio greater than or equal to 5:1 shall have one edge held in line for the entire span. Where the nominal depth-to-thickness ratio of the framing member exceeds 6:1, there shall be one line of bridging for each 8 feet (2438 mm) of span, unless both edges of the member are held in line. The bridging shall consist of not less than 1-inch by 3-inch (25 mm by 76 mm) lumber, double nailed at each end, of equivalent metal bracing of equal rigidity, full-depth solid blocking or other *approved* means. A line of bridging shall also be required at supports where equivalent lateral support is not otherwise provided.

2308.8.6 Structural floor sheathing. Structural floor sheathing shall comply with the provisions of Section 2304.7.1.

2308.8.7 Under-floor ventilation. For under-floor ventilation, see Section 1203.3.

2308.9 Wall framing.

2308.9.1 Size, height and spacing. The size, height and spacing of studs shall be in accordance with Table 2308.9.1 except that utility-grade studs shall not be spaced more than 16 inches (406 mm) o.c., or support more than a roof and ceiling, or exceed 8 feet (2438 mm) in height for exterior walls and load-bearing walls or 10 feet (3048 mm) for interior nonload-bearing walls. Studs shall be continuous from a support at the sole plate to a support at the top plate to resist loads perpendicular to the wall. The support shall be a foundation or floor, ceiling or roof diaphragm or shall be designed in accordance with accepted engineering practice.

> **Exception:** Jack studs, trimmer studs and cripple studs at openings in walls that comply with Table 2308.9.5.

2308.9.2 Framing details. Studs shall be placed with their wide dimension perpendicular to the wall. Not less than three studs shall be installed at each corner of an *exterior wall.*

> **Exception:** At corners, two studs are permitted, provided wood spacers or backup cleats of $^3/_8$-inch-thick (9.5 mm) wood structural panel, $^3/_8$-inch (9.5 mm) Type M "Exterior Glue" particleboard, 1-inch-thick (25 mm) lumber or other *approved* devices that will serve as an adequate backing for the attachment of facing materials are used. Where fire-resistance ratings or shear values are involved, wood spacers, backup cleats or other devices shall not be used unless specifically *approved* for such use.

2308.9.2.1 Top plates. Bearing and *exterior wall* studs shall be capped with double top plates installed to provide overlapping at corners and at intersections with other partitions. End joints in double top plates shall be offset at least 48 inches (1219 mm), and shall be nailed with not less than eight 16d face nails on each side of the joint. Plates shall be a nominal 2 inches (51 mm) in depth and have a width at least equal to the width of the studs.

> **Exception:** A single top plate is permitted, provided the plate is adequately tied at joints, corners and intersecting walls by at least the equivalent of 3-inch by 6-inch (76 mm by 152 mm) by 0.036-inch-thick (0.914 mm) galvanized steel that is nailed to each wall or segment of wall by six 8d nails or equivalent, provided the rafters, joists or trusses are centered over the studs with a tolerance of no more than 1 inch (25 mm).

2308.9.2.2 Top plates for studs spaced at 24 inches (610 mm). Where bearing studs are spaced at 24-inch (610 mm) intervals and top plates are less than two 2-inch by 6-inch (51 mm by 152 mm) or two 3-inch by 4-inch (76 mm by 102 mm) members and where the floor joists, floor trusses or roof trusses that they support are spaced at more than 16-inch (406 mm) intervals, such joists or trusses shall bear within 5 inches (127 mm) of the studs beneath or a third plate shall be installed.

2308.9.2.3 Nonbearing walls and partitions. In nonbearing walls and partitions, studs shall be spaced not more than 28 inches (711 mm) o.c. and are permitted to be set with the long dimension parallel to the wall. Interior nonbearing partitions shall be capped with no less than a single top plate installed to provide overlapping at corners and at intersections with other walls and partitions. The plate shall be continuously tied at joints by solid blocking at least 16 inches (406 mm) in length and equal in size to the plate or by $^1/_2$-inch by $1^1/_2$-inch (12.7 mm by 38 mm) metal ties with spliced sections fastened with two 16d nails on each side of the joint.

2308.9.2.4 Plates or sills. Studs shall have full bearing on a plate or sill not less than 2 inches (51 mm) in thickness having a width not less than that of the wall studs.

2308.9.3 Bracing. Braced wall lines shall consist of braced wall panels that meet the requirements for location, type and amount of bracing as shown in Figure 2308.9.3, specified in Table 2308.9.3(1) and are in line or offset from each other by not more than 4 feet (1219 mm). Braced wall panels shall start not more than $12^1/_2$ feet (3810 mm) from each end of a braced wall line. Braced wall panels shall be clearly indicated on the plans. Construction of braced wall panels shall be by one of the following methods:

1. Nominal 1-inch by 4-inch (25 mm by 102 mm) continuous diagonal braces let into top and bottom plates and intervening studs, placed at an angle not more than 60 degrees (1.0 rad) or less than 45 degrees (0.79 rad) from the horizontal and attached to the framing in conformance with Table 2304.9.1.

TABLE 2308.9.1
SIZE, HEIGHT AND SPACING OF WOOD STUDS

STUD SIZE (inches)	BEARING WALLS				NONBEARING WALLS	
	Laterally unsupported stud height[a] (feet)	Supporting roof and ceiling only	Supporting one floor, roof and ceiling	Supporting two floors, roof and ceiling	Laterally unsupported stud height[a] (feet)	Spacing (inches)
		Spacing (inches)				
2 × 3[b]	—	—	—	—	10	16
2 × 4	10	24	16	—	14	24
3 × 4	10	24	24	16	14	24
2 × 5	10	24	24	—	16	24
2 × 6	10	24	24	16	20	24

For SI: 1 inch = 25.4 mm, 1 foot = 304.8 mm.

a. Listed heights are distances between points of lateral support placed perpendicular to the plane of the wall. Increases in unsupported height are permitted where justified by an analysis.

b. Shall not be used in exterior walls.

2. Wood boards of $^5/_8$ inch (15.9 mm) net minimum thickness applied diagonally on studs spaced not over 24 inches (610 mm) o.c.
3. Wood structural panel sheathing with a thickness not less than $^3/_8$ inch (9.5 mm) for 16-inch (406 mm) or 24-inch (610 mm) stud spacing in accordance with Tables 2308.9.3(2) and 2308.9.3(3).
4. Fiberboard sheathing panels not less than $^1/_2$ inch (12.7 mm) thick applied vertically or horizontally on studs spaced not over 16 inches (406 mm) o.c. where installed with fasteners in accordance with Section 2306.6 and Table 2306.6.
5. Gypsum board [sheathing $^1/_2$-inch-thick (12.7 mm) by 4-feet-wide (1219 mm) wallboard or veneer base] on studs spaced not over 24 inches (610 mm) o.c. and nailed at 7 inches (178 mm) o.c. with nails as required by Table 2306.7.
6. Particleboard wall sheathing panels where installed in accordance with Table 2308.9.3(4).
7. Portland cement plaster on studs spaced 16 inches (406 mm) o.c. installed in accordance with Section 2510.
8. Hardboard panel siding where installed in accordance with Section 2303.1.6 and Table 2308.9.3(5).

For cripple wall bracing, see Section 2308.9.4.1. For Methods 2, 3, 4, 6, 7 and 8, each panel must be at least 48 inches (1219 mm) in length, covering three stud spaces where studs are spaced 16 inches (406 mm) apart and covering two stud spaces where studs are spaced 24 inches (610 mm) apart.

For Method 5, each panel must be at least 96 inches (2438 mm) in length where applied to one face of a panel and 48 inches (1219 mm) where applied to both faces. All vertical joints of panel sheathing shall occur over studs and adjacent panel joints shall be nailed to common framing members. Horizontal joints shall occur over blocking or other framing equal in size to the studding except where waived by the installation requirements for the specific sheathing materials. Sole plates shall be nailed to the floor framing and top plates shall be connected to the framing above in accordance with Section 2308.3.2. Where joists are perpendicular to braced wall lines above, blocking shall be provided under and in line with the braced wall panels.

2308.9.3.1 Alternative bracing. Any bracing required by Section 2308.9.3 is permitted to be replaced by the following:

1. In one-story buildings, each panel shall have a length of not less than 2 feet 8 inches (813 mm) and a height of not more than 10 feet (3048 mm). Each panel shall be sheathed on one face with $^3/_8$-inch-minimum-thickness (9.5 mm) wood structural panel sheathing nailed with 8d common or galvanized box nails in accordance with Table 2304.9.1 and blocked at wood structural panel edges. Two anchor bolts installed in accordance with Section 2308.6 shall be provided in each panel. Anchor bolts shall be placed at each panel outside quarter points. Each panel end stud shall have a tie-down device fastened to the foundation, capable of providing an *approved* uplift capacity of not less than 1,800 pounds (8006 N). The tie-down device shall be installed in accordance with the manufacturer's recommendations. The panels shall be supported directly on a foundation or on floor framing supported directly on a foundation that is continuous across the entire length of the braced wall line. This foundation shall be reinforced with not less than one No. 4 bar top and bottom.

   Where the continuous foundation is required to have a depth greater than 12 inches (305 mm), a minimum 12-inch by 12-inch (305 mm by 305 mm) continuous footing or turned down slab edge is permitted at door openings in the braced wall line. This continuous footing or turned down slab edge shall be reinforced with not less than one No. 4 bar top and bottom. This reinforcement shall be lapped 15 inches (381 mm) with the reinforcement required in the continuous foundation located directly under the braced wall line.

2. In the first *story* of two-story buildings, each wall panel shall be braced in accordance with Section 2308.9.3.1, Item 1, except that the wood structural panel sheathing shall be provided on both faces, three anchor bolts shall be placed at one-quarter points, and tie-down device uplift capacity shall not be less than 3,000 pounds (13 344 N).

SEISMIC DESIGN CATEGORY	MAXIMUM WALL SPACING (feet)	REQUIRED BRACING LENGTH, b
A, B and C	35′-0″	Table 2308.9.3(1) and Section 2308.9.3
D and E	25′-0″	Table 2308.12.4

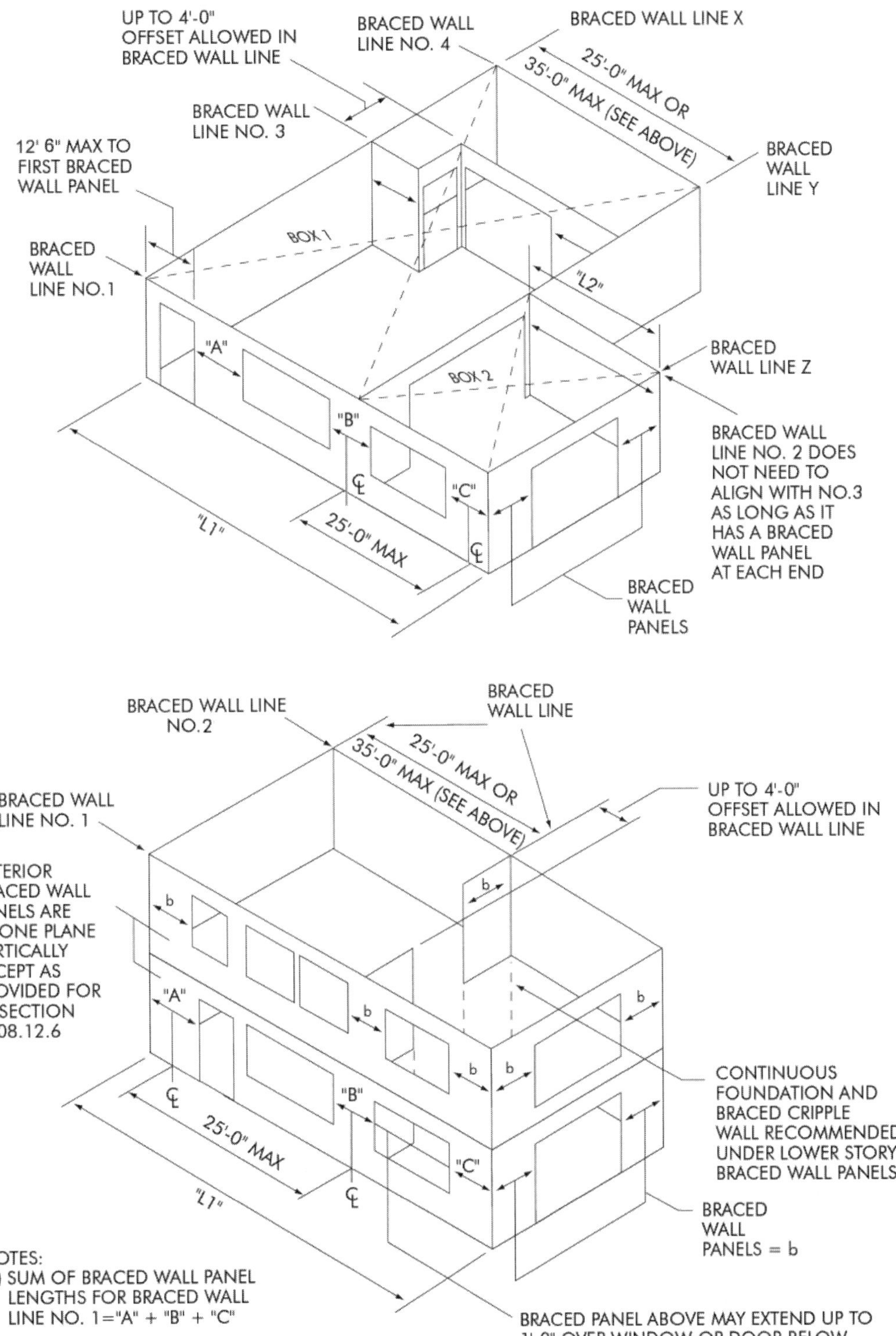

For SI: 1 inch = 25.4 mm, 1 foot = 304.8 mm.

FIGURE 2308.9.3
BASIC COMPONENTS OF THE LATERAL BRACING SYSTEM

TABLE 2308.9.3(1)
BRACED WALL PANELS[a]

SEISMIC DESIGN CATEGORY	CONDITION	CONSTRUCTION METHODS[b, c]								BRACED PANEL LOCATION AND LENGTH[d]
		1	2	3	4	5	6	7	8	
A and B	One story, top of two or three story	X	X	X	X	X	X	X	X	Located in accordance with Section 2308.9.3 and not more than 25 feet on center.
	First story of two story or second story of three story	X	X	X	X	X	X	X	X	
	First story of three story	—	X	X	X	X[e]	X	X	X	
C	One story or top of two story	—	X	X	X	X	X	X	X	Located in accordance with Section 2308.9.3 and not more than 25 feet on center.
	First story of two story	—	X	X	X	X[e]	X	X	X	Located in accordance with Section 2308.9.3 and not more than 25 feet on center, but total length shall not be less than 25% of building length[f].

For SI: 1 inch = 25.4 mm, 1 foot = 304.8 mm.

a. This table specifies minimum requirements for braced panels that form interior or exterior braced wall lines.

b. See Section 2308.9.3 for full description.

c. See Sections 2308.9.3.1 and 2308.9.3.2 for alternative braced panel requirements.

d. Building length is the dimension parallel to the braced wall length.

e. Gypsum wallboard applied to framing supports that are spaced at 16 inches on center.

f. The required lengths shall be doubled for gypsum board applied to only one face of a braced wall panel.

TABLE 2308.9.3(3)
WOOD STRUCTURAL PANEL WALL SHEATHING[b]
(Not Exposed to the Weather, Strength Axis Parallel or Perpendicular to Studs Except as Indicated Below)

MINIMUM THICKNESS (inch)	PANEL SPAN RATING	STUD SPACING (inches)		
			Nailable sheathing	
		Siding nailed to studs	Sheathing parallel to studs	Sheathing perpendicular to studs
$^3/_8$, $^{15}/_{32}$, $^1/_2$	16/0, 20/0, 24/0, 32/16 Wall–24″ o.c.	24	16	24
$^7/_{16}$, $^{15}/_{32}$, $^1/_2$	24/0, 24/16, 32/16 Wall–24″ o.c.	24	24[a]	24

For SI: 1 inch = 25.4 mm.

a. Plywood shall consist of four or more plies.

b. Blocking of horizontal joints shall not be required except as specified in Sections 2306.3 and 2308.12.4.

TABLE 2308.9.3(4)
ALLOWABLE SPANS FOR PARTICLEBOARD WALL SHEATHING
(Not Exposed to the Weather, Long Dimension of the Panel Parallel or Perpendicular to Studs)

GRADE	THICKNESS (inch)	STUD SPACING (inches)	
		Siding nailed to studs	Sheathing under coverings specified in Section 2308.9.3 parallel or perpendicular to studs
M-S "Exterior Glue" and M-2"Exterior Glue"	$^3/_8$	16	—
	$^1/_2$	16	16

For SI: 1 inch = 25.4 mm.

TABLE 2308.9.3(5)
HARDBOARD SIDING

SIDING	MINIMUM NOMINAL THICKNESS (inch)	2 × 4 FRAMING MAXIMUM SPACING	NAIL SIZE[a, b, d]	NAIL SPACING	
				General	Bracing panels[c]
1. Lap siding					
Direct to studs	$^3/_8$	16″ o.c.	8d	16″ o.c.	Not applicable
Over sheathing	$^3/_8$	16″ o.c.	10d	16″ o.c.	Not applicable
2. Square edge panel siding					
Direct to studs	$^3/_8$	24″ o.c.	6d	6″ o.c. edges; 12″ o.c. at intermediate supports	4″ o.c. edges; 8″ o.c. at intermediate supports
Over sheathing	$^3/_8$	24″ o.c.	8d	6″ o.c. edges; 12″ o.c. at intermediate supports	4″ o.c. edges; 8″ o.c. at intermediate supports
3. Shiplap edge panel siding					
Direct to studs	$^3/_8$	16″ o.c.	6d	6″ o.c. edges; 12″ o.c. at intermediate supports	4″ o.c. edges; 8″ o.c. at intermediate supports
Over sheathing	$^3/_8$	16″ o.c.	8d	6″ o.c. edges; 12″ o.c. at intermediate supports	4″ o.c. edges; 8″ o.c. at intermediate supports

For SI: 1 inch = 25.4 mm.

a. Nails shall be corrosion resistant.

b. Minimum acceptable nail dimensions:

	Panel Siding (inch)	Lap Siding (inch)
Shank diameter	0.092	0.099
Head diameter	0.225	0.240

c. Where used to comply with Section 2308.9.3.

d. Nail length must accommodate the sheathing and penetrate framing $1^1/_2$ inches.

2308.9.3.2 Alternate bracing wall panel adjacent to a door or window opening. Any bracing required by Section 2308.9.3 is permitted to be replaced by the following when used adjacent to a door or window opening with a full-length header:

1. In one-story buildings, each panel shall have a length of not less than 16 inches (406 mm) and a height of not more than 10 feet (3048 mm). Each panel shall be sheathed on one face with a single layer of $^3/_8$ inch (9.5 mm) minimum thickness wood structural panel sheathing nailed with 8d common or galvanized box nails in accordance with Figure 2308.9.3.2. The wood structural panel sheathing shall extend up over the solid sawn or glued-laminated header and shall be nailed in accordance with Figure 2308.9.3.2. A built-up header consisting of at least two 2 × 12s and fastened in accordance with Item 24 of Table 2304.9.1 shall be permitted to be used. A spacer, if used, shall be placed on the side of the built-up beam opposite the wood structural panel sheathing. The header shall extend between the inside faces of the first full-length outer studs of each panel. The clear span of the header between the inner studs of each panel shall be not less than 6 feet (1829 mm) and not more than 18 feet (5486 mm) in length. A strap with an uplift capacity of not less than 1,000 pounds (4,400 N) shall fasten the header to the inner studs opposite the sheathing. One anchor bolt not less than $^5/_8$ inch (15.9 mm) diameter and installed in accordance with Section 2308.6 shall be provided in the center of each sill plate. The studs at each end of the panel shall have a tie-down device fastened to the foundation with an uplift capacity of not less than 4,200 pounds (18 480 N).

   Where a panel is located on one side of the opening, the header shall extend between the inside face of the first full-length stud of the panel and the bearing studs at the other end of the opening. A strap with an uplift capacity of not less than 1,000 pounds (4400 N) shall fasten the header to the bearing studs. The bearing studs shall also have a tie-down device fastened to the foundation with an uplift capacity of not less than 1,000 pounds (4400 N).

   The tie-down devices shall be an embedded strap type, installed in accordance with the manufacturer's recommendations. The panels shall be supported directly on a foundation that is continuous across the entire length of the braced wall line. This foundation shall be reinforced with not less than one No. 4 bar top and bottom.

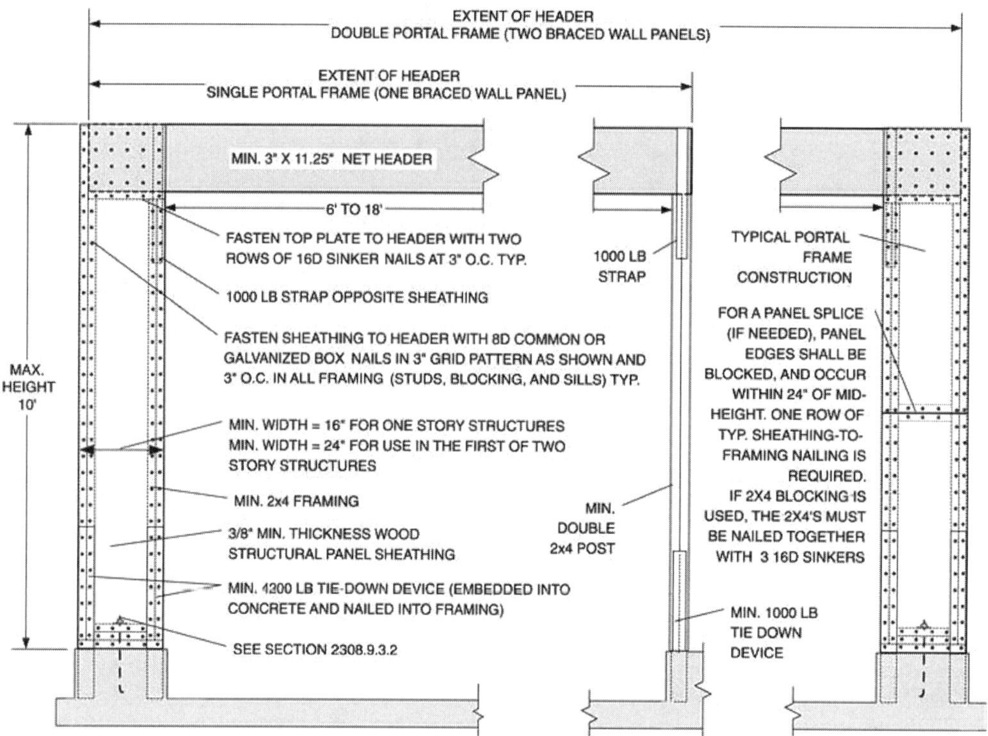

For SI: 1 foot = 304.8 mm, 1 inch = 25.4 mm, 1 pound = 4.448 N.

FIGURE 2308.9.3.2
ALTERNATE BRACED WALL PANEL ADJACENT TO A DOOR OR WINDOW OPENING

Where the continuous foundation is required to have a depth greater than 12 inches (305 mm), a minimum 12-inch by 12-inch (305 mm by 305 mm) continuous footing or turned down slab edge is permitted at door openings in the braced wall line. This continuous footing or turned down slab edge shall be reinforced with not less than one No. 4 bar top and bottom. This reinforcement shall be lapped not less than 15 inches (381 mm) with the reinforcement required in the continuous foundation located directly under the braced wall line.

2. In the first *story* of two-story buildings, each wall panel shall be braced in accordance with Item 1 above, except that each panel shall have a length of not less than 24 inches (610 mm).

2308.9.4 Cripple walls. Foundation cripple walls shall be framed of studs not less in size than the studding above with a minimum length of 14 inches (356 mm), or shall be framed of solid blocking. Where exceeding 4 feet (1219 mm) in height, such walls shall be framed of studs having the size required for an additional *story*.

2308.9.4.1 Bracing. For the purposes of this section, cripple walls having a stud height exceeding 14 inches (356 mm) shall be considered a *story* and shall be braced in accordance with Table 2308.9.3(1) for *Seismic Design Category* A, B or C. See Section 2308.12.4 for *Seismic Design Category* D or E.

2308.9.4.2 Nailing of bracing. Spacing of edge nailing for required wall bracing shall not exceed 6 inches (152 mm) o.c. along the foundation plate and the top plate of the cripple wall. Nail size, nail spacing for field nailing and more restrictive boundary nailing requirements shall be as required elsewhere in the code for the specific bracing material used.

2308.9.5 Openings in exterior walls.

2308.9.5.1 Headers. Headers shall be provided over each opening in exterior-bearing walls. The spans in Table 2308.9.5 are permitted to be used for one- and two-family *dwellings*. Headers for other buildings shall be designed in accordance with Section 2301.2, Item 1 or 2. Headers shall be of two pieces of nominal 2-inch (51 mm) framing lumber set on edge as permitted by Table 2308.9.5 and nailed together in accordance with Table 2304.9.1 or of solid lumber of equivalent size.

2308.9.5.2 Header support. Wall studs shall support the ends of the header in accordance with Table 2308.9.5. Each end of a lintel or header shall have a length of bearing of not less than $1^1/_2$ inches (38 mm) for the full width of the lintel.

2308.9.6 Openings in interior bearing partitions. Headers shall be provided over each opening in interior bearing partitions as required in Section 2308.9.5. The spans in Table 2308.9.6 are permitted to be used. Wall studs shall support the ends of the header in accordance with Table 2308.9.5 or 2308.9.6, as appropriate.

TABLE 2308.9.5
HEADER AND GIRDER SPANS[a] FOR EXTERIOR BEARING WALLS
(Maximum Spans for Douglas Fir-Larch, Hem-Fir, Southern Pine and Spruce-Pine-Fir[b] and Required Number of Jack Studs)

HEADERS SUPPORTING	SIZE	GROUND SNOW LOAD (psf)[e]											
		30						50					
		Building width[c] (feet)											
		20		28		36		20		28		36	
		Span	NJ[d]	Span	NJ[d]	Span	NJ[d]	Span	NJ[d]	Span	NJ[d]	Span	NJ[d]
Roof & Ceiling	2-2 × 4	3-6	1	3-2	1	2-10	1	3-2	1	2-9	1	2-6	1
	2-2 × 6	5-5	1	4-8	1	4-2	1	4-8	1	4-1	1	3-8	2
	2-2 × 8	6-10	1	5-11	2	5-4	2	5-11	2	5-2	2	4-7	2
	2-2 × 10	8-5	2	7-3	2	6-6	2	7-3	2	6-3	2	5-7	2
	2-2 × 12	9-9	2	8-5	2	7-6	2	8-5	2	7-3	2	6-6	2
	3-2 × 8	8-4	1	7-5	1	6-8	1	7-5	1	6-5	2	5-9	2
	3-2 × 10	10-6	1	9-1	2	8-2	2	9-1	2	7-10	2	7-0	2
	3-2 × 12	12-2	2	10-7	2	9-5	2	10-7	2	9-2	2	8-2	2
	4-2 × 8	9-2	1	8-4	1	7-8	1	8-4	1	7-5	1	6-8	1
	4-2 × 10	11-8	1	10-6	1	9-5	2	10-6	1	9-1	2	8-2	2
	4-2 × 12	14-1	1	12-2	2	10-11	2	12-2	2	10-7	2	9-5	2
Roof, Ceiling & 1 Center-Bearing Floor	2-2 × 4	3-1	1	2-9	1	2-5	1	2-9	1	2-5	1	2-2	1
	2-2 × 6	4-6	1	4-0	1	3-7	2	4-1	1	3-7	2	3-3	2
	2-2 × 8	5-9	2	5-0	2	4-6	2	5-2	2	4-6	2	4-1	2
	2-2 × 10	7-0	2	6-2	2	5-6	2	6-4	2	5-6	2	5-0	2
	2-2 × 12	8-1	2	7-1	2	6-5	2	7-4	2	6-5	2	5-9	3
	3-2 × 8	7-2	1	6-3	2	5-8	2	6-5	2	5-8	2	5-1	2
	3-2 × 10	8-9	2	7-8	2	6-11	2	7-11	2	6-11	2	6-3	2
	3-2 × 12	10-2	2	8-11	2	8-0	2	9-2	2	8-0	2	7-3	2
	4-2 × 8	8-1	1	7-3	1	6-7	1	7-5	1	6-6	1	5-11	2
	4-2 × 10	10-1	1	8-10	2	8-0	2	9-1	2	8-0	2	7-2	2
	4-2 × 12	11-9	2	10-3	2	9-3	2	10-7	2	9-3	2	8-4	2
Roof, Ceiling & 1 Clear Span Floor	2-2 × 4	2-8	1	2-4	1	2-1	1	2-7	1	2-3	1	2-0	1
	2-2 × 6	3-11	1	3-5	2	3-0	2	3-10	2	3-4	2	3-0	2
	2-2 × 8	5-0	2	4-4	2	3-10	2	4-10	2	4-2	2	3-9	2
	2-2 × 10	6-1	2	5-3	2	4-8	2	5-11	2	5-1	2	4-7	3
	2-2 × 12	7-1	2	6-1	3	5-5	3	6-10	2	5-11	3	5-4	3
	3-2 × 8	6-3	2	5-5	2	4-10	2	6-1	2	5-3	2	4-8	2
	3-2 × 10	7-7	2	6-7	2	5-11	2	7-5	2	6-5	2	5-9	2
	3-2 × 12	8-10	2	7-8	2	6-10	2	8-7	2	7-5	2	6-8	2
	4-2 × 8	7-2	1	6-3	2	5-7	2	7-0	1	6-1	2	5-5	2
	4-2 × 10	8-9	2	7-7	2	6-10	2	8-7	2	7-5	2	6-7	2
	4-2 × 12	10-2	2	8-10	2	7-11	2	9-11	2	8-7	2	7-8	2

(continued)

TABLE 2308.9.5—continued
HEADER AND GIRDER SPANS[a] FOR EXTERIOR BEARING WALLS
(Maximum Spans for Douglas Fir-Larch, Hem-Fir, Southern Pine and Spruce-Pine-Fir[b] and Required Number of Jack Studs)

HEADERS SUPPORTING	SIZE	GROUND SNOW LOAD (psf)[e]											
		30						50					
		Building width[c] (feet)											
		20		28		36		20		28		36	
		Span	NJ[d]	Span	NJ[d]	Span	NJ[d]	Span	NJ[d]	Span	NJ[d]	Span	NJ[d]
Roof, Ceiling & 2 Center-Bearing Floors	2-2 × 4	2-7	1	2-3	1	2-0	1	2-6	1	2-2	1	1-11	1
	2-2 × 6	3-9	2	3-3	2	2-11	2	3-8	2	3-2	2	2-10	2
	2-2 × 8	4-9	2	4-2	2	3-9	2	4-7	2	4-0	2	3-8	2
	2-2 × 10	5-9	2	5-1	2	4-7	3	5-8	2	4-11	2	4-5	3
	2-2 × 12	6-8	2	5-10	3	5-3	3	6-6	2	5-9	3	5-2	3
	3-2 × 8	5-11	2	5-2	2	4-8	2	5-9	2	5-1	2	4-7	2
	3-2 × 10	7-3	2	6-4	2	5-8	2	7-1	2	6-2	2	5-7	2
	3-2 × 12	8-5	2	7-4	2	6-7	2	8-2	2	7-2	2	6-5	3
	4-2 × 8	6-10	1	6-0	2	5-5	2	6-8	1	5-10	2	5-3	2
	4-2 × 10	8-4	2	7-4	2	6-7	2	8-2	2	7-2	2	6-5	2
	4-2 × 12	9-8	2	8-6	2	7-8	2	9-5	2	8-3	2	7-5	2
Roof, Ceiling & 2 Clear Span Floors	2-2 × 4	2-1	1	1-8	1	1-6	2	2-0	1	1-8	1	1-5	2
	2-2 × 6	3-1	2	2-8	2	2-4	2	3-0	2	2-7	2	2-3	2
	2-2 × 8	3-10	2	3-4	2	3-0	3	3-10	2	3-4	2	2-11	3
	2-2 × 10	4-9	2	4-1	3	3-8	3	4-8	2	4-0	3	3-7	3
	2-2 × 12	5-6	3	4-9	3	4-3	3	5-5	3	4-8	3	4-2	3
	3-2 × 8	4-10	2	4-2	2	3-9	2	4-9	2	4-1	2	3-8	2
	3-2 × 10	5-11	2	5-1	2	4-7	3	5-10	2	5-0	2	4-6	3
	3-2 × 12	6-10	2	5-11	3	5-4	3	6-9	2	5-10	3	5-3	3
	4-2 × 8	5-7	2	4-10	2	4-4	2	5-6	2	4-9	2	4-3	2
	4-2 × 10	6-10	2	5-11	2	5-3	2	6-9	2	5-10	2	5-2	2
	4-2 × 12	7-11	2	6-10	2	6-2	3	7-9	2	6-9	2	6-0	3

For SI: 1 inch = 25.4 mm, 1 foot = 304.8 mm, 1 pound per square foot = 47.8 N/m^2.

a. Spans are given in feet and inches (ft-in).

b. Tabulated values are for No. 2 grade lumber.

c. Building width is measured perpendicular to the ridge. For widths between those shown, spans are permitted to be interpolated.

d. NJ - Number of jack studs required to support each end. Where the number of required jack studs equals one, the header is permitted to be supported by an *approved* framing anchor attached to the full-height wall stud and to the header.

e. Use 30 pounds per square foot ground snow load for cases in which ground snow load is less than 30 pounds per square foot and the roof live load is equal to or less than 20 pounds per square foot.

TABLE 2308.9.6
HEADER AND GIRDER SPANS[a] FOR INTERIOR BEARING WALLS
(Maximum Spans for Douglas Fir-Larch, Hem-Fir, Southern Pine and Spruce-Pine-Fir[b] and Required Number of Jack Studs)

HEADERS AND GIRDERS SUPPORTING	SIZE	BUILDING WIDTH[c] (feet)					
		20		28		36	
		Span	NJ[d]	Span	NJ[d]	Span	NJ[d]
One Floor Only	2-2 × 4	3-1	1	2-8	1	2-5	1
	2-2 × 6	4-6	1	3-11	1	3-6	1
	2-2 × 8	5-9	1	5-0	2	4-5	2
	2-2 ×10	7-0	2	6-1	2	5-5	2
	2-2 ×12	8-1	2	7-0	2	6-3	2
	3-2 × 8	7-2	1	6-3	1	5-7	2
	3-2 ×10	8-9	1	7-7	2	6-9	2
	3-2 ×12	10-2	2	8-10	2	7-10	2
	4-2 × 8	9-0	1	7-8	1	6-9	1
	4-2 ×10	10-1	1	8-9	1	7-10	2
	4-2 ×12	11-9	1	10-2	2	9-1	2
Two Floors	2-2 × 4	2-2	1	1-10	1	1-7	1
	2-2 × 6	3-2	2	2-9	2	2-5	2
	2-2 × 8	4-1	2	3-6	2	3-2	2
	2-2 ×10	4-11	2	4-3	2	3-10	3
	2-2 ×12	5-9	2	5-0	3	4-5	3
	3-2 × 8	5-1	2	4-5	2	3-11	2
	3-2 ×10	6-2	2	5-4	2	4-10	2
	3-2 ×12	7-2	2	6-3	2	5-7	3
	4-2 × 8	6-1	1	5-3	2	4-8	2
	4-2 ×10	7-2	2	6-2	2	5-6	2
	4-2 ×12	8-4	2	7-2	2	6-5	2

For SI: 1 inch = 25.4 mm, 1 foot = 304.8 mm.

a. Spans are given in feet and inches (ft-in).

b. Tabulated values are for No. 2 grade lumber.

c. Building width is measured perpendicular to the ridge. For widths between those shown, spans are permitted to be interpolated.

d. NJ - Number of jack studs required to support each end. Where the number of required jack studs equals one, the headers are permitted to be supported by an approved framing anchor attached to the full-height wall stud and to the header.

2308.9.7 Openings in interior nonbearing partitions. Openings in nonbearing partitions are permitted to be framed with single studs and headers. Each end of a lintel or header shall have a length of bearing of not less than $1^1/_2$ inches (38 mm) for the full width of the lintel.

2308.9.8 Pipes in walls. Stud partitions containing plumbing, heating or other pipes shall be so framed and the joists underneath so spaced as to give proper clearance for the piping. Where a partition containing such piping runs parallel to the floor joists, the joists underneath such partitions shall be doubled and spaced to *permit* the passage of such pipes and shall be bridged. Where plumbing, heating or other pipes are placed in or partly in a partition, necessitating the cutting of the soles or plates, a metal tie not less than 0.058 inch (1.47 mm) (16 galvanized gage) and $1^1/_2$ inches (38 mm) wide shall be fastened to each plate across and to each side of the opening with not less than six 16d nails.

2308.9.9 Bridging. Unless covered by interior or *exterior wall coverings* or sheathing meeting the minimum requirements of this code, stud partitions or walls with studs having a height-to-least-thickness ratio exceeding 50 shall have bridging not less than 2 inches (51 mm) in thickness and of the same width as the studs fitted snugly and nailed thereto to provide adequate lateral support. Bridging shall be placed in every stud cavity and at a frequency such that no stud so braced shall have a height-to-least-thickness ratio exceeding 50 with the height of the stud measured between horizontal framing and bridging or between bridging, whichever is greater.

2308.9.10 Cutting and notching. In exterior walls and bearing partitions, any wood stud is permitted to be cut or notched to a depth not exceeding 25 percent of its width. Cutting or notching of studs to a depth not greater than 40 percent of the width of the stud is permitted in nonbearing partitions supporting no loads other than the weight of the partition.

2308.9.11 Bored holes. A hole not greater in diameter than 40 percent of the stud width is permitted to be bored in any wood stud. Bored holes not greater than 60 percent of the width of the stud are permitted in nonbearing partitions or in any wall where each bored stud is doubled, provided not more than two such successive doubled studs are so bored.

In no case shall the edge of the bored hole be nearer than $^5/_8$ inch (15.9 mm) to the edge of the stud.

Bored holes shall not be located at the same section of stud as a cut or notch.

2308.10 Roof and ceiling framing. The framing details required in this section apply to roofs having a minimum slope of three units vertical in 12 units horizontal (25-percent slope) or greater. Where the roof slope is less than three units vertical in 12 units horizontal (25-percent slope), members supporting rafters and ceiling joists such as ridge board, hips and valleys shall be designed as beams.

2308.10.1 Wind uplift. The roof construction shall have rafter and truss ties to the wall below. Resultant uplift loads shall be transferred to the foundation using a continuous load path. The rafter or truss to wall connection shall comply with Tables 2304.9.1 and 2308.10.1.

2308.10.2 Ceiling joist spans. Allowable spans for ceiling joists shall be in accordance with Table 2308.10.2(1) or 2308.10.2(2). For other grades and species, refer to the *AF&PA Span Tables for Joists and Rafters*.

2308.10.3 Rafter spans. Allowable spans for rafters shall be in accordance with Table 2308.10.3(1), 2308.10.3(2), 2308.10.3(3), 2308.10.3(4), 2308.10.3(5) or 2308.10.3(6). For other grades and species, refer to the *AF&PA Span Tables for Joists and Rafters*.

2308.10.4 Ceiling joist and rafter framing. Rafters shall be framed directly opposite each other at the ridge. There shall be a ridge board at least 1-inch (25 mm) nominal thickness at ridges and not less in depth than the cut end of the rafter. At valleys and hips, there shall be a single valley or hip rafter not less than 2-inch (51 mm) nominal thickness and not less in depth than the cut end of the rafter.

2308.10.4.1 Ceiling joist and rafter connections. Ceiling joists and rafters shall be nailed to each other and the assembly shall be nailed to the top wall plate in accordance with Tables 2304.9.1 and 2308.10.1. Ceiling joists shall be continuous or securely joined where they meet over interior partitions and fastened to adjacent rafters in accordance with Tables 2308.10.4.1 and 2304.9.1 to provide a continuous rafter tie across the building where such joists are parallel to the rafters. Ceiling joists shall have a bearing surface of not less than $1^1/_2$ inches (38 mm) on the top plate at each end.

Where ceiling joists are not parallel to rafters, an equivalent rafter tie shall be installed in a manner to provide a continuous tie across the building, at a spacing of not more than 4 feet (1219 mm) o.c. The connections shall be in accordance with Tables 2308.10.4.1 and 2304.9.1, or connections of equivalent capacities shall be provided. Where ceiling joists or rafter ties are not provided at the top of the rafter support walls, the ridge formed by these rafters shall also be supported by a girder conforming to Section 2308.4.

Rafter ties shall be spaced not more than 4 feet (1219 mm) o.c. Rafter tie connections shall be based on the equivalent rafter spacing in Table 2308.10.4.1. Where rafter ties are spaced at 32 inches (813 mm) o.c., the number of 16d common nails shall be two times the number specified for rafters spaced 16 inches (406 mm) o.c., with a minimum of four 16d common nails where no snow loads are indicated. Where rafter ties are spaced at 48 inches (1219 mm) o.c., the number of 16d common nails shall be two times the number specified for rafters spaced 24 inches (610 mm) o.c., with a minimum of six 16d common nails where no snow loads are indicated. Rafter/ceiling joist connections and rafter/tie connections shall be of sufficient size and number to prevent splitting from nailing.

TABLE 2308.10.1
REQUIRED RATING OF APPROVED UPLIFT CONNECTORS (pounds)[a, b, c, e, f, g, h]

BASIC WIND SPEED (3-second gust)	ROOF SPAN (feet)							OVERHANGS (pounds/feet)[d]
	12	20	24	28	32	36	40	
85	-72	-120	-145	-169	-193	-217	-241	-38.55
90	-91	-151	-181	-212	-242	-272	-302	-43.22
100	-131	-281	-262	-305	-349	-393	-436	-53.36
110	-175	-292	-351	-409	-467	-526	-584	-64.56

For SI: 1 inch = 25.4 mm, 1 foot = 304.8 mm, 1 mile per hour = 1.61 km/hr, 1 pound = 0.454 Kg, 1 pound per foot = 14.5939 N/m.

a. The uplift connection requirements are based on a 30-foot mean roof height located in Exposure B. For Exposure C or D and for other mean roof heights, multiply the above loads by the adjustment coefficients below.

EXPOSURE	Mean Roof Height (feet)									
	15	20	25	30	35	40	45	50	55	60
B	1.00	1.00	1.00	1.00	1.05	1.09	1.12	1.16	1.19	1.22
C	1.21	1.29	1.35	1.40	1.45	1.49	1.53	1.56	1.59	1.62
D	1.47	1.55	1.61	1.66	1.70	1.74	1.78	1.81	1.84	1.87

b. The uplift connection requirements are based on the framing being spaced 24 inches on center. Multiply by 0.67 for framing spaced 16 inches on center and multiply by 0.5 for framing spaced 12 inches on center.

c. The uplift connection requirements include an allowance for 10 pounds of dead load.

d. The uplift connection requirements do not account for the effects of overhangs. The magnitude of the above loads shall be increased by adding the overhang loads found in the table. The overhang loads are also based on framing spaced 24 inches on center. The overhang loads given shall be multiplied by the overhang projection and added to the roof uplift value in the table.

e. The uplift connection requirements are based upon wind loading on end zones as defined in Figure 6-2 of ASCE 7. Connection loads for connections located a distance of 20 percent of the least horizontal dimension of the building from the corner of the building are permitted to be reduced by multiplying the table connection value by 0.7 and multiplying the overhang load by 0.8.

f. For wall-to-wall and wall-to-foundation connections, the capacity of the uplift connector is permitted to be reduced by 100 pounds for each full wall above. (For example, if a 500-pound rated connector is used on the roof framing, a 400-pound rated connector is permitted at the next floor level down).

g. Interpolation is permitted for intermediate values of basic wind speeds and roof spans.

h. The rated capacity of approved tie-down devices is permitted to include up to a 60-percent increase for wind effects where allowed by material specifications.

2308.10.4.2 Notches and holes. Notching at the ends of rafters or ceiling joists shall not exceed one-fourth the depth. Notches in the top or bottom of the rafter or ceiling joist shall not exceed one-sixth the depth and shall not be located in the middle one-third of the span, except that a notch not exceeding one-third of the depth is permitted in the top of the rafter or ceiling joist not further from the face of the support than the depth of the member.

Holes bored in rafters or ceiling joists shall not be within 2 inches (51 mm) of the top and bottom and their diameter shall not exceed one-third the depth of the member.

2308.10.4.3 Framing around openings. Trimmer and header rafters shall be doubled, or of lumber of equivalent cross section, where the span of the header exceeds 4 feet (1219 mm). The ends of header rafters more than 6 feet (1829 mm) long shall be supported by framing anchors or rafter hangers unless bearing on a beam, partition or wall.

2308.10.5 Purlins. Purlins to support roof loads are permitted to be installed to reduce the span of rafters within allowable limits and shall be supported by struts to bearing walls. The maximum span of 2-inch by 4-inch (51 mm by 102 mm) purlins shall be 4 feet (1219 mm). The maximum span of the 2-inch by 6-inch (51 mm by 152 mm) purlin shall be 6 feet (1829 mm), but in no case shall the purlin be smaller than the supported rafter. Struts shall not be smaller than 2-inch by 4-inch (51 mm by 102 mm) members. The unbraced length of struts shall not exceed 8 feet (2438 mm) and the minimum slope of the struts shall not be less than 45 degrees (0.79 rad) from the horizontal.

2308.10.6 Blocking. Roof rafters and ceiling joists shall be supported laterally to prevent rotation and lateral displacement in accordance with the provisions of Section 2308.8.5.

2308.10.7 Engineered wood products. Prefabricated wood I-joists, structural glued-laminated timber and structural composite lumber shall not be notched or drilled except where permitted by the manufacturer's recommendations or where the effects of such alterations are specifically considered in the design of the member by a *registered design professional*.

2308.10.8 Roof sheathing. Roof sheathing shall be in accordance with Tables 2304.7(3) and 2304.7(5) for wood structural panels, and Tables 2304.7(1) and 2304.7(2) for lumber and shall comply with Section 2304.7.2.

2308.10.8.1 Joints. Joints in lumber sheathing shall occur over supports unless *approved* end-matched lumber is used, in which case each piece shall bear on at least two supports.

TABLE 2308.10.2(1)
CEILING JOIST SPANS FOR COMMON LUMBER SPECIES
(Uninhabitable Attics Without Storage, Live Load = 10 pounds per square foot, L/Δ = 240)

CEILING JOIST SPACING (inches)	SPECIES AND GRADE		DEAD LOAD = 5 psf			
			2 × 4	2 × 6	2 × 8	2 × 10
			Maximum ceiling joist spans			
			(ft. - in.)	(ft. - in.)	(ft. - in.)	(ft. - in.)
12	Douglas Fir-Larch	SS	13-2	20-8	Note a	Note a
	Douglas Fir-Larch	#1	12-8	19-11	Note a	Note a
	Douglas Fir-Larch	#2	12-5	19-6	25-8	Note a
	Douglas Fir-Larch	#3	10-10	15-10	20-1	24-6
	Hem-Fir	SS	12-5	19-6	25-8	Note a
	Hem-Fir	#1	12-2	19-1	25-2	Note a
	Hem-Fir	#2	11-7	18-2	24-0	Note a
	Hem-Fir	#3	10-10	15-10	20-1	24-6
	Southern Pine	SS	12-11	20-3	Note a	Note a
	Southern Pine	#1	12-8	19-11	Note a	Note a
	Southern Pine	#2	12-5	19-6	25-8	Note a
	Southern Pine	#3	11-6	17-0	21-8	25-7
	Spruce-Pine-Fir	SS	12-2	19-1	25-2	Note a
	Spruce-Pine-Fir	#1	11-10	18-8	24-7	Note a
	Spruce-Pine-Fir	#2	11-10	18-8	24-7	Note a
	Spruce-Pine-Fir	#3	10-10	15-10	20-1	24-6
16	Douglas Fir-Larch	SS	11-11	18-9	24-8	Note a
	Douglas Fir-Larch	#1	11-6	18-1	23-10	Note a
	Douglas Fir-Larch	#2	11-3	17-8	23-0	Note a
	Douglas Fir-Larch	#3	9-5	13-9	17-5	21-3
	Hem-Fir	SS	11-3	17-8	23-4	Note a
	Hem-Fir	#1	11-0	17-4	22-10	Note a
	Hem-Fir	#2	10-6	16-6	21-9	Note a
	Hem-Fir	#3	9-5	13-9	17-5	21-3
	Southern Pine	SS	11-9	18-5	24-3	Note a
	Southern Pine	#1	11-6	18-1	23-1	Note a
	Southern Pine	#2	11-3	17-8	23-4	Note a
	Southern Pine	#3	10-0	14-9	18-9	22-2
	Spruce-Pine-Fir	SS	11-0	17-4	22-10	Note a
	Spruce-Pine-Fir	#1	10-9	16-11	22-4	Note a
	Spruce-Pine-Fir	#2	10-9	16-11	22-4	Note a
	Spruce-Pine-Fir	#3	9-5	13-9	17-5	21-3

(continued)

TABLE 2308.10.2(1)—continued
CEILING JOIST SPANS FOR COMMON LUMBER SPECIES
(Uninhabitable Attics Without Storage, Live Load = 10 pounds per square foot, L/Δ = 240)

CEILING JOIST SPACING (inches)	SPECIES AND GRADE		DEAD LOAD = 5 psf			
			2 × 4	2 × 6	2 × 8	2 × 10
			Maximum ceiling joist spans			
			(ft. - in.)	(ft. - in.)	(ft. - in.)	(ft. - in.)
19.2	Douglas Fir-Larch	SS	11-3	17-8	23-3	Note a
	Douglas Fir-Larch	#1	10-10	17-0	22-5	Note a
	Douglas Fir-Larch	#2	10-7	16-7	21-0	25-8
	Douglas Fir-Larch	#3	8-7	12-6	15-10	19-5
	Hem-Fir	SS	10-7	16-8	21-11	Note a
	Hem-Fir	#1	10-4	16-4	21-6	Note a
	Hem-Fir	#2	9-11	15-7	20-6	25-3
	Hem-Fir	#3	8-7	12-6	15-10	19-5
	Southern Pine	SS	11-0	17-4	22-10	Note a
	Southern Pine	#1	10-10	17-0	22-5	Note a
	Southern Pine	#2	10-7	16-8	21-11	Note a
	Southern Pine	#3	9-1	13-6	17-2	20-3
	Spruce-Pine-Fir	SS	10-4	16-4	21-6	Note a
	Spruce-Pine-Fir	#1	10-2	15-11	21-0	25-8
	Spruce-Pine-Fir	#2	10-2	15-11	21-0	25-8
	Spruce-Pine-Fir	#3	8-7	12-6	15-10	19-5
24	Douglas Fir-Larch	SS	10-5	16-4	21-7	Note a
	Douglas Fir-Larch	#1	10-0	15-9	20-1	24-6
	Douglas Fir-Larch	#2	9-10	14-10	18-9	22-11
	Douglas Fir-Larch	#3	7-8	11-2	14-2	17-4
	Hem-Fir	SS	9-10	15-6	20-5	Note a
	Hem-Fir	#1	9-8	15-2	19-7	23-11
	Hem-Fir	#2	9-2	14-5	18-6	22-7
	Hem-Fir	#3	7-8	11-2	14-2	17-4
	Southern Pine	SS	10-3	16-1	21-2	Note a
	Southern Pine	#1	10-0	15-9	20-10	Note a
	Southern Pine	#2	9-10	15-6	20-1	23-11
	Southern Pine	#3	8-2	12-0	15-4	18-1
	Spruce-Pine-Fir	SS	9-8	15-2	19-11	25-5
	Spruce-Pine-Fir	#1	9-5	14-9	18-9	22-11
	Spruce-Pine-Fir	#2	9-5	14-9	18-9	22-11
	Spruce-Pine-Fir	#3	7-8	11-2	14-2	17-4

For SI: 1 inch = 25.4 mm, 1 foot = 304.8 mm, 1 pound per square foot = 47.8 N/m^2.

a. Span exceeds 26 feet in length. Check sources for availability of lumber in lengths greater than 20 feet.

TABLE 2308.10.2(2)
CEILING JOIST SPANS FOR COMMON LUMBER SPECIES
(Uninhabitable Attics With Limited Storage, Live Load = 20 pounds per square foot, L/Δ = 240)

CEILING JOIST SPACING (inches)	SPECIES AND GRADE		DEAD LOAD = 10 psf			
			2 × 4	2 × 6	2 × 8	2 × 10
			Maximum ceiling joist spans			
			(ft. - in.)	(ft. - in.)	(ft. - in.)	(ft. - in.)
12	Douglas Fir-Larch	SS	10-5	16-4	21-7	Note a
	Douglas Fir-Larch	#1	10-0	15-9	20-1	24-6
	Douglas Fir-Larch	#2	9-10	14-10	18-9	22-11
	Douglas Fir-Larch	#3	7-8	11-2	14-2	17-4
	Hem-Fir	SS	9-10	15-6	20-5	Note a
	Hem-Fir	#1	9-8	15-2	19-7	23-11
	Hem-Fir	#2	9-2	14-5	18-6	22-7
	Hem-Fir	#3	7-8	11-2	14-2	17-4
	Southern Pine	SS	10-3	16-1	21-2	Note a
	Southern Pine	#1	10-0	15-9	20-10	Note a
	Southern Pine	#2	9-10	15-6	20-1	23-11
	Southern Pine	#3	8-2	12-0	15-4	18-1
	Spruce-Pine-Fir	SS	9-8	15-2	19-11	25-5
	Spruce-Pine-Fir	#1	9-5	14-9	18-9	22-11
	Spruce-Pine-Fir	#2	9-5	14-9	18-9	22-11
	Spruce-Pine-Fir	#3	7-8	11-2	14-2	17-4
16	Douglas Fir-Larch	SS	9-6	14-11	19-7	25-0
	Douglas Fir-Larch	#1	9-1	13-9	17-5	21-3
	Douglas Fir-Larch	#2	8-9	12-10	16-3	19-10
	Douglas Fir-Larch	#3	6-8	9-8	12-4	15-0
	Hem-Fir	SS	8-11	14-1	18-6	23-8
	Hem-Fir	#1	8-9	13-5	16-10	20-8
	Hem-Fir	#2	8-4	12-8	16-0	19-7
	Hem-Fir	#3	6-8	9-8	12-4	15-0
	Southern Pine	SS	9-4	14-7	19-3	24-7
	Southern Pine	#1	9-1	14-4	18-11	23-1
	Southern Pine	#2	8-11	13-6	17-5	20-9
	Southern Pine	#3	7-1	10-5	13-3	15-8
	Spruce-Pine-Fir	SS	8-9	13-9	18-1	23-1
	Spruce-Pine-Fir	#1	8-7	12-10	16-3	19-10
	Spruce-Pine-Fir	#2	8-7	12-10	16-3	19-10
	Spruce-Pine-Fir	#3	6-8	9-8	12-4	15-0

(continued)

TABLE 2308.10.2(2)—continued
CEILING JOIST SPANS FOR COMMON LUMBER SPECIES
(Uninhabitable Attics With Limited Storage, Live Load = 20 pounds per square foot, L/Δ = 240)

CEILING JOIST SPACING (inches)	SPECIES AND GRADE		DEAD LOAD = 10 psf			
			2 × 4	2 × 6	2 × 8	2 × 10
			Maximum ceiling joist spans			
			(ft. - in.)	(ft. - in.)	(ft. - in.)	(ft. - in.)
19.2	Douglas Fir-Larch	SS	8-11	14-0	18-5	23-4
	Douglas Fir-Larch	#1	8-7	12-6	15-10	19-5
	Douglas Fir-Larch	#2	8-0	11-9	14-10	18-2
	Douglas Fir-Larch	#3	6-1	8-10	11-3	13-8
	Hem-Fir	SS	8-5	13-3	17-5	22-3
	Hem-Fir	#1	8-3	12-3	15-6	18-11
	Hem-Fir	#2	7-10	11-7	14-8	17-10
	Hem-Fir	#3	6-1	8-10	11-3	13-8
	Southern Pine	SS	8-9	13-9	18-1	23-1
	Southern Pine	#1	8-7	13-6	17-9	21-1
	Southern Pine	#2	8-5	12-3	15-10	18-11
	Southern Pine	#3	6-5	9-6	12-1	14-4
	Spruce-Pine-Fir	SS	8-3	12-11	17-1	21-8
	Spruce-Pine-Fir	#1	8-0	11-9	14-10	18-2
	Spruce-Pine-Fir	#2	8-0	11-9	14-10	18-2
	Spruce-Pine-Fir	#3	6-1	8-10	11-3	13-8
24	Douglas Fir-Larch	SS	8-3	13-0	17-1	20-11
	Douglas Fir-Larch	#1	7-8	11-2	14-2	17-4
	Douglas Fir-Larch	#2	7-2	10-6	13-3	16-3
	Douglas Fir-Larch	#3	5-5	7-11	10-0	12-3
	Hem-Fir	SS	7-10	12-3	16-2	20-6
	Hem-Fir	#1	7-6	10-11	13-10	16-11
	Hem-Fir	#2	7-1	10-4	13-1	16-0
	Hem-Fir	#3	5-5	7-11	10-0	12-3
	Southern Pine	SS	8-1	12-9	16-10	21-6
	Southern Pine	#1	8-0	12-6	15-10	18-10
	Southern Pine	#2	7-8	11-0	14-2	16-11
	Southern Pine	#3	5-9	8-6	10-10	12-10
	Spruce-Pine-Fir	SS	7-8	12-0	15-10	19-5
	Spruce-Pine-Fir	#1	7-2	10-6	13-3	16-3
	Spruce-Pine-Fir	#2	7-2	10-6	13-3	16-3
	Spruce-Pine-Fir	#3	5-5	7-11	10-0	12-3

For SI: 1 inch = 25.4 mm, 1 foot = 304.8 mm, 1 pound per square foot = 47.8 N/m^2.

a. Span exceeds 26 feet in length. Check sources for availability of lumber in lengths greater than 20 feet.

TABLE 2308.10.3(1)
RAFTER SPANS FOR COMMON LUMBER SPECIES
(Roof Live Load = 20 pounds per square foot, Ceiling Not Attached to Rafters, L/Δ = 180)

RAFTER SPACING (inches)	SPECIES AND GRADE		DEAD LOAD = 10 pounds psf					DEAD LOAD = 20 psf				
			2 × 4	2 × 6	2 × 8	2 × 10	2 × 12	2 × 4	2 × 6	2 × 8	2 × 10	2 × 12
			Maximum rafter spans									
			(ft. - in.)	(ft. - in.)	(ft. - in.)	(ft. - in.)	(ft. - in.)	(ft. - in.)	(ft. - in.)	(ft. - in.)	(ft. - in.)	(ft. - in.)
12	Douglas Fir-Larch	SS	11-6	18-0	23-9	Note a	Note a	11-6	18-0	23-5	Note a	Note a
	Douglas Fir-Larch	#1	11-1	17-4	22-5	Note a	Note a	10-6	15-4	19-5	23-9	Note a
	Douglas Fir-Larch	#2	10-10	16-7	21-0	25-8	Note a	9-10	14-4	18-2	22-3	25-9
	Douglas Fir-Larch	#3	8-7	12-6	15-10	19-5	22-6	7-5	10-10	13-9	16-9	19-6
	Hem-Fir	SS	10-10	17-0	22-5	Note a	Note a	10-10	17-0	22-5	Note a	Note a
	Hem-Fir	#1	10-7	16-8	21-10	Note a	Note a	10-3	14-11	18-11	23-2	Note a
	Hem-Fir	#2	10-1	15-11	20-8	25-3	Note a	9-8	14-2	17-11	21-11	25-5
	Hem-Fir	#3	8-7	12-6	15-10	19-5	22-6	7-5	10-10	13-9	16-9	19-6
	Southern Pine	SS	11-3	17-8	23-4	Note a	Note a	11-3	17-8	23-4	Note a	Note a
	Southern Pine	#1	11-1	17-4	22-11	Note a	Note a	11-1	17-3	21-9	25-10	Note a
	Southern Pine	#2	10-10	17-0	22-5	Note a	Note a	10-6	15-1	19-5	23-2	Note a
	Southern Pine	#3	9-1	13-6	17-2	20-3	24-1	7-11	11-8	14-10	17-6	20-11
	Spruce-Pine-Fir	SS	10-7	16-8	21-11	Note a	Note a	10-7	16-8	21-9	Note a	Note a
	Spruce-Pine-Fir	#1	10-4	16-3	21-0	25-8	Note a	9-10	14-4	18-2	22-3	25-9
	Spruce-Pine-Fir	#2	10-4	16-3	21-0	25-8	Note a	9-10	14-4	18-2	22-3	25-9
	Spruce-Pine-Fir	#3	8-7	12-6	15-10	19-5	22-6	7-5	10-10	13-9	16-9	19-6
16	Douglas Fir-Larch	SS	10-5	16-4	21-7	Note a	Note a	10-5	16-0	20-3	24-9	Note a
	Douglas Fir-Larch	#1	10-0	15-4	19-5	23-9	Note a	9-1	13-3	16-10	20-7	23-10
	Douglas Fir-Larch	#2	9-10	14-4	18-2	22-3	25-9	8-6	12-5	15-9	19-3	22-4
	Douglas Fir-Larch	#3	7-5	10-10	13-9	16-9	19-6	6-5	9-5	11-11	14-6	16-10
	Hem-Fir	SS	9-10	15-6	20-5	Note a	Note a	9-10	15-6	19-11	24-4	Note a
	Hem-Fir	#1	9-8	14-11	18-11	23-2	Note a	8-10	12-11	16-5	20-0	23-3
	Hem-Fir	#2	9-2	14-2	17-11	21-11	25-5	8-5	12-3	15-6	18-11	22-0
	Hem-Fir	#3	7-5	10-10	13-9	16-9	19-6	6-5	9-5	11-11	14-6	16-10
	Southern Pine	SS	10-3	16-1	21-2	Note a	Note a	10-3	16-1	21-2	Note a	Note a
	Southern Pine	#1	10-0	15-9	20-10	25-10	Note a	10-0	15-0	18-10	22-4	Note a
	Southern Pine	#2	9-10	15-1	19-5	23-2	Note a	9-1	13-0	16-10	20-1	23-7
	Southern Pine	#3	7-11	11-8	14-10	17-6	20-11	6-10	10-1	12-10	15-2	18-1
	Spruce-Pine-Fir	SS	9-8	15-2	19-11	25-5	Note a	9-8	14-10	18-10	23-0	Note a
	Spruce-Pine-Fir	#1	9-5	14-4	18-2	22-3	25-9	8-6	12-5	15-9	19-3	22-4
	Spruce-Pine-Fir	#2	9-5	14-4	18-2	22-3	25-9	8-6	12-5	15-9	19-3	22-4
	Spruce-Pine-Fir	#3	7-5	10-10	13-9	16-9	19-6	6-5	9-5	11-11	14-6	16-10

(continued)

TABLE 2308.10.3(1)—continued
RAFTER SPANS FOR COMMON LUMBER SPECIES
(Roof Live Load = 20 pounds per square foot, Ceiling Not Attached to Rafters, $L/\Delta = 180$)

RAFTER SPACING (inches)	SPECIES AND GRADE		DEAD LOAD = 10 pounds psf					DEAD LOAD = 20 pounds psf				
			2 × 4	2 × 6	2 × 8	2 × 10	2 × 12	2 × 4	2 × 6	2 × 8	2 × 10	2 × 12
			Maximum rafter spans									
			(ft. - in.)	(ft. - in.)	(ft. - in.)	(ft. - in.)	(ft. - in.)	(ft. - in.)	(ft. - in.)	(ft. - in.)	(ft. - in.)	(ft. - in.)
19.2	Douglas Fir-Larch	SS	9-10	15-5	20-4	25-11	Note a	9-10	14-7	18-6	22-7	Note a
	Douglas Fir-Larch	#1	9-5	14-0	17-9	21-8	25-2	8-4	12-2	15-4	18-9	21-9
	Douglas Fir-Larch	#2	8-11	13-1	16-7	20-3	23-6	7-9	11-4	14-4	17-7	20-4
	Douglas Fir-Larch	#3	6-9	9-11	12-7	15-4	17-9	5-10	8-7	10-10	13-3	15-5
	Hem-Fir	SS	9-3	14-7	19-2	24-6	Note a	9-3	14-4	18-2	22-3	25-9
	Hem-Fir	#1	9-1	13-8	17-4	21-1	24-6	8-1	11-10	15-0	18-4	21-3
	Hem-Fir	#2	8-8	12-11	16-4	20-0	23-2	7-8	11-2	14-2	17-4	20-1
	Hem-Fir	#3	6-9	9-11	12-7	15-4	17-9	5-10	8-7	10-10	13-3	15-5
	Southern Pine	SS	9-8	15-2	19-11	25-5	Note a	9-8	15-2	19-11	25-5	Note a
	Southern Pine	#1	9-5	14-10	19-7	23-7	Note a	9-3	13-8	17-2	20-5	24-4
	Southern Pine	#2	9-3	13-9	17-9	21-2	24-10	8-4	11-11	15-4	18-4	21-6
	Southern Pine	#3	7-3	10-8	13-7	16-0	19-1	6-3	9-3	11-9	13-10	16-6
	Spruce-Pine-Fir	SS	9-1	14-3	18-9	23-11	Note a	9-1	13-7	17-2	21-0	24-4
	Spruce-Pine-Fir	#1	8-10	13-1	16-7	20-3	23-6	7-9	11-4	14-4	17-7	20-4
	Spruce-Pine-Fir	#2	8-10	13-1	16-7	20-3	23-6	7-9	11-4	14-4	17-7	20-4
	Spruce-Pine-Fir	#3	6-9	9-11	12-7	15-4	17-9	5-10	8-7	10-10	13-3	15-5
24	Douglas Fir-Larch	SS	9-1	14-4	18-10	23-4	Note a	8-11	13-1	16-7	20-3	23-5
	Douglas Fir-Larch	#1	8-7	12-6	15-10	19-5	22-6	7-5	10-10	13-9	16-9	19-6
	Douglas Fir-Larch	#2	8-0	11-9	14-10	18-2	21-0	6-11	10-2	12-10	15-8	18-3
	Douglas Fir-Larch	#3	6-1	8-10	11-3	13-8	15-11	5-3	7-8	9-9	11-10	13-9
	Hem-Fir	SS	8-7	13-6	17-10	22-9	Note a	8-7	12-10	16-3	19-10	23-0
	Hem-Fir	#1	8-4	12-3	15-6	18-11	21-11	7-3	10-7	13-5	16-4	19-0
	Hem-Fir	#2	7-11	11-7	14-8	17-10	20-9	6-10	10-0	12-8	15-6	17-11
	Hem-Fir	#3	6-1	8-10	11-3	13-8	15-11	5-3	7-8	9-9	11-10	13-9
	Southern Pine	SS	8-11	14-1	18-6	23-8	Note a	8-11	14-1	18-6	22-11	Note a
	Southern Pine	#1	8-9	13-9	17-9	21-1	25-2	8-3	12-3	15-4	18-3	21-9
	Southern Pine	#2	8-7	12-3	15-10	18-11	22-2	7-5	10-8	13-9	16-5	19-3
	Southern Pine	#3	6-5	9-6	12-1	14-4	17-1	5-7	8-3	10-6	12-5	14-9
	Spruce-Pine-Fir	SS	8-5	13-3	17-5	21-8	25-2	8-4	12-2	15-4	18-9	21-9
	Spruce-Pine-Fir	#1	8-0	11-9	14-10	18-2	21-0	6-11	10-2	12-10	15-8	18-3
	Spruce-Pine-Fir	#2	8-0	11-9	14-10	18-2	21-0	6-11	10-2	12-10	15-8	18-3
	Spruce-Pine-Fir	#3	6-1	8-10	11-3	13-8	15-11	5-3	7-8	9-9	11-10	13-9

For SI: 1 inch = 25.4 mm, 1 foot = 304.8 mm, 1 pound per square foot = 47.9 N/m^2.

a. Span exceeds 26 feet in length. Check sources for availability of lumber in lengths greater than 20 feet.

TABLE 2308.10.3(2)
RAFTER SPANS FOR COMMON LUMBER SPECIES
(Roof Live Load = 20 pounds per square foot, Ceiling Not Attached to Rafters, L/Δ = 240)

RAFTER SPACING (inches)	SPECIES AND GRADE		DEAD LOAD = 10 pounds psf					DEAD LOAD = 20 pounds psf				
			2 × 4	2 × 6	2 × 8	2 × 10	2 × 12	2 × 4	2 × 6	2 × 8	2 × 10	2 × 12
			Maximum rafter spans									
			(ft. - in.)	(ft. - in.)	(ft. - in.)	(ft. - in.)	(ft. - in.)	(ft. - in.)	(ft. - in.)	(ft. - in.)	(ft. - in.)	(ft. - in.)
12	Douglas Fir-Larch	SS	10-5	16-4	21-7	Note a	Note a	10-5	16-4	21-7	Note a	Note a
	Douglas Fir-Larch	#1	10-0	15-9	20-10	Note a	Note a	10-0	15-4	19-5	23-9	Note a
	Douglas Fir-Larch	#2	9-10	15-6	20-5	25-8	Note a	9-10	14-4	18-2	22-3	25-9
	Douglas Fir-Larch	#3	8-7	12-6	15-10	19-5	22-6	7-5	10-10	13-9	16-9	19-6
	Hem-Fir	SS	9-10	15-6	20-5	Note a	Note a	9-10	15-6	20-5	Note a	Note a
	Hem-Fir	#1	9-8	15-2	19-11	25-5	Note a	9-8	14-11	18-11	23-2	Note a
	Hem-Fir	#2	9-2	14-5	19-0	24-3	Note a	9-2	14-2	17-11	21-11	25-5
	Hem-Fir	#3	8-7	12-6	15-10	19-5	22-6	7-5	10-10	13-9	16-9	19-6
	Southern Pine	SS	10-3	16-1	21-2	Note a	Note a	10-3	16-1	21-2	Note a	Note a
	Southern Pine	#1	10-0	15-9	20-10	Note a	Note a	10-0	15-9	20-10	25-10	Note a
	Southern Pine	#2	9-10	15-6	20-5	Note a	Note a	9-10	15-1	19-5	23-2	Note a
	Southern Pine	#3	9-1	13-6	17-2	20-3	24-1	7-11	11-8	14-10	17-6	20-11
	Spruce-Pine-Fir	SS	9-8	15-2	19-11	25-5	Note a	9-8	15-2	19-11	25-5	Note a
	Spruce-Pine-Fir	#1	9-5	14-9	19-6	24-10	Note a	9-5	14-4	18-2	22-3	25-9
	Spruce-Pine-Fir	#2	9-5	14-9	19-6	24-10	Note a	9-5	14-4	18-2	22-3	25-9
	Spruce-Pine-Fir	#3	8-7	12-6	15-10	19-5	22-6	7-5	10-10	13-9	16-9	19-6
16	Douglas Fir-Larch	SS	9-6	14-11	19-7	25-0	Note a	9-6	14-11	19-7	24-9	Note a
	Douglas Fir-Larch	#1	9-1	14-4	18-11	23-9	Note a	9-1	13-3	16-10	20-7	23-10
	Douglas Fir-Larch	#2	8-11	14-1	18-2	22-3	25-9	8-6	12-5	15-9	19-3	22-4
	Douglas Fir-Larch	#3	7-5	10-10	13-9	16-9	19-6	6-5	9-5	11-11	14-6	16-10
	Hem-Fir	SS	8-11	14-1	18-6	23-8	Note a	8-11	14-1	18-6	23-8	Note a
	Hem-Fir	#1	8-9	13-9	18-1	23-1	Note a	8-9	12-11	16-5	20-0	23-3
	Hem-Fir	#2	8-4	13-1	17-3	21-11	25-5	8-4	12-3	15-6	18-11	22-0
	Hem-Fir	#3	7-5	10-10	13-9	16-9	19-6	6-5	9-5	11-11	14-6	16-10
	Southern Pine	SS	9-4	14-7	19-3	24-7	Note a	9-4	14-7	19-3	24-7	Note a
	Southern Pine	#1	9-1	14-4	18-11	24-1	Note a	9-1	14-4	18-10	22-4	Note a
	Southern Pine	#2	8-11	14-1	18-6	23-2	Note a	8-11	13-0	16-10	20-1	23-7
	Southern Pine	#3	7-11	11-8	14-10	17-6	20-11	6-10	10-1	12-10	15-2	18-1
	Spruce-Pine-Fir	SS	8-9	13-9	18-1	23-1	Note a	8-9	13-9	18-1	23-0	Note a
	Spruce-Pine-Fir	#1	8-7	13-5	17-9	22-3	25-9	8-6	12-5	15-9	19-3	22-4
	Spruce-Pine-Fir	#2	8-7	13-5	17-9	22-3	25-9	8-6	12-5	15-9	19-3	22-4
	Spruce-Pine-Fir	#3	7-5	10-10	13-9	16-9	19-6	6-5	9-5	11-11	14-6	16-10

(continued)

TABLE 2308.10.3(2)—continued
RAFTER SPANS FOR COMMON LUMBER SPECIES
(Roof Live Load = 20 pounds per square foot, Ceiling Not Attached to Rafters, $L/\Delta = 240$)

RAFTER SPACING (inches)	SPECIES AND GRADE		DEAD LOAD = 10 pounds psf					DEAD LOAD = 20 pounds psf				
			2 × 4	2 × 6	2 × 8	2 × 10	2 × 12	2 × 4	2 × 6	2 × 8	2 × 10	2 × 12
			Maximum rafter spans									
			(ft. - in.)	(ft. - in.)	(ft. - in.)	(ft. - in.)	(ft. - in.)	(ft. - in.)	(ft. - in.)	(ft. - in.)	(ft. - in.)	(ft. - in.)
19.2	Douglas Fir-Larch	SS	8-11	14-0	18-5	23-7	Note a	8-11	14-0	18-5	22-7	Note a
	Douglas Fir-Larch	#1	8-7	13-6	17-9	21-8	25-2	8-4	12-2	15-4	18-9	21-9
	Douglas Fir-Larch	#2	8-5	13-1	16-7	20-3	23-6	7-9	11-4	14-4	17-7	20-4
	Douglas Fir-Larch	#3	6-9	9-11	12-7	15-4	17-9	5-10	8-7	10-10	13-3	15-5
	Hem-Fir	SS	8-5	13-3	17-5	22-3	Note a	8-5	13-3	17-5	22-3	25-9
	Hem-Fir	#1	8-3	12-11	17-1	21-1	24-6	8-1	11-10	15-0	18-4	21-3
	Hem-Fir	#2	7-10	12-4	16-3	20-0	23-2	7-8	11-2	14-2	17-4	20-1
	Hem-Fir	#3	6-9	9-11	12-7	15-4	17-9	5-10	8-7	10-10	13-3	15-5
	Southern Pine	SS	8-9	13-9	18-1	23-1	Note a	8-9	13-9	18-1	23-1	Note a
	Southern Pine	#1	8-7	13-6	17-9	22-8	Note a	8-7	13-6	17-2	20-5	24-4
	Southern Pine	#2	8-5	13-3	17-5	21-2	24-10	8-4	11-11	15-4	18-4	21-6
	Southern Pine	#3	7-3	10-8	13-7	16-0	19-1	6-3	9-3	11-9	13-10	16-6
	Spruce-Pine-Fir	SS	8-3	12-11	17-1	21-9	Note a	8-3	12-11	17-1	21-0	24-4
	Spruce-Pine-Fir	#1	8-1	12-8	16-7	20-3	23-6	7-9	11-4	14-4	17-7	20-4
	Spruce-Pine-Fir	#2	8-1	12-8	16-7	20-3	23-6	7-9	11-4	14-4	17-7	20-4
	Spruce-Pine-Fir	#3	6-9	9-11	12-7	15-4	17-9	5-10	8-7	10-10	13-3	15-5
24	Douglas Fir-Larch	SS	8-3	13-0	17-2	21-10	Note a	8-3	13-0	16-7	20-3	23-5
	Douglas Fir-Larch	#1	8-0	12-6	15-10	19-5	22-6	7-5	10-10	13-9	16-9	19-6
	Douglas Fir-Larch	#2	7-10	11-9	14-10	18-2	21-0	6-11	10-2	12-10	15-8	18-3
	Douglas Fir-Larch	#3	6-1	8-10	11-3	13-8	15-11	5-3	7-8	9-9	11-10	13-9
	Hem-Fir	SS	7-10	12-3	16-2	20-8	25-1	7-10	12-3	16-2	19-10	23-0
	Hem-Fir	#1	7-8	12-0	15-6	18-11	21-11	7-3	10-7	13-5	16-4	19-0
	Hem-Fir	#2	7-3	11-5	14-8	17-10	20-9	6-10	10-0	12-8	15-6	17-11
	Hem-Fir	#3	6-1	8-10	11-3	13-8	15-11	5-3	7-8	9-9	11-10	13-9
	Southern Pine	SS	8-1	12-9	16-10	21-6	Note a	8-1	12-9	16-10	21-6	Note a
	Southern Pine	#1	8-0	12-6	16-6	21-1	25-2	8-0	12-3	15-4	18-3	21-9
	Southern Pine	#2	7-10	12-3	15-10	18-11	22-2	7-5	10-8	13-9	16-5	19-3
	Southern Pine	#3	6-5	9-6	12-1	14-4	17-1	5-7	8-3	10-6	12-5	14-9
	Spruce-Pine-Fir	SS	7-8	12-0	15-10	20-2	24-7	7-8	12-0	15-4	18-9	21-9
	Spruce-Pine-Fir	#1	7-6	11-9	14-10	18-2	21-0	6-11	10-2	12-10	15-8	18-3
	Spruce-Pine-Fir	#2	7-6	11-9	14-10	18-2	21-0	6-11	10-2	12-10	15-8	18-3
	Spruce-Pine-Fir	#3	6-1	8-10	11-3	13-8	15-11	5-3	7-8	9-9	11-10	13-9

For SI: 1 inch = 25.4 mm, 1 foot = 304.8 mm, 1 pound per square foot = 47.9 N/m^2.

a. Span exceeds 26 feet in length. Check sources for availability of lumber in lengths greater than 20 feet.

TABLE 2308.10.3(3)
RAFTER SPANS FOR COMMON LUMBER SPECIES
(Ground Snow Load = 30 pounds per square foot, Ceiling Not Attached to Rafters, L/Δ = 180)

RAFTER SPACING (inches)	SPECIES AND GRADE		DEAD LOAD = 10 pounds psf					DEAD LOAD = 20 pounds psf				
			2 × 4	2 × 6	2 × 8	2 × 10	2 × 12	2 × 4	2 × 6	2 × 8	2 × 10	2 × 12
			Maximum rafter spans									
			(ft. - in.)	(ft. - in.)	(ft. - in.)	(ft. - in.)	(ft. - in.)	(ft. - in.)	(ft. - in.)	(ft. - in.)	(ft. - in.)	(ft. - in.)
12	Douglas Fir-Larch	SS	10-0	15-9	20-9	Note a	Note a	10-0	15-9	20-1	24-6	Note a
	Douglas Fir-Larch	#1	9-8	14-9	18-8	22-9	Note a	9-0	13-2	16-8	20-4	23-7
	Douglas Fir-Larch	#2	9-5	13-9	17-5	21-4	24-8	8-5	12-4	15-7	19-1	22-1
	Douglas Fir-Larch	#3	7-1	10-5	13-2	16-1	18-8	6-4	9-4	11-9	14-5	16-8
	Hem-Fir	SS	9-6	14-10	19-7	25-0	Note a	9-6	14-10	19-7	24-1	Note a
	Hem-Fir	#1	9-3	14-4	18-2	22-2	25-9	8-9	12-10	16-3	19-10	23-0
	Hem-Fir	#2	8-10	13-7	17-2	21-0	24-4	8-4	12-2	15-4	18-9	21-9
	Hem-Fir	#3	7-1	10-5	13-2	16-1	18-8	6-4	9-4	11-9	14-5	16-8
	Southern Pine	SS	9-10	15-6	20-5	Note a	Note a	9-10	15-6	20-5	Note a	Note a
	Southern Pine	#1	9-8	15-2	20-0	24-9	Note a	9-8	14-10	18-8	22-2	Note a
	Southern Pine	#2	9-6	14-5	18-8	22-3	Note a	9-0	12-11	16-8	19-11	23-4
	Southern Pine	#3	7-7	11-2	14-3	16-10	20-0	6-9	10-0	12-9	15-1	17-11
	Spruce-Pine-Fir	SS	9-3	14-7	19-2	24-6	Note a	9-3	14-7	18-8	22-9	Note a
	Spruce-Pine-Fir	#1	9-1	13-9	17-5	21-4	24-8	8-5	12-4	15-7	19-1	22-1
	Spruce-Pine-Fir	#2	9-1	13-9	17-5	21-4	24-8	8-5	12-4	15-7	19-1	22-1
	Spruce-Pine-Fir	#3	7-1	10-5	13-2	16-1	18-8	6-4	9-4	11-9	14-5	16-8
16	Douglas Fir-Larch	SS	9-1	14-4	18-10	23-9	Note a	9-1	13-9	17-5	21-3	24-8
	Douglas Fir-Larch	#1	8-9	12-9	16-2	19-9	22-10	7-10	11-5	14-5	17-8	20-5
	Douglas Fir-Larch	#2	8-2	11-11	15-1	18-5	21-5	7-3	10-8	13-6	16-6	19-2
	Douglas Fir-Larch	#3	6-2	9-0	11-5	13-11	16-2	5-6	8-1	10-3	12-6	14-6
	Hem-Fir	SS	8-7	13-6	17-10	22-9	Note a	8-7	13-6	17-1	20-10	24-2
	Hem-Fir	#1	8-5	12-5	15-9	19-3	22-3	7-7	11-1	14-1	17-2	19-11
	Hem-Fir	#2	8-0	11-9	14-11	18-2	21-1	7-2	10-6	13-4	16-3	18-10
	Hem-Fir	#3	6-2	9-0	11-5	13-11	16-2	5-6	8-1	10-3	12-6	14-6
	Southern Pine	SS	8-11	14-1	18-6	23-8	Note a	8-11	14-1	18-6	23-8	Note a
	Southern Pine	#1	8-9	13-9	18-1	21-5	25-7	8-8	12-10	16-2	19-2	22-10
	Southern Pine	#2	8-7	12-6	16-2	19-3	22-7	7-10	11-2	14-5	17-3	20-2
	Southern Pine	#3	6-7	9-8	12-4	14-7	17-4	5-10	8-8	11-0	13-0	15-6
	Spruce-Pine-Fir	SS	8-5	13-3	17-5	22-1	25-7	8-5	12-9	16-2	19-9	22-10
	Spruce-Pine-Fir	#1	8-2	11-11	15-1	18-5	21-5	7-3	10-8	13-6	16-6	19-2
	Spruce-Pine-Fir	#2	8-2	11-11	15-1	18-5	21-5	7-3	10-8	13-6	16-6	19-2
	Spruce-Pine-Fir	#3	6-2	9-0	11-5	13-11	16-2	5-6	8-1	10-3	12-6	14-6

(continued)

TABLE 2308.10.3(3)—continued
RAFTER SPANS FOR COMMON LUMBER SPECIES
(Ground Snow Load = 30 pounds per square foot, Ceiling Not Attached to Rafters, L/Δ = 180)

RAFTER SPACING (inches)	SPECIES AND GRADE		DEAD LOAD = 10 pounds psf					DEAD LOAD = 20 pounds psf				
			2 × 4	2 × 6	2 × 8	2 × 10	2 × 12	2 × 4	2 × 6	2 × 8	2 × 10	2 × 12
			Maximum rafter spans									
			(ft. - in.)	(ft. - in.)	(ft. - in.)	(ft. - in.)	(ft. - in.)	(ft. - in.)	(ft. - in.)	(ft. - in.)	(ft. - in.)	(ft. - in.)
19.2	Douglas Fir-Larch	SS	8-7	13-6	17-9	21-8	25-2	8-7	12-6	15-10	19-5	22-6
	Douglas Fir-Larch	#1	7-11	11-8	14-9	18-0	20-11	7-1	10-5	13-2	16-1	18-8
	Douglas Fir-Larch	#2	7-5	10-11	13-9	16-10	19-6	6-8	9-9	12-4	15-1	17-6
	Douglas Fir-Larch	#3	5-7	8-3	10-5	12-9	14-9	5-0	7-4	9-4	11-5	13-2
	Hem-Fir	SS	8-1	12-9	16-9	21-4	24-8	8-1	12-4	15-7	19-1	22-1
	Hem-Fir	#1	7-9	11-4	14-4	17-7	20-4	6-11	10-2	12-10	15-8	18-2
	Hem-Fir	#2	7-4	10-9	13-7	16-7	19-3	6-7	9-7	12-2	14-10	17-3
	Hem-Fir	#3	5-7	8-3	10-5	12-9	14-9	5-0	7-4	9-4	11-5	13-2
	Southern Pine	SS	8-5	13-3	17-5	22-3	Note a	8-5	13-3	17-5	22-0	25-9
	Southern Pine	#1	8-3	13-0	16-6	19-7	23-4	7-11	11-9	14-9	17-6	20-11
	Southern Pine	#2	7-11	11-5	14-9	17-7	20-7	7-1	10-2	13-2	15-9	18-5
	Southern Pine	#3	6-0	8-10	11-3	13-4	15-10	5-4	7-11	10-1	11-11	14-2
	Spruce-Pine-Fir	SS	7-11	12-5	16-5	20-2	23-4	7-11	11-8	14-9	18-0	20-11
	Spruce-Pine-Fir	#1	7-5	10-11	13-9	16-10	19-6	6-8	9-9	12-4	15-1	17-6
	Spruce-Pine-Fir	#2	7-5	10-11	13-9	16-10	19-6	6-8	9-9	12-4	15-1	17-6
	Spruce-Pine-Fir	#3	5-7	8-3	10-5	12-9	14-9	5-0	7-4	9-4	11-5	13-2
24	Douglas Fir-Larch	SS	7-11	12-6	15-10	19-5	22-6	7-8	11-3	14-2	17-4	20-1
	Douglas Fir-Larch	#1	7-1	10-5	13-2	16-1	18-8	6-4	9-4	11-9	14-5	16-8
	Douglas Fir-Larch	#2	6-8	9-9	12-4	15-1	17-6	5-11	8-8	11-0	13-6	15-7
	Douglas Fir-Larch	#3	5-0	7-4	9-4	11-5	13-2	4-6	6-7	8-4	10-2	11-10
	Hem-Fir	SS	7-6	11-10	15-7	19-1	22-1	7-6	11-0	13-11	17-0	19-9
	Hem-Fir	#1	6-11	10-2	12-10	15-8	18-2	6-2	9-1	11-6	14-0	16-3
	Hem-Fir	#2	6-7	9-7	12-2	14-10	17-3	5-10	8-7	10-10	13-3	15-5
	Hem-Fir	#3	5-0	7-4	9-4	11-5	13-2	4-6	6-7	8-4	10-2	11-10
	Southern Pine	SS	7-10	12-3	16-2	20-8	25-1	7-10	12-3	16-2	19-8	23-0
	Southern Pine	#1	7-8	11-9	14-9	17-6	20-11	7-1	10-6	13-2	15-8	18-8
	Southern Pine	#2	7-1	10-2	13-2	15-9	18-5	6-4	9-2	11-9	14-1	16-6
	Southern Pine	#3	5-4	7-11	10-1	11-11	14-2	4-9	7-1	9-0	10-8	12-8
	Spruce-Pine-Fir	SS	7-4	11-7	14-9	18-0	20-11	7-1	10-5	13-2	16-1	18-8
	Spruce-Pine-Fir	#1	6-8	9-9	12-4	15-1	17-6	5-11	8-8	11-0	13-6	15-7
	Spruce-Pine-Fir	#2	6-8	9-9	12-4	15-1	17-6	5-11	8-8	11-0	13-6	15-7
	Spruce-Pine-Fir	#3	5-0	7-4	9-4	11-5	13-2	4-6	6-7	8-4	10-2	11-10

For SI: 1 inch = 25.4 mm, 1 foot = 304.8 mm, 1 pound per square foot = 47.9 N/m^2.

a. Span exceeds 26 feet in length. Check sources for availability of lumber in lengths greater than 20 feet.

TABLE 2308.10.3(4)
RAFTER SPANS FOR COMMON LUMBER SPECIES
(Ground Snow Load = 50 pounds per square foot, Ceiling Not Attached to Rafters, L/Δ = 180)

RAFTER SPACING (inches)	SPECIES AND GRADE		DEAD LOAD = 10 pounds psf					DEAD LOAD = 20 pounds psf				
			2 × 4	2 × 6	2 × 8	2 × 10	2 × 12	2 × 4	2 × 6	2 × 8	2 × 10	2 × 12
			Maximum rafter spans									
			(ft. - in.)	(ft. - in.)	(ft. - in.)	(ft. - in.)	(ft. - in.)	(ft. - in.)	(ft. - in.)	(ft. - in.)	(ft. - in.)	(ft. - in.)
12	Douglas Fir-Larch	SS	8-5	13-3	17-6	22-4	26-0	8-5	13-3	17-0	20-9	24-10
	Douglas Fir-Larch	#1	8-2	12-0	15-3	18-7	21-7	7-7	11-2	14-1	17-3	20-0
	Douglas Fir-Larch	#2	7-8	11-3	14-3	17-5	20-2	7-1	10-5	13-2	16-1	18-8
	Douglas Fir-Larch	#3	5-10	8-6	10-9	13-2	15-3	5-5	7-10	10-0	12-2	14-1
	Hem-Fir	SS	8-0	12-6	16-6	21-1	25-6	8-0	12-6	16-6	20-4	23-7
	Hem-Fir	#1	7-10	11-9	14-10	18-1	21-0	7-5	10-10	13-9	16-9	19-5
	Hem-Fir	#2	7-5	11-1	14-0	17-2	19-11	7-0	10-3	13-0	15-10	18-5
	Hem-Fir	#3	5-10	8-6	10-9	13-2	15-3	5-5	7-10	10-0	12-2	14-1
	Southern Pine	SS	8-4	13-0	17-2	21-11	Note a	8-4	13-0	17-2	21-11	Note a
	Southern Pine	#1	8-2	12-10	16-10	20-3	24-1	8-2	12-6	15-9	18-9	22-4
	Southern Pine	#2	8-0	11-9	15-3	18-2	21-3	7-7	10-11	14-1	16-10	19-9
	Southern Pine	#3	6-2	9-2	11-8	13-9	16-4	5-9	8-5	10-9	12-9	15-2
	Spruce-Pine-Fir	SS	7-10	12-3	16-2	20-8	24-1	7-10	12-3	15-9	19-3	22-4
	Spruce-Pine-Fir	#1	7-8	11-3	14-3	17-5	20-2	7-1	10-5	13-2	16-1	18-8
	Spruce-Pine-Fir	#2	7-8	11-3	14-3	17-5	20-2	7-1	10-5	13-2	16-1	18-8
	Spruce-Pine-Fir	#3	5-10	8-6	10-9	13-2	15-3	5-5	7-10	10-0	12-2	14-1
16	Douglas Fir-Larch	SS	7-8	12-1	15-10	19-5	22-6	7-8	11-7	14-8	17-11	20-10
	Douglas Fir-Larch	#1	7-1	10-5	13-2	16-1	18-8	6-7	9-8	12-2	14-11	17-3
	Douglas Fir-Larch	#2	6-8	9-9	12-4	15-1	17-6	6-2	9-0	11-5	13-11	16-2
	Douglas Fir-Larch	#3	5-0	7-4	9-4	11-5	13-2	4-8	6-10	8-8	10-6	12-3
	Hem-Fir	SS	7-3	11-5	15-0	19-1	22-1	7-3	11-5	14-5	17-8	20-5
	Hem-Fir	#1	6-11	10-2	12-10	15-8	18-2	6-5	9-5	11-11	14-6	16-10
	Hem-Fir	#2	6-7	9-7	12-2	14-10	17-3	6-1	8-11	11-3	13-9	15-11
	Hem-Fir	#3	5-0	7-4	9-4	11-5	13-2	4-8	6-10	8-8	10-6	12-3
	Southern Pine	SS	7-6	11-10	15-7	19-11	24-3	7-6	11-10	15-7	19-11	23-10
	Southern Pine	#1	7-5	11-7	14-9	17-6	20-11	7-4	10-10	13-8	16-2	19-4
	Southern Pine	#2	7-1	10-2	13-2	15-9	18-5	6-7	9-5	12-2	14-7	17-1
	Southern Pine	#3	5-4	7-11	10-1	11-11	14-2	4-11	7-4	9-4	11-0	13-1
	Spruce-Pine-Fir	SS	7-1	11-2	14-8	18-0	20-11	7-1	10-9	13-8	16-8	19-4
	Spruce-Pine-Fir	#1	6-8	9-9	12-4	15-1	17-6	6-2	9-0	11-5	13-11	16-2
	Spruce-Pine-Fir	#2	6-8	9-9	12-4	15-1	17-6	6-2	9-0	11-5	13-11	16-2
	Spruce-Pine-Fir	#3	5-0	7-4	9-4	11-5	13-2	4-8	6-10	8-8	10-6	12-3

(continued)

TABLE 2308.10.3(4)—continued
RAFTER SPANS FOR COMMON LUMBER SPECIES
(Ground Snow Load = 50 pounds per square foot, Ceiling Not Attached to Rafters, L/Δ = 180)

RAFTER SPACING (inches)	SPECIES AND GRADE		DEAD LOAD = 10 pounds psf					DEAD LOAD = 20 pounds psf				
			2 × 4	2 × 6	2 × 8	2 × 10	2 × 12	2 × 4	2 × 6	2 × 8	2 × 10	2 × 12
			Maximum rafter spans									
			(ft. - in.)	(ft. - in.)	(ft. - in.)	(ft. - in.)	(ft. - in.)	(ft. - in.)	(ft. - in.)	(ft. - in.)	(ft. - in.)	(ft. - in.)
19.2	Douglas Fir-Larch	SS	7-3	11-4	14-6	17-8	20-6	7-3	10-7	13-5	16-5	19-0
	Douglas Fir-Larch	#1	6-6	9-6	12-0	14-8	17-1	6-0	8-10	11-2	13-7	15-9
	Douglas Fir-Larch	#2	6-1	8-11	11-3	13-9	15-11	5-7	8-3	10-5	12-9	14-9
	Douglas Fir-Larch	#3	4-7	6-9	8-6	10-5	12-1	4-3	6-3	7-11	9-7	11-2
	Hem-Fir	SS	6-10	10-9	14-2	17-5	20-2	6-10	10-5	13-2	16-1	18-8
	Hem-Fir	#1	6-4	9-3	11-9	14-4	16-7	5-10	8-7	10-10	13-3	15-5
	Hem-Fir	#2	6-0	8-9	11-1	13-7	15-9	5-7	8-1	10-3	12-7	14-7
	Hem-Fir	#3	4-7	6-9	8-6	10-5	12-1	4-3	6-3	7-11	9-7	11-2
	Southern Pine	SS	7-1	11-2	14-8	18-9	22-10	7-1	11-2	14-8	18-7	21-9
	Southern Pine	#1	7-0	10-8	13-5	16-0	19-1	6-8	9-11	12-5	14-10	17-8
	Southern Pine	#2	6-6	9-4	12-0	14-4	16-10	6-0	8-8	11-2	13-4	15-7
	Southern Pine	#3	4-11	7-3	9-2	10-10	12-11	4-6	6-8	8-6	10-1	12-0
	Spruce-Pine-Fir	SS	6-8	10-6	13-5	16-5	19-1	6-8	9-10	12-5	15-3	17-8
	Spruce-Pine-Fir	#1	6-1	8-11	11-3	13-9	15-11	5-7	8-3	10-5	12-9	14-9
	Spruce-Pine-Fir	#2	6-1	8-11	11-3	13-9	15-11	5-7	8-3	10-5	12-9	14-9
	Spruce-Pine-Fir	#3	4-7	6-9	8-6	10-5	12-1	4-3	6-3	7-11	9-7	11-2
24	Douglas Fir-Larch	SS	6-8	10-3	13-0	15-10	18-4	6-6	9-6	12-0	14-8	17-0
	Douglas Fir-Larch	#1	5-10	8-6	10-9	13-2	15-3	5-5	7-10	10-0	12-2	14-1
	Douglas Fir-Larch	#2	5-5	7-11	10-1	12-4	14-3	5-0	7-4	9-4	11-5	13-2
	Douglas Fir-Larch	#3	4-1	6-0	7-7	9-4	10-9	3-10	5-7	7-1	8-7	10-0
	Hem-Fir	SS	6-4	9-11	12-9	15-7	18-0	6-4	9-4	11-9	14-5	16-8
	Hem-Fir	#1	5-8	8-3	10-6	12-10	14-10	5-3	7-8	9-9	11-10	13-9
	Hem-Fir	#2	5-4	7-10	9-11	12-1	14-1	4-11	7-3	9-2	11-3	13-0
	Hem-Fir	#3	4-1	6-0	7-7	9-4	10-9	3-10	5-7	7-1	8-7	10-0
	Southern Pine	SS	6-7	10-4	13-8	17-5	21-0	6-7	10-4	13-8	16-7	19-5
	Southern Pine	#1	6-5	9-7	12-0	14-4	17-1	6-0	8-10	11-2	13-3	15-9
	Southern Pine	#2	5-10	8-4	10-9	12-10	15-1	5-5	7-9	10-0	11-11	13-11
	Southern Pine	#3	4-4	6-5	8-3	9-9	11-7	4-1	6-0	7-7	9-0	10-8
	Spruce-Pine-Fir	SS	6-2	9-6	12-0	14-8	17-1	6-0	8-10	11-2	13-7	15-9
	Spruce-Pine-Fir	#1	5-5	7-11	10-1	12-4	14-3	5-0	7-4	9-4	11-5	13-2
	Spruce-Pine-Fir	#2	5-5	7-11	10-1	12-4	14-3	5-0	7-4	9-4	11-5	13-2
	Spruce-Pine-Fir	#3	4-1	6-0	7-7	9-4	10-9	3-10	5-7	7-1	8-7	10-0

For SI: 1 inch = 25.4 mm, 1 foot = 304.8 mm, 1 pound per square foot = 47.9 N/m^2.

a. Span exceeds 26 feet in length. Check sources for availability of lumber in lengths greater than 20 feet.

TABLE 2308.10.3(5)
RAFTER SPANS FOR COMMON LUMBER SPECIES
(Ground Snow Load = 30 pounds per square foot, Ceiling Attached to Rafters, L/Δ = 240)

RAFTER SPACING (inches)	SPECIES AND GRADE		DEAD LOAD = 10 pounds psf					DEAD LOAD = 20 pounds psf				
			2 × 4	2 × 6	2 × 8	2 × 10	2 × 12	2 × 4	2 × 6	2 × 8	2 × 10	2 × 12
			Maximum rafter spans									
			(ft. - in.)	(ft. - in.)	(ft. - in.)	(ft. - in.)	(ft. - in.)	(ft. - in.)	(ft. - in.)	(ft. - in.)	(ft. - in.)	(ft. - in.)
12	Douglas Fir-Larch	SS	9-1	14-4	18-10	24-1	Note a	9-1	14-4	18-10	24-1	Note a
	Douglas Fir-Larch	#1	8-9	13-9	18-2	22-9	Note a	8-9	13-2	16-8	20-4	23-7
	Douglas Fir-Larch	#2	8-7	13-6	17-5	21-4	24-8	8-5	12-4	15-7	19-1	22-1
	Douglas Fir-Larch	#3	7-1	10-5	13-2	16-1	18-8	6-4	9-4	11-9	14-5	16-8
	Hem-Fir	SS	8-7	13-6	17-10	22-9	Note a	8-7	13-6	17-10	22-9	Note a
	Hem-Fir	#1	8-5	13-3	17-5	22-2	25-9	8-5	12-10	16-3	19-10	23-0
	Hem-Fir	#2	8-0	12-7	16-7	21-0	24-4	8-0	12-2	15-4	18-9	21-9
	Hem-Fir	#3	7-1	10-5	13-2	16-1	18-8	6-4	9-4	11-9	14-5	16-8
	Southern Pine	SS	8-11	14-1	18-6	23-8	Note a	8-11	14-1	18-6	23-8	Note a
	Southern Pine	#1	8-9	13-9	18-2	23-2	Note a	8-9	13-9	18-2	22-2	Note a
	Southern Pine	#2	8-7	13-6	17-10	22-3	Note a	8-7	12-11	16-8	19-11	23-4
	Southern Pine	#3	7-7	11-2	14-3	16-10	20-0	6-9	10-0	12-9	15-1	17-11
	Spruce-Pine-Fir	SS	8-5	13-3	17-5	22-3	Note a	8-5	13-3	17-5	22-3	Note a
	Spruce-Pine-Fir	#1	8-3	12-11	17-0	21-4	24-8	8-3	12-4	15-7	19-1	22-1
	Spruce-Pine-Fir	#2	8-3	12-11	17-0	21-4	24-8	8-3	12-4	15-7	19-1	22-1
	Spruce-Pine-Fir	#3	7-1	10-5	13-2	16-1	18-8	6-4	9-4	11-9	14-5	16-8
16	Douglas Fir-Larch	SS	8-3	13-0	17-2	21-10	Note a	8-3	13-0	17-2	21-3	24-8
	Douglas Fir-Larch	#1	8-0	12-6	16-2	19-9	22-10	7-10	11-5	14-5	17-8	20-5
	Douglas Fir-Larch	#2	7-10	11-11	15-1	18-5	21-5	7-3	10-8	13-6	16-6	19-2
	Douglas Fir-Larch	#3	6-2	9-0	11-5	13-11	16-2	5-6	8-1	10-3	12-6	14-6
	Hem-Fir	SS	7-10	12-3	16-2	20-8	25-1	7-10	12-3	16-2	20-8	24-2
	Hem-Fir	#1	7-8	12-0	15-9	19-3	22-3	7-7	11-1	14-1	17-2	19-11
	Hem-Fir	#2	7-3	11-5	14-11	18-2	21-1	7-2	10-6	13-4	16-3	18-10
	Hem-Fir	#3	6-2	9-0	11-5	13-11	16-2	5-6	8-1	10-3	12-6	14-6
	Southern Pine	SS	8-1	12-9	16-10	21-6	Note a	8-1	12-9	16-10	21-6	Note a
	Southern Pine	#1	8-0	12-6	16-6	21-1	25-7	8-0	12-6	16-2	19-2	22-10
	Southern Pine	#2	7-10	12-3	16-2	19-3	22-7	7-10	11-2	14-5	17-3	20-2
	Southern Pine	#3	6-7	9-8	12-4	14-7	17-4	5-10	8-8	11-0	13-0	15-6
	Spruce-Pine-Fir	SS	7-8	12-0	15-10	20-2	24-7	7-8	12-0	15-10	19-9	22-10
	Spruce-Pine-Fir	#1	7-6	11-9	15-1	18-5	21-5	7-3	10-8	13-6	16-6	19-2
	Spruce-Pine-Fi	#2	7-6	11-9	15-1	18-5	21-5	7-3	10-8	13-6	16-6	19-2
	Spruce-Pine-Fi	#3	6-2	9-0	11-5	13-11	16-2	5-6	8-1	10-3	12-6	14-6

(continued)

TABLE 2308.10.3(5)—continued
RAFTER SPANS FOR COMMON LUMBER SPECIES
(Ground Snow Load = 30 pounds per square foot, Ceiling Attached to Rafters, $L/\Delta = 240$)

RAFTER SPACING (inches)	SPECIES AND GRADE		DEAD LOAD = 10 pounds psf					DEAD LOAD = 20 pounds psf				
			2 × 4	2 × 6	2 × 8	2 × 10	2 × 12	2 × 4	2 × 6	2 × 8	2 × 10	2 × 12
			Maximum rafter spans									
			(ft. - in.)	(ft. - in.)	(ft. - in.)	(ft. - in.)	(ft. - in.)	(ft. - in.)	(ft. - in.)	(ft. - in.)	(ft. - in.)	(ft. - in.)
19.2	Douglas Fir-Larch	SS	7-9	12-3	16-1	20-7	25-0	7-9	12-3	15-10	19-5	22-6
	Douglas Fir-Larch	#1	7-6	11-8	14-9	18-0	20-11	7-1	10-5	13-2	16-1	18-8
	Douglas Fir-Larch	#2	7-4	10-11	13-9	16-10	19-6	6-8	9-9	12-4	15-1	17-6
	Douglas Fir-Larch	#3	5-7	8-3	10-5	12-9	14-9	5-0	7-4	9-4	11-5	13-2
	Hem-Fir	SS	7-4	11-7	15-3	19-5	23-7	7-4	11-7	15-3	19-1	22-1
	Hem-Fir	#1	7-2	11-4	14-4	17-7	20-4	6-11	10-2	12-10	15-8	18-2
	Hem-Fir	#2	6-10	10-9	13-7	16-7	19-3	6-7	9-7	12-2	14-10	17-3
	Hem-Fir	#3	5-7	8-3	10-5	12-9	14-9	5-0	7-4	9-4	11-5	13-2
	Southern Pine	SS	7-8	12-0	15-10	20-2	24-7	7-8	12-0	15-10	20-2	24-7
	Southern Pine	#1	7-6	11-9	15-6	19-7	23-4	7-6	11-9	14-9	17-6	20-11
	Southern Pine	#2	7-4	11-5	14-9	17-7	20-7	7-1	10-2	13-2	15-9	18-5
	Southern Pine	#3	6-0	8-10	11-3	13-4	15-10	5-4	7-11	10-1	11-11	14-2
	Spruce-Pine-Fir	SS	7-2	11-4	14-11	19-0	23-1	7-2	11-4	14-9	18-0	20-11
	Spruce-Pine-Fir	#1	7-0	10-11	13-9	16-10	19-6	6-8	9-9	12-4	15-1	17-6
	Spruce-Pine-Fir	#2	7-0	10-11	13-9	16-10	19-6	6-8	9-9	12-4	15-1	17-6
	Spruce-Pine-Fir	#3	5-7	8-3	10-5	12-9	14-9	5-0	7-4	9-4	11-5	13-2
24	Douglas Fir-Larch	SS	7-3	11-4	15-0	19-1	22-6	7-3	11-3	14-2	17-4	20-1
	Douglas Fir-Larch	#1	7-0	10-5	13-2	16-1	18-8	6-4	9-4	11-9	14-5	16-8
	Douglas Fir-Larch	#2	6-8	9-9	12-4	15-1	17-6	5-11	8-8	11-0	13-6	15-7
	Douglas Fir-Larch	#3	5-0	7-4	9-4	11-5	13-2	4-6	6-7	8-4	10-2	11-10
	Hem-Fir	SS	6-10	10-9	14-2	18-0	21-11	6-10	10-9	13-11	17-0	19-9
	Hem-Fir	#1	6-8	10-2	12-10	15-8	18-2	6-2	9-1	11-6	14-0	16-3
	Hem-Fir	#2	6-4	9-7	12-2	14-10	17-3	5-10	8-7	10-10	13-3	15-5
	Hem-Fir	#3	5-0	7-4	9-4	11-5	13-2	4-6	6-7	8-4	10-2	11-10
	Southern Pine	SS	7-1	11-2	14-8	18-9	22-10	7-1	11-2	14-8	18-9	22-10
	Southern Pine	#1	7-0	10-11	14-5	17-6	20-11	7-0	10-6	13-2	15-8	18-8
	Southern Pine	#2	6-10	10-2	13-2	15-9	18-5	6-4	9-2	11-9	14-1	16-6
	Southern Pine	#3	5-4	7-11	10-1	11-11	14-2	4-9	7-1	9-0	10-8	12-8
	Spruce-Pine-Fir	SS	6-8	10-6	13-10	17-8	20-11	6-8	10-5	13-2	16-1	18-8
	Spruce-Pine-Fir	#1	6-6	9-9	12-4	15-1	17-6	5-11	8-8	11-0	13-6	15-7
	Spruce-Pine-Fir	#2	6-6	9-9	12-4	15-1	17-6	5-11	8-8	11-0	13-6	15-7
	Spruce-Pine-Fir	#3	5-0	7-4	9-4	11-5	13-2	4-6	6-7	8-4	10-2	11-10

For SI: 1 inch = 25.4 mm, 1 foot = 304.8 mm, 1 pound per square foot = 47.9 N/m^2.

a. Span exceeds 26 feet in length. Check sources for availability of lumber in lengths greater than 20 feet.

TABLE 2308.10.3(6)
RAFTER SPANS FOR COMMON LUMBER SPECIES
(Ground Snow Load = 50 pounds per square foot, Ceiling Attached to Rafters, L/Δ = 240)

RAFTER SPACING (inches)	SPECIES AND GRADE		DEAD LOAD = 10 pounds psf					DEAD LOAD = 20 pounds psf				
			2 × 4	2 × 6	2 × 8	2 × 10	2 × 12	2 × 4	2 × 6	2 × 8	2 × 10	2 × 12
			Maximum rafter spans									
			(ft. - in.)	(ft. - in.)	(ft. - in.)	(ft. - in.)	(ft. - in.)	(ft. - in.)	(ft. - in.)	(ft. - in.)	(ft. - in.)	(ft. - in.)
12	Douglas Fir-Larch	SS	7-8	12-1	15-11	20-3	24-8	7-8	12-1	15-11	20-3	24-0
	Douglas Fir-Larch	#1	7-5	11-7	15-3	18-7	21-7	7-5	11-2	14-1	17-3	20-0
	Douglas Fir-Larch	#2	7-3	11-3	14-3	17-5	20-2	7-1	10-5	13-2	16-1	18-8
	Douglas Fir-Larch	#3	5-10	8-6	10-9	13-2	15-3	5-5	7-10	10-0	12-2	14-1
	Hem-Fir	SS	7-3	11-5	15-0	19-2	23-4	7-3	11-5	15-0	19-2	23-4
	Hem-Fir	#1	7-1	11-2	14-8	18-1	21-0	7-1	10-10	13-9	16-9	19-5
	Hem-Fir	#2	6-9	10-8	14-0	17-2	19-11	6-9	10-3	13-0	15-10	18-5
	Hem-Fir	#3	5-10	8-6	10-9	13-2	15-3	5-5	7-10	10-0	12-2	14-1
	Southern Pine	SS	7-6	11-0	15-7	19-11	24-3	7-6	11-10	15-7	19-11	24-3
	Southern Pine	#1	7-5	11-7	15-4	19-7	23-9	7-5	11-7	15-4	18-9	22-4
	Southern Pine	#2	7-3	11-5	15-0	18-2	21-3	7-3	10-11	14-1	16-10	19-9
	Southern Pine	#3	6-2	9-2	11-8	13-9	16-4	5-9	8-5	10-9	12-9	15-2
	Spruce-Pine-Fir	SS	7-1	11-2	14-8	18-9	22-10	7-1	11-2	14-8	18-9	22-4
	Spruce-Pine-Fir	#1	6-11	10-11	14-3	17-5	20-2	6-11	10-5	13-2	16-1	18-8
	Spruce-Pine-Fir	#2	6-11	10-11	14-3	17-5	20-2	6-11	10-5	13-2	16-1	18-8
	Spruce-Pine-Fir	#3	5-10	8-6	10-9	13-2	15-3	5-5	7-10	10-0	12-2	14-1
16	Douglas Fir-Larch	SS	7-0	11-0	14-5	18-5	22-5	7-0	11-0	14-5	17-11	20-10
	Douglas Fir-Larch	#1	6-9	10-5	13-2	16-1	18-8	6-7	9-8	12-2	14-11	17-3
	Douglas Fir-Larch	#2	6-7	9-9	12-4	15-1	17-6	6-2	9-0	11-5	13-11	16-2
	Douglas Fir-Larch	#3	5-0	7-4	9-4	11-5	13-2	4-8	6-10	8-8	10-6	12-3
	Hem-Fir	SS	6-7	10-4	13-8	17-5	21-2	6-7	10-4	13-8	17-5	20-5
	Hem-Fir	#1	6-5	10-2	12-10	15-8	18-2	6-5	9-5	11-11	14-6	16-10
	Hem-Fir	#2	6-2	9-7	12-2	14-10	17-3	6-1	8-11	11-3	13-9	15-11
	Hem-Fir	#3	5-0	7-4	9-4	11-5	13-2	4-8	6-10	8-8	10-6	12-3
	Southern Pine	SS	6-10	10-9	14-2	18-1	22-0	6-10	10-9	14-2	18-1	22-0
	Southern Pine	#1	6-9	10-7	13-11	17-6	20-11	6-9	10-7	13-8	16-2	19-4
	Southern Pine	#2	6-7	10-2	13-2	15-9	18-5	6-7	9-5	12-2	14-7	17-1
	Southern Pine	#3	5-4	7-11	10-1	11-11	14-2	4-11	7-4	9-4	11-0	13-1
	Spruce-Pine-Fir	SS	6-5	10-2	13-4	17-0	20-9	6-5	10-2	13-4	16-8	19-4
	Spruce-Pine-Fir	#1	6-4	9-9	12-4	15-1	17-6	6-2	9-0	11-5	13-11	16-2
	Spruce-Pine-Fir	#2	6-4	9-9	12-4	15-1	17-6	6-2	9-0	11-5	13-11	16-2
	Spruce-Pine-Fir	#3	5-0	7-4	9-4	11-5	13-2	4-8	6-10	8-8	10-6	12-3

(continued)

TABLE 2308.10.3(6)—continued
RAFTER SPANS FOR COMMON LUMBER SPECIES
(Ground Snow Load = 50 pounds per square foot, Ceiling Attached to Rafters, L/Δ = 240)

RAFTER SPACING (inches)	SPECIES AND GRADE		DEAD LOAD = 10 pounds psf					DEAD LOAD = 20 pounds psf				
			2 × 4	2 × 6	2 × 8	2 × 10	2 × 12	2 × 4	2 × 6	2 × 8	2 × 10	2 × 12
			Maximum rafter spans									
			(ft. - in.)	(ft. - in.)	(ft. - in.)	(ft. - in.)	(ft. - in.)	(ft. - in.)	(ft. - in.)	(ft. - in.)	(ft. - in.)	(ft. - in.)
19.2	Douglas Fir-Larch	SS	6-7	10-4	13-7	17-4	20-6	6-7	10-4	13-5	16-5	19-0
	Douglas Fir-Larch	#1	6-4	9-6	12-0	14-8	17-1	6-0	8-10	11-2	13-7	15-9
	Douglas Fir-Larch	#2	6-1	8-11	11-3	13-9	15-11	5-7	8-3	10-5	12-9	14-9
	Douglas Fir-Larch	#3	4-7	6-9	8-6	10-5	12-1	4-3	6-3	7-11	9-7	11-2
	Hem-Fir	SS	6-2	9-9	12-10	16-5	19-11	6-2	9-9	12-10	16-1	18-8
	Hem-Fir	#1	6-1	9-3	11-9	14-4	16-7	5-10	8-7	10-10	13-3	15-5
	Hem-Fir	#2	5-9	8-9	11-1	13-7	15-9	5-7	8-1	10-3	12-7	14-7
	Hem-Fir	#3	4-7	6-9	8-6	10-5	12-1	4-3	6-3	7-11	9-7	11-2
	Southern Pine	SS	6-5	10-2	13-4	17-0	20-9	6-5	10-2	13-4	17-0	20-9
	Southern Pine	#1	6-4	9-11	13-1	16-0	19-1	6-4	9-11	12-5	14-10	17-8
	Southern Pine	#2	6-2	9-4	12-0	14-4	16-10	6-0	8-8	11-2	13-4	15-7
	Southern Pine	#3	4-11	7-3	9-2	10-10	12-11	4-6	6-8	8-6	10-1	12-0
	Spruce-Pine-Fir	SS	6-1	9-6	12-7	16-0	19-1	6-1	9-6	12-5	15-3	17-8
	Spruce-Pine-Fir	#1	5-11	8-11	11-3	13-9	15-11	5-7	8-3	10-5	12-9	14-9
	Spruce-Pine-Fir	#2	5-11	8-11	11-3	13-9	15-11	5-7	8-3	10-5	12-9	14-9
	Spruce-Pine-Fir	#3	4-7	6-9	8-6	10-5	12-1	4-3	6-3	7-11	9-7	11-2
24	Douglas Fir-Larch	SS	6-1	9-7	12-7	15-10	18-4	6-1	9-6	12-0	14-8	17-0
	Douglas Fir-Larch	#1	5-10	8-6	10-9	13-2	15-3	5-5	7-10	10-0	12-2	14-1
	Douglas Fir-Larch	#2	5-5	7-11	10-1	12-4	14-3	5-0	7-4	9-4	11-5	13-2
	Douglas Fir-Larch	#3	4-1	6-0	7-7	9-4	10-9	3-10	5-7	7-1	8-7	10-0
	Hem-Fir	SS	5-9	9-1	11-11	15-12	18-0	5-9	9-1	11-9	14-5	16-8
	Hem-Fir	#1	5-8	8-3	10-6	12-10	14-10	5-3	7-8	9-9	11-10	13-9
	Hem-Fir	#2	5-4	7-10	9-11	12-1	14-1	4-11	7-3	9-2	11-3	13-0
	Hem-Fir	#3	4-1	6-0	7-7	9-4	10-9	3-10	5-7	7-1	8-7	10-0
	Southern Pine	SS	6-0	9-5	12-5	15-10	19-3	6-0	9-5	12-5	15-10	19-3
	Southern Pine	#1	5-10	9-3	12-0	14-4	17-1	5-10	8-10	11-2	13-3	15-9
	Southern Pine	#2	5-9	8-4	10-9	12-10	15-1	5-5	7-9	10-0	11-11	13-11
	Southern Pine	#3	4-4	6-5	8-3	9-9	11-7	4-1	6-0	7-7	9-0	10-8
	Spruce-Pine-Fir	SS	5-8	8-10	11-8	14-8	17-1	5-8	8-10	11-2	13-7	15-9
	Spruce-Pine-Fir	#1	5-5	7-11	10-1	12-4	14-3	5-0	7-4	9-4	11-5	13-2
	Spruce-Pine-Fir	#2	5-5	7-11	10-1	12-4	14-3	5-0	7-4	9-4	11-5	13-2
	Spruce-Pine-Fir	#3	4-1	6-0	7-7	9-4	10-9	3-10	5-7	7-1	8-7	10-0

For SI: 1 inch = 25.4 mm, 1 foot = 304.8 mm, 1 pound per square foot = 47.9 N/m^2.

TABLE 2308.10.4.1 RAFTER TIE CONNECTIONS[g]

RAFTER SLOPE	TIE SPACING (inches)	NO SNOW LOAD				GROUND SNOW LOAD (pound per square foot)							
						30 pounds per square foot				50 pounds per square foot			
						Roof span (feet)							
		12	20	28	36	12	20	28	36	12	20	28	36
		Required number of 16d common ($3^1/_2''$ x 0.162″) nails[a, b] per connection[c, d, e, f]											
3:12	12	4	6	8	10	4	6	8	11	5	8	12	15
	16	5	7	10	13	5	8	11	14	6	11	15	20
	24	7	11	15	19	7	11	16	21	9	16	23	30
	32	10	14	19	25	10	16	22	28	12	27	30	40
	48	14	21	29	37	14	32	36	42	18	32	46	60
4:12	12	3	4	5	6	3	5	6	8	4	6	9	11
	16	3	5	7	8	4	6	8	11	5	8	12	15
	24	4	7	10	12	5	9	12	16	7	12	17	22
	32	6	9	13	16	8	12	16	22	10	16	24	30
	48	8	14	19	24	10	18	24	32	14	24	34	44
5:12	12	3	3	4	5	3	4	5	7	3	5	7	9
	16	3	4	5	7	3	5	7	9	4	7	9	12
	24	4	6	8	10	4	7	10	13	6	10	14	18
	32	5	8	10	13	6	10	14	18	8	14	18	24
	48	7	11	15	20	8	14	20	26	12	20	28	36
7:12	12	3	3	3	4	3	3	4	5	3	4	5	7
	16	3	3	4	5	3	4	5	6	3	5	7	9
	24	3	4	6	7	3	5	7	9	4	7	10	13
	32	4	6	8	10	4	8	10	12	6	10	14	18
	48	5	8	11	14	6	10	14	18	9	14	20	26
9:12	12	3	3	3	3	3	3	3	4	3	3	4	5
	16	3	3	3	4	3	3	4	5	3	4	5	7
	24	3	3	5	6	3	4	6	7	3	6	8	10
	32	3	4	6	8	4	6	8	10	5	8	10	14
	48	4	6	9	11	5	8	12	14	7	12	16	20
12:12	12	3	3	3	3	3	3	3	3	3	3	3	4
	16	3	3	3	3	3	3	3	4	3	3	4	5
	24	3	3	3	4	3	3	4	6	3	4	6	8
	32	3	3	4	5	3	5	6	8	4	6	8	10
	48	3	4	6	7	4	7	8	12	6	8	12	16

For SI: 1 inch = 25.4 mm, 1 foot = 304.8 mm, 1 pound per square foot = 47.8 N/m^2.

a. 40d box (5″ × 0.162″) or 16d sinker ($3^1/_4''$ × 0.148″) nails are permitted to be substituted for 16d common ($3^1/_2''$ × 0.16″) nails.

b. Nailing requirements are permitted to be reduced 25 percent if nails are clinched.

c. Rafter tie heel joint connections are not required where the ridge is supported by a load-bearing wall, header or ridge beam.

d. When intermediate support of the rafter is provided by vertical struts or purlins to a load-bearing wall, the tabulated heel joint connection requirements are permitted to be reduced proportionally to the reduction in span.

e. Equivalent nailing patterns are required for ceiling joist to ceiling joist lap splices.

f. Connected members shall be of sufficient size to prevent splitting due to nailing.

g. For snow loads less than 30 pounds per square foot, the required number of nails is permitted to be reduced by multiplying by the ratio of actual snow load plus 10 divided by 40, but not less than the number required for no snow load.

2308.10.9 Roof planking. Planking shall be designed in accordance with the general provisions of this code.

In lieu of such design, 2-inch (51 mm) tongue-and-groove planking is permitted in accordance with Table 2308.10.9. Joints in such planking are permitted to be randomly spaced, provided the system is applied to not less than three continuous spans, planks are center matched and end matched or splined, each plank bears on at least one support, and joints are separated by at least 24 inches (610 mm) in adjacent pieces.

2308.10.10 Wood trusses. Wood trusses shall be designed in accordance with Section 2303.4.

TABLE 2308.10.9
ALLOWABLE SPANS FOR 2-INCH TONGUE-AND-GROOVE DECKING

SPAN[a] (feet)	LIVE LOAD (pound per square foot)	DEFLECTION LIMIT	BENDING STRESS (*f*) (pound per square inch)	MODULUS OF ELASTICITY (*E*) (pound per square inch)
Roofs				
4	20	1/240 1/360	160	170,000 256,000
	30	1/240 1/360	210	256,000 384,000
	40	1/240 1/360	270	340,000 512,000
4.5	20	1/240 1/360	200	242,000 305,000
	30	1/240 1/360	270	363,000 405,000
	40	1/240 1/360	350	484,000 725,000
5.0	20	1/240 1/360	250	332,000 500,000
	30	1/240 1/360	330	495,000 742,000
	40	1/240 1/360	420	660,000 1,000,000
5.5	20	1/240 1/360	300	442,000 660,000
	30	1/240 1/360	400	662,000 998,000
	40	1/240 1/360	500	884,000 1,330,000
6.0	20	1/240 1/360	360	575,000 862,000
	30	1/240 1/360	480	862,000 1,295,000
	40	1/240 1/360	600	1,150,000 1,730,000
6.5	20	1/240 1/360	420	595,000 892,000
	30	1/240 1/360	560	892,000 1,340,000
	40	1/240 1/360	700	1,190,000 1,730,000

(continued)

TABLE 2308.10.9–continued
ALLOWABLE SPANS FOR 2-INCH TONGUE-AND-GROOVE DECKING

SPAN[a] (feet)	LIVE LOAD (pound per square foot)	DEFLECTION LIMIT	BENDING STRESS (*f*) (pound per square inch)	MODULUS OF ELASTICITY (*E*) (pound per square inch)
		Roofs		
7.0	20	1/240 1/360	490	910,000 1,360,000
	30	1/240 1/360	650	1,370,000 2,000,000
	40	1/240 1/360	810	1,820,000 2,725,000
7.5	20	1/240 1/360	560	1,125,000 1,685,000
	30	1/240 1/360	750	1,685,000 2,530,000
	40	1/240 1/360	930	2,250,000 3,380,000
8.0	20	1/240 1/360	640	1,360,000 2,040,000
	30	1/240 1/360	850	2,040,000 3,060,000
		Floors		
4 4.5 5.0	40	1/360	840 950 1,060	1,000,000 1,300,000 1,600,000

For SI: 1 inch = 25.4 mm, 1 foot = 304.8 mm, 1 pound per square foot = 0.0479kN/m^2, 1 pound per square inch = 0.00689 N/mm^2.

a. Spans are based on simple beam action with 10 pounds per square foot dead load and provisions for a 300-pound concentrated load on a 12-inch width of decking. Random layup is permitted in accordance with the provisions of Section 2308.10.9. Lumber thickness is $1^1/_2$ inches nominal.

2308.10.11 Attic ventilation. For *attic* ventilation, see Section 1203.2.

2308.11 Additional requirements for conventional construction in Seismic Design Category B or C. Structures of *conventional light-frame construction* in *Seismic Design Category* B or C, as determined in Section 1613, shall comply with Sections 2308.11.1 through 2308.11.3, in addition to the provisions of Sections 2308.1 through 2308.10.

2308.11.1 Number of stories. Structures of *conventional light-frame construction* shall not exceed two *stories above grade plane* in *Seismic Design Category* C.

2308.11.2 Concrete or masonry. Concrete or masonry walls and stone or masonry veneer shall not extend above a basement.

Exceptions:

1. Stone and masonry veneer is permitted to be used in the first two *stories above grade plane* or the first three *stories above grade plane* where the lowest *story* has concrete or masonry walls in *Seismic Design Category* B, provided that structural use panel wall bracing is used and the length of bracing provided is one- and one-half times the required length as determined in Table 2308.9.3(1).
2. Stone and masonry veneer is permitted to be used in the first *story above grade plane* or the first two *stories above grade plane* where the lowest *story* has concrete or masonry walls in *Seismic Design Category* B or C.
3. Stone and masonry veneer is permitted to be used in both stories of buildings with two *stories above grade plane* in *Seismic Design Categories* B and C, provided the following criteria are met:
   3.1. Type of brace per Section 2308.9.3 shall be Method 3 and the allowable shear capacity in accordance with Table 2306.3 shall be a minimum of 350 plf (5108 N/m).
   3.2. Braced wall panels in the second *story* shall be located in accordance with Section 2308.9.3 and not more than 25 feet (7620 mm) on center, and the total length of braced wall panels shall be not less than 25 percent of the braced wall line length. Braced wall panels in the first *story* shall be located in accordance with Section 2308.9.3 and not more than 25 feet (7620 mm) on center, and the total length of braced wall panels shall be not less than 45 percent of the braced wall line length.

3.3. Hold-down connectors shall be provided at the ends of each braced wall panel for the second *story* to first *story* connection with an allowable design of 2,000 pounds (8896 N). Hold-down connectors shall be provided at the ends of each braced wall panel for the first story to foundation connection with an allowable capactiy of 3,900 pounds (17 347 N). In all cases, the hold- down connector force shall be transferred to the foundation.

3.4. Cripple walls shall not be permitted.

2308.11.3 Framing and connection details. Framing and connection details shall conform to Sections 2308.11.3.1 through 2308.11.3.3.

2308.11.3.1 Anchorage. Braced wall lines shall be anchored in accordance with Section 2308.6 at foundations.

2308.11.3.2 Stepped footings. Where the height of a required braced wall panel extending from foundation to floor above varies more than 4 feet (1219 mm), the following construction shall be used:

1. Where the bottom of the footing is stepped and the lowest floor framing rests directly on a sill bolted to the footings, the sill shall be anchored as required in Section 2308.3.3.
2. Where the lowest floor framing rests directly on a sill bolted to a footing not less than 8 feet (2438 mm) in length along a line of bracing, the line shall be considered to be braced. The double plate of the cripple stud wall beyond the segment of footing extending to the lowest framed floor shall be spliced to the sill plate with metal ties, one on each side of the sill and plate. The metal ties shall not be less than 0.058 inch [1.47 mm (16 galvanized gage)] by $1^1/_2$ inches (38 mm) wide by 48 inches (1219 mm) with eight 16d common nails on each side of the splice location (see Figure 2308.11.3.2). The metal tie shall have a minimum yield of 33,000 pounds per square inch (psi) (227 MPa).
3. Where cripple walls occur between the top of the footing and the lowest floor framing, the bracing requirements for a *story* shall apply.

2308.11.3.3 Openings in horizontal diaphragms. Openings in horizontal diaphragms with a dimension perpendicular to the joist that is greater than 4 feet (1219 mm) shall be constructed in accordance with the following:

1. Blocking shall be provided beyond headers.
2. Metal ties not less than 0.058 inch [1.47 mm (16 galvanized gage)] by $1^1/_2$ inches (38 mm) wide with eight 16d common nails on each side of the header-joist intersection shall be provided (see Figure 2308.11.3.3). The metal ties shall have a minimum yield of 33,000 psi (227 MPa).

2308.12 Additional requirements for conventional construction in Seismic Design Category D or E. Structures of *conventional light-frame construction* in *Seismic Design Category* D or E, as determined in Section 1613, shall conform to Sections 2308.12.1 through 2308.12.9, in addition to the requirements for *Seismic Design Category* B or C in Section 2308.11.

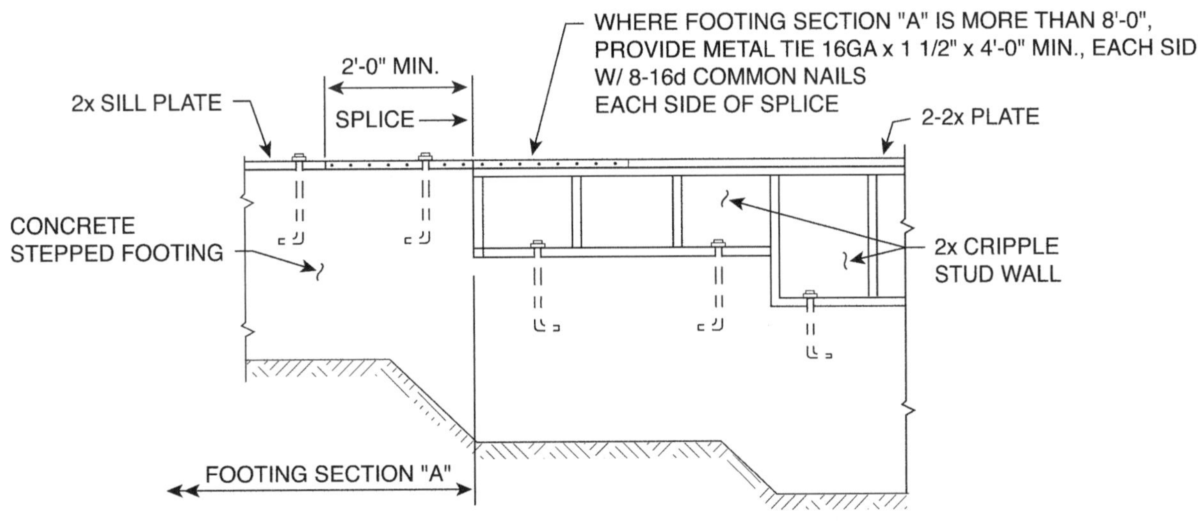

For SI: 1 inch = 25.4 mm, 1 foot = 304.8 mm.

FIGURE 2308.11.3.2
STEPPED FOOTING CONNECTION DETAILS

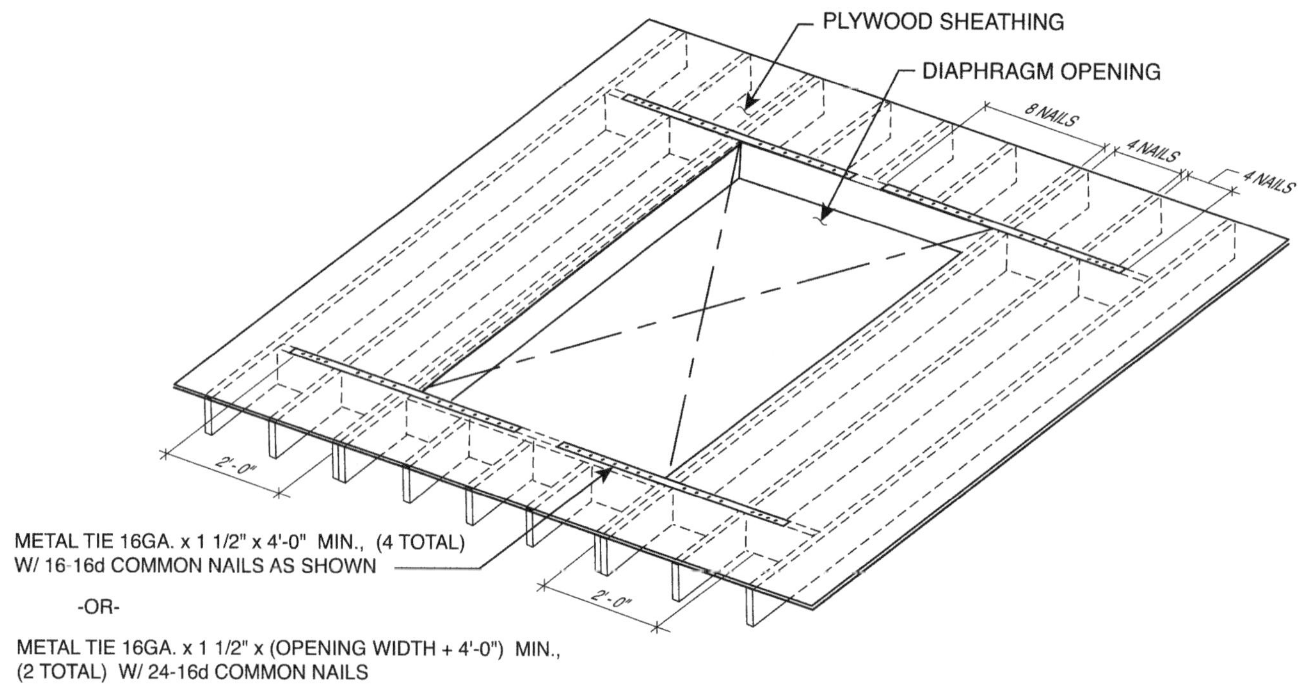

For SI: 1 inch = 25.4 mm, 1 foot = 304.8 mm.

FIGURE 2308.11.3.3
OPENINGS IN HORIZONTAL DIAPHRAGMS

2308.12.1 Number of stories. Structures of *conventional light-frame construction* shall not exceed one *story above grade plane* in *Seismic Design Category* D or E.

2308.12.2 Concrete or masonry. Concrete or masonry walls and stone or masonry veneer shall not extend above a basement.

Exception: Stone and masonry veneer is permitted to be used in the first *story above grade plane* in *Seismic Design Category* D, provided the following criteria are met:

1. Type of brace in accordance with Section 2308.9.3 shall be Method 3 and the allowable shear capacity in accordance with Table 2306.3 shall be a minimum of 350 plf (5108 N/m).
2. The bracing of the first *story* shall be located at each end and at least every 25 feet (7620 mm) o.c. but not less than 45 percent of the braced wall line.
3. Hold-down connectors shall be provided at the ends of braced walls for the first floor to foundation with an allowable capacity of 2,100 pounds (9341 N).
4. Cripple walls shall not be permitted.

2308.12.3 Braced wall line spacing. Spacing between interior and exterior braced wall lines shall not exceed 25 feet (7620 mm).

2308.12.4 Braced wall line sheathing. Braced wall lines shall be braced by one of the types of sheathing prescribed by Table 2308.12.4 as shown in Figure 2308.9.3. The sum of lengths of braced wall panels at each braced wall line shall conform to Table 2308.12.4. Braced wall panels shall be distributed along the length of the braced wall line and start at not more than 8 feet (2438 mm) from each end of the braced wall line. Panel sheathing joints shall occur over studs or blocking. Sheathing shall be fastened to studs, top and bottom plates and at panel edges occurring over blocking. Wall framing to which sheathing used for bracing is applied shall be nominal 2-inch wide [actual $1^1/_2$ inch (38 mm)] or larger members.

Cripple walls having a stud height exceeding 14 inches (356 mm) shall be considered a *story* for the purpose of this section and shall be braced as required for braced wall lines in accordance with Table 2308.12.4. Where interior braced wall lines occur without a continuous foundation below, the length of parallel exterior cripple wall bracing shall be one and one-half times the lengths required by Table 2308.12.4. Where the cripple wall sheathing type used is Type S-W and this additional length of bracing cannot be provided, the capacity of Type S-W sheathing shall be increased by reducing the spacing of fasteners along the perimeter of each piece of sheathing to 4 inches (102 mm) o.c.

2308.12.5 Attachment of sheathing. Fastening of braced wall panel sheathing shall not be less than that prescribed in Table 2308.12.4 or 2304.9.1. Wall sheathing shall not be attached to framing members by adhesives.

TABLE 2308.12.4
WALL BRACING IN SEISMIC DESIGN CATEGORIES D AND E
(Minimum Length of Wall Bracing per each 25 Linear Feet of Braced Wall Line[a])

CONDITION	SHEATHING TYPE[b]	$S_{DS} < 0.50$	$0.50 \leq S_{DS} < 0.75$	$0.75 \leq S_{DS} \leq 1.00$	$S_{DS} > 1.00$
One story	G-P[c]	10 feet 8 inches	14 feet 8 inches	18 feet 8 inches	25 feet 0 inches
	S-W	5 feet 4 inches	8 feet 0 inches	9 feet 4 inches	12 feet 0 inches

For SI: 1 inch = 25.4 mm, 1 foot = 304.8 mm.

a. Minimum length of panel bracing of one face of the wall for S-W sheathing or both faces of the wall for G-P sheathing; h/w ratio shall not exceed 2:1. For S-W panel bracing of the same material on two faces of the wall, the minimum length is permitted to be one-half the tabulated value but the h/w ratio shall not exceed 2:1 and design for uplift is required.

b. G-P = gypsum board, fiberboard, particleboard, lath and plaster or gypsum sheathing boards; S-W = wood structural panels and diagonal wood sheathing.

c. Nailing as specified below shall occur at all panel edges at studs, at top and bottom plates and, where occurring, at blocking:
For $^1/_2$-inch gypsum board, 5d (0.113 inch diameter) cooler nails at 7 inches on center;
For $^5/_8$-inch gypsum board, No. 11 gage (0.120 inch diameter) at 7 inches on center;
For gypsum sheathing board, $1^3/_4$ inches long by $^7/_{16}$-inch head, diamond point galvanized nails at 4 inches on center;
For gypsum lath, No. 13 gage (0.092 inch) by $1^1/_8$ inches long, $^{19}/_{64}$-inch head, plasterboard at 5 inches on center;
For Portland cement plaster, No. 11 gage (0.120 inch) by $1^1/_2$ inches long, $^7/_{16}$- inch head at 6 inches on center;
For fiberboard and particleboard, No. 11 gage (0.120 inch) by $1^1/_2$ inches long, $^7/_{16}$-inch head, galvanized nails at 3 inches on center.

2308.12.6 Irregular structures. *Conventional light-frame construction* shall not be used in irregular portions of structures in *Seismic Design Category* D or E. Such irregular portions of structures shall be designed to resist the forces specified in Chapter 16 to the extent such irregular features affect the performance of the conventional framing system. A portion of a structure shall be considered to be irregular where one or more of the conditions described in Items 1 through 6 below are present.

1. Where exterior braced wall panels are not in one plane vertically from the foundation to the uppermost *story* in which they are required, the structure shall be considered to be irregular [see Figure 2308.12.6(1)].

   Exception: Floors with cantilevers or setbacks not exceeding four times the nominal depth of the floor joists [see Figure 2308.12.6(2)] are permitted to support braced wall panels provided:

   1. Floor joists are 2 inches by 10 inches (51 mm by 254 mm) or larger and spaced not more than 16 inches (406 mm) o.c.
   2. The ratio of the back span to the cantilever is at least 2:1.
   3. Floor joists at ends of braced wall panels are doubled.
   4. A continuous rim joist is connected to the ends of cantilevered joists. The rim joist is permitted to be spliced using a metal tie not less than 0.058 inch (1.47 mm) (16 galvanized gage) and $1^1/_2$ inches (38 mm) wide fastened with six 16d common nails on each side. The metal tie shall have a minimum yield of 33,000 psi (227 MPa).
   5. Joists at setbacks or the end of cantilevered joists shall not carry gravity loads from more than a single *story* having uniform wall and roof loads, nor carry the reactions from headers having a span of 8 feet (2438 mm) or more.

2. Where a section of floor or roof is not laterally supported by braced wall lines on all edges, the structure shall be considered to be irregular [see Figure 2308.12.6(3)].

   Exception: Portions of roofs or floors that do not support braced wall panels above are permitted to extend up to 6 feet (1829 mm) beyond a braced wall line [see Figure 2308.12.6(4)].

3. Where the end of a required braced wall panel extends more than 1 foot (305 mm) over an opening in the wall below, the structure shall be considered to be irregular. This requirement is applicable to braced wall panels offset in plane and to braced wall panels offset out of plane as permitted by the exception to Item 1 above in this section [see Figure 2308.12.6(5)].

   Exception: Braced wall panels are permitted to extend over an opening not more than 8 feet (2438 mm) in width where the header is a 4-inch by 12-inch (102 mm by 305 mm) or larger member.

4. Where portions of a floor level are vertically offset such that the framing members on either side of the offset cannot be lapped or tied together in an *approved* manner, the structure shall be considered to be irregular [see Figure 2308.12.6(6)].

   Exception: Framing supported directly by foundations need not be lapped or tied directly together.

5. Where braced wall lines are not perpendicular to each other, the structure shall be considered to be irregular [see Figure 2308.12.6(7)].

6. Where openings in floor and roof diaphragms having a maximum dimension greater than 50 percent of the distance between lines of bracing or an area greater than 25 percent of the area between orthogonal pairs of braced wall lines are present, the structure shall be considered to be irregular [see Figure 2308.12.6(8)].

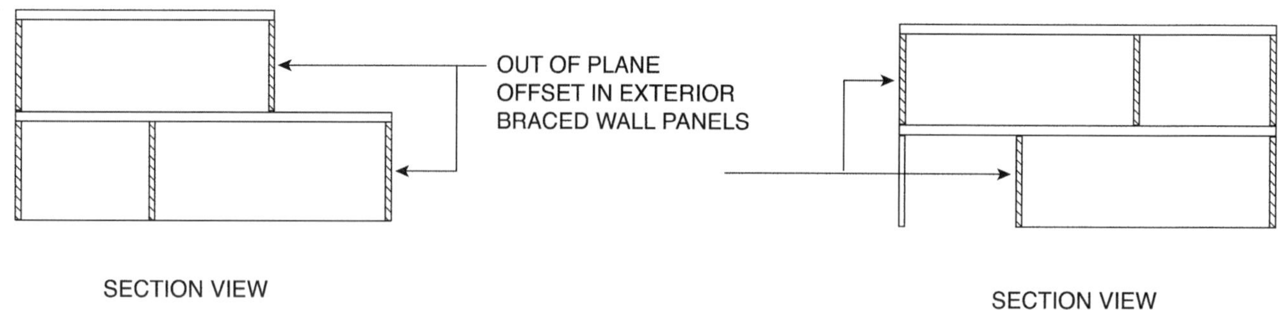

FIGURE 2308.12.6(1)
BRACED WALL PANELS OUT OF PLANE

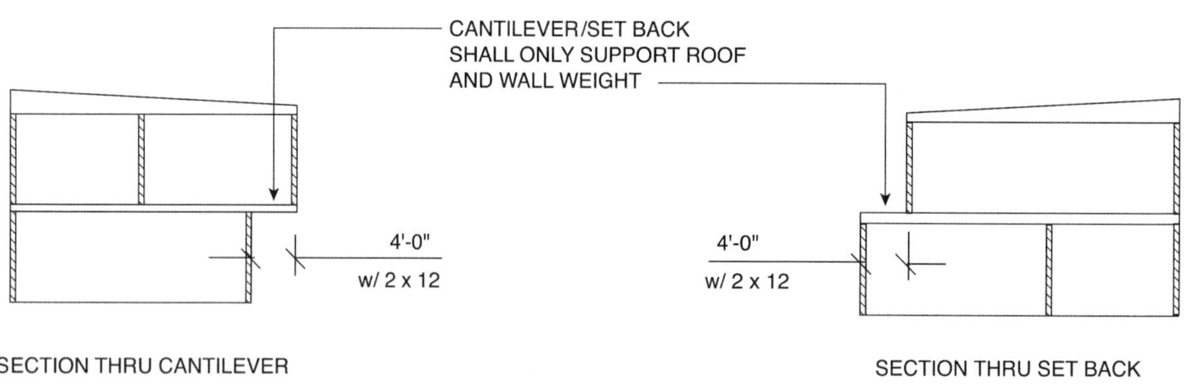

For SI: 1 foot = 304.8 mm.

FIGURE 2308.12.6(2)
BRACED WALL PANELS SUPPORTED BY CANTILEVER OR SET BACK

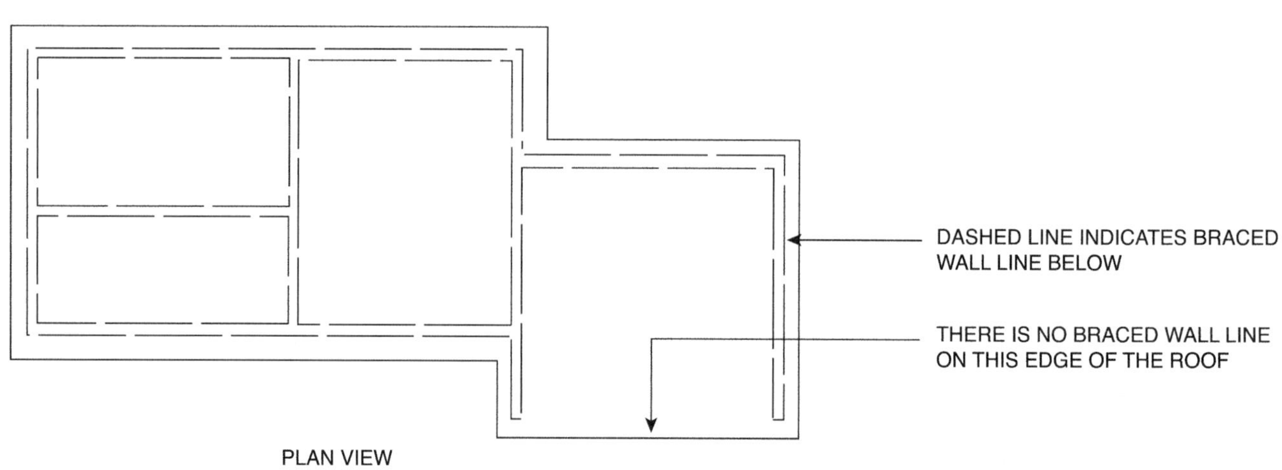

FIGURE 2308.12.6(3)
FLOOR OR ROOF NOT SUPPORTED ON ALL EDGES

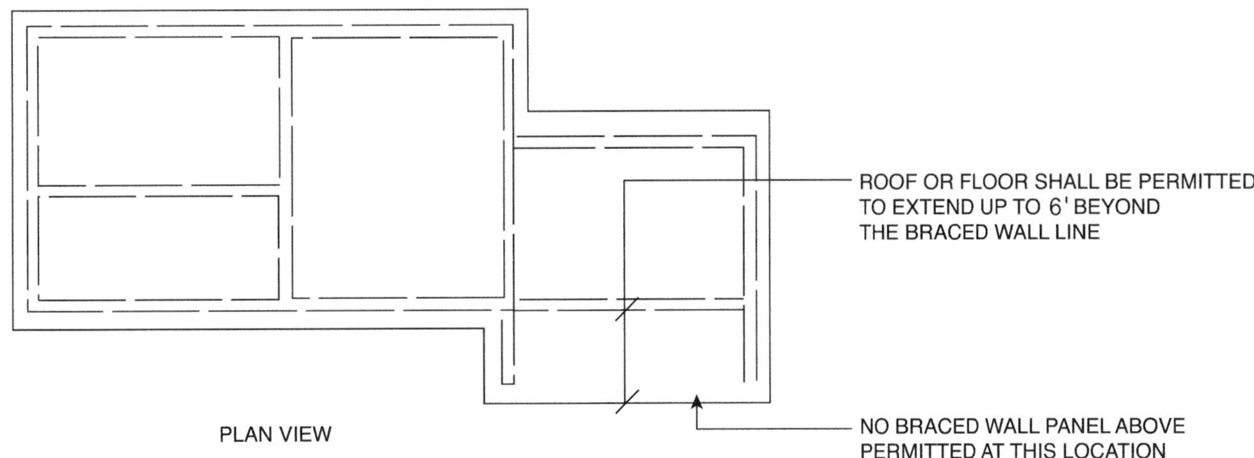

For SI: 1 foot = 304.8 mm.

FIGURE 2308.12.6(4)
ROOF OR FLOOR EXTENSION BEYOND BRACED WALL LINE

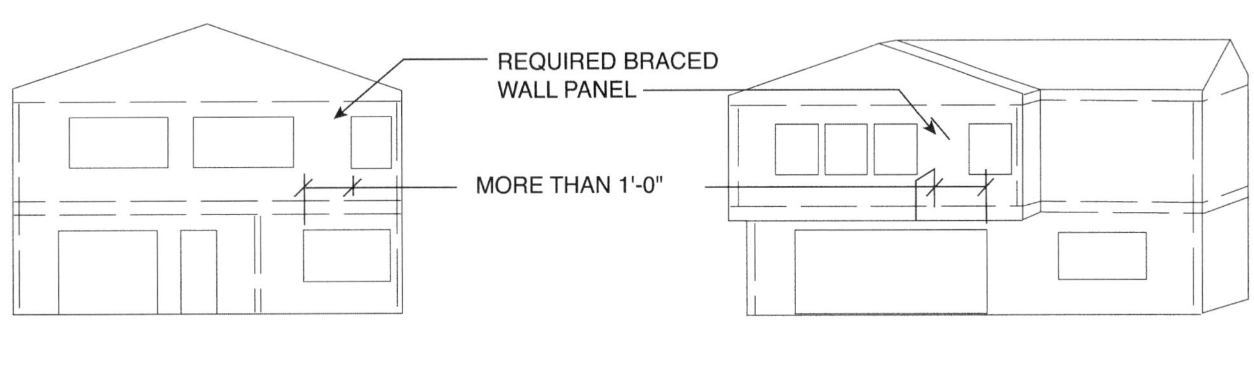

For SI: 1 foot = 304.8 mm.

FIGURE 2308.12.6(5)
BRACED WALL PANEL EXTENSION OVER OPENING

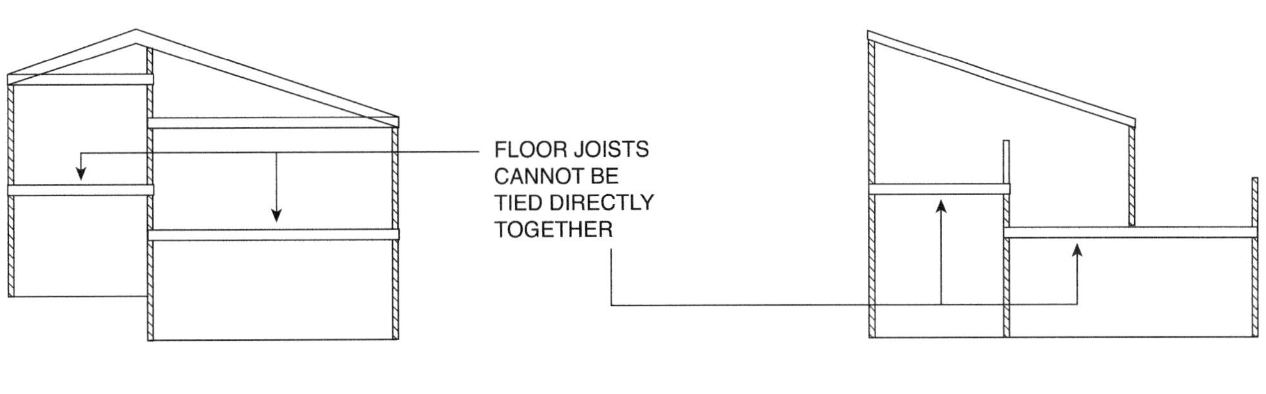

FIGURE 2308.12.6(6)
PORTIONS OF FLOOR LEVEL OFFSET VERTICALLY

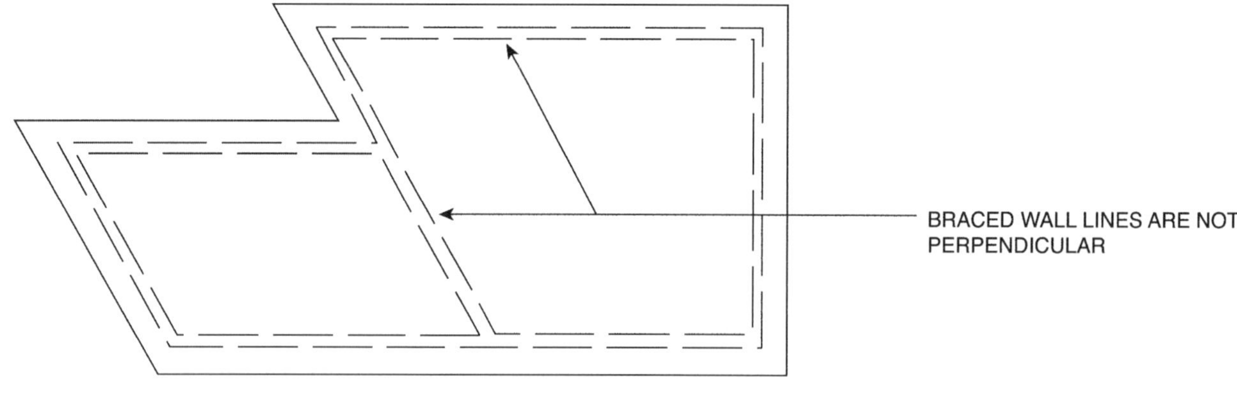

FIGURE 2308.12.6(7)
BRACED WALL LINES NOT PERPENDICULAR

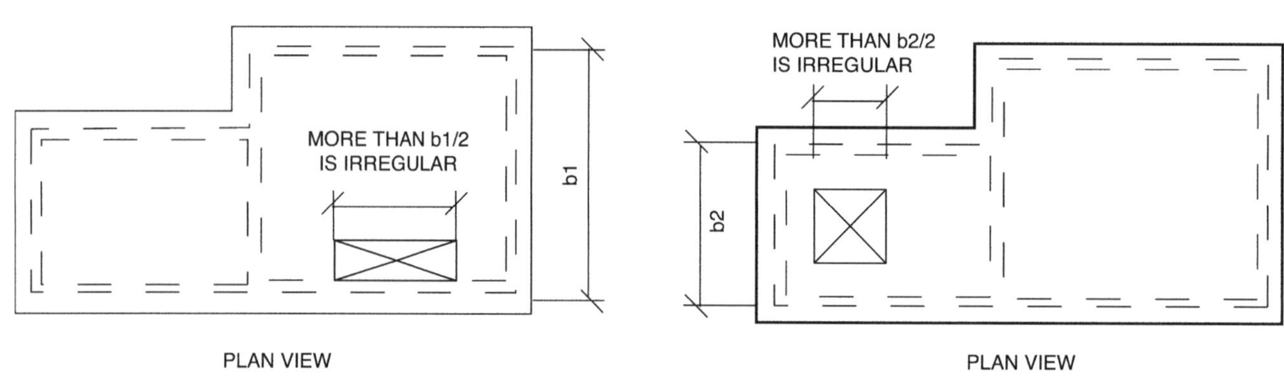

FIGURE 2308.12.6(8)
OPENING LIMITATIONS FOR FLOOR AND ROOF DIAPHRAGMS

2308.12.7 Anchorage of exterior means of egress components. Exterior egress balconies, exterior exit stairways and similar *means of egress* components shall be positively anchored to the primary structure at not over 8 feet (2438 mm) o.c. or shall be designed for lateral forces. Such attachment shall not be accomplished by use of toenails or nails subject to withdrawal.

2308.12.8 Sill plate anchorage. Sill plates shall be anchored with anchor bolts with steel plate washers between the foundation sill plate and the nut, or *approved* anchor straps load rated in accordance with Section 1716.1. Such washers shall be a minimum of 0.229 inch by 3 inches by 3 inches (5.82 mm by 76 mm by 76 mm) in size. The hole in the plate washer is permitted to be diagonally slotted with a width of up to $^{3}/_{16}$ inch (4.76 mm) larger than the bolt diameter and a slot length not to exceed $1^{3}/_{4}$ inches (44 mm), provided a standard cut washer is placed between the plate washer and the nut.

2308.12.9 Sill plate anchorage in Seismic Design Category E. Steel bolts with a minimum nominal diameter of $^{5}/_{8}$ inch (15.9 mm) or *approved* foundation anchor straps load rated in accordance with Section 1716.1 and spaced to provide equivalent anchorage shall be used in *Seismic Design Category* E.

CHAPTER 24
GLASS AND GLAZING

SECTION 2401 GENERAL

2401.1 Scope. The provisions of this chapter shall govern the materials, design, construction and quality of glass, light-transmitting ceramic and light-transmitting plastic panels for exterior and interior use in both vertical and sloped applications in buildings and structures.

2401.2 Glazing replacement. The installation of replacement glass shall be as required for new installations.

SECTION 2402 DEFINITIONS

2402.1 Definitions. The following words and terms shall, for the purposes of this chapter and as used elsewhere in this code, have the meanings shown herein.

DALLE GLASS. A decorative composite glazing material made of individual pieces of glass that are embedded in a cast matrix of concrete or epoxy.

DECORATIVE GLASS. A carved, leaded or Dalle glass or glazing material whose purpose is decorative or artistic, not functional; whose coloring, texture or other design qualities or components cannot be removed without destroying the glazing material and whose surface, or assembly into which it is incorporated, is divided into segments.

SECTION 2403 GENERAL REQUIREMENTS FOR GLASS

2403.1 Identification. Each pane shall bear the manufacturer's *mark* designating the type and thickness of the glass or glazing material. The identification shall not be omitted unless *approved* and an affidavit is furnished by the glazing contractor certifying that each light is glazed in accordance with *approved construction documents* that comply with the provisions of this chapter. Safety glazing shall be identified in accordance with Section 2406.2.

Each pane of tempered glass, except tempered spandrel glass, shall be permanently identified by the manufacturer. The identification *mark* shall be acid etched, sand blasted, ceramic fired, laser etched, embossed or of a type that, once applied, cannot be removed without being destroyed.

Tempered spandrel glass shall be provided with a removable paper marking by the manufacturer.

2403.2 Glass supports. Where one or more sides of any pane of glass are not firmly supported, or are subjected to unusual load conditions, detailed *construction documents*, detailed shop drawings and analysis or test data assuring safe performance for the specific installation shall be prepared by a *registered design professional*.

2403.3 Framing. To be considered firmly supported, the framing members for each individual pane of glass shall be designed so the deflection of the edge of the glass perpendicular to the glass pane shall not exceed $^{1}/_{175}$ of the glass edge length or $^{3}/_{4}$ inch (19.1 mm), whichever is less, when subjected to the larger of the positive or negative load where loads are combined as specified in Section 1605.

2403.4 Interior glazed areas. Where interior glazing is installed adjacent to a walking surface, the differential deflection of two adjacent unsupported edges shall not be greater than the thickness of the panels when a force of 50 pounds per linear foot (plf) (730 N/m) is applied horizontally to one panel at any point up to 42 inches (1067 mm) above the walking surface.

2403.5 Louvered windows or jalousies. Float, wired and patterned glass in louvered windows and jalousies shall be no thinner than nominal $^{3}/_{16}$ inch (4.8 mm) and no longer than 48 inches (1219 mm). Exposed glass edges shall be smooth.

Wired glass with wire exposed on longitudinal edges shall not be used in louvered windows or jalousies.

Where other glass types are used, the design shall be submitted to the *building official* for approval.

SECTION 2404 WIND, SNOW, SEISMIC AND DEAD LOADS ON GLASS

2404.1 Vertical glass. Glass sloped 15 degrees (0.26 rad) or less from vertical in windows, curtain and window walls, doors and other exterior applications shall be designed to resist the wind loads in Section 1609 for components and cladding. Glass in glazed curtain walls, glazed storefronts and glazed partitions shall meet the seismic requirements of ASCE 7, Section 13.5.9. The load resistance of glass under uniform load shall be determined in accordance with ASTM E 1300.

The design of vertical glazing shall be based on the following equation:

$$F_{gw} \leq F_{ga} \qquad \textbf{(Equation 24-1)}$$

where:

F_{gw} = Wind load on the glass computed in accordance with Section 1609.

F_{ga} = Short duration load on the glass as determined in accordance with ASTM E 1300.

2404.2 Sloped glass. Glass sloped more than 15 degrees (0.26 rad) from vertical in skylights, sunrooms, sloped roofs and other exterior applications shall be designed to resist the most critical of the following combinations of loads.

$$F_g = W_o - D \qquad \textbf{(Equation 24-2)}$$

$$F_g = W_i + D + 0.5\,S \qquad \textbf{(Equation 24-3)}$$

$F_g = 0.5\ W_i + D + S$ **(Equation 24-4)**

where:

D = Glass dead load psf (kN/m?).

For glass sloped 30 degrees (0.52 rad) or less from horizontal,

= 13 t_g (For SI: 0.0245 t_g).

For glass sloped more than 30 degrees (0.52 rad) from horizontal,

= 13 t_g cos θ (For SI: 0.0245 t_g cos θ).

F_g = Total load, psf (kN/m^2) on glass.

S = Snow load, psf (kN/m^2) as determined in Section 1608.

t_g = Total glass thickness, inches (mm) of glass panes and plies.

W_i = Inward wind force, psf (kN/m^2) as calculated in Section 1609.

W_o = Outward wind force, psf (kN/m^2) as calculated in Section 1609.

θ = Angle of slope from horizontal.

Exception: Unit skylights shall be designed in accordance with Section 2405.5.

The design of sloped glazing shall be based on the following equation:

$F_g \leq F_{ga}$ **(Equation 24-5)**

where:

F_g = Total load on the glass determined from the load combinations above.

F_{ga} = Short duration load resistance of the glass as determined according to ASTM E 1300 for Equations 24-2 and 24-3; or the long duration load resistance of the glass as determined according to ASTM E 1300 for Equation 24-4.

2404.3 Wired, patterned and sandblasted glass.

2404.3.1 Vertical wired glass. Wired glass sloped 15 degrees (0.26 rad) or less from vertical in windows, curtain and window walls, doors and other exterior applications shall be designed to resist the wind loads in Section 1609 for components and cladding according to the following equation:

$F_{gw} < 0.5\ F_{ge}$ **(Equation 24-6)**

where:

F_{gw} = Is the wind load on the glass computed per Section 1609.

F_{ge} = Nonfactored load from ASTM E 1300 using a thickness designation for monolithic glass that is not greater than the thickness of wired glass.

2404.3.2 Sloped wired glass. Wired glass sloped more than 15 degrees (0.26 rad) from vertical in skylights, sunspaces, sloped roofs and other exterior applications shall be designed to resist the most critical of the combinations of loads from Section 2404.2.

For Equations 24-2 and 24-3:

$F_g < 0.5\ F_{ge}$ **(Equation 24-7)**

For Equation 24-4:

$F_g < 0.3\ F_{ge}$ **(Equation 24-8)**

where:

F_g = Total load on the glass.

F_{ge} = Nonfactored load from ASTM E 1300.

2404.3.3 Vertical patterned glass. Patterned glass sloped 15 degrees (0.26 rad) or less from vertical in windows, curtain and window walls, doors and other exterior applications shall be designed to resist the wind loads in Section 1609 for components and cladding according to the following equation:

$F_{gw} < 1.0\ F_{ge}$ **(Equation 24-9)**

where:

F_{gw} = Wind load on the glass computed per Section 1609.

F_{ge} = Nonfactored load from ASTM E 1300. The value for patterned glass shall be based on the thinnest part of the glass. Interpolation between nonfactored load charts in ASTM E 1300 shall be permitted.

2404.3.4 Sloped patterned glass. Patterned glass sloped more than 15 degrees (0.26 rad) from vertical in skylights, sunspaces, sloped roofs and other exterior applications shall be designed to resist the most critical of the combinations of loads from Section 2404.2.

For Equations 24-2 and 24-3:

$F_g < 1.0\ F_{ge}$ **(Equation 24-10)**

For Equation 24-4:

$F_g < 0.6 F_{ge}$ **(Equation 24-11)**

where

F_g = Total load on the glass.

F_{ge} = Nonfactored load from ASTM E 1300. The value for patterned glass shall be based on the thinnest part of the glass. Interpolation between the nonfactored load charts in ASTM E 1300 shall be permitted.

2404.3.5 Vertical sandblasted glass. Sandblasted glass sloped 15 degrees (0.26 rad) or less from vertical in windows, curtain and window walls, doors, and other exterior applications shall be designed to resist the wind loads in Section 1609 for components and cladding according to the following equation:

$F_g < 0.5\ F_{ge}$ **(Equation 24-12)**

where:

F_g = Total load on the glass.

F_{ge} = Nonfactored load from ASTM E 1300. The value for sandblasted glass is for moderate levels of sandblasting.

2404.4 Other designs. For designs outside the scope of this section, an analysis or test data for the specific installation shall be prepared by a *registered design professional*.

SECTION 2405
SLOPED GLAZING AND SKYLIGHTS

2405.1 Scope. This section applies to the installation of glass and other transparent, translucent or opaque glazing material installed at a slope more than 15 degrees (0.26 rad) from the vertical plane, including glazing materials in skylights, roofs and sloped walls.

2405.2 Allowable glazing materials and limitations. Sloped glazing shall be any of the following materials, subject to the listed limitations.

1. For monolithic glazing systems, the glazing material of the single light or layer shall be laminated glass with a minimum 30-mil (0.76 mm) polyvinyl butyral (or equivalent) interlayer, wired glass, light-transmitting plastic materials meeting the requirements of Section 2607, heat-strengthened glass or fully tempered glass.
2. For multiple-layer glazing systems, each light or layer shall consist of any of the glazing materials specified in Item 1 above.

Annealed glass is permitted to be used as specified within Exceptions 2 and 3 of Section 2405.3.

For additional requirements for plastic skylights, see Section 2610. Glass-block construction shall conform to the requirements of Section 2101.2.5.

2405.3 Screening. Where used in monolithic glazing systems, heat-strengthened glass and fully tempered glass shall have screens installed below the glazing material. The screens and their fastenings shall: (1) be capable of supporting twice the weight of the glazing; (2) be firmly and substantially fastened to the framing members and (3) be installed within 4 inches (102 mm) of the glass. The screens shall be constructed of a noncombustible material not thinner than No. 12 B&S gage (0.0808 inch) with mesh not larger than 1 inch by 1 inch (25 mm by 25 mm). In a corrosive atmosphere, structurally equivalent noncorrosive screen materials shall be used. Heat-strengthened glass, fully tempered glass and wired glass, when used in multiple-layer glazing systems as the bottom glass layer over the walking surface, shall be equipped with screening that conforms to the requirements for monolithic glazing systems.

Exception: In monolithic and multiple-layer sloped glazing systems, the following applies:

1. Fully tempered glass installed without protective screens where glazed between intervening floors at a slope of 30 degrees (0.52 rad) or less from the vertical plane shall have the highest point of the glass 10 feet (3048 mm) or less above the walking surface.
2. Screens are not required below any glazing material, including annealed glass, where the walking surface below the glazing material is permanently protected from the risk of falling glass or the area below the glazing material is not a walking surface.
3. Any glazing material, including annealed glass, is permitted to be installed without screens in the sloped glazing systems of commercial or detached noncombustible greenhouses used exclusively for growing plants and not open to the public, provided that the height of the greenhouse at the ridge does not exceed 30 feet (9144 mm) above grade.
4. Screens shall not be required within individual *dwelling units* in Groups R-2, R-3 and R-4 where fully tempered glass is used as single glazing or as both panes in an insulating glass unit, and the following conditions are met:
   - 4.1. Each pane of the glass is 16 square feet (1.5 m^2) or less in area.
   - 4.2. The highest point of the glass is 12 feet (3658 mm) or less above any walking surface or other accessible area.
   - 4.3. The glass thickness is $^3/_{16}$ inch (4.8 mm) or less.
5. Screens shall not be required for laminated glass with a 15-mil (0.38 mm) polyvinyl butyral (or equivalent) interlayer used within individual *dwelling units* in Groups R-2, R-3 and R-4 within the following limits:
   - 5.1. Each pane of glass is 16 square feet (1.5 m^2) or less in area.
   - 5.2. The highest point of the glass is 12 feet (3658 mm) or less above a walking surface or other accessible area.

2405.4 Framing. In Type I and II construction, sloped glazing and skylight frames shall be constructed of noncombustible materials. In structures where acid fumes deleterious to metal are incidental to the use of the buildings, *approved* pressure-treated wood or other *approved* noncorrosive materials are permitted to be used for sash and frames. Framing supporting sloped glazing and skylights shall be designed to resist the tributary roof loads in Chapter 16. Skylights set at an angle of less than 45 degrees (0.79 rad) from the horizontal plane shall be mounted at least 4 inches (102 mm) above the plane of the roof on a curb constructed as required for the frame. Skylights shall not be installed in the plane of the roof where the roof pitch is less than 45 degrees (0.79 rad) from the horizontal.

Exception: Installation of a skylight without a curb shall be permitted on roofs with a minimum slope of 14 degrees (three units vertical in 12 units horizontal) in Group R-3 occupancies. All unit skylights installed in a roof with a pitch flatter than 14 degrees (0.25 rad) shall be mounted at least 4 inches (102 mm) above the plane of the roof on a curb constructed as required for the frame unless otherwise specified in the manufacturer's installation instructions.

2405.5 Unit skylights. Unit skylights shall be tested and labeled as complying with AAMA/WDMA/CSA 101/I.S.2/A440. The *label* shall state the name of the manufacturer, the *approved* labeling agency, the product designation and the performance grade rating as specified in AAMA/WDMA/CSA 101/I.S.2/A440. If the product manufacturer has chosen to have the performance grade of the skylight rated separately for positive and negative design pressure, then the *label* shall state both performance grade ratings as specified in AAMA/WDMA/CSA 101/I.S.2/A440 and the skylight shall comply with Section 2405.5.2. If the skylight is not rated separately for positive and negative pressure, then the performance grade rating shown on the *label* shall be the performance grade rating determined in accordance with AAMA/WDMA/CSA 101/I.S.2/A440 for both positive and negative design pressure and the skylight shall conform to Section 2405.5.1.

2405.5.1 Unit skylights rated for the same performance grade for both positive and negative design pressure. The design of unit skylights shall be based on the following equation:

$$F_g \leq PG \quad \textbf{(Equation 24-13)}$$

where:

F_g = Maximum load on the skylight determined from Equations 24-2 through 24-4 in Section 2404.2.

PG = Performance grade rating of the skylight.

2405.5.2 Unit skylights rated for separate performance grades for positive and negative design pressure. The design of unit skylights rated for performance grade for both positive and negative design pressures shall be based on the following equations:

$$F_{gi} \leq PG_{Pos} \quad \textbf{(Equation 24-14)}$$

$$F_{go} \leq PG_{Neg} \quad \textbf{(Equation 24-15)}$$

where:

PG_{Pos} = Performance grade rating of the skylight under positive design pressure;

PG_{Neg} = Performance grade rating of the skylight under negative design pressure; and

F_{gi} and F_{go} are determined in accordance with the following:

For $W_o \geq D$,
where:

W_o = Outward wind force, psf (kN/m^2) as calculated in Section 1609.

D = The dead weight of the glazing, psf (kN/m^2) as determined in Section 2404.2 for glass, or by the weight of the plastic, psf (kN/m^2) for plastic glazing.

F_{gi} = Maximum load on the skylight determined from Equations 24-3 and 24-4 in Section 2404.2.

F_{go} = Maximum load on the skylight determined from Equation 24-2.

For $W_o < D$,

where:

W_o = Is the outward wind force, psf (kN/m^2) as calculated in Section 1609.

D = The dead weight of the glazing, psf (kN/m^2) as determined in Section 2404.2 for glass, or by the weight of the plastic for plastic glazing.

F_{gi} = Maximum load on the skylight determined from Equations 24-2 through 24-4 in Section 2404.2.

F_{go} = 0.

SECTION 2406
SAFETY GLAZING

2406.1 Human impact loads. Individual glazed areas, including glass mirrors, in hazardous locations as defined in Section 2406.4 shall comply with Sections 2406.1.1 through 2406.1.4.

2406.1.1 Impact test. Except as provided in Sections 2406.1.2 through 2406.1.4, all glazing shall pass the impact test requirements of Section 2406.2.

2406.1.2 Plastic glazing. Plastic glazing shall meet the weathering requirements of ANSI Z97.1.

2406.1.3 Glass block. Glass-block walls shall comply with Section 2101.2.5.

2406.1.4 Louvered windows and jalousies. Louvered windows and jalousies shall comply with Section 2403.5.

2406.2 Impact test. Where required by other sections of this code, glazing shall be tested in accordance with CPSC 16 CFR 1201. Glazing shall comply with the test criteria for Category I or II as indicated in Table 2406.2(1).

Exception: Glazing not in doors or enclosures for hot tubs, whirlpools, saunas, steam rooms, bathtubs and showers shall be permitted to be tested in accordance with ANSI Z97.1. Glazing shall comply with the test criteria for Class A or B as indicated in Table 2406.2(2).

2406.3 Identification of safety glazing. Except as indicated in Section 2406.3.1, each pane of safety glazing installed in haz-

TABLE 2406.2(1)
MINIMUM CATEGORY CLASSIFICATION OF GLAZING USING CPSC 16 CFR 1201

EXPOSED SURFACE AREA OF ONE SIDE OF ONE LITE	GLAZING IN STORM OR COMBINATION DOORS (Category class)	GLAZING IN DOORS (Category class)	GLAZED PANELS REGULATED BY ITEM 7 OF SECTION 2406.4 (Category class)	GLAZED PANELS REGULATED BY ITEM 6 OF SECTION 2406.4 (Category class)	DOORS AND ENCLOSURES REGULATED BY ITEM 5 OF SECTION 2406.4 (Category class)	SLIDING GLASS DOORS PATIO TYPE (Category class)
9 square feet or less	I	I	No requirement	I	II	II
More than 9 square feet	II	II	II	II	II	II

For SI: 1 square foot = 0.0929 m^2.

TABLE 2406.2(2)
MINIMUM CATEGORY CLASSIFICATION OF GLAZING USING ANSI Z97.1

EXPOSED SURFACE AREA OF ONE SIDE OF ONE LITE	GLAZED PANELS REGULATED BY ITEM 7 OF SECTION 2406.4 (Category class)	GLAZED PANELS REGULATED BY ITEM 6 OF SECTION 2406.4 (Category class)	DOORS AND ENCLOSURES REGULATED BY ITEM 5 OF SECTION 2406.4[a] (Category class)
9 square feet or less	No requirement	B	A
More than 9 square feet	A	A	A

For SI: 1 square foot = 0.0929 m^2.
a. Use is only permitted by the exception to Section 2406.2.

ardous locations shall be identified by a manufacturer's designation specifying who applied the designation, the manufacturer or installer and the safety glazing standard with which it complies, as well as the information specified in Section 2403.1. The designation shall be acid etched, sand blasted, ceramic fired, laser etched, embossed or of a type that once applied, cannot be removed without being destroyed. A label as defined in Section 202.1 and meeting the requirements of this section shall be permitted in lieu of the manufacturer's designation.

Exceptions:

1. For other than tempered glass, manufacturer's designations are not required, provided the *building official* approves the use of a certificate, affidavit or other evidence confirming compliance with this code.
2. Tempered spandrel glass is permitted to be identified by the manufacturer with a removable paper designation

2406.3.1 Multi-pane assemblies. Multi-pane glazed assemblies having individual panes not exceeding 1 square foot (0.09 m^2) in exposed areas shall have at least one pane in the assembly marked as indicated in Section 2406.3. Other panes in the assembly shall be marked "CPSC 16 CFR 1201" or "ANSI Z97.1," as appropriate.

2406.4 Hazardous locations. The following shall be considered specific hazardous locations requiring safety glazing materials:

1. Glazing in swinging doors except jalousies (see Section 2406.4.1).
2. Glazing in fixed and sliding panels of sliding door assemblies and panels in sliding and bifold closet door assemblies.
3. Glazing in storm doors.
4. Glazing in unframed swinging doors.
5. Glazing in doors and enclosures for hot tubs, whirlpools, saunas, steam rooms, bathtubs and showers. Glazing in any portion of a building wall enclosing these compartments where the bottom exposed edge of the glazing is less than 60 inches (1524 mm) above a standing surface.
6. Glazing in an individual fixed or operable panel adjacent to a door where the nearest exposed edge of the glazing is within a 24-inch (610 mm) arc of either vertical edge of the door in a closed position and where the bottom exposed edge of the glazing is less than 60 inches (1524 mm) above the walking surface.

   Exceptions:

   1. Panels where there is an intervening wall or other permanent barrier between the door and glazing.
   2. Where access through the door is to a closet or storage area 3 feet (914 mm) or less in depth. Glazing in this application shall comply with Section 2406.4, Item 7.
   3. Glazing in walls perpendicular to the plane of the door in a closed position, other than the wall towards which the door swings when opened, in one- and two-family *dwellings* or within *dwelling units* in Group R-2.

7. Glazing in an individual fixed or operable panel, other than in those locations described in preceding Items 5 and 6, which meets all of the following conditions:

   7.1. Exposed area of an individual pane greater than 9 square feet (0.84 m^2);

   7.2. Exposed bottom edge less than 18 inches (457 mm) above the floor;

   7.3. Exposed top edge greater than 36 inches (914 mm) above the floor; and

   7.4. One or more walking surface(s) within 36 inches (914 mm) horizontally of the plane of the glazing.

   Exception: Safety glazing for Item 7 is not required for the following installations:

   1. A protective bar 1$^1/_2$ inches (38 mm) or more in height, capable of withstanding a horizontal load of 50 plf (730 N/m) without contacting the glass, is installed on the accessible sides of the glazing 34 inches to 38 inches (864 mm to 965 mm) above the floor.
   2. The outboard pane in insulating glass units or multiple glazing where the bottom exposed edge of the glass is 25 feet (7620 mm) or more above any grade, roof, walking surface or other horizontal or sloped [within 45 degrees (0.78 rad) of horizontal] surface adjacent to the glass exterior.

8. Glazing in *guards* and railings, including structural baluster panels and nonstructural in-fill panels, regardless of area or height above a walking surface.

9. Glazing in walls and fences enclosing indoor and outdoor swimming pools, hot tubs and spas where all of the following conditions are present:
   9.1. The bottom edge of the glazing on the pool or spa side is less than 60 inches (1524 mm) above a walking surface on the pool or spa side of the glazing; and
   9.2. The glazing is within 60 inches (1524 mm) horizontally of the water's edge of a swimming pool or spa.
10. Glazing adjacent to *stairways*, landings and ramps within 36 inches (914 mm) horizontally of a walking surface; when the exposed surface of the glass is less than 60 inches (1524 mm) above the plane of the adjacent walking surface.
11. Glazing adjacent to *stairways* within 60 inches (1524 mm) horizontally of the bottom tread of a *stairway* in any direction when the exposed surface of the glass is less than 60 inches (1524 mm) above the nose of the tread.

   Exception: Safety glazing for Item 10 or 11 is not required for the following installations where:

   1. The side of a *stairway*, landing or ramp which has a *guard* or handrail, including balusters or in-fill panels, complying with the provisions of Sections 1013 and 1607.7; and
   2. The plane of the glass is greater than 18 inches (457 mm) from the railing.

2406.4.1 Exceptions. The following products, materials and uses shall not be considered specific hazardous locations:

1. Openings in doors through which a 3-inch (76 mm) sphere is unable to pass.
2. Decorative glass in Section 2406.4, Item 1, 6 or 7.
3. Glazing materials used as curved glazed panels in revolving doors.
4. Commercial refrigerated cabinet glazed doors.
5. Glass-block panels complying with Section 2101.2.5.
6. Louvered windows and jalousies complying with the requirements of Section 2403.5.
7. Mirrors and other glass panels mounted or hung on a surface that provides a continuous backing support.

2406.5 Fire department access panels. Fire department glass access panels shall be of tempered glass. For insulating glass units, all panes shall be tempered glass.

SECTION 2407
GLASS IN HANDRAILS AND GUARDS

2407.1 Materials. Glass used as a handrail assembly or a *guard* section shall be constructed of either single fully tempered glass, laminated fully tempered glass or laminated heat-strengthened glass. Glazing in railing in-fill panels shall be of an *approved* safety glazing material that conforms to the provisions of Section 2406.1.1. For all glazing types, the minimum nominal thickness shall be $^1/_4$ inch (6.4 mm). Fully tempered glass and laminated glass shall comply with Category II of CPSC 16 CFR 1201 or Class A of ANSI Z97.1, listed in Chapter 35.

2407.1.1 Loads. The panels and their support system shall be designed to withstand the loads specified in Section 1607.7. A safety factor of four shall be used.

2407.1.2 Support. Each handrail or *guard* section shall be supported by a minimum of three glass balusters or shall be otherwise supported to remain in place should one baluster panel fail. Glass balusters shall not be installed without an attached handrail or *guard*.

Exception: A top rail shall not be required where the glass balusters are laminated glass with two or more glass plies of equal thickness and the same glass type when *approved* by the *building official*. The panels shall be designed to withstand the loads specified in Section 1607.7.

2407.1.3 Parking garages. Glazing materials shall not be installed in handrails or *guards* in parking garages except for pedestrian areas not exposed to impact from vehicles.

2407.1.4 Glazing in wind-borne debris regions. Glazing installed in in-fill panels or balusters in *wind-borne debris regions* shall comply with the following:

2407.1.4.1 Ballusters and in-fill panels. Glass installed in exterior railing in-fill panels or balusters shall be laminated glass complying with Category II of CPSC 16 CFR 1201 or Class A of ANSI Z97.1.

2407.1.4.2 Glass supporting top rail. When the top rail is supported by glass, the assembly shall be tested according to the impact requirements of Section 1609.1.2. The top rail shall remain in place after impact.

SECTION 2408
GLAZING IN ATHLETIC FACILITIES

2408.1 General. Glazing in athletic facilities and similar uses subject to impact loads, which forms whole or partial wall sections or which is used as a door or part of a door, shall comply with this section.

2408.2 Racquetball and squash courts.

2408.2.1 Testing. Test methods and loads for individual glazed areas in racquetball and squash courts subject to impact loads shall conform to those of CPSC 16 CFR 1201 or ANSI Z97.1, listed in Chapter 35, with impacts being applied at a height of 59 inches (1499 mm) above the playing surface to an actual or simulated glass wall installation with fixtures, fittings and methods of assembly identical to those used in practice.

Glass walls shall comply with the following conditions:

1. A glass wall in a racquetball or squash court, or similar use subject to impact loads, shall remain intact following a test impact.

2. The deflection of such walls shall not be greater than $1^1/_2$ inches (38 mm) at the point of impact for a drop height of 48 inches (1219 mm).

Glass doors shall comply with the following conditions:

1. Glass doors shall remain intact following a test impact at the prescribed height in the center of the door.
2. The relative deflection between the edge of a glass door and the adjacent wall shall not exceed the thickness of the wall plus $^1/_2$ inch (12.7 mm) for a drop height of 48 inches (1219 mm).

2408.3 Gymnasiums and basketball courts. Glazing in multipurpose gymnasiums, basketball courts and similar athletic facilities subject to human impact loads shall comply with Category II of CPSC 16 CFR 1201 or Class A of ANSI Z97.1, listed in Chapter 35.

SECTION 2409 GLASS IN ELEVATOR HOISTWAYS AND ELEVATOR CARS

2409.1 Glass in elevator hoistway enclosures. Glass in elevator hoistway enclosures and hoistway doors shall be laminated glass conforming to ANSI Z97.1 or CPSC 16 CFR.

2409.1.1 Fire-resistance-rated hoistways. Glass installed in hoistways and hoistway doors where the hoistway is required to have a fire-resistance rating shall also comply with Section 715.

2409.1.2 Glass hoistway doors. The glass in glass hoistway doors shall be not less than 60 percent of the total visible door panel surface area as seen from the landing side.

2409.2 Glass visions panels. Glass in vision panels in elevator hoistway doors shall be permitted to be any transparent glazing material not less than $^1/_4$ inches (6.4 mm) in thickness conforming to Class A in accordance with ANSI Z97.1 or Category II in accordance with CPSC 16 CFR. The area of any single vision panel shall not be less than 24 square inches (15 484 mm^2) and the total area of one or more vision panels in any hoistway door shall be not more than 85 square inches (54 839 mm^2).

2409.3 Glass in elevator cars.

2409.3.1 Glass types. Glass in elevator car enclosures, glass elevator car doors and glass used for lining walls and ceilings of elevator cars shall be laminated glass conforming to Class A in accordance with ANSI Z97.1 or Category II in accordance with CPSC 16 CFR.

Exception: Tempered glass shall be permitted to be used for lining walls and ceilings of elevator cars provided:

1. The glass is bonded to a nonpolymeric coating, sheeting or film backing having a physical integrity to hold the fragments when the glass breaks.
2. The glass is not subjected to further treatment such as sandblasting; etching; heat treatment or painting that could alter the original properties of the glass.
3. The glass is tested to the acceptance criteria for laminated glass as specified for Class A in accordance with ANSI Z97.1 or Category II in accordance with CPSC 16 CFR.

2409.3.2 Surface area. The glass in glass elevator car doors shall be not less than 60 percent of the total visible door panel surface area as seen from the car side of the doors.

CHAPTER 25
GYPSUM BOARD AND PLASTER

SECTION 2501
GENERAL

2501.1 Scope.

2501.1.1 General. Provisions of this chapter shall govern the materials, design, construction and quality of gypsum board, lath, gypsum plaster and cement plaster.

2501.1.2 Performance. Lathing, plastering and gypsum board construction shall be done in the manner and with the materials specified in this chapter, and when required for fire protection, shall also comply with the provisions of Chapter 7.

2501.1.3 Other materials. Other *approved* wall or ceiling coverings shall be permitted to be installed in accordance with the recommendations of the manufacturer and the conditions of approval.

SECTION 2502
DEFINITIONS

2502.1 Definitions. The following words and terms shall, for the purposes of this chapter and as used elsewhere in this code, have the meanings shown herein.

CEMENT PLASTER. A mixture of portland or blended cement, portland cement or blended cement and hydrated lime, masonry cement or plastic cement and aggregate and other *approved* materials as specified in this code.

EXTERIOR SURFACES. Weather-exposed surfaces.

GYPSUM BOARD. Gypsum wallboard, gypsum sheathing, gypsum base for gypsum veneer plaster, exterior gypsum soffit board, predecorated gypsum board or water-resistant gypsum backing board complying with the standards listed in Tables 2506.2, 2507.2 and Chapter 35.

GYPSUM PLASTER. A mixture of calcined gypsum or calcined gypsum and lime and aggregate and other *approved* materials as specified in this code.

GYPSUM VENEER PLASTER. Gypsum plaster applied to an *approved* base in one or more coats normally not exceeding $^1/_4$ inch (6.4 mm) in total thickness.

INTERIOR SURFACES. Surfaces other than weather-exposed surfaces.

WEATHER-EXPOSED SURFACES. Surfaces of walls, ceilings, floors, roofs, soffits and similar surfaces exposed to the weather except the following:

1. Ceilings and roof soffits enclosed by walls, fascia, bulkheads or beams that extend a minimum of 12 inches (305 mm) below such ceiling or roof soffits.
2. Walls or portions of walls beneath an unenclosed roof area, where located a horizontal distance from an open exterior opening equal to at least twice the height of the opening.
3. Ceiling and roof soffits located a minimum horizontal distance of 10 feet (3048 mm) from the outer edges of the ceiling or roof soffits.

WIRE BACKING. Horizontal strands of tautened wire attached to surfaces of vertical supports which, when covered with the building paper, provide a backing for cement plaster.

SECTION 2503
INSPECTION

2503.1 Inspection. Lath and gypsum board shall be inspected in accordance with Section 110.3.5.

SECTION 2504
VERTICAL AND HORIZONTAL ASSEMBLIES

2504.1 Scope. The following requirements shall be met where construction involves gypsum board, lath and plaster in vertical and horizontal assemblies.

2504.1.1 Wood framing. Wood supports for lath or gypsum board, as well as wood stripping or furring, shall not be less than 2 inches (51 mm) nominal thickness in the least dimension.

Exception: The minimum nominal dimension of wood furring strips installed over solid backing shall not be less than 1 inch by 2 inches (25 mm by 51 mm).

2504.1.2 Studless partitions. The minimum thickness of vertically erected studless solid plaster partitions of $^3/_8$-inch (9.5 mm) and $^3/_4$-inch (19.1 mm) rib metal lath or $^1/_2$-inch-thick (12.7 mm) long-length gypsum lath and gypsum board partitions shall be 2 inches (51 mm).

SECTION 2505
SHEAR WALL CONSTRUCTION

2505.1 Resistance to shear (wood framing). Wood-framed shear walls sheathed with gypsum board, lath and plaster shall be designed and constructed in accordance with Section 2306.7 and are permitted to resist wind and seismic loads. Walls resisting seismic loads shall be subject to the limitations in Section 12.2.1 of ASCE 7.

2505.2 Resistance to shear (steel framing). Cold-formed steel-framed shear walls sheathed with gypsum board and constructed in accordance with the materials and provisions of Section 2210.6 are permitted to resist wind and seismic loads. Walls resisting seismic loads shall be subject to the limitations in Section 12.2.1 of ASCE 7.

SECTION 2506
GYPSUM BOARD MATERIALS

2506.1 General. Gypsum board materials and accessories shall be identified by the manufacturer's designation to indicate compliance with the appropriate standards referenced in this section and stored to protect such materials from the weather.

2506.2 Standards. Gypsum board materials shall conform to the appropriate standards listed in Table 2506.2 and Chapter 35 and, where required for fire protection, shall conform to the provisions of Chapter 7.

TABLE 2506.2
GYPSUM BOARD MATERIALS AND ACCESSORIES

MATERIAL	STANDARD
Accessories for gypsum board	ASTM C 1047
Adhesives for fastening gypsum wallboard	ASTM C 557
Elastomeric joint sealants	ASTM C 920
Exterior soffit board	ASTM C 931
Fiber-reinforced gypsum panels	ASTM C 1278
Glass mat gypsum backing panel	ASTM C 1178
Glass mat gypsum panel	ASTM C 1658
Glass mat gypsum substrate	ASTM C 1177
Gypsum backing board and gypsum shaftliner board	ASTM C 442
Gypsum ceiling board	ASTM C 1395
Gypsum sheathing	ASTM C 79
Gypsum wallboard	ASTM C 36
Joint reinforcing tape and compound	ASTM C 474; C 475
Nails for gypsum boards	ASTM C 514, F 547, F 1667
Predecorated gypsum board	ASTM C 960
Steel screws	ASTM C 954; C 1002
Steel studs, load-bearing	ASTM C 955
Steel studs, nonload-bearing	ASTM C 645
Standard specification for gypsum board	ASTM C 1396
Testing gypsum and gypsum products	ASTM C 22; C 472; C 473
Water-resistant gypsum backing board	ASTM C 630

2506.2.1 Other materials. Metal suspension systems for acoustical and lay-in panel ceilings shall conform with ASTM C 635 listed in Chapter 35 and Section 13.5.6 of ASCE 7 for installation in high seismic areas.

SECTION 2507
LATHING AND PLASTERING

2507.1 General. Lathing and plastering materials and accessories shall be marked by the manufacturer's designation to indicate compliance with the appropriate standards referenced in this section and stored in such a manner to protect them from the weather.

2507.2 Standards. Lathing and plastering materials shall conform to the standards listed in Table 2507.2 and Chapter 35 and, where required for fire protection, shall also conform to the provisions of Chapter 7.

TABLE 2507.2
LATH, PLASTERING MATERIALS AND ACCESSORIES

MATERIAL	STANDARD
Accessories for gypsum veneer base	ASTM C 1047
Blended cement	ASTM C 595
Exterior plaster bonding compounds	ASTM C 932
Gypsum base for veneer plasters	ASTM C 588
Gypsum casting and molding plaster	ASTM C 59
Gypsum Keene's cement	ASTM C 61
Gypsum lath	ASTM C 37
Gypsum plaster	ASTM C 28
Gypsum veneer plaster	ASTM C 587
Interior bonding compounds, gypsum	ASTM C 631
Lime plasters	ASTM C 5; C 206
Masonry cement	ASTM C 91
Metal lath	ASTM C 847
Plaster aggregates Sand Perlite Vermiculite	 ASTM C 35; C 897 ASTM C 35 ASTM C 35
Plastic cement	ASTM C 1328
Portland cement	ASTM C 150
Steel screws	ASTM C 1002; C 954
Steel studs and track	ASTM C 645; C 955
Welded wire lath	ASTM C 933
Woven wire plaster base	ASTM C 1032

SECTION 2508
GYPSUM CONSTRUCTION

2508.1 General. Gypsum board and gypsum plaster construction shall be of the materials listed in Tables 2506.2 and 2507.2. These materials shall be assembled and installed in compliance with the appropriate standards listed in Tables 2508.1 and 2511.1.1, and Chapter 35.

TABLE 2508.1
INSTALLATION OF GYPSUM CONSTRUCTION

MATERIAL	STANDARD
Gypsum board	GA-216; ASTM C 840
Gypsum sheathing	ASTM C 1280
Gypsum veneer base	ASTM C 844
Interior lathing and furring	ASTM C 841
Steel framing for gypsum boards	ASTM C 754; C 1007

2508.2 Limitations. Gypsum wallboard or gypsum plaster shall not be used in any exterior surface where such gypsum construction will be exposed directly to the weather. Gypsum wallboard shall not be used where there will be direct exposure to water or continuous high humidity conditions. Gypsum sheathing shall be installed on exterior surfaces in accordance with ASTM C 1280.

2508.2.1 Weather protection. Gypsum wallboard, gypsum lath or gypsum plaster shall not be installed until weather protection for the installation is provided.

2508.3 Single-ply application. Edges and ends of gypsum board shall occur on the framing members, except those edges and ends that are perpendicular to the framing members. Edges and ends of gypsum board shall be in moderate contact except in concealed spaces where fire-resistance-rated construction, shear resistance or diaphragm action is not required.

2508.3.1 Floating angles. Fasteners at the top and bottom plates of vertical assemblies, or the edges and ends of horizontal assemblies perpendicular to supports, and at the wall line are permitted to be omitted except on shear resisting elements or fire-resistance-rated assemblies. Fasteners shall be applied in such a manner as not to fracture the face paper with the fastener head.

2508.4 Joint treatment. Gypsum board fire-resistance-rated assemblies shall have joints and fasteners treated.

Exception: Joint and fastener treatment need not be provided where any of the following conditions occur:

1. Where the gypsum board is to receive a decorative finish such as wood paneling, battens, acoustical finishes or any similar application that would be equivalent to joint treatment.
2. On single-layer systems where joints occur over wood framing members.
3. Square edge or tongue-and-groove edge gypsum board (V-edge), gypsum backing board or gypsum sheathing.
4. On multilayer systems where the joints of adjacent layers are offset from one to another.
5. Assemblies tested without joint treatment.

2508.5 Horizontal gypsum board diaphragm ceilings. Gypsum board shall be permitted to be used on wood joists to create a horizontal diaphragm ceiling in accordance with Table 2508.5.

2508.5.1 Diaphragm proportions. The maximum allowable diaphragm proportions shall be $1^1/_2$:1 between shear resisting elements. Rotation or cantilever conditions shall not be permitted.

2508.5.2 Installation. Gypsum board used in a horizontal diaphragm ceiling shall be installed perpendicular to ceiling framing members. End joints of adjacent courses of gypsum board shall not occur on the same joist.

2508.5.3 Blocking of perimeter edges. All perimeter edges shall be blocked using a wood member not less than 2-inch by 6-inch (51 mm by 159 mm) nominal dimension. Blocking material shall be installed flat over the top plate of the wall to provide a nailing surface not less than 2 inches (51 mm) in width for the attachment of the gypsum board.

2508.5.4 Fasteners. Fasteners used for the attachment of gypsum board to a horizontal diaphragm ceiling shall be as defined in Table 2508.5. Fasteners shall be spaced not more than 7 inches (178 mm) on center (o.c.) at all supports, including perimeter blocking, and not more than $^3/_8$ inch (9.5 mm) from the edges and ends of the gypsum board.

2508.5.5 Lateral force restrictions. Gypsum board shall not be used in diaphragm ceilings to resist lateral forces imposed by masonry or concrete construction.

SECTION 2509
GYPSUM BOARD IN SHOWERS AND WATER CLOSETS

2509.1 Wet areas. Showers and public toilet walls shall conform to Sections 1210.2 and 1210.3.

2509.2 Base for tile. Glass mat water-resistant gypsum backing panels, discrete nonasbestos fiber-cement interior substrate sheets or nonasbestos fiber-mat reinforced cement substrate sheets in compliance with ASTM C 1178, C 1288 or C 1325 and installed in accordance with manufacturer recommendations shall be used as a base for wall tile in tub and shower areas

TABLE 2508.5
SHEAR CAPACITY FOR HORIZONTAL WOOD FRAMED GYPSUM BOARD DIAPHRAGM CEILING ASSEMBLIES

MATERIAL	THICKNESS OF MATERIAL (MINIMUM) (inches)	SPACING OF FRAMING MEMBERS (MAXIMUM) (inches)	SHEAR VALUE[a, b] (plf of ceiling)	MIMIMUM FASTENER SIZE
Gypsum board	$^1/_2$	16 o.c.	90	5d cooler or wallboard nail; $1^5/_8$-inch long; 0.086-inch shank; $^{15}/_{64}$ inch head[c]
Gypsum board	$^1/_2$	24 o.c.	70	5d cooler or wallboard nail; $1^5/_8$-inch long; 0.086-inch shank; $^{15}/_{64}$ inch head[c]

For SI: 1 inch = 25.4 mm, 1 pound per linear foot = 14.59 N/m.

a. Values are not cumulative with other horizontal diaphragm values and are for short-term loading due to wind or seismic loading. Values shall be reduced 25 percent for normal loading.

b. Values shall be reduced 50 percent in Seismic Design Categories D, E and F.

c. $1^1/_4$-inch, No. 6 Type S or W screws are permitted to be substituted for the listed nails.

and wall and ceiling panels in shower areas. Water-resistant gypsum backing board shall be used as a base for tile in water closet compartment walls when installed in accordance with GA-216 or ASTM C 840 and manufacturer recommendations. Regular gypsum wallboard is permitted under tile or wall panels in other wall and ceiling areas when installed in accordance with GA-216 or ASTM C 840.

2509.3 Limitations. Water-resistant gypsum backing board shall not be used in the following locations:

1. Over a vapor retarder in shower or bathtub compartments.
2. Where there will be direct exposure to water or in areas subject to continuous high humidity.
3. On ceilings where frame spacing exceeds 12 inches (305 mm) o.c. for $^1/_2$-inch-thick (12.7 mm) water-resistant gypsum backing board and more than 16 inches (406 mm) o.c. for $^5/_8$-inch-thick (15.9 mm) water-resistant gypsum backing board.

SECTION 2510 LATHING AND FURRING FOR CEMENT PLASTER (STUCCO)

2510.1 General. Exterior and interior cement plaster and lathing shall be done with the appropriate materials listed in Table 2507.2 and Chapter 35.

2510.2 Weather protection. Materials shall be stored in such a manner as to protect such materials from the weather.

2510.3 Installation. Installation of these materials shall be in compliance with ASTM C 926 and ASTM C 1063.

2510.4 Corrosion resistance. Metal lath and lath attachments shall be of corrosion-resistant material.

2510.5 Backing. Backing or a lath shall provide sufficient rigidity to permit plaster applications.

2510.5.1 Support of lath. Where lath on vertical surfaces extends between rafters or other similar projecting members, solid backing shall be installed to provide support for lath and attachments.

2510.5.2 Use of gypsum backing board.

2510.5.2.1 Use of gypsum board as a backing board. Gypsum lath or gypsum wallboard shall not be used as a backing for cement plaster.

Exception: Gypsum lath or gypsum wallboard is permitted, with a *water-resistive barrier*, as a backing for self-furred metal lath or self-furred wire fabric lath and cement plaster where either of the following conditions occur:

1. On horizontal supports of ceilings or roof soffits.
2. On interior walls.

2510.5.2.2 Use of gypsum sheathing backing. Gypsum sheathing is permitted as a backing for metal or wire fabric lath and cement plaster on walls. A *water-resistive barrier* shall be provided in accordance with Section 2510.6.

2510.5.3 Backing not required. Wire backing is not required under expanded metal lath or paperbacked wire fabric lath.

2510.6 Water-resistive barriers. *Water-resistive barriers* shall be installed as required in Section 1404.2 and, where applied over wood-based sheathing, shall include a water-resistive vapor-permeable barrier with a performance at least equivalent to two layers of Grade D paper.

Exception: Where the *water-resistive barrier* that is applied over wood-based sheathing has a water resistance equal to or greater than that of 60-minute Grade D paper and is separated from the stucco by an intervening, substantially nonwater-absorbing layer or drainage space.

2510.7 Preparation of masonry and concrete. Surfaces shall be clean, free from efflorescence, sufficiently damp and rough for proper bond. If the surface is insufficiently rough, *approved* bonding agents or a portland cement dash bond coat mixed in proportions of not more than two parts volume of sand to one part volume of portland cement or plastic cement shall be applied. The dash bond coat shall be left undisturbed and shall be moist cured not less than 24 hours.

SECTION 2511 INTERIOR PLASTER

2511.1 General. Plastering gypsum plaster or cement plaster shall not be less than three coats where applied over metal lath or wire fabric lath and not less than two coats where applied over other bases permitted by this chapter.

Exception: Gypsum veneer plaster and cement plaster specifically designed and *approved* for one-coat applications.

2511.1.1 Installation. Installation of lathing and plaster materials shall conform with Table 2511.1.1 and Section 2507.

TABLE 2511.1.1 INSTALLATION OF PLASTER CONSTRUCTION

MATERIAL	STANDARD
Cement plaster	ASTM C 926
Gypsum plaster	ASTM C 842
Gypsum veneer plaster	ASTM C 843
Interior lathing and furring (gypsum plaster)	ASTM C 841
Lathing and furring (cement plaster)	ASTM C 1063
Steel framing	ASTM C 754; C 1007

2511.2 Limitations. Plaster shall not be applied directly to fiber insulation board. Cement plaster shall not be applied directly to gypsum lath or gypsum plaster except as specified in Sections 2510.5.1 and 2510.5.2.

2511.3 Grounds. Where installed, grounds shall ensure the minimum thickness of plaster as set forth in ASTM C 842 and ASTM C 926. Plaster thickness shall be measured from the face of lath and other bases.

2511.4 Interior masonry or concrete. Condition of surfaces shall be as specified in Section 2510.7. *Approved* specially prepared gypsum plaster designed for application to concrete surfaces or *approved* acoustical plaster is permitted. The total thickness of base coat plaster applied to concrete ceilings shall be as set forth in ASTM C 842 or ASTM C 926. Should ceiling surfaces require more than the maximum thickness permitted in ASTM C 842 or ASTM C 926, metal lath or wire fabric lath shall be installed on such surfaces before plastering.

2511.5 Wet areas. Showers and public toilet walls shall conform to Sections 1210.2 and 1210.3. When wood frame walls and partitions are covered on the interior with cement plaster or tile of similar material and are subject to water splash, the framing shall be protected with an *approved* moisture barrier.

SECTION 2512
EXTERIOR PLASTER

2512.1 General. Plastering with cement plaster shall be not less than three coats when applied over metal lath or wire fabric lath or gypsum board backing as specified in Section 2510.5 and shall be not less than two coats when applied over masonry or concrete. If the plaster surface is to be completely covered by veneer or other facing material, or is completely concealed by another wall, plaster application need only be two coats, provided the total thickness is as set forth in ASTM C 926.

2512.1.1 On-grade floor slab. On wood framed or steel stud construction with an on-grade concrete floor slab system, exterior plaster shall be applied in such a manner as to cover, but not to extend below, the lath and paper. The application of lath, paper and flashing or drip screeds shall comply with ASTM C 1063.

2512.1.2 Weep screeds. A minimum 0.019-inch (0.48 mm) (No. 26 galvanized sheet gage), corrosion-resistant weep screed with a minimum vertical attachment flange of $3^1/_2$ inches (89 mm) shall be provided at or below the foundation plate line on exterior stud walls in accordance with ASTM C 926. The weep screed shall be placed a minimum of 4 inches (102 mm) above the earth or 2 inches (51 mm) above paved areas and be of a type that will allow trapped water to drain to the exterior of the building. The *water-resistive barrier* shall lap the attachment flange. The exterior lath shall cover and terminate on the attachment flange of the weep screed.

2512.2 Plasticity agents. Only *approved* plasticity agents and *approved* amounts thereof shall be added to portland cement or blended cements. When plastic cement or masonry cement is used, no additional lime or plasticizers shall be added. Hydrated lime or the equivalent amount of lime putty used as a plasticizer is permitted to be added to cement plaster or cement and lime plaster in an amount not to exceed that set forth in ASTM C 926.

2512.3 Limitations. Gypsum plaster shall not be used on exterior surfaces.

2512.4 Cement plaster. Plaster coats shall be protected from freezing for a period of not less than 24 hours after set has occurred. Plaster shall be applied when the ambient temperature is higher than 40°F (4°C), unless provisions are made to keep cement plaster work above 40°F (4°C) during application and 48 hours thereafter.

2512.5 Second-coat application. The second coat shall be brought out to proper thickness, rodded and floated sufficiently rough to provide adequate bond for the finish coat. The second coat shall have no variation greater than $^1/_4$ inch (6.4 mm) in any direction under a 5-foot (1524 mm) straight edge.

2512.6 Curing and interval. First and second coats of cement plaster shall be applied and moist cured as set forth in ASTM C 926 and Table 2512.6.

TABLE 2512.6
CEMENT PLASTERS[a]

COAT	MINIMUM PERIOD MOIST CURING	MINIMUM INTERVAL BETWEEN COATS
First	48 hours[a]	48 hours[b]
Second	48 hours	7 days[c]
Finish	—	Note c

a. The first two coats shall be as required for the first coats of exterior plaster, except that the moist-curing time period between the first and second coats shall not be less than 24 hours. Moist curing shall not be required where job and weather conditions are favorable to the retention of moisture in the cement plaster for the required time period.

b. Twenty-four-hour minimum interval between coats of interior cement plaster. For alternate method of application, see Section 2512.8.

c. Finish coat plaster is permitted to be applied to interior cement plaster base coats after a 48-hour period.

2512.7 Application to solid backings. Where applied over gypsum backing as specified in Section 2510.5 or directly to unit masonry surfaces, the second coat is permitted to be applied as soon as the first coat has attained sufficient hardness.

2512.8 Alternate method of application. The second coat is permitted to be applied as soon as the first coat has attained sufficiently rigidity to receive the second coat.

2512.8.1 Admixtures. When using this method of application, calcium aluminate cement up to 15 percent of the weight of the portland cement is permitted to be added to the mix.

2512.8.2 Curing. Curing of the first coat is permitted to be omitted and the second coat shall be cured as set forth in ASTM C 926 and Table 2512.6.

2512.9 Finish coats. Cement plaster finish coats shall be applied over base coats that have been in place for the time periods set forth in ASTM C 926. The third or finish coat shall be applied with sufficient material and pressure to bond and to cover the brown coat and shall be of sufficient thickness to conceal the brown coat.

SECTION 2513
EXPOSED AGGREGATE PLASTER

2513.1 General. Exposed natural or integrally colored aggregate is permitted to be partially embedded in a natural or colored bedding coat of cement plaster or gypsum plaster, subject to the provisions of this section.

2513.2 Aggregate. The aggregate shall be applied manually or mechanically and shall consist of marble chips, pebbles or similar durable, moderately hard (three or more on the Mohs hardness scale), nonreactive materials.

2513.3 Bedding coat proportions. The bedding coat for interior or exterior surfaces shall be composed of one part portland cement and one part Type S lime; or one part blended cement and one part Type S lime; or masonry cement; or plastic cement, and a maximum of three parts of graded white or natural sand by volume. The bedding coat for interior surfaces shall be composed of 100 pounds (45.4 kg) of neat gypsum plaster and a maximum of 200 pounds (90.8 kg) of graded white sand. A factory-prepared bedding coat for interior or exterior use is permitted. The bedding coat for exterior surfaces shall have a minimum compressive strength of 1,000 pounds per square inch (psi) (6895 kPa).

2513.4 Application. The bedding coat is permitted to be applied directly over the first (scratch) coat of plaster, provided the ultimate overall thickness is a minimum of $^7/_8$ inch (22 mm), including lath. Over concrete or masonry surfaces, the overall thickness shall be a minimum of $^1/_2$ inch (12.7 mm).

2513.5 Bases. Exposed aggregate plaster is permitted to be applied over concrete, masonry, cement plaster base coats or gypsum plaster base coats installed in accordance with Section 2511 or 2512.

2513.6 Preparation of masonry and concrete. Masonry and concrete surfaces shall be prepared in accordance with the provisions of Section 2510.7.

2513.7 Curing of base coats. Cement plaster base coats shall be cured in accordance with ASTM C 926. Cement plaster bedding coats shall retain sufficient moisture for hydration (hardening) for 24 hours minimum or, where necessary, shall be kept damp for 24 hours by light water spraying.

CHAPTER 26
PLASTIC

SECTION 2601
GENERAL

2601.1 Scope. These provisions shall govern the materials, design, application, construction and installation of foam plastic, foam plastic insulation, plastic veneer, interior plastic finish and *trim* and light-transmitting plastics. See Chapter 14 for requirements for *exterior wall* finish and *trim.*

SECTION 2602
DEFINITIONS

2602.1 General. The following words and terms shall, for the purposes of this chapter and as used elsewhere in this code, have the meanings shown herein.

FIBER REINFORCED POLYMER. A polymeric composite material consisting of reinforcement fibers impregnated with a fiber-binding polymer which is then molded and hardened.

FIBERGLASS REINFORCED POLYMER. A polymeric composite material consisting of glass reinforcement fibers impregnated with a fiber-binding polymer which is then molded and hardened.

FOAM PLASTIC INSULATION. A plastic that is intentionally expanded by the use of a foaming agent to produce a reduced-density plastic containing voids consisting of open or closed cells distributed throughout the plastic for thermal insulating or acoustical purposes and that has a density less than 20 pounds per cubic foot (pcf) (320 kg/m^3).

LIGHT-DIFFUSING SYSTEM. Construction consisting in whole or in part of lenses, panels, grids or baffles made with light-transmitting plastics positioned below independently mounted electrical light sources, skylights or light-transmitting plastic roof panels. Lenses, panels, grids and baffles that are part of an electrical fixture shall not be considered as a light-diffusing system.

LIGHT-TRANSMITTING PLASTIC ROOF PANELS. Structural plastic panels other than skylights that are fastened to structural members, or panels or sheathing and that are used as light-transmitting media in the plane of the roof.

LIGHT-TRANSMITTING PLASTIC WALL PANELS. Plastic materials that are fastened to structural members, or to structural panels or sheathing, and that are used as light-transmitting media in *exterior walls.*

PLASTIC, APPROVED. Any thermoplastic, thermosetting or reinforced thermosetting plastic material that conforms to combustibility classifications specified in the section applicable to the application and plastic type.

PLASTIC GLAZING. Plastic materials that are glazed or set in frame or sash and not held by mechanical fasteners that pass through the glazing material.

THERMOPLASTIC MATERIAL. A plastic material that is capable of being repeatedly softened by increase of temperature and hardened by decrease of temperature.

THERMOSETTING MATERIAL. A plastic material that is capable of being changed into a substantially nonreformable product when cured.

SECTION 2603
FOAM PLASTIC INSULATION

2603.1 General. The provisions of this section shall govern the requirements and uses of foam plastic insulation in buildings and structures.

2603.2 Labeling and identification. Packages and containers of foam plastic insulation and foam plastic insulation components delivered to the job site shall bear the *label* of an *approved agency* showing the manufacturer's name, product listing, product identification and information sufficient to determine that the end use will comply with the code requirements.

2603.3 Surface-burning characteristics. Unless otherwise indicated in this section, foam plastic insulation and foam plastic cores of manufactured assemblies shall have a flame spread index of not more than 75 and a smoke-developed index of not more than 450 where tested in the maximum thickness intended for use in accordance with ASTM E 84 or UL 723. Loose fill-type foam plastic insulation shall be tested as board stock for the flame spread and smoke-developed indexes.

Exceptions:

1. Smoke-developed index for interior *trim* as provided for in Section 2604.2.
2. In cold storage buildings, ice plants, food plants, food processing rooms and similar areas, foam plastic insulation where tested in a thickness of 4 inches (102 mm) shall be permitted in a thickness up to 10 inches (254 mm) where the building is equipped throughout with an automatic fire sprinkler system in accordance with Section 903.3.1.1. The approved *automatic sprinkler system* shall be provided in both the room and that part of the building in which the room is located.
3. Foam plastic insulation that is a part of a Class A, B or C roof-covering assembly provided the assembly with the foam plastic insulation satisfactorily passes FM 4450 or UL 1256. The smoke-developed index shall not be limited for roof applications.
4. Foam plastic insulation greater than 4 inches (102 mm) in thickness shall have a maximum flame spread index of 75 and a smoke-developed index of 450 where tested at a minimum thickness of 4 inches (102 mm), provided the end use is approved in accordance

with Section 2603.9 using the thickness and density intended for use.

5. Flame spread and smoke-developed indexes for foam plastic interior signs in *covered mall buildings* provided the signs comply with Section 402.15.

2603.4 Thermal barrier. Except as provided for in Sections 2603.4.1 and 2603.9, foam plastic shall be separated from the interior of a building by an approved thermal barrier of $^1/_2$-inch (12.7 mm) gypsum wallboard or equivalent thermal barrier material that will limit the average temperature rise of the unexposed surface to not more than 250°F (120°C) after 15 minutes of fire exposure, complying with the standard time-temperature curve of ASTM E 119 or UL 263. The thermal barrier shall be installed in such a manner that it will remain in place for 15 minutes based on FM 4880, UL 1040, NFPA 286 or UL 1715. Combustible concealed spaces shall comply with Section 717.

2603.4.1 Thermal barrier not required. The thermal barrier specified in Section 2603.4 is not required under the conditions set forth in Sections 2603.4.1.1 through 2603.4.1.13.

2603.4.1.1 Masonry or concrete construction. A thermal barrier is not required for foam plastic installed in a masonry or concrete wall, floor or roof system where the foam plastic insulation is covered on each face by a minimum of 1 inch (25 mm) thickness of masonry or concrete.

2603.4.1.2 Cooler and freezer walls. Foam plastic installed in a maximum thickness of 10 inches (254 mm) in cooler and freezer walls shall:

1. Have a flame spread index of 25 or less and a smoke-developed index of not more than 450, where tested in a minimum 4 inch (102 mm) thickness.
2. Have flash ignition and self-ignition temperatures of not less than 600°F and 800°F (316°C and 427°C), respectively.
3. Have a covering of not less than 0.032-inch (0.8 mm) aluminum or corrosion-resistant steel having a base metal thickness not less than 0.0160 inch (0.4 mm) at any point.
4. Be protected by an *automatic sprinkler system* in accordance with Section 903.3.1.1. Where the cooler or freezer is within a building, both the cooler or freezer and that part of the building in which it is located shall be sprinklered.

2603.4.1.3 Walk-in coolers. In nonsprinklered buildings, foam plastic having a thickness that does not exceed 4 inches (102 mm) and a maximum flame spread index of 75 is permitted in walk-in coolers or freezer units where the aggregate floor area does not exceed 400 square feet (37 m^2) and the foam plastic is covered by a metal facing not less than 0.032-inch-thick (0.81 mm) aluminum or corrosion-resistant steel having a minimum base metal thickness of 0.016 inch (0.41 mm). A thickness of up to 10 inches (254 mm) is permitted where protected by a thermal barrier.

2603.4.1.4 Exterior walls—one-story buildings. For one-*story* buildings, foam plastic having a flame spread index of 25 or less, and a smoke-developed index of not more than 450, shall be permitted without thermal barriers in or on *exterior walls* in a thickness not more than 4 inches (102 mm) where the foam plastic is covered by a thickness of not less than 0.032-inch-thick (0.81 mm) aluminum or corrosion-resistant steel having a base metal thickness of 0.0160 inch (0.41 mm) and the building is equipped throughout with an *automatic sprinkler system* in accordance with Section 903.3.1.1.

2603.4.1.5 Roofing. Foam plastic insulation under a roof assembly or roof covering that is installed in accordance with the code and the manufacturer's instructions shall be separated from the interior of the building by wood structural panel sheathing not less than 0.47 inch (11.9 mm) in thickness bonded with exterior glue, with edges supported by blocking, tongue-and-groove joints or other approved type of edge support, or an equivalent material. A thermal barrier is not required for foam plastic insulation that is a part of a Class A, B or C roof-covering assembly, provided the assembly with the foam plastic insulation satisfactorily passes FM 4450 or UL 1256.

2603.4.1.6 Attics and crawl spaces. Within an *attic* or crawl space where entry is made only for service of utilities, foam plastic insulation shall be protected against ignition by $1^1/_2$-inch-thick (38 mm) mineral fiber insulation; $^1/_4$-inch-thick (6.4 mm) wood structural panel, particleboard or hardboard; $^3/_8$-inch (9.5 mm) gypsum wallboard, corrosion-resistant steel having a base metal thickness of 0.016 inch (0.4 mm) or other approved material installed in such a manner that the foam plastic insulation is not exposed. The protective covering shall be consistent with the requirements for the type of construction.

2603.4.1.7 Doors not required to have a fire protection rating. Where pivoted or side-hinged doors are permitted without a fire protection rating, foam plastic insulation, having a flame spread index of 75 or less and a smoke-developed index of not more than 450, shall be permitted as a core material where the door facing is of metal having a minimum thickness of 0.032-inch (0.8 mm) aluminum or steel having a base metal thickness of not less than 0.016 inch (0.4 mm) at any point.

2603.4.1.8 Exterior doors in buildings of Group R-2 or R-3. In occupancies classified as Group R-2 or R-3, foam-filled exterior entrance doors to individual *dwelling units* that do not require a fire-resistance rating shall be faced with wood or other approved materials.

2603.4.1.9 Garage doors. Where garage doors are permitted without a fire-resistance rating and foam plastic is used as a core material, the door facing shall be metal having a minimum thickness of 0.032-inch (0.8 mm) aluminum or 0.010-inch (0.25 mm) steel or the facing shall be minimum 0.125-inch-thick (3.2 mm) wood. Garage doors having facings other than those described above shall be tested in accordance with, and meet the acceptance criteria of, DASMA 107.

Exception: Garage doors using foam plastic insulation complying with Section 2603.3 in detached and attached garages associated with one- and two-family dwellings need not be provided with a thermal barrier.

2603.4.1.10 Siding backer board. Foam plastic insulation of not more than 2,000 British thermal units per square feet (Btu/sq. ft.) (22.7 mJ/m^2) as determined by NFPA 259 shall be permitted as a siding backer board with a maximum thickness of $^1/_2$ inch (12.7 mm), provided it is separated from the interior of the building by not less than 2 inches (51 mm) of mineral fiber insulation or equivalent or where applied as insulation with residing over existing wall construction.

2603.4.1.11 Interior trim. Foam plastic used as interior *trim* in accordance with Section 2604 shall be permitted without a thermal barrier.

2603.4.1.12 Interior signs. Foam plastic used for interior signs in *covered mall buildings* in accordance with Section 402.16 shall be permitted without a thermal barrier. Foam plastic signs that are not affixed to interior building surfaces shall comply with Chapter 8 of the *International Fire Code*.

2603.4.1.13 Type V construction. Foam plastic spray applied to a sill plate and header of Type V construction is subject to all of the following:

1. The maximum thickness of the foam plastic shall be $3^1/_4$ inches (82.6 mm).
2. The density of the foam plastic shall be in the range of 1.5 to 2.0 pcf (24 to 32 kg/m^3).
3. The foam plastic shall have a flame spread index of 25 or less and an accompanying smoke-developed index of 450 or less when tested in accordance with ASTM E 84 or UL 723.

2603.5 Exterior walls of buildings of any height. *Exterior walls* of buildings of Type I, II, III or IV construction of any height shall comply with Sections 2603.5.1 through 2603.5.7. *Exterior walls* of cold storage buildings required to be constructed of noncombustible materials, where the building is more than one *story* in height, shall also comply with the provisions of Sections 2603.5.1 through 2603.5.7. *Exterior walls* of buildings of Type V construction shall comply with Sections 2603.2, 2603.3 and 2603.4.

2603.5.1 Fire-resistance-rated walls. Where the wall is required to have a fire-resistance rating, data based on tests conducted in accordance with ASTM E 119 or UL 263 shall be provided to substantiate that the fire-resistance rating is maintained.

2603.5.2 Thermal barrier. Any foam plastic insulation shall be separated from the building interior by a thermal barrier meeting the provisions of Section 2603.4, unless special approval is obtained on the basis of Section 2603.9.

Exception: One-story buildings complying with Section 2603.4.1.4.

2603.5.3 Potential heat. The potential heat of foam plastic insulation in any portion of the wall or panel shall not exceed the potential heat expressed in Btu per square feet (mJ/m^2) of the foam plastic insulation contained in the wall assembly tested in accordance with Section 2603.5.5. The potential heat of the foam plastic insulation shall be determined by tests conducted in accordance with NFPA 259 and the results shall be expressed in Btu per square feet (mJ/m^2).

Exception: One-story buildings complying with Section 2603.4.1.4.

2603.5.4 Flame spread and smoke-developed indexes. Foam plastic insulation, exterior coatings and facings shall be tested separately in the thickness intended for use, but not to exceed 4 inches (102 mm), and shall each have a flame spread index of 25 or less and a smoke-developed index of 450 or less as determined in accordance with ASTM E 84 or UL 723.

Exception: Prefabricated or factory-manufactured panels having minimum 0.020-inch (0.51 mm) aluminum facings and a total thickness of $^1/_4$ inch (6.4 mm) or less are permitted to be tested as an assembly where the foam plastic core is not exposed in the course of construction.

2603.5.5 Test standard. The wall assembly shall be tested in accordance with and comply with the acceptance criteria of NFPA 285.

Exception: One-story buildings complying with Section 2603.4.1.4.

2603.5.6 Label required. The edge or face of each piece of foam plastic insulation shall bear the *label* of an *approved agency*. The *label* shall contain the manufacturer's or distributor's identification, model number, serial number or definitive information describing the product or materials' performance characteristics and *approved agency*'s identification.

2603.5.7 Ignition. *Exterior walls* shall not exhibit sustained flaming where tested in accordance with NFPA 268. Where a material is intended to be installed in more than one thickness, tests of the minimum and maximum thickness intended for use shall be performed.

Exception: Assemblies protected on the outside with one of the following:

1. A thermal barrier complying with Section 2603.4.
2. A minimum 1 inch (25 mm) thickness of concrete or masonry.
3. Glass-fiber-reinforced concrete panels of a minimum thickness of $^3/_8$ inch (9.5 mm).
4. Metal-faced panels having minimum 0.019-inch-thick (0.48 mm) aluminum or 0.016-inch-thick (0.41 mm) corrosion-resistant steel outer facings.
5. A minimum $^7/_8$ inch (22.2 mm) thickness of stucco complying with Section 2510.

2603.6 Roofing. Foam plastic insulation meeting the requirements of Sections 2603.2, 2603.3 and 2603.4 shall be permitted as part of a roof-covering assembly, provided the assembly with the foam plastic insulation is a Class A, B or C roofing assembly where tested in accordance with ASTM E 108 or UL 790.

2603.7 Plenums. Foam plastic insulation shall not be used as interior wall or ceiling finish in plenums except as permitted in Section 2604 or when protected by a thermal barrier in accordance with Section 2603.4.

2603.8 Protection against termites. Extruded and expanded polystyrene, polyisocyanurate and other foam plastics shall not be installed on the exterior face or under interior or exterior foundation walls or slab foundations located below grade. The clearance between foam plastics installed above grade and exposed earth shall be at least 8 inches (203 mm).

Exceptions:

1. Buildings where the structural members of walls, floors, ceilings and roofs are entirely of noncombustible materials or preservative-treated wood.
2. An approved method of protecting the foam plastic and structure from subterranean termite damage is provided.
3. On the interior side of basement walls.
4. Foam plastic less than 8 inches (203 mm) above or in contact with grade shall be installed in accordance with Section 2603.8.1.

2603.8.1 Chemical treatment. When foam plastic is in contact with the ground, the soil area shall be chemically treated in accordance with the North Carolina Structural Pest Control Committee rules.

2603.9 Special approval. Foam plastic shall not be required to comply with the requirements of Sections 2603.4 through 2603.7 where specifically approved based on large-scale tests such as, but not limited to, NFPA 286 (with the acceptance criteria of Section 803.2), FM 4880, UL 1040 or UL 1715. Such testing shall be related to the actual end-use configuration and be performed on the finished manufactured foam plastic assembly in the maximum thickness intended for use. Foam plastics that are used as interior finish on the basis of special tests shall also conform to the flame spread requirements of Chapter 8. Assemblies tested shall include seams, joints and other typical details used in the installation of the assembly and shall be tested in the manner intended for use.

SECTION 2604
INTERIOR FINISH AND TRIM

2604.1 General. Plastic materials installed as interior finish or *trim* shall comply with Chapter 8. Foam plastics shall only be installed as interior finish where approved in accordance with the special provisions of Section 2603.9. Foam plastics that are used as interior finish shall also meet the flame spread index requirements for interior finish in accordance with Chapter 8. Foam plastics installed as interior *trim* shall comply with Section 2604.2.

[F] 2604.2 Interior trim. Foam plastic used as interior *trim* shall comply with Sections 2604.2.1 through 2604.2.4.

[F] 2604.2.1 Density. The minimum density of the interior *trim* shall be 20 pcf (320 kg/m^3).

[F] 2604.2.2 Thickness. The maximum thickness of the interior *trim* shall be $^1/_2$ inch (12.7 mm) and the maximum width shall be 8 inches (204 mm).

[F] 2604.2.3 Area limitation. The interior *trim* shall not constitute more than 10 percent of the specific wall or ceiling areas to which it is attached.

[F] 2604.2.4 Flame spread. The flame spread index shall not exceed 75 where tested in accordance with ASTM E 84 or UL 723. The smoke-developed index shall not be limited.

Exception: When the interior *trim* material has been tested as an interior finish in accordance with NFPA 286 and complies with the acceptance criteria in Section 803.1.2.1, it shall not be required to be tested for flame spread index in accordance with ASTM E 84 or UL 723.

SECTION 2605
PLASTIC VENEER

2605.1 Interior use. Where used within a building, plastic veneer shall comply with the interior finish requirements of Chapter 8.

2605.2 Exterior use. Exterior plastic veneer, other than plastic siding, shall be permitted to be installed on the *exterior walls* of buildings of any type of construction in accordance with all of the following requirements:

1. Plastic veneer shall comply with Section 2606.4.
2. Plastic veneer shall not be attached to any exterior wall to a height greater than 50 feet (15 240 mm) above grade.
3. Sections of plastic veneer shall not exceed 300 square feet (27.9 m^2) in area and shall be separated by a minimum of 4 feet (1219 mm) vertically.

Exception: The area and separation requirements and the smoke-density limitation are not applicable to plastic veneer applied to buildings constructed of Type VB construction, provided the walls are not required to have a fire-resistance rating.

2605.3 Plastic siding. Plastic siding shall comply with the requirements of Sections 1404 and 1405.

SECTION 2606
LIGHT-TRANSMITTING PLASTICS

2606.1 General. The provisions of this section and Sections 2607 through 2611 shall govern the quality and methods of application of light-transmitting plastics for use as light-transmitting materials in buildings and structures. Foam plastics shall comply with Section 2603. Light-transmitting plastic materials that meet the other code requirements for walls and roofs shall be permitted to be used in accordance with the other applicable chapters of the code.

2606.2 Approval for use. Sufficient technical data shall be submitted to substantiate the proposed use of any light-transmitting material, as approved by the *building official* and subject to the requirements of this section.

2606.3 Identification. Each unit or package of light-transmitting plastic shall be identified with a *mark* or decal satisfactory to the *building official*, which includes identification as to the material classification.

2606.4 Specifications. Light-transmitting plastics, including thermoplastic, thermosetting or reinforced thermosetting plastic material, shall have a self-ignition temperature of 650°F (343°C) or greater where tested in accordance with ASTM D 1929; a smoke-developed index not greater than 450 where tested in the manner intended for use in accordance with ASTM E 84 or UL 723, or a maximum average smoke density rating not greater than 75 where tested in the thickness intended for use in accordance with ASTM D 2843 and shall conform to one of the following combustibility classifications:

Class CC1: Plastic materials that have a burning extent of 1 inch (25 mm) or less where tested at a nominal thickness of 0.060 inch (1.5 mm), or in the thickness intended for use, in accordance with ASTM D 635.

Class CC2: Plastic materials that have a burning rate of $2^1/_2$ inches per minute (1.06 mm/s) or less where tested at a nominal thickness of 0.060 inch (1.5 mm), or in the thickness intended for use, in accordance with ASTM D 635.

2606.5 Structural requirements. Light-transmitting plastic materials in their assembly shall be of adequate strength and durability to withstand the loads indicated in Chapter 16. Technical data shall be submitted to establish stresses, maximum unsupported spans and such other information for the various thicknesses and forms used as deemed necessary by the *building official*.

2606.6 Fastening. Fastening shall be adequate to withstand the loads in Chapter 16. Proper allowance shall be made for expansion and contraction of light-transmitting plastic materials in accordance with accepted data on the coefficient of expansion of the material and other material in conjunction with which it is employed.

2606.7 Light-diffusing systems. Unless the building is equipped throughout with an *automatic sprinkler system* in accordance with Section 903.3.1.1, light-diffusing systems shall not be installed in the following occupancies and locations:

1. Group A with an *occupant load* of 1,000 or more.
2. Theaters with a stage and proscenium opening and an *occupant load* of 700 or more.
3. Group I-2.
4. Group I-3.
5. Vertical *exit* enclosures and *exit* passageways.

2606.7.1 Support. Light-transmitting plastic diffusers shall be supported directly or indirectly from ceiling or roof construction by use of noncombustible hangers. Hangers shall be at least No. 12 steel-wire gage (0.106 inch) galvanized wire or equivalent.

2606.7.2 Installation. Light-transmitting plastic diffusers shall comply with Chapter 8 unless the light-transmitting plastic diffusers will fall from the mountings before igniting, at an ambient temperature of at least 200°F (111°C) below the ignition temperature of the panels. The panels shall remain in place at an ambient room temperature of 175°F (79°C) for a period of not less than 15 minutes.

2606.7.3 Size limitations. Individual panels or units shall not exceed 10 feet (3048 mm) in length nor 30 square feet (2.79 m^2) in area.

2606.7.4 Fire suppression system. In buildings that are equipped throughout with an *automatic sprinkler system* in accordance with Section 903.3.1.1, plastic light-diffusing systems shall be protected both above and below unless the sprinkler system has been specifically approved for installation only above the light-diffusing system. Areas of light-diffusing systems that are protected in accordance with this section shall not be limited.

2606.7.5 Electrical luminaires. Light-transmitting plastic panels and light-diffuser panels that are installed in approved electrical luminaires shall comply with the requirements of Chapter 8 unless the light-transmitting plastic panels conform to the requirements of Section 2606.7.2. The area of approved light-transmitting plastic materials that are used in required *exits* or *corridors* shall not exceed 30 percent of the aggregate area of the ceiling in which such panels are installed, unless the building is equipped throughout with an *automatic sprinkler system* in accordance with Section 903.3.1.1.

2606.8 Partitions. Light-transmitting plastics used in or as partitions shall comply with the requirements of Chapters 6 and 8.

2606.9 Bathroom accessories. Light-transmitting plastics shall be permitted as glazing in shower stalls, shower doors, bathtub enclosures and similar accessory units. Safety glazing shall be provided in accordance with Chapter 24.

2606.10 Awnings, patio covers and similar structures. *Awnings* constructed of light-transmitting plastics shall be constructed in accordance with the provisions specified in Section 3105 and Chapter 32 for projections. Patio covers constructed of light-transmitting plastics shall comply with Section 2606. Light-transmitting plastics used in canopies at motor fuel-dispensing facilities shall comply with Section 2606, except as modified by Section 406.5.3.

2606.11 Greenhouses. Light-transmitting plastics shall be permitted in lieu of plain glass in greenhouses.

2606.12 Solar collectors. Light-transmitting plastic covers on solar collectors having noncombustible sides and bottoms shall be permitted on buildings not over three *stories above grade plane* or 9,000 square feet (836.1 m^2) in total floor area, provided the light-transmitting plastic cover does not exceed 33.33 percent of the roof area for CC1 materials or 25 percent of the roof area for CC2 materials.

Exception: Light-transmitting plastic covers having a thickness of 0.010 inch (0.3 mm) or less or shall be permitted to be of any plastic material provided the area of the solar collectors does not exceed 33.33 percent of the roof area.

SECTION 2607
LIGHT-TRANSMITTING PLASTIC WALL PANELS

2607.1 General. Light-transmitting plastics shall not be used as wall panels in *exterior walls* in occupancies in Groups A-1, A-2, H, I-2 and I-3. In other groups, light-transmitting plastics shall be permitted to be used as wall panels in *exterior walls*, provided that the walls are not required to have a fire-resistance rating and the installation conforms to the requirements of this section. Such panels shall be erected and anchored on a foundation, waterproofed or otherwise protected from moisture absorption and sealed with a coat of mastic or other approved waterproof coating. Light-transmitting plastic wall panels shall also comply with Section 2606.

2607.2 Installation. *Exterior wall* panels installed as provided for herein shall not alter the type of construction classification of the building.

2607.3 Height limitation. Light-transmitting plastics shall not be installed more than 75 feet (22 860 mm) above *grade plane*, except as allowed by Section 2607.5.

2607.4 Area limitation and separation. The maximum area of a single wall panel and minimum vertical and horizontal separation requirements for exterior light-transmitting plastic wall panels shall be as provided for in Table 2607.4. The maximum percentage of wall area of any *story* in light-transmitting plastic wall panels shall not exceed that indicated in Table 2607.4 or the percentage of unprotected openings permitted by Section 705.8, whichever is smaller.

Exceptions:

1. In structures provided with approved flame barriers extending 30 inches (760 mm) beyond the *exterior wall* in the plane of the floor, a vertical separation is not required at the floor except that provided by the vertical thickness of the flame barrier projection.
2. Veneers of approved weather-resistant light-transmitting plastics used as exterior siding in buildings of Type V construction in compliance with Section 1406.
3. The area of light-transmitting plastic wall panels in *exterior walls* of greenhouses shall be exempt from the area limitations of Table 2607.4 but shall be limited as required for unprotected openings in accordance with Section 704.8.

2607.5 Automatic sprinkler system. Where the building is equipped throughout with an *automatic sprinkler system* in accordance with Section 903.3.1.1, the maximum percentage area of *exterior wall* in any *story* in light-transmitting plastic wall panels and the maximum square footage of a single area given in Table 2607.4 shall be increased 100 percent, but the area of light-transmitting plastic wall panels shall not exceed 50 percent of the wall area in any story, or the area permitted by Section 705.8 for unprotected openings, whichever is smaller. These installations shall be exempt from height limitations.

2607.6 Combinations of glazing and wall panels. Combinations of light-transmitting plastic glazing and light-transmitting plastic wall panels shall be subject to the area, height and percentage limitations and the separation requirements applicable to the class of light-transmitting plastic as prescribed for light-transmitting plastic wall panel installations.

SECTION 2608
LIGHT-TRANSMITTING PLASTIC GLAZING

2608.1 Buildings of Type VB construction. Openings in the *exterior walls* of buildings of Type VB construction, where not required to be protected by Section 705, shall be permitted to be glazed or equipped with light-transmitting plastic. Light-transmitting plastic glazing shall also comply with Section 2606.

2608.2 Buildings of other types of construction. Openings in the *exterior walls* of buildings of types of construction other than Type VB, where not required to be protected by Section 705, shall be permitted to be glazed or equipped with light-transmitting plastic in accordance with Section 2606 and all of the following:

1. The aggregate area of light-transmitting plastic glazing shall not exceed 25 percent of the area of any wall face of

TABLE 2607.4
AREA LIMITATION AND SEPARATION REQUIREMENTS FOR LIGHT-TRANSMITTING PLASTIC WALL PANELS[a]

FIRE SEPARATION DISTANCE (feet)	CLASS OF PLASTIC	MAXIMUM PERCENTAGE AREA OF EXTERIOR WALL IN PLASTIC WALL PANELS	MAXIMUM SINGLE AREA OF PLASTIC WALL PANELS (square feet)	MINIMUM SEPARATION OF PLASTIC WALL PANELS (feet)	
				Vertical	Horizontal
Less than 6	—	Not Permitted	Not Permitted	—	—
6 or more but less than 11	CC1	10	50	8	4
	CC2	Not Permitted	Not Permitted	—	—
11 or more but less than or equal to 30	CC1	25	90	6	4
	CC2	15	70	8	4
Over 30	CC1	50	Not Limited	3[b]	0
	CC2	50	100	6[b]	3

For SI: 1 foot = 304.8 mm, 1 square foot = 0.0929 m^2.

a. For combinations of plastic glazing and plastic wall panel areas permitted, see Section 2607.6.

b. For reductions in vertical separation allowed, see Section 2607.4.

the *story* in which it is installed. The area of a single pane of glazing installed above the first *story above grade plane* shall not exceed 16 square feet (1.5 m^2) and the vertical dimension of a single pane shall not exceed 4 feet (1219 mm).

Exception: Where an *automatic sprinkler system* is provided throughout in accordance with Section 903.3.1.1, the area of allowable glazing shall be increased to a maximum of 50 percent of the wall face of the *story* in which it is installed with no limit on the maximum dimension or area of a single pane of glazing.

2. Approved flame barriers extending 30 inches (762 mm) beyond the *exterior wall* in the plane of the floor, or vertical panels not less than 4 feet (1219 mm) in height, shall be installed between glazed units located in adjacent stories.

   Exception: Buildings equipped throughout with an *automatic sprinkler system* in accordance with Section 903.3.1.1.

3. Light-transmitting plastics shall not be installed more than 75 feet (22 860 mm) above grade level.

   Exception: Buildings equipped throughout with an *automatic sprinkler system* in accordance with Section 903.3.1.1.

SECTION 2609
LIGHT-TRANSMITTING PLASTIC ROOF PANELS

2609.1 General. Light-transmitting plastic roof panels shall comply with this section and Section 2606. Light-transmitting plastic roof panels shall not be installed in Groups H, I-2 and I-3. In all other groups, light-transmitting plastic roof panels shall comply with any one of the following conditions:

1. The building is equipped throughout with an *automatic sprinkler system* in accordance with Section 903.3.1.1.
2. The roof construction is not required to have a fire-resistance rating by Table 601.
3. The roof panels meet the requirements for roof coverings in accordance with Chapter 15.

2609.2 Separation. Individual roof panels shall be separated from each other by a distance of not less than 4 feet (1219 mm) measured in a horizontal plane.

Exceptions:

1. The separation between roof panels is not required in a building equipped throughout with an *automatic sprinkler system* in accordance with Section 903.3.1.1.
2. The separation between roof panels is not required in low-hazard occupancy buildings complying with the conditions of Section 2609.4, Exception 2 or 3.

2609.3 Location. Where *exterior wall* openings are required to be protected by Section 705.8, a roof panel shall not be installed within 6 feet (1829 mm) of such *exterior wall*.

2609.4 Area limitations. Roof panels shall be limited in area and the aggregate area of panels shall be limited by a percentage of the floor area of the room or space sheltered in accordance with Table 2609.4.

Exceptions:

1. The area limitations of Table 2609.4 shall be permitted to be increased by 100 percent in buildings equipped throughout with an *automatic sprinkler system* in accordance with Section 903.3.1.1.
2. Low-hazard occupancy buildings, such as swimming pool shelters, shall be exempt from the area limitations of Table 2609.4, provided that the buildings do not exceed 5,000 square feet (465 m^2) in area and have a minimum fire separation distance of 10 feet (3048 mm).
3. Greenhouses that are occupied for growing plants on a production or research basis, without public access, shall be exempt from the area limitations of Table 2609.4 provided they have a minimum fire separation distance of 4 feet (1220 mm).
4. Roof coverings over terraces and patios in occupancies in Group R-3 shall be exempt from the area limitations of Table 2609.4 and shall be permitted with light-transmitting plastics.

TABLE 2609.4
AREA LIMITATIONS FOR LIGHT-TRANSMITTING PLASTIC ROOF PANELS

CLASS OF PLASTIC	MAXIMUM AREA OF INDIVIDUAL ROOF PANELS (square feet)	MAXIMUM AGGREGATE AREA OF ROOF PANELS (percent of floor area)
CC1	300	30
CC2	100	25

For SI: 1 square foot = 0.0929 m^2.

SECTION 2610
LIGHT-TRANSMITTING PLASTIC SKYLIGHT GLAZING

2610.1 Light-transmitting plastic glazing of skylight assemblies. Skylight assemblies glazed with light-transmitting plastic shall conform to the provisions of this section and Section 2606. Unit skylights glazed with light-transmitting plastic shall also comply with Section 2405.5.

Exception: Skylights in which the light-transmitting plastic conforms to the required roof-covering class in accordance with Section 1505.

2610.2 Mounting. The light-transmitting plastic shall be mounted above the plane of the roof on a curb constructed in accordance with the requirements for the type of construction classification, but at least 4 inches (102 mm) above the plane of the roof. Edges of light-transmitting plastic skylights or domes shall be protected by metal or other approved noncombustible material, or the light-transmitting plastic dome or skylight shall be shown to be able to resist ignition where exposed at the edge to a flame from a Class B brand as described in ASTM E 108 or UL 790.

Exceptions:

1. Curbs shall not be required for skylights used on roofs having a minimum slope of three units vertical in 12 units horizontal (25-percent slope) in occupancies in

Group R-3 and on buildings with a nonclassified roof covering.

2. The metal or noncombustible edge material is not required where nonclassified roof coverings are permitted.

2610.3 Slope. Flat or corrugated light-transmitting plastic skylights shall slope at least four units vertical in 12 units horizontal (4:12). Dome-shaped skylights shall rise above the mounting flange a minimum distance equal to 10 percent of the maximum span of the dome but not less than 3 inches (76 mm).

Exception: Skylights that pass the Class B Burning Brand Test specified in ASTM E 108 or UL 790.

2610.4 Maximum area of skylights. Each skylight shall have a maximum area within the curb of 100 square feet (9.3 m^2).

Exception: The area limitation shall not apply where the building is equipped throughout with an *automatic sprinkler system* in accordance with Section 903.3.1.1 or the building is equipped with smoke and heat vents in accordance with Section 910.

2610.5 Aggregate area of skylights. The aggregate area of skylights shall not exceed $33^1/_3$ percent of the floor area of the room or space sheltered by the roof in which such skylights are installed where Class CC1 materials are utilized, and 25 percent where Class CC2 materials are utilized.

Exception: The aggregate area limitations of light-transmitting plastic skylights shall be increased 100 percent beyond the limitations set forth in this section where the building is equipped throughout with an *automatic sprinkler system* in accordance with Section 903.3.1.1 or the building is equipped with smoke and heat vents in accordance with Section 910.

2610.6 Separation. Skylights shall be separated from each other by a distance of not less than 4 feet (1219 mm) measured in a horizontal plane.

Exceptions:

1. Buildings equipped throughout with an *automatic sprinkler system* in accordance with Section 903.3.1.1.
2. In Group R-3, multiple skylights located above the same room or space with a combined area not exceeding the limits set forth in Section 2610.4.

2610.7 Location. Where *exterior wall* openings are required to be protected in accordance with Section 705, a skylight shall not be installed within 6 feet (1829 mm) of such *exterior wall.*

2610.8 Combinations of roof panels and skylights. Combinations of light-transmitting plastic roof panels and skylights shall be subject to the area and percentage limitations and separation requirements applicable to roof panel installations.

SECTION 2611
LIGHT-TRANSMITTING PLASTIC INTERIOR SIGNS

2611.1 General. Light-transmitting plastic interior wall signs shall be limited as specified in Sections 2611.2 through 2611.4. Light-transmitting plastic interior wall signs in *covered mall buildings* shall comply with Section 402.16. Light-transmitting plastic interior signs shall also comply with Section 2606.

2611.2 Aggregate area. The sign shall not exceed 20 percent of the wall area.

2611.3 Maximum area. The sign shall not exceed 24 square feet (2.23 m^2).

2611.4 Encasement. Edges and backs of the sign shall be fully encased in metal.

SECTION 2612
FIBER REINFORCED POLYMER AND FIBERGLASS REINFORCED POLYMER

2612.1 General. The provisions of this section shall govern the requirements and uses of fiber reinforced polymer or fiberglass reinforced polymer in and on buildings and structures.

2612.2 Labeling and identification. Packages and containers of fiber reinforced polymer or fiberglass reinforced polymer and their components delivered to the job site shall bear the *label* of an *approved agency* showing the manufacturer's name, product listing, product identification and information sufficient to determine that the end use will comply with the code requirements.

2612.3 Interior finish. Fiber reinforced polymer or fiberglass reinforced polymer used as *interior finish* shall comply with Chapter 8.

2612.4 Decorative materials and trim. Fiber reinforced polymer or fiberglass reinforced polymer used as *decorative materials* or *trim* shall comply with Section 806.

2612.5 Light-transmitting materials. Fiber reinforced polymer or fiberglass reinforced polymer used as light-transmitting materials shall comply with Sections 2606 through 2611 as required for the specific application.

2612.6 Exterior use. Fiber reinforced polymer or fiberglass reinforced polymer shall be permitted to be installed on the *exterior walls* of buildings of any type of construction when such polymers meet the requirements of Section 2603.5 and is fireblocked in accordance with Section 717. The fiber reinforced polymer or the fiberglass reinforced polymer shall be designed for uniform live loads as required in Table 1607.1 as well as for snow loads, wind loads and earthquake loads as specified in Sections 1608, 1609 and 1613, respectively.

Exceptions:

1. When all of the following conditions are met:
   1.1. When the area of the fiber reinforced polymer or the fiberglass reinforced polymer does not exceed 20 percent of the respective wall area, the fiber reinforced polymer or the fiberglass reinforced polymer shall have a flame spread index of 25 or less or when the area of the fiber reinforced polymer or the fiberglass reinforced polymer does not exceed 10 percent of the respective wall area, the fiber reinforced polymer or the fiberglass reinforced polymer shall have a flame spread index of 75 or less. The flame spread index requirement shall not be required

for coatings or paints having a thickness of less than 0.036 inch (0.9 mm) that are applied directly to the surface of the fiber reinforced polymer or the fiberglass reinforced polymer.

1.2. Fireblocking complying with Section 717.2.6 shall be installed.

1.3. The fiber reinforced polymer or the fiberglass reinforced polymer shall be installed directly to a noncombustible substrate or be separated from the *exterior wall* by one of the following materials: corrosion-resistant steel having a minimum base metal thickness of 0.016 inch (0.41 mm) at any point, aluminum having a minimum thickness of 0.019 inch (0.5 mm) or other approved noncombustible material.

1.4. The fiber reinforced polymer or the fiberglass reinforced polymer shall be designed for uniform live loads as required in Table 1607.1 as well as for snow loads, wind loads and earthquake loads as specified in Sections 1608, 1609 and 1613, respectively.

2. When installed on buildings that are 40 feet (12 190 mm) or less above grade, the fiber reinforced polymer or the fiberglass reinforced polymer shall meet the requirements of Section 1406.2 and shall comply with all of the following conditions:

2.1. Where the fire separation distance is 5 feet (1524 mm) or less, the area of the fiber reinforced polymer or the fiberglass reinforced polymer shall not exceed 10 percent of the wall area. Where the fire separation distance is greater than 5 feet (1524 mm), there shall be no limit on the area of the *exterior wall* coverage using fiber reinforced polymer or the fiberglass reinforced polymer.

2.2. The fiber reinforced polymer or the fiberglass reinforced polymer shall have a flame spread index of 200 or less. The flame spread index requirement shall not be required for coatings or paints having a thickness of less than 0.036 inch (0.9 mm) that are applied directly to the surface of the fiber reinforced polymer or the fiberglass reinforced polymer.

2.3. Fireblocking complying with Section 717.2.6 shall be installed.

2.4. The fiber reinforced polymer or the fiberglass reinforced polymer shall be designed for uniform live loads as required in Table 1607.1 as well as for snow loads, wind loads and earthquake loads as specified in Sections 1608, 1609 and 1613, respectively.

SECTION 2613 REFLECTIVE PLASTIC CORE INSULATION

2613.1 General. The provisions of this section shall govern the requirements and uses of reflective plastic core insulation in buildings and structures. Reflective plastic core insulation shall comply with the requirements of Section 2613.2 and of one of the following: Section 2613.3 or 2613.4.

2613.2 Identification. Packages and containers of reflective plastic core insulation delivered to the job site shall show the manufacturer's or supplier's name, product identification and information sufficient to determine that the end use will comply with the code requirements.

2613.3 Surface-burning characteristics. Reflective plastic core insulation shall have a flame spread index of not more than 25 and a smoke-developed index of not more than 450 when tested in accordance with ASTM E 84 or UL 723. The reflective plastic core insulation shall be tested at the maximum thickness intended for use and shall be tested using one of the mounting methods in Section 2613.3.1 or 2613.3.2.

2613.3.1 Mounting of test specimen. The test specimen shall be mounted on 2-inch-high (51 mm) metal frames so as to create an air space between the unexposed face of the reflective plastic core insulation and the lid of the test apparatus.

2613.3.2 Specific testing. A set of specimen preparation and mounting procedures shall be used which are specific to the testing of reflective plastic core insulation.

2613.4 Room corner test heat release. Reflective plastic core insulation shall comply with the acceptance criteria of Section 803.1.2.1 when tested in accordance with NFPA 286 or UL 1715 in the manner intended for use and at the maximum thickness intended for use.

CHAPTER 27

EMERGENCY AND STANDBY POWER

SECTION 2701 GENERAL

2701.1 Scope. This chapter governs the electrical components, equipment and systems used in buildings and structures covered by this code. Electrical components, equipment and systems shall be designed and constructed in accordance with the provisions of NFPA 70.

[F] SECTION 2702 EMERGENCY AND STANDBY POWER SYSTEMS

[F] 2702.1 Installation. Emergency and standby power systems required by this code or the *International Fire Code* shall be installed in accordance with this code, NFPA 110 and 111.

[F] 2702.1.1 Stationary generators. Stationary emergency and standby power generators required by this code shall be *listed* in accordance with UL 2200.

[F] 2702.2 Where required. Emergency and standby power systems shall be provided where required by Sections 2702.2.1 through 2702.2.20.

[F] 2702.2.1 Group A occupancies. Emergency power shall be provided for emergency voice/alarm communication systems in Group A occupancies in accordance with Section 907.5.2.2.4.

[F] 2702.2.2 Smoke control systems. Standby power shall be provided for smoke control systems in accordance with Section 909.11.

[F] 2702.2.3 Exit signs. Emergency power shall be provided for *exit* signs in accordance with Section 1011.5.3.

[F] 2702.2.4 Means of egress illumination. Emergency power shall be provided for *means of egress* illumination in accordance with Section 1006.3.

[F] 2702.2.5 Accessible means of egress elevators. Standby power shall be provided for elevators that are part of an *accessible means of egress* in accordance with Section 1007.4.

[F] 2702.2.6 Accessible means of egress platform lifts. Standby power in accordance with this section or ASME A 18.1 shall be provided for platform lifts that are part of an *accessible means of egress* in accordance with Section 1007.5.

[F] 2702.2.7 Horizontal sliding doors. Standby power shall be provided for horizontal sliding doors in accordance with Section 1008.1.4.3.

[F] 2702.2.8 Semiconductor fabrication facilities. Emergency power shall be provided for semiconductor fabrication facilities in accordance with Section 415.8.10.

[F] 2702.2.9 Membrane structures. Standby power shall be provided for auxiliary inflation systems in accordance with Section 3102.8.2. Emergency power shall be provided for *exit* signs in temporary tents and membrane structures in accordance with the *International Fire Code.*

[F] 2702.2.10 Hazardous materials. Emergency or standby power shall be p rovided in occupancies with hazardous materials in accordance with Section 414.5.4.

[F] 2702.2.11 Highly toxic and toxic materials. Emergency power shall be provided for occupancies with highly *toxic* or *toxic* materials in accordance with Section 414 and the *International Fire Code.*

[F] 2702.2.12 Organic peroxides. Standby power shall be provided for occupancies with silane gas in accordance with Section 414 and the *International Fire Code.*

[F] 2702.2.13 Pyrophoric materials. Emergency power shall be provided for occupancies with silane gas in accordance with Section 414 and the *International Fire Code.*

[F] 2702.2.14 Covered mall buildings. Standby power shall be provided for voice/alarm communication systems in *covered mall buildings* in accordance with Section 402.14.

[F] 2702.2.15 High-rise buildings. Emergency and standby power shall be provided in high-rise buildings in accordance with Sections 403.4.7 and 403.4.8.

[F] 2702.2.16 Underground buildings. Emergency and standby power shall be provided in underground buildings in accordance with Sections 405.8 and 405.9.

[F] 2702.2.17 Group I-3 occupancies. Emergency power shall be provided for doors in Group I-3 occupancies in accordance with Section 408.4.2.

[F] 2702.2.18 Airport traffic control towers. Standby power shall be provided in airport traffic control towers in accordance with Section 412.3.5.

[F] 2702.2.19 Elevators. Standby power for elevators shall be provided as set forth in Sections 3003.1, 3007.7 and 3008.15.

[F] 2702.2.20 Smokeproof enclosures. Standby power shall be provided for smokeproof enclosures as required by Section 909.20.6.2.

[F] 2702.3 Maintenance. Emergency and standby power systems shall be maintained and tested in accordance with the *International Fire Code.*

CHAPTER 28
MECHANICAL SYSTEMS

SECTION 2801
GENERAL

2801.1 Scope. Mechanical appliances, equipment and systems shall be constructed, installed and maintained in accordance with the *International Mechanical Code* and the *International Fuel Gas Code*. Masonry chimneys, fireplaces and barbecues shall comply with the *International Mechanical Code* and Chapter 21 of this code.

CHAPTER 29

PLUMBING SYSTEMS

SECTION 2901 GENERAL

[P] 2901.1 Scope. The provisions of this chapter and the *International Plumbing Code* shall govern the erection, installation, *alteration*, repairs, relocation, replacement, *addition* to, use or maintenance of plumbing equipment and systems. Plumbing systems and equipment shall be constructed, installed and maintained in accordance with the *International Plumbing Code*.

SECTION 2902 MINIMUM PLUMBING FACILITIES

[P] 2902.1 Minimum number of fixtures. In new construction or building additions and in changes of occupancy as defined in the North Carolina Building Code, plumbing fixtures shall be provided for the type of occupancy and in the minimum number shown in Table 2902.1. Types of occupancies not shown in Table 2902.1 shall be considered individually by the *building official*. The number of occupants shall be determined by this code. Occupancy classification shall be determined in accordance with Chapter 3.

[P] 2902.1.1 Fixture calculations. To determine the *occupant load* of each sex, the total *occupant load* shall be divided in half. To determine the required number of fixtures, the fixture ratio or ratios for each fixture type shall be applied to the *occupant load* of each sex in accordance with Table 2902.1. Fractional numbers resulting from applying the fixture ratios of Table 2902.1 shall be rounded up to the next whole number. For calculations involving multiple occupancies, such fractional numbers for each occupancy shall first be summed and then rounded up to the next whole number.

Exception: The total *occupant load* shall not be required to be divided in half where *approved* statistical data indicate a distribution of the sexes of other than 50 percent of each sex.

TABLE 2902.1
MINIMUM NUMBER OF REQUIRED PLUMBING FIXTURES[a]
(See Sections 2902.2 and 2902.3)

NO.	CLASSIFICATION	OCCUPANCY	DESCRIPTION	WATER CLOSETS (URINALS SEE SECTION 419.2 OF THE *INTERNATIONAL PLUMBING CODE*)[j]		LAVATORIES[j]		BATHTUBS/ SHOWERS	DRINKING FOUNTAIN (SEE SECTION 410.1 OF THE *INTERNATIONAL PLUMBING CODE*)[j]	OTHER[g]
				MALE	FEMALE	MALE	FEMALE			
1	Assembly (see Sections 2902.2, 2902.5 and 2902.6)	A-1[d]	Theaters usually with fixed seats and other buildings for the performing arts and motion pictures	1 per 125	1 per 65	1 per 200		—	1 per 500	—
			Theaters in K-12 schools[i]	1 per 125	1 per 100	1 per 200		—	1 per 500	1 service sink
		A-2[d]	Nightclubs, bars, taverns, dance halls and buildings for similar purposes	1 per 40	1 per 40	1 per 75		—	1 per 500	—
			Restaurants, banquet halls and food courts	1 per 75	1 per 75	1 per 200		—	1 per 500	1 service sink[h]
			Cafeterias in K-12 schools[i]	1 per 125	1 per 100	1 per 200		—	1 per 500	1 service sink
		A-3[d]	Auditoriums without permanent seating, art galleries, exhibition halls, museums, lecture halls, libraries, arcades and gymnasiums	1 per 125	1 per 65	1 per 200		—	1 per 500	—
			Gymnasiums in K-12 schools[i]	1 per 125	1 per 100	1 per 200		—	1 per 500	1 service sink
			Passenger terminals and transportation facilities	1 per 500	1 per 500	1 per 750		—	1 per 1,000	1 service sink
			Places of worship and other religious services. Churches without assembly halls[e]	1 per 150	1 per 75	1 per 200		—	1 per 1,000	—

(continued)

TABLE 2902.1—continued
MINIMUM NUMBER OF REQUIRED PLUMBING FIXTURES[a]

NO.	CLASSIFICATION	OCCUPANCY	DESCRIPTION	WATER CLOSETS (URINALS SEE SECTION 419.2 OF THE *INTERNATIONAL PLUMBING CODE*)[j]		LAVATORIES[j]		BATHTUBS/ SHOWERS	DRINKING FOUNTAIN (SEE SECTION 410.1 OF THE *INTERNATIONAL PLUMBING CODE*)[j]	OTHER[g]
				MALE	FEMALE	MALE	FEMALE			
1 *cont'd*	Assembly (see Sections 2902.2, 2902.5 and 2902.6) *cont'd*	A-4	Coliseums, arenas, skating rinks, pools and tennis courts for indoor sporting events and activities	1 per 75 for the first 1,500 and 1 per 120 for the remainder	1 per 40 for the first 1,520 and 1 per 60 for the remainder	1 per 200	1 per 150	—	1 per 1,000	—
		A-5	Stadiums, amusement parks, bleachers and grandstands for outdoor sporting events and activities[k]	1 per 75 for the first 1,500 and 1 per 120 for the remainder	1 per 40 for the first 1,520 and 1 per 60 for the remainder	1 per 200	1 per 150	—	1 per 1,000	—
			K-12 stadiums, bleachers and grandstands for outdoor sporting events and activities[i,k]	1 per 125	1 per 100	1 per 250	1 per 200		1 per 1,000	—
2	Business (see Sections 2902.2, 2902.4 and 2902.4.1)	B	Buildings for the transaction of business, professional services, other services involving merchandise, office buildings, banks, light industrial and similar uses	1 per 25 for first 50 occupants and 1 per 50 for remaining occupants exceeding 50		1 per 40 for first 80 occupants and 1 per 80 for remaining occupants exceeding 80		—	25-100 1 101-250 2 251-500 3 add 1 per 500 exceeding 500	—
3	Educational[i]	E[b]	K-8 9 through 12 Teacher/Staff	1 per 25 1 per 30 1 per 30	1 per 25 1 per 25 1 per 25	1 per 60 1 per 100 1 per 100		—	1 per 100	—
4	Factory and Industrial	F-1 and F-2	Structures in which occupants are engaged in work fabricating, assembly or processing of products or materials (see Section 403.3.1 of the *International Plumbing Code* for adjustments in occupant content)	(See OSHA 29 CFR paragraph 1910.14.1)		(See OSHA 29 CFR paragraph 1910.14.1)		(see Section 411 of the *International Plumbing Code*)	1 per 400	—
5	Institutional	I-1	Residential care	1 per 10		1 per 10		1 per 8	—	—
		I-2	Hospitals and other health-care facilities[c]	Fixture requirements are regulated and enforced by state licensing and certification jurisdictions only.						
			Employees	1 per 25		1 per 35		—	1 per 100	—
			Visitors	1 per 75		1 per 100		—	1 per 500	—
		I-3	Prisons[b]	Fixture requirements are regulated and enforced by state licensing and certification jurisdictions only.						
			Reformitories, detention centers, and correctional centers[b]	Fixture requirements are regulated and enforced by state licensing and certification jurisdictions only.						
			Employees	1 per 25		1 per 35		—	1 per 100	—
			Visitors	1 per 75		1 per 100		—	1 per 500	—
		I-4	Adult day care	Fixture requirements are regulated and enforced by state licensing and certification jurisdictions only.						
			Child care[b]	1 per 15		1 per 25		—	—	—
			Employees	1 per 25		1 per 35		—	1 per 100	—
			Visitors	1 per 75		1 per 100		—	1 per 500	—

(continued)

TABLE 2902.1—continued
MINIMUM NUMBER OF REQUIRED PLUMBING FIXTURES[a]

NO.	CLASSIFICATION	OCCUPANCY	DESCRIPTION	WATER CLOSETS (URINALS SEE SECTION 419.2 OF THE *INTERNATIONAL PLUMBING CODE*)[j]		LAVATORIES[j]		BATHTUBS/ SHOWERS	DRINKING FOUNTAIN (SEE SECTION 410.1 OF THE *INTERNATIONAL PLUMBING CODE*)[j]	OTHER[g]
				MALE	FEMALE	MALE	FEMALE			
6	Mercantile (see Sections 2902.2, 2902.4, 2902.4.1, and 2902.4.2)	M	Retail stores, service stations, shops, salesrooms, markets and shopping centers	1 per 500		1 per 750		—	100-1,000 1 greater than 1,000 require 1 more for each addition 1,000	—
7	Residential	R-1	Hotels, motels, boarding houses (transient)	1 per guestroom		1 per guestroom		1 per guestroom	—	—
		R-2	Dormitories, fraternities, sororities and boarding houses (nontransient)	1 per 10		1 per 10		1 per 8	1 per 100	—
		R-2	Apartment house	1 per dwelling unit		1 per dwelling unit		1 per dwelling unit	—	1 kitchen sink per dwelling unit; 1 automatic clothes washer connection per 20 dwelling units
		R-3[l]	One- and two-family dwellings	1 per dwelling unit		1 per dwelling unit		1 per dwelling unit	—	1 kitchen sink per dwelling unit[f]
		R-4	Residential care/unlicensed assisted living facilities	1 per 10		1 per 10		1 per 8	—	—
8	Storage (see Sections 2902., 2902.4 and 2902.4.1)	S-1 S-2	Structures for the storage of goods, warehouses, storehouse and freight depots, low and moderate hazard[m,n]	1 per 100		1 per 100		See Section 411 of the *International Plumbing Code*	—	—

a. The fixtures shown are based on one fixture being the minimum required for the number of persons indicated or any fraction of the number of persons indicated. The number of occupants shall be determined by the *International Building Code.*

b. Toilet facilities for employees shall be separate from facilities for inmates, students or patients.

c. A single-occupant toilet room with one water closet and one lavatory serving not more than two adjacent patient rooms shall be permitted where such room is provided with direct access from each patient room and with provisions for privacy.

d. The occupant load for seasonal outdoor seating and entertainment areas shall be included when determining the minimum number of facilities required.

e. The number of fixtures provided shall be based on either the capacity of the church sanctuary or the church educational building (including fellowship halls and multiple purpose rooms), whichever is larger and within 300 feet (91.44 m).

f. For attached one- and two-family dwellings, one automatic clothes washer connection shall be required per 20 dwelling units.

g. A mop receptacle with a water supply, or a hose bib and floor drain, may be used in lieu of a service sink.

h. A can wash may be used in lieu of a service sink.

i. See Section 2902.9 for additional information on plumbing fixtures for schools.

j. When the rearrangement of an area or space increases the occupant content, the plumbing facilities shall be increased in accordance with this code.

k. For baseball stadiums, the number of fixtures shall be reduced by 50 percent.

l. Service sink may be omitted when located within a single-family dwelling.

m. Self-service mini-storage facilities without an office area are exempt.

n. Unheated storage buildings which are used periodically are not required to have toilet rooms.

2902.1.2 Family or assisted use toilet and bath fixtures. Fixtures located within family or assisted use toilet and bathing rooms required by Section 1109.2.1 are permitted to be included in the number of required fixtures for either the male or female occupants in assembly and mercantile occupancies.

[P] 2902.1.3 Adjustments in occupant content. If an owner or tenant requests, the plumbing official shall make adjustments in the occupant content established by Table 2902.1 for manufacturing, workshops, loft building, foundries, storage, aircraft hangars, garages, and similar establishments. The owner or occupant shall provide written data accompanied by plans that substantiates a claim that the occupant content of a particular building or tenancy will, at all times, be less than provided in Table 2902.1. Approval of such data and accompanying claims shall not prevent the plumbing official from requiring additional facilities based on Table 2902.1, if changes are made affecting the floor plan upon which the original approval was based, whether such changes are made by the original or ultimate owner or building occupant or occupants. The remainder of the facilities requirements of Section 2902 are not affected by this section.

[P] 2902.2 Separate facilities. Where plumbing fixtures are required, separate facilities shall be provided for each sex.

Exceptions:

1. Separate facilities shall not be required for *dwelling units* and *sleeping units*.
2. Separate facilities shall not be required in structures or tenant spaces with a total *occupant load*, including both employees and customers, of 25 or less.
3. Separate facilities shall not be required in mercantile occupancies in which the maximum *occupant load* is 100 or less.
4. Except as provided in Section 504.3.2 of the *North Carolina Plumbing Code*.

[P] 2902.3 Required public toilet facilities. Customers, patrons and visitors shall be provided with public toilet facilities in structures and tenant spaces intended for public utilization. Public toilet facilities shall be located not more than one story above or below the space required to be provided with public toilet facilities and the path of travel to such facilities shall not exceed a distance of 500 feet (152 m).

[P] 2902.3.1 Location of employee toilet facilities in occupancies other than assembly or mercantile. Access to toilet facilities in occupancies other than mercantile and assembly occupancies shall be from within the employees' working area. Employee facilities shall be either separate facilities or combined employee and public facilities.

Exception: Facilities that are required for employees in storage structures or kiosks, and are located in adjacent structures under the same ownership, lease or control, shall be a maximum travel distance of 500 feet (152 m) from the employees' working area.

[P] 2902.3.1.1 Travel distance. The required toilet facilities in occupancies other than assembly or mercantile shall be located not more than one story above or below the employee's working area and the path of travel to such facilities shall not exceed a distance of 500 feet (152 m).

Exception: The location and maximum travel distances to required employee toilet facilities in factory and industrial occupancies are permitted to exceed that required in Section 2902.4.1, provided that the location and maximum travel distance are approved by the code official.

[P] 2902.3.2 Location of employee toilet facilities in mercantile and assembly occupancies. Employees shall be provided with toilet facilities in building and tenant spaces utilized as restaurants, nightclubs, places or public assembly and mercantile occupancies. The employee facilities shall be either separate facilities or combined employee and public facilities. The required toilet facilities shall be located not more than one story above or below the employees' work area and the path of travel to such facilities, in other than covered malls, shall not exceed a distance of 500 feet (152 m). The path of travel to required facilities in covered malls shall not exceed a distance of 300 feet (91.44 m).

Exception: Employee toilet facilities shall not be required in tenant spaces where the travel distance from the main entrance of the tenant space to a central toilet area does not exceed 300 feet (91.44 m) and such central toilet facilities are located not more than one story above or below the tenant space.

[P] 2902.3.3 Location of toilet facilities in covered mall buildings. In covered mall buildings, the path of travel to required toilet facilities shall not exceed a distance of 300 feet (91 440 mm). Facilities shall be installed in each individual store or in a central toilet area located in accordance with this section. The maximum travel distance to the central toilet facilities in covered mall buildings shall be measured from the main entrance of any store or tenant space.

[P] 2902.3.4 Pay facilities. Where pay facilities are installed, such facilities shall be in excess of the required minimum facilities. Required facilities shall be free of charge.

[P] 2902.4 Signage. A legible sign designating the sex shall be provided in a visible location near the entrance to each toilet facility. Signs for *accessible* toilet facilities shall comply with ICC A117.1.

2902.4.1 Directional signage. Directional signage indicating the route to the public facilities shall be posted in accordance with Section 3107. Such signage shall be located in a *corridor* or aisle, at the entrance to the facilities for customers and visitors.

2902.5 Multiplex theaters. Plumbing fixtures for multiple adjoining motion picture theaters with a common lobby shall be based upon the seating capacity of the largest single auditorium plus 50 percent of the seats in the remaining auditoriums.

2902.6 Plumbing fixtures for public schools.

2902.6.1 Occupant content. Occupant content of public schools for the purpose of determining the number of required facilities shall be the maximum legal class size multiplied by the number of classrooms. A public school classroom is a room or space 500 square feet (46.5 m^2) or larger normally used for instructional purposes. Maximum class sizes are 29 students for grades K through 9 and 33 students for grades 10-12. (GS 115C-301). The occupant load for private schools shall be as listed in Table 1004.1.1 of this code.

2902.6.2 Occupant load and distance. The total student occupant load shall be the sum of the occupant loads for all classrooms, labs, shops and vocational spaces. The total occupant load for all buildings on a campus may be utilized when calculating the total number of fixtures required. Toilet facilities for students and teachers may be located in an adjacent building but shall be located so that no person will have more than 200 feet (61 m) of accessible, covered horizontal travel distance from any classroom lab, shop or vocational space closest door for access to the required number of fixtures. The occupant content of kindergarten and first grade classrooms with internal toilet facilities is not required to be used in determining the number of group facilities for the entire school.

2902.6.3 Occupant load for teachers and staff. Fixtures provided for teachers and staff shall be determined by multiplying the number of classrooms by 1.75. Staffing ratio for grades K through 8 is 70-percent female and 30-percent male.

2902.6.4 Gymnasiums, cafeterias, auditoriums and stadiums for schools. Fixtures in group toilet facilities provided for classroom areas may be used toward satisfying the total number of required fixtures for gymnasiums, cafeterias and auditoriums provided that such facilities are located within 200 feet (61 m) from the space and cannot be locked-off from access during after-school hours use of the gymnasium, cafeteria, or auditorium. Simultaneous use of classrooms, gymnasium, cafeteria, or auditoriums shall not be considered for calculation of occupant loads for toilet fixtures. Stadium facilities shall be located within 400 (122 m) feet of the closest bleacher exit from each set of bleachers that the facility serves.

2902.6.5 Miscellaneous provisions.

2902.6.5.1 Unisex facilities. A single unisex facility may be used when the classroom area served is 1200 square feet (112 m^2) or less and is used either for grades K through 2 or is a modular classroom used for any grade level. Unisex facilities may be provided for teacher/staff if their total occupant load within 200 feet (61 m) is 15 or less.

2902.6.5.2 Student group facilities. Every public school group facility shall have a minimum of four flushing type fixtures. Four flushing male group toilets shall have a minimum of two water closets.

2902.6.5.3 Substitutions. Water closets may be substituted for urinals for grades K through 2. Urinals may be substituted for water closets in male group toilet rooms for teachers/staff and gyms, auditoriums, cafeterias or stadiums. The number of water closets shall not be reduced to less than one-third of the required total number of flushing fixtures.

2902.6.5.4 Modular classroom buildings. Toilet rooms may be omitted in a modular classroom building when facilities of sufficient capacity for the additional occupants are provided in an adjacent building and located within 200 feet (61 m) of horizontal travel distance from the modular classroom.

2902.6.5.5 Temporary modular classroom buildings. Toilet rooms may be omitted in modular classroom buildings grades 9 through 12 when these temporary buildings are to be replaced by permanent facilities which are under contract. Facilities of sufficient capacity for the additional occupants shall be provided within 450 feet (137.16 m) of horizontal travel distance from the modular classroom.

SECTION 2903
TOILET ROOM REQUIREMENTS

[P] 2903.1 Water closet compartment. Each water closet utilized by the public or employees shall occupy a separate compartment with walls or partitions and a door enclosing the fixtures to ensure privacy.

Exceptions:

1. Water closet compartments shall not be required in a single-occupant toilet room with a lockable door.
2. In toilet rooms in child care facilities in areas used exclusively by children five years of age and under, the following is permitted:
   2.1. Toilet stall enclosures, toilet stall doors and partitions between toilets may be omitted.
   2.2. Doors into toilet rooms may be omitted.
   2.3. Walls enclosing toilet rooms may be full height with vision panels, or may be partial height at least 42 inches (1067 mm) high in areas for children four and five years of age and 36 inches (914 mm) high in areas for children under four years of age.
3. This provision is not applicable to toilet areas located within Group I-3 housing areas.

[P] 2903.2 Urinal partitions. Each urinal utilized by the public or employees shall occupy a separate area with walls or partitions to provide privacy. The walls or partitions shall begin at a height not more than 12 inches (305 mm) from and extend not less than 60 inches (1524 mm) above the finished floor surface. The walls or partitions shall extend from the wall surface at each side of the urinal a minimum of 18 inches (457 mm) or to a point not less than 6 inches (152 mm) beyond the outermost front lip of the urinal measured from the finished back wall surface, whichever is greater.

Exceptions:

1. Urinal partitions shall not be required in a single occupant or family or assisted use toilet room with a lockable door.
2. Toilet rooms located in day care and child care facilities and containing two or more urinals shall be permitted to have one urinal without partitions.

[P] 2903.3 Interior finish. Interior finish surfaces of toilet rooms shall comply with Section 1210.

CHAPTER 30

ELEVATORS AND CONVEYING SYSTEMS

SECTION 3001
GENERAL

3001.1 Scope. This chapter governs the design, construction, installation, *alteration* and repair of elevators and conveying systems and their components.

3001.2 Referenced standards. Except as otherwise provided for in this code, the design, construction, installation, *alteration*, repair and maintenance of elevators and conveying systems and their components shall conform to ASME A17.1/CSA B44, ASME A90.1, ASME B20.1, ALI ALCTV, and ASCE 24 for construction in flood hazard areas established in Section 1612.3.

3001.3 Accessibility. Passenger elevators required to be *accessible* by Chapter 11 shall conform to ICC A117.1.

3001.4 Change in use. A change in use of an elevator from freight to passenger, passenger to freight, or from one freight class to another freight class shall comply with Section 8.7 of ASME A17.1/CSA B44.

SECTION 3002
HOISTWAY ENCLOSURES

3002.1 Hoistway enclosure protection. Elevator, dumbwaiter and other hoistway enclosures shall be shaft enclosures complying with Section 708.

3002.1.1 Opening protectives. Openings in hoistway enclosures shall be protected as required in Chapter 7.

Exception: The elevator car doors and the associated hoistway enclosure doors at the floor level designated for recall in accordance with Section 3003.2 shall be permitted to remain open during Phase I Emergency Recall Operation.

3002.1.2 Hardware. Hardware on opening protectives shall be of an *approved* type installed as tested, except that *approved* interlocks, mechanical locks and electric contacts, door and gate electric contacts and door-operating mechanisms shall be exempt from the fire test requirements.

3002.2 Number of elevator cars in a hoistway. Where four or more elevator cars serve all or the same portion of a building, the elevators shall be located in at least two separate hoistways. Not more than four elevator cars shall be located in any single hoistway enclosure.

3002.3 Emergency signs. An *approved* pictorial sign of a standardized design shall be posted adjacent to each elevator call station on all floors instructing occupants to use the *exit stairways* and not to use the elevators in case of fire. The sign shall read: IN FIRE EMERGENCY, DO NOT USE ELEVATOR. USE EXIT STAIRS.

Exceptions:

1. The emergency sign shall not be required for elevators that are part of an *accessible means of egress* complying with Section 1007.4.
2. The emergency sign shall not be required for elevators that are used for occupant self-evacuation in accordance with Section 3008.

3002.4 Elevator car to accommodate ambulance stretcher. Where elevators are provided in buildings four or more *stories* above, or four or more *stories* below, *grade plane*, at least one elevator shall be provided for fire department emergency access to all floors. The elevator car shall be of such a size and arrangement to accommodate an ambulance stretcher 24 inches by 84 inches (610 mm by 2134 mm) with not less than 5-inch (127 mm) radius corners, in the horizontal, open position and shall be identified by the international symbol for emergency medical services (star of life). The symbol shall not be less than 3 inches (76 mm) high and shall be placed inside on both sides of the hoistway door frame.

3002.5 Emergency doors. Where an elevator is installed in a single blind hoistway or on the outside of a building, there shall be installed in the blind portion of the hoistway or blank face of the building, an emergency door in accordance with ASME A17.1/CSA B44.

3002.6 Prohibited doors. Doors, other than hoistway doors and the elevator car door, shall be prohibited at the point of access to an elevator car unless such doors are readily openable from the car side without a key, tool, special knowledge or effort.

3002.7 Common enclosure with stairway. Elevators shall not be in a common shaft enclosure with a *stairway*.

Exception: *Open parking garages.*

3002.8 Glass in elevator enclosures. Glass in elevator enclosures shall comply with Section 2409.1.

3002.9 Pits. For dampproofing and waterproofing requirements, refer to Section 1807.

[F] SECTION 3003
EMERGENCY OPERATIONS

[F] 3003.1 Standby power. In buildings and structures where standby power is required or furnished to operate an elevator, the operation shall be in accordance with Sections 3003.1.1 through 3003.1.4.

[F] 3003.1.1 Manual transfer. Standby power shall be manually transferable to all elevators in each bank.

[F] 3003.1.2 One elevator. Where only one elevator is installed, the elevator shall automatically transfer to standby power within 60 seconds after failure of normal power.

[F] 3003.1.3 Two or more elevators. Where two or more elevators are controlled by a common operating system, all elevators shall automatically transfer to standby power within 60 seconds after failure of normal power where the standby power source is of sufficient capacity to operate all elevators at the same time. Where the standby power source is not of sufficient capacity to operate all elevators at the same time, all elevators shall transfer to standby power in sequence, return to the designated landing and disconnect from the standby power source. After all elevators have been returned to the designated level, at least one elevator shall remain operable from the standby power source.

[F] 3003.1.4 Venting. Where standby power is connected to elevators, the machine room ventilation or air conditioning shall be connected to the standby power source.

[F] 3003.2 Fire-fighters' emergency operation. Elevators shall be provided with Phase I emergency recall operation and Phase II emergency in-car operation in accordance with ASME A17.1/CSA B44.

SECTION 3004
HOISTWAY VENTING

3004.1 Vents required. Hoistways of elevators and dumbwaiters penetrating more than three *stories* shall be provided with a means for venting smoke and hot gases to the outer air in case of fire.

Exceptions:

1. In occupancies of other than Groups R-1, R-2, I-1, I-2 and similar occupancies with overnight *sleeping units*, venting of hoistways is not required where the building is equipped throughout with an *approved automatic sprinkler system* installed in accordance with Section 903.3.1.1 or 903.3.1.2.
2. Sidewalk elevator hoistways are not required to be vented.
3. Elevators contained within and serving *open parking garages* only.
4. Elevators within individual residential *dwelling units*.

3004.2 Location of vents. Vents shall be located at the top the hoistway and shall open either directly to the outer air or through noncombustible ducts to the outer air. Noncombustible ducts shall be permitted to pass through the elevator machine room, provided that portions of the ducts located outside the hoistway or machine room are enclosed by construction having not less than the *fire-resistance rating* required for the hoistway. Holes in the machine room floors for the passage of ropes, cables or other moving elevator equipment shall be limited as not to provide greater than 2 inches (51 mm) of clearance on all sides.

3004.3 Area of vents. Except as provided for in Section 3004.3.1, the area of the vents shall not be less than $3^1/_2$ percent of the area of the hoistway nor less than 3 square feet (0.28 m^2) for each elevator car, and not less than $3^1/_2$ percent nor less than 0.5 square feet (0.047 m^2) for each dumbwaiter car in the hoistway, whichever is greater. Of the total required vent area, not less than one-third shall be permanently open. Closed portions of the required vent area shall consist of openings glazed with annealed glass not greater than $^1/_8$ inch (3.2 mm) in thickness.

Exception: The total required vent area shall not be required to be permanently open where all the vent openings automatically open upon detection of smoke in the elevator lobbies or hoistway, upon power failure and upon activation of a manual override control. The manual override control shall be capable of opening and closing the vents and shall be located in an *approved* location.

3004.3.1 Reduced vent area. Where mechanical ventilation conforming to the *International Mechanical Code* is provided, a reduction in the required vent area is allowed provided that all of the following conditions are met:

1. The occupancy is not in Group R-1, R-2, I-1 or I-2 or of a similar occupancy with overnight *sleeping units*.
2. The vents required by Section 3004.2 do not have outside exposure.
3. The hoistway does not extend to the top of the building.
4. The hoistway and machine room exhaust fan is automatically reactivated by thermostatic means.
5. Equivalent venting of the hoistway is accomplished.

3004.4 Plumbing and mechanical systems. Plumbing and mechanical systems shall not be located in an elevator shaft.

Exception: Floor drains, sumps and sump pumps shall be permitted at the base of the shaft provided they are indirectly connected to the plumbing system.

SECTION 3005
CONVEYING SYSTEMS

3005.1 General. Escalators, moving walks, conveyors, personnel hoists and material hoists shall comply with the provisions of this section.

3005.2 Escalators and moving walks. Escalators and moving walks shall be constructed of *approved* noncombustible and fire-retardant materials. This requirement shall not apply to electrical equipment, wiring, wheels, handrails and the use of $^1/_{28}$-inch (0.9 mm) wood veneers on balustrades backed up with noncombustible materials.

3005.2.1 Enclosure. Escalator floor openings shall be enclosed with shaft enclosures complying with Section 708.

3005.2.2 Escalators. Where provided in below-grade transportation stations, escalators shall have a clear width of 32 inches (815 mm) minimum.

Exception: The clear width is not required in existing facilities undergoing *alterations*.

3005.3 Conveyors. Conveyors and conveying systems shall comply with ASME B20.1.

3005.3.1 Enclosure. Conveyors and related equipment connecting successive floors or levels shall be enclosed with shaft enclosures complying with Section 708.

3005.3.2 Conveyor safeties. Power-operated conveyors, belts and other material-moving devices shall be equipped with automatic limit switches which will shut off the power in an emergency and automatically stop all operation of the device.

3005.4 Personnel and material hoists. Personnel and material hoists shall be designed utilizing an *approved* method that accounts for the conditions imposed during the intended operation of the hoist device. The design shall include, but is not limited to, anticipated loads, structural stability, impact, vibration, stresses and seismic restraint. The design shall account for the construction, installation, operation and inspection of the hoist tower, car, machinery and control equipment, guide members and hoisting mechanism. Additionally, the design of personnel hoists shall include provisions for field testing and maintenance which will demonstrate that the hoist device functions in accordance with the design. Field tests shall be conducted upon the completion of an installation or following a major *alteration* of a personnel hoist.

SECTION 3006 MACHINE ROOMS

3006.1 Access. An *approved* means of access shall be provided to elevator machine rooms and overhead machinery spaces.

3006.2 Venting. Elevator machine rooms that contain solid-state equipment for elevator operation shall be provided with an independent ventilation or air-conditioning system to protect against the overheating of the electrical equipment. The system shall be capable of maintaining temperatures within the range established for the elevator equipment.

3006.3 Pressurization. The elevator machine room serving a pressurized elevator hoistway shall be pressurized upon activation of a heat or smoke detector located in the elevator machine room.

3006.4 Machine rooms and machinery spaces. Elevator machine rooms and machinery spaces shall be enclosed with *fire barriers* constructed in accordance with Section 707 or *horizontal assemblies* constructed in accordance with Section 712, or both. The *fire-resistance rating* shall not be less than the required rating of the hoistway enclosure served by the machinery. Openings in the *fire barriers* shall be protected with assemblies having a *fire protection rating* not less than that required for the hoistway enclosure doors.

Exceptions:

1. Where machine rooms and machinery spaces do not abut and have no openings to the hoistway enclosure they serve the *fire barriers* constructed in accordance with Section 707 or *horizontal assemblies* constructed in accordance with Section 712, or both, shall be permitted to be reduced to a 1-hour *fire-resistance rating*.
2. In buildings four *stories* or less above *grade plane* when machine room and machinery spaces do not abut and have no openings to the hoistway enclosure they serve, the machine room and machinery spaces are not required to be fire-resistance rated.

3006.5 Shunt trip. Where elevator hoistways or elevator machine rooms containing elevator control equipment are protected with automatic sprinklers, a means installed in accordance with NFPA 72, Section 6.16.4, Elevator Shutdown, shall be provided to disconnect automatically the main line power supply to the affected elevator prior to the application of water. This means shall not be self-resetting. The activation of sprinklers outside the hoistway or machine room shall not disconnect the main line power supply.

3006.6 Plumbing systems. Plumbing systems shall not be located in elevator equipment rooms.

SECTION 3007 FIRE SERVICE ACCESS ELEVATOR

3007.1 General. Where required by Section 403.6.1, every floor of the building shall be served by a fire service access elevator. Except as modified in this section, the fire service access elevator shall be installed in accordance with this chapter and ASME A17.1/CSA B44.

3007.2 Hoistway enclosures protection. The fire service access elevator shall be located in a shaft enclosure complying with Section 708.

3007.3 Hoistway lighting. When firefighters' emergency operation is active, the entire height of the hoistway shall be illuminated at not less than 1 footcandle (11 lux) as measured from the top of the car of each fire service access elevator.

3007.4 Fire service access elevator lobby. The fire service access elevator shall open into a fire service access elevator lobby in accordance with Sections 3007.4.1 through 3007.4.4.

Exception: Where a fire service access elevator has two entrances onto a floor, the second entrance shall be permitted to open into an elevator lobby in accordance with Section 708.14.1.

3007.4.1 Access. The fire service access elevator lobby shall have direct access to an *exit enclosure*.

3007.4.2 Lobby enclosure. The fire service access elevator lobby shall be enclosed with a *smoke barrier* having a minimum 1-hour *fire-resistance rating*, except that lobby doorways shall comply with Section 3007.4.3.

Exception: Enclosed fire service access elevator lobbies are not required at the street floor.

3007.4.3 Lobby doorways. Each fire service access elevator lobby shall be provided with a doorway that is protected with a $^3/_4$-hour *fire door assembly* complying with Section 715.4. The *fire door assembly* shall also comply with the smoke and draft control door assembly requirements of Section 715.4.3.1 with the UL 1784 test conducted without the artificial bottom seal.

3007.4.4 Lobby size. Each enclosed fire service access elevator lobby shall be a minimum of 150 square feet (14 m^2) in an area with a minimum dimension of 8 feet (2440 mm).

3007.5 Standpipe hose connection. A Class I standpipe hose connection in accordance with Section 905 shall be provided in the *exit enclosure* having direct access from the fire service access elevator lobby.

3007.6 Elevator system monitoring. The fire service access elevator shall be continuously monitored at the fire command center by a standard emergency service interface system meeting the requirements of NFPA 72.

3007.7 Electrical power. The following features serving each fire service access elevator shall be supplied by both normal power and Type 60/Class 2/Level 1 standby power:

1. Elevator equipment.
2. Elevator hoistway lighting.
3. Elevator machine room ventilation and cooling equipment.
4. Elevator controller cooling equipment.

3007.7.1 Protection of wiring or cables. Wires or cables that provide normal and standby power, control signals, communication with the car, lighting, heating, air conditioning, ventilation and fire-detecting systems to fire service access elevators shall be protected by construction having a minimum 1-hour *fire-resistance rating* or shall be circuit integrity cable having a minimum 1-hour *fire-resistance rating*.

SECTION 3008
OCCUPANT EVACUATION ELEVATORS

3008.1 General. Where elevators are to be used for occupant self-evacuation during fires, all passenger elevators for general public use shall comply with this section. Where other elevators are used for occupant self-evacuation, they shall also comply with this section.

3008.2 Fire safety and evacuation plan. The building shall have an *approved* fire safety and evacuation plan in accordance with the applicable requirements of Section 404 of the *International Fire Code*. The fire safety and evacuation plan shall incorporate specific procedures for the occupants using evacuation elevators.

3008.3 Operation. The occupant evacuation elevators shall be used for occupant self-evacuation only in the normal elevator operating mode prior to Phase I Emergency Recall Operation in accordance with the requirements in ASME A17.1/CSA B44 and the building's fire safety and evacuation plan.

3008.4 Additional exit stairway. Where an additional *means of egress* is required in accordance with Section 403.5.2, an additional *exit stairway* shall not be required to be installed in buildings having elevators used for occupant self-evacuation in accordance with this section.

3008.5 Emergency voice/alarm communication system. The building shall be provided with an emergency voice/alarm communication system. The emergency voice/alarm communication system shall be accessible to the fire department. The system shall be provided in accordance with Section 907.5.2.2.

3008.5.1 Notification appliances. A minimum of one audible and one visible notification appliance shall be installed within each occupant evacuation elevator lobby.

3008.6 Automatic sprinkler system. The building shall be protected throughout by an *approved*, electrically-supervised automatic sprinkler system in accordance with Section 903.3.1.1, except as otherwise permitted by Section 903.3.1.1.1 and as prohibited by Section 3008.6.1.

3008.6.1 Prohibited locations. Automatic sprinklers shall not be installed in elevator machine rooms and elevator machine spaces for occupant evacuation elevators.

3008.6.2 Sprinkler system monitoring. The sprinkler system shall have a sprinkler control valve supervisory switch and waterflow-initiating device provided for each floor that is monitored by the building's fire alarm system.

3008.7 High-hazard content areas. No building areas shall contain hazardous materials exceeding the maximum allowable quantities per *control area* as addressed in Section 414.2.

3008.8 Shunt trip. Means for elevator shutdown in accordance with Section 3006.5 shall not be installed on elevator systems used for occupant evacuation elevators.

3008.9 Hoistway enclosure protection. The occupant evacuation elevators shall be located in hoistway enclosure(s) complying with Section 708.

3008.10 Water protection. The occupant evacuation elevator hoistway shall be designed utilizing an *approved* method to prevent water from the operation of the *automatic sprinkler system* from infiltrating into the hoistway enclosure.

3008.11 Occupant evacuation elevator lobby. The occupant evacuation elevators shall open into an elevator lobby in accordance with Sections 3008.11.1 through 3008.11.5.

3008.11.1 Access. The occupant evacuation elevator lobby shall have direct access to an *exit enclosure*.

3008.11.2 Lobby enclosure. The occupant evacuation elevator lobby shall be enclosed with a *smoke barrier* having a minimum 1-hour *fire-resistance rating*, except that lobby doorways shall comply with Section 3008.11.3.

Exception: Enclosed occupant evacuation elevator lobbies are not required at the level(s) of *exit discharge*.

3008.11.3 Lobby doorways. Each occupant evacuation elevator lobby shall be provided with a doorway that is protected with a $^3/_4$-hour *fire door assembly* complying with Section 715.4.

3008.11.3.1 Vision panel. A vision panel shall be installed in each *fire door assembly* protecting the lobby doorway. The vision panel shall consist of fire-protection-rated glazing and shall be located to furnish clear vision of the occupant evacuation elevator lobby.

3008.11.3.2 Door closing. Each *fire door assembly* protecting the lobby doorway shall be automatic-closing upon receipt of any fire alarm signal from the emergency voice/alarm communication system serving the building.

3008.11.4 Lobby size. Each occupant evacuation elevator lobby shall have minimum floor area as follows:

1. The occupant evacuation elevator lobby floor area shall accommodate, at 3 square feet (0.28 m^2) per person, a minimum of 25 percent of the *occupant load* of the floor area served by the lobby.
2. The occupant evacuation elevator lobby floor area also shall accommodate one *wheelchair space* of 30 inches by 48 inches (760 mm by 1220 mm) for each 50 persons, or portion thereof, of the *occupant load* of the floor area served by the lobby.

Exception: The size of lobbies serving multiple banks of elevators shall have the minimum floor area *approved* on an individual basis and shall be consistent with the building's fire safety and evacuation plan.

3008.11.5 Signage. An *approved* sign indicating elevators are suitable for occupant self-evacuation shall be posted on all floors adjacent to each elevator call station serving occupant evacuation elevators.

3008.12 Lobby status indicator. Each occupant evacuation elevator lobby shall be equipped with a status indicator arranged to display all of the following information:

1. An illuminated green light and the message, "Elevators available for occupant evacuation" when the elevators are operating in normal service and the fire alarm system is indicating an alarm in the building.
2. An illuminated red light and the message, "Elevators out of service, use exit stairs" *when the elevators are in Phase I emergency recall operation in accordance with the requirements in ASME A17.1/CSA B44.*
3. No illuminated light or message when the elevators are operating in normal service.

3008.13 Two-way communication system. A two-way communication system shall be provided in each occupant evacuation elevator lobby for the purpose of initiating communication with the fire command center or an alternative location *approved* by the fire department.

3008.13.1 Design and installation. The two-way communication system shall include audible and visible signals and shall be designed and installed in accordance with the requirements of ICC A117.1.

3008.13.2 Instructions. Instructions for the use of the two-way communication system along with the location of the station shall be permanently located adjacent to each station. Signage shall comply with the ICC A117.1 requirements for visual characters.

3008.14 Elevator system monitoring. The occupant evacuation elevators shall be continuously monitored at the fire command center or a central control point *approved* by the fire department and arranged to display all of the following information:

1. Floor location of each elevator car.
2. Direction of travel of each elevator car.
3. Status of each elevator car with respect to whether it is occupied.
4. Status of normal power to the elevator equipment, elevator controller cooling equipment, and elevator machine room ventilation and cooling equipment.
5. Status of standby or emergency power system that provides backup power to the elevator equipment, elevator controller cooling equipment, and elevator machine room ventilation and cooling equipment.
6. Activation of any fire alarm-initiating device in any elevator lobby, elevator machine room or machine space, or elevator hoistway.

3008.14.1 Elevator recall. The fire command center or an alternative location *approved* by the fire department shall be provided with the means to manually initiate a Phase I Emergency Recall of the occupant evacuation elevators in accordance with ASME A17.1/CSA B44.

3008.15 Electrical power. The following features serving each occupant evacuation elevator shall be supplied by both normal power and Type 60/Class 2/Level 1 standby power:

1. Elevator equipment.
2. Elevator machine room ventilation and cooling equipment.
3. Elevator controller cooling equipment.

3008.15.1 Protection of wiring or cables. Wires or cables that provide normal and standby power, control signals, communication with the car, lighting, heating, air conditioning, ventilation and fire-detecting systems to occupant evacuation elevators shall be protected by construction having a minimum 1-hour *fire-resistance rating* or shall be circuit integrity cable having a minimum 1-hour *fire-resistance rating.*

CHAPTER 31
SPECIAL CONSTRUCTION

SECTION 3101
GENERAL

3101.1 Scope. The provisions of this chapter shall govern special building construction including membrane structures, temporary structures, *pedestrian walkways* and tunnels, automatic vehicular gates, *awnings* and canopies, marquees, signs, and towers and antennas.

SECTION 3102
MEMBRANE STRUCTURES

3102.1 General. The provisions of this section shall apply to air-supported, air-inflated, membrane-covered cable and membrane-covered frame structures, collectively known as membrane structures, erected for a period of 180 days or longer. Those erected for a shorter period of time shall comply with the *International Fire Code*. Membrane structures covering water storage facilities, water clarifiers, water treatment plants, sewage treatment plants, greenhouses and similar facilities not used for human occupancy are required to meet only the requirements of Sections 3102.3.1 and 3102.7. Membrane structures erected on a building, balcony, deck or other structure for any period of time shall comply with this section.

3102.2 Definitions. The following words and terms shall, for the purposes of this section and as used elsewhere in this code, have the meanings shown herein.

AIR-INFLATED STRUCTURE. A structure that uses air-pressurized membrane beams, arches or other elements to enclose space. Occupants of such a structure do not occupy the pressurized area used to support the structure.

AIR-SUPPORTED STRUCTURE. A building wherein the shape of the structure is attained by air pressure and occupants of the structure are within the elevated pressure area. Air-supported structures are of two basic types:

> **Double skin.** Similar to a single skin, but with an attached liner that is separated from the outer skin and provides an airspace which serves for insulation, acoustic, aesthetic or similar purposes.
>
> **Single skin.** Where there is only the single outer skin and the air pressure is directly against that skin.

CABLE-RESTRAINED, AIR-SUPPORTED STRUCTURE. A structure in which the uplift is resisted by cables or webbings which are anchored to either foundations or dead men. Reinforcing cable or webbing is attached by various methods to the membrane or is an integral part of the membrane. This is not a cable-supported structure.

MEMBRANE-COVERED CABLE STRUCTURE. A nonpressurized structure in which a mast and cable system provides support and tension to the membrane weather barrier and the membrane imparts stability to the structure.

MEMBRANE-COVERED FRAME STRUCTURE. A nonpressurized building wherein the structure is composed of a rigid framework to support a tensioned membrane which provides the weather barrier.

NONCOMBUSTIBLE MEMBRANE STRUCTURE. A membrane structure in which the membrane and all component parts of the structure are noncombustible.

3102.3 Type of construction. Noncombustible membrane structures shall be classified as Type IIB construction. Noncombustible frame or cable-supported structures covered by an *approved* membrane in accordance with Section 3102.3.1 shall be classified as Type IIB construction. Heavy timber frame-supported structures covered by an *approved* membrane in accordance with Section 3102.3.1 shall be classified as Type IV construction. Other membrane structures shall be classified as Type V construction.

> **Exception:** Plastic less than 30 feet (9144 mm) above any floor used in greenhouses, where occupancy by the general public is not authorized, and for aquaculture pond covers is not required to meet the fire propagation performance criteria of NFPA 701.

3102.3.1 Membrane and interior liner material. Membranes and interior liners shall be either noncombustible as set forth in Section 703.4 or meet the fire propagation performance criteria of NFPA 701 and the manufacturer's test protocol.

> **Exception:** Plastic less than 20 mil (0.5 mm) in thickness used in greenhouses, where occupancy by the general public is not authorized, and for aquaculture pond covers is not required to meet the fire propagation performance criteria of NFPA 701.

3102.4 Allowable floor areas. The area of a membrane structure shall not exceed the limitations set forth in Table 503, except as provided in Section 506.

3102.5 Maximum height. Membrane structures shall not exceed one *story* nor shall such structures exceed the height limitations in feet set forth in Table 503.

> **Exception:** Noncombustible membrane structures serving as roofs only.

3102.6 Mixed construction. Membrane structures shall be permitted to be utilized as specified in this section as a portion of buildings of other types of construction. Height and area limits shall be as specified for the type of construction and occupancy of the building.

3102.6.1 Noncombustible membrane. A noncombustible membrane shall be permitted for use as the roof or as a skylight of any building or atrium of a building of any type of construction provided it is at least 20 feet (6096 mm) above any floor, balcony or gallery.

3102.6.1.1 Membrane. A membrane meeting the fire propagation performance criteria of NFPA 701 shall be permitted to be used as the roof or as a skylight on buildings of Types IIB, III, IV and V construction, provided it is at least 20 feet (6096 mm) above any floor, balcony or gallery.

3102.7 Engineering design. The structure shall be designed and constructed to sustain dead loads; loads due to tension or inflation; live loads including wind, snow or flood and seismic loads and in accordance with Chapter 16.

3102.8 Inflation systems. Air-supported and air-inflated structures shall be provided with primary and auxiliary inflation systems to meet the minimum requirements of Sections 3102.8.1 through 3102.8.3.

3102.8.1 Equipment requirements. This inflation system shall consist of one or more blowers and shall include provisions for automatic control to maintain the required inflation pressures. The system shall be so designed as to prevent overpressurization of the system.

3102.8.1.1 Auxiliary inflation system. In addition to the primary inflation system, in buildings exceeding 1,500 square feet (140 m^2) in area, an auxiliary inflation system shall be provided with sufficient capacity to maintain the inflation of the structure in case of primary system failure. The auxiliary inflation system shall operate automatically when there is a loss of internal pressure and when the primary blower system becomes inoperative.

3102.8.1.2 Blower equipment. Blower equipment shall meet all of the following requirements:

1. Blowers shall be powered by continuous-rated motors at the maximum power required for any flow condition as required by the structural design.
2. Blowers shall be provided with inlet screens, belt guards and other protective devices as required by the *building official* to provide protection from injury.
3. Blowers shall be housed within a weather-protecting structure.
4. Blowers shall be equipped with backdraft check dampers to minimize air loss when inoperative.
5. Blower inlets shall be located to provide protection from air contamination. The location of inlets shall be *approved*.

3102.8.2 Standby power. Wherever an auxiliary inflation system is required, an *approved* standby power-generating system shall be provided. The system shall be equipped with a suitable means for automatically starting the generator set upon failure of the normal electrical service and for automatic transfer and operation of all of the required electrical functions at full power within 60 seconds of such service failure. Standby power shall be capable of operating independently for a minimum of 4 hours.

3102.8.3 Support provisions. A system capable of supporting the membrane in the event of deflation shall be provided for in air-supported and air-inflated structures having an *occupant load* of 50 or more or where covering a swimming pool regardless of *occupant load*. The support system shall be capable of maintaining membrane structures used as a roof for Type I construction not less than 20 feet (6096 mm) above floor or seating areas. The support system shall be capable of maintaining other membranes at least 7 feet (2134 mm) above the floor, seating area or surface of the water.

SECTION 3103
TEMPORARY STRUCTURES

3103.1 General. The provisions of this section apply to structures erected for a period of less than 180 days. Those erected for a longer period of time shall comply with all applicable sections of the *North Carolina Building Code.*

Exception: Tents, canopies and membrane structures erected for a period of less than 180 days shall comply with Chapter 24 of the *International Fire Code.*

3103.1.1 Permit required. Temporary structures that cover an area in excess of 120 square feet (11.16 m^2), including connecting areas or spaces with a common *means of egress* or entrance which are used or intended to be used for the gathering together of 10 or more persons, shall not be erected, operated or maintained for any purpose without obtaining a *permit* from the *building official.*

3103.2 Construction documents. A *permit* application and *construction documents* shall be submitted for each installation of a temporary structure. The *construction documents* shall include a site plan indicating the location of the temporary structure and information delineating the *means of egress* and the *occupant load.*

3103.3 Location. Temporary structures shall be located in accordance with the requirements of Table 602 based on the *fire-resistance rating* of the *exterior walls* for the proposed type of construction.

3103.4 Means of egress. Temporary structures shall conform to the *means of egress* requirements of Chapter 10 and shall have a maximum *exit access* travel distance of 100 feet (30 480 mm).

SECTION 3104
PEDESTRIAN WALKWAYS AND TUNNELS

3104.1 General. This section shall apply to connections between buildings such as *pedestrian walkways* or tunnels, located at, above or below grade level, that are used as a means of travel by persons. The *pedestrian walkway* shall not contribute to the *building area* or the number of *stories* or height of connected buildings.

3104.2 Separate structures. Connected buildings shall be considered to be separate structures.

Exceptions:

1. Buildings on the same lot in accordance with Section 503.1.2.

2. For purposes of calculating the number of Type B units required by Chapter 11, structurally connected buildings and buildings with multiple wings shall be considered one structure.

3104.3 Construction. The *pedestrian walkway* shall be of noncombustible construction.

Exceptions:

1. Combustible construction shall be permitted where connected buildings are of combustible construction.
2. *Fire-retardant-treated wood*, in accordance with Section 603.1, Item 25.3, shall be permitted for the roof construction of the *pedestrian walkway* where connected buildings are a minimum of Type I or II construction.

3104.4 Contents. Only materials and decorations *approved* by the *building official* shall be located in the *pedestrian walkway.*

3104.5 Fire barriers between pedestrian walkways and buildings. Walkways shall be separated from the interior of the building by not less than 2-hour *fire barriers* constructed in accordance with Section 707 or *horizontal assemblies* constructed in accordance with Section 712, or both. This protection shall extend vertically from a point 10 feet (3048 mm) above the walkway roof surface or the connected building roof line, whichever is lower, down to a point 10 feet (3048 mm) below the walkway and horizontally 10 feet (3048 mm) from each side of the *pedestrian walkway.* Openings within the 10-foot (3048 mm) horizontal extension of the protected walls beyond the walkway shall be equipped with devices providing a $^{3}/_{4}$-hour *fire protection rating* in accordance with Section 715.

Exception: The walls separating the *pedestrian walkway* from a connected building and the openings within the 10-foot (3048 mm) horizontal extension of the protected walls beyond the walkway are not required to have a *fire-resistance rating* by this section where any of the following conditions exist:

1. The distance between the connected buildings is more than 10 feet (3048 mm). The *pedestrian walkway* and connected buildings, except for *open parking garages*, are equipped throughout with an *automatic sprinkler system* in accordance with Section 903.3.1.1. The wall is capable of resisting the passage of smoke or is constructed of a tempered, wired or laminated glass wall and doors subject to the following:
   1.1. The wall or glass separating the interior of the building from the *pedestrian walkway* shall be protected by an *automatic sprinkler system* in accordance with Section 903.3.1.1 and the sprinkler system shall completely wet the entire surface of interior sides of the wall or glass when actuated;
   1.2. The glass shall be in a gasketed frame and installed in such a manner that the framing system will deflect without breaking (loading) the glass before the sprinkler operates; and
   1.3. Obstructions shall not be installed between the sprinkler heads and the wall or glass.
2. The distance between the connected buildings is more than 10 feet (3048 mm) and both sidewalls of the *pedestrian walkway* are at least 50 percent open with the open area uniformly distributed to prevent the accumulation of smoke and *toxic* gases.
3. Buildings are on the same lot in accordance with Section 503.1.2.
4. Where *exterior walls* of connected buildings are required by Section 705 to have a *fire-resistance rating* greater than 2 hours, the walkway shall be equipped throughout with an *automatic sprinkler system* installed in accordance with Section 903.3.1.1.

The previous exception shall apply to *pedestrian walkways* having a maximum height above grade of three *stories* or 40 feet (12 192 mm), or five *stories* or 55 feet (16 764 mm) where sprinklered.

3104.6 Public way. *Pedestrian walkways* over a *public way* shall also comply with Chapter 32.

3104.7 Egress. Access shall be provided at all times to a *pedestrian walkway* that serves as a required *exit.*

3104.8 Width. The unobstructed width of *pedestrian walkways* shall not be less than 36 inches (914 mm). The total width shall not exceed 30 feet (9144 mm).

3104.9 Exit access travel. The length of *exit access* travel shall not exceed 200 feet (60 960 mm).

Exceptions:

1. *Exit access* travel distance on a *pedestrian walkway* equipped throughout with an *automatic sprinkler system* in accordance with Section 903.3.1.1 shall not exceed 250 feet (76 200 mm).
2. *Exit access* travel distance on a *pedestrian walkway* constructed with both sides at least 50 percent open shall not exceed 300 feet (91 440 mm).
3. *Exit access* travel distance on a *pedestrian walkway* constructed with both sides at least 50 percent open, and equipped throughout with an *automatic sprinkler system* in accordance with Section 903.3.1.1, shall not exceed 400 feet (122 m).

3104.10 Tunneled walkway. Separation between the tunneled walkway and the building to which it is connected shall not be less than 2-hour fire-resistant construction and openings therein shall be protected in accordance with Table 715.4.

SECTION 3105 AWNINGS AND CANOPIES

3105.1 General. *Awnings* or canopies shall comply with the requirements of this section and other applicable sections of this code. For awnings or canopies that encroach into public right-of-ways, refer to Chapter 32.

3105.2 Definition. The following term shall, for the purposes of this section and as used elsewhere in this code, have the meaning shown herein.

RETRACTABLE AWNING. A retractable *awning* is a cover with a frame that retracts against a building or other structure to which it is entirely supported.

3105.3 Design and construction. *Awnings* and canopies shall be designed and constructed to withstand wind or other lateral loads and live loads as required by Chapter 16 with due allowance for shape, open construction and similar features that relieve the pressures or loads. Structural members shall be protected to prevent deterioration. *Awnings* shall have frames of noncombustible material, *fire-retardant-treated wood*, wood of Type IV size, or 1-hour construction with combustible or noncombustible covers and shall be either fixed, retractable, folding or collapsible.

3105.4 Canopy materials. Canopies shall be constructed of a rigid framework with an *approved* covering that meets the fire propagation performance criteria of NFPA 701 or has a *flame spread index* not greater than 25 when tested in accordance with ASTM E 84 or UL 723.

3105.5 Permanent canopies. Permanent canopies are permitted to extend over adjacent open spaces, provided:

1. The canopy and its supports shall be of noncombustible material, fire-retardant-treated wood, Type IV construction, or of 1-hour fire-resistance-rated construction.

   Exception: Any textile covering for the canopy shall be flame resistant as determined by tests conducted in accordance with NFPA 701 after both accelerated water leaching and accelerating weathering.

2. Any canopy covering, other than textiles, shall have a flame spread index not greater than 25 when tested in accordance with ASTM E 84 or UL 723 in the form intended for use.
3. The canopy shall have at least one long side open.
4. The maximum horizontal width of the canopy shall not exceed 15 feet (4572 mm).
5. The fire resistance of exterior walls shall not be reduced.

SECTION 3106 MARQUEES

3106.1 General. Marquees shall comply with this section and other applicable sections of this code.

3106.2 Thickness. The maximum height or thickness of a marquee measured vertically from its lowest to its highest point shall not exceed 3 feet (914 mm) where the marquee projects more than two-thirds of the distance from the property line to the curb line, and shall not exceed 9 feet (2743 mm) where the marquee is less than two-thirds of the distance from the property line to the curb line.

3106.3 Roof construction. Where the roof or any part thereof is a skylight, the skylight shall comply with the requirements of Chapter 24. Every roof and skylight of a marquee shall be sloped to downspouts that shall conduct any drainage from the marquee in such a manner so as not to spill over the sidewalk.

3106.4 Location prohibited. Every marquee shall be so located as not to interfere with the operation of any exterior standpipe, and such that the marquee does not obstruct the clear passage of *stairways* or *exit discharge* from the building or the installation or maintenance of street lighting.

3106.5 Construction. A marquee shall be supported entirely from the building and constructed of noncombustible materials. Marquees shall be designed as required in Chapter 16. Structural members shall be protected to prevent deterioration.

SECTION 3107 SIGNS

3107.1 General. Signs shall be designed, constructed and maintained in accordance with Appendix H of this code.

SECTION 3108 TELECOMMUNICATION AND BROADCAST TOWERS

3108.1 General. Towers shall be designed and constructed in accordance with the provisions of TIA-222.

> **Exception:** Single free-standing poles used to support antennas not greater than 75 feet (22 860 mm), measured from the top of the pole to grade, shall not be required to be noncombustible.

3108.2 Location and access. Towers shall be located such that guy wires and other accessories shall not cross or encroach upon any street or other public space, or over above-ground electric utility lines, or encroach upon any privately owned property without the written consent of the owner of the encroached-upon property, space or above-ground electric utility lines. Towers shall be equipped with climbing and working facilities in compliance with TIA-222. Access to the tower sites shall be limited as required by applicable OSHA, FCC and EPA regulations.

3108.3 Foundations. Footings and foundations shall be designed and constructed in accordance with the provisions of Chapter 18.

SECTION 3109 SWIMMING POOL ENCLOSURES AND SAFETY DEVICES

3109.1 General. Swimming pools shall comply with the requirements of this section and other applicable sections of this code.

3109.2 Definition. The following word and term shall, for the purposes of this section and as used elsewhere in this code, have the meaning shown herein.

SWIMMING POOLS. Any structure intended for swimming, recreational bathing or wading that contains water over 24 inches (610 mm) deep. This includes in-ground, above-ground and on-ground pools; hot tubs; spas and fixed-in-place wading pools.

3109.3 Public swimming pools. Public swimming pools (all occupancies except Group R-3) shall be completely enclosed by a fence or barrier at least 4 feet (1290 mm) in height or a screen enclosure. Openings in the fence shall not *permit* the passage of a 4-inch-diameter (102 mm) sphere. The fence or screen enclosure shall be equipped with self-closing and self-latching gates.

3109.4 Residential swimming pools. Residential swimming pools shall comply with Sections 3109.4.1 through 3109.4.3.

Exception: A swimming pool with a power safety cover or a spa with a safety cover complying with ASTM F 1346.

3109.4.1 Barrier height and clearances. The top of the barrier shall be at least 48 inches (1219 mm) above grade measured on the side of the barrier that faces away from the swimming pool. The maximum vertical clearance between grade and the bottom of the barrier shall be 2 inches (51 mm) measured on the side of the barrier that faces away from the swimming pool. Where the top of the pool structure is above grade, the barrier is authorized to be at ground level or mounted on top of the pool structure, and the maximum vertical clearance between the top of the pool structure and the bottom of the barrier shall be 4 inches (102 mm).

3109.4.1.1 Openings. Openings in the barrier shall not allow passage of a 4-inch-diameter (102 mm) sphere.

3109.4.1.2 Solid barrier surfaces. Solid barriers which do not have openings shall not contain indentations or protrusions except for normal construction tolerances and tooled masonry joints.

3109.4.1.3 Closely spaced horizontal members. Where the barrier is composed of horizontal and vertical members and the distance between the tops of the horizontal members is less than 45 inches (1143 mm), the horizontal members shall be located on the swimming pool side of the fence. Spacing between vertical members shall not exceed $1^3/_4$ inches (44 mm) in width. Where there are decorative cutouts within vertical members, spacing within the cutouts shall not exceed $1^3/_4$ inches (44 mm) in width.

3109.4.1.4 Widely spaced horizontal members. Where the barrier is composed of horizontal and vertical members and the distance between the tops of the horizontal members is 45 inches (1143 mm) or more, spacing between vertical members shall not exceed 4 inches (102 mm). Where there are decorative cutouts within vertical members, spacing within the cutouts shall not exceed $1^3/_4$ inches (44 mm) in width.

3109.4.1.5 Chain link dimensions. Maximum mesh size for chain link fences shall be a $2^1/_4$ inch square (57 mm square) unless the fence is provided with slats fastened at the top or the bottom which reduce the openings to no more than $1^3/_4$ inches (44 mm).

3109.4.1.6 Diagonal members. Where the barrier is composed of diagonal members, the maximum opening formed by the diagonal members shall be no more than $1^3/_4$ inches (44 mm).

3109.4.1.7 Gates. Access doors or gates shall comply with the requirements of Sections 3109.4.1.1 through 3109.4.1.6 and shall be equipped to accommodate a locking device. Pedestrian access doors or gates shall open outward away from the pool and shall be self-closing and have a self-latching device. Doors or gates other than pedestrian access doors or gates shall have a self-latching device. Release mechanisms shall be in accordance with Sections 1008.1.9 and 1109.12. Where the release mechanism of the self-latching device is located less than 54 inches (1372 mm) from the bottom of the door or gate, the release mechanism shall be located on the pool side of the door or gate at least 3 inches (76 mm) below the top of the door or gate, and the door or gate and barrier shall have no opening greater than $^1/_2$ inch (12.7 mm) within 18 inches (457 mm) of the release mechanism.

3109.4.1.8 Dwelling wall as a barrier. Where a wall of a *dwelling* serves as part of the barrier, one of the following shall apply:

1. Doors with direct access to the pool through that wall shall be equipped with an alarm that produces an audible warning when the door and/or its screen, if present, are opened. The alarm shall be *listed* and labeled in accordance with UL 2017. In dwellings not required to be *Accessible units*, *Type A units* or *Type B units*, the deactivation switch shall be located 54 inches (1372 mm) or more above the threshold of the door. In dwellings required to be *Accessible units*, *Type A units* or *Type B units*, the deactivation switch(es) shall be located at 54 inches (1372 mm) maximum and 48 inches (1219 mm) minimum above the threshold of the door.
2. The pool shall be equipped with a power safety cover that complies with ASTM F 1346.
3. Other means of protection, such as self-closing doors with self-latching devices, which are *approved*, shall be accepted so long as the degree of protection afforded is not less than the protection afforded by Section 3109.4.1.8, Item 1 or 2.

3109.4.1.9 Pool structure as barrier. Where an above-ground pool structure is used as a barrier or where the barrier is mounted on top of the pool structure, and the means of access is a ladder or steps, then the ladder or steps either shall be capable of being secured, locked or removed to prevent access, or the ladder or steps shall be surrounded by a barrier which meets the requirements of Sections 3109.4.1.1 through 3109.4.1.8. When the ladder or steps are secured, locked or removed, any opening created shall not allow the passage of a 4-inch-diameter (102 mm) sphere.

3109.4.2 Indoor swimming pools. Walls surrounding indoor swimming pools shall not be required to comply with Section 3109.4.1.8.

3109.4.3 Prohibited locations. Barriers shall be located so as to prohibit permanent structures, equipment or similar objects from being used to climb the barriers.

3109.5 Entrapment avoidance. Suction outlets shall be designed and installed in accordance with ANSI/APSP-7.

SECTION 3110
AUTOMATIC VEHICULAR GATES

3110.1 General. Automatic vehicular gates shall comply with the requirements of this section and other applicable sections of this code.

3110.2 Definitions. The following word and term shall, for the purposes of this section and as used elsewhere in this code, have the meaning shown herein.

VEHICULAR GATE. A gate that is intended for use at a vehicular entrance or exit to a facility, building or portion thereof, and that is not intended for use by pedestrian traffic.

3110.3 Vehicular gates intended for automation. Vehicular gates intended for automation shall be designed, constructed and installed to comply with the requirements of ASTM F 2200.

3110.4 Vehicular gate openers. Vehicular gate openers, when provided, shall be *listed* in accordance with UL 325.

CHAPTER 32

ENCROACHMENTS INTO THE PUBLIC RIGHT-OF-WAY

SECTION 3201 GENERAL

3201.1 Scope. The provisions of this chapter shall govern the encroachment of structures into the public right-of-way.

3201.2 Measurement. The projection of any structure or portion thereof shall be the distance measured horizontally from the *lot line* to the outermost point of the projection.

3201.3 Other laws. The provisions of this chapter shall not be construed to permit the violation of other laws or ordinances regulating the use and occupancy of public property.

3201.4 Drainage. Drainage water collected from a roof, *awning*, canopy or marquee, and condensate from mechanical equipment shall not flow over a public walking surface.

SECTION 3202 ENCROACHMENTS

3202.1 Encroachments below grade. Encroachments below grade shall comply with Sections 3202.1.1 through 3202.1.3.

3202.1.1 Structural support. A part of a building erected below grade that is necessary for structural support of the building or structure shall not project beyond the *lot lines*, except that the footings of street walls or their supports which are located at least 8 feet (2438 mm) below grade shall not project more than 12 inches (305 mm) beyond the street *lot line*.

3202.1.2 Vaults and other enclosed spaces. The construction and utilization of vaults and other enclosed spaces below grade shall be subject to the terms and conditions of the applicable governing authority.

3202.1.3 Areaways. Areaways shall be protected by grates, *guards* or other *approved* means.

3202.2 Encroachments above grade and below 8 feet in height. Encroachments into the public right-of-way above grade and below 8 feet (2438 mm) in height shall be prohibited except as provided for in Sections 3202.2.1 through 3202.2.3. Doors and windows shall not open or project into the public right-of-way.

3202.2.1 Steps. Steps shall not project more than 12 inches (305 mm) and shall be guarded by *approved* devices not less than 3 feet (914 mm) high, or shall be located between columns or pilasters.

3202.2.2 Architectural features. Columns or pilasters, including bases and moldings shall not project more than 12 inches (305 mm). Belt courses, lintels, sills, architraves, pediments and similar architectural features shall not project more than 4 inches (102 mm).

3202.2.3 Awnings. The vertical clearance from the public right-of-way to the lowest part of any *awning*, including valances, shall be 7 feet (2134 mm) minimum.

3202.3 Encroachments 8 feet or more above grade. Encroachments 8 feet (2438 mm) or more above grade shall comply with Sections 3202.3.1 through 3202.3.4.

3202.3.1 Awnings, canopies, marquees and signs. *Awnings*, canopies, marquees and signs shall be constructed so as to support applicable loads as specified in Chapter 16. *Awnings*, canopies, marquees and signs with less than 15 feet (4572 mm) clearance above the sidewalk shall not extend into or occupy more than two-thirds the width of the sidewalk measured from the building. Stanchions or columns that support *awnings*, canopies, marquees and signs shall be located not less than 2 feet (610 mm) in from the curb line.

3202.3.2 Windows, balconies, architectural features and mechanical equipment. Where the vertical clearance above grade to projecting windows, balconies, architectural features or mechanical equipment is more than 8 feet (2438 mm), 1 inch (25 mm) of encroachment is permitted for each additional 1 inch (25 mm) of clearance above 8 feet (2438 mm), but the maximum encroachment shall be 4 feet (1219 mm).

3202.3.3 Encroachments 15 feet or more above grade. Encroachments 15 feet (4572 mm) or more above grade shall not be limited.

3202.3.4 Pedestrian walkways. The installation of a pedestrian walkway over a public right-of-way shall be subject to the approval of the applicable governing authority. The vertical clearance from the public right-of-way to the lowest part of a *pedestrian walkway* shall be 15 feet (4572 mm) minimum.

3202.4 Temporary encroachments. Where allowed by the applicable governing authority, vestibules and storm enclosures shall not be erected for a period of time exceeding seven months in any one year and shall not encroach more than 3 feet (914 mm) nor more than one-fourth of the width of the sidewalk beyond the street *lot line*. Temporary entrance *awnings* shall be erected with a minimum clearance of 7 feet (2134 mm) to the lowest portion of the hood or *awning* where supported on removable steel or other *approved* noncombustible support.

3202.5 Space under public property.

3202.5.1 Space under sidewalk. Where space under the sidewalk is used for any purpose, a special permit shall be required.

3202.5.2 Sidewalk lights. When glass is set in the sidewalk to provide light for spaces underneath, the glass shall be supported by metal or reinforced concrete frames and such glass shall be not less than $^1/_2$ inch (12.7 mm) thick. Where such glass is over 12 square inches (7742 mm^2), it shall have wire mesh embedded in the glass. All portions of sidewalk lights shall be of not less strength than required for the load specified.

CHAPTER 33

SAFEGUARDS DURING CONSTRUCTION

SECTION 3301 GENERAL

3301.1 Scope. The provisions of this chapter shall govern safety during construction and the protection of adjacent public and private properties.

3301.2 Storage and placement. Construction equipment and materials shall be stored and placed so as not to endanger the public, the workers or adjoining property for the duration of the construction project.

SECTION 3302 CONSTRUCTION SAFEGUARDS

3302.1 Remodeling and additions. Required *exits*, existing structural elements, fire protection devices and sanitary safeguards shall be maintained at all times during remodeling, *alterations*, repairs or *additions* to any building or structure.

Exceptions:

1. When such required elements or devices are being remodeled, altered or repaired, adequate substitute provisions shall be made.
2. When the existing building is not occupied.

3302.2 Manner of removal. Waste materials shall be removed in a manner which prevents injury or damage to persons, adjoining properties and public rights-of-way.

SECTION 3303 DEMOLITION

3303.1 Construction documents. *Construction documents* and a schedule for demolition must be submitted when required by the *building official*. Where such information is required, no work shall be done until such *construction documents* or schedule, or both, are *approved*.

3303.2 Pedestrian protection. The work of demolishing any building shall not be commenced until pedestrian protection is in place as required by this chapter.

3303.3 Means of egress. A party wall balcony or *horizontal exit* shall not be destroyed unless and until a substitute *means of egress* has been provided and *approved*.

3303.4 Vacant lot. Where a structure has been demolished or removed, the vacant lot shall be filled and maintained to the existing grade or in accordance with the ordinances of the jurisdiction having authority.

3303.5 Water accumulation. Provision shall be made to prevent the accumulation of water or damage to any foundations on the premises or the adjoining property.

3303.6 Utility connections. Service utility connections shall be discontinued and capped in accordance with the *approved* rules and the requirements of the applicable governing authority.

SECTION 3304 SITE WORK

3304.1 Excavation and fill. Excavation and fill for buildings and structures shall be constructed or protected so as not to endanger life or property. Stumps and roots shall be removed from the soil to a depth of at least 12 inches (305 mm) below the surface of the ground in the area to be occupied by the building. Wood forms which have been used in placing concrete, if within the ground or between foundation sills and the ground, shall be removed before a building is occupied or used for any purpose. Before completion, loose or casual wood shall be removed from direct contact with the ground under the building.

3304.1.1 Slope limits. Slopes for permanent fill shall not be steeper than one unit vertical in two units horizontal (50-percent slope). Cut slopes for permanent excavations shall not be steeper than one unit vertical in two units horizontal (50-percent slope). Deviation from the foregoing limitations for cut slopes shall be permitted only upon the presentation of a soil investigation report acceptable to the *building official*.

3304.1.2 Surcharge. No fill or other surcharge loads shall be placed adjacent to any building or structure unless such building or structure is capable of withstanding the additional loads caused by the fill or surcharge. Existing footings or foundations which can be affected by any excavation shall be underpinned adequately or otherwise protected against settlement and shall be protected against later movement.

3304.1.3 Footings on adjacent slopes. For footings on adjacent slopes, see Chapter 18.

3304.1.4 Fill supporting foundations. Fill to be used to support the foundations of any building or structure shall comply with Section 1804.5. Special inspections of compacted fill shall be in accordance with Section 1704.7.

SECTION 3305 SANITARY

3305.1 Facilities required. Sanitary facilities shall be provided during construction, remodeling or demolition activities in accordance with the *International Plumbing Code*.

SECTION 3306
PROTECTION OF PEDESTRIANS

3306.1 Protection required. Pedestrians shall be protected during construction, remodeling and demolition activities as required by this chapter and Table 3306.1. Signs shall be provided to direct pedestrian traffic.

3306.2 Walkways. A walkway shall be provided for pedestrian travel in front of every construction and demolition site unless the applicable governing authority authorizes the sidewalk to be fenced or closed. Walkways shall be of sufficient width to accommodate the pedestrian traffic, but in no case shall they be less than 4 feet (1219 mm) in width. Walkways shall be provided with a durable walking surface. Walkways shall be *accessible* in accordance with Chapter 11 and shall be designed to support all imposed loads and in no case shall the design live load be less than 150 pounds per square foot (psf) (7.2 kN/m^2).

3306.3 Directional barricades. Pedestrian traffic shall be protected by a directional barricade where the walkway extends into the street. The directional barricade shall be of sufficient size and construction to direct vehicular traffic away from the pedestrian path.

3306.4 Construction railings. Construction railings shall be at least 42 inches (1067 mm) in height and shall be sufficient to direct pedestrians around construction areas.

3306.5 Barriers. Barriers shall be a minimum of 8 feet (2438 mm) in height and shall be placed on the side of the walkway nearest the construction. Barriers shall extend the entire length of the construction site. Openings in such barriers shall be protected by doors which are normally kept closed.

3306.6 Barrier design. Barriers shall be designed to resist loads required in Chapter 16 unless constructed as follows:

1. Barriers shall be provided with 2-inch by 4-inch (51 mm by 102 mm) top and bottom plates.
2. The barrier material shall be a minimum of $^3/_4$-inch (19.1 mm) boards or $^1/_4$-inch (6.4 mm) wood structural use panels.
3. Wood structural use panels shall be bonded with an adhesive identical to that for exterior wood structural use panels.
4. Wood structural use panels $^1/_4$ inch (6.4 mm) or $^5/_{16}$ inch (23.8 mm) in thickness shall have studs spaced not more than 2 feet (610 mm) on center (o.c.).
5. Wood structural use panels $^3/_8$ inch (9.5 mm) or $^1/_2$ inch (12.7 mm) in thickness shall have studs spaced not more than 4 feet (1219 mm) on center provided a 2-inch by 4-inch (51 mm by 102 mm) stiffener is placed horizontally at midheight where the stud spacing exceeds 2 feet (610 mm) o.c.
6. Wood structural use panels $^5/_8$ inch (15.9 mm) or thicker shall not span over 8 feet (2438 mm).

3306.7 Covered walkways. Covered walkways shall have a minimum clear height of 8 feet (2438 mm) as measured from the floor surface to the canopy overhead. Adequate lighting shall be provided at all times. Covered walkways shall be designed to support all imposed loads. In no case shall the design live load be less than 150 psf (7.2 kN/m^2) for the entire structure.

Exception: Roofs and supporting structures of covered walkways for new, light-frame construction not exceeding two *stories* above *grade plane* are permitted to be designed for a live load of 75 psf (3.6kN/m^2) or the loads imposed on them, whichever is greater. In lieu of such designs, the roof and supporting structure of a covered walkway are permitted to be constructed as follows:

1. Footings shall be continuous 2-inch by 6-inch (51 mm by 152 mm) members.
2. Posts not less than 4 inches by 6 inches (102 mm by 152 mm) shall be provided on both sides of the roof and spaced not more than 12 feet (3658 mm) on center.
3. Stringers not less than 4 inches by 12 inches (102 mm by 305 mm) shall be placed on edge upon the posts.
4. Joists resting on the stringers shall be at least 2 inches by 8 inches (51 mm by 203 mm) and shall be spaced not more than 2 feet (610 mm) on center.
5. The deck shall be planks at least 2 inches (51 mm) thick or wood structural panels with an exterior exposure durability classification at least $^{23}/_{32}$ inch (18.3 mm) thick nailed to the joists.

TABLE 3306.1
PROTECTION OF PEDESTRIANS

HEIGHT OF CONSTRUCTION	DISTANCE FROM CONSTRUCTION TO LOT LINE	TYPE OF PROTECTION REQUIRED
8 feet or less	Less than 5 feet	Construction railings
	5 feet or more	None
More than 8 feet	Less than 5 feet	Barrier and covered walkway
	5 feet or more, but not more than one-fourth the height of construction	Barrier and covered walkway
	5 feet or more, but between one-fourth and one-half the height of construction	Barrier
	5 feet or more, but exceeding one-half the height of construction	None

For SI: 1 foot = 304.8 mm.

6. Each post shall be knee braced to joists and stringers by 2-inch by 4-inch (51 mm by 102 mm) minimum members 4 feet (1219 mm) long.
7. A 2-inch by 4-inch (51 mm by 102 mm) minimum curb shall be set on edge along the outside edge of the deck.

3306.8 Repair, maintenance and removal. Pedestrian protection required by this chapter shall be maintained in place and kept in good order for the entire length of time pedestrians may be endangered. The owner or the owner's agent, upon the completion of the construction activity, shall immediately remove walkways, debris and other obstructions and leave such public property in as good a condition as it was before such work was commenced.

3306.9 Adjacent to excavations. Every excavation on a site located 5 feet (1524 mm) or less from the street *lot line* shall be enclosed with a barrier not less than 6 feet (1829 mm) high. Where located more than 5 feet (1524 mm) from the street *lot line*, a barrier shall be erected when required by the *building official*. Barriers shall be of adequate strength to resist wind pressure as specified in Chapter 16.

SECTION 3307 PROTECTION OF ADJOINING PROPERTY

3307.1 Protection required. Adjoining public and private property shall be protected from damage during construction, remodeling and demolition work. Protection must be provided for footings, foundations, party walls, chimneys, skylights and roofs. Provisions shall be made to control water runoff and erosion during construction or demolition activities. The person making or causing an excavation to be made shall provide written notice to the owners of adjoining buildings advising them that the excavation is to be made and that the adjoining buildings should be protected. Said notification shall be delivered not less than 10 days prior to the scheduled starting date of the excavation.

SECTION 3308 TEMPORARY USE OF STREETS, ALLEYS AND PUBLIC PROPERTY

3308.1 Storage and handling of materials. The temporary use of streets or public property for the storage or handling of materials or of equipment required for construction or demolition, and the protection provided to the public shall comply with the provisions of the applicable governing authority and this chapter.

3308.1.1 Obstructions. Construction materials and equipment shall not be placed or stored so as to obstruct access to fire hydrants, standpipes, fire or police alarm boxes, catch basins or manholes, nor shall such material or equipment be located within 20 feet (6096 mm) of a street intersection, or placed so as to obstruct normal observations of traffic signals or to hinder the use of public transit loading platforms.

3308.2 Utility fixtures. Building materials, fences, sheds or any obstruction of any kind shall not be placed so as to obstruct free approach to any fire hydrant, fire department connection, utility pole, manhole, fire alarm box or catch basin, or so as to interfere with the passage of water in the gutter. Protection against damage shall be provided to such utility fixtures during the progress of the work, but sight of them shall not be obstructed.

SECTION 3309 FIRE EXTINGUISHERS

[F] 3309.1 Where required. All structures under construction, *alteration* or demolition shall be provided with not less than one *approved* portable fire extinguisher in accordance with Section 906 and sized for not less than ordinary hazard as follows:

1. At each *stairway* on all floor levels where combustible materials have accumulated.
2. In every storage and construction shed.
3. Additional portable fire extinguishers shall be provided where special hazards exist, such as the storage and use of flammable and combustible liquids.

3309.2 Fire hazards. The provisions of this code and the *International Fire Code* shall be strictly observed to safeguard against all fire hazards attendant upon construction operations.

SECTION 3310 MEANS OF EGRESS

3310.1 Stairways required. Where a building has been constructed to a *building height* of 50 feet (15 240 mm) or four *stories*, or where an existing building exceeding 50 feet (15 240 mm) in *building height* is altered, at least one temporary lighted *stairway* shall be provided unless one or more of the permanent stairways are erected as the construction progresses.

3310.2 Maintenance of means of egress. Required *means of egress* shall be maintained at all times during construction, demolition, remodeling or *alterations* and *additions* to any building.

Exception: *Approved* temporary *means of egress* systems and facilities.

SECTION 3311 STANDPIPES

[F] 3311.1 Where required. In buildings required to have standpipes by Section 905.3.1, not less than one standpipe shall be provided for use during construction. Such standpipes shall be installed when the progress of construction is not more than 40 feet (12 192 mm) in height above the lowest level of fire department vehicle access. Such standpipe shall be provided with fire department hose connections at accessible locations adjacent to usable stairs. Such standpipes shall be extended as construction progresses to within one floor of the highest point of construction having secured decking or flooring.

[F] 3311.2 Buildings being demolished. Where a building is being demolished and a standpipe exists within such a building, such standpipe shall be maintained in an operable condition so as to be available for use by the fire department. Such standpipe shall be demolished with the building but shall not be demolished more than one floor below the floor being demolished.

3311.3 Detailed requirements. Standpipes shall be installed in accordance with the provisions of Chapter 9.

> **Exception:** Standpipes shall be either temporary or permanent in nature, and with or without a water supply, provided that such standpipes conform to the requirements of Section 905 as to capacity, outlets and materials.

3311.4 Water supply. Water supply for fire protection, either temporary or permanent, shall be made available as soon as combustible material accumulates.

SECTION 3312 AUTOMATIC SPRINKLER SYSTEM

[F] 3312.1 Completion before occupancy. In buildings where an *automatic sprinkler system* is required by this code, it shall be unlawful to occupy any portion of a building or structure until the *automatic sprinkler system* installation has been tested and *approved*, except as provided in Section 111.3.

[F] 3312.2 Operation of valves. Operation of sprinkler control valves shall be permitted only by properly authorized personnel and shall be accompanied by notification of duly designated parties. When the sprinkler protection is being regularly turned off and on to facilitate connection of newly completed segments, the sprinkler control valves shall be checked at the end of each work period to ascertain that protection is in service.

CHAPTER 34
EXISTING BUILDINGS AND STRUCTURES

SECTION 3401
GENERAL

3401.1 Scope. The provisions of this chapter shall control the *alteration*, repair, *addition* and change of occupancy of existing buildings and structures.

> **Exception:** Existing *bleachers*, grandstands and folding and telescopic seating shall comply with ICC 300.

3401.2 Maintenance. Buildings and structures, and parts thereof, shall be maintained in a safe and sanitary condition. Devices or safeguards which are required by this code shall be maintained in conformance with the code edition under which installed. The owner or the owner's designated agent shall be responsible for the maintenance of buildings and structures. To determine compliance with this subsection, the *building official* shall have the authority to require a building or structure to be reinspected. The requirements of this chapter shall not provide the basis for removal or abrogation of fire protection and safety systems and devices in existing buildings and structures.

3401.3 Compliance. Alterations, repairs, additions and changes of occupancy to existing buildings and structures shall comply with the provisions for alterations, repairs, buildings and additions and changes of occupancy in the *International Fire Code*, *International Fuel Gas Code*, *International Mechanical Code*, *International Plumbing* Code, *International Residential Code* and NFPA 70.

3401.4 Building materials. Building materials shall comply with the requirements of this section.

3401.4.1 Existing materials. Materials already in use in a building in compliance with requirements or approvals in effect at the time of their erection or installation shall be permitted to remain in use unless determined by the *building official* to be dangerous to life, health or safety. Where such conditions are determined to be dangerous to life, health or safety, they shall be mitigated or made safe.

3401.4.2 New and replacement materials. Except as otherwise required or permitted by this code, materials permitted by the applicable code for new construction shall be used. Like materials shall be permitted for repairs and alterations, provided no hazard to life, health or property is created. Hazardous materials shall not be used where the code for new construction would not *permit* their use in buildings of similar occupancy, purpose and location.

3401.5 Alternative compliance. Work performed in accordance with the *International Existing Building Code* shall be deemed to comply with the provisions of this chapter.

SECTION 3402
DEFINITIONS

3402.1 Definitions. The following words and terms shall, for the purposes of this chapter and as used elsewhere in the code, have the meanings shown herein.

DANGEROUS. Any building or structure or portion thereof that meets any of the conditions described below shall be deemed dangerous:

1. The building or structure has collapsed, partially collapsed, moved off its foundation or lacks the support of ground necessary to support it.
2. There exists a significant risk of collapse, detachment or dislodgment of any portion, member, appurtenance or ornamentation of the building or structure under service loads.

EXISTING STRUCTURE. A structure erected prior to the date of adoption of the appropriate code, or one for which a legal building *permit* has been issued.

PRIMARY FUNCTION. A *primary function* is a major activity for which the facility is intended. Areas that contain a *primary function* include, but are not limited to, the customer service lobby of a bank, the dining area of a cafeteria, the meeting rooms in a conference center, as well as offices and other work areas in which the activities of the public accommodation or other private entity using the facility are carried out. Mechanical rooms, boiler rooms, supply storage rooms, employee lounges or locker rooms, janitorial closets, entrances, corridors and restrooms are not areas containing a *primary function*.

SUBSTANTIAL STRUCTURAL DAMAGE. A condition where:

1. In any *story*, the vertical elements of the lateral force-resisting system have suffered damage such that the lateral load-carrying capacity of the structure in any horizontal direction has been reduced by more than 20 percent from its pre-damage condition; or
2. The capacity of any vertical gravity load-carrying component, or any group of such components, that supports more than 30 percent of the total area of the structure's floor(s) and roof(s) has been reduced more than 20 percent from its pre-damage condition and the remaining capacity of such affected elements, with respect to all dead and live loads, is less than 75 percent of that required by this code for new buildings of similar structure, purpose and location.

TECHNICALLY INFEASIBLE. An *alteration* of a building or a facility that has little likelihood of being accomplished because the existing structural conditions require the removal or *alteration* of a load-bearing member that is an essential part of the structural frame, or because other existing physical or site constraints prohibit modification or addition of elements, spaces or features which are in full and strict compliance with the minimum requirements for new construction and which are necessary to provide accessibility.

SECTION 3403 ADDITIONS

3403.1 General. Additions to any building or structure shall comply with the requirements of this code for new construction. Alterations to the existing building or structure shall be made to ensure that the existing building or structure together with the *addition* are no less conforming with the provisions of this code than the existing building or structure was prior to the *addition*. An existing building together with its additions shall comply with the height and area provisions of Chapter 5.

3403.2 Flood hazard areas. For buildings and structures in flood hazard areas established in Section 1612.3, any *addition* that constitutes substantial improvement of the *existing structure*, as defined in Section 1612.2, shall comply with the flood design requirements for new construction, and all aspects of the *existing structure* shall be brought into compliance with the requirements for new construction for flood design.

For buildings and structures in flood hazard areas established in Section 1612.3, any additions that do not constitute substantial improvement or substantial damage of the *existing structure*, as defined in Section 1612.2, are not required to comply with the flood design requirements for new construction.

3403.3 Existing structural elements carrying gravity load. Any existing gravity load-carrying structural element for which an *addition* and its related alterations cause an increase in design gravity load of more than 5 percent shall be strengthened, supplemented, replaced or otherwise altered as needed to carry the increased gravity load required by this code for new structures. Any existing gravity load-carrying structural element whose gravity load-carrying capacity is decreased shall be considered an altered element subject to the requirements of Section 3404.3. Any existing element that will form part of the lateral load path for any part of the *addition* shall be considered an existing lateral load-carrying structural element subject to the requirements of Section 3403.4.

3403.3.1 Design live load. Where the *addition* does not result in increased design live load, existing gravity load-carrying structural elements shall be permitted to be evaluated and designed for live loads *approved* prior to the *addition*. If the *approved* live load is less than that required by Section 1607, the area designed for the nonconforming live load shall be posted with placards of *approved* design indicating the *approved* live load. Where the *addition* does result in increased design live load, the live load required by Section 1607 shall be used.

3403.4 Existing structural elements carrying lateral load. Where the *addition* is structurally independent of the *existing structure*, existing lateral load-carrying structural elements shall be permitted to remain unaltered. Where the *addition* is not structurally independent of the *existing structure*, the *existing structure* and its *addition* acting together as a single structure shall be shown to meet the requirements of Sections 1609 and 1613.

Exception: Any existing lateral load-carrying structural element whose demand-capacity ratio with the *addition* considered is no more than 10 percent greater than its demand-capacity ratio with the *addition* ignored shall be permitted to remain unaltered. For purposes of calculating demand-capacity ratios, the demand shall consider applicable load combinations with design lateral loads or forces in accordance with Sections 1609 and 1613. For purposes of this exception, comparisons of demand-capacity ratios and calculation of design lateral loads, forces and capacities shall account for the cumulative effects of additions and alterations since original construction.

3403.4.1 Seismic. Seismic requirements for additions shall be in accordance with this section. Where the existing seismic force-resisting system is a type that can be designated ordinary, values of R, Ω_0 and C_d for the existing seismic force-resisting system shall be those specified by this code for an ordinary system unless it is demonstrated that the existing system will provide performance equivalent to that of a detailed, intermediate or special system.

SECTION 3404 ALTERATIONS

3404.1 General. Except as provided by Section 3401.4 or this section, alterations to any building or structure shall comply with the requirements of the code for new construction. Alterations shall be such that the existing building or structure is no less complying with the provisions of this code than the existing building or structure was prior to the *alteration*.

Exceptions:

1. An existing *stairway* shall not be required to comply with the requirements of Section 1009 where the existing space and construction does not allow a reduction in pitch or slope.
2. Handrails otherwise required to comply with Section 1009.12 shall not be required to comply with the requirements of Section 1012.6 regarding full extension of the handrails where such extensions would be hazardous due to plan configuration.

3404.2 Flood hazard areas. For buildings and structures in flood hazard areas established in Section 1612.3, any *alteration* that constitutes substantial improvement of the existing structure, as defined in Section 1612.2, shall comply with the flood design requirements for new construction, and all aspects of the *existing structure* shall be brought into compliance with the requirements for new construction for flood design.

For buildings and structures in flood hazard areas established in Section 1612.3, any alterations that do not constitute substantial improvement or substantial damage of the existing structure, as defined in Section 1612.2, are not required to comply with the flood design requirements for new construction.

3404.3 Existing structural elements carrying gravity load. Any existing gravity load-carrying structural element for which an *alteration* causes an increase in design gravity load of more than 5 percent shall be strengthened, supplemented, replaced or otherwise altered as needed to carry the increased gravity load required by this code for new structures. Any existing gravity load-carrying structural element whose gravity load-carrying capacity is decreased as part of the *alteration* shall be shown to have the capacity to resist the applicable design gravity loads required by this code for new structures.

3404.3.1 Design live load. Where the *alteration* does not result in increased design live load, existing gravity load-carrying structural elements shall be permitted to be evaluated and designed for live loads *approved* prior to the *alteration*. If the *approved* live load is less than that required by Section 1607, the area designed for the nonconforming live load shall be posted with placards of *approved* design indicating the *approved* live load. Where the *alteration* does result in increased design live load, the live load required by Section 1607 shall be used.

3404.4 Existing structural elements carrying lateral load. Except as permitted by Section 3404.5, where the *alteration* increases design lateral loads in accordance with Section 1609 or 1613, or where the *alteration* results in a structural irregularity as defined in ASCE 7, or where the *alteration* decreases the capacity of any existing lateral load-carrying structural element, the structure of the altered building or structure shall be shown to meet the requirements of Sections 1609 and 1613.

Exception: Any existing lateral load-carrying structural element whose demand-capacity ratio with the *alteration* considered is no more than 10 percent greater than its demand-capacity ratio with the *alteration* ignored shall be permitted to remain unaltered. For purposes of calculating demand-capacity ratios, the demand shall consider applicable load combinations with design lateral loads or forces per Sections 1609 and 1613. For purposes of this exception, comparisons of demand-capacity ratios and calculation of design lateral loads, forces, and capacities shall account for the cumulative effects of additions and alterations since original construction.

3404.4.1 Seismic. Seismic requirements for alterations shall be in accordance with this section. Where the existing seismic force-resisting system is a type that can be designated ordinary, values of R, Ω_0 and C_d for the existing seismic force-resisting system shall be those specified by this code for an ordinary system unless it is demonstrated that the existing system will provide performance equivalent to that of a detailed, intermediate or special system.

3404.5 Voluntary seismic improvements. Alterations to existing structural elements or additions of new structural elements that are not otherwise required by this chapter and are initiated for the purpose of improving the performance of the seismic force-resisting system of an *existing structure* or the performance of seismic bracing or anchorage of existing nonstructural elements shall be permitted, provided that an engineering analysis is submitted demonstrating the following:

1. The altered structure and the altered nonstructural elements are no less in compliance with the provisions of this code with respect to earthquake design than they were prior to the *alteration*.
2. New structural elements are detailed and connected to the existing structural elements as required by Chapter 16.
3. New or relocated nonstructural elements are detailed and connected to existing or new structural elements as required by Chapter 16.
4. The alterations do not create a structural irregularity as defined in ASCE 7 or make an existing structural irregularity more severe.

3404.6 Means of egress capacity factors. Alterations to any existing building or structure shall not be affected by the egress width factors in Section 1005.1 for new construction in determining the minimum egress widths or the minimum number of exits in an existing building or structure. The minimum egress widths for the components of the *means of egress* shall be based on the *means of egress* width factors in the building code under which the building was constructed, and shall be considered as complying *means of egress* for any *alteration* if, in the opinion of the *building official,* they do not constitute a distinct hazard to life.

SECTION 3405 REPAIRS

3405.1 General. Buildings and structures, and parts thereof, shall be repaired in compliance with this section and Section 3401.2. Work on nondamaged components that is necessary for the required repair of damaged components shall be considered part of the repair and shall not be subject to the requirements for alterations in this chapter. Routine maintenance required by Section 3401.2, ordinary repairs exempt from *permit* in accordance with Section 105.2, and abatement of wear due to normal service conditions shall not be subject to the requirements for repairs in this section.

3405.1.1 Dangerous conditions. Regardless of the extent of structural or nonstructural damage, the *building official* shall have the authority to require the elimination of conditions deemed dangerous.

3405.2 Substantial structural damage to vertical elements of the lateral-force-resisting system. A building that has sustained substantial structural damage to the vertical elements of its lateral-force-resisting system shall be evaluated and repaired in accordance with the applicable provisions of Sections 3405.2.1 through 3405.2.3.

3405.2.1 Evaluation. The building shall be evaluated by a *registered design professional*, and the evaluation findings shall be submitted to the *building official*. The evaluation shall establish whether the damaged building, if repaired to its pre-damage state, would comply with the provisions of this code for wind and earthquake loads. Evaluation for earthquake loads shall be required if the substantial structural damage was caused by earthquake effects or if the building is in Seismic Design Category C, D, E or F.

Wind loads for this evaluation shall be those prescribed in Section 1609. Earthquake loads for this evaluation, if required, shall be permitted to be 75 percent of those prescribed in Section 1613. Values of R, Ω_0 and C_d for the existing seismic force-resisting system shall be those specified by this code for an ordinary system unless it is demonstrated that the existing system will provide performance equivalent to that of an intermediate or special system.

3405.2.2 Extent of repair for compliant buildings. If the evaluation establishes compliance of the predamage building in accordance with Section 3405.2.1, then repairs shall be permitted that restore the building to its predamage state using materials and strengths that existed prior to the damage.

3405.2.3 Extent of repair for noncompliant buildings. If the evaluation does not establish compliance of the predamage building in accordance with Section 3405.2.1, then the building shall be rehabilitated to comply with applicable provisions of this code for load combinations, that include wind or seismic loads. The wind loads for the repair shall be as required by the building code in effect at the time of original construction, unless the damage was caused by wind, in which case the wind loads shall be as required by the code in effect at the time of original construction or as required by this code, whichever are greater. Earthquake loads for this rehabilitation design shall be those required for the design of the predamage building, but not less than 75 percent of those prescribed in Section 1613. New structural members and connections required by this rehabilitation design shall comply with the detailing provisions of this code for new buildings of similar structure, purpose and location.

3405.3 Substantial structural damage to gravity load-carrying components. Gravity load-carrying components that have sustained substantial structural damage shall be rehabilitated to comply with the applicable provisions of this code for dead and live loads. Snow loads shall be considered if the substantial structural damage was caused by or related to snow load effects. Existing gravity load-carrying structural elements shall be permitted to be designed for live loads *approved* prior to the damage. Nondamaged gravity load-carrying components that receive dead, live or snow loads from rehabilitated components shall also be rehabilitated or shown to have the capacity to carry the design loads of the rehabilitation design. New structural members and connections required by this rehabilitation design shall comply with the detailing provisions of this code for new buildings of similar structure, purpose and location.

3405.3.1 Lateral force-resisting elements. Regardless of the level of damage to vertical elements of the lateral force-resisting system, if substantial structural damage to gravity load-carrying components was caused primarily by wind or earthquake effects, then the building shall be evaluated in accordance with Section 3405.2.1 and, if noncompliant, rehabilitated in accordance with Section 3405.2.3.

3405.4 Less than substantial structural damage. For damage less than substantial structural damage, repairs shall be allowed that restore the building to its predamage state using materials and strengths that existed prior to the damage. New structural members and connections used for this repair shall comply with the detailing provisions of this code for new buildings of similar structure, purpose and location.

3405.5 Flood hazard areas. For buildings and structures in flood hazard areas established in Section 1612.3, any repair that constitutes substantial improvement of the *existing structure*, as defined in Section 1612.2, shall comply with the flood design requirements for new construction, and all aspects of the *existing structure* shall be brought into compliance with the requirements for new construction for flood design.

For buildings and structures in flood hazard areas established in Section 1612.3, any repairs that do not constitute substantial improvement or substantial damage of the *existing structure*, as defined in Section 1612.2, are not required to comply with the flood design requirements for new construction.

SECTION 3406
FIRE ESCAPES

3406.1 Where permitted. Fire escapes shall be permitted only as provided for in Sections 3406.1.1 through 3406.1.4.

3406.1.1 New buildings. Fire escapes shall not constitute any part of the required *means of egress* in new buildings.

3406.1.2 Existing fire escapes. Existing fire escapes shall be continued to be accepted as a component in the *means of egress* in existing buildings only.

3406.1.3 New fire escapes. New fire escapes for existing buildings shall be permitted only where exterior *stairs* cannot be utilized due to lot lines limiting *stair* size or due to the sidewalks, alleys or roads at grade level. New fire escapes shall not incorporate ladders or access by windows.

3406.1.4 Limitations. Fire escapes shall comply with this section and shall not constitute more than 50 percent of the required number of exits nor more than 50 percent of the required *exit* capacity.

3406.2 Location. Where located on the front of the building and where projecting beyond the building line, the lowest landing shall not be less than 7 feet (2134 mm) or more than 12 feet (3658 mm) above grade, and shall be equipped with a counterbalanced stairway to the street. In alleyways and thoroughfares less than 30 feet (9144 mm) wide, the clearance under the lowest landing shall not be less than 12 feet (3658 mm).

3406.3 Construction. The fire escape shall be designed to support a live load of 100 pounds per square foot (4788 Pa) and shall be constructed of steel or other *approved* noncombustible materials. Fire escapes constructed of wood not less than nominal 2 inches (51 mm) thick are permitted on buildings of Type V construction. Walkways and railings located over or supported by combustible roofs in buildings of Type III and IV construction are permitted to be of wood not less than nominal 2 inches (51 mm) thick.

3406.4 Dimensions. Stairs shall be at least 22 inches (559 mm) wide with risers not more than, and treads not less than, 8 inches (203 mm) and landings at the foot of stairs not less than 40 inches (1016 mm) wide by 36 inches (914 mm) long, located not more than 8 inches (203 mm) below the door.

3406.5 Opening protectives. Doors and windows along the fire escape shall be protected with $^{3}/_{4}$-hour opening protectives.

SECTION 3407
GLASS REPLACEMENT

3407.1 Conformance. The installation or replacement of glass shall be as required for new installations.

SECTION 3408
CHANGE OF OCCUPANCY

3408.1 Conformance. No change shall be made in the use or occupancy of any building that would place the building in a different division of the same group of occupancies or in a different group of occupancies, unless such building is made to comply with the requirements of this code for such division or group of occupancies. Subject to the approval of the *building official*, the use or occupancy of existing buildings shall be permitted to be changed and the building is allowed to be occupied for purposes in other groups without conforming to all the requirements of this code for those groups, provided the new or proposed use is less hazardous, based on life and fire risk, than the existing use.

3408.2 Certificate of occupancy. A certificate of occupancy shall be issued where it has been determined that the requirements for the new occupancy classification have been met.

3408.3 Stairways. An existing stairway shall not be required to comply with the requirements of Section 1009 where the existing space and construction does not allow a reduction in pitch or slope.

3408.4 Seismic. When a change of occupancy results in a structure being reclassified to a higher occupancy category, the structure shall conform to the seismic requirements for a new structure of the higher occupancy category. Where the existing seismic force-resisting system is a type that can be designated ordinary, values of R, Ω_0 and C_d for the existing seismic force-resisting system shall be those specified by this code for an ordinary system unless it is demonstrated that the existing system will provide performance equivalent to that of a detailed, intermediate or special system.

Exceptions:

1. Specific seismic detailing requirements of Section 1613 for a new structure shall not be required to be met where the seismic performance is shown to be equivalent to that of a new structure. A demonstration of equivalence shall consider the regularity, over strength, redundancy and ductility of the structure.
2. When a change of use results in a structure being reclassified from Occupancy Category I or II to Occupancy Category III and the structure is located where the seismic coefficient S_{DS} is less than 0.33, compliance with the seismic requirements of Section 1613 is not required.

SECTION 3409
HISTORIC BUILDINGS

3409.1 Historic buildings. The provisions of this code relating to the construction, repair, *alteration*, *addition*, restoration and movement of structures, and change of occupancy shall not be mandatory for *historic buildings* where such buildings are judged by the *building official* to not constitute a distinct life safety hazard.

3409.2 Flood hazard areas. Within flood hazard areas established in accordance with Section 1612.3, where the work proposed constitutes substantial improvement as defined in Section 1612.2, the building shall be brought into compliance with Section 1612.

Exception: *Historic buildings* that are:

1. *Listed* or preliminarily determined to be eligible for listing in the National Register of Historic Places;
2. Determined by the Secretary of the U.S. Department of Interior as contributing to the historical significance of a registered historic district or a district preliminarily determined to qualify as an historic district; or
3. Designated as historic under a state or local historic preservation program that is *approved* by the Department of Interior.

SECTION 3410
MOVED STRUCTURES

3410.1 Conformance. Structures moved into or within the jurisdiction shall comply with the provisions of this code for new structures.

SECTION 3411
ACCESSIBILITY FOR EXISTING BUILDINGS

3411.1 Scope. The provisions of Sections 3411.1 through 3411.9 apply to maintenance, change of occupancy, additions and alterations to existing buildings, including those identified as *historic buildings*.

Exception: Type B *dwelling* or sleeping units required by Section 1107 of this code are not required to be provided in existing buildings and facilities being altered or undergoing a change of occupancy.

3411.2 Maintenance of facilities. A building, facility or element that is constructed or altered to be *accessible* shall be maintained *accessible* during occupancy.

3411.3 Extent of application. An *alteration* of an existing element, space or area of a building or facility shall not impose a requirement for greater accessibility than that which would be required for new construction.

Alterations shall not reduce or have the effect of reducing accessibility of a building, portion of a building or facility.

3411.4 Change of occupancy. Existing buildings that undergo a change of group or occupancy shall comply with this section.

3411.4.1 Partial change in occupancy. Where a portion of the building is changed to a new occupancy classification, any alterations shall comply with Sections 3411.6, 3411.7 and 3411.8.

3411.4.2 Complete change of occupancy. Where an entire building undergoes a change of occupancy, it shall comply with Section 3411.4.1 and shall have all of the following *accessible* features:

1. At least one *accessible* building entrance.
2. At least one *accessible* route from an *accessible* building entrance to *primary function* areas.
3. Signage complying with Section 1110.
4. Accessible parking, where parking is being provided.
5. At least one *accessible* passenger loading zone, when loading zones are provided.
6. At least one *accessible* route connecting *accessible* parking and *accessible* passenger loading zones to an *accessible* entrance.

Where it is *technically infeasible* to comply with the new construction standards for any of these requirements for a change of group or occupancy, the above items shall conform to the requirements to the maximum extent technically feasible.

3411.5 Additions. Provisions for new construction shall apply to additions. An *addition* that affects the accessibility to, or contains an area of, a primary function shall comply with the requirements in Section 3411.7.

3411.6 Alterations. A building, facility or element that is altered shall comply with the applicable provisions in Chapter 11 of this code and ICC A117.1, unless *technically infeasible*. Where compliance with this section is *technically infeasible*, the *alteration* shall provide access to the maximum extent technically feasible.

Exceptions:

1. The altered element or space is not required to be on an *accessible* route, unless required by Section 3411.7.
2. *Accessible means of egress* required by Chapter 10 are not required to be provided in existing buildings and facilities.
3. The *alteration* to Type A individually owned *dwelling* units within a Group R-2 occupancy shall meet the provision for a Type B *dwelling* unit and shall comply with the applicable provisions in Chapter 11 and ICC A117.1.

3411.7 Alterations affecting an area containing a primary function. Where an *alteration* affects the accessibility to, or contains an area of *primary function*, the route to the *primary function* area shall be *accessible*. The *accessible* route to the *primary function* area shall include toilet facilities or drinking fountains serving the area of *primary function*.

Exceptions:

1. The costs of providing the *accessible* route are not required to exceed 20 percent of the costs of the *alterations* affecting the area of *primary function*.
2. This provision does not apply to *alterations* limited solely to windows, hardware, operating controls, electrical outlets and signs.
3. This provision does not apply to *alterations* limited solely to mechanical systems, electrical systems, installation or *alteration* of fire protection systems and abatement of hazardous materials.
4. This provision does not apply to *alterations* undertaken for the primary purpose of increasing the accessibility of an existing building, facility or element.

3411.8 Scoping for alterations. The provisions of Sections 3411.8.1 through 3411.8.14 shall apply to *alterations* to existing buildings and facilities.

3411.8.1 Entrances. *Accessible* entrances shall be provided in accordance with Section 1105.

Exception: Where an *alteration* includes alterations to an entrance, and the building or facility has an *accessible* entrance, the altered entrance is not required to be *accessible*, unless required by Section 3411.7. Signs complying with Section 1110 shall be provided.

3411.8.2 Elevators. Altered elements of existing elevators shall comply with ASME A17.1 and ICC A117.1. Such elements shall also be altered in elevators programmed to respond to the same hall call control as the altered elevator.

3411.8.3 Platform lifts. Platform (wheelchair) lifts complying with ICC A117.1 and installed in accordance with ASME A18.1 shall be permitted as a component of an *accessible* route.

3411.8.4 Stairs and escalators in existing buildings. In *alterations*, change of occupancy or *additions* where an escalator or *stair* is added where none existed previously and major structural modifications are necessary for installation, an *accessible* route shall be provided between the levels served by the escalator or *stairs* in accordance with Sections 1104.4 and 1104.5.

3411.8.5 Ramps. Where slopes steeper than allowed by Section 1010.2 are necessitated by space limitations, the slope of ramps in or providing access to existing buildings or facilities shall comply with Table 3411.8.5.

TABLE 3411.8.5
RAMPS

SLOPE	MAXIMUM RISE
Steeper than 1:10 but not steeper than 1:8	3 inches
Steeper than 1:12 but not steeper than 1:10	6 inches

For SI: 1 inch = 25.4 mm.

3411.8.6 Performance areas. Where it is *technically infeasible* to alter performance areas to be on an *accessible* route, at least one of each type of performance area shall be made *accessible*.

3411.8.7 Accessible dwelling or sleeping units. Where Group I-1, I-2, I-3, R-1, R-2 or R-4 *dwelling* or *sleeping units* are being altered or added, the requirements of Section 1107 for *Accessible* units apply only to the quantity of spaces being altered or added.

3411.8.8 Type A dwelling or sleeping units. Where 11 or more Group R-2 *dwelling* or *sleeping units* are being added, the requirements of Section 1107 for *Type* A units apply only to the quantity of the spaces being added.

3411.8.9 Type B dwelling or sleeping units. Where four or more Group I-1, I-2, R-1, R-2, R-3 or R-4 *dwelling* or *sleeping units* are being added, the requirements of Section 1107 for *Type B units* apply only to the quantity of the spaces being added.

3411.8.10 Jury boxes and witness stands. In *alterations*, *accessible* wheelchair spaces are not required to be located within the defined area of raised jury boxes or witness stands and shall be permitted to be located outside these spaces where the ramp or lift access restricts or projects into the *means of egress*.

3411.8.11 Toilet rooms. Where it is *technically infeasible* to alter existing toilet and bathing facilities to be *accessible*, an *accessible* family or assisted-use toilet or bathing facility constructed in accordance with Section 1109.2.1 is permitted. The family or assisted-use facility shall be located on the same floor and in the same area as the existing facilities.

3411.8.12 Dressing, fitting and locker rooms. Where it is *technically infeasible* to provide *accessible* dressing, fitting or locker rooms at the same location as similar types of rooms, one *accessible* room on the same level shall be provided. Where separate-sex facilities are provided, *accessible* rooms for each sex shall be provided. Separate-sex facilities are not required where only unisex rooms are provided.

3411.8.13 Fuel dispensers. Operable parts of replacement fuel dispensers shall be permitted to be 54 inches (1370 mm) maximum measured from the surface of the vehicular way where fuel dispensers are installed on existing curbs.

3411.8.14 Thresholds. The maximum height of thresholds at doorways shall be $^3/_4$ inch (19.1 mm). Such thresholds shall have beveled edges on each side.

3411.9 Historic buildings. These provisions shall apply to buildings and facilities designated as historic structures that undergo alterations or a change of occupancy, unless *technically infeasible*. Where compliance with the requirements for *accessible* routes, entrances or toilet facilities would threaten or destroy the historic significance of the building or facility, as determined by the applicable governing authority, the alternative requirements of Sections 3411.9.1 through 3411.9.4 for that element shall be permitted.

3411.9.1 Site arrival points. At least one *accessible* route from a site arrival point to an *accessible* entrance shall be provided.

3411.9.2 Multilevel buildings and facilities. An *accessible* route from an *accessible* entrance to public spaces on the level of the *accessible* entrance shall be provided.

3411.9.3 Entrances. At least one main entrance shall be *accessible*.

Exceptions:

1. If a main entrance cannot be made *accessible*, an *accessible* nonpublic entrance that is unlocked while the building is occupied shall be provided; or
2. If a main entrance cannot be made *accessible*, a locked *accessible* entrance with a notification system or remote monitoring shall be provided.

Signs complying with Section 1110 shall be provided at the primary entrance and the *accessible* entrance.

3411.9.4 Toilet and bathing facilities. Where toilet rooms are provided, at least one *accessible* family or assisted-use toilet room complying with Section 1109.2.1 shall be provided.

SECTION 3412
COMPLIANCE ALTERNATIVES

3412.1 Compliance. The provisions of this section are intended to maintain or increase the current degree of public safety, health and general welfare in existing buildings while permitting repair, *alteration*, *addition* and change of occupancy without requiring full compliance with Chapters 2 through 33, or Sections 3401.3, and 3403 through 3409, except where compliance with other provisions of this code is specifically required in this section.

3412.2 Applicability. Structures existing prior to [DATE TO BE INSERTED BY THE JURISDICTION. NOTE: IT IS RECOMMENDED THAT THIS DATE COINCIDE WITH THE EFFECTIVE DATE OF BUILDING CODES WITHIN THE JURISDICTION], in which there is work involving additions, alterations or changes of occupancy shall be made to comply with the requirements of this section or the provisions of Sections 3403 through 3409. The provisions in Sections 3412.2.1 through 3412.2.5 shall apply to existing occupancies that will continue to be, or are proposed to be, in Groups A, B, E, F, M, R, S and U. These provisions shall not apply to buildings with occupancies in Group H or I.

3412.2.1 Change in occupancy. Where an existing building is changed to a new occupancy classification and this section is applicable, the provisions of this section for the new occupancy shall be used to determine compliance with this code.

3412.2.2 Partial change in occupancy. Where a portion of the building is changed to a new occupancy classification, and that portion is separated from the remainder of the building with fire barriers or horizontal assemblies having a *fire-resistance rating* as required by Table 508.4 for the separate occupancies, or with *approved* compliance alternatives, the portion changed shall be made to comply with the provisions of this section.

Where a portion of the building is changed to a new occupancy classification, and that portion is not separated from the remainder of the building with *fire barriers* or *horizontal assemblies* having a *fire-resistance rating* as required by Table 508.4 for the separate occupancies, or with *approved* compliance alternatives, the provisions of this section which apply to each occupancy shall apply to the entire building. Where there are conflicting provisions, those requirements which secure the greater public safety shall apply to the entire building or structure.

3412.2.3 Additions. *Additions* to existing buildings shall comply with the requirements of this code for new construction. The combined height and area of the existing building and the new *addition* shall not exceed the height and area allowed by Chapter 5. Where a *fire wall* that complies with Section 706 is provided between the *addition* and the existing building, the *addition* shall be considered a separate building.

3412.2.4 Alterations and repairs. An existing building or portion thereof, which does not comply with the requirements of this code for new construction, shall not be altered or repaired in such a manner that results in the building being less safe or sanitary than such building is currently. If, in the *alteration* or repair, the current level of safety or sanitation is to be reduced, the portion altered or repaired shall conform to the requirements of Chapters 2 through 12 and Chapters 14 through 33.

3412.2.4.1 Flood hazard areas. For existing buildings located in flood hazard areas established in Section 1612.3, if the *alterations* and repairs constitute substantial improvement of the existing building, the existing building shall be brought into compliance with the requirements for new construction for flood design.

3412.2.5 Accessibility requirements. All portions of the buildings proposed for change of occupancy shall conform to the accessibility provisions of Section 3411.

3412.3 Acceptance. For repairs, alterations, additions and changes of occupancy to existing buildings that are evaluated in accordance with this section, compliance with this section shall be accepted by the *building official*.

3412.3.1 Hazards. Where the *building official* determines that an unsafe condition exists, as provided for in Section 116, such unsafe condition shall be abated in accordance with Section 116.

3412.3.2 Compliance with other codes. Buildings that are evaluated in accordance with this section shall comply with the *International Fire Code*.

3412.4 Investigation and evaluation. For proposed work covered by this section, the building owner shall cause the existing building to be investigated and evaluated in accordance with the provisions of this section.

3412.4.1 Structural analysis. The owner shall have a structural analysis of the existing building made to determine adequacy of structural systems for the proposed *alteration*, *addition* or change of occupancy. The analysis shall demonstrate that the building with the work completed is capable of resisting the loads specified in Chapter 16.

3412.4.2 Submittal. The results of the investigation and evaluation as required in Section 3412.4, along with proposed compliance alternatives, shall be submitted to the *building official*.

3412.4.3 Determination of compliance. The *building official* shall determine whether the existing building, with the proposed *addition*, *alteration* or change of occupancy, complies with the provisions of this section in accordance with the evaluation process in Sections 3412.5 through 3412.9.

3412.5 Evaluation. The evaluation shall be comprised of three categories: fire safety, means of egress and general safety, as defined in Sections 3412.5.1 through 3412.5.3.

3412.5.1 Fire safety. Included within the fire safety category are the structural *fire resistance*, automatic fire detection, fire alarm and fire suppression system features of the facility.

3412.5.2 Means of egress. Included within the means of egress category are the configuration, characteristics and support features for *means of egress* in the facility.

3412.5.3 General safety. Included within the general safety category are the fire safety parameters and the means of egress parameters.

3412.6 Evaluation process. The evaluation process specified herein shall be followed in its entirety to evaluate existing buildings. Table 3412.7 shall be utilized for tabulating the results of the evaluation. References to other sections of this code indicate that compliance with those sections is required in order to gain credit in the evaluation herein outlined. In applying this section to a building with mixed occupancies, where the separation between the mixed occupancies does not qualify for any category indicated in Section 3412.6.16, the score for each occupancy shall be determined and the lower score determined for each section of the evaluation process shall apply to the entire building.

Where the separation between mixed occupancies qualifies for any category indicated in Section 3412.6.16, the score for each occupancy shall apply to each portion of the building based on the occupancy of the space.

3412.6.1 Building height. The value for building height shall be the lesser value determined by the formula in Section 3412.6.1.1. Chapter 5 shall be used to determine the allowable height of the building, including allowable increases due to automatic sprinklers as provided for in Section 504.2. Subtract the actual *building height* in feet (mm) from the allowable height and divide by $12^1/_2$ feet (3810 mm). Enter the height value and its sign (positive or negative) in Table 3412.7 under Safety Parameter 3412.6.1, Building Height, for fire safety, means of egress and general safety. The maximum score for a building shall be 10.

3412.6.1.1 Height formula. The following formulas shall be used in computing the building height value.

$$\text{Height value, feet} = \frac{(AH)-(EBH)}{12.5} \times CF$$ **(Equation 34-1)**

$$\text{Height value, stories} = (AS - EBS) \times CF$$ **(Equation 34-2)**

where:

AH = Allowable height in feet (mm) from Table 503.

EBH = Existing *building height* in feet (mm).

AS = Allowable height in stories from Table 503.

EBS = Existing building height in stories.

CF = 1 if $(AH) - (EBH)$ is positive.

CF = Construction-type factor shown in Table 3412.6.6(2) if $(AH) - (EBH)$ is negative.

Note: Where mixed occupancies are separated and individually evaluated as indicated in Section 3412.6, the values *AH, AS, EBH* and *EBS* shall be based on the height of the occupancy being evaluated.

3412.6.2 Building area. The value for building area shall be determined by the formula in Section 3412.6.2.2. Section 503 and the formula in Section 3412.6.2.1 shall be used to determine the allowable area of the building. This shall include any allowable increases due to frontage and automatic sprinklers as provided for in Section 506. Subtract the actual *building area* in square feet (m[2]) from the allowable area and divide by 1,200 square feet (111.5 m[2]). Enter the area value and its sign (positive or negative) in Table 3412.7 under Safety Parameter 3412.6.2, Building Area, for fire safety, means of egress and general safety. In determining the area value, the maximum permitted positive value for area is 50 percent of the fire safety score as *listed* in Table 3412.8, Mandatory Safety Scores.

3412.6.2.1 Allowable area formula. The following formula shall be used in computing allowable area:

$$A_a = (1 + I_f + I_s) \times A_t$$ **(Equation 34-3)**

where:

A_a = Allowable area.

A_t = Tabular area per *story* in accordance with Table 503 (square feet).

I_s = Area increase factor for sprinklers (Section 506.3).

I_f = Area increase factor for frontage (Section 506.2).

3412.6.2.2 Area formula. The following formula shall be used in computing the area value. Determine the area value for each occupancy floor area on a floor-by-floor basis. For each occupancy, choose the minimum area value of the set of values obtained for the particular occupancy.

$$\text{Area value } i = \frac{\text{Allowable area}_i}{1{,}200 \text{ square feet}}\left[1 - \left(\frac{\text{Actual area}_i}{\text{Allowable area}_i} + \ldots + \frac{\text{Actual area}_n}{\text{Allowable area}_n}\right)\right]$$

(Equation 34-4)

where:

i = Value for an individual separated occupancy on a floor.

n = Number of separated occupancies on a floor.

3412.6.3 Compartmentation. Evaluate the compartments created by *fire barriers* or *horizontal assemblies* that comply with Sections 3412.6.3.1 and 3412.6.3.2 and are exclusive of the wall elements considered under Sections 3412.6.4 and 3412.6.5. Conforming compartments shall be figured as the net area and do not include shafts, chases, stairways, walls or columns. Using Table 3412.6.3, determine the appropriate compartmentation value (CV) and enter that value into Table 3412.7 under Safety Parameter 3412.6.3, Compartmentation, for fire safety, means of egress and general safety.

3412.6.3.1 Wall construction. A wall used to create separate compartments shall be a *fire barrier* conforming to Section 707 with a *fire-resistance rating* of not less than 2 hours. Where the building is not divided into more than one compartment, the compartment size shall be taken as

TABLE 3412.6.3
COMPARTMENTATION VALUES

OCCUPANCY	CATEGORIES[a]				
	a Compartment size equal to or greater than 15,000 square feet	b Compartment size of 10,000 square feet	c Compartment size of 7,500 square feet	d Compartment size of 5,000 square feet	e Compartment size of 2,500 square feet or less
A-1, A-3	0	6	10	14	18
A-2	0	4	10	14	18
A-4, B, E, S-2	0	5	10	15	20
F, M, R, S-1	0	4	10	16	22

For SI: 1 square foot = 0.0929 m[2].

a. For areas between categories, the compartmentation value shall be obtained by linear interpolation.

the total floor area on all floors. Where there is more than one compartment within a *story*, each compartmented area on such *story* shall be provided with a horizontal *exit* conforming to Section 1025. The *fire door* serving as the horizontal *exit* between compartments shall be so installed, fitted and gasketed that such *fire door* will provide a substantial barrier to the passage of smoke.

3412.6.3.2 Floor/ceiling construction. A floor/ceiling assembly used to create compartments shall conform to Section 712 and shall have a *fire-resistance rating* of not less than 2 hours.

3412.6.4 Tenant and dwelling unit separations. Evaluate the *fire-resistance rating* of floors and walls separating tenants, including *dwelling* units, and not evaluated under Sections 3412.6.3 and 3412.6.5. Under the categories and occupancies in Table 3412.6.4, determine the appropriate value and enter that value in Table 3412.7 under Safety Parameter 3412.6.4, Tenant and Dwelling Unit Separations, for fire safety, means of egress and general safety.

TABLE 3412.6.4
SEPARATION VALUES

OCCUPANCY	CATEGORIES				
	a	b	c	d	e
A-1	0	0	0	0	1
A-2	-5	-3	0	1	3
A-3, A-4, B, E, F, M, S-1	-4	-3	0	2	4
R	-4	-2	0	2	4
S-2	-5	-2	0	2	4

3412.6.4.1 Categories. The categories for tenant and *dwelling* unit separations are:

1. Category a—No *fire partitions*; incomplete *fire partitions*; no doors; doors not self-closing or automatic-closing.
2. Category b—*Fire partitions* or floor assemblies with less than a 1-hour *fire-resistance rating* or not constructed in accordance with Sections 709 and 712, respectively.
3. Category c—*Fire partitions* with a 1-hour or greater *fire-resistance rating* constructed in accordance with Section 709 and floor assemblies with a 1-hour but less than 2-hour *fire-resistance rating* constructed in accordance with Section 712, or with only one tenant within the floor area.
4. Category d—*Fire barriers* with a 1-hour but less than 2-hour *fire-resistance rating* constructed in accordance with Section 707 and floor assemblies with a 2-hour or greater *fire-resistance rating* constructed in accordance with Section 712.
5. Category e—*Fire barriers* and floor assemblies with a 2-hour or greater *fire-resistance rating* and constructed in accordance with Sections 707 and 712, respectively.

3412.6.5 Corridor walls. Evaluate the *fire-resistance rating* and degree of completeness of walls which create corridors serving the floor, and constructed in accordance with Section 1018. This evaluation shall not include the wall elements considered under Sections 3412.6.3 and 3412.6.4. Under the categories and groups in Table 3412.6.5, determine the appropriate value and enter that value into Table 3412.7 under Safety Parameter 3412.6.5, Corridor Walls, for fire safety, means of egress and general safety.

TABLE 3412.6.5
CORRIDOR WALL VALUES

OCCUPANCY	CATEGORIES			
	a	b	c[a]	d[a]
A-1	-10	-4	0	2
A-2	-30	-12	0	2
A-3, F, M, R, S-1	-7	-3	0	2
A-4, B, E, S-2	-5	-2	0	5

a. Corridors not providing at least one-half the travel distance for all occupants on a floor shall use Category b.

3412.6.5.1 Categories. The categories for Corridor Walls are:

1. Category a—No fire partitions; incomplete fire partitions; no doors; or doors not self-closing.
2. Category b—Less than 1-hour *fire-resistance rating* or not constructed in accordance with Section 709.4.
3. Category c—1-hour to less than 2-hour *fire-resistance rating*, with doors conforming to Section 715 or without corridors as permitted by Section 1018.
4. Category d—2-hour or greater *fire-resistance rating*, with doors conforming to Section 715.

3412.6.6 Vertical openings. Evaluate the *fire-resistance rating* of *exit* enclosures, hoistways, escalator openings and other shaft enclosures within the building, and openings between two or more floors. Table 3412.6.6(1) contains the appropriate protection values. Multiply that value by the construction type factor found in Table 3412.6.6(2). Enter the vertical opening value and its sign (positive or negative) in Table 3412.7 under Safety Parameter 3412.6.6, Vertical Openings, for fire safety, means of egress, and general safety. If the structure is a one-story building or if all the unenclosed vertical openings within the building conform to the requirements of Section 708, enter a value of 2. The maximum positive value for this requirement shall be 2.

3412.6.6.1 Vertical opening formula. The following formula shall be used in computing vertical opening value.

$$VO = PV \times CF \qquad \textbf{(Equation 34-5)}$$

where:

VO = Vertical opening value.

PV = Protection value [Table 3412.6.6(1)].

CF = Construction type factor [Table 3412.6.6(2)].

TABLE 3412.6.6(1)
VERTICAL OPENING PROTECTION VALUE

PROTECTION	VALUE
None (unprotected opening)	-2 times number floors connected
Less than 1 hour	-1 times number floors connected
1 to less than 2 hours	1
2 hours or more	2

TABLE 3412.6.6(2)
CONSTRUCTION-TYPE FACTOR

	TYPE OF CONSTRUCTION								
	IA	IB	IIA	IIB	IIIA	IIIB	IV	VA	VB
FACTOR	1.2	1.5	2.2	3.5	2.5	3.5	2.3	3.3	7

3412.6.7 HVAC systems. Evaluate the ability of the HVAC system to resist the movement of smoke and fire beyond the point of origin. Under the categories in Section 3412.6.7.1, determine the appropriate value and enter that value into Table 3412.7 under Safety Parameter 3412.6.7, HVAC Systems, for fire safety, means of egress and general safety.

3412.6.7.1 Categories. The categories for HVAC systems are:

1. Category a—Plenums not in accordance with Section 602 of the *International Mechanical Code*. -10 points.
2. Category b—Air movement in egress elements not in accordance with Section 1018.5. -5 points.
3. Category c—Both categories a and b are applicable. -15 points.
4. Category d—Compliance of the HVAC system with Section 1018.5 and Section 602 of the *International Mechanical Code*. 0 points.
5. Category e—Systems serving one *story*; or a central boiler/chiller system without ductwork connecting two or more stories. 5 points.

3412.6.8 Automatic fire detection. Evaluate the smoke detection capability based on the location and operation of automatic fire detectors in accordance with Section 907 and the *International Mechanical Code*. Under the categories and occupancies in Table 3412.6.8, determine the appropriate value and enter that value into Table 3412.7 under Safety Parameter 3412.6.8, Automatic Fire Detection, for fire safety, means of egress and general safety.

TABLE 3412.6.8
AUTOMATIC FIRE DETECTION VALUES

OCCUPANCY	CATEGORIES				
	a	b	c	d	e
A-1, A-3, F, M, R, S-1	-10	-5	0	2	6
A-2	-25	-5	0	5	9
A-4, B, E, S-2	-4	-2	0	4	8

3412.6.8.1 Categories. The categories for automatic fire detection are:

1. Category a—None.
2. Category b—Existing smoke detectors in HVAC systems and maintained in accordance with the *International Fire Code*.
3. Category c—Smoke detectors in HVAC systems. The detectors are installed in accordance with the requirements for new buildings in the *International Mechanical Code*.
4. Category d—Smoke detectors throughout all floor areas other than individual sleeping units, tenant spaces and *dwelling* units.
5. Category e—Smoke detectors installed throughout the floor area.

3412.6.9 Fire alarm systems. Evaluate the capability of the fire alarm system in accordance with Section 907. Under the categories and occupancies in Table 3412.6.9, determine the appropriate value and enter that value into Table 3412.7 under Safety Parameter 3412.6.9, Fire Alarm Systems, for fire safety, means of egress and general safety.

TABLE 3412.6.9
FIRE ALARM SYSTEM VALUES

OCCUPANCY	CATEGORIES			
	a	b[a]	c	d
A-1, A-2, A-3, A-4, B, E, R	-10	-5	0	5
F, M, S	0	5	10	15

a. For buildings equipped throughout with an automatic sprinkler system, add 2 points for activation by a sprinkler waterflow device.

3412.6.9.1 Categories. The categories for fire alarm systems are:

1. Category a—None.
2. Category b—Fire alarm system with manual fire alarm boxes in accordance with Section 907.3 and alarm notification appliances in accordance with Section 907.5.2.
3. Category c—Fire alarm system in accordance with Section 907.
4. Category d—Category c plus a required emergency voice/alarm communications system and a fire command center that conforms to Section 403.4.5 and contains the emergency voice/alarm communications system controls, fire department communication system controls and any other controls specified in Section 911 where those systems are provided.

3412.6.10 Smoke control. Evaluate the ability of a natural or mechanical venting, exhaust or pressurization system to control the movement of smoke from a fire. Under the categories and occupancies in Table 3412.6.10, determine the appropriate value and enter that value into Table 3412.7 under Safety Parameter 3412.6.10, Smoke Control, for means of egress and general safety.

TABLE 3412.6.10
SMOKE CONTROL VALUES

OCCUPANCY	CATEGORIES					
	a	b	c	d	e	f
A-1, A-2, A-3	0	1	2	3	6	6
A-4, E	0	0	0	1	3	5
B, M, R	0	2[a]	3[a]	3[a]	3[a]	4[a]
F, S	0	2[a]	2[a]	3[a]	3[a]	3[a]

a. This value shall be 0 if compliance with Category d or e in Section 3412.6.8.1 has not been obtained.

3412.6.10.1 Categories. The categories for smoke control are:

1. Category a—None.
2. Category b—The building is equipped throughout with an *automatic sprinkler system*. Openings are provided in exterior walls at the rate of 20 square feet (1.86 m^2) per 50 linear feet (15 240 mm) of *exterior wall* in each *story* and distributed around the building perimeter at intervals not exceeding 50 feet (15 240 mm). Such openings shall be readily openable from the inside without a key or separate tool and shall be provided with ready access thereto. In lieu of operable openings, clearly and permanently marked tempered glass panels shall be used.
3. Category c—One enclosed *exit stairway*, with ready access thereto, from each occupied floor of the building. The *stairway* has operable exterior windows and the building has openings in accordance with Category b.
4. Category d—One smokeproof enclosure and the building has openings in accordance with Category b.
5. Category e—The building is equipped throughout with an *automatic sprinkler system*. Each floor area is provided with a mechanical air-handling system designed to accomplish smoke containment. Return and exhaust air shall be moved directly to the outside without recirculation to other floor areas of the building under fire conditions. The system shall exhaust not less than six air changes per hour from the floor area. Supply air by mechanical means to the floor area is not required. Containment of smoke shall be considered as confining smoke to the *fire area* involved without migration to other floor areas. Any other tested and *approved* design which will adequately accomplish smoke containment is permitted.
6. Category f—Each *stairway* shall be one of the following: a smokeproof enclosure in accordance with Section 1022.9; pressurized in accordance with Section 909.20.5 or shall have operable exterior windows.

3412.6.11 Means of egress capacity and number. Evaluate the *means of egress* capacity and the number of exits available to the building occupants. In applying this section, the *means of egress* are required to conform to the following sections of this code: 1003.7, 1004, 1005.1, 1014.2, 1014.3, 1015.2, 1021, 1025.1, 1027.2, 1027.6, 1028.2, 1028.3, 1028.4 and 1029 [except that the minimum width required by this section shall be determined solely by the width for the required capacity in accordance with Table 3412.6.11(1)]. The number of exits credited is the number that is available to each occupant of the area being evaluated. Existing fire escapes shall be accepted as a component in the *means of egress* when conforming to Section 3406. Under the categories and occupancies in Table 3412.6.11(2), determine the appropriate value and enter that value into Table 3412.7 under Safety Parameter 3412.6.11, Means of Egress Capacity, for means of egress and general safety.

TABLE 3412.6.11(2)
MEANS OF EGRESS VALUES

OCCUPANCY	CATEGORIES				
	a[a]	b	c	d	e
A-1, A-2, A-3, A-4, E	-10	0	2	8	10
B, F, S	-1	0	0	0	0
M	-3	0	1	2	4
R	-3	0	0	0	0

a. The values indicated are for buildings six stories or less in height. For buildings over six stories above grade plane, add an additional -10 points.

TABLE 3412.6.11(1)
EGRESS WIDTH PER OCCUPANT SERVED

OCCUPANCY	WITHOUT SPRINKLER SYSTEM		WITH SPRINKLER SYSTEM[a]	
	Stairways (inches per occupant)	Other egress components (inches per occupant)	Stairways (inches per occupant)	Other egress components (inches per occupant)
Occupancies other than those listed below	0.3	0.2	0.2	0.15
Hazardous: H-1, H-2, H-3 and H-4	Not Permitted	Not Permitted	0.3	0.2
Institutional: I-2	Not Permitted	Not Permitted	0.3	0.2

For SI: 1 inch = 25.4 mm.

a. Buildings equipped throughout with an automatic sprinkler system in accordance with Section 903.3.1.1 or 903.3.1.2.

3412.6.11.1 Categories. The categories for Means of Egress Capacity and number of exits are:

1. Category a—Compliance with the minimum required *means of egress* capacity or number of exits is achieved through the use of a fire escape in accordance with Section 3406.
2. Category b—Capacity of the *means of egress* complies with Section 1004 and the number of exits complies with the minimum number required by Section 1021.
3. Category c—Capacity of the *means of egress* is equal to or exceeds 125 percent of the required *means of egress* capacity, the *means of egress* complies with the minimum required width dimensions specified in the code and the number of exits complies with the minimum number required by Section 1021.
4. Category d—The number of exits provided exceeds the number of exits required by Section 1021. Exits shall be located a distance apart from each other equal to not less than that specified in Section 1015.2.
5. Category e—The area being evaluated meets both Categories c and d.

3412.6.12 Dead ends. In spaces required to be served by more than one *means of egress*, evaluate the length of the *exit* access travel path in which the building occupants are confined to a single path of travel. Under the categories and occupancies in Table 3412.6.12, determine the appropriate value and enter that value into Table 3412.7 under Safety Parameter 3412.6.12, Dead Ends, for means of egress and general safety.

TABLE 3412.6.12
DEAD-END VALUES

OCCUPANCY	CATEGORIES[a]		
	a	b	c
A-1, A-3, A-4, B, E, F, M, R, S	-2	0	2
A-2, E	-2	0	2

a. For dead-end distances between categories, the dead-end value shall be obtained by linear interpolation.

3412.6.12.1 Categories. The categories for dead ends are:

1. Category a—Dead end of 35 feet (10 670 mm) in nonsprinklered buildings or 70 feet (21 340 mm) in sprinklered buildings.
2. Category b—Dead end of 20 feet (6096 mm); or 50 feet (15 240 mm) in Group B in accordance with Section 1018.4, Exception 2.
3. Category c — No dead ends; or ratio of length to width (l/w) is less than 2.5:1.

3412.6.13 Maximum exit access travel distance. Evaluate the length of *exit* access travel to an *approved exit*. Determine the appropriate points in accordance with the following equation and enter that value into Table 3412.7 under Safety Parameter 3412.6.13, Maximum *Exit* Access Travel Distance, for means of egress and general safety. The maximum allowable *exit* access travel distance shall be determined in accordance with Section 1016.1.

$$\text{Points} = 20 \times \frac{\text{Maximum allowable travel distance} - \text{Maximum actual travel distance}}{\text{Max. allowable travel distance}}$$

(Equation 34-6)

3412.6.14 Elevator control. Evaluate the passenger elevator equipment and controls that are available to the fire department to reach all occupied floors. Elevator recall controls shall be provided in accordance with the *International Fire Code*. Under the categories and occupancies in Table 3412.6.14, determine the appropriate value and enter that value into Table 3412.7 under Safety Parameter 3412.6.14, Elevator Control, for fire safety, means of egress and general safety. The values shall be zero for a single-story building.

TABLE 3412.6.14
ELEVATOR CONTROL VALUES

ELEVATOR TRAVEL	CATEGORIES			
	a	b	c	d
Less than 25 feet of travel above or below the primary level of elevator access for emergency fire-fighting or rescue personnel	-2	0	0	+2
Travel of 25 feet or more above or below the primary level of elevator access for emergency fire-fighting or rescue personnel	-4	NP	0	+4

For SI: 1 foot = 304.8 mm.

3412.6.14.1 Categories. The categories for elevator controls are:

1. Category a—No elevator.
2. Category b—Any elevator without Phase I and II recall.
3. Category c—All elevators with Phase I and II recall as required by the *International Fire Code*.
4. Category d—All meet Category c; or Category b where permitted to be without recall; and at least one elevator that complies with new construction requirements serves all occupied floors.

3412.6.15 Means of egress emergency lighting. Evaluate the presence of and reliability of *means of egress* emergency lighting. Under the categories and occupancies in Table 3412.6.15, determine the appropriate value and enter that value into Table 3412.7 under Safety Parameter 3412.6.15, Means of Egress Emergency Lighting, for means of egress and general safety.

TABLE 3412.6.15
MEANS OF EGRESS EMERGENCY LIGHTING VALUES

NUMBER OF EXITS REQUIRED BY SECTION 1015	CATEGORIES		
	a	b	c
Two or more exits	NP	0	4
Minimum of one exit	0	1	1

3412.6.15.1 Categories. The categories for means of egress emergency lighting are:

1. Category a—*Means of egress* lighting and *exit* signs not provided with emergency power in accordance with Chapter 27.
2. Category b—*Means of egress* lighting and *exit* signs provided with emergency power in accordance with Chapter 27.
3. Category c—Emergency power provided to *means of egress* lighting and *exit* signs which provides protection in the event of power failure to the site or building.

3412.6.16 Mixed occupancies. Where a building has two or more occupancies that are not in the same occupancy classification, the separation between the mixed occupancies shall be evaluated in accordance with this section. Where there is no separation between the mixed occupancies or the separation between mixed occupancies does not qualify for any of the categories indicated in Section 3412.6.16.1, the building shall be evaluated as indicated in Section 3412.6 and the value for mixed occupancies shall be zero. Under the categories and occupancies in Table 3412.6.16, determine the appropriate value and enter that value into Table 3412.7 under Safety Parameter 3412.6.16, Mixed Occupancies, for fire safety and general safety. For buildings without mixed occupancies, the value shall be zero.

TABLE 3412.6.16
MIXED OCCUPANCY VALUES[a]

OCCUPANCY	CATEGORIES		
	a	b	c
A-1, A-2, R	-10	0	10
A-3, A-4, B, E, F, M, S	-5	0	5

a. For fire-resistance ratings between categories, the value shall be obtained by linear interpolation.

3412.6.16.1 Categories. The categories for mixed occupancies are:

1. Category a—Occupancies separated by minimum 1-hour fire barriers or minimum 1-hour horizontal assemblies, or both.
2. Category b—Separations between occupancies in accordance with Section 508.4.
3. Category c—Separations between occupancies having a *fire-resistance rating* of not less than twice that required by Section 508.4.

3412.6.17 Automatic sprinklers. Evaluate the ability to suppress a fire based on the installation of an *automatic sprinkler system* in accordance with Section 903.3.1.1. "Required sprinklers" shall be based on the requirements of this code. Under the categories and occupancies in Table 3412.6.17, determine the appropriate value and enter that value into Table 3412.7 under Safety Parameter 3412.6.17, Automatic Sprinklers, for fire safety, *means of egress* divided by 2 and general safety.

TABLE 3412.6.17
SPRINKLER SYSTEM VALUES

OCCUPANCY	CATEGORIES					
	a	b	c	d	e	f
A-1, A-3, F, M, R, S-1	-6	-3	0	2	4	6
A-2	-4	-2	0	1	2	4
A-4, B, E, S-2	-12	-6	0	3	6	12

3412.6.17.1 Categories. The categories for automatic sprinkler system protection are:

1. Category a—Sprinklers are required throughout; sprinkler protection is not provided or the sprinkler system design is not adequate for the hazard protected in accordance with Section 903.
2. Category b—Sprinklers are required in a portion of the building; sprinkler protection is not provided or the sprinkler system design is not adequate for the hazard protected in accordance with Section 903.
3. Category c—Sprinklers are not required; none are provided.
4. Category d—Sprinklers are required in a portion of the building; sprinklers are provided in such portion; the system is one which complied with the code at the time of installation and is maintained and supervised in accordance with Section 903.
5. Category e—Sprinklers are required throughout; sprinklers are provided throughout in accordance with Chapter 9.
6. Category f—Sprinklers are not required throughout; sprinklers are provided throughout in accordance with Chapter 9.

3412.6.18 Standpipes. Evaluate the ability to initiate attack on a fire by making a supply of water available readily through the installation of standpipes in accordance with Section 905. Required standpipes shall be based on the requirements of this code. Under the categories and occupancies in Table 3412.6.18, determine the appropriate value and enter that value into Table 3412.7 under Safety Parameter 3412.6.18, Standpipes, for fire safety, *means of egress* and general safety.

3412.6.18
STANDPIPE SYSTEM VALUES

OCCUPANCY	CATEGORIES			
	a[a]	b	c	d
A-1, A-3, F, M, R, S-1	-6	0	4	6
A-2	-4	0	2	4
A-4, B, E, S-2	-12	0	6	12

a. This option cannot be taken if Category a or b in Section 3412.6.17 is used.

3412.6.18.1 Standpipe. The categories for standpipe systems are:

1. Category a—Standpipes are required; standpipe is not provided or the standpipe system design is not in compliance with Section 905.3.
2. Category b—Standpipes are not required; none are provided.
3. Category c—Standpipes are required; standpipes are provided in accordance with Section 905.
4. Category d—Standpipes are not required; standpipes are provided in accordance with Section 905.

3412.6.19 Incidental accessory occupancy. Evaluate the protection of incidental accessory occupancies in accordance with Section 508.2.5. Do not include those where this code requires suppression throughout the buildings, including covered mall buildings, high-rise buildings, public garages and unlimited area buildings. Assign the lowest score from Table 3412.6.19 for the building or floor area being evaluated and enter that value into Table 3412.7 under Safety Parameter 3412.6.19, Incidental Accessory Occupancy, for fire safety, *means of egress* and general safety. If there are no specific occupancy areas in the building or floor area being evaluated, the value shall be zero.

3412.7 Building score. After determining the appropriate data from Section 3412.6, enter those data in Table 3412.7 and total the building score.

3412.8 Safety scores. The values in Table 3412.8 are the required mandatory safety scores for the evaluation process *listed* in Section 3412.6.

3412.9 Evaluation of building safety. The mandatory safety score in Table 3412.8 shall be subtracted from the building score in Table 3412.7 for each category. Where the final score for any category equals zero or more, the building is in compliance with the requirements of this section for that category. Where the final score for any category is less than zero, the building is not in compliance with the requirements of this section.

TABLE 3412.6.19
INCIDENTAL ACCESSORY OCCUPANCY VALUES[a]

PROTECTION REQUIRED BY TABLE 508.2.5	PROTECTION PROVIDED						
	None	1 Hour	AFSS	AFSS with SP	1 Hour and AFSS	2 Hours	2 Hours and AFSS
2 Hours and AFSS	-4	-3	-2	-2	-1	-2	0
2 Hours, or 1 Hour and AFSS	-3	-2	-1	-1	0	0	0
1 Hour and AFSS	-3	-2	-1	-1	0	-1	0
1 Hour	-1	0	-1	0	0	0	0
1 Hour, or AFSS with SP	-1	0	-1	0	0	0	0
AFSS with SP	-1	-1	-1	0	0	-1	0
1 Hour or AFSS	-1	0	0	0	0	0	0

a. AFSS = Automatic fire suppression system; SP = Smoke partitions (See Section 508.2.5).

Note: For Table 3412.7, see next page.

TABLE 3412.8
MANDATORY SAFETY SCORES[a]

OCCUPANCY	FIRE SAFETY (MFS)	MEANS OF EGRESS (MME)	GENERAL SAFETY (MGS)
A-1	16	27	27
A-2	19	30	30
A-3	18	29	29
A-4, E	23	34	34
B	24	34	34
F	20	30	30
M	19	36	36
R	17	34	34
S-1	15	25	25
S-2	23	33	33

a. MFS = Mandatory Fire Safety;
MME = Mandatory Means of Egress;
MGS = Mandatory General Safety.

TABLE 3412.9
EVALUATION FORMULAS[a]

FORMULA	T.3410.7			T.3410.8	SCORE	PASS	FAIL
FS-MFS ≥ 0	____	(FS)	–	____ (MFS) =	____	____	____
ME-MME ≥ 0	____	(ME)	–	____ (MME) =	____	____	____
GS-MGS ≥ 0	____	(GS)	–	____ (MGS) =	____	____	____

a. FS = Fire Safety
ME = Means of Egress
GS = General Safety
MFS = Mandatory Fire Safety
MME = Mandatory Means of Egress
MGS = Mandatory General Safety

3412.9.1 Mixed occupancies. For mixed occupancies, the following provisions shall apply:

1. Where the separation between mixed occupancies does not qualify for any category indicated in Section 3412.6.16, the mandatory safety scores for the occupancy with the lowest general safety score in Table 3412.8 shall be utilized (see Section 3412.6.)
2. Where the separation between mixed occupancies qualifies for any category indicated in Section 3412.6.16, the mandatory safety scores for each occupancy shall be placed against the evaluation scores for the appropriate occupancy.

TABLE 3412.7
SUMMARY SHEET — BUILDING CODE

Existing occupancy: ____________ Proposed occupancy: ____________

Year building was constructed: ____________ Number of stories: ______ Height in feet: ______

Type of construction: ____________ Area per floor: ____________

Percentage of open perimeter increase: ______%

Completely suppressed: Yes ______ No ______ Corridor wall rating: ____________

Compartmentation: Yes ______ No ______ Required door closers: Yes ______ No ______

Fire-resistance rating of vertical opening enclosures: ____________

Type of HVAC system: ____________, serving number of floors: ____________

Automatic fire detection: Yes ______ No ______ Type and location: ____________

Fire alarm system: Yes ______ No ______ Type: ____________

Smoke control: Yes ______ No ______ Type: ____________

Adequate exit routes: Yes ______ No ______ Dead ends: ______ Yes ______ No ______

Maximum exit access travel distance: ____________ Elevator controls: Yes ______ No ______

Means of egress emergency lighting: Yes ______ No ______ Mixed occupancies: Yes ______ No ______

SAFETY PARAMETERS	FIRE SAFETY (FS)	MEANS OF EGRESS (ME)	GENERAL SAFETY (GS)
3412.6.1 Building Height 3412.6.2 Building Area 3412.6.3 Compartmentation			
3412.6.4 Tenant and Dwelling Unit Separations 3412.6.5 Corridor Walls 3412.6.6 Vertical Openings			
3412.6.7 HVAC Systems 3412.6.8 Automatic Fire Detection 3412.6.9 Fire Alarm Systems			
3412.6.10 Smoke Control 3412.6.11 Means of Egress Capacity 3412.6.12 Dead Ends	* * * * * * * * * * * *		
3412.6.13 Maximum Exit Access Travel Distance 3412.6.14 Elevator Control 3412.6.15 Means of Egress Emergency Lighting	* * * * * * * *		
3412.6.16 Mixed Occupancies 3412.6.17 Automatic Sprinklers 3412.6.18 Standpipes 3412.6.19 Incidental Accessory Occupancy		* * * * ÷ 2 =	
Building score — total value			

* * * *No applicable value to be inserted.

CHAPTER 35

REFERENCED STANDARDS

This chapter lists the standards that are referenced in various sections of this document. The standards are listed herein by the promulgating agency of the standard, the standard identification, the effective date and title, and the section or sections of this document that reference the standard. The application of the referenced standards shall be as specified in Section 102.4.

AA

Aluminum Association
1525 Wilson Boulevard, Suite 600
Arlington, VA 22209

Standard reference number	Title	Referenced in code section number
ADM1—05	Aluminum Design Manual: Part 1-A Specification for Aluminum Structures, Allowable Stress Design; and Part 1-B—Aluminum Structures, Load and Resistance Factor Design	1604.3.5, 2002.1
ASM 35—00	Aluminum Sheet Metal Work in Building Construction (Fourth Edition)	2002.1

AAMA

American Architectural Manufacturers Association
1827 Waldon Office Square, Suite 550
Schaumburg, IL 60173

Standard reference number	Title	Referenced in code section number
1402—86	Standard Specifications for Aluminum Siding, Soffit and Fascia	1404.5.1
AAMA/WDMA/CSA 101/I.S.2/A440—08	North American Fenestration Standard/Specifications for Windows, Doors and Skylights	1715.5.1, 2405.5

ACI

American Concrete Institute
38800 Country Club Drive
Farmington Hills, MI 48331

Standard reference number	Title	Referenced in code section number
216.1—07	Standard Method for Determining Fire Resistance of Concrete and Masonry Construction Assemblies	Table 720.1(2), 721.1
318—08	Building Code Requirements for Structural Concrete	1604.3.2, 1614.3.1, 1614.4.1, 1704.3.1.3, Table 1704.3, 1704.4.1, Table 1704.4, 1708. 2, 1808.8.2, Table 1808.8.2, 1808.8.5, 1808.8.6, 1810.2.4.1, 1810.3.2.1.1, 1810.3.2.1.2, 1810.3.8.3.1, 1810.3.8.3.3, 1810.3.9.4.2.1, 1810.3.9.4.2.2, 1810.3.11.1, 1901.2, 1901.3, 1901.4, 1902.1, 1903.1, 1904.1, 1904.2, 1904.3, 1904.4.1, 1904.4.2, 1904.5, 1905.1.1, 1905.2, 1905.3, 1905.4, 1905.5, 1905.6.2, 1905.6.3, 1905.6.4, 1905.6.5, 1905.7, 1905.8, 1905.9, 1905.10, 1905.11, 1905.12, 1905.13, 1906.1, 1906.2, 1906.3, 1906.4, 1907.1, 1907.2, 1907.3, 1907.4, 1907.5, 1907.6, 1907.7.1, 1907.7.2, 1907.7.3, 1907.7.4, 1907.7.5, 1907.7.6, 1907.8, 1907.9, 1907.10, 1907.11, 1907.12, 1907.13, 1908.1, 1908.1.1, 1908.1.2, 1908.1.3, 1908.1.4, 1908.1.5, 1908.1.6, 1908.1.7, 1908.1.8, 1908.1.9, 1908.1.10, 1909.1, 1909.3, 1909.4, 1909.5, 1909.6, 1912.1, 2108.3, 2205.3
530—08	Building Code Requirements for Masonry Structures	1405.5, 1405.5.2, 1405.9, 1604.3.4, 1704.5, 1704.5.1, Table 1704.5.1, 1704.5.2, 1704.5.3, Table 1704.5.3, 1807.1.6.3.2, 1808.9, 2101.2.2, 2101.2.3, 2101.2.4, 2101.2.5, 2101.2.6, 2103.1.3.6, 2106.1, 2107.1, 2107.2, 2107.3, 2107.4, 2107.5, 2108.1, 2108.2, 2108.3, 2109.1, 2109.1.1, 2109.2, 2109.2.1, 2109.3, 2110.1
530.1—08	Specifications for Masonry Structures	1405.5.1, Table 1704.5.1, Table 1704.5.3, 1807.1.6.3, 2103.8, 2103.11, 2103.12, 2103.13, 2104.1, 2104.1.1, 2104.1.2, 2104.1.3, 2104.2, 2104.3, 2104.4, 2105.2.2.1.1, 2105.2.2.1.2, 2105.2.2.1.3

AF&PA

American Forest & Paper Association
1111 19th St, NW Suite 800
Washington, DC 20036

Standard reference number	Title	Referenced in code section number
WCD No. 4—89	Wood Construction Data—Plank and Beam Framing for Residential Buildings	2306.1.2
WFCM—01	Wood Frame Construction Manual for One- and Two-family Dwellings	1609.1.1, 1609.1.1.1, 2301.2, 2308.1, 2308.2.1
NDS—05	National Design Specification (NDS) for Wood Construction with 2005 Supplement	721.6.3.2, 1716.1.1, 1716.1.4, 1809.12, 1810.3.2.4, Table 1810.3.2.6, 2302.1, 2304.12, 2306.1, Table 2306.2.1(1), Table 2306.2.1(2), Table 2306.3, Table 2306.6, 2307.1, 2307.1.1
AF&PA—93	Span Tables for Joists and Rafters	2306.1.1, 2308.8, 2308.10.2, 2308.10.3
ANSI/AF&PA PWF—07	Permanent Wood Foundation Design Specification	1805.2, 1807.1.4, 2304.9.5.2
ANSI/AF&PA SDPWS—08	Special Design Provisions for Wind and Seismic	1613.6.1, 2305.1, 2306.1, 2306.2.1, 2306.2.2, 2306.2.3, 2306.3, Table 2306.3, 2306.4, 2306.5, 2306.6, 2306.7, Table 2306.7, 2307.1, 2307.1.1

AISC

American Institute of Steel Construction
One East Wacker Drive, Suite 700
Chicago, IL 60601-18021

Standard reference number	Title	Referenced in code section number
341—05	Seismic Provisions for Structural Steel Buildings, including Supplement No. 1 dated 2005	1613.6.2, 1707.2, 1708.3, 2205.2.1, 2205.2.2, 2205.3, 2205.3.1
360—05	Specification for Structural Steel Buildings	1604.3.3, Table 1704.3, 1704.3.3, 2203.1, 2203.2, 2205.1, 2205.3

AISI

American Iron and Steel Institute
1140 Connecticut Avenue, 705
Suite 705
Washington, DC 20036

Standard reference number	Title	Referenced in code section number
S100—07	North American Specification for the Design of Cold-formed Steel Structural Members	1604.3.3, 2203.1, 2203.2, 2209.1, 2210.2, 2210.4, 2210.5
S200—07	North American Standard for Cold-formed Steel Framing—General Provisions	2203.1, 2203.2, 2210.1
S210—07	North American Standard for Cold-formed Steel Framing—Floor and Roof System Design	2210.5
S211—07	North American Standard for Cold-formed Steel Framing—Wall Stud Design	2210.4
S212—07	North American Standard for Cold-formed Steel Framing—Header Design	2210.2
S213—07	North American Standard for Cold-formed Steel Framing—Lateral Design	2210.6
S214—07	North American Standard for Cold-formed Steel Framing—Truss Design, with Supplement 2, dated 2008	2210.3.11
S230—07	Standard for Cold-formed Steel Framing—Prescriptive Method for One- and Two-family Dwellings, with Supplement 2, dated 2008	1609.1.1, 1609.1.1.1, 2210.7

AITC

American Institute of Timber Construction
Suite 140
7012 S. Revere Parkway
Englewood, CO 80112

Standard reference number	Title	Referenced in code section number
AITC Technical Note 7—96	Calculation of Fire Resistance of Glued Laminated Timbers	721.6.3.3
AITC 104—03	Typical Construction Details	2306.1
AITC 110—01	Standard Appearance Grades for Structural Glued Laminated Timber	2306.1
AITC 113—01	Standard for Dimensions of Structural Glued Laminated Timber	2306.1
AITC 117—04	Standard Specifications for Structural Glued Laminated Timber of Softwood Species	2306.1
AITC 119—96	Standard Specifications for Structural Glued Laminated Timber of Hardwood Species	2306.1

AITC—continued

AITC 200—04	Manufacturing Quality Control Systems Manual for Structural Glued Laminated Timber	2306.1
ANSI/AITC A 190.1—07	Structural Glued Laminated Timber	2303.1.3, 2306.1

ALI

Automotive Lift Institute
P.O. Box 85
Courtland, NY 13045

Standard reference number	Title	Referenced in code section number
ALI ALCTV—2006	Standard for Automobile Lifts—Safety Requirements for Construction, Testing and Validation (ANSI)	3001.2

ANSI

American National Standards Institute
25 West 43rd Street, Fourth Floor
New York, NY 10036

Standard reference number	Title	Referenced in code section number
A13.1—96 (Reaffirmed 2002)	Scheme for the Identification of Piping Systems	415.8.6.4
A108.1A—99	Installation of Ceramic Tile in the Wet-set Method, with Portland Cement Mortar	2103.10
A108.1B—99	Installation of Ceramic Tile, quarry Tile on a Cured Portland Cement Mortar Setting Bed with Dry-set or Latex-portland Mortar	2103.10
A108.4—99	Installation of Ceramic Tile with Organic Adhesives or Water-cleanable Tile-setting Epoxy Adhesive	2103.10.6
A108.5—99	Installation of Ceramic Tile with Dry-set Portland Cement Mortar or Latex-portland Cement Mortar	2103.10.1, 2103.10.2
A108.6—99	Installation of Ceramic Tile with Chemical-resistant,Water Cleanable Tile-setting and -grouting Epoxy	2103.10.3
A108.8—99	Installation of Ceramic Tile with Chemical-resistant Furan Resin Mortar and Grout	2103.10.4
A108.9—99	Installation of Ceramic Tile with Modified Epoxy Emulsion Mortar/Grout	2103.10.5
A108.10—99	Installation of Grout in Tilework	2103.10.7
A118.1—99	American National Standard Specifications for Dry-set Portland Cement Mortar	2103.10.1
A118.3—99	American National Standard Specifications for Chemical-resistant, Water-cleanable Tile-setting and -grouting Epoxy and Water Cleanable Tile-setting Epoxy Adhesive	2103.10.3
A118.4—99	American National Standard Specifications for Latex-portland Cement Mortar	2103.10.2
A118.5—99	American National Standard Specifications for Chemical Resistant Furan Mortar and Grouts for Tile Installation	2103.10.4
A118.6—99	American National Standard Specifications for Cement Grouts for Tile Installation	2103.10.7
A118.8—99	American National Standard Specifications for Modified Epoxy Emulsion Mortar/Grout	2103.10.5
A136.1—99	American National Standard Specifications for Organic Adhesives for Installation of Ceramic Tile	2103.10.6
A137.1—88	American National Standard Specifications for Ceramic Tile	2103.5
A208.1—99	Particleboard	2303.1.7, 2303.1.7.1
Z 97.1—04	Safety Glazing Materials Used in Buildings—Safety Performance Specifications and Methods of Test	2406.1.2, 2406.2, Table 2406.2(2), 2406.3.1, 2407.1, 2407.1.4.1, 2408.2.1, 2408.3, 2409.1, 2409.2, 2409.3.1

APA

APA - Engineered Wood Association
7011 South 19th
Tacoma, WA 98466

Standard reference number	Title	Referenced in code section number
APA PDS—04	Panel Design Specification	2306.1
APA PDS Supplement 1—90	Design and Fabrication of Plywood Curved Panels (revised 1995)	2306.1
APA PDS Supplement 2—92	Design and Fabrication of Plywood-lumber Beams (revised 1998)	2306.1
APA PDS Supplement 3—90	Design and Fabrication of Plywood Stressed-skin Panels (revised 1996)	2306.1
APA PDS Supplement 4—90	Design and Fabrication of Plywood Sandwich Panels (revised 1993)	2306.1

APA—continued

APA PDS Supplement 5—95	Design and Fabrication of All-plywood Beams (revised 1995)	2306.1
EWS R540—02	Builders Tips: Proper Storage and Handling of Glulam Beams	2306.1
EWS S475—01	Glued Laminated Beam Design Tables	2306.1
EWS S560—03	Field Notching and Drilling of Glued Laminated Timber Beams	2306.1
EWS T300—05	Glulam Connection Details	2306.1
EWS X440—03	Product Guide—Glulam	2306.1
EWS X450—01	Glulam in Residential Construction—Western Edition	2306.1

APSP

The Association of Pool & Spa Professionals
2111 Eisenhower Avenue
Alexandria, VA 22314

Standard reference number	Title	Referenced in code section number
ANSI/APSP 7—06	Standard for Suction Entrapment Avoidance in Swimming Pools, Wading Pools, Spas, Hot Tubs and Catch Basins	3109.5

ASABE

American Society of Agricultural and Biological Engineers
2950 Niles Road
St. Joseph, MI 49085

Standard reference number	Title	Referenced in code section number
EP 484.2 (2003)	Diaphragm Design of Metal-clad, Post-frame Rectangular Buildings	2306.1
EP 486.1 (2000)	Shallow-post Foundation Design	2306.1
EP 559 (1997)	Design Requirements and Bending Properties for Mechanically Laminated Columns	2306.1

ASCE/SEI

American Society of Civil Engineers
Structural Engineering Institute
1801 Alexander Bell Drive
Reston, VA 20191-4400

Standard reference number	Title	Referenced in code section number
3—91	Structural Design of Composite Slabs	1604.3.3, 2209.2.1
5—08	Building Code Requirements for Masonry Structures	1405.6, 1405.6.2, 1405.10, 1604.3.4, 1704.5, 1704.5.1, Table 1704.5.1, 1704.5.2, 1704.5.3, Table 1704.5.3, 1807.1.6.3.2, 1808.9, 2101.2.2, 2101.2.3, 2101.2.4, 2101.2.5, 2101.2.6, 2103.1.3.6, 2106.1, 2107.1, 2107.2, 2107.3, 2107.4, 2107.5, 2108.1, 2108.2, 2108.3, 2109.1, 2109.1.1, 2109.2, 2109.2.1, 2109.3, 2110.1
6—08	Specification for Masonry Structures	1405.6.1, Table 1704.5.1, Table 1704.5.3, 1807.1.6.3, 2103.8, 2103.11, 2103.12, 2103.13, 2104.1, 2104.1.1, 2104.1.2, 2104.1.3, 2104.2, 2104.3, 2104.4, 2105.2.2.1.1, 2105.2.2.1.2, 2105.2.2.1.3
7—05	Minimum Design Loads for Buildings and Other Structures including Supplements No. 1 and 2, excluding Chapter 14 and Appendix 11A	Table 1504.8, 1602.1, 1604.3, 1604.8.2, 1604.10, 1605.1, 1605.2.2, 1605.3.1.2, 1605.3.2, 1607.11.1, 1608.1, 1608.2, 1609.1.1, 1609.1.1.2.1, 1609.1.1.2.2, 1609.1.2, 1609.3, 1609.4.4, 1609.5.1, 1609.5.3, 1609.6, 1609.6.1, 1609.6.1.1, 1609.6.2,Table 1609.6.2(2), 1609.6.3, 1609.6.4.1, 1609.6.4.2, 1611.2, 1612.2, 1612.4, 1613.1, 1613.2,Table 1613.5.3(1), Table 1613.5.3(2), 1613.5.6, 1613.5.6.1, 1613.5.6.2, 1613.6, 1613.6.1, 1613.6.2, 1613.6.3, 1613.6.4, 1613.6.5, 1613.6.6, 1613.6.7, 1613.7, 1702.1, 1705.3.4, 1708.1, 1708.5, 1808.3.1, 1810.3.6.1, 1810.3.9.4, 1810.3.11.2, 1810.3.12, 1908.1.1, 1908.1.2, 1908.1.9, 2205.2.1, 2205.3, 2205.3.1, 2208.1, Table 2304.6.1, Table 2306.7, Table 2308.10.1, 2404.1, 2505.1, 2505.2, 3404.4, 3404.5
8—02	Standard Specification for the Design of Cold-formed Stainless Steel Structural Members	1604.3.3, 2209.1
19—96	Structural Applications of Steel Cables for Buildings	2207.1, 2207.2
24—05	Flood Resistant Design and Construction	1203.3.2, 1612.4, 1612.5, 3001.2, G103.1, G401.3, G401.4
29—05	Standard Calculation Methods for Structural Fire Protection	721.1
32—01	Design and Construction of Frost Protected Shallow Foundations	1809.5

ASME

American Society of Mechanical Engineers
Three Park Avenue
New York, NY 10016-5990

Standard reference number	Title	Referenced in code section number
A17.1—2007/ CSA B44—07	Safety Code for Elevators and Escalators	907.3.3, 911.1.5, 1007.4, 1607.8.1, 1613.6.5, 3001.2, 3001.4, 3002.5, 3003.2, 3007.1, 3008.3, 3008.12, 3008.14.1, 3411.8.2
A18.1—2005	Safety Standard for Platform Lifts and Stairway Chairlifts	1109.7, 2702.2.6, 3411.8.3
A90.1—03	Safety Standard for Belt Manlifts	3001.2
B16.18—2001 (Reaffirmed 2005)	Cast Copper Alloy Solder Joint Pressure Fittings	909.13.1
B16.22—2001 (Reaffirmed 2005)	Wrought Copper and Copper Alloy Solder Joint Pressure Fittings	909.13.1
B20.1—2006	Safety Standard for Conveyors and Related Equipment	3001.2, 3005.3
B31.3—2004	Process Piping	415.8.6.1

ASTM

ASTM International
100 Barr Harbor Drive
West Conshohocken, PA 19428-2959

Standard reference number	Title	Referenced in code section number
A 36/A 36M—05	Specification for Carbon Structural Steel	1810.3.2.3
A 153/A 153M—05	Specification for Zinc Coating (Hot-dip) on Iron and Steel Hardware	2304.9.5
A 240/A 240M—07	Standard Specification for Chromium and Chromium-nickel Stainless Steel Plate, Sheet and Strip for Pressure Vessels and for General Applications	Table 1507.4.3(1)
A 252—98 (2002)	Specification for Welded and Seamless Steel Pipe Piles	1810.3.2.3
A 283/A 283M—03	Specification for Low and Intermediate Tensile Strength Carbon Steel Plates	1810.3.2.3
A 307—04e01	Specification for Carbon Steel Bolts and Studs, 60,000 psi Tensile Strength	1911.1
A 416/A 416M—06	Specification for Steel Strand, Uncoated Seven-wire for Prestressed Concrete	1810.3.2.2
A 463/A 463M—05	Standard Specification for Steel Sheet, Aluminum-coated, by the Hot-dip Process	Table 1507.4.3(2)
A 572/A 572M—07	Specification for High-strength Low-alloy Columbium-vanadium Structural Steel	1810.3.2.3
A 588/A 588M—05	Specification for High-strength Low-alloy Structural Steel with 50 ksi (345 MPa) Minimum Yield Point to 4 inches (100 mm) Thick	1810.3.2.3
A 615/A 615M—04a	Specification for Deformed and Plain Billet-steel Bars for Concrete Reinforcement	1708.2, 1810.3.10.2
A 653/A 653M—07	Specification for Steel Sheet, Zinc-coated Galvanized or Zinc-iron Alloy-coated Galvannealed by the Hot-dip Process	Table 1507.4.3(1), Table 1507.4.3(2), 2304.9.5.1
A 690/A 690M—07	Standard Specification for High-strength Low-alloy Nickel, Copper, Phosphorus Steel H-piles and Sheet Piling with Atmospheric Corrosion Resistance for Use in Marine Environments	1810.3.2.3
A 706/A 706M—05a	Specification for Low-alloy Steel Deformed and Plain Bars for Concrete Reinforcement	Table 1704.3, 1704.4.1, 2107.4, 2108.3
A 722/A 722M—07	Specification for Uncoated High-strength Steel Bar for Prestressing Concrete	1810.3.10.2
A 755/A 755M—03	Specification for Steel Sheet, Metallic-coated by the Hot-dip Process and Prepainted by the Coil-coating Process for Exterior Exposed Building Products	Table 1507.4.3(1), Table 1507.4.3(2)
A 792/A 792M—06a	Specification for Steel Sheet, 55% Aluminum-zinc Alloy-coated by the Hot-dip Process	Table 1507.4.3(1), Table 1507.4.3(2)
A 875/A 875M—06	Standard Specification for Steel Sheet Zinc-5 percent, Aluminum Alloy-coated by the Hot-dip Process	Table 1507.4.3(2)
A 913/A 913M—04	Specification for High-strength Low-alloy Steel Shapes of Structural Quality, Produced by Quenching and Self-tempering Process (QST)	1810.3.2.3
A 924/A 924M—07	Standard Specification for General Requirements for Steel Sheet, Metallic-coated by the Hot-dip Process	Table 1507.4.3(1)
A 992/A 992M—06a	Standard Specification for Structural Shapes	1810.3.2.3
B 42—02e01	Specification for Seamless Copper Pipe, Standard Sizes	909.13.1
B 43—98(2004)	Specification for Seamless Red Brass Pipe, Standard Sizes	909.13.1
B 68—02	Specification for Seamless Copper Tube, Bright Annealed (Metric)	909.13.1
B 88—03	Specification for Seamless Copper Water Tube	909.13.1
B 101—02	Specification for Lead-coated Copper Sheet and Strip for Building Construction	Table 1404.5.3, Table 1507.2.9.2, Table 1507.4.3(1)
B 209—06	Specification for Aluminum and Aluminum Alloy Steel and Plate	Table 1507.4.3(1)
B 251—02e01	Specification for General Requirements for Wrought Seamless Copper and Copper-alloy Tube	909.13.1

ASTM—continued

Standard reference number	Title	Referenced in code section number
B 280—03	Specification for Seamless Copper Tube for Air Conditioning and Refrigeration Field Service	909.13.1
B 370—03	Specification for Cold-rolled Copper Sheet and Strip for Building Construction	1404.5.2, Table 1507.2.9.2, Table 1507.4.3(1)
B 695—04	Standard Specification for Coatings of Zinc Mechanically Deposited on Iron and Steel	2304.9.5.1, 2304.9.5.3
C 5—03	Specification for Quicklime for Structural Purposes	Table 2507.2
C 22/C 22M—00 (2005)e01	Specification for Gypsum	Table 2506.2
C 27—98 (2002)	Specification for Standard Classification of Fireclay and High-alumina Refractory Brick	2111.5
C 28/C 28M—00 (2005)	Specification for Gypsum Plasters	Table 2507.2
C 31/C 31M—06	Practice for Making and Curing Concrete Test Specimens in the Field	Table 1704.4
C 33—03	Specification for Concrete Aggregates	721.3.1.4, 721.4.1.1.3
C 34—03	Specification for Structural Clay Load-bearing Wall Tile	2103.2
C 35—01(2005)	Specification for Inorganic Aggregates for Use in Gypsum Plaster	Table 2507.2
C 36/C 36M—03	Specification for Gypsum Wallboard	Figure 721.5.1(2), Figure 721.5.1(3), Table 2506.2
C 37/C 37M—01	Specification for Gypsum Lath	Table 2507.2
C 55—06e01	Specification for Concrete Building Brick	Table 721.3.2, 2103.1, 2105.2.2.1.2
C 56—05	Specification for Structural Clay Nonload Bearing Tile	2103.2
C 59/C 59M—00 (2006)	Specification for Gypsum Casting and Molding Plaster	Table 2507.2
C 61/C 61M—00 (2006)	Specification for Gypsum Keene's Cement	Table 2507.2
C 62—05	Specification for Building Brick (Solid Masonry Units Made from Clay or Shale)	1807.1.6.3, 2103.2, 2105.2.2.1.1
C 67—07	Test Methods of Sampling and Testing Brick and Structural Clay Tile	721.4.1.1.1, 2109.3.1.1
C 73—05	Specification for Calcium Silicate Face Brick (Sand-lime Brick)	Table 721.3.2, 2103.1
C 79—04a	Specification for Treated Core and Nontreated Core Gypsum Sheathing Board	Table 2506.2
C 90—06b	Specification for Loadbearing Concrete Masonry Units	Table 721.3.2, 1807.1.6.3, 2103.1
C 91—05	Specification for Masonry Cement	Table 2507.2
C 94/C 94M—07	Specification for Ready-mixed Concrete	110.3.1
C 126—99 (2005)	Specification for Ceramic Glazed Structural Clay Facing Tile, Facing Brick and Solid Masonry Units	2103.2
C 140—07	Test Method Sampling and Testing Concrete Masonry Units and Related Units	721.3.1.2
C 150—07	Specification for Portland Cement	Table 2507.2
C 172—04	Practice for Sampling Freshly Mixed Concrete	Table 1704.4
C 199—84 (2005)	Test Method for Pier Test for Refractory Mortars	2111.5, 2111.8, 2113.12
C 206—03	Specification for Finishing Hydrated Lime	Table 2507.2
C 208—95 (2001)	Specification for Cellulosic Fiber Insulating Board	Table 1508.2, 2303.1.5
C 212—00 (2006)	Specification for Structural Clay Facing Tile	2103.2
C 216—07	Specification for Facing Brick (Solid Masonry Units Made from Clay or Shale)	1807.1.6.3, 2103.2, 2105.2.2.1.1
C 270—07	Specification for Mortar for Unit Masonry	2103.8
C 315—07	Specification for Clay Flue Liners and Chimney Pots	2111.8, 2113.11, Table 2113.16(1)
C 317/C 317M—00 (2005)	Specification for Gypsum Concrete	1914.1
C 330—05	Specification for Lightweight Aggregates for Structural Concrete	721.1.1
C 331—05	Specification for Lightweight Aggregates for Concrete Masonry Units	721.3.1.4, 721.4.1.1.3
C 406—06e01	Specification for Roofing Slate	1507.7.5
C 442/C 442M—04	Specification for Gypsum Backing Board and Coreboard and Gypsum Shaftliner Board	Table 2506.2
C 472—99 (2004)	Specification for Standard Test Methods for Physical Testing of Gypsum, Gypsum Plasters and Gypsum Concrete	Table 2506.2
C 473—06a	Test Method for Physical Testing of Gypsum Panel Products	Table 2506.2
C 474—05	Test Methods for Joint Treatment Materials for Gypsum Board Construction	Table 2506.2
C 475/C 475M—02 (2007)	Specification for Joint Compound and Joint Tape for Finishing Gypsum Wallboard	Table 2506.2
C 503—05	Specification for Marble Dimension Stone (Exterior)	2103.4
C 514—04	Specification for Nails for the Application of Gypsum Board	Table 720.1(2), Table 720.1(3), Table 2306.7, Table 2506.2
C 516—02	Specifications for Vermiculite Loose Fill Thermal Insulation	721.3.1.4, 721.4.1.1.3
C 547—06	Specification for Mineral Fiber Pipe Insulation	Table 720.1(2), Table 720.1(3)
C 549—06	Specification for Perlite Loose Fill Insulation	721.3.1.4, 721.4.1.1.3
C 552—03	Standard Specification for Cellular Glass Thermal Insulation	Table 1508.2
C 557—03e01	Specification for Adhesives for Fastening Gypsum Wallboard to Wood Framing	Table 2506.2
C 568—03	Specification for Limestone Dimension Stone	2103.4
C 578—07	Standard Specification for Rigid, Cellular Polystyrene Thermal Insulation	Table 1508.2
C 587—04	Specification for Gypsum Veneer Plaster	Table 2507.2
C 588/C 588M—01	Specification for Gypsum Base for Veneer Plasters	Table 2507.2
C 595—07	Specification for Blended Hydraulic Cements	Table 2507.2
C 615—03	Specification for Granite Dimension Stone	2103.4

ASTM—continued

C 616—03	Specification for Quartz Dimension Stone	2103.4
C 629—03	Specification for Slate Dimension Stone	2103.4
C 630/C 630M—03	Specification for Water-resistant Gypsum Backing Board	Table 2506.2
C 631—95a (2004)	Specification for Bonding Compounds for Interior Gypsum Plastering	Table 2507.2
C 635—04	Specification for the Manufacture, Performance and Testing of Metal Suspension Systems for Acoustical Tile and Lay-in Panel Ceilings	808.1.1, 2506.2.1, H107.1.1
C 636/C 636M—06	Practice for Installation of Metal Ceiling Suspension Systems for Acoustical Tile and Lay-in Panels	808.1.1
C 645—07	Specification for Nonstructural Steel Framing Members	Table 2506.2, Table 2507.2
C 652—05a	Specification for Hollow Brick (Hollow Masonry Units Made from Clay or Shale)	1807.1.6.3, 2103.2, 2105.2.2.1.1
C 728—05	Standard Specification for Perlite Thermal Insulation Board	Table 1508.2
C 744—05	Specification for Prefaced Concrete and Calcium Silicate Masonry Units	Table 721.3.2, 2103.1
C 754—04	Specification for Installation of Steel Framing Members to Receive Screw-attached Gypsum Panel Products	Table 2508.1, Table 2511.1.1
C 836—06	Specification for High-solids Content, Cold Liquid-applied Elastomeric Waterproofing Membrane for Use with Separate Wearing Course	1507.15.2
C 840—07	Specification for Application and Finishing of Gypsum Board	Table 2508.1, 2509.2
C 841—03	Specification for Installation of Interior Lathing and Furring	Table 2508.1, Table 2511.1.1
C 842—05	Specification for Application of Interior Gypsum Plaster	Table 2511.1.1, 2511.3, 2511.4
C 843—99 (2006)	Specification for Application of Gypsum Veneer Plaster	Table 2511.1.1
C 844—04	Specification for Application of Gypsum Base to Receive Gypsum Veneer Plaster	Table 2508.1
C 847—06	Specification for Metal Lath	Table 2507.2
C 887—05	Specification for Packaged, Dry Combined Materials for Surface Bonding Mortar	1805.2.2, 2103.9
C 897—05	Specification for Aggregate for Job-mixed Portland Cement-based Plaster	Table 2507.2
C 920—05	Standard for Specification for Elastomeric Joint Sealants	Table 2506.2
C 926—98a (2005)	Specification for Application of Portland Cement-based Plaster	2109.3.4.6, 2510.3, Table 2511.1.1, 2511.3, 2511.4, 2512.1, 2512.1.2, 2512.2, 2512.6, 2512.8.2, 2512.9, 2513.7
C 931/C 931M—04	Specification for Exterior Gypsum Soffit Board	Table 2506.2
C 932—06	Specification for Surface-applied Bonding Compounds Agents for Exterior Plastering	Table 2507.2
C 933—05	Specification for Welded Wire Lath	Table 2507.2
C 946—91 (2001)	Specification for Practice for Construction of Dry-stacked, Surface-bonded Walls	2103.9, 2109.2.2
C 954—04	Specification for Steel Drill Screws for the Application of Gypsum Panel Products or Metal Plaster Bases to Steel Studs from 0.033 inch (0.84 mm) to 0.112 inch (2.84 mm) in Thickness	Table 2506.2, Table 2507.2
C 955—06	Standard Specification for Load-bearing Transverse and Axial Steel Studs, Runners Tracks, and Bracing or Bridging, for Screw Application of Gypsum Panel Products and Metal Plaster Bases	Table 2506.2, Table 2507.2
C 956—04	Specification for Installation of Cast-in-place Reinforced Gypsum Concrete	1914.1
C 957—06	Specification for High-solids Content, Cold Liquid-applied Elastomeric Waterproofing Membrane with Integral Wearing Surface	1507.15.2
C 960—04	Specification for Predecorated Gypsum Board	Table 2506.2
C 1002—04	Specification for Steel Self-piercing Tapping Screws for the Application of Gypsum Panel Products or Metal Plaster Bases to Wood Studs or Steel Studs	Table 2506.2, Table 2507.2
C 1007—04	Specification for Installation of Load Bearing (Transverse and Axial) Steel Studs and Related Accessories	Table 2508.1, Table 2511.1.1
C 1019—05	Test Method of Sampling and Testing Grout	2105.2.2.1.1, 2105.2.2.1.2, 2105.2.2.1.3
C 1029—05a	Specification for Spray-applied Rigid Cellular Polyurethane Thermal Insulation	1507.14.2
C 1032—06	Specification for Woven Wire Plaster Base	Table 2507.2
C 1047—05	Specification for Accessories for Gypsum Wallboard and Gypsum Veneer Base	Table 2506.2, Table 2507.2
C 1063—06	Specification for Installation of Lathing and Furring to Receive Interior and Exterior Portland Cement-based Plaster	2109.3.4.6, 2510.3, Table 2511.1.1, 2512.1.1
C 1088—07a	Specification for Thin Veneer Brick Units Made from Clay or Shale	Table 720.1(2), 2103.2
C 1167—03	Specification for Clay Roof Tiles	1507.3.4
C 1177/C 1177M—06	Specification for Glass Mat Gypsum Substrate for Use as Sheathing	Table 2506.2
C 1178/C 1178M—06	Specification for Coated Mat Water-resistant Gypsum Backing Panel	Table 2506.2, 2509.2
C 1186—07	Specification for Flat Nonasbestos Fiber Cement Sheets	1404.10
C 1261—07	Specification for Firebox Brick for Residential Fireplaces	2111.5, 2111.8
C 1278/C 1278M—06	Specification for Fiber-reinforced Gypsum Panels	Table 2506.2
C 1280—04	Specification for Application of Gypsum Sheathing	Table 2508.1, 2508.2
C 1283—07	Practice for Installing Clay Flue Lining	2113.12
C 1288—99 (2004)	Standard Specification for Discrete Nonasbestos Fiber-cement Interior Substrate Sheets	2509.2
C 1289—07	Standard Specification for Faced Rigid Cellular Polyisocyanurate Thermal Insulation Board	Table 1508.2

ASTM—continued

C 1314—07	Test Method for Compressive Strength of Masonry Prisms	2105.2.2.2.2, 2105.3.1, 2105.3.2
C 1325—04	Standard Specification for Nonasbestos Fiber-mat Reinforced Cement Interior Substrate Sheets	2509.2
C 1328—05	Specification for Plastic (Stucco Cement)	Table 2507.2
C 1386—07	Specification for Precast Autoclaved Aerated Concrete (AAC) Wall Construction Units	2102.1, 2103.3, 2105.2.2.1.3
C 1395/C 1395M—04	Specification for Gypsum Ceiling Board	Table 2506.2
C 1396/C 1396M—06a	Specification for Gypsum Board	Table 2506.2
C 1405—07	Standard Specification for Glazed Brick (Single Fired, Solid Brick Units)	2103.2
C 1492—03	Standard Specification for Concrete Roof Tile	1507.3.5
C 1629/C 1629M—06	Standard Classification for Abuse-resistant Nondecorated Interior Gypsum Panel Products and Fiber-reinforced Cement Panels	403.2.3.1, 403.2.3.2, 403.2.3.4
C 1658/C 1658M—06	Standard Specification for Glass Mat Gypsum Panels	1810.3.2.4, Table 2506.2
D 25—99 (2005)	Specification for Round Timber Piles	2303.1.11
D 41—05	Specification for Asphalt Primer Used in Roofing, Dampproofing and Waterproofing	Table 1507.10.2
D 43—00 (2006)	Specification for Coal Tar Primer Used in Roofing, Dampproofing and Waterproofing	Table 1507.10.2
D 56—05	Test Method for Flash Point By Tag Closed Tester	307.2
D 86—07a	Test Method for Distillation of Petroleum Products at Atmospheric Pressure	307.2
D 93—07	Test Method for Flash Point By Pensky-Martens Closed Cup Tester	307.2
D 225—04	Specification for Asphalt Shingles (Organic Felt) Surfaced with Mineral Granules	1507.2.5
D 226—06	Specification for Asphalt-saturated Organic Felt Used in Roofing and Waterproofing	1404.2, 1507.2.3, 1507.3.3, 1507.5.3, 1507.6.3, 1507.7.3, Table 1507.8, 1507.8.3, 1507.9.3, 1507.9.5, Table 1507.10.2
D 227—03	Specification for Coal-tar-saturated Organic Felt Used in Roofing and Waterproofing	Table 1507.10.2
D 312—00 (2006)	Specification for Asphalt Used in Roofing	Table 1507.10.2
D 422—63 (2002)e01	Test Method for Particle-size Analysis of Soils	1803.5.3
D 448—03a	Standard Classification for Sizes of Aggregate for Road and Bridge Construction	1507.12.3, 1507.13.3
D 450—07	Specification for Coal-tar Pitch Used in Roofing, Dampproofing and Waterproofing	Table 1507.10.2
D 635—06	Test Method for Rate of Burning and/or Extent and Time of Burning of Self-supporting Plastics in a Horizontal Position	2606.4, H107.1.1
D 1143/D 1143M—07	Test Method for Piles Under Static Axial Compressive Load	1810.3.3.1.2
D 1227—95 (2007)	Specification for Emulsified Asphalt Used as a Protective Coating for Roofing	Table 1507.10.2, 1507.15.2
D 1557—02e01	Test Method for Laboratory Compaction Characteristics of Soil Using Modified Effort [56,000 ft-lb/ft^3 (2,700 KN m/m^3)]	1704.7, 1804.5, J107.6
D 1586—99	Specification for Penetration Test and Split-barrel Sampling of Soils	1613.5.5
D 1761—06	Test Method for Mechanical Fasteners in Wood	1716.1.1, 1716.1.2, 1716.1.3
D 1863—05	Specification for Mineral Aggregate Used on Built-up Roofs	Table 1507.10.2
D 1929—96 (2001)e01	Test Method for Determining Ignition Properties of Plastics	402.16.4, 406.5.3, 1407.11.2.1, 2606.4
D 1970—01	Specification for Self-adhering Polymer Modified Bituminous Sheet Materials Used as Steep Roof Underlayment for Ice Dam Protection	1507.2.4, 1507.2.9.2, 1507.3.9, 1507.5.7, 1507.8.8, 1507.9.9
D 2166—06	Test Method for Unconfined Compressive Strength of Cohesive Soil	1613.5.5
D 2178—04	Specification for Asphalt Glass Felt Used in Roofing and Waterproofing	Table 1507.10.2
D 2216—05	Test Method for Laboratory Determination of Water (Moisture) Content of Soil and Rock by Mass	1613.5.5
D 2487—06	Practice for Classification of Soils for Engineering Purposes (Unified Soil Classification System)	Table 1610.1, 1802.3.1
D 2626—04	Specification for Asphalt Saturated and Coated Organic Felt Base Sheet Used in Roofing	1507.3.3, Table 1507.10.2
D 2822—05	Specification for Asphalt Roof Cement	Table 1507.10.2
D 2823—05	Specification for Asphalt Roof Coatings	Table 1507.10.2
D 2843—99 (2004)e01	Test for Density of Smoke from the Burning or Decomposition of Plastics	2606.4
D 2850—03a	Test Method for Unconsolidated, Undrained Triaxial Compression Test on Cohesive Soils	1613.5.5
D 2898—07	Test Methods for Accelerated Weathering of Fire-retardant-treated Wood for Fire Testing	1505.1, 2303.2.4, 2303.2.6
D 3019—94 (2007)	Specification for Lap Cement Used with Asphalt Roll Roofing, Nonfibered, Asbestos Fibered and Nonasbestos Fibered	Table 1507.10.2
D 3161—06	Test Method for a Wind Resistance of Asphalt Shingles (Fan Induced Method)	1507.2.7.1, Table 1507.2.7.1(2)
D 3200—74 (2005)	Standard Specification and Test Method for Establishing Recommended Design Stresses for Round Timber Construction Poles	2303.1.11
D 3201—07	Test Method for Hygroscopic Properties of Fire-retardant-treated Wood and Wood-based Products	2303.2.7
D 3278—(2004)e01	Test Methods for Flash Point of Liquids by Small Scale Closed-cup Apparatus	307.2
D 3462—07	Specification for Asphalt Shingles Made from Glass Felt and Surfaced with Mineral Granules	1507.2.5
D 3468—99 (2006)e01	Specification for Liquid-applied Neoprene and Chlorosulfonated Polyethylene Used in Roofing and Waterproofing	1507.15.2
D 3679—06a	Specification for Rigid Poly [Vinyl Chloride (PVC) Siding]	1404.9, 1405.14
D 3689—90 (1995)	Method for Testing Individual Piles Under Static Axial Tensile Load	1810.3.3.1.5

ASTM—continued

Standard	Title	Referenced in code section number
D 3737—07	Practice for Establishing Allowable Properties for Structural Glued Laminated Timber (Glulam)	2303.1.3
D 3746—85 (2002)	Test Method for Impact Resistance of Bituminous Roofing Systems	1504.7
D 3747—79 (2007)	Specification for Emulsified Asphalt Adhesive for Adhering Roof Insulation	Table 1507.10.2
D 3909—97b (2004)e01	Specification for Asphalt Roll Roofing (Glass Felt) Surfaced with Mineral Granules	1507.2.9.2, 1507.6.5, Table 1507.10.2
D 3957—06	Standard Practices for Establishing Stress Grades for Structural Members Used in Log Buildings	2303.1.10
D 4022—07	Specification for Coal Tar Roof Cement, Asbestos Containing	Table 1507.10.2
D 4272—03	Test Method for Total Energy Impact of Plastic Films by Dart Drop	1504.7
D 4318—05	Test Methods for Liquid Limit, Plastic Limit and Plasticity Index of Soils	1613.5.5, 1803.5.3
D 4434—06	Specification for Poly (Vinyl Chloride) Sheet Roofing	1507.13.2
D 4479—07	Specification for Asphalt Roof Coatings—Asbestos-free	Table 1507.10.2
D 4586—00	Specification for Asphalt Roof Cement—Asbestos-free	Table 1507.10.2
D 4601—04	Specification for Asphalt-coated Glass Fiber Base Sheet Used in Roofing	Table 1507.10.2
D 4637—04	Specification for EPDM Sheet Used in Single-ply Roof Membrane	1507.12.2
D 4829—07	Test Method for Expansion Index of Soils	1803.5.3
D 4869—05e01	Specification for Asphalt-saturated (Organic Felt) Underlayment Used in Steep Slope Roofing	1507.2.3, 1507.5.3, 1507.6.3, 1507.7.3, 1507.8.3, 1507.9.3
D 4897—01	Specification for Asphalt-coated Glass Fiber Venting Base Sheet Used in Roofing	Table 1507.10.2
D 4945—00	Test Method for High-strain Dynamic Testing of Piles	1810.3.3.1.2
D 4990—97a (2005)e01	Specification for Coal Tar Glass Felt Used in Roofing and Waterproofing	Table 1507.10.2
D 5019—07	Specification for Reinforced Nonvulcanized Polymeric Sheet Used in Roofing Membrane	1507.12.2
D 5055—05	Specification for Establishing and Monitoring Structural Capacities of Prefabricated Wood I-joists	2303.1.2
D 5456—05a	Specification for Evaluation of Structural Composite Lumber Products	2303.1.9
D 5516—03	Test Method of Evaluating the Flexural Properties of Fire-retardant-treated Softwood Plywood Exposed to the Elevated Temperatures	2303.2.5.1
D 5643—06	Specification for Coal Tar Roof Cement, Asbestos-free	Table 1507.10.2
D 5664—02	Test Methods for Evaluating the Effects of Fire-retardant Treatment and Elevated Temperatures on Strength Properties of Fire-retardant-treated Lumber	2303.2.5.2
D 5665—99a (2006)	Specification for Thermoplastic Fabrics Used in Cold-applied Roofing and Waterproofing	Table 1507.10.2
D 5726—98 (2005)	Specification for Thermoplastic Fabrics Used in Hot-applied Roofing and Waterproofing	Table 1507.10.2
D 6083—05e01	Specification for Liquid Applied Acrylic Coating Used in Roofing	Table 1507.10.2, 1507.15.2
D 6162—00A	Specification for Styrene-butadiene-styrene (SBS) Modified Bituminous Sheet Materials Using a Combination of Polyester and Glass Fiber Reinforcements	1507.11.2
D 6163—00e01	Specification for Styrene-butadiene-styrene (SBS) Modified Bituminous Sheet Materials Using Glass Fiber Reinforcements	1507.11.2
D 6164—05	Specification for Styrene-butadiene-styrene (SBS) Modified Bituminous Sheet Metal Materials Using Polyester Reinforcements	1507.11.2
D 6222—02e01	Specification for Atactic Polypropylene (APP) Modified Bituminous Sheet Materials Using Polyester Reinforcements	1507.11.2
D 6223—02	Specification for Atactic Polypropylene (APP) Modified Bituminous Sheet Materials Using a Combination of Polyester and Glass Fiber Reinforcements	1507.11.2
D 6298—05	Specification for Fiberglass Reinforced Styrene-butadiene-styrene (SBS) Modified Bituminous Sheets with a Factory Applied Metal Surface	1507.11.2
D 6305—02e01	Practice for Calculating Bending Strength Design Adjustment Factors for Fire-retardant-treated Plywood Roof Sheathing	2303.2.5.1
D 6380—03	Standard Specification for Asphalt Roll Roofing (Organic) Felt	1507.2.9.2, 1507.3.3, 1507.6.5
D 6509—00	Standard Specification for Atactic Polypropylene (APP) Modified Bituminous base Sheet Materials Using Glass Fiber Reinforcements	1507.11.2
D 6694—07	Standard Specification for Liquid-applied Silicone Coating Used in Spray Polyurethane Foam Roofing	1507.15.2
D 6754—02	Standard Specification for Ketone Ethylene Ester Based Sheet Roofing	1507.13.2
D 6757—07	Standard Specification for Inorganic Underlayment for Use with Steep Slope Roofing Products	1507.2.3
D 6841—03	Standard Practice for Calculating Design Value Treatment Adjustment Factors for Fire-retardant-treated Lumber	2303.2.5.2
D 6878—06a	Standard Specification for Thermoplastic Polyolefin Based Sheet Roofing	1507.13.2
D 6947—07	Standard Specification for Liquuid Applied Moisture Cured Polyurethane Coating Used in Spray Polyurethane Foam Roofing System	1507.15.2
D 7158—07	Standard Test Method for Wind Resistance of Sealed Asphalt Shingles (Uplift Force/Uplift Resistance Method)	1507.2.7.1, Table 1507.2.7.1(1)
E 84—07	Test Methods for Surface Burning Characteristics of Building Materials	402.11, 402.16.4, 406.5.3, 703.4.2, 719.1, 719.4, 802.1, 803.1.1, 803.9, 806.5, 1407.9, 1407.10.1, 2303.2, 2603.3, 2603.4.1.13, 2603.5.4, 2604.2.4, 2606.4, 3105.4, D102.2.8
E 90—04	Test Method for Laboratory Measurement of Airborne Sound Transmission Loss of Building Partitions and Elements	1207.2, 1207.2.1
E 96/E 96M—05	Test Method for Water Vapor Transmission of Materials	202, 1203.2

ASTM—continued

Standard	Title	Referenced in code section number
E 108—07a	Test Methods for Fire Tests of Roof Coverings	1505.1, 2603.6, 2610.2, 2610.3
E 119—07	Test Methods for Fire Tests of Building Construction and Materials	703.2, 703.2.1, 703.2.3, 703.3, 703.5, 704.12, 705.7, 705.8.5, 707.6, 712.3.2, 713.3.1, 713.4.1.1, 714.1, 715.2, 715.4.5, 716.5.2, 716.5.3, 716.6.1, 716.6.2.1, Table 720.1(1), 1407.10.2, 2103.2, 2603.4, 2603.5.1
E 136—04	Test Method for Behavior of Materials in a Vertical Tube Furnace at 750°C	703.4.1
E 330—02	Test Method for Structural Performance of Exterior Windows, Curtain Walls and Doors by Uniform Static Air Pressure Difference	1715.5.2
E 331—00	Test Method for Water Penetration of Exterior Windows, Skylights, Doors and Curtain Walls by Uniform Static Air Pressure Difference	1403.2
E 492—04	Test Method for Laboratory Measurement of Impact Sound Transmission Through Floor-ceiling Assemblies Using the Tapping Machine	1207.3
E 605—93 (2006)	Test Method for Thickness and Density of Sprayed Fire-resistive Material (SFRM) Applied to Structural Members	1704.12.4.1, 1704.12.4.2, 1704.12.4.3, 1704.12.5
E 681—04	Test Methods for Concentration Limits of Flammability of Chemical Vapors and Gases	307.2
E 736—00 (2006)	Test Method for Cohesion/Adhesion of Sprayed Fire-resistive Materials Applied to Structural Members	704.13.2, 1704.12.6
E 814—06	Test Method of Fire Tests of Through-penetration Firestops	702.1, 713.3.1.2, 713.3.2, 713.4.1.1.2
E 970—00	Test Method for Critical Radiant Flux of Exposed Attic Floor Insulation Using a Radiant Heat Energy Source	719.3.1
E 1300—04e01	Practice for Determining Load Resistance of Glass in Buildings	2404.1, 2404.2, 2404.3.1, 2404.3.2, 2404.3.3, 2404.3.4, 2404.3.5
E 1354—04a	Standard Test Method for Heat and Visible Smoke Release Rates for Materials and Products Using an Oxygen Consumption Calorimeter	402.12.1
E 1592—01	Test Method for Structural Performance of Sheet Metal Roof and Siding Systems by Uniform Static Air Pressure Difference	1504.3.2
E 1602—03	Guide for Construction of Solid Fuel-burning Masonry Heaters	2112.2
E 1886—05	Test Method for Performance of Exterior Windows, Curtain Walls, Doors and Storm Shutters Impacted by Missiles and Exposed to Cyclic Pressure Differentials	1609.1.2
E 1966—01	Test Method for Fire-resistant Joint Systems	702.1, 714.3
E 1996—06	Specification for Performance of Exterior Windows, Glazed Curtain Walls, Doors and Impact Protective Systems Impacted by Windborne Debris in Hurricanes	1609.1.2, 1609.1.2.1
E 2072—04	Standard Specification for Photoluminescent (Phosphorescent) Safety Markings	1024.4
E 2273—03	Standard Test Method for Determining the Drainage Efficiency of Exterior Insulation and Finish Systems (EIFS) Clad Wall Assemblies	1408.4.1
E 2307—04e01	Standard Test Method for Determining Fire Resistance of Perimeter Fire Barrier Systems Using Intermediate-scale, Multistory Test Apparatus	714.4
E 2404—07a	Standard Practice for Specimen Preparation and Mounting of Textile, Paper or Vinyl Wall or Ceiling Coverings to Assess Surface Burning Characteristics	803.1.4
E 2568—07	Standard Specification for PB Exterior Insulation and Finish Systems (EIFS)	1408.2
E 2570—07	Standard Test Method for Evaluating Water-resistive Barrier (WRB) Coatings Used Under Exterior Insulation and Finish Systems (EIFS) for EIFS with Drainage	1408.4.1.1, 1704.12.1
E 2573—07	Standard Practice for Specimen Preparation and Mounting of Site-fabricated Stretch Systems to Assess Surface Burning Characteristics	803.9
F 547—01	Terminology of Nails for Use with Wood and Wood-based Materials	Table 2506.2
F 1346—91 (2003)	Performance Specification for Safety Covers and Labeling Requirements for All Covers for Swimming Pools, Spas and Hot Tubs	3109.4, 3109.4.1.8
F 1667—05	Specification for Driven Fasteners: Nails, Spikes and Staples	Table 720.1(2), Table 720.1(3), 1507.2.6, 2303.6, Table 2506.2
F 2006—00 (2005)	Standard/Safety Specification for Window Fall Prevention Devices for Nonemergency Escape (Egress) and Rescue (Ingress) Windows	1405.13.2
F 2090—01a (2007)	Specification for Window Fall Prevention Devices with Emergency Escape (Egress) Release Mechanisms	1405.13.2
F 2200—05	Standard Specification for Automated Vehicular Gate Construction	3110.3
G 152—06	Practice for Operating Open Flame Carbon Arc Light Apparatus for Exposure of Nonmetallic Materials	1504.6
G 154—05	Practice for Operating Fluorescent Light Apparatus for UV Exposure of Nonmetallic Materials	1504.6
G 155—05a	Practice for Operating Xenon Arc Light Apparatus for Exposure of Nonmetallic Materials	1504.6

AWCI

Association of the Wall and Ceiling Industry
513 West Broad Street, Suite 210
Falls Church, VA 22046

Standard reference number	Title	Referenced in code section number
12-B—98	Technical Manual 12-B Standard Practice for the Testing and Inspection of Field Applied Thin Film Intumescent Fire-resistive Materials; an Annotated Guide, First Edition	1704.13

AWPA

American Wood Protection Association
P.O. Box 361784
Birmingham, AL 35236-1784

Standard reference number	Title	Referenced in code section number
C1—03	All Timber Products—Preservative Treatment by Pressure Processes	1505.6
M4—06	Standard for the Care of Preservative-treated Wood Products	1810.3.2.4.1, 2303.1.8
U1—07	USE CATEGORY SYSTEM: User Specification for Treated Wood Except Section 6, Commodity Specification H	1403.5, Table 1507.9.6, 1807.1.4, 1807.3.1, 1809.12, 1810.3.2.4.1, 2303.1.8, 2304.11.2, 2304.11.4, 2304.11.6, 2304.11.7

AWS

American Welding Society
550 N.W. LeJeune Road
Miami, FL 33126

Standard reference number	Title	Referenced in code section number
D1.1—04	Structural Welding Code—Steel	Table 1704.3, 1704.3.1.1
D1.3—98	Structural Welding Code—Sheet Steel	Table 1704.3, 1704.3.1.2
D1.4—98	Structural Welding Code—Reinforcing Steel	Table 1704.3, 1704.3.1.3, Table 1704.4, 2107.4

BHMA

Builders Hardware Manufacturers' Association
355 Lexington Avenue, 17th Floor
New York, NY 10017-6603

Standard reference number	Title	Referenced in code section number
A 156.10—06	Power Operated Pedestrian Doors	1008.1.4.2
A 156.19—02	Standard for Power Assist and Low Energy Operated Doors	1008.1.4.2

CGSB

Canadian General Standards Board
Place du Portage 111, 6B1
11 Laurier Street
Gatineau, Quebec, Canada KIA 1G6

Standard reference number	Title	Referenced in code section number
37-GP-52M (1984)	Roofing and Waterproofing Membrane, Sheet Applied, Elastomeric	1504.7, 1507.12.2
37-GP-56M (1980)	Membrane, Modified, Bituminous, Prefabricated and Reinforced for Roofing—with December 1985 Amendment	1507.11.2
CAN/CGSB 37.54—95	Polyvinyl Chloride Roofing and Waterproofing Membrane	1507.13.2

CPA

Composite Panel Association
19465 Deerfield Avenue, Suite 306
Leesburg, VA 20176

Standard reference number	Title	Referenced in code section number
ANSI A135.4—2004	Basic Hardboard	1404.3.1, 2303.1.6

CPA—continued

ANSI A135.5—2004	Prefinished Hardboard Paneling	2303.1.6, 2304.6.2
ANSI A135.6—1998	Hardboard Siding	1404.3.2, 2303.1.6

CPSC

Consumer Product Safety Commission
4330 East West Highway
Bethesda, MD 20814-4408

Standard reference number	Title	Referenced in code section number
16 CFR Part 1201(1977)	Safety Standard for Architectural Glazing Material	2406.2, Table 2406.2(1), 2406.3.1, 2407.1, 2407.1.4.1, 2408.2.1, 2408.3, 2409.1, 2409.2, 2409.3.1
16 CFR Part 1209 (1979)	Interim Safety Standard for Cellulose Insulation	719.6
16 CFR Part 1404 (1979)	Cellulose Insulation	719.6
16 CFR Part 1500 (1991)	Hazardous Substances and Articles; Administration and Enforcement Regulations	307.2
16 CFR Part 1500.44 (2001)	Method for Determining Extremely Flammable and Flammable Solids	307.2
16 CFR Part 1507 (2001)	Fireworks Devices	307.2
16 CFR Part 1630 (2000)	Standard for the Surface Flammability of Carpets and Rugs	804.4.1

CSA

Canadian Standards Association
5060 Spectrum Way
Mississauga, Ontario Canada L4W 5N6

Standard reference number	Title	Referenced in code section number
101/I.S.2/A440—08	Specifications for Windows, Doors and Unit Skylights	1715.5.1, 2405.5

CSSB

Cedar Shake and Shingle Bureau
P. O. Box 1178
Sumas, WA 98295-1178

Standard reference number	Title	Referenced in code section number
CSSB—97	Grading and Packing Rules for Western Red Cedar Shakes and Western Red Shingles of the Cedar Shake and Shingle Bureau	Table 1507.8.5, Table 1507.9.6

DASMA

Door and Access Systems Manufacturers Association International
1300 Summer Avenue
Cleveland, OH 44115-2851

Standard reference number	Title	Referenced in code section number
ANSI/DASMA 107—1997 (R2004)	Room Fire Test Standard for Garage Doors Using Foam Plastic Insulation	2603.4.1.9
108—05	Standard Method for Testing Sectional Garage Doors and Rolling Doors: Determination of Structural Performance Under Uniform Static Air Pressure Difference	1715.5.2
115—05	Standard Method for Testing Sectional Garage Doors and Rolling Doors: Determination of Structural Performance Under Missile Impact and Cyclic Wind Pressure	1609.1.2.2

DOC

U.S. Department of Commerce
National Institute of Standards and Technology
1401 Constitution Avenue NW
Washington, DC 20230

Standard reference number	Title	Referenced in code section number
PS-1—07	Structural Plywood	2303.1.4, 2304.6.2, Table 2304.7(4), Table 2304.7(5), Table 2306.2.1(1), Table 2306.2.1(2)
PS-2—04	Performance Standard for Wood-based Structural-use Panels	2303.1.4, 2304.6.2, Table 2304.7(5), Table 2306.2.1(1), Table 2306.2.1(2)
PS 20—05	American Softwood Lumber Standard	1810.3.2.4, 2302.1, 2303.1.1

DOJ

U.S. Department of Justice
950 Pennsylvania Avenue, NW
Civil Rights Division, Disability Rights Section-NYA
Washington, DC 20530

Standard reference number	Title	Referenced in code section number
DOJ 36 CFR Part 1192	American with Disabilities Act (ADA) Accessibility Guidelines for Transportation Vehicles (ADAAG) Department of Justice, 1991	E109.2.4

DOL

U.S. Department of Labor
c/o Superintendent of Documents
U.S. Government Printing Office
Washington, DC 20402-9325

Standard reference number	Title	Referenced in code section number
29 CFR Part 1910.1000 (1974)	Air Contaminants	902.1

DOTn

U.S. Department of Transportation
c/o Superintendent of Documents
1200 New Jersey Avenue, SE
Washington, DC 20402-9325

Standard reference number	Title	Referenced in code section number
49 CFR Parts 100-185-2005	Hazardous Materials Regulations	307.2
49 CFR Parts 173.137 (2005)	Shippers—General Requirements for Shipments and Packaging—Class 8—Assignment of Packing Group	307.2
49 CFR—1998	Specification of Transportation of Explosive and Other Dangerous Articles, UN 0335, UN 0336 Shipping Containers	307.2

EN

European Committee for Standardization (EN)
Central Secretariat
Rue de Stassart 36
B-10 50 Brussels

Standard reference number	Title	Referenced in code section number
EN 1081-98	Resilient Floor Coverings—Determination of the Electrical Resistance	406.5.2

FEMA

Federal Emergency Management Agency
Federal Center Plaza
500 C Street S.W.
Washington, DC 20472

Standard reference number	Title	Referenced in code section number
FIA-TB11—01	Crawlspace Construction for Buildings Located in Special Flood Hazard Areas	1805.1.2.1

FM

Factory Mutual Global Research
Standards Laboratories Department
1301 Atwood Avenue, P.O. Box 7500
Johnston, RI 02919

Standard reference number	Title	Referenced in code section number
4450 (1989)	Approval Standard for Class 1 Insulated Steel Deck Roofs—with Supplements through July 1992	1508.1, 2603.3, 2603.4.1.5
4470 (1992)	Approval Standard for Class 1 Roof Covers	1504.7
4474 (04)	Evaluating the Simulated Wind Uplift Resistance of Roof Assemblies Using Static Positive and/or Negative Differential Pressures	1504.3.1
4880 (2005)	American National Standard for Evaluating Insulated Wall or Wall and Roof/ Ceiling Assemblies, Plastic Interior Finish Materials, Plastic Exterior Building Panels, Wall/Ceiling Coating Systems, Interior and Exterior Finish Systems	2603.4, 2603.9

GA

Gypsum Association
810 First Street N.E. #510
Washington, DC 20002-4268

Standard reference number	Title	Referenced in code section number
GA 216—07	Application and Finishing of Gypsum Panel Products	Table 2508.1, 2509.2
GA 600—06	Fire-resistance Design Manual, 18th Edition	Table 720.1(1), Table 720.1(2), Table 720.1(3)

HPVA

Hardwood Plywood Veneer Association
1825 Michael Faraday Drive
Reston, VA 20190

Standard reference number	Title	Referenced in code section number
HP-1—2004	Standard for Hardwood and Decorative Plywood	2303.3, 2304.6.2

HUD

U.S. Department of Housing and Urban Development
451 7th Street, SW
Washington, DC 20410

Standard reference number	Title	Referenced in code section number
HUD 24 CFR Part 3280 (1994)	Manufactured Home Construction and Safety Standards	G201

ICC

International Code Council, Inc.
500 New Jersey Ave, NW
6th Floor
Washington, DC 20001

Standard reference number	Title	Referenced in code section number
ICC/ANSI A117.1—09	Accessible and Usable Buildings and Facilities	406.2.2, 907.5.2.3.4, 1007.9, 1010.1, 1010.6.5, 1010.9, 1011.3, 1022.8, 1101.2, 1102.1, 1104.4, 1106.7, 1107.2, 1108.2.2, 1108.2.3, 1108.4.1.1, 1108.4.1.2, 1108.4.1.4, 1108.4.1.5, 1109.1, 1109.2, 1109.2.1.1, 1109.2.2, 1109.2.3, 1109.3, 1109.4, 1109.8, 1109.13, 2902.4, 3001.3, 3008.13.1, 3008.13.2, 3411.6, 3411.8.2, 3411.8.3, E101.2, E104.2, E104.2.1, E104.3, E104.3.4, E105.1, E105.2.1, E105.2.2, E105.3, E105.4, E105.6, E106.2, E106.3, E106.4, E106.4.9, E106.5, E107.2, E107.3, E108.3, E108.4, E109.2.1, E109.2.2.1, E109.2.2.2, E109.2.2.3, E109.2.3, E109.2.5, E109.2.6, E109.2.8, E110.2, E110.4
ICC 300—07	ICC Standard on Bleachers, Folding and Telescopic Seating and Grandstands	1028.1.1, Table 1607.1, 3401.1
ICC 400—07	Standard on Design and Construction of Log Structures	2301.2
ICC 500—08	ICC/NSSA Standard on the Design and Construction of Storm Shelters	423.1, 423.2
ICC 600—08	Standard for Residential Construction in High Wind Regions	1609.1.1, 1609.1.1.1, 2308.2.1
IEBC—09	International Existing Building Code®	3401.5
IECC—09	International Energy Conservation Code®	101.4.6, 1203.3.2, 1301.1.1

ICC—continued

IFC—09	International Fire Code®	101.4.5, 102.6, 201.3, 307.1, Table 307.1(1), Table 307.1(2), 307.1.1, 307.2, 403.4.4, 404.2, 406.5.1, 406.6.1, 410.3.6, 411.1, 412.1, 412.6.1, 413.1, 414.1.1, 414.1.2, 414.1.2.1, 414.2, 414.2.5, Table 414.2.5(1), Table 414.2.5(2), 414.3, 414.5, 414.5.1, Table 414.5.1, 414.5.2, 414.5.4, 414.5.5, 414.6, 415.1, 415.2, 415.3, 415.3.1, Table 415.3.1, Table 415.3.2, 415.6, 415.6.1, 415.6.1.4, 415.6.2, 415.6.2.3, 415.6.2.5, 415.6.2.7, 415.6.2.8, 415.6.2.9, 415.6.3, 415.6.4, 415.7, 415.8.1, 415.8.2.7, 415.8.5.1, 415.8.7.2, 415.8.9.3, 415.8.10.1, 416.1, 421.1, 421.7, 507.3, 707.1, 901.2, 901.3, 901.5, 901.6.2, 903.2.7.1, Table 903.2.11.6, 903.2.12 903.5, 904.2.1, 905.1, 905.3.6, 906.1, 907.1.8, 907.2.5, 907.2.13.2, 907.2.15, 907.2.16, 907.6.5, 907.8, 909.20, 910.2.2, 1001.3, 1203.4.2, 1203.5, 2702.1, 2702.2.9, 2702.2.11, 2702.2.12, 2702.2.13, 2702.3, 3102.1, 3103.1, 3309.2, 3401.3, 3412.3.2, 3412.6.8.1, 3412.6.14, 3412.6.14.1
IFGC—09	International Fuel Gas Code®	101.4.1, 201.3, Table 307.1(1), 415.6.3, 2113.11.1.2, 2113.15, 2801.1, 3401.3, A101.2
IMC—09	International Mechanical Code®	101.4.2, 201.3, 307.1, Table 307.1(1), 406.4.2, 406.6.3, 406.6.5, 409.3, 412.6.6, 414.1.2, 414.3, 415.6.1.4, 415.6.2, 415.6.2.8, 415.6.3, 415.6.4, 415.8.11.1, 416.3, 421.5, 603.1, 603.1.1, 603.1.2, 708.2, 716.2.2, 716.5.4, 716.6.1, 716.6.2, 716.6.3, 717.5, 719.1, 719.7, 903.2.11.4, 904.2.1, 904.11, 908.6, 909.1, 909.10.2, 1015.5, 1018.5.1, 1203.1, 1203.2.1, 1203.4.2, 1203.4.2.1, 1203.5, 1209.3, 2304.5, 2801.1, 3004.3.1, 3401.3, 3412.6.7.1, 3412.6.8, 3412.6.8.1, A101.2
IPC—09	International Plumbing Code®	101.4.3, 201.3, 415.6.4, 717.5, 903.3.5, 912.5, 1206.3.3, 1503.4, 1805.4.3, 2901.1, Table 2902.1, 3305.1, 3401.3, A101.2
IPMC—09	International Property Maintenance Code®	101.4.4, 102.6, 103.3, 3401.3, 3412.3.2
IPSDC—09	International Private Sewage Disposal Code®	101.4.3, 2901.1, 3401.3
IRC—09	International Residential Code®	101.2, 308.2, 308.5, 310.1, 2308.1, 3401.3
IWUIC—09	International Wildland-Urban Interface Code™	Table 1505.1
SBCCI SSTD 11—97	Test Standard for Determining Wind Resistance of Concrete or Clay Roof Tiles	1716.2.1, 1716.2.2

ISO

International Organization for Standardization
ISO Central Secretariat
1 ch, de la Voie-Creuse, Case Postale 56
CH-1211 Geneva 20, Switzerland

Standard reference number	Title	Referenced in code section number
ISO 8115—86	Cotton Bales–Dimensions and Density	Table 415.8.2.1.1

NAAMM

National Association of Architectural Metal Manufacturers
800 Roosevelt Road, Bldg. C, Suite 312
Glen Ellyn, IL 60137

Standard reference number	Title	Referenced in code section number
FP 1001—97	Guide Specifications for Design of Metal Flag Poles	1609.1.1

NCMA

National Concrete Masonry Association
13750 Sunrise Valley
Herndon, VA 22071-4662

Standard reference number	Title	Referenced in code section number
TEK 5-84 (1996)	Details for Concrete Masonry Fire Walls	Table 720.1(2)

NFPA

National Fire Protection Association
1 Batterymarch Park
Quincy, MA 02169-7471

Standard reference number	Title	Referenced in code section number
10—07	Portable Fire Extinguishers	906.2, 906.3.2, 906.3.4, Table 906.3(1), Table 906.3(2)
11—05	Low Expansion Foam	904.7
12—05	Carbon Dioxide Extinguishing Systems	904.8, 904.11
12A—04 Halon 1301	Halon 1301 Fire Extinguishing Systems	904.9
13—07	Installation of Sprinkler Systems	708.2, 903.3.1.1, 903.3.2, 903.3.5.1.1, 903.3.5.2, 904.11, 905.3.4, 907.6.3, 1613.6.3
13D—07	Installation of Sprinkler Systems in One- and Two-family Dwellings and Manufactured Homes	903.3.1.3, 903.3.5.1.1
13R—07	Installation of Sprinkler Systems in Residential Occupancies Up to and Including Four Stories in Height	903.3.1.2, 903.3.5.1.1, 903.3.5.1.2, 903.4
14—07	Installation of Standpipe and Hose System	905.2, 905.3.4, 905.4.2, 905.6.2, 905.8
16—07	Installation of Foam-water Sprinkler and Foam-water Spray Systems	904.7, 904.11
17—02	Dry Chemical Extinguishing Systems	904.6, 904.11
17A—02	Wet Chemical Extinguishing Systems	904.5, 904.11
20—07	Installation of Stationary Pumps for Fire Protection	913.1, 913.2.1, 913.5
30—08	Flammable and Combustible Liquids Code	415.3
31—06	Installation of Oil-burning Equipment	2113.15
32—07	Dry Cleaning Plants	415.6.4
40—07	Storage and Handling of Cellulose Nitrate Film	409.1
58—08	Liquefied Petroleum Gas Code	415.6.3
61—08	Prevention of Fires and Dust Explosions in Agricultural and Food Product Facilities	415.6.1
70—08	National Electrical Code	108.3, 415.8.2.8.2, 904.3.1, 907.6.1, 909.12.1, 909.16.3, 1205.4.1, 2701.1, 3401.3, H106.1, H106.2, K101, K111.1
72—07	National Fire Alarm Code	901.6, 903.4.1, 904.3.5, 907.2, 907.2.5, 907.2.11, 907.2.13.2, 907.3, 907.3.3, 907.3.4, 907.5.2.1.2, 907.5.2.2, 907.6, 907.6.1, 907.6.5, 907.7, 907.7.1, 907.7.2, 911.1.5, 3006.5, 3007.6
80—07	Fire Doors and Other Opening Protectives	410.3.5, 508.2.5.2, 715.4, 715.4.5, 715.4.6, 715.4.7.1, 715.4.8.2, 715.5, 715.5.5, 1008.1.4.3
85—07	Boiler and Combustion System Hazards Code (Note: NFPA 8503 has been incorporated into NFPA 85)	415.6.1
92B—05	Smoke Management Systems in Malls, Atria and Large Spaces	909.8
99—05	Standard for Health Care Facilities	407.9
101—06	Life Safety Code	1028.6.2
105—07	Standard for the Installation of Smoke Door Assemblies	405.4.2, 715.4.3.1, 909.20.4.1
110—05	Emergency and Standby Power Systems	2702.1
111—05	Stored Electrical Energy Emergency and Standby Power Systems	2702.1
120—04	Coal Preparation Plants	415.6.1
170—06	Standard for Fire Safety and Emergency Symbols	1024.2.6.1
211—06	Chimneys, Fireplaces, Vents and Solid Fuel-burning Appliances	2112.5
252—03	Standard Methods of Fire Tests of Door Assemblies	715.3, 715.4.1, 715.4.2, 715.4.3, 715.4.7.3.1
253—06	Test for Critical Radiant Flux of Floor Covering Systems Using a Radiant Heat Energy Source	402.12.1, 406.6.4, 804.2, 804.3
257—07	Standard for Fire Test for Window and Glass Block Assemblies	715.3, 715.4.3.2, 715.5, 715.5.1, 715.5.2, 715.5.9.1
259—03	Test Method for Potential Heat of Building Materials	2603.4.1.10, 2603.5.3
265—07	Method of Fire Tests for Evaluating Room Fire Growth Contribution of Textile Wall Coverings on Full Height Panels and Walls	803.1.3, 803.1.3.1
268—07	Standard Test Method for Determining Ignitibility of Exterior Wall Assemblies Using a Radiant Heat Energy Source	1406.2.1, 1406.2.1.1, 1406.2.1.2, 2603.5.7, D105.1
285—06	Standard Method of Test for the Evaluation of Flammability Characteristics of Exterior Nonload-bearingWall Assemblies Containing Combustible Components	1407.10.4, 2603.5.5
286—06	Standard Method of Fire Test for Evaluating Contribution of Wall and Ceiling Interior Finish to Room Fire Growth	402.16.4, 803.1.2, 803.1.2.1, 803.9, 2603.4, 2603.9
288—07	Standard Method of Fire Tests of Floor Fire Door Assemblies Installed Horizontally in Fire-resistance-rated Floor Systems	712.8
409—04	Aircraft Hangars	412.4.6, Table 412.4.6, 412.4.6.1, 412.6.5
418—06	Standard for Heliports	412.7.4
484—06	Combustible Metals	415.6.1

NFPA—continued

654—06	Prevention of Fire & Dust Explosions from the Manufacturing, Processing and Handling of Combustible Particulate Solids	415.6.1
655—07	Prevention of Sulfur Fires and Explosions	415.6.1
664—07	Prevention of Fires and Explosions in Wood Processing and Woodworking Facilities	415.6.1
701—04	Standard Methods of Fire Tests for Flame-propagation of Textiles and Films	402.12.1, 410.3.6, 801.1.4, 806.1, 806.1.2, 806.2, 3102.3, 3102.3.1, 3102.6.1.1, 3105.4, D102.2.8, H106.1.1
704—07	Standard System for the Identification of the Hazards of Materials for Emergency Response	414.7.2, 415.2
1124—06	Manufacture, Transportation and Storage of Fireworks and Pyrotechnic Articles	415.3.1
2001—08	Clean Agent Fire Extinguishing Systems	904.10

PCI

Precast Prestressed Concrete Institute
209 W. Jackson Boulevard, Suite 500
Chicago, IL 60606-6938

Standard reference number	Title	Referenced in code section number
MNL 124—89	Design for Fire Resistance of Precast Prestressed Concrete	721.2.3.1
MNL 128—01	Recommended Practice for Glass Fiber Reinforced Concrete Panels	1903.2

PTI

Post-Tensioning Institute
8601 North Black Canyon Highway, Suite 103
Phoenix, AZ 85021

Standard reference number	Title	Referenced in code section number
PTI—2007	Standard Requirements for Analysis of Shallow Concrete Foundations on Expansive Soils, Third Edition	1808.6.2
PTI—2007	Standard Requirements for Design of Shallow Post-tensioned Concrete Foundation on Expansive Soils, Second Edition	1808.6.2

RMI

Rack Manufacturers Institute
8720 Red Oak Boulevard, Suite 201
Charlotte, NC 28217

Standard reference number	Title	Referenced in code section number
ANSI/MH16.1—08	Specification for Design, Testing and Utilization of Industrial Steel Storage Racks	2208.1

SDI

Steel Deck Institute
P. O. Box 25
Fox River Grove, IL 60021

Standard reference number	Title	Referenced in code section number
ANSI/NC1.0—06	Standard for Noncomposite Steel Floor Deck	2209.2.2, 2209.2.2.1
ANSI/RD1.0—06	Standard for Steel Roof Deck	2209.2.3

SJI

Steel Joist Institute
1173B London Links Drive
Forest, VA 24551

Standard reference number	Title	Referenced in code section number
CJ-1.0—06	Standard Specification for Composite Steel Joists, CJ-series	1604.3.3, 2203.2, 2206.1
JG-1.1—05	Standard Specification for Joist Girders	1604.3.3, 2203.2, 2206.1
K-1.1—05	Standard Specification for Open Web Steel Joists, K-series	1604.3.3, 2203.2, 2206.1
LH/DLH-1.1—05	Standard Specification for Longspan Steel Joists, LH-series and Deep Longspan Steel Joists, DLH-series	1604.3.3, 2203.2, 2206.1

SPRI

Single-Ply Roofing Institute
411 Waverly Oaks Road, Suite 331B
Waltham, MA 02452

Standard reference number	Title	Referenced in code section number
SPRI/ANSI/ES-1—03	Wind Design Standard for Edge Systems Used with Low Slope Roofing Systems	1504.5
RP-4—02	Wind Design Guide for Ballasted Single-ply Roofing Systems	1504.4

TIA

Telecommunications Industry Association
2500 Wilson Boulevard
Arlington, VA 22201-3834

Standard reference number	Title	Referenced in code section number
TIA-222-G—05	Structural Standards for Steel Antenna Towers and Antenna Supporting Structures including-Addendum 1, 222-G-1, Dated 2007	1609.1.1, 3108.1, 3108.2

TMS

The Masonry Society
3970 Broadway, Unit 201-D
Boulder, CO 80304-1135

Standard reference number	Title	Referenced in code section number
0216—97	Standard Method for Determining Fire Resistance of Concrete and Masonry Construction Assemblies	Table 720.1(2), 721.1
0302—07	Standard Method for Determining the Sound Transmission Class Rating for Masonry Walls	1207.2.1
402—08	Building Code Requirements for Masonry Structures	1405.6, 1405.6.2, 1405.10, 1604.3.4, Table 1703.4.5.3, 1704.5, 1704.5.1, Table 1704.5.1, 1704.5.2, 1704.5.3, 1807.1.6.3.2, 1808.9, 2101.2.2, 2101.2.3, 2101.2.4, 2101.2.5, 2101.2.6, 2103.1.3.6, 2106.1, 2107.1, 2107.2, 2107.3, 2107.4, 2107.5, 2108.1, 2108.2, 2108.3, 2109.1, 2109.1.1, 2109.2, 2109.2.1, 2109.3, 2110.1
602—08	Specification for Masonry Structures	1405.6.1, Table 1704.5.1, Table 1704.5.3, 1807.1.6.3, 2103.8, 2103.11, 2103.12, 2103.13, 2104.1, 2104.1.1, 2104.1.2 2104.1.3, 2104.2, 2104.3, 2104.4, 2105.2.2.1.1, 2105.2.2.1.2, 2105.2.2.1.3

TPI

Truss Plate Institute
218 N. Lee Street, Suite 312
Alexandria, VA 22314

Standard reference number	Title	Referenced in code section number
TPI 1—2007	National Design Standards for Metal-plate-connected Wood Truss Construction	2303.4.6, 2306.1

UL

Underwriters Laboratories, Inc.
333 Pfingsten Road
Northbrook, IL 60062-2096

Standard reference number	Title	Referenced in code section number
9—2000	Fire Tests of Window Assemblies—with Revisions through April 2005	715.3, 715.4.3.2, 715.5, 715.5.1, 715.5.2, 715.5.9.1
10A—98	Tin Clad Fire Doors—with Revisions through March 2003	715.4
10B—97	Fire Tests of Door Assemblies—with Revisions through October 2001	715.4.2
10C—98	Positive Pressure Fire Tests of Door Assemblies—with Revisions through November 2001	715.4.1, 715.4.3
14B—98	Sliding Hardware for Standard Horizontally-mounted Tin Clad Fire Doors—with Revisions through July 2000	715.4
14C—06	Swinging Hardware for Standard Tin Clad Fire Doors Mounted Singly and in Pairs	715.4
103—01	Factory-built Chimneys, for Residential Type and Building Heating Appliances—with Revisions through June 2006	717.2.5.1
127—96	Factory-built Fireplaces—with Revisions through November 2006	717.2.5.1, 2111.11

UL—continued

199E—04	Outline of Investigation for Fire Testing of Sprinklers and Water Spray Nozzles for Protection of Deep Fat Fryers	904.11.4.1
217—06	Single and Multiple Station Smoke Alarms—with Revisions through August 2005	907.2.11
263—03	Standard for Fire Test of Building Construction and Materials	703.2, 703.2.1, 703.2.3, 703.3, 703.5, 704.12, 705.7, 707.7, 712.3.2, 713.3.1, 713.4.1.1, 714.1, 715.2, 716.5.2, 716.5.3, 716.6.1, Table 716.6.2(1), Table 720.1(1), 1407.10.2, 2103.2, 2603.4, 2603.5.1
268—06	Smoke Detectors for Fire Protective Signaling Systems—with Revisions through January 1999	407.7, 907.2.6.2
300—05	Fire Testing of Fire Extinguishing Systems for Protection of Restaurant Cooking Areas	904.11
305—07	Panic Hardware	1008.1.10
325—02	Door, Drapery, Gate, Louver and Window Operations and Systems—with Revisions through February 2006	406.1.5, 3110.4
555—2006	Fire Dampers	716.3
555C—2006	Ceiling Dampers	716.3, 716.6.2
555S—99	Smoke Dampers—with Revisions through July 2006	716.3, 716.3.1.1
580—2006	Test for Uplift Resistance of Roof Assemblies	1504.3.1, 1504.3.2
641—95	Type L Low-temperature Venting Systems—with Revisions through August 2005	2113.11.1.4
710B—04	Recirculating Systems—with Revisions through April 2006	904.11
723—03	Standard for Test for Surface Burning Characteristics of Building Materials—with Revisions through May 2005	402.11, 402.16.4, 406.5.3, 703.4.2, 719.1, 719.4, 802.1, 803.1.1, 803.9, 806.5, 1407.9, 1407.10.1, 2303.2, 2603.3, 2603.4.1.13, 2603.5.4, 2604.2.4, 2606.4, 3105.4, D102.2.8
790—04	Standard Test Methods for Fire Tests of Roof Coverings	1505.1, 2603.6, 2610.2, 2610.3
793—03	Standards for Automatically Operated Roof Vents for Smoke and Heat—with Revisions through April 2004	910.3.1
864—03	Standards for Control Units and Accessories for Fire Alarm Systems—with Revisions through March 2006	909.12
924—06	Standard for Safety Emergency Lighting and Power Equipment	1011.4
1040—96	Fire Test of Insulated Wall Construction—with Revisions through June 2001	1407.10.3, 2603.4, 2603.9
1256—02	Fire Test of Roof Deck Construction—with Revisions through January 2007	1508.1, 2603.3, 2603.4.1.5
1479—03	Fire Tests of Through-penetration Firestops—with Revisions through April 2007	702.1, 713.3.1.2, 713.3.2, 713.4.1.1.2
1482—96	Solid-fuel-type Room Heater—with Revisions through November 2006	2112.2, 2112.5
1715—97	Fire Test of Interior Finish Material—with Revisions through March 2004	1407.10.2, 1407.10.3, 2603.4, 2603.9
1777—04	Chimney Liners	2113.11.1, 2113.19
1784—01	Air Leakage Tests of Door Assemblies—with Revisions through December 2004	708.14.1, 711.5.2, 715.4.3.1, 715.4.6.1, 715.4.6.3, 3007.4.3
1897—04	Uplift Tests for Roof Covering Systems	1504.3.1
1975—06	Fire Test of Foamed Plastics Used for Decorative Purposes	402.11, 402.12.1, 402.16.5
1994—04	Standard for Luminous Egress Path Marking Systems—with Revisions through February 2005	411.7, 1024.2.1, 1024.2.3, 1024.2.4, 1024.4
2017—2000	Standards for General-purpose Signaling Devices and Systems—with Revisions through August 2005	3109.4.1.8
2075—2007	Standard for Gas and Vapor Detectors and Sensors	406.6.6.1
2079—04	Tests for Fire Resistance of Building Joint Systems—with Revisions through March 2006	702.1, 714.3, 714.6
2200—04	Stationary Engine Generator Assemblies—with Revisions through July 2004	2702.1.1

ULC

Underwriters Laboratories of Canada
7 Underwriters Road
Toronto, Ontario, Canada M1R3B4

Standard reference number	Title	Referenced in code section number
CAN/ULC S102.2—1988	Standard Method of Test for Surface Burning Characteristics of Flooring, Floor Coverings and Miscellaneous Materials and Assemblies—with 2000 Revisions	719.4

USC

United States Code
c/o Superintendent of Documents
U.S. Government Printing Office
Washington, DC 20402-9325

Standard reference number	Title	Referenced in code section number
18 USC Part 1, Ch.40	Importation, Manufacture, Distribution and Storage of Explosive Materials	307.2

WDMA

Window and Door Manufacturers Association
1400 East Touhy Avenue #470
Des Plaines, IL 60018

Standard reference number	Title	Referenced in code section number
AAMA/WDMA/CSA 101/I.S.2/A440—08	Specifications for Windows, Doors and Unit Skylights	1715.5.1, 2405.5

WRI

Wire Reinforcement Institute, Inc.
942 Main Street, Suite 300
Hartford, CT 06103

Standard reference number	Title	Referenced in code section number
WRI/CRSI—81	Design of Slab-on-ground Foundations—with 1996 Update	1808.6.2

CHAPTER 36

PIERS, BULKHEADS AND WATERWAY STRUCTURES

SECTION 3601 GENERAL

The intent of this chapter is to provide minimum standards for the design, construction and maintenance of piers, bulkheads and waterway structures that are not covered by other existing codes or design standards. This chapter exempts farm structures not on public waters, marine terminal or port facilities for berthing, mooring, docking and servicing ships, barges or tug boats that handle cargo of all types, including bulks, liquids, fuels and passengers.

The design of piers, bulkheads and waterway structures is essential for the protection of life and property without causing adverse effects to the shoreline. These structures by their very nature result in some modification of physical environment and therefore require minimum design standards. The guidelines in this chapter address minimum standards for foundations, design forces, structural integrity, material selection and utilization and construction techniques.

SECTION 3602 PERMITS AND APPROVALS

The construction of any pier, bulkhead or waterway structure in public waters or the placement of dredged materials in waters or wetlands, generally requires the owner to obtain permits prior to construction. A permit from the United States Army Corps of Engineers is generally required for all marine construction. In addition to the permit issued by the Corps of Engineers, additional permits may be required from municipal, county or state governments or local marine commissions. In cases of structures to be built on lakes operated by an electric utility for the generation of power, a permit from the operating utility may also be required.

SECTION 3603 MINIMUM DESIGN LOADS

3603.1 General. Every structure shall be of sufficient strength to support the imposed dead, live, wind and impact loads without exceeding the allowable stresses prescribed for the various materials elsewhere in this code. Adequate consideration shall be made for forces imposed by earth, water, docking and mooring.

3603.2 Dead loads. The weight of the component parts of a structure shall be used in the design when it will influence the strength of the structural elements.

3603.3 Live loads. Design live loads shall be the greatest load that will probably be imposed on the structure, including superimposed loads on retained material which exert horizontal loads on the structure. Where vehicles are allowed, actual weight of vehicles and wheel loads as specified in the latest edition of Standard Specifications for Highway Bridges of the American Association of State Highway and Transportation Officials shall be used. The design load shall be posed at the dock or pier approach where vehicles are allowed. Minimum live loads are:

1. Fixed piers, docks, catwalks—40 pounds per square foot (psf) (1915 Pa) or 300 pounds (1335 N) concentrated load on any area 2 foot (610 mm) square.
2. Floating piers, docks, fingers—20 psf or 300 pounds (1335 N) concentrated load on any area 2 feet (610 mm) square. Under dead load, floating piers shall have a minimum of 15 inches (381 mm) freeboard. The pier shall have not more than 6 degrees (0.11 rad) tilt from the horizontal under uniform live loading on one-half of the pier width or under concentrated load of 600 pounds (2669 N) applied on any side.
3. Bulkheads, seawalls, revetments— Design loads shall be the greatest combinations of loads exerted on the structure. Consideration shall be given to horizontal loads exerted by superimposed loads on the retained earth and by inclined surface slopes.
4. Public fishing piers
   - 4.1. Mean low waterline to land–100 psf (4788 Pa).
   - 4.2. Mean low waterline to end of pier–50 psf (2304 Pa).

3603.4 Wind loads. Design wind loads shall be as prescribed in Chapter 16.

3603.5 Impact loads. Design impact loads shall be as prescribed in Chapter 16 but not less than 1.25 times the kinetic energy exerted by a striking vessel or vehicle.

3603.6 Water loads. Hydrostatic horizontal pressures along with the equivalent fluid pressure of soil and any surcharge thereon shall be considered. Sufficient anchorage against uplift between all components and between the structure and its support of not less than 1.5 times the uplift force shall be provided. Wave forces shall be determined from wave records where available. Where no wave records are available, the design wave shall be determined from probable wind speed, direction, fetch and water depth that will yield a critical wave. Forces shall then be calculated using accepted engineering practice.

3603.7 Earth loads. Lateral earth pressures shall be determined by considering the specific soil properties and applying earth pressure theories generally accepted for soil mechanics in engineering practice. Except for simple and inexpensive structures this normally requires the services of specialists in soil mechanics or foundations design. Adequate consideration shall be given for the effect of probable varying levels of ground water, tide and flood water. Pressures exerted by the earth shall be checked for dry, saturated and submerged conditions as applicable.

3603.8 Erosion. The effects of reasonably predictable erosion and wave-induced scour shall be given ample consideration.

SECTION 3604 ENGINEERED DESIGNS

3604.1 Docks, piers and catwalks. Docks, piers and catwalks used by the public or are intended for use by vehicles shall be designed by a registered design professional.

3604.2 Bulkheads and other type retaining walls. Bulkheads and other types of retaining walls used by the public having an exposed face above the ground or above mean low water of 5 feet (1524 mm) or greater shall be designed by a registered design professional.

3604.3 Ocean-front retaining walls, bulkheads and retaining walls. Ocean-front retaining walls, bulkheads and other types of retaining walls used by the public on the coastline of the ocean or adjacent inlets shall be designed by a registered design professional.

SECTION 3605 MATERIALS

3605.1 General. The quality of materials and fastenings used for load-supporting purposes shall conform to good engineering practices. In areas subject to attack from wood borers, such as termites, teredoes or limnoria, the wood used shall be approved wood having natural resistance or shall be pressure treated with a preservative recommended by the American Wood Preservers' Association for the specific application. Piling shall comply with applicable provisions of Chapter 18. Wood components shall comply with applicable provisions of Chapter 23. Concrete components shall comply with applicable provisions of Chapter 19. Steel components shall comply with applicable provisions of Chapter 22. In areas of severe corrosion, such as salty or brackish waters, all metal components shall be protected by coating, cathodic protection or be oversized accordingly to allow for the specific exposure. Aluminum bulkhead sheets or aluminum bulkhead or dock components shall be of proper alloy to resist corrosive elements in the adjacent water and soil. Galvanized bulkhead components and dock components shall be coated by the "hot dip" process to sufficient cover to provide corrosion protection equal to the degree of exposure of corrosive elements. Masonry used in bulkheads and dock work shall comply with Chapter 21.

SECTION 3606 CONSTRUCTION OF PIERS, DOCKS, CATWALKS AND FLOATING DOCKS

3606.1 Fixed piers. Fixed piers for coastal areas shall be supported by pilings with tip penetrations of not less than 8 feet (2438 mm) dependent on the total applied load. Less penetration is approved only if other means of resisting flotation uplift is provided. Pier support by shallow piling, legs or columns with point bearing on rock shall have provisions for horizontal forces and overturn as well as flotation uplift. Connection between piling or legs to cap beams, stringers, beams and deck shall have sufficient capacity to safely support all applied loads and provide transfer of load to adjoining members. Maximum spans for pier joists shall be in accordance with the AF&PA joist and rafter span tables or may be designed in accordance with accepted engineering practice.

3606.2 Metal barrel flotation units. The use of metal barrels not specifically designed for use as flotation devices is prohibited.

3606.3 Decomposable flotation units. Floating docks or piers using exposed polystyrene billets (or other foam material) shall be designed for 125 percent of tabulated loads to allow for deterioration from environmental effects.

3606.4 Electrical service. All electrical service to marine structures shall be in accordance with the *North Carolina Electrical Code.*

3606.5 Fuel docks. Fuel docks and other marine facilities handling flammable liquids shall comply with the *Flammable and Combustible Liquids Code*, NFPA 30 and the *North Carolina Fire Code*. All fuel installations shall be designed to prevent fuel spillage from entering the water. The fuel docks or floats shall be a separate structure from berths and shall be isolated to the extent that fire or explosion would have minimal opportunity to spread to or from the fuel dock to the berths. Storage tanks for public facilities shall be located a minimum distance of 50 feet (15 240 mm) from the dispenser with a shutoff valve at the tank.

3606.6 Handrails. For walkways, access piers, steps or ranges, personnel handrails or other safety provisions shall be provided along the edges where the vertical drop to the mean low water level or mud line exceeds 6 feet (1829 mm). Edges have a primary function other than walks or access ways, such as docking frontage and swimming access shall not require railings. Railings shall be designed in accordance with Chapter 16 for balcony railings.

3606.7 Maintenance of public structures. The building official shall have the authority to condemn and close to the public any structure that is considered unsafe, and it shall not be used by the public until the deficiencies are corrected. Before the structure is reopened to the public, a certification by a registered design professional shall be required. Each owner shall be responsible for the proper and satisfactory maintenance of any public structure covered by this section. All such structures shall be subject to inspection at any time by the building official.

SECTION 3607 CONSTRUCTION: BULKHEADS, SEAWALLS AND REVETMENTS

3607.1 Bulkheads.

3607.1.1 Bulkheads shall be constructed in a manner to be effective against erosion and provide for bank stabilization. The bulkhead system may consist of either of the following combinations thereof: braced sheet pile walls with tie backs, king piles and horizontal panels, gravity walls, cantilever and counterfort retaining walls. Bulkhead walls shall be constructed to prevent passage of fine material through joints or cracks from the fill side to the stream side.

3607.1.2 Local site conditions and performance of bulkheads in service shall govern in selection of a system. The potential for erosion and scour at the mudline shall also be investigated, and compensating features shall be reflected in the construction. Bulkheads shall be terminated by either tying into adjoining structures or by extending the bulkhead-line a minimum of 10 feet (3048 mm) in a landward direction at an angle of not less than 45 degrees (0.79 rad) to the shoreline in order to protect against end erosion or flanking by wave action. No structure shall be terminated without regard for end anchorage and stabilization. Sheet pile bulkheads with an exposed vertical height of 4 feet (1219 mm) or greater shall be stabilized at the top by providing anchorage, such as the use of batter piles or tie backs. Anchor blocks for tie backs shall be located landward of the soil wedge formed by the wall and a line projected on an angle of the material being retained. The tie back anchor shall be located no closer than twice the height of the exposed vertical surface of the wall. Sheet pile embedment shall be determined by analysis and design, but shall not be less than the length of the pile exposed above ground. Cantilever and gravity wall bulkheads shall be founded on a firm foundation with consideration given to undermining and progressive instability.

3607.1.3 Where public walkways, steps or ramps run adjacent to bulkheads, personnel handrails or other safety provisions shall be provided along the top of the wall where the vertical drop to the mean low waterline or mudline exceeds 6 feet (1829 mm). Handrails shall be designed in accordance with Chapter 16 for balcony railings.

3607.1.4 Wood members used for permanent features shall be not less than 2 inches (51 mm) in nominal thickness. All steel bolts, rods and other hardware shall be hot-dipped galvanized or protected with an equivalent system. Bolts, rods and other metal materials shall be no smaller than $^1/_2$ inch (12.7 mm) in diameter or thickness. Threaded fasteners shall not be tightened directly against wood surfaces but used only in conjunction with standard ogee or flat washers.

3607.1.5 Concrete, steel and cement asbestos bulkheads shall be constructed in a manner to ensure performance. Connections shall be designed to resist the full applied load. Attention shall be given to material protection against corrosion and concrete cover for reinforcing steel. Concrete shall have a 28-day minimum compressive strength of 3,000 pounds per square inch (20 685 kPa) and shall be "air-entrained" type concrete.

3607.2 Seawalls. Seawalls may be constructed of concrete or stone rubble mound or other approved materials. They shall be founded on a firm foundation and may require the use of piling or other approved support. The face shall be shaped and supported to withstand the full force of the design wave. A provision shall be provided to prevent undermining and progressive instability by installing a sheet pile wall along the toe or by placing stone rip rap protection.

3607.3 Revetments.

3607.3.1 Rigid revetments shall be founded on a firm foundation to prevent undermining and progressive instability. Provisions shall be made to provide for adequate toe protection by extending the face a minimum of 2 feet (610 mm) below the mudline, plus a depth to compensate for known or anticipated scour. Additional protection may be needed in active areas and may consist of sheet piling along the toe or stone rip rap. An adequate pattern of weep holes shall be provided in the face to relieve hydrostatic pressure behind the wall. Joints shall be sealed to prevent loss of fines from the protected slope.

3607.3.2 Flexible revetments may be utilized where foundations will produce minor consolidation and settlement. Adequate provisions shall be made to prevent migration of fine materials through the wall. The face shall not be steeper than one unit horizontal to one unit vertical. Flatter slopes may be needed for stability depending on the construction materials and site conditions. The face may consist of stone rip rap or individual interlocking concrete units or poured concrete. Toe protection provisions shall be provided as discussed for the rigid type. Flexible revetments must be porous enough to allow for water passage and thereby relieve hydrostatic pressure behind the face.

SECTION 3608
CONSTRUCTION OF GROINS AND JETTIES

3608.1 Groins.

3608.1.1 Groins are designed and constructed for the purpose of building or maintaining a protection beach by trapping littoral drift (beach materials) or to retard the recession of an eroding shoreline. The planning and design of a groin/groin system shall be based on wave height, period and direction, characteristics of beach material and beach slope.

3608.1.2 Location. Groins shall extend landward a sufficient distance to prevent flanking.

3608.1.3 Types. Groins shall be either (1) very low, impermeable and nonadjustable or (2) impermeable and adjustable.

3608.1.4 General specifications. Adjustable groins shall be maintained at elevations in accord with actual beach needs and development of desirable changes of the beach profile, and so as to avoid damage to adjacent beaches. In no case shall the top of such groins be set higher than 2 feet (610 mm) above the beach profile. Impermeable, nonadjustable groins shall not extend seaward beyond the mean low water line, and their top elevation shall not be higher than 6 inches (152 mm) above the beach profile. Considerations of the degree of beach protection to be provided by proposed groins, and the acceptability of such installations, will be based primarily on the following factors: direction and volume of littoral drift; wave force and direction; wind force and direction; land usage; type of bulkhead; type of groin; and spacing and lengths of groins. A complete coastal engineering study may be required before approval is given to the number, type and length of groins. The design shall account for the wave and current forces focused on the beach. The groin/groin system shall not adversely modify the littoral drift to the extent to cause erosion on the lee side of the structure.

3608.2 Groins and jetties. There is no universal type of groin/groin system or jetty because of the wide variations in conditions at each location. It is incumbent on the owner of a groin or jetty type structure to recognize the legal implications of the coastal structure and to plan, design, construct and maintain the structure accordingly. It is thus prudent to seek the advice of a registered design professional with coastal engineering experience.

SECTION 3609 DEFINITIONS

BASIN, BOAT. A naturally or artificially enclosed or nearly enclosed harbor area for docking and securing small craft.

BULKHEAD. A vertical wall structure designed to retain shoreline material and prevent erosion due to wave activity.

BULKHEAD LINE. The line formed along the shore by the most seaward elements of the bulkhead.

CATWALK. A narrow footway platform extending alongside a structure.

DATUM, PLANE. The horizontal plane to which soundings, ground elevations water surface elevations are referenced.

DOCK. A pier, wharf or platform for the unloading of materials or living beings.

FETCH. The area in which waves are generated having a rather constant direction or speed.

GANGWAY. A narrow footway bridge extending from the shore, usually to a floating structure.

GROIN. A shore protection structure built (usually perpendicular to the shoreline) to trap littoral drift or retard erosion of the shore.

GROIN SYSTEM. A series of groins that function to protect a section of shoreline.

JETTY. A structure designed to protect and/or stabilize a navigation entrance.

KING PILE. The primary structural member that supports horizontal panels to form a vertical wall sometimes used in bulkhead or groin construction.

LITTORAL DRIFT. The sedimentary material transported along the shore by waves and currents.

LONGSHORE TRANSPORT. The movement of littoral drift (material) running parallel to the shoreline.

PIER. An elevated deck structure, usually pile supported, extending out into the water from the shore.

PIERHEAD LINE. The limiting line to which any pier or dock structure can extend into the water.

PILE. A cylindrical timber, concrete or metal member embedded into the ground to support or brace a structure.

PILE, SHEET. A pile with a generally slender flat cross section to be embedded into the ground or seabed and meshed or interlocked with like members to form a diaphragm, wall or bulkhead.

REVETMENT. A flexible structure usually constructed of stone or concrete and placed on a bank slope to protect it against erosion by wave and current action.

SEAWALL. A massive structure built along and parallel to a shoreline for the purpose of protecting and stabilizing the shore against erosion resulting from heavy wave activity.

WAVE, DESIGN. A wave that is potentially most damaging to an economically feasible structure, or wave for which a structure is designed.

APPENDIX A

EMPLOYEE QUALIFICATIONS

Deleted.

APPENDIX B
BOARD OF APPEALS

Deleted.

APPENDIX C

GROUP U–AGRICULTURAL BUILDINGS

The provisions contained in this appendix are adopted as part of this code.

SECTION C101 GENERAL

C101.1 Scope. The provisions of this appendix shall apply exclusively to agricultural buildings. Such buildings shall be classified as Group U and shall include the following uses:

1. Livestock shelters or buildings, including shade structures and milking barns.
2. Poultry buildings or shelters.
3. Barns.
4. Storage of equipment and machinery used exclusively in agriculture.
5. Horticultural structures, including detached production greenhouses and crop protection shelters.
6. Sheds.
7. Grain silos.
8. Stables.

SECTION C102 ALLOWABLE HEIGHT AND AREA

C102.1 General. Buildings classified as Group U Agricultural shall not exceed the area or height limits specified in Table C102.1.

C102.2 One-story unlimited area. The area of a one-story Group U agricultural building shall not be limited if the building is surrounded and adjoined by *public ways* or yards not less than 60 feet (18 288 mm) in width.

C102.3 Two-story unlimited area. The area of a two-story Group U agricultural building shall not be limited if the building is surrounded and adjoined by *public ways* or *yards* not less than 60 feet (18 288 mm) in width and is provided with an approved automatic sprinkler system throughout in accordance with Section 903.3.1.1.

SECTION C103 MIXED OCCUPANCIES

C103.1 Mixed occupancies. Mixed occupancies shall be protected in accordance with Section 508.

SECTION C104 EXITS

C104.1 Exit facilities. Exits shall be provided in accordance with Chapters 10 and 11.

Exceptions:

1. The maximum travel distance from any point in the building to an approved exit shall not exceed 300 feet (91 440 mm).
2. One exit is required for each 15,000 square feet (1393.5 m^2) of area or fraction thereof.

TABLE C102.1—BASIC ALLOWABLE AREA FOR A GROUP U, ONE STORY IN HEIGHT AND MAXIMUM HEIGHT OF SUCH OCCUPANCY

I		II		III and IV		V	
A	B	A	B	III A and IV	III B	A	B
ALLOWABLE AREA (square feet)[a]							
Unlimited	60,000	27,100	18,000	27,100	18,000	21,100	12,000
MAXIMUM HEIGHT IN STORIES							
Unlimited	12	4	2	4	2	3	2
MAXIMUM HEIGHT IN FEET							
Unlimited	160	65	55	65	55	50	40

For SI: 1 square foot = 0.0929 m^2.

a. See Section C102 for unlimited area under certain conditions.

APPENDIX D
FIRE DISTRICTS

The provisions contained in this appendix are adopted as part of this code.

SECTION D101
GENERAL

D101.1 Scope. The fire district shall include such territory or portion as outlined in an ordinance or law entitled "An Ordinance (Resolution) Creating and Establishing a Fire District." Wherever, in such ordinance creating and establishing a fire district, reference is made to the fire district, it shall be construed to mean the fire district designated and referred to in this appendix.

D101.1.1 Mapping. The fire district complying with the provisions of Section D101.1 shall be shown on a map that shall be available to the public.

D101.2 Establishment of area. For the purpose of this code, the fire district shall include that territory or area as described in Sections D101.2.1 through D101.2.3.

D101.2.1 Adjoining blocks. Two or more adjoining blocks, exclusive of intervening streets, where at least 50 percent of the ground area is built upon and more than 50 percent of the built-on area is devoted to hotels and motels of Group R-1; Group B occupancies; theaters, nightclubs, restaurants of Group A-1 and A-2 occupancies; garages, express and freight depots, warehouses and storage buildings used for the storage of finished products (not located with and forming a part of a manufactured or industrial plant); or Group S occupancy. Where the average height of a building is two and one-half *stories* or more, a block should be considered if the ground area built upon is at least 40 percent.

D101.2.2 Buffer zone. Where four contiguous blocks or more comprise a fire district, there shall be a buffer zone of 200 feet (60 960 mm) around the perimeter of such district. Streets, rights-of-way and other open spaces not subject to building construction can be included in the 200-foot (60 960 mm) buffer zone.

D101.2.3 Developed blocks. Where blocks adjacent to the fire district have developed to the extent that at least 25 percent of the ground area is built upon and 40 percent or more of the built-on area is devoted to the occupancies specified in Section D101.2.1, they can be considered for inclusion in the fire district, and can form all or a portion of the 200-foot (60 960 mm) buffer zone required in Section D101.2.2.

SECTION D102
BUILDING RESTRICTIONS

D102.1 Types of construction permitted. Within the fire district every building hereafter erected shall be either Type I, II, III or IV, except as permitted in Section D104.

D102.2 Other specific requirements.

D102.2.1 Exterior walls. Exterior walls of buildings located in the fire district shall comply with the requirements in Table 601 except as required in Section D102.2.6.

D102.2.2 Group H prohibited. Group H occupancies shall be prohibited from location within the fire district.

D102.2.3 Construction type. Every building shall be constructed as required based on the type of construction indicated in Chapter 6.

D102.2.4 Roof covering. Roof covering in the fire district shall conform to the requirements of Class A or B roof coverings as defined in Section 1505.

D102.2.5 Structural fire rating. Walls, floors, roofs and their supporting structural members shall be a minimum of 1-hour fire-resistance-rated construction.

Exceptions:

1. Buildings of Type IV construction.
2. Buildings equipped throughout with an *automatic sprinkler system* in accordance with Section 903.3.1.1.
3. Automobile parking structures.
4. Buildings surrounded on all sides by a permanently open space of not less than 30 feet (9144 mm).
5. Partitions complying with Section 603.1, Item 10.

D102.2.6 Exterior walls. Exterior load-bearing walls of Type II buildings shall have a *fire-resistance rating* of 2 hours or more where such walls are located within 30 feet (9144 mm) of a common property line or an assumed property line. Exterior nonload-bearing walls of Type II buildings located within 30 feet (9144 mm) of a common property line or an assumed property line shall have fireresistance ratings as required by Table 601, but not less than 1 hour. Exterior walls located more than 30 feet (9144 mm) from a common property line or an assumed property line shall comply with Table 601.

Exception: In the case of one-story buildings that are 2,000 square feet (186 m^2) or less in area, exterior walls located more than 15 feet (4572 mm) from a common property line or an assumed property line need only comply with Table 601.

D102.2.7 Architectural trim. Architectural *trim* on buildings located in the fire district shall be constructed of *approved* noncombustible materials or *fire-retardant-treated wood*.

D102.2.8 Permanent canopies. Permanent canopies are permitted to extend over adjacent open spaces provided all of the following are met:

1. The canopy and its supports shall be of noncombustible material, *fire-retardant-treated wood*, Type IV construction or of 1-hour fire-resistance-rated construction.

   Exception: Any textile covering for the canopy shall be flame resistant as determined by tests conducted in accordance with NFPA 701 after both accelerated water leaching and accelerated weathering.

2. Any canopy covering, other than textiles, shall have a *flame spread index* not greater than 25 when tested in accordance with ASTM E 84 or UL 723 in the form intended for use.
3. The canopy shall have at least one long side open.
4. The maximum horizontal width of the canopy shall not exceed 15 feet (4572 mm).
5. The *fire resistance of exterior walls* shall not be reduced.

D102.2.9 Roof structures. Structures, except aerial supports 12 feet (3658 mm) high or less, flagpoles, water tanks and cooling towers, placed above the roof of any building within the fire district shall be of noncombustible material and shall be supported by construction of noncombustible material.

D102.2.10 Plastic signs. The use of plastics complying with Section 2611 for signs is permitted provided the structure of the sign in which the plastic is mounted or installed is noncombustible.

D102.2.11 Plastic veneer. Exterior plastic veneer is not permitted in the fire district.

SECTION D103 CHANGES TO BUILDINGS

D103.1 Existing buildings within the fire district. An existing building shall not hereafter be increased in height or area unless it is of a type of construction permitted for new buildings within the fire district or is altered to comply with the requirements for such type of construction. Nor shall any existing building be hereafter extended on any side, nor square footage or floors added within the existing building unless such modifications are of a type of construction permitted for new buildings within the fire district.

D103.2 Other alterations. Nothing in Section D103.1 shall prohibit other alterations within the fire district provided there is no change of occupancy that is otherwise prohibited and the fire hazard is not increased by such *alteration*.

D103.3 Moving buildings. Buildings shall not hereafter be moved into the fire district or to another lot in the fire district unless the building is of a type of construction permitted in the fire district.

SECTION D104 BUILDINGS LOCATED PARTIALLY IN THE FIRE DISTRICT

D104.1 General. Any building located partially in the fire district shall be of a type of construction required for the fire district, unless the major portion of such building lies outside of the fire district and no part is more than 10 feet (3048 mm) inside the boundaries of the fire district.

SECTION D105 EXCEPTIONS TO RESTRICTIONS IN FIRE DISTRICT

D105.1 General. The preceding provisions of this appendix shall not apply in the following instances:

1. Temporary buildings used in connection with duly authorized construction.
2. A private garage used exclusively as such, not more than one *story* in height, nor more than 650 square feet (60 m^2) in area, located on the same lot with a *dwelling*.
3. Fences not over 8 feet (2438 mm) high.
4. Coal tipples, material bins and trestles of Type IV construction.
5. Water tanks and cooling towers conforming to Sections 1509.3 and 1509.4.
6. Greenhouses less than 15 feet (4572 mm) high.
7. Porches on dwellings not over one *story* in height, and not over 10 feet (3048 mm) wide from the face of the building, provided such porch does not come within 5 feet (1524 mm) of any property line.
8. Sheds open on a long side not over 15 feet (4572 mm) high and 500 square feet (46 m^2) in area.
9. One- and two-family *dwellings* where of a type of construction not permitted in the fire district can be extended 25 percent of the floor area existing at the time of inclusion in the fire district by any type of construction permitted by this code.
10. Wood decks less than 600 square feet (56 m^2) where constructed of 2-inch (51 mm) nominal wood, pressure treated for exterior use.
11. Wood veneers on *exterior walls* conforming to Section 1405.5.
12. Exterior plastic veneer complying with Section 2605.2 where installed on exterior walls required to have a *fire-resistance rating* not less than 1 hour, provided the exterior plastic veneer does not exhibit sustained flaming as defined in NFPA 268.

SECTION D106
REFERENCED STANDARDS

ASTM E 84-04	Test Method for Surface Burning Characteristics of Building Materials	D102.2.8
NFPA 268-01	Test Method for Determining Ignitability of Exterior Wall Assemblies Using a Radiant Heat Energy Source	D105.1
NFPA 701-99	Methods of Fire Tests for Flame-Propagation of Textiles and Films	D102.2.8
UL 723-03	Standard for Test for Surface Burning Characteristics of Building Materials, with Revisions through May 2005	D102.2.8

APPENDIX E
SUPPLEMENTARY ACCESSIBILITY REQUIREMENTS

The provisions contained in this appendix are adopted as part of this code.

SECTION E101 GENERAL

E101.1 Scope. The provisions of this appendix shall control the supplementary requirements for the design and construction of facilities for *accessibility* to physically disabled persons.

E101.2 Design. Technical requirements for items herein shall comply with this code and ICC A117.1.

SECTION E102 DEFINITIONS

E102.1 General. The following words and terms shall, for the purposes of this appendix, have the meanings shown herein.

CLOSED-CIRCUIT TELEPHONE. A telephone with a dedicated line such as a house phone, courtesy phone or phone that must be used to gain entrance to a facility.

MAILBOXES. Receptacles for the receipt of documents, packages or other deliverable matter. Mailboxes include, but are not limited to, post office boxes and receptacles provided by commercial mail-receiving agencies, apartment houses and schools.

TRANSIENT LODGING. A building, facility or portion thereof, excluding inpatient medical care facilities and long-term care facilities, that contains one or more dwelling units or sleeping units. Examples of transient lodging include, but are not limited to, resorts, group homes, hotels, motels, dormitories, homeless shelters, halfway houses and social service lodging.

SECTION E103 ACCESSIBLE ROUTE

E103.1 Raised platforms. In banquet rooms or spaces where a head table or speaker's lectern is located on a raised platform, an *accessible* route shall be provided to the platform.

SECTION E104 SPECIAL OCCUPANCIES

E104.1 General. Transient lodging facilities shall be provided with *accessible* features in accordance with Sections E104.2 and E104.3. Group I-3 occupancies shall be provided with *accessible* features in accordance with Sections E104.3 and E104.4.

E104.2 Accessible beds. In rooms or spaces having more than 25 beds, 5 percent of the beds shall have a clear floor space complying with ICC A117.1.

E104.2.1 Sleeping areas. A clear floor space complying with ICC A117.1 shall be provided on both sides of the accessible bed. The clear floor space shall be positioned for parallel approach to the side of the bed.

Exception: This requirement shall not apply where a single clear floor space complying with ICC A117.1 positioned for parallel approach is provided between two beds.

E104.3 Communication features. Communication features complying with ICC A117.1 shall be provided in accordance with Sections E104.3.1 through E104.3.4.

E104.3.1 Transient lodging. In transient lodging facilities, sleeping units with accessible communication features shall be provided in accordance with Table E104.3.1. Units required to comply with Table E104.3.1 shall be dispersed among the various classes of units.

E104.3.2 Group I-3. In Group I-3 occupancies at least 2 percent, but no fewer than one of the total number of general holding cells and general housing cells equipped with audible emergency alarm systems and permanently installed telephones within the cell, shall comply with Section E104.3.4.

E104.3.3 Dwelling units and sleeping units. Where *dwelling units* and *sleeping units* are altered or added, the requirements of Section E104.3 shall apply only to the units being altered or added until the number of units with accessible communication features complies with the minimum number required for new construction.

E104.3.4 Notification devices. Visual notification devices shall be provided to alert room occupants of incoming telephone calls and a door knock or bell. Notification devices shall not be connected to visual alarm signal appliances. Permanently installed telephones shall have volume controls and an electrical outlet complying with ICC A117.1 located within 48 inches (1219 mm) of the telephone to facilitate the use of a TTY.

E104.4 Partitions. Solid partitions or security glazing that separates visitors from detainees in Group I-3 occupancies shall provide a method to facilitate voice communication. Such methods are permitted to include, but are not limited to, grilles, slats, talk-through baffles, intercoms or telephone handset devices. The method of communication shall be accessible to individuals who use wheelchairs and individuals who have difficulty bending or stooping. Hand-operable communication devices, if provided, shall comply with Section E106.3.

SECTION E105
OTHER FEATURES AND FACILITIES

E105.1 Portable toilets and bathing rooms. Where multiple single-user portable toilet or bathing units are clustered at a single location, at least 5 percent, but not less than one toilet unit or bathing unit at each cluster, shall comply with ICC A117.1. Signs containing the International Symbol of Accessibility and complying with ICC A117.1 shall identify *accessible* portable toilets and bathing units.

Exception: Portable toilet units provided for use exclusively by construction personnel on a construction site.

E105.2 Laundry equipment. Where provided in spaces required to be *accessible*, washing machines and clothes dryers shall comply with this section.

E105.2.1 Washing machines. Where three or fewer washing machines are provided, at least one shall comply with ICC A117.1. Where more than three washing machines are provided, at least two shall comply with ICC A117.1.

E105.2.2 Clothes dryers. Where three or fewer clothes dryers are provided, at least one shall comply with ICC A117.1. Where more than three clothes dryers are provided, at least two shall comply with ICC A117.1.

E105.3 Depositories, vending machines, change machines and similar equipment. Where provided, at least one of each type of depository, vending machine, change machine and similar equipment shall comply with ICC A117.1.

Exception: Drive-up-only depositories are not required to comply with this section.

E105.4 Mailboxes. Where mailboxes are provided in an interior location, at least 5 percent, but not less than one, of each type shall comply with ICC A117.1. In residential and institutional facilities, where mailboxes are provided for each *dwelling unit* or *sleeping unit*, mailboxes complying with ICC A117.1 shall be provided for each unit required to be an *Accessible unit.*

E105.5 Automatic teller machines and fare machines. Where automatic teller machines or self-service fare vending, collection or adjustment machines are provided, at least one machine of each type at each location where such machines are provided shall be *accessible*. Where bins are provided for envelopes, wastepaper or other purposes, at least one of each type shall be accessible.

E105.6 Two-way communication systems. Where two-way communication systems are provided to gain admittance to a building or facility or to restricted areas within a building or facility, the system shall comply with ICC A117.1.

SECTION E106
TELEPHONES

E106.1 General. Where coin-operated public pay telephones, coinless public pay telephones, public closed-circuit telephones, courtesy phones or other types of public telephones are provided, *accessible* public telephones shall be provided in accordance with Sections E106.2 through E106.5 for each type of public telephone provided. For purposes of this section, a bank of telephones shall be considered two or more adjacent telephones.

E106.2 Wheelchair-accessible telephones. Where public telephones are provided, *wheelchair-accessible* telephones complying with ICC A117.1 shall be provided in accordance with Table E106.2.

Exception: Drive-up-only public telephones are not required to be *accessible*.

TABLE E104.3.1
DWELLING OR SLEEPING UNITS WITH ACCESSIBLE COMMUNICATION FEATURES

TOTAL NUMBER OF DWELLING OR SLEEPING UNITS PROVIDED	MINIMUM REQUIRED NUMBER OF DWELLING OR SLEEPING UNITS WITH ACCESSIBLE COMMUNICATION FEATURES
1	1
2 to 25	2
26 to 50	4
51 to 75	7
76 to 100	9
101 to 150	12
151 to 200	14
201 to 300	17
301 to 400	20
401 to 500	22
501 to 1,000	5% of total
1,001 and over	50 plus 3 for each 100 over 1,000

TABLE E106.2
WHEELCHAIR-ACCESSIBLE TELEPHONES

NUMBER OF TELEPHONES PROVIDED ON A FLOOR, LEVEL OR EXTERIOR SITE	MINIMUM REQUIRED NUMBER OF WHEELCHAIR-ACCESSIBLE TELEPHONES
1 or more single unit	1 per floor, level and exterior site
1 bank	1 per floor, level and exterior site
2 or more banks	1 per bank

E106.3 Volume controls. All public telephones provided shall have volume control complying with ICC A117.1.

E106.4 TTYs. TTYs complying with ICC A117.1 shall be provided in accordance with Sections E106.4.1 through E106.4.9.

E106.4.1 Bank requirement. Where four or more public pay telephones are provided at a bank of telephones, at least one public TTY shall be provided at that bank.

Exception: TTYs are not required at banks of telephones located within 200 feet (60 960 mm) of, and on the same floor as, a bank containing a public TTY.

E106.4.2 Floor requirement. Where four or more public pay telephones are provided on a floor of a privately owned building, at least one public TTY shall be provided on that floor. Where at least one public pay telephone is provided on a floor of a publicly owned building, at least one public TTY shall be provided on that floor.

E106.4.3 Building requirement. Where four or more public pay telephones are provided in a privately owned building, at least one public TTY shall be provided in the building. Where at least one public pay telephone is provided in a publicly owned building, at least one public TTY shall be provided in the building.

E106.4.4 Site requirement. Where four or more public pay telephones are provided on a site, at least one public TTY shall be provided on the site.

E106.4.5 Rest stops, emergency road stops, and service plazas. Where a public pay telephone is provided at a public rest stop, emergency road stop or service plaza, at least one public TTY shall be provided.

E106.4.6 Hospitals. Where a public pay telephone is provided in or adjacent to a hospital emergency room, hospital recovery room or hospital waiting room, at least one public TTY shall be provided at each such location.

E106.4.7 Transportation facilities. Transportation facilities shall be provided with TTYs in accordance with Sections E109.2.5 and E110.2 in addition to the TTYs required by Sections E106.4.1 through E106.4.4.

E106.4.8 Detention and correctional facilities. In detention and correctional facilities, where a public pay telephone is provided in a secured area used only by detainees or inmates and security personnel, then at least one TTY shall be provided in at least one secured area.

E106.4.9 Signs. Public TTYs shall be identified by the International Symbol of TTY complying with ICC A117.1. Directional signs indicating the location of the nearest public TTY shall be provided at banks of public pay telephones not containing a public TTY. Additionally, where signs provide direction to public pay telephones, they shall also provide direction to public TTYs. Such signs shall comply with ICC A117.1 and shall include the International Symbol of TTY.

E106.5 Shelves for portable TTYs. Where a bank of telephones in the interior of a building consists of three or more public pay telephones, at least one public pay telephone at the bank shall be provided with a shelf and an electrical outlet in accordance with ICC A117.1.

Exceptions:

1. In secured areas of detention and correctional facilities, if shelves and outlets are prohibited for purposes of security or safety shelves and outlets for TTYs are not required to be provided.
2. The shelf and electrical outlet shall not be required at a bank of telephones with a TTY.

SECTION E107 SIGNAGE

E107.1 Signs. Required *accessible* portable toilets and bathing facilities shall be identified by the International Symbol of Accessibility.

E107.2 Designations. Interior and exterior signs identifying permanent rooms and spaces shall be tactile. Where pictograms are provided as designations of interior rooms and spaces, the pictograms shall have tactile text descriptors. Signs required to provide tactile characters and pictograms shall comply with ICC A117.1.

Exceptions:

1. Exterior signs that are not located at the door to the space they serve are not required to comply.
2. Building directories, menus, seat and row designations in assembly areas, occupant names, building addresses and company names and logos are not required to comply.
3. Signs in parking facilities are not required to comply.
4. Temporary (seven days or less) signs are not required to comply.
5. In detention and correctional facilities, signs not located in public areas are not required to comply.

E107.3 Directional and informational signs. Signs that provide direction to, or information about, permanent interior spaces of the site and facilities shall contain visual characters complying with ICC A117.1.

Exception: Building directories, personnel names, company or occupant names and logos, menus and temporary (seven days or less) signs are not required to comply with ICC A117.1.

E107.4 Other signs. Signage indicating special accessibility provisions shall be provided as follows:

1. At bus stops and terminals, signage must be provided in accordance with Section E108.4.
2. At fixed facilities and stations, signage must be provided in accordance with Sections E109.2.2 through E109.2.2.3.
3. At airports, terminal information systems must be provided in accordance with Section E110.3.

SECTION E108 BUS STOPS

E108.1 General. Bus stops shall comply with Sections E108.2 through E108.5.

E108.2 Bus boarding and alighting areas. Bus boarding and alighting areas shall comply with Sections E108.2.1 through E108.2.4.

E108.2.1 Surface. Bus boarding and alighting areas shall have a firm, stable surface.

E108.2.2 Dimensions. Bus boarding and alighting areas shall have a clear length of 96 inches (2440 mm) minimum, measured perpendicular to the curb or vehicle roadway edge, and a clear width of 60 inches (1525 mm) minimum, measured parallel to the vehicle roadway.

E108.2.3 Connection. Bus boarding and alighting areas shall be connected to streets, sidewalks or pedestrian paths by an accessible route complying with Section 1104.

E108.2.4 Slope. Parallel to the roadway, the slope of the bus boarding and alighting area shall be the same as the roadway, to the maximum extent practicable. For water drainage, a maximum slope of 1:48 perpendicular to the roadway is allowed.

E108.3 Bus shelters. Where provided, new or replaced bus shelters shall provide a minimum clear floor or ground space complying with ICC A117.1, Section 305, entirely within the shelter. Such shelters shall be connected by an accessible route to the boarding area required by Section E108.2.

E108.4 Signs. New bus route identification signs shall have finish and contrast complying with ICC A117.1. Additionally, to the maximum extent practicable, new bus route identification signs shall provide visual characters complying with ICC A117.1.

Exception: Bus schedules, timetables and maps that are posted at the bus stop or bus bay are not required to meet this requirement.

E108.5 Bus stop siting. Bus stop sites shall be chosen such that, to the maximum extent practicable, the areas where lifts or ramps are to be deployed comply with Sections E108.2 and E108.3.

SECTION E109 TRANSPORTATION FACILITIES AND STATIONS

E109.1 General. Fixed transportation facilities and stations shall comply with the applicable provisions of Section E109.2.

E109.2 New construction. New stations in rapid rail, light rail, commuter rail, intercity rail, high speed rail and other fixed guideway systems shall comply with Sections E109.2.1 through E109.2.8.

E109.2.1 Station entrances. Where different entrances to a station serve different transportation fixed routes or groups of fixed routes, at least one entrance serving each group or route shall comply with Section 1104 and ICC A117.1.

E109.2.2 Signs. Signage in fixed transportation facilities and stations shall comply with Sections E109.2.2.1 through E109.2.2.3.

E109.2.2.1 Tactile signs. Where signs are provided at entrances to stations identifying the station or the entrance, or both, at least one sign at each entrance shall be tactile. A minimum of one tactile sign identifying the specific station shall be provided on each platform or boarding area. Such signs shall be placed in uniform locations at entrances and on platforms or boarding areas within the transit system to the maximum extent practicable. Tactile signs shall comply with ICC A117.1.

Exceptions:

1. Where the station has no defined entrance but signs are provided, the tactile signs shall be placed in a central location.
2. Signs are not required to be tactile where audible signs are remotely transmitted to hand-held receivers, or are user or proximity actuated.

E109.2.2.2 Identification signs. Stations covered by this section shall have identification signs containing visual characters complying with ICC A117.1. Signs shall be clearly visible and within the sightlines of a standing or sitting passenger from within the train on both sides when not obstructed by another train.

E109.2.2.3 Informational signs. Lists of stations, routes and destinations served by the station which are located on boarding areas, platforms or mezzanines shall provide visual characters complying with ICC A117.1 Signs covered by this provision shall, to the maximum extent practicable, be placed in uniform locations within the transit system.

E109.2.3 Fare machines. Self-service fare vending, collection and adjustment machines shall comply with ICC A117.1, Section 707. Where self-service fare vending, collection or adjustment machines are provided for the use of the general public, at least one accessible machine of each type provided shall be provided at each accessible point of entry and exit.

E109.2.4 Rail-to-platform height. Station platforms shall be positioned to coordinate with vehicles in accordance with the applicable provisions of 36 CFR, Part 1192. Low-level platforms shall be 8 inches (250 mm) minimum above top of rail.

Exception: Where vehicles are boarded from sidewalks or street level, low-level platforms shall be permitted to be less than 8 inches (250 mm).

E109.2.5 TTYs. Where a public pay telephone is provided in a transit facility (as defined by the Department of Transportation) at least one public TTY complying with ICC A117.1, Section 704.4, shall be provided in the station. In addition, where one or more public pay telephones serve a particular entrance to a transportation facility, at least one TTY telephone complying with ICC A117.1, Section 704.4, shall be provided to serve that entrance.

E109.2.6 Track crossings. Where a circulation path serving boarding platforms crosses tracks, an accessible route complying with ICC A117.1 shall be provided.

Exception: Openings for wheel flanges shall be permitted to be $2^1/_2$ inches (64 mm) maximum.

E109.2.7 Public address systems. Where public address systems convey audible information to the public, the same or equivalent information shall be provided in a visual format.

E109.2.8 Clocks. Where clocks are provided for use by the general public, the clock face shall be uncluttered so that its elements are clearly visible. Hands, numerals and digits shall contrast with the background either light-on-dark or dark-on-light. Where clocks are mounted overhead, numerals and digits shall comply with ICC A117.1, Section 703.2.

SECTION E110 AIRPORTS

E110.1 New construction. New construction of airports shall comply with Sections E110.2 through E110.4.

E110.2 TTYs. Where public pay telephones are provided, at least one TTY shall be provided in compliance with ICC A117.1, Section 704.4. Additionally, if four or more public pay telephones are located in a main terminal outside the security areas, a concourse within the security areas or a baggage claim area in a terminal, at least one public TTY complying with ICC A117.1, Section 704.4, shall also be provided in each such location.

E110.3 Terminal information systems. Where terminal information systems convey audible information to the public, the same or equivalent information shall be provided in a visual format.

E110.4 Clocks. Where clocks are provided for use by the general public, the clock face shall be uncluttered so that its elements are clearly visible. Hands, numerals and digits shall contrast with their background either light-on-dark or dark-on-light. Where clocks are mounted overhead, numerals and digits shall comply with ICC A117.1, Section 703.2.

SECTION E111 REFERENCED STANDARDS

DOJ 36 CFR Part 1192	Americans with Disabilities Act (ADA) Accessibility Guidelines for Transportation Vehicles (ADAAG). Washington, D.C.: Department of Justice, 1991	E109.2.4
ICC/ANSI A117.1-03	Accessible and Usable Buildings and Facilities	E101.2, E104.2, E104.2.1, E104.3, E104.3.4, E105.1, E105.2.1, E105.2.2, E105.3, E105.4, E105.6, E106.2, E106.3, E106.4, E106.4.9, E106.5, E107.2, E107.3, E108.3, E108.4, E109.2.1, E109.2.2.1, E109.2.2.2, E109.2.2.3, E109.2.3

APPENDIX F
RODENTPROOFING

The provisions contained in this appendix are adopted as part of this code.

SECTION F101
GENERAL

F101.1 General. Buildings or structures and the walls enclosing habitable or occupiable rooms and spaces in which persons live, sleep or work, or in which feed, food or foodstuffs are stored, prepared, processed, served or sold, shall be constructed in accordance with the provisions of this section.

F101.2 Foundation wall ventilation openings. Foundation wall ventilator openings shall be covered for their height and width with perforated sheet metal plates no less than 0.070 inch (1.8 mm) thick, expanded sheet metal plates not less than 0.047 inch (1.2 mm) thick, cast iron grills or grating, extruded aluminum load-bearing vents or with hardware cloth of 0.035 inch (0.89 mm) wire or heavier. The openings therein shall not exceed $^{1}/_{4}$ inch (6.4 mm).

F101.3 Foundation and exterior wall sealing. Annular spaces around pipes, electric cables, conduits, or other openings in the walls shall be protected against the passage of rodents by closing such openings with cement mortar, concrete masonry or noncorrosive metal.

F101.4 Doors. Doors on which metal protection has been applied shall be hinged so as to be free swinging. When closed, the maximum clearance between any door, door jambs and sills shall not be greater than $^{3}/_{8}$ inch (9.5 mm).

F101.5 Windows and other openings. Windows and other openings for the purpose of light or ventilation located in exterior walls within 2 feet (610 mm) above the existing ground level immediately below such opening shall be covered for their entire height and width, including frame, with hardware cloth of at least 0.035 inch (0.89 mm) wire or heavier.

F101.5.1 Rodent-accessible openings. Windows and other openings for the purpose of light and ventilation in the exterior walls not covered in this chapter, accessible to rodents by way of exposed pipes, wires, conduits and other appurtenances, shall be covered with wire cloth of at least 0.035 inch (0.89 mm) wire. In lieu of wire cloth covering, said pipes, wires, conduits and other appurtenances shall be blocked from rodent usage by installing solid sheet metal guards 0.024 inch (0.61 mm) thick or heavier. Guards shall be fitted around pipes, wires, conduits or other appurtenances. In addition, they shall be fastened securely to and shall extend perpendicularly from the exterior wall for a minimum distance of 12 inches (305 mm) beyond and on either side of pipes, wires, conduits or appurtenances.

F101.6 Pier and wood construction.

F101.6.1 Sill less than 12 inches above ground. Buildings not provided with a continuous foundation shall be provided with protection against rodents at grade by providing either an apron in accordance with Section F101.6.1.1 or a floor slab in accordance with Section F101.6.1.2.

F101.6.1.1 Apron. Where an apron is provided, the apron shall not be less than 8 inches (203 mm) above, nor less than 24 inches (610 mm) below, grade. The apron shall not terminate below the lower edge of the siding material. The apron shall be constructed of an approved nondecayable, water-resistant rodentproofing material of required strength and shall be installed around the entire perimeter of the building. Where constructed of masonry or concrete materials, the apron shall not be less than 4 inches (102 mm) in thickness.

F101.6.1.2 Grade floors. Where continuous concrete grade floor slabs are provided, open spaces shall not be left between the slab and walls, and openings in the slab shall be protected.

F101.6.2 Sill at or above 12 inches above ground. Buildings not provided with a continuous foundation and which have sills 12 or more inches (305 mm) above the ground level shall be provide with protection against rodents at grade in accordance with any of the following:

1. Section F101.6.1.1 or F101.6.1.2;
2. By installing solid sheet metal collars at least 0.024 inch (0.6 mm) thick at the top of each pier or pile and around each pipe, cable, conduit, wire or other item which provides a continuous pathway from the ground to the floor; or
3. By encasing the pipes, cables, conduits or wires in an enclosure constructed in accordance with Section F101.6.1.1.

APPENDIX G
FLOOD-RESISTANT CONSTRUCTION

The provisions contained in this appendix are adopted as part of this code.

SECTION G101 ADMINISTRATION

G101.1 Purpose. The purpose of this appendix is to promote the public health, safety and general welfare and to minimize public and private losses due to *flood* conditions in specific *flood hazard* areas through the establishment of comprehensive regulations for management of *flood hazard areas* designed to:

1. Prevent unnecessary disruption of commerce, access and public service during times of *flooding*;
2. Manage the alteration of natural *flood* plains, stream channels and shorelines;
3. Manage filling, grading, dredging and other development which may increase *flood* damage or erosion potential;
4. Prevent or regulate the construction of *flood* barriers which will divert floodwaters or which can increase flood hazards; and
5. Contribute to improved construction techniques in the flood plain.

G101.2 Objectives. The objectives of this appendix are to protect human life, minimize the expenditure of public money for *flood* control projects, minimize the need for rescue and relief efforts associated with *flooding*, minimize prolonged business interruption, minimize damage to public facilities and utilities, help maintain a stable tax base by providing for the sound use and development of flood-prone areas, contribute to improved construction techniques in the flood plain and ensure that potential owners and occupants are notified that property is within flood hazard areas.

G101.3 Scope. The provisions of this appendix shall apply to all proposed development in a flood hazard area established in Section 1612 of this code.

G101.4 Violations. Any violation of a provision of this appendix, or failure to comply with a permit or variance issued pursuant to this appendix or any requirement of this appendix, shall be handled in accordance with *the North Carolina Admintrative Code and Policies*.

SECTION G102 APPLICABILITY

G102.1 General. This appendix, in conjunction with the *International Building Code*, provides minimum requirements for development located in flood hazard areas, including the subdivision of land; installation of utilities; placement and replacement of manufactured homes; new construction and repair, reconstruction, rehabilitation or additions to new construction; substantial improvement of existing buildings and structures, including restoration after damage, temporary structures, and temporary or permanent storage, and utility and miscellaneous Group U buildings and structures.

G102.2 Establishment of flood hazard areas. *Flood hazard areas* are established in Section 1612.3 of the *International Building Code*, adopted by the applicable governing authority on [INSERT DATE].

SECTION G103 POWERS AND DUTIES

G103.1 Permit applications. The *building official* shall review all *permit* applications to determine whether proposed development sites will be reasonably safe from flooding. If a proposed development site is in a flood hazard area, all site development activities (including grading, filling, utility installation and drainage modification), all new construction and substantial improvements (including the placement of prefabricated buildings and manufactured homes) shall be designed and constructed with methods, practices and materials that minimize flood damage and that are in accordance with this code and ASCE 24.

G103.2 Other permits. It shall be the responsibility of the *building official* to assure that approval of a proposed development shall not be given until proof that necessary permits have been granted by federal or state agencies having jurisdiction over such development.

G103.3 Determination of design flood elevations. If design flood elevations are not specified, the *building official* is authorized to require the applicant to:

1. Obtain, review and reasonably utilize data available from a federal, state or other source, or
2. Determine the *design flood elevation* in accordance with accepted hydrologic and hydraulic engineering techniques. Such analyses shall be performed and sealed by a *registered design professional*. Studies, analyses and computations shall be submitted in sufficient detail to allow review and approval by the *building official*. The accuracy of data submitted for such determination shall be the responsibility of the applicant.

G103.4 Activities in riverine flood hazard areas. In riverine *flood hazard areas* where *design flood elevations* are specified but *floodways* have not been designated, the *building official* shall not permit any new construction, substantial improvement or other development, including fill, unless the applicant demonstrates that the cumulative effect of the proposed development, when combined with all other existing and anticipated flood hazard area encroachment, will not increase the design flood elevation more than 1 foot (305 mm) at any point within the community.

G103.5 Floodway encroachment. Prior to issuing a *permit* for any *floodway* encroachment, including fill, new construction, substantial improvements and other development or land-disturbing activity, the *building official* shall require submission of a certification, along with supporting technical data, that demonstrates that such development will not cause any increase of the level of the base *flood*.

G103.5.1 Floodway revisions. A *floodway* encroachment that increases the level of the base *flood* is authorized if the applicant has applied for a conditional Flood Insurance Rate Map (FIRM) revision and has received the approval of the Federal Emergency Management Agency (FEMA).

G103.6 Watercourse alteration. Prior to issuing a permit for any alteration or relocation of any watercourse, the *building official* shall require the applicant to provide notification of the proposal to the appropriate authorities of all affected adjacent government jurisdictions, as well as appropriate state agencies. A copy of the notification shall be maintained in the permit records and submitted to FEMA.

G103.6.1 Engineering analysis. The *building official* shall require submission of an engineering analysis which demonstrates that the flood-carrying capacity of the altered or relocated portion of the watercourse will not be decreased. Such watercourses shall be maintained in a manner which preserves the channel's flood-carrying capacity.

G103.7 Alterations in coastal areas. Prior to issuing a permit for any alteration of sand dunes and mangrove stands in flood hazard areas subject to high velocity wave action, the *building official* shall require submission of an engineering analysis which demonstrates that the proposed alteration will not increase the potential for flood damage.

G103.8 Records. The *building official* shall maintain a permanent record of all *permits* issued in *flood hazard areas*, including copies of inspection reports and certifications required in Section 1612.

SECTION G104 PERMITS

G104.1 Required. Any person, owner or authorized agent who intends to conduct any development in a flood hazard area shall first make application to the *building official* and shall obtain the required *permit*.

G104.2 Application for permit. The applicant shall file an application in writing on a form furnished by the *building official*. Such application shall:

1. Identify and describe the development to be covered by the permit.
2. Describe the land on which the proposed development is to be conducted by legal description, street address or similar description that will readily identify and definitely locate the site.
3. Include a site plan showing the delineation of flood hazard areas, floodway boundaries, flood zones, design flood elevations, ground elevations, proposed fill and excavation and drainage patterns and facilities.
4. Indicate the use and occupancy for which the proposed development is intended.
5. Be accompanied by construction documents, grading and filling plans and other information deemed appropriate by the building official.
6. State the valuation of the proposed work.
7. Be signed by the applicant or the applicant's authorized agent.

G104.3 Validity of permit. The issuance of a *permit* under this appendix shall not be construed to be a permit for, or approval of, any violation of this appendix or any other ordinance of the jurisdiction. The issuance of a *permit* based on submitted documents and information shall not prevent the *building official* from requiring the correction of errors. The *building official* is authorized to prevent occupancy or use of a structure or site which is in violation of this appendix or other ordinances of this jurisdiction.

G104.4 Expiration. A *permit* shall become invalid if the proposed development is not commenced within 180 days after its issuance, or if the work authorized is suspended or abandoned for a period of 180 days after the work commences. Extensions shall be requested in writing and justifiable cause demonstrated. The *building official* is authorized to grant, in writing, one or more extensions of time, for periods not more than 180 days each.

G104.5 Suspension or revocation. The building official is authorized to suspend or revoke a *permit* issued under this appendix wherever the permit is issued in error or on the basis of incorrect, inaccurate or incomplete information, or in violation of any ordinance or code of this jurisdiction.

SECTION G105 VARIANCES

G105.1 General. The *board of appeals* established pursuant to Section 112 shall hear and decide requests for variances. The *board of appeals* shall base its determination on technical justifications, and has the right to attach such conditions to variances as it deems necessary to further the purposes and objectives of this appendix and Section 1612.

G105.2 Records. The building official shall maintain a permanent record of all variance actions, including justification for their issuance.

G105.3 Historic structures. A variance is authorized to be issued for the repair or rehabilitation of a historic structure upon a determination that the proposed repair or rehabilitation will not preclude the structure's continued designation as a historic structure, and the variance is the minimum necessary to preserve the historic character and design of the structure.

Exception: Within *flood hazard areas*, *historic structures* that are not:

1. Listed or preliminarily determined to be eligible for listing in the National Register of Historic Places; or
2. Determined by the Secretary of the U.S. Department of Interior as contributing to the historical significance of a registered historic district or a district preliminarily determined to qualify as an historic district; or
3. Designated as *historic* under a state or local historic preservation program that is approved by the Department of Interior.

G105.4 Functionally dependent facilities. A variance is authorized to be issued for the construction or substantial improvement of a functionally dependent facility provided the criteria in Section 1612.1 are met and the variance is the minimum necessary to allow the construction or substantial improvement, and that all due consideration has been given to methods and materials that minimize flood damages during the design flood and create no additional threats to public safety.

G105.5 Restrictions. The *board of appeals* shall not issue a variance for any proposed development in a floodway if any increase in flood levels would result during the base flood discharge.

G105.6 Considerations. In reviewing applications for variances, the *board of appeals* shall consider all technical evaluations, all relevant factors, all other portions of this appendix and the following:

1. The danger that materials and debris may be swept onto other lands resulting in further injury or damage;
2. The danger to life and property due to flooding or erosion damage;
3. The susceptibility of the proposed development, including contents, to flood damage and the effect of such damage on current and future owners;
4. The importance of the services provided by the proposed development to the community;
5. The availability of alternate locations for the proposed development that are not subject to flooding or erosion;
6. The compatibility of the proposed development with existing and anticipated development;
7. The relationship of the proposed development to the comprehensive plan and flood plain management program for that area;
8. The safety of access to the property in times of flood for ordinary and emergency vehicles;
9. The expected heights, velocity, duration, rate of rise and debris and sediment transport of the floodwaters and the effects of wave action, if applicable, expected at the site; and
10. The costs of providing governmental services during and after flood conditions including maintenance and repair of public utilities and facilities such as sewer, gas, electrical and water systems, streets and bridges.

G105.7 Conditions for issuance. Variances shall only be issued by the *board of appeals* upon:

1. A technical showing of good and sufficient cause that the unique characteristics of the size, configuration or topography of the site renders the elevation standards inappropriate;
2.. A determination that failure to grant the variance would result in exceptional hardship by rendering the lot undevelopable;
3. A determination that the granting of a variance will not result in increased flood heights, additional threats to public safety, extraordinary public expense, nor create nuisances, cause fraud on or victimization of the public or conflict with existing local laws or ordinances;
4. A determination that the variance is the minimum necessary, considering the flood hazard, to afford relief; and
5. Notification to the applicant in writing over the signature of the building official that the issuance of a variance to construct a structure below the base flood level will result in increased premium rates for flood insurance up to amounts as high as $25 for $100 of insurance coverage, and that such construction below the base flood level increases risks to life and property.

SECTION G201
DEFINITIONS

G201.1 General. The following words and terms shall, for the purposes of this appendix, have the meanings shown herein. Refer to Chapter 2 for general definitions.

G201.2 Definitions.

DEVELOPMENT. Any manmade change to improved or unimproved real estate, including but not limited to, buildings or other structures, temporary structures, temporary or permanent storage of materials, mining, dredging, filling, grading, paving, excavations, operations and other land-disturbing activities.

FUNCTIONALLY DEPENDENT FACILITY. A facility which cannot be used for its intended purpose unless it is located or carried out in close proximity to water, such as a docking or port facility necessary for the loading or unloading of cargo or passengers, shipbuilding or ship repair. The term does not include long-term storage, manufacture, sales or service facilities.

MANUFACTURED HOME. A structure that is transportable in one or more sections, built on a permanent chassis, designed for use with or without a permanent foundation when attached to the required utilities, and constructed to the Federal Mobile Home Construction and Safety Standards and rules and regulations promulgated by the U.S. Department of Housing and Urban Development. The term also includes mobile homes, park trailers, travel trailers and similar transportable structures that are placed on a site for 180 consecutive days or longer.

MANUFACTURED HOME PARK OR SUBDIVISION. A parcel (or contiguous parcels) of land divided into two or more manufactured home lots for rent or sale.

RECREATIONAL VEHICLE. A vehicle that is built on a single chassis, 400 square feet (37.16 m^2) or less when measured at the largest horizontal projection, designed to be self-propelled or permanently towable by a light-duty truck, and designed primarily not for use as a permanent dwelling but as temporary living quarters for recreational, camping, travel or seasonal use. A recreational vehicle is ready for highway use if it is on its wheels or jacking system, is attached to the site only by quick disconnect-type utilities and security devices and has no permanently attached additions.

VARIANCE. A grant of relief from the requirements of this section which permits construction in a manner otherwise prohibited by this section where specific enforcement would result in unnecessary hardship.

VIOLATION. A development that is not fully compliant with this appendix or Section 1612, as applicable.

SECTION G301 SUBDIVISIONS

G301.1 General. Any subdivision proposal, including proposals for manufactured home parks and subdivisions, or other proposed new development in a flood hazard area shall be reviewed to assure that:

1. All such proposals are consistent with the need to minimize flood damage;
2. All public utilities and facilities, such as sewer, gas, electric and water systems are located and constructed to minimize or eliminate flood damage; and
3. Adequate drainage is provided to reduce exposure to flood hazards.

G301.2 Subdivision requirements. The following requirements shall apply in the case of any proposed subdivision, including proposals for manufactured home parks and subdivisions, any portion of which lies within a flood hazard area:

1. The flood hazard area, including floodways and areas subject to high velocity wave action, as appropriate, shall be delineated on tentative and final subdivision plats;
2. Design flood elevations shall be shown on tentative and final subdivision plats;
3. Residential building lots shall be provided with adequate buildable area outside the floodway; and
4. The design criteria for utilities and facilities set forth in this appendix and appropriate *International Codes* shall be met.

SECTION G401 SITE IMPROVEMENT

G401.1 Development in floodways. Development or land disturbing activity shall not be authorized in the *floodway* unless it has been demonstrated through hydrologic and hydraulic analyses performed in accordance with standard engineering practice that the proposed encroachment will not result in any increase in the level of the base *flood*.

G401.2 Flood hazard areas subject to high-velocity wave action. In *flood hazard areas* subject to high-velocity wave action:

1. New buildings and buildings that are substantially improved shall only be authorized landward of the reach of mean high tide.
2. The use of fill for structural support of buildings is prohibited.

G401.3 Sewer facilities. All new or replaced sanitary sewer facilities, private sewage treatment plants (including all pumping stations and collector systems) and on-site waste disposal systems shall be designed in accordance with Chapter 7, ASCE 24, to minimize or eliminate infiltration of floodwaters into the facilities and discharge from the facilities into floodwaters, or impairment of the facilities and systems.

G401.4 Water facilities. All new or replacement water facilities shall be designed in accordance with the provisions of Chapter 7, ASCE 24, to minimize or eliminate infiltration of floodwaters into the systems.

G401.5 Storm drainage. Storm drainage shall be designed to convey the flow of surface waters to minimize or eliminate damage to persons or property.

G401.6 Streets and sidewalks. Streets and sidewalks shall be designed to minimize potential for increasing or aggravating flood levels.

SECTION G501 MANUFACTURED HOMES

G501.1 Elevation. All new and replacement manufactured homes to be placed or substantially improved in a *flood hazard area* shall be elevated such that the lowest floor of the manufactured home is elevated to or above the design flood elevation.

G501.2 Foundations. All new and replacement manufactured homes, including substantial improvement of existing manufactured homes, shall be placed on a permanent, reinforced foundation that is designed in accordance with Section 1612.

G501.3 Anchoring. All new and replacement manufactured homes to be placed or substantially improved in a *flood hazard area* shall be installed using methods and practices which minimize flood damage. Manufactured homes shall be securely anchored to an adequately anchored foundation system to resist flotation, collapse and lateral movement. Methods of anchoring are authorized to include, but are not limited to, use of over-the-top or frame ties to ground anchors. This requirement is in addition to applicable state and local anchoring requirements for resisting wind forces.

SECTION G601 RECREATIONAL VEHICLES

G601.1 Placement prohibited. The placement of recreational vehicles shall not be authorized in *flood hazard areas* subject to high velocity wave action and in *floodways*.

G601.2 Temporary placement. Recreational vehicles in *flood hazard areas* shall be fully licensed and ready for highway use, and shall be placed on a site for less than 180 consecutive days.

G601.3 Permanent placement. Recreational vehicles that are not fully licensed and ready for highway use, or that are to be placed on a site for more than 180 consecutive days, shall meet the requirements of Section G501 for manufactured homes.

SECTION G701 TANKS

G701.1 Underground tanks. Underground tanks in *flood hazard areas* shall be anchored to prevent flotation, collapse or lateral movement resulting from hydrostatic loads, including the effects of buoyancy, during conditions of the design *flood*.

G701.2 Above-ground tanks. Above-ground tanks in flood hazard areas shall be elevated to or above the design *flood* elevation or shall be anchored or otherwise designed and constructed to prevent flotation, collapse or lateral movement resulting from hydrodynamic and hydrostatic loads, including the effects of buoyancy, during conditions of the design *flood*.

G701.3 Tank inlets and vents. In *flood hazard areas*, tank inlets, fill openings, outlets and vents shall be:

1. At or above the design flood elevation or fitted with covers designed to prevent the inflow of floodwater or outflow of the contents of the tanks during conditions of the design *flood*.
2. Anchored to prevent lateral movement resulting from hydrodynamic and hydrostatic loads, including the effects of buoyancy, during conditions of the design *flood*.

SECTION G801 OTHER BUILDING WORK

G801.1 Detached accessory structures. Detached accessory structures shall be anchored to prevent flotation, collapse or lateral movement resulting from hydrostatic loads, including the effects of bouyancy, during conditions of the design *flood*. Fully enclosed accessory structures shall have flood openings to allow for the automatic entry and exit of *flood* waters.

G801.2 Fences. Fences in floodways that may block the passage of floodwaters, such as stockade fences and wire mesh fences, shall meet the requirement of Section G103.5.

G801.3 Oil derricks. Oil derricks located in *flood hazard areas* shall be designed in conformance with the flood loads in Sections 1603.1.7 and 1612.

G801.4 Retaining walls, sidewalks and driveways. Retaining walls, sidewalks and driveways shall meet the requirements of Section 1803.4.

G801.5 Prefabricated swimming pools. Prefabricated swimming pools in *floodways* shall meet the requirements of Section G103.5.

SECTION G901 TEMPORARY STRUCTURES AND TEMPORARY STORAGE

G901.1 Temporary structures. Temporary structures shall be erected for a period of less than 180 days. Temporary structures shall be anchored to prevent flotation, collapse or lateral movement resulting from hydrostatic loads, including the effects of buoyancy, during conditions of the design *flood*. Fully enclosed temporary structures shall have flood openings to allow for the automatic entry and exit of floodwaters.

G901.2 Temporary storage. Temporary storage includes storage of goods and materials for a period of less than 180 days. Stored materials shall not include hazardous materials.

G901.3 Floodway encroachment. Temporary structures and temporary storage in floodways shall meet the requirements of G103.5.

SECTION G1001 UTILITY AND MISCELLANEOUS GROUP U

G1001.1 Utility and miscellaneous Group U. Utility and miscellaneous Group U includes buildings that are accessory in character and miscellaneous structures not classified in any specific occupancy in the *International Building Code*, including, but not limited to, agricultural buildings, aircraft hangars (accessory to a one- or two-family residence), barns, carports, fences more than 6 feet (1829 mm) high, grain silos (accessory to a residential occupancy), greenhouses, livestock shelters, private garages, retaining walls, sheds, stables and towers.

G1001.2 Flood loads. Utility and miscellaneous Group U buildings and structures, including substantial improvement of such buildings and structures, shall be anchored to prevent flotation, collapse or lateral movement resulting from flood loads, including the effects of buoyancy, during conditions of the design *flood*.

G1001.3 Elevation. Utility and miscellaneous Group U buildings and structures, including substantial improvement of such buildings and structures, shall be elevated such that the lowest floor, including basement, is elevated to or above the design *flood* elevation in accordance with Section 1612 of the *International Building Code*.

G1001.4 Enclosures below design flood elevation. Fully enclosed areas below the design flood elevation shall be at or above grade on all sides and conform to the following:

1. In *flood hazard areas* not subject to high-velocity wave action, enclosed areas shall have flood openings to allow for the automatic inflow and outflow of floodwaters.
2. In *flood hazard areas* subject to high-velocity wave action, enclosed areas shall have walls below the design flood elevation that are designed to break away or collapse from a water load less than that which would occur during the design flood, without causing collapse, displacement or other structural damage to the building or structure.

G1001.5 Flood-damage-resistant materials. Flood-damage-resistant materials shall be used below the design *flood* elevation.

G1001.6 Protection of mechanical, plumbing and electrical systems. Mechanical, plumbing and electrical systems, including plumbing fixtures, shall be elevated to or above the design *flood* elevation.

> **Exception:** Electrical systems, equipment and components, and heating, ventilating, air conditioning, and plumbing appliances, plumbing fixtures, duct systems and other service equipment shall be permitted to be located below the design *flood* elevation provided that they are designed and installed to prevent water from entering or accumulating within the components and to resist hydrostatic and hydrodynamic loads and stresses, including the effects of buoyancy, during the occurrence of flooding to the design flood elevation in compliance with the flood-resistant construction requirements of this code. Electrical wiring systems shall be permitted to be located below the design flood elevation provided they conform to the provisions of NFPA 70.

SECTION G1101
REFERENCED STANDARDS

ASCE 24–05	Flood Resistance Design and Construction	G103.1, G401.3, G401.4
HUD 24 CFR Part 3280 (1994)	Manufactured Home Construction and Safety Standards	G201
IBC—06	International Building Code	G102.2
NFPA 70—08	National Electrical Code	G1001.6

APPENDIX H
SIGNS

The provisions contained in this appendix are adopted as part of this code.

SECTION H101 GENERAL

H101.1 General. A sign shall not be erected in a manner that would confuse or obstruct the view of or interfere with exit signs required by Chapter 10 or with official traffic signs, signals or devices. Signs and sign support structures, together with their supports, braces, guys and anchors, shall be kept in repair and in proper state of preservation. The display surfaces of signs shall be kept neatly painted or posted at all times.

H101.2 Signs exempt from permits. The following signs are exempt from the requirements to obtain a permit before erection:

1. Nonilluminated wall signs.
2. Temporary signs.
3. Signs erected by transportation authorities.
4. Projecting signs not exceeding 6 square feet (0.56 m^2).
5. The changing of moveable parts of an approved sign that is designed for such changes, or the repainting or repositioning of display matter shall not be deemed an alteration.

SECTION H102 DEFINITIONS

H102.1 General. Unless otherwise expressly stated, the following words and terms shall, for the purposes of this appendix, have the meanings shown herein. Refer to Chapter 2 of the *International Building Code* for general definitions.

COMBINATION SIGN. A sign incorporating any combination of the features of pole, projecting and roof signs.

DISPLAY SIGN. The area made available by the sign structure for the purpose of displaying the advertising message.

ELECTRIC SIGN. A sign containing electrical wiring, but not including signs illuminated by an exterior light source.

GROUND SIGN. A billboard or similar type of sign which is supported by one or more uprights, poles or braces in or upon the ground other than a combination sign or pole sign, as defined by this code.

POLE SIGN. A sign wholly supported by a sign structure in the ground.

PORTABLE DISPLAY SURFACE. A display surface temporarily fixed to a standardized advertising structure which is regularly moved from structure to structure at periodic intervals.

PROJECTING SIGN. A sign other than a wall sign, which projects from and is supported by a wall of a building or structure.

ROOF SIGN. A sign erected upon or above a roof or parapet of a building or structure.

SIGN. Any letter, figure, character, mark, plane, point, marquee sign, design, poster, pictorial, picture, stroke, stripe, line, trademark, reading matter or illuminated service, which shall be constructed, placed, attached, painted, erected, fastened or manufactured in any manner whatsoever, so that the same shall be used for the attraction of the public to any place, subject, person, firm, corporation, public performance, article, machine or merchandise, whatsoever, which is displayed in any manner outdoors. Every sign shall be classified and conform to the requirements of that classification as set forth in this chapter.

SIGN STRUCTURE. Any structure which supports or is capable of supporting a sign as defined in this code. A sign structure is permitted to be a single pole and is not required to be an integral part of the building.

WALL SIGN. Any sign attached to or erected against the wall of a building or structure, with the exposed face of the sign in a plane parallel to the plane of said wall.

SECTION H103 LOCATION

H103.1 Location restrictions. Signs shall not be erected, constructed or maintained so as to obstruct any fire escape or any window or door or opening used as a *means of egress* or so as to prevent free passage from one part of a roof to any other part thereof. A sign shall not be attached in any form, shape or manner to a fire escape, nor be placed in such manner as to interfere with any opening required for ventilation.

SECTION H104 IDENTIFICATION

H104.1 Identification. Every outdoor advertising display sign hereafter erected, constructed or maintained, for which a permit is required shall be plainly marked with the name of the person, firm or corporation erecting and maintaining such sign and shall have affixed on the front thereof the permit number issued for said sign or other method of identification *approved* by the *building official*.

SECTION H105
DESIGN AND CONSTRUCTION

H105.1 General requirements. Signs shall be designed and constructed to comply with the provisions of this code for use of materials, loads and stresses.

H105.2 Permits, drawings and specifications. Where a permit is required, as provided in Chapter 1, construction documents shall be required. These documents shall show the dimensions, material and required details of construction, including loads, stresses and anchors.

H105.3 Wind load. Signs shall be designed and constructed to withstand wind pressure as provided for in Chapter 16.

H105.4 Seismic load. Signs designed to withstand wind pressures shall be considered capable of withstanding earthquake loads, except as provided for in Chapter 16.

H105.5 Working stresses. In outdoor advertising display signs, the allowable working stresses shall conform to the requirements of Chapter 16. The working stresses of wire rope and its fastenings shall not exceed 25 percent of the ultimate strength of the rope or fasteners.

Exceptions:

1. The allowable working stresses for steel and wood shall be in accordance with the provisions of Chapters 22 and 23.
2. The working strength of chains, cables, guys or steel rods shall not exceed one-fifth of the ultimate strength of such chains, cables, guys or steel.

H105.6 Attachment. Signs attached to masonry, concrete or steel shall be safely and securely fastened by means of metal anchors, bolts or approved expansion screws of sufficient size and anchorage to safely support the loads applied.

SECTION H106
ELECTRICAL

H106.1 Illumination. A sign shall not be illuminated by other than electrical means, and electrical devices and wiring shall be installed in accordance with the requirements of NFPA 70. Any open spark or flame shall not be used for display purposes unless specifically approved.

H106.1.1 Internally illuminated signs. Except as provided for in Sections 402.16 and 2611, where internally illuminated signs have facings of wood or approved plastic, the area of such facing section shall not be more than 120 square feet (11.16 m^2) and the wiring for electric lighting shall be entirely enclosed in the sign cabinet with a clearance of not less than 2 inches (51 mm) from the facing material. The dimensional limitation of 120 square feet (11.16 m^2) shall not apply to sign facing sections made from flame-resistant-coated fabric (ordinarily known as "flexible sign face plastic") that weighs less than 20 ounces per square yard (678 g/m^2) and that, when tested in accordance with NFPA 701, meets the fire propagation performance requirements of both Test 1 and Test 2 or that when tested in accordance with an approved test method, exhibits an average burn time of 2 seconds or less and a burning extent of 5.9 inches (150 mm) or less for 10 specimens.

H106.2 Electrical service. Signs that require electrical service shall comply with NFPA 70.

SECTION H107
COMBUSTIBLE MATERIALS

H107.1 Use of combustibles. Wood, approved plastic or plastic veneer panels as provided for in Chapter 26, or other materials of combustible characteristics similar to wood, used for moldings, cappings, nailing blocks, letters and latticing, shall comply with Section H109.1, and shall not be used for other ornamental features of signs, unless approved.

H107.1.1 Plastic materials. Notwithstanding any other provisions of this code, plastic materials which burn at a rate no faster than 2.5 inches per minute (64 mm/s) when tested in accordance with ASTM D 635 shall be deemed approved plastics and can be used as the display surface material and for the letters, decorations and facings on signs and outdoor display structures.

H107.1.2 Electric sign faces. Individual plastic facings of electric signs shall not exceed 200 square feet (18.6 m^2) in area.

H107.1.3 Area limitation. If the area of a display surface exceeds 200 square feet (18.6 m^2), the area occupied or covered by approved plastics shall be limited to 200 square feet (18.6 m^2) plus 50 percent of the difference between 200 square feet (18.6 m^2) and the area of display surface. The area of plastic on a display surface shall not in any case exceed 1,100 square feet (102 m^2).

H107.1.4 Plastic appurtenances. Letters and decorations mounted on an approved plastic facing or display surface can be made of approved plastics.

SECTION H108
ANIMATED DEVICES

H108.1 Fail-safe device. Signs that contain moving sections or ornaments shall have fail-safe provisions to prevent the section or ornament from releasing and falling or shifting its center of gravity more than 15 inches (381 mm). The fail-safe device shall be in addition to the mechanism and the mechanism's housing which operate the movable section or ornament. The fail-safe device shall be capable of supporting the full dead weight of the section or ornament when the moving mechanism releases.

SECTION H109
GROUND SIGNS

H109.1 Height restrictions. The structural frame of ground signs shall not be erected of combustible materials to a height of more than 35 feet (10668 mm) above the ground. Ground signs constructed entirely of noncombustible material shall not be erected to a height of greater than 100 feet (30 480 mm) above the ground. Greater heights are permitted where approved and located so as not to create a hazard or danger to the public.

H109.2 Required clearance. The bottom coping of every ground sign shall be not less than 3 feet (914 mm) above the ground or street level, which space can be filled with platform decorative trim or light wooden construction.

H109.3 Wood anchors and supports. Where wood anchors or supports are embedded in the soil, the wood shall be pressure treated with an approved preservative.

SECTION H110 ROOF SIGNS

H110.1 General. Roof signs shall be constructed entirely of metal or other approved noncombustible material except as provided for in Sections H106.1.1 and H107.1. Provisions shall be made for electric grounding of metallic parts. Where combustible materials are permitted in letters or other ornamental features, wiring and tubing shall be kept free and insulated therefrom. Roof signs shall be so constructed as to leave a clear space of not less than 6 feet (1829 mm) between the roof level and the lowest part of the sign and shall have at least 5 feet (1524 mm) clearance between the vertical supports thereof. No portion of any roof sign structure shall project beyond an exterior wall.

Exception: Signs on flat roofs with every part of the roof accessible.

H110.2 Bearing plates. The bearing plates of roof signs shall distribute the load directly to or upon masonry walls, steel roof girders, columns or beams. The building shall be designed to avoid overstress of these members.

H110.3 Height of solid signs. A roof sign having a solid surface shall not exceed, at any point, a height of 24 feet (7315 mm) measured from the roof surface.

H110.4 Height of open signs. Open roof signs in which the uniform open area is not less than 40 percent of total gross area shall not exceed a height of 75 feet (22 860 mm) on buildings of Type 1 or Type 2 construction. On buildings of other construction types, the height shall not exceed 40 feet (12 192 mm). Such signs shall be thoroughly secured to the building upon which they are installed, erected or constructed by iron, metal anchors, bolts, supports, chains, stranded cables, steel rods or braces and they shall be maintained in good condition.

H110.5 Height of closed signs. A closed roof sign shall not be erected to a height greater than 50 feet (15 240 mm) above the roof of buildings of Type 1 or Type 2 construction, nor more than 35 feet (10 668 mm) above the roof of buildings of Type 3, 4 or 5 construction.

SECTION H111 WALL SIGNS

H111.1 Materials. Wall signs which have an area exceeding 40 square feet (3.72 m^2) shall be constructed of metal or other approved noncombustible material, except for nailing rails and as provided for in Sections H106.1.1 and H107.1.

H111.2 Exterior wall mounting details. Wall signs attached to *exterior walls* of solid masonry, concrete or stone shall be safely and securely attached by means of metal anchors, bolts or expansion screws of not less than $^3/_8$ inch (9.5 mm) diameter and shall be embedded at least 5 inches (127 mm). Wood blocks shall not be used for anchorage, except in the case of wall signs attached to buildings with walls of wood. A wall sign shall not be supported by anchorages secured to an unbraced parapet wall.

H111.3 Extension. Wall signs shall not extend above the top of the wall, nor beyond the ends of the wall to which the signs are attached unless such signs conform to the requirements for roof signs, projecting signs or ground signs.

SECTION H112 PROJECTING SIGNS

H112.1 General. Projecting signs shall be constructed entirely of metal or other noncombustible material and securely attached to a building or structure by metal supports such as bolts, anchors, supports, chains, guys or steel rods. Staples or nails shall not be used to secure any projecting sign to any building or structure. The *dead load* of projecting signs not parallel to the building or structure and the load due to wind pressure shall be supported with chains, guys or steel rods having net cross-sectional dimension of not less than $^3/_8$ inch (9.5 mm) diameter. Such supports shall be erected or maintained at an angle of at least 45 degrees (0.78 rad) with the horizontal to resist the *dead load* and at angle of 45 degrees (0.78 rad) or more with the face of the sign to resist the specified wind pressure. If such projecting sign exceeds 30 square feet (2.8 m^2) in one facial area, there shall be provided at least two such supports on each side not more than 8 feet (2438 mm) apart to resist the wind pressure.

H112.2 Attachment of supports. Supports shall be secured to a bolt or expansion screw that will develop the strength of the supporting chains, guys or steel rods, with a minimum $^5/_8$-inch (15.9 mm) bolt or lag screw, by an expansion shield. Turn buckles shall be placed in chains, guys or steel rods supporting projecting signs.

H112.3 Wall mounting details. Chains, cables, guys or steel rods used to support the live or dead load of projecting signs are permitted to be fastened to solid masonry walls with expansion bolts or by machine screws in iron supports, but such supports shall not be attached to an unbraced parapet wall. Where the supports must be fastened to walls made of wood, the supporting anchor bolts must go through the wall and be plated or fastened on the inside in a secure manner.

H112.4 Height limitation. A projecting sign shall not be erected on the wall of any building so as to project above the roof or cornice wall or above the roof level where there is no cornice wall; except that a sign erected at a right angle to the building, the horizontal width of which sign is perpendicular to such a wall and does not exceed 18 inches (457 mm), is permitted to be erected to a height not exceeding 2 feet (610 mm) above the roof or cornice wall or above the roof level where there is no cornice wall. A sign attached to a corner of a building and parallel to the vertical line of such corner shall be deemed to be erected at a right angle to the building wall.

H112.5 Additional loads. Projecting sign structures which will be used to support an individual on a ladder or other servicing device, whether or not specifically designed for the servicing device, shall be capable of supporting the anticipated additional load, but not less than a 100-pound (445 N) concentrated horizontal load and a 300-pound (1334 N) concentrated vertical load applied at the point of assumed or most eccentric loading. The building component to which the projecting sign is attached shall also be designed to support the additional loads.

SECTION H113 MARQUEE SIGNS

H113.1 Materials. Marquee signs shall be constructed entirely of metal or other approved noncombustible material except as provided for in Sections H106.1.1 and H107.1.

H113.2 Attachment. Marquee signs shall be attached to approved marquees that are constructed in accordance with Section 3106.

H113.3 Dimensions. Marquee signs, whether on the front or side, shall not project beyond the perimeter of the marquee.

H113.4 Height limitation. Marquee signs shall not extend more than 6 feet (1829 mm) above, nor 1 foot (305 mm) below such marquee, but under no circumstances shall the sign or signs have a vertical dimension greater than 8 feet (2438 mm).

SECTION H114 PORTABLE SIGNS

H114.1 General. Portable signs shall conform to requirements for ground, roof, projecting, flat and temporary signs where such signs are used in a similar capacity. The requirements of this section shall not be construed to require portable signs to have connections to surfaces, tie-downs or foundations where provisions are made by temporary means or configuration of the structure to provide stability for the expected duration of the installation.

TABLE 4-A
SIZE, THICKNESS AND TYPE OF GLASS PANELS IN SIGNS

MAXIMUM SIZE OF EXPOSED PANEL		MINIMUM THICKNESS OF GLASS (inches)	TYPE OF GLASS
Any dimension (inches)	Area (square inches)		
30	500	$^1/_8$	Plain, plate or wired
45	700	$^3/_{16}$	Plain, plate or wired
144	3,600	$^1/_4$	Plain, plate or wired
> 144	> 3,600	$^1/_4$	Wired glass

For SI: 1 inch = 25.4 mm, 1 square inch = 645.16 mm^2.

TABLE 4-B
THICKNESS OF PROJECTION SIGN

PROJECTION (feet)	MAXIMUM THICKNESS (feet)
5	2
4	2.5
3	3
2	3.5
1	4

For SI: 1 foot = 304.8 mm.

SECTION H115 REFERENCED STANDARDS

ASTM D 635—03	Test Method for Rate of Burning and/or Extent and Time of Burning of Self-Supporting Plastics in a Horizontal Position	H107.1.1
NFPA 70—08	National Electrical Code	H106.1, H106.2
NFPA 701—99	Methods of Fire Test for Flame Propagation of Textiles and Films	H106.1.1

APPENDIX I
PATIO COVERS

The provisions contained in this appendix are adopted as part of this code.

SECTION I101 GENERAL

I101.1 General. Patio covers shall be permitted to be detached from or attached to *dwelling units*. Patio covers shall be used only for recreational, outdoor living purposes and not as carports, garages, storage rooms or habitable rooms. Openings shall be permitted to be enclosed with insect screening, approved translucent or transparent plastic not more that 0.125 inch (3.2 mm) in thickness, glass conforming to the provisions of Chapter 24 or any combination of the foregoing.

SECTION I102 DEFINITIONS

I102.1 General. The following word and term shall, for the purposes of this appendix, have the meaning shown herein.

PATIO COVERS. One story structures not exceeding 12 feet (3657 mm) in height. Enclosure walls shall be permitted to be of any configuration, provided the open or glazed area of the longer wall and one additional wall is equal to at least 65 percent of the area below a minimum of 6 feet 8 inches (2032 mm) of each wall, measured from the floor.

SECTION I103 EXTERIOR OPENINGS

I103.1 Light, ventilation and emergency egress. Exterior openings required for light and ventilation shall be permitted to open into a patio structure. However, the patio structure shall be unenclosed if such openings are serving as emergency egress or rescue openings from sleeping rooms. Where such exterior openings serve as an exit from the dwelling unit, the patio structure, unless unenclosed, shall be provided with exits conforming to the provision of Chapter 10.

SECTION I104 STRUCTURAL PROVISIONS

I104.1 Design loads. Patio covers shall be designed and constructed to sustain, within the stress limits of this code, all dead loads plus a minimum vertical live load of 10 pounds per square foot (0.48 kN/m^2) except that snow loads shall be used where such snow loads exceed this minimum. Such patio covers shall be designed to resist the minimum wind and seismic loads set forth in this code.

I104.2 Footings. In areas with a frost depth of zero, a patio cover shall be permitted to be supported on a concrete slab on grade without footings, provided the slab conforms to the provisions of Chapter 19 of this code, is not less than 3$^1/_2$ inches (89 mm) thick and further provided that the columns do not support loads in excess of 750 pounds (3.36 kN) per column.

APPENDIX J
GRADING

The provisions contained in this appendix are adopted as part of this code.

SECTION J101 GENERAL

J101.1 Scope. The provisions of this chapter apply to grading, excavation and earthwork construction, including fills and embankments. Where conflicts occur between the technical requirements of this chapter and the geotechnical report, the geotechnical report shall govern.

J101.2 Flood hazard areas. The provisions of this chapter shall not apply to grading, excavation and earthwork construction, including fills and embankments, in *floodways* within *flood hazard areas* established in Section 1612.3 or in *flood hazard areas* where design *flood* elevations are specified but floodways have not been designated, unless it has been demonstrated through hydrologic and hydraulic analyses performed in accordance with standard engineering practice that the proposed work will not result in any increase in the level of the base flood.

SECTION J102 DEFINITIONS

J102.1 Definitions. For the purposes of this appendix chapter, the terms, phrases and words listed in this section and their derivatives shall have the indicated meanings.

BENCH. A relatively level step excavated into earth material on which fill is to be placed.

COMPACTION. The densification of a fill by mechanical means.

CUT. See Excavation.

DOWN DRAIN. A device for collecting water from a swale or ditch located on or above a slope, and safely delivering it to an approved drainage facility

EROSION. The wearing away of the ground surface as a result of the movement of wind, water or ice.

EXCAVATION. The removal of earth material by artificial means, also referred to as a cut.

FILL. Deposition of earth materials by artificial means.

GRADE. The vertical location of the ground surface.

GRADE, EXISTING. The grade prior to grading.

GRADE, FINISHED. The grade of the site at the conclusion of all grading efforts.

GRADING. An excavation or fill or combination thereof.

KEY. A compacted fill placed in a trench excavated in earth material beneath the toe of a slope.

SLOPE. An inclined surface, the inclination of which is expressed as a ratio of horizontal distance to vertical distance.

TERRACE. A relatively level step constructed in the face of a graded slope for drainage and maintenance purposes.

SECTION J103 PERMITS REQUIRED

J103.1 Permits required. Except as exempted in Section J103.2, no grading shall be performed without first having obtained a *permit* therefor from the *building official*. A grading *permit* does not include the construction of retaining walls or other structures.

J103.2 Exemptions. A grading *permit* shall not be required for the following:

1. Grading in an isolated, self-contained area, provided there is no danger to the public, and that such grading will not adversely affect adjoining properties.
2. Excavation for construction of a structure permitted under this code.
3. Cemetery graves.
4. Refuse disposal sites controlled by other regulations.
5. Excavations for wells, or trenches for utilities.
6. Mining, quarrying, excavating, processing or stockpiling rock, sand, gravel, aggregate or clay controlled by other regulations, provided such operations do not affect the lateral support of, or significantly increase stresses in, soil on adjoining properties.
7. Exploratory excavations performed under the direction of a registered design professional.

Exemption from the permit requirements of this appendix shall not be deemed to grant authorization for any work to be done in any manner in violation of the provisions of this code or any other laws or ordinances of this jurisdiction.

SECTION J104 PERMIT APPLICATION AND SUBMITTALS

J104.1 Submittal requirements. The applicant shall state the estimated quantities of excavation and fill.

J104.2 Site plan requirements. In addition to the provisions of Section 107, a grading plan shall show the existing grade and finished grade in contour intervals of sufficient clarity to indicate the nature and extent of the work and show in detail that it complies with the requirements of this code. The plans shall show the existing grade on adjoining properties in sufficient detail to identify how grade changes will conform to the requirements of this code.

J104.3 Geotechnical report. A geotechnical report prepared by a *registered design professional* shall be provided. The report shall contain at least the following:

1. The nature and distribution of existing soils;
2. Conclusions and recommendations for grading procedures;
3. Soil design criteria for any structures or embankments required to accomplish the proposed grading; and
4. Where necessary, slope stability studies, and recommendations and conclusions regarding site geology.

Exception: A geotechnical report is not required where the building code official determines that the nature of the work applied for is such that a report is not necessary.

J104.4 Liquefaction study. For sites with mapped maximum considered earthquake spectral response accelerations at short periods (S_s) greater than 0.5g as determined by Section 1613, a study of the liquefaction potential of the site shall be provided, and the recommendations incorporated in the plans.

Exception: A liquefaction study is not required where the building official determines from established local data that the liquefaction potential is low.

SECTION J105 INSPECTIONS

J105.1 General. Inspections shall be governed by Section 110 of this code.

J105.2 Special inspections. The special inspection requirements of Section 1704.7 shall apply to work performed under a grading permit where required by the *building official*.

SECTION J106 EXCAVATIONS

J106.1 Maximum slope. The slope of cut surfaces shall be no steeper than is safe for the intended use, and shall be no steeper than two units horizontal to one unit vertical (50-percent slope) unless the owner or authorized agent furnishes a geotechnical report justifying a steeper slope.

Exceptions:

1. A cut surface shall be permitted to be at a slope of 1.5 units horizontal to one unit vertical (67-percent slope) provided that all of the following are met:
   - 1.1. It is not intended to support structures or surcharges.
   - 1.2. It is adequately protected against erosion.
   - 1.3. It is no more than 8 feet (2438 mm) in height.
   - 1.4. It is approved by the building code official.
   - 1.5. Ground water is not encountered.
2. A cut surface in bedrock shall be permitted to be at a slope of one unit horizontal to one unit vertical (100-percent slope).

SECTION J107 FILLS

J107.1 General. Unless otherwise recommended in the geotechnical report, fills shall comply with the provisions of this section.

J107.2 Surface preparation. The ground surface shall be prepared to receive fill by removing vegetation, topsoil and other unsuitable materials, and scarifying the ground to provide a bond with the fill material.

J107.3 Benching. Where existing grade is at a slope steeper than five units horizontal to one unit vertical (20-percent slope) and the depth of the fill exceeds 5 feet (1524 mm) benching shall be provided in accordance with Figure J107.3. A key shall be provided which is at least 10 feet (3048 mm) in width and 2 feet (610 mm) in depth.

J107.4 Fill material. Fill material shall not include organic, frozen or other deleterious materials. No rock or similar irreducible material greater than 12 inches (305 mm) in any dimension shall be included in fills.

J107.5 Compaction. All fill material shall be compacted to 90 percent of maximum density as determined by ASTM D 1557, Modified Proctor, in lifts not exceeding 12 inches (305 mm) in depth.

J107.6 Maximum slope. The slope of fill surfaces shall be no steeper than is safe for the intended use. Fill slopes steeper than two units horizontal to one unit vertical (50-percent slope) shall be justified by a geotechnical report or engineering data.

SECTION J108 SETBACKS

J108.1 General. Cut and fill slopes shall be set back from the property lines in accordance with this section. Setback dimensions shall be measured perpendicular to the property line and shall be as shown in Figure J108.1, unless substantiating data is submitted justifying reduced setbacks.

J108.2 Top of slope. The setback at the top of a cut slope shall not be less than that shown in Figure J108.1, or than is required to accommodate any required interceptor drains, whichever is greater.

J108.3 Slope protection. Where required to protect adjacent properties at the toe of a slope from adverse effects of the grading, additional protection, approved by the *building official*, shall be included. Such protection may include but shall not be limited to:

1. Setbacks greater than those required by Figure J108.1.
2. Provisions for retaining walls or similar construction.
3. Erosion protection of the fill slopes.
4. Provision for the control of surface waters.

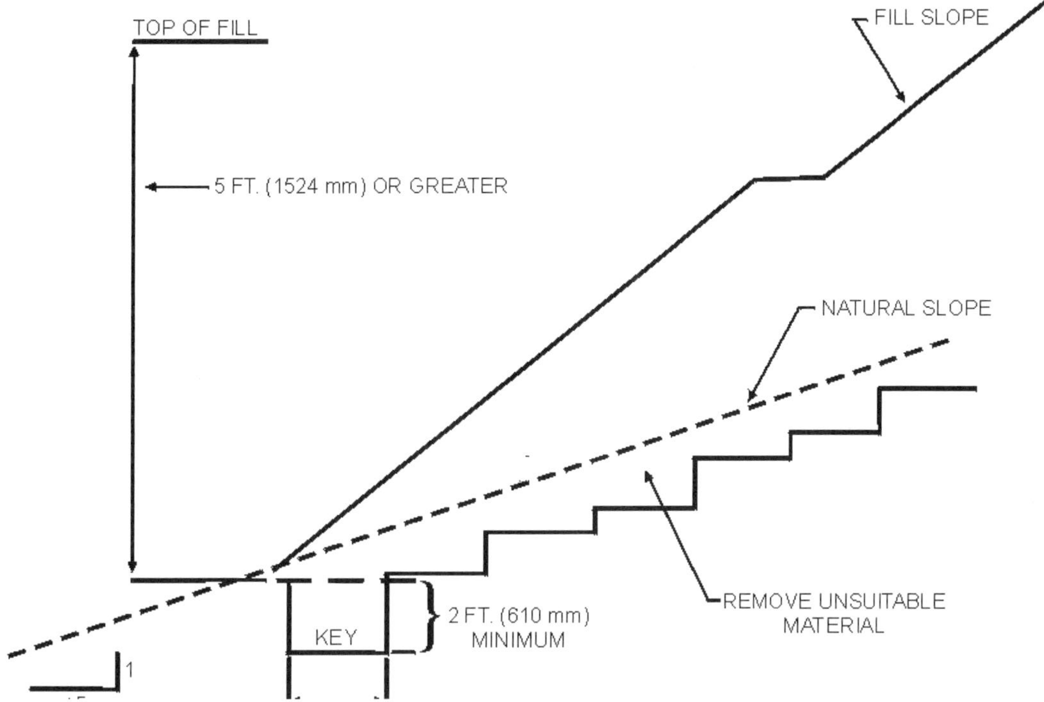

For SI: 1 foot = 304.8 mm.

FIGURE J107.3
BENCHING DETAILS

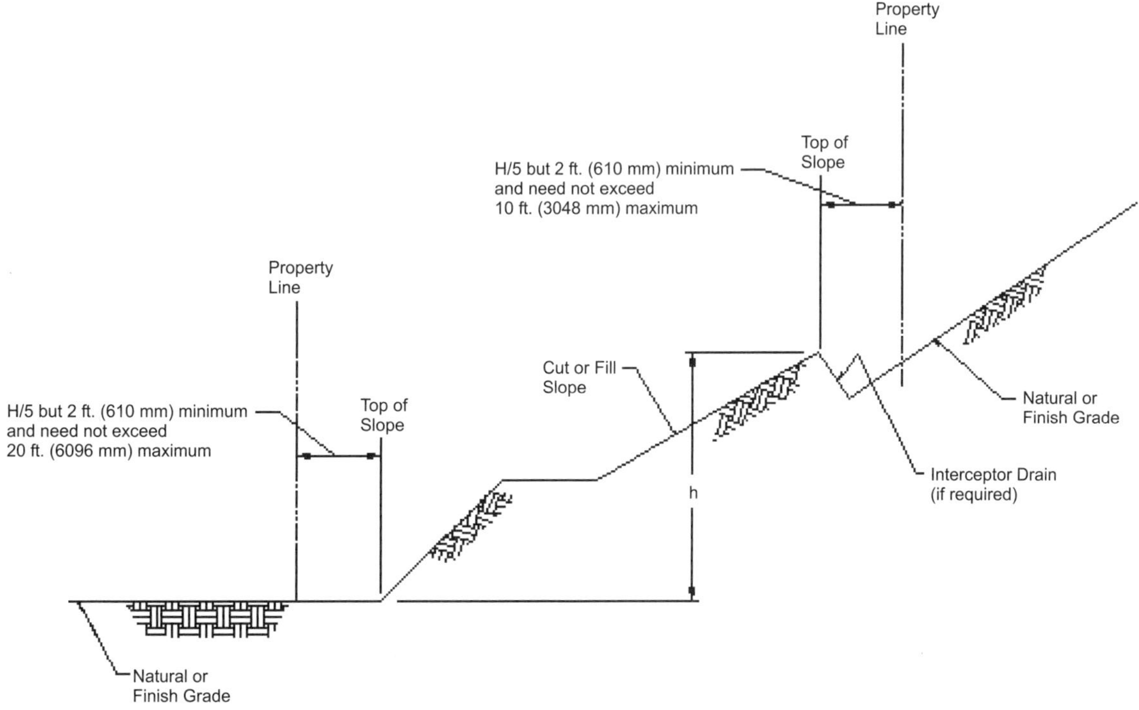

For SI: 1 foot = 304.8 mm.

FIGURE J108.1
DRAINAGE DIMENSIONS

SECTION J109 DRAINAGE AND TERRACING

J109.1 General. Unless otherwise recommended by a *registered design professional*, drainage facilities and terracing shall be provided in accordance with the requirements of this section.

Exception: Drainage facilities and terracing need not be provided where the ground slope is not steeper than 3 horizontal to 1 vertical (33 percent).

J109.2 Terraces. Terraces at least 6 feet (1829 mm) in width shall be established at not more than 30-foot (9144 mm) vertical intervals on all cut or fill slopes to control surface drainage and debris. Suitable access shall be provided to allow for cleaning and maintenance.

Where more than two terraces are required, one terrace, located at approximately mid-height, shall be at least 12 feet (3658 mm) in width.

Swales or ditches shall be provided on terraces. They shall have a minimum gradient of 20 horizontal to 1 vertical (5 percent) and shall be paved with concrete not less than 3 inches (76 mm) in thickness, or with other materials suitable to the application. They shall have a minimum depth of 12 inches (305 mm) and a minimum width of 5 feet (1524 mm).

A single run of swale or ditch shall not collect runoff from a tributary area exceeding 13,500 square feet (1256 m^2) (projected) without discharging into a down drain.

J109.3 Interceptor drains. Interceptor drains shall be installed along the top of cut slopes receiving drainage from a tributary width greater than 40 feet (12 192 mm), measured horizontally. They shall have a minimum depth of 1 foot (305 mm) and a minimum width of 3 feet (915 mm). The slope shall be approved by the *building official*, but shall not be less than 50 horizontal to 1 vertical (2 percent). The drain shall be paved with concrete not less than 3 inches (76 mm) in thickness, or by other materials suitable to the application. Discharge from the drain shall be accomplished in a manner to prevent erosion and shall be approved by the building official.

J109.4 Drainage across property lines. Drainage across property lines shall not exceed that which existed prior to grading. Excess or concentrated drainage shall be contained on site or directed to an approved drainage facility. Erosion of the ground in the area of discharge shall be prevented by installation of nonerosive down drains or other devices.

SECTION J110 EROSION CONTROL

J110.1 General. The faces of cut and fill slopes shall be prepared and maintained to control erosion. This control shall be permitted to consist of effective planting.

Exception: Erosion control measures need not be provided on cut slopes not subject to erosion due to the erosion-resistant character of the materials.

Erosion control for the slopes shall be installed as soon as practicable and prior to calling for final inspection.

J110.2 Other devices. Where necessary, check dams, cribbing, riprap or other devices or methods shall be employed to control erosion and provide safety.

SECTION J111 REFERENCED STANDARDS

ASTM D 1557-e01	Test Method for Laboratory Compaction Characteristics of Soil Using Modified Effort [56,000 ft-lb/ft^3 (2,700kN-m/m^3)].	J107.6

APPENDIX K

ADMINISTRATIVE PROVISIONS

Deleted.

INDEX

B

C

D

G

H

J

K

L

M

N

R

T

Y